The World Today Series®

Stryker-Post Publications, Harpers Ferry, WV, USA

Latin America

Robert T. Buckman

2010

44th edition

Next Edition: August 2011

Robert T. Buckman . . .

A journalism professor at the University of Louisiana at Lafayette, he graduated from Texas Christian University where he earned his bachelor's degree in journalism and political science and his master's in political science. He holds a doctorate in journalism from the University of Texas. His writings on Latin America have been widely published in books, newspapers, magazines, and scholarly journals. He has lived and worked in Chile, where he served a Fulbright Fellowship in 1991, Panama, and Paraguay. A retired lieutenant colonel in the U.S. Army Reserve, he was Reserve military attaché to Colombia until his retirement in 1998. He was recalled to active duty in June 2008 for a one-year tour with the Multi-National Security Transition Command-Iraq in Baghdad.

Adapted, rewritten and revised annually from a book entitled *Latin America 1967,* published in 1967 and succeeding years by

Stryker-Post Publications
P.O. Drawer 1200
Harpers Ferry, WV 25425
Telephones: 1–800–995–1400 (U.S.A. and Canada)
   Other: 1–304–535–2593
   Fax: 1–304–535–6513
   www.strykerpost.com
VISA–MASTERCARD–AMERICAN EXPRESS

The World Today Series has thousands of subscribers across the U.S. and Canada. A sample list of users who annually rely on this most up-to-date material includes:

Public library systems
Universities and colleges
High schools
Federal and state agencies
All branches of the armed forces & war colleges
National Geographic Society
National Democratic Institute
Agricultural Education Foundation
Exxon Corporation
Chevron Corporation
CNN

International Standard Book Number: 978-1-935264-12-5

International Standard Serial Number: 0092-4148

Library of Congress Catalog Number 73-647061

Cover design by nvision graphic design

Cartographer: William L. Nelson

Typography by Barton Matheson Willse & Worthington Baltimore, MD 21244

Printed in the United States of America by United Book Press, Inc. Baltimore, MD 21207

Photographs used to illustrate *The World Today Series* come from many sources, a great number from friends who travel worldwide. If you have taken any which you believe would enhance the visual impact and attractiveness of our books, do let us hear from you.

ACKNOWLEDGMENTS

Un montón de gracias to five people who help ensure the quality of this volume every year: Mario Antonio Sandoval of Guatemala, Orlando López and Alejandro Kounin of Paraguay and Chris Mueller, a Canadian expatriate in Honduras, who keep me apprised of behind-the-scenes developments in those countries and who review those countries' chapters to offer suggestions or corrections; and Dave Sessoms of the U.S. Army Special Warfare Center and School at Fort Bragg and Dr. William Spracher, editor and adjunct faculty member at the Center for Strategic Intelligence Research, National Defense Intelligence College in Washington, both of whom keep me updated on new titles for the bibliography. I also wish to salute the courageous journalists in Mexico and other Latin American countries who have been murdered this year in pursuit of the truth.

São Paulo, Brazil, in 1930 . . .

. . . and today

CONTENTS

Stone piece, Tiahuanaco culture, Bolivia

The UN has received into its ranks many small countries, such as those of the Caribbean region. The purpose of this series is to reflect *modern world dynamics.* Thus, we mention only briefly the beautiful nations of the Lesser Antilles and concentrate our attention on the growth of the larger, developing countries.

Latin America Today

Latin America, always a land of color and conflict, is undergoing the most dramatic changes of its post-colonial history. These changes—political, economic, technological and cultural—are accelerating as the 21st century progresses. Latin America in 2000 bore little resemblance to the Latin America of 1900. Despite some notable exceptions, Latin America gave rise to a stereotype that persists to this day of tropical republics mired in squalor, ruled by self-serving autocrats and lagging decades if not centuries behind the economically advanced societies of Europe and North America.

Such a view ignores the fact that Argentina at the turn of the 20th century was an industrialized and agriculturally rich society boasting a higher per capita income than that of the United States or France. Sadly, as is true of many stereotypes, there was enough element of truth throughout the rest of the region to reinforce the perception of dictators, destitution and depression. Since World War II, this picture has been slowly, painfully, and sometimes violently evolving into a collection of societies entering the modern world. Some have evolved more than others, but the trend is inexorable. This evolution involves four discrete elements: a democratic revolution; economic diversification and expansion; technological acceleration; and cultural growth and projection.

Democratic Revolution

The sudden collapse of communism and the emergence of democracy in Eastern Europe at the beginning of the 1990s was one of the watershed events of world history. Less dramatic but no less historic was the slow, inexorable shift of Latin America away from its past of *caudillo* strongmen, military juntas and revolving-door regimes and toward constitutionally elected civilian governments. As recently as 1977, only three of the 20 true "Latin" American republics had genuinely democratic systems with free elections involving two or more political parties and peaceful trans-

fers of power from one to another: Colombia, Costa Rica and Venezuela.

Two other nations had what could be charitably described as imperfect civilian democracies. Mexico had enjoyed civilian rule since the promulgation of its 1917 constitution and peacefully transferred power from one president to another like clockwork every six years, with re-election strictly forbidden. But until 2000, all those presidents were of one party, the *Partido Revolucionario Institucional (PRI)*, which held government at all levels in a vise-grip and was not above rigging elections to quash the aspirations of upstart opposition parties. In the Dominican Republic, the late President Joaquín Balaguer was elected in 1966, 1970 and 1974 and attempted to hang onto power indefinitely through extra-constitutional means.

Fourteen other republics were governed by military juntas or strongmen. The

longest-ruling despot was Paraguay's Gen. Alfredo Stroessner, who kept himself in power through rigged "elections" from 1954 until overthrown by one of his own generals in 1989. Even the once-envied democracies of Chile and Uruguay opted for order over chaos in 1973.

Finally, Cuba was—and still is—distinguished by the peculiar totalitarian experiment of Fidel Castro, a model that was once viewed as a beacon by guerrilla movements and left-wing political parties throughout the region. The model is still embraced by new left-wing leaders like Venezuela's Hugo Chávez and Bolivia's Evo Morales, even as Fidel Castro's brother and successor, Raúl, has begun implementing some lukewarm reforms.

Democracy in Latin America, it seemed, was a concept that was unfeasible at best and unwanted at worst. But in 1978, the tide slowly began to turn, until by the late 1980s it had become a tidal wave in favor of duly elected civilian government. This transition to democracy in all but one of the Latin American Republics is described in detail in the sections on each nation, together with an indication of things to come.

Lest this picture of emerging democracy be misconstrued as overly rosy, it must be noted that two or more consecutive elections, no matter how honest in the eyes of international observers, do not in and of themselves guarantee that the mortar of democratic institutions will set properly. It often takes generations before adherence to liberal principles becomes woven into a nation's social fabric. True democracy flowers best in a climate characterized by such principles as co-equal executive, legislative and judicial branches; tolerance of opposition parties and viewpoints, whether expressed on the floor of a congress, in free and independent mass media or peacefully in the streets; unquestioned civilian control over the military; workable constitutions that endure more than a decade or two; eschewal of the temptation to resort to political violence; accountability for official wrongdoing; and

Latin America Today

A Guatemalan woman shows her finger stained with indelible ink to show she has voted in the 2007 presidential election. The ink prevents duplicate voting, a safeguard employed throughout Latin America.

Photo by the author

public confidence in the integrity of governmental institutions and leaders. Most Latin American countries are still lacking in this regard.

In fairness, Latin America should be cut some slack. There is not yet a Utopian society anywhere on Earth. Even in the United States, which has long held a paternal attitude toward its wayward Latin American neighbors, political assassinations and attempted assassinations have occurred with alarming frequency, and local pockets of political corruption, complete with vote fraud, influence peddling and kickbacks, are legendary.

But the United States, Canada and the English-speaking states of the Caribbean enjoyed an advantage over their Latin American neighbors in having had a colonial master that had experienced its Glorious Revolution in 1688. The Enlightenment came late, if at all, to Spain, Portugal and France. The abuses of George III that Jefferson enumerated in the Declaration of Independence seem little more than nitpicks in contrast to the absolute power wielded by divine right by the monarchs of the other colonial powers. When Great Britain granted independence to its colonies, whether voluntarily or involuntarily, it left in place viable political institutions

rooted in parliamentary democracy and common law upon which they could build. Washington and Jefferson learned much in the House of Burgesses of colonial Virginia. The press was privately owned. Spain, Portugal and France, by contrast, bequeathed a legacy of power concentrated in the hands of one man.

To put it another way, no Spanish king ever signed a Magna Carta.

Although the newly independent Latin America emulated the U.S. Constitution with its three branches of government and checks and balances, in practice the executive enjoyed disproportionate power. Latin America became the living embodiment of the adage that absolute power corrupts absolutely, and such traditions are not easily discarded. In just the past few years, despite the aforementioned advances in Latin American democracy, we have witnessed attempts by several elected presidents to play fast and loose with constitutional rights in the name of expediency. We also have seen the assassinations of prominent political activists in Colombia, Mexico, Brazil, Paraguay and elsewhere.

Another troubling factor is the willingness of democratically elected presidents to employ legal and extralegal measures once employed by their dictatorial prede-

cessors to curtail freedom of the press, especially critical editorials and investigative reporting.

Under the Spanish legal system, the principle of *desacato,* or criminal libel, is often used as a cudgel against journalists by thin-skinned public officials offended by critical reporting or editorials; truth is not a defense. Other methods that have been frequently employed to intimidate the press include tax audits, licensing of journalists, alleged labor code violations, the withdrawal of advertising by government-owned utility or transportations companies, revocation of broadcast licenses for opposition stations or revocation of work visas for aggressive foreign journalists.

Another tactic for dealing with nettlesome journalists remains widespread in Latin America: murder. According to the Inter American Press Association (IAPA), 369 journalists were martyred in the performance of their duties in the Americas from 1987 to mid-2010, including 124 in Colombia, 83 in Mexico, 32 in Brazil, 23 in Guatemala, 19 in Peru, and 16 in El Salvador. Another 11 journalists disappeared during that time, nine of them in Mexico. Twenty-three journalists were murdered just in 2009, the deadliest year since 1991; 11 of those were in Mexico. Many of the murders can be linked to drug traffickers or guerrillas, but a suspicious number— many of them still unsolved and unpunished—were of journalists who were investigating official corruption or who had written critical editorials or exposés. Independent journalism in Latin America remains a high-risk occupation, and until it can be practiced without fear, true democracy cannot take root.

The Declaration of Chapultepec, promoted by the IAPA and signed in Mexico

Veracruz, Mexico: The largest of the colossal heads found from the Olmec civilization

2

City in 1994 by representatives of 22 nations of the hemisphere, acknowledges the importance of freedom of the press and freedom of expression for democratic societies and denounces acts of violence against journalists. Yet, abuses continued to occur—and still do—even in the signatory countries. The plight of the media was serious enough that it appeared on the agenda of the Second Summit of the Americas in Santiago, Chile, in 1998. The 34 hemispheric leaders (Castro was not invited) agreed to establish an office within the Inter-American Commission for Human Rights to investigate attacks against journalists. As of February 2010, 55 successive heads of government from 32 countries and Puerto Rico had endorsed the Declaration of Chapultepec, and 83 people had been convicted of crimes against journalists as of April 2010.

In its annual rating of press freedom around the world, New York-based Freedom House rated the press of only three Latin American countries as "free" in 2009: Chile, Costa Rica and Uruguay. It is probably not a coincidence that Transparency International rated those same three countries as the least corrupt of Latin America. Freedom House rated Cuba and Venezuela as "not free" and the other 15 Latin republics as "partly free." The press of the English-speaking Caribbean countries was generally rated as "free."

There have been encouraging signs during the past few years that executive branches, and the once-omnipotent military establishments, no longer wield unchecked power. Two presidents, Brazil's Fernando Collor and Venezuela's Carlos Andres Pérez, were impeached and removed from office by their congresses for political corruption. In Paraguay, President Raúl Cubas was impeached by the Chamber of Deputies for abuse of power in 1999 and resigned and went into exile in the face of certain conviction and removal by the Senate.

The leaders of the former Argentine junta were prosecuted for human rights abuses committed during the "dirty war" of 1976–83. Chile's Augusto Pinochet was arrested for human rights violations and spent the remaining nine years of his life resisting efforts to bring him to trial. Jorge Serrano's attempt to stage a Fujimori-style self-coup in Guatemala in 1993 failed because the army remained loyal to the constitution, and he fled into exile. A coup attempt by a Paraguayan army general, Lino Oviedo, also fizzled out for lack of support in 1996. During the constitutional crisis over the 1998 removal, justifiable or not, of Ecuador's President Abdalá Bucaram, the military remained in its barracks and allowed the civilians to effect a reasonably smooth transition.

Not all signs have been encouraging, however. There were the 1991 military coup that toppled the elected government of Jean-Bertrand Aristide in Haiti; the temporary suspension of constitutional guarantees in 1992 by Peru's Fujimori for reasons of expediency, and his shamelessly rigged "re-election" in 2000; the constitutionally questionable removal by Congress of Ecuador's Bucaram in 1998 on the ostensibly justifiable (but unproven) charge of "mental incompetence;" the unquestionably unconstitutional barracks revolt in Ecuador that overthrew President Jamil Mahuad in 2000 for the unjustifiable reason that his public popularity was too low; the rigged election in Haiti in 2000 that brought Aristide back to power; the almost successful military coup in Venezuela in 2002 that had President Chávez under house arrest for 24 hours; and the combined congressional-military overthrow of Honduran President Manual Zelaya in 2009.

Another disturbing antidemocratic trend has been the use of mob violence to force the resignations of democratically elected presidents who have subsequently become unpopular. There were the violent street protests in Argentina that led to the resignation of the elected president, Fernando de la Rua, in 2001 and his eventual replacement with the man he had defeated at the polls, Eduardo Duhalde; the violent demonstrations in Bolivia that forced President Gonzalo Sánchez de Lozada from office in 2003 after 14 months in office, and forced his successor, Carlos Mesa, to step down in 2005 after 19 months; and the street protests in Ecuador that forced Congress to remove President Lucio Gutiérrez in 2005 after 27 months in office.

Two other presidents forced from office by public protests evoke less sympathy: Fujimori of Peru in 2000 and Aristide in Haiti in 2004. Both had been re-elected fraudulently.

A possible indicator of growing self-confidence in the viability of these new democratic institutions is a willingness to permit re-election of popular, successful presidents. In a region with its tradition of Stroessners and Balaguers, who remained in control through orchestrated elections, virtually all of these new democracies, and some of the old ones, incorporated a prohibition against re-election, or at least immediate re-election, into their constitutions. Since then, however, Peru, Argentina, Brazil, Venezuela, Colombia, the Dominican Republic, Bolivia and Ecuador amended their constitutions—or wrote new ones—to permit immediate re-election. Yet, in Panama, when President Pérez Balladares called a referendum in 1998 to seek approval for a second term, a resounding 64% of the voters rejected the idea.

A related trend is the return to power of former presidents after one or more intervening terms. Sánchez de Lozada of Bolivia did so in 2003. After the Dominican Republic lifted its ban on re-election, former President Leonel Fernández returned to power in 2004; in 2008, he was elected to a *third* term. In 2006 alone, Oscar Arias of Costa Rica, René Préval of Haiti, Alan García of Peru and Daniel Ortega of Nicaragua (after three unsuccessful re-election bids) all staged comebacks to reclaim the presidencies of their countries.

Still another peculiarity is the number of presidents in recent years elected on their second or subsequent attempt. Presidents Álvaro Colom of Guatemala and Tabaré Vázquéz of Uruguay were both elected on their third attempts, and Brazil's da Silva on his *fourth*. Bolivia's Morales, Panama's Martín Torrijos and Ricardo Martinelli, Honduras' Porfirio Lobo Sosa and Chile's Sebastián Piñera all had run once unsuccessfully.

An encouraging trend in Latin American democracy that cannot be ignored is the increasing influence of women in a region once characterized by its *machismo*. Voters in five countries have elevated women to their presidencies: Violeta Barrios de Chamorro in Nicaragua (1990), Mireya Moscoso de Arias in Panama (1999), Michelle Bachelet in Chile (2006), Cristina Fernández de Kirchner in Argentina (2007) and Laura Chinchilla in Costa Rica (2010). In May 2010, Kamla Persad-Bessessar became the first female prime minister of Trinidad and Tobago.

On the down side, it appears some of the old dangers may be resurfacing. After Peru and Argentina opened the door to re-election, Fujimori and Menem sought Rooseveltian third consecutive terms. When Peru's electoral court rejected that as unconstitutional, Fujimori made an end-run around the judiciary, maintaining that his first election in 1990 was under the pre-1993 constitution and thus did not count. Opinion polls showed overwhelming sentiment against a third term, but when Fujimori's opposition in Congress attempted to call for a referendum to decide the issue as was done in Panama, Fujimori's allies squelched the initiative. Fujimori was "re-elected" in May 2000 in an election so blatantly fraudulent that the opposition boycotted it and international observers withdrew rather than participate in a flawed vote count. Fujimori was inaugurated for his third term, but public indignation and mounting evidence of scandal forced him to resign that November.

In Argentina, Menem disavowed another run in 1999, but bombastically vowed a comeback in 2003. He tried, but received only 24% of the vote and dropped out. He

Latin America Today

vowed to retake the presidency in the 2007 election; he did not.

In Venezuela, President Hugo Chávez wrote a new constitution that allowed him to serve two consecutive six-year terms, then sought to amend the constitution to allow him to run indefinitely. In December 2007, voters narrowly rejected that idea by 51%. Not one who enjoys being denied what he wants, Chávez called another referendum in February 2009, and this time 54.4% voted to allow him to run again—and again and again.

In Colombia, President Álvaro Uribe persuaded Congress to amend the constitution *again* to allow him to seek a third consecutive term, but on February 26, 2010, the Constitutional Court overturned the proposed amendment as a threat to democracy that violated the spirit of the 1958 constitution.

Another curious trend is the public's fascination in several countries with former strongmen or charismatic military figures who have entered politics. In Bolivia, former strongman Hugo Banzer was elected to the presidency by the Congress in 1997 after he won a plurality of the popular vote. He resigned after four years because of cancer, but he respected democratic institutions while in power.

In Guatemala, opinion polls once showed that the most popular political figure in the country was former military dictator Efraín Ríos Montt, a pariah in human rights circles for his alleged massacre of thousands of Indian peasants during his 1982–83 regime. He was barred by the

constitution from serving again as head of state, but he successfully appealed that restriction and ran for president in 2003, at the age of 77. When push came to shove, however, the Guatemalan people decided they weren't all that nostalgic for his jack-booted rule after all, and he ran a poor third.

A similar situation occurred in Paraguay. Former General Lino Oviedo, who had attempted a coup in 1996 and who was convicted and placed under house arrest, won the Colorado Party nomination for president over the opposition of incumbent civilian President Juan Carlos Wasmosy—himself of the Colorado Party. Polls indicated that Oviedo, who could not even leave his quarters to campaign, would win the 1998 election hands-down, causing Wasmosy to threaten to postpone the vote. The Supreme Court intervened and declared Oviedo's candidacy illegal, whereupon his running mate, Raúl Cubas, was elected president. Cubas then ordered the release of Oviedo, widely seen as the power behind the throne, a move that sparked a governmental crisis.

The public's fascination with Oviedo, however, dimmed after the 1999 assassination of Vice President Luis María Argaña, Oviedo's leading opponent within the Colorado Party. The day after President Cubas' resignation under threat of impeachment, Oviedo fled to Argentina, then to Brazil, where he was arrested in 2000. The Supreme Court ordered his release in 2001, and he vowed to return to Paraguay and run for the presidency.

Faced with imminent arrest, he remained in Brazil and again ran a surrogate candidate in 2003, who received only 13.5% of the vote, finishing fourth. Oviedo eventually returned to Paraguay, served his time in a military prison and at last ran for president in the 2008 election. Like Ríos Montt in Guatemala, he ran a distant third.

The most dramatic case of a modern-day *caudillo* continues to unfold in Venezuela. Former Lieutenant Colonel Hugo Chávez, who spent two years in prison for leading a failed attempt to overthrow President Carlos Andres Pérez in 1992, capitalized on public disgust with the corruption of the two traditional parties to run for president in 1998 as an independent populist. Chávez won a landslide victory. Upon assuming office in February 1999, he expressed his contempt for the legislative and judicial branches, then called for an election for a constituent assembly to rewrite the 1962 constitution. His adherents won 90% of the seats in that assembly, which then forged a new organic law that allowed Chávez to serve for two consecutive six-year terms, besides granting him broad new powers. Voters overwhelmingly approved the new constitution in 1999, whereupon Chávez called for a new presidential election in 2000. Chávez won with 59% of the vote, an even greater landslide than in 1998. An open admirer of Cuba's Fidel Castro, Chávez has openly expressed contempt for freedom of the press and the voices of dissent. He has voiced the familiar siren song of *caudillos* past who assume dictatorial powers: It is the only way to solve the country's problems.

Mounting opposition to Chávez's heavy-handed methods erupted into violence in April 2002, which led to an abortive military coup. Within 48 hours, additional violence by pro-Chávez mobs effected his return to power. Ironically, Chávez, like Argentina's Juan Perón, is an elected autocrat, a political oxymoron if there ever was one.

In 2004, Chávez's opponents succeeded in collecting more than the 2.4 million signatures needed for a recall election, but Chávez emerged stronger than ever when 59% of the voters chose not to remove him. In December 2006, he won another six-year term with 63%, showing just how polarized Venezuela remains between pro- and anti-Chávez camps. He plans to run again in 2012—and beyond.

A Chávez-like phenomenon occurred in troubled Ecuador, where Lucio Gutiérrez, a flamboyant colonel who spent six months in jail for his role in overthrowing Mahuad in 2000, was elected president in 2002 on a platform to clean up corruption and effect social justice. But then Gutiérrez fell from public favor when he

The Tikal Altar Stone, Guatemala

View of Montevideo, Uruguay

himself came under suspicion for corruption. In the face of mounting street protests demanding Gutiérrez's resignation, Congress removed him from office in 2005 and sent him into exile in Brazil, the third Ecuadorian president to be removed either by Congress or the military within eight years.

In Peru, a left-wing former lieutenant colonel, Ollanta Humala, who pledged the same type of radical reforms as Chávez, made it into the 2006 presidential runoff and was narrowly defeated by former President García.

There is nothing new about people in struggling societies turning to a strong-willed, charismatic leader who promises to bring order out of chaos, in Latin America or elsewhere. It evokes memories of the infamous explanation by an Italian woman for why Mussolini remained popular for so long: "Because he made the trains run on time." The fact that a former strongman is elected president in a free, honest popular vote does not in and of itself represent a threat to democracy; Brazil's Getulio Vargas (a civilian) and Chile's Carlos Ibáñez (a soldier) both were returned to power in free elections. Indeed, it is the very manifestation of the people's will. It can be argued that the United States has elevated a number of military heroes to the presidency—most recently in 1952 and 1956—without undermining its democracy. But the United States and Latin America have vastly different traditions where military presidents are concerned, and the question that remains unanswered at this juncture is whether military men who win power through the ballot box are committed democrats or Trojan horses who will disregard the democratic process if it becomes inconvenient to them.

Even when civilians are elected, Latin Americans have shown themselves incredibly impatient with new presidents who do not prove themselves to be Super-men (or women) who can solve all their countries' problems quickly.

An ambitious periodic 17-nation survey begun in 1996 by the Chilean polling firm *Latinobarómetro* for the British newsmagazine *The Economist* on Latin Americans' attitudes toward their young democracies gives cause for both cheer and alarm. Respondents are asked each year whether they agree with the statements, "Democracy is preferable to any other kind of government," and "In certain circumstances, an authoritarian government can be preferable to a democratic one." The Dominican Republic became the 18th nation in the survey in 2004.

In the 2008 survey, support for democracy since 1996 had increased in only five countries and decreased in 12; in the 2009 survey, it had increased in seven countries since 1996. Moreover, in 2007 support for democracy was below 50% in *nine* countries, in 2008 and 2009, in only five. It increased in 12 countries between 2008 and 2009, and decreased in six. The greatest one-year increase came in El Salvador: 18 percentage points, to 68%. The largest one-year decrease, 13 points, was in Colombia

FREEDOM RANKINGS, 2010		
Country	Score	Rating
Bahamas	2	Free
Barbados	2	Free
Canada	2	Free
Chile	2	Free
Costa Rica	2	Free
Uruguay	2	Free
USA	2	Free
Belize	3	Free
Granada	3	Free
Panama	3	Free
Argentina	4	Free
Brazil	4	Free
Dom. Rep.	4	Free
Suriname	4	Free
Trinidad-Tobago	4	Free
El Salvador	5	Free
Guyana	5	Free
Jamaica	5	Free
Mexico	5	Free
Peru	5	Free
Bolivia	6	Partly Free
Ecuador	6	Partly Free
Paraguay	6	Partly Free
Colombia	7	Partly Free
Honduras	8	Partly Free
Guatemala	8	Partly free
Nicaragua	8	Partly Free
Venezuela	9	Partly Free
Haiti	9	Partly free
Cuba	13	Not Free

SOURCE: Freedom House

and Ecuador. Interestingly, the highest support for democracy in 2009 was in Chávez's Venezuela, at 84%. The lowest support, 42%, was in Guatemala and—another surprise—Mexico.

Meanwhile, tolerance of authoritarian government increased in eight countries and decreased in eight between 1996 and 2010; El Salvador was 12% both years. The highest tolerance for authoritarianism is still Paraguay, at 31%, followed closely by Guatemala at 30%.

Overall, when the Latin America of 2008 is compared with the Latin America of 1977, there can be no disputing the advances that have been made toward democracy, so in fairness, the Latin American glass should be viewed as four-fifths full rather than one-fifth empty. In its 2010 report on overall freedom, in which it rates political rights and civil liberties on seven-point scales, Freedom House rated 10 of the 20 Latin American republics and all the English-speaking Caribbean as "free," nine Latin American countries as "partly free" and just one—Cuba—as "not free" (see "Freedom Rankings" table). The long-range prospects for democracy ultimately will depend on economic stability and development—and the patience and determination of the Latin Americans themselves.

Economic Diversification and the Trend Toward Free Trade

For more than a hundred years, most of the post-colonial Latin American countries languished in the economic doldrums while North America experienced robust economic growth and prosperity. Only Argentina experienced growth similar to that of the United States and Canada. Several factors condemned Latin America to the poverty from which it is only now beginning to emerge.

Just as Spain, Portugal and France failed to bequeath a democratic tradition to their former colonies, neither did they leave behind sound economic infrastructures. Sadly, these colonial powers were more concerned with exploitation than with development. Spain in particular was obsessed with how much precious metal could be extracted from the ground, not with agriculture or with building roads, schools or financial institutions.

Granted, the Jamestown colonists had come in search of gold, but when it became apparent that there was no gold in Virginia, the English recognized that the fecund soil offered other opportunities. The demand created for tobacco and later cotton generated the wealth that gold did not. Subsequent English and Scottish immigrants to the New World, whether to escape debtors' prison or religious per-

Latin America Today

secution, came prepared to exploit the wealth of the soil or to engage in mercantilism. This fostered an independent, entrepreneurial spirit that was carried over into the post-independence period.

In addition, the Industrial Revolution was exported successfully from Britain to America. Industry, agriculture and the advent of public education led in the 19th century to the rise of a literate middle class of independent farmers and merchants with political rights sandwiched between those who amassed great wealth and those left behind in destitution. The unique concept of homesteading, providing free title to land in return for working it, further broadened the base of the independent-minded middle class in the English colonies and later the United States. The opportunities it offered for self-advancement also sparked a wave of immigration that brought with it new zeal and new ideas.

There was no corresponding industrialization, democratization or mass education in Spain, Portugal and France or in most of their erstwhile colonies in the 19th

century. The result was a dual class structure in which a tiny, educated, wealthy elite, a disproportionate number of them Caucasian, held absolute economic and political power over a mass of desperately poor, illiterate Indian and *mestizo* peons or, in Brazil and Haiti, black slaves. This structure was enforced in some countries for decades by a lone dictator, such as Paraguay's Rodrigo Gaspar de Francia or Mexico's Porfirio Díaz. Thus, social inequality enforced at bayonet point and usually condoned by the Catholic Church, became the second major obstacle to Latin American development. Industrial growth requires a literate workforce.

The third major obstacle was monocultural dependency, the reliance of a country's economy on a single resource for export. This handicap persisted throughout the late 19th century and in some cases well into the 20th. Thus, Brazil and Colombia depended on coffee, Bolivia on tin, Chile on copper, Peru on guano fertilizer, Cuba, the Dominican Republic and Haiti on sugar, Venezuela on petroleum and Ecuador and the Central American republics on bananas. The derogatory term "banana republic" is another unfortunate Latin American stereotype, but again, it had some basis in fact. The products upon which these countries depended for foreign exchange were at the mercy of the world market. To use an old analogy, when the world tin market sneezed, Bolivia caught pneumonia.

Compounding this situation was a fourth obstacle, undercapitalization, which could only be overcome by surrendering control of the nation's one valuable resource to those who *did* have capital: foreign investors. Consequently, foreign-owned companies, mostly British and U.S., came to dominate these underdeveloped economies, exercising considerable political influence over their host governments. Probably the most egregious example was that of the United Fruit Company of the United States, which treated the Central American countries as private fiefs.

These deplorable conditions persisted decade after decade, as those with the power and money were able to maintain the status quo through force if necessary. Those lacking power could only submit. In those countries where democracy did manage to gain a temporary foothold in the late 19th and early 20th centuries—Argentina, Brazil, Chile and Uruguay—it is not surprising that socialist, communist and anarchist movements won adherents, much as they did in the United States during the same era. If misery existed under a capitalist system, the logic went, capitalism must be the enemy. Foreign capitalists were especially popular whipping boys. Expropriation of foreign holdings came

into vogue, beginning with Mexico's nationalization of the oil industry in 1938. Guerrilla movements also targeted foreign companies.

Latin American intellectuals, from the 1960s until the early '90s, almost universally followed like sheep a school of thinking known as "dependency theory," which held that Latin America was economically and culturally "dependent" upon the developed countries, especially the United States. Occasionally even reform-minded military officers would seize power with a promise to redress social wrongs, such as the military government in Peru from 1968–80 that sought to impose a socialist system based on the Yugoslav model. Marxism came to power by force of arms in Cuba in 1959 and in Nicaragua in 1979 and through the ballot box in Chile in 1970. Fidel Castro became an enticing role model.

Even conservative military regimes created state-owned corporations to run utilities, airlines, railroads, ports, mines and oil refineries. The realization that a cumbersome bureaucracy was a woefully inefficient way to provide reliable telephone or electrical service came slowly.

Other economic experiments like high protective tariffs and regional trade blocs were aimed at what were seen as sinister outside forces. Alas, these also proved a disappointment. Tariffs designed to protect fledgling local industries often created bloated monopolies that produced substandard and overpriced products. Trade blocs such as the Central American Common Market and the Andean Pact proved ineffectual because the member countries were not producing products for export that the other members wanted to import.

The right-wing Pinochet government in Chile proved to be the regional maverick when it withdrew from the Andean Pact and scuttled its protective tariffs to create a free-market economy based on the theories of Nobel Prize-winning U.S. economist Milton Friedman. Many of Pinochet's economic brain trust studied under Friedman at the University of Chicago, earning them the sobriquet, "Chicago Boys." The initial result was a disastrous recession as local businesses proved unable to compete with better and cheaper foreign imports. But gradually the economy equalized, showing real growth with single-digit inflation, something unattainable under the Marxist government of Salvador Allende. Pinochet also broke Chile's dependency on copper exports, promoting the export of fresh fruits. Chile's free-market strategy proved so successful that Pinochet's civilian successors have left it in place and it has been emulated by its neighbors. Alas, the Pinochet's regime's record in human rights is far less admirable.

PER CAPITA INCOME, 2008	
USA	$47,930
Canada	$43,640
Bahamas	$21,390
Trinidad-Tobago	$16,590
Mexico	$9,990
Chile	$9,370
Venezuela	$9,230
Uruguay	$8,260
Brazil	$7,300
Argentina	$7,190
Panama	$6,690
Costa Rica	$6,060
Grenada	$5,880
Jamaica	$4,800
Suriname	$4,760
Colombia	$4,620
Dom. Rep.	$4,330
Peru	$3,990
Cuba	$3,856*
Belize	$3,740
Ecuador	$3,690
El Salvador	$3,460
Guatemala	$2,680
Paraguay	$2,110
Honduras	$1,740
Bolivia	$1,460
Guyana	$1,450
Nicaragua	$1,080
Haiti	$975**
Barbados	N/A

* estimated min.; $11,905 max.
** or less
Latin America and Caribbean
Average: $6,768

SOURCE: World Bank (Atlas Method)

Not long after the creation of Chile's free-market model, the Soviet Bloc collapsed, taking down with it the discredited notion of a state-run economy. Like a chain of dominoes, Latin American countries began privatizing decades-old, state-owned corporations: Argentina, Brazil, Mexico, Peru and others. New policies, some of them draconian, also permitted Argentina, Brazil, Mexico and Peru to tame the hyperinflation that had become a seemingly permanent fixture throughout the 1970s and '80s.

Two presidents who were the very embodiments of Latin America's conversion from public sector to private sector dominance were Brazil's Fernando Henrique Cardoso (1995–2003), an erstwhile Marxist economist and leading dependency theorist, and Argentina's Carlos Saúl Menem (1989–99), a Peronist who steered the country on a course 180 degrees from that set by his patron saint, Juan Perón.

By the mid-1990s, Latin America was in the midst of an economic boom that had U.S. and European economists predicting that the region could repeat the success story of the robust export-oriented economies of Asia. This expectation was heightened by the catastrophic collapse of the Asian stock markets in late 1997. Mexico joined the North American Free Trade Agreement (NAFTA) in 1993, while Argentina, Brazil, Paraguay and Uruguay formed *Mercosur,* a trade bloc that showed moderate signs of success. The bloc almost collapsed in the wake of the economic crises in Argentina and Brazil, then showed signs of revitalization. So has the Andean Pact, composed of Bolivia, Colombia, Ecuador, Peru and Venezuela. In mid-2004, the two blocs discussed creating a South American free-trade area. In 2006, Venezuela became a member of *Mercosur,* but it seceded from the Andean Pact because Colombia and Peru signed bilateral trade agreements with the United States.

In the late 1990s, Latin America was experiencing regional economic growth that averaged a healthy 3% per year. In 1998, however, uncertainty over the Russian ruble caused a chain-reaction market panic that hit the United States, the major Asian stock markets, and then Brazil, Argentina and Mexico. The crisis worsened in January 1999 when the bottom dropped out of the Brazilian stock market; its government allowed its currency, the *real,* to float, and it lost 46% of its value. The panic spread to neighboring stock markets, and for a time it appeared a massive regional recession was likely. The market crisis coincided with a dramatic drop in the world market price of petroleum, which affected the economies of Venezuela, Ecuador and Mexico. The situation eventually stabilized.

No longer seen as bogeymen, foreign investors were not only welcome but openly courted, and the political stability spreading through the region made it an attractive target for investment. In addition, tourism continued to expand, providing jobs and a pollution-free source of foreign exchange.

Following up on the concept of NAFTA and *Mercosur,* U.S. President Bill Clinton invited the Western Hemisphere's heads of state, minus Cuba's Fidel Castro, to Miami in 1993 for the First Summit of the Americas. There, the idea of establishing a hemisphere-wide Free Trade Area of the Americas (FTAA), with membership limited to democratic countries, was first advanced.

At the Second Summit of the Americas in Santiago, Chile, in 1998, the 34 heads of state (once again, Castro was not invited), approved blueprints to establish the FTAA by 2005. Also recognizing that true economic development is dependent upon an educated workforce, the summit's communiqué called for the expenditure of $6.1 billion over three years to improve education. It also set a goal that 100% of the hemisphere's children would have access to elementary education and 75% would have access to secondary education by 2010.

The Third Summit of the Americas was held in Quebec City, Canada, in 2001, and once again the FTAA was the top agenda item. The new U.S. president, George W. Bush, was an even more enthusiastic advocate of the FTAA than Clinton. The heads of state set a target date of January 1, 2005, for establishment of what would become the world's largest free-trade bloc, encompassing 800 million people and accounting for an estimated $15 trillion in trade. The concept was not without its nay-sayers. In the streets of Quebec, protesters representing labor unions, environmental groups and various anti-capitalist organizations engaged in violent protests in an attempt to break up the summit. Inside the summit, Venezuela's Chávez charged that the lofty goals of the Miami and Santiago summits of reducing poverty had not been met, while Brazilian President Cardoso complained about U.S. anti-dumping laws.

A harbinger of doom for the FTAA came at a 2003 meeting of the World Trade Organization in Cancun, Mexico, which collapsed largely because of the opposition of Latin American members. At a "mini" Summit of the Americas in Monterrey, Mexico, in 2004, Chávez was joined by two powerful new anti-FTAA allies, Luiz Inácio "Lula" da Silva of Brazil and Néstor Kirchner of Argentina. Besides the anti-dumping issue, they demanded a reduction in U.S. agricultural subsidies so

their exports could compete. The United States, meanwhile, pressed for greater protection for intellectual property.

Meanwhile, *Mercosur* embarked on concluding free-trade pacts with the Andean Pact, Mexico, and the European Union, though the talks with the EU broke down. The target date for the FTAA quietly passed, and even Bush acknowledged the FTAA was moribund when the Fourth Summit of the Americas convened in Mar del Plata, Argentina in 2005. The summit accomplished nothing of substance.

At the Fifth Summit of the Americas in Port-of-Spain, Trinidad in 2009, the climate was even more hostile to the FTAA, and the new U.S. president, Barack Obama, prudently avoided the subject.

As with the trend toward democracy, the dramatic improvement in the Latin American economy has had its negative aspects, as well as nagging, unremedied problems: the continued gap between the very wealthy and the very poor; endemic corruption; environmental pollution; urban overpopulation; and an underground economy based on the illegal traffic of drugs.

According to a report released in 1996 by the U.N. Economic Commission for Latin America and the Caribbean (ECLA), one third of Latin Americans lived in poverty and 18 percent of them lived in *dire* poverty, earning less than $1 a day. Even in comparatively affluent countries such as Uruguay, the wealthiest 10 percent of the population had access to 15 times the resources of the poorest 10 percent; in Honduras and Peru, the figure was 80 times.

Ten years later, the overall economic picture had improved dramatically. In 2006, according to ECLA, regional economic growth was a healthy 5.3%, the

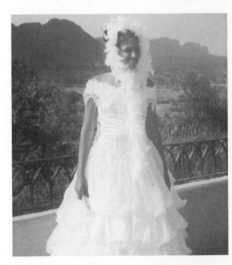

Quinceañera, a special 15th birthday celebration
Photo by Gary Seldomridge

Latin America Today

third consecutive year of strong growth, while once-feared inflation was only 4.8%; per capita income had risen 11.7% since 2003. The percentage of Latin Americans living in poverty had declined from 44% in 2002 to 38.5% in 2006. However, the fact that poverty still afflicts more than a third of the population remains a nagging social, economic and political issue.

In these emerging democracies, the impatient masses now have access to the ballot box, and they have been using it. Latin America has seen a rebirth of the once-discredited movements of the left, with their siren song of help for the underprivileged. The election of Chávez in Venezuela in 1998 was followed by the elections of such populists as da Silva in Brazil and Lucio Gutiérrez in Ecuador in 2002; Néstor Kirchner in Argentina in 2003; Tabaré Vázquez in Uruguay in 2004; Evo Morales in Bolivia and Manuel Zelaya in Honduras in 2005; Alan García in Peru, Rafael Correa in Ecuador and Daniel Ortega in Nicaragua in 2006; Álvaro Colom in Guatemala in 2007; Fernando Lugo in Paraguay in 2008; and Mauricio Funes in El Salvador in 2009.

Such newly industrialized countries as Mexico, Argentina, Brazil and Chile are learning quickly what it took the United States and other developed economies more than a century to discover: that industrialization carries an expensive environmental price tag. The air pollution in Mexico City, Santiago and São Paulo is notorious, as well as a serious health hazard. Rivers and coastlines have become dumping grounds for the toxic waste byproducts of heavy industry. Brazil did not begin to take action until 1998 to slow the destruction of the vast Amazon rain forests in the name of agriculture, an environmental rape that had raised international concerns for its exacerbation of global warming.

In most of these still-underprivileged countries, this is a price they have been willing to pay in order to provide jobs for growing urban populations. But unless some solutions are found soon, those who are "lucky" enough to find work in the major cities may find that they have condemned themselves and their children to early graves.

An encouraging economic and environmental trend is the growth of ethanol plants in sugar-producing countries to meet the world's growing demand for the alternative fuel in the face of escalating petroleum prices. Brazil pioneered the manufacture of ethanol from sugar cane and of ethanol-powered vehicles in the 1970s to reduce its dependence on imported petroleum, and other tropical countries have begun to realize the potential of the fuel, which burns cleaner than gasoline. Moreover, ethanol made from sugar cane has a greater yield per acre and is less expensive to produce than the corn-based ethanol produced in the United States. Latin America stands to be a major exporter, as well as consumer, of ethanol, in the coming years, although critics, such as Venezuela's Chávez, warn that diverting food crops to ethanol will worsen world-wide hunger.

Unchecked population growth has been problematical in countries ranging from industrial giants such as Mexico and Brazil to desperately poor agrarian Haiti. Too often social scientists in developed countries, many of whom apparently never visit Latin America, are too quick to single out the Roman Catholic Church's ban on contraception as the primary culprit. Although this is a factor, the urban middle classes in Latin America have proven just as willing to practice birth control in defiance of the pope as Roman Catholics in North America or Europe. Most of the population growth occurs in the lower economic strata, but not because they are more devout Catholics.

There are long-standing cultural factors at play as well. The *macho* ethic holds that the number of children a man sires is an outward manifestation of his virility, his very manhood. Moreover, as is the case in Africa and Asia, poor Latin Americans dependent upon agriculture for their existence see children as future field hands, someone to help carry their burdens as they themselves age. Such traditions cannot be overcome by government decree, but until some way is found to ensure that the number of new job-seekers does not exceed supply, Latin America's newly affluent cities will continue to be ringed by slums populated by those with high expectations, waiting their turn for a better life that may never come.

The drug trade has created in some areas the illusion of prosperity. In reality, it has brought back the monocultural dependence of poor farmers on a single cash crop. In the cities, it has brought fabulous wealth to a tiny cadre of drug lords, wealth that has trickled down in droplets to the veritable army of lab processors, transporters, security personnel and others who have been enticed away from legitimate pursuits by the promise of quick, if venal, wealth.

It has been estimated that the Rodríguez Orijuela brothers, Gilberto and Miguel, the leaders of the Cali Cartel of Colombia who were extradited to the United States in 2004, are worth $250 billion. But the wealth drugs generate is illusionary—there is so much of it there is nothing left on which to spend it. Further, the real economies within which the drug trade operates cannot officially incorporate it. Governments cannot tax billions in revenue that is not legal and not claimed. Moreover, it proves a drain on the economy because governments must spend millions on enforcement that proves futile, while the very governmental institutions that seek vainly to bring this illicit industry to bay are themselves corrupted from the top down by the drug barons.

The futility is exacerbated by the rather naive counter-narcotics policies of the consuming countries of the north. For years, the hope has been that somehow impoverished peasants can be made to see that they are endangering lives in Los Angeles or Chicago and that they can be persuaded to substitute cultivating coca with another cash crop—whose yield per hectare may be one tenth as much. Unless the insatiable demand for narcotics can be curbed in the consuming countries, there will be poor Latin Americans willing to run the risks to cultivate, process and transport drugs.

Technological Emergence

Yet another stereotype of Latin America, persistently reinforced by Hollywood, is of a backward region with muddy streets and antiquated technology. In the rural areas, that is still too often the case. But in the major cities, the economic boom has led inevitably to investment in modernizing the technological infrastructures. The impetus is the very essence of free-market capitalism: the necessity to compete. Visitors to even the poorer capital cities of most Latin American capitals will find computers literally everywhere, in hotels, banks, newspapers, universities and even small businesses. Internet cafés are trendy. To ignore computerization is to fall behind the competition.

The communications revolution also has pervaded Latin America. For example, the tallest structure on the Santiago, Chile, skyline, just two blocks from the Moneda (presidential) Palace along Avenida Bernardo O'Higgins, is the Entel Tower, bristling with antennas and satellite dishes linking Santiago with the interior and with the rest of the world. Guests at even mid-priced hotels in a country like Guatemala may be surprised to find CNN and HBO on their television sets. Again, competition demands this. Cell phone use exploded in Latin America in the 1990s, largely because it was quicker and cheaper to subscribe to cell phone service that to wait for weeks or months to have a more expensive conventional telephone installed by a cumbersome state-owned utility.

As is the case in developed countries, the technological revolution has been an upward spiral, with innovation breeding innovation. Some of these countries, such as Brazil and Chile, now manufacture their own computer hardware and software. Free-trade agreements facilitate the transfer of technology across international boundaries.

If there is a negative picture at all in the technological emergence of Latin America, it is that there is still a long way to go. If public investment is made in upgrading public transportation, perhaps with modern subway systems such as Santiago's, it could help lessen the air pollution crises in the capital cities; as bad as Santiago's air quality is, it would be worse if the subway had not supplanted hundreds of buses belching oily exhaust from the combustion of cheap fuel. Despite advances in medical technology, more funds need to be invested in that sector to acquire state-of-the-art equipment. If the current economic expansion continues, it is inevitable that technological expansion will continue in its wake.

Cultural Growth and Projection

There is no more a "Latin American culture" than there is a homogenous U.S. or European culture. Which music, for example, is indicative of U.S. culture: jazz, blues, country-western, bluegrass, rock 'n' roll, rap, or grunge rock? The answer, of course, is all of the above. Is there a typically European art, literary style, music, architecture, fashion or cuisine? They vary, of course, from country to country.

Latin American culture—or better described, cultures—also are regionalized.

The stereotype of the Latin American as a devout Catholic *mestizo* who speaks Spanish, wears white *campesino* cotton clothing, listens to mariachi music and eats spicy food is as far from reality as the Latin American stereotype of the "typical" gringo as a rich, Anglo-Saxon Protestant who wears Calvin Klein jeans, listens to rock music and eats nothing but steak or hamburgers. (All right, maybe there's a kernel of truth to the rock and hamburger part.)

The North American view of Latin America understandably has been geographically influenced by neighboring Mexico. As Don Podesta of the *Washington Post* once wrote, Mexico is "a prism through which all Latin culture is viewed." But it is a woefully distorted view. In reality, the majority of South Americans are Portuguese-speaking Brazilians. Chile has a Lutheran minority of more than 10% stemming from German immigration in the 19th century, while nearly 40% of Guatemalans are converts to evangelical Protestantism. Mariachi music is no more, nor less, representative of Latin America than are Argentina's tango, Brazil's samba, the salsa of the Caribbean countries, the flute music of the Andean highlands, Chile's *huaso* music or the harp-based folk music of Paraguay. An Argentine accustomed to his bland meat-and-pasta diet would probably gag on chili-pepper-laced *ceviche*, a concoction of raw fish and lime juice peculiar to the Pacific coast countries.

Ethnically, the Hispanic colonies evolved far differently from their counterparts in North America, or for that matter, in Brazil. The English colonizers pushed the Indian tribes back beyond the ever-expanding frontier, or simply exterminated them, while for manual labor in the fields they imported black slaves from West Africa. The Portuguese followed a roughly similar policy in Brazil. The Spanish, meanwhile, enslaved the Indian populations they found there, pressing them into service in the mines and on the *haciendas*. But while miscegenation was limited between the English on the one hand and the Indians and black slaves on the other, it was widespread in Brazil and the Spanish colonies, producing a mixed race of *mestizos* in the Hispanic realm, and of *mulattos* in Brazil.

This ethnic mosaic was not woven evenly, which resulted in the cultural discreteness of today. The Argentines, like their counterparts in the United States, followed a shameless policy of genocide against the indigenous inhabitants, with the result that its culture is preponderantly Caucasian-European. So is that of Costa Rica, but there the white settlers found the land largely uninhabited. In Guatemala, Peru and Bolivia, the undiluted Indian races are in the majority. Perhaps the most diversified cultural tapestry is that of Panama, where apart from whites, *mestizos* and Indians there are the descendants of black laborers brought

A Garifuna band performs in Tegucigalpa, Honduras. The Garifunas are descendants of escaped African slaves who settled along the Caribbean coast of Central America.   *Photo by the author*

Latin America Today

from the Caribbean early in this century to construct the canal, and the Orientals who came later.

Just as the Anglo-Saxon stereotype is fading in the United States, so is the Hispanic stereotype no longer *apropiado* in Latin America, and for the same reason: successive waves of massive immigration beginning in the late 19th century and continuing to the present. Roughly half of all Argentines and Uruguayans, for example, are of Italian lineage, descendants of migrant farmworkers who came to harvest grapes because of the reversed seasons and decided to stay. Germans, British and other Europeans also flocked to Argentina, Uruguay and Chile, as did European Jews seeking escape from persecution. Spanish Republicans seeking refuge after their defeat in the 1936–39 civil war settled throughout the region. Most Latin American countries also have unassimilated colonies of Arabs, Gypsies, blacks, and Orientals.

To underscore just how much of a melting pot Latin America has become, we have only to consider the surnames of some of the recent elected presidents in more than one half of the former Spanish colonies over the past two decades: Sanguinetti in Uruguay and Martinelli in Panama (Italian); Fujimori in Peru (Japanese); Aylwin in Chile (Welsh); Frei in Chile (Swiss); Wasmosy in Paraguay (Hungarian); Menem in Argentina, Bucaram and Mahaud in Ecuador and Saca in El Salvador (Arab); Fox in Mexico (English), Kirchner in Argentina (German), Berger in Guatemala (Belgian) and Bachelet in Chile (French). By contrast, of its 43 presidents, the United States has had but seven without Anglo-Saxon surnames: Van Buren and the two Roosevelts (Dutch), Kennedy and Reagan (Irish), Eisenhower (German) and Obama (Kenyan).

Language, religion and ethnicity may be the roots of a culture, but its flowers are thoughts, ideas and expressions. In this regard, Latin America represents a veritable cultural nursery, one that finally has begun achieving recognition from the rest of the world. To be sure, U.S. and European cultural influences are much in evidence, ranging from Coca-Cola, McDonald's and Calvin Klein to the *plan europeo* practiced by the hotels and the architecture that makes cities like Buenos Aires, Rio de Janeiro and Santiago appear like New World copies of Madrid, Milan or Lisbon.

The dependency theorists who warned that Latin America was economically subjugated by the United States also wrung their hands over perceived U.S. cultural intrusion; for some reason, they never seemed threatened by European influences. Despite Coca-Cola, McDonald's, Calvin Klein, Rambo, rock music and the ubiquitous "I Love Lucy" reruns, the *dependentistas* wasted a great deal of bile for nothing. The Latin American cultures not only were not supplanted, but Latin American art, music, literature, cinema and television have grown into distinctive genres in their own right, and these cultural expressions have been projected to the developed world.

Five Latin Americans have received the Nobel Prize for Literature: Gabriela Mistral of Chile (1945), Miguel Angel Asturias of Guatemala (1967), Pablo Neruda of Chile (1971), Gabriel García Márquez of Colombia (1982), and Octavio Paz of Mexico (1990), all of whose works have been translated into several languages.

Because Latin American art, music, literature and cinema are so individualistic according to nation, they are described more fully under the "Culture" section of each nation contained in this book.

Latin American television development lagged well behind that of the United States and Europe, and because of its higher price tag it was usually the governments that led the way. This made television, like radio, an important political tool and a pawn in the quest for power. An exception was in Chile, where the first three stations were licensed to major universities. In recent years, state-owned television stations have yielded increasingly to privatization; in several countries, as in Britain, privately owned stations compete with the government station or network. In its early days, television programming in Latin America was crude, unreliable and heavily dependent on translated imported programs from the United States, which were cheaper than producing programs locally. This reality lent grist to the argument of the cultural dependency theorists.

That has changed dramatically since the 1970s, with Mexico, Brazil, Argentina, Venezuela, Colombia and Chile all producing that uniquely Latin American soap opera, the *telenovela*, both for domestic consumption and for export. Variety shows are reminiscent of those of the United States in the 1950s and 1960s. One that reaches a hemispheric audience is *Sábado Gigante,* transmitted every Saturday from Miami but emceed by a Chilean, Mario Krutzberger, better known by the stage name Don Francisco.

Latin America has embraced U.S.-style sitcoms and news magazine shows, and some U.S. imports are still in evidence, but the dependency theorists' fears that they would outpace demand for programs produced in the native language have not been realized.

Latin American high culture and pop culture have received increasing acceptance in the United States and other developed countries. Novelists like García Márquez, Mario Vargas Llosa of Peru, Carlos Fuentes of Mexico and Isabel Allende of Chile are widely translated into English and other languages. Film stars like Salma Hayek of Mexico regularly are cast in U.S. films, while pop singers like Colombia's Shakira are winning Grammy Awards. U.S. baseball has witnessed a huge infusion of Latin American talent, like Sammy Sosa of the Dominican Republic and "El Duque" Hernández of Cuba.

Looking Forward . . .

In attempting to digest this description of the political, economic, technological

The home of Nobel Laureate Pablo Neruda (1904–73) at Isla Negra, Chile, is now a museum visited by tens of thousands of Chilean and foreign visitors a year. Neruda, whose poetry has been translated into several languages, was one of five Latin Americans to have won the Nobel Prize in Literature.
Photo by the author

and cultural realities of Latin America today, one must invariably return to the analogous glass that is half full rather than half empty. Unquestionably, advances have been made, but the remaining shortcomings must be acknowledged and addressed.

Another indicator of hope is Latin America's seeming abandonment of its policy of paranoia vis-à-vis its neighbor to the north. Granted, the United States did much to warrant paranoia with its policy of gunboat diplomacy and CIA-sponsored intrigue. A sardonic joke underscored the Latin American view of the United States: Why are there never military coups in the United States? Because they don't have an American Embassy!

The most recent U.S. military intervention in the region, in Haiti in 1994, however well intentioned it may have been, inevitably raised eyebrows anew in Latin American capitals. For that reason, virtually all Latin American governments opposed in principle the U.S. invasion of far-off Iraq in 2003. Still, the United States is not seen quite as the bogeyman it once was, and country after country has elected presidents who earned undergraduate or graduate degrees in the United States, something that is no longer a political stigma.

Meanwhile, the relationship of old that bordered on paternalism has yielded to one of a more equitable partnership in terms of trade. The stubborn resistance of Venezuela, Brazil and Argentina to the FTAA underscores the region's growing independence. But even leftist presidents who oppose the FTAA have welcomed bilateral trade with the U.S. and, of course, U.S. investments.

Another encouraging sign of growing Latin American independence from the United States since the advent of democracy has been the trend toward regional cooperation and integration. In 1986, 19 democratic countries established the so-called Rio Group—17 of the Spanish-speaking republics (less Cuba), Brazil and Guyana. Unlike the Organization of American States (see U.S.-Latin American Relations), the United States is not a signatory. The Rio Group was created to promote democracy within the region, but its annual summits provide the heads of state of these nations an opportunity to discuss issues of mutual concern, including all those listed in the previous paragraph plus regional trade, drug trafficking, terrorism and political unrest.

An even newer organization, the South American Union of Nations, or *UNASUR* in Spanish, was established in Cuzco, Peru, in 2004. The presidents of six countries and foreign ministers of six others signed the accord: the 10 Spanish- or Portuguese-speaking countries of South America, plus Guyana and Suriname. The group was the outgrowth of talks between South America's two free-trade blocs, *Mercosur* and the Andean Pact, to create a continent-wide free-trade zone, which has a combined gross domestic product of about $1 trillion. The presidents of Brazil and Peru also announced their countries would collaborate to construct the first east-west highway across the continent from ocean to ocean, which they said would further integration even more. The new community is largely the brainchild of Brazilian President da Silva. Citing the European Union as a model, da Silva said he envisions, eventually, a unified continent with a central government, one foreign policy and a common currency. At a summit in Buenos Aires in May 2010, attended by 10 of the 12 presidents, former Argentine President Kirchner was unanimously elected *USASUR*'s secretary-general, and the organization will be headquartered temporarily in Buenos Aires.

Other issues must be addressed, however, if Latin America is to continue to develop democratically, socially and economically. Mob rule to force out duly elected presidents must be eschewed. Otherwise, political anarchy will lead to the type of instability that invites a return to authoritarianism. Press freedom must be respected as an independent check on would-be autocrats. Environmental pollution, that inevitable by-product of development, threatens the health of the next generation. Institutionalized corruption is still a political and economic leech on the lifeblood of almost all the countries of the region (see Corruption Perceptions Index). Hygiene and health care still lag far behind those of the developed world. Most importantly, that next generation needs to be provided with better education. Latin America continues to trail the developed world and the emerging countries of Asia in educational quality. The next generation must be more than merely literate; it must join the computer age.

The hemisphere's greatest remaining blight, the anachronistic totalitarian system in Cuba, must inevitably acquiesce to the weight of history. Fidel Castro has imprisoned dissenters—78 alone in the crackdown of 2003, bringing the total to more than 300—and has resisted international calls for reform. In response to the "Varela Project," a petition signed by 11,000 courageous dissenters in 2002 that called for a referendum on free elections and freedom of expression, Castro responded with a "petition" of his own, signed by a suspicious 8.2 million people, for a constitutional amendment that would make his dogmatic Marxist system "untouchable." The National Assembly dutifully passed this constitutional amendment-to-outlaw-constitutional amendments, 557-0. Castro thus threw down his gauntlet before the domestic and international chorus for reform, raising the specter of a violent struggle for power when he finally dies. That death now appears imminent, and in 2008 he resigned as president and relinquished much of his power to his brother, Raúl. There are small but encouraging signs that Raúl Castro may at least be open to new ideas, and he released about 60 of the prisoners of conscience. Yet, Cuba remains the least-free nation of the hemisphere.

The overall trend in Latin America toward greater political freedom, economic development, technological expansion, cultural individuality and regional integration is evident. There have inevitably been setbacks. There will be more. But for the moment, Latin America appears to be investing in its future, and its stock is clearly on the rise.

CORRUPTION PERCEPTIONS INDEX 2009		
Country	World Rank	Score
New Zealand	9.4	1
Canada	8.7	8
USA	7.5	19
Barbados	7.4	20
Chile	6.7	25
Uruguay	6.7	25
Puerto Rico	5.8	35
Costa Rica	5.3	43
Cuba	4.4	61
Brazil	3.7	75
Colombia	3.7	75
Peru	3.7	75
Suriname	3.7	75
Trinidad-Tobago	3.6	79
El Salvador	3.4	84
Guatemala	3.4	84
Panama	3.4	84
Mexico	3.3	89
Dominican Republic	3.0	99
Jamaica	3.0	99
Argentina	2.9	106
Bolivia	2.7	120
Guyana	2.6	126
Honduras	2.5	130
Nicaragua	2.5	130
Ecuador	2.2	146
Paraguay	2.1	154
Venezuela	1.9	162
Haiti	1.8	168
Somalia	1.1	180
Bahamas, Grenada		not ranked

SOURCE: Transparency International

Robert T. Buckman
Lafayette, Louisiana, June 2010

The Early Americans

THE GEOGRAPHICAL FACTOR

The development of few civilizations have been so influenced by geographical factors as those in Latin America. Contrary to long held beliefs, the land of Central and South America is neither young nor generally fertile. Old and trampled by several civilizations, large territories had already been abandoned by the Indians, even before the arrival of the Spaniards. The Mayas probably exhausted their initial homeland, and the Incas called the vast desert regions between Peru and Chile "the land of hunger and death." Furthermore, the continent had few and scattered ports and is internally divided by rugged mountains, jungles, turbulent rivers and arid zones, which constitute formidable obstacles for communication or exploitation of natural resources.

Thus, since pre-Columbian times, human societies developed in sort of isolated clusters having little contact with other communities. The Spanish policy of building cities as centers of political power increased this basic pattern of concentration and regionalism. Consequently, once the unifying authority of the Spanish king collapsed, it was impossible to keep all those remote and distant cities under a common authority. Immediately, almost every important urban center felt capable of demanding and asserting its own independence.

Geography not only contributed to this fragmentation, but also greatly determined the acceleration of two negative social trends which continue to hinder Latin American progress: (1) the abnormal growth of cities, especially capitals, constantly attracting masses of impoverished peasants—Mexico City's population jumped from less than 5 million in 1963 to 13.1 million in 2000—and (2) the lack of balance in the national population distribution. In almost every Latin country, the population is concentrated in one-third to one-half of its national territory, leaving large zones almost totally uninhabited. Such conditions make the exploitation of the hinterland's resources a difficult and costly enterprise.

Indian Civilizations

When the Spaniards and other Europeans reached the New World, they found the native Americans in various stages of cultural development. Thinly scattered nomadic tribes of hunters and fishermen who also practiced simple farming populated much of the region. In contrast, three groups of natives—the Mayas, the Aztecs and the Incas—developed comparatively sophisticated and complex civilizations. They constructed large cities with imposing architectural styling, organized empires, acquired a knowledge of mathematics and astronomy and worked in pre-

cious stones and metals. The majority of these Indian civilizations had a sort of fatalistic concept of life and the universe; their worship halls and temples were full of terrifying gods who incessantly demanded sacrifices, usually human. Their societies were stratified by class division and were based more on communal interest and units than on individual achievements. Furthermore, vast distances and geographical obstacles hindered enlightening inter-cultural relations, while the absence of horses, cows or any pack animals limited their economic expansion or mass mobility. Perhaps because of such limitations, only one of these civilizations, the Mayas, developed some form of primitive writing, while none discovered the practical use of the wheel. In spite of intense research by scientists and archaeologists, we don't have yet a clear picture of the intricate aspects of the social systems and collective beliefs of pre-Columbian Indian society. Many questions remain to be answered.

The Mayas (Guatemala, Mexico, Belize, Honduras, El Salvador)

As the most advanced and sophisticated of the early American civilizations, Mayan culture flourished for more than 1,000 years, reaching the peak of its development in the 7th and 8th centuries A.D. Mayan life was sustained by a single basic crop: corn, which grew in such abundance that it allowed them time to engage in a multitude of activities other than raising food, thus raising their lifestyles above that of the other Indian societies which remained tied to the soil in order simply to exist. Apparently the Mayas lived mostly in independent city states, tied together by an extensive road system and a common culture. A warlike people, the Mayas placed most political power in the hands of an extended royal family and priests. Mayan religion was based on the worship of many gods, but the practice declined with the growing sophistication of the society. Initially, religious ceremonies called for frequent human sacrifices. Art and architecture were not greatly inferior to that of Europe at the time. As pioneers in the use of mathematics and astronomy, the Mayas refined an advanced calendar as early as the 4th century B.C. They also devised the mathematical concept of *zero* and developed a highly complex form of writing based on hieroglyphics (picture writing) which until today remains partially undeciphered.

Among the greatest achievements of the Mayas was art, including sculpture, pottery and textiles. Foremost was architecture. Major reminders of the Mayan civilization survive today in the form of thousands of monumental temples, soaring pyramids and majestic palaces. Many of these impressive structures have been discovered only recently, enveloped in the lush, tropical jungles of Central America and southern Mexico. These vestiges of the past, however, have yet to reveal why the Mayas suddenly abandoned their great cities long before the arrival of the Spaniards. Was it due to massive crop failure? Was it pestilence? Military defeat? Rebellion by slaves? The answer to this question is slowly being revealed—it probably involved the split-up of a large empire because of rivalries, followed by succession of unnumbered small states each with its own fortification and the fascination of the people with constant warfare. The techniques of siege were probably perfected, and they killed each other off to an extent that those remaining simply disappeared into the thick foliage to live as primitives.

The Aztecs (Mexico)

When Hernán Cortés landed on the Mexican coast in 1519, the Aztec empire

Aztec goddess *Coatlicue*

was at the very height of its power and development. Assimilating the knowledge and achievements of previous civilizations such as the Olmecs and the Toltecs, the Aztecs developed into a harsh and efficient military society which allowed them to conquer all of central Mexico from the Atlantic to the Pacific. This brutal form of domination provoked constant rebellions among the tribes they subjugated, from whom they extracted slaves and human victims for sacrifice to their gods. In one especially dry season, Montezuma I, claiming that "the gods are thirsty," sacrificed 20,000 human beings on Aztec altars.

The Aztec social system rested on a rigid class structure with most manual work being performed by slaves captured during military campaigns. The economy was based on corn. Aztec architecture was impressive and their capital city of Tenochtitlán, now the site of Mexico City, was described by the conquering Spaniards as being equal to any in Europe. Although not as advanced as the Mayas had been in the use of science, mathematics or writing, the Aztecs did develop a more cohesive empire, even though it was based on force. The widespread resentment among enslaved neighboring groups was shrewdly exploited by Cortés to topple the Aztec empire.

Incas (Peru, Ecuador, Bolivia)

The empire carved out of the rugged Andes by the Incas reached its greatest level of development about a century before the arrival of the Spaniards. Through conquest of weaker Indian tribes in the region, the Incas expanded their realm from Peru through southern Colombia, Ecuador and Bolivia, and northern Chile—a

Mayan ruins at Tikal, Guatemala

The Early Americans

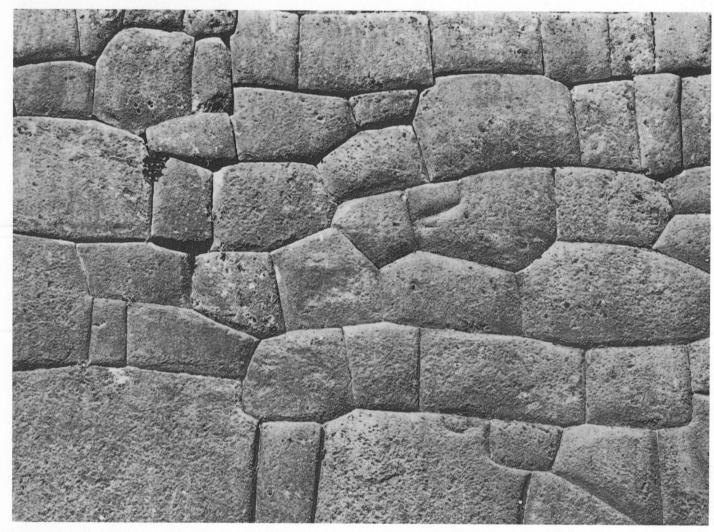

Detail of an Inca stone wall in Cuzco, Peru

combined area of more than 350,000 square miles. Facilitated by an efficient administrative command, a courier communications network and an impressive road system rivaling that of the Roman Empire, the Incas were able to weave their vast domain into the most highly organized and efficient civilization of all the native Americans.

At the head of the entire system was the ruling god-emperor called Inca. Under him was a highly structured noble class and priests, followed by lower level officials. The rigid chain of command permeated every corner of the empire. The Incas integrated newly conquered tribes into the realm by imposing a single language, *Quechua*, religion and social structure. Except for the highly rigid caste system of the ruling elite, the Inca state came close to being a totalitarian socialist state. All property was owned by the state and all work was organized on a communal basis. Through a system called "mita" (which the Spaniards later immediately

adopted in the region) all members of the lower classes were obliged to work free for the empire for a period of four months every year. In return, the empire provided for the needs of its citizens. The result was a rather dull life for the masses—with little incentive, capability or effort to rebel.

The heart of the empire was the capital of Cuzco (literally "navel" in Quechua). A magnificent city by almost any standard, Cuzco glistened with enormous palaces and temples (many of which were lavishly decorated with gold) and other imposing dwellings which housed the elite. Even today, some of these structures are still in use, having withstood for centuries the abuses of man and the elements.

Although the Incas were less developed than the Mayas in the skills of writing, mathematics and astronomy, they surpassed the Mayas in architecture, water works, stonework and engineering. Indeed, some lengthy Inca suspension bridges were found when the Europeans reached the area and remained in use un-

til the middle of the 19th century. Inca systems of irrigation, pottery, textiles, medicines and even surgical techniques were remarkable. The Incas' greatest gift to the world, however, was the potato, which in time would save tens of thousands of Europeans from starvation. Despite its vast power, the Inca empire quickly fell to the *conquistadores*. The reasons for the sudden collapse of America's greatest Indian civilization were numerous: the Spaniards possessed superiority in firearms, employed advanced military tactics, exploited the advantage of horses and were relentlessly driven onward by the lure of gold. In contrast, the Inca empire was mortally weakened by a rigid social system in which the vital administrative structure was paralyzed once the top Inca was captured. In addition, a devastating war of succession between two royal Inca brothers had left the empire exhausted and divided. As a result, the Incas fell easy prey to a band of only 184 conquerors led by a cunning Francisco Pizarro.

Major Native Cultures About 1500

The Early Americans

from the colonial period; its influence is waning as Indians migrate to the larger cities.

Scattered remnants of Indian civilization retreated from Spanish influence to the mountains of Guatemala, Ecuador, Peru and Bolivia, while the majority remained under Spanish rule. Until recent times, many of the Indians have succeeded in preserving their ancient communal life and customs. Today, the Quechua-speaking Indians still number some 6 million in Bolivia and 2 million in Ecuador. Although their living conditions have scarcely improved since Pizarro's time, Andean Indians have remained detached and suspicious of meager government efforts to incorporate these survivors of the Inca Empire into a modern social and economic structure.

Efforts to modernize traditional Indian lifestyles have also been painfully slow in Central America and Mexico. In Guatemala, the descendants of the Mayas have largely continued to cling to their traditional customs despite government programs to encourage change. Even in Mexico, the most *mestizo* country in Latin America, many of Aztec and Mayan ancestry, particularly in the southern area, still have only marginal contact with the 20th century—even though modernization of Indian lifestyles has been a nominal objective of the Mexican government.

The process of social change has accelerated since World War II with the aid of modern communications—particularly the transistor radio—which have helped to penetrate the isolation that has allowed outmoded social, economic and political conditions to persist in the remote hinterlands.

Recently some Latin American governments, particularly those of Mexico and Peru, have begun to show an increasing appreciation of the contributions and heritage of the early American civilizations. This growing interest has not been without cost. The rising appeal for Indian art has led to large-scale looting of ancient monuments and graves. In Central America and in the Andes, art thieves have stolen priceless stonework, jewelry and pottery—irreparably damaging some of it in the process—in an effort to satisfy the modern demand for genuine ancient art. In that sense, today's art thieves are continuing the same traditions of the *conquistadores* who plundered the early American Indian civilizations.

Other Indian civilizations that reached a high level of development were the Chibchas of northern Colombia and the Pueblo Indians of New Mexico. Indeed, the 16th century Spanish conquerors of Latin America—in contrast to the 17th century English, French and Dutch settlers in North America—encountered civilized natives whose social level was not greatly inferior to their own.

The impact of the conquest destroyed the Indian civilizations and looted their priceless treasures. To this was added the seizure of their valuable lands, forced labor and the spread of diseases unknown to the Indians, which decimated their population. The Spanish intermarried with the women of the former Indian ruling classes and built their empire on the social and economic foundations of the vanquished civilizations. Unsuited to plantation labor, especially in the tropics, the Indians were replaced by slaves imported from Africa and indentured laborers from Asia.

One of the most impressive and lasting achievements of the Spaniards was the conversion of the Indians to Catholicism. Devoted missionaries, still imbued with the religious fervor of the "glorious crusade" which had expelled the Arabs from Spain, risked their lives to preach the new faith among the Indians, learned their languages and defended them from the greed of the *conquistadores* and even the Spanish crown. Thanks to their examples and sacrifices, Catholic religion, or at least some variation of Catholicism, penetrated deeply among the Indian masses, transforming the Church into a powerful and influential institution in Latin America

The ruins of Machu Picchu, the remote mountainous retreat of the Inca rulers, so well hidden that it was not until discovered in 1911.

15

Conquest, Colonization, and the Challenge of Independence

Cortés and the ambassadors of Moctezuma

Cortés began his conquest of Mexico in 1519; Pizarro invaded Peru in 1531 and Quesada and others began the conquest of Colombia in 1536. The Spaniards' superiority in weaponry and cavalry does not fully explain the victory of so few over so many. The decisive factor was the different character of the contending armies. Based on individual initiative, the Spanish regiments could face and fight formidable odds no matter what the losses. Based on strict authority and command, the Indian armies usually disintegrated when the general or high priest was captured or killed. In the battle of Otumba, Cortés had no gunpowder and only sixteen horsemen, while the Aztecs were 20,000 strong. When a desperate Spanish charge killed the Aztec commander, the Indian army remained paralyzed while Cortés and his small group marched toward the safety of Tlaxcala, the capital of a powerful Indian tribe which had become Cortés' ally.

The conquest and colonization of Brazil followed a different pattern. By the Treaty of Tordesillas of 1494, Spain and Portugal divided South America between them along the 45th Meridian—Spain to the west, Portugal to the east. As early as April 22, 1500, Admiral Pedro Alvares Cabral established Portugal's authority over the region, but as further explorations found no traces of gold and silver, and since Portugal was then fully engaged in its profitable Asian trade, Brazil received scant attention. For many years, colonists occupied only a narrow belt of coastal land. The *"bandeirantes,"* rough adventurers and *mestizos* organized in groups called "bandeiras," were the ones who in their search for Indians and wealth slowly opened the interior of Brazil, pushing the nomadic Indian tribes into further remote areas. Portugal's declining Asian trade ultimately stimulated emigration to Brazil. In 1549, after the appointment of the first royal governors, a better system of land distribution was established and the Jesuits opened their first schools.

The strategic position and potential of Brazil attracted foreign attacks. French and Dutch attempts to hold Brazilian territories failed, however, and by 1645 the expanding colony was under Portugal's firm control. Initially sugar production flourished in the north, but the discovery of gold in what is today the state of Minas

Gerais made the south the economic and political center of the colony, a position consolidated by subsequent discoveries of diamonds and precious stones. At the beginning of the 19th century, Brazil was a growing but still basically rural colony, with a vast and untouched hinterland.

During the colonial period, Spain created a highly centralized government, with most power concentrated in the monarch, and an internal balance of power which functioned remarkably well for three centuries. The region was divided into four viceroyalties: New Spain (capital, Mexico City), New Granada (capital, Bogotá), Peru (capital, Lima), and Rio de la Plata (capital, Buenos Aires). Several captains-general ruled less important territories. All judicial matters were dealt with by the *audiencias*, and the designation of ecclesiastical posts remained in the king's hands. At the end of his term, every viceroy had to submit to a *juicio de residencia*, a sort of trial where everyone could accuse him of improprieties or abuses of power. Although initially some authority had been granted to city councils (*cabildos*), eventually their autonomy was greatly reduced by royal control. Conse-

16

Conquest, Colonization, and the Challenge of Independence

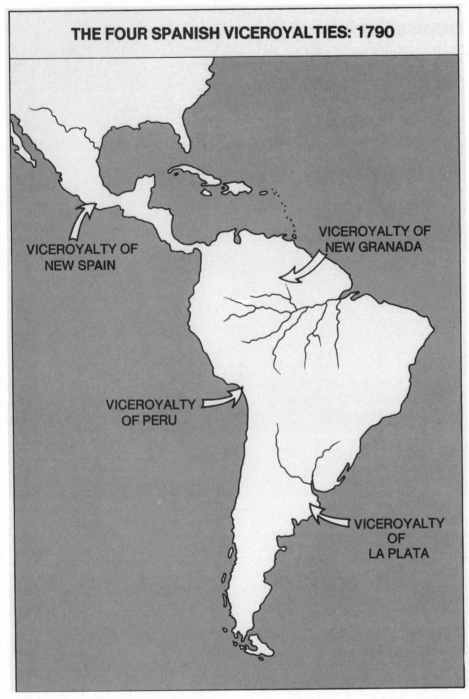

THE FOUR SPANISH VICEROYALTIES: 1790

VICEROYALTY OF NEW SPAIN

VICEROYALTY OF NEW GRANADA

VICEROYALTY OF PERU

VICEROYALTY OF LA PLATA

oles to be treated as equals and to share political power intensified the friction between the two groups. Aware of Spain's and Portugal's decline as European powers, the creoles turned to France for cultural guidance.

Thus, the French Revolution had more impact in Latin America than did the American one. In Haiti, the division of the French white ruling elite brought about by France's political turmoil, sparked a rebellion of the black slaves under Toussaint L'Overture, which after a bloody and devastating war, ended with the liberation of the island. In the rest of Latin America, though, the creoles were far from being *Jacobins* (revolutionaries). A minority sympathized with the Declaration of Human Rights, but the majority was aware of the dangers which an open rebellion against Spain and Portugal could bring. Fearful of the surrounding masses of Indians and *mestizos*, most of the creoles wanted reforms, not revolution. Only the collapse of the Iberian monarchies could prompt them into action. In 1808 Napoleon gave them the opportunity. Invading the Iberian peninsula, he imprisoned the Spanish king and forced the Braganças, Portugal's royal family, to escape to Rio de Janeiro. Confronted with this political crisis, the creoles were forced to act.

Independence and Its Aftermath

While the Spanish people rebelled against Napoleonic armies, and the Brazilians proudly received their sovereigns, Hispanoamericans were left in a political vacuum. Their initial reaction was to swear fidelity to Ferdinand, the captured Spanish king. Soon, however, *they* realized their power. Deprived of legitimacy and without hope of receiving reinforcements

quently, the colonies gained little experience in self-government or administration of public affairs.

The Church was in charge of education, but private religious orders, especially the Jesuits, made determined efforts to modernize learning. Nevertheless, a humanistic, non-scientific type of education became traditional in Ibero-America. Under the patronage of the Church and the Crown, architecture and schools of painting flourished, and the Baroque style, perfectly suited to dazzle the masses, became dominant in all artistic expression. By the middle of the 18th century, while Brazil,

whose development was much slower, had only scattered rural towns, Hispanic America displayed important cities like Mexico and Lima, impressive cathedrals, a few universities and even famous writers like Sor Juana Inés de la Cruz and Carlos de Siguenza y Gongora.

At the beginning of the 18th century, the ruling elite became increasingly divided between the *criollos*, or creoles (those born in America) and the *peninsulares* (mainly functionaries recently arrived from Spain or Portugal). The creoles generally controlled the land, the *peninsulares* wielded political power. The aspiration of the cre-

Cathedral of Cuzco, built about 1535

17

Conquest, Colonization, and the Challenge of Independence

General José de San Martín proclaims Peru's independence, July 1821

from Spain, colonial authorities were practically paralyzed. By 1810 the creoles had moved from tentative autonomy to open independence. Significantly, Mexico and Peru, the two viceroyalties where Indian population was in greater proportion, remained under Spanish control. Immediately, regionalism and individualism began to fragment colonial unity. In the principal cities of the continent, hastily formed governments adopted republican constitutions and strove to extend their shaky authority over the surrounding territories.

In 1814, Napoleon's defeat brought absolutist Ferdinand back to the Spanish throne. The prestige of the restored king, and some military reinforcements, gave the colonial authorities the upper hand. By 1816, with the exception of Buenos Aires, including the Viceroyalty of Rio de la Plata, Spanish rule had been reestablished over most of the empire. Absolutism, however, could no longer appeal to the creoles. Furthermore, Spain's political troubles had not ended: in 1820 a poorly equipped army destined to fight in America rebelled against the king, occupied Madrid and imposed a liberal constitution. In the meantime, inspired by the leadership of Simón Bolívar and José de San Martín, the creoles renewed the war.

After organizing an army in Argentina, San Martín crossed the Andes and defeated the Spaniards in Chile. Bolívar obtained similar victories in Venezuela and Colombia. After invading Peru and meeting Bolívar, San Martín abandoned the struggle and retired to France, the first in a long list of disillusioned liberators. Bolívar marched into Peru and on December 9, 1824, his best commander, Antonio José de Sucre, defeated the last royalist army in the battle of Ayacucho.

Two years before that decisive battle, with less violence, Mexico and Brazil achieved independence. In Mexico, the successive rebellions of two priests, Father Miguel Hidalgo and Father José María Morelos, backed mostly by Indians and *mestizos*, had been defeated by an alliance of conservative creoles and Spanish forces. In 1820 the proclamation of a liberal constitution in Spain induced those conservative allies to seek independence. Their instrument was a creole army officer, Agustín de Iturbide, whose mission was to defeat the remnant republican guerrillas and to proclaim a conservative empire. Instead, Iturbide gained popularity by appealing to *all* factions, entered Mexico City in triumph and was proclaimed Emperor Agustín I. In Brazil, Portugal's liberal revolution produced simi-

lar consequences. The new government in Lisbon recalled the king, and tried to reduce Brazil back to a colonial status. Before departing Brazil, the king designated his son Pedro as regent and gave him sound advice: if the Brazilians want independence, don't *oppose* them, *lead* them. Shortly after his father's departure Pedro received a peremptory summons from the Lisbon parliament. Encouraged and supported by the Brazilians, he refused to go. When Portugal sent him a rash ultimatum, Pedro answered by proclaiming the independence of Brazil. On December 1, 1822, he was crowned emperor of Brazil. By 1825, Portugal had lost its American colony and only Cuba and Puerto Rico remained under Spanish rule.

The Challenge of Independence

The first 50 years of independence were marked by political turmoil, regional confrontations and economic decline. The only exceptions to this were Chile, where a small territory and a rather homogenous population allowed the creole elite to develop a strong and stable government, and Brazil, where the monarchy provided a moderate unifying force. In the rest of Latin America, the lack of concensus on who should rule, massive ignorance,

ACTA DE INDEPENDENCIA

DEL

IMPERIO MEXICANO,

PRONUNCIADA POR SU JUNTA SOBERANA,

CONGREGADA EN LA CAPITAL DE EL, EN 28 DE SETIEMBRE DE 1821.

La Nacion Mexicana, que por trescientos años, ni ha tenido voluntad propia, ni libre el uso de la voz, sale hoy de la opresion en que ha vivido.

Los heróicos esfuerzos de sus hijos han sido coronados, y está consumada la empresa, eternamente memorable, que un génio, superior a toda admiracion y elogio, amor y gloria de su patria, principió en Iguala, prosiguió y llevó al cabo, arrollando obstáculos casi insuperables.

Restituida, pues, esta parte del Septentrion al ejercicio de cuantos derechos le concedió el Autor de la naturaleza, y reconocen por inenagenables y sagrados las naciones cultas de la tierra, en libertad de constituirse del modo que mas convenga á su felicidad, y con representantes que puedan manifestar su voluntad y sus designios, comienza á hacer uso de tan preciosos dones, y declara solemnemente, por medio de la Junta Suprema del imperio, que es Nacion soberana é independiente de la antigua España, con quien, en lo sucesivo no mantendrá otra union que la de una amistad estrecha, en los términos que prescribieren los tratados: que entablará relaciones amistosas con las demas potencias, ejecutando, respecto de ellas, cuantos actos pueden y están en posesion de ejecutar las otras naciones soberanas: que va a constituirse con arreglo a las bases que en el plan de Iguala y tratado de Córdoba estableció sabiamente el primer gefe del ejército imperial de las tres garantías; y en fin, que sostendrá a todo trance, y con el sacrificio de los haberes y vidas de sus individuos, si fuere necesario, esta solemne declaracion, hecha en la capital del imperio a veintiocho de setiembre del año de mil ochocientos veintiuno, primero de la independencia mexicana.

Mexico's Declaration of Independence with Iturbide's signature, top left-hand corner

Conquest, Colonization, and the Challenge of Independence

racial differences and a tradition of authoritarianism, opened the doors for *caudillos*, strong leaders who temporarily commanded the loyalty of armed groups and imposed their authority over congresses and constitutions. There were *caudillos* of all sorts: enigmatic men like Gaspar Rodríguez de Francia, who closed Paraguay to foreign influences; barbarians like Bolivian Mariano Melgarejo, who "executed" his uniform for hurting his neck; ultra Catholics like Ecuadorian García Moreno and liberals like Venezuelan Gusmán Blanco. But almost all of them, even Argentine Juan Manuel de Rosas, represented more a consequence than a cause. They filled a political vacuum and, to a certain extent, contributed to uniting the nations they ruled.

Around 1870, Latin America entered a period of political stability and economic progress. In Argentina, Buenos Aires' liberal oligarchy finally imposed its authority over the provinces. Brazil became a republic in 1889 and even Mexico, a land plagued by internal dissension and foreign military interventions, attained political stability under the firm control of dictator Porfirio Díaz. Almost simultaneously, expanding European markets, especially England's, which had become the dominant economic power in Latin America, increased the demands for Latin American products, ushering in a period of growth and economic dependence.

During this period, waves of European immigrants poured into Argentina, Brazil, Chile and, in lesser numbers, into other Latin American nations. Political parties appeared, government control over the remote territories expanded thanks to better communication and the creation of professional armies, and large towns like Buenos Aires, Rio de Janeiro and Mexico became burgeoning cities.

In 1898, the United States intervened in the Cuban war of independence, defeated Spain and occupied Cuba and Puerto Rico. Cuba became "independent" in 1902, while the following year, Panama severed itself from Colombia (an event orchestrated by the United States) and signed a treaty with Washington authorizing the construction of a canal in an "American" territorial zone that was to extend from the Atlantic to the Pacific, physically dividing Panama. In spite of those ominous notes, which sent a wave of anti-imperialism throughout Latin America, at the beginning of the 20th century a mood of optimism reigned in the hemisphere.

Many of the old problems, though, remained unsolved. Unequal distribution of wealth, economic dependence, landless peasants, regional concentration of power, all hampered genuine development. Very soon, hemispheric and international events demonstrated the fragility of Latin American political stability. In 1910, the Mexican Revolution began; four years later, World War I exposed the vulnerability of the hemispheric economies; after the Russian Revolution of 1917, Communist parties appeared in almost every Latin American country. Another economic crisis shook the continent in 1919; thus, the 1920s were years of political turmoil crowned by the devastating economic crisis of the worldwide depression of 1929–1939.

U.S. troops camp in front of the Presidential Palace in Havana, 1898

Conquest, Colonization, and the Challenge of Independence

View of the Zocalo, Mexico City's main square

Few Latin American governments survived the impact of the Great Depression. Only World War II and the emergence of the United States as a global power temporarily revitalized the economy of the hemisphere. But the period after the war also brought the economic competition of new underdeveloped nations, the decline of Latin exports, and, finally, with Cuba's revolution, the entrance of Latin America into the ideological struggle between the U.S. and the Soviet Union.

In 1961, Castro's Cuba, the first socialist regime in the Western Hemisphere, launched a continental offensive under Marxist banners. The emergence of Castroite guerrillas in almost every corner of the continent disrupted the slow but steady progress toward democracy experienced in the 1950s, when military regimes were toppled in Argentina, Venezuela, Colombia, Brazil, Guatemala and Peru. Threatened by this new enemy, Latin American armies, occasionally backed or tacitly supported by equally alarmed civil-

ians, responded with a series of military coups, which reduced the number of democratic governments to only four. Simultaneously, Washington initiated an ambitious "Alliance for Progress" to lessen Latin American economic and social problems, and increased its military aid to the armies. By 1975, the guerrillas had been defeated, but dictatorial regimes dominated most of the continent. Under new authoritarian economic guidelines, there was some progress toward industrialization and agricultural development. In the 1970s Latin America spent more money on education (in relative terms of national budgets) than any other region in the world.

The stormy economic winds of the early 1980s brought a sudden halt to that effort. The oil crisis, accompanied by the subsequent economic recession in the United States and Western Europe, hit Latin America hard. With astronomical external public debts, plummeting prices for its products and sources for further loans drying up, Latin America plunged into its

worst economic crisis of the last five decades. While austerity measures triggered popular protests in several countries, the emergence of the Marxist-oriented *Sandinista* regime in Nicaragua brought forth an oblique U.S. intervention.

By the end of the 1980s, however, military regimes had yielded to elected civilian governments in Argentina, Bolivia, Brazil, Chile, Ecuador, El Salvador, Guatemala, Honduras, Paraguay, Peru and Uruguay, while Mexico initiated political reform that led to a pluralist party system in place of one-party dominance.

Latin America entered the 21st century in the midst of impressive economic expansion that was giving rise at long last to a middle class. But it also was experiencing political growing pains as the young democracies sought to cope with perennial woes such as widespread poverty, drug trafficking and institutionalized corruption. Developing strong, viable democratic institutions for the future remains the challenge for the present.

U.S.-Latin American Relations

The history of the relationship between the United States and Latin America can be divided into five relatively distinct periods: **1820–80**, the era of the Monroe Doctrine and U.S. paternalism; **1880–1934**, the era of open U.S. imperialism, intervention, and the policies of gunboat diplomacy and the "big stick;" **1934–45**, the "Good Neighbor Policy;" **1945–90**, the Cold War, the Alliance for Progress, the Cuban and Nicaraguan revolutions and U.S. support for anti-communist dictators; and **1990–present**, the post Cold War era, the emergence of democracy in Latin America and a growing U.S.-Latin American trade partnership.

Even a brief summary of U.S.-Latin American relations usually begins by mentioning how the example of American independence stirred rebellious ideas among the Creole elites in colonial Latin America. Actually, geographical, cultural and political barriers greatly reduced the impact of American "revolutionary" wars in the southern hemisphere. Only the tiny minority of cultivated Creoles had some notion of what had happened in North America.

Following President Washington's isolationist policy, the United States for years remained indifferent to the affairs of the southern neighboring nations. While Latin America struggled and achieved independence, the United States concentrated on purchasing Florida from Spain in 1821 and avoided any act or declaration that could endanger those negotiations.

In 1823, President James Monroe delivered his famous message to Congress, quickly raised to the rank of a "doctrine," warning European powers that any attempt to extend their system to any portion of this hemisphere would be considered as a threat to the United States. Despite its significance, the Monroe Doctrine was a U.S. unilateral declaration that did not imply any concern or interest in Latin American problems. When Simón Bolívar, dreaming of unifying the newly born Latin American states, convened the ill-fated first Pan-American Congress three years later, the United States reacted with little enthusiasm. The United States did not invoke the Monroe Doctrine in 1833 when Britain occupied the Falkland Islands claimed by Argentina, nor in 1838–40, when France took military actions against Mexico and Buenos Aires. In 1848, its victory in the war with Mexico allowed the United States to acquire vast territories from that country and to extend its territory to the Pacific Ocean.

Historical circumstances prevented Latin America from expressing any strong criticism of the United States during Mexico's debacle. Fragmented into several fledgling states, facing almost continuous internal political turmoil and poorly informed of international events, Latin America was not ready for continental solidarity. Furthermore, during almost the entire 19th century, the dominant power in Latin America was Great Britain, not the United States. By 1880, the situation had changed. Political stability and economic progress in Latin America coincided with the emergence of expansionist or imperialist trends in the United States.

In 1889, the United States showed its growing economic interest in the southern regions by holding in Washington the first Pan-American Conference and establishing the basis for an inter-American regional system under U.S. domination. Shortly after that conference, American expansionism transformed the image of the United States from a "model" to be copied by Latin America into an aggressive "Colossus of the North," bent on dominating the entire hemisphere. The Pan-American Union later evolved in 1948 into the Organization of American States (OAS).

In 1898, the United States intervened in the Cuban rebellion against Spain, defeated Spain and occupied Cuba, Puerto Rico and the Philippines. Cuba proclaimed its independence in 1902 only after accepting an amendment in its constitution (the Platt Amendment) that gave the United States the right to intervene in Cuban affairs under certain conditions (determined by the United States). The United States also leased the naval base at Guantanamo, which it still occupies.

Meanwhile, President Theodore Roosevelt, famed for his motto "speak softly but carry a big stick," utilized intrigue and the threat of military intervention to help Panama gain its independence from Co-

International Conference of American States, Washington, D.C., 1889

22

lombia in 1903. The acquisition of rights to build the Panama Canal and the Roosevelt Corollary to the Monroe Doctrine, by which the United States maintained the right to decide when a "flagrant wrong-doing" had occurred in a Latin America state that merited "preventive intervention," defined a new imperialist U.S. policy nicknamed "gunboat diplomacy."

Woodrow Wilson, a self-professed progressive on domestic policy, soon proved that he could be as jingoistic as Roosevelt in the name of imposing his vision of democratic morality on the nations to the south. After the odious Victoriano Huerta overthrew and murdered the democratic reformer Francisco Madero in Mexico just days before Wilson's inauguration in 1913, Wilson soon signaled that it would be U.S. policy to promote democracy in Mexico and elsewhere. When U.S. intelligence determined that a shipment of German arms was bound for Veracruz, Wilson ordered U.S. Marines to seize the Mexican port in 1914 to prevent the guns from reaching Huerta, a move that backfired by causing Mexican public opinion to rally around the dictator.

After Huerta was toppled in 1915, Wilson threw his support behind the new president, Venustiano Carranza, who was opposed by such rebel leaders as Emiliano Zapata in the south and Francisco "Pancho" Villa in the north. Wilson could do little in the south, but he allowed Carranza's troops to use U.S. railroads to outflank Villa. Enraged, Villa attacked the town of Columbus, New Mexico, in 1916, killing 19 Americans and prompting Wilson to dispatch Gen. John J. Pershing on a "punitive expedition" into Mexico to pursue Villa. Once again, the U.S. intervention had the effect only of galvanizing the various Mexican warring factions against the *gringo* invaders. The expedition was a total failure, and even long after the end of the Mexican Revolution, Mexico's distrust of its trigger-happy northern neighbor lingered.

Also during his first term, before he became more preoccupied with the threat from Germany that led to U.S. entry into World War I, Wilson sent the Marines at one time or another to occupy Nicaragua, Honduras, Costa Rica, the Dominican Republic and Haiti. The Marines remained in Nicaragua throughout much of the 1920s, battling a rebel leader who was to become a martyr and would lend his name to a Marxist movement 50 years later: Augusto César Sandino. The occupation of Haiti endured for 19 years, under five presidents of both parties, until 1934.

World War I diminished Great Britain's influence and facilitated U.S. economic expansion in the hemisphere. Between 1913 and 1920, U.S. commerce with Latin

The President of Colombia addresses the OAS conference, Bogotá, March 1948.

America increased by 400%. In 1929, U.S. investment in the region amounted to more than $5 billion, exceeding Britain's by almost $1 billion. Latin American bitterness, however, worried Washington. By 1928, the time of the sixth Conference of American States in Havana, Nicaraguan guerrilla leader Sandino, then fighting the Marines in his country, had become a Latin hero and the United States began to reconsider the wisdom of the "big stick" policy. The economic crash of 1929 increased interest in a policy change. In 1933, President Franklin Roosevelt proclaimed the Good Neighbor Policy.

From 1933–45, U.S.-Latin relations experienced a considerable improvement. Economic recovery and better trade agreements, the rise of fascism, adoption by the Communist parties of a conciliatory tactic known as the "popular front" and the

spirit of solidarity provoked by World War II, contributed to raising the Good Neighbor Policy and Panamericanism to a real level of continental unity.

Roosevelt died in 1945, the war ended, and the United States once more relegated Latin America to a secondary position. From the end of World War II to the Cuban Revolution, U.S.-Latin American relations steadily declined. While Washington concentrated its attention on Europe and Korea to confront the Soviet global challenge, Latin America confronted old and pressing economic, political and social problems: Population growth, unstable economies, populist movements and military interventions. Latin America soon became a pawn in the Cold War, as the United States sought to create a solid anti-communist bloc in the hemisphere.

U.S.-Latin American Relations

In 1954, when the elected but leftist government of President Jacobo Arbenz in Guatemala posed a perceived threat to the unity of the bloc, the United States used the first conference of the new Organization of American States (OAS), created in Bogotá in 1948, to pressure Latin delegates into an anti-Guatemalan declaration. A few months later, Arbenz was toppled by a U.S.-backed invasion from Honduras.

Democratic leaders and parties in Latin America denounced what they considered U.S. favoritism toward anti-communist dictators. This criticism found a favorable echo when a powerful upsurge of democratic movements swept the continent. The *MNR (Movimiento Nacionalista Revolucionario)* came to power in Bolivia in 1952; in 1955, Juan Perón fell in Argentina, and in the following years, Generals Odría, Rojas Pinilla and Pérez Jiménez were toppled in Peru, Colombia and Venezuela, respectively. "Democracy is on the march," proclaimed Costa Rican leader José Figueres in 1959. That year, General Fulgencio Batista was forced to abandon Cuba as Fidel Castro entered Havana in triumph, hailed as a democratic hero. Contrary to general expectations in and outside the island, the Cuban revolution moved radically to the left, creating an entirely new situation in Latin American history.

Immediately after seizing power, Castro demonstrated his decision to revolutionize Latin America by encouraging and aiding guerrilla groups in several countries. This policy, the rapid socialization of the revolutionary regime and increasing anti-American propaganda, strained relations with the United States. In 1960, when President Eisenhower reduced the quota of Cuban sugar allowed to enter the United States, the Soviet Union announced it would purchase the total amount of the reduction, and arms from the communist bloc began pouring into Cuba. In January 1961, after much mutual recrimination, President Eisenhower broke diplomatic relations with Cuba; they have never been restored.

John F. Kennedy, inaugurated just days later, inherited from Eisenhower a CIA plan for an invasion of Cuba by anti-Castro exiles. The force of 1,200 men had been training clandestinely in Guatemala, again governed by a president friendly to the United States. At the last minute, however, Kennedy withdrew crucial air support for the operation, fearing a Soviet response. The Bay of Pigs (Playa Girón) invasion was a disaster, raising Castro to the level of an international hero in the eyes of some, and damaging the United States' reputation as a military power.

Emboldened by this U.S. failure, the Soviets secretly began placing nuclear missiles in Cuba capable of striking deep inside the continental United States. A dangerous Soviet-American confrontation followed. In October 1962, the United States imposed a naval "quarantine" around Cuba to prevent the delivery of more missiles, and demanded the removal of those already there. The world teetered closer to the brink of nuclear war than at any time during the Cold War. After a tense standoff, the Soviets pulled the missiles out of Cuba, but at the same time, obtained a guarantee from Washington that no further aggressive action would be taken against Castro. The anti-communist bloc in the Western Hemisphere seemingly had been broken.

Protected by the U.S.-Soviet pact, Castro increased his guerrilla campaign in Latin America. The United States, which had managed to isolate Cuba diplomatically in 1961, answered with the Alliance for Progress, to promote economic progress in Latin America, and with renewed military aid to friendly Latin American countries. The second aspect of the strategy proved more successful than the first. Although few economic advantages were accomplished by the Alliance for Progress, Latin American armies defeated the guerrillas everywhere in the region. Unfortunately, victory was usually preceded or followed by military coups. By the end of the 1960s, only a few democracies had survived the military onslaught.

The guerrillas' defeat, and the deterioration of Cuba's economy, rescued by Soviet aid, forced Castro to abandon his independent guerrilla path and to accept tacit Soviet control of Cuba. Yet, from 1973–75, U.S.-Cuban relations improved slightly. Many Latin American nations reestablished relations with Cuba, while several influential voices in the United States asked for an end to the commercial embargo imposed on the island. In 1975, the conciliatory trend was halted when Castro sent troops to Angola to aid a faltering socialist regime, and publicly denounced American "colonialism" in Puerto Rico.

Castro was not the only crisis facing the United States in Latin America during the 1960s. In January 1964, less than two months after Lyndon Johnson succeeded the assassinated Kennedy, riots erupted in Panama when foolhardy American high school students in the U.S.-controlled Canal Zone tore down the Panamanian flag which, under a decree from President Eisenhower, flew beside the U.S. flag in the Zone. U.S. troops opened fire on the rioters as they spilled over into the Zone; a total of 22 Panamanians and six Americans were killed in the bloodshed. Panama still honors its slain citizens on every anniversary of the riots, and Fourth of July Avenue in Panama City was renamed "Avenue of the Martyrs."

The following year, the left-wing Juan Bosch came to power in the Dominican Republic, sparking civil unrest, and an alarmed Johnson feared that the country would become "another Cuba." He dispatched the 82nd Airborne Division to restore order, but not before there was considerable fighting and loss of life. When an adviser suggested that the OAS assume the peace-making role in the Dominican Republic, the earthy LBJ was reported to have commented, "Those people couldn't pour piss out of a boot if they had instructions written on the heel." True or not, it epitomized what Latin Americans regarded as U.S. arrogance and condescension.

The back-to-back incidents of U.S. military force in Panama and the Dominican

Panama Canal locks

Republic reinforced Latin America's distrust of its powerful neighbor, and greatly enhanced Castro's prestige among left-leaning, anti-U.S. movements in the region.

In 1967, Johnson enjoyed a modest triumph with a CIA operation to train a Bolivian ranger battalion that ultimately tracked down and killed the legendary revolutionary Ernesto "Che" Guevara.

Republican President Richard Nixon did little to dissipate Latin American distrust in 1970 when the CIA made a clumsy attempt to bribe Chilean congressmen into blocking the election of the Marxist Salvador Allende as president after he had received a narrow plurality, but not a majority, of the popular vote. As another example of both the prevailing Cold War mentality and traditional U.S. arrogance toward Latin America, National Security Adviser Henry Kissinger reportedly said, "I see no reason to allow a country to go communist because of the irresponsibility of its own people."

Allende was elected, and he promptly nationalized most U.S. businesses. Nixon responded with an economic embargo against Chile, which brought Allende sympathy even from non-Marxist Latin

Americans. Like Castro, he was viewed as a heroic David standing up to the American Goliath. It wasn't revealed until 1975 that Nixon's CIA also waged a clandestine effort to destabilize the Allende government by instigating public protests and strikes by independent truck drivers. The CIA also was tangentially involved in the military coup that overthrew Allende in September 1973. Allende died in the bloody coup, and although it is still debated whether it was by his own hand or the hands of the military, another anti-U.S. martyr had been created.

That same year, the Uruguayan military overthrew that country's long-standing democracy, which had proven incapable of dealing with the *Tupamaros*, an urban revolutionary movement. U.S. complicity was also suspected in the Uruguayan coup. The military regime succeeded in crushing the *Tupamaros*—along with Uruguayan democracy in the process.

Democratic President Jimmy Carter reversed long-standing U.S. policy of supporting military dictatorships in the name of anti-communism and embarked on a moralistic crusade reminiscent of Woodrow Wilson's. He appointed ambassadors

who aggressively confronted the right-wing generals in Brazil, Chile, Argentina, Uruguay, El Salvador, Nicaragua and Paraguay for alleged human rights violations and curtailed or cut military aid to those countries. He also strained relations with Brazil just weeks into his presidency in 1977 by condemning its nuclear program, which provoked Brazil into canceling its mutual-defense treaty with the United States.

At the same time, Carter sought to ameliorate long-standing distrust of the United States by signing the historic Panama Canal treaties—somewhat hypocritically—with a left-wing dictator, Omar Torrijos. The signing ceremony at OAS headquarters in Washington in 1977 was a major hemispheric event, with all the Latin American heads of state except Castro in attendance.

The *Sandinistas* toppled strongman Anastasio Somoza—a West Point graduate—in Nicaragua on Carter's watch in 1979, but they exhibited little gratitude to the United States for withdrawing its traditional support for Somoza. They vilified the United States, turned to Cuba and the Soviet Union for support and began establishing a Marx-

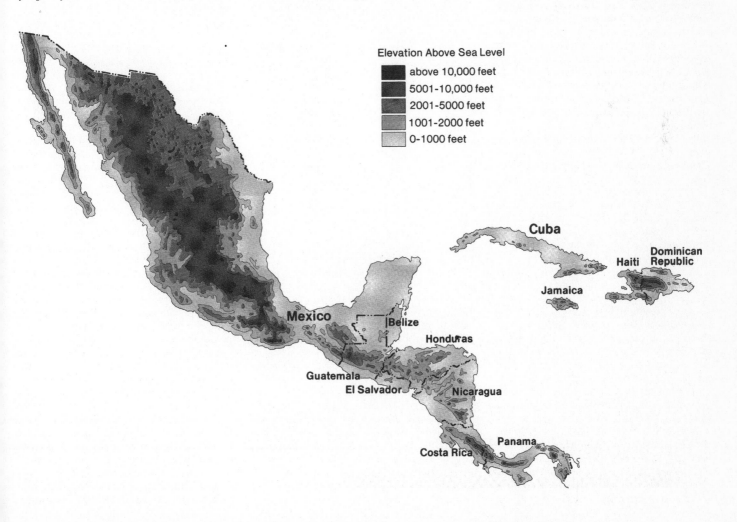

Elevation Above Sea Level

- above 10,000 feet
- 5001-10,000 feet
- 2001-5000 feet
- 1001-2000 feet
- 0-1000 feet

U.S.-Latin American Relations

ist state with little regard for the human rights that Carter professed to cherish.

Carter faced another Latin American crisis in 1980 with the so-called Mariel boatlift, named for a small Cuban port. When Castro declared that anyone who wished to leave Cuba was free to do so, thousands of boats owned by Cuban-American expatriates in Florida sailed to Mariel in a Dunkirk-like evacuation and carried about 125,000 Cubans to the United States. Too late was it discovered that thousands of them were common criminals and lunatics Castro had removed from prisons and asylums and forced onto the boats. Carter's inept handling of the crisis was a major issue in the 1980 election.

In that election, Republican Ronald Reagan defeated Carter in a landslide and immediately ordered a 180-degree course change in Latin American policy. He reversed Carter's human-rights policy and began patching up relations with the military strongmen. He restored military aid and enlarged the training programs for Latin American officers and noncommissioned officers at the U.S. Army's School of the Americas (which Carter had relocated from Panama to Georgia) to combat Marxist insurgencies. Despite congressional objections, he lavished military aid on the military regime in El Salvador to combat that insurgency, and he fired the Carter-appointed ambassador there who had the audacity to criticize the regime after four American nuns were raped and murdered by right-wing death squads.

In October 1983, Reagan ordered U.S. forces into the Caribbean island nation of Grenada after its Marxist president, Maurice Bishop, was overthrown and murdered by a cabal of pro-Cuban, Marxist-Leninist soldiers. The invasion, all too reminiscent of the era of gunboat diplomacy, was denounced throughout Latin America, even by the anti-communist strongmen Reagan had been courting.

Moreover, Reagan provided military and financial aid to the Nicaraguan *Contras*, who were battling to topple the *Sandinistas* and whom Reagan praised as "the moral equivalent of our founding fathers." All this was part of Reagan's overall strategy of defeating the Soviet Union and winning the Cold War with a massive military buildup and confronting the Soviets vicariously with surrogate warriors on such far-flung battlefields as Afghanistan, Angola and Central America.

Reagan's support for the *Contras* almost proved the undoing of his presidency, however. When the Democratic-controlled Congress prohibited any further aid to the *Contras*, Reagan's minions made an end-run around Congress by secretly selling

Elevation Above Sea Level

■ above 10,000 feet
▨ 5001–10,000 feet
▨ 2001–5000 feet
▨ 1001–2000 feet
□ 0–1000 feet

arms to Iran, then at war with Iraq, and diverting the profits to the *Contras*. When the deal became public in late 1986, a major scandal erupted that lingered until Reagan left office in 1989. By then, however, Reagan's strategy of out-spending the Soviet Union into oblivion was well on its way to success.

With the collapse of the Soviet Union, Reagan's successor, Republican George H. W. Bush, had the opportunity to usher in a new era of mutual understanding and cooperation between the United States and Latin America without the old issue of communism vs. anticommunism hanging over both parties. He attended an anti-drug summit in Cartagena, Colombia, and promised closer ties with Latin America in return for its cooperation on drug control.

However, Bush's military intervention in Panama in December 1989, no matter how justifiable in light of strongman Manuel Noriega's provocations, was denounced throughout the hemisphere as just another example of the naked application of U.S. power to enforce its will in Latin America.

Another obstacle in U.S.-Latin American relations left over from the Reagan era was effectively eliminated when the *Sandinistas* finally were removed from power—by free election—in 1990.

Toward the end of his single term in office, Bush negotiated the North American Free Trade Agreement (NAFTA) with Canada and Mexico, and he openly advocated a hemisphere-wide free trade zone.

By the time Democrat Bill Clinton took office in 1993, virtually all the dictatorships had been replaced by democratically elected civilian governments. He had to contend neither with gross abuses of human rights, as Carter had, nor with the problem of communist insurgencies, as Reagan had. In his first year in office, Clinton invited the heads of state of all the nations of the hemisphere except Cuba to a Summit of the Americas in Miami. There, he resurrected Bush's proposal for a Free Trade Area of the Americas (FTAA), open to any country with a democratic form of government. Toward that end, he made a state visit to Brazil, Uruguay, Argentina and Chile in 1997.

Nonetheless, Clinton found himself resorting to armed intervention just as his two Republican predecessors had. After the military strongmen who had overthrown the democratically elected Haitian President Jean-Bertrand Aristide refused to acquiesce to international pressure to restore Aristide, Clinton ordered the 82nd Airborne Division to Haiti in September 1994 to keep order and to effect the transition back to democracy. Although this invasion was a benevolent one and there was minimal loss of life, the televised images of American paratroopers landing in Haiti in full battle dress evoked the old specter of Theodore Roosevelt's "big stick." The Americans withdrew in 1995 and were replaced by U.N. peacekeepers, who remain there today a decade and a half hence.

Clinton turned his attention toward the upcoming Second Summit of the Americas in Santiago, Chile, in April 1998. The 34 hemispheric leaders (once again, Castro had been excluded) issued a communiqué that called for establishment of the FTAA by 2005. Clinton praised Latin America's advances in democracy, but called for "a second generation of reforms" to consolidate the region's fragile democracies.

Although the Santiago summit was marked by unprecedented good will between the U.S. president and his Latin American counterparts, there were still nagging complaints about U.S. hegemony. Among these were the continued U.S. embargo against Cuba, with which nearly all the Latin American countries by then had diplomatic and trade relations, and the U.S. policy of "certifying" countries as cooperating allies in the war against drugs as a condition for financial aid, which the Latin Americans saw as demeaning. The drug issue as a whole continues to strain North-South relations today, with the United States pushing for support at eradicating coca, marijuana and heroin poppy cultivation at their sources, while Latin America argues that there would be no market for illegal drugs if the United States would curb the demand for them at home. Both sides, of course, have a point.

Clinton's successor in 2001, Republican George W. Bush, at first showed a greater interest in, and sensitivity toward, Latin America than most of his predecessors, including his father. In fact, he declared the 21st century "the century of the Americas." A former governor of Texas, he was fluent in Spanish and openly courted Hispanic votes in the 2000 presidential race. Indeed, the Cuban-American vote in Florida provided the narrow victory in that state that gave him an Electoral College victory over the Democratic candidate, Al Gore.

Accustomed to dealing with Mexican authorities as governor, Bush made a state visit to Mexico weeks after his inauguration to meet with the newly inaugurated President Vicente Fox; in the past, new U.S. presidents made their first trip abroad to Western Europe. Both conservatives, Bush and Fox got on well. Bush also hosted Chilean President Ricardo Lagos and Brazilian President Fernando Henrique Cardoso at the White House soon after the visit to Mexico.

In April 2001, Bush attended the Third Summit of the Americas in Quebec, where he conversed in Spanish with his Latin American counterparts and voiced his strong commitment to the FTAA. The leaders agreed to a target date of January 1, 2005, and made adherence to representative democracy a condition for participation. The only major opposition came from Cardoso, who accused the United States of protectionism, and Venezuela's Hugo Chávez, who said the FTAA would do nothing to alleviate poverty.

Bush concluded a bilateral free-trade pact with Chile in 2003, which was seen as a precursor to the FTAA. He also pushed for a free trade agreement with Central America and the Dominican Republic; in 2009, Costa Rica became the final country to sign on.

Five months after Quebec, U.S. Secretary of State Colin Powell flew to Lima, Peru, to attend the periodic summit of OAS foreign ministers, ostensibly to emphasize again the Bush administration's commitment to regional integration and democracy.

The date: September 11, 2001.

Within hours of his arrival, Powell hastily returned to Washington to deal with the crisis of the terrorist attacks on New York and Washington. Although his Latin American colleagues were sympathetic and understanding, there could have been no more symbolic reminder that U.S. priorities in the world lay elsewhere.

Perhaps mindful of the need to mend fences in the wake of the shift of global priorities after 9/11, Bush made a whirlwind, four-day tour of Mexico, El Salvador and Peru in 2002. In Mexico, he attended a U.N. summit on poverty in Monterrey, to assure Latin America and other developing regions that the United States was concerned with more than the war on terror. In El Salvador, he held a summit with several Central American presidents to assure them of his commitment to a U.S.-Central American-Dominican Republic free-trade pact. In Lima, Bush told his Andean counterparts that he was trying to get a recalcitrant Democratic-controlled Senate to reinstate preferential tariffs that had expired the month before, and he urged their continued cooperation on combating terrorism and drug trafficking. On all three stops, he reiterated his support for democracy.

Despite Bush's wooing of Latin America, more and more newly elected leaders began echoing Brazil's and Venezuela's skepticism toward the FTAA. In December 2001, Argentine President Fernando de la Rua, an FTAA advocate, was forced to resign because of an economic crisis and deadly riots. He was replaced by an interim president, Eduardo Duhalde, who was cool to the FTAA; his elected successor, Néstor Kirchner, was hostile. Brazil's president, Luiz Inácio da Silva, elected in 2002, was a longtime critic of the FTAA, more so even than his predecessor, Cardoso. Da Silva and Kirchner instead called for strengthening the *Mercosur* trade bloc (Argentina, Brazil, Uruguay and Paraguay) and for increased regional economic integration in preference to the FTAA, which they argue would be dominated by the United States.

Mexico's Fox, despite his conservatism and warm relations with Bush, met with da Silva at the Rio Group summit in Peru in 2002 and came away committed to greater Mexican trade with *Mercosur*.

Opposition to the FTAA has grown steadily since then, with the elections of Nicanor Duarte Frutos, and later Fernando Lugo, in Paraguay; Tabaré Vázquez and later Jorge Mujíca in Uruguay; Evo Morales in Bolivia; Rafael Correa in Ecuador; Manuel Zelaya in Honduras; Daniel Ortega in Nicaragua; and Mauricio Funes in El Salvador.

In 2002, the 10 presidents from South America's two major trading blocs, *Mercosur* and the Andean Pact, (Bolivia, Colombia, Ecuador, Peru and Venezuela) met in Guayaquil, Ecuador; the president of Chile, an associate member of *Mercosur*, also attended. In the so-called "Guayaquil Consensus," the presidents agreed that strengthened trade between the two South American blocs must precede implementation of the FTAA, and there was more grumbling that the United States preaches free trade while practicing protectionism. In 2003, Peru joined Bolivia and Chile as associate members of *Mercosur*, and Venezuela became a full member in 2006.

U.S.-Latin American Relations

In December 2004, 12 countries signed an accord in Cuzco, Peru, creating the South American Union of Nations. It was ratified in 2008, and at a summit in Buenos Aires in May 2010, former Argentine President Kirchner was elected secretary-general.

The January 1, 2005 deadline for establishing the FTAA came and went, and when the Fourth Summit of the Americas was held in Mar del Plata, Argentina, in November 2005, even Bush acknowledged that the idea was stalled. A total of 29 of the 34 nations still favored an FTAA, but the other five—Argentina, Brazil, Paraguay, Uruguay and Venezuela—effectively blocked it. Mexico's Fox suggested at the summit that the 29 countries move ahead on their own, but without the participation of major economies like Brazil and Argentina, it would serve little purpose. As usual, the summit was made contentious by violent anti-Bush demonstrations and by Chávez's strident anti-U.S. comments. The summit accomplished nothing other than a photo opportunity; the leaders did not even see the need to issue a communiqué.

Meanwhile, Castro and Chávez began lobbying for what they call the "Bolivarian Alternative for Latin America;" its Spanish acronym, *ALBA*, also means "dawn." They envision Latin American integration that excludes the United States. President Morales of Bolivia, elected in 2005, eagerly signed on to the idea, as did Correa of Ecuador, Ortega of Nicaragua, Zelaya of Honduras and Lugo of Paraguay.

Despite Bush's declaration of "the century of the Americas," drug certification and four other practices or incidents strained U.S.-Latin American relations on his watch and called into question the depth of his administration's commitment to Latin America in general or to its democratization in particular.

The first was the abortive military coup in Venezuela in 2002 that had President Chávez under house arrest for 48 hours. Chávez had long been—and remains today—a thorn in the side of the United States because of his close ties to Cuba, Iran, Saddam Hussein's Iraq and Libya as well as for his opposition to the FTAA (see Venezuela). The statements emanating from the State Department within hours of the coup clearly conveyed the idea that the Bush administration regarded the overthrow of Chávez, who had twice been elected by overwhelming majorities, as the will of the Venezuelan people. The administration said, essentially, that Chávez had it coming. When Chávez was reinstalled two days later, President Bush's then-national security adviser, Condoleezza Rice, said in a televised interview that she hoped Chávez had learned something from his experience. The message

regarding U.S. policy toward Latin America was unmistakable: We're all for democracy—as long as you don't elect someone we don't like.

The second was what apparently had been the official policy of the Bush administration to have its ambassadors openly electioneer for presidential candidates it favors, a stunning breach of diplomatic protocol. The first such instance came in the 2001 Nicaraguan campaign, when the U.S. ambassador appeared at functions for the Liberal candidate, Enrique Bolaños, whose opponent was the former *Sandinista* president, Daniel Ortega. The ambassador even invited Bolaños to distribute U.S. food aid, and he actually warned Nicaraguan voters that U.S. aid could be jeopardized if Ortega won. Bolaños won the election.

A few months later, the U.S. ambassador used the same tactics in Bolivia, where one of the candidates was Morales, leader of the coca farmers, who had pledged to reverse the incumbent administration's coca-eradication policy. The ambassador appeared at campaign rallies for the favored U.S. candidate, former President Gonzalo Sánchez de Lozada, and he publicly hinted that a Morales victory could jeopardize U.S. aid. This time, this clumsy policy almost backfired. Bolivians were justifiably furious over this interference in their internal political affairs. The result: Morales, whom polls had predicted would receive no more than 12% of the vote, was catapulted into second place, with about 21% (see Bolivia). Congress then had to choose between Morales and Sánchez, and the ambassador lobbied members of Congress to vote for Sánchez, who ultimately won, but U.S. interference left a bitter taste in the mouths of Bolivians.

In the 2005 elections, Morales won a first-round victory in Bolivia, while in October 2006, Ortega was elected in Nicaragua.

The third unpopular episode was the U.S. intervention in Iraq in 2003, which for many Latin American countries was just too reminiscent of U.S. gunboat diplomacy. Even those countries morally opposed to Saddam Hussein's regime and generally friendly to the United States, such as Mexico and Chile, publicly criticized the war. Chile's opposition on the U.N. Security Council briefly delayed the U.S.-Chilean free-trade agreement. Four countries—the Dominican Republic, El Salvador, Honduras and Nicaragua—did send contingents of several hundred troops each to participate in the allied coalition in Iraq. All but El Salvador decided to pull their troops out, however, after Spain withdrew its troops from Iraq in the wake of the Madrid terrorist bombings in March 2004. El Salvador kept a contingent in Iraq until early 2009.

The fourth has been the practice—which in fairness did not originate with Bush—to send lower-echelon representatives to the inaugurations of democratically elected presidents. When a dozen or more heads of state from Latin America, and sometimes elsewhere, attend an inauguration and the United States sends a cabinet secretary who happens to have a Hispanic surname—as it did in Argentina—or an unpopular trade representative—as it did in Brazil—the contrast does not go unnoticed and can only be seen as offensive. Fidel Castro regularly attended inaugurations before age and illness kept him at home.

This souring of U.S.-Latin American relations was acutely evident when Powell once again attended the OAS foreign ministers' summit, in Santiago, Chile, in 2003. He urged his 33 colleagues to denounce Cuba's crackdown on dissent that April (see Cuba) and to support the transition to a democratic Cuba. Powell's plea met an icy reception. Just a month earlier, the United States had failed to persuade the OAS to adopt a resolution condemning the crackdown, winning support from only 17 of the 34 member countries. Even countries opposed to Castro's dictatorship also oppose the U.S. trade embargo. The rejection of the U.S. position against Cuba appeared to be a case of Latin American blood being thicker than Western Hemisphere water and general resentment against a paternalistic U.S. attitude.

Another indication of this is the fact that the Ibero-American summits (see Latin America and the World), which include Cuba but exclude the United States, have been far more critical of Cuba's human rights record than has the OAS. In other words, Latin America seems to be saying, we don't need you to tell us right from wrong.

Bush's second secretary of state, Condoleezza Rice, visited Chile, Brazil, Colombia and El Salvador in 2005 in yet another attempt to soothe ruffled feathers in the region, to discuss the war on terrorism and to reiterate U.S. support for democracy.

In 2004, the pro-U.S. Miguel Angel Rodríguez, who served as president of Costa Rica from 1998–2002, was elected secretary-general of the OAS. Just two weeks later, however, Rodríguez resigned in the face of allegations that as president he received $900,000 in foreign payoffs or kickbacks. This reopened the jockeying for the OAS leadership, which lasted six months. The United States' preferred candidate was Mexican Foreign Secretary José Luis Derbez—which may have doomed his candidacy. When the first vote in April 2005 ended in a 17–17 tie between Derbez and Chilean Interior Minister José Miguel Insulza, Derbez dropped out in the interest of unity. Rice declared she was pleased with the selection of Insulza, who stressed his commitment to promoting democracy in the region.

The 2005 annual meeting of the OAS foreign ministers was held in Fort Lauderdale, Florida, the first time the meeting had been held on U.S. soil since 1971. Both Bush and Rice addressed the meeting, urging the OAS to grant the secretary-general greater power to deal with countries drifting back toward authoritarianism. Venezuela responded that the idea was obviously directed at it. Most members agreed the language had Venezuela in mind, and in a major rebuff of the United States, the final resolution was a watered-down version that stressed "the right of self-determination and the principle of non-intervention" over worries about would-be dictators.

Apparently in response to growing anti-U.S. sentiment in the region, Bush made a goodwill visit in 2007 to Brazil, Uruguay, Colombia, Guatemala and Mexico, but he was met with anything but goodwill. His stops in each country were met by large, sometimes violent protests, and Chávez made rival visits to Argentina and Bolivia, where he addressed large, enthusiastic anti-Bush rallies. In Guatemala, Mayan Indians performed an "exorcism" after Bush's visit to an archeological site to rid it of evil spirits. About the only substantive accomplishment of the visit was an ethanol-promotion agreement Bush signed with Brazil's da Silva. Even that was marked by discord when da Silva, at a news conference, called on the U.S. Congress to repeal the 54-cent-a-gallon tariff on Brazilian ethanol, which is designed to protect U.S. corn-based ethanol. Bush responded bluntly that the law would not be repealed before it expires in 2009.

Democrat Barack Obama succeeded Bush in January 2009, and his appearance at the Fifth Summit of the Americas in Trinidad and Tobago that April served as his much-anticipated debut on the hemispheric stage. Even before then, Obama sent Vice President Joseph Biden to Santiago for a mini-summit with the center-left presidents of Chile, Brazil, Argentina and Uruguay and the prime ministers of Britain and Spain to discuss the international financial crisis and environmental issues as a precursor to the G-20 Summit in London. Biden also visited Peru and Costa Rica.

On the eve of his departure to Port-of-Spain, Trinidad, Obama fulfilled a campaign promise—which helped him carry the key state of Florida—to rescind the Bush Administration's restrictions on Cuban Americans traveling to Cuba and on the amount of money they could remit to families in Cuba. Fidel Castro grumbled that this wasn't enough, that Obama should lift the trade embargo, but Obama said the next move was up to Cuba.

The day before the summit, Cuban President Raúl Castro—ironically while attending a summit of the left-wing *ALBA* countries in Caracas—reversed decades of Cuban policy by saying, "We are prepared, wherever they want, to discuss everything—human rights, freedom of the press, political prisoners—everything, everything, everything that they want to discuss." Obama replied cautiously that "the United States seeks a new beginning with Cuba," but suggested that Cuba demonstrate its willingness by releasing political prisoners. Within days, Fidel Castro threw cold water on his brother's dramatic overture, saying in his newspaper column that Raúl didn't really mean "everything" was open to discussion, even though Raúl said it three times. Fidel said Raúl only meant Cuba was willing to talk but that it would not compromise the principles of the Revolution—such as suppressing freedom of thought. Raúl then quickly clarified his remarks, removing any doubt over who was still in charge in Cuba.

Obama made his first state visit to Mexico en route to the Trinidad summit, promising President Felipe Calderón he would do more to stop the traffic of weapons to Mexico in an effort to curtail the alarming rise in drug-related violence, but he said immigration reform would not be on his agenda until the end of 2009. (He later moved it back to the end of 2010). Simultaneously, Secretary of State Hillary Clinton visited Haiti and the Dominican Republic on her way to the summit.

At the summit, Obama remained statesmanlike as Nicaragua's Ortega delivered a 50-minute anti-American harangue straight out of the Cold War. Obama countered that he had not come to rehash "stale debates" but to look to the future, and he quipped that at least Ortega "did not blame me for things that happened when I was three months old."

The greatest anticipation centered on how Chávez would behave toward the new U.S. president, whom he had already called an "ignoramus" who had "the same stench" as Bush. The two leaders perfunctorily shook hands during a brief encounter, which was captured by photographers and disseminated worldwide. During a business session, the grandstanding Chávez approached a surprised Obama to present him a copy of a leftist book, *Latin America's Open Veins—Five Hundred Years of the Pillage of a Continent* by Uruguayan author Eduardo Galeano. They shook hands again, as the TV cameras rolled. At both encounters, Chávez told Obama in English, "I want to be your friend." Toward the end of the summit, Chávez approached Hillary Clinton to voice his willingness to restore ambassadorial-level relations, which he had disrupted the previous September by expelling the U.S. ambassador; the United States responded by booting out the Venezuelan ambassador. Ambassadors were exchanged in June.

At a post-summit news conference, Obama said he found the summit "very productive," and assured Latin America that he wanted to be equal partners. He said he had been struck by how many of his counterparts had mentioned the role that Cuban doctors have played in their countries, while U.S. involvement had been in the form of drug interdiction or military aid. "If our only interaction with many of these countries is drug interdiction—if our only interaction is military—then we may not be developing the connections that can over time increase our influence and have a beneficial effect," Obama said. However, he also chided Chávez for his tendency to play to the TV cameras and for years of "inflammatory" rhetoric toward the United States. Ultimately, he said, "The test for all of us is not simply words but also deeds."

As a follow-up to the summit, Secretary Clinton said in a town hall meeting at the State Department that the Obama administration would not continue the Bush administration's policy of attempting to isolate hostile nations like Cuba and Venezuela, a policy she said had failed, but would seek dialogue with even its harshest critics. At the same time, she said the United States expects reciprocal gestures from Cuba. She also pointed to growing Chinese, Russian and Iranian influence in the region, which she called "quite disturbing."

Since then, however, her meetings with Latin American leaders *have*, in fact, appeared aimed at isolating Chávez. During a visit to Washington by Uruguayan President Vázquez in September 2009, Clinton expressed her concern that the $2.2 billion arms credit extended to Venezuela by Russia could provoke an "arms race" in the region.

Interestingly, Obama was not in a hurry to replace Bush's assistant secretary of state for Western Hemisphere affairs, Thomas A. Shannon Jr., who remained in the post until November, when Obama replaced him with the Chilean-born Arturo Valenzuela; Shannon was named ambassador to Brazil.

In sum, if U.S. policy toward Latin America seems paradoxical and pendular, so do Latin American attitudes toward the United States. Despite the election of a succession of pro-Chávez presidents in the region, even such left-wing presidents as da Silva, Vázquez of Uruguay and Morales of Bolivia demonstrated they realize their countries' economic well-being

U.S.-Latin American Relations

depends in no small part to access of their goods to U.S. markets. Even as they echoed Chávez's anti-imperialist rhetoric, they eagerly signed bilateral trade agreements with the United States and pleaded with the U.S. Congress to extend the preferential tariffs on their non-traditional products, which represent billions of dollars in sales and hundreds of thousands of jobs. In other words, Latin Americans are saying, we detest your paternalistic attitude, your trade embargo of Cuba, your drug certification, your restrictive immigration quotas and the war in Iraq, but business is business.

Latin America and the World

One of the most dramatic changes taking place in Latin America is its progressive integration into the rest of the world. Almost totally isolated during most of the 19th century and until World War II under the tutelage first of Britain and then of the United States, Latin America has since then experienced a progressive "opening to the world."

After 1960, Canada increased its economic and cultural ties with Latin countries, principally Brazil, Cuba and, with NAFTA in 1994, Mexico. The most important nations of Western Europe, especially Germany, Italy and Spain, reinforced their influence in the hemisphere through economic aid, cultural programs and support for political groups or parties attuned to their predominant ideologies.

During the Cold War, the Soviet Union eagerly sought to extend its influence, and enjoyed some degree of success. The Castro regime, which transformed Cuba into a formidable military base, opened the door for further Soviet influence in Latin America. The Peruvian military regime of 1968–80 enjoyed close ties with the Soviet Union, which re-equipped the Peruvian army with T-62 tanks and its air force with MiGs. The Nicaraguan army under the *Sandinistas* also received Soviet weapons, including tanks, helicopter gunships, surface-to-air missiles and other modern armaments. Every year, thousands of Latin American students received grants to study in Moscow, and Marxist publications multiplied on the continent. Latin America, a region once relegated by the Kremlin to a secondary position, became one of its top priorities (as foretold by Lenin before his death). With the fall of communism, Russia has maintained warm relations with Latin America, especially Cuba and Venezuela.

In recent decades, there has been increased Japanese interest in investment in Latin America. With its huge surplus from a favorable balance of foreign trade for years, the supply of money is ample.

Needless to say, the Japanese insist on control and security of their investments and, above all, efficiency and productivity.

During much of the Cold War, Latin American countries other than Cuba joined the United States in recognizing the Nationalist Chinese government on Taiwan as the legitimate government of China. Mexico recognized the communist regime in Beijing in 1971, seven years before the United States did. One by one, most other Latin American countries followed suit. However, of the 23 nations that still maintain full diplomatic relations with Taiwan, 10 are developing nations of the Western Hemisphere that have benefited greatly from Taiwan's generosity with foreign aid: Belize, Costa Rica, the Dominican Republic, Guatemala, Haiti, Honduras, Nicaragua, Panama and Paraguay.

Over the past decade, however, the economically resilient People's Republic of China has greatly expanded its political and economic influence among the other Latin American nations. Chinese President Hu Jintao made an unprecedented state visit to Chile, Argentina and Brazil in 2004, signing letters of intent to invest tens of billions of dollars in those countries' infrastructures and to greatly expand trade. China, meanwhile, has great demand for Chilean copper and South American agricultural products, especially Argentine soybeans. Venezuela's Chávez visited Beijing in 2004; China pledged to invest in Venezuela's oil industry and to double bilateral trade. Hu returned to Latin America in late 2008, to to sign a $70 million investment agreement with Cuba and to sign a free-trade agreement (FTA) with Peru on the eve of the APEC summit (see below). China has extended billions of dollars worth of loans to Argentina, Brazil and Ecuador, among others. China's trade with Latin America mushroomed from $10 billion in 2000 to $140 billion in 2008.

Latin America has two rotating seats on the 15-member U.N. Security Council, but in 2005 Brazil joined with Germany, Japan and India in sponsoring a resolution to expand the council to 25 members and make those four countries permanent members along with the United States, Russia, Britain, France and China. Permanent members have veto power. Their petition still has not been approved, however, in part because of Mexican and Argentine resentment of Brazil's ambition.

Latin America's two rotating seats have sometimes placed Latin America in the forefront of world events, as when Chile and Mexico voted to oppose the U.S. resolution authorizing its invasion of Iraq in 2003. The two-year seats have since become coveted political prizes, leading to intra-regional contention. In 2006, Venezuela's Chávez made a controversial speech before the U.N. General Assembly equating President Bush with the devil, and he announced Venezuela would bid for one of the Security Council seats to advance his anti-U.S. agenda. Guatemala, with U.S. backing, also bid for the seat, but neither country could obtain the two-thirds majority of the General Assembly. After more than 20 ballots, the 32 Latin American and Caribbean ambassadors compromised on Panama. Latin America's current members are Brazil, until 2011 and, again, Mexico, through 2010.

Latin America also has played a leading role in the so-called G-15, a group of developing countries, most of them rich in natural resources or with large industrial bases, which was organized in Belgrade, Yugoslavia in 1989 as a counterpart to the G-7 (later G-8) group of highly industrialized countries. Originally the bloc had 15 members, but has expanded to 18. Seven Latin American or Caribbean countries belong to the G-15: Argentina, Brazil, Chile, Jamaica, Mexico, Peru and Venezuela. The other members are Algeria, Egypt, India, Indonesia, Iran, Kenya, Malaysia, Nigeria, Senegal, Sri Lanka and Zimbabwe. Venezuela hosted the 12th G-15 summit in 2004 and Cuba, which is not a member, hosted the 13th in 2006 to coincide with a meeting of the 118-nation Non-Aligned Movement.

Overlapping with the G-15 is the G-21, an organization of developing countries designed to present a unified stance in trade negotiations with the developed countries, particularly over the thorny issue of agricultural subsidies in the developed countries, which developing countries complain is hypocritical and makes their agricultural exports uncompetitive. The organization's 22 countries encompass half the globe's population and most of its farmers. Thirteen of those countries are Latin American: Argentina, Bolivia, Brazil, Chile, Colombia, Costa Rica, Cuba, Ecuador, Guatemala, Mexico, Paraguay, Peru and Venezuela. The others are China, Egypt, India, Indonesia, Nigeria, Pakistan, the Philippines, South Africa and Thailand.

At the G-8 summit in France in 2002, the leaders of Latin America's two largest economies—Brazil's da Silva and Mexico's Fox—attended for the first time. At the expanded G-20 summit in London in April 2009, the presidents of Brazil, Mexico and Argentina participated.

Mexico, Peru and Chile are among the 21 countries with robust economies around the Pacific Rim that comprise the so-called Asia-Pacific Economic Cooperation (APEC) group. Other members include the United States, Canada, Japan, China, South Korea, Thailand, Malaysia and Australia. Chile hosted the annual summit in 2004, where the United States proposed a free-trade zone that would dwarf the European Union or the ill-fated FTAA. Such a bloc is far in the future, however. Peru hosted the 2008 summit, where the members condemned trade protectionism.

Since 1991, the heads of government and key ministers of Spain, Portugal and the 19 Latin American countries they once colonized have met every October or November for the Ibero-American Summit. Unlike the OAS and the Summits of the Americas, the United States is not included but Cuba is. The former Spanish colony of Equatorial Guinea in Africa began attending in 2005. The agendas usually include such topics as trade and human rights. Although these summits have accomplished little of substance, such as persuading Cuba to clean up its human rights act, they have provided a forum for a healthful exchange of ideas of mutual importance to the Latin American leaders and their Iberian counterparts, such as health, education and the environment. They also have helped give Latin America a toehold in European trade, as Spain and Portugal are both members of the European Union.

With the election of more and more left-wing leaders in Spain and Latin America, the summits have been less critical of Cuba's human rights record and more critical of the United States. At the 15th summit in Salamanca, Spain, in 2005, a resolution called on the United States to ease its economic embargo against Cuba. That summit also approved the establishment of the group's first permanent general secretariat.

U.N. Secretary-General Kofi Annan attended that summit for the first time, as well as the 16th summit in Montevideo, Uruguay, in 2006. That summit dealt largely with migration issues, and the leaders condemned U.S. plans to build a security fence along the Mexican border. Attendance at that summit was unusually poor; six presidents were absent, which upset the summit's host, Uruguay's Tabaré Vázquez.

The Ibero-American summits usually attract little attention outside the member countries, but the 2007 summit in Santiago, Chile, splashed into world headlines when Venezuela's Chávez used his allotted time to launch into an diatribe against former conservative Spanish President José María Aznar, calling him a "fascist" and accusing him of complicity in the 2002 coup attempt against him. His tirade proved too much even for incumbent Spanish President José Luis Rodríguez Zapatero, Aznar's political arch-rival, who used his allotted time to rebut Chávez's attack on a duly elected Spanish chief of government and to admonish Chávez for his undiplomatic lan-

guage. Chávez, not known for his tolerance of criticism at home, repeatedly tried to interrupt Zapatero, a violation of the summit's parliamentary procedure. Finally, Spain's King Juan Carlos leaned forward and told Chávez, *"Por qué no te callas?"* (Why don't you shut up?). Chávez briefly threatened to sever diplomatic relations with Spain, which up until then had been friendly to him under Zapatero; meanwhile, the king became an overnight hero in Spain. (Chávez later reconciled with the king on a visit to Spain.)

The 2008 summit in El Salvador was far less contentious, with members again calling on the United States to lift the trade embargo against Cuba. But the 2009 summit in Estoril, Portugal, which was supposed to deal primarily with technological innovation and advancement, degenerated into a squabble over the presidential election held in Honduras the day before. The representatives unanimously passed a resolution condemning the ouster of Honduran President Manuel Zelaya that June, but they were divided over whether to recognize his duly elected successor, Porfirio Lobo Sosa. Honduras' interim president, Roberto Micheletti, did not attend the summit, and most certainly would not have been welcome if he had.

The 2010 Ibero-American Summit will be held in Buenos Aires, and Argentine President Cristina Fernández de Kirchner announced her intention at the 2009 summit to again raise Argentina's claim over the British-held Falklands (Malvinas) Islands.

As an outgrowth of the Ibero-American summits, the first summit of leaders of the European Union, Latin America and the Caribbean was held in Rio de Janeiro, Brazil, in 1999. Spain hosted another two-day summit in Madrid in 2002, which was attended by about 50 heads of government and their foreign and economy ministers. Trade and terrorism dominated the agenda. The EU and Chile ended their "association" agreement, the first step to beginning a FTA signed later that year; Mexico already had such an agreement, and its trade with Europe had grown from $19 billion to more than $48 billion. The EU pledged to initiate separate free-trade talks with the Andean, Caribbean and Central American trade blocs. *Mercosur* then entered into an "association" agreement with the EU like Chile had. The EU also acceded to a request from the Colombian president to add the Revolutionary Armed Forces of Colombia *(FARC)* to its list of terrorist organizations.

The Third EU-Latin American-Caribbean summit, held in Guadalajara, Mexico, in 2004, proved more political and more contentious. The major agreement was a resolution calling for a strengthening of the

United Nations, which the delegates said should be the sole entity to resolve international conflicts. It was seen as an oblique criticism of U.S. intervention in Iraq. Less obliquely, the delegates condemned the abuse of Iraqi prisoners by U.S. forces. As often happens, however, Cuba introduced a note of discord by complaining that the resolution wasn't harsh enough. It attacked the EU for allegedly blocking a resolution against the U.S. economic embargo and was the only nation of the 58 represented to withhold its approval of the summit's final declaration. The Cuban government then issued a statement referring to the EU as "a flock of sheep" that follows the U.S. lead. EU President Romano Prodi chided Cuba for its confrontational attitude.

Also at the summit, representatives of the EU and *Mercosur* fine-tuned some of the points for a FTA, which would have represented $40 billion in trade. The EU and *Mercosur* had concluded a FTA earlier that year, but it soon became unraveled as the two blocs quibbled over a wide array of issues. *Mercosur* wanted greater access to Europe for its agricultural products, while the EU wanted greater access for its industrial goods. The deal went nowhere.

The Fourth EU-Latin America-Caribbean Summit in Vienna in May 2006 opened under a cloud. Days earlier, new Bolivian President Evo Morales had nationalized the natural gas operations of several foreign companies, including British, French, Spanish, U.S. and Brazilian. The developed countries warned Morales and Venezuela's Chávez that such nationalizations discourage investment and in the end harm the developing countries. Morales claimed he would guarantee investors "long-lasting security." The other agenda items for the 58 leaders were trade and energy. By 2005, trade among the 58 countries had increased 13%, to $152 billion. British Prime Minister Tony Blair urged Chávez and Brazil's da Silva to use their countries' vast energy resources "responsibly," an apparent reference to the mushrooming price of crude oil.

The Fifth Summit was held in Lima, Peru, in 2008, attended by representatives of 60 countries, including 37 heads of state. The two primary agenda items were poverty and the environment and climate change, but the leaders' attention also turned to the stalled FTAs between the EU and *Mercosur* and Andean Pact blocs. The EU opted instead for bilateral trade deals with individual countries. In the final declaration, the leaders also expressed concern for skyrocketing world food prices, with particular attention to Haiti, which had just experienced food riots.

The Sixth Summit, held in Madrid, Spain May 18–19, 2010, appeared doomed

U.S.-Latin American Relations

before it started when 12 South American countries announced they would boycott it over the invitation to Honduran President Lobo, whom they deemed as illegitimate even though elected by a landsluide in a fair election. The 12 leaders continued to demand the reinstatement of Zelaya. In the end, Lobo declined to attend, but Venezuela's Chávez and Cuba's Raúl Castro still stayed away. The summit went ahead, with leaders or representatives of 60 nations participating. The global recession and the devastating earthquake in Haiti were major topics, as were technology, innovation, trade and immigration. Among the positive results of the summit was the creating of the EUROLAC Foundation, designed to promote bi-regional understanding and development, and the creation of a fund, initially with $150 million, for infrastructure projects in Latin America. Also noteworthy were the holding of numerous "mini-summits," in which trade between individual nations or blocs was discussed. As a result, the EU entered into a trade association agreement with Central America and agreed to resume the long-delayed free-trade talks with *Mercosur*. The EU also signed a trilateral trade agreement with Colombia and Peru.

The Seventh Summit will be held in Chile in 2012.

Even as the trade deal between *Mercosur* and the EU fell apart, a new window of opportunity opened with the First South American-Arab Summit in Brasilia, Brazil, in 2005. Heretofore, trade between Latin America and the Middle East had been meager, despite the blood ties that date back to the Moorish occupation of the Iberian Peninsula before 1492 and, more recently, to 19th and 20th century Arab emigration to Latin America (see Latin America Today). An estimated 20 million Latin Americans are of Arab descent, and they have achieved economic success and influence disproportionate to their numbers. The summit, organized and hosted by Brazil's da Silva, brought together representatives of 12 South American and 22 Arab countries of the Middle East and North Africa. Many of those were heads of state, including new presidents Mahmoud Abbas of the Palestinian Authority and Jalal Talabani of Iraq (in reality a Kurd, not an Arab).

A tangible result of the summit was an agreement between the four-nation *Mercosur* and the six-nation Gulf Cooperation Council (Bahrain, Kuwait, Oman, Qatar,

Saudi Arabia and the United Arab Emirates) to initiate negotiations for a FTA. But the summit had more far-reaching results as a forum for the disdain both regions harbor toward U.S. economic and military hegemony. Da Silva, in fact, rejected a U.S. request for observer status at the summit. The Declaration of Brasilia did denounce terrorism and expressed support for Iraq's battle against insurgents, but it also endorsed resistance to "foreign occupation." The declaration called for a sovereign Palestinian state and called on Israel to withdraw to its pre-1967 borders and to dismantle its settlements in Palestinian territory, including East Jerusalem. The declaration embraced the concept of free trade, but said it should be geared toward the benefit of the world's poor and should not widen the gap between developed and developing nations.

Trade between the two regions almost tripled, from $8 billion to $21 billion, by the time the Second South American-Arab Summit was held in Doha, Qatar, on March 31, 2009, on the heels of an Arab League meeting there and on the eve of the G-20 Summit in London. Three of the summit participants—Argentina, Brazil and Saudi Arabia—also attended the G-20. Once again, 22 Arab and 12 South American countries attended the second summit, including 16 Arab and eight South American heads of state. And once again, the summit declaration called for creation of an independent Palestinian state, while condemning Israel for its invasion of Gaza. Venezuela and Bolivia had severed diplomatic relations with Israel over the invasion.

The international financial crisis also was a major agenda item, and Venezuela's Chávez suggested replacing the U.S. dollar as an international currency with an oil-based "petro-currency." The final communiqué called for the "necessity of establishing an international financial system that prevents financial speculation and takes into account adequate regulations." The participants side-stepped the thorny issue of Sudan's alleged genocide in Darfur, although Argentine President Fernández avoided being photographed with Sudanese President Omar al-Bashir, subject of an international arrest warrant. The two regions agreed to continue their cooperation in international forums.

The potential for trade agreements between Latin America, on the one hand, and the EU, the Middle East or China, on the other, remains enormous. They also signal a lessening of Latin America's traditional dependence on the United States and its increasing involvement in world affairs.

The Republic of Argentina

Downtown Buenos Aires

Capital City: Buenos Aires (Pop. 13 million, including suburbs)
Climate: The northern *Chaco* region is wet and hot; the central plains, or *Pampas*, are temperate with moderate rain-fall; southern Patagonia is arid, becoming wet and cold in the southernmost part
Neighboring Countries: Uruguay and Brazil (East); Paraguay and Bolivia (North); Chile (West)
Official Language: Spanish
Other Principal Tongues: English, German, Italian
Ethnic Background: European (predominantly Spanish and Italian) 98%; *Mestizo* (mixed Spanish and Indian ancestry) 2%
Principal Religion: Roman Catholicism
Chief Commercial Products: Meat, grain, oilseed, hides, wool
Currency: Peso
Gross Domestic Product: U.S. $304.9 billion in 2009, est., ($7,455 per capita)
Former Colonial Status: Spanish Crown Colony (1580–1816)
Independence Date: July 9, 1816
Chief of State: Cristina Elisabet Fernández Wilhelm de Kirchner (b. February 19, 1953), president (since December 10, 2007)
National Flag: Sky blue, white and sky blue equal horizontal stripes with "the sun of May" centered in the white stripe.

Argentina varies widely in terrain and climate. Four main regions are generally recognized. The northern region (*Chaco*) is heavily forested, low, wet and hot; the central plains (*Pampas*) are flat, fertile and temperate, well watered along the coast and increasingly dry to the west; the southern region (*Patagonia*) is an arid, windswept plateau, cut through by grassy valleys; the fourth region (Andes) runs the length of the Argentine-Chilean frontier—the mountains are low and glaciated in the south, high and dry in the central part and gradually widen into the high plateau of Bolivia in the north.

Argentina's most important river is the Paraná, with tributaries that flow into the Rio de la Plata estuary north of Buenos Aires. Three-quarters of Argentina's land is too dry for cultivation without irrigation. The capital city and adjoining *Pampas* have 98% of the population. Temperatures vary from the hot, humid *Chaco* to the cold and damp Patagonia in the south.

History: The Río de la Plata estuary was first visited in 1516 by Spanish explorers who were driven off by hostile Indians. Magellan visited the region in 1520 and Spain made unsuccessful efforts to establish colonies on the Paraná River in 1527 and 1536. The Spanish moved up river to the Paraná's junction with the Paraguay

Area: 1,072,745 square miles (2,771,300 sq. km.) Argentina claims 1,084,120 square miles, including the Falkland Islands, in dispute with Great Britain, and other territories claimed by Chile. Its claims in Argentina total 373,774 square miles (965,597 sq. km.)
Population: 40.9 million (2009 est.)

Argentina

River, where they founded Asunción, the center of Spanish operations in southeastern South America for the succeeding 50 years. In 1573, an expedition from Asunción established a settlement in the vicinity of modern Buenos Aires and subsequently Spain transferred its base of colonial government from Asunción to the new town.

Argentina was settled by two main streams of colonists: one crossed the Andes from Peru and occupied the fertile oases along the areas on the eastern slopes of the Andes, founding Córdoba and Tucumán; the other arrived directly from Europe and settled in and around the port of Buenos Aires. Thus, from the start, two distinct groups of Argentine people developed. The people of the interior, a mixture of Spanish and Indian heritage, were dependent on the grazing of cattle on the plains of the central *Pampas* and upon small home manufactures. These isolated people developed a rude, self-sufficient civilization fiercely resistant to encroachment and disdainful of the ruling authority established in Buenos Aires by urban intellectuals.

The people of Buenos Aires, a mixture of Europeans (Spanish, French, English, Italian and German) who came to the port for trade, to defend the region or to govern it, had little interest in the Latin Americans and re-created in Buenos Aires the standards of living of the European cities

from which they originated. The nobility, which governed the defending military, and the clergy, retained special privileges; they could neither be tried in the local courts nor be held accountable to the people for their actions.

Under the Spanish colonial system, Latin America was held by a few people who administered their grants as feudal holdings. Far removed from the restraints of the Spanish court, the Argentine people evolved into a somewhat wild and free

civilization that allowed the development of community and regional pride. In 1806 and 1807, British expeditions attacked and temporarily occupied Buenos Aires; in both cases, almost without Spanish aid, the Creoles rallied and defeated the British. The following year, Napoleon's invasion of Spain turned the British into allies, but the exhilaration of those victories did much to imbue self-confidence among the Creoles.

On May 25, 1810, the *cabildo* of Buenos Aires declared it would govern the vice-

royalty of La Plata in the name of the deposed King Fernando VII; rebel envoys and armies were sent to the provinces to forge national unity, but, as in the rest of Hispanic America, attempts to hold the former viceroyalty's territories under Buenos Aires' control were far from successful. A provincial assembly eventually declared independence on July 9, 1816. Paraguay proclaimed its own independence and Uruguay, under the guidance of its popular hero José Manuel Artígas, insisted on autonomy, ushering in a long

Argentina

City Hall in Buenos Aires, 1846

period of Brazilian-Argentine conflict over the region, which culminated in a precarious Uruguayan independence in the 1840s. Even in the interior of what is today Argentina, the provinces constantly rebelled against Buenos Aires. The first 50 years of Argentine history is the history of the struggle between Buenos Aires and the provinces, and of political turmoil in the capital, where different types of government were tried in a desperate search for stability.

Argentina's greatest hero, General José de San Martín, refused to be dragged into such internecine disputes and concentrated on organizing an army to invade and liberate Chile. Like Bolívar in the north, San Martín was convinced that independence could not be assured until no Spanish stronghold remained in South America. Subsequently he crossed the Andes with his army, battling the Spanish into submission in Chile. He then turned to Peru, where he linked up with the liberator of northern South America, Simón Bolívar. Disappointed by Bolívar's refusal to take command of the two armies, San Martín, feeling that his presence as a military man might adversely affect the Peruvian revolution, retired and left for France, where he remained for the rest of his life.

Argentina started its independent history with great territorial losses and a division between its social groups—those of the port and the interior, the metropolis and the countryside. The elimination of Spanish control created a series of conflicts among the regional contenders for power. There was immediate strife between the ranchers controlling large estates on the

coast and the merchants in Buenos Aires, who insisted that all trade pass through the port, with duties and taxes used for the capital city rather than for the country. The interior provinces in turn demanded a federal form of government, with autonomous sovereign states and a national capital outside Buenos Aires.

To foster economic development, the leaders of Buenos Aires wanted to promote agriculture and expand European immigration to farm the land as was being done in the United States. The coastal ranchers, knowing that small farms would destroy their great *estancias*, made common cause with the interior to overthrow the Buenos Aires leaders and installed their own leader in 1835, Juan Manuel de Rosas. In the name of federalism, he brutally imposed "national unity" and stubbornly opposed French and British intervention in Río de la Plata, preserving Argentina for future generations. Unfortunately, his enemies belonged to one of the most brilliant generations in Argentine history, one that produced quantities of great literature. These eminent writers included Domingo Faustino Sarmiento and Bartolomé Mitre, both destined to become presidents of the republic (see Culture). A combination of Brazilian forces and Argentine caudillos finally overthrew Rosas' government in 1852.

The constitution of 1853 provided for a federal system and moved the seat of government to Paraná, 150 miles north of Buenos Aires. The former capital seceded from the union, was defeated, renewed the war and was again defeated by national forces. In 1861, the provinces ac-

cepted Buenos Aires' supremacy and the first constitutional president, Mitre, assumed office. During the years of the non-urban leadership, the fertile *Pampas* lands were seized and distributed to large estate holders, a policy that continued for several years; the governments used the army "to open" the interior of Argentina, which meant eliminating the Indians. Argentina became a cattle-raising country, while importing all manufactured goods and even food from Europe.

In the late 19th century, the demand for chilled beef led to changes in the meat industry, requiring better cattle and grains for both cattle-feeding and human consumption. Despite the changes in production, Argentine economic and political power remained in the hands of a small group of planters, ranchers and the merchants in Buenos Aires.

Contemptuous of the cattle-herding *gauchos*, the *porteños*, as residents of Buenos Aires are called, opened Argentina to European immigrants. From 1852 to 1895, hundreds of thousands of Italians, Spanish, Germans and British poured in. In 1852, of a total population of 1.2 million, non-Argentines were less than 5%, but by 1895, of almost 4 million inhabitants, more than 1 million were foreigners.

By the beginning of the 20th century, the demands for political equality by this mass of immigrants transformed the political scene. The Radical Party had become the most popular among the immigrants and emerged into the first really populist party of Argentina. Organized by an enigmatic leader, Hipólito Irigoyen, the Radical Party has maintained its influence, in one form or another, up to the present day.

General José de San Martín

Argentina

General Bartolomé Mitre

Industrialization came late to Argentina and was largely due to British investment during the last half of the 19th century. Concentrated in Buenos Aires and in the hands of a few large investors, industry centered on the supply of local needs and the transportation and processing of Argentina's export commodities. Although industrialization changed the ratio of national earnings from agriculture and cattle raising to include industrial products, it provided little increase in total earnings.

The formation of labor unions, largely through the efforts of immigrants, posed the first threat to the historic domination of the country by landed interests and industrialists, both Argentine and foreign. The unions also included displaced agricultural laborers and were initially disorganized and effectively excluded from participation in political or economic power until the first decades of the 20th century.

The ruling elite chose compromise. In 1912, electoral laws were liberalized, providing for a secret ballot and minority party representation. The first elections held under this system in 1916 resulted in a Radical Party victory under Irigoyen and the defeat of the large land-owners' and industrialists' Conservative Party. The Radical Party governed from 1916–30. Its programs included expansion of the democratic system and social reforms to benefit workers, but these fell short of expectations.

Political and social unrest soon appeared. In 1918 there was a student rebellion at the University of Córdoba; a year later, widespread strikes provoked bloody confrontations with the police. Social unrest soon caused the downfall of the Radical Party. A restless army, weary of turmoil and fascinated by Italian dictator Benito Mussolini and his totalitarian efficiency, found its opportunity in 1930 when the international depression gripped the country. An elderly Irigoyen was deposed and the armed forces seized the government "to save the nation from chaos." These "saviors" remained in or behind power for more than five decades and remain a force to be reckoned with to this day.

The Conservative Party was restored to power. For the next 13 years, a combination of landowners, bankers, merchants and generals controlled the government. But in 1943, a group of pseudo-fascist army officers, who feared the government's progressive inclinations toward the Allied powers, used "official corruption" as a pretext to seize power. Lacking a program, and with limited leadership abilities, the government failed to cope with internal problems and mismanaged foreign relations.

The Perón Eras

From the rubble of political confusion there emerged a new leader, Colonel Juan Domingo Perón, a classic charismatic *caudillo* who, wittingly or unwittingly, united forces that had resisted conservative efforts to reestablish political dominance. He brilliantly saw that no government could exist without the support of the middle class, which had grown substantially, and, more important, the laboring class.

Named labor minister under the conservative military government, Perón devoted his efforts toward seizing control of the labor unions from the Radical and Conservative parties. Tremendous assistance came from popular radio personality María Eva Duarte. The military-conservative element sensed too late that he had acquired an immense power base. When an attempt was made to remove Perón in 1945, masses rallied to his support and forced the government to desist. In the elections of 1946, Perón became president with a substantial majority.

Perón married the glamorous and even more charismatic Duarte, popularly called "Evita," and they used their abilities well, gaining firm control of labor and creating a popular mass organization called the *descamisados* ("shirtless ones"). Despite the fact that Perón threatened conservative interests, he was able to gain and hold vital army support through pay raises and military expenditures. He also received support of the clergy through advocacy of programs for religious education and by adopting a moderate position on church-state relations.

Perón and Evita built their strength through propaganda and blatant patronage, but some of their accomplishments were significant. The working class was brought into the political arena and made aware of its massive power. Evita's charitable social works provided health and welfare benefits to the poor (all, of course, widely publicized). The increased wages paid to labor and the practice of "featherbedding" in the government of Buenos Aires was deceiving, as rising prices canceled increased earnings. Mass housing, schools and hospitals and a flood of labor laws favorable to the workers dominated Perón's programs.

There was a dark side to this seeming largesse. The regime used various forms of intimidation against real or perceived opponents. Businessmen who failed to toe the line found themselves threatened with tax audits or health and safety inspections. Outspoken opponents were jailed on one pretext or another or forced into exile. The influential and nettlesome opposition newspaper *La Prensa* was expropriated in 1951. Good squads regularly resorted to physical violence to stifle opposition. Argentina was, in effect, an elected dictatorship. Just as Perón's idol, Mussolini, had proclaimed himself *Il Duce,* Perón became *El Líder* (The Leader).

Costly and often inefficient industries were created to provide jobs for the thousands streaming into the cities. Agriculture, the backbone of the economy, was taxed heavily to pay for ill-planned industrialization. The natural result was a drop in farm output, which in turn caused a drop in exports and foreign trade. Trade deficits have been perennial in Argentina.

Perón's handling of foreign relations was astute and restored Argentina's international prestige. However, his efforts to establish Argentine political leadership in Latin America were resented and resisted by most of the other nations of the continent.

The death of Evita in 1952 from cancer marked the beginning of the decline of Perón's power. Within a short time, the bankrupt state of the economy became apparent and thereafter the moral bankruptcy was difficult to hide. Popular unrest and increasing economic problems gave the armed forces, which had resisted Perón's attempts to control them, an opportunity to intervene. In September 1955, a military insurrection ended his rule, and Perón went into exile in Spain. *La Prensa* was reported to its rightful owners.

The army installed an honest but timid provisional president, who proved unable to cope with the overwhelming problems

President and Mrs. Perón

inherited from Perón. After two months, he was replaced by another general who was able to restore civil order and hold elections in 1958.

Arturo Frondizi, a civilian elected in 1958, was capable, but also a stern disciplinarian who sought to repair the damage created by Perón. He lasted until 1962, when he was overthrown by the military and replaced by Dr. Arturo Illia, who lasted until 1966 when he, too, was deposed by another military coup.

Lieutenant General Carlos Ongania was installed as the next president. He was nicknamed *"El Caño"* (The Pipe), because he was said to be straight on the outside but hollow within. His solution for Argentina's problems was to ban political parties, dismiss the Congress and neutralize the courts. It was not long before he envisioned another regime modeled after that of Mussolini with himself (of course) as permanent head. By 1969, however, his dream turned into a nightmare, replete with riots, strikes and general unrest, and he was overthrown.

Three years of near-anarchy and frequent changes in military government leadership ensued. The generals ordered elections for March 1973, and most political parties were legalized, including Perón's *Justicialista* movement. Long-standing criminal charges against Perón were dropped to permit his return from Spain. He had maintained control of his movement by balancing one rival faction against another and issuing vague political statements.

When the military refused to permit Perón to run for the presidency, he instructed his party to nominate Héctor J. Cámpora, a colorless party worker. Campaigning on the slogan "Cámpora to the presidency, Perón to power," the *Justicialistas* gained 49.5% of the vote, plus large majorities in congressional and provincial races.

Inaugurated in May 1973, Cámpora pledged to revitalize the economy, increase benefits for labor and seek closer ties with "neutralist" countries. However, Cámpora's efforts to cooperate with the restive leftists within the party quickly alienated its conservative members. Street fighting between rival factions became common; when one bloody shootout left 25 dead and hundreds wounded at an airport reception for Perón, Cámpora and his entire Cabinet were forced to resign after only 49 days in power. New elections were set for September. With anti-Perón military leaders having been forced into retirement, Perón, then 77, was free to run for president.

Ironically, many of those who supported *El Líder* included such former enemies as the military, the large landowners and business leaders—all of whom welcomed his increased conservatism. Perón's main support, however, came from his traditional base of power: organized labor. As his running mate, Perón chose his wife, Isabel, a 42-year-old former cabaret dancer. Certain of victory, he ran a

leisurely campaign based on vague promises of national unity. He received 61.9% of the vote, while the candidate of the opposition Radical Civic Union received 24.3%. A third center-right coalition candidate won less than 15%.

The problems facing Perón were immense. The economy was plagued with low growth and high inflation; leftist terrorism was rampant and his own political movement was badly divided. Perón concocted an unrealistic mixture of a leftist foreign policy and a conservative domestic program. He sought closer economic and political ties with Marxist and Third World countries. Huge credits ($1.2 billion) were offered to Cuba; at the same time, greater restrictions were placed on foreign private investments in Argentina.

Perón's domestic policies, however, were staunchly conservative. He openly courted right-wing union and political leaders. At his direction, left-wing government and school officials were dismissed and leftist publications closed. He publicly berated leftist *Peronista* youths as "mercenaries at the service of foreign forces." These conservative policies merely widened the rift within his movement. Having played an important role in bringing Perón back to power through their struggles with the military government, the leftists now refused to be pushed out. Left-wing guerrillas continued their attacks against conservative union leaders, right-wing government officials and foreign businessmen. Conservatives responded with counter-terror. The basic functions of the government ground to a halt as the rift between the right and the left, as well as between *Peronistas* and anti-*Peronistas*, fragmented the nation.

Perón's hapless plight was perhaps best seen in his 1974 May Day speech: while he was calling for "peace and conciliation" among his followers, rival *Peronista* factions broke into bloody street fighting even before his speech ended. The continued jockeying for position became even more intense as Perón's health began to fail; in hindsight, he was senile when he returned from Spanish exile. Each faction hoped to be able to seize control of the party should *El Líder* die in office.

The aging Perón tired easily and had difficulty concentrating for more than brief periods. In November, he suffered a mild heart attack from which he never recovered; death came from heart failure on July 1, 1974.

With Perón's passing, most national leaders quickly pledged their *oral* support for constitutional government and the new president, María Estela Martínez de Perón, widely known simply as "Isabel" or "Isabelita." However, a crucial difference existed between the loyalty the peo-

Argentina

ple showed toward *El Presidente Perón* on the one hand and *La Presidente Perón* on the other. She lacked his personal magnetism and the immense power base he had held, and she was totally unimaginative. Moreover, Argentines could not help but draw unfavorable references between her and the much more popular and charismatic Evita. Actually, Perón reportedly had selected her as his running mate only to allow him additional time to choose a more likely successor.

Occupying the highest office ever held by a woman in the Western Hemisphere, Isabel held conservative views that were bitterly opposed by leftists, while old-line *Peronistas* resented her because she was not Evita. More ominous, the old guard regarded her background as a nightclub dancer with a sixth-grade education as woefully inadequate—which it was. The upper classes dismissed her as a commoner, as they had Evita. Feeling herself thus isolated from traditional sources of power, Isabel began to rely heavily on the advice and counsel of José López Rega, minister of social welfare, a close confidant of the late president and somewhat mysterious practitioner of the occult. He, too, favored staunch conservative measures which, needless to say, were opposed by moderates and bitterly resisted by leftists.

La Presidente **Isabela Perón**

Frail and reclusive, Isabel delegated broad power to López Rega and other key officials in the hope of pulling the nation out of an economic nosedive caused by runaway inflation, growing shortages of industrial and consumer goods, a thriving black market, huge budget and foreign trade deficits, declining domestic and foreign investments and a disastrous drop in farm output. Isabel worsened the fiscal plight by permitting large wage increases in violation of an earlier wage-price freeze. Although the move was popular with the large labor movement, it triggered widespread business losses which, in turn, led to a further escalation of inflation, which by 1975 was at an annual rate of 330%.

Meanwhile, the policy of overtaxing farmers to subsidize the immense urban population had caused a major decline in farm exports, which traditionally furnished the bulk of Argentina's foreign exchange earnings. As a result, the nation faced a trade deficit of $600 million in 1975. Worse, some $2 billion in foreign debts were due the same year; although foreign reserves stood at $1 billion when the *Peronistas* took office in 1973, they plummeted to an all-time low of only $2 million by early 1976. To finance the government, the money supply was expanded by 200%.

In spite of further attempts at austerity (which failed), the economic picture worsened until there was virtual paralysis. Political conditions also declined—violence became the worst in the nation's history. Assassinations by left-wing and right-wing terrorists claimed 1,100 lives during 1975. One leftist group, the *Montanaros*, collected huge fees by kidnapping business leaders. One kidnapping netted the guerrillas $60 million.

During the 21 months she was in office, Isabel reorganized the Cabinet 10 times. The conservative labor movement—long a pillar of support for Perón—continued to increase the distance between itself and Isabel. The loss of this vital support paved the way for the collapse of the Perón presidency. Increasingly erratic, *La Presidente* took a leave of absence from her job in late 1975.

Compounding the economic and political malaise was a growing public resentment against increasing reports of widespread political corruption. Among those implicated was Isabel, who was accused of transferring half a million dollars from a public charity to her own bank account. The *Peronista*-controlled Congress voted along strict party lines to block an inquiry. At the same time, López Rega's Rasputin-like influence over the president was the subject of widespread gossip.

Government corruption, rising terrorism, a reeling economy and disintegrating

Lt. Gen. Jorge Rafael Videla

government control of national affairs prompted a long expected military coup on March 24, 1976—the sixth within the prior 21 years. Isabel was whisked away from the roof of the presidential palace by helicopter—under military arrest. Army Lieutenant General Jorge Rafael Videla, 50, was named president and head of the three-man junta.

The "Dirty War"

To combat Argentina's mounting problems, the generals vowed to fight for three key goals: an end to political terrorism, a drastic cut in the inflation rate and economic development.

To control inflation, wages were frozen, taxes were increased and prices were allowed to rise to their natural levels. Also, the peso was devalued by 70%, government spending was reduced and farm prices were raised to stimulate agricultural growth. These measures helped cut inflation from 35% *a month* to about 10% by early 1978. Political corruption was a special target, and the *junta* moved swiftly to prosecute those who profited illegally under the *Peronista* government; Isabel Perón was so charged and remained under house arrest.

The junta was able to boast of some dramatic improvements in the economy. Foreign reserves jumped from $20 million in 1976 to $10 *billion* by mid-1980. Farm output also grew, paced by a 52% rise in wheat production during the 1978–79 season over the previous harvest. Oil and natural gas exploration was increased as the government sought to attain self-sufficiency in energy. Nonetheless, the liberalization of monetary policy helped to undermine confidence in the peso.

The cost in human lives was even greater. Hoping to improve domestic stability—and thereby stimulate economic investments—the government unleashed a terror campaign against the leftists. Between 1976 and 1981, some 6,000 to 15,000 persons simply "disappeared" after having been arrested by security forces. To protest these human rights abuses, the Carter administration suspended military aid to Argentina.

For their part, however, the leftists didn't have the words "human rights" in their vocabulary. Summary executions of military personnel using clandestine, terrorist and guerrilla tactics were ordinary occurrences at the time. Terrorist bombings claimed many innocent lives.

Retaliation by the military was equally grisly. It was revealed in 1995 that a naval mechanics school converted into a prison was the destination for many of those arrested by the military. A prison guard wielding a hypodermic loaded with a hypnotic drug would inject a shackled prisoner. When he became unconscious, he was loaded aboard an airplane that flew over the Atlantic for an appropriate distance. The unconscious (but not dead) prisoner would be unceremoniously dumped overboard. Dissidents thus did indeed disappear, without a trace. The school also served as a torture center.

Economic Woes

The nation's economic boom proved short-lived, and by 1981 the country was mired in a recession and disenchanted with military rule. To enhance its public image, the junta tried several moves. In 1981, Videla was replaced by a more moderate general, Roberto Viola. The government bowed to the demands of the *Peronistas* and freed Isabel; she promptly took up a luxurious and quiet exile in Spain.

Still, the opposition to military rule persisted. In December 1981 the junta fired

ARGENTINAZO: ¡LAS MALVINAS RECUPERADAS!

ACCION CONJUNTA DE NUESTRAS FUERZAS ARMADAS; MARCHAN AVIONES Y BARCOS EN GRAN OPERATIVO; EL TIEMPO CONSPIRA

Buenos Aires' *Cronica* (April 2, 1982) hails Argentina's "recovery" of the Malvinas (Falkland Islands)

Viola, replacing him with hard-line Army Commander Leopoldo F. Galtieri. In contrast to Viola, who attempted to deal with the banned political parties, the new president sought to reaffirm the military's control of the government and its commitment to free-market economic policies. Although Galtieri pledged to deal more firmly with the nation's economic problems, the recession intensified, driving inflation to 130% and unemployment to 13–16%. By March 1982, labor unrest was spreading and the outlawed political parties were agitating for a return to constitutional government.

The Falkland Islands War

At that point, Galtieri and some top military commanders made a momentous decision. Taking advantage of a dispute between Argentina and Britain over the sparsely populated but British-held Falkland Islands (*Malvinas* to the Argentines), the president ordered the armed forces to seize them in April 1982. After an absence of 149 years, the Argentine flag once again flew over this disputed territory. Overnight, Galtieri and his military conquerors were the heroes of Argentina. For the next 74 days, Argentina and Britain were at war.

General Leopoldo F. Galtieri

Argentine troops man the Falkland beaches

Argentina

The dispute over the Falklands started in the 1500s. On the basis of initial occupation, the Argentine historical claim did seem to have somewhat greater validity.

Despite treaties, the British established colonies on the islands in the 1770s, but they were soon abandoned. The Spanish claims to the islands were transferred to Argentina when it achieved independence in 1816. Four years later, Argentina reaffirmed its sovereignty over the archipelago as parts of the islands were settled and land grants were awarded.

At the urging of the U.S. consulate in Buenos Aires, the British forcibly occupied the islands in 1833 and all Argentine residents were deported. For the next 149 years, Argentines were prevented from living on the islands, and until 1999 Argentine citizens had to buy a round-trip ticket before they were even allowed to *visit* the islands. Since 1851 the islands had been largely controlled by the Falkland Islands Company, a London-based firm that owns 40% of the main two islands.

Economically, the Falklands have little to offer except offshore oil deposits. Charles Darwin called them "the miserable islands" when he visited them in 1833. Most of the residents today are engaged in sheep ranching and wool production.

The Argentine invasion of 1982 *did* violate two basic principles of international law: use of force to settle international disputes and the right of self-determination. As a result, the U.N. Security Council voted to demand that they withdraw. There was widespread sentiment in Latin America in favor of returning the islands to Argentina, and the United Nations had voted overwhelmingly in the 1960s and 1970s to ask Great Britain to negotiate on the islands' "decolonization." The British position in 1982 was for 25 more years of control over the islands. Argentina warned that it might seek "other means" to resolve the dispute.

It was this frustration with diplomacy that set the stage for the invasion. The conflict quickly escalated. The Argentine air force crippled a British destroyer with an Exocet missile and sank a conveyer ship, while a British submarine torpedoed and sank the Argentine battleship Belgrano, with a loss of more than 300 lives. The British army landed in the Falklands, quickly defeating the Argentine defenders, most of them poorly trained conscripts.

After 10 weeks, there were 1,700 Argentine casualties, including 650 dead or missing. The beaten Argentines left enormous amounts of military equipment worth millions of dollars. The British held 11,000 POWs. After a lengthy delay, they were returned to remote ports in Argentina where they were received amid great security (in part to prevent media

coverage) and with little fanfare. The battle cost the British $2 billion—$1 million for each Falklander.

For Argentina, the war was a disaster. The army was humiliated, the military dictatorship was discredited and the economy was pushed toward bankruptcy. In Buenos Aires, fickle, angry crowds marched on the Plaza de Mayo demanding to nail "Galtieri to the wall!" In order to prevent elimination of its power, the *junta* promptly fired him.

For the next week, the government remained virtually paralyzed while the three armed forces quarreled over a successor. Having just lost on the battlefield, the army—the largest of the three services—had no intention of going down in defeat on the home front as well. Unable to reach an agreement, it named retired Major General Reynaldo Benito Antonio Bignone as president. In dismay, the navy and air force said they would not actively participate in the new government.

The United States was put in an awkward position by the conflict. Its endorsement of a 1947 Inter-American Treaty of Mutual Defense (better known as the Rio Treaty) was questioned when it refused to side with Argentina, but Secretary of State Al Haig that the Rio Treaty did not apply because the first use of force had not come from outside the hemisphere. Argentina's support of President Reagan's efforts against communists in Nicaragua and El Salvador was terminated.

Return to Democracy

Demoralized by defeat and besieged by monumental social and economic problems, the Argentine military government had no other expedient but to allow the electoral process to run as fast and smoothly as possible while attempting a rear-guard action to protect the armed forces from future judicial action. Encouraged by political freedom, human rights activists demanded more information about the *desaparecidos* (disappeared ones) during the "Dirty War" and stern punishment for those responsible for the crimes. The military *junta* answered with a declaration that the *desaparecidos* should be considered dead and with a law granting amnesty to military security personnel involved in the anti-terrorist campaign of 1976–1982. An outraged public opinion forced the presidential candidates to announce they would repeal the law as soon as civilian authority was reestablished.

On October 30, 1983, general elections were held. The winner, Raúl Alfonsín of the Radical Civic Union (*UCR*), represented a more moderate tendency in the Argentine political spectrum. The *Peronistas*, poorly organized, were waiting for

Isabel to return, but she preferred her more peaceful life in Spain.

The new democratic government faced a multitude of urgent problems, but three were especially pressing: control of the armed forces, labor demands and a depressed economy. The full extent of the military's crackdown became clear in late 1985 when nine military leaders, including Videla, Viola, Galtieri and Admiral Emilio Massera were placed on trial. Furious with an attempt by the military to whitewash the gruesome activities of elite military and paramilitary units, the civilian courts assumed jurisdiction. The trial furnished lively media material, describing in detail methods of torture and execution. The defense presented by the generals was predictable: they were fighting a war against a subversive enemy financed from abroad, and they did not know the extent of the excesses being perpetrated by their subordinates. In typical military fashion, those subordinates claimed they were simply following orders.

Videla and Massera (the Navy member of the Videla *junta*) were sentenced to life for 62 murders; three others were given nominal sentences. Galtieri and two other principals were acquitted, but Galtieri was sentenced by a court martial to 12 years imprisonment for "negligence" in directing the armed forces during the Malvinas war. His son, killed in the conflict, was buried on one of the islands.

Thousands of human rights activists, led by the Mothers of the Plaza de Mayo, who sought information as to their absent loved ones, paraded to protest the leniency of the sentences. This illustrated a well-known fact about the military in Argentina—the country cannot exist without it and cannot stand living with it. Nevertheless, prosecution of thousands of former military and police strongmen began in 1986, with orders that they be expedited. This led to extreme unrest within the ranks and, in 1987, a serious threat of military revolt. To dispel this, Alfonsín asked Congress to grant amnesty to all military personnel below the rank of colonel—an action which the liberals (but not the *Peronistas*) denounced. The president was obviously under heavy pressure from the military. The net result was that of 7,000 potential defendants who could have been tried for atrocities, perhaps 50 actually were charged; there were few convictions.

In 1985, there began action as well against former *Montanaro* leaders who had touched off the "Dirty War" of the 1970s. The defense to charges of murder and kidnapping was also predictable: the organization was only exercising political rights and responsibilities.

It was on the international economic front that Argentina scored its most im-

40

pressive, if indecisive, success. Under the burden of a public debt estimated at about $48 billion, Argentina threatened to ignore a 1984 deadline for paying $500 million in interest to creditors around the world. After several complicated maneuvers, the alarmed bankers agreed to new terms and better payment conditions. Argentina temporarily gained a respite and showed other debtor nations they were not without bargaining power.

The austerity program, necessary to support economic reorganization on even a modest level, sharply lowered living standards. A basic problem involved investment funds. The trade surplus was eaten up by the need to pay interest. It was necessary to borrow additional funds to pay that interest, pushing the external debt to $64 billion.

Although Alfonsín initially appeared to be an astute politician, his knowledge of economic policy was meager, and he had

Raúl Alfonsín

no competent advisers. The result was hyperinflation caused by spiraling wages and prices (as much as 400% per month!). A new currency, the *austral*, was introduced, but it was devalued so many times it became worthless.

Alfonsín tried repeated wage-price freezes that didn't work. Strikes became commonplace. Although the country could have been self-sufficient in oil production, he demanded 50% of production from potential foreign producers as the price of exploration.

The *Peronista* movement splintered into two factions, but in 1988 they agreed on the nomination of Carlos Saúl Menem, popular governor of the impoverished province of La Rioja in the northwest, for president. His running mate was Eduardo Duhalde, from Buenos Aires. Years later,

they would become bitter rivals for control of the party.

Menem, of Syrian descent, proved to be a colorful and charismatic candidate, promising everything to everybody. He was known for his love of movie starlets and fast cars. He trounced his opponent from Alfonsín's *UCR*, receiving 47.4% of the vote to 32.5%. Alfonsín had vowed to serve until the end of his term in November, but, beset with riots and a host of unsolvable problems, he stepped down in July; Menem was sworn in. He was faced with a debt of $69 billion.

The Menem Presidency

What those attending the inaugural heard was quite different from that which they heard before the election. "I do not bring easy or immediate promises ... I can only offer my people work, sacrifice and hope," he said, sounding rather Churchillian. "We must tell the truth, once and for all: Argentina has broken down." He announced a number of controversial measures calculated to restore order.

The early days of Menem's presidency were stormy. Prices went up, restaurants emptied and pasta became a disliked meat substitute. By the end of 1989, all military were pardoned, including Galtieri and later, Videla, infuriating many; 1 million signed a resolution of protest. Menem normalized relations with Britain. His popularity plummeted sharply. He took an ominous step in 1990, signing a decree authorizing the military to act in the event of "social upheaval." Further, it would command all state and local police in such an event. The economy continued its downward spiral and the middle class became poor.

In an ingenious move, Menem privatized about 90 state monopolies. Part of the purchase price was the purchase of a portion of Argentina's external debt, worth about 30 cents to the dollar. The first to go was the antiquated telephone system, which fetched more than $1.8 billion in hard currency. In 1992, Menem effectively tied the latest Argentine currency, again called the peso, to the U.S. dollar to slow inflation and to encourage North American and European investment.

The economy turned sharply upward, at least on the surface, but the improvement did not affect all sectors. In a hurry to placate union workers and the economic elite, the government tended to overlook the small business sector and the white-collar workers. Privatization took its toll among relatives and party favorites—or as economists call them, "redundancies." In other words, unless a person actually did something productive, he or she was fired. In the past, this was unheard of. Favoritism had not been limited

Carlos Saúl Menem

to the elite; unions also had benefited. The result was the same: low productivity.

Foreign investors remained wary, so Menem energetically set about changing age-old employment patterns. The result spoke for itself. Both the gross national product and the annual per capita income more than *doubled* after 1990, while inflation was in single digits.

Meanwhile, scandals and corruption involving Menem's in-laws tarnished his image (although he never pretended to be an angel). When a dispute arose with his wife in 1990, he threw her out of the presidential palace. She provided exciting copy for the media, particularly the tabloids.

Menem moved to repeal the constitutional limitation that forbade a president more than one consecutive term. His constitutional six-year term was to end in 1995. To do this, it was necessary to have the cooperation of the *UCR*. A deal was made (the Olivos Pact) between Menem's *Justicialista* Party and the *UCR* for a constituent assembly, the prime purpose of which was to enable Menem to run for a second term. The two parties had the two-thirds majority (211 of 305 seats) adequate to adopt the constitutional amendment. The bill also reduced the presidential term to four years, created the office of prime minister and gave the president the power to nominate Supreme Court justices, subject to a two-thirds vote in the Senate.

Menem easily won re-election in May 1995 with about 50 percent of the vote, thus avoiding a runoff. Vice President Duhalde left the ticket to win the governorship of Buenos Aires Province. No sooner did Menem win his second term than the effects of the Mexican peso deval-

Argentina

Edición
Internacional
Vía Aérea

LA NACION

Una selección
de la semana

Año 120 - Nros. 42.255 al 42.261 - Ed. Int. Nº 1502 - Año 28   Buenos Aires, lunes 3 de julio de 1989   Bouchard 557, C. P. 1106, Tel. 313-1003, 1453 y 312-3021/9

Menem dispondría la libertad de militares

Lo reveló implícitamente, al sostener que no puede ver encerrados "ni a los pájaros"; viajará a los EE. UU., en septiembre, por el problema de la deuda externa

Por César Ivancovich

(Enviado especial de LA NACION)

Jueves 29

LA RIOJA.- El presidente electo, Carlos Menem, reiteró que hay que cerrar las heridas entre militares y civiles y reveló implícitamente que todos los hombres de armas condenados por la Justicia recuperarán su libertad, al utilizar la expresión: "Yo no puedo ver encerrados ni a los pájaros".

También anunció que viajará en septiembre próximo a los Estados Unidos, en un intento por revertir la "extrema dureza" advertida en los medios financieros internacionales respecto de la Argentina.

"No hay vuelta que darle, todo pasa por allí", comentó el todavía gobernador riojano al justificar la aceptación del convite formulado por el presidente norteamericano, Georges Bush.

Menem no sólo se refirió a las dificultades que enfrenta la economía en el plano externo -en su reciente viaje a Washington, el canciller-designado, Domingo Cavallo, se estrelló contra una dura muralla construida por los centros financieros-, sino también en el ámbito local.

Admitió, por ejemplo, que esos 2500 millones de dólares que según versiones aportarían empresas locales para el arranque de su plan económico son, por ahora, algo así como un espejismo en el medio del desierto. Nadie sabe, empero, si al seguir avanzando la imagen corresponderá efectivamente a un oasis.

Por lo que dicen los allegados de

Lo que sí dijo ayer el presidente electo es que la dureza que implica va a ser mayor después de los cien días que al comienzo de su gestión. Cree que las medidas de shock por aplicarse de entrada serán efectivas para bajar la inflación, pero que las requeridas para mantenerla en ese nivel, después de los tres primeros meses, podrían llegar a ser mucho más duras.

Este enviado le preguntó si creía que los operadores retirarían su capital del circuito financiero para invertirlo en la producción. "Sí. Los especuladores deberán replegarse, pues habrá créditos baratos para la producción. Las mesas de dinero tendrán que adaptarse o desaparecer", sentenció el futuro presidente.

Formalizaron sus renuncias Alfonsín y Víctor Martínez

Las presentaron en el Congreso; serán aceptadas el 8, antes de que jure Menem

Sábado 1

El presidente Raúl Alfonsín y el vicepresidente Víctor Martínez presentaron ayer al Parlamento sus renuncias, para que la Asamblea Legislativa del 8 del actual las acepte momentos antes de que preste juramento como nuevo mandatario el doctor Carlos Saúl Menem.

Se formalizaron así las dimisiones anunciadas por Alfonsín en su discurso del 12 de junio, cuando anticipó su decisión de resignar el cargo a partir de ayer.

El sobre lacrado con la renuncia del jefe del Estado llegó al Congreso en manos del secretario general de la Presidencia, Carlos Becerra, quien lo entregó a Víctor Martínez en su carácter de titular del Senado.

Al recibir la renuncia -en una breve ceremonia realizada en su despacho- Martínez sumó la suya, también en sobre cerrado. Ambos fueron entregados al secretario parlamentario de la Cámara alta, Antonio Macris, y sólo serán

a la formalidad o un mensaje extenso con consideraciones o pronunciamientos políticos.

"Misión histórica"

"Presentar la renuncia me apena un poco, pero nos complace saber que esto lo hacemos en beneficio del país", dijo Víctor Martínez a los periodistas tras el acto en su despacho.

Becerra, por su parte, declaró que se sentía "muy honrado por esta misión histórica que me encomendó el Presidente: este acto cierra el capítulo de la consolidación de la democracia".

Agregó que el radicalismo acompañará "con alta responsabilidad" la nueva etapa política que comienza el 8 del actual.

Alfonsín en el Congreso

Martínez confirmó, asimismo, que pasado mañana Alfonsín concurrirá al Congreso, a las 17, para saludar protocolarmente al nuevo titular provisional

La Nación headlines two watershed events on July 3, 1989: President–elect Menem's declaration that he would release jailed military officers as a gesture of reconciliation, and the resignations of President Alfonsín and Vice President Martínez, which allowed Menem to take office five months early.

---

uation struck Argentina, plunging it into recession. Unemployment soared to 18%.

Menem kept his promises to modernize the economy through privatization and other free-market reforms, and he accomplished the unthinkable by keeping inflation to single digits. Still, the painful remedies cost Menem his popularity. In 1996, the *Peronistas* were dealt a severe blow when Fernando de la Rua, the *UCR* candidate for mayor of Buenos Aires, won a decisive victory in that *Peronista* stronghold.

In 1997, the Radicals entered into an opposition alliance with *Frepaso*, a *Peronist* splinter group, to contest the October congressional elections. The Alliance wisely chose not to attack Menem's successful free-market policies, because the economy was still growing at a robust 8%. Instead, the Alliance hit the president where he was most vulnerable: the rampant corruption within his administration, which had grown so bad that Economy Minister Domingo Cavallo, the architect of the new economic miracle, resigned in disgust in 1996. In the elections for 127 of the 257 seats in the lower house, the *Peronistas* suffered another serious setback by losing their absolute majority, dropping from 131 seats to 119; their share of the popular vote plummeted from 43% in 1995 to 36%. The Alliance won 106 seats, while other parties held 32 and the balance of power.

There was a hostile relationship between Menem and the press. Unlike years

past, the Argentine media now enjoy unprecedented freedom and they dutifully exposed scandal after scandal in the Menem government. In January 1997, José Luis Cabezas, an investigative photographer who was probing alleged police corruption, was found beaten, shot and burned to a cinder in his car. The crime shocked the nation and brought international pressure on Menem to bring the killers to justice. The scandal reached a head in 1998 when the wife of one of two policemen arrested in connection with Cabezas' murder publicly revealed that they had been hired by Alfredo Yabrán, a powerful, influential and secretive tycoon rumored to have Mafia ties and who for good measure was a close friend of Menem's. Cabezas had surreptitiously taken the first published photographs of the reclusive Yabrán, who, like Menem, was of Arab descent. As police closed in on Yabrán's *estancia* to arrest him for Cabezas' murder, the tycoon apparently shot himself to death. There was no autopsy, and rumors circulated that the Mafia had silenced him. Quipped the U.S. ambassador: "Yabrán committed suicide, but we don't know who did it yet."

Yabrán's mysterious death was not to be the last to rivet the attention of the press and public. In 1998, former navy Captain Horacio Estrada, who had just been subpoenaed to testify in controversial and illegal arms sales to Ecuador and Croatia, was

found dead in his apartment with a gunshot wound to his head. Two months later, businessman Marcelo Cattaneo, who was expected to appear in court in connection with another high-profile scandal involving alleged bribes by Banco Nación and the U.S. computer firm IBM, was found hanged on a communications tower. Both deaths were ruled suicides, but the press raised allegations of organized crime connections. A defensive Menem responded, "We can't jump to conclusions."

The Elections of 1999

Duhalde, as governor of Buenos Aires Province, regarded himself as the logical heir apparent to Menem. But Menem shocked the country—and infuriated Duhalde—by hinting in 1998 that he would be amenable to a constitutional amendment permitting him to run for a *third* term. For most it seemed a moot point; the Peronists had lost their majority in the Chamber of Deputies. Menem was faced with increasing opposition within the party, a chorus of criticism from the press, the near-impossibility of pushing such an amendment through Congress and opinion polls showing him running in the single digits.

Tension between Menem and Duhalde mounted, and Duhalde pulled off an astute political maneuver: a referendum in Buenos Aires Province on whether or not

42

... and the socially elite at the glittering Colón Theater
in Buenos Aires

the constitution should be amended to allow Menem to run again. It was a classic poker player's bluff; it could have backfired if the vote were yes, but Duhalde was confident the vote would go against Menem. Menem realized it, too, and folded. He withdrew from the race, but boasted he would return to power in 2003. Duhalde easily won the party primary.

The Alliance, meanwhile, had a schism of its own between the *UCR*'s Fernando de la Rua, mayor of Buenos Aires, and *Frepaso*'s Senator Graciela Fernández Meijide, mother of one of the "desaparacidos" of the Dirty War. In the Alliance's primary in November 1998, de la Rua handily defeated her 63% to 36%. De la Rua chose as his running mate a *Frepaso* strategist, Carlos Alvarez. As a consolation, Fernández Meijide became the Alliance's candidate to succeed Duhalde as governor of Buenos Aires Province. Her opponent was Menem's retiring vice president, Carlos Ruckauf.

The disgruntled Domingo Cavallo, Menem's erstwhile economic adviser, launched an independent candidacy for president.

The ensuing campaign was the most dramatic the country had seen since the restoration of democracy. But 10 years of Peronist rule, coupled with nagging public concerns over official corruption and an alarming 14.5% unemployment, proved too much of an encumbrance for Duhalde.

In the balloting in October, de la Rua scored a decisive first-round victory, receiving 48.5% of the vote to Duhalde's 38% and Cavallo's 10.2%. With characteristic bombast, Menem declared on election night, "I could have won easily," a claim that was highly debatable.

The Alliance also increased its number of seats in the Chamber of Deputies from 106 to 123, just six short of a majority, while the *Justicialistas* fell from 122 seats to 101, their worst showing since 1985. The *Justicialistas* did win a number of governorships, among them Buenos Aires, where Ruckauf defeated Fernández Meijide. Moreover, they still controlled the Senate, which required de la Rua to govern by consensus.

In July 1999, Foreign Minister Guido di Tella and British Foreign Secretary Robin Cook signed a bilateral agreement that in effect ended the diplomatic hostilities over the Falkland Islands. Argentine nationals were once again permitted to visit the islands.

Even before he took office, de la Rua also found himself involved in foreign affairs. He and Menem both denounced Spanish Judge Garzón's charges against 98 former Argentine officers (see Ghosts from the Past) as an infringement on Argentine sovereignty and refused to recognize them.

Faced with a strained relationship with an old European friend, de la Rua made an effort to further improve relations with a long-time European foe. While in Paris in November to represent the Alliance in the Socialist International convention, he held a 20-minute dialogue with British Prime Minister Tony Blair. The two men agreed in principle to expand upon the bilateral agreement reached in July on the Falkland Islands. Prince Andrew, a Falklands War veteran, represented Britain at de la Rua's inauguration.

De la Rua's Aborted Presidency

De la Rua was sworn in on December 10, 1999. The new president soon demonstrated that his administration represented not merely a change in parties and personalities but in style as well. He sold Tango 1, the ostentatious presidential jet, a Boeing 757 that cost Argentine taxpayers $66 million and a small fortune to fly and maintain as well. De la Rua took trips by commercial jet.

De la Rua advocated a $2.5 billion tax increase to reduce the $7.1 billion budget deficit. The IMF responded with a $7.4 billion loan, but the tax increase was unpopular with the public. Nonetheless, polls showed that while his government had only a 42% approval rating, the president's was 63%. That would soon change.

De la Rua then introduced a controversial labor reform bill to allow more flexibility in labor contracts, a gesture to wary foreign investors and to the IMF. The still-powerful trade unions took to the streets to protest the new measure after it passed the Chamber of Deputies. In April 2000, union militants surrounded the Congress and clashed with police. It was merely a taste of what was to come.

The Senate passed, 57–4, a compromise version. De la Rua slyly promised entrenched labor bosses that he would not probe their operations if they would support it. The Chamber of Deputies passed it 121–84.

Fissures appeared in the Radical-*Frepaso* Alliance after de la Rua announced $938 million in budget cuts and reductions of up to 15% in civil service salaries. *Frepaso* members of Congress revolted, as did Fernández Meijide, who had become social development minister. Left-wing members of the Alliance also grumbled over what they regarded as undue influence on de la Rua by his close friend Fernando de Santibañes, a prominent and conservative banker de la Rua had named head of the National Intelligence Service (*SIDE*).

A one-day work stoppage was called in June 2000, the most serious expression of public disapproval yet of de la Rua's aus-

Argentina

terity measures, which the public nicknamed *"el Ajuste,"* or, the Adjustment.

De la Rua shuffled his Cabinet in October 2000. But when he retained Santibañes, Vice President Alvarez resigned in protest. Alvarez denounced corruption in the government, but insisted he and his party would remain loyal to de la Rua. Fernández Meijide remained in the Cabinet, prolonging the illusion that *Frepaso* was a partner in the government. Alvarez's resignation would confront Argentina with a constitutional crisis 14 months later.

At year's end, de la Rua admitted that the country's economic performance had been disappointing in 2000, with GDP down by 5% and unemployment remaining around 15%. About the only bright spot was a $40 billion IMF economic rescue package. Among the terms: Argentina had to reduce its budget deficit from more than $9 billion to $6.5 billion by the end of 2001.

In March 2001, de la Rua appointed a new economy minister, a conservative technocrat, Ricardo López Murphy, trusted by investors but detested by the Peronists and *Frepaso*. He lasted only two weeks, but he provoked the last remaining *Frepaso* Cabinet members, including Fernández Meijide, to resign by announcing $4.5 billion in budget cuts. De la Rua stunned the country—but delighted international financial markets—by resurrecting Domingo Cavallo to replace López.

Cavallo came up with a series of offbeat ideas designed to placate the IMF and, in theory, to jumpstart the flagging economy. One proposal: Granting emergency powers for one year to the president—in reality, to Cavallo—to deal with the crisis by decree. Congress and the IMF approved these "superpowers."

Cavallo then offered another offbeat idea: Instead of pegging the peso solely to the dollar, the inflation-busting technique he had fathered a decade earlier, he proposed pegging the peso to the average of the dollar and the Euro, the European Union's new monetary unit.

Argentina suspended issuance of $700 million in treasury bills, and its international risk rating jumped more than 10% to 1,049—a rate worse than Russia's. Cavallo insisted his recovery plan was "on track."

In a separate development, a federal prosecutor accused Menem of being the intellectual author of illegal arms sales in 1991 to Ecuador, then in a virtual state of war with Peru, and to Croatia, then under a U.N. arms embargo. Menem denied it.

Always flamboyant, the 70-year-old Menem splashed back into the international headlines in 2001 by marrying Cecilia Bolocco, a 36-year-old former Miss

Fernando de la Rua

Universe from Chile. He made headlines again when he was placed under house arrest on the arms sale charges. He was indicted, but the Supreme Court threw out the charges.

In July 2001, de la Rua announced another austerity plan to trim the deficit and stave off defaulting on the $128 billion foreign debt. The plan included a 13% pay cut for civil servants, which sparked labor protests. Argentina's country risk indicator jumped to 1,616 points—worse than troubled Ecuador's.

The austerity plan may have pleased the IMF, but it proved highly unpopular to the Argentines. By October, de la Rua's approval rating was 18% and Cavallo's was 16%. In the October elections for the entire Senate and half the Chamber of Deputies, the Peronists strengthened their majority in the Senate and increased from 102 to 116 in the lower chamber, becoming the largest bloc. The *UCR* dropped from 84 seats to 71, while *Frepaso* dropped from 23 to 17. In the popular vote, the Peronists received 40%, the Alliance only 23%. Duhalde won a Senate seat from Buenos Aires. But 30% of Argentines angrily cast blank ballots or nullified them. The public mood was dangerously ugly.

For the next two months, de la Rua and Cavallo desperately tried to deal with the deepening crisis and to avoid default on the national debt, which had increased to $132 billion; it would be the largest default in history, one that threatened to generate global shock waves. In November, he announced a "debt swap," that traded $95 billion worth of existing bonds that paid 11% for longer-term bonds that paid only 7%; for investors, it was a no-brainer. Then the Peronist governors rejected his proposed reduction in federal remittances to the state governments, something he

needed to meet the terms for a $22 billion international rescue plan.

Descent into Chaos

By December 2001, fears of an imminent default and economic meltdown had Argentines in a near-panic. De la Rua infuriated them by reducing the monthly limit on savings withdrawals from $1,500 to $1,000. The IMF did not help matters by freezing a scheduled $1.3 billion installment on its $22 billion line of credit because of the government's lack of progress in meeting demands on deficit reduction and because it felt the peso had become overvalued by the dollar peg.

Events then exploded in chain reaction. On December 11, the government pleaded for consensus with the Peronists to cut the budget 14% to obtain the desperately needed IMF help. The deficit was $11 billion, double what de la Rua had assured the IMF it would be by year's end. The Peronists demanded de la Rua's resignation as their price for cooperation. On December 13, there was a massive general strike to protest the 18.3% unemployment rate. The next day, the government announced it had allayed defaulting on the debt by making a loan payment of more than $700 million.

For the next six days, Argentina was a powder keg. On December 19, it exploded.

The spark was a demonstration by mostly middle-class Argentines, frustrated over the decline in their living standards and weary of their financial insecurity. The demonstrations began peacefully with the traditional *cacerolazo*, the banging on pots and pans, but soon there were violent clashes with police. Full-scale rioting erupted in the capital and other cities. Rioters looted grocery stores. Five people were killed that first day, and de la Rua declared a 30-day state of siege—the first since the 1989 riots that shortened the Alfonsín presidency. The riots continued on December 20. Demonstrators tried to storm de la Rua's office. More people were killed, as de la Rua pleaded for calm. With the republic literally falling apart, the entire Cabinet, including Cavallo, resigned in a vain attempt to quell the violence. The number of rioters in Buenos Aires alone was estimated at 20,000. Thousands of people rushed to banks to withdraw their monthly limit.

That evening, de la Rua himself resigned, two years and 10 days after he was inaugurated, and at sunset he was ignominiously whisked away from the Casa Rosada by helicopter, a scene eerily like that in 1976 when the military overthrew Isabel Perón. The mobs cheered, but it was a hollow celebration. The death toll had climbed to 22, many of them looters shot

The next hapless interim president was Eduardo Carmoña, speaker of the Chamber of Deputies, who like Puerta would keep the presidential chair warm for 48 hours until a joint session of Congress met on New Year's Day 2002 to select the nation's fifth president in 12 days. Meanwhile, on New Year's Eve, Congress canceled the March election and decided to appoint an interim president. The initial plan was for the interim president to fill out de la Rua's term, which would have expired on December 10, 2003.

Caretaker Government

The unfortunate "winner" of the January 1 balloting: Duhalde, the losing presidential candidate in 1999. The vote was 262–21, with 18 abstentions. Duhalde was sworn in on January 2, 2002. He told Congress and the nation that he was scrapping the "exhausted model" of free markets and neoliberal economic policies that he blamed for the country's plight and that he would "recreate the conditions" to attract investors. "Argentina is bankrupt," he bluntly told his countrymen, "Argentina is destroyed. This model destroyed everything." He called for a return to the pre-Menem Peronist ideals of populism and protectionism. He promised to guarantee deposits to prevent further panic—or violence. He also continued the moratorium on foreign debt payments. But he avoided mention of the two most sensitive topics—a possible peso devaluation and whether he would lift the detested restriction on bank withdrawals, which Argentines had nicknamed "*el corralito,*" or little corral.

Duhalde appointed a bipartisan Cabinet but with the key posts going to Peronists. As economy minister, he named Jorge Remes Lenicov, an internationally respected economist. Duhalde and Remes submitted to Congress an emergency economic plan that granted Duhalde and Remes *carte blanche,* authorized devaluation of the peso and froze job layoffs for six months. On January 3, Argentina missed an interest payment on a $28 billion loan; the country was officially in default. Congress quickly approved it. Remes ended the decade-old peg of the peso to the dollar and devalued the peso 40%, saying it would be allowed to float freely.

The IMF denounced Duhalde's economic plan as incoherent, while U.S. President George W. Bush told the OAS in Washington that Argentina would face a "bleak and stagnant future" if it returned to the old Peronist protectionism.

The Supreme Court declared the restrictions on savings unconstitutional. Remes responded with another bank holiday, as depositors armed themselves with court

Rounding up sheep for market

not by police but by shopkeepers defending their property.

Despite de la Rua's resignation, the rioting continued, as a leaderless government tried to cope with the violence as well as with a constitutional crisis. With the vacancy in the vice presidency caused by Alvarez's resignation in 2000, de la Rua's constitutional successor was the Senate president, Ramón Puerta, a Peronist. But Puerta eschewed his constitutional mandate, which he said made him president for only 48 hours. It was hard to blame him.

Thus, Argentina was literally on the brink of anarchy by December 22, when Congress called new elections for March and the Peronists tapped their governor of San Luis, Adolfo Rodríguez Sáa, as their choice for interim president until then. He was elected on a 169–138 vote in a joint session of Congress and sworn in on December 23. Rodríguez Sáa lifted the state of siege, suspended payment on the foreign debt, and channeled the money into the creation of 1 million new jobs, the first 24,000 to be public service jobs.

It seemed that the country at least was no longer rudderless, as calm temporarily returned; the final death toll from the ri-

ots was 27, with hundreds more injured or arrested.

On December 29, pot-beating protesters took to the streets again to protest Rodríguez Sáa's decision to continue the limit on savings withdrawals. Again, the protests turned violent, although not deadly. Protesters coined a popular new slogan that summed up the national mood: *Que se vayan todos!* (Throw all of them out!) They tried to storm their way into the Casa Rosada and the Congress, but were expelled by riot police.

If Rodríguez Sáa had thought he would have more success than de la Rua at achieving a consensus, he was soon disappointed. He urged the Peronist leaders to offer solutions that might quell the popular uprising without worsening the economic crisis and to reach a consensus on how to select the Peronist candidate for the March election. They could not—or would not.

On December 30, after exactly one week in office, Rodríguez Sáa resigned in disgust, bitterly lashing out at the members of his own party for failing to support him on the tough decisions that had to be made. Mob rule, it seemed, was close to prevailing in Argentina.

Argentina

orders directing the banks to give them their money. Remes also declared that bank withdrawals and government transactions would henceforth be in pesos. This announcement led to more violent demonstrations. (A year later, the Supreme Court ruled the conversion of bank accounts from dollars to pesos was an unconstitutional infringement of private property rights.)

Duhalde finally persuaded the Peronist governors to agree to a revenue-sharing plan the IMF demanded. But the economic situation worsened. Unemployment increased to an alarming 23.8% in April 2002—about what it was in the United States during the depths of the Great Depression. The peso hit an all-time low of 4.00 to the dollar. The percentage of Argentines living below the $200-a-month poverty line mushroomed to 57%. Then, suddenly, another old enemy returned: inflation. In April 2002 alone, prices rose 10%. The combination of double-digit unemployment and double-digit inflation defied the laws of economics and renewed a climate of desperation. The government then devised a scheme requiring depositors to accept five- and 10-year bonds in exchange for some accounts. Depositors reacted with fury.

In April, Remes abruptly resigned after Congress rejected his proposed bank reform plan. Duhalde appointed Roberto Lavagna, a trade expert and former ambassador to the European Union and the World Trade Organization, as economy minister—the country's sixth in 14 months.

In a separate, unrelated development, Cavallo was arrested in connection with the alleged sale of illegal arms to Ecuador and Croatia that had implicated Menem. At the same time, an appeals court ordered the presiding judge in the case to reopen the investigation of Menem and several others.

In May, Duhalde finally received some good news: the IMF agreed to give Argentina another year to pay a $136 million loan that was due. The IMF also agreed to postpone a $2.8 billion loan payment, but it rejected Argentina's request for an aid package unless several reforms were adopted. The talks broke down. In January 2003, the IMF relented and agreed to a $6.8 billion loan to prevent a default on the $141 billion debt, which would have had global financial repercussions that nobody wanted.

The Election of 2003

A frustrated Duhalde advanced the presidential elections by six months, from September to March 2003, then moved them back again to April 27. For the first time, a runoff would be held on May 18

if no candidate received a majority. The new president would be inaugurated on May 25.

A new intra-party turf battle quickly erupted between the Menem and Duhalde factions over who the Peronist candidate would be. Duhalde succeeded in getting party backing to scrap the Peronist primary altogether, obviously because he knew Menem might win. Instead, the election became a free-for-all, with rival Peronists, Radicals and independents winding up on the same ballot, Louisiana-style.

Rodríguez Sáa declared his candidacy, as did a dark horse, Néstor Kirchner, the populist Peronist governor of Santa Cruz Province in remote, sparsely populated Patagonia. Duhalde endorsed Kirchner, which infuriated both Menem and Rodríguez Sáa. Kirchner scored points by promising to retain the popular Lavagna as economy minister. With three strong candidates who were slinging mud at each other, it seemed the Peronists were in the process of disemboweling themselves.

The opposition was fragmented, too, however. Former Economy Minister Ricardo López Murphy, a Radical who survived his association with de la Rua with his reputation intact, announced as an independent and became the preferred choice of the country's business sector. Another new face, Elisa Carrió, elected to Congress as a Radical, launched a new movement with an anti-corruption platform. The poor, discredited *UCR*, meanwhile, offered up a political lightweight, Leopoldo Moreau, as its sacrificial lamb.

The vote totals stunned everyone:

Menem	4,686,646	24.36%
Kirchner	4,232,052	22.0%
López Murphy	3,144,528	16.34%
Carrió	2,720,692	14.14%
Rodríguez Sáa	2,715,799	14.12%
Moreau	450,489	2.34%

Far from feeling elated over his first-place showing, the once-popular Menem was shocked that he had failed to poll even a fourth of the vote. He was shocked even more when polls showed Kirchner would humiliate him by more than 2–1 in the runoff. Faced with his first-ever electoral defeat, what Menem did next was generated by pure ego: On May 14, he withdrew from the runoff and made Kirchner president by default. It was more than just an egotistical move designed to avoid humiliation; it was pure Machiavellian politics, Menem-style. Kirchner, denied an electoral victory, would have to govern for four years—if he lasted—on a shaky second-place mandate from only 22% of the voters. Menem, meanwhile, would be reminding Argentines of that every step of the way.

Eduardo Duhalde

Kirchner Shakes Up the System

Kirchner, 53, a lawyer, was sworn in on May 25, 2003. Shaky mandate or not, he began rattling the country's institutions and its foreign policy. At least 12 Latin American presidents attended the inauguration, including Cuba's Fidel Castro, Venezuela's Hugo Chávez and Brazil's Luiz Inácio da Silva—all critics of the U.S.-supported Free Trade Area of the Americas. Kirchner repeated his opposition to the FTAA after he was sworn in, and the inauguration became something of a festival of the Latin American left. Kirchner also let it be known he sided with da Silva in stressing regional Latin American integration, and touted a concept he called "national capitalism." The Bush administration snubbed Kirchner by sending only the secretary of housing and urban development, Mel Martínez.

Just three days into his term, Kirchner forced 27 army generals and 13 navy admirals into retirement. The upper echelons of the armed forces reacted angrily, but meekly complied. What else could they do? They obtained little sympathy from the senior field-grade officers who stood in line for promotion to general and admiral. Then Kirchner began cashiering top-ranking federal police officers as well.

The same month, Kirchner turned on the judiciary, asking Congress to impeach "some" of the nine Supreme Court justices. In unusually blunt language in a nationally televised address, Kirchner accused the justices of corruption and cronyism and of holding the nation "hostage" by decisions that had hamstrung many of Duhalde's economic reform plans. The Argentine justice system is notoriously corrupt, and Duhalde had tried unsuccessfully to impeach the justices. Kirchner focused on justices appointed by, and still loyal to, Menem, especially Supreme Court President Julio Nazareno. He

Ghosts from the Past

The past came back to haunt Argentina in 1998, beginning with controversial statements by two former naval officers that scraped open the still-healing wounds of the Dirty War. One, Adolfo Scilingo, voluntarily traveled to Spain, where he was wanted for human rights violations against Spanish citizens in Argentina, and served three months in jail. Upon his release, he openly expressed remorse in a press interview that he had participated in the so-called "death flights," in which an estimated 1,000 naked prisoners were thrown to their deaths into the ocean from aircraft. He called for war-crimes trials for his fellow officers.

The other officer, Alfredo Astiz, known by the sobriquet "the Blond Angel of Death," was arrogant and unrepentant. Astiz had been sentenced in absentia to life in prison by France in 1990 for the murder of two nuns, and he was also wanted by Spain and Italy for Dirty War atrocities against nationals of those countries. He, too, admitted in a magazine interview that he had killed prisoners, but justified it as necessary. His remarks sparked an outcry. Jailed briefly, he remained defiant. Menem stripped him of his rank. In 2001, Astiz was arrested at the request of Sweden, which wanted him to try him for the death of a Swedish girl during the Dirty War. He was later released and has yet to stand trial—anywhere.

The Astiz incident prompted a move to repeal the amnesty granted to military officers after the return to civilian rule. In the end, Congress passed a watered-down version.

Almost simultaneously, the public expressed outrage over Menem's plan to raze the Navy Mechanics School, the most notorious of the military's torture centers during the Dirty War, and replace it with a park containing a memorial to the victims. Most Argentines preferred to convert the school into a museum, like those dedicated to Holocaust victims. A judge issued an injunction against plans to demolish the building, not on sentimental grounds but on the pretext that destruction might destroy criminal evidence.

Former President Videla was re-arrested in 1998, this time on charges he participated in selling the babies of "disappeared" dissidents to adoptive parents. Videla's 1990 pardon on war crimes charges did not cover these new allegations. The so-called "baby-stealing" probe widened after Videla's arrest. Former Admiral Emilio Massera, navy chief during the Dirty War, was re-arrested after DNA tests showed that two women adopted as babies were children of parents who had disappeared after being arrested; one of them was adopted and raised by an aide of Massera's. Massera suffered a debilitating stroke in 2004 and the next year was ruled mentally incompetent to stand trial.

The case against Videla languished until 2010. Videla, who turns 85 on August 21, is now scheduled to stand trial in September, not only on the baby kidnapping charges but for the kidnapping and torture of 40 prisoners.

Former President Reynaldo Bignone was arrested in 1999 for possible involvement in the baby-kidnapping scheme but was not charged with a specific crime. Several more officers were detained in the baby-stealing investigation. His case, too, languished until 2009, when he and six other elderly former officers finally went on trial in November, not on the old baby-stealing allegations, but for the kidnapping and torture of 56 prisoners at the Campo de Mayo detention center in Buenos Aires. More than 100 people testified in the five-month trial. In April 2010, they were convicted and sentenced to 25 years in prison—not house arrest, as had been requested because of their age. Bignone by then was 82.

Spanish Judge Baltasar Garzón, the same judge who had requested the arrest of former Chilean strongman Augusto Pinochet by the British in 1998, charged 98 former Argentine officers with alleged human rights abuses in 1999.

In 2001, a federal judge ruled that the amnesty laws absolving the military of wrongdoing in human rights cases were unconstitutional. A judge then ordered the arrests of 12 former military men and six civilians at the request of Judge Garzón. In 2002, former President Galtieri and 41 others were detained in connection with the disappearance of 20 *Montanaro* suspects during his presidency. Galtieri died in 2003.

Néstor Kirchner, who became president in 2003, accelerated investigations into, and arrests for, human rights abuses. At Kirchner's urging, Congress repealed two of Alfonsín's amnesty laws that had blocked further prosecutions of military officers.

A federal judge quickly ordered the arrests of 45 former officers. Forty of them had been charged by Garzón and Spain sought their extradition, but Kirchner's government insisted on bringing them to justice in Argentina The notorious Astiz was arrested. France sought his extradition for the murder of the two French nuns. But his indictment in Argentina in 2004 served notice that he would face an Argentine court.

Kirchner then recalled the Argentine attaché to Italy, Horacio Losito, in connection with the massacre of 22 dissidents in Chacó in 1976. A retired brigadier general and two retired colonels were arrested as part of the investigation into torture centers operated in Buenos Aires during the Dirty War, including the Navy Mechanics School. Kirchner had the school turned into a human rights museum in 2004. Kirchner also ordered police files opened and an investigation into whether the army was still abusing prisoners three years after the return to democracy.

Scilingo, the navy captain who had voluntarily surrendered to Spanish authorities and had admitted participation in the "death flights," finally went on trial in Madrid in 2005. Scilingo abruptly recanted his confession, but the court found him guilty of 30 counts of murder and of torture and illegal detentions. He was sentenced to 640 years.

Later that year, the Supreme Court declared an amnesty granted to lower-level police officials unconstitutional, making possible the prosecutions of nearly 800 people. In 2006, federal judges also nullified the pardons Alfonsín had granted to Videla and Massera in 1990; they appealed.

One of the few Argentine officers Spain actually had behind bars was Ricardo Miguel Cavallo, a former lieutenant at the Navy Mechanics School, who was arrested in 2003. Inexplicably, Spain extradited him to Argentina in 2008.

Other ghosts pre-date the Dirty War. In 2007, former President Isabel Perón was arrested in her exile in Spain in connection with the disappearance of a Peronist activist during her presidency in 1976. She was released, but Argentina subsequently sought her extradition. In a court appearance in 2008, Perón, then 77, argued that she is immune from extradition because she has Spanish as well as Argentine citizenship; her attorneys also argued she is in poor health. Two weeks later, the Spanish court rejected the extradition request on the curious grounds that the allegations did not constitute an abuse of human rights.

In August 2008, two prominent retired generals, Antonio Bussi and Luciano Menendez, were sentenced to life imprisonment—both are in their 80s—for the kidnap-murder of Senator Guillermo Vargas on the day of the 1976 military coup. Both men were unrepentant. Menendez had been sentenced to life the month before for the murder of four activists in 1977. Menendez went on trial again in October 2009 for illegal detentions, torture and homicide. But a key witness, Jesús González, a former detention camp guard, was found dead in his bathtub in Cordoba with a stab wound in his heart. Numerous other witnesses in human rights trials have died under mysterious circumstances in recent years.

A forensic anthropology team spent seven months searching through a former detention center in the city of La Plata and in December 2008 announced they had recovered 10,000 human bone fragments. It was the first time human remains had been recovered at a detention center.

In 2009, two former navy pilots were arrested in connection with the "death flights." Captain Emir Sisul Hess was arrested in Bariloche for the deaths of 56 prisoners, while Lieutenant Julio Alberto Poch was arrested in Spain, accused of pilotinmg flights from which 950 prisoners may have been thrown tomtgheirm deaths. Poch was extradited to Argentina in May 2010.

The disappearances and torture and the anguish of families searching for missing loved ones during the Dirty War inspired Lawrence Thompson's novel *Imagining Argentina*, made into a motion picture in 2003 starring Antonio Banderas and Emma Thompson. Another novel about the Dirty War, Eduardo Sacheri's *El secreto de sus ojos (The Secret in Their Eyes)*, was made into an internationally acclaimed movie by Argentine director Juan José Campanella in 2009 (see Culture).

Estimates of the numbers of "disappeared" range from 9,000 to 30,000, although the official number is 13,000. Their families continue to seek answers and justice, and their ghosts seem destined to haunt Argentina for years to come.

Argentina

and four more Menem appointees resigned in the face of likely impeachment.

Kirchner then shook up taxpayers by announcing a crackdown on tax evasion—a time-honored tradition in Argentina. Reliable estimates indicate that revenue could be increased by 50% if all the tax cheaters paid what they owe.

Kirchner simultaneously made a splash in international circles. U.S. Secretary of State Powell belatedly visited Argentina after the OAS foreign ministers' meeting in Santiago, Chile. Kirchner assured Powell he wanted amicable relations with the United States, but also insisted that Washington maintain a respectful distance. The next day, Kirchner flew to Brasilia, where he and da Silva repeated their call for greater Latin American integration. Kirchner also reiterated Argentina's claim of sovereignty over the Malvinas (Falkland Islands), and called on Britain to resume talks on the islands' future. Britain summarily rejected the suggestion.

Horst Köhler, managing director of the IMF, came to Buenos Aires to meet with Kirchner and Lavagna on the conditions for debt restructuring. Kirchner bluntly told Köhler that he would not agree to any further conditions that would cause more suffering, and Köhler just as bluntly replied that the suffering would end only if there were an economic climate that again attracted foreign investors and encouraged Argentines to bring their money back from foreign accounts. Köhler conceded that "Argentina needs to deepen and broaden its structural reforms, but this cannot be done in six months." Köhler also agreed that some of the IMF-demanded reforms could be delayed. The two sides agreed to start negotiations on a three-year plan to repay the $13.5 billion that would be coming due between 2003 and 2006. Köhler left saying he was "impressed" with Kirchner.

Nonetheless, in September 2003, Argentina defaulted on a $3 billion payment to the IMF on its $90 billion debt, the largest single missed payment in IMF history. A day later, Kirchner negotiated a deal with the IMF that allowed Argentina to restructure payment of $21 billion of the debt over three years. Kirchner addressed the United Nations in New York, where he laid part of the blame at the feet of the IMF itself and of developed nations that block the exports of developing nations.

Relations with the IMF had improved immeasurably by January 2004, when the IMF announced that it was satisfied with Argentine compliance with the 2003 agreement. But in August, Kirchner suddenly and inexplicably canceled the agreement with the IMF. For good measure, Kirchner defiantly informed the holders of the $102.6 billion in outstanding Argentine bonds that he would exchange them for new bonds worth only about 30-35% of the value of the originals and, in essence, told them to take it or leave it. Creditors screamed foul and demanded that Kirchner compromise on a less painful figure. He refused. Faced with recovering 30 cents on the dollar or nothing, more than 70% of the bondholders decided to take it when the deadline for the so-called debt-swap deal expired on February 25, 2005. Officially, the world's largest debt default in modern history was over, but Argentina had no international credit.

Ironically, one effect of the reneging on debt obligations was a huge budget surplus, which Kirchner invested in infrastructure and social programs. Thus, although his actions and his rhetoric made Kirchner a pariah to the IMF, he became enormously popular with the Argentines. He became the first president since Menem who could boast of an *improving* economy.

In 2004, a crime wave, much of it attributed to increasingly organized gangs of unemployed or homeless people, had the capital in a grip of fear. Residents took to the streets again in mass demonstrations to demand that something be done. The law-and-order demonstrators proved not much better than the criminals. In July, hundreds of them stormed city hall in Buenos Aires and held it for several hours before police finally acted. Kirchner sacked the police chief for not acting more expeditiously. When the justice minister publicly criticized the chief's firing, the pugnacious president fired him as well. Concern over crime continues today.

Another crisis was an acute energy shortage, blamed on frozen electricity rates that led to increased demand. The foreign-owned utility companies complained that inflation made the current rates unrealistic and prevented further investment, but Kirchner steadfastly refused to raise the rates on residential customers. The water supply system also was affected, and the freeze strained relations with France, because the French company Suez owned a 40% share of Aguas Argentinas. Some local blackouts occurred. Like crime, energy remains a political issue.

Menem, the perennial bad penny of Argentine politics, remained a force his detractors, including Kirchner, could not ignore. In 2004, an Argentine judge issued an arrest warrant for Menem, who was living in Chile with his Chilean wife and their baby, for allegedly embezzling $60 million from two prison construction projects. A Chilean judge rejected Argentina's extradition petition, ostensibly because the stated reason for the extradition, Menem's failure to appear in court, is not an extraditable offense. Two Argentine judges rescinded the warrant, and the flamboyant Menem triumphantly and with great media fanfare returned to Argentina days, vowing to defeat his fellow Peronist Kirchner in 2007.

Kirchner experienced the same kind of break with his mentor Duhalde that Duhalde had had earlier with his mentor Menem, as both grappled for control of the *Peronista* movement. The crucial test of their strength came in the mid-term congressional elections in October 2005, in which a third of the 72 Senate seats and almost half the seats in the 257-member Chamber of Deputies were contested. The most symbolic showdown came in the Senate race in Buenos Aires Province, which pitted the two rivals' wives against each other. It turned into the political equivalent of a female mud-wrestling match. Cristina Fernández de Kirchner soundly defeated Hilda González de Duhalde, 46% to 20%. Kirchner's allies also won 15 of the 16 Senate seats, giving the Kirchner faction a majority. His faction also emerged as the largest in the Chamber of Deputies. Kirchner had finally received the electoral mandate Menem had denied him in 2003.

Emboldened, Kirchner announced a Cabinet shakeup, stunning the country by removing Lavagna, who was largely credited for Argentina's near-miraculous economic recovery. Probably the most controversial new face was that of Defense Minister Nilda Garré, who had been involved with the leftist *Montanaro* guerrillas during the Dirty War.

In a dramatic development, Kirchner announced in December 2005 that Argentina was repaying its entire $9.8 billion debt to the IMF, using currency reserves that had accumulated during the economic recovery. The repayment saved Argentina 4.5% interest payments, further fattening the budget surplus for domestic programs that had made Kirchner so popular. The announcement came two days after Brazilian President da Silva made a similar announcement—and almost four years to the day after the riots that precipitated de la Rua's resignation. Argentina had indeed come a long way back from the brink of the abyss. However, Kirchner paid nothing toward a $6.7 billion debt owed to the so-called Paris Club of creditor countries, including the United States, Japan, Germany and Italy.

Congress granted Kirchner virtual *carte blanche* in August 2006 to reallocate government spending, causing concern in some circles over such a concentration of power. Kirchner also began re-nationalizing some companies, including the postal service, the Buenos Aires water system and an airline.

A Dynastic Power Play

The economy grew by 9.2% in 2006 and remained robust as the country prepared

Former President Néstor Kirchner

President Cristina Fernández de Kirchner

for the presidential election on October 28, 2007. The man Menem had thought would collapse from his shaky 22% mandate in 2003 enjoyed a 70% approval rating, phenomenal for Latin America—or any democracy anywhere. Yet, he coyly insisted, as he had from the beginning, that he would not seek a second term, although few believed him.

Kirchner's sacked economy minister, Lavagna, announced his candidacy under the banner of a movement called An Advanced Nation, hoping voters would credit him with Argentina's economic miracle. He was endorsed by former presidents Alfonsín and Duhalde, for whatever that was worth. Elisa Carrió announced she would try again, as candidate of the Civic Coalition Confederation; anticorruption remained her theme. Former interim President Rodríguez Sáa also ran, as did 10 lesser candidates. Still, polls showed Kirchner to be unbeatable.

Then, the always enigmatic president did something every bit as Machiavellian as Menem had done in 2003: He announced he was yielding the Peronist presidential nomination to his wife, Cristina, 54. The apparent motive: If elected to a second term, he would have to yield power in 2011; if his wife could keep the presidential chair warm for four years, he could run again in 2011 and stretch their rule to 12 years—or longer. Political pundits immediately began comparing Senator Cristina Fernández de Kirchner to Senator Hillary Rodham Clinton in the United States. Because of her stylish manner, others compared her to Eva Perón. Indeed, Fernández herself publicly stated she identified with Evita.

This nepotistic power play would have offended voters in most countries, but it

was indicative of Kirchner's popularity for taking Argentina from economic bust to boom and from chaos to confidence that Argentines enthusiastically rallied around his wife.

Although the Peronists were split between Fernández and Lavagna, the *UCR* had virtually ceased to exist as a viable political force, as some Radicals supported Carrió, others backed Lavagna, while one, Julio Cobos, the governor of Mendoza, became Fernández's running mate.

Polls consistently showed the outcome to be a foregone conclusion. More than 19 million Argentines went to the polls, a turnout of 74.14%. Fernández received 8.2 million votes, or 44.9%, to 4.2 million, or 23%, for Carrió. Because the difference was greater than 10 percentage points, Fernández was elected without a runoff. The once-popular Lavagna was a distant third with 3.1 million votes, or 16.9%.

Argentina's first elected woman president—and Latin America's fourth—was sworn in on December 10, 2007.

Any hope that relations with the United States would improve under Fernández were dashed when the U.S. Justice Department in Miami arrested and indicted two Venezuelan businessmen for allegedly funneling $800,000 in illegal campaign contributions to Fernández's campaign in a suitcase. The money reportedly originated with the state-owned Venezuelan oil company, *Petroven*. Fernández angrily denounced the U.S. allegations as "garbage," but she soon became reticent in the face of damning evidence. The indictments widened, and two Venezuelans and an Uruguayan pleaded guilty in federal court in Miami in 2008 of failing to register as foreign agents. Another went on trial, while a fifth testified that another suitcase containing $4.2 million from the Venezuelan government made it through customs to Fernandez's campaign. The Argentine media labeled the matter "Suitcasegate."

In March 2008, the president found herself faced with a more serious challenge close to home after she abruptly and drastically raised the export tariffs on agricultural products; the tax on soybeans alone was hiked from 27% to 44%. Farmers went on strike and blockaded roads leading into the capital, and grocery store shelves emptied. The beef-loving Argentine middle class resorted to the traditional form of protest, the *cacerolazo*, the pounding on pots and pans. Protests erupted throughout the country, including in the Plaza de Mayo, the first *cacerolazo* there since the economic meltdown of 2001. Fernández denounced the farmers' strike as "extortion." After 21 days, the farmers voluntarily suspended their strike, apparently

fearful the privation it was causing could backfire on their cause. The crisis nonetheless forced the resignation of Fernández's economy minister, Martín Lousteau. After talks with the government failed to resolve the impasse, the farmers announced another eight-day stoppage. The public generally sympathized with the farmers, and Fernández's approval rating plummeted to 20%.

The farmers next took the tax to court, and the Supreme Court agreed to rule on the constitutionality of the president's imposing a tax by decree instead of by statute. Apparently sensing she would lose, she then introduced the necessary legislation to Congress. It narrowly passed in the Chamber of Deputies despite cloakroom deal-making, and the Senate vote ended in a 36–36 tie. Vice President Cobos, the Radical whom Fernández had chosen as her running made in the interest of unity, cast the tie-breaking vote—*against* the bill. A furious Fernández retaliated against her vice president's disloyalty by sacking six of his loyalists from their government posts.

Fernández turned her attention to the economy, which was impacted by the worldwide market slump in late 2008 and went into recession. In a dramatic reversal of her husband's policy, she announced in September 2008 that she would repay the $6.7 billion owed to the Paris Club. This not only saved money on interest payments, but it also made Argentina eligible for new loans for infrastructure improvements at reduced interest rates. This in turn lessened Argentina's growing dependence on Venezuela, to which Argentina was paying a usurious 15% interest rate on bonds.

Argentina

Fernández made another dramatic announcement in November 2008: The re-nationalization of the unpopular private pension system, which amounted to $23 billion. Critics accused her of raiding the pension system to meet a budget deficit caused by the falling price of soybeans. The move has had a negative effect on private investment.

In March 2009, Fernández and the farmers seemed to have reached an agreement to end their long-simmering tax standoff, but when Congress failed to obtain a quorum to reduce the taxes, the farmers used trucks to blockade highways throughout the country. Vice President Cobos broke with the president over the issue.

Former President Alfonsín died on March 31, 2009, at the age of 82. The accolades from all political parties and the outpouring of public grief at his state funeral for the man who brought Argentina from dictatorship to democracy in 1983 was in sharp contrast to the denunciations and riots that forced him to leave office early in 1989.

In the latest of their Machiavellian power plays, the Kirchners pushed Congress to move forward the date of the mid-term congressional elections, from October to June 28, 2009. The president's popularity was 30%, and the couple evidently feared it would sink even lower by October. In addition, the global recession was causing the economy to slow dramatically after the boom years, and the Kirchner faction of the *Justicialista* Party concluded it would suffer voter reprisals by October. It was a major high-stakes political gamble, in which Kirchner himself ran for the Chamber of Deputies to head his faction's ticket in Buenos Aires, putting his reputation and very political future on the line. The anti-Kirchner faction entered into an alliance with Buenos Aires Mayor Mauricio Macri and nominated wealthy businessman Francisco de Narváez to go head-to-head against Kirchner.

Kirchner, the erstwhile president who had boasted a 70% approval rating, narrowly lost to de Narváez, although he was awarded a seat through proportional representation. The pro-Kirchner faction, Front for Victory, lost its majority in both houses of Congress. Kirchner resigned as president of the party the day after the election. His Peronist faction now has 35 Senate seats to 37 for the opposition alliance. Senator Carlos Ruckemann, a leader of the anti-Kirchner faction, was narrowly re-elected in Santa Fe, while an ally of Vice President Cobos won a landslide victory for the Senate in Mendoza. In the Chamber of Deputies, the Front for Victory won only 87 of the 257 seats. The *UCR* won 42, the anti-Kirchner Peronist faction (Federal Peronism) won 29 and the rest are fragmented among a bewildering 31 other movements.

Recent Developments

Instead of being cowed by their humiliating defeat, the Kirchners appear to have grown more combative. In August, President Fernández introduced the controversial Audio-Visual Communication Bill, which is ostensibly designed to diversify the country's broadcast outlets. In reality, it seemed aimed directly at breaking up the powerful Grupo Clarín, a media conglomerate that owns the influential newspaper of the same name and controlled two thirds of the country's cable television market. The newspaper has been one of the Kirchners' most nettlesome critics; probably not coincidentally, de Narváez is a member of its board of directors. "Freedom of expression cannot turn into freedom of extortion," she rationalized in a speech. In September, tax auditors raided the newspaper's offices, but found nothing incriminating.

The media bill mandated that the nation's radio and television outlets would be divided into thirds among the government, private companies and "non-profit" organizations. It was debated furiously in the lower house, where the president succeeded in winning the support of enough independent deputies to ensure passage. Opponents walked out in protest, and it passed 147–4. In October, it passed the Senate 44–24. International journalism organizations denounced it as a Chávez-like measure to intimidate opposition media and to extend government control over mass communication.

By January 2010, the once-plump budget surplus and turned into a yawning deficit. To alleviate it, Fernández ordered the Central Bank to transfer $6.6 billion in foreign reserves to a special fund designed for debt service. The bank's director, Martín Redrado, demurred, protesting that the Central Bank was independent of presidential mandates and that only Congress could authorize such a transfer. Fernández forced him out and replaced him with Mercedes Marcó del Pont, who complied with her order, but then the opposition-controlled Congress stymied her.

Nonetheless, Congress granted her authorization to lift the ban her husband had imposed on debt restructuring and began ardent overtures to try to mend the shattered fences with foreign—and domestic—holders of Argentine bonds. With the sour economy, she needs to make Argentine bonds attractive again by lowering their risk factor, but as this book went to press, her efforts were showing no signs of success.

Even as their popularity plummets at home, the Kirchners have been enhancing their stature on the world stage. Fernández was accorded the honor of delivering the closing address at the 2009 Ibero-American Summit in Estoril, Portugal, which she used as a forum to announce that she intended to make Argentina's renewed claim to the Falkland Islands an agenda item when she hosts the 2010 summit in Buenos Aires. In April 2010, she attended President Barack Obama's Nuclear Security Summit in Washington, where she and Obama engaged in bilateral talks on non-proliferation and apparently came away in agreement. A month later, Fernández also took center stage at the Sixth EU-Latin American-Caribbean Summit in Madrid. She hosted Russian President Dmitry Medvedev on his first state visit to Argentina in April 2010. Fernández's foreign ministry issued a sharply worded protest to Iran in September 2009 when President Mahmoud Ahmadinejad appointed as defense minister Ahmad Vahidi, who Argentina believes is the mastermind of the 1994 terrorist bombing of the Israeli-Argentina Mutual Association in Buenos Aires that killed 85 people. This issue is another that has distanced Fernández from her one-time ally and benefactor, Chávez, who enjoys close ties with Iran.

In May, Kirchner was elected the first secretary-general of the six-year-old South American Union of Nations (*UNASUR*). Until the organization sets up its permanent headquarters in Quito, Ecuador, it will be seated in Buenos Aires. Kirchner's acceptance of the *USASUR* post seemed peculiar, as he has publicly indicated he intends to stand for president again in May 2010 (see The Future).

Culture: Unlike most of the South American colonies, Argentina did not develop a *mestizo* race (European-Indian) because the indigenous inhabitants were driven ever westward beyond the expanding frontier or were exterminated outright. This genocidal military policy extended into the late 19th century. While the United States and neighboring Brazil imported African slaves, what was to become the laboring class in Argentina stemmed from a wave of European immigrants, chiefly from Spain and Italy, who were attracted during the 19th century by work on the cattle ranches and in the wheat fields, vineyards and emerging industries.

Consequently, Argentina's ethnic make-up today is almost wholly European, with Italian descendants accounting for nearly half the population. This also has given Argentine Spanish a distinctly Italian inflection, an unmistakable accent that is the butt of jokes in other Latin American countries.

Carlos Gardel

Lesser influxes of British and German settlers, many of them well-to-do investors, also have colored Argentina's social fabric, as have Jews, Arabs and Gypsies.

Which is not to say that Argentina lacks a rich cultural heritage of its own. As occurred in the United States, the romanticism associated with the conquest of the frontier and the development of vast stretches of rich farming and grazing lands of the *Pampas* gave rise to a uniquely Argentine folk hero: the *gaucho*, or cowboy. As with the North American cowboy, it is difficult to separate myth from reality, but unquestionably the raw-boned *gauchos* with their baggy cotton pants, sheepskin chaps and *bolas*, (the device used to ensnare the legs of running calves) greatly shaped Argentine culture and folklore. Their drum-based music, *malambo*, is as identifiable with Argentine culture as the tango.

One of the great works of the so-called golden age of Argentine literature of the late 19th and early 20th centuries was the epic poem *El gaucho Martín Fierro*, written by José Hernández in two installments in 1872 and 1879. Martín Fierro occupies much the same place in Argentine folklore as do Paul Bunyan or Pecos Bill in the United States. It is not uncommon to see truck stops in northern Argentina today named for this folk hero. The legacy of the *gauchos* also is exploited today for tourist purposes in such Buenos Aires steakhouses as *La Estancia*, where waiters dress in traditional *gaucho* garb and *malambo* groups provide live music.

The wealth of the *estancias*, or ranches, also shaped Argentines' meat-based diets. The most popular eating places in Argentina, except perhaps for the ubiquitous pasta bars, are *parrilladas*, which specialize in assorted meats grilled over wood embers; often an entire goat is staked out on a metal frame and roasted in front of a *fogón*, or bonfire. The most common social gathering is the *asado*, a barbecue on a massive scale in which sometimes dozens of guests consume a variety of meats and wash them down with copious amounts of domestic wine, which can be excellent.

The relative enlightenment that followed the Rosas dictatorship in the mid-19th century allowed a rich literary tradition to take root. Two of the greatest writers of this period also were leaders in the struggle for democracy. Bartolomé Mitre served as president of the republic during the pivotal period of 1862–68, and two years after leaving the presidency he founded the daily newspaper *La Nación*, still published by his descendants today and regarded as one of the world's great newspapers.

Domingo Faustino Sarmiento was forced into exile during the Rosas era and nettled the dictatorship from neighboring Chile, where he edited *El Mercurio*, then based in Valparaiso. Sarmiento's writings proved inspirational not only for Argentines but for other Latin Americans saddled with dictatorship, and he is revered as one of the premier figures of Latin American letters. He succeeded Mitre in the presidency, serving from 1868–74.

Another great newspaper of record, *La Prensa*, was established in 1869; it served as a conduit for the poems, stories and essays of the great writers of the golden age. Both it and *La Nación* also developed a reputation for resisting the will of dictators; *La Prensa*, published by several generations of the Gainza and Paz families, was closed by Perón from 1951–55.

This tradition continued into the 20th century, when *La Nación* made space available for the verse of a blind man acknowledged as Argentina's greatest poet: Jorge Luis Borges (1899–1986). His reputation was global, although the Nobel Prize eluded him all his life. Like many of Latin America's great writers, artists and musicians, he spent much of his career in Europe, in part because of Argentina's periodic reversions to dictatorship and the chilling effect that invariably had on the arts. He died in Switzerland in 1986.

Other notable 20th century Argentine writers include Julio Cortázar (1914–84), a novelist, playwright and poet, perhaps best remembered for the plays *Los reyes* (1949) and *Bestiario* (1951) and the novels *Los premios* (1960), *Rayuela* (1963), *62/Modelo para armar* (1968), and *Libro de Manuel* (1973); and Ernesto Sábato (b. 1911), a renowned

essayist and author of three memorable novels: *El túnel* (1948), *Sobre héroes y tumbas* (1961), and *Abbadón el exterminador* (1974). Both Cortázar and Sábato achieved recognition throughout the Spanish speaking—and reading—world, and their works have been translated into numerous other languages. Manuel Puig (1932–90), wrote a tale of two political prisoners sharing a cell that was adapted to the stage and the screen: *El beso de la mujer araña* ("The Kiss of the Spider Woman.") Another Argentine writer, Adolfo Pérez Esquivel, received the Nobel Peace Prize in 1980 for his courageous opposition to military rule.

In music, Argentina has produced its share of classical composers, the most renowned being Alberto Ginastera (1916–83). Argentina also has partial claim to Carlos Kleiber (1930–2004), one of the world's most eminent 20th century composers. His father, Erich Kleiber, also a noted composer, emigrated from Austria to Argentina in 1935 to escape the Nazis. Carlos Kleiber divided his career between Argentina and Europe, where he died and is buried.

But when one thinks of Argentine music, one thinks of the tango. The dance and music that has become synonymous with Argentina emerged as an erotic art form in the sleazy nightclubs and brothels of La Boca, the port district of Buenos Aires. Its contagious rhythm and sexual innuendo won it ready acceptance in the *avante-garde* circles of Paris during the 1920s, and from the Left Bank its popularity spread throughout the bistros and cabarets of Europe and the Prohibition-era U.S. nightclubs and speakeasies. Ironically, the tango composer and singer who came to be most identified with the genre was an immigrant from France at age 3: Carlos Gardel (1890–1935). Killed in a plane crash in Colombia at age 45, Gardel even today is the center of an Elvis-like cult following in Argentina. Posters of the forever-young Gardel, his slick black hair parted in the middle, are a ubiquitous symbol of the nation's cultural identity.

Eventually, through the talents of the internationally renowned composer Astor Piazzolla (1921–92), the tango emerged into a classical form acceptable in polite society. One literally cannot escape the sounds of the tango in Argentine restaurants, so ingrained is it in the life of the nation. Two U.S.-made movies, "Scent of a Woman" and "Evita," have revived interest in the tango abroad. In fact, the tango performed in "Scent of a Woman" was *Por una cabeza*, written by Gardel and Alfredo Le Pera shortly before they perished together in Colombia.

Argentine cinema, established in the 1930s, enjoyed something of a boom during the first Perón era, but lapsed into mediocrity during subsequent military re-

Argentina

gimes, particularly that of 1976–83, when political repression and artistic censorship forced many leading actors and directors into exile. Since 1983 it has enjoyed a renaissance and has won some international accolades.

Luis Puenzo's *La historia oficial, (The Official Story)*, the account of a middle-aged housewife who comes to realize that her adopted daughter was taken from two slain dissidents during the "Dirty War," won the Golden Palm at the Cannes Film Festival in 1985 and became the first Argentine film to win the U.S. Academy Award for Best Foreign Film.

Argentina's second Oscar came in 2010 for Juan José Campanella's *El secreto de sus ojos (The Secret in Their Eyes)*, which also won Spain's Goya Award for Best Spanish Language Film for 2009. Based on a novel by Eduardo Sacheri, it involves a detective in 1999 who tries to solve the rape and murder of a dissident in 1974. In Argentina, it became the second-greatest box office success since Leonardo Favio's *Nazareno Cruz y el lobo (Nazareno Cruz and the Wolf)* in 1975.

Another noted director was María Luisa Bemberg (1946–94), whose films that achieved acclaim abroad included *Miss Mary*, with Julie Christie, a story set in the 1930s, which Bemberg both wrote and directed; and *Camila*, the true story of a girl and her lover priest who were executed for their forbidden love during the Rosas regime in the 1840s.

Radio in Argentina enjoyed a golden age in the 1920s and '30s, just as it had in the United States, the exception being that tango enjoyed equal billing with that of the Big Band sounds. Soap operas were popular, and provided the boost to stardom of an ambitious young actress named Eva Duarte—later Eva Perón. Television began as a state venture and wallowed in mediocrity for decades for much the same reason as did the cinema: the flight of talent from the censorship of military regimes. The result was a dependence on dubbed imported programs, mostly from the United States. Today's less-encumbered Argentine television has seen a boom in locally produced programs, many of them the ever-popular telenovelas, which often are exported.

Economy: Argentina is well-endowed with some of the richest farmland in the world and as a result, the economy has traditionally been based on agriculture, primarily cattle, wheat and wine. A favorable balance of trade led to industrialization as well, and at the turn of the 20th century, Argentina was one of the four wealthiest nations in the world.

After World War II, the economy was plagued by the fiscal policies of the first Perón administration. When he took office in 1946, reserves stood at a respectable $1.5 billion. By 1955 that surplus had vanished and the nation was deeply in the red. Every government since then has added to the debt. Agriculture was penalized in order to promote industrialization. Food prices were held artificially low and taxes were placed on farm exports in order to finance the construction of factories.

The government role in the economy also expanded. The state controlled more than half of all heavy industry—most of which has been inefficient, overstaffed and unprofitable. Because of a lack of capital investment in newer techniques, it became the equivalent of the "rust belt" industry of the northeast United States, which has been undergoing replacement by facilities erected in the southern United States because of onerous taxes, wages and workers' benefits in the North.

Argentina for more than half a century enjoyed the most evenly distributed and largest per capita income in Latin America. Much of this wealth, however, was eroded by runaway inflation, particularly during the 1980s. Perón taught the nation to live beyond its means, printing more and more pesos, establishing a precedent which was repeated over and over.

Once the *Peronistas* returned to power in 1973, the economy was harassed by widespread strikes, a shortage of consumer goods and high job absenteeism. Even more damaging was the disastrous drop in farm exports, which usually had counted for 70% of the nation's foreign earnings. Although poor weather was a contributing factor, most farm problems stemmed from government policies that maintained low food prices for the people of Buenos Aires and the cities, where 80% of the nation lives. Beef exports dropped to their lowest level of the century when the European Common Market reduced Argentine meat imports. At the same time, beef consumption rose because of lowered prices. By 1975 Argentines consumed 220 pounds of beef per person annually, twice the U.S. figure.

Industrial output fell in Argentina, partially due to a shortage of parts, frequent strikes and low capital reinvestment. The nation's once-mighty auto industry also broke down, with eight foreign-owned assembly plants losing $160 million on their Argentine operations in 1975. During that period, the growth in the nation's gross national product dropped to zero. It went as low as –9% in the late 1980s.

The military rulers in power from 1976–83 sought to return Argentina to a free-market system—a dramatic about face from the state planning that had dominated the economy since Perón first took office. The impact of the changes was limited—partly because 60% of the economy was under government control or ownership.

The worst depression, coupled with hyper-inflation, corruption, overspending, a bulging bureaucracy in Buenos Aires and the provinces, and the excessive demands of labor unions, all took the starch out of the economy during the presidency of Raúl Alfonsín, of the Radical Civil Union (1983–89). One observer noted, "In the U.S. and Europe, things are either automatic or predictable. Here, nothing is automatic or predictable." Riots forced Alfonsín to relinquish power to his successor several months early.

Under Peronist President Carlos Menem (1989–99), things at last began changing (although a bitter pill for many). In 1992, he announced he was pegging the peso to the U.S. dollar, one-to-one. The effect was almost immediate. Inflation dropped from 40% per month to less than 10% per year, which enabled Argentina at last to engage in intelligent financial planning. It also attracted foreign investment in quantities necessary for renewed growth. Menem also abandoned protectionism and embraced free-market economics, which for a Peronist was heretical. But there was no questioning its success.

Capital that used to migrate abroad began staying within Argentina, and funds began returning there from overseas. The return on investment was attractive in the 1990s, and Argentina imposed fewer and fewer restrictions on withdrawal of profits by investors, in stark contrast to much of the rest of Latin America.

The devaluation of the Mexican peso in 1994 presented a major threat to Argentine economic stability since it, just as Mexico, had been presumed to be a place for safe investment. Menem responded energetically to preserve Argentina's reputation, and did so successfully. He almost immediately instituted an austerity program to reduce imports and wages, two unpopular moves which had to be made just before the May 1995 elections. The program enabled Argentina's banking system to defend its currency.

By 1998, Argentina had successfully overcome the effects of the 1994–95 Mexican peso crisis, only to begin feeling the effects of the crisis in the Asian markets. Growth was still in the neighborhood of 8%, and though unemployment was down it was still an uncomfortable 13%. Inflation for 1998 was a mere 1%. Overall, these were the best economic times Argentina had seen in decades. But it was not to last.

Foreseeing a coming slump, the IMF approved a three-year, $2.8 billion loan for Argentina in February 1998. Nonetheless, the country slid into recession. Meanwhile, in a surprise move apparently aimed at shoring up his traditional support among the once-powerful labor unions, Menem swung the pendulum back from his policy of appeasing the needs of big business by proposing new labor regulations that essentially left in place the *Peronistas'* liberal severance benefits

Year-end figures for 1999 graphically demonstrated the severity of the recession incoming Radical President Fernando de la Rua had inherited from Menem. Real GDP declined by 3.5%, and unemployment was 14.5%. About the only good news was that inflation *declined* by 2%. De la Rua's painful austerity measures and the labor reform bill were needed to obtain funds from the IMF, but experts warned that it could be some time before the benefits were felt. Those experts proved correct. De la Rua made an ill-advised prediction that Argentina would end 2000 with positive growth of 3.5% to 4%, a prediction that returned to haunt him. The economy *shrank* another 0.5%. Unemployment was still a troubling 14.7% and it grew steadily worse.

De la Rua publicly called for *Mercosur* to emulate the European Union by adopting a common currency for the trade bloc. He predicted monetary union could be in place within three years, but financial experts said it could take 10. De la Rua also was an advocate of the Free Trade Area of the Americas (FTAA).

In late 2001, the recession deepened as unemployment grew to 18.3% and de la Rua sought desperately to meet the deficit-reduction goals he had set to ensure continued IMF support so Argentina could avoid default on its $132 billion foreign debt. When he imposed strict limits of $1,000 a month on savings withdrawals, angry Argentines took to the streets. The demonstrations erupted in violence that left 27 people dead and forced de la Rua to resign (see Descent into Chaos).

The new interim president, Eduardo Duhalde, pushed an emergency economic reform package through Congress, after which he revoked Menem's 10-year-old dollar-parity plan.

The crisis had plunged more and more Argentines into poverty. A 2000 study by the Social Development Ministry had reported that 37% of Argentines lived below the poverty line of $200 a month. By 2002, that figure was a staggering 57%, and in mid-2003 it had increased to 58.5%; 28% were classified as living in extreme poverty, double the percentage from before the meltdown. Bartering became commonplace, as did eking a living by scavenging from garbage dumps.

GDP growth was down 1% in 2001 and a near-cataclysmic 13.6% in 2002 before it finally bottomed out. Unemployment

abated to 18%, and the peso rebounded from 4.0 to about 2.8 to the dollar.

The newly elected president, Néstor Kirchner, who took office on May 25, 2003, still had an economic nightmare to deal with. He rejected Menem's free-market approach and returned to the populism of Juan Perón. He also joined forces with Brazil's new center-left president, Luiz Inácio da Silva, in calling for a revival of the *Mercosur* trade bloc.

Kirchner's hard-ball tactics in negotiating with the IMF bore fruit with an agreement reached in 2004, but Kirchner later canceled the agreement. In a bold maneuver, he bluntly made a take-it-or-leave it offer to creditors to exchange $102.6 billion in Argentine bonds for new ones worth only about 35% of the original indebtedness, and he gave them a deadline of February 25, 2005, to decide. Unhappy creditors had little choice but to accept and take the loss; those who did accounted for 76% of the debt. In December 2005, Argentina repaid its entire remaining debt to the IMF of almost $9.8 billion.

Without a doubt, the diversion of resources from debt servicing led to a dramatic resurgence in the economy. Argentina showed growth in 2003 for the first time in five years, a robust 8.7%, and has averaged 8.6% since then, something Argentina has not experienced since its Golden Age at the turn of the 20th century. In 2006, growth was 9.2%, third-highest in Latin America, behind the Dominican Republic and Venezuela, and in 2007 it was 8.7%. The poverty rate also dropped from 58% in 2002 to 27% in 2007. Unemployment, still about 16% for both 2003 and 2004, dropped to 11% at the end of 2005 and to 10% in 2006 and 2007. On the other hand, inflation was 12%, the highest since 1992 if the 2002 peso devaluation is discounted.

Much of the improvement could be attributed to high market prices for agricultural products, Argentina's traditional export, especially corn and soybeans, which have joined wheat as the major cash crops. Argentina is currently the world's second-largest exporter of corn and the third-largest of soybeans.

In December 2007, Kirchner turned the reins of government over to his wife, Cristina Fernández de Kirchner, who was faced with the uncharacteristic problem for Argentina of trying to moderate an overheated economy. In 2008, the government claimed inflation was 9%, but experts accused the government of "cooking" inflation figures by eliminating products that were rising in price the steepest, on the dubious premise that people would put their spending priorities on other products. More reliable estimates put the rate for 2008 at 25%, and it had not tapered off by mid-2009.

Economic growth remained a robust 7.1% in 2008, but a 40% drop in the international price of soybeans, coupled with the international market crisis, led to a –2.5% drop in 2009. It was expected to grow back by that same amount in 2010.

In March 2008, Fernández attempted to increase export tariffs on agricultural products by more than 50%, provoking a serious strike by farmers that has not been resolved (see History).

The Future: For three years, Argentina has had what amounts to a co-presidency. But Kirchner simply could not transfer his 70% popularity to his wife, whose approval ratings have sunk to 20%. Their losing gamble in moving forward by four months the mid-term congressional election, in which their Peronist faction suffered a humiliating defeat and lost their congressional majorities, means she is limping along as a lame duck for the remainder of her term. The once-popular Kirchner had seemed a shoo-in to win a second term in 2011, but all bets now seem off.

Belize

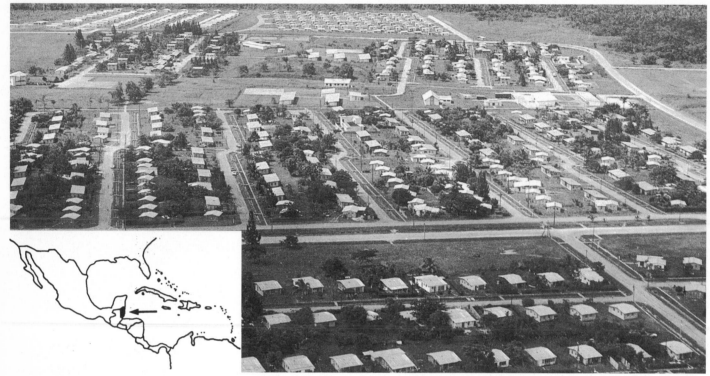

Aerial view of Belmopan

(pronounced Beh-lees)

Area: 8,866 sq. mi., somewhat larger than Massachusetts.

Population: 307,899 (2009 est.).

Capital City: Belmopan (Pop. 13,500).

Climate: Hot and humid.

Neighboring Countries: Mexico (North); Guatemala (West); Honduras lies 50 miles to the southeast across the Gulf of Honduras.

Official Language: English.

Other Principal Tongues: Spanish and some Indian dialects.

Ethnic Background: African (65%); Mestizo, Creole and those of Mayan ancestry, European.

Principal Religions: Roman Catholicism, Anglican Protestant Christianity.

Chief Commercial Products: Sugar, citrus fruit, lobster, shrimp, forest products.

Currency: Belize Dollar.

Gross Domestic Product: U.S. $1.424 billion (est.) in 2009 ($4,625 per capita);

Former Colonial Status: British Colony (1862–1981).

National Day: September 21 (Independence Day).

Chief of State: Queen Elizabeth II of Great Britain, represented by Sir Colville Young, governor general.

Head of Government: Dean Barrow (born March 2, 1951), prime minister (since February 8, 2008).

National Flag: A white circle on a blue field, with red horizontal bars at top and bottom. The circle shows two workers and symbols of agriculture, industry and maritime activity.

Wedged between Mexico's Yucatán Peninsula to the north and Guatemala to the west and south, and calmed by placid waters of the Caribbean Sea on its eastern coastline, Belize is a warm to hot and humid country about 174 miles long and 69 miles wide at its widest point. Flat and swampy on the coast, but mercifully relieved by pleasant sea breezes, the beaches are unspoiled and beautiful. The terrain slowly rises toward the interior to about 3,000 feet above sea level into pine forests and pasturelands. At lower altitudes, tropical growth predominates.

Some 15 miles offshore there is the longest barrier reef in the Western Hemisphere, stretching 190 miles, offering a spectacular variety of tropical fish and coral formations, a delight for the experienced snorkel diver. The land is thinly inhabited; the largest town is Belize City with a population of about 50,000—which, however, has an international airport.

History: Belize was part of the Mayan domain, which declined about 1000 A.D. It was settled about 1638 by bands of British woodcutters illegally harvesting the timber in Spanish domains. These settlers

managed their own affairs and government, although the Spanish tried many times to eject them. In 1786 Britain finally appointed a superintendent for the territory; in 1840 it was termed a colony, called British Honduras, although it was not officially a colony until 1862 when it was made subordinate to Jamaica. In 1884 it was made a separate crown colony.

Colonial status continued until 1964 when the colony was granted full internal

Belize

Former Prime Minister Said Musa

unpopular measures returned to haunt Esquivel, and in the general election in August 1998, the pendulum swung sharply back to the PUP, which had chosen Said Musa, a former attorney general under Price, as its standard bearer. Musa is of Palestinian descent.

In the campaign, Musa denounced Esquivel's "killa taxes," which he said were frightening away foreign investors. He pledged to cut utility rates and to create 15,000 new jobs. The appeal paid off; the PUP won in a landslide, taking 23 of the 29 seats in the lower house. The PUP carried some districts by 3–1. This time, Esquivel was defeated in his own district by the mayor of Belize City. He was replaced as opposition leader by Dean Barrow, who is of African descent and had served as deputy prime minister and foreign minister.

The PUP became the first party since independence to win two consecutive mandates, albeit with a slightly reduced majority, winning 22 of the 29 seats in the general elections in March 2003.

Musa's popularity waned because of alleged corruption. In August 2004, it was disclosed that $3 million had been taken from the country's social security fund to cover the debts of a company owned by the finance minister. Seven cabinet ministers resigned, demanding that Musa fire the finance minister, which he did. Musa then assumed the finance portfolio himself.

In 2005, Musa did what he had denounced Esquivel for doing in 1998—proposed a dramatic tax increase, as well as a cut in services. He said the measures were necessary to service the country's

self-government. In June 1973, its name was changed to Belize. Following an outbreak of rioting, the colony was given its independence in September 1981.

Guatemala long had claimed Belize as an integral part of its territory. It protested the granting of independence and refused to recognize it. Britain maintained a force of some 1,800 troops to maintain Belize's security. Guatemalan President Vinicio Cerezo generally conceded that Belize's independence was negotiable, provided Guatemala obtained access to the Atlantic via one or more of its ports. The dispute was settled in late 1992 when such rights were granted, and Guatemala formally recognized Belize.

Government consists of a 31-member House of Representatives, expanded from 29 in 2008, and an eight-member Senate; in a 2008 referendum, voters changed it from appointed to elected.

The People's United Party (PUP) of George Price held power from independence until 1984, when it was defeated by the United Democratic Party (UDP) led by Manuel Esquivel, running on a free-trade platform. But in late 1989, the Price and the PUP returned to power by a narrow majority of 15–14, later increased to 16–13 when a UDP member deserted his party.

Price introduced the "clinic day" on Wednesdays, whereby any Belizean could drop in his office in Belize City and tell him of his concerns. His successors have continued this popular tradition.

In early 1993 Britain announced that it would withdraw its force from Belize within 15 months. Price, hoping to gain from the recent years of prosperity, held elections in June 1993, 15 months before they were due. Security was the main is-

sue. Guatemala had repudiated the treaty recognizing Belize. The UDP seized the issue, typified by a song: "We don't want no Guatemala!" It won narrowly, 16–13 seats, and Esquivel again became prime minister.

Belize repudiated the treaty with Guatemala. British troops departed on January 1, 1994, and security became the responsibility of the Belize Defense Force.

The UDP government, alleging mismanagement by the PUP, raised taxes early in its five-year mandate. Most controversial was a 15% value-added tax; the government also raised utility rates. These

A sleepy weekday in Belize City

Photo by Karen Bubenheim

55

Belize

Prime Minister Dean O. Barrow

staggering debt, one of the highest in the world as a percentage of GDP (see Economy). Under Musa alone, the debt rose to 90.4% of GDP in 2007. Demonstrations outside the House of Representatives during the tax debate turned violent, a rarity in Belize.

The violence intensified in April and May 2005 when Musa announced plans to sell the government's shares in the telephone company, BTL, to U.S. interests. Saboteurs, apparently union workers, cut down telephone poles and severed power lines, disrupting the country's power and communications grids. Looting broke out in Belize City that left one dead, 27 injured and 100 arrested. Teachers and civil servants staged strikes. Three UDP leaders were arrested in confrontations with police. The UDP demanded that Musa resign, but he steadfastly refused.

In July 2006, the government announced it could not service its debt. On January 31, 2007, a historic agreement was reached with Belize's foreign creditors to swap 98% of the existing debt for bonds that will mature in 2029. Belize paid 4.5% to service the bonds for the first three years, 6% for the next two years, then 8.5% per year until maturity.

Musa called new elections for the House of Representatives, which had been expanded by two seats, on February 7, 2008. He simultaneously called a referendum on changing the Senate from an appointed to an elected body, which the UDP denounced as a gimmick to help the PUP in the parliamentary election. If so, it failed, because the UDP scored a landslide victory, winning 25 of the 31 seats; voters also approved an elected Senate by a margin of 61%–39%. The following day, Dean Barrow, 56, who holds a law degree from

the University of Miami, became Belize's first black prime minister. He also assumed the finance portfolio.

Barrow married his long-time girlfriend, Kim Simplis, on the first anniversary of his becoming prime minister.

The leading issue that has preoccupied the Barrow government has been its nationalization of Belize Telemedia, the country's largest telephone company, in August 2009. Barrow alleged that Telemedia and other companies had benefited from a "sweetheart deal" under Musa's PUP government. Barrow said he intended the takeover to be only temporary until a new buyer can be found. The takeover put Barrow at odds with Lord Michael Ashcroft, a member of the British House of Lords who is believed to be the largest single investor in Belize, including of Belize Bank, which was a shareholder in Telemedia. Barrow claimed that Ashcroft's net worth was greater than Belize's GDP. Ashcroft spent part of his youth in Belize and has made no secret of his financial stake there. From 1998–2000, he served as Musa's ambassador to the United Nations, but in an interview in late 2009 he claimed to be the greatest single contributor to the UDP's 2008 campaign, which brought Barrow to power. He insisted he always had regarded Barrow as a friend.

Barrow's efforts to undo the sweetheart arrangements, which he said stifled competition, landed his government in court in Belize and in arbitration in Britain. Barrow prevailed in court, but the British arbitrators levied awards of $41 million against the Belizean government, which Barrow has vowed not to pay. Meanwhile, Telemedia has been losing tens of thousands of subscribers under government tutelage, making it more difficult to sell. According to Belizean media, Telemedia has engaged in heavy-handed tactics against its major private competitor, Smart Speednet, such as reneging on an interconnectivity agreement. The issue was ongoing when this book went to press.

Barrow also has generated controversy by submitting Belize's long-standing border dispute with Guatemala to the World Court in The Hague, Netherlands.

Culture: About 65% of Belizeans are Garifunas, descendants of shipwrecked slaves of African origin, who speak a distinct dialect that is a mix of English, Carib and Spanish; another 25% are of Mayan and mestizo background. Most of the remainder is primarily of European extraction. A colony of German-speaking Mennonites produces almost all the country's dairy products. There also are colonies of Taiwanese, Sri Lankans and Arabs in this harmonious ethnic gumbo. Former Prime Minister Said Musa is of Palestinian de-

scent, and in 2008 Dean Barrow became the first black prime minister.

Belmopan, the capital city, was built in 1971 in the center of the country about 50 miles west of Belize City, which is the largest urban area with a population of about 50,000. For the tourist, the city is not safe for a lone pedestrian, especially after dark. This also is true of those traveling alone to remote tourist facilities. Armed robbery and muggings are growing in number in spite of efforts by the government to control crime.

U.S. baseball is immensely popular; both men and women spend hours watching games.

There are roughly 700 Mayan ruins about 1,000 years old, which can be seen on guided tours, and unusual wildlife is prolific. The result has been that Belize has become a popular destination for adventuresome tourists.

Belize's best-known cultural figure in international circles was probably the Punta musician Andy Palacio (1960–2008). Punta is the genre associated with Palacio's Garifuna culture, and Palacio devoted his short life to preserving that culture and language. He recorded five albums, his last being *Watina* in 2007. He served as head of the Natioinal Institute of Culture and History for a time.

Economy: Until recent times, forestry was the most important activity in Belize, but as the timber supply grew sparse, sugar cane growing took on more importance and now is the leading industry. Although the country has a great deal of land which is well suited for agriculture, only a small portion is farmed, and it is necessary for Belize to import millions of dollars in foodstuffs. Belize's major trading partners are the United States and the United Kingdom—about two thirds of its exports and imports are with these nations. It is a member of the Caribbean Community (CARICOM).

The lush lower altitudes of Belize, with their tropical climate, are favorable locations for two crops: marijuana and oranges for juice. The first presented a problem both to Belize and the United States in the 1980s. Production rose quickly to more than 1,000 tons annually and Belize became the second-largest supplier to U.S. dealers. After 1984 this was curtailed and virtually eliminated by a spraying program, but not before a high government official was arrested and indicted in Miami (1985) on charges of conspiring to export 30,000 tons annually to the United States. Production is now closely monitored and is less than 100 tons per year.

Cocaine proved to be a far more serious problem. As alternative routes of transportation from Colombia to the United

States were restricted, Belize took up the slack. Small airplanes would land on rural roads for refueling. In order to stop this, the government erected poles on the sides of the roads to break the wings of the craft. Local people bent the poles to eliminate their effectiveness.

Belize is relatively more prosperous than its Spanish-speaking neighbors, with an estimated per capita GDP of about $4,625 in 2009. Real GDP was estimated at $ 1.424 billion in 2009. Inflation in 2009 was was only 0.3%. Major exports are sugar, bananas and citrus fruit.

Real economic growth had been healthy: 9.2% in 2003 and 2004, 5.1% in 2005 and 5.6% in 2006, thanks largely to tourism. The number of tourists in 2006 was 247,000, roughly equal to the country's population, an increase of 4.5% over 2005. New hotel construction is booming, but investment in infrastructure is badly needed. Several cruise lines now make port calls in Belize, and its reef is a favorite spot for snorkeling. Belize also has been promoted in recent years for ecotourism and as a retirement location.

GDP growth dropped to 1.6% in 2007, rebounded to 4.8% in 2008 but shrank by an estimated –1.5% in 2009. Unemployment dropped from 9.4% in 2006 to 8.1% in 2008.

A succession of governments has sought to boost the economy with drunken-sailor spending and heavy borrowing. The public debt in 2007 was $1.17 billion, nearly 100% of GDP, among the highest in the world. Standard & Poor's downgraded Belize's bonds in 2006 and called the country's financial situation "dire." The debt restructuring agreement announced in January 2007 (see History) will do little more than buy time. But the picture has improved slightly; the debt in 2008 was down slightly to $954.1 million, or 67% of GDP—ranking it 148 th worst aming the world's roughly180 nations.

The Future: It is tempting to draw an analogy between Belize and the American frontier of the 19th century. Belize harks back to an earlier, less hurried time, a place where "civilization" has not yet taken over with fast-food chains and computers. Tourists and immigrants have flocked here to take advantage of the legendary scuba diving in the longest coral reef in the Western Hemisphere, to enjoy the unspoiled beaches, to soak up the culture of the Mayan ruins and to experience the unique ecological wonders. But the real allure is that Belize is an anachronism, a laid-back, English-speaking enclave in the tropics just two hours by air from Houston, a place that has eschewed the frenetic pace of the 21st century, where visitors can "get away from it all" for a few days and settlers can find a new life in an unspoiled, underpopulated paradise.

But there is trouble in paradise. Corruption, drug trafficking, banditry in the rural areas and a crushing public debt threaten Belize's greatest asset: its peacefulness. Greater transparency would go a long way toward establishing confidence in governmental institutions, but political cronyism is entrenched in both parties. A poll in 2005 suggested that 49% of Belizeans would be willing to vote for a third party, but in the general elections of February 7, 2008, when there were three new alternative parties, they collected only 2% of the vote among them.

Ironically, Belize is hampered by the very thing that has made it so appealing: resistance to change. It has yet to be seen whether Prime Minister Dean Barrow will have any more success than his predecessors.

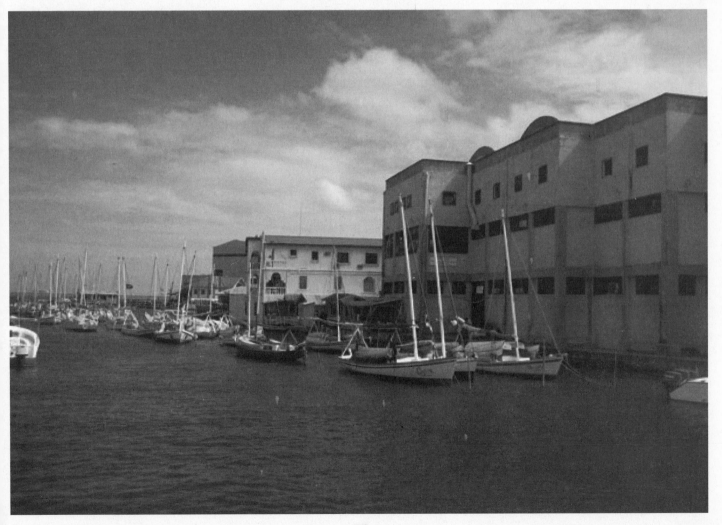

Plurinational State of Bolivia

Nestled in the rugged mountains is a shimmering Andean lake

Area: 424,052 sq. mi.

Population: 9.775 million (2009 est.)

Capital Cities: La Paz (Pop. 835,000), seat of the executive and legislative branches; and Sucre (247,000), the judicial seat.

Climate: The eastern lowlands are hot all year round; they are wet from November through March, dry from May through September. The highland climate varies greatly with the altitude. The high plateau, or *altiplano*, is dry and cold all year round.

Neighboring Countries: Brazil (North and East); Paraguay (Southeast); Argentina (South); Chile (Southwest); Peru (Northwest).

Official Language: Spanish

Other Principal Tongues: Quechua, Aymara and Guaraní

Ethnic Background: Indian (70%); *mestizo* (mixed European and Indian (25%); European (5%)

Principal Religion: Roman Catholic Christianity

Chief Commercial Products: Tin, lead, zinc, silver, tungsten, gold, natural gas, agricultural products. Coca production, used to make cocaine, is a major source of income.

Currency: Bolivian Peso (subject to erratic valuation)

Gross Domestic Product: U.S. $17.76 billion in 2009 ($1,817 per capita).

Former Colonial Status: Spanish colony known as Upper Peru (1538–1825)

Independence Date: August 6, 1825

Chief of State: Juan Evo Morales Ayma (b. October 26, 1959), president (since January 22, 2006).

National Flag: Equal red, yellow and green horizontal stripes.

Bolivia, the fifth-largest nation in South America, is landlocked. Stretching 1,000 miles from north to south and 800 miles east to west, it is divided into two highly contrasting regions—the *altiplano* (a high mountain plateau) and the eastern lowlands. The Andean mountain range reaches its greatest width—some 400 miles—in

Bolivia

Bolivia. The *Western Cordillera*, which separates Bolivia from Chile and Peru, contains snowy peaks of 19,000 to 21,240 feet, with numerous rough volcanoes along the crest. The narrow passes to the Pacific coast exceed 13,000 feet in altitude. The *altiplano*, lying to the east of the *Western Cordillera*, is an arid, windswept, treeless plateau some 85 miles wide and 520 miles in length and much of it is above 13,000 feet.

Split into basins by spurs from the *Western Cordillera*, the southern portion is parched desert, uninhabited except for mining camps; the northern portion, containing chilly Lake Titicaca (3,400 square miles at 12,500 feet), has many small settlements along the river flowing into the lake, and around the shore there is a large and prosperous Indian farming population. The eastern *cordillera*, separating the *altiplano* from the lowlands, reaches 20,000 feet in the north, but is much lower in the south.

The mountains drop sharply to the northeast and the hot, humid Amazon basin. Further to the south they form a stepped descent to a region called the *Puno* and then into the *Chaco* plains of Paraguay and Argentina. The valleys that cut into the eastern slopes of the mountains are fertile, semi-tropical and densely inhabited. These valleys, called *yungas*, produce a wide variety of cereals and fruits, but the task of transporting them to the cities of the *altiplano* is formidable. The lowland tropical plains of the northeast, once heavily populated, are now largely abandoned because of their inaccessibility.

History: The Aymara Indians of the Lake Titicaca region had a relatively high level of development between 600 and 900 A.D. This civilization disappeared from some undetermined disaster and the Quechua-speaking Inca invaders found the surviving Aymaras living among ancient monuments and ruins they could not explain.

Bolivia was still in Inca hands when the Spaniards arrived from Peru in 1538.

The Spanish development of Bolivia began with the discovery of a silver mountain at Potosí in 1545, followed by additional discoveries at Oruro. The capital, Sucre, was founded in 1539. La Paz, founded in 1548, was an important terminal for treasure convoys preparing for the difficult passage to Peru; it became the seat of government in 1898 after the silver played out near Sucre, which remains the judicial seat.

The Inca social and economic organizations were abandoned in a mad effort to extract and process the metallic wealth of the mountains—tin, silver, lead and zinc. Jesuit missionaries penetrated the tropical lowlands, gathering the Indians into prosperous farming communities that endured into the 18th century. However, they aroused little interest on the part of the Spanish authorities and had even less influence on the social and political development of the country. The Spaniards intermarried with the Indians, producing a large group of multi-ethnic *mestizos* that would affect the course of Bolivian history.

Revolutionary movements against Spanish rule began early in Bolivia; revolts by *mestizos* broke out in La Paz in 1661 and at Cochabamba in 1730. Indian revolts occurred in Sucre, Cochabamba, Oruro and La Paz from 1776 to 1780. The University of San Francisco Xavier in Sucre issued a call in 1809 for the liberation of all colonies from Spain. Although several attempts were made to free Bolivia, they were unsuccessful until 1825, when Simón Bolívar sent General Antonio José de Sucre to free Upper Peru. Independence was declared on August 6 of that year.

Exacting Inca stonework

Bolivia

Few South American nations faced greater initial handicaps than Bolivia. There were few competent patriotic leaders among the landed aristocracy, and there was no middle class. The apathetic Indians and the *mestizos* were simply pawns in a game they did not understand. The military, which had been trained in the campaigns of San Martín and Bolívar, seized power. The history of independent Bolivia's first 50 years is a dismal recitation of misrule and violence as jealous rivals struggled for power. Following its defeat in The War of the Pacific (1879–83), Bolivia lost its Pacific provinces to Chile and became a landlocked nation.

During the 1880s and 1890s, several able men occupied the presidency. Silver mining was revived, a few schools were opened and political parties were established. Traditional Liberal and Conservative titles were adopted, but their memberships represented little more than opposing factions of the nation's ruling elite. One of the principal Liberal demands was for the transfer of the capital from Sucre to La Paz. After seizing the presidency by revolt, a Liberal regime made La Paz the seat of government.

Under Liberal leadership, Bolivia achieved a degree of stability in the first two decades of the 20th century. Economic reforms were undertaken, disputes with Chile and Brazil were resolved—with losses of territory but with receipt of indemnities—mining was expanded and roads and railroads were built. The motive behind this limited "modernization" was the increasing world demand for tin, a mineral that quickly became Bolivia's basic export, transforming the small group that controlled its extraction—the "tin barons"—into powerful international millionaires. In the 1920s, a party carrying the Republican label came to power, and it sought foreign capital for mining and petroleum interests, attracting U.S. investors.

By the 1930s, U.S. interests controlled most of Bolivia's mineral concessions. Although some of the investment capital went into roads, railroads and agriculture, much of it was wasted by irresponsible spending. When the world depression of the 1930s hit Bolivia, its economy collapsed, the treasury defaulted on its bonds and the Republican president was ousted.

In 1931 elections, Daniel Salamanca, a competent businessman, became president amid hopes that he could bring order out of chaos. This optimistic mood was shattered the following year with the outbreak of the Chaco War with Paraguay. Blame for this senseless conflict lies with the miscalculation of the leadership of both countries. Humiliated by a long series of military disasters, both nations overestimated their own capabilities and underestimated those of the other. Though ostensibly more powerful than Paraguay, Bolivia, in a monumental display of military incompetence, suffered a crushing defeat in which 52,000 of its soldiers were killed. Fought to exhaustion on both sides, the war ended with Paraguay in possession of the disputed Chaco region in 1935. Soldiers returning home, angered by their shabby treatment during the war, joined with university students and labor agitators in demanding social reforms.

In 1936, a group of socially conscious military officers led by Colonel David Toro overthrew the civilian government and proclaimed Bolivia a "socialist republic." This shortlived government established the first labor ministry and expropriated the holdings of Standard Oil. After only a year and a half, Toro was overthrown by an even more radical officer, Colonel Germán Busch, a hero of the Chaco War. He implemented the first labor code, encouraged organization of the tin miners and imposed governmental control over the tin companies. Busch died suddenly in 1939, and it remains a mystery whether he died by his own hand or those of conservative economic interests alarmed by the pace of his reforms. At any rate, his death temporarily halted social reform.

Conservative military elements took control of the ballot boxes in 1940 elections and installed their man as president. For the next three years, the country was ruled by these right-wing elements, but there arose a number of civilian-based political parties and movements, ranging from Trotskyite on the left to the Bolivian Falange, modeled after the movement of Spain's Generalissimo Francisco Franco, on the right.

The one that was to have the most profound impact on the country, however, one that endures to this day, was the Revolutionary Nationalist Movement, or *MNR*, led by Víctor Paz Estenssoro, who had been an economic adviser to Busch. When another group of military reformers overthrew the conservatives in 1943 and installed Major Gualberto Villarroel as president, they invited the *MNR* to participate in the new government. Although Villarroel was enlightened in his treatment of the Indian population and was sympathetic to the miners, he proved too conservative for ultra-leftwing elements that overthrew him and publicly hanged him in 1946.

The 1952 Revolution

The following six years were marked by exceptional political turbulence and instability, even for Bolivia. The end of this volatile period, in which Bolivia was ruled by a wearisome series of military *juntas*,

A Bolivian miner gazes into the icicled entrance of a tin mine near La Paz

60

Bolivia

View of La Paz

was marked by the beginning of what scholars regard as one of Latin America's four genuine social revolutions, along with those of Mexico, Cuba and Nicaragua.

In 1952, the *MNR* led a revolt that left about 3,000 dead and led to the installation of Paz Estenssoro as president. His revolutionary government took three remarkable steps: it temporarily abolished the army and replaced it with armed militias of Indians and tin miners; it extended universal suffrage to the illiterate masses, giving them genuine political power for the first time; and it implemented true land reform, breaking up huge estates and giving Indian peasants title to their own plots. The *MNR* also established itself within the unions and Indian communities, making it then the country's premier civilian political force for decades.

The revolution was hampered by a lack of trained administrators, by inadequate financial resources, by opposition from both internal and external elements and, above all, by a steady decline in tin prices that put Bolivia in chronic economic crisis. Nonetheless, for its first 12 years the revolution gave power to the powerless and brought an end to revolving-door governments. When Paz Estenssoro's four-year term expired in 1956, he was succeeded by another *MNR* leader, Hernán Siles Suazo. Paz Estenssoro returned to power in the 1960 election, but when he made overtures toward re-election in 1964, the newly organized revolutionary army proved as skillful at staging a *coup d'etat* as had its predecessors. The vice president and for-

mer air force commander, General René Barrientos, came to power in November 1964 and forced Paz Estenssoro into exile. Despite the *MNR's* failure to retain power, its 12 years of revolution proved to be a *fait accompli* from which there was no turning back to the "old order."

The flamboyant and charismatic Barrientos, a moderate conservative, proved a highly popular president, and he was given a resounding mandate in a 1966 election. In 1967, he promulgated a new constitution that would last for 42 years, venerable for a Bolivian organic law. That same year, a U.S.-trained counter-insurgency battalion captured and executed the legendary Argentine-born revolutionary, Ernesto "Che" Guevara, who had attempted to launch a Cuban-style revolution among Bolivia's rural Indians. Barrientos was fond of making personal visits to the interior by helicopter, and on one such trip, in April 1969, he died in a helicopter crash.

Military Rule, 1969–82

Barrientos was succeeded by his vice president, who was quickly overthrown by General Alfredo Ovando, a leftist and nationalist who expropriated the holdings of Gulf Oil Co. He was in turn overthrown by the even more left-wing General Juan José Torres in 1970. Torres replaced the Congress with a Soviet-style "People's Assembly" and forged a coalition of Marxist intellectuals and tin miners. However, he failed to win the support of the peasants, as Barrientos had, or most workers. Even worse, he alienated the U.S. Embassy.

Coup No. 187 (the best estimate) in 145 years of independence came in 1971, bringing to power a more conservative military strongman, Colonel Hugo Banzer Suárez. By 1975, Banzer had fended off 13 coup attempts, and by 1978, after seven years, he had held power continuously longer than any Bolivian president of the 20th century. The formula for his longevity was a three-point strategy: elimination of major political opposition, economic improvement and increased emphasis on foreign affairs to divert popular attention from unsolved domestic problems. Perhaps the best example of this last strategy was Bolivia's renewed demand for access to the sea through Chile.

In July 1978 Banzer called for an open presidential election in which he had intended to relinquish power to his handpicked successor, Colonel Juan Pereda Asbún. But in the balloting, former President Siles Suazo won a plurality, while Pereda ran a poor third. Congress was to decide the outcome, but rather than risk the antimilitary Siles Suazo coming to power, Banzer suddenly resigned and Pereda proclaimed himself president. Banzer's departure thus created a power vacuum that was to return Bolivia to political turmoil for two years.

The usurpation of power lasted only four months. General David Padilla, the latest reform-minded officer, overthrew Pereda in November and pledged to pave the way for yet another free election in July 1979. In that contest, Siles Suazo again polled a plurality but not a majority, throwing the decision to Congress. Under the ever-watchful eye of the jittery military, Congress opted for a compromise choice for president: Walter Guevara Arce, a civilian leader of the 1952 revolution who later split from the *MNR* and therefore was acceptable to conservative military elements. This good-faith effort at restoring civilian rule also would last only four months, when an overly ambitious colonel, Alberto Natusch Busch, led a successful coup.

Busch, whose only apparent motive was personal gain, immediately found himself faced with overwhelming domestic and international opposition to his naked power play. After only 19 days in power, he was forced to resign and he fled into exile, taking an undetermined amount of cash from the national treasury with him. Congress then chose Lidia Gueiler as Bolivia's first woman president. She had no sooner taken office, of course, before speculation began as to when she would be overthrown and by which officer. She called still another election in June 1980 to choose a president, and once again the victor was Siles Suazo. Coup No. 191 took place and General Luis García Meza seized control of the government.

Bolivia

General García Meza

Thus, in the 24 months between Banzer's resignation in July 1978 and García Meza's coup in July 1980, Bolivia had a total of seven presidents.

García Meza's 13 months in power marked the harshest crackdown on personal freedom in Bolivia's modern history. Hundreds were arrested, some labor leaders were murdered and strict censorship was imposed on the press. The new military regime seemed determined to muzzle—and if possible to exterminate—the opposition in the labor movement. Reports held that 500 to 2,000 political prisoners were jailed. The Carter Administration suspended all aid and Bolivia had to turn to neighboring military governments for assistance.

Seeking to consolidate his control, García Meza jailed his opponents and allegedly bribed key members of the armed forces with payoff money from drug traffickers. Such heavy-handed tactics, combined with depressed economic conditions, fomented widespread opposition to the military. In August 1981, reformist military officers forced García Meza to resign.

Named as the new head of the three-man military *junta* was General Celso Torrelio Villa. Political conditions remained unstable as the nation chafed under harsh military rule. Tin workers mounted widespread strikes to demand a return of their union and political rights which the *junta* suspended in 1980. Hoping to ease criticism of the regime, Torrelio promised to reduce human rights violations, to slow the rampant flow of illegal cocaine out of the country and to reduce the state's role in the economy while expanding the opportunities for private enterprise.

Although such policies pleased the United States, which resumed full diplomatic ties after a 16-month delay, the promises prompted skepticism at home. Efforts to impose austerity measures touched off widespread strikes. When the peso was allowed to float, it promptly fell 76% in value. This was only a precursor of that which was to come.

Return to Democracy

To reduce growing criticism, the *junta* promised to lift its ban on political activity and to hold elections for a constituent assembly early in 1983, but as the economic crisis worsened and popular agitation spread, the government was forced to lift the ban on the activities of parties and unions. Torrelio resigned in mid-1982 and the remainder of the democratically elected Congress of 1980 confirmed Siles Suazo's 1980 election victory; in late 1982 he and Jaime Paz Zamora, a Socialist and the nephew of Paz Estenssoro, were installed as president and vice president.

The situation inherited by the civilian government bordered on total chaos. The public debt amounted to about $3 billion, inflation was out of control, unemployment was rampant and the corruptive influence of the drug traffic had reached alarming proportions. The government made valiant, but disorganized, attempts to impose a program of economic austerity and public honesty. Its partial success provoked opposition and social unrest.

Battered by strikes and coup rumors, the civilian government survived against formidable odds. Exemplifying the extent of the regime's troubles, in 1984 Siles Suazo encouraged private sectors to invest in the country, rejected a demand for a 500% rise in workers' wages, proclaimed a new war against drug dealers, promised to reduce inflation to 45%, reaffirmed his confidence in the loyalty of the armed forces and appealed to international institutions to lend more money to Bolivia to save the nation from a "desperate economic situation."

The president was abducted one month later and held for some hours before being released in what appeared to be a clumsy attempt to stage a military coup.

Social unrest, several more strikes and inflation, which at the beginning of 1985 was running at an astronomical annual rate of 24,000%, led Siles Suazo to advance presidential elections to 1985. It appeared that General Hugo Banzer would win, and he actually received more votes than the runner–up in an election riddled with corruption, particularly in the La Paz area. Although former President Paz Estenssoro, age 77, received 26.4% of the vote, about 2% less than Banzer, he was elected president by the new Congress, in which Paz Estenssoro's party received more seats Banzer's.

Paz Estenssoro successfully undertook renegotiation of Bolivia's foreign debt when he took office in August 1985. He also promised decentralization of the economy, particularly the state mining and petroleum monopolies. These moves and others increased food prices ten-fold and provoked strikes and violence that led to the declaration of a state of siege. About 1,500 hunger-striking trade unionists were arrested and sent into internal exile. Surprisingly, Banzer and his supporters joined Paz Estenssoro's efforts for economic reform. As a result of the dramatic changes, the International Monetary Fund, the World Bank, the United States, Japan, China and European countries resumed loans to Bolivia.

The 1985–88 period was not kind to Bolivia. Part of this was because of internal human factors, but most were natural or external in nature. The bottom dropped out of world tin prices in 1985. The basic causes were a vast stock oversupply and, more ominously, increased substitution of aluminum. Further complicating Bolivia's problems was the discovery of Brazilian deposits that were mined much more easily. Bolivia wound up in the position of marketing tin for less than one third the price of production. By 1989, a single province of western Brazil was producing more tin than all of Bolivia, using modern technology in contrast to Bolivia's antiquated methods. The government had no choice but to close the most inefficient mines, causing unemployment to rise to 32%. Huge numbers of workers marched in protest.

Finally, the United States decided to tackle its growing cocaine problem by eliminating the source—coca leaf cultivation. At first, a mild approach was attempted: an offer of $350 for every hectare of coca leaf taken out of production. Because coca growers, mostly peasants, can make up to $10,000 per hectare, the plan was poorly received and actively resisted by farmers. Then, in "Operation Blast Furnace," the United States persuaded the Bolivian government to cooperate, with the assistance of American helicopters and armaments, in destroying facilities used to process coca into cocaine. The result: crowds demonstrated in front of the U.S. Embassy shouting *"Viva coca!"*

U.S. anti-coca efforts from 1986–97 were hampered for several reasons. First, there was the demand for cocaine. If Bolivian coca production went down, it rose in neighboring nations. Second, coca production was an informal government industry, an elaborate, ever-changing system of bribery that had invaded even the Supreme Court. Third, paid informants were useless because drug figureheads had counter-informants up to the highest level of the military and police.

Coca production underwent two important changes. First, it was no longer a "cottage" industry—plantations were used for production, which hired help at low wages for the menial work (they would otherwise be unemployed). The growers could easily raise large crowds for anti-government demonstrations. Second, instead of producing coca paste using kerosene and shipping it to Colombian cartels, Bolivia developed a tremendous number of "factories" producing the treasured final product—white powder.

The 1989 presidential elections produced two top candidates out of nine—Gonzalo Sánchez de Lozada, candidate of the *MNR*, received 23% of the vote and Banzer received 22%. Jaime Paz Zamora, a leftist, received 19.5%. Three months of meetings in smoke-filled rooms ensued. Finally, in August, the third-place Paz Zamora was declared the new president. Why? Banzer, who while in power had jailed and exiled Paz Zamora in the 1970s, threw his support behind his former arch foe in exchange for 10 out of 17 cabinet posts that virtually assured his control of the government.

Paz Zamora pledged to continue his uncle's style of government and did so. Unrest did not cease; his term was marred by a nationwide teacher's strike and a murky plot to assassinate him, the chief drug enforcement officer and the U.S. ambassador in 1990. Drug raids with U.S. assistance were only moderately successful and highly resented.

In the 1993 elections, Cabinet ministers resigned to support Banzer. In spite of this, Sánchez de Lozada won a plurality of 36%; Banzer then threw his support to his rival, and Congress decreed Sánchez de Lozada president.

Like many other Latin American presidents of the 1990s, Sánchez de Lozada, popularly—and unpopularly—known as "Goni," undertook a pragmatic program of privatizing cumbersome state-owned enterprises, including the national airline, the oil company and the telecommunications infrastructure. He also sought to decentralize power, placing unprecedented control in the hands of the departments. He also welcomed foreign investors with red-carpet incentives.

Faced with strikes and protests by the majority Indian community for this seeming betrayal of the 1952 revolution, Sánchez reached a new land-reform agreement with Indian leaders in 1996, the most significant such law since the transcendental land-reform law of 1952. Unlike the earlier law, the new statute not only gave peasants title to their land but also permitted them to sell it. Previously, they could only bequeath it to their children, with the result that individual plots became too small to be economically viable.

Banzer Returns to Power

The reforms proved to be the leading issue of the 1997 elections, which drew 10 candidates. All the major candidates embraced Sánchez's reforms, but Banzer capitalized on the discontent among the poor by running on a foggy populist platform that included his promise to "humanize" the reforms. The ploy worked, and Banzer, now a zealous democrat who pledged to respect human rights, emerged as the frontrunner with 22% of the vote. The *MNR* candidate was second with 18% and former President Paz Zamora was third with 17%. There was a 70% turnout of 3.2 million voters.

Congress again was required to select the president, but this time Banzer's right-wing Nationalist Democratic Alliance (*ADN*) forged an unusual alliance with populist and left-wing parties to assure him of victory. Banzer, then 71, received the necessary majority of 79 of the 157 deputies after only two thirds of them had voted. The new vice president was Jorge Quiroga, 37, a previous finance minister under Paz Zamora, a former IBM executive and an engineering graduate of Texas A&M who was married to a Texan. They were sworn in the next day, August 6, Independence Day, for a term that had been constitutionally extended from four to five years.

Banzer issued a controversial pledge to eradicate Bolivia's coca production before the end of his term in 2002, news that gladdened the Clinton administration.

The powerful Confederation of Bolivian Workers (*COB*) soon began engaging in the country's second most popular pastime after soccer: general strikes. The *COB* demanded an increase in the monthly minimum wage from $45 to an unreasonable and inflationary $667. The government counter-offered $54, which the *COB* rejected. It called three 48-hour general strikes in 1997 and 1998. When the government refused to budge, an open-ended strike began in April 1998. Coupled with this, coca-growing peasants in the Chapare region, furious over the government's decision to eliminate their livelihood, joined the strike by setting up roadblocks on the Santa Cruz-Cochabamba highway. Hundreds of troops and police were dispatched to disperse them, and violence erupted.

Negotiations between the government and the *COB* broke down when the government refused to accept the participation of Evo Morales, the leader of the coca growers, who had been elected to Congress in 1997. Morales proposed that the government offer incentives for the peasants to switch to alternative crops, which, in fact, already had been done; non-traditional crops in Chapare by then

Hugo Banzer Suárez

outnumbered coca acreage 3–1. The government also had paid farmers up to $2,500 per hectare—almost all of it provided by the United States—to uproot coca plants, but the incentive program was not to be extended beyond 1998. Cooperate now and get paid, or be an outlaw, was the strategy.

Miffed, Morales accused Banzer of having had ties to drug traffickers, which the president denied. The strike turned violent, with 18 fatalities. But in the test of wills, Banzer prevailed. He reported to Congress that of the estimated 40,000 hectares of coca cultivation, 7,000 were eradicated in 1997 and 11,620 in 1998. Critics maintained that new cultivation reduced the net eradication in those years to only 2,000 and 8,000, respectively. Moreover, Morales and younger, less moderate spokesmen for the growers complained that the ostensible markets for the alternative crops did not exist.

Banzer faced another challenge in 1998 when former President Sánchez de Lozada called for an investigation into Banzer's role in the human rights abuses committed during his military regime, when an estimated 200 people were killed. The call no doubt was inspired by the arrest in London days earlier of former Chilean strongman Augusto Pinochet and by the ongoing investigation of Argentine military men for atrocities committed during the "Dirty War." Banzer accused the *MNR* of hypocrisy and called on the opposition party to examine its own complicity with military regimes.

In 1999, the government announced even more impressive figures in the coca-eradication program than it had the year

Bolivia

before: 14,000 hectares removed that year, compared with 11,670 in 1998, which left only 16,000 hectares under cultivation.

General strikes continued to plague the country. In April 2000, a seemingly routine local protest in Cochabamba against an increase in water prices turned violent and presented Banzer with his gravest domestic crisis yet. The protests spread to five of the nine departments; five people were killed and 40 injured, dozens were arrested, and the president issued a 90-day state of siege, the seventh since the restoration of democracy. The unrest quickly spread, as angry farmers erected roadblocks in five departments. Negotiations between the government and the protesters, mediated by the Catholic Church, defused that crisis.

New, more broadly based protests flared up again, principally by coca farmers protesting the eradication programs, but they were joined by other peasant farmers, teachers and transport workers. Banzer's response was relatively measured, leaving "only" about 10 people dead.

In late 2000, Banzer declared the successful culmination of the coca eradication program, claiming 40,000 hectares had been removed from cultivation; 12,000 hectares in Yungas were allowed to be cultivated for "traditional" purposes, a concession to the sentiments of local Indians. Still, the peasants complained that other crops, such as coffee, would earn them only a fraction of what they made from coca.

A new variable was added into the Bolivian political equation in November 2000, when a new Indian-based political party, *Movimiento Indígeno Pachacuti* (the Aymara word for "revival"), was established by Felipe Quispe, the head of a peasant labor confederation.

Banzer pushed through Congress in 2001 an ambitious, 50-point constitutional reform to broaden, in principle at least, Bolivian democracy. The reforms targeted election fraud by removing local elections from the control of local kingpins, providing for referenda, and by empowering the Supreme Court rather than Congress with the decision to revoke congressional immunity in corruption investigations. The opposition *MNR* grudgingly supported the plan.

A political era came to an end in Bolivia on June 7, 2001, when four-time former president Paz Estenssoro, the intellectual author of the 1952 revolution, died at 93 on the 59th anniversary of the founding of the *MNR*. His funeral in Tarija attracted thousands of peasants, who mingled with the elite of various parties who came to pay tribute to the man and his legacy.

The incumbent president would soon follow him. Banzer, a heavy smoker, was diagnosed with lung and liver cancer. He resigned effective August 6, 2001, Independence Day and the fourth anniversary of his inauguration, and Vice President Quiroga was sworn in the following day for the remaining year of his term. Banzer, 75, died nine months later. Thousands filled the streets to pay homage to this dictator-turned-democrat.

A lame duck from the start, Quiroga seemed determined to make a mark during his brief occupancy of the presidential palace. He pledged to continue Banzer's coca eradication policy, and he pushed several reform measures through Congress, including a civil service, non-partisan electoral courts, expanded powers for the comptroller-general and financial accountability for public officials. Armed with his new power, the comptroller-general began investigating other congressmen and other public officials without regard to party. One problem that still went unaddressed, however, was the rampant corruption in the national police.

When Quiroga issued a decree that outlawed the drying, shipping or sale of coca leaves in open markets, Morales denounced the decree as unconstitutional. When police attempted to close such a market near Cochabamba in January 2002, the protests flared into violence that left nine people, including four policemen, dead. A congressional panel sought to strip Morales of his seat for allegedly inciting the violence, but Quiroga and Morales compromised.

The Cliffhanger of 2002

The 2002 presidential race was the usual free-for-all. Two former presidents, Sánchez de Lozada of the *MNR* and Paz Zamora of the Movement of the Revolutionary Left (*MIR*) entered the race. As Quiroga was barred from running, the *ADN* nominated Ronald MacLean. Morales entered the race as the candidate of the Movement to Socialism (*MAS*), while Felipe Quispe stood for the Pachacuti Indigenous Movement (*MIP*). Rounding out the cluttered field of major contenders was the long-time mayor of Cochabamba and a former army captain, Manfred Villa Reyes, standard-bearer of the populist-oriented New Republican Force (*NFR*).

Sánchez, then 72, pledged to continue free-market reforms and to make Bolivia more attractive to investors, initiatives he had taken as president. Paz and Morales both denounced free-market capitalism. Paz said he would return some of the country's vast natural gas wealth to state control, while Morales, who chewed coca leaves at his rallies as a political statement, vowed to discontinue the coca eradication program and bombastically declared he would expel the *"yanquis."* Reyes offered only vague generalities.

U.S. Ambassador Manuel Rocha, in a stunning breach of diplomatic protocol, warned during a ceremony he attended with President Quiroga that voting for Morales could jeopardize continued U.S. aid. The reaction was immediate and ferocious, as Bolivians of all political stripes denounced this U.S. intrusion into domestic politics. (Many Bolivians already were sensitive to U.S. intrusion, as the first lady, Virginia Gillum de Quiroga, still held U.S. citizenship.)

Sánchez took an early lead on June 30, with Reyes Villa close behind. But to everyone's surprise, Morales surged into third place. For nine days, the country—and the Bush administration—held their breaths. After the votes trickled in from the remote altiplano—coca-growing country—Morales finished in second place just 721 votes ahead of Reyes!

A total of 2,993,708 Bolivians had voted, a respectable turnout of 72.04%. The complete official count gave Sánchez de Lozada 624,126 votes, 22.46%; Morales, 581,884 votes, 20.94%; Reyes, 581,163, 20.91%; and Paz, 453,375, 16.31%. Sánchez and Morales each carried four of the nine departments; Paz carried one.

Congress then had to choose from between Sánchez and Morales, and frantic jockeying began. The press reported again that Ambassador Rocha was thrusting himself into domestic politics by participating in an inter-party meeting and that he was applying "pressure" on behalf of Sánchez and against Morales.

For his part, Morales suddenly began sounding conciliatory. He insisted there was a difference between coca cultivation and narcotrafficking, which he said he had always opposed, but he blamed the problem on the demand for cocaine in the developed countries. He also made conciliatory remarks about the World Bank and the IMF.

Yet, on August 4, Congress elected Sánchez de Lozada, over Morales, 84–43.

An Abortive Presidency

Sánchez and Vice President Carlos Mesa were inaugurated on August 6, 2002. In his address, Sánchez made conciliatory overtures to the Indian-based movements that constituted much of the congressional opposition for the first time, promised to launch massive public works projects to create jobs and warned his countrymen that they "must choose between progress and collapse."

With his shaky 22% mandate, there was little Sánchez could accomplish, and even that meager base of support quickly eroded. Long-simmering tensions over

Former President Jorge Quiroga

the coca eradication program erupted into violence again in 2003, when troops sought to clear roadblocks that angry farmers had erected on the La Paz-Cochabamba highway. The farmers kept the highway closed for two weeks, and the resulting violence left 10 civilians and two soldiers dead before the government and the farmers agreed to negotiate. But the worst was yet to come.

Sánchez announced plans for a new progressive income tax of up to 12.5% to augment the value-added tax, in order to meet IMF demands to reduce the budget deficit from 8.5% to 5.5%. The reaction was immediate, and violent. First, 7,000 La Paz police officers, who were demanding a 40% salary increase, went on strike to protest the new tax. They were joined by thousands of other protesters, who besieged the presidential palace. Protesters chanted, "Resign or die, those are your choices," apparently a parody of Sánchez's inaugural address.

Sánchez called out the troops. Policemen and soldiers confronted each other. In the ensuing exchange of gunfire, 14 people died. Chaos erupted as mobs looted and burned department stores; others occupied or set fire to 12 government buildings, including the vice president's office. The fires raged out of control as firefighters joined the striking policemen. Other riots broke out in Cochabamba and other cities.

Sánchez himself escaped from the presidential palace in an ambulance. Shaken, he agreed to rescind the income tax. After two days of violence, policemen returned to work and order was restored. The final

toll was 32 dead and at least 102 injured, the worst civil violence since the implementation of democracy in 1982. A peaceful mass protest demanded Sánchez's resignation, and the president responded two days later by purging his cabinet of his most unpopular ministers and reduced the number of ministries from 18 to 13 to reduce expenditures. The IMF subsequently moderated its budget deficit demand to 6.5%.

By mid-2003, Sánchez's approval rating was 19%, the second-lowest of any Latin American leader; it would plummet still lower. Bolivia remained a powder keg, which exploded again in September 2003.

The spark was something that should have been heralded as a major boost to the economy: a $5 billion pipeline to Chile by which natural gas could be sold for export to the western United States. Nationalists were furious that the pipeline would pass through the territory that Bolivia lost to Chile in the War of the Pacific of 1879–84, and Morales and other peasant leaders objected to selling Bolivia's natural resources to the hated *yanquis*. Clashes between peasants and security forces left seven dead, and angry peasants once again blockaded La Paz. Sánchez offered to negotiate with the peasants, but Quispe rebuffed the offer. Teachers and street vendors in La Paz joined the protests, followed by the miners. Their demand: Sánchez's resignation.

Another 16 people died over the next two weeks; the El Alto suburb of La Paz was placed under martial law. A desperate Sánchez agreed to cancel the pipeline project, which would have created hundreds of badly needed jobs and brought in $1.5 billion a year in foreign exchange. The cancellation failed to placate the protesters, however, and on October 13 La Paz was paralyzed by a transportation strike. Fifteen people died in clashes in La Paz, El Alto and Santa Cruz, two of them soldiers. Morales joined those demanding that Sánchez resign, and in a stunning development, Vice President Mesa withdrew his support for the president because of the use of deadly force against the protesters and urged him to change course.

The embattled president, whose approval rating had dropped to a pitiful 9%, addressed the nation, but in unconciliatory language he refused to resign and blamed the unrest on "foreign" elements, apparently a reference to Venezuela's Hugo Chávez and Libya's Muammar Qadhafi, with whom Morales has close ties. The speech only inflamed the situation.

Thousands of miners marched on La Paz to join protesters who had besieged the capital with burning tires and rock barricades; the death toll mounted. Morales called the president and his cabinet

"butchers," and Quispe went into hiding, claiming his life was in danger.

On October 17, with his allies abandoning him, the death toll at 74 and the country on the brink of chaos, Sánchez bitterly submitted his resignation to Congress. He and his wife flew to Miami. The violent street protests were transformed immediately into mass celebrations.

Mesa Seeks Consensus

Hours later, Mesa, a 50-year-old historian and a respected journalist, was sworn in as Bolivia's 82nd president, providing some constitutional trappings to the third overthrow by mob rule of an elected South American president in less than

**Former President
Gonzalo Sánchez de Lozada**

four years. Addressing Congress, Mesa pledged a "period of historic transition" and said he would appoint a non-partisan cabinet. He advocated resolving the gas pipeline issue through a popular referendum; the gas-producing areas that stood to benefit from it were solidly in favor of its construction.

Morales, widely seen as the man who orchestrated Sánchez's downfall, suddenly became statesmanlike and pledged to give Mesa a grace period to restore order.

Mesa, who constitutionally was entitled to serve out the remainder of Sánchez's five-year term, at first said he would serve only as interim president until he called a new election. But he changed his mind and decided to last out his term. Few

Bolivia

seemed to object; by mid-2004, his approval ratings were above 70%, a dramatic contrast to the detested Sánchez.

Mesa was under pressure from Morales and other Indian leaders to call a constituent assembly to revise the country's constitution. Mesa agreed in principle.

Mesa held the promised referendum on the gas pipeline in July 2004. Voters approved all five issues on the ballot, one of them by 92%, handing the president a major vote of confidence. The referendum, a new experience for Bolivians, increased taxes at the wellhead on the foreign companies and trimmed some of their rights.

But that did not defuse the gas issue. The left pushed for either re-nationalization of oil and gas companies or at least greater state control. The gas-producing provinces of Santa Cruz and Tarija, however, had stood to benefit greatly from the pipeline deal. In November, there was a 24-hour general strike in the two departments to demand autonomy from La Paz so they could close the deal themselves, the beginning of a separatist movement that still threatens to tear Bolivia in two.

A town-hall meeting was held in Santa Cruz, Bolivia's largest city with 1.4 million people, in January 2005 to demand popular election of the local governor; the president still appointed departmental governors. Tarija Department, where 85% of the gas reserves are located, also backed the separatist movement. This provoked a warning from the armed forces that they fully supported the constitutional president and would not sit idly by to watch the country break apart. Mesa acceded to the *cruzeños'* demand rather than risk bloodshed. He agreed to elections for all nine departmental governors in 2005, and he said he would call another referendum to decide the autonomy issue.

The next flash point was a controversial energy bill. Morales advocated raising the royalty on oil and gas extraction from 18% to 50%. Mesa sought a compromise that would put a 32% maximum tax on top of the 18% royalty. Morales and the various indigenous groups rejected the compromise, erected roadblocks and precipitated yet another crisis that came to a head in March 2005, when Mesa announced he would resign unless the demonstrations ended. Morales' *MAS* refused, and Mesa submitted his resignation to Congress. His bluff worked. Thousands of pro-Mesa demonstrators converged on the Congress, which unanimously rejected the resignation. Even Morales admitted he did not want Mesa to quit—yet.

Mesa agreed to stay if the roadblocks were dismantled, and if Congress passed his energy bill and approved elections for August to choose his successor as well a new Congress. Mesa warned that Bolivia

was headed toward "collective suicide," but vowed he would not resort to violence. Congress rejected Mesa's call for an early election as unconstitutional. Meanwhile, the roadblocks continued. For a second time, Mesa threatened to resign. After a tense two days, Mesa went on national television to declare, "I will not run away from my responsibilities."

By May, Congress had passed a compromise energy bill. At first, Mesa indicated he would sign it as the price for domestic peace, then stunned the country by refusing to either sign or veto it. The indigenous movements reacted with more protests. Mesa had kept his promise not to use deadly force, but he threatened again to resign if the protests turned violent.

The Senate president signed the bill into law, as provided for in the constitution. Morales continued to demand a 50% tax, and an "indefinite" strike began in El Alto to demand outright nationalization and even the dissolution of Congress. Tens of thousands of protesters besieged La Paz. Police fired tear gas and rubber bullets,

Former President Carlos Mesa

but not live ammunition. Police sealed off Murillo Plaza, site of the presidential palace. Mesa suddenly proclaimed he would serve out the remainder of his term and not cave in to pressure. It was ominously reminiscent of October 2003.

In Santa Cruz, the autonomy movement was revived when Congress failed to call for a referendum. Leaders of the movement called a referendum themselves.

With Congress deadlocked on resolving the crisis, Mesa signed a decree that set an election in October for members of a constituent assembly that would rewrite the constitution to give more power to the Indian communities, one of the militants' key demands. Mesa set the same day for a referendum on departmental autonomy. Neither side was placated. The militants refused to call off their siege of La Paz, while Santa Cruz separatist leaders said they would forge ahead with plans for their own referendum. Both U.N. Secretary-General Kofi Annan and Pope Benedict

XVI urged Bolivians to resolve the crisis peacefully.

On June 6, 2005, Mesa went on television to announce his resignation for a second time. He suggested that neither of the presidents of the Senate or Chamber of Deputies, who were next in the line of succession, should accept the presidency, which would require a new election within 150 days. Only the electoral process, Mesa warned, could save the nation, which he said was "on the brink of civil war."

The Congress abandoned La Paz for an emergency session in the judicial capital of Sucre. Protests quickly erupted there as well. On June 9, Congress voted to accept Mesa's resignation. Morales said his party would refuse to recognize either the Senate president or the Chamber president; consequently, both men refused to accept the presidency. Under the constitution, that left Supreme Court Chief Justice Eduardo Rodríguez next in line. He was sworn in late that night as Bolivia's 83rd president—and the fourth in less than two years.

Morales pledged his support to Rodríguez until new elections. The next day, the protesters lifted the siege of La Paz, where life returned to normal. Clearly, Morales had become the new power in Bolivia. That same day, the so-called "Paris Club," composed of the eight largest creditor nations, announced it was canceling $40 billion in Bolivian debt.

New Elections

The various factions in Congress set December 4, 2005, as the date for new presidential elections for president, Congress and, for the first time, the departmental governors, and July 2, 2006, as the date for elections for the constituent assembly. The presidential vote was later changed to December 18.

Morales stood again as the *MAS* candidate. The other now-discredited established parties all but disappeared. A total of seven other candidates entered the fray, but the conservative, pro-free trade forces eventually coalesced around the candidacy of former interim President Jorge Quiroga and a hastily assembled movement called Democratic and Social Power, or *Podemos* (We Can).

Morales was an even more bombastic campaigner than in 2002, vowing to become the "nightmare" of the United States. He made ambiguous declarations, saying he would nationalize oil and gas but honor contracts with foreign-owned firms, and vowing to end the coca eradication program while promising to work with the United States against cocaine production. His motto was "zero cocaine, but not zero coca." He also pledged to implement a "democratic revolution" along the lines of that of Venezuela's Chávez. He also embraced what he called "21st century socialism."

On December 18, almost 2.8 million Bolivians went to the polls, a turnout of 84.5%. Morales surged ahead by a convincing plurality, but after the votes trickled in from the remote coca-growing regions over the next few days, the final tally stunned the nation and the world:

| Morales | 1,544,374 | 53.7% |
| Quiroga | 821,745 | 28.6% |

The vote was truly historic. For the first time in their 23-year-old democracy, Bolivians had given a president a majority electoral mandate, and for the first time in Bolivia's 180 years as an independent republic, a member of the indigenous majority had been elevated to the presidential palace.

The *MAS* won 64 of the 130 seats in the Chamber of Deputies, just two short of an absolute majority, to 44 seats for Quiroga's *Podemos*. In the Senate, however, *Podemos* won 13 of the 27 seats to 12 for the *MAS*. Pro-Morales governors won in only three of the nine departments.

Morales Takes Charge

President-elect Morales embarked on a whirlwind 10-day world tour. The first two legs were Havana and Caracas to celebrate his win with his ideological heroes, Castro and Chávez. From there he went to Europe, South Africa, China and Brazil. In Brazil, he promised President da Silva, his friend and, like him, a socialist and former union leader, that he would not nationalize the holdings of *Petrobras*, Brazil's state-owned oil and gas firms, which had been one of the four companies responsible for discovering and exploiting Bolivia's rich gas deposits. Washington was pointedly excluded from Morales' itinerary.

On January 22, 2006, Washington's "nightmare" came true as Evo Morales,

46, assumed the presidential sash. Alvaro García was sworn in as vice president. Morales wore an open-necked jacket, and thousands of Indians attended the inauguration. So did Chávez and 10 other Latin American presidents (Castro was uncharacteristically absent), while the United States was represented only by Bush's assistant secretary of state for Western Hemisphere affairs.

The world waited to see whether Morales would pragmatically abandon his fiery leftist rhetoric once in office, like Brazil's da Silva, or become another loose cannon like Chávez. He chose the loose cannon option.

First, he loaded his cabinet with left-wing members of his indigenous movement and a handful of left-wing intellectuals with little or no administrative experience. Next, he tripled the minimum wage, which threatened to cripple small businesses and return Bolivia to the hyperinflation of the 1980s. At the same time, he slashed his own salary and those

Bolivia

of even mid-level government bureaucrats, sparking mass resignations.

Morales saved his 100th day in office for his greatest bombshell. On May 1, 2006, International Labor Day, Morales declared Bolivia's gas deposits under state control and dispatched troops to seize the fields being exploited by French, British, Brazilian and Spanish-Argentine firms. Morales, clad in a hard hat, went to the largest gas field, operated by *Petrobras,* to read the decree; so much for his promise to da Silva. He declared that the firms would have to sign new contracts within six months or forfeit their property, a Mafia-like ultimatum.

He also increased the government's take of revenue from the gas from the 50% agreed to the year before to 82%, and declared that *YPFB,* Bolivia's state-owned oil company, would have majority control not only of the companies drilling for oil and gas in Bolivia but of refineries and pipelines as well. The heretofore friendly governments of Brazil, Spain and Argentina were stunned. Ironically, those socialist leaders were now on the receiving end of a nationalization. One of da Silva's responses was to embark on an expansion of Brazil's hydroelectric potential to reduce the dependence on Bolivian gas for electricity generation—much to Morales' chagrin.

Morales returned to Havana, where he, Castro and Chávez signed a pact declaring the Bolivarian Alternative for Latin America, or *ALBA,* which is also the Spanish word for "dawn." *ALBA* is designed as an alternative to the Free Trade Area of the Americas (FTAA) advocated by the United States.

Morales' natural gas power play cast a pall over the Fourth European Union-Latin American-Caribbean Summit that opened in Vienna a few days later. Morales was warned that such draconian actions would serve only to discourage further foreign investment. Morales continued to insist in Vienna, not very convincingly, that he would respect the rights of investors.

Morales took another page from Chávez's Bolivarian Revolution by announcing the redistribution of 9,600 square miles of state-owned land to peasant farmers, mostly in the agriculture-rich east, as part of his "agrarian revolution." The plots are about 124 acres and are to have the titles guaranteed. Morales said he planned to distribute 77,000 square miles over his five-year term, raising fears among agricultural business interests.

Just as it was with Chávez in 1999, the next step for Morales was the election in July for the 255 members of the constituent assembly, who would draw up a new constitution revamping Bolivian in-

stitutions to guarantee the rights of the indigenous majority, and the concurrent referendum on regional autonomy. Unlike Cháves, Morales was dealt a muted victory. His *MAS* won a majority of 137 seats in the assembly to 65 for *Podemos,* but that was well short of the two-thirds he needed for his rubber-stamped revolutionary constitution. A majority of 55% of the voters opposed regional autonomy, but it carried handily in the four eastern departments, putting them on a collision course with La Paz.

Lacking the needed two-thirds majority, Morales decided in good Marxist fashion to change the rules. His delegates to the constituent assembly insisted that articles to the new constitution could be approved by a simple majority, although the final document would require a two-thirds vote and ratification by the voters. Squabbling between the pro- and anti-Morales factions led to fistfights in the assembly.

Meanwhile, Morales discovered that to nationalize oil and gas fields was one thing, to operate them something else. By August 2006, he admitted that the state-owned firm, *YPFB,* was desperately short of operating capital and was on the brink of shutting down. As the six-month deadline he had given the foreign companies approached, he pragmatically compromised. To appease the Brazilians, he fired his energy minister and reduced the taxes and royalties on *Petrobras'* two largest fields from 82% to 50%—still more than it had paid before. He reached agreements with the other companies that were essentially the same as the deal Mesa had struck that Morales had opposed so vigorously. *YPFB* has a majority 51% stake in the firms' operations, far from the full nationalization Morales had promised.

That October, Morales was suddenly on the receiving end of violent protests when rival groups of salaried and independent tin miners at the huge Huanuni mine clashed with one another. Both groups had been supportive of Morales, who did not send police to intervene until the second day. In the confrontation, 16 people were killed and more than 80 wounded; independent miners withdrew their support for Morales.

Opposition to Morales continued to simmer in the four eastern departments as well. An anti-Morales hunger strike at the governor's palace in Santa Cruz was attacked by Morales partisans. Morales' popularity rating, like those of his predecessors, began to plummet, from 82% in May 2006 to 58% in October.

Morales suddenly ceased his anti-*yanqui* rhetoric when the realized that the preferential tariff the United States had granted Bolivian textiles was due to expire in December 2006. Hat in hand, the

Bolivians lobbied the new Democratic-controlled Congress to renew the accords. The pro-union Democrats were cool to the idea, but granted a six-month extension. In May 2007, a Bolivian delegation headed by the deputy trade and exports minister was back in Washington to plead for another extension. The textile agreement brought in so much foreign exchange and created so many jobs in Morales' core constituency that he was forced to swallow his pride (see Economy).

Morales resorted to decidedly undemocratic tactics to ramrod his constitution through the constituent assembly in December. Pro-Morales demonstrators in Sucre blocked access to the assembly of anti-Morales delegates, whereupon the Morales faction quickly passed a constitution that, among other things, imposed heavy new taxes on the four wealthy eastern provinces, gave new powers to the indigenous majority at the expense of the Caucasian and *mestizo* minorities and lifted the ban on re-election that would allow Morales to run again. The assembly set May 4, 2008 as the date for the referendum on the new organic law.

The governors of Santa Cruz, Beni, Panda and Tarija responded by declaring their autonomy. Santa Cruz went a step further by scheduling a referendum on autonomy for May 4, the same day as the national referendum on the constitution.

Perhaps in part because of widespread criticism of the mob-rule tactics in Sucre, the government decided to postpone the May 4 referendum. Santa Cruz, however, proceeded with its autonomy referendum, which Morales angrily declared to be illegitimate and said La Paz would not recognize the results. Congress passed a resolution to that effect, with the government employing the same mob-rule tactics to prevent opposition members from entering.

The autonomy referendum went off as planned, and 86% of *cruzeños* voted in favor of autonomy, despite intimidation by government supporters, who burned ballot boxes in some areas. Morales declared the vote a failure.

Days after the May 4 referendum, Morales called yet another referendum for August 10 on whether he, Vice President García and eight departmental governors would remain in office. In a peculiar twist of Chávez's victory in the recall election in Venezuela, Morales called this recall election on *himself.* With a turnout of 84%, Morales received a convincing vote of confidence with 67.4%, 13 percentage points higher than his 2005 election victory. Two anti-Morales governors, including former presidential candidate Manfred Reyes Villa of Cochabamba, were ousted and replaced by Morales appointees. But the vote may only have sharpened the country's growing polarization. The anti-Morales governors of the four eastern departments also were retained with strengthened majorities.

The vote seemed to both embolden the government to move forward on the new constitution in a heavy-handed manner and to make the opposition more desperate. On August 28, Morales announced there would be yet another referendum, this time on his new constitution, on December 7, 2008. The four anti-Morales governors who had survived recall called for civil disobedience, including a general strike, in the so-called "Media Luna" departments (for their crescent-moon shape) to demand their share of oil and gas revenues that Morales had diverted to his social programs. On September 10, hundreds of opposition protesters seized a major gas field. One pipeline exploded, cutting off lucrative gas exports to Brazil. Anti-government and pro-government demonstrators opened fire on each other in Pando. In a separate incident in El Porvenir, 15 peasants were slain in an ambush.

Morales, who now found himself on the other side of the barricades, dispatched troops, declared martial law and arrested Pando Governor Leopoldo Fernández despite his constitutional immunity. Troops killed two protesters. Fernández has been held without trial ever since. (He was scheduled to face trial beginning in June 2010 on a litany of charges, including alleged "genocide" for the "El Porvenir Massacre.")

The violence flared for three weeks, leaving an estimated 30 dead. U.S. Ambassador Philip Goldberg met with the regional governors, prompting Morales to declare him *persona non grata* and expel him from Bolivia. The Bush administration responded by expelling the Bolivian ambassador and declaring Bolivia "noncompliant" in the war on drugs, threatening the cutoff of $30 million in aid. Morales later expelled U.S. Drug Enforcement Agency (DEA) agents.

Both sides prudently backed away from the brink of civil war, which neither really needed or wanted. Mediators from neighboring nations were called in. Some compromises were reached on the new constitution, including shifting the referendum date to January 25, 2009, but in the end, the 411-article document gave Morales most of what he wanted: The right to run for re-election for another five-year term, greater state control over the economy and enhanced rights for the indigenous majority. The various Indian "nations" would be granted greater control over their own natural resources. The opposition, weakened by the president's two-

President Evo Morales

thirds mandate on August 10 and frightened by the arrest of the Pando governor, could do little but howl in protest.

The outcome of the January 25 constitutional referendum was a foregone conclusion. The turnout was 3.5 million voters, or 90.3%, 61.4% of whom voted for the new organic law. Morales had yet another mandate for his "21st century socialism." Voters also approved limiting landholdings to 5,000 hectares.

Relations with the United States went from deplorable to abysmal. Just weeks after expelling the U.S. ambassador and a month after visiting Libya and Iran, Morales displayed the height of diplomatic *chutzpah* by sending a delegation to Washington to plead for continuation of the preferential tariffs for Bolivian goods! Even as the Bolivians arrived, Secretary of State Condoleezza Rica announced the preferences would be allowed to expire on December 31, 2008. The move was expected to cost Bolivia an estimated 30,000 jobs and to price an estimated $300 million in Bolivian goods off the U.S. market. Morales bombastically declared that Bolivia did not need the drug aid or the preferential tariffs, apparently in the belief that his friend in Caracas would come to his rescue.

In November 2008, Bolivia demanded the extradition of former President Sánchez for "genocide" in the violence of 2003; the United States has taken no action on the request. Morales expelled

another U.S. diplomat in March 2009 for allegedly conspiring with opposition groups, and in April he accused the DEA of conspiring to assassinate him, but produced no convincing evidence.

To further annoy Washington, in November 2009 Morales hosted another visit by Iranian President Mahmoud Ahmadinejad, who also visited Brazil and Venezuela. The two presidents signed a "mutual cooperation" agreement and made it a media event. In reality, the agreement served no purpose other than to irritate the United States. The agreement certainly does little to make up for the loss of Bolivia's preferential tariffs with the United States. Women members of the Bolivian Congress objected to an earlier treaty signed by the two presidents in 2007 because of Iran's treatment of women.

In March 2009, Morales went on a hunger strike to intimidate Congress into setting the date for the election in which he expected to coast to a second term. Congress acquiesced and set December 6 as the date for the presidential election and April 4, 2010, as the date for regional and municipal elections.

Re-Election

The anti-Morales forces feebly coalesced around a new alliance, the Plan Progress for Bolivia. It nominated former Cochabamba Governor Reyes Villa, whom Morales had nudged out of second place in the 2002 cliffhanger election. Six other candidates appeared on the ballot. But the opposition knew from the start that mathematics was against them.

In the balloting on December 6, Morales received 2,943,209 votes, or 64.2%, to only 1,212,795, or 26.5%, for Reyes Villa. Morales' *MAS* received 88 of the 130 seats in the Chamber of Deputies and 26 of the 36 Senate seats. The Plan Progress for Bolivia won 37 seats in the lower house and 10 in the Senate.

There were few surprises in the departmental elections in April, either; what they did was reinforce Bolivia's growing polarization. The *MAS* won the governorships of Chuquisaca, Cochabamba, La Paz, Oruro, Pando and Potosí. The opposition won in the eastern "Media Luna" departments of Beni, Santa Cruz and Tarija.

Since his second inauguration in January, Morales has used his power as a cudgel to intimidate his political opponents under the rubric of judicial reform and anti-corruption. His leading presidential opponent, Reyes Villa, was accused of fraud and fled to the United States, saying he could not g et a fair trial in Bolivia. Four former presidents also are facing various charges; Sánchez de Lozada, still in the United States, is being tried *in ab-*

Bolivia

sentia on the genocide charges. Former Pando Governor Leopoldo Fernández, who has been in jail since September 2008, is facing trial for treason and genocide. Morales' new judicial reform, which provides for popular election of judges, also places the burden of proof on the defendant in corruption cases.

Culture: The Spanish conquerors and settlers of Bolivia built new cities and tended to concentrate there, leaving the interior to the indigenous Aymara Indians. Today, the majority of Bolivians still speak Aymara as their first language, learning Spanish as a necessity to conduct official business. A substantial minority of the population also speaks Quéchua, the ancient tongue of the Incas. The populations of the cities of La Paz and Potosí are about 70% indigenous Indian, 25% *mestizo* and only 5% European.

Bolivian culture, consequently, remains essentially Indian with only a thin veneer of European Christianity superimposed upon it. Bolivia has produced few cultural figures of international note, although the flute–based folk music of the *altiplano* has become internationally popular. It is not unusual to see *altiplano* flute bands in colorful Indian dress playing on street corners from New Orleans to New York to Paris to Venice. Bolivians insist that the Brazilians "stole" the music for the mega-hit dance *Lambada* from Bolivia.

Because of the abysmally low literacy rate, Bolivia never developed a strong literary tradition. There were two newspapers of note, however, both published in *La Paz*: *El Diario*, founded in 1904, and *Presencia*, established by the Catholic Church during the revolutionary year 1952. *Presencia* ceased publication in 2001. Other current independent dailies now include *Los Tiempos, El Deber, La Prensa* and *La Razón*. The government of Evo Morales began publishing the daily newspaper *Cambio* in 2008.

Economy: Bolivia's economy has been based on the extraction of its mineral wealth for more than 400 years. The vast sums produced were exported, with little or no benefit accruing to the Bolivian people. Mismanagement and the decline of world demands for its minerals resulted in the *de facto* bankruptcy of the Bolivian government. While the 1952 revolution largely ended serfdom, a lack of technical and financial resources limited a more even distribution of wealth and income. The nation's major source of income, the tin mines, are largely a thing of the past and has been replaced at least in part by exports of petroleum and natural gas.

The other mainstay of the Bolivian economy is coca leaf. President Banzer's program to eradicate coca cultivation between 1997 and 2002 was largely successful, but it created social unrest among the impoverished peasants who depend on it for their livelihood. This program ceased with the election of the coca growers' leader, Evo Morales, as president in 2005.

Bolivia remains one of the hemisphere's poorest nations, and its agricultural- and mineral-based economy has shown modest growth in recent years. Growth has risen from 1.5% in 2001 to 4.5% in 2006, 4.6% in 2007 and an estimated 6.1% for 2008, but it dropped back to 2.8% in 2009.

GDP stood at $13.12 billion in 2007, 11.3% of it from agricultural products in the fertile eastern departments, 11% from mineral products, principally natural gas and tin. Per capita income surpassed the $1,000 mark for the first time in 1999, but it dropped back to $953 in 2002 and to $914 in 2004. It was back up to $1,030 in 2006 and $1,460 in 2008. That was still the third-poorest in Latin America.

President Sánchez de Lozada sought to boost the economy with the potentially lucrative sale of natural gas to the United States. Bolivia has estimated gas reserves of 53.4 trillion cubic feet, second only to Venezuela in South America. This move encountered furious opposition from the left. Public protests against the planned construction of a $5 billion gas pipeline to a Chilean port led to Sánchez's resignation in October 2003 and to the resignation of his successor, Carlos Mesa, in June 2005 (see History). In 2007, Bolivia's natural gas production was an estimated 14.7 billion cubic feet, of which it exported 11.7 bcf. Brazil is its major customer.

On May 1, 2006, President Evo Morales, elected on the campaign slogan of "21st century socialism," decreed the nationalization of oil and gas deposits, which affected the holdings of Brazil's *Petrobras*, France's Total and the Spanish-Argentine firm Repsol S.A., among others, which had invested $5 billion in exploration and in developing Bolivia's natural gas industry (see History). Morales found himself forced to compromise with the foreign companies when the new state-owned firm, *YPFB*, found itself in need of $180 million in operating capital, as well as technological expertise.

In addition to its natural gas wealth, Bolivia suddenly finds itself sitting atop another potential windfall: lithium. Bolivia has an estimated 5.4 million tons of lithium, the demand for which has mushroomed because it is a key ingredient for the batteries used to power hybrid and electric cars. Bolivia's deposits represent

just over half the world's known reserves; Chile is a distant second. Several Japanese and European companies have expressed an interest in mining the deposits, but the Morales government is resisting foreign exploitation. The state-owned firm *COMIBOL* has invested $6 million in a small lithium plant.

A trade preference accord with the United States Bolivia had enjoyed under the Andean Trade Protection and Drug Eradication Act of 1991 expired on December 31, 2008, representing a potential loss of $300 million in annual exports to the U.S., mostly textiles, and 30,000 jobs, most of them in factories in the impoverished El Alto suburb of La Paz, which is one of Morales' core constituencies. The United States did not renew them in retaliation for Morales' expulsion of the U.S. ambassador in September 2008 (see History).

Gas production declined in 2009, both because of mismanagement and the dearth of new foreign investment.

The Future: Evo Morales' election in 2005 was analogous to the ascension to power of Nelson Mandela in South Africa after decades of apartheid. Alas, Morales has shown himself to be no Nelson Mandela. Mandela effected reconciliation between the black majority and white minority, which was, and still is, the country's economic powerhouse. The same is true of Bolivia's Caucasian minority. Unlike Mandela, Morales has set about to create a "tyranny of the majority" on the model of his mentor, Venezuela's Hugo Chávez. Moreover, the white population of South Africa is diffused throughout the country, while Bolivia is regionally polarized between the indigenous western departments and the Caucasian- and mestizo-dominated eastern departments. Instead of effecting reconciliation, Morales has chosen to bleed the affluent eastern departments of the income from their natural gas resources and alienate their people.

Morales' lack of statesmanship and vision has also unnecessarily earned Bolivia enemies abroad, alienating not only the United States, which responded by suspending Bolivia's preferential tariffs at the end of 2008, but even erstwhile friends like Brazil and Spain, whose companies he has nationalized. He seems to be banking on the largess of Chávez to keep his economy afloat in the wake of the loss of the U.S. market, but sagging petroleum prices have jeopardized that hope.

The outbreak of violence in September 2008 brought Bolivia perilously close to outright civil war. That possibility persists. The unknown variable in this complex equation is the officer and NCO corps in the Bolivian military. If the eastern departments secede, will these soldiers then choose sides, as happened at the outbreak of the U.S. Civil War? Such a civil war could result in appalling bloodshed if both sides have professional military leadership and weaponry.

Yet, despite his divisiveness and heavy-handedness, Morales' rise to power, his constant holding of referenda (which he knows he has the votes to win) and his landslide re-election victory in December 2009, seem to have elevated his countrymen's faith in democracy. According to the annual *Latinobarómetro* surveys published by the British newsmagazine *The Economist,* the percentage of Bolivians who believe that democracy is preferable to any other form of government plummeted from 64% in 1996 to 50% in 2003 (when Sánchez fell) to just 45% in chaotic 2004. In 2006, Morales' first year in office, it was back up to 62%; in 2008, it was 68%; in 2009, it was 71%, fourth-highest in Latin America behind Venezuela, Uruguay and Costa Rica.

What remains to be seen is whether democracy Morales-style will be an emulation of the dictatorship of the proletariat his friend Chávez has implanted in Venezuela, or whether, as in a genuine democracy, the rights of the minority will be respected. Recent developments, such as the filing of criminal charges against four of his presidential predecessors and his 2009 opponent, and his so-called judicial "reform," which appears to be designed to effect retribution rather than justice, are not encouraging.

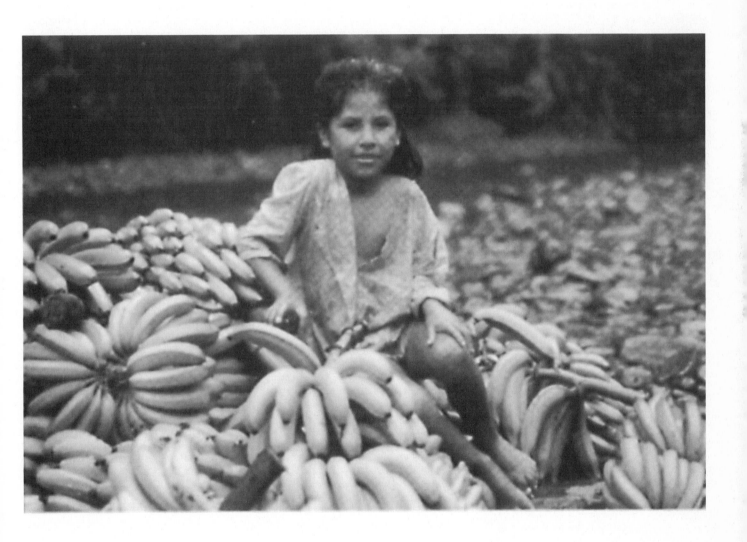

The Federative Republic of Brazil

Iguazu Falls (Brazil, Argentina, Paraguay)

Area: 3,286,500 square miles

Population: 198.7 million (2009 est.).

Capital City: Brasilia (Pop. 2.5 million, estimated).

Climate: The northern lowlands are hot, with heavy rainfall; the central plateau and northeastern regions are subtropical and dry; the southern regions are temperate with moderate rainfall.

Neighboring Countries: French Guiana, Suriname, Guyana, Venezuela, Colombia (North); Peru, Bolivia (West); Paraguay, Argentina, Uruguay (Southwest).

Official Language: Portuguese.

Other Principal Tongues: English, French, German and other European languages.

Ethnic Background: Black African/Mulatto (48%), European White (48%); Other (3%); Native Indian (1%).

Principal Religion: Christianity (Roman Catholic 75%, Protestant Evangelical 20%).

Chief Commercial Products: Coffee, refined metal ores, chemicals, cacao, soybeans, sugar, cotton, wood, automobiles and parts, shoes.

Currency: Real (established July 1, 1994).

Gross Domestic Product: U.S. $1.499 trillion in 2009 (est.) ($7,544 per capita);

Former Colonial Status: Colony of Portugal (1500–1815); Kingdom of the Portuguese Empire (1815–1822).

Independence Date: September 7, 1822.

Chief of State: Luiz Inácio "Lula" da Silva (b. October 27, 1945), president (since January 1, 2003).

National Flag: Green, with a yellow lozenge enclosing a blue sphere with 21 stars, five of which form the Southern Cross, and the motto *Ordem e Progresso* (Order and Progress).

Brazil occupies almost half of the South American continent and is almost as large as the continental United States. It stretches some 2,700 miles from the Guiana highlands in the North to the plains of Uruguay in the South and an equal distance from the "hump" on the Atlantic Coast to the jungles of Bolivia and Peru in the West. Almost half of this area is the hot, humid basin of the mighty Amazon River and its thousands of winding tributaries.

The northeast Bahia region, the interior of the "hump," is a semi-arid region; to the south and inland is a plateau drained to the northeast by the São Francisco River. This is a region of forests and plains which attracts migrants from other parts of Brazil and from abroad. The plains of the extreme south drain into the Paraná River valley. The southern states from Minas Gerais to Rio Grande do Sul comprise the effective Brazil, where approximately 90% of the population lives on less than 30% of the land. In an effort to draw settlers into other areas of the interior, the capital was moved in 1960 from pleasant and coastal Rio de Janeiro to inland and not so pleasant Brasilia. A modern city as planned, the capital is now surrounded by outlying shantytowns with almost one million people within 12 miles of the central area.

History: Pedro Alvares Cabral first raised the Portuguese flag in Brazil on April 22, 1500 after having been blown off course while en route (he thought) from Portugal to India. The Portuguese government, preoccupied with its India trade, took little interest in the American claim until 1530, when it established a colony at Rio de Janeiro and in 1532 founded São Vincente. The land was quickly divided into vast estates with frontages on the Atlantic Ocean and ran west to the line of demarcation between Spanish and Portuguese areas for discovery and colonization—approximately the 45th meridian west, set by the Treaty of Tordesillas in 1494. These estates, called *capitanias*, were granted as feudal holdings to the nobles who were to build towns and forts, explore, settle colonists and enrich the mother country. Thirteen estates were laid out, but the poor quality of the colonists sent out and the oppressive climate gave them a poor start.

In spite of this, several towns were founded—Olinda in 1535, Santo Amaro, Itamarca and Pernambuco in 1536, Bahia in 1549—and from these towns expeditions explored the interior.

72

Brazil

From 1580 to 1640, Brazil was under Spanish control—Philip II of Spain had inherited the Portuguese throne. During this period, explorations were pushed beyond the demarcation line, but few towns were established in the dense interior. From 1630 to 1654, the Dutch briefly held the northeast coast from Pernambuco to Parnaiba. During most of its colonial period, Brazil was in reality a coastal colony with an immense, unexplored interior. That the colonies prospered and remained under Portuguese control was largely due to the politics of Europe and to the efforts of two capable leaders—General Tomé de Souza and General Mem de Sá—and to the efforts of a few Jesuit missionaries.

For almost one and a half centuries following Spanish rule, Brazil was neglected by the Portuguese government. It did, however, benefit from the liberal policies of the Marquis of Pombal, the Portuguese prime minister under Joseph I (1749–77), who did much to improve public services. In general, Brazil's communities were ruled by municipal councils with little interference from Lisbon. By the end of the colonial period, cities had developed power and prestige reminiscent of the feudal ones of Europe. The smaller municipalities were at the mercy of the militia commanders, and the great estates were under the absolute rule of their owners.

Probably the most cohesive force in the Brazilian colonies was the Catholic Church, and the most influential of the churchmen were the Jesuits. The Portuguese church had been influenced by modifying cultures at home, both Moslem and Oriental, and was subject to still more change in Brazil because of the native Indian and imported African cultures. The Jesuits took as their first responsibility the protection of the Indians. Despite the opposition of the planters, who needed labor, they gathered their charges into fortified villages, taught them useful arts and crafts, and improved methods of agriculture simultaneously with the fundamentals of Christianity.

The ouster of the Jesuits in 1759 was simply political reaction to the fact that they were so successful in their work of protecting the native Indians that they were bad for the colony's businessmen.

The settling of Brazil's interior was the work of a few pioneers, the celebrated *bandeirantes*, the boldest of whom were the missionaries and the slave raiders of São Paulo. The latter were foremost in establishing Portuguese rule in the interior; their raids forced the remaining Indians to withdraw deeper inland and served as a counter-force against Spanish penetrations. In their wake came planters and, later, gold prospectors. As African slaves were introduced, the slave raiders turned

to commerce and industry, making São Paulo the most prosperous Brazilian state. The colonial economy was based on sugar and forest products until the end of the 17th century, when the lure of gold depopulated the plantations as owners and their slaves migrated to Minas Gerais. Gold was also found in Mato Grosso and Goiás; about the same time it was learned that the bright stones found in Minas Gerais were diamonds. This wealth brought an influx of immigrants and pushed the frontier further inland. In 1763 the capital of Brazil

was transferred from the north to Rio de Janeiro.

The cities furnished only the middlemen, the brokers and the hucksters in the development of colonial Brazil. Its theoretically rigid class society was in fact for many decades a bizarre mixture of aristocracy, democracy and anarchy. At the top was the ruling class from Portugal; next came those of Portuguese origin born in Brazil—which included a majority of the estate owners; then followed in descending order mixed bloods, slaves and native Indians.

Actually, the system was elastic. The mulatto children born of the owner and his slaves might be reared equally with his legitimate children, and the Negro with the capacity to win wealth or influence took precedence with the elite. By the end of the colonial period, the whites had declined in number and influence, while those of mixed ancestry showed strength and a high degree of adaptation to the Brazilian environment. Brazil's society was tolerant, and the freedom from interference from Portugal allowed it to develop a one-class people—Brazilians.

Brazil's history as an independent state may be divided into two periods: Empire and Republic, and these in turn have their subdivisions. Certainly, loyalty to the

Brazil

Rio de Janeiro about 1825

crown kept the regional factions from creating small states, as happened in the Spanish states of Gran Colombia and Central America.

Empire and Republic

In 1822, Pedro I, crown prince of Portugal and titular prince of Brazil, refused an order to return to Portugal and on September 7 declared Brazil independent. Surviving republican and separatist movements, he was able to create a constitutional monarchy. With his father's death in 1826, he inherited the throne of Portugal, which he renounced in favor of his five-year-old daughter to appease those Brazilians who feared a reunion with Portugal. However, through mismanagement and corruption, Pedro alienated the Brazilians, who in 1831 forced his abdication in favor of his five-year-old son, Pedro II. Fortunate in his tutors and regents, Pedro II proved to be a capable leader who retained the affection of the Brazilian people for a period of 49 years.

Although the abdication of Pedro I left Brazil on the verge of anarchy, the regents who governed during Pedro II were able to suppress rebellions. They made many liberal changes in the constitution, and Brazil avoided the series of tyrannical dictatorships experienced by many of the former Spanish colonies.

From his coronation in 1841 until 1850, Pedro II was occupied with establishing his authority to rule. The Brazil of this era consisted of population centers at Rio de Janeiro, Minas Gerais, São Paulo and Pernambuco. The population numbered

some 7 million—between 1 and 2 million whites, 3 to 4 million Negro slaves, a million free Negroes and people of mixed blood and a half million Indians. The immense Amazon River basin was largely unexplored and while the cattle-raising south and the states of São Paulo and Minas Gerais were showing progress, the remainder of Brazil was still little more than a fringe of Atlantic coast settlements.

Although Pedro II's government was patterned after that of Great Britain, it lacked the popular base of the British government; the illiterate mass of Brazilians had no vote, and effective control fell to landowners, merchants and the learned men of the cities. Pedro's government was conducted by his ministers, while he exercised the role of arbitrator. The 1840s were devoted to the suppression of separatist movements and consolidation of the nation; the 1850s and 1860s were spent in resolving Brazil's foreign disputes and in enlarging the national territory. The 1870s and 1880s were marked by much liberal legislation, the growth of republican ideas, the abolition of slavery and the end of the Empire.

From the 1850s to the 1870s, Brazil's economy expanded in a manner similar to that of the United States. Railroads, industry, agriculture and land speculation attracted large amounts of capital and a stream of immigrants who brought technical skills missing from Brazil's own population. By the mid-1870s, Brazil was earning a net profit of some $20 million from its foreign trade. During this period, Pedro II fostered education and Brazilian cultural expression developed. Through

the 1860s his popularity and support were such that he could have governed under any title—king, emperor or president.

Liberal in his religious views, he respected freedom of worship; when in 1865 the pope published a ban against Freemasonry, Pedro refused to permit its adoption in Brazil. Despite his stand, the conflict between church and Masonry grew to the point that he personally became involved, losing support from the church and the clergy without satisfying the Masons. Following the Paraguayan War (1865–70), the Emperor became involved in a dispute between the army and the

Dom Pedro II, Emperor of Brazil

74

Liberal Party; while keeping the army under civilian control, he insisted upon supporting its legitimate needs for maintaining professional competence. These measures satisfied neither group and cost him the support of the elements whose interests he was defending.

The support of landowners was lost when slavery was abolished in 1871; the law also safeguarded the owners' economic interests and provided for the training of the emancipated slaves. Again, neither side was satisfied with Pedro's moderation and he was forced to abdicate in 1889 in the face of an impending military coup.

General Deodoro da Fonseca announced by decree the creation of the Federative Republic of Brazil, composed of 20 states. Pledged to recognize and respect the obligations created under the empire, the new government won popular acclaim. A constitution based on that of the United States was imposed on the country by decree in 1891. Although theoretically founded under democratic principles, the constitution gave less voice to the populace than it had under Pedro II. Fonseca later proved to be an inept leader and was replaced in 1893 by Marshal Floriano Peixoto, an even more capricious figure who provoked the navy into a rebellion which was followed by a short-lived civil war.

A reign of terror, heretofore unknown in Brazil, followed the rebellion. In 1894, Peixoto peacefully turned the government over to a more moderate civilian president, Prudente de Morais Barros, the first of three consecutive presidents from São Paulo.

The government was badly demoralized and had an empty treasury, while the people were widely split during a military-civilian standoff. Further complicating the scene were the *conselheiros*, a group of fanatics in the northeast who held out against the army until the last man was killed. The president spent his last year in office in peace.

The years to 1910 saw the republic develop under a series of three capable presidents, but two decades of turmoil then ensued, testing the strength of the federal republic. Problems centered around political meddling by the military, anarchic regionalism and an ailing economy, all of which were complicated by World War I. The military-civilian division worsened and continued for some 20 years, while loyalty to individual states was greater than national loyalty and was compounded by various militia loyal to local political leaders.

The Vargas Era

Asian rubber production, the decline of coffee prices and the loss of foreign mar-

kets, rubbed salt in already sore wounds. Foreign debts and unwise fiscal policies in Brazil brought it to the verge of bankruptcy. The world-wide depression and political blunders of the government brought on military intervention in 1930 and the installation of the populist governor of Rio Grande do Sul, Getulio Vargas, who ruled as dictator for 15 years. He combined a shrewd sense of politics with managerial ability and personal honesty. Sometimes compared with the Jesuits who defended the Indians against the landlords, Vargas posed as a defender of Brazil against the military and the powerful state governors, while trying to unify the laboring classes and grant the right to vote to the entire population. He was also compared to Italy's Benito Mussolini and Portugal's dictator, Antonio de Oliveira Salazar.

Vargas rehabilitated the economy and forced state cooperation with the new national government. A new pseudo-fascist

Getulio Vargas, 1934

constitution in 1934 enfranchised women and provided social legislation to protect workers. Peace endured for a year, but was followed by communist and fascist attempts to seize power. Profiting from the scare, Vargas suspended the constitution in 1937, extended his term and ruled by decree. He called his regime the *Estado Novo* (New State), after Salazar's.

An amiable but forceful dictator, he selected capable men to administer government services and accomplished much to improve the living standards of the poor. His management of the national economy was sound and Brazil made notable progress in industrialization and production. He also brought Brazil into World War II on the side of the Allies and sent troops to fight in Italy. Despite the generally popular nature of his rule, by the end of the

war, opposition had developed to the point that Vargas could only retain his position by the use of force.

On October 29, 1945, a committee of military officers persuaded Vargas to resign. Vargas already had ordered free elections for December, in which General Eurico Gaspar Dutra won the presidency by a decisive margin. Colorless and inept, he was unable to control the economy. Overspending and corruption and inflation spelled the end of his career.

In the elections of 1950, Vargas entered the competition as a candidate of the Labor Party and announced himself to be the champion of democratic government. The National Democratic Union was unable to stop his demagogic appeal. But his new term in office was not impressive; his appointees were largely incompetent and many were corrupt.

By 1954, general discontent was highly apparent; both the military and civilian elements were in a mood to unseat Vargas— events were triggered by an attack on the editor of a leading Rio newspaper. Faced with the evidence that his own bodyguard was implicated, and under military pressure for his resignation, Vargas instead committed suicide in his office.

Juscelino Kubitschek was elected in 1955, and it was he who initiated work on the new capital city of Brasilia. The government formally moved from Rio de Janeiro to Brasilia in 1960. There were also a flurry of strikes and refusals of the International Monetary Fund and Washington to advance further sums to a seemingly extravagant Brazil.

Campaigning on a platform of austerity and competent government, Jãnio Quadros won the 1960 elections by the largest plurality of any president in Brazilian history. However, he was embarrassed by a last-minute round of wage increases granted by Kubitschek and the election of a controversial leftist, João Goulart, as vice president. Quadros faced staggering problems, including large foreign debts, mounting inflation, widespread opposition to his plan for trade with the communist bloc and moderation toward Cuba. This led to feelings of frustration and his sudden resignation in August 1961.

Goulart was permitted to take office the following month only after agreeing to demands by conservative military officials to a drastic limitation of presidential powers. Brazil thus became a rudderless ship, headed by a president with no authority and a congress bitterly divided among 12 political parties. Faced with a stagnant economy, inflation that had reached an annual rate of 100% by 1964 and deepening social division, Goulart fought for and obtained greater power through a plebiscite in 1963. Relying increasingly on leftist

Brazil

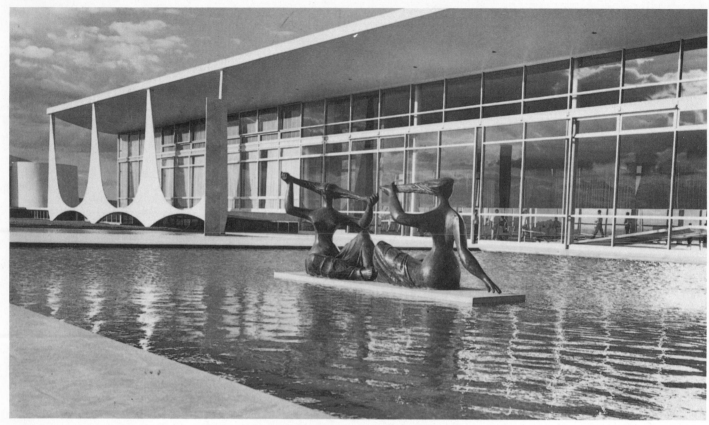

Brasilia's Alvorada Palace, the presidential residence

support, he sought to divide the military and use mass demonstrations to intimidate his opposition.

Military-*ARENA* Rule, 1964–85

Fearing the nation might be plunged into chaos, the armed forces ousted Goulart on April 1, 1964, and replaced him with General Humberto Castelo Branco. This began a series of military governments that altered the political and economic face of Brazil.

Regarding themselves as authentic "revolutionaries," the military imposed a presidential government controlled by the high command of about 12 top officers better known as the *Estado Maior* or general staff. Their basic goal was not a social revolution, but an industrial revolution to enable Brazil to become a major world power. Relying heavily on technicians, the military government was relatively honest and nonpolitical. Indeed, the traditional politicians were suspect, "social" programs had low priority and human rights were respected only when they did not interfere with the "revolution."

The military quickly imposed austere economic measures to control inflation. In addition, all political parties were disbanded and replaced by two new ones: the Alliance for National Renovation (*ARENA*),

and the Brazilian Democratic Movement (*MDB*).

In theory, *ARENA* was to be the dominant, government party, while the *MDB* was to furnish token opposition. In reality, both parties were powerless to challenge the military. The military saw to it that *ARENA* won a large majority in carefully supervised 1966 elections. Following instructions, legislators then chose as the next president Marshal Arthur da Costa e Silva in 1967. In late 1968 he dissolved Congress, instituted press censorship and jailed prominent political opponents, including Kubitschek. In addition he suspended judicial "interference" with prosecution for "crimes against the state."

When Costa e Silva suffered a paralyzing stroke in mid-1969, General Emilio Garrastazu Médici was named president. Prosperity and repression were the two prominent traits of his regime, which believed that the first is possible only because of the latter. Under his tutelage, Brazil developed a prosperous economy, forcing even critics to compare the "Brazilian economic miracle" with the postwar boom in Germany and Japan, albeit at tremendous loss of liberty.

The expanding economy helped finance ambitious government projects in education, health and public works. The Trans-Amazonian highway linked Brazil's At-

lantic coast with the Peruvian border, hacked 3,250 miles through vast empty stretches of the national heartland. The cost of economic boom was high; industrial growth was financed largely through exploitation of workers. During the first 10 years of military rule, the economy grew by 56% while real wages dropped by 55%. The result was a severe decrease in purchasing power for the lower classes.

In the same period, government expenditures for education were reduced by half and investments in health and social services also declined in real terms. While the upper 5% of the population saw its share of the national wealth jump to a total of 36%, the lower half's share dropped to 14%. Although Brazilian business executives were among the world's best paid, the bottom 40% of the people were underfed.

The political situation was even more rigidly controlled—the 1967 constitution, imposed by the military, provided for a strong executive and a powerless congress. Through Institutional Acts Nos. 5, 13 and 14, the regime systematically silenced its critics. Torture of political opponents was condemned by the Human Rights Commission of the Organization of American States. Prior censorship was imposed on the print media and the arts. Yet, some criticism of the regime seeped out.

Brazil

Most outspoken was the Catholic Church. The regime in turn charged that church work with the poor was communist-oriented. Paramilitary secret police frequently raided church offices, seizing property and harassing leaders. The regime conducted a major crackdown in 1973 on church activities that offended it.

A shamelessly rigged presidential election was held in early 1974. The official government candidate—selected by the military high command—was retired Army General Ernesto Geisel, a portly 68-year-old former head of the Brazilian oil monopoly, Petrobras. The only opposition candidate was denied meaningful access to the media during the campaign; he could not speak out against the regime,

but he called the election a "farce." There was no direct vote for president in Brazil; the "electoral college" formalized the selection of the new president by a vote of 400–76.

Although he promised a degree of moderation, Geisel cautioned that social reform must wait until the nation's economic problems were solved. Nevertheless, press censorship was greatly reduced, although not eliminated, and police repression was also less evident. Efforts were made to improve strained relations with the Catholic Church and organized labor; small steps were taken to increase wages for the workers.

After allowing politicians a greater voice in national affairs, despite objections from hardliners within the ruling military

councils, Geisel went ahead with plans to hold congressional elections in late 1974. The results proved to be a disaster for the regime and *ARENA*. The opposition *MDB* received twice the vote of the military-backed slate, winning 16 of 22 Senate seats and a third of the Chamber of Deputies.

Geisel tried to walk a tightrope between the two sides—he decided not to overturn the election results, but at the same time he appeared to have placated the conservative military by permitting a rise in right-wing "vigilante" acts against suspected leftists and petty criminals. Reports of torture of political opponents continued to circulate; most of this activity was conducted by the government's Intelligence Operations Detachment (*DOI*). The president revoked the

STATES AND TERRITORIES

Brazil

political rights of three opposition legislators who charged that Brazil was being run by "an aristocracy wearing uniforms." The regime also brought charges against 21 critical journalists.

Economic decline had a dramatic impact on both Brazil's domestic and foreign policy. The quadrupling of oil prices by the Organization of Petroleum Exporting Countries (OPEC) in 1973–74 had a dramatic impact on Brazil, which then imported nearly 90% of its petroleum. Geisel's pragmatic response was to begin production of ethanol from expanded cultivation of sugar cane, and he decreed Brazilian auto manufacturers to begin producing ethanol-burning engines (see Economy). Brazil thus became a trendsetter in the production of alternative fuels, although the rest of the world did not catch on for another 30 years.

In foreign affairs, Brazil in 1975 became the first Latin American nation (aside from Cuba) to recognize the Soviet- and Cuban-backed revolutionaries in the Angolan civil war. This surprising move by the staunchly anti-communist regime was largely due to economics, as Brazil hoped to buy Angolan oil and wanted to include that country in an international coffee cartel to raise the price of that commodity. It also viewed this Portuguese-speaking African nation as a potential customer for Brazilian products.

Although Brazil always had maintained cordial relations with the United States, there was a strain in 1975. Besides recognizing Angola, Brazil voted in the UN to equate Zionism with racism. (Brazil imported much of its oil from Arab states).

Further questions centered around development of atomic power based on West German technology. Although Brazil said it would not build an atomic bomb, the United States and other countries feared Brazil's entry into the nuclear field would accelerate the race for nuclear weapons then shaping up in the Third World.

In 1977, the new Carter administration reduced military aid until Brazil showed greater respect for human rights and called on Brazil to terminate its nuclear program. Brazil's response was cancellation of the entire 25-year-old military pact with the United States.

Geisel faced a serious conflict with the business community, which openly complained that it was being elbowed aside by huge, state-run industries and fast-growing multi-national corporations. Small farmers (as in the United States) were forced off their land by huge farm combines and other modern agricultural techniques. Political tensions mounted.

After the Congress dismissed Geisel's proposal for judicial changes in 1977, the president dismissed Congress for two weeks. By decree, he ordered changes that made Brazil a one-party state. Under the plan, the president, all state governors and a third of the Senate would be elected indirectly, and in a manner so as to force them to remain under permanent control of *ARENA* and the military. The measure further gave the president another year in office.

Geisel chose his successor, announcing in early 1978 that General João Baptista de Oliveira Figueiredo, head of the national intelligence agency, would become the

next chief executive. Virtually unknown to the public at the time of his nomination, Figueiredo sought to project the image of a Harry Truman-style "man in the street"— a campaign model that sharply contrasted with Brazil's normally stern, colorless military leadership. The obedient electoral-college officially named Figueiredo to a six-year term. In contrast, unusually free congressional elections were held in late 1978. To the chagrin of the military, the opposition *MDB* won a majority of the 45 million popular votes, largely because of big margins in urban areas. Nevertheless, since Brazilian law prohibited any opposition party from winning control of Congress, *ARENA* wound up with 231 of the 420 seats in the lower house and 42 of the 67 Senate seats. All 21 state governors and most city mayors were appointed directly by the military.

Installed in March 1979, Figueiredo pledged to "open this country up to democracy"—a promise that dismayed some army officers who distrusted civilian government. Under a new plan, free, direct elections were to be held for every office except president. Brazil suddenly came alive with political activity. For the first time, government opponents were allowed access to the news media, and the last political prisoner was released. At least six parties fielded candidates. The plan put all Chamber of Deputies seats and one-third of the Senate seats up for grabs.

Maintaining the government-proclaimed policy of gradually returning the country to democratic rule, on November 15, 1982, peaceful elections were held for 479 seats in the Chamber of Deputies, one third of the seats in the Senate, the state governorships and assemblies, and the municipalities. Five parties participated—one pro-government, the *Partido Democratico Social* (PDS), and four opposition groups, the most important of which was the *Partido Movimento Democratico Brasileiro* (PMDB). The *PDS* gained an overall victory, retaining vital control of Congress, but the opposition, mainly the *PMDB* and the *Partido Trabalhista Brasileiro* (PTB)—Brazilian Labor Party—managed to win the governorships of the three most important states: São Paulo, Rio de Janeiro and Minas Gerais.

Public attention then became focused on the presidential elections. The majority of the opposition leaders favored direct presidential elections. The military-backed *PDS* convention in Brasilia nominated Paulo Salim Maluf, a wealthy businessman of Lebanese heritage. At the same time, a coalition of the *PMDB* and dissident *PDS* delegates calling itself the Democratic Alliance met and selected a widely known and revered public figure, Dr. Tancredo Neves.

Cattle-drawn cart

This elderly gentleman had the unique ability to attract the support of not only military elements, but communists and leftists. José Sarney, who had recently resigned as head of the *PDS*, was named his vice presidential candidate.

Figueiredo, beleaguered by both illness and the military, correctly foresaw a Neves victory. He made peace with him in an unwritten agreement. Sensing the tide running against him, Maluf attempted to make party allegiance binding on all delegates of the electoral college. The effort failed.

Return to Democracy

In January 1985, indirect presidential elections were held, and an 686-member electoral college representing most political parties elected Neves by a majority of 480–180 for Maluf.

Neves would have been sworn into office for a five-year term on March 15, officially ending a period of military rule of 21 years. Popular celebrations were cut short by the president-elect's sudden illness. Neves was rushed to the hospital the day before his inauguration; he died on April 21, 1985, plunging the country into mourning.

Vice President Sarney, who had been acting president during Neves' illness, assumed the presidency and proclaimed that he would follow "the ideas and plans of Tancredo Neves." He inherited a coalition of Neves' center-left *PMDB* and the smaller rightist Liberal Front Party (*PFL*), formed by a faction of the *PDS* of which Sarney had been president. Bickering between the two factions erupted almost immediately. Sarney initially ruled somewhat timidly and it appeared that he lacked the leadership necessary to move Brazil forward.

Labor unrest was rampant; a strike by a half million truckers, who in early 1986 blocked highways, threatened the food supply of the cities. This was topped by 1985 strikes by 2 million other workers, many under the leadership of a trade union firebrand destined to play a major role in Brazilian politics for the next two decades: Luiz Inácio da Silva, better known by his sobriquet "Lula."

Sarney did nothing to lessen corruption, that which had grown worse under the military. He spent the nation into virtual bankruptcy but did nothing for the impoverished masses.

Nature was not kind to Brazil, either. A killing frost in the 1970s destroyed millions of coffee trees; as soon as the industry had recovered, a murderous drought killed or stunted the plants, reducing production by 50%. Floods in the northeast and southeast in the 1980s followed by a

Former President and Mrs. Figueiredo

five-year drought in the northeast left more than a million homeless. In late 1994, killing frosts again hit the coffee trees, resulting in a 100% rise in the price of Brazil's favored Arabica coffee. These natural disasters increased migration of unskilled, penniless people to the cities.

Economic Reforms and External Debt

Sarney's only attempt at economic reform was "The Cruzado Program," which froze prices and decreed wage increases of 20% in many sectors. The cruzeiro was abolished and the cruzado took its place, at a ratio of 1,000:1. An ostensible freeze on government hiring commenced at both the federal and state level.

The staggering foreign debt (the largest in the world at $108 billion) was hesitantly rescheduled by the "Paris Club," a group of creditor nations representing commercial and national banks that had lent money to Brazil. The IMF, accustomed to inspections of and "recommendations" to debtor nations, was told it had to keep these activities to a minimum in Brazil.

A watered-down land reform plan permitted the purchase only of sub-marginal land, yet landowners sometimes hired gunmen to drive out peasants who had resettled. "Liberation theology" priests and bishops of the Roman Catholic Church who supported the poor fomented unrest. Pope John Paul II had to remind the National Conference of Brazilian Bishops that the clergy had to stay out of politics, although he, too, supported land reform in Brazil.

High interest rates were established to discourage capital flight. Taxes were raised, including on the purchase of U.S. dollars (25%), on the purchase of cars, and

on compulsory "loans" to the government. These reforms were generally greeted with acceptance by a country that had been sapped economically for so long. But the "maharajas"—persons with low or nonexistent work at government "jobs"—remained a parasite.

The *PMDB* and *PFL* increased their majority in the Chamber of Deputies in 1986 elections to a total of 374 out of 487 seats.

Because of inflation and currency instability, a vigorous black market developed. Brazil sank into actual bankruptcy. Sarney made it official in early 1987: Brazil would suspend payment of principal and interest on its foreign debt indefinitely, which disrupted international credit. The moratorium lasted a year and cost far more than had been gained. Further, the moratorium worsened economic chaos within Brazil to the extent that there was a genuine threat of resumed military control.

Although heavily indebted, Brazil became the 10th-largest industrial nation in

Former President José Sarney

Brazil

Glamorous Rio de Janeiro from the ocean . . .

the world. It developed a lively business in aircraft and armaments worldwide, selling products of good quality and easily repairable. It surpassed Bolivia in tin production and experimented in enriched nuclear fuels, while avowing not to develop weapons. Nevertheless, it insisted on classifying itself as a Third World nation.

Fernando Collor de Mello

After five years of economic chaos under Sarney, capped by an inflation rate of 1,700% in 1989, it was inevitable that the 1989 elections would center on the economy. Although 30 candidates entered the fray, three emerged as the frontrunners. Because candidates of the left-wing *PTB* had been so successful in municipal elections in 1988, its leader, "Lula" da Silva, was initially the front-runner. Leonel Brizola of the also leftist Democratic Worker's Party was second. Both were quickly outpaced by Fernando Collor de Mello, of the hastily organized, right-of-center National Reconstruction Party (*PRN*).

This wealthy, tall, handsome governor of poverty-stricken Alagoas State on the central Atlantic Coast, trained as an econ-

omist, began his career as a reporter and went on to own a number of media organizations. He contrasted sharply with da Silva, a lathe operator with a fifth-grade education. Collor made a bold promise: 7% annual economic growth. If there was anything left over, it would be used to retire foreign debt.

The campaign for the November election was dirty and spirited. When the dust settled, Collor had 28.5% of the vote and da Silva 16%. About 17% cast blank ballots (voting is compulsory over the age of 18 in Brazil). After an equally heated runoff in December, which had a turnout of 88.1%, Collor won 50% to da Silva's 44.2%; the rest were void or blank.

Collor took office on March 15, 1990. If the people thought Collor's campaign promises were stiff medicine, they gasped when decrees started to issue from the presidential palace. All banks were closed for three days and all savings accounts were limited to withdrawals of the equivalent of $1,200. Industries were allowed to withdraw only enough to pay current salaries; this resulted in wholesale layoffs. Although this initially landed about $88 billion, it quickly dwindled to about $16

billion through corruption. The cruzeiro was reconstituted the national currency at a vastly increased value. Much of Brazil reverted to a barter economy because of currency shortages. Yet, 80% of the people stood solidly behind Collor despite personal sacrifices.

The president had vowed to get rid of 360,000 unneeded government workers. He reached the figure of 260,000, but the Supreme Court overturned him. Civil servants had tenure under the constitution and could not be fired. Collor also oversaw the sale of 4,675 government limousines.

Things began to fall apart in 1992, when Collor was caught up in an unprecedented four-part storm.

First, the righteousness he displayed in his campaign inflamed the passions of his supporters to a degree he never anticipated. Second, his loose-cannon younger brother decided to play to the tabloid media in a series of exposés that became a media frenzy. Third, Collor had virtually no support in either house of the Congress, and his Cabinet turned out to have the loyalty of hyenas. Finally, he had used about $2.5 million in campaign contributions for personal purposes.

The attacks by non-Collor-owned media were vicious. The alleged offenses he was charged with had been commonplace and overlooked in Brazil for more than a century. But incited particularly by a national TV network, popular demonstrations against Collor became commonplace.

Congress impeached Collor in 1992, which some felt was like the pot indicting the kettle. He resigned rather than face a televised, months-long trial, but was convicted of "lack of decorum."

The Supreme Court dismissed criminal charges because of "insufficient evidence." Collor benefited from the unwritten Brazilian law that no former political leader is convicted—of anything. In 2006, he was elected to the Senate.

Itamar Franco

Collor's successor, Itamar Franco, was an unintelligent, colorless, temperamental hack who had bubbled to the top of the Brazilian political cauldron. He showed poor judgment in personal matters while in office, permitting himself to be shown on TV holding hands with and kissing a young pornography actress.

During most of Franco's 27-month tenure, Brazil went from disorganized to chaotic. Inflation neared 40% per month, devaluing the currency to the point that it was virtually worthless. About half the people lived outside the wage economy. The authority of the state virtually disappeared. Murder, which had been frequent, became ordinary. The killing of homeless "street children" in Rio and other large cities reached dreadful levels. They were almost all black and were kicked out of their homes as early as age 6 because there was not enough to feed them. Prostitution at age 8 was common. Shantytowns around the cities (*favelas*) were, and still are, controlled largely by drug gangs.

An effort was made in 1994 to assert control by sending the military with armored vehicles into areas close to Rio de Janeiro, which has the third largest slums in Latin America. This was done when it became apparent that innocent people were being frequently killed during police forays in pursuit of drug dealers.

The Congress wallowed eyeball deep in its own scandals; with Collor disposed of, the media turned on it. The judiciary and police also remained openly corrupt.

After wearing out four finance ministers, Franco appointed Fernando Henrique Cardoso in 1994. It was an unlikely choice; Cardoso was a longtime Marxist economist and one of the loudest of the *dependentistas*, who viewed foreign investments as a threat to national identity. His book, *Dependency and Underdevelopment in Latin America*, was the Koran of dependency theorists. When it was published, Cardoso was exiled by the military government.

Once in office as finance minister, equipped with power rather than theories, Cardoso underwent a conversion as dramatic as that of St. Paul on the road to Damascus. He pragmatically replaced the inflation-riddled and devaluation-prone *cruzeiro* with a new currency, the *real*, which was pegged to the U.S. dollar. Cardoso also began welcoming foreign investors and dismantling inefficient and costly state-owned utilities and other enterprises. Under Cardoso's guidance, inflation plummeted from 2,500% annually to double-digits. He became a national hero, an economic David who had slain the Goliath of hyperinflation. In October 1994, Cardoso was the presidential candidate of a coalition of his own Social Democratic Party and Franco's larger *PMDB*. He handily defeated da Silva, the perennial candidate of the left, 54.3% to 27%; turnout was 82.2%.

The Cardoso Era

Cardoso was inaugurated in January 1995 to a reduced four-year term, and he forged a record as an able and effective president. His policies stabilized the *real* and provided real GDP growth that was a steady 3–4% throughout his first term. He also followed through with his privatization program, as billions in foreign investment flowed into the country. At the end of 1997, unemployment was a mere 4.84%. On the negative side, corruption remained ingrained, resisting attempts to combat it from the top.

An important political development in 1996 was the election of Celso Pitta as the first black mayor of São Paulo, although his administration, too, would be marred by corruption.

Riding a crest of popularity, Cardoso persuaded Congress in 1997 to amend the constitution to allow him to seek a second term, arguing that no president could successfully deal with the country's prodigious problems in one four-year term. His popularity was only marginally affected by the impact of the Asian market crisis that October that caused him to impose a tough, painful austerity plan to shore up the *real*. Even so, unemployment shot up sharply in 1998.

. . . seen from Corcovado crowned by Christ the Redeemer, and then to . . .

Brazil

... the city's dark side where poverty and desperation live side by side in the favelas

Former President Franco sought the nomination of the *PMDB* for president in the October 1998 elections, but the party opted to nominate Cardoso. That left da Silva, again, as his only major opponent. The campaign between Cardoso and da Silva took a nasty turn when da Silva accused Cardoso of offering to sell off the state-owned communications firm, *Telebras*, below market value: Cardoso responded by suing da Silva for defamation.

In September, the world financial jitters, stemming from the previous year's Asian market crisis and uncertainty over the Russian ruble and debt payments, came crashing down on Brazil. Rumors spread that Brazil would devalue the *real*, which caused a market panic in São Paulo. On one day, the market dropped 13%, and the panic quickly spread to the markets in Ar-

gentina, Mexico, Venezuela and Colombia; shock waves also were felt in New York, Europe and Asia.

To defend the *real*, the government sold off $30 billion of its reserves of dollars. Interest rates were raised from 29.75% to 49.75%. Cardoso announced an austerity program to reduce the huge budget deficit, a move sure to reassure the IMF and nervous foreign investors, but highly risky for a politician nine days away from an election.

Yet, on October 4, voters gave Cardoso a resounding mandate for another four years. He crushed da Silva, 53% to 32%. He put off details of the austerity program until after the governor's races on October 25, in which mhis friend and ally, Mario Covas, was re-elected in São Paulo, but two leftists were elected in Rio de

Janeiro and Rio Grande do Sul. More ominously, former President Franco, now Cardoso's bitter enemy, was elected governor of Minas Gerais.

The 1999 Economic Crisis

Cardoso was inaugurated for his second term on January 1, 1999; the same day, Franco was inaugurated as governor of Minas Gerais. Cardoso's austerity plan seemed to have quieted the fears of foreign investors and lending institutions. The slide of the *real* had stopped, and it was still pegged to the dollar; sanity had returned to the stock market, and inflation had remained under control.

Suddenly, the willful Franco, known to be consumed with jealousy against Cardoso, tossed a boulder into this tranquil pond and precipitated a financial crisis with global repercussions. On January 6, Franco announced a 90-day moratorium on the payment of his state's $13.5 billion debt, triggering another market panic that far surpassed the one in September. World markets responded negatively, and international condemnation was heaped upon Franco, who actually seemed to relish the attention. It backfired on him, however; the World Bank froze $209 million in development loans for Minas Gerais.

This time, the central government could not keep propping up the *real* by selling dollars so it abandoned the five-year-old *Real* Plan—which Franco and Cardoso had introduced together—and announced that the *real* would float against foreign currencies. At one point, the *real* plummeted 46% in value, before beginning a slow climb. The devaluation raised the specter of renewed inflation. On the other hand, it made Brazilian exports more attractive.

Brazil slid into recession, but by March, international fears that the Brazilian economy would collapse proved unfounded. Cardoso's painful austerity measures dragged down his approval rating in the polls, especially as unemployment remained stubbornly high.

In 1999, the economy shrank by .4%, not as bad as Cardoso had predicted, and grew by 2.6% in 2000. In April 2000, Brazil paid off the last of the $41.5 billion of the international loan package the IMF and other institutions had advanced during the January 1999 market panic. Clearly, the economy was back on track.

There was a historic governmental restructuring in 1999. Cardoso created a new defense ministry, consolidating the three armed services and placing them under a civilian minister for the first time. The three chiefs of the uniformed services simultaneously were removed from the cabinet. The change showed how far the country had emerged from the 1964–85 dictatorship.

Former President Itamar Franco

On April 22, 2000, Brazil observed the 500th anniversary of the landing of Portuguese sailor Pedro Alvares Cabral in Brazil in 1500. But what Cardoso had intended as a major celebration of national identity and unity turned ugly when nearly 200 Indian tribes protested the event as an insult to their own cultural identity. They had a point; there were 6 million indigenous inhabitants when Cabral landed, but there were only 700,000 left. One of their banners asked a logical question: "Who says Brazil was discovered?" The Indians were soon joined by some African Brazilians, who said that to celebrate the Portuguese arrival was to celebrate the legacy of slavery. The protests turned violent as poliuce and Indians clashed. Cardoso cut short his appearance in Porto Seguro, his carefully planned party in ruins.

An even more violent confrontation occurred between authorities and landless peasants who squatted on unused lands and even forcibly occupied government buildings in Brasilia. About 30,000 peasants of the Landless Rural Workers Movement, or *MST*, took part in the protests, which left one peasant dead and 47 injured. Cardoso organized a special police force to deal with illegal squatters, at the same time agreeing to parcel out 5 million more acres in addition to the 40 million that already had been distributed during his administration. The landless issue remains volatile in Brazil.

Voters went to the polls on October 1 and 29, 2000, to elect mayors and councilmen in more than 5,500 municipalities, a closely watched quadrennial bellwether of the public mood midway between presidential elections. For the first time, reelection was permitted. Da Silva's Workers Party (*PT*) increased its share of the popular vote from 10.6% in 1996 to 14.1%

and the number of mayors from 112 to 174. In the 31 cities holding runoffs on October 29, the *PT* won 13 of the 16 that it contested. Marta Suplicy, a former television sex psychologist in the 1980s who later served in Congress, was elected mayor of São Paulo.

For the remainder of Cardoso's term, his political troubles came not from the opposition but from scandals within his coalition.

Congress approved a long-debated revision to the country's archaic 1916 civil code in 2001, legitimizing the civil status of people born out of wedlock, lowering the age of majority for marrying or signing contracts from 21 to 18, and eliminating the preferential legal status of men over women. Previously, a man could annul his marriage if he discovered his bride was not a virgin. Under the new code, neither spouse can go into debt without the consent of the other, and divorced fathers have equal custody rights.

Meanwhile, Brazil's alarming crime problem, and the methods being used to deal with it, remained in the international spotlight. Reports of extrajudicial executions of criminal suspects, especially youths in the country's squalid *favelas*, were commonplace—and still are. In 2001, the London-based human rights group Amnesty International alleged that torture was still a widespread practice by Brazilian security forces nearly two decades after the end of military rule.

Brazilians were reminded of the evil nature of the problem in 2002 when Tim Lopes, an award-winning investigative reporter for the *Globo* network, was murdered while conducting an undercover in-

**Former President
Fernando Henrique Cardoso**

vestigation into sex abuse and drug use in a Rio de Janeiro *favela*. His burned and desecrated corpse was found in a cave. The killing outraged the country. Four people were arrested, including a drug lord.

Lula Finally Prevails

Da Silva declared his fourth candidacy in 2002, and this time the polls consistently showed him in the lead against a field of lesser known candidates. Among those were Health Minister José Serra, of the *PSDB* and Cardoso's acknowledged choice as his successor; Rio de Janeiro State Governor Anthony Garotinho of the Brazilian Socialist Party, a mellowed Marxist and a former agnostic who became an evangelical Presbyterian; former President Franco of the *PMDB*, then governor of Minas Gerais but still a pariah; Ciro Gomes of the moderate-left Popular Socialist Party, a former governor of Ceará and a finance minister under Franco; and Maranhão State Governor Roseana Sarney, daughter of former President José Sarney of the *PFL*, then still part of the governing coalition. Sarney later dropped out because of a financing scandal.

The increasing possibility of a da Silva victory sent a chill through international financial markets, prompting the candidate to engage in some frantic public relations maneuvering. The *PT* pointed to the sound fiscal records of the states and municipalities under its control, and da Silva pledged to continue Cardoso's rational policies and to continue servicing the $274 billion debt; he even began wearing suits and ties at his campaign appearances! Moreover, in a bold shift toward the political center, the *PT* entered into an alliance with the center-right Liberal Party in June, and da Silva named José Alencar, a Liberal senator, as his running mate.

Sensing a chance to win without a runoff, da Silva largely ignored his opponents and decided to play statesman, seeking to dispel his international image as a leftist bogeyman. Pundits labeled the new da Silva "Lula Light." Da Silva's bandwagon then attracted latecomers. The sudden rush of supporters to what appeared to be the winning candidate even spawned a new verb: *Lular*.

On October 6, 82.2% of the 115.1 million registered voters in the world's fourth-largest democracy turned out. The results:

Da Silva	39,443,876	46.44%
Serra	19,700,470	23.20%
Garotinho	15,175,776	17.87%
Gomes	10,167,650	11.97%

The runoff campaign was largely anticlimactic, and Da Silva's bandwagon quickly took on the appearance of an M-1

Brazil

tank. Serra bravely continued, insisting he would do a better job of rescuing the stagnant economy and predicting a return to hyperinflation if da Silva won. Even Cardoso began distancing himself from his own candidate.

The voters gave da Silva the expected present for his 57th birthday on October 27:

Da Silva	52,777,919	61.28%
Serra	33,354,230	38.72%

Turnout was 79.5%. Serra graciously conceded defeat in a telephone call to his rival, as congratulations poured in from Cardoso, George W. Bush and other world leaders. Millions of da Silva's supporters poured into the streets for a Carnaval-like celebration.

On January 1, 2003, the one-time shoeshine boy, metal lathe operator and trade union leader who never went beyond the fifth grade finally realized the goal that had eluded him in three previous elections as he was sworn in as president. He was the first avowed leftist to serve as president since Goulart, overthrown by the military in 1964, and the first one elected directly. Brazilians, and the world, waited anxiously to see whether he would prove to be another statesman like South Africa's Nelson Mandela—or another loose cannon like Venezuela's Hugo Chávez.

Da Silva performed a dexterous balancing act between the fire-breathing leftists in his own party on the one hand and the IMF, the Brazilian business community and the conservative opposition in Congress on the other. He had little choice but to try to govern by consensus; his *PT* had only 91 seats in the 513-member Chamber of Deputies, although it was the largest bloc in the lower house, and 14 in the 81-member Senate.

In one of his first acts of statesmanship, da Silva struck an unlikely deal and made former President Sarney of the *PSDB*, once the target of da Silva's strikes, president of the Senate. Da Silva hammered together a coalition of nine of the 16 parties in the Congress, but the opposition still enjoyed a comfortable majority in both houses. The opposition, fortunately, opted for cooperation over confrontation.

To mollify his core constituency on the left, da Silva led his entire cabinet on a visit to one of Rio's worst *favelas*. He delayed for one year a contract to purchase 12 new jet fighters for the air force. He hosted the assembly of the left-wing World Social Forum in Pôrto Alegre. He created a Council for Economic and Social Development, a town-hall-style body the *PT* had used successfully at the local level to forge a consensus among government, business and labor leaders. And he made elimination of hunger his top priority through the estab-

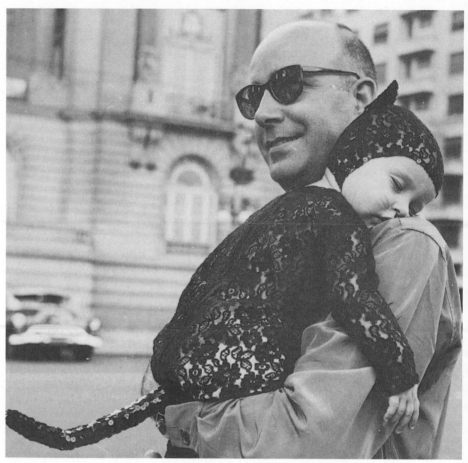

Dancing in the streets . . . then after Carnaval

lishment of *Fome Zero* (Zero Hunger), an ambitious nutrition program that incorporated governmental and nongovernmental social organizations.

Although he toned down his rhetoric against the FTAA, which he once said would amount to U.S. "annexation" of Latin America, he continued to insist on greater "reciprocity" in U.S.-Latin American trade and indicated his intention to try to reinvigorate *Mercosur* as a regional alternative.

Still, Da Silva successfully downplayed his bogeyman image. Three weeks after his election, he had a meeting with IMF representatives regarding a $30 billion loan package, and the IMF people left pleased. His key appointments were far from frightening: As chief of staff he appointed José Dirceu, the *PT* president who engineered the party's move to the center; as finance minister he appointed Antônio Palocci, a physician, who pursued a Reaganesque fiscal policy that exceeded IMF expectation on the budget surplus and stressed higher interest rates to ward off inflation; as foreign minister he named a career diplomat, Celso Amorim; and as head of the Central Bank he named Henrique Meirelles, former director of global

banking for FleetBoston Financial Corporation. He pragmatically undertook critically needed reforms in taxation and the cumbersome public pension system, which caused grumbling on the left but which were straining public finances. In June 2003, he flew to Washington to meet with President Bush, and the two leaders got on so amicably that one would never had suspected their earlier ideological antipathy.

After 100 days in office, da Silva's approval rating was 75%.

Da Silva pushed for two major reforms in 2003. One was a restructuring of the overly generous civil service pension system, which was $19 billion in debt and had become a luxury Brazilians couldn't afford. The president forged a consensus with centrist parties to obtain the necessary three-fifths majority in both houses of Congress. The financial markets responded favorably, but fringe elements within da Silva's own party, and the civil service union that had long supported the *PT*, did not.

The other major reform was an overhaul of the cumbersome and complex tax system that had confusing overlaps between the states and the federal government. The reform did not make much difference in revenue collections, but it greatly simplified the process.

In January 2004, da Silva reshuffled his cabinet and brought the *PMDB* into the governing coalition.

The Landless Movement *(MST)*, which had helped elect da Silva by curtailing its activities during the campaign, charged that da Silva had reneged on his promise to give titles to 60,000 families in his first year in office. Indeed, the government itself admitted it had given titles to only 36,000 families. Peasants invaded more than 200 parcels of land in 2003, and 63 of them were killed in the resulting clashes with the landowners' hired militias; it was the bloodiest year since 1990.

Da Silva pledged to provide land to 115,000 families in 2004 and to 400,000 before the end of his term (Cardoso resettled 526,400 families in eight years). Instead, the promise merely emboldened the peasants, and squatters began invading parcels of unused land, mostly in the impoverished northeast. The government ministry in charge of the land program exacerbated the problem by giving priority to peasants in existing camps on unused land, which served as an incentive for more invasions.

By May 2005, only 117,500 families had received land, and 12,000 landless farmers staged a protest march from Goiania to Brasilia that ended in violent clashes with police. The Pastoral Land Commission reported that the 1,801 violent incidents stemming from land disputes in 2004 was the highest in 20 years. The commission put the number of people killed in land disputes since democracy was restored in 1985 at 1,400. Meanwhile, the centrist parties in da Silva's governing coalition pressured da Silva to show more backbone against the *MST*. Clearly, the president was *entre a cruz e a espada*, as the Brazilians say.

In 2004, the *PT* found itself embroiled in a series of corruption scandals, something the self-righteous party once boasted it was above. The most serious involved Da Silva's chief of staff, José Dirceu, who had appointed the head of Rio de Janeiro's state lottery, Waldomiro Diniz, as deputy secretary of parliamentary affairs. The media aired a video showing Diniz apparently accepting campaign funds from a local numbers racketeer in exchange for political favors when he was head of the lottery. Diniz was fired, and Dirceu offered to resign, but da Silva rejected the offer.

In international affairs, da Silva sought to give Brazil an ever-higher profile. He visited Washington again, and he and Bush again spoke glowingly of their relationship. That was remarkable, given the on-going battle over U.S. tariffs, da Silva's close friendships with Cuba's Castro and Venezuela's Hugo Chávez, and da Silva's outspoken criticism of the U.S. invasion and occupation of Iraq.

In 2004, da Silva visited China, and the two countries announced they would launch their third joint satellite and concluded a $5 billion deal for China to purchase Brazilian iron ore.

Brazil's own fledgling space program, meanwhile, was plagued by technical failures and, in August 2003, a disaster. A 100-

The Cathedral, Brasilia

Brazil

Fishing in the waters of the mighty Amazon River near Manaus

foot VLS-3 rocket exploded on the launch pad at the Alcantara Launch Center on the Atlantic Coast, three days before it was to have been launched. Twenty-one people died.

In 2004, Brazil contributed a force of 1,200 troops to the U.N. peacekeeping mission in Haiti. It was the largest national contingent, and the peacekeeping mission was under Brazilian command.

Brazil's nuclear program sparked an international controversy in 2004 when *The Washington Post* reported Brazil had denied U.N. inspectors access to a new uranium enrichment facility under construction at Resende. Brazil is the world's sixth-largest producer of uranium, but must send it abroad for enrichment. The new centrifuges would permit Brazil to enrich its own uranium for its Angra I and II nuclear power plants, which provide 4.3% of Brazil's electricity. There are plans to make a third plant operational by 2014.

Brazil denied the report and said it would allow inspectors access to part of the facility, but not to the centrifuges on the grounds that it would compromise industrial secrecy. Brazilian Science and Technology Minister Eduardo Campos struck an accord with the IAEA whereby its inspectors would examine the pipes leading to the centrifuges, but would not make a visual inspection of the centrifuges. The IAEA inspection was required before enrichment could begin. The IAEA said its inspection was to ensure that no material has been removed illegally and to ensure that no weapons-grade fuel can

be produced. Brazil insisted that it has no intention of producing weapons-grade fuel.

The influential newspaper *O Estado de São Paulo* then published a story quoting a former U.S. Defense Department source that the IAEA suspected Brazil had obtained a centrifuge on the black market from a notorious Pakistani scientist who has sold nuclear technology to rogue states like Iran, Libya and North Korea. U.S. Secretary of State Colin Powell visited Brasilia and expressed his confidence that Brazil did not intend to build nuclear weapons. Then the U.S. magazine *Science* reported that the enrichment facility would provide Brazil with enough weapons-grade fuel to produce six warheads per year and 63 per year by 2014. An IAEA team revisited the Resende plant, after which the agency gave the green light for Brazil to begin enriching fuel.

Da Silva found himself at the center of another international incident in 2004. *The New York Times*' bureau chief in Rio de Janeiro, Larry Rohter, wrote an article quoting da Silva's 1998 running mate, Leonel Brizola, and others as saying da Silva has a drinking problem that could affect his performance. Da Silva angrily denounced the article as "slander" and, in a fit of pique, revoked Rohter's work visa for "offending the honor of the president." It would be the first time a foreign journalist had been expelled since the military regime was in power. The domestic and international reaction from human rights and journalism organizations was swift. Cardoso labeled da Silva's overreaction as undemocratic. The Supreme Court blocked the revocation, and a chastened da Silva then rescinded it.

Da Silva again raised doubts about his commitment to press freedom after magazines reported leaked documents suggesting that Henrique Meirelles, head of the central bank, had evaded taxes. Da Silva introduced a bill to Congress to create a national press council that would require licenses to practice journalism, would impose a code of conduct and would have the power to discipline journalists who violate the code. The council also would prevent leaks and require reporters to show respect for people they write about and to do nothing "contrary to human values." In short, the council would prevent the press from reporting freely, as guaranteed in the constitution. Media organs called the idea a throwback to the military regime, which had once jailed da Silva. Faced with massive domestic and international condemnation, da Silva withdrew the bill.

The closely watched quadrennial elections for the 5,562 municipalities were a muted victory for da Silva's *PT*. In the first round of voting on October 3, 2004, the *PT*

more than doubled its number of mayoralties from 187 to 389, including six of the 26 state capitals. But it lost the biggest prize of all when São Paulo Mayor Marta Suplicy was trounced for re-election by former presidential candidate José Serra of the *PSDB*. The *PT* won 11 of the cities contested in the runoff, but it lost 12, including the stronghold of Pôrto Alegre, which the *PT* had governed for 16 years.

Ghosts from the military dictatorship returned to haunt Brazil in 2004, when newspapers published gruesome pictures purported to be the body of Vladimir Herzog, a journalist accused of Communist sympathies slain by the military in a 1975 incident that garnered worldwide attention. Without consulting Defense Minister José Viegas, the army issued a statement that seemed to justify Herzog's death. Human rights groups, one of da Silva's core constituencies, reacted angrily. The army retracted its statement and da Silva's government maintained that the pictures were not of Herzog. Viegas resigned in protest. Apparently seeking to maintain amicable relations with the armed forces, da Silva appointed Vice President Alencar as the new defense minister; he remained vice president. Da Silva issued a decree permitting declassification of files from the dictatorship era, when about 400 dissidents were killed. Cardoso had ordered them classified forever.

Da Silva then had to face the long-simmering dispute between Brazilian farmers of the Amazon region and the indigenous tribes there. The government had acceded to many of the Indians' demands by guaranteeing them enclaves from which white settlers would be excluded. In 2004, a band of about 40 farmers torched three Indian villages, one of them in a 6,370-square-mile enclave in the Sun Fox Mountains that was to be presented to five tribes totaling 15,000 people. The presentation was formally made in 2005.

On February 12, 2005, Sister Dorothy Stang, a 73-year-old American nun who had championed the rights of Indians and landless peasants of Para state and had opposed ranching and illegal logging in the Amazon rain forest, was shot to death following a dispute with a rancher. She became an international martyr overnight.

Da Silva ordered an investigation and dispatched 4,000 troops into the area. Three men were initially arrested and charged with killing Stang. Also charged was the rancher who allegedly ordered the murder, who went into hiding, but surrendered six weeks later. A fourth alleged accomplice was arrested later. Two of the suspects were convicted in 2005 after recanting their original confessions. They were accused of accepting $25,000 from ranchers to kill Stang. The actual hitman admitted killing Stang, but said he did so when she reached for her Bible and he mistakenly thought she was reaching for a gun. He contended he shot her in self-defense—six times! Both men denied accepting money. One was sentenced to 28 years, the other to 17. In 2007, a rancher was convicted of ordering Stang's murder and sentenced to 30 years, but in 2008 he was retried and acquitted when a witness said he had given false testimony against the rancher. The same jury upheld one of the hitmen's conviction. In May 2010, a second rancher was convicted of ordering Stang's murder and sentenced to 30 years.

Amnesty International issued a scathing report in 2005 accusing the government of not doing enough to protect Indian rights. In a remarkable ceremony at the presidential palace on April 19, Indian Day, the da Silva government officially apologized to the Indians for all past abuses and injustices.

Da Silva suffered a major political blow in late 2004 when two key parties withdrew from his coalition, including the *PMDB*, the largest party in Congress, and the Popular Socialist Party (*PPS*).

In 2005, Brazil joined Germany, Japan and India in introducing a U.N. resolution that would expand the 15-member Security Council to 25 and make those four countries permanent members along with the United States, Russia, China, Britain and France. But Brazil's regional rivals, Argentina and Mexico, oppose a permanent seat for Brazil, as do Colombia and Costa Rica. Secretary-General Kofi Annan said the issue needed further study, and no further action has been taken.

Da Silva was instrumental in creating the IBSA (India-Brazil-South Africa) Dialogue Forum, designed to promote cooperation among Southern hemisphere nations, and he hosted its first summit in Brasilia in September 2006.

Da Silva could boast a robust 5.2% growth in GDP for 2004, while inflation declined from 12.5% in 2003 to 7.6% in 2004. He remained one of the few South American presidents whose popularity was consistently above 50%.

However, new scandals involving the *PT* erupted in 2005 that threatened da Silva's re-election. The respected newsmagazine *Veja* accused a postal manager of accepting a bribe in exchange for a construction contract. It published images of him accepting the money. The magazine also accused Roberto Jefferson, leader of the *PT*, of involvement.

Jefferson admitted that the *PT* had paid monthly "allowances" totaling $12,000 to unnamed lawmakers in return for their participation in the shaky coalition. Congress launched an investigation. Jefferson admitted he didn't have proof and said da

President Luiz Inácio da Silva

Silva himself was unaware of the payments, but that Dirceu was. Dirceu denied the charges, but he resigned as chief of staff to return to his congressional seat. He was replaced as chief of staff by Dilma Roussef.

Da Silva went on the offensive, addressing the nation on television. In a comment reminiscent of Richard Nixon's "I am not a crook" speech, da Silva angrily insisted that his government "has not swept dirt under the rug," challenged his party's accusers to produce evidence and pledged to fight corruption.

The vote-buying scandal, nicknamed the *"mensasão"* by the media, became the subject of congressional and media scrutiny. Months later, the Chamber of Deputies expelled Dirceu and three other members after concluding they were guilty of taking the monthly payments; four other members resigned, and eight were exonerated. Da Silva's approval rating dropped to its lowest point, but it rose when the multi-party congressional investigative panel concluded in its report that he had not been implicated.

Meanwhile, Finance Minister Palocci, who had won high marks for engineering steady, moderate economic growth without inflation, was accused of having collected illegal campaign contributions for the *PT*, including one from the Cuban government, while he was mayor of Ribeirão Preto in São Paulo State. For months, Palocci denied the accusations, as da Silva stood by him. Gradually, the evidence became more convincing and the denials more hollow. Palocci was brought down by a new allegation, supported by witnesses, that he attended meetings with lobbyists at a house at which the lobbyists provided Palocci and others in power

with prostitutes and paid them off with briefcases filled with cash. Palocci resigned, and da Silva replaced him with Guido Mantega.

Lula's Second Term

With his party and himself under a cloud, da Silva did not declare his intention to seek re-election before the congressional report clearing him of wrongdoing in the *mensasão* scandal. The *PSDB* nominated São Paulo State Governor Geraldo Alckmin, a 53-year-old anesthesiologist, as its candidate over São Paulo Mayor José Serra, who announced he would seek to replace Alckmin as governor instead of taking on Lula again.

Five other candidates entered the race, but it soon narrowed to Lula and Alckmin.

This time, da Silva did not have to defend himself against the charges of being a left-wing boogeyman. He had strengthened his support among the poor with his anti-hunger program and, in 2006, by increasing the minimum wage by 17%, but he had not proven a loose cannon like Venezuela's Chávez. Yet, he was encumbered by the scandals within his own party and lackluster economic growth of 2.4% in 2005, well below the Latin American and world averages, both of which Alckmin exploited. Still, polls showed that da Silva would win re-election outright.

As usual in Brazilian politics, something happened to defy the predictions. Days before the October 1 election, *PT* operatives were caught with $780,000 in cash that was to have been used to purchase damaging information to use against Serra, da Silva's 2002 opponent, who was running for governor of São Paulo. Da Silva chose, unwisely, to ignore the embarrassment. Even more unwisely, he bowed out of the final presidential debate, which many voters regarded as cowardly and arrogant.

They delivered a rebuke by denying him the expected first-round win:

Da Silva	46,662,365	48.61%
Alckmin	39,968,369	41.64%
Helena	6,575,393	6.85%

In the four-week runoff campaign, da Silva rebounded, and he and Alckmin exchanged increasingly acrimonious charges. In the end, da Silva successfully portrayed Alckmin as too pro-business and too zealous to privatize state-owned entities. The results:

Da Silva	58,295,042	60.8%
Alckmin	37,543,178	39.2%

After four years in office, Lula was given a new mandate that was only half a per-

Brazil

centage point less than his 2002 runoff victory, but he received 4.5 million more votes. It was a convincing vote of confidence.

Da Silva's *PT* won 83 of the 513 seats, a loss of eight from 2002, but still the second-largest bloc after the *PMDB*'s 89. The *PT* had fewer dogmatic leftists and more pragmatists than before. The *PSDB* and *PFL* each had 65, and 16 other parties comprised the remainder of the usual patchwork quilt. The Senate was almost evenly divided between supporters and opponents of the government. Once again, da Silva had to hammer out a fragile coalition. Serra easily won the São Paulo governorship.

Da Silva's inauguration on January 1, 2007, was much more low-keyed than the one in 2003, with no foreign heads of state invited. Da Silva promised greater economic growth and continued reform of the cumbersome bureaucracy.

He was faced almost immediately with the renewed crisis of rampant street crime, especially in Rio de Janeiro. With nearly 50 murders annually per 100,000 people, it was officially one of the world's most dangerous cities, and renegade policemen and soldiers had formed vigilante groups that murdered suspected drug dealers, reminiscent of the notorious death squads of the 1950s. The week before the inauguration, drug gangs in Rio launched a bold attack on police stations and set buses on fire in reprisal for vigilante attacks; 19 people were killed. Da Silva dispatched 500 members of an elite anti-crime unit to Rio at the request of the governor.

Da Silva turned to his other great concern, the sluggish economy. In 2006, GDP grew by only 2.8%, again well below the average for Latin America and the world. He unveiled a "growth acceleration package," which reduced interest rates to 13.25%, still higher than neighboring

countries; in booming Chile, it was only 5%. It also called for investing $236 billion in infrastructure projects and housing over four years, a reduction in taxes by $5.4 billion during the same period and continued reduction of the bloated public payroll.

Da Silva welcomed George W. Bush on a state visit to Brazil in March 2007, which was marred by large demonstrations. The two leaders signed an accord encouraging greater worldwide production of ethanol, although da Silva failed to get Bush to agree to repeal the 54-cent-a-gallon tariff on Brazilian ethanol. Da Silva visited Bush at Camp David a month later.

Ironically, even as relations were growing warmer with Bush, they became strained with his erstwhile philosophical ally, Chávez. In April 2007, da Silva attended a Latin American energy summit in Caracas, where Chávez lashed out at his ethanol-promotion plan, saying it would take land away from producing food for the poor. (Chávez, of course, was also concerned that his petroleum exports would be jeopardized.) Da Silva responded that Latin America still has sufficient arable land to produce both food and ethanol. Da Silva made the same argument during a two-day state visit to the Netherlands in 2008, where he denied ethanol production contributes to world hunger and suggested that impoverished tropical countries like Haiti could themselves benefit from ethanol production.

In 2007, da Silva announced he had instructed supporters in Congress not to introduce a constitutional amendment that would allow him to seek a third term, but he said he hoped to designate his successor.

The *mensasão* scandal returned to haunt the president and his party in 2007 when the Supreme Court indicted 40 people, among them Dirceu and Genoino. In addition, the Senate president, Renan Cal-

heiras, became the focus of a sex-and-pay-off scandal when it was reported he had an affair with a journalist, who bore him a child.

As another example of da Silva's effort to cast Brazil—and himself—in the role of an international leader, he hosted the third summit of the 12 South American presidents in Brasilia in May 2008, where a new continental organization was established: the Union of South American Nations (*UNASUR* in Spanish and *UNASUL* in Portuguese). It is an outgrowth of the South American Community established in Cuzco, Peru, in 2004. Modeled after the European Union, *UNASUR* incorporates the *Mercosur* and Andean Pact trade blocs and will have a headquarters in Quito, Ecuador, a parliament in Cochabamba, Bolivia and a Bank of the South located in Caracas, Venezuela. The eventual goal is to have a common South American currency and passport.

Da Silva hosted Russian President Dmitry Medvedev in November 2008, and in December, he hosted a summit in Salvador attended by 33 leaders of the Western Hemisphere; unlike the Summits of the Americas, Cuba was invited while the United States was not. Da Silva was adroitly statesmanlike, holding the middle ground against *yanqui*-haters like Chávez. The leaders discussed the global economic downturn and defense issues, but little of substance was achieved except a photo-op.

Da Silva had an amicable meeting with new U.S. President Barack Obama at the White House in March 2009, where he restated his belief that major developing countries like Brazil, China and India should have a greater voice in world affairs. A month later, Da Silva carried that message to the G-20 Summit in London.

In September 2008, da Silva visited an offshore oil platform in the rich new Tupi field, where he ceremoniously coated his hands with the first crude oil extracted from the field that could make Brazil a major oil exporter (see Economy).

Although da Silva continued to enjoy approval ratings of 75-80%, his scandal-plagued *PT* scored only minor gains in the important municipal elections of October 2008. Marta Suplicy, seeking to regain the São Paulo mayoralty, lost to an ally of Governor José Serra, Gilberto Kassab.

Recent Developments

The financial windfall from the Tupi oil-field permitted Brazil to become a serious contender to host the 2016 Olympic Games in Rio de Janeiro. Da Silva was among a host of world leaders who flew to Oslo, Norway, in October 2009 to lobby for the games. His efforts paid off, and the

A rural church in Curitiba World Bank Photo

Destruction of the Amazon: A global catastrophe

During the late 1990s, it seemed Brazil was finally willing to deal with a problem that had brought it international condemnation for more than a decade: the destruction of the Amazon rain forest, which encompasses 1.6 million square miles and is believed to be home to 30% of the world's plant and animal species. The wholesale destruction of this priceless resource continues at a much reduced but still alarming pace.

In their zeal to foster growth, a succession of Brazilian presidents, both military and civilian, gave agricultural development of the vast, virgin Amazon Basin a high priority. Developers were given *carte blanche* to use slash-and-burn methods to cut away trees to make room for cultivation, despite protests by national and international ecologists that such destruction could have a global impact. The clearing of vast areas of oxygen-producing trees, they argued, would contribute to the worldwide buildup of greenhouse gases and contribute to global warming, as would the carbon dioxide produced by the fires.

Brazilian environmental activist Chico Mendes was murdered in 1988 for his high-profile efforts to save the forest, while president after president ignored the issue in the name of development.

In 1998, the Cardoso government released a report with the bittersweet finding that deforestation had reached its peak in 1994–95 of 11,621 square miles, double the 5,958 square miles cleared in 1993–94, and had begun tapering off. The rate in 1995–96 was down to 7,200 square miles, and 5,200 in 1996–97. Since 1978, the report said, 200,000 square miles, or one eighth of the forest, had been lost.

Congress approved legislation giving the federal environmental agency power to enforce protective laws and providing criminal penalties for violators. Ironically, a devastating fire in Roraima state, exacerbated by an El Niño-related drought, destroyed the forest at a pace even more rapid than man's.

In 2001, another 7,014 square miles was lost through logging or fires. The government banned mahogany logging altogether, and in 2002 it made operational a huge, $1.4 billion radar network, called the System for the Vigilance of the Amazon, or *SIVAM*, designed to maintain surveillance to thwart drug trafficking and illegal logging and mining.

Nonetheless, a report released by a group of environmental experts stated that deforestation accelerated by an alarming 40% in 2002, to 9,840 square miles, the worst year since 1995. The government's own official figures were 8,983 square miles.

The loss slowed dramatically in 2002–03, according to the government, to 2.1%, which still meant a loss of 9,496 square miles.

The government's figures for 2003–04 were grimmer: 10,088 square miles, an accelerated increase of 6.2%, the second-worst loss on record. That meant that an area larger than New Jersey had been lost each year for three years. The government acknowledged in 2004 that burning of the rain forest accounted for three fourths of Brazil's greenhouse gas emissions, while Brazil accounted for 3% of the world's greenhouse gases.

The seven members of the Green Party in the lower house of Congress withdrew from the governing coalition of President da Silva in 2005 to protest his government's failure to stop the destruction. The party complained that while the government has set aside preserves, it also has promoted dams, roads and farming.

In 2005, the loss was about 7,256 square miles, a 31% decrease; in 2006, it was 5,421 square miles, a 49% decrease; and in 2007 it was 3,865 square miles, another 47% decrease.

According to the World Wildlife Fund, more than 17% of the Amazon rain forest has been destroyed. A report released by the International Center for Forestry Research in Indonesia in 2004 blamed much of the increased deforestation on cattle ranching, while a report by the group Friends of the Earth cited construction of a highway through the Amazon, BR-163, which illegal loggers were using to gain access. Still others blamed soybean farming; Blairo Maggi, then governor of Mato Grosso state, where three fourths of the destruction has taken place, is the world's largest soybean producer.

Environmentalists had another martyr in February 2005 when Dorothy Stang, a 73-year-old American nun who agitated against ranching and illegal logging in the rain forest, was murdered in a dispute with a rancher in Para state (see History). Largely in response to Stang's murder, the da Silva government mandated a reserve of 32,000 square miles of rain forest in Para, Mato Grosso and Roraima that would be off-limits to illegal loggers and ranchers; controlled logging would be strictly monitored. An estimated 350 logging companies now operate in the Amazon.

The international environmental organization Greenpeace hailed the move as historic, but also faulted the government for failing to do more. In 2005 it whimsically nominated da Silva, his chief of staff, his finance and agriculture ministers and the governors of Mato Grosso and Para for

its first annual "Golden Chainsaw" award. The "winner" was Governor Maggi.

In a positive and dramatic development in 2005, federal investigators arrested 90 people, about half of them officials of the federal environmental protection ministry, *Ibama*, and the rest businessmen, in a crackdown on bribery by illegal logging companies. The officials were accused of accepting bribes in return for documents certifying that trees had been cut legally. Much of the illegal logging had taken place on Indian enclaves and in national parks. Such corruption is understandable; the value of wood harvested illegally since the early 1990s is estimated at $370 million.

A federal law enacted in 2006 set aside —over 10 years—3% of empty rainforest as "public forest" in which logging will be strictly controlled. The da Silva government has now set aside about 60,000 square miles of conservation area. In late 2006, the government placed 57,915 square miles of the Guyana Shield, dense forest bordering Guyana, Suriname and French Guiana, under protection.

In February 2008, da Silva dispatched troops to Para state after logging companies were physically prevented from inspecting their facilities.

Brazil's hunger for energy now threatens the Amazon, not from burning, but from flooding. The government was faulted in 2006 for failure to consider the environmental impact of four new hydroelectric dams on the upper Amazon along the borders with Peru and Bolivia. The National Institute for Amazon Research said the dams would flood twice the area of 200 square miles the government claims.

Da Silva's environment minister, Marina Silva, resigned in May 2008 in frustration over opposition to conservation from other ministries, which favored development, and over what she said was the president's lack of commitment. She later defected from the president's political party and is currently the Green Party candidate for president (see History—Recent Developments).

Her successor was Carlos Minc, like her an environmental activist, who accepted on the condition that his efforts would be taken seriously. On his watch, the Brazilian government, acting on evidence supplied by Greenpeace, sued three British supermarket chains in 2009 for selling meat allegedly from illegal ranching operations in the Amazon.

According to Brazil's National Institute for Space Research (*INPE*), the deforestation rate accelerated by 11% in 2008, to 4,984 square miles, but for 2009 it was estimated to be "only" 2,705 square miles or less—little cause for cheer.

Brazil

announcement that the International Olympic Committee had chosen Rio, despite fears over its crime rate, set off rejoicing in Brazil. It will mark the first time the Olympics have been held in South America. Brazil has pledged to spend $14.4 billion to build an Olympic village and on new infrastructure to assure access among the various sites.

Da Silva has continued to attract attention on the world stage, not all of it favorable. In November 2009, he hosted a visit by Iranian President Mahmoud Ahmadinejad, who was seeking Brazilian support in the U.N. against sanctions for Iran's uranium enrichment program. Pictures of the two smiling leaders embracing raised eyebrows around the world and sparked criticism at home. U.S. Secretary of State Hillary Clinton was concerned enough over Brazil's unusual new friendship with Iran that she flew to Brasilia in March 2010 to discuss it with Foreign Minister Celso Amorin. At a joint news conference, however, Amorin said Brazil "would not bend" to U.S. pressure to support sanctions against Iran.

Working with Prime Minister Recap Tayyip Erdogan of Turkey—like Brazil a current member of the U.N. Security Council—da Silva flew to Teheran in May for three-cornered talks with Ahmadinejad and brokered a compromise deal by which Iran would ship 1,200 kilograms of its low-grade enriched fuel to Turkey in exchange for 120 kilos of fully enriched fuel for Iran's nuclear reactor. The swap was hailed as proof that Iran was not interested in having enough enriched uranium to produce a nuclear weapon. The Obama administration and much of the world community appeared less than enthusiastic, and when this book went to press the issue was ongoing.

Da Silva remained in Teheran for the latest summit of the Group of 15. In April, he hosted the fourth summit of the IBSA (India-Brazil-South Africa) Dialogue Forum.

Brazil is now focused on the October 3, 2010 presidential election. In 2009, Da Silva anointed his chief of staff, Dilma Rousseff, as his chosen successor. But that August, her campaign, and the *PT*, were dealt a seeming setback when Senator Marina Silva, a longtime *PT* loyalist, defected to join the Green Party over dissatisfaction with da Silva's centrist domestic policy. She is now its presidential candidate.

Serra was regarded as the inevitable opposition candidate, and for almost a year polls showed him as the strong frontrunner, leading Rousseff by as much as 20 percentage points. In early 2010, however, the still-popular Lula began campaigning earnestly with his chosen candidate, while Serra delayed announcing his own candidacy and resigning as governor. He

may have waited too long. In late April, a Vox Populi poll showed Rousseff in the lead for the first time, 38%–35%, and Silva with 8%. If the race remains close, Silva could well throw it into a runoff (see The Future).

Culture: Brazil is culturally unique among the Latin American republics, with its mix of Portuguese and African accents in religion, music, architecture and food. There was little interplay between the invading Portuguese colonizers and the indigenous Indians, and what scattered tribes remain are isolated and unassimilated in the vast interior Amazon rain forest. It was the influx of African slaves that shaped modern Brazil's ethnic and cultural composition.

It can be argued that Brazilian culture today is tripartite. In the far southern temperate zone, characterized by wheat farming, cattle ranching and coffee production, the population is predominantly Caucasian, a cross-current of European immigration. As in Argentina, the cattle culture produced a distinct sub-culture with a meat-based diet. The Brazilian equivalent of the Argentine *asado* is the *churrasco*, a variety of grilled meats and sausages. This region is the home of Brazil's national dish, *feijoada*, a culinary orgy traditionally served on Wednesdays and Saturdays and consisting of various smoked meats and sausages, black beans (*feijão*), rice, greens and orange slices.

In the northeast, on the "hump" of Brazil, the population is predominantly black and the culture has its roots in Africa, a mere 1,000 miles across the Atlantic. Despite the ostensible dominance of the Roman Catholic Church in Brazil, blacks still practice *macumba*, a voodoo-like tribal religion based on black magic. In this equatorial climate, there is little cattle ranching, and the diet is based more on seafood and the universal Brazilian staples, black beans and rice. The Bahian style of cooking is characterized by stewing fish, shellfish or chicken in dende oil, derived from a palm nut, and coconut milk. Perhaps the region's greatest contribution to Brazilian culture, however, is its music. Here is where the samba was born, and like Argentina's tango it began in the slums and won mainstream acceptance and an international following.

The third element of Brazilian culture is in the cosmopolitan and industrial urban centers, chiefly Rio de Janeiro and São Paulo, where the other two cultures converge. Here, Catholicism and *macumba* have intertwined to give the world one of its most distinctive cultural offerings: *Carnaval*, the Brazilian version of *Mardi Gras*, the great explosion of revelry and hedonism before the onset of the somber season of Lent.

Officially, Brazil is the largest Roman Catholic country in the world, and there was speculation that a Brazilian cardinal, Claudio Hummes, would be elected pope when Pope John Paul II died in April 2005. However, census figures show that the number of practicing Catholics has declined from 84 million in 1991 to 74 million in 2000, while the number of evangelical Protestants has soared from 9 million to 15 million in the same period. Recent polls indicate that 125 million Brazilians still consider themselves Catholic, even though they do not attend Mass, but an overwhelming majority of them disagree with the church on contraception and abortion.

Perhaps in response to this, Pope Benedict XVI visited Brazil in May 2007, one of his few foreign trips. He canonized Brazil's first native-born saint, Friar Antonio de Sant'Anna Galvão, a Franciscan monk who lived in the 18th and 19th centuries and is credited with 5,000 miracle cures.

One of Brazil's great social and cultural anomalies is that although racial tolerance has been practiced for generations and intermarriage between whites and blacks is relatively commonplace, the country's social elite and its political power structure remain virtually entirely Caucasian, while blacks still occupy a disproportionate share of the bottommost rung of Brazil's social and economic ladder. Mulattos are caught somewhere in between.

While the Portuguese influence is most keenly felt in Brazil's architecture and literature, the African contribution has been greatest to Brazilian folklore, art and music. Moreover, there was considerable French influence during the immediate post-independence period. During the reign of Emperor Dom Pedro I (1825–31), the French-founded Royal School of Science, Arts and Crafts was incorporated into the Academy of Fine Arts. French influence on Brazilian art was especially strong.

Nineteenth century Brazilian literature also was influenced by French naturalism. The two leading Brazilian representatives of this style were Aluísio de Azevedo, author of the novels *Ó mulato* and *O Cortico* (*The Slum*); and the mulatto novelist, poet, playwright and story writer Joaquim Maria Machado de Assis. In the early 20th century were published two novels that remain classics of Brazilian—and Latin American—literature: *Os sertões*, by Euclides da Cunha, and *Canaã*, by Jose Pereira de Graça Aranha, for whom one of Brazil's modern literature prizes is named.

Arguably the country's most internationally renowned writer of the 20th century was Jorge Amado, (1912–2001), whose novels *Terra do sem fin*, *Dona Flor e seus dois maridos* and *Gabriela, cravo e canela*, have been translated and marketed worldwide. His death in August 2001, four days before his 89th birthday, was a cause for national mourning, and his passing was noted around the world. Other noteworthy contemporary writers include the poet and essayist Carlos Drummond de Andrade and playwright Nelson Rodrigues.

In music, the samba and other styles of African origin bridge the gap between folk and popular. Brazilian classical composers whose works incorporated Brazilian folk styles included Claudio Santoro and the better-known, and internationally renowned, Heitor Villa-Lobos (1887–1959). Villa-Lobos is best remembered for his 14 *Chôros*, composed while working in *avant-garde* Paris from 1925–30. *Chôros* were popular street serenades in Rio de Janeiro in the early 20th century, and they inspired Villa-Lobos' classical compositions much the way the tango inspired those of Astor Piazzolla in neighboring Argentina or jazz influenced those of George Gershwin in the United States.

Brazilian popular music, or *MPB* as it is called in the press, is a major domestic industry. Perhaps the best known abroad were Sergio Mendes, whose group Brasil 66 was especially popular in the United States in the 1960s during the *Bossa Nova* craze, and Antonio Carlos Jobim, (1927–94) who wrote such internationally popular tunes as *Desafinado, Meditacão, Insensatez (End of a Love Affair), Garota de Ipanema (Girl from Ipanema)* and *The One-Note Samba*. Brazilian pop singers whose popularity spread throughout Latin America included Roberto Carlos and the late Elis Regina. Regina's daughter, Maria Rita, splashed onto the international scene in 2005 when she was named best new artist in the Latin Grammy Awards ceremony in Los Angeles.

Internationally known Brazilian artists included Waldemar Cordeiro, sculptor Mario Carvo Jr., and the naturalist painter Candido Portinari. In the field of architecture Brazil boasts the internationally famous Oscar Niemeyer, whose most enduring creation is Brazil's futuristic capital city, Brasilia, constructed in the 1950s during the presidency of Juscelino Kubitschek.

The Brazilian film industry, one of the region's oldest, received an impetus in the 1960s and 1970s through the creative genius of director Glauber Rocha and his *Cinema Novo* movement. Brazilian films, long exported to other Latin American countries and to Portugal, have won increasing critical acclaim elsewhere. Two outstanding examples are the comedy *Dona Flor e seus dois maridos*, adapted from the Jorge Amado novel, and *Pixote*, a dark film about the lives of Brazil's street chil-

dren, which won actress Marilia Pera the New York Film Critics' Award for best actress in 1982.

After that, Brazilian cinematic creativity went into a slump that lasted nearly a decade. After the state-owned firm *Embrafilme* was abolished in 1990, ending government subsidies, only a handful of films was produced each year in the 1990s and only 1% of the films shown in Brazil were domestically produced, compared with 40% during the era of *Cinema Novo*. But in the late 1990s, a new law allowed film companies a tax write-off if they invested up to 3% in new films.

The incentive helped spark a revival. Thirty films were produced in 2000, and Brazil has seen a new generation of directors achieve international acclaim. For example, *O Quatrilho*, a story about Italian immigrants to Brazil directed by Fabio Barreto, and *O Que E Isso Companheiro*, whose English title is *Four Days in September*, the true story of the kidnapping of a U.S. ambassador directed by Barreto's brother, Bruno, were nominated for Oscars in 1996 and 1998. In 1999, *Central do Brasil (Central Station)*, a story of an elderly woman who befriends an orphan boy directed by Walter Salles, was nominated for Best Foreign Film and its star, Fernanda Montenegro, was nominated for Best Actress. *Eu, Tu, Eles (Me, You, Them)*, a true story of polygamy in the Brazilian outback directed by Andrucha Waddington, received widespread acclaim at the 2001 Cannes Film Festival and won prizes at festivals in Cuba and the Czech Republic.

In 2002–03, another Brazilian film that won box office success at home and critical acclaim abroad was *Cidade de Deus (City of God)*, the name of an infamous Rio de Janeiro *favela*, or slum. Adapted from a novel by Paulo Lins and directed by Fernando Meirelles, the film examines the drug gang culture there. It received four Oscar nominations in the United States in 2004. The Brazilian Culture Ministry selected the film "Olga," by Jayme Monjardi, as Brazil's entry for best foreign film in the 2005 Oscars, but it was not nominated. It is the true story of Olga Benario, a German Jew who emigrated to Brazil, married a Communist activist and was deported back to Germany, where she died in a concentration camp in 1942.

A different sort of phenomenon was the 2004 film "Mary, Mother of the Son of God," directed by the charismatic Catholic priest and pop music sensation Marcelo Rossi. It had the same sort of impact as Mel Gibson's "The Passion of the Christ" in the United States, and by March had been seen by 2.5 million Brazilians. Columbia, the distributor, planned to translate it into Spanish.

Brazilian radio and television developed along U.S. lines, though in its early days Brazilian television depended heavily on U.S. imports. That has changed, and Brazil now exports its translated *telenovelas* throughout Latin America. The mammoth *Globo* Network, with 75 million viewers, claims the largest audience of any network in the world.

Educational reform was late in coming to Brazil, and it lags behind some of its neighbors in literacy and newspaper readership per 1,000 people. For decades Brazil's most respected daily has been *O Estado de São Paulo*, owned by the Mesquita family, which resisted the press controls imposed by both Getulio Vargas and the military regimes of 1964–85. Rio's two elite newspapers are *Jornal do Brasil*, founded in 1891, and the circulation leader, *O Globo*, which also owns the like-named television network. Numerous tabloid newspapers boast large circulations throughout the country. There are several high-quality magazines, including *Manchete, Veja* and *Isto É*.

Economy: In 2009, Brazil boasted the world's eighth-largest economy. Occupying half the continent, Brazil has immense natural wealth, including a diverse agricultural sector in which tropical and subtropical products flourish. A significant cattle industry in the south provides meat for domestic consumption and leather for export. The country also has been blessed with mineral wealth, including gold, iron, manganese, chromium, tin and in recent years, petroleum. Brazil also is the world's third-leading producer of bauxite, the raw material from which aluminum is refined.

Manufacturing began early in the 20th century, but domestic industry, protected from imports by high tariffs, failed to match that of neighboring Argentina. Like many Latin American countries, Brazil adopted a quasi-socialist mixed economy, characterized by public sector control of utilities and transportation. Brazil's economic growth has long been hamstrung by one of the world's highest birthrates, which largely accounts for the high percentage of people living below the poverty line.

The military governments that ruled the country from 1964–85 reversed policy in the late 1960s by inviting foreign investors into Brazil, offering attractive tax incentives. The resulting capitalization led to a boom that international economists referred to as the "Brazilian economic miracle." Foreign automobile manufacturers put Brazil on wheels, and Volkswagen and General Motors remain major manufacturers today. An aggressive effort was made to increase nontraditional exports, including automobiles, tractors, military

Brazil

vehicles, weapons, aircraft and shoes. In 1967 the government declared the port of Manaus near the mouth of the Amazon a free-trade zone, which still produces consumer items for export.

The miracle abruptly halted in 1974–75 because of a dual blow: OPEC's quadrupling of petroleum prices, which sparked a worldwide recession that was felt especially keenly in Brazil, which then imported 90% of its oil; and a devastating frost in the south that virtually destroyed Brazil's coffee crop, the leading export item. The military rulers sought a twofold solution. Because coffee trees require seven years to produce marketable beans, farmers were encouraged to replant much of the destroyed coffee acreage with soybeans, an annual crop that provided immediate export earnings. The second was to begin manufacturing automobiles designed to burn pure alcohol, distilled from domestically grown sugar cane. Ethanol production fell to *Petrobras,* the state-owned oil firm. Exploitation of newly discovered offshore oil deposits, coupled with the ethanol program, eventually led to independence from oil imports.

Also in response to energy needs, Brazil joined with Paraguay to build the Itaipu dam, the world's second-largest, in the late 1970s.

As in Argentina, efforts by the military to deal with the recession sparked hyperinflation, which continued into the democratic period. Inflation peaked in 1994, when then-Finance Minister Cardoso implemented the *"Real* Plan," named for the new currency unit. Inflation dropped to double-digit, then single-digit levels by 1997, when the Asian economic crisis forced President Cardoso to adopt a drastic austerity plan that included a 40% increase in interest rates and $18 billion worth of public savings, paid for through a combination of spending cuts and tax increases. Still, unemployment jumped to 7.25%, the highest in 13 years. In order to further shore up the *real* and prevent a flight of foreign capital, Cardoso streamlined the civil service and made social security cuts, which sparked violent protests.

By mid-2000, there were clear signs that Brazil had weathered the crisis. It finished 1999 with a slight GDP growth of about 1%. The growth rate for 2000 was an encouraging 4.5%, but in 2001 in dropped back to 3% and in 2002 it fell even further to 1.5%, barely enough to keep up with the growth in the workforce. The *real* stabilized, though it experienced fluctuations. As another positive indicator, the Central Bank announced in 2000 that it was repaying $10.5 billion of the $41.5 billion emergency loan package the IMF had extended in 1999 to rescue the economy,

bringing to $18.2 billion the amount that had been repaid.

Unemployment remained about 8% from 1999–2002, although urban unemployment still was only half that of Argentina.

Cardoso met with U.S. President George W. Bush at the White House in 2001. Bush proposed a U.S.-Brazilian free-trade pact, but a skeptical Cardoso questioned Bush's sincerity by pointing out protectionist U.S. anti-dumping measures aimed at Brazilian steel and produce. Cardoso repeated his criticism at the Third Summit of the Americas in Quebec. The steel dispute worsened in 2002 when Bush, yielding to demands from domestic steelmakers, imposed a 30% tariff on most steel imports. Brazil protested the U.S. tariff before the World Trade Organization.

The predicted election of the socialist former union leader Lula da Silva as president in 2002 caused jitters in world financial markets. Da Silva met with the IMF to dispel the notion he was a reckless left-wing firebrand. The IMF took da Silva at his word and approved a new $30 billion loan package shortly before the election. He was fre-elected in 2006. He has carefully followed a pragmatic economic policy not unlike that of Cardoso's, which is ironic given that he twice ran against Cardoso and vilified his policies.

Da Silva had little to boast about on the economy at the end of his first term. GDP, which had increased by 1.9% in 2002, declined by –0.2% in 2003, the economy's worst showing in a decade. Moreover, unemployment at year-end stood at 12.2%, while inflation was 9%. Inflation dropped to 3% by 2006.

GDP growth for 2004 rebounded to an impressive 5.2%, which temporarily boosted da Silva's popularity. He also enjoyed a huge budget surplus, much of which was used to create dead-end public service jobs. GDP growth in 2005 slid back to 2.4%, but inflation remained in the single digits and unemployment continued to decline. At the same time, Finance Minister Palocci, widely regarded as the engineer of this rosy economic picture, was forced to resign in March 2005 because of scandal (see History). The stock market plummeted when he resigned.

Brazil attained two significant economic milestones in 2005 and 2006. In December 2005, Brazil announced it was repaying its entire $15.5 billion debt to the IMF in full, which saved on interest payments and freed up revenue for da Silva's promised domestic programs. The early repayment was ironic considering the fears the IMF and foreign banks had of a da Silva presidency.

In April 2006, Brazil announced it had achieved petroleum self-sufficiency,

through a combination of new offshore discoveries and the 30-year-old ethanol substitution program. *Petrobras* produced 15 billion liters of ethanol in 2005, 17 billion in 2007 and an 24.9 billion in 2009. *Petrobras* announced a 50–50 partnership with the Japanese firm Nippon Alcohol Hanbai to produce 1.8 billion liters of ethanol annually for the Japanese market.

The 54-cent-per-gallon U.S. tariff on Brazilian ethanol remains a bone of contention between the two countries. U.S. agribusiness, which receives billions of dollars in subsidies to produce corn-based ethanol, does not want competition from the cheaper, sugar-based Brazilian fuel. Currently, about 3.5 million hectares are devoted to sugar cultivation devoted to ethanol, and experiments are underway to develop cane with higher sucrose yields and that require less water. Brazil has indeed come a long way since the 1970s, when it imported 90% of its petroleum.

GDP growth in 2006 was a still-lackluster 3.7%, and the average for da Silva's first term was 2.6%. Da Silva made economic growth a major priority as he began his second term in 2007. Growth was a healthy 6.1% in 2007, one of the highest in Latin America, and 5.1% in 2008, but it declined –0.2% in 2009 because of the global recession. Despite the recession, unemployment declined from 7.9% in 2008 to 7.4% in 2009. Inflatiion was 4.2% in 2009.

Petrobras announced another exciting offshore discovery in November 2007, a deep field called Tupi that it said could contain 5–8 billion barrels of oil and that would give Brazil the world's eighth-largest oil and gas reserves. Brazil may for the first time become an oil *exporter.* In 2009, *Petrobras* signed a $10 billion contract with China's oil company to provide 200,000 barrels per day from the Tupi field for 10 years. Yet, Brazil turned down Saudi Arabia's invitation to join OPEC. Da Silva was present for the extraction of the first crude oil from the Tupi field. He has since upset private shareholders who control 60% of *Petrobras* by proposing legislation to create a new state-owned company, *Petrosal,* that would be devoted exclusively to the Tupi exploitation; half the revenue would go to the government. Coastal states had benefited greatly from the oil windfall, but in 2009 non-coastal states successfully lobbied Congress for a greater share.

The decision by Bolivian President Evo Morales in May 2006 to nationalize that country's natural gas fields—in which *Petrobras* had invested heavily and from which Brazil imports much of its natural gas—and to increase the tax from 50% to 82% strained relations between the two previously friendly governments and greatly increased the cost of gas for Brazilian consumers. To meet rising energy demands, the government in 2007 announced plans for a third Angra nuclear generating plant.

Work also has begun two new dams on the Madeira River in Rondonia state to be completed by 2012 and for a third dam, Belo Monte, on the Xingu River, which would become the world's third largest. It would produce up to 11.2 billion kilowatt hours during the rainy season.

Internationally, Da Silva has placed greater emphasis on the *Mercosur* trade bloc and sought to forge a merger of *Mercosur* with the Andean Pact and a free-trade agreement with the European Union. Negotiations for the latter collapsed in 2004 but were revived in 2010.

The Future: "Lula" da Silva's stewardship of the world's fourth-largest democracy and the eighth-largest economy has been impressive. He has performed a delicate high-wire act, placating his natural constituency on the left with ambitious social programs while reassuring the right and center by keeping the shaky economy on at least an even keel. In the process, he has made enemies on both sides—something that statesmen sometimes must do. But he has obviously made friends, as opinion polls consistently place his popularity at around 80%, phenomenal for a Latin American president after seven and a half years.

He has done the same on the world stage, where he seems equally comfortable talking with George W. Bush, Fidel Castro, Hugo Chávez, Barack Obama or Mahmoud Ahmadinejad. He is the key force behind the new Union of South American Nations, and he envisions a European Union model for the continent, with one foreign policy, one currency—and Brazilian leadership (see Latin America Today). In the process, he has countered the growing influence of Venezuela's Chávez. He promoted his anti-hunger campaign at international forums, and has lobbied, thus far unsuccessfully, for Brazil, China and India to turn the G-8 into the G-11, and for Brazil, India and Japan to become permanent members of the U.N. Security Council. He has steadfastly defended Brazil's nuclear program in the face of justifiable international concerns, while at the same time brokering a compromise on Iran's nuclear program to avoid international sanctions.

At home, da Silva succeeded in implementing meaningful social and environmental reforms without upsetting the economy. Brazil's ethanol program has been a beacon for the rest of the world to emulate as it deals with staggering energy costs.

The da Silva presidency is historic in Latin America: an elected leftist who has not caused even a stir within the ranks of the armed forces. Of course, much has changed in Brazil since the military overthrew the last leftist president in 1964. But then, da Silva has changed, too, since he led strikes against the military government in the 1980s.

By dragging the *PT* to the political center, he brought it out of the political wilderness to respectability and to victory, much as Tony Blair did with Britain's long-discredited Labour Party. Da Silva's cautious and balanced course has allowed him to succeed where Juan Perón, Fidel Castro, Salvador Allende and Hugo Chávez failed, by bringing about genuine social reform without wreaking economic disaster or political upheaval or both. In doing so, he alienated hard-core elements in his own party. He may be destined to hold a revered place in Brazilian and Latin American history, and other struggling Third World countries may seek to embrace the Lula Alternative.

The question in Brazil now is, who will follow Lula? The October 3, 2010 election pits his anointed candidate, Dilma Rousseff, against São Paulo Governor José Serra, who lost to da Silva in 2002. Serra held a strong lead in the polls for months, but at mid-year Rousseff had pulled slightly ahead. She would become Brazil's first woman president, and Latin America's sixth elected woman president. A third candidate, Marina Silva, a *PT* loyalist who defected to the Green Party in 2009 because da Silva's domestic policy was not leftist enough for her, could throw the outcome into a runoff on October 24. Silva is ideologically closer to Rousseff, and her voters would logically turn to Rousseff against Serra, but in Brazilian politics, anything can happen—and often has.

Grinding corn to be used for Pamonha, a typical dish in Minas Gerais.   Clotilde Soares Guilbeau

Chile

La Moneda (presidential palace) in Santiago

Area: 286,322 square miles; Chile also claims sovereignty over a tract in Antarctica totaling 478,444 square miles.

Population: 16.6 million in 2009 (est.).

Capital City: Santiago (Pop. 5.1 million, estimate).

Climate: Northern coastal lowlands are very hot and dry; the central valley is warm and dry from October through April and mild and damp through September; the southern regions are wet and cold.

Neighboring Countries: Peru (Northwest); Bolivia (Northeast); Argentina (East).

Official Language: Spanish

Other Principal Tongues: German, Quechua and Araucana.

Ethnic Background: The majority are mestizo (mixed European and Indian).

Principal Religion: Roman Catholic Christianity.

Chief Commercial Products: Copper, nitrates, iron, steel, foodstuffs, processed fish, agricultural products.

Currency: Peso.

Gross Domestic Product: U.S. $152.1 billion in 2009 ($9,163 per capita).

Former Colonial Status: Spanish Crown Colony (1541–1818).

Independence Day: September 18, 1810.

Chief of State: Sebastián Piñera Echenique, Ph.D. (born December 1, 1949), president (since March 11, 2010).

National Flag: White, blue and red, with a white star in the blue stripe.

Chile, a name derived from an old Indian word meaning "land's end," sixth in size among the South American countries, is a strip of land 2,600 miles long and averaging 110 miles wide, lying between the Andes and the Pacific Ocean. Nearly one-half of this territory is occupied by the Andes Mountains and a coastal range of peaks. Because of its north-south length, Chile has a wide range of soils and climates; the country's frontier with Peru runs from Arica on the Pacific coast east to the crest of the Andes. The frontier with Bolivia and Argentina follows the crest of the Andes—18,000 feet high in the north, rising to 23,000 feet in the center and dropping to 13,000 feet in the south. The coastal range runs from the north to deep south, dropping abruptly into the sea with few ports. The heartland of Chile is the central valley between the two ranges.

Chile is divided into five natural regions. The northern, extending 600 miles south from the Peruvian border to Copiapo, is one of the driest regions of the world. Here are found rich nitrate deposits and major copper mines for which Chile has been famous. From Copiapo 400 miles south to Illapel, there is a semi-arid region; however, there is sufficient rainfall to permit the raising of crops in the valleys. Chile's iron ore is found in this region. From Illapel 500 miles south to Concepción is the fertile area of the lush, green central valley. With adequate rainfall in the winter (May to August) the valley is intensively cultivated. Here also are the three principal cities and the major portion of the population. From Concepción to Puerto Montt there is a forest region, with large, sparkling lakes and rivers where rainfall is oppressively heavy during the fall and winter. The fifth and last zone stretches south 1,000 miles from Puerto Montt. This is an almost uninhabited wild region of cold mountains, glaciers and small islands. Rainfall is torrential and the climate stormy, wet and chilling.

History: Prior to the arrival of the Spaniards, Chile was the home from time immemorial of the Araucanas, a loosely grouped civilization that was completely isolated from the rest of mankind. Their origins remain a mystery.

In the early 15th century, the Incas pushed across the desert and conquered the tribes of Mapuche Indians in the

Chile

northern half of the fertile valley where present-day Santiago is located. However, they were unable to penetrate south of the river Maule because of Araucana resistance. The Spaniards founded Santiago in 1541. About a century later, the Indians entered into a treaty with the Spanish to retain the land south of Concepción. Despite the treaty, war continued between the Araucanas and their would-be conquerors until late in the 19th century.

During the conquest, the land was divided into great estates among the army officers; soldiers and settlers married Indian women captives, producing a *mestizo* population with qualities of both conquerors and the conquered. The colonial period was one of savage warfare and internal dissension. Particularly sharp were clashes between landowners and the clergy over the practice of holding Indians in slavery. During the 17th century, slavery was replaced by a system of sharecropping which prevailed until the late 20th century.

To the wars and dissensions that marked Chile's history must be added a long list of natural disasters. Earthquakes and tidal waves have repeatedly destroyed its cities. Moreover, from the end of the 16th century until independence in 1817, Chile's coasts were infested with British and French pirates.

For the entire Spanish period, Chile was part of the Viceroyalty of Peru, governed from Lima; trade with areas other than the colony was forbidden, which led to wholesale smuggling. Reports in the early 18th century indicated some 40 French ships engaged in illegal trade with Chile. Not until 1778 was trade permitted between Chile and Spain. Neglected by both Spain and Lima, the landowning aristocracy felt little

loyalty to their own overlords and developed their estates as semi-independent fiefs.

Chile declared its independence from Spain on September 18, 1810, while Spain was occupied by the French under Napoleon. Seven years of bitter war between the Chileans and Spanish forces followed. Final victory was achieved in 1817 when General José de San Martín led an army from Argentina across the Andes to support the Chileans. The Chilean revolutionary hero, General Bernardo O'Higgins, became the first president of the republic, and under his leadership the first constitution was drafted. Almost revolutionary in its liberal democratic ideas, it served as a model for the famous constitution adopted in 1833.

Opposition of the landowners to O'Higgins' efforts to redistribute land to small farmers, to separate church and state and

Punta Arenas, the only city on the Strait of Magellan

Courtesy: Mr. & Mrs. Schuyler Lowe

95

Chile

General Bernardo O'Higgins

to encourage free education resulted in his ouster in 1823. For nearly 100 years, the country was ruled by a small oligarchy of landowners, or *latifundistas* who still own the major share of valuable land. Conservatives, advocating a strong central government, dominated the political scene until 1861. Their autocratic rule enlarged the economy and united the country, but the repression of the Liberal Party laid the basis for years of bitter conflict.

Liberals came to power in 1861 and were successful in modifying some of the more restrictive measures of the conservative regime. However, they made little progress against the landowners or the church. Liberals ruled until 1891, during which time longstanding disputes with Peru and Bolivia led to the War of the Pacific (1879–1884). Although unprepared for war, Chile quickly defeated Bolivia, overran the disputed nitrate fields and occupied Lima from 1881 to 1884.

Dictating the victor's terms, Chile took possession of both Bolivian and Peruvian provinces and the ports of Arica and Antofagasta. Liberal José Balmaceda, elected to the presidency in 1886, decided the time was ripe for major reforms to improve the lot of the poor and to curb the power of the landlords and the church. By 1890, he had created a crisis in urging these programs and in 1891 the Congress voted to depose him and installed a naval officer to head a provisional government. With the support of the army, Balmaceda resisted the action; the result was a civil war resulting in the deaths of some 10,000, with widespread damage. Balmaceda was ultimately forced to seek asylum in the Argentine Embassy, where he committed suicide.

Balmaceda's death also marked the death of the Liberal era and ushered in the phenomenon of congressional rule that predominated over the executive—definitely an anomaly for Latin America. The

conservative oligarchy wielded virtually unchecked control for the next three decades through a political machine known as *La Fronda*. This same period witnessed a proliferation of political parties that supplanted the traditional Liberals and Conservatives: Radical, National, Democratic, Socialist and Communist, among others. Moreover, there was an industrial revolution that led to greater agitation for reform by organized labor movements. World War I saw a boom in the demand for Chilean nitrates, although the wealth that flowed into the country, as usual, failed to trickle down to the lower economic strata. At the end of the war, the same social ferment that led to the Bolshevik Revolution in Russia erupted in Chile in the form of strikes. Revolution seemed imminent.

Alessandri and Ibáñez

In 1920, a so-called Liberal Alliance of Radicals, Democrats, some Liberals and other factions, coalesced behind the nomination of Arturo Alessandri Palma for president. Like Franklin D. Roosevelt and John F. Kennedy, Alessandri was a handsome, wealthy patrician with a charismatic personality who convinced the working classes that he had their interests at heart. His message paralleled that of President Hipólito Irigoyen in neighboring Argentina, whose social reforms had defused a revolution there and caught the fancy of Chileans. Alessandri advocated separation of church and state, women's suffrage and increased taxes on the wealthy, including an income tax, to fund social welfare programs. Alessandri's popular appeal was such that he eked out a narrow plurality despite the *latifundistas'* control of the rural vote. Faced with the prospect of a genuine revolution, such as the one that had just unfolded in Mexico, the oligarchy's representatives in Congress pragmatically realized that Alessandri represented the lesser of two evils and voted to ratify his victory.

It was a largely hollow victory, because although the Liberal Alliance controlled the Chamber of Deputies, the right still controlled the Senate and frustrated virtually all of Alessandri's reform measures save the income tax. Congress' obstinance, however, was to prove its undoing, because one of the measures that was tied up was the army's appropriation, always a mistake in Latin America. In September 1924, a band of officers invaded Congress and demanded that it approve Alessandri's reform package (as well as their back pay). The officers then demanded that the president sign the measures. He complied, but to protest this undemocratic intervention, he resigned and left for self-imposed exile, first to Argentina, then to his parents' native Italy.

A power vacuum resulted, into which stepped in January 1925 a young colonel who would have a direct or indirect influence on Chilean government for more than 30 years: Carlos Ibáñez del Campo. Ironically, it was this military man who would implement much of the remainder of the reforms Alessandri had called for in 1920, and he somehow did so without alarming the oligarchy. Moreover, he promulgated the 1925 constitution, largely inspired by Alessandri, which returned power to the executive and served as the cornerstone for a reborn but shaky democracy that would last until 1973. Hardly a democrat himself, however, Ibáñez ruled from behind the throne for two years until he was "elected" in a highly suspect election in 1927. Although he enjoyed widespread public approval for a time, not even this military strongman could control events in New York. With the Stock Market Crash of 1929, the world price of copper plummeted, dragging Chile into the Great Depression. Ibáñez was overthrown in 1931, and there was a bewildering succession of revolving-door governments, including a socialist one, for the next 15 months. During this period of chaos, Alessandri returned from Italy and his leadership-starved countrymen returned him to the presidency for a six-year term in October 1932.

The Alessandri of the 1930s, however, was a changed man from the fiery reformer of the 1920s. His exile in Benito Mussolini's Italy had taught him the value of order and stability. He skillfully placated the discrete elements of the power structure—the military, the church, the wealthy landowners and industrialists, the middle class—when necessary; he resorted to a heavy hand to keep the social ferment from exploding. Yet, he gave women the right to vote in 1935. He once dissolved Congress, and he threw strike leaders in jail, causing the Socialists and Communists to break away and form a European-style Popular Front then in vogue.

The Popular Front's presidential candidate in 1938, Pedro Aguirre Cerda, an intellectual, won by a narrow plurality. His government was responsible for the creation of Latin America's most comprehensive social welfare program, made possible largely by the jump in copper and nitrate prices caused by the outbreak of World War II, and it became something of a model for the left-wing reformers in Latin America and Europe. It also proved a training ground for a generation of left-wing politicians at home; Aguirre Cerda's minister of health, for example, was a young physician named Salvador Allende. The war also caused a breakup of the Popular Front because of the nonaggression pact between Hitler and Stalin.

President Aguirre died in 1941 and a Radical, Juan Antonio Ríos, defeated Ibáñez, the candidate of the right, in the ensuing election. Ríos, who was considerably to the right of his predecessor, oversaw a booming wartime economy and, largely because of German influence, maintained a neutral course until just before the end of the war, when Chile declared war on the all-but-defeated Axis.

Ríos, too, died in office, and in the election to choose a successor in 1946 the vote was fragmented among several candidates. Congress then selected another Radical, Gabriel González Videla, who formed a coalition government that included Socialists and Communists. Not only did the United States exert pressure on González Videla because of the Communist influence, but the Communists began engaging in intrigues aimed at seizing absolute power. In 1948, González Videla purged the Communists not only from his cabinet but from Congress, including the world-renowned poet and future Nobel Laureate, Pablo Neruda.

Chile swung even farther to the right in the election of 1952 when Ibáñez, then 75, finally succeeded in finishing in first place in another fragmented election. Labeling himself above politics, this quasi-fascist managed to draw votes from poor laborers and farm workers. Congress, following its tradition to ratify the top vote-getter, returned him to power. Despite fears that he would seek to become another Juan Perón, whom he admired, Ibáñez presided over a largely do-nothing government for six years. When he failed to take strong action to deal with spiraling inflation, the populace became bitterly disillusioned with this once-dynamic leader.

In 1958, the Socialists and Communists, in their most determined effort, united behind the candidacy of Salvador Allende, a committed Marxist. The Liberals and Conservatives rallied behind a moderate, Jorge Alessandri, son of Arturo, while a new force, the Christian Democrats, nominated Eduardo Frei Montalva. Alessandri finished just 1% ahead of Allende, giving the establishment a scare. Alessandri proved quite conservative, and although he helped stabilize the economy, he failed to address the perennial social ills that were providing grist for the far left.

By 1964, it seemed the impatience of the lower classes for some remedies to their plight could well give Allende a plurality of the popular vote and, if Congress followed tradition, the presidency. Fearing that eventuality, the rightists gradually abandoned their own candidate and rallied behind the Christian Democrats' Frei, who represented a middle course of reform without revolution. Frei easily defeated Allende with 55% of the vote, the

first time in decades that a candidate had won with an absolute majority. Frei made good on many of his promises, initiating land reform and making the first steps toward nationalization of the foreign-owned copper mines. But he found himself in a damned-if-you-do-damned-if-you-don't dilemma. The right vilified him for going too far, the left for not going far enough.

Allende and Pinochet

In 1970, Allende was again a candidate, this time of a Socialist-Communist-Radical coalition called Popular Unity. But this time the right split with the Christian Democrats and nominated former President Alessandri, by then quite elderly, while the Christian Democrats nominated a left-of-center candidate, Rodomiro Tomic, who tried unsuccessfully to steal Allende's thunder. Polls showed the race a tossup between Allende and Alessandri, and the world watched with expectation to see if Allende would usher in the world's first democratically elected Marxist government. Ironically, only 29% of the electorate turned out for what would become the most fateful election in Chile's history. Allende won by an eyelash, 36.4% to Alessandri's 35.2%. Under the 1925 constitution, the choice fell again to Congress.

Despite a clumsy attempt by the CIA to bribe Christian Democratic congressmen to vote for Alessandri, Congress confirmed Allende, and Frei placed the presidential sash over the shoulders of his Marxist successor on November 3, 1970.

The victory of Popular Unity seemed to have caught even Allende and his dogmatic supporters by surprise. Despite their shaky mandate, they set off to turn Chile into a Marxist state, gradually alienating the centrist Christian Democrats who initially provided them with the congressional votes they needed to pass legislation. The government implemented a hastily devised economic program that nationalized the U.S.-owned copper mines and telephone system. Virtually no compensation was offered, which resulted in economic sanctions by the Nixon Administration. The Soviet Union and China, for a time, willingly came to Chile's economic rescue. In other action, the government increased wages and froze prices, which temporarily created the illusion of prosperity; Chileans went on a spending spree, and in 1971 municipal elections voters expressed their gratitude by giving Popular Unity 49% of the vote.

The Soviet Union started to worry about being burdened with supporting a second Latin American nation. Fidel Castro warned Allende in 1973 during a state

View of downtown Santiago

Chile

Salvador Allende

General Augusto Pinochet Ugarte

visit that Chile's economic plans were the opposite of Marxism, in which consumption is held to a minimum. Allende replied that he was working in a system where he had to win re-election until a "dictatorship of the proletariat" could be established, and rejected Castro's advice.

Although general disintegration of the economy was well underway by the time of 1973 congressional elections, thirst for continued consumerism resulted in an increased share of the vote for Allende's coalition to 44%. Voter enthusiasm could not save the economy, which was experiencing a "domino" style collapse in which one sector brought down others. First to fall were the retail stores. With prices fixed and wages raised, stores could not afford to restock sold items; when everything on the shelves was gone, the stores closed, idling thousands.

The result in agriculture was the same. Instead of orderly land redistribution, Allende simply broke up plantations of wealthy persons regardless of productivity. Owners refused to plant crops which would be harvested by others. Political cronies were appointed to administer the nationalized farms. As production dropped 20%, it became necessary for Chile to increase food imports.

Spurred on by widespread public support for his expropriation of the copper mines, Allende ordered the nationalization of other key industries—including those owned by Chileans. Taking their cues from the government, workers (and outside agitators) began seizing farms and factories throughout the country. To the great dismay of Allende's economic planners, workers did not hesitate to strike against newly expropriated state industries. These work stoppages—combined with inept management of nationalized

firms, led to a catastrophic decline in economic output.

Allende isolated Chile in foreign affairs and trade. The availability of loans from non-communist nations and institutions predictably disappeared. The Soviets and Chinese heaped praise on Chile, but offered little monetary support. The United States even declined Chilean offers to buy food for cash.

The people found themselves standing for hours in lines to buy what few consumer goods were left. As the government continued to "finance" itself by printing more money, inflation ran wild. Food was scarce; spare parts for machinery were nonexistent; only the black market flourished. Strikes and street fights between rival political factions became common. Political bickering in the Congress froze all constructive activity.

As things crumbled, the opposition became more unified. The right-wing National Party and the fascist Fatherland and Freedom Party began to sabotage operations of the government. The culmination of resistance came when a two-month strike by the nation's truck owners opposing nationalization—a strike a U.S. congressional inquiry later determined to have been partly financed by the CIA—virtually cleared the roads at the same time protesting housewives were filling the streets banging pots and pans.

With civil war imminent, the military staged its long-expected coup on September 11, 1973. Quickly seizing control, they announced that Allende had killed himself with a machine gun given to him as a gift by Castro.

During his brief but stormy term as president, Allende left a lasting mark on the nation. He sought to increase the living standards of the poor, to distribute farms to those who worked the land and to provide a full spectrum of social and economic benefits. He might possibly have succeeded if a unified, workable plan had first been developed and if at the same time he had been given enough time and had control of his followers.

Although Allende was unable to control his supporters, civil liberties were largely respected. A small number of political opponents was sent into exile, but none was killed. The vigorous opposition press (two-thirds of the total) remained free, but endured government harassment. Opposition parties thrived while critics of the government spoke out without fear of reprisal. Congress and the courts continued to function normally. Yet his administration was a disaster. When the Congress and courts opposed his policies, Allende felt free to ignore them.

Allende never received a majority of votes in any election, thus he lacked the

necessary public support for changes that were so radical. He came to power because of a divided opposition rather than because of his own popularity.

Once it decided to move against the Allende government, the *junta* left no holds barred. Leftists and suspected opponents of the *junta* were promptly exterminated or rounded up in huge detention centers. Catholic Church officials in Chile estimated that one out of every 100 Chileans was arrested at least once during the 16½ years the military held power. Many, according to the government, were "shot while trying to escape." Others simply disappeared while under detention. Other opponents of the regime were exiled. By 1980, the government allowed many to return.

General Carlos Prats, Pinochet's predecessor as army commander, who had opposed the coup, went into self-imposed exile in Argentina. A year later, he and his wife were killed in a car bombing that two decades later was linked to Pinochet's infamous National Intelligence Directorate, or *DINA*. Another prominent exile, Orlando Letelier, who had served as Allende's defense and foreign ministers, was killed in an almost identical car bombing in Washington, D.C. in 1976. That assassination, also linked to *DINA*, strained relations with the United States because it occurred in Washington and because Letelier's American secretary also was killed in the bombing. Four men, including one American, ultimately were convicted of Letelier's death.

A major victim of military repression was Chile's long-standing tradition as a pioneering Latin American democracy. Upon seizing power the *junta* immediately closed Congress and pointedly used its chambers to store records of political prisoners. The constitution was suspended and the courts neutralized. Freedom of the press disappeared and suspected books and publications were destroyed. Schools, factories and the nation itself were placed under rigid control to discourage dissent and—most importantly—to "root out Marxism."

Political parties (except selected rightwing groups) were placed "in suspension." The Christian Democratic Party newspaper was closed and its leader, former President Frei, was forced to muzzle his biting criticism. Not surprisingly, Marxists suffered most. Socialist and Communist leaders were arrested, killed, exiled or forced into hiding.

The only group that continually dared to speak out against the generals was the Catholic clergy. The *junta* responded by banning some religious festivals and arresting priests and nuns suspected of leftist sympathies. When the Catholic Church published a book by former President Frei in 1976 calling for a return to democracy, the government quickly outlawed public discussion of it. In his sermons, Raúl Cardinal Silva Henríquez condemned the regime's austerity program, which he said was pushing the nation's poor to the edge of starvation.

A major goal of the military rulers had been to pull Chile out of an economic tailspin caused by the Allende administration. Skilled managers were sent to farms and factories while property seized by the previous government was returned. Taxes and interest rates were increased and the amount of currency in circulation was reduced by cuts in government spending of 15% to 20%. Strikes were strongly "discouraged," while the nation's high unemployment rate in the months following the coup forced wage levels downward.

To increase farm output and industrial production, prices of consumer goods—including food—were allowed to rise to their natural levels. Soaring food costs, however, threatened fully a third of the nation with hunger. To prevent starvation, the government provided the most destitute with limited food handouts and low-paying public works jobs.

Although the *junta* consisted of four military men, real power was in the hands of General Augusto Pinochet Ugarte. Pinochet initially said democracy could not be restored during his lifetime or the lifetime of his successor. Military rule, he had insisted, could not be lifted until "the ills of democracy" had been erased. On freedom of expression, Pinochet was once quoted as saying, "We're not against ideas; we're just against people spreading them."

Still, his economic program was a tremendous success. Pinochet surrounded himself with a clique of civilian economic technocrats, many of whom had studied under free-market guru Milton Friedman at the University of Chicago, and who quickly won the monicker, "los Chicago Boys" (see Economy).

Chileans surged to the polls in 1978 to give a simple "sí" or "no" vote in a plebiscite testing support for the military rulers. The *junta* received a lopsided 75% approval.

Even as Pinochet savored his electoral triumph, however, he was confronted with a serious threat from abroad. Neighboring Argentina suddenly revived an old territorial claim over three rocky, uninhabited islands at the mouth of the Beagle Channel in faraway Tierra del Fuego. At Argentina's suggestion, the two countries submitted their competing claims to the islands—Lennox, Picton and Nueva—to the British Crown for arbitration. The British ruled that Chile had legitimate sovereignty over all three islands, whereupon the Argentine military government of General Jorge Rafael Videla renounced the decision it itself had sought and threatened to seize the islands by force. By December 1978, both countries were on a war footing, and hostilities appeared imminent. Literally at the 11th hour, the two military strongmen, who were bound philosophically by their hatred of communism and democratic institutions, agreed to a second arbitration, this time by the Vatican. The Italian cardinal assigned to review the matter also concluded that Chile had the stronger claim. Despite occasional saber-rattling, Argentina eventually dropped the matter. But Pinochet had the last laugh. When Argentina foolishly invaded the Falkland Islands in 1982, precipitating war with Britain, Pinochet secretly allowed the Royal Navy to use Chilean territorial waters and islands, even as Chile was echoing the denunciation of other Latin American countries of the perceived British aggression against their sister republic.

Despite widespread national and international criticism of its harsh political and rigid economic policies, the *junta* could point to some dramatic successes: the inflation rate dropped from 600% per year in 1973 to just under 10% in 1981—one of the lowest in Latin America. In addition, foreign investment rose rapidly.

Repression had also been reduced. The regime became increasingly tolerant of public criticism, and arrests of political opponents declined. At the same time, a limited number of Chileans sent into exile following the coup were allowed to return home.

Another "*sí*" or "*no*" plebiscite was put before the voters in September 1980. By a 2–1 margin, they approved Pinochet's desire to remain in power for another eight years. His term was technically scheduled to end in 1990 after an election to choose his successor. But the strongman still enjoyed an added insurance policy: the *junta* had the power to reappoint him for *another* eight years—which in theory could stretch his term until 1997, the year that constitutional safeguards were slated to become effective. His intentions were made known in 1986 when he scheduled another plebiscite to be held in October 1988. A yes vote would have returned him to power for another eight years.

Human rights violations by Chile's military rulers touched off widespread international protests and complicated relations with the United States. After Chilean secret police were linked to the 1976 assassination of Letelier, the Carter administration cut off most military aid to the Pinochet regime in 1979. When a member of the military involved in the murder identified the masterminds of the plot in 1986, the United States demanded their extradition; Pinochet ignored the demand.

By then the Reagan administration, favorably impressed with the *junta*'s anticommunist leanings, had sought to improve ties between the two countries. In 1981, some trade barriers were removed and the United States invited Chile to participate in joint naval exercises. The U.S.

Entrance of La Moneda, the presidential palace

Chile

Senate voted in 1981 to resume military aid to Chile—on the condition that Santiago comply with "internationally recognized standards of human rights."

Chile suffered a severe recession in 1981–83, resulting in a reduction of about 13% in GDP and forcing the government to intervene in private enterprise to prevent an increasing number of bankruptcies. By May 1983, it was estimated that 21% of the urban force was unemployed. The following month, a strike of truck drivers and copper miners—the first important labor challenge to the military government since 1973—appeared to be the beginning of a deep social crisis. The government's swift reaction, combining repression with conciliation, defused the danger.

When the *Alianza Democrática* (Democratic Alliance), a group of five opposition parties formed in 1983, tried in 1984 to expand tenuous dialogue with the government and to pressure Pinochet for more political concessions, the government answered by declaring a stage of siege (the first in its 11 years in power), imposing a curfew and tightening its control over the media. By 1985, the regime softened its stand and was willing to listen to the group's more moderate members. Another attempt at reconciliation was attempted, this time spearheaded by "liberation theology" Catholic priests and bishops.

In September 1986, Pinochet narrowly escaped death in an ambush by left-wing terrorists on his motorcade that left five of his bodyguards dead. The radical Manuel Rodríguez Patriotic Front (*FPMR*) claimed responsibility; predictably, Pinochet responded with a new 90-day state of siege and announced he would "expel or lock up all those people talking about human rights and all those things."

Pinochet announced the legalization of political parties in March 1987 (except Marxists). But there was a catch: no party could be affiliated with one that had existed before. A visit by Pope John Paul II in 1987 was marred by clashes between dissidents and forces of the regime.

Return to Democracy

As the October 7, 1988 plebiscite drew near, Pinochet underwent a marked change. Instead of his former elitist, aloof style, he promoted the image of a kindly old grandfather-figure. He counted on the division of the opposition (17 parties) and confidently predicted he would win. The *junta* voted him in for another eight-year term as provided for in the 1980 constitution. This met with widespread disfavor. The numerous political parties were highly united into The Command for No by a single ambition: to oust Pinochet.

The voting was relatively close because of a single reason: economic prosperity. By 1988, inflation had descended to 8% and Chile enjoyed a trade surplus of more than $1.5 billion. The outcome was 54% to 43% against Pinochet. The country held its breath, wondering what the elderly leader would do. Somewhat hesitantly, he announced that as provided for by law, elections would be held in December 1989.

Patricio Aylwin, a centrist Christian Democrat who had been a senator when the 1973 coup occurred, was the presidential candidate of a coalition of 17 center-left parties called the *Concertación*. The Communists were not part of the coalition but gave tacit support to Aylwin. In a three-way contest, Aylwin received 55% against Pinochet's hand-picked candidate, who received only 29%, and a tycoon who polled 15% as an independent. Election night saw an outpouring of jubilation as *Concertación* supporters filled the streets to celebrate the end of 17 years of authoritarian rule. On March 11, 1990, Pinochet placed the presidential sash on the shoulders of his civilian successor, marking a major milestone in the life of the country.

Not surprisingly, friction soon developed between the two over the issue of civilian control. Aylwin asked Pinochet to resign as army commander, but the general refused, saying his presence provided stability for the transition to democracy. There was little Aylwin could do, as the 1980 constitution permitted Pinochet to remain in command until the end of 1997, and the *Concertación* lacked the votes in Congress to amend the constitution.

Fish market in Puerto Montt

In fact, the constitution also allowed Pinochet to name nine permanent "institutional" senators to the 47-member upper house of Congress when he left office, which gave the conservative opposition a narrow majority and effective veto power over legislation passed by the *Concertación*-controlled Chamber of Deputies. The opposition also enjoyed a disproportionate number of elected seats in both houses because of the peculiar double-member districts, in which the top two vote-getters are both elected. It created gridlock. Among other things, the opposition-controlled Senate repeatedly blocked executive branch efforts to abolish the national holiday for September 11, the anniversary of the coup. The holiday was finally abolished in 1999.

Aylwin was pressured to try all major military figures responsible for disappearances. In the style of a skilled politician, he appointed a commission to investigate and study the matter. The commission found that 3,197 people had been killed outright or disappeared at the hands of the military following the coup, but in the midst of prosperity, most Chileans seemed to prefer to let the past rest in peace.

The Supreme Court, in an unusual and imaginative decision, heard a case involving the validity of the amnesty laws that protected the military. It was argued that because Chile was in fact at war, criminal charges could not be sustained. The court agreed, but held that even so, the terms of the Geneva Convention forbidding the murder of prisoners was applicable.

Chile prospered under Aylwin, and its economy expanded at a rate approaching an average of 10% per year. It still had a thorny problem with the perpetually poor, but the government attempted to tackle that problem, too. Prosperity and growth were the products of free trade (few, if any tariffs); foreign investment, the latter flowing in at a rate of more than U.S. $1 billion a year; and booming exports of Chilean agricultural products.

Another Frei Presidency

In December 1993, voters affirmed their satisfaction with the status quo by electing Eduardo Frei Ruiz-Tagle, son of the president who preceded Allende, to the presidency by a resounding 59 percent of the vote against five opponents. Arturo Alessandri, grandson and namesake of the president of the 1920s and 1930s and nephew of the late President Jorge Alessandri, was second with 29 percent. The once-mighty Communist Party received only about 3 percent.

Almost simultaneously, Congress extended the presidential term from four to six years, as it was before the military

The author with General Augusto Pinochet following an interview at his office in 1991, the year after Pinochet relinquished power. He remained commander in chief of the army.

Photo by Melissa Buckman

coup. Like Aylwin, Frei was a Christian Democrat who was the candidate of the *Concertación*.

The *Concertación* retained its majority in the lower house, but the eight remaining "institutional senators" named by Pinochet (one had died) allowed the conservative opposition to keep control of the upper chamber and serve as a brake on the majority.

Following the counsel of a group of influential advisers, Frei wisely kept the successful economic policies in effect, and Chile's economic growth continued to be the envy of Latin America. The combination of stable civilian government and free-market economics made Chile a favorite target of foreign investors, who increasingly sought new opportunities in the region as they once did in the Pacific Rim countries of Asia. Frei also emerged as a leader of regional importance, hosting the Second Summit of the Americas in 1998.

Like Aylwin, Frei experienced friction with Pinochet, who successfully resisted efforts to curtail the extraordinary authority granted to him in his personalized 1980 constitution. Pinochet finally retired as army commander, at age 82, in March 1998 in a fanfare-filled ceremony in which he tearfully bade farewell to the troops he had commanded for nearly 25 years and

to the institution to which he had belonged for more than 60.

But Pinochet's long-awaited retirement did not mean he was withdrawing from public life—or from controversy. The day after his retirement ceremony, and still adhering to a right given to him in the constitution as a former head of state, he assumed a lifetime seat in the Senate, joining the other non-elected "institutional senators" who gave the conservative opposition a majority. Pinochet's transfer to the Senate angered left-wing lawmakers, and there were demonstrations to protest such an antidemocratic measure. Efforts to block Pinochet by judicial means failed, as did an impeachment motion in the Chamber of Deputies, which was rejected in an unusual secret ballot 62–52. Once again, the aging general demonstrated he was still a force to contend with.

Congressional elections in December 1997 failed to alter the balance of power, but voters sent some confusing signals. The lineup in the Chamber of Deputies remained 70–50 in favor of the *Concertación*, but it lost one Senate seat, giving it 20 of the elected seats to 18 for the conservatives. With the "institutional" senators, including Pinochet, the opposition held a majority. There were two major surprises: the ultra-rightwing (Independent Democratic Union (*UDI*) became the second

ranking party in the Senate, moving ahead of its opposition partner, the National Renewal (*RN*).

The Pinochet Case

Chilean government and society were suddenly thrust into turmoil in October 1998 when Pinochet flew to London for back surgery. As he was recuperating in a clinic, the British government formally placed him under arrest, acting on an extradition request from Spain.

A Spanish judge, Baltasar Garzón, on his own initiative, requested Pinochet's extradition to account for Spanish citizens tortured and killed during the military regime. But the warrant eventually was broadened to take advantage of the 1988 U.N. International Convention Against Torture, by which a country can seek the arrest in a second country of someone accused of torture committed in a third country. Judges in Switzerland and France soon submitted similar extradition requests for Pinochet, while Chilean exiles-by-choice in France, Denmark, Italy and Belgium also filed petitions against Pinochet.

The news of Pinochet's arrest made headlines around the world. In Chile, the news was greeted with glee by Pinochet's detractors and with outrage by his supporters. But the Spanish warrant and the British arrest also struck at the core of Chilean nationalism, and moderate Chileans, even some Pinochet-haters, denounced the action as a violation of Chilean sovereignty.

President Frei, despite his own personal animosity to the general, dutifully urged Pinochet's release on the grounds that as a member of the Chilean Senate he enjoyed diplomatic immunity. In a case of delicious irony, Foreign Minister José Miguel Insulza, who himself had been arrested after the coup and spent years in exile, went to London to plead Pinochet's cause.

The Pinochet case then began a torturous (no pun intended) 16-month journey through the British court system. The case was heard before a panel of five Law Lords, jurists who are members of the House of Lords, Britain's court of last resort. On November 25—Pinochet's 83rd birthday—the Law Lords voted 3–2 that Pinochet's arrest was legal. The decision then fell upon Home Secretary Jack Straw whether to grant Spain's extradition request.

The proud general was required to undergo the ignominy of appearing in court for a bail hearing. He huffily declared in Spanish that he did not recognize the jurisdiction of a non-Chilean court, and the judge remanded him on bail. The House of Lords agreed that Pinochet was entitled to a new hearing before a seven-judge panel.

Chile

**Former President
Eduardo Frei Ruiz-Tagle**

In March 1999, the Law Lords this time ruled 6–1 that Pinochet's arrest was legal and that the extradition request could proceed, but they agreed with Pinochet's lawyers that he could not be held accountable for any crime allegedly committed before September 29, 1988—the date that Britain incorporated the international torture convention into its criminal laws. This effectively dismissed 29 of the 32 charges in the Spanish warrant. The general remained under arrest on the other three counts. Judge Garzón began raising new allegations of cases committed after 1988.

In April 1999, Straw decided to proceed with the extradition request. That September, Pinochet's lawyers argued that Spain lacked jurisdiction to try the general for alleged crimes that occurred in Chile and also that he was too ill to stand trial. A magistrate rejected Pinochet's arguments and declared that he could be extradited. Once again, the decision fell upon Straw, who had to choose between releasing what the international community regarded as a war criminal or sending a feeble old man to Spain, where in all likelihood he would die in captivity.

Straw vacillated three months before ordering that Pinochet undergo a series of medical examinations to determine whether he were too ill to be extradited. The general, by then 84, underwent the exams in January 2000, after which Straw decided that Pinochet was indeed too ill to be extradited, setting off a torrent of outrage by human rights groups.

A Chilean air force plane was dispatched to Britain, and in March 2000, the once-proud Pinochet returned to his native soil—in a wheelchair.

His travails continued, however, and in May 2000 the Santiago Court of Appeals

voted 13–9 to strip him of his legislative immunity as senator-for-life to allow him to stand trial. Pinochet's lawyers appealed to the Supreme Court, arguing again that he was too frail. Moreover, the U.S. government announced in March it planned to investigate whether Pinochet were the intellectual author of the 1976 assassination of Letelier.

That August, the Supreme Court voted 14–6 to uphold the decision to strip Pinochet of his immunity. Judge Juan Guzmán found a loophole around the amnesty law that protected members of the military from being tried for atrocities committed following the coup. He decided to try him for the *kidnappings,* not murders, of 18 prisoners who disappeared and were never accounted for during the infamous "Caravan of Death," a helicopter-borne squad of soldiers that scoured the country after the coup and carried dissidents away to their deaths.

Guzmán generated world headlines by announcing that Pinochet would stand trial and placed him under house arrest. An appeals court overturned his order, on the grounds that Guzmán never interrogated Pinochet before arresting him. Pinochet ignored his lawyers and agreed to let Guzmán interrogate him in his seaside home. As a result, the judge declared Pinochet mentally competent to stand trial and issued an arrest warrant, which was served on Pinochet at his home. In July, an appeals court ruled that Pinochet was mentally incompetent to stand trial. But in August, the Supreme Court overturned that decision.

The lawyers wrangled until the Supreme Court ruled 4–1 in July 2002 that Pinochet was mentally incompetent. Three days later, Pinochet resigned his lifetime Senate seat. His 29-year political career and an era in Chilean history were over.

But Pinochet's legal problems persisted. Argentina requested his extradition in connection with the 1974 car bomb assassination there of the exiled General Carlos Prats and his wife. The Supreme Court, citing its incompetence ruling, blocked the request.

In November 2003, Pinochet granted an interview to a Spanish-language network in Miami, in which he laid the blame on the human rights abuses on his subordinates. In the interview, Pinochet came across as quite lucid. Suddenly, he was facing charges again, not only for the Prats assassination, but for nine kidnappings and one murder committed as part of the so-called "Operation Condor," a joint effort by South American military regimes of the 1970s to kill or imprison leftists.

In a 14–9 decision in May 2004 that stunned both sides, the Santiago Court of Appeals stripped Pinochet of his immunity, leaving him vulnerable not only to prosecution but to about 200 civil lawsuits. The Supreme Court upheld the appeals court. His lawyers again appealed on the grounds that Pinochet was incompetent, and he was examined by three doctors: one appointed by Pinochet's lawyers, one by the families of victims, one by Guzmán. In their report, the doctors appointed by the judge and the defense agreed Pinochet was incompetent, while the third said he was competent. Guzmán decided to go with the doctor who said he was competent and issued an indictment against Pinochet in the Condor case. Five days later, Pinochet was hospitalized with a stroke. In January 2005, a panel of the Supreme Court upheld the indictment by a 3–2 vote.

As if Pinochet did not have enough legal problems with the human rights charges, in August 2004 a U.S. Senate committee report alleged that the Washington-based

Torres del Paine

Riggs Bank had allowed Pinochet and his wife to illegally stash $8 million in accounts there from 1994–2002. Although most Chileans had come to accept the reality that Pinochet was the intellectual author of human rights abuses, it was widely believed, even by some of his opponents, that he was personally honest.

The Chilean government compared the amount of money Pinochet had stashed abroad and the amount he claimed for taxes; they didn't add up, and the government sued him for back taxes. Pinochet's long-time nemesis, Spanish Judge Garzón, charged the Pinochets and eight others with money laundering. The Chilean government froze $5 million of Pinochet's assets. Two days before Pinochet's 90th birthday in November 2005, a judge ordered him placed under house arrest for the fraud and tax evasion charges; he was later fingerprinted and mugshots were taken at his house. In January 2006, Pinochet, his wife and four of their children were indicted. The case dragged on until the feeble old general finally died on December 10, 2006.

The armed forces were caught in a dilemma with Pinochet's arrest. Although the military protested vigorously, it seemed to realize that it is a new day in Chile, and that it would be bad public relations to undermine a duly elected government. Moreover, the military felt compelled to own up to the whereabouts of the bodies of many of the "disappeared." Once a death is confirmed, it is covered by the amnesty law and can no longer be treated as a kidnapping. Alas, the military acknowledged that many victims were dumped at sea.

The Lagos Presidency

As the Pinochet drama unfolded in 1999, Chileans elected their third president since the restoration of democracy. In a coalition primary, the *PPD*'s Ricardo Lagos, 61, a neo-socialist economist, defeated Andrés Zaldivar, a moderate Christian Democrat, with 70% of the vote. The two right-wing opposition parties, *RN* and the *UDI*, also held a joint primary, and the overwhelming winner was the *UDI*'s Joaquín Lavín, also an economist and a former mayor of the affluent Santiago suburb of Los Condes. During the Pinochet regime, Lavín had been one of the "Chicago Boys," the University of Chicago-educated economists who engineered Chile's free-market economic miracle. The Communist Party leader Gladys Marín mounted a separate candidacy, while three lesser candidates completed the field.

The results of the first round on December 12 were breathtakingly close: 3,359,679, or 47.96 percent, for Lagos, to 3,328,652,

The front page of the Santiago daily *La Tercera* the morning after the January 16, 2000, presidential runoff shows the victorious Ricardo Lagos, right, with his defeated opponent, Joaquín Lavín, in a display of gracious goodwill.

or 47.52 percent, for Lavín. Marín received only 223,000 votes, or 3.2 percent, but those votes would prove crucial in the January 16, 2000 runoff.

This author spent two weeks in Chile observing the runoff campaign as a freelance journalist. By then, Lagos had heeded the advice of his advisers and was beginning to campaign in a more laid-back style, addressing crowds without a coat, although he still wore a tie. Both candidates tried to outdo each other with lavish, U.S.-style campaign promises that left analysts wondering how they expected to pay for them.

The runoff was almost as dramatic as the first round: 3,677,968 or 51.31% for Lagos, to 3,490,561, or 48.69% for Lavín.

The loser stunned the winner by coming personally to his hotel to congratulate him, then the two of them went to the balcony together where, to the delight of the cheering Lagos supporters, Lavín magnanimously pledged his support to the president-elect. Lagos was inaugurated on March 11, 2000.

In the municipal elections in October 2000 for 341 local governments, the *Concertación* polled 52% of the popular vote nationwide, down from 56% in the 1996 municipal elections. Moreover, it lost about 40 cities and towns to the opposition. In the Santiago mayor's race, Lavín was elected with 62%.

The next major showdown came in the congressional elections in December 2001.

Chile

Former President Ricardo Lagos
Photo by the author

The *Concertación* received 51.4% of the 1.7 million votes cast, compared with 44% for the conservative coalition *Alianza para Chile* and 2.6% for the Communists. But in the tabulation of seats, the *Concertación* lost ground. Even with former President Frei assuming a lifetime Senate seat, and the continued absence of Pinochet, the election resulted in a tie in the upper chamber. In the Chamber of Deputies, the *Concertación* dropped from 70 to 63 deputies.

In January 2003, Chile suddenly found itself in the world spotlight when it assumed one of the rotating seats on the 15-member U.N. Security Council just as debate began over the proposed U.S. resolution to authorize the use of force against Iraq. Chile opposed the war resolution, straining relations with the United States, with which it had just concluded a long-sought free-trade agreement (see Economy).

In October 2003, police arrested a wealthy, politically connected gymnasium owner, Claudio Spiniak, and charged him with operating a pedophile ring in which street children of both sexes were procured to provide pleasure for his friends at orgiastic parties. At first, it seemed like just a sensational news story. But then *RN* Deputy Pía Guzmán, a children's rights advocate, declared at a news conference that three senators were among those who frequented Spiniak's parties, two from the *UDI* and one from the *Concertación*, although she declined to name them. Guzmán's allegation caused a rift between the *RN*'s president, Sebastián Piñera, and Pablo Longueira, the *UDI* president. Their squabbling became so caustic that Lavín declared he would pursue a presidential candidacy independent of the two parties.

Meanwhile, *"el Caso Spiniak"* became a veritable media circus, which this author witnessed first-hand during an eight-day visit to Chile in December. By early 2004, polls showed Lavín losing ground to two female cabinet ministers seen as potential *Concertación* candidates: Defense Minister Michelle Bachelet of the Socialist Party, and Foreign Minister Soledad Alvear, a Christian Democrat.

Two institutional changes of historic proportions were implemented in 2004 and 2005. In 2004, Lagos signed into law a bill legalizing divorce in Chile, the last Latin American country do so. Then the opposition-controlled Senate agreed to reform Pinochet's 1980 constitution to abolish the eight appointed senators, to repeal the provision giving former presidents Senate seats for life and to give the president the power enjoyed in other democracies to remove the heads of the armed forces. Still in place, however, is the double-member district system that guarantees the opposition virtual parity in both houses. In 2005, the two chambers finally agreed on the amendment, which also shortened the presidential term back to four years. The change left the Senate with 38 members, all elected.

Virtually as historic was the remarkable statement issued in 2004 by General Juan Emilio Cheyre, commander of the army, acknowledging for the first time the army's institutional responsibility for the "morally unacceptable actions of the past." Lagos praised the army's decision, and said it represented the army's "integration into today's democratic Chile." A presidential commission interviewed 35,000 people and issued a definitive report in 2004 in which the government admitted that torture was state policy during the military regime and that 28,000 people had been tortured. Chile finally came to terms with its past to heal old wounds.

Lagos hosted the annual summit of the Asia-Pacific Economic Cooperation (APEC) group in 2004, and he called for a free-trade agreement by 2020 of the 21 signatories, which represent 60% of the world's economy.

Bachelet Makes History

Responding to opposition complaints that Foreign Minister Alvear and Defense Minister Bachelet were campaigning for president on company time, Lagos replaced both of them in 2004.

In October 2004 the *Concertación* made its poorest showing to date in municipal elections. In the popular vote, it led the opposition coalition *Alianza* 45% to 39%, and it won 199 of the 345 municipal governments. Although the government claimed the elections were a triumph, it was the first time the *Concertación* had failed to poll a majority in municipal elections, and its six-point winning margin was half of what it was in 2000. The *Alianza* retained the mayoralty of Santiago. Lavín decided not to run so he could focus on his presidential candidacy.

Two major developments in 2005 changed the electoral landscape. First, the long-simmering opposition rivalry between the *UDI* and *RN* came to a head. Instead of endorsing Lavín's candidacy again as expected, *RN* abruptly voted to

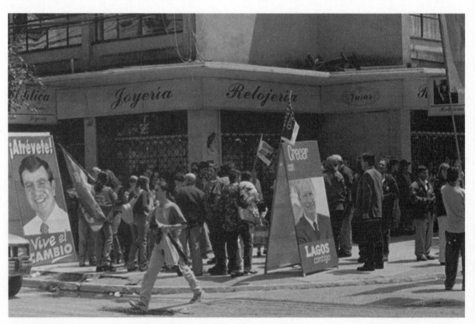

Supporters of rival presidential candidates Ricardo Lagos and Joaquín Lavín compete for space on the same street corner in downtown Puerto Montt in January 2000.
Photo by the author

run its leader, Sebastián Piñera, as its candidate. Days later, Alvear dropped out of the race, assuring that Bachelet would be the *Concertación* candidate.

The only drama for the December 11, 2005 election was whether Bachelet would win outright and, if not, whether she would face Lavín or Piñera in the runoff. She was an unlikely frontrunner in a conservative, devoutly Catholic country, an agnostic who separated from her husband and bore a child by a lover. She also had had an extra-marital affair with a leader of the notorious Manuel Rodríguez Revolutionary Front, a left-wing terrorist group responsible for the 1986 assassination attempt on Pinochet, which became a campaign issue.

Voter turnout was 87.7%. The results:

Bachelet	3,190,691	46%
Piñera	1,763,964	25.4%
Lavín	1,612,608	23.2%

Lavín graciously pledged his support to Piñera for the January 15, 2006 runoff, and Piñera quixotically campaigned to try to overtake Bachelet's huge lead. The runoff, which had a turnout of 87.1%, was closer than some had predicted, but Bachelet's mandate was convincing:

Bachelet	3,723,019	53.5%
Piñera	3,236,394	46.5%

On March 11, 2006, Bachelet, 54, made history not only by becoming Chile's first woman president, but unlike Nicaragua's Violeta Chamorro and Panama's Mireya Moscoso, she was the first elected Latin American female president who is not the widow of a prominent political figure. With the changes to the constitution, the *Concertación* also won a majority in both houses of Congress.

Bachelet captured the fancy of the global media because of her peculiar, mixed background. She is the daughter of an air force general and attended school in Washington when her father was assigned to Chile's military mission there in the 1960s. Following the 1973 coup, which her father refused to support, he was arrested for treason and died in prison of a heart attack. Bachelet and her mother were also arrested and tortured. Bachelet went into exile in Communist East Germany, where she studied pediatrics and married her husband, also a Chilean exile, by whom she had two children. She completed her medical degree after she returned to Chile in 1979.

Despite her leftist background and her medical training, Bachelet also studied military strategy and graduated from the Inter-American Defense College in Washington in 1998. She later earned the praise

Former President Michelle Bachelet

of armed forces officers during her tenure as Lagos' defense minister. She earlier had served as his health minister.

Bachelet pledged to continue the moderate, free-market economic policies of her three predecessors and met with President Bush at the White House. During that visit, she paid a nostalgic visit to her former middle school.

The End of an Era

On Pinochet's 91st birthday on November 25, 2006, at a party held for him by admirers, the ever-unpredictable general had his wife read a prepared statement in which he suddenly acknowledged the human rights abuses committed during his years in power.

"Today, near the end of my days, I want to say that I harbor no rancor against anybody, that I love my fatherland above all and that I take political responsibility for everything that was done, which had no other goal than making Chile greater and avoiding its disintegration," the statement read. "I assume full political responsibility for what happened."

Two days later, he was again arrested, but the general apparently knew he would elude further prosecution. On December 3, he suffered an acute heart attack; on December 10, he died.

Even in death, Pinochet proved a polarizing figure for his countrymen; some mourned and praised him, others celebrated his demise. Bachelet denied him a state funeral, although he was accorded full military honors at the Military Academy; Bachelet declined to attend, saying it would be "a violation of my conscience." At his request, he was cremated so that vandals could not desecrate his tomb. An era in Chilean—and world—history was finally at an end.

But the legal battle surrounding his wealth did not die with him. In October 2007, Pinochet's widow, his five children and several of his former associates were detained for two days and indicted on embezzlement charges. The Supreme Court later threw out the charges against his widow and four of the children on the grounds that they had not been government employees and could not have committed embezzlement. Charges against eight associates also were dismissed, but the court upheld the indictments against Pinochet's oldest son, Augusto, and two associates. The court also ordered an investigation of the Pinochets' assets.

With the Pinochet factor literally laid to rest, Bachelet found herself beset with her countrymen's growing disillusionment with her governing ability. She had to contend with a crippling strike at a copper mine, street protests by students and teachers demanding to know why the boom in revenue from high copper prices was not being channeled into education, and commuters' anger over a newly reorganized bus system in Santiago that turned into a nightmare from poor planning. She also rankled men in this *macho* country by arbitrarily appointing half the Cabinet posts to women, regardless of merit, and introducing legislation that would mandate all parties to designate 30% of their candidates for Congress as women. A poll in the Santiago daily *La Tercera* in 2007 showed that 61% of respondents lacked confidence in her ability to handle a crisis.

She reshuffled her Cabinet and made a remarkable, televised apology to her countrymen for her poor performance, but it did not defuse the situation. Days later, hundreds of high school students went on a rampage in Santiago, erecting burning barricades and looting supermarkets. Thirty-two policemen were injured in the melee and more than 800 people were arrested. Exactly what the students were protesting was unclear, other than their general dissatisfaction with the status quo in what is still Latin America's strongest economy.

There were more violent outbursts on September 11, 2007, the 34th anniversary of the coup. Demonstrations marking the coup occur every year, but this time hundreds of protesters, their motive unclear, began looting and burning stores. A policeman was killed, 41 people were injured and 216 were detained.

As if she didn't have enough problems at home, Bachelet suddenly had one with Peru. The two countries' long-standing animosity, which dates to Chile's annexation of Peruvian territory after the War of the Pacific of 1879–84, was strained further by Chile's delay in extraditing for-

Chile

mer Peruvian President Alberto Fujimori, wanted in Peru for a host of charges (see Peru).

It seemed relations had improved with the signing of a bilateral free-trade agreement in 2006, but then, in 2007, Peru abruptly renounced a maritime boundary agreement dating to the 1950s. It had extended due west into the Pacific from the point where their land border reaches the coast. Peru now claims the maritime boundary is an extension of the land border, which points southwesterly. In January 2008, Peru published a map claiming a 14,630-square-mile tract of Chilean waters that is rich in fish. Chile withdrew its ambassador from Lima and said it would exercise its territorial rights over the area. Peruvian President Alan García said Peru would take its claim to the International Court of Justice in the Hague, Netherlands, which could take years to rule on the matter.

Bilateral relations worsened further in November 2009 when Peru announced it had arrested an air force officer for spying for Chile. Ironically, Bachelet and García were both in Singapore for the annual APEC summit when the news broke. García canceled a scheduled workshop with Bachelet and flew back to Lima.

By 2008, in part because of an economic boom fueled by record high prices for copper on the world market, Bachelet's esteem in the eyes of her countrymen suddenly soared, with an approval rating of 75% or more. Nonetheless, in the closely watched bellwether municipal elections in October 2008, the conservative opposition *Alianza* won 144 mayor's races to only 101 for the *Concertación,* including Santiago, Valparaiso and Concepción. Voter turnout was 7 million, or 86%. The *Alianza* received 40.7% to only 28.7% for the *Concertación.* Broken down by party, the *PDC* won 59 mayoralties, the *UDI* 58, *RN* 55 and Bachelet's *PS,* 30. It was an ominous harbinger for the *Concertación* going into the 2009 presidential campaign.

Political and Geological Earthquakes

Bachelet and the *Concertación* had hoped they could parlay her new popularity into a fifth consecutive victory, but after 20 years of center-left presidents, voters seemed ready for a change. Also, the booming economy went into a slump in 2009 because of the global recession. The ruling alliance may have made two fatal errors, first by not holding an open primary as in the past, and second by turning to the past rather than to the future by nominating former President Frei, 67. In protest, Socialist Party Deputy Marco Enríquez-Ominani, 36, bolted from the *Concertación* and launched an independent candidacy.

President Sebastián Piñera Echenique

The conservative opposition, now under the Obama-like banner Coalition for Change, again nominated Sebastián Piñera, 59, a billionaire whose business interests include the *Chilevisión* TV channel and a fourth of LAN Chile, the formerly state-owned airline. He holds a master's degree and a doctorate in economics from Harvard.

The Communist Party nominated Jorge Arrate.

Piñera campaigned on a platform of restoring 6% economic growth and making Chile a First World developed country by 2018. He sought to downplay his wealth and adroitly pledged to continue the social welfare programs of the *Concertación* that Chileans had come to expect. He came across well in televised debates, while Frei appeared dour and uninspiring. Enríquez-Ominami also came across as more charismatic than Frei, and he cut deeply into the *Concertación*'s base.

The results of the first round on December 13:

Piñera	3,074,164	44.1%
Frei	2,065,061	29.6%
Enríquez-Ominami	1,405,124	20.1%
Arrate	433,195	6.2%

Clearly, it was up to Enríquez-Ominami to play the role of kingmaker in the January 17, 2010 runoff, but he steadfastly refused to endorse either Piñera or Frei. To close the wide gap with Piñera, Frei would need all of Arrate's voters and at least 80% of Enríquez-Ominami's. But many of Enríquez-Ominami's voters apparently chose to stay home, while exit polls showed that 36% of them opted for change over ideology and voted for Piñera. The results on January 17:

Piñera	3,591,182	51.6%
Frei	3,367,790	48.4%

After 20 years of wandering in the political wilderness, the conservative opposition was finally given a chance to show it was ready to move from its Pinochet-tainted past and to lead Chile into the future. It was the first time the right had won the presidency since Jorge Alessandri in 1958.

Bachelet would bequeath to Piñera an improving economy and a discretionary fund of $1.1. billion that she had wisely set aside from the copper windfall. It would prove vital to face a challenge neither Piñera, his coalition nor his countrymen anticipated.

On February 27, just 12 days before the transfer of power, central Chile was struck by a magnitude 8.8 earthquake that killed 500 people and inflicted billions of dollars in damage to the infrastructure. A tsunami washed away entire villages. It was reminiscent of the earthquake of comparable historic magnitude that derstroyed Puerto Montt in 1960. Concepción was the largest city near the epicenter, and it sustained major damage. An estimated 400,000–500,000 homes were totally destroyed or sertiously damaged, leaving a staggering 2 million people homeless—almost one eighth of the country's population. But it was indicative of Chilean engineering that the percentage of homes and office buildings destroyed, and the death toll, were not higher.

Several presidents came to Santiago for Piñera's inauguration on March 11, but the ceremony was literally shaken by a severe aftershock, and the newly installed president eschewed the usual post-inaugural festivities to tour the devastated areas by helicopter.

Piñera demonstrated a take-charge approach, mandating that schools re-open within a week at temporary facilities. He decided to use $400 million of the discretionary fund for reconstruction, but imposed a $2 billion corporate tax increase to help pay the rest, a move that did not go over well with his core constituency. When this book went to press, the full extent of the damage to wineries and other export industries was still being assessed (see Economy), but the vital copper mines are well to the north of the affected zone.

Culture: One of Spain's least-developed colonies, since independence Chile has made cultural contributions far out of proportion to its size, particularly in literature. During the 19th century, Chile's intellectual climate produced not only outstanding writers but attracted others seeking greater freedom of expression. Two outstanding examples are Venezuela's Andrés Bello, whose statue stands in front of the University of Chile, which he founded, and Argentina's Domingo

Faustino Sarmiento, who spent several years in exile as editor of *El Mercurio* during the dictatorship of Juan Manuel de Rosas in his native land. During this era Chile produced a number of its own realist prose writers, the best known of whom was probably the novelist Alberto Blest Gana, author of such enduring classics as *El niño que enloqueció de amor.* The late 19th century also produced a golden age in art, though it was heavily influenced by contemporary French impressionism.

In the 20th century, Chile enjoyed the distinction of being the only Latin American country to have produced two Nobel Prize-winning poets, Lucía Godoy Alcayaga (1886–1957) and Naftalí Reyes (1904–73). But the world does not remember them by those names; it remembers them as Gabriela Mistral and Pablo Neruda. Both achieved international acclaim, and both represented Chile abroad for a time as diplomats. Mistral taught for several years in the United States. Their verse has been translated into several languages, and Neruda especially has become a global icon. The centennial of his birth on July 12, 2004, was marked by observances in Chile and throughout the Spanish-speaking world. His home overlooking the Pacific at Isla Negra is a popular pilgrimage destination for his admirers.

Chile's poetic tradition remains strong. Gonzalo Rojas, a contemporary of Neruda's, received Spain's prestigious Cervantes Prize in Literature in December 2003 at the age of 85. Another Chilean poet, Jorge Edwards, won the award several years earlier.

Two of Chile's best-known prose writers today are the novelist Isabel Allende, a distant cousin of the Marxist president, who now lives in California, and Ariel Dorfman. Two of Allende's novels, *La casa de los espíritus,* and *De amor y sombras,* were adapted for the English-language films *The House of the Spirits* and *Of Love and Shadows.* Dorfman's play, *La muerte y la doncella,* was adapted for the U.S. movie *Death and the Maiden.*

Probably the premier figure in music in the 20th century was the internationally renowned concert pianist Claudio Arrau (1903–91), who spent most of his career in Europe. In popular music, a folk singer who achieved cult-legend status much as Elvis Presley did in the United States was Violeta Parra (1917–67), like Arrau born in Chillán but who remained in Chile. Probably best remembered for the song, *Gracias a la vida,* Parra committed suicide over an unhappy love affair in 1967. Like Neruda, her likeness is still seen everywhere in Chile, and her voice or her songs remain popular throughout the Hispanic world.

Chile's folklore is grounded in the tradition of the *huaso,* a trans-Andean version of Argentina's gaucho. Its guitar-based music is similar to Mexican ranchero. Distinctly Chilean, however, is the national folk dance, the *cueca,* which traditionally is performed in conjunction with Chilean independence day on September 18 but is performed in touristy cafes year-round.

Chile's reputation as a haven for political and artistic expression disappeared during the 1973–90 military regime. Many of its own artistic, literary and musical figures were either killed or exiled. One of Chile's best-known popular singers, Victor Jara, was killed in the Santiago stadium after the 1973 coup. Film director Miguel Littín fled to Cuba. After 1990 many such artists returned, but a new generation emerged, less tied to the Marxist traditions of its predecessors. A promising young film director is Ricardo Larraín, whose 1991 movie, *La frontera,* won international acclaim.

Television came to Chile in 1960, but rather than the first stations being private or government-owned as in other Latin American countries, the first three stations were put on the air by the University of Chile, Catholic University of Santiago and Catholic University of Valparaíso; these universities still operate the stations today. The government launched *TV Nacional* in 1967. It wasn't until the early 1990s that the first two private franchises were awarded. Chilean television has become increasingly less dependent on foreign programming and has produced a number of creditable programs of its own, some of which are exported to other Latin American countries.

Chile was the birthplace of the Latin American press. The region's first regularly published newspaper, *La Aurora de Chile,* appeared in 1810 and lasted nearly a decade. The press used to print it is on display in the National Library. Chile also is the home of the oldest continually published newspaper in Latin America, *El Mercurio,* which began as a weekly in Valparaiso in 1837, became a daily a few years later, and began publishing in Santiago in 1900. Today six dailies are published in the capital, and the provincial press also flourishes.

Economy: Few countries in the world have been whipsawed as violently from one political or economic extreme to another as has Chile. The country was long dependent on copper for foreign exchange, which as late as the 1970s still accounted for 60 percent of exports. It is mstill the leading export. As with Bolivia's dependence on tin, fluctuations in the world copper market often led to recessions in Chile. Moreover, the copper mines, as well as many of the country's utilities, were owned by foreign corporations, a fact that provided the Communist and Socialist parties with election-year ammunition. The elder Eduardo Frei tried to steer Chile on a middle course between Marxism and capitalism in the 1960s, an effort rewarded by President Lyndon Johnson, who lent Chile substantial foreign aid. Frei's halfway economic and social reforms proved of limited success, however, and in the end were criticized by the right as too radical and by the left as inadequate.

The result was the narrow minority victory of Salvador Allende's Popular Unity coalition in 1970, which jerked the country abruptly to the left. Allende nationalized the copper mines and utilities, moves that were applauded even by Allende's opponents at first because of nationalist pride. But signing a decree nationalizing an industry is one thing; running it efficiently and profitably proved quite another. The result was one of the many economic disasters of the Allende regime.

Another was land reform, through the breaking up of the huge *latifundias* of wealthy and often absentee owners. On the surface, such reform seemed a long-overdue application of social justice. In reality, it destroyed agricultural operations that often were operating well, replacing them with small communal plots that were not commercially useful and run by peasants with little or no knowledge of efficient agricultural techniques.

Marxist distribution policies also resulted in severe, Cuban-style shortages, which eroded what little confidence the regime still enjoyed. To compound its woes, the regime was beset by hyperinflation of 1,000 percent annually. The country was on the verge of social and economic chaos when the military intervened on September 11, 1973.

The military government of General Pinochet quickly restored order and reversed virtually every policy of the Marxist experiment. Land holdings were restored to their original owners, although a new homesteading law was implemented to provide land to small farmers who were able to demonstrate they planned to make it produce something beyond the basic needs of their families. For a time, nationalized industries were run by the state, but by the 1980s they were privatized.

The Pinochet government made it clear it intended a dramatic break with the past, that it would not merely restore the *status quo ante* Allende. With the government's encouragement, Chilean entrepreneurs began to exploit the extraordinarily rich nitrate deposits. Because of the reversal of seasons in the Southern Hemisphere, Chile began exporting enormous quantities of produce to the United States,

Chile

A visitor to the Pablo Neruda museum adjacent to his home in Isla Negra gazes at a larger-than-life portrait of the Nobel-laureate poet.   *Photo by the author*

Europe and Japan during the Northern Hemisphere winter. By the time Pinochet relinquished power in 1990, agricultural exports exceeded those of copper, thus breaking the traditional dependence. Yet, even copper contributed to the Chilean economy as never before in the 1990s as exports from other copper-mining countries, such as Zaïre and Zambia, declined because of inefficiency and instability and the world markert price soared.

The most dramatic economic transition of the Pinochet regime, however, was the move to almost pure free-market economics. Pinochet surrounded himself with a "kitchen cabinet" of civilian economic technocrats, many of whom had been schooled under Milton Friedman at the University of Chicago. Thus, the press quickly dubbed this team of economists "los Chicago Boys." Chile withdrew from the Andean Pact in the late 1970s and slashed its high protective tariffs, which led to a flood of cheap imported goods. At the same time, government subsidies that had kept inefficient domestic industries afloat were eliminated, forcing them to sink or swim; more than a few sank. After a brief period of seeming prosperity, the new policies plunged Chile into a severe recession in 1981. Large and small industries, unable to compete with foreign imports, foundered. So did many banks. The economic crisis lasted more than three years before the new economic realities took hold.

New Chilean industries proved capable of holding their own in the international marketplace. One such example was Chile's new arms industries, born out of necessity from the cutoff of U.S. military aid because of Pinochet's human rights violations. Chilean wineries are another international marketing success story, and there are now computer hardware and software industries.

By 1990, when Pinochet turned over power to Patricio Aylwin, Chile was in the midst of an economic boom. Ironically, while the new civilian government publicly reviled Pinochet for his human rights abuses, it grudgingly acknowledged the success of his free-market policies by retaining them. It was an especially bitter pill for the Socialists who were part of the governing coalition. The result, however, was an economy that for several years was the envy of Latin America—and the world. Real GDP growth between 1990 and 1997 averaged a dazzling 8% annually, exceeding 12% in 1992 and 10% in 1995. Contributing to Chile's success, and to its attractiveness to foreign investors, are wage costs lower than Mexico's or South Asia's and an educated workforce; the literacy rate is 96%, compared with Brazil's 83%. In addition to robust growth, inflation was trimmed to 6% and unemployment to 4%. Chile also became widely admired for its private pension fund administrator *(AFP)* system, implemented during the Pinochet era and continued since, which provided retirees far greater returns than the government's social security system. U.S. congressmen eyed Chile's retirement system as a possible model.

Chile is an associate member of the four-nation *Mercosur* free-trade pact (Argentina, Brazil, Uruguay and Paraguay),

Gabriela Mistral

but because its tariff policies differ so sharply from the other four, it has opted against full membership. Chile was expected to become the fourth member of NAFTA. President Eduardo Frei discussed the issue with President Clinton during a state visit to Washington in 1997.

A major success story in recent years has been Chile's wines, long recognized for their quality. Wine exports skyrocketed 5,000%, from $10.9 million in 1985 to $526 million in 1999, accounting for 5.4% of total exports. The trend continues upward, although subject to periods of drought, as large new tracts in the central region have been planted with grapes.

In 1997, the economy became a victim of its own success. Frei was twice forced to raise interest rates to prevent the economy from overheating and to keep inflation under control. The price of copper, which despite diversification still accounted for 42% of export earnings, dropped from $1.19 to 75 cents a pound,

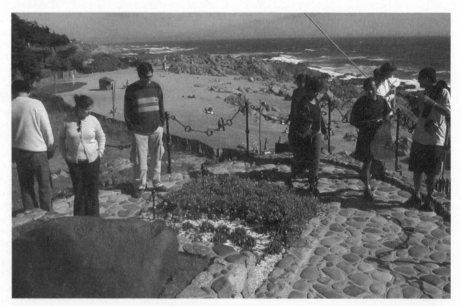

Visitors pay their respects at the graves of Pablo Neruda and his third wife, Matilde Urrutia, at his home overlooking the Pacific at Isla Negra.   *Photo by the author*

and the October market panic in Asia, which buys about a third of Chile's exports, had repercussions in Chile. GDP growth for 1998 was only 3.3%, compared with the steamroller of 7.1% in 1997 and 7.2% in 1996. Worse still, the economy shrank 2.7% in 1999, while unemployment leaped from 6% to 11% and per capita income fell slightly from $5,100 to $5,000. meaning Chile officially was in recession for the first time in 15 years.

The recession almost proved the undoing of the ruling *Concertación* in the presidential elections of 1999–2000. President Ricardo Lagos of the *Concertación*, who had barely squeaked into office, saw real GDP growth snap back from the negative column to a healthy 5.4% in 2000; it was up 4.0% in 2001 but only 2.1% in 2002, reflecting the economic crisis in neighboring Argentina and the recession in the United States, the leading market for its exports.

Like Brazil's Fernando Henrique Cardoso, the Socialist Lagos underwent a dramatic conversion to free-market principles and followed an economic course that was so conservative the opposition had little to quibble with. He traveled to Quebec in 2001 for the third Summit of the Americas and embraced the concept of a Free Trade Area of the Americas. He concluded a $9 billion free-trade agreement (FTA) with the European Union in 2002. The United States and Chile resumed free-trade talks that had begun 11 years earlier. After reaching some compromises over environmental issues and capital investment out-flows among others, the two countries signed a $6 billion FTA in 2003. In 2004, Chile concluded a $1.1 billion FTA with South Korea. Since then, Chile has concluded FTAs with China, India, Japan, New Zealand, Singapore, Peru and, in 2008, with Australia.

Growth for 2003 was 3.3%, and it jumped to 6.1% in 2004—the best showing since 1997, largely because of a high international market price for copper—and 6.3% in 2005. It dropped to 4% in 2006, in part because of a strike at a copper mine and the decision of energy-starved Argentina to suspend natural gas exports to Chile, requiring more expensive fuels to generate electricity. Growth was back up to 5.1% in 2007, again due to record high copper prices. The copper windfall also gave Chile a budget surplus, and it is debt-free, a rarity in Latin America.

Growth for 2008 was down to 3.2%, reflecting the impact of the global recession on export-dependent Chile, and in 2009 the economy *shrank* by –1.7%.

Inflation has remained steady in recent years, dropping from 4.5% in 2000 to only 1.1% in 2003, the lowest rate since 1935. In 2008 it was at 8%, but with the recession it dropped to 1.7% in 2009.

Unemployment has fluctuated little: 9% in 2004, 7.8% in 2006, 7.8% in 2008 and 10% in 2009.

The devastating earthquake that struck Chile in February 2010 caused an estimated $4 billion to $7 billion in damage and disrupted the wine industry, which suffered an estimated $250 million in damage. Ironically, however, the influx of international aid, coupled with reconstruction activity, will almost certainly lower unemployment and enhance revenues from increased sales and income taxes. On the down side, the influx of foreign money may cause Chile's strong peso to become undervalued, requiring a revaluation that would make Chilean exports more expensive.

The Future: Chile has slowly laid its tragic past to rest. This author covered the 1989, 1993 and 1999–2000 presidential elections as a free-lance journalist and spent a semester in Chile as a Fulbright Scholar in 1991. In 1989, I had been struck by the lingering hatred between right and left, even by Chileans who had been born after the Allende period. The bitterness I heard in conversations with scores of Chileans from all classes and political persuasions reminded me of the century-long resentment of Southerners after the U.S. Civil War, which I experienced as a boy in Texas.

Now, at last, things seem to be changing. On a visit to Santiago in 2003, I saw

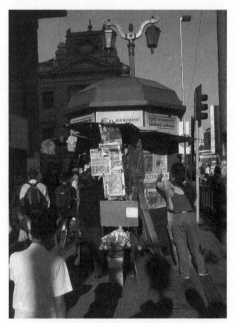

The ubiquitous news kiosks in Santiago and all Chilean cities and towns boast a wide variety of daily and weekly newspapers and magazines. *Photo by the author*

something that once would have been unthinkable: a statue of Salvador Allende in the *Plaza de la Constitución*, right across the street from the Moneda, where he died.

The army's dramatic confession of its sins during the dictatorship, and the government's come-clean report on torture, were transcendental, but not as dramatic as the death's door confession of Pinochet two weeks before his death on December 10, 2006. The historic changes to the 1980 constitution that eliminate the unelected senators have made Chile a genuine democracy.

With Pinochet's death, the governing *Concertación* lost a unifying factor, and after 20 years in power, the governing coalition was showing its age. The narrow election of billionaire businessman Sebástián Piñera in the January 2010 runoff is as historic a change as when Patricio Aylwin replaced Pinochet. Yet, although he is the first conservative elected president since Jorge Alessandri in 1958, Piñera seems to be as prudently committed to retaining the *Concertación's* popular social welfare programs as the *Concertación* was committed to retaining Pinochet's successful free-market economic policies. Although the conservative opposition has finally won power, it is unlikely Chile will see a drastic swerve to the right. The ghost of the Pinochet era may finally be laid to rest.

In a perverse way, the devastating 2010 earthquake could spark a building boom that will have positive ripple effects on a sluggish economy that was heavily affected by the 2008–09 global market panic and recession. It could lower the current 10% unemployment rate and, as happened in Louisiana after Hurricanes Katrina and Rita in 2005, the government's coffers could be filled by value-added tax revenues from the sales of construction materials. Higher employment also means higher income tax collections. Armed also with the discretionary fund President Bachelet created from the copper windfall, Piñera will likely follow an entrepreneur-friendly policy that could, as he hopes, place Chile in the ranks of First World countries by 2018.

Earthquake recovery will occupy Piñera for the short term, but for the long term he needs to focus on one of the *Concertación's* glaring failures: the need to reform Chile's public education system. It is also time to amend the constitution to abolish the last of Pinochet's undemocratic legacies, the peculiar double-member district system for electing senators and deputies. If he allies his center-right coalition with centrist Christian Democrats, Piñera could prove as successful in getting things done as president as he did as a businessman.

The Republic of Colombia

Area: 439,405 square miles.

Population: 44.2 million (2010 est.).

Capital City: Bogotá (Pop. 8.25 million, estimate).

Climate: The lowlands are generally hot, with heavy rainfall except for the Guajira Peninsula, which is arid. Highland climate varies with altitude, becoming quite temperate and pleasant in the higher elevations.

Neighboring Countries: Venezuela (East and Northeast); Brazil (Southeast); Peru and Ecuador (South); Panama (Northwest).

Official Language: Spanish.

Other Principal Tongues: Isolated Indian dialects.

Ethnic Background: *Mestizo* (mixed European and Indian, 58%), European (20%) Mulatto (mixed Black and White, 14%), Negro (4%), Mixed Negro-Indian and Indian (4%).

Principal Religion: Roman Catholic Christianity.

Chief Commercial Products: Refined cocaine, a technically illegal export worth over $10 billion U.S., coffee, petroleum, cotton, tobacco, sugar, textiles, bananas, fresh-cut flowers.

Currency: Peso.

Gross Domestic Product: U.S. $231.3 billion in 2009, est. ($5,233 per capita). This does not include money from drug trafficking, which, if included, would increase this figure by an estimated 25%.

Former Colonial Status: Spanish Crown Colony (1525–1819)

Independence Date: July 20, 1810.

Chief of State: Álvaro Uribe Vélez, (b. July 4, 1952), president (since August 7, 2002); Juan Manuel Santos Calderón (b. August 10, 1951), president-elect, to be inaugurated August 7, 2010.

National Flag: Yellow, blue and red horizontal stripes.

Colombia is the fourth largest nation in South America and the only one with both Atlantic and Pacific coasts. The high Andes mountains divide the country into four ranges and occupy about two fifths of the land. To the east of the mountains are the great plains (*llanos*) and the western tip of the Guiana Highland. The majority of Colombia's population is concentrated in the green valleys and mountain basins that lie between the ranges of the Andes.

Eleven of Colombia's 14 urban centers are in the mountain valleys; the remainder are on the Caribbean coast. The vast plains along the base of the eastern range contain cattle ranches, but the extensions of the plains into the jungle-filled Amazon Basin are almost unpopulated. The northern ends of the mountain valleys, which fan out to the Caribbean coast, are wet, hot and almost uninhabited.

Colombia's people comprise communities that vary from white, Indian and black populations to combinations of mixed ancestry. Rivers have been Colombia's most important means of communication; the Magdalena is navigable for nearly 1,000 miles and still is the principal means of transporting cargo to and from Bogotá. The second great river is the Cauca, not important for transportation but for furnishing water for irrigation and power for industry in the Cauca Valley. A major construction program, similar to that of the Tennessee Valley project, was undertaken to further develop the Cauca Valley's resources.

As in all countries near the Equator, altitude is the principal factor, modifying an otherwise oppressive climate. Throughout the country rainfall is ample. There are no seasons applicable to the whole country. Summer is generally considered the dry season and the rainy season is winter; however, in some regions along the Pacific, rains, either violent thunderstorms or warm, steady showers, fall every day of the year. From sea level to 3,000 feet the climate is tropical; from 3,000 to 6,500 feet it is temperate; above 6,500 feet it is chilly. Crops are grown at elevations up to 10,000 feet, but above this level trees thin out and tall peaks are covered by snow year around.

History: The Spaniards discovered the coast of Colombia about 1500, but the Indians proved so hostile that the explorers quickly withdrew. The first settlement was later established at Santa Marta in 1525, and Cartagena was subsequently founded in 1533. The interior was not penetrated until 1536, when Gonzalo Jiménez de Quesada explored the Magdalena River seeking its source. Climbing the eastern range, he found the Chibcha Indians in several of the mountain valleys, conquered them and founded Bogotá, the present capital. The Chibchas were sedentary, agricultural people who had developed a fairly high level of civilization.

An expedition from Ecuador under Sebastián de Belalcazar discovered the Cauca Valley and founded Pasto, Popayán and Cali in 1536. Nicolaus de Federmann led an expedition toward the site of Bogotá from Venezuela. Belalcazar reached

Bogotá in 1538 and came into contact with Federmann in 1539. Similar to other conquests, the period of settlement was marked by conflict among the various groups of conquerors. The Spaniards introduced sugarcane, wheat, cattle, sheep and horses and established a royal government at Bogotá in 1550 for the administration of most of the land in modern Colombia.

Gold was discovered in Antioquía about 1550, rapidly reducing further interest in the agricultural regions around Bogotá and Cali. Almost simultaneously with the start of gold shipments to Spain, English and Dutch pirates started their attacks on Spanish shipping and the Caribbean ports. However, the interior of the country was at peace and, unmolested, gradually developed. Descendants of the conquerors amassed large estates, worked by Indian or black slaves and established a semi-feudal system of agriculture that still persists in the remote parts of Colombia.

During the colonial period, what is modern-day Colombia was part of the viceroyalty of New Granada. The movement for independence started in the 1790s following publication of the French Revolution's Declaration of the Rights of Man. This was not a popular movement, but rather one of young intellectuals from the aristocratic families of Bogotá.

Revolts erupted in Venezuela in 1796 and 1806, followed by an abortive attempt to set up an independent government at Bogotá. However, the provinces were divided and the Spanish re-established control. When news reached New Granada in 1810 that Spain's King Fernando VII had been deposed by Napoleon, the restive creoles revolted again. This time they seized Cartagena, then town after town in the Cauca and Magdalena valleys. On July 20, 1810, today observed as independence day, the *cabildo* in Bogotá arrested the viceroy and assumed control. Independence came after eight years of see-saw warfare in which Simón Bolívar and his generals, José Antonio Páez, Francisco de Paula Santander and Antonio José de Sucre victoriously marched and countermarched across Colombia, Venezuela and Ecuador. Following the defeat of the Spanish forces at the Battle of Boyacá, the Republic of Gran Colombia was proclaimed December 17, 1819, incorporating Venezuela, Colombia and Ecuador in a political union.

The allies in the war for independence divided over the form of government that should be established for the new state. Bolívar advocated a strong central government, while Páez and Santander pressed for a federation of sovereign states. Later, this discord would lead to the establishment of two political parties that still control the country today: the

Bolívar crossing the Andes

Conservatives, in favor of central government and close relations with the Catholic Church, and the Liberals, favoring a federation of states and separation of church and state.

The Republic of Gran Colombia lasted only 10 years. Venezuela separated from the union in 1829 and Ecuador declared its independence a year later; the remaining provinces took the name of New Granada. The name Colombia was restored in 1861 as the United States of Colombia and became the Republic of Colombia in 1886.

From its inception, the new republic was torn with dissent. Bolívar sought to create a "Great Colombia;" Santander believed there was little hope for uniting diverse people with few common interests into an effective union. Dissent grew during the period of the wars of liberation of Peru and Bolivia (1822–24). In 1826, Bolívar assumed dictatorial power. By 1830, opposition to him led to revolt, the republic was broken up, and the *el Libertador* died on his way into exile.

Santander became the actual founder of Colombia. Recalled from exile in 1832, he brought a degree of order from the chaos of war. Despite his own championing of democratic ideas, he imposed a strict discipline, organized finances and set up central government services with an iron hand. He and his successor pursued moderate policies concerning the church and the differences between the Conservatives and Liberals on the form of government. However, the radicals of both sides, as well as regional interests, sought their goals by force of arms; from 1839 to 1842

civil war was waged intermittently by constantly changing forces.

By 1840 the gap between the Conservative and Liberal views had widened; the Liberals were characterized as blasphemous and disorderly, while the Conservatives gained power as defenders of order, godliness and good government. The Conservatives (as usual during this period) represented an alliance of the landowners, the church and the army.

From 1840 to 1880, the two parties alternated in power, each using its position to persecute the other and generally provoking recurrent strife bordering on civil war. In spite of this turmoil, by 1880 the economy had broadened, the population had doubled since independence, communication and trade were improved and Colombia had few international problems.

The election of Rafael Núñez in 1880 marked a major change in Colombia's history. A long-time Liberal, he united the moderates of his party with the more moderate Conservatives and formed the National Party. Surviving another Conservative-Liberal civil war in 1884–85, Núñez secured adoption of Colombia's 10th constitution and brought order to the country. The Liberal regime became progressively conservative and subsequently dictatorial. The privileges of the church were restored, peace was maintained and political dissent was suppressed. His death in 1899 left the government in the hands of Conservatives without a leader capable of avoiding the consequences of 20 years of repression. Civil war raged for three years as the Liberals sought to oust

Colombia

the Conservatives. The so-called Thousand Day War left more than 100,000 dead, widespread destruction, a ruined economy and a demoralized people. These losses were soon followed by the revolt of the province of Panama in 1903 (arranged by the United States; see Panama).

The Colombians demanded a leader capable of reuniting the country and rebuilding the economy. A Conservative seemed to fit the bill; a proud and energetic man, Rafael Reyes assumed dictatorial powers. His five-year term was stormy—despite an empty treasury and a bitter people, he was able to reorganize the national finances, restore Colombia's credit, initiate construction of roads and railroads and encourage development of the coffee industry. Opposition forced his resignation in 1909.

Five Conservative presidents followed him (1909–1930). This era was marked by advances in political realism and cooperation. Elections became more honest, a semblance of a two-party government was developed and censorship of the press was reduced. During the same period, the economy improved, production rose, petroleum was discovered and business grew with the boom years of the 1920s. The ready money brought on an expansion of industry: railroads and power plants were built and coffee production expanded. The affluence also corrupted public officials and led to over expansion and inflation.

The Great Depression produced a financial disaster that discredited the Conservatives, and in 1930 a Liberal government came to power.

The peaceful transfer of power in 1930 was in marked contrast to the violence found in other parts of Latin America and to Colombia's own past. So, too, the Liberals of 1930 were quite distinct from their predecessors. Most of the issues that had produced the civil wars of the previous century were dead or no longer important. The Liberal Party of 1930 was interested in economic and social reforms to protect the interests of labor and of the growing middle class.

The first of three elected Liberal presidents who would govern for the next 16 years, Enrique Olaya Herrera (1930–34), satisfied reform-minded Liberals while his moderation reassured Conservatives. The second, Alfonso López (1934–38), a wealthy publisher and intellectual, was far more outspoken and dynamic. To secure needed social reforms, he implemented radical changes in the constitution that frightened Conservatives. However, he tempered their fears with more moderate legislation. His successor, Eduardo Santos (1938–42), publisher of the influential Liberal daily *El Tiempo*, moved the country sharply back to the right, bringing denunciation from López and creating the first signs of the growing schism between the left and right wings of the party.

López returned to power in the 1942 election and brought the country into World War II on the side of the Allies, much to the displeasure of pro-Axis Conservatives and neutralists within his own party. Compounding López's problems, a corruption scandal erupted during his second administration that embroiled members of his own family. Increasingly, moderate Liberals joined with Conservatives in Congress to block his proposals. There were numerous plots against him, and he faced discontent from underpaid government employees. Under mounting pressure, he resigned in 1945 and was replaced by an interim president until the 1946 election.

La Violencia

The Liberal split led to the election of a Conservative, Mariano Ospina Pérez, in 1946 with a plurality of 42% of the vote. A timid man in the wrong job at the wrong time, he was incapable of controlling either the growing militancy of the Liberal left or the fanaticism of the crypto-fascists in his own party. Bloodshed erupted between elements of these two political extremes, and there were revolts in several departments.

The murder in April 1948 of Jorge Eliécer Gaitán, a popular leader of the Liberal left, touched off a riot in the capital of such violence that the term *Bogotazo* was coined to describe a situation in which a whole people rioted. Some 2,000 deaths resulted as mobs roamed the streets, burning, looting and shooting. The conflict spread throughout the country as Liberals and Conservatives fought for control of villages and rural communities. The president declared martial law and gradually restored an appearance of order. It was in this atmosphere that the elections of 1950 were held. The Liberal Party, badly split, expected trouble at the polls and stayed away; the Conservatives elected their candidate, Laureano Gómez.

President Gómez was an admirer of Franco and Hitler, and installed an ultra-rightist regime. Ruling as a dictator, he used the army and police to hunt down and exterminate the Liberals. From his regime there developed an undeclared civil war that caused an estimated 200,000 deaths and a way of life known as *La Violencia* (The Violence). In 1953, he was ousted by a military coup, and General Gustavo Rojas Pinilla was installed as president. The change, accompanied by an amnesty, brought a lull in the fighting. However, his administration proved cruel and incompetent. The sole redeeming feature of his rule was that he did not discriminate between Liberals and Conservatives, forcing these enemies to arrange a truce in order to oust him in 1957.

Democracy Takes Root

There followed a Liberal-Conservative coalition, known as the National Unity Agreement, which would alternate Liberal and Conservative presidents for 16 years. A Liberal, Alberto Lleras Camargo, took office on August 7, 1958. Having to cope not only with the conflict between the parties but with the equally bitter internal party strife, Lleras Camargo nonetheless succeeded in separating the politi-

Coffee plantation

cal antagonists from rural bandits who were capitalizing on a continuing reign of terror. He pursued moderate policies in social and economic matters while seeking political unity. His moderation restored a degree of stability, but the government, lacking a majority, was unable to enact any of the needed reforms.

Lleras Camargo's Conservative successor in 1962, Guillermo León Valencia, unable to obtain legislative cooperation for even the routine functions of government, was forced to rule by decree.

The Liberal regime that followed from 1966 to 1970 was forced to use the same system. Under President Carlos Lleras Restrepo, Colombia enjoyed a comfortable rate of economic growth and continued decline in traditional rural banditry and violence.

Misael Pastrana Borrero, a Conservative, was elected by a slim 1.5% majority over former dictator Rojas Pinilla in 1970. A politically unknown Conservative economist, Pastrana sought to diversify the farm-based economy. Although exports soared and certain sectors of the economy improved, runaway inflation and increasing unemployment became major issues in the 1974 election campaign.

With the National Unity Agreement expiring at the presidential level in 1974, Colombians voted in the nation's first open election in more than 20 years. Alfonso López Michelsen, a Liberal, was elected with 52% of the vote. In second place was the Conservative candidate, while Rojas Pinilla's daughter ran a strong third as an independent. Although the Liberals also had won large majorities in both houses of Congress, the Constitution required that all appointive offices be divided equally between the Liberals and Conservatives until 1978; this requirement was extended informally through 1986.

To carry out his program, the president declared a "national economic emergency" just five weeks after taking office in August 1974. Permitted under a 1968 law, the action allowed López to bypass the slow-moving Congress and institute by decree certain economic reforms. His plan included raising the daily wage by 40% to $1.50, imposing a hefty tax increase on the wealthy and on luxury imports and instituting a special tax on idle farmland to encourage greater agricultural output. In addition, various steps were taken to cut the inflation rate from 30% in 1974 to an estimated 20% in 1976.

These bold economic measures met stiff opposition. Conservatives charged that the new taxes were causing a recession and discouraging new investments. Leftists demanded even more radical change, particularly in the rural sector. The top 4% of the population owned 68% of the farm-

land while the bottom 73% of the people held just 7%. consisting of small plots that provided a living only for a small family. Largely as a result Two thirds of the nation's youth suffered from malnutrition.

The Liberal Party candidate, Julio César Turbay Ayala, defeated his Conservative opponent in 1978 by 140,000 votes. He immediately implemented his law-and-order promises by ordering an all-out military campaign against political violence, drug smuggling and general lawlessness.

Harsher tactics against guerrillas led to worldwide charges of human rights violations. Yet, the M-19 guerrilla front continued its sensational terrorism throughout 1980: seizure of 15 diplomats, murder of an American missionary and a 300-man attack on two provincial towns. In a murderous shoot-out with government troops in 1981 in which much of the M-19 high command died, more than 400 people were killed.

Liberal infighting ultimately resulted in a Conservative victory in the 1982 presidential election. The new president, Belisario Betancur, adopted a populist domestic policy to help the lower classes and a foreign policy more independent of the United States. The government was able to persuade some guerrillas to become part of the lawful political process.

Return to *La Violencia*

The next several administrations found themselves trying to deal with escalating violence from guerrillas, drug traffickers and right-wing paramilitary elements that was to make Colombia one of the most dangerous countries on Earth. Betancur ordered a crackdown on rampant drug trafficking in 1984. The powerful drug barons retaliated against the judiciary, and contributed heavily to the various guerrilla movements active in the country. When the president in turn authorized the extradition of the drug lords to the United States for trial, the cocaine producers hired guerrillas to wipe out the judges involved.

During the 1980s, about 100 revolutionary groups or coalitions were active, all dedicated to terrorism. Their threat was amply illustrated in 1985 when the *M-19* stormed the Palace of Justice using mortar fire and grenades. Betancur ordered the army to storm the building, resulting in the deaths of 11 Supreme Court justices and several other people. After the event, one Colombian judge said, "You either have the choice of accepting a $500,000 bribe from these people or be killed." In all, 350 judges and prosecutors were killed during the 1980s. Frozen with fear, the Colombian Supreme Court ruled the extradition treaty unconstitutional.

The next president, Virgilio Barco, a Liberal (1986–90), also declared war on the drug barons. Fearful of being extradited, the drug barons paralyzed efforts to control leftist guerrillas. They bribed or killed uncounted local police and eluded the national police and army. Crusading journalists also were assassinated. When a leading Liberal candidate for president, Luis Carlos Galán, was gunned down in 1989, Barco responded by reinstating the extradition laws. The terrified justice minister resigned, going into hiding in the United States with her son, fearful for their lives.

However, the lives of *Los Extraditables* also was hell on Earth. They increasingly became interested in a trial in Colombia and the possibility that bribes and favors would produce a lenient sentence in a country-club prison. In the interim, their drug business could be operated by their lieutenants.

Disillusioned by events in the former Soviet Union and Eastern Europe, *M-19* guerrillas began laying down their arms in 1989. Presidential elections were held in May 1990. After the notoriously bloodthirsty Medellín Cartel of Pablo Escobar assassinated Galán, yet another candidate, Carlos Pizarro, a former guerrilla commander, was assassinated by right-wing elements. Abandoning a promise to continue the war on drug leaders, César Gaviria of the Liberal Party won with less than a majority.

The war on the cartels was costly—there were 40 or more murders a day in Colombia. The cost of having a policeman killed was $4,000 and a judge was $20,000—pocket change for the drug barons. All officials traveled in armored vehicles in motorcades. The drug cartels proclaimed a unilateral truce in mid-1990 and the level of violence abated sharply. Gaviria decreed that any drug baron who surrendered and confessed would not be extradited to the United States and would have his Colombian jail sentence cut in half. These promises would prove costly.

In 1991, several kingpins, including Escobar and the Ochoa brothers, surrendered. Escobar was allowed to build his own luxurious "jail" close to Medellín, his home town. It was virtually an open house. Rated as one of the wealthiest men in the world, he enjoyed the company of 11 of his associates, claiming that the walls of the "jail" were in place to keep his enemies out. A deal obviously had been struck.

But even these pleasant conditions bored Escobar. He started running his cocaine business from the "jail," and used it as a site for the execution of real and imagined rivals. This was too much for the government and, exasperated, it sent a force to seize the "jail" and its prime oc-

Colombia

cupant. But Escobar was forewarned and escaped in July 1992. He was hunted not only by federal forces, but by an impromptu group of former henchmen turned into reward-seekers (the United States and Colombia had posted $8.7 million for his capture). Loosely organized, they were known as *"Los Pepes"* (People Persecuted by Pablo Escobar).

Weary, he offered to surrender in the spring of 1993, but the terms were impossible. He hid for several weeks in Medellín in late 1993, but was located by means of a traced telephone call. He and his bodyguard "offered resistance" and were shot dead on December 2 trying to elude pursuers on the rooftop of the building in which he had hidden. His funeral was sheer pandemonium as thousands paid him tribute; he had given generously to many people and causes. The fact was, he had a huge surplus of money that *had* to be given away.

After 1990, Cali replaced Medellín as the center of the cocaine trade with its own cartel of drug overlords, chiefly the Rodríguez Orejuela brothers. It eventually controlled 80% of the world's cocaine production and trade. Its leadership has changed several times in theory. When jailed, the drug kingpins operate from cells and their orders are carried out by an constantly changing army of lieutenants. An elaborate system of distribution and money laundering is in place and functions smoothly. The profits are enormous, and now are no longer being made by distribution using small aircraft. There are many remote airports in Mexico where a 747 can land and quickly unload at night. Mexico is now the route of transport of an estimated 70% of the cocaine entering the United States.

A new prosecutor general, Gustavo de Greiff, angered both U.S. Attorney General Janet Reno and many Colombian officials by suggesting that drug legalization be given serious consideration. He met with three kingpins of the Cali Cartel to discuss a plea bargain, whereby none of them would receive more than five years in a country-club prison. U.S. and Colombian officials were dismayed. De Greiff resigned when he reached the mandatory retirement age in 1994 and the Supreme Court named as his replacement Alfonso Valdivieso. The new special prosecutor's tenure thus began at precisely the same time as a new president's, one who was shrouded with scandal even before taking office and who never shook it off.

The Samper Presidency

Ernesto Samper, the Liberal candidate in 1994, bragged in his campaign that he bore 11 bullet wounds from an assassination attempt by drug traffickers. Indeed, he had survived an attempt on his life in 1989 by the Medellín Cartel. He emerged the front-runner in the first round of voting in May 1994, and he was elected president in the June runoff by a razor-thin margin over his Conservative opponent, Andrés Pastrana.

Between his election victory and his inauguration in August, however, a series of audiotapes of telephone conversations between Samper or members of his campaign staff and kingpins of the Cali Cartel were leaked to the press, which quickly dubbed them the "narcocassettes." Thus, Samper was sworn into office under a cloud. In his first year in office, his defense minister, who had been his campaign manager, was arrested and admitted that

the Samper campaign had accepted about $6 million in assistance from the Cali Cartel. Samper became a pariah to the United States, and in 1996 the Clinton Administration revoked Colombia's certification as an ally in the war against drugs.

Samper also was under pressure at home to resign because of the embarrassing revelations. When he refused, the lower house of Congress brought impeachment charges. But the House of Representatives voted decisively not to impeach; even the opposition Conservatives voted by a two-vote margin against impeachment. Why? Some observers contended that the House of Representatives was fearful of the political turmoil that would result from removing a president. Still others believed that Congress wanted to send a signal to the United States not to interfere in Colombia's internal affairs.

Samper's exoneration, despite convincing evidence, infuriated the United States. The U.S. ambassador waged an almost daily war of words, not only against Samper but the Colombian government as a whole. The United States took an extraordinary step when it revoked Samper's visa to visit the United States, a stunning rebuke of a sitting chief of state.

Samper was again humiliated when a stash of heroin was discovered on the presidential aircraft just as it was about to take the president to New York to address the United Nations—on the war against drugs! Authorities impounded his plane, and he had to fly to New York on a commercial aircraft. (Three Colombian Air Force soldiers were later charged with having smuggled the heroin onto the aircraft.)

In 1997, the Clinton Administration again refused to certify Colombia as an ally in the drug war. Still, Samper hung tough, and vowed to serve until the end of his term.

Meanwhile, Valdivieso began to enjoy some success in his campaign against the Cali Cartel. In 1996, the Rodríguez Orejuela brothers, Gilberto and Miguel, surrendered separately to authorities and were incarcerated in La Picota, a country-club prison, to await trial. A third Cali Cartel kingpin, José Santacruz Londoño, also surrendered but later opted to escape. He subsequently was gunned down, ostensibly by a rival drug gang. A judge sentenced Gilberto Rodríguez Orejuela to 10½ years in prison; Miguel subsequently was sentenced to terms of nine and 22 years. Both the U.S. and Colombian governments expressed outrage over the lightness of the sentences. The sentences were another factor in the continued decertification of Colombia as an ally in the drug war.

Another major kingpin, Helmer "Pacho" Herrera, was sentenced in 1998 to six

A view of Medellín

years and eight months in prison. Herrera was murdered in his jail cell seven months later, apparently in a contract killing by a rival drug gang.

In December 1997, the Clinton administration lifted its ban on military aid, suspended because of alleged human rights abuses by the army and the paramilitary groups it was accused of supporting. But the United States stipulated the $37 million could be used only for operations against guerrillas suspected of dealing with narcotics traffickers, and those operations were to be confined to an area in the south referred to as "the Box." In 1998, for the first time in three years, the Clinton administration "certified" Colombia as an ally in the drug war.

Guerrilla Warfare Stalemates

Coupled with the Colombian government's inability to come to grips with drug trafficking has been its stalemated war against the guerrilla groups, principally the Revolutionary Armed Forces of Colombia (*FARC*) and the National Liberation Army (*ELN*). Another once-nettlesome group, *M-19*, abandoned its armed struggle to participate in the electoral system, with minimal success. The *FARC* and *ELN* continued to hold sway over vast areas of the rugged interior, but with a new twist. In the wake of the collapse of the Soviet Union, the two groups appeared to have become motivated less by ideology and more by greed, and that they have become mercenary forces in the hire of the drug traffickers. In other words, they have become common outlaws, much as Jesse James and other former Confederate guerrillas did after the U.S. Civil War.

More than 40,000 people, military and civilian, have been killed since the insurgency erupted in the early 1960s. The rebels have disrupted the country's vital oil pipeline to the Caribbean coast regularly, they continue to assassinate or kidnap local, state and national officials, and they frequently kidnap domestic and foreign businessmen for astronomical ransoms that help them purchase sophisticated arms on the international black market. However, the rebels lack the military strength to take Bogotá by storm. It has been a classic military stalemate.

In municipal elections in 1997, guerrillas murdered dozens of candidates and frightened hundreds of others into withdrawing. Tens of thousands of voters, intimidated by rebel threats of violence, stayed home.

In 1998, the *FARC* launched a Tet-like offensive designed to disrupt the congressional elections. The rebels inflicted the worst defeat to date on the army in 30 years. The brunt of the fighting took place in Caquetá. At least 83 soldiers were killed and another 61 captured.

The guerrillas and the armed forces are not the only key players in this protracted guerrilla war. Another is the various right-wing paramilitary groups that have committed numerous atrocities against civilians, mostly peasants, who are suspected of rebel sympathies. International human rights groups have alleged that these groups have the tacit support of the army, which the army continues to deny. In 1997, Carlos Castaño, leader of the most notorious of these groups, brought 5,000 paramilitary fighters together under the umbrella of the so-called United Self-Defense Forces of Colombia (*AUC*). In 1997 and 1998, the *AUC* was responsible for several civilian massacres in different departments, many of which brought reprisals from the guerrillas. By 2003, the *AUC* was believed to have 10,000 fighters under arms.

Pastrana Seeks Peace

The Liberals nominated President Samper's hand-picked candidate, former Interior Minister Horacio Serpa, for president in 1998. But Serpa's nomination threatened to split the party as anti-Samper reformers, led by Representative Ingrid Betancourt of the so-called Liberal Oxygen faction, denounced him.

The Conservatives, meanwhile, renominated Andrés Pastrana, who narrowly lost to Samper in 1994, while retired General Harold Bedoya, whom Samper had sacked the previous July, launched an independent candidacy, as did Noemí Sanín, who had served as a cabinet minister under both Betancur and Gaviria.

In the congressional elections in March, the Liberals won 53 of the 102 Senate seats to 27 for the Conservatives and about the same proportion of seats in the 161-member House of Representatives. Turnout was a higher-than-expected 44%, despite the backdrop of a guerrilla offensive and the usual voter apathy. The maverick Betancourt won her Senate seat by the largest majority of any candidate.

Polls for the first round on May 31 showed Pastrana with a strong lead. But on election day, which this author covered as a free-lance journalist, Serpa emerged with a razor-thin first-place finish of 34.3% to Pastrana's 34.0Sanín drew 26.6%, the largest vote for an independent candidate since Rojas Pinilla in 1970. The guerrillas behaved themselves, permitting a record turnout of 10.7 million voters.

Four days before the June runoff, the media reported that a Pastrana representative had met with Manuel "Tirofijo" Marulanda of the *FARC*, who declared that Pastrana was the candidate with the greater chance of negotiating peace. This crippled Serpa, whose slogan was "the road to peace." In a record turnout of 12 million voters, 59% of those eligible, Pastrana won with 50.4% to Serpa's 46.5%, almost the identical margin by which Pastrana had lost to Samper four years before. The remaining 3.1% cast blank ballots in protest.

Pastrana, 44, took office on August 7, 1998. He was the son of former President Misael Pastrana. He was schooled as a lawyer but eschewed that profession in favor of broadcast journalism, which he practiced until he was elected to the Bogotá city council in the 1980s. He was elected mayor in 1988 and a senator in 1991.

Plaza de Bolívar, Bogotá

Colombia

Shortly after his inauguration, Pastrana met again with Marulanda. Much to the army's displeasure, Pastrana agreed to the *FARC*'s demand to demilitarize an area the size of Switzerland in Caquetá as a pre-condition to peace talks. Pastrana fired the army commander because of his opposition. Pastrana rejected, however, a guerrilla proposal to exchange captured soldiers and policemen for 452 rebel prisoners.

Those who had hoped for a cessation of hostilities in anticipation of the peace talks were cruelly disillusioned in late 1998 when the *FARC* launched its biggest push since the Caguan offensive, this time in coca-rich Vaupes Department in the southeast. The rebels overran the departmental capital, Mitu, near the Brazilian border, killing 60 policemen and 10 civilians; another 40 policemen were taken prisoner. The army suffered heavy casualties retaking the town. Despite the rebel offensive, the army meekly completed the demilitarization in Caquetá.

In a separate development, the U.S. Congress tripled the amount of aid to the Colombian police for its drug-fighting efforts, to $289 million. In 1999, the Clinton administration, which had not requested the dramatic increase in counterdrug aid, recertified Colombia as an ally in the drug war.

The peace talks began on schedule in January 1999, but days later the *AUC* killed 130 alleged guerrilla sympathizers. Pastrana flew to Havana and met with Fidel Castro and Venezuelan President-elect Hugo Chávez to solicit their intercession with the guerrillas. Nonetheless, the *FARC* broke off the talks, demanding that Pastrana clamp down on the paramilitaries.

Perhaps as part of an effort to placate the *FARC* and jump-start the peace talks, Prosecutor General Alfonso Gómez ordered the arrest of an army lieutenant colonel in connection with the grisly 1997 massacre by paramilitary forces of about 30 peasants in the town of Mapiripán, in Meta Department.

Peace talks and warfare dragged on simultaneously. In November 1999, government and *FARC* representatives met in Sweden, and Pastrana suggested a ceasefire for the holiday season. Within days, the *FARC* responded with one of its largest offensives in months, launching coordinated attacks in six departments. Still, government and *FARC* representatives met again at the Vatican in February 2000 with a representative of Pope John Paul II, with inconclusive results. By May, a frustrated, angry Pastrana was threatening to break off the talks. The *FARC*'s blasé response: If you want to. That November, the *FARC* suspended the talks indefinitely, ostensibly to protest the government's failure to curtail army involvement with the paramilitaries. Pastrana offered to extend the terms of the euphemistically named demilitarized zone—in reality a safe haven for the highly militarized guerrillas—if the *FARC* would return to the bargaining table. Pastrana met with Marulanda again in the jungle and agreed to an eight-month extension of the safe haven and a purging of the army's ranks of suspected collaborators with the *AUC*.

In February 2001, an army tribunal sentenced a brigadier general to only 40 months for failing to stop the 1997 Mapiripán massacre. Pastrana pushed through a law mandating that armed forces personnel accused of human rights violations would henceforth be tried in civilian, not military, courts.

Yet, the killing continued. Although the armed forces scored a few impressive tactical victories, they also suffered humiliating setbacks. In October 2000, 800 *FARC* guerrillas attacked a town in Urubá Department. Five Blackhawk helicopters brought elite troops to the rescue. One was shot down by ground fire, killing all 22 men on board; a second was grounded by mechanical failure; the other three reached their landing zone, but the 60 troops were annihilated after they landed. In March 2001, the *FARC* killed 17 marines in an attack in the south. In another incident, the *FARC* "executed" 13 policemen it had taken prisoner in the town of Roncesvalles. Apparently, the *FARC* was competing with the *AUC* to seize the moral low ground.

A prisoner exchange occurred in June 2001, when the *FARC* released a badly wounded police colonel and three other officers. In exchange, the government released 73 ill prisoners. The *FARC* then released 242 more prisoners, leaving only an estimated 42 still in its hands. Some hailed the exchange as the most positive product of the two and a half years of "peace" talks, while some skeptics claimed the *FARC* was only ridding itself of a logistical burden.

The public had good reason to be skeptical. A report released by the president's human rights office showed that in the first four months of 2001, the number of killings by non-governmental forces had actually *increased* by 75% over the previous year. Of those deaths, 529 were attributed to the *AUC*, 190 to the *FARC* and 50 to the *ELN*.

For its part, the *ELN* demanded that the government create a demilitarized zone for it in the north as it had for the *FARC*

Bogotá, Colombia

in the south, although it was more modest in its demand: "only" 2,300 square miles. Amazingly, despite the failure of the concessions to the *FARC* to bring peace, Pastrana agreed to demilitarize three municipalities in Bolívar and Antioquía departments, a total of about 1,800 square miles, to appease the *ELN*.

Government and *ELN* representatives met in Geneva in 2000, but the talks were unproductive. Pastrana at first refused to yield to the demands for a safe haven, but after the *ELN* staged some spectacular kidnappings as a show of force, the jelly-spined Pastrana acquiesced in 2001, agreeing to a reduced area of about 1,100 square miles, still larger than Rhode Island. Residents in the area, spurred in part by the *AUC*, protested their government's surrendering them and their lands to the *ELN*'s control in exchange for—nothing.

The *AUC's* strength was estimated at 8,000 in 2001. It flouted the rules of warfare by massacring civilians to achieve its nebulous goals. One such atrocity was a raid in Cauca state in 2001 in which 32 civilians were reported killed; the arms of a 17-year-old girl were severed with a chain saw. The U.S. government formally declared the *AUC* a terrorist organization in 2001, and added it to the list of terror organizations to which Americans may be prosecuted for contributing money.

A milestone for the *AUC* came with Castaño's supposed resignation in 2001, ostensibly because he could not control the more bloodthirsty elements. In reality he merely yielded the *AUC*'s military command to Salvatore Mancuso, perceived as more of a hardliner than Castaño. In a 2002 interview at a mountain hideout, Mancuso boasted that the *AUC* numbered 14,000 effectives and promised even greater bloodshed.

The *FARC* broke off talks again in early 2002 and Pastrana gave it 48 hours to abandon the demilitarized zone. He then dispatched troops into the area. The *FARC* responded with a 14-point negotiating plan, which Pastrana at first rejected, but then acquiesced again. The *FARC* responded to the president's show of good faith by setting off bombs in a town 30 miles from Bogotá and by attacking a prison and freeing 39 rebels, killing four soldiers. Yet, Pastrana caved in again and agreed to resume cease-fire negotiations, to be brokered by the United Nations. The *FARC* responded by setting off a car bomb in Bogotá that killed five people; then it dynamited 50 electrical towers and the dam that provides Bogotá with its water supply. Thousands of *capitalinos* poured into the streets for a mass demonstration against the *FARC*, banging on pots and pans in the traditional Latin American form of nonviolent protest, the *cacerolazo*.

Former President Andrés Pastrana

Events then exploded in a dramatic and violent chain reaction. In February 2002, after the *FARC* hijacked a domestic airliner and forced it to land, kidnapping a prominent senator on board, Pastrana finally realized the futility of attempting to negotiate with people of bad faith and broke off the peace talks. He sent the army into the safe haven and ordered the air force to bomb and strafe *FARC* base camps and landing strips in the zone; the military met surprisingly feeble resistance.

In response, the *FARC* kidnapped independent presidential candidate Ingrid Betancourt. She remained a hostage until she was rescued in 2008. The *FARC* then went on a rampage of assassinations, bombings and kidnappings. It made an unsuccessful attempt to assassinate the front-running presidential candidate Alvaro Uribe, who was calling for a military victory over the *FARC* (see The Elections of 2002), and it kidnapped the governor of Antioquía. But the worst was yet to come.

In May 2002, about 1,000 *FARC* and 600 *AUC* fighters engaged in a bloody battle for the village of Bella Vista in Chocó Department. More than 500 civilians were huddled in a church for safety during the battle when a *FARC* gas-cylinder mortar shell crashed through the roof and exploded, killing and dismembering 117 people, including 40 children. The *FARC* admitted firing the mortar round but claimed the church had been hit by accident. It cynically blamed the *AUC* for the appalling death toll, saying the civilians should not have been in the town—where they lived. It took the army eight days to reach the area. The Bella Vista atrocity shocked an already numbed Colombia, as well as the international community.

The U.N. human rights representative to Colombia called it a "war crime."

Pastrana asked a U.N. human rights investigating team to visit the area. In a scathing report, it concluded the *FARC* was directly responsible for the deaths, but it blamed the *AUC* for putting the civilians in harm's way and it assailed the Pastrana government for ignoring warnings the United Nations had given it that a violent confrontation was imminent. It also castigated the army for its tardiness in reaching the town. The U.S. Congress, meanwhile, demanded to know why the army, which was the beneficiary of so much U.S. aid, had responded so slowly.

Because of Bella Vista, the European Union acceded to a request from Pastrana to follow the U.S. lead in declaring the *FARC* a terrorist organization.

The guerrilla war soured Colombia's relations with neighboring Venezuela. In 2001, the government of President Hugo Chávez, long suspected of being sympathetic to the Colombian guerrillas, admitted it had captured, then released, an *ELN* member suspected in a 1999 airplane hijacking. Pastrana and Chávez met at the Venezuelan town of Puerto Ordaz. By then Venezuela had rearrested the hijack suspect, and Pastrana was pressing for his extradition. The two presidents announced that Venezuela would serve as an active partner in the negotiations between the Colombian government and the guerrillas and that their two armed forces would exchange intelligence information. However, Colombian intelligence was aware that aircraft regularly flew between Venezuela's border region and the *FARC* safe haven.

A potentially important new variable was added to this already complex equation in 2002 when the Bush administration asked Congress to approve additional military aid for Colombia. In a major policy shift, Secretary of State Colin Powell said the aid should be used against the guerrillas, not just against the drug traffickers. The United States saw the *FARC* as just another international terrorist organization to be included in its war on terrorism in the wake of the September 11, 2001 attacks. The *FARC*'s alleged international links had been spotlighted when three suspected members of the Irish Republican Army were arrested in Colombia, accused of providing the *FARC* with terror training. In fact, the *FARC*'s bombings in Bogotá had distinct IRA fingerprints.

"Plan Colombia"

As the peace talks and the fighting both droned on, Pastrana outlined a six-year, $7.5 billion plan to destroy the drug trade. Called *"Plan Colombia,"* it included ex-

Colombia

panded enforcement as well as incentives to farmers to plant alternative crops. The Clinton administration had asked Congress in 2000 for $1.6 billion for aid to both the Colombian police and army for their counter-drug operations. Among the hardware included for *Plan Colombia* were 30 sophisticated Blackhawk helicopters. As usual, the administration insisted that the new aid money for the army would be used only against drug traffickers, not against the guerrillas, thus seeking to perpetuate the myth that the two were distinguishable and unrelated.

The U.S. Congress approved a reduced $1.3 billion aid package, which Clinton quickly signed into law. Colombia thus became the third-largest recipient of U.S. military aid after Israel and Egypt. Clinton met with Pastrana in Cartagena.

U.S. Special Forces, or "Green Berets," trained a special counter-drug brigade of three battalions, totaling 3,000 men. The brigade received 16 Blackhawks and 25 SuperHueys. The *FARC* denounced *Plan Colombia*, using it as a convenient pretext for scuttling the peace talks. Clearly, they were feeling the pinch.

The new U.S. president, George W. Bush, upped the ante for *Plan Colombia*. In 2001, Congress approved an additional $676 million to battle the Colombian drug trade, a 50% increase. However, with all that money, some of it was bound to go bad. In 2002, the U.S. Congress partially suspended further aid for the drug war when Colombian media and the U.S. Embassy reported that $2 million had disappeared. Six officers of the national police's anti-drug unit were fired, and the commander himself resigned.

A major event in the drug war occurred in 2001 when Fabio Ochoa, an alleged kingpin of the old Medellín cartel, was extradited to the United States. It was a major departure for Colombia, which had not extradited such a notorious suspect in more than 10 years. Ochoa was convicted in Miami in 2003.

According to the U.N. Drug Control Program, the number of hectares under coca cultivation in Colombia declined by 11% from 2000 to 2001, to 145,000, and by another 30% in 2002. There were even greater inroads under the new government of President Alvaro Uribe, who took office in August 2002.

The Elections of 2002

Meanwhile, the hapless president's Conservative Party lost badly in the departmental and municipal elections in 2000, a bellwether for the presidential contest in May 2002. The Conservatives failed to win a single governorship, while the Liberals and independents each won 15.

The campaigns were marked by the usual violence and intimidation; more than 20 candidates were killed either by left-wing guerrillas or right-wing paramilitaries.

In the presidential race, the Liberals again nominated Horacio Serpa. The Conservatives nominated Juan Camilo Restrepo, who had been Pastrana's finance minister. Once again, there were several independent candidates, seemingly assuring the race would be thrown into a runoff again: Noemí Sanín, who polled over a fourth of the vote in 1998; Senator Ingrid Betancourt, a prominent Liberal renegade who had supported Pastrana in 1998; and Álvaro Uribe, a former Liberal governor of Antioquía, candidate of a movement called *Primero Colombia*, who pledged to get tough with the guerrillas. Rounding out the field was Luis Eduardo Garzón of the far-left Social and Political Front. It looked like Colombian politics as usual—but this election would not be usual.

As the peace talks droned on and the *FARC* outrages continued, Uribe suddenly broke from the pack by promising to double the size of the military and seek an all-out victory over the guerrillas. His campaign slogan was *"mano firme, corazón grande"* (firm hand, big heart). After the peace talks collapsed and Betancourt was kidnapped, he soared to 59% in the polls.

In the congressional elections, the Liberals retained their majorities in both houses, but at least 27 new senators publicly declared their support for Uribe (the *AUC* claimed that 35% of the new Congress were its sympathizers). Voters clearly were in a get-tough mood.

Restrepo dropped out, leaving the Conservative Party without a presidential candidate for the first time since it was founded in 1849.

Uribe's tough anti-*FARC* rhetoric was not lost on the guerrillas. They attempted to assassinate him by setting off a remote-controlled bomb under a bridge on a highway near Barranquilla as his motorcade passed. He escaped unhurt, but three bystanders were killed and 15 injured. For Uribe, the attack was *déjà vu*; in 1983, his father had been killed when he resisted a *FARC* kidnap attempt.

The attempt on Uribe's life only boosted his standing in the polls. A desperate Serpa alleged that Uribe was drawing support from the right-wing paramilitaries; Uribe denied it.

The results on May 26 were a veritable landslide, not just a mandate in favor of the hawk, Uribe, over the dove, Serpa, but a repudiation of the guerrillas. A total of 11.2 million Colombians voted, a turnout of 46.3%. Uribe scored a decisive first-round victory with 5.7 million votes, or 52.9%; Serpa received 3.5 million, or 31.7%. Garzón was a distant third, fol-

lowed closely by Sanín; Betancourt, still in *FARC* captivity, was a poor fifth.

The president-elect announced he still favored a U.N.-brokered peace with the guerrillas but that he was willing to engage in peace talks with the paramilitaries. He promised to continue the war against drugs, to reduce corruption and increase efficiency in government, and to increase social spending.

A Harvard-educated lawyer, Uribe, 50, had a positive record as an efficient governor of Antioquía. He met with President Bush in Washington and other senior officials and in New York with U.N. Secretary-General Kofi Annan. Back home, he advocated a constitutional amendment to allow him to declare a state of emergency to deal with the guerrillas, which gave chills to human rights advocates.

Uribe Gets Tough

Uribe was inaugurated on August 7, 2002—indoors for security reasons. Pastrana, an Andean version of Neville Chamberlain, left office a pitiful failure, with an approval rating of 20%. The *FARC* launched a mortar attack near the National Palace in an attempt to disrupt the inauguration, killing 19 people and injuring 60.

Uribe soon made it clear he would be as tough as Pastrana had been spineless. He declared a 90-day state of emergency to crack down on the guerrillas, the paramilitaries and the narcotraffickers, though human rights advocates feared an erosion of civil liberties. Roadblocks, ID checks and warrantless arrests became commonplace, and some parts of the country were placed under martial law. The state of emergency was twice extended, until May 2003.

Uribe proposed equipping 1 million citizens with two-way radios so they could report guerrilla activity; recruiting for volunteers was brisk. Uribe also introduced an emergency war tax to pay for his promised military buildup. In Antioquía, he gave local military commanders a dressing down—reported on national television—for failing to take action against reported guerrilla activity in the area, in effect telling them to shape up and fight or resign. He ordered the training of young farmers to create a rural militia that numbered 12,000.

The first major battles between the army and the *FARC* after Uribe's inauguration came in September in Meta and Tolima departments. Both were decisive army victories that left 100 guerrillas dead in Meta and 22 in Tolima. Later clashes near Bogotá and in Antioquía left another 21 guerrillas dead. Army casualties were light.

Uribe visited Washington again to lobby for $450 million in military and counternarcotics aid, assuring liberal U.S. senators

Santuario (sanctuary) de las Lajas in Nariño State in southwestern Colombia, partially built into the rock of the mountain
Courtesy: Embassy of Colombia

Colombia

he would respect human rights. He visited again with Annan, who admonished him to clean up Colombia's human rights act. Bush's State Department certified that Colombia passed muster under a U.S. law that denies aid to countries that violate human rights, and it released the first $41.6 million in aid. The United States already had announced it would step up its training of Colombian officers and NCOs and a new brigade for pipeline security. Secretary of State Powell visited Bogotá in 2002 and sent mixed signals by praising Uribe's get-tough policy, while warning Colombia that the United States would not tolerate human rights abuses.

Uribe's policy was not to negotiate with the *FARC*, the *ELN* or the *AUC* as long as they were engaging in combat, but he held out the promise of renewed talks to any group that declared a unilateral cease-fire. It paid off; the *AUC* declared a unilateral cease-fire beginning December 1, 2002.

The *AUC* leadership felt the heat not only of the army and the *FARC*, but of the U.S. Justice Department. U.S. Attorney General John Ashcroft unsealed indictments against Castaño and Mancuso in 2002 alleging they were instrumental in the shipment of 17 tons of cocaine to the United States since 1997 and calling them a threat to U.S. national security.

Talks between the government and the *AUC* began, but at least 1,500 *AUC* renegade members refused to participate. Castaño warned them that they face "annihilation" if they did not. The talks broke down in 2003 after the *AUC* accused the army of "massacring" 12 *AUC* members. The army said they were killed in an ambush.

The *AUC* suffered another blow in 2003 when one of its most notorious commanders, Said Sepulveda, believed responsible for the deaths of 450 people, was captured by the army. That July, Mancuso announced the *AUC* would lay down its arms because of the army's successes against the *FARC*, promising a complete demobilization by the end of 2005.

The *FARC* and *ELN* remained in the field, although tenuous lines of communication to the government remained open through third parties—France for the *FARC*, Cuba for the *ELN*.

In February 2003, the *FARC* set off a powerful car bomb that gutted a 10-story social club in Bogotá frequented by the capital's elite. The death toll of 35 included six children; another 168 people were injured. It was the worst act of terrorism in Bogotá since the bloody days of Pablo Escobar, and it sparked national outrage. Another *FARC* atrocity turned into an international incident when a small counterdrug aircraft carrying four American "contractors" for the U.S. Southern Command and

one Colombian crashed behind *FARC* lines. The Colombian sergeant and one American were apparently executed by the rebels, who took the other three Americans prisoner. The Colombian government bristled, however, when the Bush administration sent a reported 150 troops to search for the three Americans, calling it an interference in Colombia's internal affairs. It was an incredible windfall for the *FARC*, which announced it was holding the Americans as "prisoners of war" and said they would be released in exchange for dozens of rebel prisoners. They were eventually rescued by Colombian special forces in 2008.

In an even bolder act, the *FARC* executed 10 hostages, including former Antioquía Governor Guillermo Gaviría, who had been kidnapped in 1997, when the army attempted a raid to rescue them in 2003. The army and air force retaliated, bombarding *FARC* positions in Cauca and Meta, killing 67 rebels.

The government claimed a major political victory over the *FARC* in 2003 when Rafael Rojas, commander of the *FARC's* 46th Front, surrendered and, in a nationally televised event with Uribe in Cartagena, urged his former comrades to do the same.

The already tense relations with Venezuela over Chávez's alleged support for the guerrillas were strained further when Colombian peasants reported that Venezuelan air force jets and helicopters crossed the border in March 2003, providing close air support for *FARC* rebels battling paramilitaries in North Santander Department. Uribe ordered an investigation, and confronted Venezuela with the evidence. Venezuelan Vice President José Vicente Rangel dismissed the reports as "an arsenal of lies." Uribe and Chávez met face-to-face in Puerto Ordaz, Venezuela, but the meeting produced little of substance.

A low-ranking judge suddenly created an international incident in 2002 when he ordered the release of Gilberto and Miguel Rodríguez Orejuela, the imprisoned leaders of the Cali cocaine cartel, after they had served only about half their terms. Uribe tried to block their release by appealing to another court. That judge ordered that Miguel, 59, be retained in prison, but agreed that Gilberto, 63, should be released for "good behavior." This infuriated Uribe—and U.S. authorities who had long sought the brothers' extradition. They watched helplessly as the elder kingpin walked free. However, he was rearrested in 2003 on an outstanding charge that he shipped 330 pounds of cocaine to the United States—in 1995. Both were extradited to the United States, Gilberto in 2004 and Miguel in 2005.

In a major development in the guerrilla war—and possibly a sign that Uribe's

crackdown was having an effect—the *FARC* and the *ELN* in 2003 re-established an alliance that had dissolved nearly 20 years before and declared they would engage in joint military actions against the Uribe government. But the momentum clearly remained on the side of the army, which continued to win victories in the field.

In 2004, the *FARC's* Ricardo Palmera, alias Simón Trinidad, was arrested in Ecuador, the highest-ranking *FARC* leader to be captured to date.

Uribe then made a new peace overture to the *ELN*, probably hoping to drive a wedge between the two guerrilla movements. In 2005, the *ELN* agreed to meet with Uribe's representatives in Havana in talks brokered by Colombian Nobel Laureate novelist Gabriel García Márquez (see Culture).

Meanwhile, security forces continued to inflict battlefield losses on the paramilitaries as well, even as negotiations continued. In 2003, 800 *AUC* effectives laid down their arms in Medellín, and in 2004, the *AUC* signed an agreement with the government's peace negotiator by which they would move into a 230-square-mile safe haven as a first step toward demobilization. The inducement was a generous amnesty offer and even cash rewards, which had human rights groups protesting that some of the *AUC* leaders should be tried for war crimes. The United States, meanwhile, wanted some of them extradited for drug trafficking. Uribe compromised and agreed that *AUC* members could be tried for atrocities before a special war crimes tribunal and would face five to 10 years in prison. But he did not agree to extradite them.

Castaño mysteriously vanished in 2004 and was believed killed by a rival faction that opposed demobilization. Former *AUC* leader Carlos Mauricio García, who had opposed the *AUC's* involvement in drug trafficking, was gunned down in a Bogotá neighborhood in 2004.

Defense Minister Jorge Alberto Uribe, no relation to the president, announced that 16,000 members of the *FARC*, *ELN* or *AUC* had been killed or captured or had surrendered during 2003. Moreover, the murder rate in 2003, though still high by most international standards, was the lowest since 1986. By 2006, it was lower still.

Uribe also could claim a major victory in the "third war," the war on drugs. The U.N. Office on Drugs and Crime stated in a report that in the first seven months of 2003, 81,500 acres of coca had been destroyed, mostly through the U.S. fumigation program, an increase of 32% from the acreage destroyed in 2002.

Nonetheless, the Colombian electorate dealt Uribe an unexpected setback in the

2003 municipal elections. A major winner was Lucho Guzmán of the moderate left movement Democratic Pole, who was elected mayor of Bogotá.

In addition, a group of 80 human rights organizations issued a scathing report in 2003 titled "The Authoritarian Curse," which accused Uribe of sanctioning human rights abuses and of undermining civil liberties. Uribe accused his critics of being sympathetic to "terrorists." He defended his approach to combating the guerrillas and *narcos* in a speech to the U.N. General Assembly.

In its 2004 annual report, the Office of the U.N. High Commissioner for Human Rights called the human rights situation in Colombia "critical." However, the report also praised the government for restoring law and order in wide areas once held by the guerrillas, and it also assailed the guerrillas and the paramilitaries. Jan Egeland, U.N. under-secretary for humanitarian affairs, called the situation in Colombia a "humanitarian catastrophe." Egeland noted that the number of displaced persons had risen to 1 million, third highest in the world behind Congo and Sudan; by 2006, the number of displaced persons was second only to Sudan, some 2.5 million.

Bush, however, continued to support Uribe. The Bush administration asked Congress in 2004 to increase aid to Colombia by nearly $700 million, while the Pentagon asked Congress to double the limit on military and civilian advisers to Colombia to 800 each.

The armed forces continued to make gains in the wars against the guerrillas and the paramilitaries, although victory remained elusive. James LeMoyne, the U.N. negotiator who had been trying since 2001 to negotiate an agreement between the government and the *FARC*, finally gave up in frustration in 2005.

A major *FARC* leader, Ricardo Palmera, was extradited to the United States in 2005 to face drug charges. In 2006, Ramón Isaza, head of the *AUC*'s Medio Magdalena Bloc, and 1,000 of his operatives laid down their arms in a public ceremony. That brought to 22,000 the number of paramilitaries who had accepted amnesty.

Colombian authorities discovered a cache of 13.8 tons of cocaine worth $400 million in a wooden underground chamber near the Pacific coast in 2005, the largest seizure of cocaine ever on Colombian soil. Some of the cocaine belonged to the *FARC* and some to the *AUC*; the two battlefield rivals had actually contracted with the same trafficker!

On the down side, the White House Office for National Drug Control Policy admitted that the number of hectares of coca eradicated in 2004, 114,000, was es-

President Álvaro Uribe Vélez

sentially unchanged from 2003, although it is still one third less than in 2001. Moreover, the street value of cocaine in the United States and Europe had actually *decreased*, suggesting that supply had not been affected.

Relations between Colombia and Venezuela grew tense again in 2004 after Colombia announced the capture of Rodrigo Granda, the *FARC*'s foreign affairs representative. Colombia claimed Granda had been arrested in Cucuta, a Colombian town near the border. Soon, however, Colombian and Venezuelan newspapers reported that Granda had, in fact, been abducted in Caracas by Colombian agents aided by some Venezuelans. Chávez called for an investigation, and Uribe acknowledged that Granda had been captured in Caracas. Chávez denounced the violation of Venezuelan sovereignty, canceled bilateral trade agreements, recalled his ambassador and demanded that Uribe apologize, without offering an explanation of why or how Granda was in Venezuela in the first place and was given Venezuelan citizenship. Uribe did not apologize. The two presidents held an amiable, even jovial meeting in Santa Marta, Colombia, in December 2005, during which Uribe acknowledged that several Colombian officers had been conspiring with anti-Chávez Venezuelan officers and vowed to prevent such intrigue.

Re-election

Uribe's approval rating soared to 80% in late 2003, and he introduced a constitutional amendment that would permit him to run for re-election in 2006, but the Senate rejected it. He tried again. A poll indicated that 72% of Colombians favored it, and both major parties endorsed it. The

amendment faced a total of eight votes in the Senate and Chamber of Representatives, then it was submitted to the Constitutional Court, which finally approved it in 2005.

A faction of pro-Uribe Liberals defected and formed the Social National Unity Party, nicknamed the "U Party." Traditional Liberals reacted to the news predictably, saying it smacked of *personalismo*. The old Conservative Party by then was also allied with Uribe's movement.

In congressional elections in 2006, Uribe's party or its allies won roughly two thirds of the 102 Senate seats and a majority in the 163-member House. The "U Party" alone won 20 Senate seats and 29 House seats, while the Conservatives staged a comeback from near-oblivion, winning 18 Senate seats (up from 13) and 30 in the House. The Liberals won 17 in the Senate (down from 29) and 36 in the House. The left-wing Alternative Democratic Pole won 11 in the Senate and nine in the House. Six new members were suspected of having paramilitary links.

In the presidential campaign, the pro-Uribe parties nominated him under an umbrella coalition called *Colombia Primero* (Colombia First). The Liberals again nominated the two-time loser, Horacio Serpa. The Democratic Pole, in a party primary, nominated Senator Carlos Gaviría, 69, no relation to the former president. Antanas Mockus, a flamboyant former Bogotá mayor, launched an independent bid. There were three minor candidates.

There was little suspense as to the outcome. The major surprises were the size of Uribe's mandate, the strong showing by Gaviría, and the drop in support for Serpa. Voter turnout on May 28 was normal—45.1%. The results:

Gaviría	2,609,412	22.0%
Serpa	1,401,173	11.8%
Mockus	146,540	1.2%
Others	87,126	.8%

Uribe's unprecedented landslide mandate sent a clear signal to the guerrillas, the paramilitaries and the drug traffickers that Uribe has the support of the Colombian people for his no-nonsense approach. His victory was also celebrated in Washington; Uribe is about the only friend the United States had left on the continent. He was inaugurated for his second term on August 7.

Uribe found himself *entre la espada y la pared*, trying to get the disbanded paramilitaries to fulfill their promises to cooperate with investigators and prosecutors in exchange for leniency and to avoid extradition to the United States, while at the same time placating domestic and international human rights advocates who be-

Colombia

lieve he is being *too* lenient with alleged war criminals.

The Constitutional Court amended the Peace and Justice Law in 2006 to provide, among other provisions, that assets of the surrendered paramilitaries be used to compensate their victims. The paramilitaries angrily charged a double-cross and threatened to take up arms again; as many as 3,600 were believed to have done so.

Uribe attempted to disarm his human rights critics by continuing his get-tough policy on the paramilitaries. Although 31,000 of them had laid down their arms by the end of 2006, they remained politically influential. About 60 of the political leaders at all levels unveiled as having links to the *AUC* were members of Uribe's own party. In 2007, eight members of Congress had been arrested for alleged paramilitary ties. Most embarrassing to Uribe was the fact that one of them, Senator Alvaro Araújo, was the brother of his foreign minister, María Consuelo Araújo. Evidence against them was found on a confiscated laptop belonging to an aide of the *AUC*'s Rodrigo Tovar, better known by the *nom de guerre* "Jorge." At first, Uribe defended his minister, but she acquiesced to the chorus of criticism and resigned. She was replaced by Fernando Araújo, no relation to her, who just six weeks earlier had escaped from *FARC* captivity after six years.

Also embarrassing to Uribe was the arrest of his intelligence chief, Jorge Noguera. But while Uribe's supporters argued that the arrests showed that the government was serious about exposing the paramilitaries' connections no matter where they led, domestic and foreign skeptics, including the new Democratic-controlled U.S. Congress, countered that there are still too many unanswered questions about the president's own possible complicity.

New talks with the *FARC* to exchange hostages for guerrilla prisoners came to naught when the *FARC* set off a bomb in October 2006 at the Military Academy, injuring 23 people. Uribe broke off the talks.

In March 2007, President George W. Bush, amid tight security, made a six-hour stop in Bogotá, the first sitting U.S. president to visit the capital since Ronald Reagan in 1982. Thousands protested the visit. Uribe visited Bush a month later at Camp David, where they discussed military aid, Senate ratification of a proposed bilateral free-trade agreement signed in 2006 and extension of the preferential tariff agreement under which Colombia has exported hundreds of millions of dollars worth of fresh flowers and other non-traditional products. But a hostile Democratic Congress, skeptical not only of Uribe's possible ties to paramilitaries

but also concerned about the 1,300 trade unionists murdered in Colombia over the past 10 years, delayed action. Uribe even hired a public relations firm co-founded by President Clinton's one-time press secretary, Joe Lockhart, to lobby Democratic congressmen.

In October 2007, after a two-year trial that riveted the attention of the country, Alberto Santofimio, a one-time Liberal Party luminary, was convicted of conspiring with the Medellín Cartel in the assassination of Luis Carlos Galán, his rival for the Liberal presidential nomination, in 1989. Santofimio was sentenced to 24 years.

Colombian warplanes bombed a *FARC* camp just across the border in Ecuador in March 2008, killing 22 guerrillas, among them Luis Edgar Devia, better known by his *nom de guerre*, Raúl Reyes, who was one of the *FARC*'s seven-member general secretariat and its international press spokesman. For good measure, Colombian troops entered Ecuador to recover Reyes' body and three of his laptop computers, which proved an intelligence bonanza.

An angry Ecuadorian President Rafael Correa ordered 3,200 troops to the border and broke diplomatic rerlations. Chávez went on national television and bombastically ordered 10 battalions to the Colombian border; he also broke diplomatic relations with Colombia. So did Nicaraguan President Daniel Ortega. Actual warfare appeared imminent. Correa called on the Organization of American States to condemn Colombia's raid. The OAS responded with a lukewarm resolution labeling the raid a violation of Ecuadorian sovereignty and territorial integrity. This did not mollify Correa. The OAS decided to send a four-member delegation headed by Secretary-General José Miguel Insulza to Colombia and Ecuador to investigate the raid and to defuse the crisis.

Meanwhile, Colombia released information that the captured laptops showed that Correa had received a $20,000 campaign contribution from the *FARC*; that Chávez had given the *FARC* $300 million, proving him to be a liar; and that the *FARC* were seeking the technology to build a radioactive "dirty bomb." Uribe vowed to take the evidence against Chávez before an international court; in Washington, President Bush declared his support for Uribe and denounced Chávez's alleged provocations.

Uribe, Correa and Chávez met in Santo Domingo, Dominican Republic. After a reportedly contentious exchange between Uribe and Correa, the three presidents signed a declaration ending the crisis. Uribe, in effect, apologized for the raid and said he would never again violate a neighbor's sovereignty; Correa and Chávez ac-

cepted the apology and agreed to work together with Colombia to control the *FARC*.

The *FARC* leadership received a series of other blows in 2008. Six days after Reyes' death, another member of its secretariat, Iván Ríos (real name Manuel de Jesús Muñoz) was murdered by his bodyguard, apparently to collect the $2.7 million reward; he did. It suffered a third blow in May when Nelly Avila Moreno, also known as Karina, a senior *FARC* commander in Antioquia and the suspected mastermind of the murder of Uribe's father in 1983, accepted an invitation from the president to turn herself in. She held a news conference and urged other rebels to follow her example, saying the answer to Colombia's problems is through "dialogue," not war. She had fought in the *FARC* ranks for 24 years.

Finally, in May, the *FARC* announced that Marulanda (real name Pedro Antonio Marín), had died of a heart attack in a hideout on March 26. His successor was Guillermo León Sáez, who goes by the *nom de guerre* Alfonso Cano.

Uribe's popularity in Colombia soared even higher as a result of the border incursion, but he was soon embarrassed by growing evidence of involvement by members of his party—and his family—with the paramilitaries. Investigations began in 2006, and the Colombian media dubbed the growing scandal "parapolitics." By April 2008, 30 members of Congress were facing charges of links to the paramilitaries. Uribe's second cousin, Mario Uribe, was forced to resign as Senate president in 2007. After an unsuccessful attempt to obtain political asylum at the Costa Rican embassy, Mario Uribe was arrested for questioning about an alleged meeting with the *AUC*'s Mancuso in 2002. He spent only four months in jail before a prosecutor released him for lack of evidence. Another 60 political figures were investigated.

The "parapolitics" scandal did little to persuade the Democratic-controlled U.S. Congress to look kindly upon Uribe. In June 2007, the U.S. House of Representatives voted to *cut* military aid to Colombia from $590 million to $530 million. In January 2008, Secretary of State Condoleezza Rice brought a delegation of nine Democratic congressmen to Colombia in an attempt to overcome opposition to discuss the proposed bilateral free-trade agreement. The Democrats continue to be leery of the murders of labor union leaders; more are killed in Colombia than in any other country, although the number has declined sharply since Uribe became president. Both Democratic candidates for president, Hillary Rodham Clinton and Barack Obama, as well as House Speaker Nancy Pelosi, all said they opposed approval of the FTA. Clinton was embarrassed when it was revealed that one of her campaign staffers had been a paid lobbyist for the Colombian government to secure approval of the FTA.

The plight of the 750-odd hostages still held by the *FARC* garnered greater international attention in 2007 and 2008, especially the fate of Ingrid Betancourt, who holds dual Colombian and French citizenship and was reported to be gravely ill with hepatitis and suffering from chronic depression.

In a desperate attempt to secure the release of at least 45 of the most ill hostages, Uribe swallowed his pride and solicited the help of Venezuela's Chávez. Always hungry for the international spotlight, Chávez eagerly accepted. But three months later, Uribe, impatient and annoyed that Chávez's grandstanding had produced nothing, rescinded the request.

Chávez annoubnced in December 2007 that the *FARC* had agreed to release two female legislators and the 3-year-old son of one of them. Chávez asked his friend, former Argentine President Néstor Kirchner, to go to the Colombian city of Villavicencia to receive the freed captives on New Years Eve; he even arranged for U.S. filmmaker Oliver Stone to film the event. But Chávez's carefully planned media event fell apart when the *FARC* reneged, accusing the army of disrupting the release. Chávez was acutely embarrassed, although he did obtain the release of the two women and two other former legislators in February 2008. The former hostages related horror stories of the conditions in which the hostages exist, and they confirmed that Betancourt was very frail.

French President Nicholas Sarkozy declared Betancourt's release a top priority. In June 2007, he persuaded Uribe to release Rodrigo Granda, the *FARC* leader whose arrest in Caracas had provoked the 2004 diplomatic crisis, in an attempt to secure her release. Granda went to Cuba, but the *FARC* did not reciprocate by releasing Betancourt. Sarkozy dispatched a humanitarian delegation to Colombia in 2008 in an attempt to persuade the *FARC* to release her or to at least allow her to be treated by a physician. The mission failed.

The world was electrified on July 2, 2008 by the stunning news that Colombian intelligence agents posing as *FARC* guerrillas and as members of an international humanitarian organization had rescued Betancourt, the three American contractors captured in 2003 and 11 other hostages. The commandos flew into the *FARC* camp by helicopter with a cover story they had orders from the new *FARC* commander, Alfonso Cano, to move the hostages to another camp. The bluff worked, and once airborne the comman-

dos overpowered the two *FARC* guards assigned to accompany the hostages. Not a shot was fired.

The Defense Ministry did not bask for long in the international glow of the audacious rescue. In October 2008, media reports in Colombia and the United States alleged the army commander, General Mario Montoya, had practiced a system of officer promotions based on a unit's body counts, which in turn had led to innocent civilians being killed on the pretext that they were guerrillas. The claiming of civilian bodies as guerrillas killed in combat became known internationally as the "false-positives scandal." In one controversial incident involving three army units, 11 young unemployed men from the Bogota slum of Soacha were recruited for supposed well-paying jobs, then taken to North Santander Department and murdered. Their bodies were found in a mass grave. A U.N. investigator called the murders of civilians by the army "widespread and systematic." Amnesty International claimed security forces carried out 330 "extrajudicial executions" in 2007, a one-third increase over previous years.

Uribe sacked three generals and 24 other officers or sergeants and disavowed the promotion policy. A CIA memo leaked to the press alleged that Montoya had followed the promotion policy when he was a brigade commander. Montoya resigned and was replaced by General Freddy Padilla, who himself was tainted by suspected human rights abuses. Uribe ordered the army and police to undertake investigations into the slayings of civilians. The United States suspended military aid to selected brigades, but did not specify how much. U.S. military aid to Colombia totaled $615 million in 2007. As of May 2009, 22 soldiers had been arrested in connection with the false-positives scandal and almost 1,200 were under investigation. The scandal continued to generate headlines in 2010 as new revelations surfaced.

The Administrative Directorate of Security *(DAS)*, the Colombian equivalent of the FBI, became the target of an investigation after allegations that it had illegally wiretapped politicians of both Uribe's coalition and the opposition, judges and journalists. Uribe disavowed any knowledge of the wiretaps. The deputy director of the *DAS* resigned, and in 2009 Uribe transferred the responsibility for legal wiretaps to the National Police.

In January 2009, the always unpredictable *FARC* set off a bomb at a Blockbuster store in an upscale Bogota neighborhood that killed two people, then released a total of six of their remaining 700 hostages. Among those released were Alan Jara, governor of Meta Department

when he was abducted in 2001, and Sigifredo López, who was one of 12 departmental legislators abducted in a brazen *FARC* raid in 2002. Interviewed after his release, López alleged the *FARC* murdered the other 11 lawmakers in cold blood.

In March 2009, police foiled a *FARC* plot to assassinate Defense Minister Eduardo Santos and captured 10 guerrillas. The *FARC* was clearly showing signs of being worn down by attrition. Its strength is believed to have diminished from 20,000 to about 8,000.

The government claimed a major victory in the war against drug traffickers in April 2009 when an elite police unit captured Daniel Rendón Herrera, who had emerged as Colombia's most-wanted kingpin. His brother, Freddy Rendón Herrera, was already behind bars.

Uribe first met with his new U.S. counterpart, Barack Obama, at the Summit of the Americas in Trinidad and Tobago in April 2009, and it soon became apparent Uribe would enjoy as close a relationship with Obama as he had with Bush. Uribe visited Washington June 29–30, 2009, ostensibly to advance the stalled free-trade agreement, but within days it was announced that the two countries also were discussing a defense cooperation agreement (DCA) by which the United States would have access to several Colombian bases to make up for Ecuador's termination of the base agreement at Manta (see Ecuador).

The reports immediately raised a firestorm of criticism both in Colombia and abroad. Both conservative and left-wing members of the Colombian Congress voiced concern about a supposed influx of U.S. soldiers, while every president in South America expressed opposition to the idea. Chávez, of course, was loudest in his denunciation, saying "the winds of war" had been unleashed. He reduced trade with Colombia by 70% in reprisal. But even moderate presidents like Brazil's da Silva and Chile's Michelle Bachelet criticized the deal.

Nonetheless, the two sides announced the details of the agreement in August. There was a hastily called summit of the South American Union of Nations (UNASUR) in Bariloche, Argentina, to discuss the issue on August 30, but Uribe did not attend. The DCA was formally signed in Bogota on October 30. Under the terms, U.S. personnel would utilize three Colombian air bases, Palanquero, Apjay and Malambo; two naval bases, including Malaga; and two army bases. The duration of the DCA is 10 years. It stipulates that the U.S. access would be limited to drug interdiction and support for Colombian forces against guerrillas, but that U.S. forcers could not act against a third coun-

Colombia

**President-elect
Juan Manuel Santos Calderón**

try. It continues the current cap on U.S. personnel at 600 military and 800 civilian contractors. Nonetheless, the agreement continues to affect Colombia's relations with the rest of South America.

The U.S.-Colombian base pact, among other issues, led to a dramatic shouting match between Uribe and Chávez during the periodic Rio Pact summit, held on February 24, 2010, in Cancun, Mexico. Chávez shouted *"Véte al carajo!"*—somewhat stronger language than "Go to hell"—at Uribe and was about to stomp out of the meeting, when Uribe shouted for Chávez to "be a man" and defend his arguments.

The Elections of 2010

Whether or not Uribe would be allowed to run for a third term, and if he would run if he could, continued to be the country's major guessing game for almost a year. To hedge his bets, Defense Minister Santos, with Uribe's blessing, resigned in May 2009 in order to run for president in the event Uribe could not or would not. In mid-2009, Uribe was still enjoying a phenomenal approval rating of 70%.

On August 19, the Senate voted 56–2 to call a referendum on whether the constitution should be amended to permit a third consecutive term. On September 2, the Chamber of Representatives followed suit, 85–5. The opposition boycotted both votes. That left the matter in the hands of the Constitutional Court, which took no action for almost six months, leaving the campaign in a state of flux. The suspense ended on February 27, 2010, when the court, composed of Uribe appointees, nonetheless voted 7–2 that a third term would be an unconstitutional threat to Colombian democracy. It barred Uribe and future presidents not just from a third

consecutive term but from a third term, *period*.

Santos, scion of the prominent Liberal family that owns the newspaper *El Tiempo* and grand-nephew of President Eduardo Santos (1938–40), then put his campaign in high gear as the candidate of Uribe's U Party. Eight other candidates entered the race, but only four were given a serious chance of making it into a runoff: Antanas Mockus, the flamboyant two-time mayor of Bogota, who campaigned on a moderate populist platform; Noemí Sanín, a Conservative who ran a strong independent campaign for president in 1998; Germán Vargas of the Radical Change party, which is pro-Uribe; and Gustavo Petro, a 39-year-old left-wing senator of the Alternative Pole party, who had belonged to the M-19 guerrilla group in his teens. Despite her earlier declared intentions, Betancourt decided not to run. For the first time in memory, there was no candidate running under the Liberal banner.

As always, the congressional elections, held on March 14, 2010, proved a bellwether for the presidential election. The U Party won 25.2% of the votes and 27 of the 102 Senate seats, up from 20. The Conservatives, part of Uribe's coalition, finished second with 20.6% of the vote and 23 seats, a gain of four. Another coalition partner, Radical Change, received 7.9% of the vote and fell from 15 to eight seats. That gave Uribe's coalition a strengthened Senate majority. The Liberals were unchanged with 18 seats, winning 15.8% of the votes, but the new Party of National Integration *(PIN)*, acknowledged to be linked to the right-wing paramilitaries, sent a chill through the establishment by finishing in fourth place with 8.1% of the votes and eight seats. Petro's Alternative Pole fell from 10 to eight seats and received 7.6% of the vote.

In the Chamber of Representatives, the U Party won 47 of the 166 seats, the Conservatives 38, and Radical Change, 15, again, an absolute coalition majority. The Liberals won 37, the *PIN* 12 and Alternative Pole, only four.

In the campaigning for the first round of the presidential election on May 30, the race quickly narrowed to Santos and Mockus. The two men, both 58, held similar beliefs except that Mockus advocated conciliation with Venezuela while Santos favored Uribe's confrontational approach. In a new twist for Colombian politics, Santos' official Web site had links to his Facebook and Twitter pages. Santos' strategy was to generally wrap himself in the mantle of the still-popular Uribe, which apparently paid off. Polls had showed the two men in a statistical dead heat, but an unusually high turnout of 49% surprised everyone. The virtually complete official results:

Santos	6,758,539	46.56%
Mockus	3,120,716	21.50%
Vargas	1,471,377	10.13%
Petro	1,329,512	9.16%
Sanin	892,323	6.15%

The headline in *El Tiempo* on June 21, 2010, quotes President-elect Juan Manuel Santos Calderón, declaring, "The hour of unity has arrived."

124

Both major guerrilla groups endeavored to mar the manifestation of democracy on June 20. The *FARC* killed three soldiers and the *ELN* killed seven policemen in an ambush. Nonetheless, more than 13.3 million Colombians turned out for the runoff. The results, according to virtually complete but unofficial returns when this book went to press, were:

Santos	9,004,221	65.1%
Mockus	3,588,819	27.5%

Another 444,330 voters cast blank ballots and 119,302 ballots were null.

Santos declared that under his administration, Colombia "will be an ally of all the countries in the world." Congratulations poured in to Santos from the presidents of Brazil, Spain, the United States and other countries—but his victory was greeted by stony silence from Venezuela and Ecuador.

Santos was to be inaugurated on August 7.

Culture: The blend of the European and Indian races was more thorough in Colombia than in the nations of the southern areas of Latin America. Moreover, refugee blacks from the Caribbean settled along the northern coast and, as elsewhere, have made their contribution to Colombian music and art. However, the so-called Bolivarian countries of the northwestern tier of South America, those liberated by Simón Bolivar, have not been characterized by the comparative freedom of expression and political stability of the countries of the southern part of the continent.

Colombia's long history of dictatorship, political turmoil and domestic violence conspired to retard its cultural development until the latter half of the 20th century. The overthrow of the Rojas Pinilla dictatorship, and the truce reached between the warring Liberal and Conservative parties in 1958, marked a watershed in Colombian cultural expression. Bogotá's self-proclaimed title of "the Athens of South America" is a bit boastful, but there is no question that the country has made a regional impact.

This is especially true in the plastic arts, as a visit to the top floor of the *Museo Nacional* in Bogotá will attest. As in Chile, the influence of France on 19th century Colombian art is unmistakable, but in the late 20th century a number of talented Colombian painters and sculptors have won international reputations. Perhaps the three best known are Edgar Negret, the abstractionist Alejandro Obregón and Fernando Botero.

The premier figure of Colombian literature remains Gabriel García Márquez (b. 1927), who received the Nobel Prize in 1982. His landmark novel was *Cien años de soledad*, but later novels that have won international critical acclaim include *Crónica de una muerte anunciada* and *El amor en los tiempos de cólera*. In 2002, he released the first of three installments of his memoirs, *Vivir para conratla (Live to Tell It)*. García Márquez's leftist policies have brought him controversy. He is a close friend of Fidel Castro's and maintains a residence in Havana as well as in Paris. Despite his international prestige, he was denied a visa to visit the United States during the Reagan Administration.

Another Colombian literary star is Álvaro Mutis (b. 1923), a novelist and poet who has achieved acclaim in the Spanish-speaking world with the fictitious character, Maqroll el Gaviero; such novels as *La última escala del Tramp Steamer* and *Amirbar*; and the book of poetry, *La mansión de Araucaíma*. At the age of 79, he received Spain's coveted Cervantes Prize in 2002, becoming the first writer from any country to win all three of Spain's most prestigious literary awards.

Bogotá and the major provincial capitals of Medellín, Cartagena, Cali and Barranquilla have active theatrical and musical communities, though much is still borrowed from abroad. Colombian popular music has definite Caribbean influence.

Colombian cinema is still in the developmental stage, compared with the more established industries of Mexico, Brazil and Argentina, but a few feature-length films are produced each year. Colombian television has become largely self-sufficient in programming, and some of its *telenovelas* are exported.

In popular music, the beautiful young singer Shakira Ripoll (b. 1977) has won international renown in recent years, including U.S. Grammy Awards for Best Latin Pop in 2001 and Best Latin Rock 2006, and seven Latin Grammys. But even Shakira is eclipsed by Juan Esteban Arristazábal (b. 1972), internationally known by the stage name Juanes. As of 2009, Juanes had a record 17 Latin Grammys, including eight in 2008, and in 2010 he shared a "mainstream" U.S. Grammy with Taylor Swift for best rap song collaboration. He gained notoriety as one of 12 Latin pop singers who appeared at the "Peace Concert" in Havana in September 2009, which critics said implied a lack of concern for Cuba's human rights violations.

Colombia's leading recording artist and songwriter was once Diomedes Díaz (b. 1957), popularly known as *"El Jefe"* and as *"El Cacique de la Junta."* Díaz has written and/or recorded 33 popular songs since 1976. He was convicted in 2002 of the wrongful death by cocaine overdose of his 22-year-old lover but spent only 37 months in jail. He has been banned from performing in Cali after he snorted cocaine on stage in 2005. His failure to appear for a performance in Santa Marta sparked a riot. He recorded two more songs in 2009.

The Colombian press, like so much else in the country, has been shaped by the Liberal-Conservative rivalry and in recent years has been the target of drug-related violence. Involvement of newspaper owners in politics has been commonplace, most notably former Presidents Laureano Gómez, who established the Conservative mouthpiece *El Siglo*, and Eduardo Santos, whose family still publishes the prestigious pro-Liberal daily *El Tiempo*. Ironically, these two rival newspapers both were intimidated by the Rojas Pinilla dictatorship, forcing them to collaborate editorially against the dictator. The dean of the Colombian press and its circulation leader is another pro-Liberal paper, *El Espectador*, which has won international plaudits for its courageous editorial attacks against the drug cartels. Its editor, Guillermo Cano, was murdered by the Medellín Cartel in 1986, just one of scores of Colombian journalists who have given their lives in the line of duty. *El Espectador* has since become a weekly.

Several high-quality news magazines are published, the most widely read being *Cromos, Revista Cambio* and *Semana*. Nobel laureate Garbrel García Márquez (see above) has owned *Cambio* since 1999.

Economy: The informal economy of Colombia is based on production and smuggled export of refined cocaine and far outweighs the formal economy based on agriculture. The coca leaves are not generally grown in Colombia, but come from Peru, Ecuador and Bolivia, where an acre can yield $10,000 a year. The final stage of processing takes place in Colombia, which traditionally has had but loose control over illicit activities. Small "factories" are easily moved, and with police double-agents abounding, when there is a raid on a facility, no one is home.

Most of the population, however, was employed in agriculture, which is handicapped by inefficient techniques and misuse of resources—produce and labor. Rural violence is common and has stimulated migration to the cities since 1948 where many of the newcomers are unemployable because of lack of education and skills. Now, only 1.7% of the people work the land. An estimated 60% are engaged in the cocaine traffic in one capacity or another. The resources of Colombia are capable of supporting the growing population without the cocaine industry, but numerous problems, principally poor distribution of wealth, must be resolved before there can be major economic gains.

Colombia

Government programs were undertaken to end the traditional dependence on coffee exports, and by 1973 other goods and products produced more foreign income than coffee. Manufactured goods are slowly gaining a larger share of total exports.

The López Michelsen (1978–82) administration sought to revitalize the rural sector through agrarian reform and government investment. Tighter controls over foreign-owned firms and banks, together with new taxes on the wealthy increased government revenues 50%.

Colombia has a thriving coal industry; it is not only self-sufficient in oil, but is an exporter. Honda makes motorcycles here, with production exceeding 50,000 units per year.

One bright spot for the economy in 1996, albeit temporary, was a disastrous frost in Brazil that destroyed much of its coffee harvest. The result was skyrocketing coffee prices on the world market, much to the benefit of Colombia, whose coffee growers already had embarked on an aggressive marketing campaign with its "Juan Valdez" character in the industrialized countries. In 2005, the Colombian Federation of Coffee Growers, which holds the trademark to Juan Valdez, began opening specialty coffee shops in the United States to compete with companies like Starbucks.

The overall economic picture in Colombia was bleak for several years. Chronic high unemployment, along with the endemic corruption within the Samper government, was one of the major issues in the 1998 presidential election that saw an end to 12 years of Liberal rule. The jobless rate that year was 16%, second only to Haiti among the 20 Latin republics, while inflation also was among the highest in the region at 18%. The picture did not improve much under Conservative President Pastrana, however. Real GDP growth was up 3% in 1998, 4.3% in 1999, and 2.8% in 2000, bottoming out at 1.9% in 2002.

Growth improved under the administration of President Álvaro Uribe, both because of his hard-nosed fiscal policy and because of the dramatic improvement in public security. Growth was 3.2% in 2003, 4% in 2004 and 5.1% in 2005. It jumped to a robust 6.7% in 2006 and 7.7% for 2007. Then the global recession hit in late 2008. Colombia's growth in 2008 was down to 2.6%, and it 2009 it *shrank* by 0.1%.

The unemployment picture was dismal for years: 18.1% in 1999, 19.7% in 2000 and 20.5% in 2001, the worst in Latin America. At the end of 2003, the first full year of Uribe's administration, it was down to 14%, and at the end of 2005, it was 10.2%. It dropped to 9.4% in 2007, but it was back up to 11.8% in 2008 and 12% in 2009.

Inflation was estimated at 7.7% in 2008 and only 2% in 2009, remarkably low by Latin American standards.

The combination of sluggish economic growth, population increase, joblessness and inflation have affected Colombians' living standards. Per capita GDP declined from $2,440 in 1997 to $2,087 in 2001. In 2003, it plummeted to $1,844, but it rebounded to $3,250 in 2007 and $4,620 in 2008.

Two major recent developments have been the free-trade agreements Colombia signed with the *Mercosur* trade bloc in 2004 and with the United States in 2006. The *Mercosur* deal gives Colombian exports duty-free entry to Brazil and Argentina over eight to 10 years, while tariffs will be eliminated on those countries' exports to Colombia over a period of 12 to 15 years. The bilateral agreement with the United States made Colombia the ninth Latin American country to reach one. Peru signed one the previous month. Bilateral trade with the United States totaled $14.3 billion. However, the U.S. Senate has failed to ratify the FTA (see History). Colombia has since concluded a FTA with Canada, which is pending approval by the Canadian Parliament. Colombia's political problems with neighboring Venezuela, Colombia's second-largest trading partner after the United States, led Venezuela to restrict Colombian imports. Consequently, in 2009 China became Colombia's second-largest trading partner. Because of the shrinking economy from the global recession, Uribe urged exporters to search for non-traditional buyers in Europe and the Far East.

Because of bilateral FTAs with the United States, the old Andean Pact, composed of Colombia, Venezuela, Ecuador, Peru and Bolivia, became largely irrelevant as a result. As one consequence, Colombia now buys its soybeans from the United States instead of from Bolivia.

The reduction in violence has led Colombia to promote tourism, and in 2006 tourism revenues were up almost 50% above 2005. It also has encouraged foreign oil companies to engage in new exploration, which has borne fruit. Colombia was to have become a net oil importer by 2007, but that transition has been postponed to at least 2011. Net reserves have been revised upward to 1.51 billion barrels.

The Future: The Álvaro Uribe phenomenon was a classic example of not arguing with success. The contrast between him and his hapless, spineless predecessor, Andrés Pastrana, was as dramatic as that between Winston Churchill and his predecessor, Neville Chamberlain. He largely brought order out of what once was chaos and brought the left-wing guerrillas and right-wing paramilitaries to bay.

Uribe's countrymen rewarded him with a landslide vote of confidence of 62.2% in 2006, the first time a Colombian president has been permitted immediate re-election, and he almost certainly would have been given a third term in 2010 if the Constitutional Court had not declared it unconstitutional.

Uribe also may be responsible for reversing the slide of public confidence in Colombia's 50-year-old democracy, according to the annual surveys by the Chilean firm *Latinobarómetro* published in the British newsmagazine, *The Economist.* In 2002, the year Uribe assumed office, the survey showed that only 39% of Colombians believed that democracy was preferable to any other form of government, compared with 60% in 1996. In 2008, it was up to 62%, the highest it has ever been. However, in 2009 it dropped back to 49%, for inexplicable reasons. At the same time, 20% of Colombians in 1996 said in the survey that authoritarianism was sometimes preferable to democracy. In 2006, that was down to 16%; it 2009, it was only 5%.

Juan Manuel Santos Calderón' landslide victory in the June 20 runoff was an unmistakable mandate for continuity of Uribe's hard-nosed approach toward the guerrillas and toward Venezuela. Santos, like Uribe, was educated abroad, having studied at Harvard, Tufts, the University of Kansas and the London School of Economics. He pledged that Colombia would be an ally of all countries, but didn't explain how he would mend fences with Venezuela or with Ecuador—where he is wanted for murder in the raid on the *FARC* camp when he was defense minister. He is unlikely to make any goodwill visits to Quito anytime soon.

The Republic of Costa Rica

Costa Rican cowboys—campesinos

tive. Mount Irazú, close to the capital, littered the city with ashes and cinders in 1962. Arenal erupted in 1998.

Costa Rica's coffee is grown on the slopes of the hills and volcanoes which rim the valley. The Atlantic coastal plains are moist and low, heavily forested and sparsely settled. Costa Rica's main port in the east is Puerto Limón, the only city of commercial importance in the area.

The Pacific lowlands, drier than the Atlantic plains, are quite narrow except for the Nicoya and Osa peninsulas. Thinly settled, the region produces bananas and fiber on large plantations. The port of Golfito on the Pacific coast handles most of the country's exports. Lying in the tropical rainbelt, Costa Rica has more than abundant rainfall, particularly in the rainy season from April to December of each year. Some parts of the oppressive Atlantic coast region have rain during 300 days of the year.

History: The Spaniards discovered the Nicoya Peninsula in 1522, settling in the Central Valley, where a few sedentary Indian farmers were found. They organized into a hacienda system of independent farm communities. The Spaniards inter-married with the Indians, who were assimilated into the Spanish culture. Cartago was founded in 1563, but no expansion of this settlement occurred for 145 years, during which time the Costa Ricans evolved as a community of small farmers. With the assimilated Indians and a few slaves, the Costa Rican worked his own land, developing a system of small, efficient and independent landowners and a tradition of industry not usually found in colonial Hispanic society. Settlers from Cartago founded Heredia in 1717 and San José in 1737; by 1750 the population had reached approximately 2,500, divided into some 400 family groups.

Independence from Spain was achieved on September 15, 1821 as a result of actions in Guatemala, Mexico and other colonies. Costa Rica fell victim to the civil wars which followed the separation of the Central American Republics from the short-lived Mexican Empire. However, remoteness from the scene of the bitter quarrels between conservatives and liberals in Guatemala and El Salvador minimized the effects of the civil war in Costa Rica. The most significant events of Costa Rica's history as an independent state have been its efforts to develop the economy to provide the revenues required to support the people.

The government encouraged the production of coffee in 1825, offering free land for development. From 1850, the coffee trade attracted new settlers and inspired the development of roads and the

Area: 19,647 square miles.
Population: 4.516 million (2010 est.).
Capital City: San José (Pop. 800,000, estimated).
Climate: The coastal lowlands are hot and tropical, with heavy rains from April to December. The valley of the central highlands is temperate, with moderate rains during the wet season.
Neighboring Countries: Nicaragua (North); Panama (Southeast).
Official Language: Spanish
Ethnic Background: Overwhelmingly Spanish European descent, blended with some Indian lineage. A few Indians with African heritage are found along the Atlantic coast; some pure-blood Indians live in the highlands.
Principal Religion: Roman Catholic Christianity.
Chief Commercial Products: Coffee, bananas, sugar and cacao.
Currency: Colón.
Gross Domestic Product: U.S. $29.64 billion in 2009 ($6,563 per capita).
Former Colonial Status: Spanish Crown Colony (1522–1821).
Independence Date: September 15, 1821.

Chief of State: Laura Chinchilla Miranda de Rico (b. March 28, 1959), president (since May 8, 2010).
National Flag: Blue, white and red horizontal stripes.

Costa Rica, literally *Rich Coast*, is next to the smallest of the Central American republics. Lying between Nicaragua and Panama with coasts on both the Atlantic and Pacific oceans, the distance from ocean to ocean varies from 75 to 175 miles.

The country is divided into three distinct regions: the Atlantic coastal plains, the central highlands and the Pacific coast. The central highlands are part of a chain of scenic mountains rising in Nicaragua and running southeast through Costa Rica into Panama. They contain lofty peaks reaching 12,500 feet and several steep-sided inter-mountain valleys. The green central valley, some 40 miles wide and 50 miles long, lying between 3,000 and 6,000 feet above sea level, is the most densely populated part of Costa Rica.

The two principal cities, San José and Cartago, share the valley with four volcanoes, two of which are still violently ac-

Costa Rica

settlement of areas outside the central valley. The building of railroads between the 1870s and 1890s introduced banana growing to provide traffic for the new system. At the same time, West Indians were brought in to build the railroads, clear the forests and work the Atlantic coast plantations.

Subsequently, irrigated banana plantations were developed on the Pacific coast, resulting in the building of ports at Golfito and Puntarenas. On the Nicoya Peninsula and in the northwest, cattle raising became and remains an important industry.

Politically, the Costa Rican experience was tranquil. The first experiments in government were hardly more than gentlemanly agreements among the principal families. The constitution of 1848 abolished the army and replaced it with a civil guard. Costa Rica has had only one major experience with dictatorial government. Tomás Guardia came to power in 1870 and ruled as dictator until 1882. Exiling opposition leaders and spending money with a lavish hand, he broke up the traditional parties, installed his friends in office but also undertook to modernize the rural agricultural state. He built roads, railroads, schools and public buildings, increased the production of sugar and coffee and encouraged international trade.

Political freedom was restored by free and honest elections in 1889. Three subsequent attempts were made to seize the government: in 1917, which lasted two years; an unsuccessful attempt in 1932; and the refusal of the National Assembly to recognize the election victory of Otilio Ulate over former President Rafael Calderón in 1948. This led to a six-week civil war that left 2,000 people dead.

José Figueres, founder of the National Liberation Party (*PLN*), which is still one of the country's major parties, led a band of 700 revolutionaries that prevented Calderón from regaining power. Figueres, whom Calderón had sent into exile from 1942–44, served for 18 months as head of a revolutionary junta, during which time he granted women the right to vote, abolished the standing army and implemented the Uruguay-like social welfare system still in place today. He relinquished power in 1949 to the duly elected Luis Rafael Ulate, a respected journalist and member of the National Union Party, whose name has changed several times and is today the Social Christian Unity Party (*PUSC*). This began an uninterrupted period of two-party, democratic government, peacefully alternating between the *PLN* and the Social Christians, until the scandal-plagued *PUSC* went into eclipse in 2006.

Figueres was elected to succeed Ulate in 1953. A successful coffee grower and businessman, he expanded public works and

increased government revenues. An outspoken critic of Caribbean dictatorships, he was denounced as a "communist" and an invasion force from Nicaragua moved to unseat him. An appeal to the Organization of American States ended the conflict. Dominican dictator Rafael Trujillo plotted to assassinate him. Figueres served another term as president from 1970–74, and is still revered as the patriarch of Costa Rica's democracy. His son and namesake was president from 1994–98. He died in 1990.

Daniel Oduber of the *PLN* was elected to succeed Figueres in 1974 with 42% of the vote. Oduber promised agrarian reform and constitutional changes to increase the power of the executive branch. However, in 1978, voters ousted the *PLN*, electing Rodrigo Carazo of the Democratic Renovation Party. He won by 50% to 49% over the *PLN* candidate, Luís Alberto Monge.

The right-of-center president soon found his administration beset by scandals and fiscal problems. For years, Costa Ricans imported more than they exported and spent more than they earned. Somehow, it worked until 1980, when the nation's imported oil bills and international

interest charges skyrocketed while earnings from exports nosedived.

Rather than impose needed austerity measures (the government subsidized food, fuel and luxury imports), Carazo sought to stave off disaster by printing more paper money. International lenders responded by cutting off credit.

Carazo became the most unpopular president in recent years. In 1982, voters elected Monge, a former labor organizer, who this time took 58% of the vote. His popularity remained high in spite of an unpleasant task: austerity measures to bolster a sagging economy.

By 1984, Costa Rica was besieged by other problems. The armed conflicts in neighboring Nicaragua and El Salvador threatened to interfere with the national political process at a time when economic conditions in the nation reached a dangerously low level; the national public debt increased to $4.4 billion by 1986, placing the government on the brink of bankruptcy. Significantly, the government asked the United States for $7.3 million in order to improve its military capability to resist increasing *Sandinista* pressure on its Nicaraguan border. By 1985, U.S. military advisers were training the Costa Rican National Guard.

In 1986, voters elected Oscar Arias Sánchez of the *PLN* president by a majority of 52.3%. A highly educated and respected man, he performed admirably in the face of adversities affecting the country, including communist infiltration of the labor movement. His performance was mostly steady, and sometimes erratic. During a visit to Washington in 1987, he urged President Reagan to discontinue aid to the anti-communist *contras* of Nicaragua, stating that they were fomenting unrest in Central America. But a few days later, he declared that so long as the *Sandinista* regime of Nicaragua existed, there would be a danger that communism would spread throughout Central America.

Arias was the architect in 1987 of a peace plan for Central America, a scheme immediately embraced by liberals in the U.S. Congress who had been trying to end aid to the *contras*. With the demise of the Soviet Union, the *Sandinistas* found the economic rug abruptly yanked out from under their regime, and grudgingly accepted the Arias plan, which included democratization of Nicaragua. Arias received the Nobel Peace Price for his efforts.

Arias was succeeded in 1990 by Rafael Angelo Calderón, a lawyer from the *PUSC*. He significantly cut the number of civil employees and undertook a number of measures to modernize the economy.

In the 1994 election, the *PLN* returned to power with the candidacy of José María Figueres, son of the former president. He narrowly defeated Miguel Angel Rodríguez of the *PUSC*. Each attacked the other's allegedly shady past.

Although the Harvard-educated Figueres was elected on a promise to retain the Uruguayan-style social welfare system his father had engineered, once in office he did what so many other Latin American presidents have done in recent years. Confronted with economic reality, including a cumbersome public debt of $3.5 billion that represented 40% of GDP, he abandoned his party's idealistic social principles and sought pragmatic solutions to the country's economic woes. His greatest feat was in touting Costa Rica's low labor costs and highly literate work force to persuade transnational high-tech firms to locate assembly plants in Costa Rica. His major prize was Intel Corp., which agreed to build a $300 million assembly plant that has since exported $2–3 billion per year in Pentium processors. By 2009, Intel accounted for 20% of Costa Rica's exports.

Among Figueres' other economic successes, he lowered the unemployment rate from 6.2% in 1996 to 5.4% in 1997, cut inflation to 11.2% in 1997, the lowest in four years, and oversaw a modest GDP growth rate of 4% in 1997. Yet, Figueres proved the most unpopular president since Carazo. Despite Figueres' economic successes, Costa Ricans still grumbled that their glass was half empty rather than half full. The Figueres administration was plagued by a number of low-level scandals, hardly more than peccadillos by Latin American standards but which undermined public confidence. The public also was concerned over an alarming increase in common crime, including violent crime, once rare. Finally, Figueres was faulted for neglecting the nation's infrastructure, especially the sorry condition of streets and highways.

The time was ripe for the *PUSC*'s Rodríguez to make a comeback in 1998. The *PLN* candidate, former soccer star José Miguel Corrales, sought to distance himself from the unpopular Figueres and to seize the moral high ground by purging the party of congressional and municipal candidates with allegedly questionable backgrounds, which alienated Corrales from the rank and file of his own party. Rodríguez's strategy might well have been summed up, "It's the potholes, stupid." At times, he sounded more like a candidate for county commissioner than for president, promising to repave highways, to expand water purification systems, even to remove the hated turnstiles from buses and to allow passengers to exit from the rear. The outcome was closer than the polls had predicted, with Rodríguez winning by a 46–43% margin over Corrales.

Former President and Mrs. Abel Pacheco

Rodríguez managed to do something unusual for a Latin American president: keep his promises. He expanded the San José airport and embarked on an ambitious road-building and repaving program. He was aggressive in luring more foreign investors, an initiative that appeared to pay off (see Economy). However, Rodríguez was met with vigorous street protests when he attempted to privatize state-owned companies as has been done in virtually every other Latin American country except Cuba and Uruguay. Rice farmers protested his free-trade initiatives.

The 2002 election reflected Costa Ricans' growing disenchantment with what they regarded as a lack of choice between the two major parties. For the first time in Costa Rica's venerable 53-year-old democracy, a third-party candidate emerged who threatened the traditional parties' grip on power. In 2001, Ottón Solís, a 48-year-old economist and *PLN* dissident, formed the Citizen Action Party (*PAC*). The *PUSC* nominated a 68-year-old psychiatrist and congressional deputy, Abel Pacheco, while the *PLN* nominated Rolando Araya, a chemical engineer. Both Pacheco and Araya had high name recognition from having been television commentators.

Solís attacked what was widely perceived as the two main parties' corruption; Pacheco pledged to crack down on common crime, which had become a major problem and a threat to the all-important tourist industry; Araya placed his emphasis on improving education.

Solís prevented either major party candidate from receiving the necessary 40% to avoid a runoff. Pacheco received 38.5%, Araya was second with 30.9% and Solís was a strong third with 26.3%. Besides throwing the election into a runoff for the first time, Solís' *PAC* also emerged as the kingmaker in the new Congress with 14 seats; the *PUSC* won 19 and the *PLN*, 17. Voter turnout was 69%.

In the runoff, Araya attempted to win over Solís' voters by pledging a crackdown on official corruption, but he had little success because of the bitter attacks he had made on Solís in the first round. Pacheco won with a resounding mandate of 58%. It was the first time the *PUSC* had won two successive elections.

In 2004, Costa Rica belatedly agreed to join El Salvador, Guatemala, Honduras, Nicaragua and the Dominican Republic in creating a Central American Free Trade Agreement (CAFTA) with the United States. Costa Rica at first balked at opening up its state-owned insurance and telecommunications industries to competition with U.S. firms. Under a compromise reached with the United States, those two sectors would not become fully competitive until 2011. Still, the National Assembly hesitated to ratify the treaty, which was opposed by the powerful unions.

Costa Ricans were stunned when a series of events began unfolding in 2004 that implicated the current and three former presidents, from both major parties, in alleged financial improprieties.

There were 13 days of street protests when it was reported that the lucrative contract for vehicle inspections was awarded to a Spanish firm in which a political adviser of President Pacheco had part ownership. But this relatively mild conflict of interest was nothing compared to two later bombshells.

First, prosecutors announced they were investigating two payments from the Tai-

Costa Rica

wan government totaling $400,000 in 2001 and 2002 to a company controlled by former President Rodríguez, who just two weeks earlier had been elected secretary-general of the Organization of American States. At the same time, the former head of the state-owned power and telephone company, *ICE*, testified that he had accepted a $2.4 million "prize," a euphemism for kickback, from the French firm Alcatel for a $149 million cell phone contract in 2001 and that he had passed $550,000 of it to then-President Rodríguez. Rodríguez resigned his OAS post and returned to Costa Rica to answer the charges. He was briefly handcuffed and jailed, then sentenced to house arrest, then jailed again pending trial.

Then former President Calderón was also jailed, accused of taking $9 million in kickbacks from a $39 million loan from Finland for medical equipment to upgrade the state health care system. He allegedly brokered the deal in 2001, seven years after leaving office. Calderón and Rodríguez are both of the *PUSC*. He later stood accused of embezzling funds from the social security system.

Next it was the turn of former President Figueres of the *PLN*, who had become head of the World Economic Forum, a Swiss-based think tank. He was accused in Costa Rica of failing to report as income about $1 million he received from Alcatel for supposed "consulting fees." Figueres admitted receiving the money, which violated the terms of his contract with the WEF. He resigned and returned to Costa Rica to face possible tax evasion charges.

Almost simultaneously, Pacheco stood accused of illegally accepting foreign contributions for his 2002 campaign. Nine officials resigned from Pacheco's government, while the public works minister was caught running a loan-shark operation.

In 2005, judges agreed to release both Calderón and Rodríguez, who had complained of health problems, from jail and placed them under house arrest pending trial. Rodríguez had to post $430,000 in bond and Calderón, $500,000.

Figueres was exonerated by a judge in 2005 and by the attorney general in 2007. Calderón finally went on trial in November 2008. In October 2009, he was convicted of the embezzlement charges and sentenced to five years, as was the former head of the social security system.

Rodríguez went in trial in April 2010.

At the height of the scandals, Oscar Arias, the only recent president *not* to be under investigation, announced he would run for president again in 2006 for the *PLN*. The *PUSC* had no candidate with the stature of the respected Nobel laureate and settled for a veteran party hack, Ricardo Toledo. Solís was again the candi-

Former President Oscar Arias Sánchez

date for the *PAC*. A new player on the field was the Libertarian Movement *(ML)*, which nominated Otto Guevara.

Besides corruption, the major issue proved to be Costa Rican ratification of CAFTA; Costa Rica's failure to do so delayed CAFTA's formal establishment beyond the January 1, 2006 target date. Arias and Guevara strongly supported ratification, while Solís, backed by the labor unions, opposed it.

Voter turnout was only 65.4%, the lowest in the history the 57-year-old democracy. A slow count produced a cliffhanger between Solís and Arias, prompting a manual recount. The official results were not announced for 17 days:

Arias	664,551	40.9%
Solís	646,382	39.8%
Guevara	137,710	8.5%

In the balloting for the National Assembly, Arias' *PLN* fell just short of a majority, winning 25 of the 57 seats, an increase of eight. Solís' *PAC* became the second largest bloc with 17 seats. The Libertarian Movement won six, while the *PUSC* was humiliated, dropping from first to fourth place with five seats.

CAFTA ratification remained stalled by endless legislative and judicial wrangling. CAFTA opponents tried and failed to persuade the Supreme Electoral Tribunal *(TSE)* to approve a referendum on the issue.

In 2007, tens of thousands of CAFTA opponents, mostly farmers and trade unionists, staged a peaceful protest march in San José. The *TSE* suddenly reversed itself and gave the go-ahead for a referendum, which the Assembly approved 48–5. It was held on October 7, 2007. Voter turnout was 59.2%, and the outcome, so close it wasn't validated for days, showed

how sharply divided Costa Ricans were on CAFTA:

Sí	805,658	51.56%
No	756,814	48.44%

CAFTA opponents refused to recognize the results. Nonetheless, CAFTA came into existence on January 1, 2009.

Recent Developments

As he did in the 1980s, Arias again sought to play peacemaker by brokering negotiations in 2009 between deposed Honduran President Manuel Zelaya and interim President Robertto Micheletti. The talks in San José proved futile. After the election and inauguration of Porfirio Lobo Sosa, Costa Rica became one of only four Latin American countries to join the United States in recognizing the new Honduran president; the others were Colombia, Panama and Peru.

Arias threw his support behind Vice President Laura Chinchilla for the *PLN* presidential nomination for 2010, and the party nominated her. She also had served as justice minister before resigning both posts to run. Ottón Solís faced a challenge for the *PAC* nomination from Epsy Campbell, a 46-year-old economist of Jamaican parentage, but the party nominated him for a third time. Otto Guevara stood again at the *ML* candidate. Former President Calderón declared his intention to run despite his pendingt corruption trial, but the *PUSC* eventually nominated Luis Fishman, who had little name recognition. Five minor party candidates also were on the ballot.

Despite a slight downturn in the economy from the global recession, Arias and the *PLN* enjoyed the continued goodwill of the voters, upon which Chinchilla capitalized. Moreover, gradual acceptance of CAFTA had deprived Solís of his major issue. Turnout on February 7 was up somewhat from 2006 to 69.1%, and this time there was no cliffhanger:

Chinchilla	863,803	46.8%
Solís	464,454	25.6%
Guevara	384,540	20.8%
Fishman	71,330	3.9%

Although elected without a runoff, Chinchilla will have to govern by consensus as the *PLN* lost two of its 25 seats in the Assembly. The *CAC* won 11, the *ML* 10 and the *PUSC* six, a gain of one. Two other parties claimed the other five seats.

On May 8, Chinchilla, 51, made history as she was sworn in as Costa Rica's first woman president and as Latin America's fifth elected female president. She holds a master's degree in public policy from Georgetown University in Washington and worked as a consultant for several years on judicial and public security reform for various governmental and non-governmental organizations.

Although the *PLN* is a member of the Socialist International and she promised to continue Costa Rica's traditional welfare model, Chinchilla is also a social conservative who opposes abortion and gay marriage. Nonetheless, she has been divorced and bore a son out of wedlock by the Spaniard to whom she is now married. She is also environmentally conscious, and on her first day in office signed an executive order prohibiting strip-mining for gold.

Culture: Costa Ricans are predominantly Roman Catholic. Basically they are of European, primarily Spanish, ancestry; the country has the lowest percentage of Indians and mestizos of any Central American country. Early in the colonial era, the few Indians native to the area were assimilated into a uniform, friendly society of middle class merchants and small farmers. The pure Spanish descendants emerged as a small, rich elite controlling the wealth of Costa Rica.

Popular cultural expression is found in music and dance. The most characteristic art expression is the brilliantly decorated ox carts like those still found in rural Spain and Portugal; they are accepted as a national symbol, although they have been replaced by trucks and tractors in the national economy.

Through energetic promotion of education, Costa Rica has achieved the highest literacy rate in Central America—96%—greater than that of the United States. There is a vigorous free press. The country's newspaper of record is *La Nación*. Fifteen television stations provide a wide variety of entertainment.

This is one of the most pleasant of the Central American countries to visit. Of course, the usual precautions against thievery must be taken where there is great disparity in wealth, particularly in the city of Limón.

Economy: Costa Rica's sources of external income are coffee and bananas. Industrial activity once was limited to processing agricultural products for market and the production of import substitutes for domestic consumption. In recent years, foreign firms have established assembly plants, such as Motorola and Intel.

Improved economic conditions have encouraged the upper class to retain more capital funds within Costa Rica, which before would have been invested abroad. There is no immediate threat to the econ-

President Laura Chinchilla Miranda

omy, and there is also a growing sense within the elite that the wealth of the nation must be shared more widely.

Tourism is a rapidly growing industry, thanks to beautiful beaches on both coasts and a number of rain forest reserves. Costa Rica also has proven an ideal site for a relatively luxurious retirement at a modest cost for U.S. citizens. Stability and lower prices for everything but imported goods are attractive to middle-class retirees. Costa Rica advertises itself in U.S. media as an excellent place for individual (not communal) retirement, attracting widespread interest. About 30,000 Americans already have settled here.

Motorola announced in 1998 it would begin scaling back the output of its Costa Rican plant, but the impact was more than neutralized by the opening of Intel's Pentium processor plant. The plant's $2–3 billion in exports since 1999 have helped Costa Rica trade surpluses, compared with earlier huge deficits. It still accounts for 20% of Costa Rica's exports, and Intel has begun investing another $800 million in its Costa Rica operations.

After the initial construction was over, GDP growth for 2000 was a meager 1.4%, only .7% in 2001, and 3.0% in 2002.

These positive factors, plus political stability, an educated labor force and the Rodríguez administration's eight-year tax exemption for manufacturers of export products, proved attractive to foreign investors. One target: the cumbersome government-owned electricity and telecommunications company, which Rodríguez attempted unsuccessfully to privatize. Costa Ricans have proven stubbornly reluctant to dismantle the quasi-socialist public sector, apparently out of fear of the unknown and despite the privatization trend that has swept Latin America. Even cellular telephone service and insurance are state-owned in Costa Rica. In the next

few years, high-tech and ecotourism are expected to transform the Costa Rican economy, replacing the far more market-sensitive coffee and bananas as the mainstays of the economy.

In 2003, GDP growth was back up to 5.6%, but tapered back off to 3.9% in 2004, then rose to 8.8% in 2006 and 7.8% for 2007. With the beginning of the global recession, it dropped to 2.6% in 2008, the lowest since 2002. In 2009, the economy shrank by –1.6%

Unemployment has remained steady and quite low by Latin American standards: 6.7% in 2003, 4.6% in 2007 and 4.9% in 2008. With the recession, it jumped to 6.4% in 2009.

Inflation remained at about 9% for several years, but jumped to 11.5% in 2007 and 13.4% in 2008. It fell to 8.3% in 2009

In 2004, Costa Rica became a signatory to the Central American Free Trade Agreement with the United States, El Salvador, the Dominican Republic, Guatemala, Honduras and Nicaragua, but ratification was opposed by labor unions and some business sectors because of concerns over the state-owned insurance and telecommunications industries, which are sacred cows. Ratification became an issue in the 2006 presidential election. The winner, Oscar Arias, favored ratification, which was narrowly approved in a referendum on October 7, 2007 (see History).

In his second administration, President Oscar Arias oversaw a reduction in the once crushing public debt, although in 2008 it was still 42.2% of GDP, climbing to 49.3% in 2009. In 2007, Costa Rica enjoyed its first budget surplus in 50 years.

The Future: Although Costa Ricans grumbled for years about suspected corruption by their politicians, they were nonetheless boastful that their political system was still far more circumspect than those of most other Latin American countries. Indeed, Transparency International consistently rates Costa Rica in its annual corruption perceptions index among the three least corrupt countries in Latin America; only Chile and Uruguay are regarded as less corrupt (see Latin America Today).

The jailing of former Presidents Calderón and Rodríguez in 2004, and the investigations against President Pacheco and former President Figueres, shook Costa Ricans' pride in their country's perceived rectitude. They are now like parents who thought their teenage daughter had done nothing worse than smoke cigarettes and drink beer, only to discover she had been smoking marijuana and charging the soccer team for sexual favors. Calderón became the first Costa Rican president to be convicted of anything; he was sentenced to five years in 2009. Rod-

Costa Rica

ríguez's trial began in April 2010, shortly before this book went to press.

Oscar Arias' second term in office, 2006–10, was the first in almost two decades that was almost untainted by scandal, an encouraging and refreshing change.

The Costa Ricans' attitude toward their once-envied democracy has consequently taken a roller-coaster ride in recent years. Even before the scandals broke, the annual *Latinobarómetro* survey showed a 10-point drop from 2003 to 2004 in the percentage of Costa Ricans who believed democracy is preferable to any other form of government, from 77% to 67%; in 1996 it was 80%. In 2006, with Arias' election to a second term, it recovered to 75%, and in 2007 it rose to 83%, the highest in Latin America. But in 2008, perhaps because of the impending corruption trials, it plummeted again back to 67%; the 16-point drop in one year was the greatest of any nation in the survey. In 2009, it was back up to 74%, the third highest after Venezuela and Uruguay.

The February 7, 2010 presidential election made history with the election of Costa Rica's first woman president, Laura Chinchilla of the *PLN*. Other than bearing a child out of wedlock—little more than a peccadillo in Latin America—she apparently has been free of scandal in her public career as a judicial reform consultant for various organizations in Latin America and Africa. She later married José María Rico Cueto, a Spanish lawyer and the father of their now 14-year-old son. A centrist, she likely will prove a moderating force, as Arias did, in the ideological struggle in the hemisphere between Washington on the one hand and leftist Venezuelan President Hugo Chávez on the other.

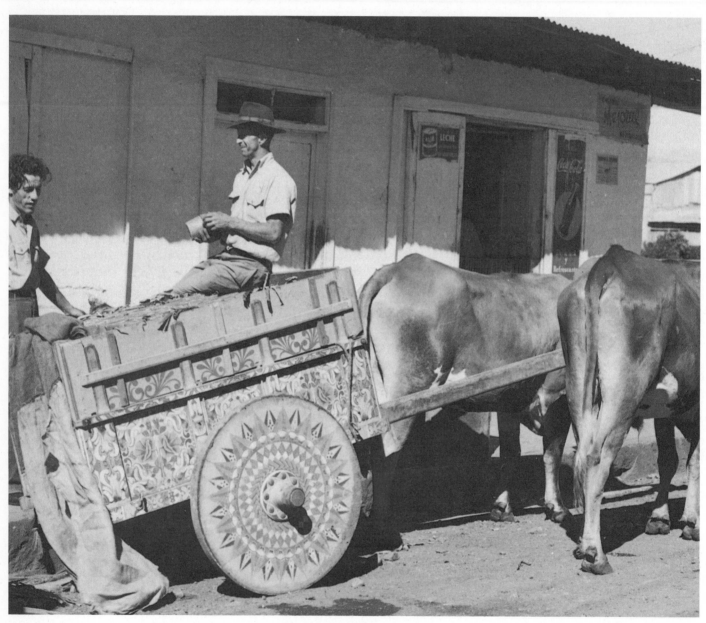

Typical Costa Rican ox cart

"Señores Imperialists: We are not in the least afraid of you!"   *Photo by Sheila Curtin*

Area: 44,217 square miles; with the Isle of Youth, 45,397 square miles.

Population: 11.477 million in 2010 (est.).

Capital City: Havana (Pop. 2.4 million, estimated).

Climate: Tropical with little daily or seasonal change. Cuba is buffeted by occasional tropical hurricanes from July to October.

Neighboring Countries: Cuba is an island, the largest and most westerly of the Greater Antilles islands, lying 90 miles south of Florida and separated from Hispaniola by 40 miles.

Official Language: Spanish.

Ethnic Background: Mulatto (mixed black and white), 51%; white, 37%; black, 11%; other, 1%.

Principal Religion: Roman Catholic.

Chief Commercial Products: Sugar, minerals and tobacco.

Currency: Peso.

Gross Domestic Product: U.S. $56.52 billion (est.) in 2009 ($3,856–$11,905 per capita in real terms in 2008, according to World Bank; $9,700 in so-called purchasing power parity, which factors in social benefits, in 2009.)

Former Colonial Status: Spanish Crown Colony (1492–1898).

Independence Date: May 20, 1902. (Spanish rule ended on December 10, 1898).

Chief of State: Raúl Modesto Castro Ruz (b. June 3, 1931), president of the Council of State (since February 28, 2008)

National Flag: Three blue and two white horizontal stripes; a white star in a red triangle at the staff.

Cuba, an island 745 miles long and not over 90 miles wide at any point, lies east and west across the Gulf of Mexico, 90 miles south of Key West, Florida. Cuba is gifted with moderate temperatures, adequate rainfall and excellent soils. While the general impression of Cuba is one of rolling hills, it is in fact quite mountainous in parts. To the west of Havana is the Sierra de los Organos, with elevations of up to 2,500 feet; toward the center of the island are the Trinidad Mountains rising to 3,700 feet; in the east the Sierra Maestra has peaks reaching 6,500 feet. About one sixth of the land is forested. The rough, stony headlands east of Guantanamo Bay are semi-arid and the source of copper, nickel, chrome and iron ores.

History: Columbus discovered Cuba in 1492 and conquered by the Spanish in 1511. Indians offered little resistance and, decimated by hard labor and epidemics, disappeared fairly rapidly. By the end of the 16th century only small, dwindling groups survived in the mountainous areas of the island.

The Spanish conquest of the continent relegated Cuba and the other islands in the Caribbean to a secondary position in the rapidly expanding empire. Lured by the news of gold and glory coming from Mexico and Peru, Spanish immigrants abandoned Cuba to join further exploration and conquests. Two factors, though, compelled Spain to pay special attention to Cuba: its strategic geographical location, dominating the entrance to the Gulf of Mexico, and the increasing attacks by pirates, which forced Spain to concentrate its naval resources in "convoys," or fleets, for better protection of its rich cargoes. These fleets, one departing from Veracruz, Mexico, and the other from Cartagena, Colombia, joined in Havana and then, under the protection of the Spanish navy, sailed for Europe. Consequently the port of Havana had to be extremely well fortified, and the sporadic presence of these fleets allowed for a flourishing degree of commerce.

During the 18th century the development of the island gained some momentum. The decline of gold and silver production on the continent convinced many Spaniards to remain in Cuba. Garrisons protected several ports besides Havana; smuggling with other islands—principally

Cuba

Jamaica and Haiti, by then British and French possessions—increased trade. The rising demand for the island's first valuable export, tobacco, created favorable conditions for steady economic growth. The strategic importance of Cuba was highlighted in 1762 when Havana was attacked and captured by a large British expeditionary force. The British did not expand their occupation beyond the port, and they stayed less than two years. However, the attack jolted Spain. More fortifications were built on the island, more capable officials were sent to govern the colony and a program of road construction began into the interior. Almost simultaneously, the island's sugar production began to demonstrate its rich potential.

The independence of the United States in 1783 opened a close and expanding market, and the collapse of Haiti's sugar production in 1799–1801 during its devastating war for independence gave Cuba a truly golden opportunity. In the first three decades of the 19th century, the island changed rapidly into the world's leading sugar producer. Sugar production, however, required a growing number of black slaves, who would alter Cuban culture.

Fearing a repetition of Haiti's experience, and enjoying unhindered prosperity—the Napoleonic wars and affairs in South America had kept Spain occupied in other areas—Cubans were not eager to risk all in an attempt to break with the mother country. After 1830, this situation began to change. Concentrating her attention on Cuba, Spain increased taxation, imposed arbitrary rules for its own benefit and completely alienated the creoles (native-born Cubans of Spanish ancestry), by denying them any voice in the government. Seeking annexation to the United States, many slave owners promoted armed expeditions from southern American ports, but the North's resistance to the incorporation of another slave territory into the Union, and the eventual defeat of the South in the American Civil War, put an end to those efforts.

By 1865, the majority of the creoles still held hopes of obtaining reforms from Madrid. Only a minority still advocated independence. But an international economic crisis in 1866 and Madrid's dismissal in 1867 of a Cuban delegation demanding reforms set the stage for the *independentistas*. In 1868, in the town of Yara, Carlos Manuel de Céspedes raised the banner of independence.

Using guerrilla tactics, and under the guidance of able military leaders, the Cubans fought valiantly against an increasing number of Spanish troops for 10 years. Their failure to invade the rich western provinces (the struggle was limited to the eastern regions), internal dissension, exhaustion of resources and renewed Spanish promises of reforms, brought peace in 1878. But despite the Cuban Autonomist Party's efforts, few reforms materialized. By 1890, Cuban discontent was growing and a new, exceptional leader had appeared: José Martí. Poet, essayist and patriot, Martí managed to unite almost all Cuban exiles, organized a conspiracy on the island and prepared to renew the struggle. He dreamed of a short, popular war that would avoid the destruction of wealth, the rise of military *caudillos* and U.S. intervention. In 1895 the war began and Martí was killed in one of its first skirmishes.

U.S. Domination

From 1895 until 1898, the Cubans fought Spain's military might. This time, able to carry the war throughout the entire island, the rebels torched much of Cuba's sources of wealth. Increasingly alarmed, and stimulated by imperialist groups and a "yellow" (sensationalist) press, the United States finally intervened in 1898 after the explosion of the battleship *Maine* in Havana harbor raised the clamor for war to a peak. The "splendid little war" against an exhausted Spain lasted a few months and ended with U.S. military occupation of Cuba.

After reorganizing a country ravaged by war and disease, the U.S. military forces abandoned the island in 1902. That year, the Cuban people proclaimed a constitution, although the Platt Amendment enacted by the U.S. Congress gave the United States the right to intervene in case of crisis and the use of a naval base at Guantanamo Bay. Tomás Estrada Palma was elected the first democratic president.

Estrada Palma's honest administration was marred by political turmoil when the president sought re-election in 1906, and the United States reoccupied the island for two years. After building a Cuban army and overseeing the election of Liberal José Miguel Gómez, the United States once more pulled out its military forces.

The next 20 years witnessed rapid expansion of sugar production, increased U.S. investment, persistent political corruption and instability of a one-product economy. Nevertheless, the republic progressed in many areas. Education improved, communication was expanded and a new nationalistic awareness matured. An economic crisis in 1919–21 resulted in a rising crescendo of popular demands for the abrogation of the Platt Amendment and strong protests against official corruption.

134

President Batista deposits his ballot

Liberal Gerardo Machado was elected president in 1925 and initiated a vast program of national regeneration and public construction. His popularity declined in 1928 when he sought re-election. It plunged even more after the economic collapse of 1929–30. Faced with widespread misery and with violent opposition spearheaded by university students and an underground dissident group known as *ABC*, Machado responded with brutality. By 1933, despite increased terrorism on the part of the government, the struggle had reached a stalemate; the opposition had no realistic hopes of toppling Machado, and the government was unable to eliminate its opponents. Washington again intervened.

Constrained by his own "Good Neighbor Policy," which precluded the use of military force, the recently elected President Franklin Roosevelt sent his trusted aide Sumner Welles to seek a legal solution for Cuba; his mission was to prevent a revolution and avoid U.S. military intervention. Posing as a mediator, Welles pressured Machado into making concessions, encouraged the opposition and eroded the army's loyalty to the president. A general strike forced Machado to flee the island. Immediately Welles organized a provisional government with the cooperation of the *ABC* and the majority of the opposition. But the revolutionary momentum disrupted his plan.

There followed a military insurrection of army sergeants, headed by Fulgencio Batista, which was transformed by university students into a revolutionary movement that toppled the provisional government. For four turbulent months under a temporary president, the students

and the sergeants (by then *colonels*) tried to enforce a radical and ambitious program of social reforms. Sternly opposed by Welles, the government collapsed in January 1934 when Batista shifted to the opposition. As soon as a moderate president was installed, Washington abrogated the Platt Amendment. For the following decade, *real power* centered around Batista.

Batista was neither a bloodthirsty dictator nor a counter-revolutionary. A man of humble origins, both shrewd and ambitious, he preferred bribery and corruption over brutality. Well aware of the importance of the nationalistic and social forces unleashed by the revolutionary episode of 1933, he tried to use them for his own benefit.

Encouraging the emergence of political parties and the return to the island of political exiles, he quickly restored stability. Labor unions were legally protected, social legislation approved and a modest plan for national recovery announced. After Batista harshly repressed a general strike in 1935, the Cuban political atmosphere became calm. Supported by several parties, including, ironically, the Communist Party, Batista convened a constitutional assembly, and in 1940 promulgated one of the most advanced social constitutions in all of Latin America. That same year, Batista was elected president.

With the price of sugar climbing during World War II, Batista's term coincided with a return to economic prosperity. In 1944, Batista crowned his accomplishments by allowing free elections. Ramón Grau San Martín, a hero of 1933 and head of the *Auténtico* Party, obtained an overwhelming majority. The *Auténticos* ruled

from 1944–48 with a positive record of benefits for workers, respect for democratic values, a more equitable distribution of wealth, continuing economic recovery and rising living standards, but they were tarnished by public corruption on an unprecedented scale.

Grau was succeeded in 1948 by a fellow *Auténtico*, Carlos Prío Socarrás, who proved equally venal. Before the people

---

The U.S. and Cuba
1902–1959

Despite the unevenness of U.S.–Cuban relations politically, the two nations developed close economic ties during the post-independence period through the 1959 Cuban Revolution. U.S. investment was encouraged and protected, and in fact became a mainstay of the Cuban economy. In spite of domestic Cuban upheavals, there was an unwritten understanding that neither U.S. investments nor Cuban tourist facilities calculated to attract Americans would be disturbed.

Some aspects of this relationship were resented by many Cubans, particularly the common U.S. notion that Cuba was a paradise for those seeking sexual adventures not explicitly described, but well-known. Many "French" postcards (pornography, judged by then-prevailing standards in the United States) had their origin in Cuba. Numerous films "for private exhibition" were produced and made in the island nation. Tourists relished the decadence offered by the casinos and nightclubs, many controlled by organized crime figures, chief among them Meyer Lansky.

Havana and other coastal resorts and towns were favored ports of call for resort and cruise ships and there was regular steamship service catering to vacationers. A luxurious train regularly departed from New York—"The Havana Special"—which ran down the east coast through Miami and went on to Key West over a rail causeway. From there, the cars were loaded onto seagoing ferries which took them to their ultimate destination, loaded with fun-seeking vacationers. This ended in 1936 when a devastating hurricane wiped out the causeway.

As airline traffic came into its own after World War II, Havana was a favorite destination of tourists and vacationers. This pleasant state of affairs continued right up to 1960, with all political considerations being put aside.

Cuba

could repudiate the *Auténticos* in 1952 elections, Batista disrupted the political process with a military coup.

Trying to keep up democratic appearances, Batista promised elections in 1954. But the illegitimacy of his government prompted political parties and numerous sectors of the population to demand a return to "true democracy." Soon more radical opponents appeared. The students organized violent acts and on July 26, 1953—now a holiday in Cuba—a group of young men under the leadership of Fidel Castro made an unsuccessful attack on the Moncada Barracks in Santiago de Cuba. The sheer brutality of its repression mobilized popular support for the rebels. With Castro and his surviving group in prison, Batista renewed his futile effort to gain legitimacy.

Batista was "elected" to the presidency in 1954 and he allowed *all* political prisoners to go free—including young Castro. But opposition to Batista increased. While a Student Revolutionary Federation resorted to terrorism to achieve Batista's overthrow, Castro, who had been in self-exile in Mexico, landed an expedition of 86 men in Oriente Province in December 1956—among them his brother Raúl and an Argentine Marxist named Ernesto "Che" Guevara—and took refuge in the Sierra Maestra mountains of eastern Cuba.

Weakened by adverse propaganda and its own corruption, with a demoralized army incapable of mounting any serious operation, the regime consistently lost ground. When in 1958 Washington showed its disapproval by proclaiming an arms embargo, Batista was doomed. On December 31 he fled the island (with millions of dollars stashed safely in Swiss banks), and Castro's rebel army entered Havana in triumph on January 1, 1959.

The Cuban Revolution

For the vast majority of the Cuban people, Batista's downfall promised an end to an illegitimate and violent episode in their history and a quick return to the democratic process. Castro, and other leaders of the 26th of July Movement (named after the attack on the Moncada Barracks) had repeatedly promised the restoration of the 1940 constitution, freedom of expression, elections within 18 months and an end to political corruption. Thus, the 32-year-old leader, enhanced by his heroic image, received the almost unanimous applause of the Cuban people. Batista had fallen into such disrepute in the eyes of the world that Castro was considered a liberating hero; the Eisenhower administration hoped that firm and friendly ties with the new government on the island could be forged, to-

Ché Guevara, 1959

gether with enhanced U.S. investment. Castro, however, had other ideas.

The son of a wealthy Spanish landowner who studied for a time in a Jesuit seminary, Castro had very early shown inclinations toward violence and unlimited ambition: he wanted unrestricted, absolute power. Increasing his power with a series of laws which, at least temporarily, benefited the masses—agrarian reform, increased wages, a reduction of the cost of public services—he simultaneously used his popularity, or his charisma, as a weapon to crush his opponents.

Dr. Manuel Urrutia, the same man he had appointed president six months before, was forced to resign under a barrage of insults. A new slogan appeared: "Revolution first, elections later!" Special tribunals dealt harshly with *Batistianos* and later with anyone accused of counter-revolution; about 550 were executed by firing squads. In late 1959, one of the heroes of the revolution, Major Huber Matos, resigned to protest an increasing communist influence in the government. He was sentenced to 20 years in prison. By the end of that year, almost all of the media were under government control. Ominously, another slogan proclaimed that "to be anti-communist is to be counter-revolutionary."

Quietly, Castro also began building a formidable military apparatus, commanded by his brother, Raúl. He also appointed "Che" Guevara as minister of industry. Guevara embarked on a disastrous plan to communize Cuba's means of production. Tens of millions of dollars worth of U.S. land and business holdings were expropriated, further souring bilateral relations. In 1960, the United States retaliated with an economic embargo of the Castro regime, still in effect four decades later, and in January 1961 the outgoing Eisenhower administration severed diplomatic relations.

Meanwhile, there was widespread disillusionment in Cuba. Tens of thousands left

the island (with their descendants, the figure is now more than 2 million); others organized resistance. Anti-communist guerrillas appeared in the central mountains and acts of sabotage became common.

Encouraged by this show of resistance, the U.S. CIA and Cuban exiles in Florida hatched a scheme for Cuban expatriates to invade. The people, supposedly fed up with Castro, were anticipated to join the invaders in a groundswell movement that would envelop and suffocate the newborn regime. In April 1961, an expedition of about 1,200 Cuban exiles invaded at the Playa Girón, known in English as the Bay of Pigs, on the southern coast of Cuba. Although the size of the force, the anticipated response by Castro's forces and the terrain involved all mandated the use of air support, no provision in the plans had been made for this. Further, no coordination had been undertaken with internal Cuban resistance forces, which had little, if any, organization. The invasion force was a sitting duck target for Castro's army. The whole plan was, in the words of Sir Winston Churchill, "a wretched half-measure." About 100 of the invaders were killed and the remainder captured.

Castro triumphantly announced that total victory had been won against "American imperialism," and he proceeded to wipe out all remaining internal resistance and to pose as a conquering hero. Defiantly, he proclaimed Cuba a socialist state. Emboldened by what appeared to be an indication of U.S. weakness, the Soviet Union, which until then had refrained

Fidel pursuing his passion for baseball, 1960

Cuba

from any military commitment, began sending advisers and vast amounts of military equipment to Cuba—including intermediate-range ballistic missiles with nuclear warheads.

In October 1962, President John F. Kennedy, still smarting from the Bay of Pigs fiasco, imposed a naval "quarantine" of Cuba, placed U.S. military forces on alert and demanded withdrawal of the missiles. For 13 days, the world teetered on the brink of thermonuclear war. Soviet Premier Nikita Khrushchëv, furious, grudgingly complied with the U.S. demands, but only after obtaining a costly oral promise from Kennedy: the U.S. would never invade Cuba. Kennedy thus verbally abrogated a cornerstone of U.S. Latin American policy—the long-standing Monroe Doctrine. Emboldened by that assurance, Castro embarked on a series of continental revolutionary adventures.

Castro's formula for revolutionary success was guerrilla warfare modeled on the Cuban experience. From 1962 to 1968, Havana became a center of support for leftist revolutionaries who spread their activities from Mexico to Argentina. Nevertheless, the formula failed. Opposed by communist parties that rejected *any* revolution they did not control as the "vanguard of the proletariat," and confronted by armies much better trained than Batista's, the guerrillas were defeated everywhere. In 1967, "Che" Guevara was killed in Bolivia, thus becoming an international Marxist icon and martyr. A dangerous deterioration of Cuba's economy forced Castro to fold the guerrilla banner and to accept the orthodox communist line demanded by the Soviet Union. Castro applauded the 1968 Soviet invasion of Czechoslovakia and publicly criticized China's Mao Tse-tung.

Consolidating Communism's Grip

Nothing resembling the structures of government envisioned in the Marxist dogma came about in Cuba, nor did anything similar to the dual party-government structure of the Soviet Union emerge under Castro. Instead, Cuba became a personality cult under Castro, much as China did under Mao. However, three stated goals of 20th century communism were achieved with remarkable success: the eradication of illiteracy, universal medical care and public housing. The centrally planned economy of the Soviet Union did not appear. Even though he had no skills in economics, Castro waded in without hesitation, quickly wrecking the economy. Erratic planning, concentration of total power in Castro's hands and burgeoning bureaucracies, capped by the maintenance of a huge military force (once about 450,000) resulted in declining sugar pro-

ductivity and failure to develop other resources for trade and income.

Increased Soviet aid became vital for the survival of the revolution. When in 1968 Moscow was forced to apply a minimum of economic pressure to avoid pouring increasing amounts of economic aid into what seemed to be a bottomless chasm, Castro surrendered more of what had become Cuba's limited independence. He made an urgent effort in 1970 to obtain desperately needed hard currency by mobilizing urban residents, sending thousands of them into the fields to harvest sugar cane with machetes, hoping for a 10-million-ton crop. The effort failed, and it disrupted the economy for months. The next year, Castro began a process of "institutionalization" (creating organizations theoretically capable of sharing his power) while yielding increasing control over economic planning to Soviet advisers.

The Cuban debt to the Soviet Union, despite its annual purchases of the sugar crop at a level above the prevailing world price, gradually rose to more than $5 billion. In an effort to repay the Soviets, Castro was receptive to a request for the use of his troops for international communist adventures. In 1975, Castro deployed 20,000 soldiers to Angola to prop up that tottering communist regime; by 1989, that force had grown to almost 60,000. Having no stake in the outcome of Angola's ongoing struggle, the Cubans turned out to be lackluster fighters. Many returned home infected with AIDS and without a "vic-

Cuban militia woman, 1960

tory," ending an unfortunate chapter in communist adventurism. Cuban involvement in Ethiopia, Yemen, Nicaragua, El Salvador and Guatemala also occurred during the 1970s and 1980s.

Both the United States and Cuba were humiliated in early 1980. Hundreds of Cubans stormed into the compound of the Peruvian Embassy in Havana, begging for political asylum. In a bold and unprecedented move, Castro suddenly announced that any Cuban who wished to leave the country was free to do so. The result was a frantic exodus, as thousands of small privately owned boats crossed the Florida Straits to the port of Mariel to pick up refugees in a Dunkirk-like evacuation. About 125,000 so-called *Marielitos* departed the island. Most were honorable and were assimilated into the Florida Cuban community as well as in other places. But a significant number were lunatics and criminals, some forced onto the waiting boats at gunpoint, who wound up in already overcrowded U.S. federal prisons. Many others were homosexuals, considered undesirable in Cuba.

It had been a master stroke by Castro, a means of emptying his prisons and asylums as well as getting rid of potentially troublesome dissenters. But even he realized that he had overplayed his hand. After tedious indirect negotiations with the United States, Castro agreed to accept the undesirables back. Many of the prisoners rioted, however, preferring life as detainees in the United States to life in Cuba. The so-called "Mariel Boatlift" became a political issue in the 1980 U.S. presidential campaign, one of several foreign policy fiascos of President Jimmy Carter that contributed to Ronald Reagan's landslide victory.

There followed eight years of increased bilateral hostility and U.S. military opposition to Cuban adventurism in Nicaragua, El Salvador and Grenada, among other places. The U.S. invasion of Grenada in 1983 and the increasing presence of U.S. advisers and troops in Central America made Castro more cautious. As a further demonstration of its submission to the Soviets, Cuba declined to attend the 1984 Summer Olympics in Los Angeles. Relations with the United States appeared to thaw briefly in 1984, but then resumed their frozen state when "Radio Martí" started broadcasting from Miami with U.S. government support. Cuba quickly jammed it.

Fall of the Soviet Benefactor

The ascension to power of Mikhail Gorbachëv in the Soviet Union was fateful for communist Cuba. In 1986, Soviet trade terms became tougher, and subsidies shrank. Soviet aid had been as much as $6

Cuba

"We are dignified and revolutionary Cubans." Propaganda in Viñales

Photo by Wayne Thompson

billion a year. In 1989, Gorbachëv visited the island. He had already concluded that overlaying the Castro regime with Soviet technicians and advisers had not and would not work. Moreover, the Soviets by then had to borrow money from Western banks and to import food from the United States. The deterioration accelerated rapidly, and by 1991–92 Cuba was in the grip of economic disaster.

Castro's response was to get rid of all elements of dissent, particularly Carlos Aldana, formerly No. 3 in the Cuban hierarchy, who represented a moderate trend corresponding to the Soviet Union's *glasnost* and *perestroika*.

At the 1991 Politburo meeting, Castro heaped praise on the achievements of Cuba under socialism. Then his mood turned to one of rage—he berated the assemblage, lashed out at the shortcomings of the Cuban people, vilified capitalism and vented his anger on the United States, the trade embargo in particular, Americans in general and all the presidents from Kennedy to Bush. He blamed all of Cuba's problems on these sources, not on poor Cuban leadership. Later added to his list of pariahs was the former Soviet Union and Gorbachëv.

Cuba's foreign interests had been identical to those of the Soviet Union. Since then, they have been centered upon the cautious wooing of capitalist nations perceived as unthreatening, such as Canada and Spain.

Between 1989 and 1992, Cuba's annual purchasing power dropped from $8.1 billion to $2.2 billion. Sugar production descended to 7 million tons, even with rationing and dispatching urban workers to harvest the cane by hand (there was no fuel). The 1992 harvest was 4.2 million tons and less was produced in 1993–94.

The administration of President George H.W. Bush tightened the 1960 embargo in late 1992 with the Torricelli Amendment. No U.S. company, affiliate or subsidiary in the United States or abroad, could trade with Cuba in any form. U.S. ports are closed to any ship of any nation or registry that has, within the previous six months, called at a Cuban port. These tightened screws, together with the disappearance of $300 million a year in Soviet aid, left the Cuban people in near-destitution. Increasing numbers of Cubans attempted to flee the island in flimsy boats or inner-tube rafts. There may never be an accurate accounting of how many have drowned, died of dehydration or been eaten by sharks in a desperate attempt to escape their misery.

Cuba's economic prostration brought some basic changes the 1990s. Possession of the U.S. dollar was legalized in 1993 and for 11 years was virtually the only hard currency on the island (see Economy). The peso officially traded at 1:1 with the dollar, but it took more than 100 pesos to buy a dollar on the open market. With the advent of the dollar came a system of black markets that still pervades everything.

Persons in certain trades and professions were allowed to become "self-employed" in a variety of enterprises, but only if they first secured permits. Of course, a permit that is granted can be revoked, which they later were. Small enterprises bloomed, particularly in urban areas. A large number of "mom and pop" restaurants were known for delicious food in Havana, for fees payable in U.S. dollars. Bicycle repair, plumbing, and similar services were by contract with one of the entrepreneurs. Physicians were not allowed the same freedom.

Several events occurred in 1994 that suggested, falsely, that basic change was on the horizon. Cuba decided to use the threat of a renewed flood of refugees to lessen or abate the U.S. embargo. Severe shortages of just about everything led to increased pressures to migrate to the United States. When these were resisted, there were anti-government riots in and near Havana. The Clinton administration, dealing with a flood of Haitian refugees, tried to discourage the Cuban refugees, but refused to alter the tight embargo. A stop-gap "solution" of interning refugees in the U.S. base at Guantanamo Bay failed. The attempts to leave Cuba for Florida resulted in the loss of many lives. Castro threatened to unleash another wave of boat people in the summer of 1995; this was averted by a U.S. plan to gradually admit the Cubans remaining at Guantanamo.

The Helms-Burton Act

On February 24, 1996, in an unexplainable and stupid act, Cuban air force jets shot down two unarmed small aircraft that were patrolling the waters off the coast of Cuba to protect the "boat people" from mishap. Three men, who were members of the Miami-based exile organization Brothers to the Rescue, were killed. There was an immediate outcry in the U.S. Congress; the result was the Helms-Burton Act, strengthening the embargo. Any foreign firm doing business with Cuba could be penalized in the United States. The avowed purpose was to stifle even minuscule investment and loans to Cuba.

In some respects, the Helms-Burton Act backfired on the United States in that it appears to have done more to anger traditional U.S. allies, Canada in particular, than to punish Cuba.

Castro observed his 70th birthday in 1996. The once-flamboyant revolutionary made a number of state visits, including a tour of Europe and to the Latin American summit in Chile, dressed in stylish business suits rather than the fatigue uniform of old. In Rome, the avowed atheist visited Pope John Paul II, and the two announced that the pontiff would visit Cuba in 1998.

A visit to Havana in 1996 by Democratic U.S. Representative Bill Richardson of New Mexico succeeded in winning release of a number of political prisoners. As a further sign of an easing of tensions, the Clinton administration approved a request by 10 U.S. news organizations to establish bureaus in Cuba.

No foreign media, however, were allowed to cover Castro's seven-hour speech in October 1997 before the Fifth Communist Party Congress, the first in six years. The aging dictator squelched any hopes

Cuba would deviate further from its dogmatic Marxism. He blamed the United States for a series of terrorist bombings at Cuba's tourist-oriented hotels, accusing the Clinton administration of trying to undermine the Revolution by frightening away badly needed foreign tourists (see Economy).

Castro tied the congress to the week-long ceremony to rebury the skeletal remains of Che Guevara that had been recovered from the Bolivian jungle after 30 years. On the eve of the congress, however, four dissidents, among them Vladimoro Roca, a former air force pilot and son of revolutionary hero Blas Roca, issued a document titled "Homeland for Us All," which ridiculed the congress for focusing on the past glories of the revolution without offering solutions for the problems of the present. All four were sentenced to prison.

Cuba suffered another public relations disaster with the defection to Costa Rica in 1997 of the talented pitcher Orlando "El Duque" Hernández, half-brother of the Florida Marlins' Livan Hernández. Livan Hernández had defected in Mexico in 1995, and in 1996, his half-brother was banned from playing baseball in Cuba. Orlando Hernández was given a U.S. visa and was recruited into the Majors. It was yet another humiliation for the baseball-loving Castro. So was the much-publicized request of his 41-year-old daughter, Alina Fernández-Revuelta, for political asylum in Spain during the papal visit.

The Papal Visit of 1998

Another public relations gimmick was even more stunning: Castro's invitation to Pope John Paul II to visit Cuba, which the pope accepted. This was a major gamble for Castro, because he would not be able to censor the strong-willed pope the way he controls his own people's thinking. On the other hand, he apparently reasoned, the gesture might bring a relaxing of the U.S. trade embargo.

Enigmatic as ever, Castro declared at the 1997 Ibero-American Summit in Venezuela that Cuba would never deviate from its revolutionary course, rejecting calls from his peers for more respect for human rights. Yet, as a gesture to the pope, Castro permitted the first Christmas holiday Cubans had had since 1969 (the declaration of atheism as official state doctrine had been rescinded in 1992). He also eased restrictions on religious worship, and suddenly Catholic churches were filled for Mass; other sects received increased interest as well from a people starved for spirituality, including young people born after the Revolution.

The pope's four-day visit in January 1998 was truly historic, with hundreds of thousands of Cubans attending open-air Masses. Castro, true to his word, welcomed the pontiff at the airport and even attended a Mass; he also addressed John Paul as "holy father" and recalled that he had been schooled by Jesuits. Hundreds of exiles were granted special permission to return for the event, many of whom were reunited with loved ones they had not seen for nearly 40 years.

The pope's public declarations must have made Castro cringe. He denounced human rights violations and the denial of religious freedom, and called for the release of political prisoners. At the same time, he noted that the Vatican and the Cuban Revolution find common ground in their concern for the poor. More importantly for Fidel, he lamented the human suffering on the island and called for a lifting of the U.S. embargo. The pope privately presented Castro with the names of 270 jailed dissidents and requested their release. In February, all were released but 70, who remained jailed for "security reasons." At the same time, the government reiterated that the laws against political dissent remained in effect, raising doubts as to whether there has been any meaningful move toward greater freedom of expression.

Nonetheless, Castro's gamble at least partly paid off. After the dissidents were freed, President Clinton resumed sales of medical goods and of airline service that had been severed after the 1996 downing of the two unarmed planes. He also renewed permission for dollars to be sent to Cuba. Since then, however, U.S.-Cuban relations resumed their usual roller-coaster course, while continued repression brought more international condemnation.

Dissent and Baseball Diplomacy

The government implemented a new sedition law in 1998, aimed primarily at independent journalists and political dissidents. One of its first victims was journalist Mario Viera, who sent abroad a column, "Morals in Underwear," that lampooned the Cuban justice system and poked fun at Foreign Minister José Peraza Chapeau. Viera was jailed for "defaming" Peraza Chapeau, and his trial drew about a dozen courageous protesters.

Still another independent journalist, Jesús Joel Díaz Hernández, was sentenced to four years in 1999 for "dangerous social behavior." The New York-based Committee to Protect Journalists named Castro as one of the world's 10 "enemies of the press."

The so-called "Group of Four," meanwhile, was sentenced in 1999 to jail terms ranging from three and a half to five years for issuing the 1997 document criticizing the party congress. The sentences sparked protests on the island and brought denunciations from human rights groups abroad.

Cuban dissidents continued their courageous activities, which are reminiscent of the non-violent movements of Gandhi, Martin Luther King Lech Walesa and Aung San Suu Kyi. In 1999, they opened a "school" for teaching the tactics of civil disobedience. Two opposition movements boldly delivered to the Council of State a document that detailed plans for a peaceful transition to a democratic Cuba.

Dr. Oscar Elías Biscet, a well-known physician and dissident, was sentenced to three years in prison for "public disorder

Varadero Beach—a protected area that the Cuban government would like all to believe is "typical."

Photo by Sheila Curtin

Cuba

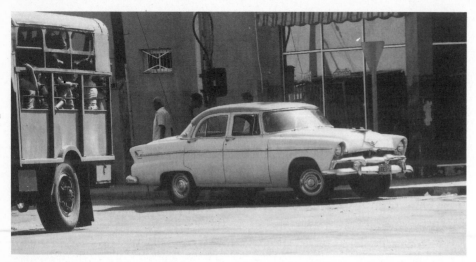

Transportation in Cuba: bus (left) or rare private automobile   *Photo by Katherine Dickson*

and instigating crime." His offense: He hung three Cuban flags upside down as a symbol of protest!

Meanwhile, international pressure against Castro's repression continued. The Inter American Press Association, the Committee to Protect Journalists and Reporters Sans Frontières in France all sent notes to Castro demanding he release jailed independent journalists and stop harassing others. One such independent journalist, Raúl Rivero, was named the recipient of the prestigious Maria Moors Cabot Award by Columbia University in 1999, but of course the Cuban government refused to grant him a visa to accept it.

Another leading dissident, Elizardo Sánchez, formed the Commission for Human Rights and National Reconciliation, which monitors dissidents' arrests and reports them to the outside world.

The dissidents received some encouraging news in 2000 when the government unexpectedly granted an early release to three of four dissidents imprisoned in 1997 for criticizing a Communist Party document to foreign journalists. The case had sparked international condemnation, even from Castro's friend, the Colombian Nobel Laureate Garbriel García Márquez. One of those released, Marta Beatríz Roque, an economist, had staged a two-month hunger strike in 1999.

It was not a harbinger of a Cuban *glasnost,* however. On February 24, 2001—the fifth anniversary of the shoot-down of the two Cuban exile planes—Cuban security briefly jailed about 40 dissidents to ensure there were no demonstrations marking the event.

José González Bridón, leader of the dissident labor group Confederation of Democratic Workers, wrote an article in 2000 reporting that a dissident had been killed by her ex-husband, which was published on the Web site of the Miami-based Cuba

Free Press. He was sentenced to two years in May 2001 for reporting "false news" about Cuba.

On a happier note, Castro approved an exhibition baseball game in Havana between the Baltimore Orioles and the Cuban All-Stars. Castro attended the historic, invitation-only game in March 1999, the first time a U.S. Major League team had played in Cuba since 1959. Some observers compared the initiative with the "ping-pong diplomacy" in the early 1970s that presaged U.S. recognition of the People's Republic of China. Much to Castro's chagrin, the Orioles won the game in the 11th inning, 3–2. The All-Stars redeemed themselves in a second game in Baltimore in May, defeating the Orioles 12–6. The victory was muted, however, by yet another embarrassing defection; a pitching coach went to a Baltimore police station and requested asylum. The Cuban team was abruptly ordered home.

The Elián González Controversy

On November 25, 1999, a five-year-old Cuban boy, Elián González, was found clinging to an inner-tube off the east coast of Florida. In the ensuing days, the boy was turned over to an uncle in Miami, and it was learned that he was one of just three survivors of a raft that left Cuba with 11 people on board. Among those lost were the boy's mother and her boyfriend.

The case became a media sensation in the United States, while Castro exploited it for propaganda value. He declared the boy had been "kidnapped" by his mother and demanded that he be returned to his father in Cuba. He organized mass demonstrations to focus world attention on the case. Counter-demonstrations soon occurred in the exile community in Miami to demand that the boy be granted political asylum and be allowed to stay with his

Miami relatives. (The difference between the mass demonstrations, of course, was that participation at the ones in Miami was purely voluntary.) Castro also paraded the boy's tearful father, Juan Miguel González, before television cameras, to plead for his son's return.

Legally, Castro had a strong case. Under U.S. and international laws, a surviving parent is the presumptive custodian. There began a tortuous legal battle, after the Immigration and Naturalization Service declared that the boy should be returned to his father. Attorney General Janet Reno supported that position, whereupon the Miami relatives filed suit in federal court seeking an immigration hearing.

The case became a political football in the United States. The Republican-controlled Congress suggested either granting the boy U.S. citizenship so he could not be deported or granting resident alien status to the father. Juan Miguel González, a Castro loyalist, indignantly refused, and Castro gleefully milked his refusal for propaganda value. The case also became an issue in the 2000 U.S. presidential campaign when Vice President Al Gore, hoping to carry Florida, dramatically broke with the Clinton administration and advocated giving the boy resident alien status. Opinion polls, however, showed that a majority of Americans nationwide favored returning the boy to Cuba.

Tensions increased after a U.S. district judge rejected the family's suit. The United States granted a visa to Juan Miguel González, who arrived in Washing-

The bicycle is the only sure method of transportation in this gas-and-car starved nation.   *Photo by Sheila Curtin*

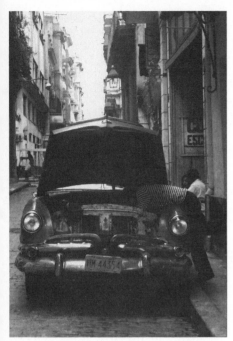

From a street scene in Old Town Havana, to . . .

ton in April. But his Miami relatives and their attorneys continued to file legal motions to delay surrendering Elián. Her patience wearing thin, Reno demanded that they surrender the boy, but still they stonewalled. Finally, in the pre-dawn hours of April 22, INS agents in SWAT gear stormed into the González house in Miami and hustled the terrified child into a waiting van.

Cuba's totalitarian leader praised Reno for the forcible seizure, praise that must have made Reno squirm. Father and son finally were reunited in Washington. That June, a U.S. circuit court ruled that the INS had acted properly when it had rejected an asylum hearing and that only a parent should have the right to make such a decision for a child that age. Although the decision was what Elián's father (and Castro) wanted, Castro nonetheless summoned more mass demonstrations in Cuba to protest it. Why? Because Elián and his father had to wait until the Miami relatives exhausted their appeals. On June 28, after the U.S. Supreme Court rejected the Miami relatives' appeal, Juan Miguel and Elián returned to Cuba to a heroes' welcome.

Cuba's Isolation Worsens

Cuba continued to experience diplomatic triumphs and embarrassments. In 1999, Havana hosted the Ibero-American Summit for the first time. But Castro soon became annoyed when some of the participants, including the king of Spain and the leaders of Portugal, Panama and even onetime defender Mexico, called for

greater democratization on the island. Several leaders met with dissidents, and Castro lashed out at the international media for what he termed disproportionate coverage of the dissidents.

Whatever public relations value Castro may have gleaned from the summit was effectively nullified in April 2000 when the U.N. Commission on Human Rights in Geneva approved, 21–18, with 14 abstentions, to censure Cuba for its repression of political dissent and religious freedom. Especially galling for Castro was the fact that two of Cuba's erstwhile allies, Poland and the Czech Republic, had sponsored the motion.

U.S.-Cuban relations turned chillier with the election of the new U.S. president, George W. Bush in 2000. The fact that Bush owed his razor-thin election victory to the overwhelming vote he received from the Cuban exile community in Florida, thus giving him Florida's 25 electoral votes, was not lost on the Castro brothers.

In 2001, Senators Jesse Helms—coauthor of the Helms-Burton Act—and Joseph Lieberman—the losing Democratic vice presidential candidate—co-sponsored a bill to allocate $100 million to Cuban dissidents over four years. In an apparent case of reverse psychology, Cuban Foreign Minister Felipe Pérez Roque endorsed the measure, saying it would demonstrate to the world that the United States is seeking to subvert Cuba.

Despite the harder line toward Castro of the Bush administration, the president angered Cuban exiles by doing the same thing that President Clinton had done every six months for four years: He exercised the executive prerogative granted

under the Helms-Burton Act to block lawsuits against foreign companies occupying expropriated U.S. property in Cuba. Bush tightened the screws in other areas, including stricter enforcement of the trade embargo and greater support for dissenters. The United States offered scholarships to Cuban prisoners of conscience, and the U.S. Interests Section in Havana distributed radios and information about free-market capitalism.

Castro denounced this as interference in Cuba's internal affairs and threatened to expel the U.S. diplomats. One explanation for the harsher U.S. stance: Bush had appointed Otto Reich, a Cuban exile and hard-line Castro critic, as assistant secretary of state for Western Hemisphere affairs. Still another: The president's brother, Jeb, was running for re-election as governor of Florida in 2002.

Despite souring relations, Castro condemned the September 11, 2001, terrorist attacks on the United States, and more surprisingly, he was conciliatory toward the imprisonment of al-Qaeda and Taliban prisoners at Guantanamo Bay. Castro even offered to provide medical and sanitary support, and pledged to return any prisoners who escaped. In response, Bush permitted the historic sale of food to Cuba in November 2001 as a humanitarian gesture in the wake of Hurricane Michelle, which caused widespread suffering. Cuba purchased a total of $30 million worth of food. Both governments stressed that the sale did not herald a change in policy by either side.

As if Cuba did not have enough problems from the United States, by 2002 Cuba was becoming increasingly isolated dip-

. . . typical apartment housing in Havana

Photo by Sheila Curtin

Cuba

lomatically and encountered serious problems in its relations with two traditional friends, Russia and Mexico. In 2001, Russian President Vladimir Putin announced Russia was closing an electronic surveillance station it had operated near Havana since 1964. Castro denounced the decision, saying he had not been asked for his "permission"and arguing it would create security problems for Cuba. He accused Putin—probably correctly—of trying to curry favor with Bush, whom Putin needed far more than he needed Castro. What Castro probably lamented the most, however, was the loss of the $200 million annual rent Russia paid for the station.

In 2002, Mexican President Vicente Fox, the first opposition president in 70 years and a conservative businessman who enjoyed a warm working relationship with Bush, made his first state visit to Cuba. Fox and Castro engaged in cordial talks, aimed primarily at trade. During the visit, Mexican Foreign Minister Jorge Castañeda assured the Cubans that Mexico would neither "sponsor nor co-sponsor" a resolution before the U.N. Human Rights Commission in Geneva, implying that Mexico would abstain as it had in previous years. The visit turned sour when Fox, unlike previous visiting Mexican presidents, agreed to meet with Cuban dissidents.

Later that month, Castañeda said in Miami that "the doors of the Mexican Embassy are open to all Cubans," a remark paraphrased by Radio Martí as an invitation to seek political asylum. Days later, 25 young men crashed a bus through the embassy gates. Police forcibly prevented hundreds of others from entering the embassy compound; foreign journalists were pushed back, cursed or manhandled. The Cubans inside the compound yelled anti-Castro slogans from the roof. The incident prompted a phone call from Fox to Castro. When the men did not seek asylum and refused to leave, Fox allowed Cuban security forces to enter the embassy to arrest them.

Next, Fox hosted an international poverty summit in Monterrey, which Castro decided at the last minute to attend, posing another dilemma for Fox because Bush was scheduled to attend. Castro left in a huff after his prepared speech to the conference, accusing Fox of asking him to leave; Fox denied it.

Then Mexico joined eight other Latin American nations in voting for a resolution, proposed by Uruguay, calling on Castro to permit democratic reforms; the resolution passed 23–21, with nine abstentions. Castro denounced Mexico for its "betrayal." In a stunning breach of diplomatic protocol, he called Fox a liar for denying Castro had been unwelcome at the Monterrey conference, and he played

for international journalists a recording of his telephone conversation with Fox, which did imply that Fox was concerned about Castro's presence. Such a betrayal of confidence was grounds for Mexico to sever diplomatic relations, but it did not. In fact, that May the two countries marked the 100th anniversary of their diplomatic relations. However, Mexico replaced its ambassador in Havana, who was seen as too friendly with Castro for the Fox administration's taste.

Castro also antagonized Uruguay for the U.N. resolution by calling President Jorge Batlle a "lackey" of the United States. Batlle broke diplomatic relations that had been re-established in 1986 after a 25-year break, giving the Cuban ambassador 72 hours to leave the country.

Castro received another international rebuke in 2002 when the European Union balked at an aid initiative by Barbados on behalf of Cuba, which had just joined the 63-member African-Pacific-Caribbean group of former European colonies. Under the Cotonou Agreement, signed between the EU and the APC countries in 2000, the EU made a $12.7 billion aid package available to the APC over five years. But the EU demurred on speeding up Cuba's access to the aid funds, citing its lack of commitment to democracy and human rights. Cuba correctly labeled the EU decision a "humiliation and a slap in the face."

It was followed by another slap from the EU. The European Parliament named Cuban dissident Osvaldo Payá, organizer of the Varela Project (see next section) and founder of the Christian Liberation Movement, the recipient of the 2002 Sakharov Award for Human Rights and Freedom of Thought. Other recipients for the presti-

gious award have included Nobel Peace Laureates Nelson Mandela of South Africa and Aung San Suu Kyi of Burma.

In 2002, Cuba for the first time hosted a meeting of the 15-member Caribbean Community (CARICOM), for which Cuba has only observer status. Castro announced Cuba would reapply for inclusion in the Cotonou Agreement, and the CARICOM states pledged to support Cuba. Poul Nielson, EU commissioner for development and humanitarian aid, met with Cuban authorities. Some Cuban dissidents favored Cuba's inclusion in Cotonou, believing Cuba would be under more pressure to adhere to democratic principles, while others argued that it would merely reward Castro's government for its repression. Nielson concluded that Cuba's inclusion could help bring about democratic reform. However, the EU quickly saw the prospects for Cuban democratization for what they are: an illusion (see Crackdown and Aftermath).

Perhaps in response to its growing international isolation and alienation, Cuba suddenly declared it was willing to sign the Nuclear Non-Proliferation Treaty, which it had always refused to do on the grounds that it somehow needed to "defend" itself against nuclear aggression from the United States.

Castro witnessed first-hand just how isolated his archaic system is when he visited another old friend, China, in 2003, his first visit in seven years. Castro confessed to his amazement at the changes since his last visit, changes that have made China an economic powerhouse by virtue of market reforms. But Castro made it clear when he returned home that he did not intend to institute similar reforms.

Relaxing in Santiago

Photo by Wayne Thompson

Cuba's three propaganda "newspapers"

The Varela Project

In 2002, Castro stunned the world, as he had with the invitation to the pope in 1998, by inviting former U.S. President Jimmy Carter to visit Cuba; Carter, long a champion of Latin American democracy, accepted.

Carter spent five days in Cuba, the highest-ranking American to visit Cuba since 1959. Castro kept his word to allow Carter to address the Cuban people in his unpracticed Spanish without censorship. In his live address on radio and television, which was reported verbatim in the next day's issue of the official newspaper *Granma*, Carter denounced Cuba's restrictions on human rights, and he endorsed the Varela Project, a petition drive initiated by dissidents and signed by 11,020 Cubans, for a referendum on free elections and free expression. Of course, his puzzled listeners had read or heard nothing about the Varela Project through the Cuban media. Carter also called for an end to the U.S. embargo. Castro trumpeted Carter's call for an end to the embargo, while ignoring his calls for democratization.

Almost as if in response to Carter's call for an end to the embargo, Bush flew to Miami to deliver a policy address on the 100th anniversary of Cuban independence on May 20. Bush rejected any notion of rescinding the embargo, and called on Castro to impose long-overdue reforms.

Castro cynically launched a petition drive of his own, one calling for a constitutional amendment declaring the principles of the Cuban Revolution "untouchable"—in effect, a constitutional amendment forbidding constitutional amendments. The government claimed that 8.2 million of the country's 11 million people—statistically, virtually everyone of voting age and then some—had signed the petition, which went before the National Assembly. The 557 deputies, of course, approved the amendment unanimously, without discussion. There was one major difference between the two petition drives: it did not require any courage to sign Castro's petition.

The fact that Castro launched his own petition drive to make the revolution "untouchable" was an indication that the dissidents' efforts were striking a raw nerve. The world soon learned how raw that nerve was.

Crackdown and Aftermath

Undeterred by the predictable rejection of the Varela Project, the dissident movement organized the Assembly to Promote Civil Society. Organized by economist Marta Beatríz Roque, the group comprises 321 discrete opposition movements and touted itself as a shadow parliament. Many in the group did not support the Varela Project, arguing that it is lukewarm, the first indication of a schism within the opposition.

In October 2002, Dr. Oscar Elías Biscet, the dissident sentenced to three years for hanging Cuban flags upside down, was released three months before his term was up, but he was rearrested in December for participating in a protest in Matanzas.

Oswaldo Payá, the organizer of the Varela Project, was granted a travel visa at the last minute to go to Europe to receive the Sakharov Award from the European Parliament (see Cuba's Isolation Worsens), but not before his home was vandalized. The visa was granted after Spain, Cuba's window to the EU, applied diplomatic pressure. Over 48 days,

Cuba

Payá visited eight countries and met with Pope John Paul II, Czech President Vaclav Havel, Mexican President Fox and U.S. Secretary of State Colin Powell, which did little to endear him to the Cuban government. Neither did Payá's nomination for the Nobel Peace Prize by Havel, himself a writer who had once opposed—and help topple—a Communist government.

Cuba held its latest "election" for the real parliament and provincial assemblies in January 2003. Turnout was reported to be 97.6%, which the government and party hailed as "proof" of support for the Revolution. Dissidents boycotted the election, and a few courageously put up banners ridiculing it.

The chief of the U.S. Interests Section in Havana, James Cason, visited with 20 members of the Assembly to Promote Civil Society at Roque's home, declared the Castro government was "afraid" to grant civil liberties and called for Biscet's release. Castro denounced Cason's action as a "blatant provocation."

Then, the ax fell. On March 11, 2003, Roque and other dissidents began a hunger strike. Almost simultaneously, during the five-day visit by EU Commissioner Nielson to discuss Cuba's inclusion in the Cotonou Agreement, by which Cuba stood to benefit by as much as $100 million, Vladimiro Roca and other leading dissidents petitioned the EU to deny Cuba's admission. Coincidentally or not, it was the same week the United States was preparing to invade Iraq. On March 18, with the attention of the world's media focused on Iraq, authorities rounded up some of the country's best-known dissidents, whom the government labeled "mercenaries," including Roque. When the roundup was completed, 78 people had been jailed, 21 of them independent journalists, including the best-known journalist, Raúl Rivero, and Hector Palacios, who had been active in the Varela Project. The predictable charge: subversive activities. As significant as the list of those who had been arrested was the list of those who had not: Payá, Roca and Elizardo Sánchez.

Meanwhile, the government imposed a new rule requiring foreign diplomats to obtain advance permission before traveling outside Havana. The United States imposed a similar restriction on Cuban diplomats.

Justice would prove swift if not just. Trials began in April, as Western media focused on the U.S. drive to Baghdad, and prosecutors indicated at first they would seek life terms for some of the dissidents. Foreign journalists were barred from the kangaroo-court proceedings, but news quickly leaked out. Among the startling revelations was that one well-known inde-

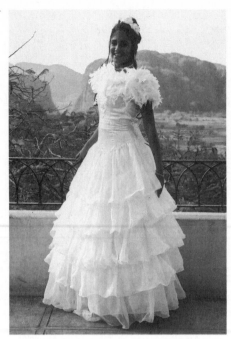

La Quinceañera—turning 15.
Photo by Gary Seldomridge

pendent journalist, Manuel David Orrío, was in fact an undercover agent assigned to infiltrate the dissident movement. He had attended meetings at the U.S. interests section, and he testified that Rivero and other journalists were conspiring with Cason to undermine the government.

The sentences also were handed down behind closed doors, but news of them soon reached the international media: Roque and Rivero, 20 years; Palacios and Biscet, 25. The heaviest sentence, 27 years, was meted out to journalist Omar Rodrí-

guez Saludes. His crime: launching Cuba's first independent magazine! The dissidents went immediately to prison; 60 reportedly were held in solitary confinement. The Supreme Tribunal, the regime's highest court, upheld the verdicts.

Some Cuban dissidents continued to defy Castro despite the crackdown, while as many as 40 independent journalists courageously continued to e-mail free-lance articles to foreign news organizations.

Coinciding with the crackdown and the sham trials was a wave of hijackings, two of airliners and one of a ferry. Both airliners were hijacked to Key West, and 25 of the 50 passengers and crews chose to remain in the United States.

Then eight hijackers commandeered a ferry with 50 passengers and attempted to take it to Florida, but low fuel forced it back to the port of Mariel. Cuban troops stormed the ferry and arrested the hijackers, who were tried within days even as the trials of the dissidents were unfolding. Three were sentenced to death and executed by firing squad.

If Castro had thought that the world's preoccupation with Iraq would cause the crackdown, the trials of the dissidents and the executions of the hijackers to go unnoticed, he was quickly disillusioned and no doubt stunned by the ferocity of the reaction. All were widely reported abroad, and media groups like the Committee to Protect Journalists, Society of Professional Journalists, Inter American Press Association, American Society of Newspaper Editors and Reporters Sans Frontières all called on the Cuban government to release the independent journalists. International human rights groups like Amnesty

Special show for children in Havana's National Museum of Fine Arts

144

International, Human Rights Watch and the Carter Center also denounced the arrests and stiff sentences.

Bush was joined by the EU and Pope John Paul II in condemning the crackdown; even longtime friend Canada sternly called upon Cuba to release the prisoners. The execution of the hijackers days later intensified the chorus of denunciations from countries where capital punishment is banned, including Mexico. Nonetheless, Castro defiantly shrugged off the world's condemnation.

As another indication of Castro's growing isolation, Costa Rica, a member of the U.N. Human Rights Commission, reversed its traditional opposition to a strongly worded resolution denouncing Cuba's human rights violations. Costa Rica, which in the past had supported resolutions that called only for a U.N. human rights monitor to visit Cuba, indicated it would support a U.S.-backed resolution expressing "deep concern" over the crackdown and calling on Cuba to release the dissidents. EU representatives also supported the resolution.

But the 53-member commission was still dominated by countries with despotic regimes, such as Sudan; it rejected the harsh resolution 31–15. Instead, it approved 24–20 the same resolution it passed the year before for Cuba to allow a human rights monitor, French judge Christine Chanet, to visit the island. Castro had rejected Chanet's visit, calling her post "illegitimate." Foreign Minister Felipe Pérez Roque said Cuba would not abide by the resolution. As had happened the year before when Castro alienated Uruguay, the Cuban delegate to the commission called Peru, Nicaragua, Uruguay and Costa Rica "repugnant lackeys" of the United States for voting for the resolution.

"The Cocktail War"

Days later, Cuba was awarded one of Latin America's six seats on the commission, prompting the U.S. delegate to walk out in disgust. The 15-nation EU—later increased to 25—not only unanimously rejected Cuba's participation in the Cotonou Agreement but voted to impose diplomatic sanctions that limited high-level visits to Cuba and reduced the EU's participation in Cuban cultural events. Even more galling to Castro, the EU announced it would begin inviting Cuban dissidents to receptions on European national days. The media quickly dubbed the Cuban-EU dispute the "cocktail war."

Defiant to the end, Castro alluded to the EU, which buys 35% of Cuba's exports and had provided about $160 million in aid to Cuba during the previous 10 years, as "a gang, a mafia" that had caved in to U.S.

pressure. During a four-hour televised address, he called Spanish Prime Minister José María Aznar a "little Führer" and Italian Prime Minister Silvio Berlusconi a "fascist" and a "clown." Spain for years had been Cuba's leading apologist before the EU, even under conservative governments like Aznar's.

The next day, Fidel and Raúl led hundreds of thousands of people in a mass protest outside the Spanish and Italian embassies. Cuba also annulled a 1997 agreement with Spain for a Spanish cultural center in Havana. Castro used the occasion of the 50th anniversary of the July 26, 1953, attack on the Moncada Barracks, the spark of the Cuban Revolution, to reject further aid from the EU under the Cotonou Agreement. He castigated Europe as the United States' "Trojan horse," and railed against its "shameful past" of colonization and exploitation.

Castro's tirades against the EU and Cuba's mother country served only to further alienate himself from the community of nations. The European Parliament responded with a resolution formally condemning Cuba for its human rights abuses.

Another humiliation came in 2004 when the U.N. Educational, Scientific and Cultural Organization (UNESCO) awarded the Guillermo Cano World Press Freedom Award to Raúl Rivero, the imprisoned journalist. The Cuban foreign ministry denounced the award as "deplorable and embarrassing." Yes, but for whom?

In April 2004, the regime suddenly invited a delegation of international journalists to tour the prison where the dissidents were incarcerated, but they were allowed to speak only with inmates chosen by the government. They did not meet with Rivero.

That same month, the U.N. commission once again voted, 22–21 with 10 abstentions, to urge Cuba to guarantee freedom of expression, to undertake dialogue with the dissidents and to allow Charet to visit Cuba.

Cuba again cast itself in the role of outcast at the third summit of 53 EU, Latin American and Caribbean countries in Guadalajara, Mexico, in 2004, which Castro did not attend. For once, Cuba was on the same side with the EU and its neighbors on a resolution condemning U.S. abuse of Iraqi prisoners. But the resolution wasn't harsh enough for Foreign Minister Pérez Roque, and he accused the EU of scuttling a resolution condemning the U.S. trade embargo. Cuba was the only country at the summit not to vote for the final declaration.

Even as Castro was alienating old friends, he cultivated two new ones: newly elected presidents Luiz Inácio da Silva of Brazil and Néstor Kirchner of Argentina,

Farm family in Viñales
Photo by Wayne Thompson

who both assumed office in 2003. Castro attended both inaugurations. Kirchner re-established diplomatic relations with Cuba, which former President Fernando de la Rua had severed in 2001 because of Castro's insults. Da Silva, a longtime friend of Castro's, visited Havana to sign bilateral agreements and a deal to stretch out Cuban repayment of its $40 million debt to Brazil. Argentina and Brazil abstained on the U.N. Human Rights Commission vote condemning Cuba in 2004, and neither da Silva nor Kirchner expressed any qualms over Castro's 2003 crackdown.

In 2005, Uruguay's new left-wing president, Tabaré Vázquez, restored diplomatic relations with Cuba as his first official act, although Castro did not attend the inauguration.

Cuba's relations with Spain also improved dramatically with the election victory of the Socialists in March 2004. José Luis Rodríguez Zapatero replaced Aznar as prime minister, and Zapatero began interceding on Castro's behalf with the EU. He argued that the freeze in diplomatic relations was not having the desired effect. Spain, Hungary and Belgium re-established normal relations with Cuba after Castro released five dissidents, including Rivero, on health grounds; Rivero went into exile in Spain. Over the next three months, he released nine more. Austria, Britain, France, Germany, Greece, Italy, Portugal and Sweden then resumed full relations, and the rest of the EU soon followed suit. It seemed the "cocktail war" was over.

Self-Alienation Grows

Poland and the Czech Republic were the only EU members still skeptical of appeasing Castro without reciprocity; they would soon be proved right. When a meeting of EU foreign ministers announced the EU would continue to monitor Cuba on human rights, Castro responded with another

Cuba

arrogant four-hour speech, in which he ridiculed the EU and said he had no intention of changing his policies. "What are they going to forgive us for?" he asked sarcastically, adding for good measure, "Cuba does not need Europe." Instead of improving his human rights record, Castro ordered Cubans to minimize the amount of time they spend associating with foreigners.

Britain's deputy foreign secretary for Latin America visited Havana and urged Castro to release all the jailed dissidents. Castro bluntly told him that while he welcomed improved relations with the EU, he would not release the dissidents and told the EU to stop interfering in Cuba's internal affairs. So much for Chamberlain-style appeasement of dictators.

Then EU Development Commissioner Louis Michel, a Belgian, arrived in Havana for talks with Castro as well as with Payá and other dissidents. Castro said the talks were "very frank," while Michel called them "very optimistic and positive." He proclaimed Castro "a very kind man." Michel noted that Castro had released 14 of the 75 dissidents and asked him politely to please release the remaining 61.

He did not, however, and Charet, still barred from visiting Cuba, submitted to the U.N. Human Rights Commission her scathing report on Cuba's refusal to free prisoners of conscience and its harassment of other dissidents. In 2005, for the sixth consecutive year, the commission voted to condemn Cuba, 21–17 with 15 abstentions. Castro responded this time that he "couldn't care less" about the vote.

Meanwhile, "Cocktail War II" erupted in 2005 when Cuba expelled five European parliamentarians—three Spanish, one German and one Czech—who had gone there to attend a rally of the Assembly to Promote Civil Society, the dissident group. Entry was denied to two Polish members of the European Parliament and four European journalists were arrested.

The EU expressed its "concern," while Italy and even Spain summoned the Cuban ambassadors to express their displeasure. Castro had alienated his best friend in Europe.

Cuban authorities permitted the rally of the Assembly to Promote Civil Society in May 2005, but forbade coverage by foreign journalists. About 200 people attended, led by Roque, who had been released from prison. Not attending was Payá, now Roque's rival within the dissident movement. In February 2005, Payá had called for a "National Dialogue" on the transition for post-Castro Cuba that included 57 exiles, but some anti-Castro hardliners opposed Payá's offer to include members of the government in the dialogue.

Meanwhile, the wives of the jailed dissidents, nicknamed the "Ladies in White," staged marches and candlelight vigils to focus attention on the plight of their husbands. Their protests, usually harassed by pro-government supporters, were still continuing in 2010.

While relations with the EU went from bad to good to worse than ever, Castro hosted an amicable visit by his fellow autocrat, Chinese President Hu Jintao, in 2004, during which the two countries signed new trade agreements. China accounts for 10% of Cuba's trade and is Cuba's third-largest trading partner after Venezuela and Spain. China also pledged to invest $500 million in a new nickel plant, while Cuba agreed to export 4,400 tons of nickel to China for its hungry industries.

When Pope John Paul II died on April 2, 2005, the always unpredictable Castro declared three days of mourning and even attended a memorial Mass at Havana Cathedral—the first time he had entered the building since his sister's wedding in 1959.

An amusing episode in the on-going battle for human rights was the appearance in 2005 of an underground video, titled "Monte Roque," that satirized the

government's electronic surveillance of its citizens. Other underground videos have spoofed such things as chronic shortages, but this is the first that actually poked fun at official policy.

Growing Cuban-U.S. Tension

The 2003 crackdown derailed, at least temporarily, the growing sentiment in the U.S. Congress to lift the trade embargo. After the easing of the embargo in 2000, Cuba imported 600,000 tons of U.S. agricultural products, paid for in cash. In 2002, a shipment of $750,000 worth of brand-name grocery items arrived in Cuba, the first such transaction in 40 years. Despite objections from the Bush administration, U.S. agricultural executives held a food fair in Cuba in 2002, also the first in 40 years. Cuba concluded $66 million in food contracts with the executives.

Cuba was an issue again in the 2004 U.S. presidential election. Bush reiterated his hard-line policy to please Cuban-American voters in Florida. Bush unveiled a 500-page report by a presidential commission he had named to study the post-Castro succession. Bush declared he would not wait for Castro's death to begin planning for a democratic transition. To tighten the economic screws, Bush changed the regulations for visits by Cuban Americans to family members in Cuba from one a year to one every three years, and he lowered the per diem allowance for expenditures during those visits from $160 to $50. He retained the current $1,200-a-year cap on remittances to the island.

To Bush's surprise, some leading dissidents, including Payá, Sánchez and Gutiérrez, denounced the report as U.S. interference and argued that Cubans and Cubans alone should decide the succession. Meanwhile, Democratic presidential contender John Kerry went to Florida to charge that Bush had given only "lip service" to Cuban Americans over four years, while he promised to work "full-time" to bring about a democratic transition in Cuba.

Castro's response was to suspend sales of all but essential items at the island's 5,300 dollars-only stores, ostensibly for "inventory," inflicting a hardship on his own people that he blamed on the United States. Castro abruptly ordered the dollar stores reopened, but with prices about 15% higher than before, which he also blamed on the United States.

On the eve of the U.S. election, and in an apparent attempt to influence the outcome, Castro ordered the Central Bank to declare that effective November 8, the U.S. dollar would no longer be accepted at Cuban stores, even the so-called dollar stores. Instead, only the "convertible peso"

Farming in Cuba

Photo by Katherine Dickson

Cuba

would be accepted. Castro also told his countrymen to ask relatives living abroad to begin sending remittances in Euros, British pounds or Swiss francs. Cubans could still exchange dollars for pesos, but with a 10% surcharge; other currencies were not subject to the surcharge.

Castro apparently hoped the measure would intimidate Cuban Americans to vote for Kerry, but Bush was re-elected, and this time he carried Florida decisively.

By 2005, according to the Cuban government, purchases of U.S. food had passed the $1 billion mark, and ever since then, the United States has been the largest source of imported food. Although the U.S. government permitted the sales as "humanitarian" exceptions to the embargo (and profitable for Republican campaign contributors), the Treasury Department made things tougher on Cuba. Effective March 31, 2005, Cuba had to pay for all shipments in cash in advance, before the ships are loaded, instead of upon delivery in Cuba.

The U.S. Coast Guard reported that the number of Cubans it had intercepted at sea had more than doubled from 2004 to 2005. Meanwhile, the number of Cubans who actually succeeded in reaching shore—and thus guaranteed asylum—totaled more than 2,500, compared with fewer than 1,000 in 2004. Dozens more were confirmed to have died at sea. An estimated 6,000 more entered the United States through Mexico.

In 2005, Michael Parmly replaced Cason as head of the U.S. interests section. At first, Castro heralded the change, but Parmly soon made it apparent he would continue Cason's support for the dissidents. He also erected an electronic billboard outside the interests section to post messages nettlesome to the government.

The Posada Carriles Case

The most serious U.S.-Cuban conflict since the Elián González controversy exploded in May 2005. The United States detained Luis Posada Carriles, a 77-year-old anti-Castro firebrand who had bribed his way out of a Venezuelan prison in 1985 while awaiting retrial for allegedly masterminding the 1976 bombing of a Cuban airliner that killed 73 people off Barbados. Arrested in Miami, where he had many supporters, Posada had apparently been in the United States for two months, entering illegally through Mexico. Reportedly, he had intended to seek political asylum, but went into hiding. He came out of hiding to hold a news conference, which led to Cuban and Venezuelan demands for his arrest.

Posada spent four years in prison in Panama, where he attempted to assassinate Castro during a summit in Panama in 2000; he was pardoned in 2004 (see Panama). Cuba also accuses him of the bombings of hotels in the 1990s, one of which killed an Italian tourist.

Venezuelan President Hugo Chávez demanded that the United States extradite Posada to Venezuela. He had already been twice acquitted of charges stemming from the airliner bombing. Posada, a renegade former CIA agent turned terrorist, holds Venezuelan citizenship, and the bombing was believed to have been planned in Caracas. Two other Venezuelans were convicted for their roles. Posada's supporters in Miami argued against extradition, saying Chávez could send him to Cuba, where he would face execution.

For his part, Castro termed Posada's arrest a "farce," questioning how such a high-profile fugitive could have entered and spent two months in the United States undetected. He also accused Bush of having a double standard toward terrorists. For once, Castro had not one but two valid points, and like the Elián González case, he milked the Posada case for its propaganda value. What especially outraged Castro and Chávez was that Posada was arrested not as a fugitive from justice, but for illegally entering the country.

The U.S. government played into Castro's hands by its clumsy handling of the case. At first, authorities said they would decide what to do with Posada within 48 hours, then began stalling. He remained in custody in El Paso, Texas, then in a county jail in New Mexico. In 2007, a federal judge ruled he could be released on $250,000 bond, provoking outrage in Havana and Caracas; an appeals court upheld the granting of bail. Posada went to Miami, and in May 2007, a district judge dismissed the immigration fraud charges, saying the Justice Department had railroaded Posada. Not to be deterred, the Justice Department obtained a perjury indictment from a federal grand jury in El Paso in April 2009, charging Posada with lying about his knowledge of the tourist hotel bombings as well as lying to immigration officials. In June, the El Paso district judge postponed his trial until February 2010 to give his attorneys time to prepare his defense, but it has since been delayed twice more.

Transition. . .

On August 1, 2006, Castro stunned the nation and the world, announcing he had undergone surgery for intestinal bleeding and was relinquishing power "temporarily" as president of the Council of State to his brother Raúl. Fidel remained head of the party. The transition to Raúl generated headlines worldwide, as well as celebra-

tions in Miami's exile community, as rumors spread that Fidel was actually dead or comatose. Neither Fidel nor Raúl appeared in public for two weeks, when Raúl greeted Venezuela's Chávez at the airport for Fidel's 80th birthday on August 13. Fidel still did not appear in public, but a video was released showing Chávez visiting him in his hospital room.

Fidel underwent two more operations. Another "proof of life" video was to reassure the Cuban people, but his shockingly gaunt, cadaverous appearance only fueled speculation that death was imminent. Castro's physician announced that, although his condition remained a state secret, he was suffering from diverticulitis, a swelling of the intestine common among the elderly.

There was speculation that Fidel would make his first public appearance at the 2007 May Day celebration, as was his custom. U.S. networks sent news crews to Havana to report on that eventuality, but he failed to appear, generating still more speculation.

For 18 months, it was widely believed both in Cuba and abroad that Raúl's stewardship was largely window-dressing and that Fidel was still running things from his sickbed. Indeed, Fidel himself had declared that he would continue to be consulted on major political, military and economic matters, and he was writing a column, "Reflections by Comrade Fidel," for *Granma* several days a week.

Constitutionally, Raúl was next in the line of transition, but Fidel's duties were parceled out among six other top officials as well. Among them were Carlos Lage, the vice president, a de facto prime minister and a popular and able administrator, who took charge of the overhaul of the crumbling electric system; Felipe Pérez Roque, the foreign minister; Francisco Soberón, head of the central bank; and Ricardo Alarcón, president of the National Assembly, who is fluent and articulate in English and is frequently interviewed by U.S. television networks. They muzzled any appearance of a power struggle, although Raúl publicly expressed an interest in Chinese-style economic reforms, while Lage publicly opposed them.

In July 2007, Raúl publicly acknowledged that the economy was badly in need of "structural and conceptual changes," and he encouraged a dialogue to discuss suggested reforms. With some understatement, he said Cuba's $15 monthly wage was "insufficient," and he called the state-run dairy production system "absurd." He has long been known to be impatient with the shortcomings of Cuba's cumbersome bureaucracy, and he evidently listened to the suggestions he received with an open mind. It was a dramatic departure from his brother's single-mindedness and resistance

Cuba

to change. Raúl also showed an inclination to delegate responsibility, in sharp contrast to Fidel's micromanagerial style.

Raúl also loosened the restrictions on private enterprise, and paid debts to dairy farmers and others private producers. He scored points with the Cuban people by replacing the aging, gas-guzzling Russian-built public transit buses with modern, more fuel-efficient Chinese models. With Venezuelan help, he augmented the electrical system with thousands of diesel-powered generators and mandated replacing incandescent bulbs with fluorescent bulbs, which reduced the endemic blackouts. Lacking his brother's oratorical skills, Raúl has eschewed Fidel's mass rallies and long-winded speeches. Perhaps most dramatically, he reduced the number of political prisoners from roughly 300 to 240, including one jailed for 13 years, although 61 of the 75 people jailed in the 2003 crackdown remained behind bars. Harassment of dissidents eased for a time.

A turning point in Cuban, and world, history came on February 18, 2008, when Fidel formally relinquished all power in a letter to the Cuban people published in *Granma*, which read in part:

"Dear compatriots:

"The moment has come to nominate and elect the State Council, its President, its Vice Presidents and Secretary. . .

"My wishes have always been to discharge my duties to my last breath. That's all I can offer. . .

"It would be a betrayal to my conscience to accept a responsibility requiring more mobility and dedication than I am physically able to offer. This I say devoid of all drama. . .

"This is not my farewell to you. My only wish is to fight as a soldier in the battle of ideas. I shall continue to write under the heading of 'Reflections by Comrade Fidel.' It will be just another weapon you can count on. Perhaps my voice will be heard. I shall be careful.

"Thanks.

"Fidel Castro Ruz"

On February 24, the 614-member National Assembly unanimously elected Raúl as president of the Council of State, ushering in a new but uncertain era in Cuban, and Latin American, history (see The Future). As his first vice president, he named José Ramón Machado, nearly a year older than himself, quashing expectations about grooming the next generation to take over. Few of his seven appointees to the Politburo's executive committee were under 70. Moreover, Fidel remained first secretary of the party.

Raúl continued his reform of what he called "excessive restrictions," beginning with lifting the prohibition against Cubans staying in hotels reserved for for-

eigners, a restriction most Cubans found offensive. Of course, few Cubans can afford to stay in the resort hotels on their $15 monthly salaries. He also pragmatically agreed to expand the acreage allocated to private farmers in the hopes of reducing food imports.

Raúl also announced he wanted to lift the restriction on Cubans' Internet access, but complained that the U.S. embargo prevented Cuba from tying in to U.S.-controlled undersea fiber-optic cables. Venezuela's Chávez promised to provide Cuba with access to its fiber-optic network. Like so many other things, Internet access in Cuba had become a black-market commodity. He also said Cubans may now use cell phones.

The Bush White House expressed skepticism toward Raúl's changes, but Bush said if Raúl were serious, he would allow Americans to send cell phones to Cuba.

Raúl also announced he would call a party congress for late 2009, the first since 1997, with the express purpose of discussing the eventual post-Castro—both of them—leadership. But in August 2009, he abruptly changed his mind, saying, "The party is not ready."

Cuba's struggling economy was dealt a dual blow by Hurricanes Gustav and Ike in August and September 2008. The government decided to expand the existing program that permits private farming, increasing existing plots to 40 hectares (100 acres), while opening up new plots of 13 hectares on unused state land. More than 5,500 people applied for the new plots.

As a sign of a possible thaw in relations between the communist government and the Catholic Church, Raúl Castro attended the beatification ceremony in November 2008 for Friar José Olallo, a 19th century monk known for his work with the poor and elderly. A miracle was credited to Olallo in 1999, qualifying him for beatification, the first step toward sainthood. It was the first beatification ceremony ever held in Cuba.

Cuba observed the 50th anniversary of the Revolution on January 1, 2009, and once again international media descended on Havana in the expectation that Fidel would use the occasion to make a public appearance. But he did not show, fueling further speculation as to whether he was incapacitated. Fidel continued to receive, and to be photographed with, visiting heads of state, such as Russian President Dmitry Medvedev in September 2008 and Argentine President Cristina Fernández de Kirchner in January 2009.

Raúl delivered a hard-line speech for the 50th anniversary celebration that reasserted Cuba's hostility toward the United States and seemed to throw cold water on expectations that more reforms would be forth-

coming. Yet, just three weeks later, the enigmatic brothers suddenly began sounding conciliatory to the United States. Raúl said he would be willing to meet with President-elect Barack Obama, while the Argentine president quoted Fidel as saying that Obama is "a sincere man with good ideas."

On the eve of the Summit of the Americas in Trinidad and Tobago in April 2009, Obama kept a campaign promise by announcing the lifting of restrictions on travel and monetary remittances by Cuban Americans to Cuba (Obama had carried Florida). Days later, in Caracas for a meeting of the left-wing *ALBA* countries, Raúl reiterated his willingness to meet with Obama, and in a stunning reversal of long-standing Cuban policy, said he was willing to discuss "everything, everything, everything," including such heretofore non-negotiable topics as release of political prisoners and freedom of the press. Before Washington could respond to this overture, however, Fidel quickly quashed the initiative in his newspaper column, saying the media had "misinterpreted" Raúl's words and that the basic principles of the Revolution were not negotiable. Raúl subsequently issued his own "clarification."

Obama stopped well short of lifting the trade embargo, saying it was up to Cuba at this point to show good faith by releasing prisoners of conscience. A CNN poll that April said two thirds of Americans favor lifting the embargo and three fourths favor renewing diplomatic relations. But both brothers have retreated to their traditional intransigence, saying the embargo should be lifted without any Cuban *quid pro quo*. In late May, Havana and Washington did agree to resume immigration talks that had been suspended five years earlier.

In a dramatic development in June 2009, the OAS, meeting in Honduras, abruptly rescinded the 47-year-old expulsion of Cuba and invited Cuba to apply for renewed membership, contingent upon acquiescing on such issues as the remaining 220 prisoners of conscience. Any lingering doubts as to who is really calling the shots in Cuba were dispelled when Fidel declared Cuba would not apply to rejoin the OAS; Raúl's opinion on the issue was not reported.

Recent Developments

The thaw in U.S.-Cuban relations under an Obama administration that had been anticipated on both sides of the Florida Straits still has not materialized. Besides lifting the restriction on remittances, Obama authorized a resumption of bilateral immigration talks Bush had halted. However, he did not lift the travel ban as many had expected, pending some show of good faith from the Cuban side. It never came.

In December 2009, Cuba arrested Alan Gross, a contractor for the U.S. Agency for International Development, accusing him of spying. The White House denied it. A month later, the United States angered Cuba by including it among 14 nations on a terrorist "watch list," under which airline passengers undergo more rigorous screening. In this poisoned atmosphere, bilateral talks resumed in February 2010, but they broke down quickly when Cuba refused to release Gross or to release political dissidents. Secretary of State Hillary Clinton blamed Cuba for the impasse, accusing it of using the U.S. embargo as an "excuse" for its economic failures.

But other issues overshadowed the talks as well. In October 2009, Cuba refused to grant an exit visa to Yoani Sánchez, who writes the controversial dissident blog *Generation Y* (see Culture), so she could fly to New York to accept the prestigious Maria Moors Cabot Award, presented each year by Columbia University to a courageous journalist. In November, she alleged that government security agents abducted and beat her.

Also in November, 10 prominent dissidents, including Beatríz Roque, holed up in a Havana house and went on a liquids-only hunger strike that garnered international media attention—but none at home, of course. Then Orlando Zapata, one of the remaining prisoners from the 2003 crackdown, also went on a total hunger strike to protest his conditions. After 85 days, he died in February 2010, prompting denunciations from around the world. A chastened Raúl Castro claimed he "lamented" Zapata's death, even as he continued to insist he was a "common criminal."

In April 2010, Cardinal Jaime Ortega published an unusually harsh attack on the government in the church's monthly magazine, *Palabra Nueva (New Word)*, calling on it to negotiate in good faith with the United States to obtain a lifting of the embargo and alleviate the suffering of the Cuban people. Surprisingly, in May Raúl held a four-hour meeting with Ortega and Havana Archbishop Dionisio García. The Vatican foreign minister visited Cuba in June. Raúl also agreed to allow the Ladies in White to march without harassment. When this book went to press, it was unclear whether they did.

(Another dissident, Guillermo Farinas, a 48-year-old writer and psychologist, began a hunger strike in February when Zapata died. He was at the point of death in July as this book went to press when the government acceded to a request by Cardinal Ortega to release 52 imprisoned dissidents and allow them to go to Spain. Farinas then ended his hunger strike.)

Besides the mounting domestic and international pressure for reform, Raúl also

President Raúl Modesto Castro Ruz

has been hamstrung by an ever-worsening economy in 2009 and 2010, including a soaring trade deficit from fuel imports, a downturn in tourism and GDP growth because of the global recession, damage from the 2008 hurricanes and the worst sugar harvest since 1905; and by revelations of corruption within the government, which he has acknowledged. He has recently fired a number of high-level officials for poor performance, such as his education minister and the rector of the University of Havana in 2009, and the sugar and transport ministers in 2010, or for outright corruption, such as an aviation offical who was renting out state-owned planes and pocketing the money. He mandated creation of a new auditor general's office to probe corruption. In 2009, the government eliminated free hot lunches for workers, saving $350 million in mostly imported food, but granting workers a 15-peso-a-day (60 cents) increase as compensation. Offices were ordered to run air conditioning only for five hours daily, during the afternoon, to ease demand for diesel fuel for the generators.

Raúl also allowed private barber shops and hair salons to begin operating again, as well as small cafés where workers could buy their lunches, which will stimulate tax collections.

Culture: Cuba is an ethnic peculiarity in Latin America. The Spaniards largely exterminated the native Carib Indians, but the influx of blacks from the British West Indies has given Cuba a distinctive Euro-African culture. About 62% of Cubans today are black or mulatto. Although Roman Catholicism took root in colonial times and has survived the repression of the communist government, thousands of Cubans of African descent, both before and after the Revolution, practice a hybrid religion called *santería* that blends elements of

Catholicism with ancient Yoruban tribal rites. Santeria rituals have actually become a lucrative tourist attraction.

Although independence came to Cuba eight decades later than it did to its sister republics, some Creole writers and poets gained recognition during the 19th century. Best known of these is the poet José Martí (1853–95), a leader in Cuba's quest for independence, who was martyred in a battle against the Spanish. Cuba's best known 20th century poet was Nicolás Guillén (1902–87), whose verse celebrated the island's African cultural heritage.

Another celebrated 20th century Cuban writer in the Hispanic world and beyond was the novelist Guillermo Cabrera Infante (1929–2005), but the current Cuban government does not claim him because he fell out of favor with Castro in 1962 and did most of his acclaimed work after leaving Cuba in 1967. He won Spain's coveted Cervantes Prize in Literature in 1997. Most critics regard his most famous work as *Tres Tristes Tigres* (English title *Three Trapped Tigers)*, published in 1967, which was a sketch of pre-revolutionary Havana night life. Also well known were the autobiographical *Habana para un infante difunto (Infante's Inferno)* (1979) and *Mea Cuba* (1993). He obtained British citizenship and died in London.

A young contemporary writer who has received several domestic and international literary awards is Amir Valle (b. 1967), who first gained attention in 2006 with his detective novel, *Santuario de Sombras (Sanctuary of Shadows)*, published in Spain. But another, non-fiction book, *Jineteras*, published in Spain, Argentina, Colombia and the United States the same year, provoked the displeasure of the Cuban government because it dealt with the sensitive topic of prostitution on the island. In 2006, while on a book tour in Europe, Valle overstayed his Cuban exit visa. He declared he had not defected but his intent was to assert his right to come and go as he pleased. He went into self-imposed exile in Berlin, where he remains. His Web site states: "I am a Cuban writer: this is my cross . . . I do not inhabit Cuba: Cuba inhabits me. And I love my island with the same rage that makes me suffer. I love her diversity and I suffer from her blindness." His latest novel, *Largas Noches con Flavia (Long Nights With Flavia)* was published in Spain in 2008.

Cuba's leading cultural export has been its music. The African-based rhythms of *son*, the *mambo*, the *rumba* and the *cha-cha-cha* were the rage in the United States and Europe during the 1940s and 1950s, and brought stardom to such bandleaders as Xavier Cugat and Desi Arnaz. The Cuban genre *son* is the cornerstone of the Caribbean's popular *salsa*.

Cuba

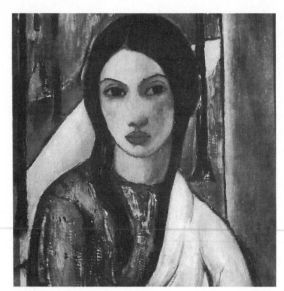

"Gitana Tropical" by Victor Manuel García, 1929. In Museo National de Bellas Artes, Cuba

The Cuban Revolution proved to be a cultural tradeoff. On the one hand, the repressiveness of the totalitarian system caused many of Cuba's most talented writers, artists, singers, musicians and actors to abandon Cuba for the United States, Spain or another Latin American country to more freely express themselves.

None was better known than Celia Cruz (1925–2003), the acknowledged "queen of salsa." In prerevolutionary Cuba she won fame as the lead singer for the band, *La Sonora Matancera*. She resumed singing after she emigrated to the United States, eventually becoming a pop icon as salsa won acceptance among *anglos* as well as *latinos*. She won a Grammy Award in 1990. So great was her hemispheric recognition that when she died in New York City in 2003, thousands turned out for her funeral, and her obituary was carried all over Latin America—even, grudgingly, in the Cuban media.

Perhaps the best-known singer who has remained in Cuba is Silvio Rodríguez (b. 1946), a folk singer and songwriter known as the leader of the so-called *nueva trova* movement. He has enjoyed special privileges for traveling abroad and earning money, including a tour in the United States in mid-2010, his first U.S. tour since 1979; he performed at Carnagie Hall in June. Usually a darling of the Cuban regime and the bane of the exiles in Miami, Rodríguez performed with Colombian pop icon Juanes at the "Concert for Peace" in Havana in September 2009, but in February 2010 he released a new album that called on the regime to release political prisoners and overhaul the way the country is run. The regime evidently was not pleased. He was scheduled to sing at a "Concert for the Mortherland" in April,

but instead he read a prepared statement defending the regime from the negative international fallout following the death of Orlando Zapata, a jailed dissident who died after an 85-day hunger strike (see History—Recent Developments). He left the stage without singing. He may have had to cut a deal to go on the U.S. tour.

Ironically, one of the people most responsible for renewing international interest in Cuban music was an American composer and guitarist, Ry Cooder, an *aficionado* of Cuban sounds. He obtained permission to travel to Cuba in 1996 in quest of some of the aging figures of prerevolutionary music. He assembled pianist Rubén González, singer Ibrahim Ferrer and singers-guitarists Eliades Ochoa and Compay Segundo for a recording session under the name, the Buena Vista Social Club. The 1997 CD became a hit and won a Grammy Award, and the group's new fame led German director Wim Wenders to make a movie, "The Buena Vista Social Club," which received an Oscar nomination. Segundo and González died in 2003, Ferrer in 2005; their passing made headlines all over Latin America as well as the United States. Ochoa, by far the youngest, turned 64 in 2010. His last recordings were *Se saltó un león* and *La colección cubana* in 2006.

A newer genre that has become popular in Cuba is a blend of rap and reggae known as "raggaeton." It has become something of an underground movement, as many of its songs touch upon *tabú* subjects and poke fun of the system. Probably the most popular rapper in Cuba is Aldo Rodríguez of the group, *Los Aldeanos* (The Villagers). The regime has sought unsuccessfully to control rap music, but thus far *Los Aldeanos* have not gone to jail.

While many cultural figures fled Cuba, previously banned leftist writers and other intellectuals were free to come. The Castro regime has taken great pride in its commitment to fostering arts and preserving the indigenous culture, particularly art, music, literature, theater and cinema. Several Cuban films have achieved international recognition in high-brow circles, but naturally they convey subtle—or not so subtle—ideological messages.

Some outstanding talent remained in Cuba after the Revolution, including the composer José Ardévol and Latin America's prima ballerina, Alicia Alonso. But other creative minds felt the heavy hand of the communist system. At least two cases of repression brought international condemnation upon the regime even from its sympathizers. When the writer Herberto Padilla was jailed in 1971, there was an outcry from such leftist intellectuals as Jean-Paul Sartre, Colombian novelist Gabriel García Márquez and the Mexican poet Octavio Paz. Castro ordered Padilla released, but only after the writer signed a confession of his "errors against the Revolution," which he was obligated to read before the Cuban Congress on Education and Culture.

As an indicator of postrevolutionary culture, the congress passed a resolution that said, in part, that the mass media, writers and artists "are powerful instruments of ideological education whose utilization and development should not be left to spontaneity and improvisation." Padilla worked in obscurity as a translator before being allowed to emigrate to the United States in 1980. In 1981, the poet Armando Valladares was imprisoned, provoking more international pressure. He, too, was allowed to resettle in the United States. Several intellectuals remain imprisoned in Cuba, although a visiting U.S. congressional delegation won the release of a few in 1996.

Cuba's literary community had cause to celebrate in 2002 when writer and poet Cintio Vitier, 80, received Mexico's coveted Juan Rulfo Literature Prize. He had received Cuba's National Literature Prize in 1988.

The history of the Cuban press is not a happy one, either before or since the Revolution. There was an eight-year period of relative press freedom during the constitutional administrations of Ramón Grau San Martín and Carlos Prío Socarrás prior to Batista's imposition of dictatorship in 1952. The Cuban government subsidized the press, which placed an economic sword of Damocles over newspapers critical of Batista. There were several independent dailies before the Revolution, the most prestigious being *Diario de la Marina*.

By 1962, Castro had expropriated all the independent newspapers and magazines,

Yoani Sanchéz, the Cuban blogger
Photo by Generación Y

and only one daily newspaper remained: *Granma*, the official *Communist Party* and government mouthpiece, named for the boat that brought Castro and his revolutionaries from Mexico in 1956. *Granma*, of course, is more of a propaganda organ than a genuinely informative newspaper. The regime retained the name of one confiscated magazine, *Bohemia*, which is somewhat less propagandistic and more of a literary and artistic review.

All things considered, the term "revolutionary journalism" is an oxymoron, because everything that appears in print or is transmitted over the airwaves is tightly controlled by the regime. Meaningful intellectual freedom and pluralism of thought expressed in opinion-editorial pieces remain non-existent, and modern Cuban cultural expression has been rendered quadriplegic for nearly four decades. About a third of the people sentenced to prison in the crackdown on dissent in 2003 (see History) were independent journalists, such as Raúl Rivero, who was later released and is now in exile in Spain.

A new independent journalist who has thus far evaded retribution is Yoani Sánchez, now 34, who in 2007 began clandestinely posting the now-popular blog, *Generación Y*, which satirizes and criticizes life in Cuba. The blog was receiving 1.2 million hits monthly in 2008, and the government blocked access to it within Cuba. Sánchez was awarded Spain's coveted Ortega y Gasset Prize in the category of digital journalism in 2008, but the government refused her permission to attend. (Rivero received an Ortega y Gasset Prize in 2007). She sent a tape recording of her acceptance speech, which read in part: "The fact that I am not there is more revealing of the Cuban reality than all of the posts I have written in my blog in all these months. But

some day, it won't take courage to put down in writing all these things we are living today." *Time* magazine named her one of the world's 100 most influential people in 2008, and in November 2009, she scored a journalistic coup by interviewing President Obama online for her blog. In 2009, Columbia University gave her the prestigious Maria Moors Cabot Award for courageous journalism, but again the government denied her permission to leave Cuba. *Generación Y* can be found at www.desdecuba.com/generaciony. It is translated into 17 languages and now has millions of hits per month.

Economy: Like so many Latin American countries, Cuba was condemned to a monocultural dependency on a given commodity, in Cuba's case, sugar cane. Nickel deposits and Cuba's famous black tobacco provided some economic diversity, but for the most part Cuba's prosperity or lack of it depended largely on the world market price for sugar. Even so, Cuba enjoyed a generally higher standard of living than did most of its sister republics, and it was somewhat ironic that Marxism took root here rather than in one of the more destitute nations.

The Marxist experiment proved no more feasible in this tropical setting than it did in Eastern Europe. As industry minister in the early 1960s, the legendary Ché Guevara set out to convert Cuba into an industrialized state, with disastrous results. What Cuba became, and what it still is today, is an illusion of self-sufficiency, with housing, education and medical care all provided "free." But it was the infusion of nearly $1 million a day worth of Soviet aid for 30 years, and guaranteed Soviet purchases of Cuban sugar, that made this smoke-and-mirrors economy viable. The dependency on sugar continued, the difference being that with collectivized agriculture, crop yields dropped precipitously after the Revolution.

On paper, the Cuban peso was proclaimed to be worth more than the U.S. dollar, while in reality it was worthless. Official per capita GDP figures were disregarded by international economists, and largely still are (see below). The classic communist method of distribution of goods and services resulted in chronic food shortages, which the regime blamed solely on the U.S. embargo rather than face the reality of the system's design flaws.

When the Soviet sugar daddy (pun intended) began collapsing in the late 1980s and the aid stopped pouring in, the plight of the people became increasingly desperate. The unpredictable Castro suddenly shifted policy during what he euphemistically termed Cuba's "special period" of readjustment. In a desperate bid to al-

leviate the destitution, Castro decided to allow private agricultural plots and fruit markets and permitted some skilled workers, such as mechanics, to moonlight as entrepreneurs, called *cuentapropistas*. The Cubans eagerly responded. When many of these small entrepreneurs and farmers began showing signs of bourgeois prosperity, Castro just as unpredictably terminated the experiment in limited capitalism temporarily. At the Fourth Communist Party Congress in 1991, again motivated by desperation to alleviate food shortages, he resumed limited private and cooperative cultivation. He also permitted the U.S. dollar to circulate, in effect creating a dual currency system.

In 1993, Castro expanded limited entrepreneurship to 157 discrete areas of endeavor. For example, he permitted the licensing of mom-and-pop restaurants called *paladares*, and small pensions called *casas particulares*. By 1995, more than 200,000 tiny restaurants and hotels had been licensed, but they faced such stringent regulation and fees that the number dropped to 150,000 in 2001. Those that remained have proven popular with customers and modestly lucrative for their owners.

By 1997, the private agricultural plots and co-ops were providing more food than the state farms. By 2002, there were 65,000 such small farms, grouped into 1,116 cooperatives. In a remarkable concession to their success, the National Assembly voted in 2002 to increase the amount of profits rebated to member farms from 50% to 70%.

In another seemingly counterrevolutionary move in 1994 that stemmed from raw desperation, Castro ordered the old decadent hotels, casinos and nightclubs to reopen under state tutelage. Cubans were not permitted to frequent such bourgeois establishments, of course, only to work there. The fun spots are reserved for foreign tourists, Canadians mostly, who are encouraged to pay with dollars. The gimmick to bring in desperately needed foreign exchange was successful, so much so that anti-Castro dissidents—whether from Florida or Cuba has not been determined—set off bombs in three of the hotels in 1997, killing one tourist and injuring four, in an obvious attempt to frighten other tourists away.

Cuba remains the world's eighth-largest sugar producer, but the sugar industry has deteriorated dramatically in recent years, in part because of natural factors, but also because of outdated equipment and low world market prices. Hurricane Georges was a factor in the 24% drop in sugar production in 1998, from 4.2 to 3.4 million metric tons. The sugar crop was hit again in 2001 by Hurricane Michelle, which destroyed an estimated 35% of the crop.

Cuba

Nonetheless, official figures released in 2002 put the harvest at 3.61 million tons, up slightly from the record low of 3.53 million in 2001, but a far cry from the record of 8.1 million in 1989. Because of lower market prices, the 2002 crop brought in about $120 million less in export earnings than the $561 million from the 2001 crop. Faced with grim economic realities, the government grudgingly and quietly closed 71 of the island's 156 sugar mills and said it plans to modernize the remaining ones. It also announced plans to replace about half of the 3.5 million acres devoted to sugar cultivation with crops that will help feed the Cuban people, such as rice.

On the remaining land, using improved techniques, the government hoped to increase the sugar yield from 16 tons per acre to 23. But the 2002–03 harvest showed a cataclysmic drop of 45%, to 2 million tons, a new record low. Still, Castro stubbornly clung to the collectivist model. The 2003–04 harvest was up slightly to 2.5 million tons, but the worst drought in a century devastated the sugar crop of 2004–05. A glum Castro admitted the harvest would be no more than 1.7 million tons, possibly only 1.5 million, the lowest since 1909—before mechanization. The 2005–06 and 2006–07 harvests were equally disappointing, 1.2 million tons each year, due to both bad weather and mechanical breakdowns at the 39 remaining mills, although the high international price for sugar helped boost GDP growth somewhat. Despite increasing the number of mills to 44, the government media admitted that the 2009–10 harvest fell 850,000 tons short of its goal and that the harvest was the worst since 1905. Low production prevents Cuba from capitalizing on the current international boom in sugar because of ethanol production. It is estimated Cuba could produce 1.6 billion gallons of ethanol from sugar cane a year, but Fidel Castro refused to divert sugar from a foodstuff to ethanol. That could change if Raúl becomes desperate enough and is willing to accept Brazilian help to set up ethanol distilleries.

Cuba is the world's sixth-largest producer of nickel and holds 30% of the world's reserves. Its exports of nickel and cobalt in 2001 exceeded $600 million. It produced 75,200 tons in 2002 and has the potential for 100 million, but because of the 2003 crackdown on dissent it has had difficulty finding European, Canadian or Australian mining firms willing to make the necessary $1.2 billion investment. In 2004, Chinese President Hu Jintao visited Cuba and agreed to invest $500 million in Cuba's nickel industry, not out of the goodness of his heart but because China's booming industries need the nickel. China is to import 4,400 tons annually. Record high nickel

prices on the international market in 2007 helped boost Cuba's export revenue.

Cuba has hoped tourism would be its economic savior, and to a degree, it has been. In 1999, Vice President Carlos Lage admitted the country was relying increasingly on foreign tourism for development. He said tourism brought in $1.7 billion in badly needed foreign exchange in 1998 and that it showed a 30% increase in the first quarter of 1999. An estimated 1.8 million tourists visited Cuba in 2000, bringing in $1.9 billion, dwarfing the amount from sugar exports. In 2001, the number of tourists dropped by 5% to 1.7 million, reflecting the global drop in tourism as a consequence of the September 11, 2001 terror attacks on the United States and a devastating hurricane, and in the first quarter of 2002 it was down by 14%. During the winter of 2001–02, several Cuban hotels actually closed up for lack of business, while prices at dollar stores skyrocketed.

Most of Cuba's tourists are from Canada and Europe, and in response to that fact, Cuba officially began accepting the Euro as well as the dollar in 2002. By 2003, it seemed the crisis had been weathered, with 1.9 million tourists bringing in $2.1 billion. In 2003, Castro himself presided at the opening of a 944-room resort on Cuba's northeast coast, the largest resort yet. The total number of hotel rooms on the island is now about 40,000. The government reported that in 2004, the number of tourists hit the 2 million mark, bringing in 15% more in foreign exchange than in 2003. The reports added tourism accounted for 4% of foreign exchange in 1990 and 41% in 2004. The number of tourists peaked in 2005 at 2.32 million, then declined by 4.3% in 2006; in 2007, it declined again, to 2.15 million. For 2008, the government announced a record 2.35 million visitors, who brought in a record $2.7 billion, up $326 million from 2007. The figures were expected to drop significantly for 2009 because of the global recession.

So desperate has Cuba been for foreign exchange that Venezuela, about the best friend Cuba still has and the source of a third of its oil, was forced to suspend oil shipments in 2002 when Cuba was unable to pay more than $63 million it owed for past shipments. The shipments resumed five months later under a deferred payments plan.

Cuba produces about 75,000 barrels of crude oil a day, about half its needs. Fidel Castro himself announced in 2004 the discovery of a deposit off the north coast containing an estimated 100 million barrels; estimates since then have placed it at perhaps 4 billion barrels. However, U.S. deep-water technology will be needed to fully exploit most of the deposits, and U.S. firms are still prohibited from drilling in Cuba.

Also dwarfing sugar earnings as a source of foreign exchange in recent years, now second only to tourism, have been remittances from Cubans living abroad, primarily the United States, Mexico and Spain. They are estimated at about $1 billion.

Since the collapse of the Soviet Union, Cuba has come to rely on foreign—i.e., capitalist—investors for economic development. By the end of 2001 there were nearly 400 joint ventures with the state, about 60% of them with Canadian, Spanish, French and Italian firms, specializing primarily in tourism, construction and biotechnology. Such investments have totaled an estimated $5 billion. But the drop in tourism, coupled with an unfavorable business climate, led to a dramatic decline in foreign investments. From an annual average of $268 million from 1996–2000, including $488 million in 2000, it plunged to only 38.9 million in 2001. The number of joint ventures dropped to about 300 in 2004, in part because the government abruptly began stiffening bureaucratic rules to drive out smaller businesses. By 2009, several foreign companies were complaining that the cash-strapped government had not been paid them their share of the profits from the joint ventures. One executive who complained publicly had his contract revoked.

Since 1998, growth has averaged a respectable 4.7% per year, thanks almost wholly to the foreign capitalist investors, who are theoretically anathema to the Marxist-Leninist model. Growth was estimated at a robust 6.9% for 1999, 5.6% for 2000 and 3% for 2001, but plummeted to 1.1% in 2002 and 1.3% in 2003, largely as a result of the drops in sugar production and in tourism after 9/11. The government claimed growth in 2004 was 5%, while the Economist Intelligence Unit in London put it at 3%. In 2006, reliable estimates put growth at a healthy 9.5%, largely because of unusually high international prices for both sugar and nickel. In 2007 it was estimated at 7.3%, dropping to 4.3% in 2008. Withn the global recession, it dropped to 1.4% min 2009.

On paper, the country claimed a per capita income of $2,800 in 2003, which was suspicious considering that the average monthly wage is only about $15. This is accomplished through a smoke-and-mirrors technique called "purchasing power parity," or PPP, which factors in such benefits as free rents and medical care. In 2005, the figure was raised to $3,300, even as destitute Cubans continued to flee the country, and to a questionable $9,500 in 2007. The World Bank placed it at "$3,706 or more" in 2007. In 2008, the World Bank said Cuban per capita income in real terms could be anywhere between $3,856 and $11,905, while the CIA World Factbook put PPP at $9,600 in 2008 and $9,700 in 2009.

In 2004, Castro ordered one of his periodic crackdowns on entrepreneurship, which many Cubans rely on to survive. Among those affected were private auto mechanics and even clowns who perform at birthday parties. He also froze new licenses for the popular *paladores*, or private restaurants, and *casas particulares*, a kind of Cuban bed-and-breakfast. He placed the existing establishments under onerous new restrictions and fees that could only be seen as disincentives. His logic was analogous to shutting off the engines once a plane had attained cruising altitude. Yet, in 2005, he confidently declared an end to the "special period" of austerity and readjustment following the Soviet collapse. In 2008, his brother Raúl replaced him as president. In 2009, faced with a desperately troubled economy, Raúl again expanded private agricultural plots, including some close to Havana, and permitted small enterprises such as barber shops and beauty salons to start operating again.

For a decade, Fidel Castro pragmatically allowed U.S. dollars to be spent at certain stores, appropriately tagged "dollar stores." That ended abruptly in 2004, when Castro ordered the Central Bank to prohibit circulation of the dollar at stores and businesses. In its place, there was the so-called "convertible peso," with an exchange rate to the dollar of 1:1. For government paychecks and most everyday uses, Cubans still used the regular peso, which Castro devalued in 2005 from 27 to the dollar to 25. The Central Bank now levies a 10% surcharge to convert dollars to either kind of peso, while the Euro and other hard foreign currencies are exempt.

In sum, Cuba today remains an economic basket case, a destitute society with an economy propped up only by a flourishing black market for almost everything, including parts for the prerevolutionary Fords and Chevrolets that still chug along on Havana's streets as in a scene from a 1950s movie. Prostitution is widespread despite revolutionary disapproval, and begging, something Fidel Castro once boasted he had eliminated, is back. A beggar, in fact, is what the entire country has become, totally reliant on pity from friendly countries, but even they are finding it increasingly difficult to ignore the Castros' appalling abuse of human rights.

Although the U.S. government is under increased pressure from its friends abroad and from some members of Congress and businessmen at home to lift the 1960 economic embargo—the argument being that it penalizes the average Cuban more than it does the Castro regime—an end to the embargo would not prove to be the panacea that many assume. Only thorough economic reform, such as occurred in China or in Hungary and other former East

Cuban state-owned media released this picture of a sweatsuit-clad Fidel Castro talking with unidentified people at the national Center for Scientific Research in Havana on July 10, 2010, apparently to dispel rumors that he was dead or incapacitated.
Photo by Alex Castro/Cubadebate

Bloc nations, will bring significant improvement. The ascension to power of Castro's brother, Raúl, in February 2008 has not augured a new era. He has indicated a greater tolerance toward entrepreneurship and a pragmatic interest in foreign investment, but he has intransigently refused to budge on the human rights issue.

The Future: One of the world's great guessing games for years was: How much longer can Fidel Castro last? On February 18, 2008, he ostensibly relinquished power to his brother, Raúl, who had governed as caretaker since Fidel fell critically ill in August 2006.

The obvious questions now are, what next, and is Raúl *really* in charge? Raúl, who turned 79 on June 3, had shown some encouraging signs that major change was in the offing. He detests bureaucratic inefficiency and took steps to combat it. He showed himself to be open to new ideas, encouraging suggestions for economic reform, in contrast to his brother's inflexibility. He has eased the restrictions on entrepreneurship and is willing to encourage foreign investment. He even released some political prisoners and reduced, but did not eliminate, harassment of dissidents, such as the Ladies in White, but he intransigently refused to free more. He suffered a major public relations fiasco when Orlando Zapata, one of the dissidents jailed in the 2003 crackdown, died in February after an 85-day hunger strike.

Raúl obviously remains a hard-core Marxist. Missing thus far from the winds of change sweeping Cuba is a willingness to engage in meaningful dialogue with the dissidents. That is a grave mistake, as they are likely to become far more assertive, especially after Zapata's death. The dissident movement encompasses some coura-

geous individuals, who may form a cadre from which post-Castro leadership could be drawn, as was the case in Poland and the Czech Republic. But the internal squabble between Oswaldo Payá and Beatríz Roque is ominous. Another variable is the exile community in Miami, which may expect a piece of the action, but their 50-year absence deprives the exiles of legitimacy in the transition.

Also missing is any suggestion of contested elections or a free and independent press; about 20 independent journalists continue to rot in prison because of the ideas they printed. Raúl apparently does not intend to introduce a Cuban *glasnost*. The latest sham election for the 169 Assembly seats was held in April 2010 and—surprise!—the Communist Party won all 169. A demonstration by the Ladies in White in March was broken up by pro-government goons. Some reform.

The Obama administration, which indicated early-on it felt the time was ripe for a new era in U.S.-Cuban relations, has discovered to its chagrin and dismay what 10 earlier administrations learned from bitter experience: Fidel's concept of "negotiations" means the United States lifts its embargo and Cuba yields nothing in return, such as releasing the 220 remaining prisoners of conscience. (The sudden release of 52 prisoners as this book went to press in July could represent a major policy shift; time will tell.)

On more than one occasion, Fidel has made it clear he still has veto power over Raúl's decisions. Only Fidel's death will truly lead to any meaningful transition. Although Raúl is reported to be in excellent health, at his age he cannot expect to be much more than a bridge in leadership to whoever comes after him. His election was analogous to the College of Cardinals electing the 78-year-old Pope Benedict XVI to succeed John Paul II. Raúl suggested that the transition to a new generation of Communist Party leaders would be the principal purpose of the party congress he said would be held in late 2009, but then he canceled the congress, saying the party "is not ready." Not ready for *what?* Entering the 21st century, now a decade old?

Hopefully, after both Castros are gone, that transition will be peaceful rather than violent, and the new leadership will seek to embrace something along the Uruguayan or Costa Rican models, allowing Cubans to enjoy the impressive social services they have come to expect, while at the same time enjoying the right to freely elect their leaders, to read, watch and listen to what they choose, to practice their religion without intimidation, to pursue a profession of their choosing, to own property and to live or travel where they want—in short, to live as a *free* people at last.

The Dominican Republic

Panorama of Santo Domingo with the Presidential Palace in the foreground

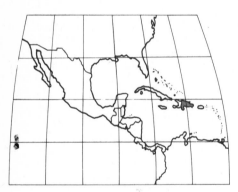

Area: 18,811 square miles
Population: 9.79 million (2010 est.)
Capital City: Santo Domingo (Pop. 2.25 million, est.).
Climate: Tropical, tempered by sea breezes; moderate rainfall is heaviest from April to December.
Neighboring Countries: The Dominican Republic occupies the eastern two thirds of the island of Hispaniola, the second largest of the Greater Antilles; the Republic of Haiti occupies the western one-third of the island.
Official Language: Spanish.
Other Principal Tongues: There are small French and English-speaking groups.

Ethnic Background: Mixed European, African and Indian origin (73%), White (16%), Negro (11%).
Principal Religion: Roman Catholic Christianity.
Chief Commercial Products: Tourism, sugar, bananas, cacao, coffee, nickel, gold, textiles, clothing.
Currency: Peso.
Gross Domestic Product: U.S. $45.24 billion in 2009 ($4,617 per capita).
Former Colonial Status: Spanish Crown Colony (1492–1795); French Possession (1795–1808); Spanish Control (1808–21); occupied by Haiti (1822–44).
Independence Date: February 27, 1844.
Chief of State: Leonel Fernández Reyna (b. December 26, 1953), president (since August 16, 2004).
National Flag: Blue and red, quartered by a white cross.

The Dominican Republic occupies the eastern two-thirds of the island of Hispaniola, also known by its Indian name, *Hayti*, which means place of mountains. Majestically cresting at 10,000 feet in the center of the island, mountain spurs run south to the Caribbean Sea and to the east, dropping to rolling hills before reaching the coast. A separate range, with peaks reaching 4,000 feet, runs along the north coast of the Dominican Republic. The Cibao Valley, lying between the central range and north coast hills, and the southern coastal plains, are the most productive agricultural lands of the island and the most heavily populated regions. The

154

slopes of the mountains, green throughout the year, are forested and well watered and are the locale of most of the country's coffee production.

The climate, while tropical, is moderated by invigorating sea breezes. During the dry season, December to March, the trade winds cool the air, making the southern coast beaches a major tourist attraction.

History: The island of Hispaniola was discovered by Columbus on his first voyage and selected as the site for his first colonization effort. The city of Santo Domingo, founded in 1496, is the oldest European-established city in the Americas. The native Indians were described as peaceful by Columbus and were absorbed into the Spanish population; they became virtually extinct as a race within 30 years of the Spanish discovery. Slaves from Africa were introduced in the 1520s. The discovery of more valuable domains on the mainland and the exhaustion of gold deposits on the island caused the Spanish to lose interest in Hispaniola at an early date after it was settled by them.

The island was frequently attacked by pirates and privateers—Santo Domingo was held for ransom by the English privateer Sir Francis Drake in 1585. Buccaneers took the western part of the island in 1630, and French settlers arrived shortly thereafter. The western portion of Hispaniola was ceded to France in 1697. With the outbreak of the French Revolution in 1789, a series of rebellions occurred on the island. The French section of the island, Haiti, was overrun by British and Spanish forces in 1791; they were expelled by the French in the same year and France was given possession of the entire island by treaty in 1795. Returned to Spain in 1806, the Spanish-speaking Dominicans declared themselves independent in 1821, but were conquered by the neighboring Haitians in the following year, and did not achieve final independence until 1844.

The independent history of the Dominican Republic has been a continuation of internal war, foreign intervention and misrule. From 1844 to 1861, the country was governed by a succession of military men who were put in office by various factions of the island's upper class. Constant unrest and invasions from Haiti caused General Pedro Santana to invite the Spanish to return in 1861; however, the Spanish discipline was no more welcome than it had been earlier, and the Spaniards were again ousted in 1865. The second republic was as restless as the first, and the government passed from one dictator to another in an unbroken series of corrupt administrations which had little or no governing ability.

By 1905, the Dominican Republic was largely bankrupt and threatened with occupation by European powers seeking to collect bad debts; the United States intervened under a 50-year treaty to administer the island's finances. There were more or less continuous revolts—in 1914 the United States landed Marines to bolster the government; nevertheless, the president was ousted in 1916. From 1916 to 1922, the country was administered by the U.S. Navy.

A provisional government was reestablished in 1922 and in 1924 U.S. troops were withdrawn. It soon became apparent that the Dominicans' political habits had not changed by the six years of military occupation; following a reasonably effective administration, revolt again broke out in 1930. General Rafael Leonidas Trujillo Molina, commandant of the military, seized power and brought a semblance of order to the country.

The Trujillo Era

The era of Trujillo provided a 31-year respite in a long history of violence and dissension. Ruthlessly suppressing all opposition, Trujillo dominated the island as its absolute ruler. Tyrannical as his rule was, no other dictator in Latin America approached his material benefits.

In 1930 he assumed control of a nation which had never known anything but lawlessness, banditry, bankruptcy and foreign intervention. With the treasury empty, the people poverty-stricken, the capital city destroyed by a hurricane and foreign debts almost three times the total annual income, Trujillo took on the herculean task of rebuilding his country. Twenty years later, internal and foreign debts had been paid; the national income had multiplied to 40 times the level of 1930 and the nation had a balanced budget for most of the period.

**General Rafael Leonidas
Trujillo Molina, 1930**

Schools, roads and numerous public buildings were constructed during the Trujillo years. *"El Benefactor"* also built a huge personal fortune, valued at an estimated $800 million and comprising 60% of all land in the nation. The cost of his rule was the total loss of personal liberty for the Dominican people, who were held in check by Trujillo's efficient and merciless secret police force. Trujillo's assassination in mid-1961 ended an era of one of Latin America's most brutal dictatorships. Attempts by his son to retain control of the country were unsuccessful and the family fled the island in late 1961.

The Balaguer 'Democracy'

Joaquín Balaguer, titular president at the time of the assassination, maintained a semblance of order after the flight of the Trujillo family by promising to step down when provisions for elections could be made. Balaguer was overthrown by a military coup in early 1962 and a few days later, a counter-coup installed the vice president.

The first experiment in democratic government was undertaken in late 1962; Juan Bosch, a moderate leftist, was chosen president in honest elections. He was inaugurated with feelings of optimism; honest, well-intentioned but politically inexperienced, he was overthrown by a military coup six months later as he attempted to limit the power of the armed forces.

A new regime was soon dominated by a former car salesman, but in April 1965 a civil war erupted when dissident elements in the armed forces sought to return Juan Bosch to office. As the toll in human lives quickly mounted (an estimated 2,000 were killed), fearing the imminent defeat of the conservative faction and creation of a new Castro-style government, the United States intervened with 22,000 combat troops.

The Organization of American States agreed to send in additional troops and to take over the task of preserving order and conducting elections. Nevertheless, the fact that the United States intervened unilaterally—in apparent violation of existing inter-American agreements—caused widespread discontent in Latin America.

Carefully supervised by the OAS, free elections were held in mid-1966 and Balaguer, supported by a centrist coalition, won the presidency. He followed a moderate economic policy, satisfying few of the demands of the warring factions. The U.S. intervention solved none of the social or economic problems—it merely postponed the day when these questions would be resolved.

After amending the constitution so that he could succeed himself, Balaguer was re-

Dominican Republic

elected to a second term in 1970. Unable to unite, the rival candidates provided only token resistance. Bosch boycotted the elections because he knew the military would overrule his left-wing policies.

Under Balaguer, the economy achieved the most spectacular growth of any Latin American nation. Gross domestic product rose by an impressive 12.5% in 1972 and 1973—the world's highest rate in those years. Virtually every key sector of the economy set records in 1973, particularly agriculture, tourism and mining. Pacing the growth was the nation's revitalized sugar industry, where workers responded to a profit-sharing plan by increasing output.

The significant factor in the nation's economic boom was the political stability enforced by the soft-spoken Balaguer. The president's conservative Reformist Party pursued a policy called *continuismo*, which meant a strong emphasis on law and order and economic development. However, opposition parties often received heavy-handed treatment in the name of political stability. Balaguer obtained the all-important loyalty of the armed forces by granting the military special favors.

During 1971, the administration was linked to a right-wing vigilante group called "The Gang," which terrorized and murdered several hundred suspected and real leftists. When a tiny group of 10 Cuban-trained guerrillas entered the country in early 1973, they were quickly eliminated by the efficient Dominican forces. Balaguer then used the occasion to polish off the rest of his opposition; political opponents were jailed, the university was closed and opposition newspapers and media were seized. Major political leaders were forced into hiding or exile.

The repression of political opponents set the stage for the 1974 elections. Although the opposition was divided among about 20 small parties, the two major groups (one liberal, the other conservative) formed a coalition and nominated Silvestre Antonio Guzmán Fernández, a wealthy cattle rancher.

Although Balaguer was at first regarded as a shoo-in for re-election despite his promise during the 1970 campaign to seek a constitutional change banning the re-election of presidents, a sudden groundswell of support for Guzmán clearly alarmed the administration. When Balaguer hurriedly implemented a new voting rule, the opposition boycotted the election, charging that the new rules would permit administration supporters to vote more than once. With the opposition boycott and the military openly supporting his re-election, Balaguer coasted to an easy "victory."

Major problems facing him at the start of his third term were inflation, which had

Joaquín Balaguer

reached an annual rate of 20% by mid-1974, and high unemployment. A more fundamental problem was the fact that although the Dominican Republic was enjoying the most prosperous period in its history, the benefits of the boom were confined largely to the upper class, while fully 80% of the people remained trapped in poverty. The annual per capita income hovered at $350 while the population growth was increasing at a dangerous 3.6%.

Interregnum

Balaguer suffered a stunning upset in the 1978 presidential election when he was defeated by Guzmán of the Dominican Revolutionary Party (*PRD*). Balaguer supporters in the army temporarily halted vote tabulation when early returns showed him losing. However, strong protests at home and abroad, especially from the Carter administration, forced the military to allow the results to stand.

Guzmán's program to promote domestic peace and a strong economy was generally successful during the first three years of his term, with gains in health, education and rural development. However, a dramatic increase in the price of imported oil, plus a sharp drop in sugar export earnings as the United States and the Western Hemisphere were gripped by recession, plunged the economy into a recession by late 1980. Guzmán declined to run for re-election in 1982—the first time a Dominican chief of state had offered to step down *voluntarily*.

The May 1982 elections saw the ruling *PRD* presidential candidate, moderate social democrat Salvador Jorge Blanco, win with 46% of the vote. His two main opponents were Balaguer (39.14%) and Bosch (9.69%). Blanco, a 55-year-old constitutional lawyer affiliated with the Socialist International, saw his *PRD* also win con-

trol of Congress and most local governments. Although 12 people died in campaign violence, the election was generally the most honest and peaceful in the nation's history. Unfortunately, the last victim proved to be President Guzmán himself, who committed suicide a month before leaving office.

At the insistence of the International Monetary Fund and creditor banks, Blanco imposed economic austerity, reducing luxury imports and limiting government expenditures. This led to a slow increase in GDP growth, still slower than that of the population growth, and the per capita income fell slightly. The situation became tense in May 1984 when a series of popular demonstrations led to bloody confrontations with police. Because of the sagging economy, Blanco's popularity sagged equally in 1985.

Balaguer Returns

The elections in both 1986 and 1990 pitted an elderly Balaguer against an energetic opponent. Both campaigns were heated, replete with personal insults and slanderous statements. Notwithstanding an attempt by the military to halt ballot-counting in 1986, Balaguer won even though his opponent was considered a shoo-in and despite the fact that Balaguer was virtually blinded by glaucoma.

The contest in 1990 was between Balaguer and Bosch, only four years younger than he; Balaguer won by a margin of 22,000 votes out of 1.9 million. The reason for the two victories of the aging Balaguer was simple: relative prosperity.

Both elections were tainted with the usual irregularities. Balaguer carefully paved the way for yet another run for the presidency in 1994. This time, the favored opponent was José Francisco Peña Gómez, leader of the *PRD* and former Santo Domingo mayor. The campaign was extraordinarily dirty. Because Peña Gómez was black, and Dominicans harbor a deep fear and distrust of black Haitians, Balaguer successfully capitalized on these emotions. A video was used allegedly showing Peña Gómez practicing voodoo in Haitian style. Balaguer won by an estimated 30,000 votes amid charges of fraud. Many supporters of Peña Gómez somehow hadn't been registered even though they had.

The Clinton administration, trying to enforce an embargo of Haiti and needing Dominican help, chose to ignore the irregularities. Balaguer cooperated with the embargo, with the tacit understanding that the Clinton administration would not protest the 1994 election results. The matter quietly faded, and the 87-year-old Balaguer was inaugurated in August; by then he was totally blind.

Fernández and Mejía

Tacitly acknowledging irregularities, Balaguer, then 89, agreed to step down mid-way through his term and new elections were held in 1996. Meanwhile, Congress amended the constitution in 1994 to prohibit immediate re-election for president.

In the first round of voting in May 1996, Peña Gómez of the *PRD* led with 46% of the vote to 39% for Leonel Fernández Reyna of Bosch's *PLD*. Balaguer, though the longtime rival of Bosch, disliked Peña Gómez even more, and threw his support behind Fernández, a 42-year-old lawyer who grew up in New York City. In the runoff election, Fernández edged out Peña Gómez with 51.25% of the vote in a contest that international observers proclaimed fair and untainted by the traditional Balaguer trickery. The new president promised to take the Dominican Republic down a "new road."

Fernández found that "new road" a bumpy one. In the 1996 elections, his party won only one seat in the 30-member Senate and 12 of 120 seats in the lower house. In the May 1998 congressional elections, the *PRD* swept all but five seats in the Senate and won an absolute majority in the Chamber of Deputies. Peña Gómez, however, died before he could savor his party's triumph. The *PRD*-controlled Congress passed, and Fernández signed, a prohibition against immediate re-election, clearly a reaction to Balaguer's electoral abuses.

Tension among the political parties took a violent turn in January 1999. At issue was the election of a new secretary-general of the Dominican Municipal League, the organization that distributes revenues totaling 4% of the national budget to the local governments. The *PLD* and Balaguer's newly named Social Christian Reform Party (*PRSC*) joined forces once again to elect a secretary-general, prompting the dominant *PRD* to meet separately and "elect" its own candidate. Pro-*PRD* demonstrators surrounded the headquarters of the municipal league and soon clashed with police. In the ensuing melee, several demonstrators were injured by police shotgun pellets, including two *PRD* senators. Soldiers also surrounded the Congress building in a show of force, prompting the *PRD* to denounce Fernández as a would-be dictator.

A truly historic event occurred in August 1998 when Fidel Castro visited the Dominican Republic for the first time, shortly after Fernández re-established diplomatic relations. Officially, Castro's visit was to attend the 14-nation Caribbean Forum summit. Few were surprised when Castro paid a call on his old ally, Bosch, then 89. But Castro astonished everyone by also paying a visit to the 92-year-old Balaguer at his home. The two aging Cold War antagonists sat side-by-side on a sofa for nearly an hour and engaged in a cordial, even jocular conversation.

By 1999, the Fernández administration could boast a 40% increase in economic growth in its four years and Latin America's second-highest growth rate of 7% per year (see Economy). Such booms usually favor the party in power, but Fernández could not run for re-election in 2000, barred by the law aimed at Balaguer. Thus, he engineered the nomination of an economic adviser, Danilo Medina, 47, as the *PLD*'s standard bearer. Within the *PRD*, meanwhile, a 59-year-old agricultural economist, Hipólito Mejía, assumed Peña's mantle and became the party's nominee. The venerable and resilient Balaguer, by then 93, once again became the nominee of the *PRSC*.

Balaguer proved to be a spoiler for the *PLD*, dividing the conservative vote. Mejía, meanwhile, preached a populist message, vowing that the poor would begin enjoying the fruits of the burgeoning economy through expanded public works and improved education, a persuasive message to those who felt left out of the growing prosperity evident all around them. He fostered his image as a simple farmer, and charmed voters with Lincolnian folk wisdom and humor.

As usual, the campaign turned violent. As Mejía's car passed the house of a local *PLD* official in Moca, gunfire erupted, and Mejía's bodyguards shot and killed the *PLD* official and another man, claiming an assassination attempt. The *PLD* maintained that the bodyguards had fired first.

In the vote results of May 16, certified as fair by more than 100 international observers, Mejía received 49.87% of the vote—tantalizingly close to a first-round victory. Medina and Balaguer finished in a dead heat for second place—but with Medina slightly ahead, 24.94% to 24.61%. On May 18, Balaguer announced he was accepting Mejía's election, meaning he would not endorse Medina in a runoff. Medina, faced with the near-impossibility of closing a 25-point gap with Mejía, withdrew, handing the presidency to Mejía. Scattered gunfire that night marred the celebrations of Mejía's victory.

Mejía was inaugurated on August 16, 2000. He inherited from Fernández the most robust economic growth in Latin America, which benefited Mejía's *PRD* in the mid-term congressional elections of May 16, 2002. The party swept 29 of the 32 Senate seats, a gain of 10; strengthened its lead in the 150-member Chamber of Deputies; and won control of 104 of the 125 municipalities. Election-related violence was minimal by Dominican standards; "only" one person was killed and seven injured. Armed with these overwhelming majorities, the *PRD* amended the constitution to permit the immediate re-election of a president for a second term, largely because Mejía insisted that he was not interested in running again.

On February 7, 2002, the *PLD* lost its patriarch when Bosch died at the age of 92. He was buried with full state honors, and diplomatic representatives of six countries and Puerto Rico—but not the United States—attended the funeral, as did thousands of Dominicans. Bosch was followed in death five months later by his arch-rival, Balaguer, who died on July 14 at the age of 95. An colorful era in Dominican history was over.

Mejía's popularity plummeted after the mid-term elections as the once-vibrant economy turned sour (see Economy). Power blackouts, created when the privatized power companies could not keep up with demand, led to protests in September 2002 that left two people dead and 50 injured. Mejía responded by renationalizing the power companies, which cost about $600 million, causing the IMF to cancel a loan for that amount in October 2002.

In February 2003, Mejía announced a series of austerity measures designed to halt an alarming increase in inflation and the decline in the value of the peso, which lost 40% of its value against the dollar in just the first two months of 2003. By February 2004, it was down by 65%. Among the austerity measures was a reduction in the number of government jobs and of gov-

Former President Hipólito Mejía

Dominican Republic

ernment salaries. Unlike in other Latin American countries, where the opposition launches general strikes and confrontational street demonstrations to protest austerity measures, the opposition charged that the measures did not go far enough and called for street protests to demand even greater spending cuts.

The reeling economy was then delivered a knockout blow when Banco Intercontinental, or Baninter, the country's third-largest private bank, went bankrupt in April 2003 as the result of an embezzlement and fraud scandal. The central bank was legally obligated to pay only 500,000 pesos, or $12,000, to each depositor, but it generously compensated the depositors for their entire losses, a total of $2.4 billion that the economy could not absorb. The bank's owners went to jail, but that did not prevent the ripple effects of the bailout on the economy.

By early 2004, inflation was running at 42%, and unemployment was 16%. Dominicans began joining Cubans and Haitians in trying to reach the United States—or at least Puerto Rico—in search of a better life. It was a stark contrast to the boom times of the 1990s.

Fernández Makes a Comeback

Mejía made an abrupt about face and announced he planned to run again in 2004. He met with immediate opposition from within his own *PRD*, whose rules still precluded immediate re-nomination. Mejía arrogantly pressed on with his re-election plans despite polls that showed 73% of Dominicans opposed a second term.

He did not increase his popularity by contributing 370 Dominican troops to the allied coalition in Iraq. He began withdrawing them in April 2004, after Spain withdrew its troops following the al-Qaeda terror attacks in Madrid.

In December 2003, an anti-re-election faction chose *PRD* president Hatuey de Camps as its candidate, but in January, party regulars dutifully re-nominated Mejía at a convention boycotted by the de Camps faction. Mejía then attempted a Byzantine maneuver, pushing through Congress a bill that would allow each party to nominate up to five candidates, with the one receiving the most votes to receive all the party's votes. In the face of a public outcry, he declared that "power is there to be exercised." This only inflamed public opinion further.

Former President Fernández, meanwhile, announced his own comeback bid as the *PLD* candidate, and polls showed him a heavy favorite over Mejía. Rounding out the field was Eduardo Estrella of Balaguer's *PRSC*.

President Leonel Fernández

Mejía was so unpopular at that point he was booed at baseball games. Businessmen staged a two-day strike in January, in which 20 people were injured. The IMF, meanwhile, re-approved the desperately needed loan, but parceled it out in increments. Gradually, however, as polls showed Mejía ahead of the other factions in the *PRD*, the party faithful gradually coalesced around his candidacy as the only way to prevent a Fernández comeback.

There was a new twist to the 2004 campaign: The three candidates campaigned in Miami and New York, because Dominicans living abroad were allowed to vote for president for the first time; more than 52,000 were registered to do so. An estimated 1 million Dominicans reside in the United States, another 100,000 in Puerto Rico. Polling centers also were established in Montreal, Caracas, Madrid and Barcelona.

In the end, on May 16, Dominicans chose between a president who had presided over a boom and another who had presided over a bust. The turnout was 72% of the 5 million registered voters, compared with 76% in 2000. The results were pretty much what the polls had predicted:

Fernández	2,063,871	57.11%
Mejía	1,215,928	33.65%
Estrella	312,493	8.65%

Days after the election, the worst torrential rains in recent Caribbean history hit the Dominican Republic and Haiti. The human toll on the Dominican side was 395 dead and 274 missing.

Fernández was inaugurated for his second term on August 16, 2004. He named four men to high-level posts who were

under investigation for allegedly embezzling $100 million during his first term from a fund created to establish jobs and mediate strikes. Fernández dismissed the charges as "politically motivated."

Fernández tackled the economic crisis with a series of painful austerity measures. He pushed through the *PRD*-controlled Congress increases in various taxes, including the VAT, or sales tax, from 12% to 16% to reduce a $490 million budget deficit and to prevent a default on the $7.9 billion debt. He also began ending subsidies on gas and electricity, but eased that blow by concluding an agreement for low-cost Venezuelan oil for electricity generation. Power blackouts remained a problem.

At the same time, he declared he would cut 20% from the budget reduce the size of the bloated public payroll, which Mejía had increased by 30% to 400,000. Among those losing their jobs were 97 of the army's 202 generals; Fernández said the country didn't need, and couldn't afford, that many generals.

There was some grumbling over the austerity measures, but they began turning the economy around. At the height of the crisis, the peso dropped to 51 to the dollar; by the end of 2004, it was back up to 29. The country recorded a modest increase in the GDP for 2004 after posting a loss in 2003. Fernández reinforced his reputation as an economic wizard in 2005 with GDP growth of 9.3%. In 2006, it was 10.7%, the highest in Latin America, and in 2007 it was a still-robust 7.9%.

In 2005, the corruption investigation shoe was on the foot of the other party. Charges were filed against two of Mejía's former ministers and several businessmen in an alleged scheme to divert $60 million worth of buses and minivans for the public transportation system into their own pockets. However, Fernández was less than aggressive in dealing with corruption on his predecessor's watch, apparently because he needed the *PRD*'s support in Congress.

That changed with the congressional elections of 2006, in which the *PLD* obtained 52% of the vote and won a majority in both houses. The *PLD* won 96 seats in the Chamber of Deputies to 60 for the *PRD* and 22 for the *PRSC*; in the Senate, the *PLD* won 22 seats, the *PRD* 7, the *PRSC*, 3.

In 2005, the Dominican Republic ratified the Dominican Republic-Central American Free Trade Agreement with the United States. It went into effect on March 1, 2007.

Re-Election

Besides having brought back the boom times of his first term, Fernández in his second term began construction of the first subway system in the Caribbean for Santo Domingo, which will cost $700 million. The first 11-mile segment opened on the eve of the 2008 presidential election campaign. Although there were still nagging problems, such as 16% unemployment, a high poverty rate and chronic blackouts, Fernández was the hands-down favorite for the May 16 election, now that immediate re-election was permitted. The only real suspense was whether he could win without a runoff.

The *PRD* unwisely nominated its leader, Miguel Vargas Maldonado, a civil engineer and businessman who had been Mejía's public works minister. He was still under a cloud of suspicion for alleged financial irregularities. The *PRSC* nominated a flamboyant populist, Amable Aristy Castro, former general-secretary of the Dominican Municipal League. Although the *PRSC* was still the most conservative of the three major parties, Aristy billed himself the champion of the poor and tossed out salamis at his campaign rallies. There were four minor candidates.

Four people were killed in the customary election-related violence. Voter turnout was 70.67%. Fernández scored a convincing first-round victory with 2.2 million votes, or 53.8%. Vargas had 1.65 million votes, or 40.5%, while Aristy polled only 188,000 votes, or 4.6%, a pitiful showing for Balaguer's old party. Fernández was sworn in for his third term on August 16.

Fernández continued to enjoy respectable economic growth until the global recession hit in late 2008. In February 2010, the president visited neighboring Haiti in the wake of the devastating earthquake there and pledged immediate medical and reconstruction aid. It may not have been out of pure benevolence; Dominicans feared a new migration of desperate Haitians across the border.

Culture: The succession of lengthy dictatorships since independence has not proven conducive to the development of Dominican culture. Ethnically, the island is a mix of European, Indian and African, and the domestic culture is a hybridization that has influenced its music. A dance that has won popular acceptance abroad is the meringue, with its contagious Caribbean rhythm.

The absence of educational reform and the resulting low literacy rate crippled the Dominican Republic's literary growth. The prose fiction writer Juan Bosch, who served briefly as president in the 1960s and remains influential in Dominican politics, is one of only a handful of Dominicans who have obtained international recognition in literature or the arts. Perhaps the country's most notable cultural contribution has been the fashion designer, Oscar de la Renta.

The independent Dominican press often has felt the pressure of dictators. The dean of the press is the daily *Listín Diario*, founded in 1889, which flourished until shut down by the Trujillo dictatorship. It resumed publication in 1963 and has followed a left-of-center editorial line, counterbalanced by the country's other "respectable" newspaper, *El Caribe*. *Listín Diario* was taken over by the government in 2003, not for criticizing the government but because its owner, Ramón Baéz, was arrested for fraud and embezzlement following the collapse of Banco Intercontinental, of which he was an owner (see History). A judge ruled in September 2004 that the newspaper was not connected to

Partial view of the port of Santo Domingo

Dominican Republic

the bank collapse and ordered it returned to Baéz's family.

Sports is a national obsession, particularly soccer and baseball. Numerous Dominican baseball players have gone on to play in the U.S. major leagues, most notably Sammy Sosa of the Chicago Cubs, a source of great national pride, who along with Mark McGwire broke Roger Maris' single-season home run record of 61 in 1998; McGwire hit 70, Sosa hit 66.

Economy: The Dominican economy has been traditionally based on agriculture, with sugar being the main cash crop. However, now tourism produces more income than sugar as sugar prices fell and the U.S. reduced the Dominican quota allowed for importation. New hotels and tourist facilities have sprung up throughout the nation. In 2002, tourism revenue amounted to $2 billion.

An aggressive government program to place unused farmland into production has increased the output of other cash products such as meat, coffee, tobacco and cacao. Thanks to an ambitious irrigation program centering around a four-dam system on the Nizao River, some farm regions are now producing up to three crops a year in contrast to a single crop in previous years.

Also gaining in importance is the nation's mining industry. A Canadian-based consortium exports Dominican ferro-nickel ingots worth $75 million a year; other important exports include bauxite, salt and gypsum. Gold and silver are mined in small quantities. Three huge new oil refineries have also boosted the economy. Intensive efforts are being made to increase the output from the nation's own small oil fields. The Dominican Republic continues to attract record amounts of investment, partly because of the comparatively stable political conditions. Foreign investment in luxury hotels and resorts, textiles, clothing and assembly-for-re-export plants, like Mexico's *maquiladoras,* created about 200,000 new jobs. The result was what could only be called a boom during the presidency of Leonél Fernández (1996–2000) of the conservative, business-oriented Democratic Liberation Party *(PLD)*. Even as some of the major economies of the region slipped into recession after the Brazilian market meltdowns of 1998 and 1999, the Dominican Republic maintained the highest sustained GDP growth in Latin America from 1997–2000, above 7% a year. Per capita GDP rose from $1,572 in 1996 to $2,486 in 2001.

Mid-way through the presidency of Hipólito Mejía (2000–04), a populist of the Democratic Revolutionary Party *(PRD)*, the economy went into a tailspin. Unemployment jumped to 16%, inflation soared to 42% and the foreign debt more than doubled, from $3.7 billion to $7.6 billion. The value of the peso fell from 18 to the dollar to 51. The government generously paid out $2.4 billion to depositors in the bailout of Banco Intercontinental in 2003. The country's third-largest bank collapsed because of fraud and embezzlement, which exacerbated the crisis and caused an estimated $2 billion in foreign capital to be withdrawn from Dominican banks in the wake of the scandal.

Real GDP growth slumped to 3% in 2001 and 4.1% in 2002, then *declined* by 0.4% in 2003. Per capita GDP dropped to $2,320 in 2002 and $1,896 in 2003. Boom had turned to bust.

The downturn was largely responsible for the return to power in 2004 of former President Fernández. He quickly imposed a number of austerity measures, which turned the economy around (see History).

GDP growth in 2004 was a meager 1.8%, a far cry from the boom years, but at least positive rather than negative. In 2005 it was back up to the boom level of 9.3%, while inflation was reduced to 7.4%. In 2006, growth was 10.7%, the highest in Latin America, while inflation was only 5%; growth in 2007 was a still-high 8.5%, and per capita income was back up to $3,850. Ironically, the strengthened peso against the dollar led to a 17% decline in textile exports and the loss of 41,000 jobs. Growth slowed to 5.3% in 2008 and 1.8% in 2009, largely because of the global recession and growing unemployment in the United States, which has affected the ever-vital remittances from Dominicans working there. Unemployment rose to 14.1% in 2008 abnd 15.1% in 2009. With the recession, inflation dropped from 10.6% in 2008 to 1.4% in 2009.

Remittances from Dominicans living abroad, mostly the United States, leaped from $1.5 billion in 1999 to $2.7 billion in 2004, roughly 17% of GDP. In 2008, they were a record high $3.1 billion, but the global recesiion was expected to significantly reduce remittances in 2009.

The Dominican Republic ratified its membership in the U.S.-Central American Free trade Agreement (CAFTA-DR) in March 2007. The United States accounts for 66.4% of Dominican exports and 46% of Dominican imports.

The Future: The Dominican Republic went from boom under Leonel Fernández to bust under Hipólito Mejía back to boom under Fernández. He is now in his third term, and he has coyly suggested he may amend the constitution to run again in 2012, conjuring up memories of the six-term Balaguer, to whose legacy Fernández has begun to lay claim as he shifts his party to the right. Indeed, his *PRD*'s campaign slogan for the May 16, 2008, election was "Four more years, then we'll talk."

Fernández's major shortcoming has been failure to channel the booming growth rate to reduce nagging 16% unemployment, to reduce the 42% poverty rate, or to revamp the infrastructure other than to build a $700 million subway system for Santo Domingo, which many criticize as a boondoggle, while electrical blackouts remain chronic. If he is as wise as he is politically astute, he will address these problems and establish a legacy far better than that of Balaguer, who is remembered for fraudulent elections and repression. The Dominican Republic does not need another Balaguer.

Ecuador

Fishermen out from Guayaquil, Ecuador

Area: 104,749 square miles.

Population: 14.79 million (2010 estimate).

Capital City: Quito (Pop. 1.5 million estimated).

Climate: The eastern lowlands are hot and wet; the coastal plains receive seasonally heavy rainfall; the highland climate becomes increasingly temperate with altitude.

Neighboring Countries: Colombia (north); Peru (east and south).

Official Language: Spanish.

Other Principal Tongues: Quechua and Jívaro.

Ethnic Background: Predominantly Indian, with small groups of European and African origin.

Principal Religion: Roman Catholic Christianity.

161

Ecuador

Chief Commercial Products: Petroleum, coffee, bananas, cacao, shrimp, sardines.

Currency: U.S. Dollar (formerly the *sucre*).

Gross Domestic Product: U.S. $56.27 billion, 2009, est. ($3,805 per capita).

Former Colonial Status: Spanish Crown Colony (1532–1821); a state of *Gran Colombia* (1822–1830).

Independence Date: May 13, 1830.

Chief of State: Rafael Vicente Correa Delgado (b. April 6, 1963), president (since January 15, 2007).

National Flag: A top yellow stripe, center blue stripe and a lower red stripe.

Because of disputes with Peru over boundaries, and territorial losses in the 1942 settlement of a war with Peru, Ecuador's area is uncertain. It has three distinct zones: the vast Andean highland, with lofty, snow-capped peaks and green valleys; the narrow coastal plain between the Andes and the Pacific, from 50 to 100 miles wide; and the *Oriente* (East), consisting of tropical jungles in the upper Amazon Basin. The high mountain valleys have a temperate climate, rich soils and moderate rainfall suitable for dairy farming and the production of cereals and vegetables. The Pacific coastal plains are tropical and devoted to plantation farming of bananas, cotton, sugar and cocoa. The *Oriente* is more than one third of the agricultural land of Ecuador and is a thick, virgin forest and jungle land containing valuable timber, although much of it cannot be transported to market at a profit.

Lying about 650 miles off the coastline are the Galapagos Islands, an archipelago situated on the Equator. Consisting of 14 islands and numerous islets, it is a haven for many species of waterfowl and giant turtles. With a population of 650, it is regularly visited by tour groups interested in its unspoiled setting.

History: Shortly before Spanish penetration of Ecuador, the ancient Inca Empire had been united under a single chief, Huayna Cápac, in 1526. Francisco Pizarro, the Spanish conquistador, touched along the coastline in 1528 at about the time Cápac died.

After returning temporarily to Spain, Pizarro came back to Ecuador with a larger force seeking the treasures he believed were in the interior. Huayna Cápac had divided his empire between two sons—Huáscar, who ruled the Cuzco area, and Atahualpa, who ruled over Quito.

After holding him for a huge ransom of gold and silver, Pizarro executed Atahualpa and mercilessly started the suppression of the Incas.

The invasion of Ecuador followed the pattern of other Spanish conquests. As the Incas and their subject tribes were de-

feated, the land was awarded in large grants to the successful leaders; the Indians were enslaved to work the estates and the Spaniards built strategically located cities to administer the territory. The low, unhealthy coastal plains had been shunned by the Incas, who lived in the temperate highland and valleys. The Spanish followed the same pattern building their cities of Quito, Ona, Cuenca and Loja above the 5,000-foot level.

The Spanish made little effort to improve the port of Guayaquil or to farm its valley, leaving the fever-ridden region to later arrivals and outcasts from the highlands. Thus, the colonial period continued a regionalism well established in the Inca period and which still divides the highlander from the coastal dweller.

Spanish rule was not challenged for several harsh, uneventful centuries. Antonio José de Sucre, a brilliant military leader under Simón Bolívar, united Ecuador with neighboring Colombia and Venezuela from 1822 to 1830. This union dissolved when Ecuador and Venezuela withdrew. Bolívar died at the age of 47 shortly thereafter.

Ecuador's history as an independent state has been an alternating swing from near anarchy under weak governments to the enforced peace established by dictators. The first president of Ecuador, Juan José Flores, a brave soldier but an indifferent governor, appealed to the Conservatives in Quito and aroused the opposition of the Liberals in Guayaquil. However, he worked out a scheme to alternate as president with Vicente Rocafuerte, a Guayaquil Liberal—a device that remained in effect until 1845.

In the next 15 years, Ecuador had 11 changes of administration, most of them Liberal; there were three constitutions and sporadic civil wars as well as border wars with Peru and Colombia. By 1860 there was little semblance of a central government—local strongmen ruled the communities with the support of their gunmen. Popular opposition to the cession of Guayaquil and the southern provinces to Peru in 1860 brought a Conservative to power, who established a theocratic Catholic dictatorship which lasted until his assassination in 1875. However, he did more for the unification of the country and for its economy than any other 19th century leader.

For 20 years, Ecuador returned to civil war and anarchy, banditry, and economic deterioration. Conservatives regularly won the elections and were regularly ousted by Liberals from Guayaquil until the revolution of 1895; this brought 50 years of Liberal rule to Ecuador, highlighted by three more constitutions, the passage of 28 presidents and uninterrupted political, social and economic crises. While the power of the Conservatives and the church were

curtailed, the Liberal promises of free elections and honest government had little meaning, by and large. Galo Plaza Lasso (1948–52) was a notable exception. He became secretary-general of the Organization of American States in 1968.

From 1952–63, Conservatives alternated in power with Liberal José María Velasco Ibarra until a reform military government seized power; it was promptly overthrown by the Liberals it sought to assist.

A constituent assembly elected an interim president in 1966; he was succeeded by the aging Velasco, elected for a fifth time. Always controversial, he soon grew restless with his inability to win congressional approval for his economic policies. With the approval of the armed forces, he seized dictatorial power in mid-1970, dismissing the Congress and replacing the moderate constitution (Ecuador's 16th) with a more conservative 1946 version.

Velasco vowed to surrender power to his legally elected successor in 1972. But, fearing a free election would be won by Assad Bucaram, a left-leaning former mayor of Guayaquil, the armed forces seized power in early 1972 and installed General Guillermo Rodríguez Lara as president. Modeling itself after the reformist Peruvian military government, the new regime pledged its policies would be "revolutionary and nationalistic."

The regime concentrated on how best to spend the huge tax royalties pouring into the treasury from Ecuador's newly developed oil fields; most funds were spent on public works (education, highways and hospitals) and fancy military hardware.

Despite the oil boom, dissatisfaction arose against the center-right regime. Leftists denounced inaction of promised social and economic reforms, while Conservatives condemned swollen civil service rolls (one in every 10 workers) and new taxes on luxury imports. The oil revenue-fed inflation, high unemployment and continuing government corruption and repression heightened the discontent.

Democracy, Ecuadorean Style

An unsuccessful attempt by dissident soldiers to oust Rodríguez Lara in 1975 left 22 dead and 100 injured. But after widespread student and labor unrest in early 1976, the strongman was finally toppled by a *junta* headed by Admiral Alfredo Poveda. The new rulers promptly movec to restore civilian rule. In January 1978, voters approved another constitution; elections were held six months later, followed by a run-off in April 1979.

Jaime Roldós Aguilera, a mild-mannered populist attorney from Guayaquil, was elected president for a four-year term by 59% of the vote. At 38, he was the youngest chief executive in Latin America. Although his own Concentration of Popular Forces party and the allied Democratic Left party won 45 of the 69 seats in the unicameral Congress, the new president was unable to build a ruling coalition. Ironically, his bitterest rival was Assad Bucaram, his father-in-law and leader of Congress. Because Roldós rejected Bucaram's populist program in favor of a more conservative approach, the two quickly became enemies and Bucaram blocked virtually all of Roldos' proposals. Austerity measures further damaged Roldós' effectiveness, leading to widespread disorder and the threat of another coup.

A border clash with Peru in 1981 temporarily diverted attention from Ecuador's economic problems. Although the basic dispute dates back to 1830, the latest crisis centered around the 1942 border treaty between the two nations, which Ecuador later disavowed.

On May 24, 1981, Roldós, his wife and seven others were killed in a plane crash while on a trip to the troubled border region. He was succeeded by Vice President Osvaldo Hurtado. The late president's brother, León, was named vice president.

In May 1984, León Febrés Cordero, of the conservative Social Christian Party, a businessman and candidate of the Front for National Reconstruction, was elected president. His first year saw modest economic growth, but also worker unrest and often bitter friction between the president and Congress. Febrés Cordero, an energetic, free-market capitalist, provided Ecuador with strong if heavy-handed leadership. He packed a .45 automatic pistol. When the choice of 18 members of the judiciary by the opposition-controlled Congress didn't suit him, he had the Supreme Court surrounded by tanks so they could not take the oath of office. He chose 18 others, more to his liking. Opposition members were fired from government positions and critical newspapers suffered a drop in public advertising. Difficulties with the military, punctuated by two attempts at mutiny, led to an unsuccessful effort to impeach Febrés Cordero for "disgracing the national honor."

Adverse economic conditions led Ecuadorians to turn to two leftists in 1988 elections. The contest was hot, with charges such as "alcoholic atheist" and "drug-trafficking fascist" commonplace. Rodrigo Borja ultimately won. Political bickering and infighting, corruption and a stale economy were the main features of the Borja years.

Apparently tired of the "same old thing," voters turned to a conservative in 1992:

Sixto Durán Ballén, a 71-year-old architect born in Boston, who promised basic reforms. He wasted no time in putting them into effect. He devalued the sucre by 27.5%, and auctioned off inefficient, money-losing state-owned enterprises. Subsidies on commodities were sharply reduced or eliminated, but to prevent hardships, Durán raised wages modestly. Ecuador dropped its membership in OPEC and announced it would establish its own quotas to market its petroleum. Production rose 18% in 1993, but lower international oil prices decreased income.

Higher fuel and electricity prices, reduced state spending and a freeze on government employment combined to create serious unrest in 1992. Payment on the $13 billion external debt was suspended, freezing international credit. Strikes and bombings by terrorist groups added to Ecuador's difficulties.

On January 29, 1995, the long-simmering border dispute with Peru finally erupted into open warfare in an isolated, mountainous area. Several times before there had been minor border clashes close to the anniversary of the January 29, 1942, Rio Accords by which Ecuador had been forced to cede nearly half its territory. This time, however, the incident quickly escalated into full-scale war with mortar attacks and

Quito—the modern and the colonial

Ecuador

airstrikes. Ecuadorian gunners shot down a Peruvian helicopter and three jet fighter-bombers. Frightened civilians fled their villages. Two tentative cease-fires in February failed to hold. The four guarantor countries—Argentina, Brazil, Chile and the United States—finally succeeded in effecting a definite cease-fire on July 25. In the three weeks of heavy fighting at the outset of the hostilities, 73 people were killed and at least 200 wounded; each side took a number of prisoners, later expatriated.

The economy became generally better-organized during the Durán years, but scandal detracted from its successes and little attention was paid to the poor. This neglect was to influence the 1996 presidential election.

The Bucaram Fiasco

In the first round of voting in May 1996, Jaime Nebot of the Social Christian Party led Abdalá Bucaram of the *Roldosista* Party, 30% to 26%. The July runoff thus presented voters with a clear choice: Nebot, a conservative who favored continuation of privatization of key economic sectors, and Bucaram, a populist who opposed privatization or reform of the cumbersome social security system. Bucaram also displayed a flamboyance on the campaign trail that startled, and apparently amused, voters. He unabashedly proclaimed himself *"El Loco."* The unorthodox appeal worked: Bucaram defeated Nebot 54.1% to 45.9%.

What followed in the six months after Bucaram's inauguration in August 1996 marked the most bizarre episode in modern Ecuadorian political history, as the unpredictable Bucaram shocked Ecuadorians almost daily with his strange public antics and even stranger governmental measures. He made international headlines when he invited Lorena Bobbitt, the Ecuadorian-born woman infamous for severing her husband's penis in the United States, to the presidential palace for lunch. He took to singing in a rock band, and an Associated Press photo of the president, clutching a microphone and flanked by buxom, scantily clad beauties, was published all over the world. When a presidential helicopter crashed and burned, Bucaram denounced it as an assassination attempt.

He shocked almost everyone by hiring Argentina's sacked economy minister, Domingo Cavallo, to be his economic adviser. More shocking still, he discarded his populist campaign promises and imposed an austerity program that included geometric price increases for public services, such as public transport (200%), electricity (more than 100%) and natural gas (250%). Bucaram's draconian measures sparked widespread protests, some of them violent. His approval rating dropped out of sight.

The main marketplace in Guayaquil

In February 1997, as Bucaram came under intense pressure to resign, Ecuador plunged into semi-chaos. The beleaguered president imposed a state of emergency that allowed him to take extra-constitutional measures, such as banning demonstrations and imposing press censorship. In a move that delighted the public but which totally disregarded the constitution, Congress removed Bucaram from office on the grounds of "mental incapacity," despite the absence of any authoritative medical or psychiatric testimony.

Bucaram's peculiar behavior proved to be the least of his transgressions. He went into self-imposed exile in Panama (long a dumping ground for deposed and disgraced rulers), denouncing Congress for its unconstitutional actions. Evidence then surfaced that he may have absconded with as much as $26 million from the treasury. Some estimates placed the total that Bucaram and his entourage withdrew illegally from the treasury during his six months in power at $80 million. The Supreme Court formally charged Bucaram and four of his aides with corruption, influence peddling, embezzlement and nepotism, and unsuccessfully sought his extradition. (Guatemala, it should be noted, has tried unsuccessfully since 1993 to extradite former President Jorge Serrano from Panama, who also allegedly stole millions from the treasury.) One of the aides was arrested in Peru, carrying $3.4 million.

Revolving-Door Presidency

The post-Bucaram transition also proved chaotic—and probably unconstitutional. At first, Vice President Rosalia Arteaga was duly sworn in as Ecuador's first woman president, with the tacit blessing of the armed forces. But within days Congress "elected" one of its leaders, Fabián Alarcón, to serve as interim president until a new presidential election could be called. In a referendum in May, 74% of Ecuadorian voters "ratified" Alarcón's interim presidency until August 1998. On another of the 14 referendum issues, 65% of voters indicated that they approved of Bucaram's removal from office. Interviewed by CNN in Panama, Bucaram ridiculed the plebiscite as a "political show."

Ecuadorians again were distracted from domestic concerns by renewed border tensions with Peru, which in July 1997 had begun acquiring advanced Russian MiGs. Unlike 1995, however, sanity prevailed and the two countries sent representatives to Brasilia to negotiate a timetable for demarcation of the 48-mile stretch of disputed frontier. In January 1998, the representatives signed an accord that set a deadline for reaching a final agreement. Also signing were representatives of the four peace guarantors—Brazil, Argentina, Chile and the United States.

Ecuadorians went to the polls in November 1997 to elect a constituent assembly charged with overhauling the 1978 organic law in the wake of the Bucaram fiasco and to prepare for the election of a new president. The Social Christian Party of former President Febrés Cordero won a plurality of 24 of the 70 seats. Former President Hurtado's Popular Christian Party was a distant second with nine seats, while 11 other parties split the remainder, ensuring that whatever emerged from the assembly would be by broad consensus.

In February 1998, the assembly voted 60–7 to preclude anyone convicted of cor-

Ecuador

ruption, embezzlement or other misuse of public funds, from running for public office, a move aimed squarely at Bucaram, who already had announced from Panama that he planned to run in the next presidential election. He soon relinquished his candidacy and endorsed the country's leading banana exporter, Álvaro Noboa, as the *Roldosista* candidate. The first round of voting was another free-for-all, with five other candidates vying with Noboa. The frontrunner was Quito Mayor Jamil Mahuad of the Popular Democracy movement.

In the first round of balloting on May 31, Mahuad placed first with 36.6% and Noboa came in second with 29.7%. In the July 12 runoff, Mahuad pulled off a narrow victory, receiving 51% of the valid votes, or 2,242,836 to Noboa's 2,140,628. Mahuad took office on August 10.

Mahuad presented a sobering change from Bucaram; apparently the only thing they had in common was Lebanese ancestry. He was well prepared professionally, having served as labor minister under Roldós, then as a member of Congress before being elected mayor of Quito in 1992 and re-elected in 1996. In between, he earned a master's degree in public administration from Harvard.

On the diplomatic front, Mahuad and Peruvian President Alberto Fujimori signed the peace accord in Brasilia in October 1998, which definitively delineated the disputed stretch of frontier that led to the 1995 war. The agreement was almost entirely along the lines Peru had demanded, that the border would follow the divide of the Cordillera del Condor range. As a gesture to Ecuador, however, Peru acquiesced Tiwintza Hill, which Ecuadorian soldiers had successfully defended against the Peruvians in 1995.

The next step of the peace process came in January 1999, when Mahuad and Fujimori met again along the border to dedicate the first border post at Lagartococha. They met again in Washington, where they worked out the final details of the peace agreement and of a $3 billion cross-border international loan package. Fujimori pledged not to buy any new weapons, while Mahuad announced he was cutting the draft by 60% and converting 8,000 soldiers—a fourth of the army—into policemen. Under the 10-year border development plan, the two countries were to make the border region accessible by new roads, to integrate their electrical grids and to embark on joint irrigation and resource-exploitation projects. Moreover, Peru was to allow Ecuador to use its oil pipeline. President Bill Clinton hosted the two presidents at the White House to toast them on their achievement, the peaceful resolution of the last major border conflict in Latin America.

Former President Jamil Mahuad

Back at home, Mahuad had to face the ever-present economic crisis. No longer a member of OPEC, Ecuador could only watch helplessly as the price of oil on the world market plummeted in 1998, at one point diving to just over $11 a barrel. The price of Ecuador's other major export, bananas, also remained depressed. Ecuador then sustained $2.6 billion in damage from the floods of the 1997–98 *El Niño* and suffered financial fallout from Brazil's economic meltdown in 1998. Mahuad delivered grim economic news: a $1.5 billion budget deficit and a projected growth rate of 1.7 percent for 1999, with inflation estimated at 22%. Public discontent over the inevitable austerity measures erupted again into street demonstrations.

Several banks foundered. Mahuad declared a week-long bank holiday and imposed a 60-day state of emergency. The value of the *sucre* went into a free-fall, losing 60% of its value at one point. As part of a new austerity plan, Mahuad tripled the price of gasoline and raised the value-added tax from 10% to 15%. Transit workers went on strike. The Social Christian Party, the coalition partner of Mahuad's Popular Democracy party, denounced the austerity plan as "inhuman." Mahuad's public approval rating fell to 16%.

Mahuad caved in to the public outcry and struck a deal with the left-of-center parties in Congress for a watered-down plan. The price of gasoline was rolled back, and in place of the VAT increase the Congress reinstated the income tax, with a 15% ceiling.

Over the next 10 months, the political and economic situations deteriorated from bad to worse to impossible. Every time Mahuad sought to impose austerity measures to win IMF approval for desperately needed capital, street protests forced him to back down. He sought a $1.2 billion bailout of 18 defunct banks, but then the head of one bank, who had been arrested for fraud, revealed he had donated more than $3 million to Mahuad's campaign.

In August 1999, Mahuad announced Ecuador could not make the $98 million interest payment on its $6 billion in Brady bonds, which the U.S. Treasury had extended to 18 countries to help them restructure their debts (Ecuador's total foreign debt by then was a ponderous $13.6 billion). A month later, Ecuador became the first nation to default on its Brady bonds. By the end of 1999, the *sucre* had fallen from 7,000 to 25,000 to the dollar; inflation had hit 61%; foreign creditors pounded on the door; and military officers were publicly criticizing the civilian government's inaction, prompting rumors of an imminent coup. Moreover, a poll showed that 91% disapproved of Mahuad's performance and that 53% wanted him to resign.

Dollarization and Downfall

On January 9, 2000, the desperate president unveiled a desperate plan: He would replace the *sucre* with the U.S. dollar—not merely peg the *sucre* to the dollar as the Argentines had done, but make the dollar the official currency, as it is in Panama. The dramatic proposal seemed to have a popular consensus. The Social Christians, *Roldosista* Party and Mahuad's own Popular Democracy party reached a rare agreement in support of dollarization. One poll showed that 59% of the public supported the idea.

Not so with the rural Indians who make up 40% of the population. Within days, the Ecuadorian Confederation of Indigenous Communities (*CONAIE*), reportedly the most powerful Indian-rights group in the Americas, not only declared its opposition to dollarization but demanded that Mahuad resign and mobilized thousands of peasants to march on Quito. Violence appeared imminent.

Matters came to a head on January 21, when *CONAIE* protesters stormed and occupied the Congress building. They were joined by about 150 field-grade military officers, led by Colonel Lucio Gutiérrez, who echoed the Indians' demand that the president resign. Faced with open rebellion, Mahuad fled the presidential palace and took refuge at a military base, but he steadfastly refused to resign. His defense minister, General Carlos Mendoza, announced he was assuming power at the head of a three-man junta, which also included *CONAIE* leader Antonio Vargas.

Ecuador

With the backing of the military, the ouster of Mahuad became a *fait accompli*. It was Latin America's first military *coup d'etat* since the overthrow of Jean-Bertrand Aristide in Haiti in 1991. After 22 years of tenuous democracy, Ecuador's constitutional system finally had broken down, a victim of mob rule.

For 24 tense hours, the junta faced intense diplomatic pressure from the United States, Canada, the Organization of American States, the European Union, U.N. Secretary-General Kofi Annan and most Latin American presidents. Even Bucaram, who had long denounced Mahuad as a usurper, condemned his overthrow. In a stunning turnabout, Mendoza declared he would yield power to the constitutional vice president, Gustavo Noboa, apparently to maintain some semblance of constitutional niceties.

Though the transfer of power was undemocratic, the new president was at least a respectable figure. Noboa, 62, was a lawyer and former dean of Catholic University, who gained fame as one of the negotiators of the border settlement with Peru. The hapless Mahuad, who still refused to resign, lamely expressed his backing for Noboa. "A deposed president doesn't resign," he said wanly, "he's just deposed." Congress confirmed Noboa to fill out the remainder of Mahuad's term, to 2003.

Ironically, Noboa announced he would push forward with dollarization, which had precipitated Mahuad's downfall. Under pressure from the IMF and other international lending institutions, which had promised $2 billion in loans, Congress approved the plan. The IMF approved a $304 million loan package, with more contingent upon further concessions. Noboa announced that Ecuador would resume payments on its Brady bonds.

In another hypocritical attempt at constitutional window-dressing, the government moved quickly to "punish" the people who had brought about Mahuad's overthrow. The defense ministry arrested four colonels and 12 lieutenant colonels and began investigating the roles of hundreds more junior officers. The ministry narrowed the number to be court-martialed to 16 officers and one sergeant.

To bring this farce to an end, Noboa asked Congress to declare an amnesty to those who participated in the coup. The head of the Joint Chiefs of Staff and the commanders of the navy and the air force (but not the army) resigned their posts to protest the president's recommendation for amnesty. Nonetheless, Congress approved amnesty for all 117 military rebels. Public opinion polls, which seem to govern Ecuador, showed that 67% of the public supported the amnesty.

Not so with the dollarization plan. A majority, according to the polls, now opposed it. *CONAIE*, labor unions and students called a one-day strike to demand that the government revoke its agreement with the IMF, and the usual 10,000 demonstrators peacefully turned out in the streets of the capital.

Nonetheless, dollarization went into effect as planned in September 2000. The stability of the currency, coupled with the rising international price of petroleum and a $2 billion international loan package arranged by the IMF, led to a surprisingly rosy economic picture by the end of the year. Noboa enjoyed a relative—and rare—popularity.

But defections gave a center-left bloc a majority in Congress, which resisted Noboa's privatization plans for electricity, petroleum and telecommunications that the IMF—and foreign investors—expected. Moreover, the Constitutional Tribunal ruled 44 points of the privatization program unconstitutional. In February 2001, when Noboa acceded to IMF demands and doubled the price of cooking gas and raised the price of gasoline by 22% to offset the reduction of subsidies, *CONAIE* and other groups besieged the capital. Noboa declared a state of emergency, and in the ensuing violence four protesters were killed. Noboa caved in to demands to scale back the increases. The IMF reluctantly agreed.

Congress thumbed its nose again at the IMF by rejecting an increase in the VAT from 12% to 15%. It also rejected other revenue-raising measures, assuring a crushing budget deficit. The Constitutional Tribunal hamstrung the president's fiscal reform efforts by declaring unconstitutional a tax he had proposed to satisfy IMF demands; international financial markets reacted negatively.

To compound Noboa's domestic problems, in May 2000 members of a dissident faction of the Revolutionary Armed Forces of Colombia (*FARC*) encroached into Ecuadorian territory. Two of the rebels were killed in a firefight with the Ecuadorian army. The army beefed up its 1,500-man border forces with an additional 2,000 troops.

On the positive side, the dismal economic picture improved dramatically in 2001, although the improvement was in part illusionary.

The Elections of 2002

The presidential and congressional campaign in October and November 2002 turned into the customary Ecuadorian donnybrook. Former President Febrés Cordero of the Social Christian Party, still the country's largest, decided against making a comeback bid because of ill health. The party nominated its congressional leader and former trade minister, Xavier Neira.

The field became crowded as former presidents Borja of the Democratic Left and Hurtado both entered the race, as did, once again, the banana millionaire Álvaro Noboa, no relation to President Noboa. León Roldós, brother of the late president, entered as a Socialist. Another former president's brother, Jacobo Bucaram, became the *Roldosista* candidate.

But the race suddenly became unconventional with the entry of two leaders of the 2000 coup: Indian activist Antonio Vargas, and cashiered army Colonel Lucio Gutiérrez, who had spent time in jail and who became the candidate of the newly organized January 21 Patriotic Society. The parallels between Gutiérrez and Venezuela's Hugo Chávez were unmistakable. The results of the first round stunned everyone and sent a chill through Ecuador's political establishment—and the U.S. State Department. About 5.1 million, or 63%, of Ecuador's registered voters turned out. The results:

Gutiérrez	943,123	02.3%
Noboa	794,614	17.4%
Roldós	703,593	15.5%
Borja	638,142	14.1%
Neira	553,106	12.2%
Bucaram	544,688	11.9%

Gutiérrez and Noboa sought to mend political fences with the losers for the November runoff. Because both Noboa and Gutiérrez were political outsiders with populist messages, the political establishment was lukewarm to both of them. As the country's wealthiest man, Noboa appeared less frightening than Gutiérrez, who had the support of *CONAIE* and of Marxist-Leninist and other far-left elements.

The race came down to personalities. Noboa unconvincingly tried to persuade the country's impoverished masses that as a millionaire, he could serve their interests better than Gutiérrez by luring foreign investors to Ecuador. Like Chávez in Venezuela, Gutiérrez pledged to combat corruption as well as to increase funding for education and health.

Gutiérrez won a decisive mandate with more than 2.7 million votes, or 54.4%, to less than 2.3 million, or 45.6%, for Noboa.

President-elect Gutiérrez suddenly sounded conciliatory and toned down his leftist rhetoric; he even apologized for saying that all the former presidents deserved to be in jail. He had little choice; Ecuador still desperately needed IMF and World Bank assistance. Moreover, the Social Christians and Democratic Left formed a peculiar right-left opposition bloc of 62 members of the 100-seat Congress. Gutiérrez's party and its allies had but 17 seats.

Another Abortive Presidency

Gutiérrez, 45, a civil engineer and an erstwhile pentathlete, was sworn in as Ecuador's sixth president in as many years on January 15, 2003. His vice president was Alfredo Palacio, a 64-year-old heart surgeon and a populist who had served as health minister under Durán. The new president's task was unenviable: a $300 million budget deficit, $2.6 billion in foreign debt payments, an intransigent congressional opposition, a wary IMF, a resentful military high command and a notoriously impatient and fickle electorate.

The new president bewildered his constituency by undertaking a chameleon-like ideological transformation. He made some obligatory gestures to his Indian supporters, such as appointing an Indian activist as foreign minister and reducing his own salary by 20%. But he appointed a mainstream, investor-friendly economist as finance minister.

Gutiérrez met with President Bush in Washington both before and after his inauguration and pledged Ecuador's cooperation against drug traffickers and terrorists. He also persuaded the IMF to make a $205 million loan available. Back home, he sought to placate the IMF by proposing tax increases; he increased the price of gasoline by a third and of electricity by 10%, seeking to create a $250 million budget surplus. A third of the $6.7 billion budget for 2003 was earmarked for debt reduction, only a fourth to promised social programs; it also increased military spending by 40.5%. Moreover, Gutiérrez pledged to retain the dollar, the root cause of his 2000 coup.

Gutiérrez's abandonment of the principles he had campaigned on cost him allies. Vice President Palacio broke with him, but wisely did not resign. CONAIE's political arm, Pachakutik, withdrew its congressional support because of Gutiérrez's cuts to the civil service and subsidies for basic commodities, leaving him with only six seats. He turned to the conservative Social Christians for support. It was an unlikely match, but it held for a time. CONAIE and affiliated Indian groups pressured Gutiérrez to resign.

Gutiérrez also faced hostility from his generals, no doubt resentful over taking orders from a former colonel. Seventeen generals and admirals resigned, allowing Gutiérrez to appoint officers he could trust.

Five of his civilian appointees also resigned because of allegations of past unethical conduct.

As Gutiérrez's approval rating slid to 18% in November 2003, he himself became embroiled in a scandal. A former governor arrested on cocaine trafficking charges reported that he gave $30 million to Gutiérrez's campaign. Gutiérrez denied involvement in drug trafficking. He also was accused of accepting illegal donations from Mexico's Labor Party.

As if he didn't have enough problems with the IMF, opposition politicians, disgruntled generals, betrayed supporters and corruption accusations, Gutiérrez found himself in a nasty public controversy with his estranged wife, Ximena Bohorquéz, a prominent physician and a member of Congress for Gutiérrez's January 21 Patriotic Society. Bohorquéz complained in a newspaper interview that her husband had not lived up to his campaign promise to appoint well-qualified and uncorrupted officials. The president accused her of engaging in "cheap politics." It was reminiscent of the vocal opposition by the wives of former presidents Menem of Argentina and Fujimori of Peru; both of their husbands divorced them while in office. Bohorquéz lived in the family's home rather than the presidential palace. In September 2003, the couple announced a reconciliation, but then she began criticizing his economic policies. Their marriage provided Ecuadorians with a real-life *telenovela*.

In 2003, former President Noboa became the third former president to go into exile to avoid prosecution. Mahuad already had taken up residence in the United States, accused of corruption. Bucaram was still in Panama. Noboa allegedly schemed to use government bonds to shore up state-owned banks, among other sins. He proclaimed his innocence, but asked for and received political asylum in the Dominican embassy. Gutiérrez issued him a safe-conduct, and Noboa flew to the Dominican Republic.

In 2004, the Social Christian Party withdrew its support and announced it would seek impeachment proceedings against Gutiérrez, ostensibly for misusing public funds for political purposes in the municipal elections. The party collected the necessary 51-vote majority to begin impeachment hearings, although it was well short of the necessary two thirds for removal. Gutiérrez forged an unusual new 52-member coalition in Congress with the *roldosistas* and the party of millionaire Alvaro Noboa. This ended the impeachment effort.

Gutiérrez should have left well enough alone. But he had Congress remove the 31 justices of the Supreme Court, most of them Social Christians, accusing them of being biased against him. He introduced a bill that would broaden his powers, including dissolving Congress. The move was widely regarded as revenge for the impeachment effort. He packed the court with "temporary" appointees and said he would call a referendum to choose a new method for selecting Supreme Court justices.

That smacked too much of dictatorship for the Ecuadorians, who already had enough grievances against him. By early 2005, demonstrations demanding the president's resignation gripped the country. It was reminiscent of January 2000.

The first indication that Gutiérrez was losing his congressional majority came when nine members of the Gutiérrez coalition voted with the opposition to reject, 60–40, a list of possible nominees for attorney general. Feeling increasingly cornered, Gutiérrez suggested that Congress remove the temporary justices and establish an electoral college to appoint new ones, provided that the new body be approved by referendum. The opposition rejected the proposal.

Gutiérrez's list of attorney general nominees came before Congress again, and it was rejected again, 56–44. Outside the building, pro-Gutiérrez demonstrators hurled eggs and sticks at opposition congressmen.

A new wrinkle developed when the head of the "temporary" Supreme Court and a *Roldosista*, suddenly declared all charges against former President Bucaram "null and void," paving the way for "*El Loco*" to return to the country. He also dropped pending charges against former President Noboa, and both exiled presidents returned to the country. Bucaram made his usual bombastic and eccentric statements, vowing to run for president and lead a "revolution of the poor."

Then mayor of Quito, a former army commander, urged the armed forces not to recognize Gutiérrez, in effect, calling for another coup. But the defense minister said the armed forces would continue to support the constitutional president.

Bucaram, a Gutiérrez ally, did his friend an unwitting disservice when in a radio interview he said cavalierly that Gutiérrez should dissolve Congress and declare a state of emergency. Rumors spread that Gutiérrez was planning to do just that, sparking a mini-panic in financial markets and causing the value of Ecuadorian bonds to drop. The interior minister frantically denied Gutiérrez planned to dissolve Congress.

But the damage was done. Gutiérrez's opponents had the pretext they needed to fill the streets of Quito again, banging pots and pans and honking horns, demanding that he resign. Gutiérrez declared a state of emergency, fired his hand-picked Supreme Court justices who were causing the crisis and vowed in an interview that he would not resign. After all, he said with some validity, the economy was booming compared with the crisis that led to Mahuad's ouster in 2000 (see Economy).

In an attempt to pacify the demonstrators, Gutiérrez lifted the state of emergency after less than 24 hours. He addressed the nation on television, insisted

Ecuador

he had achieved his primary objective of removing the Supreme Court and that "tranquillity is returning."

But it was not. The streets remained filled with thousands of unmollified, noisy but non-violent protesters—but no soldiers. On April 18, thousands of demonstrators also filled the streets of Guayaquil. Back in Quito, 30,000 protesters shouted *"Fuera, Lucio!"* ("Lucio, out!"). Police fired tear gas to drive them back from the presidential palace.

On April 20, 2005, Congress voted 62–0 to remove Gutiérrez from office on the peculiar pretext that he had "abandoned his post." Gutiérrez flew from the roof of the palace by helicopter and sought asylum at the Brazilian embassy. He flew to Brazil four days later, becoming the latest of several Ecuadorian presidents forced into exile. He later obtained asylum in Colombia.

The Palacio Interregnum

Vice President Palacio, a populist who had become critical of Gutiérrez's move to the right, was sworn in. But this did not pacify some of the protesters, who trapped him in the building where he took the oath, demanding that he dissolve Congress and call new elections. Palacio said he would call a referendum on constitutional reforms before calling any election, and he received the all-important pledge of support from the armed forces.

The OAS expressed concern whether Gutiérrez's removal was constitutional, and sent a high-level delegation to investigate. After meetings with Palacio and the opposition, the OAS concluded that Palacio's government was legitimate.

Meanwhile, Bucaram, sensing the shifting political winds could be unhealthy for him, quickly fled to Peru and then back to Panama, which again granted him asylum. Noboa chose to remain in Ecuador, and was placed under house arrest on the charges that he had mishandled debt negotiations.

Palacio demonstrated his constitutional muscle by appointing new armed forces commanders.

As economy minister, Palacio named a leftist economist, Rafael Correa, who announced that the government was reversing Gutiérrez's policy and would spend more oil revenue on social programs and less on debt servicing. But Correa resigned after only four months when Palacio sought to appease the World Bank.

Palacio's shift to the left did not save him from the usual public protests. In August, protesters shut down the vital oilfields in the Amazon region for a week, dynamiting pipelines and destroying pumps, demanding that more of the government's revenue windfall from the high price of petroleum on the world market

Former President Lucio Gutiérrez

be spent on social programs there. But the protesters' disruption of the oil supply and the damage they caused cost the government an estimated $400 million.

Gutiérrez gave up his asylum in Colombia and returned to Ecuador in October 2005, vowing to take legal action to reclaim the presidency against what he called an illegal takeover. Palacio promptly ordered Gutiérrez jailed as "a threat to national security." He remained in prison five months, when the Supreme Court ordered him released for lack of evidence. The Supreme Court also reduced the charges against former President Noboa and ordered him released from house arrest.

In May 2006, Palacio stunned foreign investors by expropriating the lucrative holdings of Occidental Petroleum for alleged breach of contract. He may have been inspired by Bolivian President Evo Morales' nationalization of foreign oil companies 15 days earlier.

Palacio hosted a summit with Presidents Uribe of Colombia, Toledo of Peru and Morales of Bolivia, to reiterate the right of members of the all-but-defunct Andean Pact to negotiate bilateral free-trade agreements (FTAs) with the United States. Venezuela's Chávez, a fierce critic of such pacts, was not invited; he angrily withdrew from the Andean Pact in April after Colombia and Peru signed FTAs with the United States. The meeting represented an abrupt about face for Morales, who earlier had agreed with Chávez. Uribe, a key U.S. ally, promised to urge Washington to renew free-trade talks with Ecuador to extend the trade preferences granted Andean nations in 1991 in return for substituting coca with other crops, which were due to expire at the end of 2006. Without FTAs, Washington had indicated it would not ex-

tend the highly beneficial preferences, under which Ecuador sells avocados and artichokes to the United States. For Palacio and Morales to continue seeking FTAs after nationalizing foreign oil companies was seen as a bit erratic.

The Elections of 2006

The next presidential campaign was the usual circus, with 13 candidates. As usual, there were some old names, and as happened in 2002, a newcomer came out of nowhere to break from the back of the pack. Only this time, the new would-be *caudillo* sprang not from the barracks, but from academe.

Alvaro Noboa, the billionaire banana magnate, launched his third presidential attempt, this time as candidate of a movement with the grandiose name Institutional Renewal Party of National Action, or *PRIAN*. Gilmar Gutiérrez, brother of the deposed president, was the standard bearer of their January 21 Patriotic Society. Once again, former President Roldos' brother León was the *roldosista* candidate, while the Social Christians nominated Cynthia Viteri. Among the remaining nine candidates was former Economy Minister Rafael Correa, a left-wing economics professor who had hammered together a movement called Alliance for Change. It did not field a congressional slate, however, probably because Correa was planning to scrap the institution, which he called a "sewer of corruption."

Like Gutiérrez four years earlier, Correa sounded a Chávez-like message that rejected free trade with the United States, promised to spend more oil wealth on social programs and even hinted darkly that Ecuador should default on its foreign debt. He said he disliked dollarization, but would grudgingly continue it. He sounded like Chávez with his anti-U.S. rhetoric, once calling President Bush "dimwitted," and he said he would not renew the lease on the U.S. counterdrug base at Manta when it expired in 2009. (Ironically, Correa earned his doctorate in economics at the University of Illinois.) Correa also pledged, like Chávez, to call a constituent assembly to revamp Ecuador through what he called a "citizens' revolution" that would rid the country of its "partyocracy." Also like Gutiérrez, Correa was young and charismatic.

The results on October 15 were:

Noboa	1,464,251	26.83%
Correa	1,246,333	22.84%
Gutiérrez	950,895	17.42%
Roldós	809,754	14.84%
Viteri	525,728	9.63%

The six-week runoff campaign was pure political theater, even by Ecuadorian stan-

Interim President Alfredo Palacio

dards. Correa charged that the computer breakdown on election night experienced by the Brazilian firm contracted to tabulate the results was nothing less than fraud and that he had finished ahead of Noboa. But a team from the OAS investigated the incident and declared the vote results were accurate.

Noboa, as before, used his wealth to give away presents to voters at his rallies. Like Correa, he ran on a populist platform, although unlike Correa he advocated a FTA with the United States. Correa, meanwhile, like many other Latin American leftist firebrands who find themselves in Both candidates had messianic messages; Correa declared himself a "Christian leftist," while Noboa proclaimed himself to be "a messenger of God." Noboa was humiliated days before the runoff when the list of voters who had signed up for 1.2 million homes he had promised was discovered in the trash.

On November 26, voters spoke decisively:

| Correa | 3,517,635 | 56.67% |
| Noboa | 2,689,418 | 43.33% |

With his third consecutive runoff defeat, Noboa was becoming the William Jennings Bryan of Ecuadorian politics. A disturbing factor in the election was that more than a million voters cast null or blank ballots, which are no longer included in the vote totals.

The "Citizens' Revolution" Begins

Correa, just 43, was sworn in on January 15, 2007. Although he had toned down his fiery rhetoric in the runoff campaign, he soon demonstrated he intended to move full speed ahead with his "citizens' revolution," first by electing a constituent assembly that would scrap the 1998 constitution and compose a new one that would transform Ecuador's political system to create what he called "21st century socialism." It was the same courser taken by Chávez in Venezuela and Morales in Bolivia.

Congress approved Correa's call for the assembly, but inserted a proviso that it could not dissolve the existing Congress. Correa turned to the Supreme Electoral Tribunal, packed with his appointees, which ruled that the constituent assembly would have absolute power, including to supersede the Congress. Congress responded by removing the president of the electoral tribunal, which responded in turn by "firing" 57 members of Congress who had approved the constituent assembly only if it didf not have the authority to dissolve the existing Congress.

Although the dismissed legislators were replaced by members of their own party, the new members proved to be more compliant with Correa's wishes. Congress then approved a referendum for April 15 on the issue of calling elections for a constituent assembly, just as Chávez had done in Venezuela and Morales had in Bolivia.

A judge declared the legislators' dismissal unconstitutional and ordered they be reinstated. The president of the Congress agreed, provoking a negative reaction from the Correa backers. The case went before the Constitutional Court, which upheld the dismissal. Fifteen of them opted for exile when Correa threatened them with arrest on trumped-up charges; he later relented. Congress responded by voting to dismiss the judges, but without the backing of the executive, there was no way they could enforce it.

Ecuadorians went to the polls again for the *sí o no* referendum on whether to elect a 130-member constituent assembly. Correa threatened to resign if voters rejected the idea, but they approved it with a resounding 80%.

In September 2007, voters returned to the polls to elect the constituent assembly; Correa's newly renamed movement, *Acuerdo País*, won 80 of the 130 seats. Gutiérrez's faction won 18. High on Correa's agenda was the removal of the restriction of immediate re-election of the president, the dissolution of Congress and the stripping of power from the traditional elite. It appeared to be the next step toward a Venezuelan-style elected autocracy.

Meanwhile, for all his railing against corruption, Correa was acutely embarrassed when a clandestine video surfaced showing his finance minister, Ricardo Patiño, meeting with three bond investors shortly before Patiño hinted Ecuador would not meet a $135 million interest payment, which led to uncertainty in the bond market. Ecuador made the interest payment, the market stabilized, and the investors allegedly benefited to the tune of $200 million; the government reportedly made $50 million. The scandal forced Correa to cashier Patiño—to another job.

Border Incident

At the height of the assembly's six-month tenure, Correa found himself in the midst of a foreign policy crisis, which he milked for political value. On March 1, 2008, Colombian warplanes bombed a camp of the Revolutionary Armed Forces of Colombia *(FARC)* in heavy jungle a few kilometers inside Ecuador. Correa maintained later that Colombian President Álvaro Uribe had called him to say Colombian forces had entered Ecuador in hot pursuit of the rebels. Uribe later admitted that the attack was not in hot pursuit but a raid, and that Colombian ground forces had encroached on Ecuadorian territory after the airstrike to seize the camp. Twenty-two *FARC* guerrillas were killed in the operation.

Correa angrily broke off diplomatic relations with Colombia and moved 3,200 troops to the border. His ally Chávez then moved troops to the Venezuelan-Colombian border. A two-front border war appeared imminent. Correa called on the OAS to condemn Colombia, but the OAS approved instead a watered-down resolution admonishing Colombia for violating Ecuador's sovereignty and territorial integrity and promised to investigate the incident. Uribe, meanwhile, announced that three laptop computers confiscated at the *FARC* camp contained evidence of the complicity of both Correa and Chávez with the *FARC*, among other things, a $20,000 laundered donation to Correa's campaign from the *FARC*.

In May, Correa, Uribe and Chávez met in the Dominican Republic, where Correa and Uribe reportedly engaged in a heated discussion. Ultimately, to defuse the crisis, Uribe apologized for the incursion and promised not to repeat it, while Correa and Chávez pledged to cooperate with Colombia in its battle against the *FARC*.

New Constitution, New Election

Correa's steamroller was in high gear in 2008 and 2009. The constituent assembly supplanted the Congress and assumed the country's legislative function. In July 2008, it overwhelmingly approved the new 444-article constitution, Ecuador's 20th, which among other things permits two successive four-year presidential terms, increases the

Ecuador

power of the executive over a 124-seat National Assembly, reduces the size of the Supreme Court from 31 to 21 justices and makes it subordinate to a new Constitutionality Court, bans foreign military bases and greatly increases state control over the economy. Voters ratified the constitution in yet another referendum on that September by 64%. It received only 45% in Guayaquil, however, which remains a hotbed of anti-Correa sentiment.

Flushed with his latest election victory, and buoyed at least temporarily by an economic windfall of record-high petroleum prices, Correa generated international headlines in November 2008 by threatening to default on the foreign debt if an investigative commission found parts of the debt to be "illegitimate." In December, he followed through on the threat, refusing interest payments on $3.6 billion in bonds on the grounds that previous presidents had exceeded their authority in agreeing to the "immoral" terms. Appearing on national television, Correa declared defiantly, "We know full well who we are up against: real monsters who will not hesitate to try to crush the country and to try to make an example of Ecuador. We accept that responsibility, we know what we are going up against, but it was impossible with all the conclusions of the debt audit for me as president of the republic to allow continued payment of this immoral debt."

The impetuous move made Ecuador, once again, a pariah in international lending circles, at a time when oil prices had dropped from $140 a barrel to $35, killing the goose that laid the golden eggs to finance Correa's ambitious social programs. He desperately turned to China for loans, and offered oil drilling rights in return for a $1.2 billion concession up front.

But Correa's actions only seemed to enhance his own popularity going into the first presidential election under his new constitution. His approval ratings remained in the 70% range. Both former President Gutiérrez and the thrice-defeated Noboa launched quixotic bids against Correa in the April 26, 2009 election, as did five candidates of the traditional parties. Former President Febres Cordero had died in December 2008. The traditional movements were so discredited that the outcome was a foregone conclusion. A total of 7.1 million voters, a turnout of 75.3%, went to the polls, but 1.2 million of them, fully 15.5% of the total, cast blank or null votes in protest. The remainder gave Correa a resounding first-round victory:

Correa	3,586,439	52%
Gutiérrez	1,947,830	28.4%
Noboa	786,718	11.4%

Correa's again-renamed *Alianza País* movement fell just short of a majority in the balloting for the National Assembly, winning 59 of the 124 seats. Gutiérrez's January 21 Patriotic Pole was a distant second with 19 seats and the Social Christians won 11. Eight other parties or movements split the remainder. Correa had already declared before the election that if the legislative branch blocked his proposals, he would simply dissolve it in accordance with his new constitution and call a new election.

Correa's second inaugural was on August 10, 2009. The "Chávezization" of Ecuador was thus well underway, but with some notable differences. Correa has not sought to nationalize key industries like electricity and telecommunications. He has not moved to confiscate large landholdings, although the new constitution contains language about land being used for "social" purposes. Despite his refusal to extend U.S. rights to use the base at Manta, he has not engaged in inflammatory anti-U.S. rhetoric and seems intent on preserving the preferential trade tariffs Ecuador enjoys.

Recent Developments

Correa has moved to resolve his differences with Colombia's Uribe and to normalize bilateral relations. In September 2009, Foreign Ministers Jaime Bermúdez of Colombia and Fander Falconi of Ecuador met for talks, which ended with Colombia signing a pledge not to attack across Ecuador's border. But a low-ranking judge, acting on his own volition, unexpectedly muddied the diplomatic waters a month later by issuing an arrest warrant for Colombian General Freddy Padilla, the armed forces commander, in connection with the 2008 border incident. An earlier arrest warrant had been issued against Juan Manuel Santos, then Colombia's Defense Minister but who was elected president in June 2010. Colombia has rejected both warrants, saying Ecuador has no jurisdiction over the actions of Colombian officials, but the latest warrant caused Padilla to cancel a visit to Ecuador to meet with his counterpart, General Fabián Varela.

Although he professes to champion Ecuador's indigenous population and speaks Quechua, Correa has begun to have the same difficulties with Indian militants as his predecessors. On September 28, 2009, Indians blockaded a highway in the edge of the Amazon basin to protest Correa's water resources plan, which would divert water for the economically important mining in that area. Violence erupted between the protesters and security forces two days later that left a woman schoolteacher dead.

President Rafael Correa

Correa met the next day with representatives of the Confederation of Indigenous Nationalities 0f the Ecuadorian Amazon *(CONFENIAE)*, but each side blamed the other for the violence. Correa insisted the police were not armed and that the teacher had been shot to death by other protesters. *CONFENIAE* not only wants the water plan scrapped, but wants the mining and petroleum activities on indigenous lands ended. The dispute is ongoing.

At about the same time, Correa devised a controversial "carbon reduction" scheme by which developed countries would pay Ecuador *not* to develop oil deposits in the Amazon, thus reducing the carbon emissions believed to contribute to global warming. With the fall of oil prices and a 5% drop in Ecuadorian oil production in 2009, Correa has been desperately trying to obtain credit from China and other foreign sources to continue financing his social revolution, but his default has now backfired on Ecuador—and him.

As was true with his predecessors, Correa's once phenomenal popularity has begun to slide, from a 72% approval rating at the time of his re-election to 42% by the end of 2009. Besides losing the support of the indigenous population, Correa has alienated his supporters in the middle class with his increasing emulation of Chávez's dictatorial policies. He ordered creation of Cuban-style "committees for the defense of the revolution," which is in effect a network to spy on political opponents. In early 2010, he tried to pass a Venezuelan-style media law that would greatly have restricted freedom of the press and expression, but his own party balked at the idea and came up with a watered-down version, much to the president's annoyance.

One reason Correa has called the media his "worst enemy" was because of an exposé by the venerable Guayaquil daily *Ex-*

preso in October 2009 that Correa's older brother, Fabricio, had received $167 million in construction contracts despite a law that prohibits relatives of officials from benefiting from government contracts. The president at first castigated the newspaper for spreading lies about his family, but when the charges appeared to have validity, he disavowed his brother and called him "unbalanced by greed." Fabricio Correa counter attacked against his brother, stating publicly that corruption was rife in the administration and turning over to the attorney general a "corruption file" that supposedly documents high-level wrong-doing.

Culture: Ecuador is the quintessential mestizo country, with pure European and Indian descendants being heavily outnumbered by their ethnic hybrid. Of the two cultures, it is the Indian that has had the greater influence on the country's cultural identity. Ecuador is a remnant of the Inca Empire, and Quéchua is still widely spoken. The 200-odd Quéchua-based dialects serve as a unifying thread among the rural people. The Indian roots are visible and audible in the country's art and traditional folk music and dances.

Like other Bolivarian countries of northern South America, Ecuador has been whipsawed by dictatorship and political instability that has had a negative impact on cultural growth. Ecuadorian culture attracted little attention outside its borders until the 20th century. Its outstanding literary figure remains Jorge Icaza, whose 1934 novel, *Huasipungo*, is a Latin American classic and has been translated into at least 17 languages. Another prominent novelist was José de la Cuadra.

Ecuador's principal cultural contribution has come from its many talented artists, the best known of whom have been Oswaldo Guayasamín, a revolutionary painter in the style of Mexico's Diego Rivera, and Kingman Riofrío, whose works stress indigenous subjects. Guayasamín died in 1999, and a museum containing his works was dedicated in Quito in November 2002.

The high illiteracy rate has hampered development of the printed media. There are a number of mid-sized dailies, centered in Quito and Guayaquil. The oldest is the elite *El Telégrafo*, founded in 1884 and located in Guayaquil. The nation's circulation leader with about 200,000 daily is *El Universo*, which dates to 1921 and also is published in the port city. The capital's leading paper is *El Comercio*. There also are a number of magazines.

Economy: Ecuador's economy was always dependent upon the sale of agricultural products (bananas) and minerals abroad to pay for needed imports. It remains dominated by oil exportation.

The agricultural/mineral exports are produced by illiterate, poorly paid labor in economic bondage to the land, who live on a subsistence income.

Ecuador's economic future improved dramatically with the discovery of rich oil deposits, estimated at 5 billion barrels of high-grade petroleum, in the jungles east of the Andes. Oil income quadrupled government revenues with royalties reaching about $500 million by 1975, and Ecuador became a member of OPEC. Nationalistic oil policies later forced most private firms to leave the country—thereby reducing exploration for new deposits. As a result, production declined; domestic oil consumption came close to outstripping production.

In 1981, oil output rose 27% to a total of 77 million barrels. However, the country's unfriendly attitude toward foreign oil companies prior to 1984 made it difficult to obtain foreign expertise needed to develop its resources. This was remedied by the administration of Febrés Cordero and additional exploration began in 1986.

But in 1985, Saudi Arabia increased its production because other OPEC nations were cheating on their oil quotas. This allowed the price for the product to "float," and the worldwide market went into a steep decline. The price descended to one-third of its 1980 level in 1986 (less than $10 a barrel), rebounding to $17 by 1995. Ecuador withdrew from OPEC.

As of 2007 and 2008, oil production was not sufficient to capitalize on the skyrocketing price of petroleum, and ironically, the high prices actually hurt Ecuador because it lacks refining capacity and must import its fuel. In 2009, it dropped by 5%.

Ecuador, together with Peru and Bolivia, is a major producer of raw cocaine paste, which is processed into powder in Colombia. Numerous "factories" are located within Ecuador (owned by Colombian cartels) where the paste is processed because of control measures within Colombia. Distribution is still via Colombia.

The devastating effects of *El Niño* in 1997, the drastic drop in world oil prices in 1998 and the simultaneous meltdown of the Asian and Brazilian financial markets all contributed to an economic crisis that President Mahuad declared to be the worst in 70 years. But OPEC's decision in 1999 to boost the price of oil augured well for Ecuador. Meanwhile, a panel of WTO experts sided with the United States, Ecuador, Guatemala, Honduras and Panama in their complaint that the European Union's banana import policy was discriminatory. The five plaintiff countries had charged that the EU showed favoritism to bananas imported from former Caribbean colonies and against Latin American producers and U.S. distributors, in violation of international trading regulations. Ecuador exports 16% of its bananas to the EU, or $238 million of its $1.05 billion 1998 production, amounting to more than 650,000 tons.

Mahuad and the Congress compromised on an austerity plan, which deepened the recession in 1999, leading a desperate Mahuad to recommend replacing the *sucre* with the dollar. Real GDP declined by a devastating 7.5%, unemployment jumped from 11.5% in 1998 to 16.9%, per capita income fell from $1,619 to $1,164, and inflation was again the highest in Latin America: 50.4%.

The dollarization scheme led to massive protests, which in turn led to Mahuad's ouster in January 2000, but his vice president and successor, Gustavo Noboa, also embraced dollarization and put it into effect (see H. The dollar replaced the *sucre* as Ecuador's legal tender that September.

Giant tortoises of the Galápagos Islands

Ecuador

The resulting currency stabilization, coupled with the fortuitous rise in international oil prices, led to a growth rate for 2000 of 2.0%. Inflation, however, nearly doubled to a crippling 96.6%, again the highest in Latin America, while unemployment dropped slightly to 14.7%.

The figures for 2001 were dramatically better, although deceptive. The good news was that real GDP increased by 5.6%, the fastest growth in Latin America. In reality, this only recovered the ground lost in 1999. Inflation, meanwhile, plummeted to "only" 22.4%.

There were two factors responsible for the strong showing in 2001. Noboa signed a $1.3 billion contract for an oil pipeline that was expected to create 50,000 jobs and, when completed, to boost petroleum exports by 50%. But a more important factor was a peculiar demographic phenomenon. During the 1999–2000 economic meltdown, an estimated 1 million Ecuadorians abandoned the country, legally and illegally, seeking work abroad in the United States, Spain, Italy and other countries. In 2001, the government actually created a program to expedite the exit visas of its citizens to work abroad. Year-end figures for 2001 showed that this both cut domestic unemployment almost by half to 8.8% (although 40% were still considered underemployed) and generated $1.4 billion in remittances from abroad, accounting for 8% of GDP, second only to oil exports. By 2003, the figure was $1.5 billion, or 5.6% of GDP.

By 2004, the economy grew at a rate of 6.9%, among the highest in Latin America, while inflation was only 1.95%. The spike in international oil prices in 2004 was largely responsible for the growth. Income from oil exports totaled $2.13 billion, accounting for 43% of national revenue, definitely an over-reliance. Despite the even higher price for crude oil in 2005 and 2006, growth was only 3.9% in 2005 and 2006 and 2.5% in 2007. Growth in 2008 was a healthy 6.5%, almost exclusively because of the skyrocketing world price of oil, which reached more than $140 a barrel. Then the global recession began, oil dropped to $35, and growth declined by –1.0% in 2009.

Tourism has increased dramatically, largely because of the popularity of the Galapagos Islands for foreign visitors. Tourism in 2007 was the third-largest generator of foreign exchange. Per capita GDP has risen steadily since the 1999 crisis, jumping from $1,450 per capita in 2002 to $2,424 in 2005 and $3,080 in 2008.

Something Ecuador must address if it is ever to get a permanent handle on its economy is the entrenched corruption that costs the economy an estimated $2 billion a year—more than 10% of GDP. Tax evasion alone costs the public treasury an estimated $600–$800 million a year. In 2006, 2007 and 2008, Transparency International, the corruption watchdog group, rated Ecuador the third most corrupt country of the 20 Latin American republics; only Venezuela and Haiti were ranked worse. All the presidents since 1997 have been accused iof enriching themselves in one way or another. President Rafael Correa, inaugurated in 2007, promised reform through his new constitution approved by voters in 2008. But his own finance minister was fired in a bond manipulation scheme (see History). In 2009, Ecuador had "improved" to the fourth most corrupt Latin American country.

Another problem that needs to be addressed is illegal logging in Ecuador's rain forests, a precious natural resource. The government estimates that 370,000 acres of virgin forest fall to the saws each year, but environmental groups indicate it could be twice that. An estimated 70% of the lumber sold is cut illegally. In 1999, the government, unable to regulate the logging effectively itself, wisely contracted with a Swiss firm to monitor the logging and to tax legal logging. Under pressure from the logging industry, the Constitutional Tribunal overturned the outsourcing agreement in 2003, for unclear legal reasons.

Environmentalists also are concerned with illegal shark fishing and harvesting of sea cucumbers in the Galapagos Islands, considered a world heritage site by the United Nations. In 2007, UNESCO placed the Galapagos Islands on its list of endangered world heritage sites.

The Future: Three elected Ecuadorian presidents were ousted by the military, the Congress or the mobs in the streets in just eight years. Rafael Correa is the latest would-be savior to climb to the top of the greased pole that the Ecuadorian presidency has become. He has promised to revamp Ecuador's notoriously corrupt system, the fourth most corrupt in Latin America, but now his own brother is accused of corruption and has begun to sing about corruption in the Correa administration (see History).

In 2008, Correa could finance his social programs with record-high oil prices. But the price of oil since 2009 has remained steadily at $70–$80 a barrel, half what it was in mid-2008, and Correa's bond default, though popular at home, has dried up international credit. Correa's popularity has already begun heading south. Moreover, Ecuadorians seem to be losing what little faith they had in democracy. The annual *Latinobarómetro* poll by *The Economist* showed that in 1996, 52% of Ecuadorians believed that democracy was preferable to any other form of government. In 2008, the year voters overwhelmingly approved Correa's new constitution, it was 56%. But in 2009, the year Correa's approval rating dropped from 72% to 42%, belief in democracy dropped to 43%, the second-lowest of the 18 nations in the survey. The 13-point one-year drop tied with neighboring Colombia as the sharpest in the survey. Meanwhile, the percentage of Ecuadorians who believe authoritarianism is sometimes preferable to democracy jumped from 16% in 2008 to 25% in 2009, the third-highest in the survey.

Authoritarianism appears to be where Correa would like to lead his country.

The Republic of El Salvador

Street scene in San Salvador

Area: 8,260 square miles.

Population: 6.1 million in 2010, est. (excluding expatriates).

Capital City: San Salvador (Pop. 1.75 million, estimated).

Climate: Tropical in the coastal plain, becoming temperate at higher altitudes.

Neighboring Countries: Honduras (North and East); Guatemala (West).

Official Language: Spanish.

Ethnic Background: *Mestizo* (mixed Spanish and Indian).

Principal Religion: Roman Catholic Christianity.

Chief Commercial Products: Coffee, Cotton, Sugar.

Currency: U.S. Dollar (formerly the *Colón*).

Gross Domestic Product: U.S. $22.43 billion in 2009 ($3,706 per capita).

Former Colonial Status: Spanish Crown Colony (1524–1821).

Independence Date: September 15, 1821

Chief of State: Mauricio Funes Cartagena (b. October 18, 1959), president (since June 1, 2009).

National Flag: Blue, white and blue horizontal stripes with the national coat of arms on the white stripe.

El Salvador is the smallest and most densely populated of the Central American republics. Most of the country is a volcanic upland with two parallel rows of volcanoes running east to west. Fourteen of the cones exceed 3,000 feet and three reach more than 7,000 feet. Lowlands lie north and south of the volcanic ranges. El Salvador's principal river, the Lempa, drains the northern lowlands by cutting through the volcanic region to reach the Pacific.

El Salvador's soils are rich and easily accessible from the Pacific coast; thus it is one of the few Latin American countries in which the whole of the national territory is settled. Various estimates are given for the percentages of European, Indian and African ancestry in the national population, but the most obvious facts are that there are no tribal Indians and few blacks, and that the white minority claiming pure European origins is indistinguishable from the admittedly *mestizo*, a mixture of Spanish and Indian. Cotton and sugar are raised on the coastal plains and the Lempa River valley, while the slopes of the volcanoes produce coffee. The climate is healthful and the rainfall abundant, with the rainy season running from May through October.

History: El Salvador was conquered by Pedro de Alvarado with a force from Mexico in 1524. Defeating the Indians and capturing their capital, Cuscutlán, he joined the region to the Captaincy-General of Guatemala. The small number of Spanish settlers intermarried with the Indians and established large agricultural and cattle-raising estates in the fertile valleys of the volcanic uplands, a pattern of land holding which exists today, and the root of much of El Salvador's present-day social problems. The remnants of the Indian population still farm village-owned lands in the mountains.

El Salvador declared its independence from Spain on September 15, 1821, with the other countries of Central America. Joining in a short-lived federation until its breakup in 1838, El Salvador was a center for the liberal republican opposition to the conservatives of Guatemala. It sought admission to the United States at one time and participated in several attempts to

El Salvador

unite with Honduras and Nicaragua. As was true in most of the Central American republics, the political history of El Salvador during the 19th century after independence was one of turbulence, revolution, dictators, military governments and civil strife. Added to the internal difficulties of the nation were frequent periods of conflict with neighboring states.

The first quarter of the 20th century was relatively peaceful, but this was followed by period of virtual anarchy until the seizure of power by an absolute ruler, Hernández Martínez, from 1931 to 1944. The low point of his regime came in 1932, when a peasant uprising in protest against the landed elite cost 20,000 lives, almost all of them peasants, an event remembered today as *"La Matanza"* (the slaughter).

Various factions have been labeled conservative (favoring central government and close church-state relations) and liberal (anti-clerical federalists); however, those represented only blocs within the elite landowning class and were not truly different political entities. A degree of political stability was existed from 1948–60, but popular opposition to the elite's domination of politics and continuing economic inequality centered around a small number of wealthy and a comparatively huge number of poor.

This led to minor change in October 1960, when a provisional military-civilian *junta* took power, promising to reform the nation's political structure and hold elections. A new constitution was adopted in 1962 and in presidential elections held the same year there was but one candidate, Adalberto Rivera of the *Partido de Conciliación Nacional (PCN)*, a movement controlled by the oligarchy and the military. Although he and his party were supposed to be "middle-of-the-road," there was no such thing in El Salvador. There were right-wing, elitist elements and communist-leftist rebels, with little in between. Providing capable and honest leadership, Rivera encouraged the development of light industry and supported the nation's participation in the Central American Common Market.

Starting about 1960, a culture of violence gripped the country. Right-wing vigilante groups, such as the White Warrior's Union, often joined with government forces—including rightist members of the army, the National Guard and the Treasury Police—to torture and execute peasant leaders and other advocates of social reform. Leftist groups—including Marxist-led guerrilla units such as the People's Revolutionary Army, the Popular Forces of Liberation, and the Armed Forces of National Resistance—responded in kind with attacks against military forces and their conservative supporters. Generally, leftist groups tended to pin-

point specific targets, while right-wing terrorists employed random violence. As a result, a large percentage of the political deaths in El Salvador have been linked to conservative forces.

Another *PCN* "moderate" candidate, Colonel Fidel Sánchez Hernández, won the 1967 election. His policies included an unheard-of land ownership reform proposal that infuriated conservatives, businessmen and wealthy landowners. The brief but bitter "Soccer War" was fought with Honduras in 1969 (see Honduras).

Great controversy surrounded the presidential elections of 1972. Christian Democrat José Napoleón Duarte, a nominal moderate, apparently outpolled *PCN* candidate Colonel Arturo Armando Molina. However, a subsequent "official" count gave the ruling *PCN* party a 22,000-vote victory; Molina's "election" was confirmed by Congress, where the *PCN* enjoyed a two-thirds majority. The military used a similar tactic for the presidential elections of 1977 when the ruling *PCN* candidate, General Carlos Humberto Romero, was declared the winner by a two-to-one margin over his opponent, another right-wing officer. When riots broke out against the rigged elections, the government imposed martial law. Before order was restored, an estimated 100 protesters were killed.

A staunch conservative, Romero was involuntarily faced immediately with urgent

problems of land reform, human rights and the Catholic Church, which had become reformist. He equated change from the old order with communism. Most of the fertile farmland in the valleys and lowlands (about 60% of the total) continued to be owned by a handful of families who were closely allied to the ruling armed forces. In contrast, more than 65% of the population lived in abject poverty. Backed by the military, the conservative aristocracy had traditionally blocked disorganized peasant demands for land and reform. Wealthy landowners (including military officers who owned large estates) feared a repetition of the unsuccessful peasant uprisings against the landed elite of 1932.

The pace of fighting between rightists and leftists rose dramatically after Romero became president. Hoping to wipe out all opposition, he launched a bitter campaign against leftists and their sympathizers.

Coup and Civil War

As the nation moved toward complete chaos, a group of liberal army officers led by Colonel Adolfo Arnoldo Majano ousted Romero in a bloodless coup in November 1979. Power then shifted to a progressive five-man *junta* that included Majano and two members of the "centrist" Christian Democratic Party. The new rulers promised sweeping economic and social reforms that provided nationalization of key parts of foreign trade industries, including coffee marketing; nationalization of many banks, which traditionally provided loans only to the upper class; and land reform.

On paper, the land reform proposal was comparable in scope to those of Mexico, Bolivia and Peru. The first phase, affecting 400 estates containing more than 1,235 acres each, would have redistributed about 600,000 acres of land (about 25% of the nation's arable land) to peasants. A second phase, planned for 1981, was to involve all farms larger than 370 acres.

A major catalyst for reform was the Carter administration in Washington, which supplied El Salvador with economic and military assistance. Washington feared that unless fundamental reforms were enacted, El Salvador would slide into a disastrous class war. Such a conflict might well be won by leftists, who could then be expected to combine with radicals in Nicaragua to force Marxist governments onto neighboring Honduras and Guatemala.

Conservative opposition to the *junta's* reforms proved overwhelming, however, and right-wing violence rose dramatically. The assassination of Archbishop Oscar Romero in 1980 shocked the nation and the world, and in 1980 conservatives murdered the head of the country's Human Rights Commission (its report had embarrassed the government). The top six leaders of a "centrist" political front that included the Christian Democratic Party were killed in late 1980, and the following month four U.S. women Catholic missionaries were murdered. Two U.S. agricultural agents associated with the nation's land reform program were murdered as well.

Appalled by this violence, President Carter halted all aid to El Salvador in late 1980. The Salvadoran military responded by taking aim at the *junta*, but the result was unexpected. Majano was replaced by a new four-member *junta* under the leadership of José Napoleón Duarte of the Christian Democratic Party. A graduate of Notre Dame University, the 55-year-old civil engineer pledged to move forward with social reform while taking steps to

José Napoleón Duarte

control right-wing terrorism. Duarte quietly retired some right-wing military leaders while others were reassigned to isolated posts.

Convinced that the time was ripe for revolution, the guerrillas launched a full-scale "final assault" against government forces in January 1981. Although supplied with Nicaraguan and Cuban arms, the rebels found no popular support in the countryside, and the offensive soon foundered.

In Washington, the new Reagan administration issued a hastily prepared report claiming to have "concrete" evidence that the Salvadoran guerrilla front was a part of a "worldwide communist conspiracy"

masterminded by the Soviet Union. Insisting that it was necessary to "draw the line" against communism, President Reagan soon ordered a resumption of large-scale military and economic assistance to El Salvador. He also fired the Carter-appointed ambassador.

Despite such aid, Duarte's regime found itself increasingly dependent on the military for survival. To placate powerful right-wing critics, Duarte shelved many of his promised reforms. Hoping to increase domestic support for the government and to improve El Salvador's international image, Washington pressured Duarte to hold elections for a Constituent Assembly in 1982 as the first step toward a return to constitutional government. While almost all leftists boycotted the elections—and the guerrillas sought to disrupt the balloting—voter turnout was heavy. Official returns showed 1.3 million votes cast.

Duarte's centrist-left Christian Democratic Party (*PDC*) won 40% of the vote and 24 seats in the 60-seat Constituent Assembly, the largest total of any single party. But right-wing tickets led by the National Republican Alliance (*ARENA*) and the National Conciliation Party (*PCN*) gained nearly 60% of the vote and 34 seats in the Assembly.

Much to the chagrin of Duarte and his supporters in Washington, the rightists promptly formed a coalition and voted to exclude the *PDC* from participation in the new government. Named president of the Assembly was arch-conservative Roberto D'Aubuisson, an ex-army intelligence officer allegedly linked with the right-wing death squads. In 1980 he had been arrested for plotting a coup against the government.

Under strong pressure from the army's influential defense minister, General José Guillermo García, the Assembly elected a moderate U.S.-educated economist and banker as provisional president: Alvaro Alfredo Magaña, 56. The Assembly also named three vice presidents, one each for *ARENA*, *PCN*, and the *PDC*.

As the first democratically elected president in 50 years, Magaña was expected to have only a limited impact on the country's destiny. The rightist-controlled Assembly sought to strip the president of any real power while Assembly President D'Aubuisson tried to repeal many of the reforms planned by the Duarte regime. In one of its first acts, the Assembly voted to dismantle Phases II and III of the land reform program longed for by the poor. (By mid-1982, provisional land titles had been given to more than 7,000 peasants under the program.) D'Aubuisson boasted he would wipe out the nation's guerrilla movement "in no more than six months." Although weakened by the failures of its 1981 "final assault," the guerrillas were

Salvadoran guerrillas, Usulátan Province

El Salvador

A young rural mother does the family wash

not dislodged. The insurgents controlled most of Chalatenango and Morazán provinces in the mountainous north part of the country near the Honduran border.

The nation's five major Marxist groups continued to quarrel among themselves, but joined under a single umbrella organization, the Farabundo Martí National Liberation Front (*FMLN*). Most of the groups, which trace their common roots to the communist-inspired peasant uprising in 1932, became active in the late 1960s and early 1970s. Both France and Mexico recognized the rebels in 1981 as a "representative political force"—a move which could only alienate the United States.

As full-scale civil war unfolded, the government began to improve its military capabilities. The United States was drawn increasingly into the anti-communist war in El Salvador. The Reagan administration effectively wrote a blank check to those in charge, a military establishment whose loyalty was consistently identified with the elite. U.S. advisers took their place alongside the Salvadoran military, quickly training and developing rapid-response battalions that were quite effective, but which soon acquired the dubious label of "death squads." The most notorious was the Atlacatl Battalion. The U.S. Congress, however,

repelled by government-sponsored atrocities, rigidly limited the number of advisers to 55.

The military faced an insurgency initially of poor guerrillas, who rapidly came to be supported by Soviet-via-Cuba resources, military and financial. Alongside the government forces were private forces that frequently perpetrated atrocities. But it was not one-sided by any means. Both sides resorted to the worst sort of warfare, using any tactic or method necessary to instill total fear in innocent bystanders. Public torture, mutilation and murder of innocents, all became acceptable tools.

The U.S. Senate Foreign Relations Committee voted to cut $100 million from the Reagan administration's $226 million aid package in 1982. The House of Representatives passed a resolution requiring the president to certify that the Salvadoran government was making "good faith efforts" to prosecute five National Guard personnel accused of the 1980 murders of the three American nuns and a lay worker.

El Salvador's civil war increasingly spilled over into other parts of Central America. Thousands of Salvadoran peasants fled to Honduras to escape the terror from the guerrillas and the right-wing death squads, including *ORDEN*, a rural

civil defense force feared even more than the regular army. An estimated 2 million Salvadorans lived outside the country; 1 million of them, mostly illegal immigrants, were in the United States.

Guatemala, Honduras, Costa Rica and El Salvador formed a common front to exchange intelligence and coordinate strategy against Nicaraguan and Salvadoran guerrillas. Both Honduras and Guatemala maintained large troop concentrations along their common borders with El Salvador. Honduran troops controlled a contested zone along the border of the two countries, partly to prevent the communist rebellion from spreading into its territory.

The *FMLN* sought to disrupt elections in 1984, but Salvadorans went to the polls under the eyes of scores of international observers. Duarte defeated D'Aubuisson for president, and immediately traveled to Washington to ask for more economic aid for both social programs and military assistance. In 1985, legislative and municipal elections, the *PDC*, in an upset, captured a majority of seats in the National Assembly and municipal councils.

The Catholic Church announced it would try to mediate in the civil war. This eased the cautious attitude of the U.S. Congress, which in 1984 appropriated additional emergency and military aid. But in 1985, the communists kidnapped Duarte's daughter at San Salvador University. The president had to agree to the release of 22 rebels and safe passage for 96 wounded guerrillas to Cuba (and then to Eastern Europe for medical treatment) to win her release. He sent his family to the United States to avoid further kidnappings. The military and rightists were furious at his apparent weakness, but talk about a coup rapidly faded. He was, after all, necessary for continued U.S. military aid.

The years 1986–87 saw a beefed-up military achieve greater successes. Ultimately the conflict cost $6 billion in U.S. aid. Periodic negotiations failed, as both sides negotiated with ultimatums. In 1988 the *FMLN* flatly rejected a proposal that the organization participate in municipal and legislative elections. When it finally tried this in 1991, in spite of successfully blocking observation at 30 polling places it controlled, only one of its candidates was sent to the National Assembly.

But in 1989 the communists agreed to take part in and respect the outcome of presidential elections *if* they were postponed for six months. They demanded a multitude of other conditions that made the offer impossible. They resorted to terrorism to disrupt the electoral process, and the right-wing death squads retaliated, committing their own atrocities. As usual, the innocent suffered.

The *PDC* had unwisely divided into two factions. *ARENA*, well unified under D'Aubuisson, was able to mount an upset in local and legislative elections, and was the decisive victor in a contest marred by charges of ballot box stuffing.

Six candidates vied for president in 1989. The *FMLN* nominally supported one, but did its best to keep voters away from the polls. *ARENA* candidate Alfredo Cristiani won with almost 54% of the vote.

By late 1989, it was apparent that Soviet-Cuban aid was going to dry up. Deciding that negotiations were the best course, the *FMLN* tried two super-offensives as last-ditch efforts in 1989 and 1990 to win as much territory as possible and thereby be in a better negotiating position. The guerrillas held parts of San Salvador for several days, but could not consolidate their gains. Nine members of a death squad murdered seven pro-guerrilla Jesuit priests in cold blood, together with their servant and her daughter in the melee. Two of the soldiers later were sentenced to 30 years imprisonment for following orders.

Peace at Last

After the last-gasp rebel offensive of 1989, both sides were forced to acknowledge a stalemate. Neither could achieve full victory, and each side was willing to make peace; all that was needed was an appropriate broker. In September 1991, the U.S. ambassador and his military group commander seized that initiative by traveling boldly into guerrilla territory in a four-wheel-drive vehicle to confront an astonished *FMLN* leadership. Essentially, the two U.S. officials asked what it would take for the *FMLN* to make peace.

Former President Armando Calderón Sol

It turned out that two of the rebels' key expectations for a post-war El Salvador were relatively reasonable ones: rural electrification and an end to death-squad atrocities. The ambassador brought these and other bargaining points back to the capital. On December 31, the two sides signed a truce that ended 12 years of slaughter that had claimed an estimated 75,000 lives, a grim toll in a country of only 6 million people.

The formal signing of the peace accords followed on January 16, 1992. Under the terms of the peace agreement, guaranteed by the United Nations, the *FMLN* laid down their arms and agreed to participate in the democratic process. The army ceased its sponsorship of death-squad activities. Despite an occasional low-level violation, the desire for peace superseded the deep-seated class hatreds that had led to the bloodbath. Less realistic was the establishment of a "truth commission" to investigate the atrocities committed during the war. Among the recommendations in its 211-page report was that the entire Supreme Court be sacked. President Cristiani chose to ignore these and other recommendations, but the mood of the country was one of forgive and forget. Despite some pessimism and a few setbacks, the tenuous armistice took hold.

The first postwar elections revealed a great deal about the conflict in El Salvador. Both Duarte and D'Aubuisson had died of cancer since 1989. Armando Calderón Sol was the *ARENA* presidential candidate of in 1994; Rubén Zamora was the choice of a leftist coalition that included the *FMLN*. Campaigning was vigorous. People were incredulous at seeing once-feared guerrillas suddenly soliciting their votes. In the first round, Calderón scored not quite 50% of the vote in balloting that was free of irregularities; Zamora received 25%. *ARENA* sailed to an easy victory in the runoff.

ARENA and an allied party took 43 seats, a bare majority in the 84-seat Assembly, while the *FMLN* won 21 and the *PDC* fell to 18. The *PDC* soon fragmented again.

Nagging problems remained. Former *FMLN* guerrillas had been promised jobs and stipends to enable them to live decently, but no one planned where the funds would come from. They split into numerous factions and groups, many of which practiced thievery, kidnapping and demolition of homes to obtain and extort money from small villages and the countryside. This illustrated an age-old problem: what is done with the revolutionaries when the revolution is over?

The lower echelon army troops also went frequently unpaid, but were promised tracts in the rich, upper highlands, to

be taken from the land barons. Anticipating this, many squatted on the large *estancias*, but were driven from them. They became embittered and restive.

The political and economic elites received a scare in the municipal and congressional elections of 1997. *ARENA* lost its absolute majority in the National Assembly, winning just 28 of the 84 seats, while the *FMLN* shocked the country—and the world—by winning 27. *ARENA* was forced to govern in coalition with small conservative parties. Moreover, the *FMLN* won the mayoralties of most of the major cities, including San Salvador. The winner in the capital was Hector Silva, a Boston-born gynecologist, who became highly popular for his public works improvements. The *FMLN* had an unlikely ally in President Calderón, who had become unpopular because of a stagnant economy, allegations of corruption and an alarming increase in violent crime that he seemed impotent to control. By mid-1998, it seemed possible that the former guerrillas would win through the ballot box what they had failed for 12 years to win on the battlefield. But two things happened to blunt the pro-*FMLN* trend.

First, *ARENA* wisely cleaned up its act by nominating as its presidential candidate Francisco "Paco" Flores, an unthreatening, 39-year-old former philosophy professor who had no link to the dark days of D'Aubuisson's death squads. In fact, he was an undergraduate at Amherst College in Massachusetts when the civil war erupted in 1979, then stayed in the United States to study for a year at Harvard before traveling to India to study Hindu philosophy. After returning to El Salvador, he taught at Central American University, where he became friends with the Jesuit priests later slain by the army during the 1989 guerrilla offensive. He taught philosophy at a small college in the capital before becoming an adviser to President Cristiani. He was then elected to the National Assembly, becoming the chamber's president after the 1997 elections.

Second, the *FMLN* began disemboweling itself with nasty intra-party bickering between Marxist hardliners and moderates. In a party caucus, the popular Silva, a moderate, deadlocked with another popular moderate, Victoria Aviles, who had served as U.N. human rights ombudsman. They both acquiesced in favor of yet another moderate, Facundo Guardado, a former commander-in-chief of the rebel army, who was best remembered for his seizure of the Sheraton Hotel during the 1989 offensive on the capital. But the public squabble within the *FMLN* ranks, which at times resembled a barroom brawl, was shown to the country on television, creating grave doubts about the party's ability

El Salvador

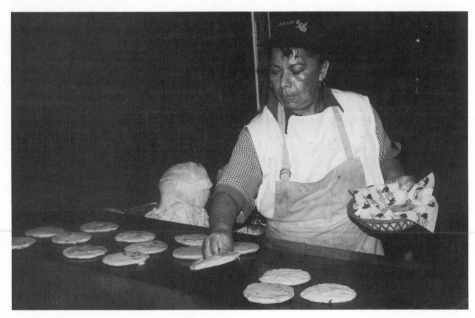

Making *pupusas* (a *tortilla* made of cornmeal, onion, pork rinds, and shortening) at a sidewalk restaurant in San Salvador

Photo by the author

to govern the country. Five other candidates entered the race, but the race boiled down to Flores and Guardado.

The Flores Presidency

This author covered the 1999 election campaign as a freelance journalist, interviewing both the major candidates. The consensus among the people I interviewed on both right and left was that Guardado was handicapped by his image as a guerrilla commander, which stood out in especially sharp contrast with the intellectual and urbane Flores, as well as by the infighting within the *FMLN* ranks.

"People understand that there has been a deep change within *ARENA*," Flores told me. "It's not only a generational change, but it's a change in the way we do things and the way we relate to other politicians, to other political parties and to the Salvadoran people."

In a separate interview, Guardado agreed that the campaign has been respectful, but insisted that *ARENA* has not changed its spots and that the *FMLN* better represents the middle class.

In the end, the polls and the pundits proved correct in their forecasts of the outcome. In the March 7 balloting, Flores avoided a runoff by receiving just under 52% of the vote, to 29% for Guardado.

The *FMLN* soon rebounded from its electoral loss. In 2000, they shocked the establishment once again by winning 31 seats in the National Assembly, while *ARENA's* seats remained unchanged at 29. *ARENA* still enjoyed a small majority

through a coalition with the PCN and smaller conservative parties.

Two major but unrelated events occurred in 2001. On January 1, El Salvador joined Panama and Ecuador in abandoning its currency and embracing the dollar. On January 13, the country was hit by a devastating earthquake that killed 1,200 people and caused an estimated $1 billion in damage—about half the national budget. A second quake struck exactly a month later, on February 13, which added to the damage but mercifully claimed far fewer lives.

A potentially significant political event occurred in November 2001. Salvador Sánchez Cerén, who under the *nom de guerre* Leonel González had commanded the largest of the *FMLN's* guerrilla factions during the civil war and who adheres to

Former President Francisco Flores

the party's traditional socialist roots, scored a decisive victory, 45% to 22%, over a reformist candidate to lead the *FMLN*. In the wake of Sánchez's victory, some *FMLN* moderates, including six members of the Assembly, defected from the party to form their own movement, thus fragmenting the opposition to *ARENA*.

In March 2002, U.S. President George W. Bush included El Salvador on his itinerary for a three-nation visit to Latin America. His visit became the occasion for a summit with the other presidents of Central America, at which Bush preached his gospel of free trade.

Despite an improvement in the economy, the *FMLN* again won 31 Assembly seats to 27 for *ARENA* in 2003, recovering the six seats it had lost from defections. *ARENA* still enjoyed a working majority through its alliance with the *PCN*, which won 16 seats. The *FMLN* also retained the mayoralty of San Salvador under the candidacy of a political newcomer, Carlos Rivas Zamora.

In 2003, Flores dispatched a contingent of 380 troops to participate in the allied coalition in Iraq, under Spanish command. El Salvador decided to keep its troops in Iraq, even after Spain withdrew its forces.

The waning days of the Flores administration were clouded by graft scandals at a private bank and a water company.

The Saca Presidency

ARENA and the *FMLN* presented voters with an even sharper choice in 2004 than they had in 1999. *ARENA* once again presented a youthful, post-civil war candidate by nominating Elías Antonio "Tony" Saca, 39, a former sportscaster who had become a media executive. The *FMLN*, which apparently had not learned anything about not frightening voters, chose Schafik Hándel, 73, a well-known leader of the Communist faction of the guerrilla movement. About the only thing the two men had in common was that they were born of Palestinian immigrant parents, who were from Bethlehem. Two minor candidates rounded out the field.

ARENA used the usual scare tactics against the Communist Hándel, hinting that the United States could begin restricting remittances by Salvadorans living in the United States, as they do with remittances by Cuban Americans, if Hándel won. The *FMLN* candidate did little to downplay his past, pledging to establish diplomatic relations with Cuba and the People's Republic of China, to pull Salvadoran troops out of Iraq, to heavily tax businesses and the wealthy, to bring back the *Colón* to circulate alongside the dollar and to oppose a Central American free-trade agreement with the United States.

Former President Elias Antonio Saca

On March 21, 67.3% of the Salvadoran electorate turned out to vote; the outcome was little different from that of 1999:

Saca	1,314,436	57.7%
Hándel	812,519	35.7%
Others	150,518	6.6%

Hándel, reflecting his antidemocratic background, ungraciously blamed his defeat on *ARENA*'s "lies and blackmail." He died in 2006.

Saca continued Flores' commitment to the Allied Coalition in Iraq even after Honduras, Nicaragua and the Dominican Republic brought their troops home. Saca sent new contingents of 380 troops to Iraq every six months, the last Latin American nation to have troops there. He ended El Salvador's participation in the coalition on December 31, 2008, the date the U.N. mandate expired.

As another indication of El Salvador's pro-U.S. policy, the National Assembly voted 49–35 in December 2004 to ratify the proposed Central American Free Trade Agreement. It was the first country to do so. It went into effect on March 1, 2006, despite public protests.

A major multinational problem that Saca faced is the growing threat in El Salvador, the United States, Mexico, Guatemala and Honduras of *maras*, or street gangs. These groups, formed by Central American, mostly Salvadoran, emigrants in Los Angeles, constitute a serious form of organized crime. Perhaps the most infamous is *Mara Salvatrucha-13*, or *MS-13*, believed to have 100,000 members in 31 states and five countries, including Canada. Another is called *Mara-18*. So serious is the threat that the FBI opened a special anti-gang office in San Salvador in 2005.

In 2006, El Salvador had the unfortunate distinction of having the highest murder rate in the entire world, 55.3 per 100,000 inhabitants. In 2007, is was second-highest after Honduras, with 49 murders per 100,000.

In the 2006 legislative and municipal elections, *ARENA* and the *FMLN* were virtually tied in the popular vote with about 39% each, but *ARENA* regained a slight lead in the Assembly, 34 seats to 32. *ARENA* also fared better than the *FMLN* in the municipal races. The *FMLN* barely held on to the mayoralty of San Salvador.

A violent incident reminiscent of the dark days of civil war shocked the country in February 2007. Three Salvadoran members of the Central American Parliament, which sits in Guatemala City, were abducted when their three-car convoy was attacked between the Salvadoran-Guatemalan border and Guatemala City. They were shot and then set on fire, apparently while still alive. Their charred bodies were found on a farm the next day. All three were members of *ARENA*. Among them were Eduardo d'Aubuisson, son of the late founder of the party, and Ramón González, a co-founder. Making the incident even more bizarre, four Guatemalan police officers were jailed on suspicion of complicity in the murders. Just three days later, hitmen entered the Guatemalan jail and killed all four suspects. The hitmen had to get past eight locked doors, suggesting official complicity. The motive for the *ARENA* members' assassination was unclear, but drug traffickers were believed involved.

Mauricio Funes Makes History

By 2009, *ARENA* had won four consecutive elections and had held the presidency for 20 years, unusual in any democracy. Voters were in the mood for a change, and this time the *FMLN* wised up and nominated a moderate, a television journalist named Mauricio Funes, 49. Funes, who had hosted a popular interview show in El Salvador and also worked as a freelancer for *CNN en Español*, had not fought as a guerrilla and was not an ideological hardliner, although his brother was a guerrilla who was killed in action. *ARENA* nominated Rodrigo Ávila.

The triennial legislative and municipal elections held in January 2009 failed to serve as a clear bellwether for the March 15 presidential election. The *FMLN* gained three seats to again become the largest party in the Assembly with 35 seats to 32 for *ARENA*. The *FMLN* also had a four-point plurality of the popular vote and won most of the municipalities, but *ARENA* won the mayoralty of the capital for the first time in 12 years.

Although the mild-mannered Funes was hardly the bogeyman previous *FMLN*

President Mauricio Funes

candidates had been, *ARENA* attacked his running mate, Salvador Sánchez Cerén, the hardline former guerrilla commander, and even his wife, Vanda Pignato, a Brazilian who had been an activist in the Workers Party there. Ávila sought to persuade voters that Funes would become another Hugo Chávez, while Funes insisted he would not abandon the dollar and would keep El Salvador in CAFTA. About his most radical proposal was a tax increase on the rich to fund social programs.

On March 15, voters decided to finally give the former guerrillas a shot at national power:

Funes	1,349,142	51.3%
Ávila	1,280,995	48.7%

Funes was sworn in on June 1, 2009. He is but the latest of a long string of leftist Latin American presidents. Oddly enough, U.S. Secretary of State Hillary Clinton attended the inauguration, while Chávez and Bolivia's Evo Morales did not. After the ceremony, Funes made a symbolic visit to the tomb of the assassinated Archbishop Romero, and one of his first official acts was to restore diplomatic relations with Cuba, the last Latin American nation to do so. He discussed severing El Salvador's long-standing relations with Taiwan and establishing relations with the People's Republic of China, but as of mid-2010 he had not done so. He named his wife minister of "social inclusion," while Vice President Sánchez is doubling as education minister.

Funes joined the majority of Latin American presidents in refusing to recog-

El Salvador

nize the elected government of President Porfirio Lobo Sosa of neighboring Honduras as a protest against the forced removal of President Manuel Zalaya in June 2009 (see Honduras).

The world was reminded of El Salvador's rampant gang violence when Christian Poveda, a French film director who had just released a documentary about the *Mara-18* titled *La Vida Loca*, was shot to death in a town north of San Salvador on September 4, 2009. Within days, a member of the national police and four *Mara*-18 members were arrested. A *Mara*-18 member who allegedly ordered the murder was already in prison.

Culture: The people of El Salvador have adopted European customs for the most part—pure Indians are hard to find in the Republic. Their lives revolve around the family as the primary social, economic and political unit.

El Salvador (The Savior) has perhaps some of the most beautiful churches found in Latin America—the people devote a full 12 days of the year to a festival in honor of their Christian namesake.

Ancient ruins of Mayan civilization have yielded treasures from the countryside which are being intensely studied, and there are explorations in progress for traces of even earlier inhabitants. One invaluable site near San Salvador has been bulldozed for a housing development and a brand-new (bulletproof) American embassy.

A rising star in Latin American literature is the Salvadoran novelist Horacio Castellanos Moya (b. 1957), best known for *El asco* (1997) and *La diabla en el espejo* (2000). His latest novels are *Donde no estén ustedes* (2003), *Insensatéz* (2004), *Desmoranamiento* (2006) *and Tirana memoria* (2008). He is currently a visiting professor at the University of Pittsburgh.

Economy: Agriculture is the dominant factor, with the major cash crops being coffee, sugar and cotton. Despite its small size, El Salvador ranks among the top five coffee producers in the world. Farming remains largely under the control of a small group of wealthy landowners; the large peasant population lives in virtual serfdom. Serious overcrowding and limited economic opportunities in rural regions have caused many peasants to migrate to the already congested cities.

Since World War II, light industry has gained steadily, making El Salvador the most industrialized nation in Central America. The civil war was costly in spite of U.S. assistance and seriously undermined economic growth.

The state banking industry was been privatized after the war. A major portion of the budget formerly devoted to the military is now being used for health and welfare.

Salvadorans love to grumble about the state of their economy, but in relative terms, their lot is not that bad. While El Salvador is plagued by widespread poverty, and although its economy is far from booming, it is certainly nowhere near the basket cases of neighboring Honduras, which has slightly over half the per capita income of El Salvador, or Nicaragua, where it is one third as much. In reality, peace has brought greater foreign investment in the form of *maquiladora* assembly plants for textile products, which in turn have created jobs. Tourism has risen modestly since the killing stopped. Moreover, Salvadoran expatriates still living in the United States send billions of dollars in remittances to their families back home.

Real GDP growth has been sluggish for years, only 2.8% per year or less from 1997 to 2005. Some of the blame during those years can be attributed to the damage wrought by Hurricane Mitch in 1998 and the twin earthquakes of 2001. Growth was a more encouraging 4.2% in 2006 and 4.7% in 2007. It dropped back to 2.5% in 2008, and with the gloobal recession, it shrank by –3.0% in 2009.

Unemployment has remained about 6–7%. The poverty rate has been reduced from 66% in 1991, the year before the civil war ended, to 30.7% in 2006. Inflation has been stabilized as a result of replacing the *Colón* with the dollar on January 1, 2001. The dollarization made sound economic sense; tens of thousands of Salvadorans live and work in the United States, and the bil-lions of dollars in remittances they send home to their families annually have become an important pillar of the economy since the exodus of refugees during the civil war. In 2006, the Central Bank placed the value of remittances at $3.3 billion; nearly a fourth of Salvadoran families receive them.

In March 2006, El Salvador became the first country formally to be incorporated into the U.S.-Dominican Republic-Central American Free Trade Agreement (DR-CAFTA). It is expected to boost Salvadoran exports, although the *FMLN* argues that it threatens domestic manufacturers and street vendors and others with low-cost U.S. imports.

The Future: The former guerrillas of the FMLN finally achieved national power at the ballotbox in 2009 with the election of President Mauricio Funes, and ARENA peacefully relinquished that power after 20 years in control. Funes is expected to rule as apragmatist, like Brazil's Lula, rather than as an ideological firebrand like Venezuela's Chávez. Closer ties with Cuba and Venezuela are likely, as Funeshas to appease his core constituency of leftists, but dollarization has provided monetary stability, CAFTA has opened up U.S. markets to Salvadoran products and about 1 million Salvadoran expatriates in the United States remit more than $3 billion a year back home. Ideology is one thing, economic realities are another.

Funes and the *FMLN* control only 35 of the 84 National Assembly seats, so unlike Chávez, he is having to govern by consensus rather than by fiat. But his peaceful ascension to office was an auspicious indication of the maturation of El Salvador's democracy 17 years after the bloodletting ended.

It may also have boosted his countrymen's faith in the democratic process, according to the annual *Latinobarómetro* poll in *The Economist*. In 1996, the first year of the survey, 56% of Salvadorans said they agreed that democracy is preferable to any other form of government. It plummeted to 25% by 2001, then rebounded to 50% in 2008. In 2009, the year Funes won the presidency and was inaugurated, it jumped to 68%. The 18-point one-year increase was the greatest of the 18 nations in the survey.

Like his predecessors, Funes is faced with a sagging economy, even worse now because of the global recession, which has affected remittances from Salvadorans, and with the still-rampant gang-related crime, which has given El Salvador one of the world's highest murder rates per capita. The *FMLN* struggled for 20 years to win power; now it needs to deliver on the expectations it has created that it can do a better job overcoming these problems than *ARENA* did. Thus far it has not.

Children in an alleyway in San Salvador

The Republic of Guatemala

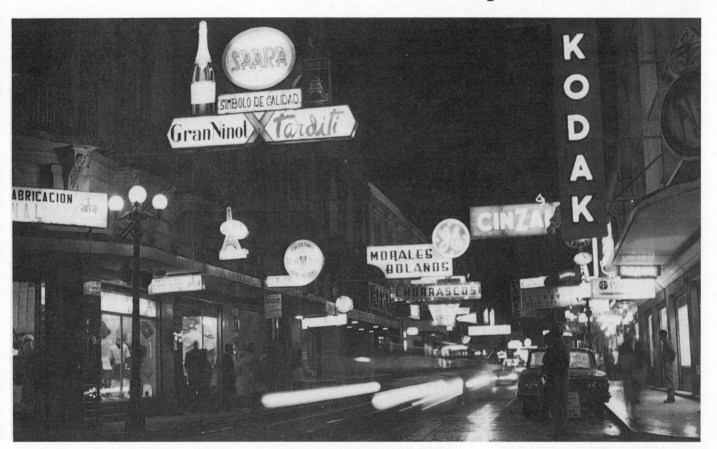

Guatemala City in the late evening

Area: 42,031 square miles.

Population: 13.55 million (2010 estimate).

Capital City: Guatemala City (Pop. 2.5 million, including surrounding areas).

Climate: Tropical on the coastal plains, temperate at the higher altitudes; heaviest rainfall is from May to October.

Neighboring Countries: Mexico (north and west); Belize (northeast); Honduras, El Salvador (east).

Official Language: Spanish.

Other Principal Tongues: Twenty distinct Maya-based dialects; Quiché is the most important.

Ethnic Background: Maya Indian origin (55%), *mestizo or Ladino* (mixed Spanish and Indian, (42%) European or African (3%).

Guatemala

Principal Religion: Roman Catholic Christianity. A substantial number of people have converted to evangelical Protestantism (about 25–30%).

Chief Commercial Products: Coffee, cotton, bananas, corn and other agricultural products.

Currency: *Quetzal.*

Gross Domestic Product: U.S.$36.9 billion in 2009, estimated ($2,723 per capita)

Former Colonial Status: Spanish Crown Colony (1524–1821).

Independence Date: September 15, 1821.

Chief of State: Álvaro Colom Caballeros (b. June 15, 1951), president (since January 14, 2008).

National Flag: Blue, white and blue vertical stripes with national crest in the center white stripe.

Guatemala, the most populous of the Central American republics, is a mountainous highland bordered by coastal plains in the North and South. The southern Pacific coast plain is a 200-mile ribbon of land reaching a maximum of 30 miles in width. The highland rises abruptly from this plain to an elevation of 8,000 to 10,000 feet with a string of volcanoes on the southern rim. Three of these volcanoes are above 13,000 feet and three of them are still quite active.

The highland is interspersed with basins ranging from 5,000 to 8,000 feet in elevation, which are the most heavily populated regions of Guatemala. The northeastern lowlands are more extensive than the southern, and include the valleys of the Motagua River, which originates in the southern volcanoes and flows 185 miles into the Gulf of Honduras; the Polochic

River drains the more westerly mountains along a 200-mile course into Lake Izabal, a salty lagoon extending some 50 miles west from the Gulf of Honduras.

The Petén, a low, poorly drained plain, extending north 100 miles into the Yucatán Peninsula, is heavily forested and sparsely populated.

History: Guatemala was conquered by Spanish forces from Mexico in 1523 and the first Spanish settlement was established in 1524. Finding little precious metal and a land peopled by a sedentary agricultural folk, the Spanish governor rapidly lost interest in the region. Left to their own devices, the Spanish settlers intermarried with the Indians. The missionaries sought to Christianize the Mayas, whose culture began centuries before the birth of Christ. The fertile mountain valleys were developed into semi-independent estates worked by virtually enslaved Indians. The majority of the Maya, Quiché and other peoples of Mayan origin simply withdrew from the Spanish-speaking community and maintained their traditional way of life. The efforts of the missionaries to Christianize the Indians did not fully displace their pagan gods—rather, the Indians tended to add the Christian God to their own deities.

Before independence, the Captaincy-General of Guatemala included the modern Central American states and the southern provinces of present-day Mexico. Sparsely settled by the Spanish, the region contained subdued tribes in the highlands and poor settlements on the Pacific coast, while the Caribbean coast was in the hands of buccaneers, native Indians who

had retained their independence and a few illegal British settlers.

Augustín de Iturbide, emperor of Mexico, invited the patriot committee of Guatemala to join Mexico in 1821. Despite considerable opposition, the Central American states were annexed in 1822; with Iturbide's abdication in 1823 they declared themselves independent. The northern state of Chiapas elected to remain with Mexico; Soconusco later joined that nation in 1842.

The independent states formed a federation known as the United Provinces of Central America. Two parties appeared in the formation of a government—the *Serviles* (conservatives) who wanted a strong central government and close ties with the Church, and the *Radicales*, who favored a federal republic and curtailment of the privileges of the landowners and the clergy. A constitution based on that of the United States was adopted and a liberal president was installed. The liberal-conservative conflict resulted in a series of wars, and the confederation collapsed in 1838.

Independence and Dictatorship

From the time of dissolution of the union to 1944, Guatemala was dominated by four dictators. The first was Rafael Carrera (1838–65), who was an illiterate but popular *mestizo* leader, beloved of the Indians, but a religious fanatic of conservative persuasion. Hating liberals, he intervened in neighboring countries, seeking the overthrow of liberal presidents.

After his death, another conservative was elected, but liberal Justo Rufino Barrios gained control of the government in 1871 and ruled until his death in 1885 in the battle of Chalchuapa, El Salvador, while trying to reunite Central America by military force. A man of progressive ideas, Rufino fostered public education, built railroads and achieved a measure of economic development. He also curtailed the privileges of the landowners and destroyed the political power of the clergy.

Manuel Estrada Cabrera (1897–1920), a cultured but ruthless man, ruled as a despot with no effort to conceal his absolute power. Jorge Ubico came to power in 1931 and ruled until 1944. Honest and hard-working, he suppressed the previous corruption in government, bolstered the economy and carried out many social reforms of benefit to the laboring classes.

Opposition to Ubico's strict discipline resulted in public disorder and he ultimately resigned in the so-called "October Revolution" in 1944. Following two short-lived military governments, a liberal intellectual and novelist, Juan José Arévalo, was elected president in a genuinely free

Panorama of Guatemala City with the civic center in the foreground

182

election, taking office in 1945. He implemented a number of reforms, including social security, university autonomy and labor laws, and is still remembered as one of Guatemala's most enlightened presidents.

In the elections of 1950, Jacobo Arbenz Guzmán won as the candidate for the Revolutionary Action and National Regeneration parties. Inexperienced, with a government infiltrated by communists, he was overthrown in 1954 by Colonel Carlos Castillo Armas in a coup promoted by the U.S. CIA. Basically corrupt and ineffective, the latter was assassinated in 1957 in the presidential residence.

Following inconclusive elections, Miguel Idígoras Fuentes was appointed president in 1958; also corrupt and arrogant, he was in turn overthrown by a military coup in 1963. Colonel Enrique Peralta Azúrdia, who assumed the power of chief of state, suspended the constitution, dismissed Congress and ruled by decree until 1966, when in free and apparently honest elections, Julio César Méndez Montenegro,

General Jorge Ubico

a liberal, was elected. This was an effort to return constitutional government to Guatemala. In reality, it was the beginning of 20 years of military-dominated governments. It was also in the 1960s that a guerrilla insurgency began that lasted until 1996.

The single most impressive accomplishment of President Méndez Montenegro was his ability to stay in office until the end of his term. Beset by radicals and powerful conservatives, Méndez was forced to abandon reform programs and concentrate instead on pleasing traditionally powerful elements.

With virtual civil war between right-wing and leftist extremists continuing unabated, voters turned to conservative Colonel Carlos Arana in the 1970 presidential elections. Promising "bread and peace,"

the noted counter-insurgency expert nearly wiped out the leftist guerrilla movement by indiscriminately repressing all opposition political groups. His term was marked by a reduction in political violence and improved economic conditions.

As the 1974 presidential election approached, the military stipulated that any candidate would be acceptable—so long as he was in the armed forces. The ruling coalition thus nominated as its candidate the moderate former defense minister, General Kjell (pronounced "shell") Eugenio Laugerud García of the *Partido Institucional Democrático (PID)*. But when the early election returns gave National Opposition Front candidate Brigadier General Efraín Ríos Montt a formidable lead, the government suddenly halted the tabulation. Several days later the regime announced that Laugerud had won with 41% of the vote. Although such blatant fraud caused an uproar, the military refused to permit a recount.

The election also catapulted Ríos Montt into national—and international—prominence and notoriety, where he remains to this day.

Relations between the new president and ultra-conservative elements in the ruling coalition—led by former President Arana and the right-wing *Movimiento de Liberación Nacional (MLN)*—soon soured when Laugerud suggested mild reforms to ease the plight of the impoverished highland Indians. The *MLN*, representing the wealthy landowners, bitterly accused the president of being a "communist" for encouraging the formation of rural peasant cooperatives to increase production from inefficient, small peasant plots.

Guatemala was devastated in early 1976 when a violent earthquake in 17 of the 22 provinces killed 24,000 people. In addition, 76,000 were injured and 1.5 million left homeless. Although large amounts of foreign aid quickly poured into the country, little of it filtered down to the peasants because of bureaucratic bungling and political corruption.

None of the presidential candidates received a majority of votes in the 1978 election; 60% of the electorate ignored or boycotted the balloting. Congress elected the government-supported candidate, General Fernando Romeo Lucas García, but only 35 of the eligible lawmakers participated in the congressional vote. The new president promptly reversed the previous administration's policy of supporting limited reforms. Thus began an all-out campaign against both moderates and leftists.

Right-wing paramilitary "death squads," such as the Secret Anti-Communist Army, which drew most of its support from army and police units, systematically wiped out thousands of government opponents. Key

targets included student, labor, peasant and political leaders. During its four years in office, Lucas García's regime was widely regarded as the most repressive and corrupt in Latin America. London-based Amnesty International accused him of operating "murder and torture" chambers in an annex of the Presidential Palace.

A 1981 report by the Human Rights Commission of the Organization of American States found the Lucas García regime responsible for the "great majority" of political murders in the country at the time. Evangelical Church officials estimated that at least 11,000 civilians died from political violence in 1981 alone. The Catholic Church reported that 200,000 Guatemalan peasants fled to neighboring Central American countries to escape the violence.

In an attempt to halt rural support for the guerrillas, Lucas García sought to wipe out key segments of the Indian population. Such repression, however, induced many peasants to join the insurgents. As a result, warfare spread to seven provinces and the number of guerrillas increased from 1,500 in 1980 to about 4,000 in 1982.

Because of Guatemala's dismal human rights record, the Carter administration in Washington halted most military and economic aid to the country in 1977. Lucas García angrily responded by rejecting all U.S. military assistance. The subsequent election of Ronald Reagan was warmly applauded by Lucas García's supporters, who hoped that Washington would resume assistance. Yet, the Reagan administration also kept its distance, although

General Fernando Romeo Lucas García

Guatemala

$3.2 million in military aid was provided in 1981.

Unbridled repression by the regime was not limited to its battle against peasants and leftists. When moderate Christian Democracy (*DC*) party members urged in late 1980 that all political groups be allowed to participate in upcoming March 1982 elections, right-wing terrorists responded by assassinating 76 *DC* members.

Not surprisingly, only conservatives dared to run for president in the March 7, 1982 elections. When the balloting failed to produce a winner with a majority, Congress again voted to elect the government-supported candidate, General Angel Aníbal Guevara—who had received a bare 16% of the popular vote. The three losing candidates were arrested when they protested that the election was a fraud.

The 1982 Coup

On March 23, 1982, as the political crisis escalated, a core group of 20 junior officers in the barracks decided to vote with their guns. Early in the morning, they surrounded the Presidential Palace, forcing Lucas García to flee from a side door.

The bloodless coup was attributed to a variety of factors: the administration's heavy-handed treatment of opponents that had offended nearly all segments of the population; the perceptions of the president-elect as a clone of the unpopular Lucas García; and the rising dissatisfaction of junior officers in the army. Indeed, while these men were being sent to the field to fight against the guerrillas, senior officers were frequently given safe, cushy jobs in the rear. The widespread corruption that permeated the regime and the military high command was galling, even by Guatemalan standards. Vast public works projects initiated by the regime seemed to have been created for the sole purpose of providing a source of graft for top government officials. Of the 900 or so officers in the Guatemalan army, fully 240 were colonels or generals!

The coup created a temporary political vacuum; three different *juntas* were proclaimed the first day before the military finally settled on one led by Ríos Montt, then 55 and retired. His participation tended to give the *junta* some legitimacy, as Ríos Montt had probably won the 1974 elections, only to see the prize stolen.

Within hours of assuming power, the new *junta* annulled the March elections, abolished Congress, suspended the 1965 constitution, barred activities by political parties, reaffirmed Guatemala's age-old claim to Belize, arrested various civilians for corruption, ruled out elections in the near future and announced that the new government would rule by decree.

In the hope of dealing with the country's insurgency, the *junta* proposed an amnesty plan to leftist guerrillas. When the offer was rejected, Ríos Montt ordered an all-out "final assault" against the guerrillas in mid-1982, wiping out about 400 villages in the process.

Finding the three-member *junta* cumbersome, Ríos Montt fired his partners in mid-1982 and proclaimed himself president—breaking his pledge not to do so. The new president was a curiosity. A "born-again" evangelical Christian, he loved to quote the Bible to friends and foes alike when enunciating government policy. Thus, when asked about the nation's civil strife, he answered that the best way to combat it was with "love." On Sundays he gave spiritual pep-talks on national television. He was fond of saying that he "had lunch with God today."

His moralistic approach produced some positive results. He ordered a rare public campaign against corruption and cracked down on right-wing paramilitary vigilante groups. As a result, violent urban crime subsided dramatically, although political violence continued unabated in the countryside. Impressed by his efforts to reduce human rights violations, the Reagan administration offered Guatemala $4.5 million in military aid and $50 million in economic assistance in 1982.

Ríos Montt's grip on the presidency was tenuous. Some powerful elements in the military opposed his anti-corruption campaign, which reduced lucrative supplementary income sources for high-ranking officials. Others disliked his moralistic approach, dubbing him "Ayatollah." His evangelical beliefs made him extremely unpopular among the majority Catholics. General Oscar Humberto Mejía Victores overthrew Ríos Montt in mid-1983 and proclaimed himself president.

General Oscar Humberto Mejía Victores

Democracy Returns

Mejía promised a return to democracy. Elections for a constituent assembly were held in mid-1984; 71% of the electorate voted, which remains the record voter turnout. The *DC* led by a narrow plurality. A new constitution was adopted on May 31, 1985, and congressional and presidential elections were held that November.

In honest elections, Vinicio Cerezo, a Christian Democrat who proclaimed himself "left of center," won the presidency—a dubious honor. During the military years, immense debts were run up and the treasury was empty. The International Monetary Fund suspended loan agreements. Military and state police death squads had caused the disappearance of about 100,000 people.

Victorious leftists insisted on punishing the military, but Cerezo wisely announced that although investigations would be conducted into human rights violations, no punishments would result, infuriating many of his supporters. Mejía had decreed a general amnesty for the military during his final days in office. Underlining this, during the first three weeks of civilian government, five dozen bodies, some mutilated, were scattered throughout the country. More selective killings followed.

But "Vinicio," as the then-popular young president was known, carefully planned and executed a single raid and mass arrest of the Department of Technical Investigation, a military unit devoted to "counter-insurgency." Two hundred agents were fired and 400 were dispatched for "additional training." He also made substantial changes in the military leadership.

A committee on human rights was formed. But the civilian government had the same problems experienced in Argentina and in El Salvador: self-protection by the military. The matter was "resolved" when the Supreme Court issued more than a thousand writs of habeas corpus.

General José Efraín Ríos Montt

As might have been expected, no one had any genuine desire to go around digging up dead bodies.

The right-wing military, police and vigilante groups did not have a monopoly on cruel violence. Three left-wing guerrilla groups joined into the Guatemalan National Revolutionary Union (*URNG*); in 1990 they moved their operations from remote, rural areas and were operating in the more populous regions around Guatemala City. They were bold enough to stop traffic on the Pan-American Highway to collect "taxes."

Inconclusive talks were held in Madrid in 1987 and 1988 between the government and rebel representatives. The rebels were down to 1,000 men from a high of 10,000, and only operated in remote areas where they were equally despised by local Indian inhabitants, who just wanted to be left alone by both sides.

Military coups were aborted without violence in 1988 and 1989. But murders and disappearances at the hand of right-wing groups continued at the rate of more than 1,000 a year. Cerezo's popularity dwindled as his inability to control the military became increasingly apparent; further, he justifiably acquired the reputation as a playboy, spending much of his time during the week away from the capital or jetting abroad.

The country was in a state of near-anarchy by 1990. Countless paramilitary groups and the army operated freely, murdering at will virtually anyone suspected of being a leftist, the definition of which sometimes included anyone found outside after dark at night. In this setting, Ríos Montt campaigned in the 1990 elections on a "no-nonsense" platform; he was ruled ineligible to run under the 1986 constitution in a provision, directed against him, that forbade anyone from serving more than once as chief of state.

The Serrano Presidency

Jorge Serrano Elías, an evangelical Protestant, was elected president in a January 1991 runoff with 68% of the vote, which this author covered as a freelance journalist. Only about one third bothered to vote, however. He pledged to end the 30-year-old civil war.

While Cerezo had proved inept, Serrano proved venal and power-hungry. In May 1993, he attempted to effect a Fujimori-style "self coup" that initially had the backing of the armed forces. Serrano announced that he was dissolving Congress and ruling by decree on the familiar pretext that only in this way could he come to grips with the serious socio-economic problems facing the country. To make sure the Guatemalan people received only the information he wanted them to, he imposed prior censorship on the print and broadcast media, which immediately began collaborating with one another to outwit the censors and get information to the public.

For a week, it appeared that Guatemala would experience a throwback to the bad old days of strongman rule. But thousands of demonstrators flooded the streets of the capital to protest Serrano's power grab, among them such eminent figures as 1992 Nobel Peace Prize Laureate Rigoberta Menchú and U.N. Human Rights Ombudsman Ramiro de León Carpio. Moreover, the U.S. State Department hinted not very subtly that aid to Guatemala would likely evaporate. Simultaneously, the Constitutional Court declared Serrano's actions illegal.

The armed forces, realizing they were backing the wrong side, refused further to support the coup attempt. For a change, the military found itself hailed as a champion of democracy! Serrano fled the country to a life of luxurious exile in Panama with an estimated $25 million in "retirement funds" from the treasury. (Guatemala is still trying unsuccessfully to have Serrano extradited.)

Congress then named de León Carpio interim president, which proved to be a sound choice. As was the case with the interim presidency of Gerald Ford after the power abuses of Richard Nixon, de León Carpio proved fair and just, albeit a bit lackluster.

Legislative elections in mid-1994 (14% voted) resulted in a plurality for the Guatemalan Republican Front (*FRG*) led by Ríos Montt, who became president of the Congress. Four other parties split the remainder of the 80-seat body. The *FRG* repeatedly found itself outmaneuvered by the other parties in Congress.

Most of the next two years in Guatemala were even more turbulent than ever. The president turned to the army for support. The insurgency continued in spite of an agreement supposedly ending it. Torture and murder remained commonplace.

The Arzú Presidency and Peace

In November 1995, 12 candidates vied for president, whose term had been reduced from five to four years. The top two vote-getters were former Guatemala City Mayor Alvaro Arzú of the Party of National Advancement (*PAN*), and Alfonso Portillo of the *FRG*, the political vehicle of the still-popular Ríos Montt, whom the Constitutional Court again had ruled could not run. The court also prohibited the former strongman's wife from running, leaving Portillo as the stand-in candidate. Portillo unabashedly declared that Ríos Montt would serve in a high-level advisory capacity if he were elected.

In the January 1996 runoff, Arzú squeaked into office with only 52% of the vote; he lost 18 of the 21 departments outside his power base in the capital, an indicator of the lingering popular appeal of Ríos Montt. Arzú's *PAN* won 43 of the 80 seats in the unicameral Congress, though

Woman picking corn　　　　　World Bank Photo

Guatemala

Former President Ramiro de León Carpio

Ríos Montt's *FRG* remained a potent opposition. The *URNG*, in its first test at the polls, elected two deputies.

The new president pledged to respect human rights and insisted, not altogether convincingly, that the armed forces would be subordinate to the civilian authority. However, Arzú was mainstream enough, coming from a wealthy and prominent business family, that he posed no threat to the generals and seemed adept at working with them.

Above all else, Arzú pledged to continue the peace talks and see them through to fruition. The two sides met throughout 1996 in Mexico City and finally reached an historic truce, though some grumbled over the amnesty given to members of the security forces for past human rights abuses. On December 27, 1996, several Latin American presidents and UN Secretary-General Boutros Boutros-Ghali came to Guatemala City to witness the momentous signing of the accords that ended Central America's longest civil war. The peace took hold, with no serious violations by either side. The war-weary country at last had reason for some optimism regarding its future.

Arzú, smooth and charming while courting votes, proved ornery and arrogant as president. Days after his inauguration in January 1996, while Arzú was horseback riding near Antigua, a milk truck suddenly headed toward him. Halted by the bodyguards, the driver fled from the vehicle. The bodyguards then opened fire, killing him. The presidential palace described the incident as an assassination attempt. But when the media looked deeper, they concluded that the driver was a drunken milkman who had panicked.

A furious Arzú accused the media, most of which were critical of him, of attempting to discredit him. He then took mea-

sures aimed at curtailing the independent press. He used the government-subsidized television program, *Avances*, as a vehicle to vilify his editorial critics in the press and investigative reporting that had proved embarrassing to his administration. Arzú also cajoled wealthy friends to stop advertising in specified print media, particularly the country's leading daily, *Prensa Libre*, and the weekly newsmagazine *Crónica*. For business people who were not his friends, he extended a Godfather-like offer: Stop advertising, or face tax audits. *Prensa Libre* was too economically viable to be seriously hurt by the campaign, but *Crónica* was driven to the point of bankruptcy. In 1998, *Crónica* was bought out by a group of businessmen loyal to Arzú; its editorial staff was fired and its editorial tone changed overnight. It's credibility gone, it eventually folded.

On the positive side, the peace process took hold, although the public found itself polarized between those who demanded justice for past atrocities and those who preferred to forget the horrors of the past. Unfortunately, horrors kept occurring.

The Gerardi Murder

In April 1998, a Roman Catholic bishop, Juan José Gerardi Conedera, head of the church's human rights office, released a controversial report that laid the blame for most of the human rights abuses squarely at the feet of the army. Days later, Gerardi was found bludgeoned to death in his quarters. The crime stunned the country and reverberated abroad.

The official, secular investigation into the murder resembled a Keystone Kops farce. First, a local drunk who had been a laborer for Gerardi was arrested, but eventually was released for lack of evidence. Then authorities arrested a priest and accused him of killing Gerardi in a homosexual crime of passion, and the bishop's cook for complicity; both were released days later.

To make this comic-opera spectacle complete, the suspect priest's dog was "arrested" on suspicion of mauling Gerardi to death. However, Gerardi's body was exhumed for a second autopsy, which ruled out the canine theory. In a touch of irony worthy of a Greek comedy, Gerardi's successor as head of the church's human rights office was none other than Bishop Mario Ríos Montt, brother of the former strongman.

The Gerardi investigation ground on throughout 1999, largely because of intense public and media pressure, domestic and international. Authorities announced that DNA from blood samples taken at the scene matched one of the suspects. Still, there were no arrests.

**Former President
Alvaro Enrique Arzú Irigoyen**

Guatemalan public opinion already had indicted the same culprit that Gerardi had named: the army. These suspicions were intensified when the prosecutor in the case, who had been following the military lead, fled to the United States because of death threats.

In 2001, police arrested army Captain Byron Lima Oliva and his father, retired Colonel Disrael Lima Estrada, in connection with the murder. Police also rearrested Gerardi's cook and issued a warrant for the priest, Mario Orantes, both of whom had been arrested and released in 1998. An intelligence NCO with the presidential guard, Sergeant Major José Obdulio Villanueva, was arrested the next day. It was Villanueva who had killed the milkman in 1996, for which he had been sentenced to five years in prison but arranged to pay a $1,500 fine instead. Orantes was arrested when he returned from the United States to face the charges. A judge subsequently freed Villanueva because of an apparently iron-clad alibi. He was later rearrested, but and the four accused men went on trial in March 2002.

The trial absorbed Guatemala's attention—and that of human rights activists around the world—before the historic verdicts were handed down on June 8, 2002: guilty! The judge sentenced the two Limas and Villanueva to 30 years and Orantes to 20; the cook was acquitted.

The elation of human rights groups over the conviction proved short-lived. Six weeks later, the judge fled the country because of death threats. In September 2002, the four convicted men formally ap-

The author interviews Nobel Laureate Rigoberta Menchú in Guatemala City, December 1999.
Photo by Mario Antonio Sandoval

pealed, and an appeals court overturned their convictions and ordered a new trial, ostensibly because of questionable testimony from one eyewitness. They were not set free, however. In February 2003, Villanueva was killed and decapitated when rival gangs of inmates at his prison north of the capital went on a rampage. It took 800 riot police to quell the disturbance.

The Gerardi case is the subject of the 2007 book, *The Art of Political Murder* (see Bibliography).

Quest for Justice

Some measure of justice for past atrocities also was meted out in November 1998, when three former members of an army-organized civilian militia force were convicted and sentenced to death by lethal injection for their roles in the so-called Rio Negro Massacre in March 1982—during the first days of the Ríos Montt regime—in which 130 Indian peasants were slain. An appeals court overturned the sentences, but they were reinstated in 1999.

Guatemala moved even closer to its long-sought catharsis in February 1999 when the three-member Historical Clarification Commission issued its report after 18 months of investigation into the human rights abuses committed during the civil war. Among its more controversial findings: the More than 200,000 people had been killed during the civil war; there had been 42,000 individual human rights violations, 29,000 of them fatal; 92% of these

violations had been committed by the army; and U.S. businesses and the CIA had pressured the successive Guatemalan governments into suppressing the guerrilla movement by ruthless means, particularly when Ríos Montt was in power.

When the commission presented its report at the National Theater before a crowd of about 2,000 people, mostly relatives of victims, the crowd chanted, *"justicia! justicia!"* President Arzú dutifully attended the ceremony and shook hands with the commission members, but studiously avoided accepting a copy of the report, citing "protocol." This led to cat-calls from the crowd for him to accept the report. Some observers concluded that Arzú's actions were intended to distance the government from the report. Just days later, President Clinton visited Guatemala during his tour of countries affected by Hurricane Mitch and, while stopping short of a formal apology, expressed "regret" for the U.S. role in the human rights abuses.

The quest for justice became an international issue in December 1999 when Guatemala's most illustrious human rights champion, 1992 Nobel Peace Laureate Rigoberta Menchú, flew to Madrid to file a lawsuit before the Spanish Supreme Court against eight past military and civilian figures, including former military strongmen Ríos Montt, Lucas García and Mejía Victores. It was the same court that had requested the extradition of former Chilean dictator Augusto Pinochet from

Britain for alleged human rights abuses the year before.

This author interviewed Menchú in Guatemala shortly before she returned to Spain to testify. She explained that she chose Spain because it had shown its commitment to human rights in the Pinochet case and others. (Ironically, Ríos Montt had served as Guatemala's military attaché to Spain during the 1970s, a consolation prize for having been cheated out of the presidency in the fraudulent 1974 election.)

Among Menchú's complaints was the assault by security forces on the Spanish Embassy in Guatemala in 1980 after it was seized by guerrillas. In the ensuing fire, 39 Spanish diplomats and guerrillas perished, including Menchú's father. She also cited the deaths of her mother and two brothers between 1980 and 1982, and for the deaths of four Spanish priests during the same period. Menchú's eyes filled with tears as she explained that her mother's remains were never found. "I just want to recover my mother's bones and give her a decent burial," she said. Asked if a dialogue between her and Ríos Montt were possible, she said bitterly, "I'd have to wait 2,000 years."

Another milestone in the quest for justice was reached in 2002 when Colonel Juan Valencia, a former assistant director of the presidential guard, was convicted and sentenced to 30 years for ordering the 1990 murder of U.S. anthropologist and human rights activist Myrna Mack. Two of his superiors, however, were acquitted, much to the chagrin of human rights advocates. The Guatemalan government officially acknowledged to the Inter-American Human Rights Commission in Costa Rica in 2003 that the government bore "institutional responsibility" for Mack's death. However, the country's human rights record continued to come under international scrutiny.

The Elections of 1999

The country was focused in 1999 on both a referendum, called the *"Consulta Popular,"* held to ratify the constitutional changes agreed upon in the peace agreement between the government and the guerrillas, and on the upcoming November presidential election. In the *Consulta Popular,* there was an almost unprecedented consensus reached among the *PAN,* the *FRG* and the *URNG.* About 50 complex issues were boiled down to four separate referendum items, including a restructuring of the role of the armed forces in society and the granting of far greater cultural and political autonomy to the indigenous Mayas. Only about 18% of the electorate bothered to vote, and those who

Guatemala

Alfonso Portillo addresses an *FRG* rally a week before the December 26, 1999, runoff.

Photo by the author

Portillo acknowledged candidly, however, that he was seen internationally as the surrogate of a former dictator. "The people in human rights circles don't believe my speeches," he said. "All I ask is, give me the benefit of the doubt. Judge me by my actions." He also assured me he would "not tolerate harassment of the press" by members of his government, something for which Arzú was notorious. It was a promise he would break.

Berger seemed resigned to defeat. "We're going to be a constructive opposition," he said, "not the kind of opposition they were. Anyway, it's only for four years, then the voters will do the same thing to them they did to us." That proved prophetic.

Turnout was predictably low: 40.9%. Portillo won by the anticipated landslide: 1,184,932 of the valid votes, or 68.32%, to 549,407 votes, or 31.68% for Berger. Portillo thus became the first Guatemalan presidential candidate to poll more than 1 million votes.

The Portillo Presidency

The 48-year-old Portillo was inaugurated on January 14, 2000, joining a growing list of Latin American presidents who won on their second attempts. In his address, he vowed to fulfill reforms promised in the peace accords, which the Arzú government had failed to implement, and he pledged to bring the killers of Bishop Gerardi to justice, calling the failure to do so after two years a "disgrace."

did rejected all the initiatives by more than a 2–1 margin. The voters seemed to be saying they were not quite ready for their society to be overhauled by politicians, but with a turnout of 18%, it was clear most Guatemalans didn't care one way or the other.

In the presidential race, Alfonso Portillo, the Ríos Montt stand-in who almost upset Arzú in the 1996 runoff, was renominated by the *FRG*. He had been campaigning for three years, as had Ríos Montt on his behalf.

The *PAN*, meanwhile, dutifully nominated Arzú's hand-picked choice, Guatemala City Mayor Oscar Berger, who quickly had a falling-out with the president when he demonstrated he intended to be his own man.

The *URNG* experienced intra-party bickering between moderates and hardliners, eventually nominating a moderate, Álvaro Colom, an Indian rights advocate and nephew of a well-known leftist politician and mayor of Guatemala City who was assassinated during the presidency of Lucas García. An engineer, Colom himself is Caucasian. The *URNG* became part of a left-wing coalition called the New Nation Alliance (*ANN*).

The campaign took an interesting twist in July when Portillo admitted he shot two men to death in self-defense while teaching in Mexico in 1982. He said had become involved in a local political dispute and that when two members of the rival faction attacked him with firearms. The Mexican authorities declined to prosecute Portillo. Berger (pronounced bear-ZHAY), who is of Belgian descent, tried to make political capital out of this confession, but the polls showed that it had no effect.

This author spent 10 days in Guatemala observing the campaign and interviewing the three major candidates as a freelance journalist. It was obvious voters were more concerned about the blatant corruption and cronyism of the Arzú administration and about the sour economy than they were about the possible influence of Ríos Montt. I sensed a clear shift in public opinion since the last election toward Portillo, whom the public called *"Pollo Ronco,"* or "Hoarse Chicken," because of his raspy, Godfather-like voice.

On November 7, an unexpectedly high 53% turned out to vote. Portillo almost won an outright victory with 48% to 30% for Berger and 12% for Colom; nine lesser candidates split the remainder. The *FRG* won an absolute majority in the newly expanded Congress, 63 of the 113 seats, ensuring Ríos Montt's return to the speaker's chair. (His daughter, Zury, was No. 2 on the party's proportional representation list of deputies.) The *PAN* won 37 seats, the *ANN* nine.

The campaign for the *segunda vuelta* on December 26 seemed almost anticlimactic, as polls showed a Portillo victory inevitable. It drew international attention, however, because of Menchú's lawsuit against Ríos Montt and others. This author spent eight days in Guatemala in December and again interviewed the two candidates.

When I asked Portillo about what impact the lawsuit would have, he said, "None. None. It's a show. There's not a country in the world that can judge something that happened in Guatemala. Rigoberta Menchú doesn't even have followers in her hometown so she's looking for some in Europe."

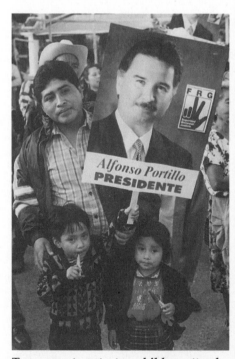

Too young to vote, two children attend a campaign rally with their father

Photo by the author

188

Just four days later, Portillo stunned the Guatemalan political and military establishments as well as the international community by appointing as defense minister a mere colonel, bypassing 19 generals and one admiral. He later appointed Ríos Montt's son to command the army.

Portillo also introduced a military reform package allowing him to appoint a civilian as defense minister. He also promised to abolish the infamous presidential guard, another promise that went unkept.

As many had expected, Portillo and Ríos Montt soon became tangled in a power struggle within the *FRG*, in both the executive and legislative branches. Ríos Montt and 22 other *FRG* deputies were caught up in a scandal involving the illegal altering of the percentage on a revenue bill on liquor from 20% to 10%—after it had passed. Ríos Montt and the other deputies denied they had changed the figure, but a reporter for the daily *Prensa Libre* produced an audiotape of a committee meeting in which the amount had been set at 10%. The press dubbed the scandal "Boozegate." Portillo apparently was not involved, but the allegations against members of his party embarrassed him.

The power struggle continued into 2001. Portillo vetoed five bills supported by Ríos Montt; in apparent retribution, Congress slashed the appropriations for the ministries headed by members of the Portillo faction of the party.

Portillo's image was further tarnished when the daily newspaper *Siglo Veintiuno* and the Panamanian daily *La Prensa* reported they had documentation that the president and Vice President Francisco Reyes had used dummy companies to open Panamanian bank accounts in 2001 designed to receive $1.5 million monthly in deposits. Days later, 3,000 protesters banging pots and pans demonstrated in front of the government palace demanding that Portillo and Reyes resign. Portillo denied the allegations, calling them a smear campaign by "the oligarchy."

Meanwhile, past atrocities kept on surfacing—literally. In 2002, the bodies of 47 people, apparently Indian peasants massacred during the civil war, were unearthed from a mass grave found beneath a school in Rabinal, 120 miles north of the capital.

In 2003, Ríos Montt traveled to Rabinal to attend an *FRG* meeting even as local Mayas were preparing to rebury the remains of 66 of the people who had been excavated from the mass grave. When he arrived, the furious Indians began hurling rocks at him. He escaped unhurt, and with a touch of bitter irony, his legislator-daughter Zury termed the stoning incident a "violation of human rights."

Human rights advocates continued to fault Portillo for failing to keep his promise to abolish the presidential guard. At first, he merely embellished the guard with 70 trained civilians. Sensitive to criticism on the issue, he said he would reduce the guard by 25%, reassign half the remaining members to other duties and remove the guard from army control. The changes were to have been completed in 2003. They were not.

In 2001, the international rights group Amnesty International charged that threats against human rights workers in Guatemala had increased on Portillo's watch.

In April 2002, Guillermo Ovalle, an administrator of the Rigoberta Menchú Foundation, was slain in a hail of automatic weapons fire in broad daylight in the capital. Authorities maintained—as they had in the Gerardi murder almost four years to the day earlier—that it was a common crime, an apparent robbery attempt. Human rights workers excavating the mass graves of victims of army massacres in the 1980s received death threats. Then, in December 2002, two prominent Indian rights activists were abducted and murdered. According to the UN human rights ombudsman in Guatemala, there were 70 murders, attempted murders or death threats against human rights workers in 2002.

In 1999, Portillo had told this author that human rights groups should "judge me by my actions." They did.

On a brighter note, Pope John Paul II made his third visit to Guatemala in late July 2002 to canonize Pedro de San José Betancur (1619–67), son of a shepherd in the Canary Islands, who lived humbly in Antigua, Guatemala and who became a Franciscan brother and preached to prison inmates. He also raised money for orphans, established a hospital for the poor and founded the Antigua-based Bethlehemite Congregation. His grave in Antigua is a place of pilgrimage, and thousands have claimed miracles were granted after touching the tomb.

The Elections of 2003

Berger sought the *PAN* nomination again in 2003, but the party broke up into three factions, with the party regulars nominating Leonel López Rodas, who had labored to keep the party afloat after Berger's poor showing in 1999. A faction loyal to former President Arzú split off and resurrected an old party, the Unionist Party *(PU)*, choosing as its candidate Guatemala City Mayor Fritz Garcia-Gallont. Berger became the candidate of three tiny parties that comprised the Grand National Alliance *(GANA)*. Colom entered the race again, this time as head of a coalition of

Former President Alfonso Portillo

left-wing parties called the National Union of Hope *(UNE)*. There were six minor candidates.

With the judicial appointments Portillo had made over three and a half years, Ríos Montt, by then 77, embarked on a Machiavellian maneuver to circumvent the constitution through the courts and run for the presidency as the *FRG* candidate. The Supreme Electoral Tribunal again barred him from running. He appealed to the Supreme Court, which upheld the electoral tribunal's decision. He then appealed to the Constitutionality Court, which for the first time had a majority of *FRG* justices. In a stunning reversal, the Constitutionality Court voted 4–2 to allow his candidacy.

Ríos Montt's opponents appealed that decision back to the Supreme Court, which granted a stay. What happened next shocked the country and the world, and may have turned the tide irreversibly against Ríos Montt. In an obviously well-orchestrated show of force, hundreds of pro-*FRG* peasants were bused to the capital from the country in exchange for a promise of $40 and three meals a day for two days. They were issued clubs and ski masks.

On Thursday, July 24, they went on a rampage, erecting barricades, burning tires, smashing store windows and demonstrating outside the Supreme Court and the Constitutionality Court. They turned on journalists covering the disturbances, beating some of them or dousing them with gasoline. A 65-year-old television reporter, ironically with a pro-*FRG* station, died of a heart attack while being chased by club-wielding goons. Through it all, the police failed to intervene. Under public

Guatemala

pressure, Portillo announced he would send in troops to maintain order; they never arrived. The disturbances, which the media named *Jueves Negro* (Black Thursday), spilled over into Friday. Then, Ríos Montt gave the order to end the demonstrations, and the goons dispersed.

Incredibly, the *FRG* insisted that it had not instigated *Jueves Negro,* even after newspaper photographs showed well-known *FRG* leaders, including Jorge Arévalo, a high-ranking congressman, and Ríos Montt's niece, involved in the disturbances. Polls for years had suggested that Ríos Montt could win the presidency if he were allowed to run. Now, faced with the reality of Ríos Montt's candidacy, voters began to get cold feet after *Jueves Negro.* He slipped to third, then fourth, then fifth place in the polls.

This author spent six days in Guatemala as a freelance journalist and interviewed Berger, López Rodas and the spokeswoman for the U.N. Verification Mission to Guatemala, who maintained that the *FRG* was in fact responsible for the disturbances as well as threats against opposition journalists.

Ríos Montt, ever wary of foreign journalists, refused me an interview. But his daughter Zury, the *FRG*'s second-ranking figure in Congress after her father, agreed. She accused the "oligarchy" of manipulating the polls. She continued to insist that the *FRG* was blameless for *Jueves Negro,* saying that "the U.N. Mission has become very politicized."

Berger told me he was frankly worried because the *FRG* controlled not only the national government but many municipal governments in the interior.

The campaign continued to be marred by mysterious murders in the interior. Ríos Montt never recovered the ground he lost from *Jueves Negro* to make it into the runoff. On November 9, 55.2% of the electorate went to the polls. The results:

Berger	904,533	34.5%
Colom	694,734	26.5%
Ríos Montt	503,994	19.2%
López Rodas	218,577	8.3%
García-Gallont	79,784	3.0%
Others	222,423	8.6%

Under the complicated proportional representation formula, Berger's new *GANA* coalition emerged as the largest movement in the newly enlarged Congress, with 48 of the 158 seats. The *FRG* was still a major force, finishing second with 42 seats. Colom's *UNE* won 33, the *PAN* won 15 and five other parties won 18.

Berger and Colom embarked on what was a gentlemanly campaign for the *segunda vuelta,* or runoff, in December. The turnout was 46.8%. The results:

Berger	1,235,303	54.13%
Colom	1,046,868	45.87%

It was the closest the Guatemalan left had ever come to tasting victory. Berger's *GANA,* Colom's *UNE* and the *PAN* an-

Former President Oscar Berger

nounced an unorthodox right-center-left legislative coalition, giving them a working majority of 96 seats. The *FRG* was once again in opposition, with Zury Ríos its leader in Congress. She made international headlines a year later by marrying U.S. Representative Jerry Weller, a Republican from Illinois; it was her fourth marriage.

Berger Makes Changes

Berger was sworn in on January 14, 2004, the latest in a growing list of Latin American president elected on their second or subsequent attempts. In his address, Berger promised to crack down on corruption and human rights abuses, something the jaded Guatemalans had heard time and again. In a gesture reminiscent of Andrew Jackson, he flung open the doors of the presidential palace on inauguration day, allowing thousands of ordinary people to visit.

Berger quickly set out to make good on his promises. The day after his inauguration, he appointed Nobel Laureate Rigoberta Menchú as a "goodwill ambassador" to help monitor the 1996 peace accords, something that would have been unthinkable under Portillo. Berger seemed sensitive about his Belgian heritage and his reputation as a member of the ruling elite in the overwhelmingly Mayan country. He appointed Frank LaRue, a leftist activist, as human rights commissioner.

In March 2004, a court ordered Ríos Montt placed under house arrest, not for genocide, but for the death of the journalist on *Jueves Negro.* Six years later, he remains under house arrest, awaiting trial in both Guatemala and Spain.

In a move that once would have provoked a military coup, Berger cut the size

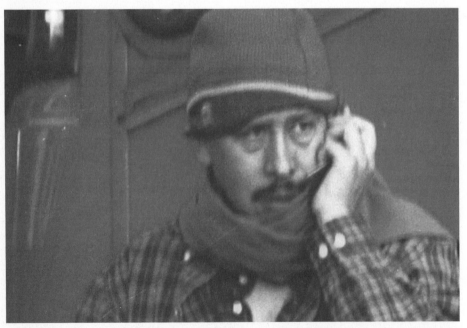

A photographer for the Guatemala City daily *Prensa Libre* snapped this tell-tale photo of Jorge Arévalo, the high-ranking *FRG* congressional deputy who successfully appealed the ban on Efrain Ríos Montt's candidacy, as he lifted his ski mask to use his cell phone during the bloody riots of *Jueves Negro,* July 24, 2003. The *FRG* had denied instigating the disturbances.
Photo courtesy Prensa Libre

of the army almost in half, from 27,000 to 15,500; the savings went to welfare and education. Berger and members of his government received death threats over the cuts. He also did what Arzú and Portillo promised to do but didn't: He disbanded the notorious presidential guard.

Under Berger, both the executive and legislative branches declared war on the country's endemic corruption—a formidable enemy indeed. Transparency International ranked Guatemala as the third most corrupt country in the Western Hemisphere in 2004 (only Haiti and Paraguay were worse) and one of the 23 worst in the world. By 2007, Berger's final year in office, Guatemala had "improved" to the eighth most corrupt in the Western Hemisphere and ranked as 111th most corrupt in the world out of 179 nations.

The government also launched an investigation into Portillo's Panamanian bank accounts. The U.S. government revoked the former president's visa; Portillo fled the country, surfacing in Mexico on a one-year work visa. The auditor released a report stating that $600 million in public funds was unaccounted for over a 12-year period, which also implicated the presidencies of Arzú and de León Carpio, as well as Serrano, whose crookedness was well known. The auditor said about half that amount was bilked from the public health system. Mexico eventually agreed to extradite Portillo in October 2008 in connection with $15 million worth of military kickbacks to him and others while he was president. But instead of Portillo standing trial in Guatemala, in March 2010 a judge granted a U.S. extradition request for him to stand trial there for money laundering.

Racial discrimination had been officially outlawed in 2002 during Portillo's presidency, but no one had ever been prosecuted for it until 2004. Five men with *FRG* ties, including Ríos Montt's grandson, were charged with abuse against Rigoberta Menchú in 2003 when she testified at a hearing against allowing Ríos Montt to run for president. They allegedly shoved her and verbally insulted her, saying, "Go back to selling tomatoes in the market, Indian." In 2005, the five were convicted and sentenced to 38 months each

Although U.N. Secretary-General Kofi Annan warned that the country still had a long way to go in providing rights to the Indian majority, the U.N. Verification Mission for Guatemala was closed in 2004. In its place, however, the U.N. established the International Commission Against Impunity in Guatemala *(CICIG)* in 2006 to investigate past or present human rights violations. It has a staff of 180 and works to assist Guatemalan law enforcement and judicial institutions rather than supplant

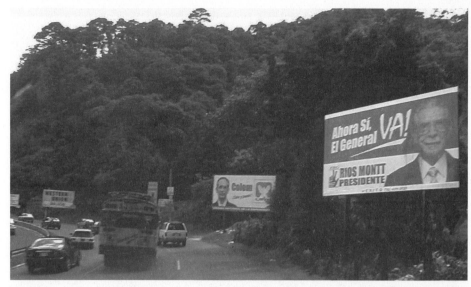

A billboard for former strongman Efrain Ríos Montt looms over the highway between Guatemala City and Antigua. In the background is a billboard for the left-wing presidential candidate Álvaro Colom, who bumped Ríos Montt out of the runoff in the November 9, 2003 election. *Photo by the author*

them. Its two-year mandate was later extended to 2011.

Besides coming to terms with the corruption and rights abuses of the past, Berger had to contend with the growing problem of street crime and an alarmingly high murder rate. In 2005, Guatemala tied with Venezuela for the world's third-highest murder rate, 42 per 100,000 inhabitants; in 2006, it increased to 45. It became so critical that he ordered 1,600 army troops to augment the police in patrolling the streets of the capital and fired his interior minister and police chief. Much of the crime is believed linked to the international *maras,* or street gangs, with roots in

El Salvador and Los Angeles, California (see El Salvador). Drug trafficking also remains a menace. According to some estimates, 75% of the cocaine that enters the United States passes through Guatemala.

The Congress ratified, and Berger signed into law, Guatemala's membership in the proposed Dominican Republic-Central America Free Trade Agreement (DR-CAFTA) with the United States in 2005. The CAFTA vote was briefly delayed in Congress when 4,000 left-wing demonstrators outside the legislative building hurled rocks and bottles at police, who responded with tear gas. Guatemalan participation in CAFTA took effect on July 1, 2006.

The author interviewing winning presidential candidate Oscar Berger in Guatemala City in August 2003. *Photo by Berger staff*

Guatemala

Guatemala was one of the stops on President Bush's five-nation tour of Latin America in March 2007. The brief visit was purely of a goodwill nature, although the extraordinary security resulted in traffic jams that caused more anger than goodwill. Bush visited a Mayan archeological site, after which some Mayan shamans performed an "exorcism." The report that Bush brought his own drinking water offended Guatemalan sensibilities.

The Elections of 2007

As always, the field for the September 9, 2007 presidential and congressional elections was fragmented, with 15 candidates on the presidential ballot. President Berger threw his support behind Alejandro Giammatei, a Christian Democrat who was his prison director, for the *GANA* nomination. Retired General Otto Pérez Molina, who was presidential chief of staff under De León Carpio and was a negotiator for the 1996 peace accords, became the candidate of a new conservative movement called the Popular Party *(PP)*. Colom again became the standard bearer for *UNE*. The *FRG* nominated Luis Rabbé, who was Portillo's minister of communication and had a reputation for corruption. Former Guatemala City Mayor Fritz García-Gallont was again the candidate of Arzú's Unionist Party. Nobel Laureate Rigoberta Menchú declared her candidacy, but the various Indian groups would not coalesce around her.

As usual, the campaign was marred by violence. Between the beginning of the campaign in May and the first round of voting, 40 candidates or party officials, activists or their relatives were killed, 18 of them from Colom's *UNE*. Amnesty International called on the candidates to conduct their campaigns "in a manner consistent with respect for the rule of law and human rights standards." It also attacked "clandestine groups that operate with absolute impunity." Colom said 14 of the *UNE* members killed were slain by "organized crime," a reference to the notorious *maras* that still operate virtually unchecked.

The climate of fear that common crime had created in Guatemala was the overriding issue when five of the candidates appeared for an unprecedented televised debate, which CNN aired throughout the hemisphere. Pérez Molina, whose campaign slogan was *"mano dura"* (stern hand), promised a get-tough approach to the *maras*. Colom, whose kindler, gentler slogan was *"vida, desrarollo y paz"* (life, development and peace), argued that economic reforms and greater socioeconomic equality would help eliminate the root causes of crime.

A total of 3,280,609 valid ballots were cast in the first round, an unusually high turnout of 60.5%. The results:

Colom	926,244	28.23%
Pérez Molina	771,244	23.51%
Giamattei	565,270	17.23%
Rabbé	239,208	7.29%

There were three notable results of the first round: the left had finished in first place for the first time with the tenacious Colom; Ríos Montt's once powerful *FRG* finished in a pitiful fifth place; and Menchú had placed a dismal seventh with a mere 3% of the vote.

In the simultaneous election for the 158 congressional deputies through proportional representation, Colom's *UNE* finished first with 48 seats; *GANA* received 37; Pérez Molina's *PP,* 30; the *FRG,* 15; seven other parties accounted for the remaining 28 seats.

This author covered the November 4 runoff between Colom and Pérez Molina for two newspapers. Polls almost universally favored Pérez Molina, but two factors made the outcome uncertain. One is the reluctance of poll respondents in Guatemala to tell the truth, and Colom's voters were mindful of the retribution directed against *UNE*. Another was the fact that Thursday, November 1, All Saints Day, was a national holiday, and thousands of affluent residents of Guatemala

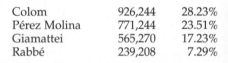

The front page of *Prensa Libre* for November 21, 2004, was bittersweet for the Guatemalan Republican Front (*FRG*) of former strongman Efraín Ríos Montt. At right is a photo from the wedding of his daughter, Zury, the FRG's leader in Congress, who married U.S. Representative Jerry Weller of Illinois. At the left is a headline that reads, "The FRG: Divided and affected by corruption."

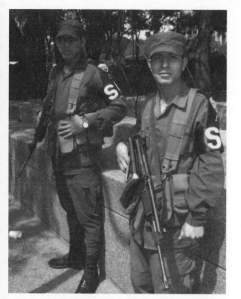

Guatemalan soliders guard the entrance to a polling station in an underground parking garage near the government palace in Guatemala City. *Photo by author*

| Colom | 1,449,153 | 52.82% |
| Pérez Molina | 1,294,645 | 47.18% |

Colom swept 20 of the 22 departments, although Pérez Molina carried the capital handily. Pérez Molina conceded defeat, but without congratulating Colom. Colom's supporters partied well into the night, celebrating the end to their wandering for years in the political wilderness.

The next day, this author attended the president-elect's traditional morning-after press conference. He was flanked by Vice President-elect Rafael Espada, a prominent heart surgeon in Houston, Texas. Colom seemed to bend over backward to dispel any suggestions that he is a left-wing firebrand in the style of Venezuela's Hugo Chávez. Asked whether he would be closer to Washington or to Chávez, Colom replied cautiously that relations with the U.S. "will be more or less as they are now. I hope to strengthen the relationship. We've always been good partners." He said he hoped to visit Washington "when the opportunity arises." (President Bush hosted him at the White House for talks on trade, drugs and immigration in April 2008.)

Colom added that Guatemala also enjoys friendly relations with Venezuela, which he said will continue, but he insisted, "We don't have any special connection." He said he also will maintain friendly relations with Cuba as well with conservative leaders like Colombian President Álvaro Uribe and especially with Mexican President Felipe Calderón, "because we share a common border and are brother peoples."

President Álvaro Colom
Photo by the author

I asked Colom if he were surprised by his upset victory. He smiled sardonically and said, "Polls in Guatemala have often been wrong before. You just have to look at who owns them," a reference to the monied oligarchy. His supporters in the room laughed and applauded.

Colom Battles Crime, Scandal and Hunger

The 56-year-old Colom was inaugurated on January 14, 2008, ushering in what many hoped would be a new era in Guatemalan history. As Colom had suggested, both Chávez and Uribe attended. Colom promised that "today marks the beginning of privileges for the poor and those without opportunity."

In April, Colom fired Victor Rivera, a Venezuelan who had been hired a decade

City—Pérez Molina's core constituency—had opted to take off Friday as well and leave the capital for a four-day weekend.

The overconfident Pérez Molina, like Aesop's hare, made a serious tactical blunder by failing to show up for a televised debate with Colom. Pérez Molina was unquestionably handsomer and more charismatic than Colom, who has gaunt, Lincolnesque features and speaks in a dull, nasal monotone. But Pérez Molina's no-show rubbed many voters the wrong way. So did his *mano dura* slogan, which conjured up ugly memories of the military's past human rights abuses, although Pérez Molina's own hands were apparently clean.

Street crime remained the burning issue in the runoff, and I saw first-hand a disturbing change since my last visit in 2003: coils of razor wire, often electrified, topped the walls around homes, businesses, even churches. The ubiquitous small shops are now fronted with bars, and customers place their orders through them. According to U.N. figures, Guatemala's murder rate of 47 per 100,000 people is the second-highest in the hemisphere's after Colombia's, but Colombia's is declining, while Guatemala's had risen from 31.5 in 2003.

Army troops with automatic weapons and national policemen stood guard outside polling places for Sunday's voting to discourage electoral violence, while army helicopters patrolled overhead. A total of 2,743,798 voters cast ballots, a greatly reduced turnout of 48.3%, which, as expected, was to Colom's advantage. The historic results:

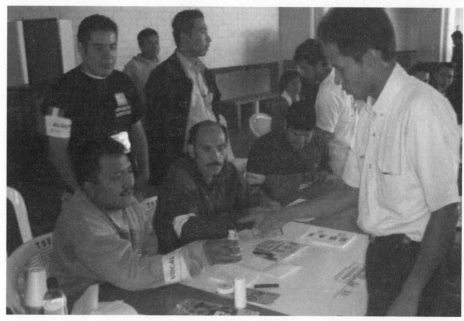

A polling official applies indelible ink to the forefinger of a man who has just cast his ballots for president and Congress on November 4, 2007. It is a traditional Latin American method of preventing repeat voting. *Photo by author*

193

Guatemala

earlier as a security consultant and kidnapping negotiator, but whom human rights groups accused of killing gang members without due process. Colom agreed with Rivera's critics that he had become too powerful. A week after he was fired, Rivera was himself murdered.

The crime situation continued to worsen, and Mexican President Calderón's crackdown on the drug cartels apparently has forced some of them to shuffle their operations into Guatemala, whose institutions are weaker. In 2009, 6,451 murders were recorded in Guatemala; by comparison, 1,951 civilians and 498 U.S. soldiers, a total of 2,449, were killed in Iraq in 2009. Anti-Colom posters appeared showing the president bare-chested with trademark *mara* tattoos.

In September 2008, Colom announced in a CNN interview that hidden microphones and cameras had been discovered in the presidential palace, and he accused drug cartels of planting them to learn of the government's counter-drug efforts.

But of all the killings, the one that shook the Colom administration to its core was the bizarre death of a prominent attorney, Rodrigo Rosenberg, who was gunned down by two assailants while riding a bicycle in the capital on May 10, 2009. A security video showed two gunmen; the second one fired a *coup de grace* into Rosenberg's head. The next day, a video surfaced that Rosenberg had made three days before his death in which he declares, "Unfortunately, if you are watching this message, it is because I was assassinated by President Álvaro Colom, with help from Gustavo Alejos."

Alejos is Colom's private secretary. Rosenberg also accused the president's wife, Sandra Torres, other presidential aides and various bankers and businessmen of involvement in the April 2009 murders of businessman Khalil Musa, Rosenberg's client, and Musa's daughter, who was Rosenberg's girlfriend. Rosenberg alleged on the video the Musas were killed because they refused to participate in a corruption scheme involving the government's Rural Development Bank, which he called a "den of thieves, drug traffickers and murderers." Rosenberg said he himself was marked for death for publicly alleging the government's involvement in the Musa murders.

"El caso Rosenberg" became an overnight media sensation in Guatemala and was picked up by international media; the video also was aired on YouTube. Colom went on national television the same night to plaintively deny any complicity in Rosenberg's death by himself, his wife or others. The government Web site blamed Rosenberg's death on "organized crime" and accused Colom opponents of exploiting Rosenberg's death to discredit him. Nonetheless, Rosenberg's death became a *cause célèbre* that brought hundreds of thousands of violence-weary Guatemalans into the streets to protest. The U.N.'s International Commission Against Impunity in Guatemala *(CICIG)*, headed by a Spanish judge, began a six-month investigation into Rosenberg's death that involved more than 300 crime experts from 11 countries.

Seven men, including a policeman and several *mara* members, were arrested in September 2009 in connection with Rosenberg's murder, but still unsolved was who hired them or why. In January 2010, the commission released its findings, which concluded that Rosenberg, despondent over his girlfriend's murder, his impending second divorce and his mother's death, and bitter against the Colom government for failing to apprehend the Musas' killers, engineered an elaborate suicide scheme to discredit the government. The report found he paid for his own hitmen. Two brothers wanted in connection with the hit turned themselves in in June. Colom expressed relief over what he saw as his and his wife's exoneration, but some Guatemalans remained skeptical.

Guatemala's violent crime again made international headlines in April 2009, when five policemen were killed in a shootout with drug traffickers; the police were allegedly trying to *steal*, not seize, 750 kilos of cocaine. In August, Colom sacked his national police chief for allegedly stealing drugs and cash and replaced him with Baltazar Gómez. In September, four prison

The front pages of *Prensa Libre*, *Siglo Veintiuno* and *Nuestro Diario* on **Monday, November 5, 2007**, proclaim the upset election victory of Álvaro Colom the day before.

Photo by author

194

officials—an assistant director, a warden and two guards—were shot to death within five hours in an obviously coordinated gang attack. Interior Minister Raúl Velásquez attributed the assassinations to *mara* members in reprisal for the transfer of gang members to a higher-security prison and for a crackdown on the smuggling of goods and weapons into prisons. Ten similar attacks occurred over the next month, leaving nine policemen and other people dead and nine wounded. Velásquez himself was later fired and has remained in hiding.

The *CICIG* investigated the deaths of the five police officers, and in March 2010 the jaded country was stunned again by the news that Police Chief Gómez and Nelly Bonilla, the top counter-narcotics official, had been arrested for drug trafficking and conspiring to thwart the investigation into the fatal incident.

In a case of awkward timing, U.S. Secretary of State Hillary Clinton visited Guatemala a few days later to discuss the drug trafficking crisis.

In other matters, Colom went on national television in September 2009 to declare a "state of national calamity" because of widespread malnutrition, which had become exacerbated by a drought. Colom theorized that the declaration would facilitate international food aid to 300,000 needy people. He cited U.N. statistics showing Guatemala with the highest rate of malnutrition in Latin America and fourth-highest in the world, although its per capita income is higher than many other countries with lower rates of malnutrition. Half of Guatemala's children under the age of 5 were undernourished, he said. UNICEF estimates that in the predominantly indigenous rural areas, child undernourishment could be as high as 80%, and stunted growth is widespread.

Also in September, the government released a report that concluded that at least 333 children had been stolen by the army during the civil war and sold through international adoption agencies, similar to what happened during the Dirty War in Argentina.

Culture: The culture of modern Guatemala represents a composite of traditional Mayan and colonial Spanish. Although the mixing of the two bloods has produced a *mestizo* element called by the locals *"Ladino,"* the majority of the population remains unassimilated, pure-blood Indians of Mayan descent who speak a number of dialects, the most widely spoken being Quiché. The Mayan heritage has largely shaped the country's rich folklore in art and music, much to the benefit of the country's tourist industry. Guatemalans take special pride in their *marimba*

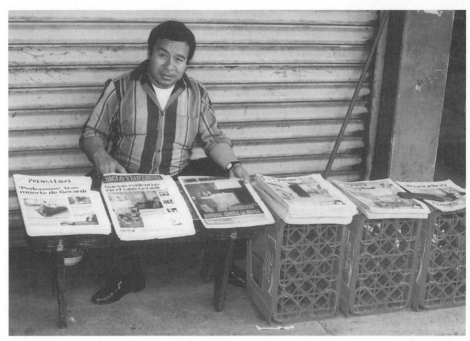

A street vendor hawks copies of six different daily newspapers. *Photo by the author*

bands, which often greet arriving visitors at the capital's airport.

Guatemala's religious practices are among the most curious in Latin America. Roman Catholicism never firmly took root, despite efforts by zealous colonial-era priests to force or entice the Indians away from their pagan practices. Eventually, the Church came to realize that it would have better results with a little more tolerance. Today, in towns such as Chichicastenango, visitors can see Indians practicing their tribal rites inside the Catholic cathedral. The shallow roots of Catholicism also made Guatemala a promising target for the proselytizing of U.S.-based evangelical Protestantism. Today an estimated one third of the population are zealous, "born-again" fundamentalists; among the converts were former strongman Efraín Ríos Montt and former President Jorge Serrano.

An abysmally low literacy rate, combined with chronic dictatorship and political violence, forced many of Guatemala's talented writers, artists and musicians to work abroad. But the cultural glass is far from empty. The country's most eminent writer was Miguel Angel Asturias (1899–1974), probably best remembered for his novel, *El Señor Presidente*. In 1967, Asturias became only the second Latin American to receive the Nobel Prize for Literature.

Former President Juan José Arévalo (1904–90) was a noted literary figure as well, and also served as ambassador to Israel.

Another internationally acclaimed literary figure was short story writer Augusto Monterroso, who went into exile to Mexico in 1944 during the Ubico dictatorship and remained there until his death in 2003 at the age of 81. He received Spain's prestigious Prince of Asturias Award, and his story *El dinosaurio (The Dinosaur)* is reputed to be the shortest story in any language. It contained seven words: *"Cuando despertó, el dinosaurio todavía estaba allí."* ("When he awoke, the dinosaur was still there.")

Illiteracy and political violence also took its toll on the development of the Guatemalan press. Dozens of journalists, from newspaper publishers to reporters, were murdered by one side or the other during the 36-year civil war that ended in December 1996. There is only a handful of daily newspapers, all of them relatively young and all published in the capital, and even fewer magazines. The oldest, most prestigious newspaper, and the circulation leader until 2000, is *Prensa Libre*, founded in 1951. *Siglo Veintiuno* began publishing in 1991 and has become the country's second prestigious daily, winning high marks for its quality and reliability. Both papers now publish sensational, working-class tabloids as well. *Nuestro Diario*, published by *Prensa Libre*, has a circulation of 300,000, the greatest in Central America and a phenomenal number given the high illiteracy rate.

Radio is a popular, and influential, medium in Guatemala because of the poverty and illiteracy. The three privately owned over-the-air television stations are monopolized by a Mexican, Angel González, who is married to a Guatemalan; critics charge that his ownership, and the monopoly, are illegal, but he has managed to remain friendly with all the powers that

Guatemala

be, no matter what their political leanings. In 2003, a new cable channel, Guatevisión, broke González's television monopoly and reaches 300,000 homes. Its independent news reporting is especially popular. More than 90% of Guatemalan homes now have cable television, exceeded in Latin America only by Argentina.

Economy: Guatemala's economy is based almost entirely on agriculture. Major cash crops include coffee, bananas, beef and cotton, with coffee the main export crop. Most farmland is controlled by huge estates—the top 2% of the population owns more than 60% of the farmland. The large Indian population lives outside the formal economy on small plots in the highlands.

Light industry has grown, but economic development remains handicapped by the traditional, largely feudal economic system. Also impeding development are communications problems caused by the large number of Indian dialects used in Guatemala.

Although the devastating earthquake of 1976 affected the nation's productivity by damaging the infrastructure, economic output survived largely intact. Major cash crops, produced mostly along the coastal regions, were unaffected.

Efforts to root out corruption, a national pastime in Guatemala, have shown some results. Officials who heretofore would have gotten away with enriching themselves have been going to jail. In 2004, Transparency International ranked Guatemala the third most corrupt nation in the Western Hemisphere and one of the 23 most corrupt in the world; by 2008, it had "improved" to 10th most corrupt in the region, and in 2009, it was 14th most corrupt.

Guatemala was heavily affected by Hurricane Mitch in 1998. The human toll was 268 dead, 121 missing and 734,198 adversely affected. Ninety-eight bridges were destroyed, 60% of the roads were damaged and 45–60% of the corn crop, so vital for domestic consumption, was destroyed.

The hurricane could be only partially blamed for the grave downturn in the economy in 1998–99, sparked by a drop in coffee prices. Real GDP dropped by –6.2%.

GDP showed modest but steady growth of 3.3% in 2000, 2.3% in 2001 and 2.2% in 2002, which barely recovered the ground lost in 1999 and failed to keep up with population growth. Growth remained meager until 2006, when it increased by 12.1%. Growth was 6.3% in 2007 and 4% in 2008, but as elsewhere in Latin America, the global recession led to a decline in 2009 of –0.5%. Tropical Storm Agatha in May 2010 was expected to have a negative impact on the economy.

Guatemala remains the seventh poorest nation in the Western Hemisphere, and it has one of the world's greatest disparities in distribution of wealth. An estimated 75% of the population lives below the poverty line.

Since 2003, the dollar has circulated alongside the *quetzal* and is accepted as legal tender.

In 2005, Guatemala ratified the Dominican Republic-Central American Free Trade Agreement with the United States. Guatemala's participation went into effect on July 1, 2006. As a result, foreign direct investment increased from $353 million in 2006 to $535 million in 2007.

The Future: Guatemalans now have elected six presidents since the restoration of democracy; they were bitterly disillusioned with the first four and blasé about the fifth. They have never returned a ruling party to power. It is hard to blame them. The first president was a playboy who showed little interest in improving the country. The second tried to become a dictator and remains in Panama after fleeing with $25 million from the treasury. The third succeeded in ending the civil war, but was disliked for his handling of the economy and for his elitism. The fourth was the stand-in for a former dictator accused of genocide and went into self-imposed exile in Mexico, extradited in 2008 to stand trial for corruption.

Oscar Berger, the most able and most honest of the five elected presidents, came the closest to overcoming his countrymen's cynicism and establishing their faith in their democracy and their institutions, although the problem of violent, organized crime is worse than ever.

In the periodic *Latinobarómetro* poll published in the British newsmagazine *The Economist*, the percentage of Guatemalans who say that democracy is preferable to any other form of government nosedived from 50% in 1996 to just 33% in 2003, the last year of the corrupt and repressive Portillo presidency. Under Berger, support for democracy rose to 41% in 2006, but in 2007, an election year, it dropped again to 32%, the lowest of the 17 Latin American countries in the survey. At the same time, the percentage who believe authoritarianism is sometimes preferable to democracy rose from 21% in 1996 to 33% in 2007—the second-highest after Paraguay. Guatemala and Paraguay were the only nations in the survey where support for authoritarianism was actually *higher* than that for democracy. In 2008, the first full year of the presidency of Álvaro Colom, support for democracy rose slightly to 34% while support for authoritarianism dropped to 27%—hardly a cause for cheering. In 2009, support for democracy jumped to 42%, but support for authoritarianism also climbed, to 30%, one point behind Paraguay.

Colom, elected on his third attempt, is the first candidate of the left to win since Jacobo Arbenz in 1950. But just how "leftist" is Colom? He is a civil engineer and small businessman who comes from the country's ruling Caucasian minority. When I interviewed him in 1999 during his first run for the presidency and asked him how a man of European ancestry became the candidate of a coalition championing Indian rights, he replied, "One man can serve as a bridge." From what this author has seen, Colom is no bogeyman like Hugo Chávez but a man of even temperament and deliberate judgment who is pragmatic enough to know he must learn to coexist with the military and the ruling business elite for whom he has expressed such hostility.

Colom's eventual victory was foretold in 1999 by my friend and consultant on Guatemalan politics, Mario Antonio Sandoval of the prestigious daily *Prensa Libre* and its cable TV affiliate, *Guatevisión*, an objective and respected journalist. He predicted Guatemala would elect a candidate of the left in 2007 "because it's the only thing they haven't tried."

Sandoval also proved a prophet by expressing serious concern about the growing influence of Colom's wife, Sandra Torres de Colom, and sister-in-law, Gloria Torres. Colom appointed his wife as head of the Social Cohesion Council, which gives her a great deal of authority over government officials and which oversees a $250 million budget, 5% of the total budget. He named his sister-in-law as his liaison to the country's municipal governments. Sandoval described Sandra Torres as "the real power behind the throne, a Guatemalan Cristina Kirchner or Hillary Clinton." Now she is widely believed to harbor her own presidential ambitions for 2011, although legal opinions vary on whether the 1985 constitution's provision against nepotism would preclude her candidacy. Media commentaries have been critical of the idea.

Colom is making a valiant effort to combat Guatemala's violent crime and the corruption that has permeated law enforcement. He also deserves credit for his efforts to tackle Guatemala's inexcusably shocking rate of malnutrition and undernourishment, especially among indigenous children, who look as emaciated as those of Somalia or Sudan. The fact that no prior democratic president, all from the ruling oligarchy, made such an effort is a national disgrace. Whether the people benefiting from Colom's food distribution will reward his party in 2011 is an open question. Polls show the indigenous majority is still more concerned with the violent crime wave. Besides not feeling hungry, they desperately want to just feel *safe*.

The Cooperative Republic of Guyana

A diver prepares to look for diamonds in the Essequibo River

Area: 82,978 square miles.

Population: 772,298 in 2009 (estimated).

Capital City: Georgetown (Pop. 215,000, estimated).

Climate: Tropically hot and humid; there are heavy rains from April to August and from November to January.

Neighboring Countries: Suriname (East); Brazil (South and West); Venezuela (West).

Official Language: English.

Other Principal Tongues: Various East Indian dialects.

Ethnic Background: East Indian (about 52%), African and mulatto (about 41%), European and mixed (about 7%).

Principal Religion: Christianity (Anglican Protestant).

Other Principal Religions: Roman Catholic Christianity, Hinduism, Islam.

Chief Commercial Products: Bauxite, sugar, rice, aluminum, shrimp, molasses, timber, rum, diamonds.

Currency: Guyana Dollar.

Gross Domestic Product: U.S. $1.21 billion in 2009, estimated ($1,566 per capita).

Former Colonial Status: Colony of the Dutch West India Company (1616–1796); British Colony (1796–1966).

Independence Date: May 26, 1966.

Chief of State: Bharrat Jagdeo (b. January 23, 1964), president (since August 11, 1999).

National Flag: A yellow field bordered in green with black, red and white triangles from top to bottom along the staff.

Guyana lies on the northeast coast of South America. A narrow (5 to 10 miles wide) ribbon of swampy plain extends along the 200-mile length of the coastline. Much of this land lies below sea level and is intersected by large rivers requiring a complex system of dikes and canals to protect it from both floods and drought. Annual rainfall averages 80 to 100 inches and the country is hot the year round; the daily temperature variation of 10° F is greater than the seasonal changes. This coastal region is the country's principal agricultural area and contains some 90% of the population.

Inland from the coastal plains, the land rises to natural grassy plains with poor soils and scrub bush. It is here that gold, diamonds and bauxite are found. Further inland, heavily forested hills rise to the base of the Guiana Highlands, with elevations of over 8,000 feet on the Guyana-Venezuela border, rising out of the forests in vertical red cliffs of 2,000 feet. Rivers flowing out of the highland produce spectacular falls as they drop to the lowlands.

Guyana's principal rivers, the Corantijn on the Suriname frontier, the Berbice and the Essequibo, which flow into the Atlantic at Georgetown, are navigable for only short distances because of falls and rapids—yet they are of major importance as means of communication in the roadless interior.

History: The Dutch first settled on the banks of the Essequibo River as early as 1596, but permanent settlements were not established until the Dutch West India Company started its operations about 1620. The Dutch drained the swamps and lagoons and initiated the system of dikes and canals which make the coastal plain habitable. The Spanish and Portuguese conquerors of the lands to the west and south saw no apparent value in the Guianas and did not molest the British, French and Dutch settlers of the region.

British forces captured the Dutch settlement in 1796, and the territory now incorporated into Guyana was ceded to the British in 1814. In 1831, the colony was officially named British Guiana. The British confined themselves to plantation operations along the coast and some lumbering along the rivers. Sugar, rice and cotton were the principal crops.

Forebears of the current population arrived in two different groups. Africans came in the 17th and 18th centuries to work the plantations. With the abolition of slavery in 1830, Asian peoples migrated from India, China and southeast Asia, and they now account for the largest element in the population. During the 19th century, the British further developed the drainage system and built roads and railroads in an effort to open the interior for settlement and exploitation of the mineral wealth. However, few people moved to that area. Descendants of the Africans have tended to gather in the urban areas as mechanics and tradesmen; the Asians have remained on the farms and plantations along the coast. Despite Guyana's size, the habitable land is overcrowded and the interior is uninhabited except for a few aboriginal Indians.

Politically, the British started tutoring the people of Guyana for independence after World War II. Self-government, which was planned for 1962, had to be postponed until 1966 because of bitter

Guyana

racial friction between the Asian and African sectors. Cheddi Jagan, leftist leader of the Asian people, was premier during most of these four years. His open sympathy with world communism and policies directed against those of African descent led to his defeat, and Forbes Burnham, of African descent, became prime minister. A constitutional change of 1965 provided for proportional representation of the two communities in the parliament, called the National Assembly, and the election of moderate leaders in 1964 made possible the granting of independence in 1966.

Under Burnham's leadership, racial tensions eased, although scattered disturbances surfaced occasionally. Burnham was re-elected in 1968, easily defeating Jagan. During his second term, he emphasized broadening the base of the economy and a neutral foreign policy. To reduce dependence on sugar exports, he gave more attention to development of other crops.

Burnham started moving toward the political left in 1970, declaring Guyana to be a "cooperative republic" and establishing 1,200 small worker cooperatives. The government began taking over the foreign-owned bauxite mining operations in 1971. Burnham was elected in 1973 to a third term, again defeating Jagan. His People's National Congress (PNC) won 37 seats in the 57-member Assembly to 14 for Jagan's People's Progressive Party (PPP).

Burnham's main strength came from blacks who live in the cities, while Jagan dominated the East Indian vote in the rural areas. Although Asians comprised 52% of the population compared to 40% who were black, Burnham skillfully garnered his winning margins through political patronage and by espousing ideas originally proposed by his opponent.

Both Burnham and Jagan were dedicated Marxists. In 1976, the government nationalized the huge British-owned sugar industry—the last remaining major foreign investment in Guyana. Steps were taken to control the insurance, banking and rum industries, so that the state ultimately controlled 85% of the economy.

With Burnham continuing his swing to the left, he gained the unexpected endorsement of Jagan for his economic programs. This political accommodation brought an unfamiliar tranquility to Guyana, which was short-lived.

World attention of an unwanted sort was focused on Guyana in November 1978 when 913 members of a bizarre religious cult from California living in an isolated, newly constructed jungle settlement of Jonestown, named for its messianic leader, Jim Jones, committed suicide after drinking a concoction laced with cyanide.

Burnham decreed a new constitution in 1980 that gave him increased control over opposition political parties and the judicial system. Three months later, he won another five-year term in office.

A 140-year-old border dispute with Venezuela erupted anew in 1982 with Venezuelan incursions into Guyana. This latest dispute had been smoldering since 1962, when Venezuela suddenly declared the 1899 accords (which the United States helped to arrange between Britain and Venezuela) void. The dispute has quietly faded into the background since 1988, which marked state visits by the heads of the respective nations to each other. It threatens to flare up again, however, because of vast untapped oil desposits believed to lie in the disputed zone.

Burnham died of heart failure in 1985 after minor throat surgery in Moscow. Although he had made plans for his family to take over Guyana, surprisingly the party endorsed his vice president, Desmond Hoyte. Balloting in a subsequent election gave the PNC 42 of the 53 seats in the National Assembly; Jagan claimed the contest was rigged.

President Hoyte, realizing that the collapsing Soviet Union offered no economic hope for Guyana, dropped all pro-Soviet rhetoric and traditional communist pronouncements and actively sought closer ties with Western nations. He personally visited the United States to encourage investment (without results). Energetic plans were initiated to get the state out of business and to drastically cut govern-

Guyana

ment personnel. Credit became available from the International Monetary Fund and the United States as a result. Hoyte wisely began including talented Asians at top levels within his administration.

Elections in October 1992, considered the fairest ever held in Guyana, ended the PNC's 28 years in power. The outcome was totally unexpected, because in 1991–92 Guyana's economy had hummed along well, and conditions had improved considerably. Usually in times of prosperity voters settle for what they have. But Jagan led the PPP to an upset victory, gaining a working majority of 35 seats in the Assembly. This was *not* the old Cheddi Jagan. He also had dropped all illusions of Marxism and was able to portray himself as a moderate progressive rather than as a radical leftist.

With the typical zeal of the newly converted, Jagan implemented sweeping economic changes. From its high of 105% in 1989, inflation was reduced to 4.5% in 1996. That same year, he signed an agreement to reduce Guyana's debt to the Paris Club of creditor nations by two thirds. The erstwhile Marxist also opened Guyana's agricultural, mining and forestry sectors to foreign investors. Foreign economists praised Guyana's example as one of the most successful adjustments from a state-controlled to a free-market system. That legacy proved to be Jagan's requiem. On February 16, 1997, the 78-year-old president suffered a serious heart attack. He was taken to Washington, where he died on March 6. Prime Minister Samuel Hinds was sworn in to succeed Jagan. Hinds then named Jagan's widow, Chicago-born Janet Rosenberg Jagan, as Guyana's first woman prime minister.

For the presidential and parliamentary elections of December 15, 1997, Hoyte again stood as presidential candidate for the PNC, but President Hinds stood aside to allow Mrs. Jagan to be the standard-bearer of the PPP. Mrs. Jagan insisted she was running reluctantly to fulfill a deathbed wish of her husband. But Hoyte accused her of nepotism and of seeking to establish a nation of "Jagana." Race also played a role in the campaign, with Hoyte supporters denouncing her as "that Caucasian old lady" and alleging that she still carries a U.S. passport. In reality, Mrs. Jagan's Guyanese credentials were impeccable. She had lived there for 54 years and had lost her U.S. citizenship when she voted in British Guiana in 1947. She had served time in jail with her husband during the independence struggle in the 1950s.

In balloting that the PNC immediately denounced as rigged, Mrs. Jagan unofficially received 191,332 votes to 144,359 for Hoyte. She was hastily inaugurated just four days later, publicly defying a court injunction the PNC had obtained to block the ceremony. Hinds became prime minister. Although observers from the Organization of American States pronounced the elections fair, PNC loyalists embarked on a month of street protests, some quelled by army troops and police using tear gas. To help defuse the volatile situation, a negotiating team from the Caribbean Community (Caricom), headed by former Barbados Prime Minister Henry Forde, brokered an agreement between Mrs. Jagan and Hoyte that called for an end to street demonstrations and the institution of constitutional reforms.

The deal was a remarkable concession for Mrs. Jagan's government, because it called for new elections within three years, two years short of her constitutional mandate. Under the agreement, the constitutional reforms would be worked out within 18 months, and the elections would come within 18 months after that. Although the unrest quieted down, the personal animosity between Jagan and Hoyte lingered.

Hoyte and other critics of Jagan blamed her unreconstructed Marxism for discouraging badly needed foreign investments; her government, they noted, steadfastly refused to consider tax incentives, which drove potential investors to other, more inviting countries. Despite her life-long devotion to Marxism, however, Jagan pragmatically but grudgingly moved to privatize some cumbersome state-controlled enterprises, including the airline and a bauxite operation. Such economic reforms paid dividends in 1999, when the World Bank and the IMF granted Guyana $256 million in relief for its $1.09 billion national debt under the Heavily Indebted Poor Countries initiative that rewards countries that implement painful but needed reforms. Guyana was only the third country to receive such debt relief under this program.

President Bharrat Jagdeo

A New Generation

A chronic heart condition forced Jagan to undergo treatment in the United States, and on August 11, 1999, she resigned. Although Prime Minister Hinds was in line to succeed her, he deferred in favor of the finance minister, Bharrat Jagdeo, who, at 35, became the youngest head of state in the hemisphere. The departure of Jagan did little to defuse the tense political rivalry between the PNP and the PPP, however, as Hoyte refused to recognize Jagdeo's government.

But in 2000, Jagdeo's main preoccupation was the long-simmering border disputes with both Venezuela to the west and Suriname to the east. In May, Venezuela issued a formal protest over a concession that Guyana had granted to a Texas company to construct a $100 million satellite launching facility in the disputed Essequibo region. Venezuela called the concession an "unfriendly act" and called on the Guyanese government to "review" it. The site was chosen because of its proximity to the Equator, which makes it easier to launch heavy payloads into geosynchronous orbits. The European Space Agency has a similar facility in nearby French Guiana.

Then, in June 2000, Suriname ordered a Canadian oil drilling company to tow its offshore platform from what it claimed was Surinamese territorial waters in the Atlantic Ocean. Like the Essequibo dispute with Venezuela, this dispute dates to colonial times. At issue is which bank of the Corantijn River forms the boundary between the two countries. The river empties into a V-shaped gulf, and the border is extended into the Atlantic Ocean. It was in that narrow disputed corridor that Guyana had granted a drilling concession to the Toronto-based company, which reluctantly towed its expensive platform into undisputed Guyanese waters and waited for the two countries to resolve the matter diplomatically.

Hugh Desmond Hoyte

Guyana

Each country accused the other of moving troops up to their common land border. The two governments then agreed to a series of talks, first in Georgetown, then in Paramaribo, which ended in failure. Another round of talks in July also failed, and further talks were put on hold because of the campaign for the March 2001 election in Guyana. Meanwhile, each country made tragicomic attempts to build up its minuscule military force. Guyana, which has no navy, purchased two aging British and three U.S. warships, while Suriname beefed up its existing navy. There is far more at stake in the 7,700 square-mile disputed zone than water and fish; it sits atop an estimated 15 billion barrels of oil which, at a time of rising oil prices, could prove a jackpot for both of these impoverished nations. On September 21, 2007, a U.N. tribunal awarded most of the disputed tract to Guyana. The Canadian firm was planning to resume operations in 2009.

The Elections of 2001

The general elections originally had been scheduled for January 2001, but an independent electoral commission, headed by the highly respected retired Major General Joseph Singh, concluded they could not be held before March. In December 2000, Jagdeo, after consulting with Hoyte, moved them back to March 19. Because of the ugliness of the disputed 1997 elections, the 2001 contest drew an unusual amount of international scrutiny: 170 observers from six organizations and 45 nationalities. The election was carried out with a minimum of discord.

The results were a resounding victory for the incumbent Jagdeo and his PPP, which had an electoral alliance with the small Civic Party: 209,031 votes, or 53% to 164,074, or 42%, for Hoyte's PNC. In the 65-seat Assembly, the PPP-C won an outright majority of 35 seats, the PNC won 27 and minor parties took the remaining three. Despite the clear-cut results, which the international observers termed fair and honest, the PNC filed a formal complaint with the electoral commission, claiming thousands of opposition voters had been turned away at the polls. Meanwhile, disgruntled PNC supporters went on a rampage in Georgetown, looting shops and torching a gas station. Police used tear gas to restore order. It was politics as usual in Guyana.

Not long after the election violence, the international human rights group Amnesty International accused Guyanese police of operating death squads that had allegedly summarily executed as many as 15 criminal suspects. The government denied the allegations.

Political violence erupted once again in July 2002 when pro-PNC demonstrators staged protests outside Jagdeo's office, apparently in an effort to embarrass the president, who was hosting a summit of leaders of the 14 Caribbean Community countries. In the ensuing violence, two protesters were killed and six wounded. Jagdeo called the incident an assassination attempt.

The political landscape changed dramatically with Hoyte's sudden death in December 2002. The partisan tension was evident even at his funeral, when Bagdeo magnanimously delivered a eulogy to his fallen rival but was sometimes drowned out by PNP hecklers.

Early in 2003, the PNP members of Parliament staged a boycott that lasted several months. The stalemate between the two parties ended when the PNP elected Robert Corbin as leader of the opposition. On May 2, 2003, which President Bagdeo termed an "historic" day, he and Corbin sealed a pact that they termed "Constructive Engagement," by which the PNP ended its parliamentary boycott and Bagdeo appointed a nine-member Ethnic Relations Commission with powers to investigate and punish incidents of racial injustice. It was not to last, however.

In March 2004, the PNP staged a mass demonstration to investigate the mysterious killings of 40 black criminals by what was believed to be a death squad called the Phantom Gang, allegedly headed by Home Affairs Minister Ronald Gajraj. Supposedly, firearms and telephone records were traced to Gajraj's office. The United States and Canada, without explanation, revoked his visas. Gajraj denied the allegations and offered to step aside. Bagdeo at first declined his offer. Corbin, meanwhile, withdrew from the Constructive Engagement agreement and resumed the PNP's boycott of Congress.

Bagdeo appointed an investigative commission, but Corbin, still dissatisfied, refused to cooperate with it or to abide by its results. The situation became more volatile in June 2004, when George Bacchus, an Afro-Guyanese rancher who had made the initial accusation of a death squad on national television, was shot to death at his home by unknown assailants. Bacchus was about to testify in the trial of two men accused of killing Bacchus' brother. Bacchus had claimed that his brother was slain by death-squad members who mistook his brother for him. Meanwhile, the magistrate hearing the case resigned because of death threats. The PNP accused the government of complicity in Bacchus' death.

Gajraj eventually stepped down pending the outcome of the commission's inquiry. In April 2005, the commission formally exonerated Gajraj of any direct complicity in

the death squads although it acknowledged he had an "unhealthy" relationship with organized crime figures and had illegally interfered with firearms licenses. He was reinstated as home affairs minister, which sparked complaints from the U.S. State Department, the European Union and the Guyana Human Rights Association.

The latest killing to shock the country was that of Bagdeo's agriculture minister, Satyadeo Sawh, in April 2006. Several gunmen burst into Sawh's home and killed him, his brother and sister and a security guard. It was not clear whether it was a common robbery or a political assassination.

Guyana achieved some international prestige in 2006 when it assumed chairmanship of the 20-member Rio Group.

The Elections of 2006

After the violence of 2001, the nation braced itself for the worst in the presidential-parliamentary elections of August 28, 2006. A new element was a third force, the Alliance for Change, which apparently expected to become a power broker between the two major parties. It did well, but not well enough to become a kingmaker. The results:

PPC	183,867	54.6%	36 seats
PNC	114,608	34.0%	21 seats
Alliance	28,366	8.4%	5 seats
Others	9,514	8%	2 seats

Lesser parties took the remaining two seats. The turnout was 70%, high by U.S. and Latin American standards, but a disappointing drop from the 92% in 2001. Contrary to expectations, the 2006 election was relatively peaceful.

Local elections have not been held since 1994. They were finally scheduled for April 2010, but were postponed again.

Culture: The people of Guyana have adopted the culture of the British ruling elite of the past century. Schooled through the elementary grades, their literacy rate is higher than those in neighboring nations. There are few cultural traits reflecting the origin of the African community; the Asian community still retains some of its original customs, especially in marriage and family relations.

Economy: Despite large mineral and forest resources, Guyana's economy is agricultural and severely limited to foreign markets. Much of the nation's sparsely settled but potentially rich interior is also claimed by Venezuela. Efforts to populate this inhospitable region have been unsuccessful.

Although the ambitious Burnham sought to convert Guyana into a Marxist state, change was initially gradual in an attempt to avoid the disruptions that occurred in Cuba and in Chile. But after 1982, all curbs in the march toward socialism disappeared. The result was disastrous. The purchasing power of the average citizen declined by 40% compared to 1976 figures.

The state-owned bauxite operation, called *Guybau*, showed a profit largely because of high world prices, which have since declined. Before the romance with communism, farm output was constant; rice and sugar exports initially rose after independence. In 1977, Guyana applied for formal association with *Comecon*, the communist bloc's common market. Yet, Guyana also became a member of the Inter-American Development Bank, a Washington-based organization of the OAS.

Strikes in 1983 and 1984 resulted in a sharp decline in bauxite production. Guyana's economic situation deteriorated dreadfully in 1984–86. Negotiations with the International Monetary Fund were suspended and the IMF declared Guyana ineligible for further assistance. There initially was no improvement under Hoyte, who inherited an economy that had de-scended to primitive agriculture. Eventually, the Hoyte administration brought some modest prosperity. Although strict conditions imposed by the IMF were resented, they were successful.

The Omai gold mine was Guyana's largest enterprise, but it closed in 2005.

Throughout most of the 1990s, Guyana experienced extraordinary GDP growth averaging 7% a year. Unlike many of its Latin American neighbors that were cursed by dependence on one export commodity, Guyana was blessed with diversified exports, including bauxite (aluminum ore), gold, timber, sugar, shrimp and rice. But the robust growth halted abruptly in 1998, when the Asian financial crisis and *El Niño* both hit Guyana. World market prices for timber, gold, bauxite and sugar all fell; timber exports alone dropped 35% because of the crisis in Asia, the major consumer of Guyanese wood. Only rice exports showed an increase. As a result, GDP growth for 1998 declined by 1.3% and grew only .3% in 1999 and another .5% in 2000, 2001 and 2002. It was still a sluggish 1.9% in 2004, but in 2006 and 2007 it was an encouraging 6.3%, thanks largely to favorable prices for bauxite, rice and sugar. It slowed to 4% in 2008. Because of the global recession, growth was negative for 2009, –1.7%.

In 2004, Guyana had the dubious distinction of having a public debt that was 200% of GDP, the highest in the entire world. Thus, when the so-called Paris Club of the wealthiest creditor nations met in 2005 to discuss debt forgiveness, Guyana was one of the 18 countries—four of them in the Western Hemisphere—that qualified. In 2006 and 2007, the World Bank, Inter-American Development Bank and Japan forgave a total of $700 million in debt.

Two bright spots in Guyana's economy are its growing diamond production and the potential for an oil boom now that the maritime dispute with Suriname has been resolved (see History).

The Future: Any future for Guyana, one of the four poorest countries in the hemisphere, depends on the PPP and PNC getting their act together and defusing the country's long-simmering racial tension between blacks and Asians. The potential for an oil boom is there if the suspected vast deposits off the coast can be tapped—and assuming it doesn't enhance the country's already notorious corruption.

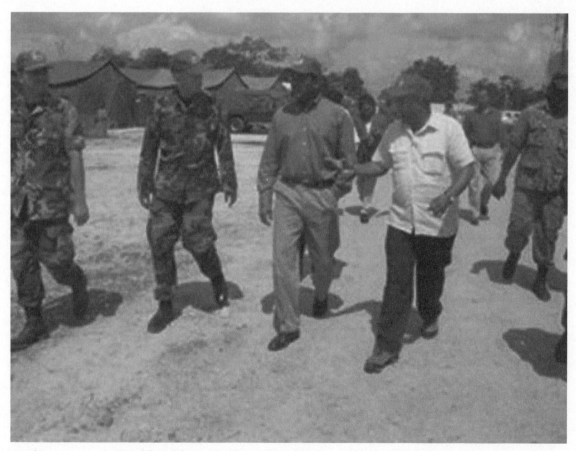

President Bharrat Jagdeo at New Horizons Timehri Base Camp.

The Republic of Haiti

Emperor Henri Christophe's *La Citadelle*, **the mountaintop fortress in the north that took 13 years and the labor of 200,000 men to build.**

Area: 10,711 square miles.

Population: 10,035,536 (2009; growth rate 2.5% annually).

Capital City: Port-au-Prince (Pop. 2.5 million, estimated).

Climate: Tropical, moderate at higher elevations; rainy season from May to December.

Neighboring Countries: Haiti occupies the western third of Hispañola, the second-largest of the Greater-Antilles; the Dominican Republic occupies the eastern two thirds of the island.

Official Languages: French and Creole, a mixture of French and African origin spoken by almost all Haitians.

Other Principal Tongues: Creole, a dialect of French and African origin spoken by a majority of the rural Haitians.

Ethnic Background: African Negro (90%), mixed African and European (10%).

Principal Religion: Officially Roman Catholic Christianity, but a majority of Haitians practice *voodoo*, a variety of animism similar to African native religions, but with a greater emphasis on mysticism.

Chief Commercial Products: Coffee, light industrial products, sisal, sugar and textiles.

Currency: Gourde.

Gross Domestic Product: U.S. $6.966 billion in 2009 ($696 per capita).

Former Colonial Status: Spanish Colony (1492–1697); French Colony (1697–1804).

Independence Date: January 1, 1804.

Chief of State: René García Préval (b. January 17, 1943), president (since May 14, 2006).

National Flag: Blue and red vertical stripes, coat of arms on white square in center.

The Haitian western one third of the island of Hispaniola is covered by tropically green mountains rising to heights of 9,000 feet. The narrow coastal plains and river valleys, one fifth of the total territory of the nation, are arable, but irrigation is necessary in many of the fields. Of these areas, the Artibonne River valley and the north coastal plains are most suited to agriculture. The mountains that divide Haiti and the Dominican Republic prevent the moisture-laden trade winds from reaching Haiti, thus its lands are generally drier than those of its neighbor.

History: Haiti was discovered by Columbus in 1492 and remained under Spanish control for the following 200 years. Because of the limited number of settlers, the Spanish exploited the eastern part of Hispaniola, neglecting the western portion, which became a popular base for French-speaking pirates. The western portion of the island was ceded to France in 1697, and ultimately became one of that country's most profitable colonies. African slaves had been brought in by the Spanish and their numbers increased during French rule. The slaves obtained their freedom during the period of the French Revolution in a confusion of slave rebellions and civil wars that involved blacks, mulattos, French, Spanish and English on the island of Hispaniola.

Toussaint L'Ouverture, a former slave, rose rapidly to the rank of general during this period. He fought with the Spanish against the French, later joined the French against the English, and ultimately forced them from the island. Napoleon sent a large force under his brother-in-law, General Victor-Emmanuel Leclerc, which captured L'Ouverture and attempted to restore slavery. Independence was finally achieved in 1804 after a dozen years of bit-

Haiti

ter bloodshed when the French forces were defeated and expelled by the Haitians.

General Jean Jacques Dessalines, commander of the black army, was named governor-general for life. An ex-slave, illiterate, brutal and arrogant, he lacked the qualifications for ruling his newborn nation and was unable to secure aides capable of compensating for his ignorance. The few whites left in Haiti were slaughtered by Dessalines' order—the war had been fought not only to obtain freedom, but also to destroy anything that would remind the blacks of serfdom and forced labor.

Drafting a constitution abolishing slavery, prohibiting land ownership by whites and making the term *Negro* synonymous with Haitian, Dessalines was enthroned as Emperor Jacques I. By use of conscripted labor and enforced discipline, he made some progress in restoring order and in rebuilding the economy until he was assassinated in 1806 by his two trusted military commanders, Henri Christophe and Alexandre Pétion. Haiti then split into two states—the north ruled from Cap-Haitien by Henri Christophe and the south ruled as a republic by Alexandre Pétion. Christophe styled himself emperor; he constructed a massive castle and established an elaborate circle of courtiers, dukes, duchesses and barons who were former slaves. In contrast, Pétion governed the south as an independent republic, and his rule was relatively moderate and progressive. He was at war with Henri Christophe from 1811–18, when the latter, faced with rebellion caused by his cruelty, shot himself with a silver bullet.

Haiti was reunited between 1818 and 1820 by Jean Pierre Boyer, a French-educated mulatto who was able to dominate the entire island by 1822. Initially of moderate outlook, the declining economy and disruption of society induced Boyer to resort to harsh tactics to till the land and restore governmental authority. When he was overthrown in 1844, the Spanish-speaking eastern portion of the island regained its independence and Haiti again fell into the hands of illiterate leaders.

The period from 1843 to 1915 was one of disorder, tyranny and bloodshed under 22 dictators. It was a period of economic and social deterioration. The only occupants of the presidential palace who accomplished any beneficial acts were Fabre Geffrard (1859–67), who cut the army in half, built a few schools and signed a concordat with the Vatican to revitalize the church. Lysius Salomon (1879–88) created a national bank, built rural schools and imported French school teachers. The last, Florvil Hyppolite (1889–96), built bridges, docks and public buildings and opened telephone and telegraph services.

U.S. Intervention, 1915–34

The country degenerated into anarchy in 1908, culminating in the killing and dismemberment of President Guillaume Sam by an angry mob on July 28, 1915. Sailors and Marines on a U.S. naval vessel offshore promptly seized Port-au-Prince to restore order. The occupation was to last for 19 years under five U.S. presidents of both parties, during which the military high commissioner, Marine Brigadier General John H. Russell, oversaw the successive "elections" of puppet presidents. The president from 1922–30 was Louis Borno, who collaborated so well with Russell that a U.S. financial adviser to Haiti called the arrangement a "joint dictatorship." The United States also imposed a new constitution on Haiti in 1918, written by the assistant secretary of the Navy—Franklin Delano Roosevelt. FDR later was to boast of its authorship. Under Russell's tutelage, there was no freedom of the press or other basic civil liberties. Several newspaper editors, in fact, were jailed in the name of establishing democracy, something that Thomas Jefferson would have frowned upon.

In 1919, the *cacos*, or peasants, under the leadership of the charismatic Charlemagne Peralte, revolted against U.S. rule.

In an operation that has become part of Marine Corps folklore, Major Smedley Butler disguised himself, infiltrated Peralte's camp, killed him with his revolver and forced the other *cacos* to flee. The revolt was crushed, with more than 3,000 Haitians killed in the process.

On the positive side, the Marines greatly improved Haiti's infrastructure. From 1919–22 they built 365 miles of roads and improved 200 miles of existing road. Irrigation systems were repaired and experimental farms set up. The Marines also established the *Garde d'Haiti*, a constabulary that had American officers, to maintain law and order. This force, however, later would become little more than the personal goon squad for a succession of dictators. Moreover, the Americans made no effort to diversify the coffee-dependent economy or to train schoolteachers, with the result that Haiti remained the poorest and least literate nation of the Americas.

When a strike led to another outbreak of violence in 1929 that the Marines ruthlessly crushed, President Herbert Hoover dispatched an investigative commission to inspect the U.S. role in Haiti. In its report, the commission concluded: "The failure of the occupation to understand the social problems of Haiti, its brusque attempt to plant democracy there by drill and harrow, its determination to set up a middle class—however wise and necessary it may seem to Americans—all these explain why, in part, the high hopes of our good works in this land have not been realized."

A new legislative assembly was elected in October, 1930, General Russell resigned on November 1, and legislators chose an opposition newspaper editor, Stenio Vincent, as president. Haitians reassumed con-

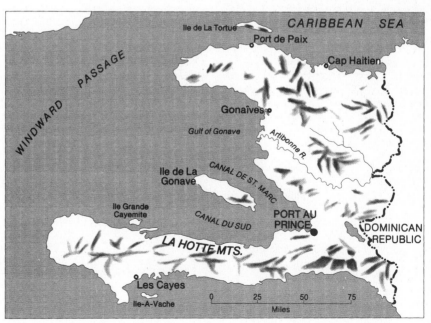

Haiti

trol of key public agencies a year later. On August 15, 1934, President Roosevelt, who had once boasted of writing Haiti's constitution, withdrew the Marines. It would be 60 years, one month and four days before the next U.S. military intervention.

The departure of the U.S. Marines in 1934 was hailed as Haiti's second emancipation. Haitian politicians and military officers were restored to their former privileges, and the following three decades revealed that Haiti had profited little from U.S. military rule. The Marines had sought to place the educated mulatto minority in power, but the *Garde d'Haiti,* consisting principally of mulattos, emerged as the dominant force.

The Duvalier Era

The election of Dr. Francois "Papa Doc" Duvalier as president in 1957 began a new era of dictatorial rule. A devoted voodoo practitioner, Duvalier ruled Haiti by a combination of superstition and brutality. He created an incredibly cruel and imaginative force known as the *Tonton Macoutes* (rough translation: "Uncle's Boogeymen"), which had the capability of dispensing instant justice (usually death or unbelievable torture). This force became an all-pervasive instrument of Haiti's "government."

The single most significant accomplishment of Duvalier's administration was his durability and longevity—he died apparently of natural causes in April 1971. Before his death, Duvalier named his portly, naïve, childish, fun-loving son, Jean-Claude ("Baby Doc") as Haiti's next president for life. Assuming a serious attitude not considered possible, the youthful ruler immediately began reshaping Haiti's horror-filled image with a semblance of political stability and programmed economic growth under the tutelage of his older sister Simone and his mother. New foreign investments created more than 80,000 low-paying jobs.

Although Haiti received more per capita foreign aid than any other Western Hemisphere nation, most benefits were diluted by corruption. Half of all foreign loans and grants were funneled into secret accounts controlled by government leaders. The nation's stagnant economy prompted thousands to flee—often in unsafe boats—to the Bahamas and the United States in search of work. At one time, one out of every 10 persons in the Bahamas was said to be an illegal alien from Haiti.

To improve its international image, Haiti permitted limited free elections in 1979. The so-called "liberalization program" was short-lived; in November 1980 opposition political and intellectual leaders were arrested and deported in the worst government purge since 1963. Although it was not initially apparent to the outside world, "Baby Doc" apparently had become estranged from his mother and "divorced" his sister as the "first lady" of Haiti in favor of a light-skinned charmer, Michèle Bennett. Her father, on the verge of bankruptcy, quickly became the coffee export baron on Haiti and the family attached itself firmly to the inner circles of government. Michèle tried to emulate the late Evita Perón of Argentina.

To outward appearances, Michèle Duvalier was the soul of charity and kindness, opening orphanages, providing relief for the poor and tirelessly working against injustice. But the palace life she created was another story. Luxuries piled upon luxuries and she "ran" Jean-Claude with an iron fist. Worst of all, she had television sets placed in every small town and settlement to show all of her charitable works and, foolishly, to broadcast the festivities from the marble palace. Her father and family graduated from the edge of bankruptcy to rich, elite exporters and businessmen. Goose liver paté contrasted sharply with garbage, and anger started to smolder.

The Revolt of 1986

Perhaps the straw that broke Haiti's back occurred when Michèle went on a Paris shopping spree that cost more than $1 million. Among the items purchased in profusion were fur coats to be given as gifts to close friends. When this appeared on Haitian television, it proved the beginning of the end.

The final insult came with the arrival of 1,200 money-laden passengers for the inauguration of a much-celebrated (and criticized) new tourist haven on the island of Labadie at a resort developed under questionable financial circumstances. They were not to be exposed to Haiti's "backward" atmosphere, but rather, to luxury.

Rioting erupted in January 1986. Duvalier made tentative efforts to disband the *Tonton Macoutes* and undertook some other reforms—all too late. The rioting continued and intensified. Amid chaos, "Baby Doc" and his wife were flown out of Haiti in a U.S. plane for France in early February; no other country would receive him. He is still there, living opulently until the money reportedly ran out in 2006.

Meanwhile, "Papa Doc's" tomb was raided (his body wasn't there) and others were broken open; skulls were paraded through the streets. The Bennett family was all but wiped out. Shopkeepers closed their shops, frozen with fear, in spite of governmental threats. Among the prime movers behind the revolt were the "liberation theology" priests of the Roman Catholic Church who from the pulpit regularly condemned the government. One of them was a charismatic firebrand named Jean-Bertrand Aristide.

A military regime under General Henri Namphy emerged to lead Haiti. Assets of the Duvaliers in various parts of the world, including the United States, France and Switzerland, were frozen. However, enough remained untouched to apparently enable "Baby Doc" to live in comfort for life.

The ouster of Duvalier did not end the violence. Mobs sought out the members of the *Tonton Macoutes* and brutally murdered them. There were riots when the head of that organization was allowed to leave for Brazil instead of facing trial.

After a new constitution was adopted in 1987, there followed a procession of presidents averaging eight months in office before being overthrown. They all had initial approval of the military and the elite Haitians, which quickly soured as they tried to expand the bases of their popularity. The last one in early 1990 took the offensive: he had all significant rivals for power seized and beaten, then exiled to Florida. He also went there after the U.S. ambassador persuaded him that there was no choice—either he left or Haiti faced unbridled violence.

Elections were again attempted in late December 1990. Jean-Bertrand Aristide, the "liberation theology" priest who had been thundering anti-Duvalier, anti-elite rhetoric from his pulpit (and was defrocked by the Catholic Church for meddling in politics), was elected president. This was by a majority of 70%, despite the opposition of the army, the elite, the Catholic Church and what was left of the *Tonton Macoutes*. But he was revered by the poor. The army commander was able to coerce his men into inaction and silence to ensure free elections.

Lacking military support, President Aristide imported 60 Swiss officers to train a new palace guard loyal to him. Fearing loss of power, the military ousted him on September 30, 1991, and only the intervention of the United States, Canada, France and Venezuela prevented his assassination. He went initially to Venezuela, later entering the United States in early 1992, where he spent large sums of money from frozen Haitian assets without accounting for them. General Raoul Cedras became chief of state.

French, EC and U.S. aid to Haiti was immediately suspended. An uneven trade embargo was imposed, dampened by President George H. W. Bush and by Europeans eager to profit from Haiti's misfortune. Acting in spite of the embargo, they shipped petroleum to Haiti, which was immediately snapped up by the mili-

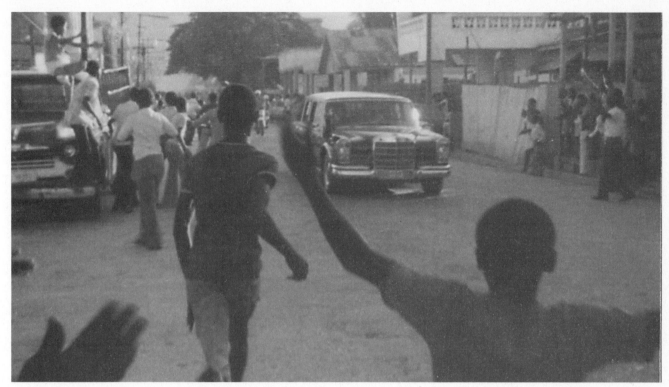

Haitians greet car of former president "Baby Doc" Duvalier, who is throwing money out of the car windows

Photo by Susan L. Thompson

tary and the elite. The poor of the island became even more desperate, and began leaving by home-made boats for Florida and Guantanamo Bay, Cuba. The United States immediately blocked this with the Coast Guard, even outside the coastal limits of the United States.

Of the Haitians who made it to the United States or Guantanamo, only about 11% were admitted as political refugees. Incredibly poor and uneducated, many of them infected with AIDS and other diseases, they were considered undesirables. Meanwhile, the Black Caucus of the U.S. Congress demanded that Aristide be returned and installed in office by U.S. troops, if necessary.

One of the cruelest hoaxes occurred during the U.S. presidential campaign of 1992. Democratic candidate Bill Clinton flatly promised that, if elected president, he would immediately admit refugee Haitians to the United States without limit. When Clinton was elected in November, countless numbers of Haitians began building boats, using any materials they could find, legally or illegally, awaiting the day of Clinton's inaugural so they could set sail from misery to hope. Literally within hours of taking the oath of office, Clinton decided that it was "wise" after all to continue the policies of the defeated Bush.

The question of Haiti appeared to have been solved in mid-1993 when an agreement was signed in New York by Aristide,

Cedras and the head of the national police that Aristide would return by October 31. Training officers for the Haitian police appeared at Port-au-Prince aboard U.S. and Canadian vessels, but were prevented from landing by the Haitian military. Cedras did not abide by the agreement.

When President Clinton received black support in Congress on the NAFTA treaty and other measures, he was called upon to respond with more energetic action to remove the military from power in Haiti and to reinstall Aristide. On the refugee

problem, the United Nations adopted directives that they be received by all nations (actually meaning the United States).

U.S. Intervention, 1994

Pressures for action mounted and there was increased talk from Clinton threatening invasion. The U.N. Security Council authorized intervention in July 1994. Troops were readied in September, and in a last-ditch effort, Clinton dispatched former President Jimmy Carter, Senator Sam

A wedding near Port-au-Prince

Haiti

Panoramic view of Port-au-Prince

Nunn and retired General Colin Powell to Haiti. They persuaded the military leadership to stand down and leave Haiti, which they did within days.

A force overwhelmingly of U.S. troops entered the island peacefully on September 19 and took up a triple role: janitors, policemen and, later, presidential guard after Aristide returned to the island. Little in their combat training prepared them for such roles.

Both before and after his return on October 15, Aristide modified his former radical positions to become acceptable to the elite. He undertook a disarmament program, but for every weapon obtained, at least 10 were hidden by their owners. Almost 4,000 Haitian refugees were repatriated from Guantanamo Bay. The army, seen as an obstacle to democracy, was disbanded. That move would backfire on Aristide a decade later.

Aristide appointed Smarck Michel as prime minister; together they devised plans for election of a new Parliament in 1995. There were plans to withdraw U.S. forces by the fall of 1995, which proved impossible. Aristide's supporters started behaving as goons, not as saviors of their nation. A well-known opponent of Aristide was gunned down in March 1995, the first of many murders of anti-Aristide Haitians; his personal involvement was suspected.

The Préval Presidency

Aristide floated the idea of canceling presidential elections scheduled for the fall of 1995 so he could remain in office—a proposition that even liberals in the U.S. Congress shrank from in horror. René Pré-

val won in an election with a light turnout; although Aristide hated him, he embraced him at his inauguration in February 1996.

Préval undertook the unenviable task of trying to govern a country still beset by economic, political and social conditions that have made it the basket case of the Western Hemisphere. As if he didn't have problems enough, he inherited a palace guard that was loyal to Aristide and that he did not trust. The United States dispatched a special security team to guard him.

Like so many other recent Latin American leaders, Préval faced economic reality and launched a program aimed at privatizing the inefficient state-owned enterprises. He had the added incentive of meeting requirements of the International Monetary Fund to qualify for additional loans, which accounted for 60 percent of Haiti's budget. Part of the painful austerity program was the elimination of 7,000 of 43,000 public employees. As usually happens, the austerity measures sparked a series of protest demonstrations in 1997. Préval also undertook an effort to distribute parcels of land to peasants, but the tracts were so tiny—1.2 acres—that they could not be commercially viable, and while he won meager appreciation from the recipients of the parcels, he was condemned by those who were left out.

A wave of political violence claimed about 50 lives in early 1997. Préval attributed the killings to remnants of the *Tonton Macoutes*.

The democratic process came close to total breakdown following Senate elections in 1997. Aristide had established an offshoot of his *Lavalas* (Avalanche) Politi-

cal Organization, or *OPL*, called the *Fanmi* (Family) *Lavalas*, as a vehicle for his re-election in 2000. The Aristide faction was accused of rigging the election, which would have given *Famni* a majority in the Senate. Préval indefinitely postponed the runoff elections. Prime Minister Rosny Smarth resigned to protest Aristide's power play, but agreed to remain until Parliament confirmed a successor. But the 83-member Chamber of Deputies, in which the *OPL* was the largest bloc with 33, rejected Préval's nominee.

Préval then nominated Hervé Denis, an economist committed to privatization of nine state-owned companies. The Chamber voted 34–33 to confirm Denis, but abstentions left him short of the needed majority. Préval stubbornly re-nominated Denis in March 1998, and the *OPL* just as stubbornly vowed not to confirm any nominee until the president dismissed the nine members of the electoral council and had the election results revised. Préval refused, and while this petty contest of wills continued, as much as $300 million in foreign aid packages was tied up because there was no one to negotiate them. It also frightened away foreign investors.

U.S. Secretary of State Madeleine Albright visited Haiti and chided both sides for their failure to resolve the impasse. It seemed the logjam was broken when the Chamber finally confirmed Denis. But the nomination was blocked in the Senate when it received approval by eight of the 16 senators—not an absolute majority.

While the domestic crisis was unfolding, the three-year mandate of the U.N. peacekeeping force, composed of Canadians and Pakistanis, expired on November 30, 1997; the foreign troops withdrew the next day. It was the worst possible timing. Political violence and common street crime engulfed the country, while drug traffickers swarmed into Haiti like cockroaches into a dark, filthy kitchen. Not only did the 5,200-member police force established under U.S. and U.N. auspices prove incapable of maintaining order, but the new police force killed about 100 people, roughly half of them without any apparent justification. Two of Préval's bodyguards and two of his chauffeurs were gunned down (even his dog was stabbed to death), and he asked the United Nations to protect the presidential palace. Two days before the peacekeeping force left, the U.N. Security Council voted to establish a 290-member civilian police force with a one-year mandate. There also were 500 U.S. military "engineers" still in Haiti engaged in public works projects. They left in early 2000.

With the Denis nomination twice rebuffed, Préval nominated his minister of education, Jacques Edouard Alexis. For months, Parliament took no action, and

Haiti at top.

the crisis rumbled on. Meanwhile, the Senate, facing the imminent expiration of the terms of eight of its remaining 16 elected members, voted in November 1998 to extend those terms until November 1999, apparently expecting new elections before then. It was an act of dubious constitutionality, and the Chamber of Deputies took no similar action to extend its own expiring mandate.

It suddenly seemed the logjam would be broken when, in December 1999, the Senate unexpectedly confirmed Alexis 12–1, with three abstentions. The Chamber followed suit, with 46–78. The country—as well as the United Nations and the U.S. government—breathed a collective sigh of relief.

Alas, Préval ignored his own deadline and failed to appoint the electoral council. The crisis flared anew on January 11, 1999, the date of the expiration of parliamentary mandates. Declaring that in the absence of new elections there was no longer a parliamentary quorum, Préval announced that he would rule by decree. The reaction was immediate and violent, as pro-*OPL* demonstrators, denouncing the move as a ploy by Préval to assume dictatorial powers, took to the streets. So did pro-Préval demonstrators, who blockaded local municipal councils on the pretext that their terms, too, had expired. Members of Parliament showed up for work in a largely symbolic gesture, but the Finance Ministry had severed their operating funds.

Alexis assumed the post of prime minister and named a cabinet in the absence of Parliament. Once again, Préval set a deadline of February 2, 2000, to name a new electoral council that would call new elections, and once again he let his own deadline pass. Denying he was setting himself up as Haiti's latest dictator, he insisted, "It is democracy we are building."

The Electoral Farces of 2000

If so, the architect and carpenters should have been fired. Three times in 1999 and 2000, the Provisional Electoral Council (*CEP*) set parliamentary election dates only to postpone them. The *CEP* then set new dates for the first and second rounds, but Préval disapproved those dates.

At that point, the United States and the EU impatiently reminded Préval that $500 million in aid desperately needed aid was contingent upon his calling the long-overdue parliamentary elections. The Haitian people responded with mass demonstrations in March 2000 that left four people dead.

The *CEP* and Préval agreed on a fourth date: May 21, with runoffs on June 25, later moved to July 8. At stake were 19 of the 27 Senate seats and all 83 members of the Chamber of Deputies, plus about 7,500 local offices. During the six-week campaign that followed, at least 15 candidates or campaign workers for various parties were murdered, some hacked to death with machetes in traditional fashion.

Another casualty was Jean Dominique, the country's most prominent radio commentator, who was gunned down as he arrived at work on April 3, 2000. Dominique had made enemies on both the far right and the far left. Six men believed to be the triggermen were arrested and eventually indicted two years later, but the investigation into who ordered Dominique's death was stymied by intimidation, including the murders of two witnesses. It remains unsolved a decade later, though theories abound.

Six opposition groups hastily formed an alliance in a last-ditch effort to prevent a predicted landslide by Aristide's *Lavalas* movement. The election was marred by poor organization and outright manipulation. Many polling places opened late, and at others, the ballots were still being printed.

In the department of Grand Anse, the election was postponed altogether because inter-party bickering had prevented voter registration. OAS observers reported cases of vote fraud and intimidation of voters by pro-Aristide militants, which the U.N.-trained police force seemed uninterested in stopping. A policeman and a gunman were killed at one polling place. An opposition candidate for a local office was stoned to death.

When polls closed, armed goons, presumably from *Lavalas*, stormed several polling places and made off with the ballot boxes. Marked ballots, representing about 10% of those cast, were found lying in the street; workers swept up about 90% of them. It was Haitian "democracy" under construction.

The OAS official in charge of the 200 international observers, speaking with considerable understatement, termed the irregularities "most unfortunate." Former U.S. President Carter, whose Atlanta-based Carter Center also participated in observing the election, told this author in Caracas, Venezuela, six days later: "It is obvious to me that the election in Haiti was seriously flawed." About the only thing to cheer was the record voter turnout: An estimated 60% of the 4 million eligible voters—a far cry from the 5% who voted in the annulled 1997 elections. Unfortunately, not all their votes were counted.

According to the "results" released by the *CEP* days after the election, *Lavalas* won 16 of the 19 Senate seats and 23 deputy seats without a runoff. But on June 2, the deputy chief of the OAS observation

Former President Jean-Bertrand Aristide

mission reported that the *CEP* apparently had miscalculated the final percentages for the Senate by counting only the votes for the top four candidates for each seat. Eliminating the votes for lesser candidates gave several *Lavalas* candidates outright majorities they did not actually have. The opposition and the observers claimed that 10 "winning" *Lavalas* Senate candidates should have faced a runoff. When the official results were finally announced, *Lavalas* held all but one of the 27 Senate seats and more than 80% of the seats in the Chamber of Deputies; it also controlled almost all the municipal governments.

This creative tabulating brought international demands that the *CEP* count the votes properly. Even U.N. Secretary-General Kofi Annan urged a clean count. But the government refused to budge. Two weeks before the runoffs, the president of the *CEP* fled the country, saying government officials had threatened him with death if he did not certify the flawed results. He had refused. Aristide supporters took to the streets to burn tires and to demand that the government release the results. It did—the flawed ones.

This farce continued into the presidential election of November 26, 2000, which the major opposition parties boycotted to protest the parliamentary elections. (In a peripheral farce, two days before the election Parliament finally confirmed Alexis in the office he had held for 20 months.) Aristide, who almost certainly would have won anyway, was thus opposed only by six unknown candidates, and even they did not campaign because of threats. In the usual pre-election violence, nine pipe bombings killed two people and injured at least 16. The United States, Canada and the EU withdrew their observers rather than

Haiti

participate in a sham. In the balloting, Aristide predictably received 92% of the vote. The government declared that the turnout had been 60.5%, but more objective assessments put it at between 15% and 20%, depriving Aristide of a meaningful mandate.

Three weeks later, 15 opposition parties, calling themselves the Democratic Convergence, declared they would form an "alternative government" and even urged *Lavalas* to join them. Aristide brushed aside their call, and he was sworn in on February 7, 2001. Just as the opposition parties had boycotted the election, the international community largely snubbed the inauguration.

Governing a Cauldron

The opposition rebuffed Aristide's invitation to join his government, saying his election was illegitimate and demanding new elections. An opposition demonstration at the local headquarters of the OAS, which had sought to broker a truce between the government and the opposition, was broken up by Aristide supporters. Three people died.

In April 2001, OAS Assistant Secretary-General Luigi Einaudi arrived in Haiti to jumpstart talks. Aristide supporters staged a tire-burning demonstration and blocked traffic, apparently to impress the OAS team that while Aristide is open to new talks with the opposition, they would be on his terms.

The talks broke down in July. Under U.S. and OAS pressure, *Lavalas* and the opposition agreed in principle for a new parliamentary election to be held in November, but the opposition rejected Aristide's "nonnegotiable" demand that the incumbent lawmakers be allowed to serve out their terms, which made new elections pointless.

In December 2001, a band of about 30 armed men stormed the National Palace in an attempted *coup d'etat*, killing two guards and two bystanders. Forces loyal to Aristide recaptured the palace, killing one of the gunmen and capturing seven; another was apprehended as he attempted to cross the Dominican border.

Although the attackers appeared to be disgruntled former soldiers from the army Aristide had disbanded in 1994, rather than Convergence activists, Aristide supporters around the country used the palace attack as a pretext to go on a rampage against the opposition. A Convergence headquarters and the homes of three Convergence leaders were burned; four people were burned alive by mobs. Pro-Convergence radio stations received threats. Much of the violence was believed linked to Aristide's personal goon squads, called *chimères*, or ghosts. They hacked to

death another prominent radio journalist, Brignol Lindor, after he allowed opposition representatives on his talk show.

In March 2002, Prime Minister Jean-Marie Cherestal resigned amid mounting public pressure from Aristide supporters, who faulted him for not doing enough for the economy, which shrank by 1.2% in 2001. As his replacement, Aristide nominated, and Parliament approved, Senate President Yvon Neptune, who promised new talks with the opposition. Aristide met with Convergence leaders for the first time in two years and assured them he would move to satisfy their demands, including reparations for the property destroyed by mobs. But the stalemate, and the public unrest, continued, with each side blaming the other for the continued freeze on $500 million in international aid.

In May, Aristide ordered the imprisonment of Amiot Metayer, leader of one of his own *chimères*, the "Cannibal Army." Metayer, who allegedly had burned down houses of a rival gang, was charged with arson. Metayer then turned against Aristide, and his gang used a bulldozer to smash into his jail in Gonaives and free him and about 150 other inmates. Anti-Aristide demonstrations then broke out around the country, while Metayer disappeared—for 13 months.

International pressure increased on Aristide to clean up his act. Haiti joined the Caribbean Community (Caricom) in 2002, and at a summit that December the leaders of the other 14 member nations called for new elections to end the stalemate.

In March 2003, Einaudi tried again to resolve the impasse and clear the way for a resumption of aid. Einaudi led a delegation of representatives from the United States, Canada, the EU and OAS and insisted that Aristide disarm the *chimères*, respect human rights and overhaul the police. The delegation set a deadline of March 30 to set up a new electoral council to pave the way for new elections. The deadline was ignored.

Aristide Falls

Two events set things in motion that would eventually bring down Aristide. The first was a meeting of representatives of 180 civic groups that demanded Aristide's resignation in Cité Soleil, a teeming slum near the capital that is a stronghold of Aristide supporters. When the opposition sought to assemble in July 2003, pro-Aristide mobs pelted them with rocks, injuring dozens. The opposition countered with mass anti-Aristide demonstrations in Cap-Haitien, the second-largest city, which turned violent.

In September, Metayer's bullet-riddled body was found near the coastal town of

St. Marc. The identity of the assassins was a mystery, but Metayer's supporters accused Aristide of silencing him because of his knowledge of the government's sins. Aristide denied complicity, but it was too late; a large, well-organized, well-armed band of thugs that had been loyal to Aristide now took up arms against him.

Metayer's death sparked more than a week of tire-burning in the capital and in Gonaïves, where gangs burned or ransacked four government buildings and captured weapons. Over the next three months, about 50 people died in sporadic political violence.

Then, in January 2004, even as the country observed the bicentennial of its independence, all hell broke loose. Once again, the mandate of the Chamber of Deputies expired and no elections were forthcoming, so Aristide began ruling by decree as Préval had done. First came a general strike by shopkeepers. On January 18, the funeral of a student shot to death during an anti-Aristide demonstration turned into another violent confrontation between demonstrators and police that left one person dead and six injured. Another violent confrontation on January 29 left an Aristide partisan dead.

Political attempts to resolve the impasse came to nothing. A delegation of 14 opposition representatives, calling themselves the Democratic Platform, met with several Caribbean prime ministers during a Caricom summit in the Bahamas. A Caricom delegation came to Haiti and met with Aristide in Kingston, Jamaica. Aristide agreed to disarm his *chimères* and to reform the police. Now it was the opposition that became intransigent, saying Aristide must step down.

Armed groups would determine the course of events. On February 5, insurrection broke out in at least a dozen towns, and rebels soon captured Gonaïves, symbolic as the cradle of Haitian independence. Metayer's brother, Butheur, declared himself the new police chief there. The first week of the insurrection, 47 people died. Neptune admitted that the 5,000-man police force was incapable of dealing with the uprising—even if it had been so inclined. Many policemen simply fled as the rebels took town after town. The army, of course, had been disbanded in 1994—by Aristide. It literally became gang warfare, the rebels against the *chimères*.

The rebels, who named their movement the National Resistance Front for the Liberation of Haiti, were far from an army of liberation. They were a rag-tag, unappetizing and improbable collection of disgruntled Aristide loyalists, former soldiers from the army Aristide had disbanded, even former members of the Duvaliers' *Tonton Macoutes*. The only thing they had in common was a belief in violence as a means for achieving their ends, and this they wielded skillfully. At first, the Democratic Platform disavowed the violence and distanced itself from the rebels, many of whose leaders were known killers. But when the rebels began achieving victories, they could not be ignored. Eventually, Guy Philippe, a more respectable former army officer and the former police chief in Cap-Haitien, emerged as their leader.

Meanwhile, U.S. Secretary of State Colin Powel admonished Aristide for continuing to unleash gangs of thugs to attack peaceful demonstrations, but he insisted that the United States stood by the elected president. Aristide finally yielded to a U.S.-brokered power-sharing plan that would have allowed him to remain in office. But the opposition, sensing imminent victory, turned it down.

Then 200 rebels overran Cap-Haitien, and looters went wild. The death toll rose to 80. The rebels moved on Port-au-Prince. A siege mentality gripped the capital as the Aristide gangs erected barricades. Foreign nationals left in droves. U.S. Marines entered Port-au-Prince to safeguard the embassy—just as they had in 1915. Philippe vowed to take the presidential palace and arrest Aristide. On February 27, the rebels captured Mirebalais, just 30 miles from the capital. There also was an uprising in Les Cayes, the third-largest city.

Aristide remained defiant and pleaded for international troops to keep him in power, but by now Powell was questioning whether the man the United States had reinstalled in 1994 should in fact continue to misgovern his country. The United Nations said it would send peacekeeping forces only if Aristide and the opposition could agree on a power-sharing arrangement, which, of course, the opposition had no intention of doing, and no incentive to accept. Chaos reigned in Port-au-Prince, as Aristide's supporters even ransacked a hospital in search of wounded rebels. Looting was widespread.

On Sunday, February 29, 2004, Aristide resigned and fled the country, flying to the Central African Republic. The jubilation in the streets was immediate. Under the constitution, Supreme Court Chief Justice Boniface Alexandre became interim president, but the menacing rebel gangs on the outskirts of the capital had not yet agreed to lay down their arms. Anti-Aristide mobs went in search of retribution, and exacted it. There were several execution-style slayings in the ensuing days. A contingent of 100 U.S. Marines and 300 French Foreign Legionnaires arrived as the vanguard of the latest U.N. peace-keeping mission.

The rebel army entered Port-au-Prince on March 2, peacefully, as the U.S.

Marines watched warily. Philippe announced that he was not interested in political power but wanted to be "military chief." Meanwhile, 1,500 more Marines entered Haiti, as did 500 more French and 130 Chilean troops, to maintain order and, unofficially, to prop up the new government. Philippe claimed he welcomed the intervention.

In March, Haiti moved a step closer to establishing a semblance of a government when a seven-member "Council of Sages" bypassed the Democratic Platform to agree on a new prime minister: Gérard Latortue, a former U.N. official who had served briefly as foreign minister during one of the revolving-door presidencies in 1988. Unlike Aristide's figurehead prime ministers, Latortue was given some genuine authority. He stated his top priorities were to establish law and order and to arrange new elections.

Meanwhile, in a bizarre postscript, Aristide told journalists in his temporary exile that the United States had forcibly removed him from the presidential palace, in effect, not just abetting but staging a *coup d'etat*. The State Department denied the allegation, but its official declarations made it clear that the United States was glad to get rid of this embarrassment. Caricom leaders tended to accept Aristide's version and demanded that the U.N. General Assembly and the OAS investigate. They also were unhappy with what they saw as Latortue's kowtowing

to the rebels. Despite objections from the United States and the new Haitian government, the OAS General Assembly voted to invoke Section 20 of the charter to determine whether the government of a member country was subverted through unconstitutional means.

Aristide flew to Jamaica, where he announced his final destination: South Africa. He had developed a friendship with President Thabo Mbeke, who had once tried to broker a dialogue with Aristide and the opposition. Aristide arrived in Johannesburg, insisting he was still the legitimate president of Haiti and that the United States had forced him to leave.

The United States increased its aid to Haiti for the year to $160 million. That would not have happened had Aristide remained.

In June, the U.N. peacekeeping mission, 8,000 strong, set up its headquarters. The largest contingent was 1,200 Brazilian troops, augmented by 500 Argentines, along with Canadians and Nepalese. The United States withdrew by June 30. The United Nations authorized a force of 5,700, but by August there were only 2,300 U.N. peacekeepers left, far too few to deal with the lawlessness and political turmoil that was to come.

The new Haitian government let the foreigners know it was in no hurry for them to leave, especially after devastating floods in May that killed 1,191 Haitians and left 1,484 unaccounted for. In September, Hur-

Former President Boniface Alexandre

Haiti

Palm trees along the northern coast of Haiti

ricane Jeanne slammed into Haiti, killing an estimated 3,000 people and leaving thousands more homeless. It seemed that Haiti was indeed living under a curse. A group of donor nations pledged $1.3 billion in aid.

Futile Quest for Stability

Aristide's fall was not the panacea for the country's ills his opponents had hoped. The unelected Alexandre-Latortue interim government was viewed by many Haitians, and in some international circles, as illegitimate. Meanwhile, Aristide's *chimères* launched a low-grade insurgency roughly analogous to the insurgency in Iraq; indeed, they dubbed their effort "Operation Baghdad." Like the Iraqi insurgents, they hoped for a return to the *ancien régime*.

The first major clash in the insurgency came in Port-au-Prince in September 2004,

when Aristide supporters demonstrated to commemorate the 13th anniversary of his 1991 overthrow. By the time the violence subsided five days later, the overall death toll was 45. At least seven were policemen, three of whom were beheaded. In October, Haitian police and Brazilian troops staged a counteroffensive by raiding *chimère*-controlled slums. Amnesty International charged that the interim government was little better than the insurgents, accusing it of illegal detentions and at least 11 summary executions.

The *chimères* were not the only threat to the interim government, or to U.N. peacekeepers. The former soldiers of the old army who had helped bring down Aristide, themselves still heavily armed, began demanding that the interim government reconstitute the army and restore them to their old positions—with back pay. In December 2004, Brazilian troops

stormed an estate once owned by Aristide, which some of the former soldiers had converted into a fortress. The ex-soldiers surrendered and laid down their weapons. Hundreds of them were allowed to join the new national police force.

The U.N. contingent was boosted to 7,400 to deal with the mounting violence. Brazil again played the leading role.

Latortue announced that elections would be held for president and Parliament, but postponed the date twice until setting a firm date of February 7, 2006. A total of 91 parties originally organized to contest the elections, including Aristide's *Lavalas*. The United States, Canada, the EU and the United Nations funded the elections.

Still, the violence continued. In March 2005, two U.N. peacekeeping troops, from Nepal and Sri Lanka, were killed, and three others wounded in separate gun battles with former soldiers. Two of the former soldiers also were killed in the fierce firefights. Violence committed by rival gangs of pro- and anti-Aristide partisans continued unabated, a lawless scenario reminiscent of the Lincoln County War in New Mexico of the 1870s, only with a much higher death toll. The U.N. peacekeepers and the 3,500 Haitian police found themselves battling both groups. In April 2005, police killed Remissainthe Ravix, one of the key leaders of the former soldiers, while police and Jordanian troops invaded Cité Soleil and clashed with the Aristide partisans, killing 10.

A new wave of violence in June left nine people dead, including a French diplomat, bringing the death toll since September 2004, to about 750, including 40 policemen. The U.N. Security Council approved an additional 1,000 troops to safeguard the election. A U.S.-sponsored "peace" rally designed to discourage gang violence itself turned into a bloodletting that killed an estimated 20 people.

One who did not die violently, as his brother did, was Butteur Metayer, one of the key instigators of the 2004 revolt against Aristide. He died of kidney failure in June 2005.

The Return of Préval

The election of a new president began to resemble the electoral farce of 2000, as the election was postponed again and again. This time it was international advisers who kept urging the delay, warning that the mechanism for an election was not ready.

Former President Préval declared his candidacy at the head of his new *Lespwa* (Hope) Party, and rejected accusations that he was merely Aristide in sheep's clothing who would allow Aristide to return. Indeed, the two men apparently had had an irrevocable falling-out. Aristide's own *Lavalas,* meanwhile, broke into two factions, one that fielded a candidate, and one that called for boycotting an election they believed Préval would win. His only two reasonably serious opponents were former President Leslie Manigat, overthrown by the military after five months in 1988, and Charles Henri Baker, who represented the business establishment.

The only real suspense when the long-postponed election finally took place on February 7 was whether Préval would obtain the majority needed to avoid a runoff. Gang-related violence threatened to disrupt the electoral process. Two Jordanian peacekeepers were killed, whereupon the U.N. contingent was increased to 9,000 to guarantee the election.

The turnout was a healthy 63%, about 2.2 million voters, but the vote-counting turned into another sham of democracy. About 85,000 blank ballots—about 4% of

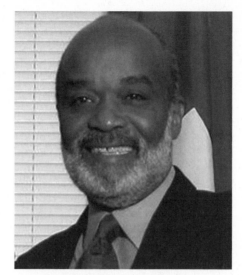

President René Préval

the total—were stuffed into ballot boxes, apparently in an effort to deprive Préval of a majority. Other ballots were stolen and burned. The initial count showed Préval with 63%, but when the tedious count continued and it dropped below 50%, Préval alleged fraud and urged his supporters to protest. They dutifully went on a tire-burning rampage that paralyzed Port-au-Prince.

The United Nations oversaw the vote count, during which the head of the electoral council fled the country because of death threats for discarding the blank and suspicious ballots. About 125,000 ballots were disallowed. A compromise was reached on the blank ballots, allotting them to the candidates on the basis of the percentages they had obtained without them. That put Préval over the top. The final tally on February 15 gave him 51.5%. Manigat was a distant second with 11.8%.

That left the also-postponed parliamentary elections. Under the constitution, the new National Assembly had to be in place before Préval could be inaugurated. The elections finally took place in April, and *Lespwa* emerged as the largest bloc in both the Senate and Chamber of Deputies.

Préval was inaugurated for his second term on May 14. 2006. Even before then, he played the role of statesman, visiting Washington, Cuba, Venezuela and Brazil, seeking help for his destitute country. Cuba's Castro, also head of a destitute nation, offered the usual medical aid, while Venezuela's Chávez offered the usual fuel at discounted prices. Brazil promised to help develop an ethanol program.

For prime minister, Préval nominated, and the Senate quickly confirmed, Jacques Edouard Alexis, who had been prime minister during his first term.

In a bizarre postscript to the fall of Aristide in 2004, Guy Philippe, the onetime

rebel leader, became a fugitive in 2007 after U.S. and Haitian drug agents raided his house. He is accused of drug trafficking.

A total of 9,500 peacekeepers—7,500 military and 2,000 police—in the U.N. Stabilization Mission in Haiti have remained in Haiti during Préval's second term. Their role has been to patrol the violence-torn slums to try to quell the armed gangs. Gun battles frequently erupt, many resulting in fatalities. Haitians began to chafe at the U.N. presence, accusing the troops of firing indiscriminately and wounding civilians during clashes with gangs. However, when the U.N. Security Council unanimously voted in October 2007 to extend the peacekeeping mission, the Haitian government expressed relief and gratitude. The U.N. also named former U.S. President Bill Clinton as its special envoy to Haiti.

Violence in Haiti again made international news in April 2008 when mobs in towns around the country began protesting the high cost of food, leaving at least five people dead. The protests spread to Port-au-Prince, where rioters stormed the presidential palace to demand Préval's resignation. Repulsed from the palace, they went on a rampage through the capital, looting stores for food. Préval delivered a national address, asking the National Assembly to cut taxes to provide relief and ordering the protesters to stop looting stores. The riots, in which a Nigerian peacekeeper was killed, died out after a few days. The National Assembly forced Alexis to resign as prime minister, apparently to appease the restive population. Haiti became an international *cause célèbre* over escalating food prices as food crops worldwide were diverted to ethanol production.

The Chamber of Deputies rejected two of Préval's nominees to succeed Alexis. In June 2008, he nominated Michèle Pierre-Louis, 60, a U.S.-educated economist who for 13 years had been executive director of liberal American billionaire George Soros' Foundation of Knowledge and Liberty (FOKAL). She was confirmed by both houses and assumed office in September. A leftist and former Aristide supporter who broke with him, she tried to follow a pragmatic economic course and attempted to crack down on drug-based corruption—which won her more political enemies than friends.

Haitian economic recovery was the subject of a conference in Bridgetown, Barbados in April 2009 attended by U.N. Secretary-General Ban Ki-moon, Prime Minister Pierre-Louis, U.S. Secretary of State Hillary Clinton and the representatives of more than 30 countries. The new Obama administration implemented a new trade law, called Hope II, that extends preferential tariffs to Haitian products for nine years. Ban urged developed nations to in-

Haiti

crease investment in Haiti, but also called on Haiti to reform its institutions.

Recent Developments

On October 30, 2009, a majority of 18 senators—most of them of Préval's *Lepswa*—passed a resolution demanding the dismissal of Prime Minister Pierre-Louis because of her perceived failure to come to grips with the country's prodigious problems, especially poverty. Observers speculated the real reason was that some senators were positioning themselves to run for president. It was widely believed that the prime minister had stepped on too many toes in her zeal to combat corruption The next day, Préval nominated Jean-Max Bellerive, the minister of planning and external cooperation, to succeed her. He formally assumed office in November.

Bellerive soon found himself facing not only the problems Pierre-Louis allegedly failed to overcome, but with one that has left Haiti devastated and even more desperate. At 5 p.m. on January 12, 2010, a massive 7.0-magnitude earthquake struck Haiti, leveling thousands of poorly constructed homes and office buildings—including many government ministries—killing tens of thousands of people and leaving hundreds of thousands homeless. The presidential palace and Parliament were badly damaged, and the executive branch set up an emergency office in a police station. The archbishop of Port-au-Prince was among those killed when the building where he was holding a meeting collapsed. Hillside slums were swept away.

International relief efforts were immediate and generous, but the magnitude of the human tragedy was more than even disaster-relief experts had bargained for. Compared with Chile, which suffered an even more powerful quake six weeks later (see Chile), Haiti simply lacked the institutional or physical infrastructures to cope with a disaster on this scale, even with the outpouring of funds, supplies and personnel from around the world.

Because of primitive logistics, food, bottled water and relief supplies, such as tents and medical supplies, sat in airport hangers or in ships offshore as thousands went hungry and without shelter. Port-au-Prince's major port was put out of commission by the quake. The electrical grid was disrupted, which temporarily halted air traffic control. Landslides blocked roads into the interior. Lack of running water and sewerage sparked outbreaks of disease.

The collapse of several hospitals magnified the suffering. The thousands of unburied corpses rotting in the tropical heat also componded the nightmare. Mass burials and cremations followed. Looting broke out, as did gunfights. The parliamentary elections scheduled for February 28 were postponed. About the only good news was that the quake occurred during the dry season, which would end in April.

About 22,000 U.S. military personnel, and 2,000 from Canada, were deployed and gradually brought order to the logistical impasse and helped maintain order. A month after the quake, more than 300 tent communities were housing 550,000 people. It was estimated that 25,000 buildings had been destroyed; the number damaged was even higher. The U.S. joint task force withdrew on June 1, leaving about 850 personnel, mostly engineers. Reconstruction is now in the hands of various non-governmental organizations.

When this book went to press, the generally accepted death toll from the quake was 230,000. The cost of reconstruction was estimated at between $8 billion and $14 billion—twice the country's entire GDP for 2009. At a meeting in New York in March, donor nations pledged $9.9 billion in assistance. On May 28, the World Bank forgave Haiti's $36 million debt to the Internatioinal Development Association. What remained unanswered six months after the quake was whether the billions of dollars in international aid would be spent wisely.

Préval set November 28 as the date for both the presidential and parliamentary elections.

Culture: Haiti's culture is a singular blend of African and European influences. A minority, the mulattos, relatively better educated in the French-language schools, boast of their European culture and superiority. Educated in medicine and law, they patronize the arts and disdain most manual work. Most are Christian.

The Haitians are, for the most part, an illiterate peasant society. Poor and neglected, they practice *voodoo*, a type of animism with African roots with many spirits and deities, and great emphasis on the powers of evil and good spirits. Voodoo, or *voudou* as the Haitians spell it, was sanctioned in the 1987 constitution but was not officially recognized as a religion with legal authority to perform marriages and baptisms until 2003.

Their language is a dramatic indication of their culture. Called *Creole*, it is a blend of French, Spanish, English and Dutch, the foreign influences to which Haiti has been exposed, with a distinct basis in African dialects and tongues.

Creole is the basic language of the country; in addition to their French, the mulattos also speak this tongue. Some of its terms baffled troops sent by the United States to help Haiti. An important, wealthy person in Creole is a *gros neg*—"big nigger"—and a foreigner, regardless of race, is a *blanc*—"white." Most artistic expression has *voodoo* overtones. Traditional African designs blend with imaginative contemporary motifs in cloth, wood carving and basketry. Such crafts are valued internationally.

Economy: Haiti's economy, based on peasant survival at unbelievably low levels, is almost nonexistent. Deforestation, soil erosion, periodic hurricanes and overpopulation all combine to limit agricultural production. The leading cash crops are coffee, cotton, sisal, cacao and sugar.

Low wage scales attract some foreign investment in light industry such as electronic assembly, finished leather goods and tourism. Clothing assembly has been moderately successful. Precut materials are sent from the United States and sewn into garments in Haiti. This substantially lowers import duties when the finished product is shipped to the United States. When former President George H. W. Bush watered down the embargo on Haiti, he did so not out of consideration of Haitians, but because of extreme pressure from the U.S. garment makers and merchants.

During the 1980s the economy suffered from expensive fuel imports, low prices for coffee exports and hurricane damage to crops. Continued U.S. assistance kept the nation economically afloat—barely—before 1987. The already prostrate economy was further stricken by Hurricane Georges in 1998.

Beginning in the 1980s, the desperate economic conditions led to a massive exodus of economic refugees by boat, bound for Florida, the Bahamas, or anywhere they might find a better life; untold numbers died at sea.

Economic growth declined each year from 2001 to 2004. In 2005, growth was positive, but only 1.5% Growth was 2.5% in 2006, 3.2% in 2007, and 2.3% in 2008, below the Latin American average and only slightly ahead of the birth rate. In 2009, growth was 2%, higher than the Latin American average, surprising given the global recession and the damage to the economy from the 2008 storms. Unemployment remains about 70%. The per capita income of $975 in 2008 was the lowest in the hemisphere, while the infant mortality rate of 70 per 1,000 births is the highest. In 2003, the most recent year with reliable statistics, 80% of the population lived below the poverty line.

The January 12, 2010 earthquake caused even more human suffering and damage to the economic infrastructure for the already destitute country, but reconstruction could, ironically, prove beneficial for the economy (see The Future). The United Nations has already spent millions in relief funds to hire 220,000 Haitians to clear rubble.

The Future: The Haitian people have discovered the cruel fact that political democracy is not a panacea for two centuries of tenacious poverty and political misrule. Even before the tragic 2010 earthquake, Haiti was the Western Hemisphere's basket case: destitute, illiterate, lawless and virtually ungovernable. Its per capita income is the lowest in Latin America, 80% of the population lives below the poverty level and economic growth has averaged 2% a year for the past five years. Haiti desperately needs an enlightened leader, but it has not found one. It appeared for a time it had found one in Prime Minister Michèle Pierre-Louis, who showed spunk, skill and honesty. Those traits may have been the very reason the Senate ordered her dismissal in October 2009. She has no political base to stand up to such political machinations.

About the best thing that can be said about President René Préval is that he is at least better than Aristide. His first term was unspectacular, by his own admission. His countrymen desperately needed a better performance this time around, but after four and a half years, they haven't received it. His performance in dealing with the January 12 earthquake has been about as impressive as then-Mayor Ray Nagin of New Orleans after Hurricane Katrina. Préval was rarely seen in public, but he insisted he was accomplishing more in his temporary office in a police station than by going out to check on the suffering of his people first-hand. If it hadn't been for the United Nations, international non-governmental organizations and the temporary presence of 24,000 U.S. and Canadian military personnel, the country would have deteriorated into chaos once again.

In a perverse way, the earthquake *could* represent Haiti's salvation. At least $10 billion in international relief funds already has been pledged toward a reconstruction that is expected to cost between $8 billion and $14 billion. Haiti will literally be rebuilt from the ground up, which should be viewed as an unprecedented opportunity. That will put hundreds of thousands of Haitians to work in reconstruction projects, at least temporarily lowering unemployment and stimulating the overall economy, as it did in Louisiana after Hurricanes Katrina and Rita in 2005. If reconstruction is planned properly, the new homes, office buildings, hospitals and schools will be built with affordable techniques that have been used elsewhere, such as Chile, to make them more resistant to earthquakes—and hurricanes. The outdated telecommunications system could be replaced with 21st-century technology. Generators burning imported diesel fuel and gas-guzzling buses could be replaced with those burning locally produced ethanol, and homes and offices could be fitted with new, low-cost solar panels to harness the tropical sunshine. Education *must* be a priority. "Nation-building" would not be merely a metaphor in Haiti's case.

Alas, how much of that $10 billion will be spent wisely and invested in Haiti's future, and how much will be channeled into the pockets of venal politicians and businessmen? In 2007, the second year of Préval's mandate, Transparency International rated Haiti as tied with Iraq and Somalia as the three most corrupt countries on the planet. In 2009, Haiti had "improved" to the world's 12th most corrupt out of 180 nations, but it remains the most corrupt of the Western Hemisphere.

Préval's successor was supposed to have been elected in November 2010, but the Senate has now extended his term up to three months beyond the expiration of his five-year term on February 7, 2011, if the election cannot be held. The parliamentary elections are already four months overdue, and no date has been set for them, either. Préval has called for international assistance to conduct the elections, and the U.N. Stabilization Mission has already promised to provide security.

No candidates of any real stature or vision have emerged in the November 28 elections to oversee the daunting responsibility of rebuilding Haiti from scratch.

God save Haiti.

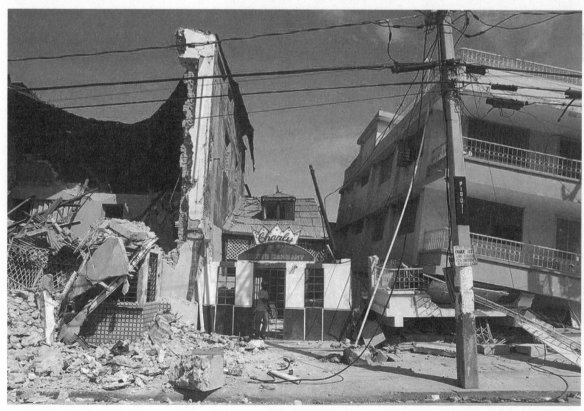

Haiti after the earthquake.

The Republic of Honduras

Detail from a carved stone pillar at the Mayan ruins of Copán in western Honduras

Area: 43,266 square miles.
Population: 7.989 million (2009).
Capital City: Tegucigalpa (Pop. 1.25 million, 2005 est.).
Climate: Tropical, with clearly marked wet and dry seasons. Heaviest rains occur from May to December.
Neighboring Countries: Nicaragua (Southeast); El Salvador (South); Guatemala (West).
Official Language: Spanish.
Other Principal Tongues: Various Indian dialects.
Ethnic Background: *Mestizo* (Mixed Spanish and Indian, 90%) African (5%), Indian (4%) European (1%).
Principal Religion: Roman Catholic Christianity.
Chief Commercial Products: Coffee, bananas, lumber, meats, petroleum products.
Currency: Lempira.
Gross Domestic Product: U.S. $14.75 billion in 2009 ($1,846 per capita).
Former Colonial Status: Spanish Colony (1524–1821).

Independence Date: September 14, 1821.
Chief of State: Porfirio "Pepe" Lobo Sosa (b. December 22, 1947), president (since January 27, 2010).
National Flag: Blue, white and blue horizontal stripes, 5 blue stars in a cluster on the center stripe.

Honduras is the second largest of the Central American republics and one of the most thinly populated. Much of the country is mountainous; an irregular plateau in the southwest has peaks approaching 8,000 feet near Tegucigalpa and La Esperanza. The plateau drops to a narrow plain on the Pacific Coast (Gulf of Fonseca). To the north there also is a narrow coastal plain broadening to the east. The valleys of the Ulúa (N.W.) and Aguán (N.E.) rivers extending south from the Atlantic coast (Gulf of Honduras), are important agricultural regions. Running south from the Ulúa to the Gulf of Fonseca is an intermountain valley which is the principal route of communications from the Atlantic to the Pacific oceans. The eastern plains along the Patuca River are covered with jungle and only partially explored.

The central plateau descends into several basins at 2,000 to 4,000 feet, in which are located the principal urban centers. The southern and western highlands contain the majority of the native Indian societies. The black population is found in the banana-raising section along the Atlantic coast. Prevailing winds are from the east, and the Atlantic coastal plain, receiving heavy rainfall, is covered with forests that are also found on the eastern slopes of the plateau and mountains.

History: Honduras was settled by Spanish treasure seekers from Guatemala in 1524. The mainstream of movement and settlement was along the Guatemala trail, a pattern that today governs the population distribution. The Spaniards ignored the Atlantic coast and the region was untouched until the U.S. fruit companies set up banana plantations in the late 19th century.

Honduras achieved independence from Spain with the other Central American states in 1821, and joined with them in a short-lived federation. Going its own way as a separate state in 1838, Honduras has been subjected to interference from Guatemala, El Salvador and Nicaragua as these countries sought Honduran support in conflicts among and between them. Honduran politics has followed the Central American pattern—two-party conflict between liberal and conservative factions of the elite, little popular participation in the political process and a long list of ever-changing dictatorial regimes.

However, Honduras' dictatorships have been somewhat more benign than those of its neighbors, and several governments have been committed to social and economic reform. Less inclined toward revolution than its neighbors, sparsely populated and with few roads, Honduras has been able to avoid the large-scale bloodshed of its neighbors. Still, during its first 161 years of independence, Honduras witnessed 385 armed rebellions, 126 governments and 16 constitutions. Generally regarded as the most capable presidents were Policarpo Bonilla (1894–99) and Tiburcio Carías Andino (1932–48). Neither made any pretense of democratic rule, governing instead as benevolent despots.

During his 16 years, Carías did more to advance the social and economic well-being of the country than any of his predecessors. Some roads and a few schools were built, and modern agricultural methods were introduced. His regime was maintained by jailing or exiling his critics.

After peacefully surrendering power following 1948 elections, Carías was followed by a series of mediocre presidents.

Honduras

The military seized power in 1963 in a coup led by General Oswaldo López. Honduras joined the Central American Common Market, trade was improved and an industrial development program was initiated in the northern plains region around San Pedro Sulaq and Puerto Cortés. Presidential balloting held in 1965 resulted in López's election at the head of the National Party to a six-year term.

A long-simmering dispute between Honduras and El Salvador, stemming from the fact that tiny El Salvador is badly overpopulated, erupted into a brief, but bloody war in 1969 over a contentious soccer match. Since the 1940s, some 300,000 landless peasants have settled illegally on vacant land near the border inside under-populated Honduras. Some Salvadorans fled their homeland to escape the horrors of prolonged civil strife. Others came to Honduras in search of a better life. In time, these highly industrious people were living better than many native Hondurans in the region.

Alarmed by what it viewed as a growing flood of "squatters," Honduras enacted a new land reform law which, among other things, distributed to native Hondurans plots that had been cleared and brought under cultivation by the Salvadorans. All too often, the immigrants would be evicted just before their crops were ready for harvest. The mass deportation of 17,000 Salvadorans created more tension between the two countries.

Although the North American press tended to joke about the 100-hour "soccer war" between the two "banana republics," the conflict claimed more than 2,000 lives and devastated the economies of both countries. Because of the strife, Honduras withdrew from the Central American Common Market, causing further economic damage to both nations.

Capitalizing on his role as a "wartime" leader, President López sought to remain in office by amending the constitution to permit his re-election in 1971. When that effort failed, López persuaded the Liberal and National parties to divide equally most national offices. Under this "Pact of National Unity," Ramón Ernesto Cruz was elected president.

Unable to cope with the nation's growing economic and political problems, the elderly Cruz was ousted in a coup led by López in 1972. To gain popular support, he promised a major land reform program. The plan was opposed by both the land-owners, who rejected any change in the tenure system, and by peasants, who felt the concept was too little, too late. López was himself ousted in a coup in 1975 as a result of a "bananagate" scandal in which high-level government officials were accused of accepting a $1.25 million bribe

from the U.S.-owned United Brands Company to lower taxes on banana exports.

The new chief of state, Colonel Juan Alberto Melgar Castro, sought to implement various social and economic development projects. Partly as a result of these efforts, the country enjoyed a healthy GNP growth rate of 6%–8% annually until 1980. Pledging to enact the land reform program promised earlier by López, Melgar also found himself in a deadly crossfire between wealthy farmers and landless peasants.

The heart of the dispute was land. Much of Honduras is extremely mountainous; only 22% is arable. Most has traditionally been controlled by just 667 families (0.3% of the population) and by two U.S. banana firms. In contrast, the peasants (87% of the people) lived as peons on small, difficult-to-till plots. The end result was often widespread malnutrition, particularly among the young. Still, the recent land reform program, while not meeting all expectations, permitted a larger number of peasants to be resettled on their own property.

Melgar was replaced in 1978 by a three-member *junta* headed by General Policarpo Paz García. Yielding to pressure from the Carter administration, Paz appointed a civilian-dominated cabinet to direct the transition to civilian govern-

ment. Elections in April 1980 for the 71-seat constituent assembly gave the reform-minded Liberal Party 35 seats, while the conservative Nationalists took 33.

The Return to Democracy

General elections in 1981 marked the return of democracy and resulted in the presidency of the Liberal Roberto Suazo Córdova, who took office in early 1982. A country doctor, he tried to revive a patient that was suffering from backwardness, a declining economy and growing security problems caused by events in neighboring countries. More than 25,000 Salvadoran refugees flooded into Honduras to escape that nation's war. Many were relocated away from the border and were placed under the U.N. high commissioner for refugees.

After the Marxist *Sandinista* movement came to power in neighboring Nicaragua in 1979, Honduras unwillingly became a sanctuary for the Nicaraguan *Contra* forces opposed to the *Sandinistas*. During the 1980s, there were repeated raids into Honduras from Nicaragua as the *Sandinistas* periodically tried to destroy *Contra* encampments in the remote, inaccessible mountains and jungle along the common border. Losses in coffee production in areas abandoned by farmers because of the conflict were substantial.

The Reagan administration stepped up its military aid commitment to Honduras in response to the *Sandinista* threat. In addition to weaponry, military personnel were sent. Economic aid in large amounts was insufficient to alleviate economic woes, however, because of fluctuations in the prices of bananas and coffee.

Cuba, meanwhile, used Honduras as a transport route to dispatch Soviet-bloc arms and munitions to the *FMLN* rebels

Honduras

in El Salvador. Friction with Nicaragua increased because of the *Contra* presence. In an effort to control the situation, a combined U.S.-Honduran military force established permanent American military bases close to the Nicaraguan border. Some thought this was an effort by President Reagan to provoke the *Sandinistas*, justifying direct intervention in Nicaragua.

An incident did occur—*Sandinista* troops entered Honduras in 1988 to wipe out a *Contra* base after a cease-fire had been negotiated between the warring parties. When 3,000 additional U.S. troops were sent into the country, the *Sandinistas* retreated.

With the collapse of the Soviet Union and the end of its support to the *Sandinistas*, a semblance of peace finally came to Central America. But this left a burgeoning, expensive military in Honduras with little purpose. Releasing them would not help in a country where the unemployment-underemployment rate has been close to 50% for more than a generation.

Despite financial and security woes, democracy proceeded reasonably well in Honduras with the elections and peaceful transitions to power of José Azcona (Liberal) in 1985, Rafael Leonardo Callejas (Nationalist) in 1989 and Carlos Roberto Reina (Liberal) in 1993. All was not tranquil, however. Ethnic Indians, largely ignored by the government, became more politically aware and began expressing their dissatisfaction with their status. Vague guerrilla groups periodically appeared and disappeared.

As U.S. aid dwindled to less than $100 million annually, other sources of funding were sought. The International Monetary Fund agreed to loans, but attached a host of conditions that were difficult, including reduction of the size of the legislature and military.

Reina raised eyebrows in 1994 when he launched an anticorruption campaign that saw charges brought against 18 former officials, including former President Callejas, who was immune from prosecution as a member of the Central American Parliament. But it was the paring of the once-omnipotent military that may be regarded as Reina's enduring legacy. He ended the draft, obtained executive control over the armed forces' budget, removed the national police from military control and reduced troop strength; some units were only 20% of their former size. Moreover, there were Argentine-style efforts to hold the military accountable for human rights abuses during the 1970s and 1980s.

The armed forces complained that the downsizing emasculated their ability to defend Honduras, but to defend against whom? The guerrilla wars in neighboring Nicaragua and El Salvador, which once

Former President Carlos Flores Facussé

threatened to embroil Honduras, had ended. Before leaving office in 1998, Reina signed a long-sought border agreement with Salvadoran President Armando Calderón Sol that formally delineated the disputed frontier areas that led the two countries to war in 1969.

Carlos Flores

The presidential and congressional elections in November 1997 proved to be the most colorful yet for this fledgling democracy. To succeed the 71-year-old Reina, the Liberal Party made a generational leap to the president of the Congress, 47-year-old Carlos Flores Facussé, who lost an earlier bid to Callejas. The National Party, meanwhile, nominated Alba Nora de Melgar, widow of erstwhile military strongman Juan Alberto Melgar Castro and a former mayor of Tegucigalpa. Her link to the days of dictatorship, plus her decision to hire as her campaign adviser Dick Morris, U.S. President Bill Clinton's onetime aide, brought the campaign international attention. Three minor parties fielded candidates.

Flores distanced himself from Reina and from the Liberal Party's traditional middle-class base and reached out to the country's impoverished masses, although he had little in common with them as the scion of two of the country's wealthiest families. He received a degree in industrial engineering from Louisiana State University and held a master's degree in international economics and finance; his wife was American.

While Melgar pledged to promote economic growth by making Honduras a free-trade zone and by reducing illiteracy from 30% to 5% by 2001, Flores issued a 10-point plan that stressed women's rights, child care and health improvement. Ultimately, his populist approach and youthful appeal

proved successful, as he defeated Melgar, 53% to 42.4%. Flores was inaugurated on January 27, 1998.

Like his predecessors since the restoration of democracy, Flores found his will tested by the military. The armed forces commander promoted a list of officers without clearing them with the president—who objected to the men chosen and who nullified the promotions.

That problem, however, was trivial compared with the blow dealt to poverty-plagued and debt-ridden Honduras in October 1998 by Hurricane Mitch, one of the most powerful storms in recorded history. Entire villages on the Caribbean coast were swept away by the winds and floods. In human terms, 5,657 Hondurans were confirmed dead, another 8,058 missing and uncounted thousands more left homeless. The storm also destroyed 170 bridges and damaged 70% of the country's roads; property losses were in the billions of dollars, and 90% of the vital banana crop was destroyed. International relief efforts to alleviate the immediate human misery were quick in coming. The World Bank approved a $200 million loan, and the IMF extended a $215 million credit.

But these were little more than bandaids, and a bewildered President Flores declared to the world that Honduras's debt was "unpayable."

Ricardo Maduro

Hondurans were in the mood for change in 2001 as they prepared to elect their sixth president since the establishment of democracy. The Liberal Party nominated a veteran political insider, Rafael Piñeda, 71, president of the Congress. The Nationalists gambled on a 55-year-old businessman, Ricardo Maduro, whose only political office had been head of the Central Bank under the 1990–94 Nationalist administration of Callejas.

As both major parties are center-right, the campaign focused on personalities and the issues of who could better combat crime and promote foreign investment. Maduro, whose own son had been killed in a kidnap attempt in 1997, focused on the crime issue. He visited New York City and promised the "zero-tolerance" approach of then-Mayor Rudolph Giuliani, not only against violent crime but against such petty offenses as littering, vagrancy and defacing public property, all of which, Maduro argued, discouraged tourism and foreign investment. Piñeda, a former elementary schoolteacher, countered that enhanced education was the solution to the crime problem, which had become exacerbated by violent gangs known as "*maras*."

In a country plagued by more than 2,000 murders a year, a staggering figure for a nation of only 6.2 million, Maduro's proposal enjoyed widespread support. The violence issue was underscored just two days before the election when a Nationalist candidate for Congress was assassinated; police later arrested three employees of a Liberal deputy.

On November 25, voters gave Maduro a convincing mandate of 53% to Piñeda's 44%. The Nationalists also won the mayoralty of Tegucigalpa, but minor parties kept either of the two major parties from gaining a majority in the 128-seat Congress.

Maduro told his cheering supporters from the balcony of the party headquarters, "We are not just going to administer the country; we are going to effect significant reform." He also vowed "to enforce the laws as never before." He also promised to reduce the bloated government payroll, to streamline the bureaucracy and to make it more efficient, and to crack down on abuses of privileges and frivolous spending by government officials.

The *maras* evidently took Maduro's promises seriously. In January, police foiled a plot by one gang to assassinate the president-elect two days before his inauguration. He was sworn in on January 27, 2002.

In 2002, the divorced Maduro married a Spanish diplomat, Aguas Ocaña, Honduras' second consecutive foreign-born first lady. News reports soon circulated that the couple already had become estranged.

Maduro sought to reform the state-owned water utility in order to facilitate a line of credit from the IMF, which was placed on hold in 2002. As Congress considered the proposal, a demonstration by 10,000 people became uncharacteristically violent. The crowd clashed with police, then stormed inside the Congress.

Former President Ricardo Maduro

The president also created controversy 2003 when he contributed a contingent of 370 troops to the allied coalition in Iraq for a one-year tour. However, after Spain withdrew its contingent following the 2004 terrorist attacks in Madrid, Maduro ordered the troops home.

Gang-related violence remained the country's major problem, other than the endemic poverty that spawns it. But the problem is not Honduras' alone. The *maras*, organized by Central American expatriates in Los Angeles, mostly Salvadorans, have become a serious form of international organized crime, a Mafia with tattoos. The most infamous are the *Mara Salvatrucha*, better known as *MS-13*, and *Mara 18*. So serious have they become that the United States, Mexico and most Central American countries launched a joint offensive against them (see El Salvador). In 2003, the Honduran Congress passed a law that provides 12-year prison terms for gang membership.

In Honduras, *maras* established control over local areas, posing a greater threat to the central government than did the guerrilla groups of the 1980s. They specialize in spectacular, grisly murders and even massacres to instill terror. In 2003, 13 people were killed and 17 wounded when gangs assaulted two buses in San Pedro Sula. In an even more shocking and senseless attack, the *MS-13* attacked a bus full of Christmas shoppers in 2004 in San Pedro Sula and killed 28 people, six of them children, and wounded 14. The gang's rationale for the attack, left on a note on the windshield: to protest a bill to reinstitute the death penalty! Three *MS-13* leaders were arrested. The government began investigating possible links between the gangs and major drug-trafficking organizations.

In March 2005, Honduras became the second country, after El Salvador, to ratify the Dominican Republic-Central American Free Trade Agreement with the United States. More than 100 left-wing protesters briefly occupied the Congress building to protest the ratification.

Manuel Zelaya

The gang problem again dominated the campaign for the 2005 presidential election. In the two parties' primaries in February 2005, Porfirio "Pepe" Lobo Sosa, the president of the Congress and an advocate of capital punishment, won the National Party nomination. Manuel Zelaya, a wealthy rancher who opposes the death penalty, easily won the Liberal nomination.

Lobo Sosa pledged to continue Maduro's get-tough approach toward the gangs. Zelaya, who cut a flamboyant cowboy figure with boots, Stetson hat and black mustache, also pledged to get tough with the gangs but advocated life imprisonment rather than the death penalty for criminals deemed "beyond rehabilitation." Zelaya also pledged to create 400,000 new jobs in four years. He campaigned on the populist slogan "citizen power."

The election became the most dramatic cliffhanger of any of the seven since democracy was restored in 1981. Turnout was the usual lethargic 46%, about 1.83 million voters. On election night, the Liberal member of the electoral tribunal declared Zelaya the winner after only 1% of the votes were counted, which infuriated the Nationalists. Meanwhile, the vote count all but stopped, ostensibly because of computer problems, and 3,000 Nationalists marched on the offices of the tribunal to demand to know why the count was so slow. Zelaya claimed victory, but Maduro and Lobo Sosa refused to concede. Zelaya said Maduro was "playing with fire," and rumors circulated that Maduro had placed the army on alert,

In this mountainous nation, passengers and freight share a flight

Honduras

which he denied. Finally, after 10 days, the tribunal released its official tally:

Zelaya	915,075	49.9%
Lobo Sosa	846,493	46.2%
Others	72,142	3.9%

For the first time, members of Congress were elected directly instead of by proportional representation. The Liberals won 62 seats, the Nationalists 55, and three small parties made up the balance of power with 11.

Zelaya was inaugurated on January 27, 2006. He moved quickly to deal with an alarming increase in deaths inside the country's 22 prisons—180 in the previous year—which the president blamed on overcrowding because of Maduro's policy of prosecuting anyone with gang associations. Zelaya also initiated a program to offer job training to gang members who turn in their weapons.

On the negative side, Zelaya demonstrated a decidedly undemocratic attitude toward the country's independent press. In 2007, he introduced legislation that would have outlawed news reports on violent crime, on the theory that such reports "glorify evil." Congress rejected it. He then used his executive authority to require the privately owned television stations to carry two and a half hours of conversation programs a day between government officials and pro-Zelaya journalists. Zelaya said the move was required because the stations were biased against him. It was the most serious attack on freedom of the press under Honduras' 22-year-old democracy.

In 2006, Honduras recorded the fifth-highest murder rate in the entire world, 43 per 100,000 inhabitants; El Salvador was in first place. By March 2008, the wave of gang-related violence became so severe that Zelaya ordered a major crackdown, "Operation Hunter," dispatching 5,000 soldiers and policemen in a nationwide sweep that rounded up hundreds of suspected gang members. Meanwhile, a U.N. report estimated there are 36,000 gang members in Honduras alone. Not only did it prove ineffective, in 2008 Honduras had the world's *highest* murder rate, 58 per 100,000 people.

Zelaya moved increasingly to the left, bringing Honduras into Venezuelan President Hugo Chávez's so-called *ALBA* organization, a left-wing group that also includes Cuba, Bolivia and Nicaragua. Honduras benefited by receiving discounted Venezuelan oil.

Vice President Elvin Ernesto Santos, a 46-year-old engineer and construction company CEO educated at Lamar University in Texas, easily won the Liberal Party nomination for the November 29, 2009 presidential election in a party primary in

November 2008. He then resigned the vice presidency in accordance with the constitution. A month later, the Nationalists renominated "Pepe" Lobo Sosa, now 61, who narrowly lost to Zelaya in 2005. Lobo Sosa is a wealthy businessman and landowner who earned his business degree at the University of Miami. Both candidates discussed the problem of the 1 million undocumented Hondurans living in the United States with Secretary of State Hillary Clinton when she attended the OAS General Assembly session in Tegucigalpa in June 2009.

A Constitutional Coup?

Zelaya provoked a constitutional crisis, which eventually led to his overthrow by the Congress and the military, when he called a referendum for June 28, 2009, on whether to place on the November 29 ballot a proposition to elect a constituent assembly to rewrite the 1982 constitution. It was viewed as an attempt to emulate the models of Venezuela's Chávez, Bolivia's Evo Morales and Ecuador's Rafael Correa. Congress rejected the idea; his own Liberal Party was cool to it.

Zelaya defied Congress and proceeded with plans for the referendum, even ordered the ballots printed. His critics saw the constituent assembly plan as a ploy to perpetuate himself in power by lifting the ban on re-election, as Chávez, Morales and Correa all had done, and they took him to court. The Supreme Court ruled the referendum unconstitutional. Zelaya then defied the Supreme Court and ordered the army to distribute the ballots to polling stations. General Romeo Velásquez, the army commander, refused to comply on the grounds that it was an illegal order. Zelaya fired him. The Supreme Court, on a 5–0 vote, ordered Zelaya to reinstate Velásquez, ruling that he had been dismissed without cause. The same day, the Supreme Electoral Council also ruled the referendum illegal.

At odds with both the legislative and judicial branches as well as the armed forces, Zelaya *still* attempted to proceed with the referendum. On June 25, he and hundreds of supporters removed boxes of ballots from a military base and took them to the presidential palace. Before daylight on June 28, however, soldiers raided Zelaya's residence outside Tegucigalpa and placed him under arrest. Within hours, still in pajamas, he was flown to exile in Costa Rica, where he denounced what he called a *coup d'etat*. It was the first forcible removal of an elected president by the military in Latin America since the overthrow of Ecuador's Jamil Mahuad in 2000.

Back in Tegucigalpa, both major parties applauded Zelaya's ouster, and Congress

Deposed President Manuel Zelaya

stripped him of his powers through a resolution that said he had "provoked confrontations and divisions," although it was questionable whether that was an impeachable offense. Congress then elected its Liberal speaker, Roberto Micheletti, 65, who had opposed Santos for the party's presidential nomination, as interim president. Micheletti denied what had happened was a *coup d'etat*, saying civilian control and constitutional order were intact and that it was "absolutely a legal transition process," although power had not been passed to the interim vice president. Zelaya supporters protested, but were dispersed by police firing tear gas and water cannons and wielding truncheons. Micheletti declared an indefinite curfew.

International reaction was swift. There were the predictable denunciations from Zelaya's allies, Chávez and Morales, but OAS General-Secretary José Miguel Insulza of Chile also condemned the overthrow, as did U.N. General Assembly President Miguel D'Escoto, of neighboring Nicaragua, and the European Union. President Barack Obama said he was "deeply concerned," declared the overthrow "not legal" and called it "a step backward." He did not recall the U.S. ambassador, but he suspended some aid.

The day after his ouster, Zelaya flew to Nicaragua to meet with Chávez and Nicaraguan President Daniel Ortega to plan their next move. From there, he flew to New York to seek support from the U.N. and to Washington to plead his case to the OAS. The OAS issued a 72-hour deadline for Honduras to reinstate Zelaya. When the deadline expired on July 4, the OAS expelled Honduras.

Presidents Cristina Fernández of Argentina, Rafael Correa of Ecuador and Fernando Lugo of Paraguay joined Zelaya in Washington and at first said they would fly with him to Tegucigalpa to oversee his reinstatement. Citing security concerns, they changed their minds and flew in separate planes. Zelaya attempted to return on July 5—in a Venezuelan plane—but Micheletti denied him permission to land. Thousands of pro-Zelaya protesters had assembled to welcome him at the airport, where security forces opened fire with tear gas and live ammunition, killing one demonstrator and wounding eight. Zelaya and the other presidents, as well as OAS Secretary-General Insulza, diverted to El Salvador.

Costa Rican President Oscar Arias, a Nobel peace laureate, then offered to mediate between Zelaya and Micheletti. He met separately with both at his home in San José, but Micheletti returned to Honduras before meeting face-to-face with Zelaya. Zelaya insisted that the only solution to the impasse was his reinstatement. Arias' attempts to broker an agreement failed.

Micheletti said if Zelaya returned to Honduras he would be arrested to face 18 charges, including treason and dereliction of duty for failing to enforce more that 80 laws passed by Congress. However, he lost the chance to arrest Zelaya when he denied his plane permission to land. No Latin American nation had recognized Micheletti's government, not even the conservative governments of Mexico and Colombia, and some had recalled their ambassadors. The United States, the United Nations, the European Union and the World Bank all were applying pressure for Zelaya's reinstatement. In Honduras, pro- and anti-Zelaya demonstrations continued for months, and pro-Zelaya graffiti appeared on buildings all over the capital.

New Election and the Quest for Legitimacy

Ignoring the swirl of international condemnation, Micheletti held fast and proceeded with the regularly scheduled presidential and congressional elections on November 29 to choose a constitutional successor to Zelaya and himself. The major candidates remained Lobo Sosa for the Nationalists and Santos for the Liberals; there were three minor party candidates on the ballot.

Zelaya, meanwhile, slipped back into the country and took refuge in the Brazilian Embassy, from where he exorted his supporters to boycott the election and continued to demand his reinstatement. Micheletti ordered the closure of two pro-Zelaya radio stations; one was allowed to return to the air after it promised to tone down criticism of the government. Zelaya's supporters were hardly champions of free expression, however. They resorted to violence to intimidate would-be voters, attacking radio and television stations that encouraged people to vote. This

President Porfirio "Pepe" Lobo Sosa

author covered the election as a freelance journalist and was awakened by a grenade blast at a radio station a block away two nights before the election. The country was dangerously polarized.

Philosophically, there was little difference between Lobo and Santos. Both had supported Congress' ouster of Zelaya. Consequently, graffiti in the capital labeled the Liberal Santos *"traidor"* (traitor). Each gave the usual pledges to combat violent crime and to improve the dismal economy, which had grown worse with the global recession (see Economy.)

Despite the boycott campaign, voter turnout actually *increased*, from 46% in 2005 to 50%. The results were a convincing mandate:

Lobo Sosa	1,212,846	56.6%
Santos	816,874	38.1%
Others	114,740	5.4%
Null	92,534	4.0%
Blank	61,086	2.7%

The Nationalists also won a clear majority in Congress with 71 of the 128 seats; the Liberals won 45 and three other parties a total of 12.

In his victory statement, Lobo appealed to the community of nations to respect the will of the Honduran voters and recognize his elected government, saying the United States, France, Germany, Italy, Japan, Indonesia, Switzerland and the United Arab Emirates had assured him they would. In his concession, even Santos called on the world to recognize the new government, saying, "Today Honduras tells the world that we Hondurans, who may live in a little country in the heart of Central America but who have big hearts, know how to solve our problems peacefully and democratically."

At first, only four Latin American countries—Colombia, Costa Rica, Panama and Peru—recognized the outcome of the election. Micheletti, obviously aware he was a pariah, opted not to try to attend the annual Ibero-American Summit, which coincidentally convened the day after the election in Estoril, Portugal.

Lobo was inaugurated on January 27, 2010. That same day, under a safe-conduct agreement Lobo had agreed to, Zelaya left the Brazilian Embassy and went into exile in the Dominican Republic. Since then, Honduras has re-established diplomatic relations with about 30 countries, including Canada, El Salvador, Guatemala and Mexico. However, 10 of the 12 presidents in the South American Union of Nations (UNASUR)—all but Colombia's Álvaro Uribe and Peru's Alan García, both pro-U.S.—threatened to boycott the Sixth EU-Latin American-Caribbean Summit held May 18-19 in Madrid if Lobo attended. Even Chile's new conservative, pro-U.S. President Sebastián Piñera joined in the threat. Lobo

Pro-Zelaya graffiti appeared all over Tegucigalpa after his overthrow on June 28, 2009. This says "No to the elections, yes to the constituent assembly, eliminate the armed forces." Zelaya had called for a boycott of the November 29 presidential and congressional elections.

Photo by the author

Honduras

The major Honduran newspapers proclaim Lobo Sosa's victory in the November 29 election the day before. *El Heraldo*'s headline says "Honduras Spoke to the World." *La Tribuna*'s says "Massive Turnout," a reference to Zelaya's call for a boycott.

Photo by the author

the subject of intensive research and archaeological exploration for more than 100 years, had declined many centuries prior to the arrival of the Spaniards. The Caribbean coast has a significant population of Garifunas, descendants of escaped African slaves. Immigration has further broadened the country's ethnic makeup, including a colony of Palestinian Christians who have thrived in business and banking.

Moorish-Spanish architecture prevails throughout most of the nation, particularly in the beautiful churches built during the centuries since the arrival of Roman Catholicism. Education is compulsory through the age of 15, but there is a serious shortage of trained teachers, a lack of schools and little effort to enforce the educational law. Higher education is available, including that offered by the National University of Honduras, established in the capital city in 1847. Only a small percentage of Hondurans engage in such studies.

The folklore and music of Honduras are not distinctive, bearing a close resemblance to those of the other Central American nations. Culture division exists between the bustling cities and the isolated, mountainous rural areas—the people of the lonely countryside have been almost completely bypassed by the civilization of the more mundane city people.

The high illiteracy rate has hindered the development of newspapers, magazines and book publishing. The leading newspapers are *Tiempo* of San Pedro Sula and *El Heraldo* and *La Tribuna* in Tegucigalpa. Newspapers remain politically influential, and are owned by familes of the ruling elite. *Tiempo* tends to be pro-Liberal and *El Heraldo* and *La Tribuna*, owned by the same family, pro-Nationalist. Radio and television are the most popular media and have become well-developed for such an impoverished country. They, too, are owned primarily by wealthy, politically connected families.

took the hint and stayed away. Honduras remained a hemispheric outcast.

The legitimacy of Lobo's government and Honduras' reinstatement into the OAS did not even appear on the agenda of the 40th OAS General Assembly, held in Lima, Peru, on June 6-8. Nonetheless, U.S. Secretary of State Hillary Clinton, in her address to the plenary session, noted that the United States had joined the rest of the OAS in condemning Zelaya's overthrow, saying, "these interruptions of democracy should be completely relegated to the past." However, she added, "Now it is time for the hemisphere as a whole to move forward and welcome Honduras back into the Inter-American community ... We saw the free and fair election of President Lobo, and we

have watched President Lobo fulfill his obligations under the Tegucigalpa-San Jose Accord–including forming a government of national reconciliation and a truth commission. This has demonstrated a strong and consistent commitment to democratic governance and constitutional order."

But the delegates demurred on voting on Honduras' reinstatement, instead passing a resolution saying they needed "more information" and calling on Secretary-General Insulza to appoint a high-level commission to go to Honduras and make a report on the situation by July 30.

Culture: Honduran culture is almost entirely based on that of its colonial conquerors. The ancient Mayan civilization,

Economy: Honduras is a classic example of a "banana republic," with a small aristocracy, almost no middle class and a large peasant population that lives on a per capita income of less than $800 per year. Most of the nation's farmland is controlled by U.S.-owned banana firms and by a few huge cattle ranches. Mountainous terrain and periodic droughts limit farm output and methods are primitive. Most industry is foreign-owned. Coffee production has recently replaced bananas as the chief source of foreign exchange, followed by lumber, meat, sugar, cotton and tobacco. Continued balance-of-payments problems left the treasury nearly bankrupt by 1987, while the nation's debt grew to $3 billion—the size of the annual GNP.

Honduras

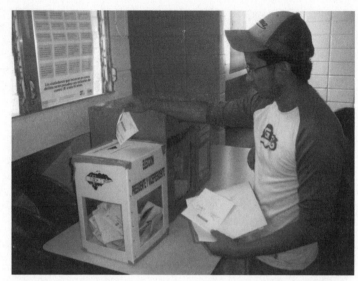

A man casts his ballot for president and Congress in 2009.

Photo by the author

Honduras remains one of the three poorest countries of Latin America, along with Haiti and neighboring Nicaragua, and all three were buffeted by powerful hurricanes in 1998—Honduras and Nicaragua by Mitch.

Largely because of the devastation caused to the banana crop, real GDP growth declined –3% in 1999. It rebounded to 6.3% in 2000, then dipped before returning to 6.3% in both 2006 and 2007. In 2008 it was 4%, but with the global recession, and perhaps because of the political unrest of 2009 (see History), growth declined in 2009 by –3.0%.

Remittances from Hondurans working abroad, mostly in the United States, amounted to $2.56 billion in 2007, more than 25% of GDP. They were expected to shrink because of the 2008–09 global recession.

Per capita income has grown slowly, from $643 in 1998 to $1,740 in 2007, the fifth-lowest in the Western Hemisphere, and 59% of the population was below the poverty line in 2008. Child prostitution is a growing social problem in Honduras.

Honduras also is saddled with a high external debt that was equal to 74.1% of GDP in 2005. It was one of 18 countries—and one of four in the Western Hemisphere—that qualified for a debt-forgiveness program when the so-called Paris Club of creditor nations met in June 2005. Since 2005, it has received about $4 billion in debt relief. At the end of 2008 its debt was still $3.6 billion, which was only about 25% of GDP.

Unemployment in 2008 was estimated at 27.8%. Compounding the economic woes is the country's gang-related crime problem, which was blamed for a devastating 30% decrease in foreign investments in 2001 alone. More than 200 business people have been the targets of kidnappers since 1997; several of them of them were murdered, including the son of former President Ricardo Maduro (see History).

The Future: It almost appeared that democracy had taken root in this impoverished republic since 1982. The military had confined itself to its barracks, and the Liberal and National parties demonstrated in seven elections that they could alternate peacefully in power. Of course, there are few real philosophical differences between them.

The overthrow of President Manuel Zelaya on June 28, 2009, called all that into question, even though his own party and the Congress insisted his removal was legal and necessary to prevent him from staging a Chávez-like power play to ramrod through a new constitution that would allow him to remain in power. Zelaya's Chávez-like pressure on opposition news media also was troubling.

That said, there is little doubt that the election of President Porfirio Lobo Sosa, which this author observed in November 2009, was fair and honest and that his 56.6% mandate represented the will of the Honduran people. Even working-class Hondurans with whom I chatted over five days said that it was time for Zelaya to accept the inevitable and depart the scene—which he has. He is now in self-imposed exile in the Dominican Republic.

The periodic *Latinobarómetro* survey published in *The Economist* shows that the percentage of Hondurans who believe democracy is preferable to any other form of government dropped from 42% in 1996 to just 33% in 2005, the year Zelaya was elected. Perhaps because of that campaign, it rebounded to 51% in 2006, but dropped back to 38% in 2007. In 2008 it rose to 44%, hardly a ringing endorsement. But in 2009, despite the ouster of Zelaya or because if it, the percentage jumped to 55%. The one-year increase of 11 percentage points was the second-highest of the 18 nations in the survey.

It was a peculiar endorsement of the seemingly undemocratic removal of an elected president. But unlike the interim president, Roberto Micheletti, Lobo has a clear mandate, and there is little to be gained by the world community's refusing to recognize his constitutional ascension to power as a *fait accompli*. The refusal of the 40th OAS General Assembly even to put Honduras' reinstatement on its agenda in Lima in June was a travesty. Last year, the OAS voted to reinstate Cuba! Cuba turned down the invitation, but for the OAS to suggest that Cuba is more democratic than Honduras is perverse logic.

Lobo may never obtain recognition from some hard-line leftist presidents like Chávez and Ortega, but he has bigger problems to face at home, namely gang violence and the world's highest murder rate.

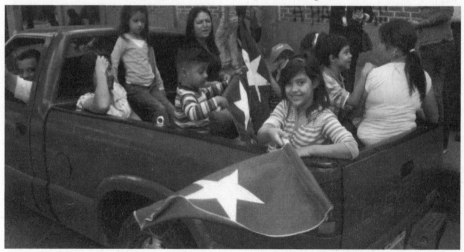

Children fly National Party flags in Tegucigalpa on election day, 2009.

Photo by the author

Jamaica

Dunn's River Falls near Ocho Rios on the north-central coast, a 600-foot stairstep waterfall that is one of the island's favorite attractions.

Area: 4,470 square miles.

Population: 2,847,232 million (2010 estimate); another 2–3 million live abroad.

Capital City: Kingston (Pop. 700,000, estimated).

Climate: The coastal climate is hot and humid; the uplands are moderate, variable and pleasant.

Neighboring Countries: This island state, the third largest of the Greater Antilles, lies about 100 miles south of Cuba and 100 miles west of the southwestern tip of Haiti.

Official Language: English.

Other Principal Tongues: A distinct variety of English spoken with a very rhythmic pattern.

Ethnic Background: African Negro and mulatto, with a very small European minority. There are prominent Chinese and East Indian minorities.

Principal Religion: Protestant Christianity (Anglican); the Roman Catholic Church and other Protestant sects are very active, as is Rastafarianism (Rasta), which holds that former Ethiopian Emperor Haile Selassie was the reincarnation of Jesus Christ.

Chief Commercial Products: Alumina (partially refined bauxite), bauxite, sugar, bananas and other tropical fruits, rum. Tourism is a very important source of income.

Currency: Jamaica Dollar.

Gross Domestic Product: U.S. $12.06 billion in 2009 ($4,236 per capita).

Former Colonial Status: Spanish Colony (1494–1655); British Colony (1655–1962).

Independence Date: August 6, 1962.

Chief of State: Queen Elizabeth II of Great Britain, represented by Dr. Patrick Allen, governor-general (since February 26, 2009).

Head of Government: Orette Bruce Golding (b. December 5, 1947), prime minister (since September 11, 2007).

National Flag: A gold diagonal Cross of St. Andrew, with black triangles at each side and green triangles at the top and bottom.

Jamaica is a picturesque, mountainous island about 145 miles long by 50 miles in width. The mountains run east and west, with spurs to the north and south reaching 7,420 feet in the east and descending in the west. The coastal plains are intensively cultivated and are the most densely populated. The Jamaican people are descendants of African slaves imported by Spanish and English planters. Rich soils and adequate rainfall encouraged sugar and cotton production during the colonial period, while the small valleys provided fruits and vegetables for local consumption. Jamaica possesses large deposits of bauxite and gypsum which are commercially exploited.

History: Jamaica's history is inextricably interwoven with the struggle between Spain and England for domination of Atlantic trade in the 16th and 17th centuries. The island was discovered by Columbus

222

Jamaica

in 1494 during his second voyage to the New World; the Spanish adventurer, Juan de Esquivel, settled the island in 1509, calling it Santiago. Villa de la Vega, (later, Spanish Town) was founded in 1523 and served as the capital until 1872. The native Arawak people were rapidly exterminated and Negro slaves were imported to provide labor.

When Jamaica was taken by the British in 1655, the total population was about 3,000. The Spanish were completely expelled by 1660, at which time their slaves fled to the mountains. These people, known as *Maroons*, resisted all efforts to recapture them, and maintained a state of guerrilla warfare against the British through the 18th century.

British title to Jamaica was confirmed in 1670, and from 1672 on, the island became one of the world's largest slave markets. By the end of the 18th century, Jamaica had a slave population in excess of 3 million, working 70 sugar, 60 indigo and 60 cacao plantations. With a profitable trade with London and an equally great illegal trade with Spanish America, the Jamaican planters were extremely wealthy. The prohibition of slave trade in 1807, freedom of the Spanish colonies by 1821 and the abolition of slavery in 1833–38, ended the plantation economy as the freed slaves took to the hills, occupying small plots of land, where their descendants are found today.

The 19th century was marked by increasing resistance to colonial rule as the economic situation deteriorated. Riots in 1865 brought about changes in the government, while disturbances in 1938 led to the establishment of dominion status in 1944 and an advance preparation for independence, granted in 1962.

Jamaica's history has also been influenced by natural disasters. An earthquake in 1692 destroyed Port Royal and led to the founding of Kingston. It in turn was destroyed by a 1907 earthquake, but was rebuilt. Hurricanes have also exacted their toll and revised the island's agricultural patterns.

The island nation has a parliamentary system of government with a two-chamber legislature consisting of a 21-member Senate and 60-member House of Representatives. The prime minister, selected from the majority party, chooses 13 senators and the remaining 8 are selected by the governor-general with advice from the leader of the opposition party. Technically, Jamaica is still a member of the British Commonwealth and a constitutional monarchy with the queen of Great Britain as the titular head of state. The queen appoints the governor-general (a Jamaican recommended by the prime minister) as her local representative.

By law, elections must be held every five years, but can be called by the party in power sooner. The two major political parties in Jamaica are the Jamaica Labour Party (JLP) and the People's National Party (PNP).

The Manley-Seaga Years

The ensuing two decades after 1972 were dominated by Michael Manley, whose father, Norman Manley, founded the PNP and played a key role in the independence movement, and Edward P.G. Seaga of the JLP. Both were Caucasian. Their policies were energetically directed toward improving Jamaica, and both tried a number of ideas to accomplish this, Manley from the left and Seaga from the right. Both, however, were hamstrung by deep-seated social and economic woes.

Manley, who won the 1972 elections, by 1976 had established a centrally planned economy and forged close ties with the Soviet Union via Castro's Cuba. Government spending increased tremendously and production fell sharply. By 1980, the prime minister's spending habits had all but bankrupted the country, and his popularity, even among the poor, plummeted. Although he counted on subsidies from the Soviet Union like Cuba did, the money and goods never seemed to make it beyond Cuba if, indeed, it had been sent at all by an overextended Soviet Union.

Manley scheduled elections in 1980. Campaign violence claimed an estimated 650 lives. Seaga, despite his party's liberal-sounding name, was right of center. Impoverished Jamaicans listened to his message and gave the JLP 57% of the popular vote and 51 of the 60 House seats.

Seaga established close ties with the new Reagan administration while distancing Jamaica from Cuba. He was instrumental in the creation of Reagan's Caribbean Basin Initiative. Economic growth resumed, although Seaga was criticized

Michael Manley

Errol Harvey

over a currency devaluation in 1983. He called elections abruptly late that year, catching the PNP off balance. The PNP boycotted the election and the JLP won all the seats in the House.

Another devaluation followed, but the economy continued to falter. Export prices for bauxite (aluminum ore) dropped in large part because of widespread recycling of the metal. Discontent over the lack of progress led to a resurgence of Manley's party in 1986, when it captured all but one of the municipal governments. After two more devaluations, the country was plagued by riots in 1987 and 1988, and it sustained widespread damage from Hurricane Gilbert in 1988, which left half a million homeless.

Seaga called new elections in 1989, but he was battling a new edition of Manley, who foresaw the imminent worldwide collapse of communism. Manley had discarded all the old rhetoric and concentrated on attacking Seaga's record and the miserable state of the Jamaican economy. The PNP and Manley returned to power, capturing 44 seats.

Jamaica

Edward P.G. Seaga
Elizabeth Marshall

Faced with continued discontent and in failing health, the 67-year-old Manley retired in 1992. Despite allegations of earlier questionable dealing, his deputy prime minister, Percival James "P.J." Patterson succeeded. Pattersonbecame the first post-independence black prime minister.

Patterson called elections in 1993. Patterson and the PNP waged an openly racist campaign against Seaga, appealing to the 75% black population of the island ("He is one of us"). He and his party won in a landslide, but the PLP alleged there was wholesale fraud. It initially boycotted the Parliament, but returned to claim the eight seats it won.

The JLP fared little better in the general elections of 1997, in which it raised its number of seats only to 10. Overall, the PNP polled 56% of the vote to 39% for the JLP and 5% for the National Democratic Movement, which won no seats. Turnout was low, but so was the traditional political violence. A 60-member team of international observers, headed by former U.S. President Jimmy Carter, declared the elections generally fair, although Carter admitted there had been "serious problems." Chief among these was the peculiar Jamaican tradition of "garrison constituencies" controlled by one party or the other, a practice Carter said he had never seen in monitoring 22 elections in 15 countries.

A political era, and a dynasty, ended when Manley died of prostate cancer on March 6, 1997. Fidel Castro was among those attending his funeral. Manley was buried next to his father.

In July 2001, Patterson was forced to mobilize the entire 3,000-man army to quell violence between gangs suspected of ties to the two major parties that left 28

dead in and around Kingston. He and Seaga held an unusual three-hour meeting aimed at reducing the violence, but there were new outbreaks in September and October and in January 2002 that left scores dead, including several children. There was a total of 1,140 murders in Jamaica in 2001, a 28% increase over 2000, and the violence affected the all-important tourism industry as hotels reported a wave of cancellations.

A special commission investigating the 2001 outbreak concluded its work in March 2002, but Amnesty International criticized the report as one-sided because it relied solely on the testimony of the police and military. Not surprisingly, the report concluded that the security forces had acted properly. For his part, Seaga was called to testify before the commission, but he refused.

Patterson also responded to the growing violence by advocating creation of a Caribbean Court of Justice, based in Trinidad, to replace Britain's Privy Council, currently the court of last resort for Jamaica and other British Commonwealth countries in the Caribbean. The new court is seen as a means of expediting hangings of murderers.

Patterson called new elections in 2002. In the three-month campaign, there were 17 politically related deaths—relatively low for Jamaica. Both parties pledged to combat the alarming crime rate. The PNP vowed to seek a 6% growth in GDP, while the JLP stressed education. Patterson won an unprecedented third term, but with a greatly reduced majority: 34 seats to 26. Patterson, then 68, said he would retire before the end of his five-year mandate. Meanwhile, Seaga, 72, said before the election that he would step aside as opposition leader if the JLP lost again and make way for new leadership.

Jamaica received an unsavory distinction in 2004 when two Jamaican nationals, Norris Nembhard and Leebert Ramcharan, were among a group of eight people from five countries placed on a sanctions list by the U.S. government as known international drug kingpins. A Jamaican court ordered Ramcharan extradited, while Nembhard was arrested and held without bail.

The murder of two prominent businessmen in 2005 led to a one-day shutdown of Jamaican businesses to protest the crime problem. Meanwhile, the murder rate for 2004 was 50% higher than in 2003, exceeding 100 per month.

In 2005, Jamaica attained another unwanted distinction: the highest homicide rate in the entire world, 58 per 100,000 people. The number of murders hit a record of 1,671, up another 25%. Patterson launched a major crackdown on drug smuggling, which was feeding much of the gang vio-

Former Prime Minister P. J. Patterson

lence, and brought crime consultants from Britain, the United States, Canada and Australia. In 2006, Jamaica's homicide rate dropped slightly to 49, still the second-highest in the world after El Salvador.

An old era ended and a new one began in Jamaican politics in 2005 and 2006. Keeping his promise, Seaga stepped down as leader of the JLP in January 2005, and on February 24 Orette Bruce Golding, 57, was elected to succeed him in a party convention, becoming the JLP's first black leader. A former member of the House of Representatives who had become a senator, Golding had long been considered Seaga's heir apparent, but he had impatiently bolted the party in 1995 when Seaga declined to retire. However, Golding could not officially become leader of the opposition until he won a House seat, which he did in a by-election in West Kingston in April. Seaga took a faculty position at the University of the West Indies.

Patterson, meanwhile, announced he would retire, and the PNP held a convention in February 2006 to elect a new president, who would automatically become prime minister. In the balloting, Portia Simpson-Miller, a veteran member of Parliament and former minister of labor and of tourism, was elected over Peter Phillips, the security minister. On March 30, Simpson-Miller, 60, widely known as "Sister P," was sworn in as Jamaica's first woman prime minister. She pledged to combat the endemic violence and corruption, to reform education and to expand the economy.

The Elections of 2007

Simpson-Miller's stewardship was to be short-lived. She called a general election for September 3, 2007. Golding made a

Prime Minister Bruce Golding

surprisingly strong showing in a televised debate with her, emphasizing corruption scandals within the PNP. Unlike past elections, violence was minimal.

The vote was so close the counting went on for two days before Simpson-Miller conceded defeat. The JLP won 50.5% of the popular vote and 32 House seats to 28—a tenuous mandate. Golding was sworn in as prime minister on September 11, ending 18 years of PNP rule. Later that year, faced like other Third World leaders with escalating oil prices, Golding took a page out of Seaga's book and devalued the currency.

Jamaica recorded another 1,574 murders in 2007, an increase of 17% over 2006; 65 were children.

Golding moved forward with his promise to crack down on corruption, appointing special auditors to investigate the customs service, the National Housing Trust and the Jamaica Urban Transit Company. One auditor, Douggie Chambers, uncovered padded payrolls in the transit company and ordered the dismissal of several managers and almost 500 unneeded employees. On June 27, 2008, Chambers was assassinated in Spanish Town. The prime suspect was a gang called the Klansmen, which has an extortion racket with roots in the transit union. Although Jamaicans had almost become inured to common gang violence, they are unaccustomed to high-level assassinations by contract killers.

Recent Developments

In 2009, Jamaica recorded a record 1,671 murders, moving its homicide rate back up to 58 per 100,000, tying with Honduras as the highest in the world. It may be even higher in 2010 after the events of May 23–29.

In March 2010, the United States submitted an extradition request for Christopher "Dudus" Coke, 41, the reputed top crime lord in Jamaica, who had been indicted the previous August by a federal grand jury in New York for trafficking in marijuana and cocaine, especially crack cocaine. The aptly named Coke is the alleged leader of an international drug- and gun-smuggling organization called the "Shower Posse" that he inherited from his father, Lester Lloyd Coke, who was burned to death in prison under mysterious circumstances in 1992. The organization has tentacles in several major U.S. cities. Like Colombia's late drug kingpin Pablo Escobar, Coke is revered among the poor in the garrison community he controls as a benevolent Robin Hood- or Godfather-like figure who provides such services as free food and who pays medical bills and other expenses. The Shower Posse is also widely believed to have shadowy ties to Golding's JLP; indeed, his garrison community of Tivoli Gardens in West Kingston is in Golding's parliamentary district.

That may help explain why Golding, who had routinely agreed to 15 earlier extradition requests, at first rejected the one for Coke, saying the evidence against Coke was based on an illegal wiretap. Under U.S. pressure, he relented, and on May 18 he announced that his justice minister would sign the request and issue an arrest warrant.

No effort was made to arrest Coke for five days. When that effort did begin, Coke's supporters resisted violently. On May 23, two policemen were killed and six wounded in a gun battle with Coke supporters near the Kingston airport. The next day, hundreds of police and army soldiers stormed into Tivoli Gardens to apprehend him. Full-scale combat ensued with Coke loyalists, who were well armed. By the end of the first day, two policemen, one soldier and 26 civilians had been killed. By the end of that week, the death toll had climbed to 74, the overwhelming number of them civilians.

Coke partisans alleged to the parliamentary ombudsman that the security forces had engaged in summary executions, which the government denied, while Amnesty International called for an investigation. Dozens more people on both sides were wounded, and about 500 people were arrested. The impact on the all-important tourism industry was devastating (see Economy).

Coke remained at large until he was apprehended in Kingston on June 22 and turned over to U.S. authorities.

Culture: The Jamaican people have inherited a vibrant culture. Their musical expression is found in the hypnotic rhythms of "reggae," a style popularized by Bob Marley, Jimmy Cliff and Peter Tosh. Reggae, grounded in the Rastafarian religion, is the basis of a thriving recording industry in Jamaica and has achieved international acclaim.

Rastafarianism, or "Rasta," as its adherents call it, is a Christian cult with African roots. Its central tenet is that Haile Selassie, the late emperor of Ethiopia, was the reincarnation of Jesus Christ. Rasta also permits the ritual smoking of marijuana. The "dreadlock" hair style is a distinctive feature of this faith.

Performing arts have been exemplified by such groups as the National Dance Theatre and the Jamaica Folk Singers, which take the country's dance and song abroad. Kingston and almost all of the larger resort towns have excellent theatrical presentations.

The Daily Gleaner, established in 1834, is one of the oldest continually published newspapers in the hemisphere.

The National Gallery of Art, established in 1974, houses a collection of priceless works executed by Jamaican artists, but also contains representative works centuries old and new ones from many nations. Local artists, potters, sculptors and weavers produce works that encompass all schools and techniques. They range in price from $10 into the thousands. Many art galleries and craft shops are found throughout the island.

Lamentably, Jamaica is characterized by a culture of violence, some political, some common crime. Handguns abound in Jamaica and are the favored means of "settling" all disputes. A "Gun Court" was established to hand down stiff sentences for illegal firearm activity. Capital punishment was discontinued in 1988, but reinstituted in 1999. All appeals must be completed within six months; execution is by hanging.

Economy: Rich bauxite deposits, sugar and tourism have dominated Jamaica's economy, and the financial conditions of the nation have been traditionally closely tied to these assets. The long-range outlook for the island's economy is linked to diversification and expansion. The Seaga government focused upon agricultural development. The goal was to become self-sufficient in food production as well as to capture a share in the lucrative U.S. market for winter vegetables.

Although Jamaica's business community was buoyed by the election of pro-business Seaga and private investment did rise somewhat, foreign capital for economic development was slow in responding. A lowered annual inflation rate (5%) of the 1980s climbed back to 22% in the 1990s.

Jamaica

An invisible economy revolves around the drug trade, and the gang culture affects politics as well as the economy. Marijuana is plentiful in Jamaica and is exported to the United States informally. Its availability is a large factor in Jamaica's astronomical crime rate. Jamaica is also a way station for an estimated 100–120 tons of cocaine per year en route to the United States, Canada and Europe. The gangs also engage in protection rackets, particularly in the construction sector, which increases construction costs by as much as 40%.

Tourism, the third largest industry after sugar and mining, is centered around popular resorts like Montego Bay and Ocho Rios on the north coast (far from crime-ridden Kingston) that cater to U.S., Canadian and European vacationers, especially during the Northern Hemisphere winter. It accounts for about $2–$3 billion a year, which represents 20% of GDP, 50% of foreign exchange and 25% of the jobs. It fluctuates according to the global economy and outbreaks of violence. The events of 2009–10 were a "perfect storm" for Jamaican tourism, a global recession and the outbreak of violence surrounding the ef-

fort to arrest and extradite reputed drug lord Christopher Coke in May 2010 (see History). The violence caused hundreds of hotel cancellations, and the government estimated losses could reach $350 million.

On a par with tourism as a source of foreign exchange are the remittances that the estimated 2–3 million Jamaicans living in the United States, Britain, Canada and other developed countries send home to their families. However, that also means that the country's brightest minds are living and working elsewhere. The recession of 2009–10 was expected to cause a sharp decline in remittances.

An economic dilemma that has no immediate solution is the crushing external debt, which in 2009 was 131.7% of GDP, the fifth-highest in the world. About 70% of government revenues are used just to service the debt.

The per capita GDP of $4,800 for 2008 is deceptively high, because it is inequitably distributed. An estimated 14.8% lived below the poverty line in 2003, the most recent year with reliable statistics, but the economy has not improved appreciably since then. Unemployment has remained

stubbornly high for years, and was 14.5% in 2009. This is at least partially responsible for the alarming crime rate.

GDP growth shrank in 1996 and 1997 and was 2% or less from 1998–2004. An increase in the world price of bauxite and an increase in hotel building in 2005–06 increased growth for 2005 to 2.5%. The skyrocketing price of imported fuel and Hurricane Felix were serious drags on the economy in 2007, which saw growth slip back to 1.5%. Then the global recession began in late 2008, with the predictable drop in tourism and remittances. GDP shrank by –.6% in 2008 and –4.2% in 2009.

Inflation was a cumbersome 22% in 2008, largely because of the high world price for petroleum, but it fell back to 8.6% in 2009.

An exciting new venture is Excel Motors, which produced its first 22 "Island Cruiser" automobiles in 2003. It exports them throughout the Caribbean.

In 2008, the money-losing state-owned sugar company became a joint venture with a Brazilian ethanol company, which could lower Jamaica's dependence on expensive foreign oil.

Jamaica signed a 27-month stand-by agreement with the International Monetary Fund in February 2010 to ease its chronic balance of payments deficit.

The Future: A cynic might well ask, *what future?* Jamaica is plagued by a moribund economy based on market-sensitive commodities such as bauxite ore and sugar, a crushing external debt that is the fifth-highest in the world as a percentage of GDP (131.7%), and a culture of political violence and common crime that is threatening the third-largest source of foreign exchange: tourism.

Jamaica needs visionary leadership, but it does not appear to have found it. Prime Minister Bruce Golding is already facing opposition calls to resign in the wake of the bloodshed in May that stemmed from the belated attempt to arrest drug kingpin Christopher Coke, who is known to be politically connected with Golding's JLP. Golding at first rejected the U.S. extradition request for Coke, then waited five days before executing the warrant, during which time Coke disappeared until his arrest on June 22. More than 70 lives were lost in the resulting violence, which frightened away hundreds of tourists and may have cost the economy $350 million in lost tourism exchange.

In short, Jamaica remains a mess. Moreover, Jamaica's best and brightest continue to gain their educations abroad, and remain there. Perhaps that is where a visionary leader for the future can be found—if he or she can be persuaded to return.

Mexico

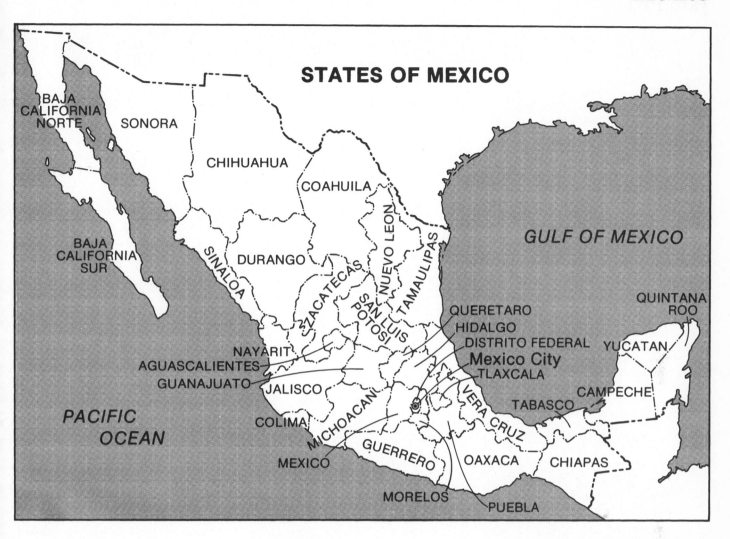

STATES OF MEXICO

BAJA CALIFORNIA NORTE

SONORA

CHIHUAHUA

COAHUILA

NUEVO LEON

BAJA CALIFORNIA SUR

SINALOA

DURANGO

ZACATECAS

SAN LUIS POTOSI

TAMAULIPAS

GULF OF MEXICO

QUINTANA ROO

QUERETARO

HIDALGO

DISTRITO FEDERAL

Mexico City

TLAXCALA

YUCATAN

NAYARIT

AGUASCALIENTES

GUANAJUATO

JALISCO

CAMPECHE

TABASCO

VERA CRUZ

PACIFIC OCEAN

COLIMA

MICHOACAN

MEXICO

GUERRERO

OAXACA

CHIAPAS

MORELOS

PUEBLA

Area: 767,919 square miles.

Population: 112,468,855 (2010 est.; growth, 1.12% per year, est.).

Capital City: Mexico City (Population 8.8 million, 19.5 million in metropolitan area, 2008 est.).

Climate: Hot, wet on the coast; milder winters, hot summers in the dry north; mild, dry winters in the central highlands.

Neighboring Countries: United States (North); Guatemala and Belize (South).

Official Language: Spanish.

Other Principal Tongues: Various Indian dialects (the census of 1960 identified 52 non-Spanish-speaking groups); English.

Ethnic Background: *Mestizo,* (mixed Spanish and Indian, 60%); Indian and predominantly Indian, (30%); White or predominantly white (9%); other (1%).

Principal Religion: Roman Catholic Christianity.

Chief Commercial Products: Petroleum, petroleum products, border assembly plants, tourism, cotton, coffee, nonferrous metals, shrimp, sulfur, fresh fruit and vegetables, clothing.

Currency: Peso.

Gross Domestic Product: U.S. $1.017 trillion in 2009 ($9,043 per capita).

Former Colonial Status: Spanish Colony (1510–1821).

Independence Date: September 16, 1810 (observed); September 27, 1821 (achieved).

Chief of State: Felipe de Jesús Calderón Hinojosa (b. August 18, 1962), president (since December 1, 2006).

National Flag: Green, white and red vertical stripes with the national coat of arms (an eagle strangling a snake) in the white stripe.

Mexico is a vast upland plateau lying between the two branches of the Sierra Madre Mountains plus the low-lying Yucatán Peninsula. The Sierra Madre range enters Mexico in the south from Guatemala at elevations from 6,000 to 8,000 feet, then dips to low hills in the Isthmus of Tehuantepec and then rises abruptly to a jumble of scenic high peaks and intermountain basins. Mexico City is located in one of the most beautiful of these. From this point northward, the Sierra Madre Occidental (west) runs to Arizona in the U.S. and the Sierra Madre Oriental (east) proceeds northeast to the border of Texas. The eastern mountains are not as high as their counterparts in the west.

Mountains and their plateaus occupy two thirds of the land area of Mexico. The highest elevations are found south of Mexico City, where Citlaltepetl (the highest 18,696 feet) with an almost perfect conical shape, is reminiscent of Fujiyama in Japan. Mountains and plateaus drop gradually toward the north. The western range descends steeply to the Pacific Ocean with few passes, while the eastern range is

Mexico

more gentle, with gaps to the Gulf of Mexico at Tampico and Veracruz.

The western mountain slopes, the northern plateau and the peninsula of Lower California (*Baja California*) are arid; the southern inter-mountain valleys receive moderate rainfall; the eastern slopes and the Gulf of Mexico coast receive up to 100 inches of rainfall between the months of June and December.

The whole of Mexico lies in the tropical and subtropical zones; however, climatically, altitude is a more important influence than latitude. Temperatures are hot between sea level and 3,000 feet, temperate between 3,000 feet and 6,000 feet and cold above the latter height. The majority of Mexico's population is found in the southern part of the plateau at elevations between 3,000 and 7,000 feet.

History: Mexico has a rich, dramatic and colorful history that for the purposes of this chapter can be divided roughly into four periods: pre-Conquest, colonial, post-independence and post-revolutionary. Modern Mexico remains heavily influenced by its past, which must be explored if the current realities and dynamics there are to be understood.

The Pre-Conquest Period

A number of succeeding civilizations thrived in the land area that is now Mexico south of the Tropic of Cancer for more than a millennium before the arrival of the Spanish, among them the Toltecs, Mixtecs, Zapotecs and Olmecs. The Toltecs, who flourished on the central plateau in about the ninth and 10th centuries of the Christian era, are remembered for their development of metallurgy as well as for worshiping a deity known as Quetzalcoatl, or the feathered serpent. When the Toltec civilization collapsed, it was attributed to the departure of Quetzalcoatl to the lands beyond the eastern sea, though he promised to return one day to reclaim his dominions. Six centuries later, it was to become a self-fulfilling prophecy.

Perhaps the greatest of these early peoples, however, were the Mayas, whose empire extended from central Mexico as far south as modern-day Honduras. They were an advanced, if somewhat barbaric, people, paradoxically developing remarkable mathematical, astronomical, engineering, agricultural and medical knowledge even as they practiced rituals that included human sacrifice. The ruins of some of their greatest cities lie in present-day Mexico, such as Chichén Itzá on the Yucatán Peninsula and Palenque in the state of Oaxaca. This great empire suddenly and mysteriously disappeared in about the 15th century.

The ruins of the Maya civilization's temple of Chichén-Itzá near Mérida, Yucatán.

To the north, even before the decline of the Mayas, another great civilization began to flower: the Aztecs. They, too, developed advanced knowledge in the sciences and medicine, but also practiced a barbaric cruelty to vassal tribes that eventually would lead to their undoing. According to legend, the Aztec god Huitzilopochtli instructed the tribal priests that their capital should be established where they found an eagle perched upon a cactus devouring a serpent. This omen was seen on an island in Lake Texcoco in the great central valley of Mexico in the early 14th century, and consequently the Aztecs began building their great city, Tenochtitlán, upon man-made islands in the lake connected by causeways to the mainland. With its network of canals for streets, the Spanish later dubbed Tenochtitlán, the "Venice of the New World," but the venue also explains why parts of modern-day Mexico City are sinking. The omen, of course, later became the basis for the modern-day symbol of the Mexican Republic, which graces the national flag.

The Aztec empire had reached its zenith by the end of the 15th century, and Tenochtitlán was as resplendent as any city of the Old World. In 1503, Moctezuma II ascended the throne, destined to be the last of the Aztec emperors. In February 1519, a force of 500 Spaniards landed first in Yucatán, then in Tabasco, and finally at Vera Cruz, on the Gulf coast. In command was a young nobleman and soldier-of-fortune determined to make himself rich and famous in this new, unexplored land: Hernán Cortés. Unlike earlier Spanish freebooters who had robbed the coastal

Indians, Cortés treated them benevolently and soon found in them willing allies against their oppressors, the Aztecs. Unknown to Cortés, he also had another ally in the legendary Quetzalcoatl. When this bearded, fair-skinned stranger from across the eastern sea landed in Mexico, the superstitious Indians immediately assumed that he was the reincarnation of the feathered serpent, returning as promised to reclaim his land.

Cortés and his band marched to Tenochtitlán, where Moctezuma, also influenced by the legendary prophecy, greeted him al-

Moctezuma II

Retreat of the Spanish on *"la noche triste."*

most as a deity. The wily Cortés, sensing an incredible opportunity, seized the emperor and, through him, issued orders to the Aztecs. The plan unraveled, however, when the Aztecs revolted against these uninvited "gods," and in the resulting melee Moctezuma was hit in the head by a rock and killed. On the night of June 30, 1520—remembered in Spanish and Mexican history as *la noche triste*—Cortés and his men had to fight their way across the narrow causeway to the mainland, suffering heavy losses. Reinforced by later arrivals from Cuba, however, he again marched on the Aztec capital with 900 men in early 1521. Meanwhile, Moctezuma had been succeeded by his 20-year-old nephew, Cuauhtémoc, who was to prove less amenable to the invaders than was his uncle. Cortés besieged the capital for three months, but despite starvation and disease, Cuauhtémoc refused to surrender. The Spaniards finally took Tenochtitlán by storm on August 13, 1521, and set it ablaze; Cortés reportedly wept at the destruction of such a beautiful city. Cuauhtémoc was

captured trying to escape by canoe and brought before Cortés, who angrily blamed him for the capital's destruction. Cuauhtémoc requested that Cortés kill him, and the conqueror complied. The remainder of Mexico was subdued quickly, and the Spanish would remain for precisely 300 years.

The Colonial Period

The viceroyalty of New Spain was a vast territory extending from Central America to modern-day California, Colorado and Texas. As was true in Spain's other American colonies, the colonial experience in Mexico differed sharply from that in England's colonies farther north. For example, the wealth of the English colonies lay primarily in their fertile agricultural land, which gave rise to a class of independent small-scale farmers. Mexico, too, had rich farmland in the central plateau, which attracted Spanish fortune-seekers willing to work it. These were not small-scale farmers, however; they were

the first of the *hacendados*, who ruled over vast estates like feudal lords.

Moreover, Mexico, like Peru, was blessed—or cursed, depending on one's standing in colonial society—with fabulously wealthy deposits of gold and silver, which filled the coffers of the royal treasury in Madrid and gave rise to a class of idle rich who occupied the top 1% of the social pyramid. Unlike their English counterparts, however, the Spanish did not drive the indigenous peoples from their lands and either exile or exterminate them and import African slaves or indentured servants to perform the heavy labor. Instead, the Spanish drove the Indians from their lands and enslaved them for labor on the *haciendas* and in the mines.

Besides the soldiers and the fortune hunters, the Spanish Crown had another ally in its quest to establish its dominion over this new territory: the Catholic Church. The first priests arrived in tandem with Cortés and set about converting the pagan inhabitants to Christianity. At first, the Indians were loathe to abandon

Mexico

their tribal gods in favor of the one worshiped by their oppressors, and they resented the destruction of their idols. At the same time, the veneration of saints and relics was not terribly unlike their pagan idolatry.

But in 1531, just 10 years after the Conquest, an event occurred that was to accelerate dramatically the conversion of the aborigines and would provide Mexico with an institution that remains part of its national identity. An Indian peasant named Juan Diego reported to the bishop that the Virgin Mary had appeared to him on a hillside outside the City of Mexico and had instructed him to return to gather the roses he would find there. Diego did as he was bidden and found roses lying among the cactus. He gathered them in his cloak and carried them to the bishop, but when the cloak was opened, the roses had disappeared and on the cloak was an image of the Virgin. At first skeptical, the church authorities accepted this version, which the Vatican later recognized as a bona fide miracle. The news that the Mother of God had appeared to a humble Indian peasant electrified the Indians and greatly facilitated the priests' job of bringing them into the bosom of the church. Below the hill where the roses were found was constructed the Shrine of Our Lady of Guadalupe, and over its altar still hangs the cloak of Juan Diego with the mysterious image that modern-day art experts have pronounced unexplainable. In December 2001, the Vatican canonized Juan Diego as a saint, which was a cause for national celebration. Pope John Paul II came to Mexico for the formal canonization in the Shrine of Guadalupe in August 2002.

Apart from the conversion of the Indians, there would be few changes in Mexico during the three centuries of Spanish colonial rule. There was, however, a gradual demographic change that was to have a major impact on the subsequent history of the country. Slowly, the Spanish conquerors began to pass their seed to their Indian subjects, and within a few generations a new, *mestizo* race began to grow and which would constitute a majority by the end of the colonial period. Yet, they were to be a race without any real identity, relegated by the Spanish to second-class citizenship, while resented by the Indians for their mixed ancestry. Although amorous dalliances with Indian women and the spawning of bastard children were commonly accepted, the Spanish men married women of their own race and social position, producing yet another class, the *criollos*, or creoles, people of pure European ancestry born in the New World.

The Spanish colonial experience in Mexico can only be described as exploita-tive. Her land and peoples were seen to exist only for the enrichment of the Crown. While England experienced the Renaissance, the Protestant Reformation, the Enlightenment and the Glorious Revolution, whose ideals were exported to its American colonies, Spain wallowed in the fear, tyranny and superstition of the Inquisition, which also was exported to America. Unlike the English colonies, there was no large middle class of well educated planters, merchants, craftsmen and intellectuals. Eventually the ideas of Locke, Rousseau and Voltaire did trickle into Mexico via a most unlikely source— the king himself. The sole exception to the succession of reactionary, divine-right monarchs was Carlos III, a reasonably enlightened sovereign who reigned from 1758–1788. Appalled when he learned of the abuses of power that characterized colonial rule in Mexico, Carlos instituted a number of reforms that improved local administration and facilitated trade. He also encouraged science and the arts, expanded education and appointed competent viceroys to carry out his ideas. At the same time, his French-inspired anticlericalism, exemplified by his expulsion of the Jesuits from Mexico, caused alarm within the church, which had heretofore enjoyed great wealth and privileges in the colony. As often happens when reforms are undertaken, there can be no turning back the clock. When Carlos died—on the eve of the French Revolution—he was succeeded by his pathetic son, Carlos IV, who was dominated by his wife who, in turn, was dominated by her unscrupulous paramour, Manuel de Godoy.

The misrule of Carlos IV contrasted so sharply with the enlightened rule of his father that resentment soon set in. Mexico already had enough reason for resentment

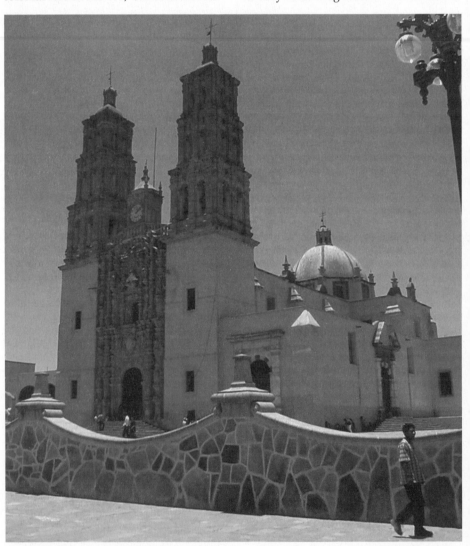

This cathedral was erected on the site of the humble church in the town of Dolores— now Dolores Hidalgo-Guanajuato, where on September 16, 1810, Father Miguel Hidalgo rang the bell to summon the peasants to take up arms against their Spanish oppressors.

Photo by the author.

Father Miguel de Hidalgo

by the end of the 18th century. The *criollos* resented the social superiority of the Spanish-born elite, whom they referred to disparagingly as *gachupines*, or the ones with spurs. The *mestizos* and the Indians, meanwhile, chafed under the oppression of their Spanish masters. For 20 years after Carlos III's death, these resentments continued to ferment, while news of the American and French revolutions gave rise to talk of independence. Ironically, it was the French themselves, in the form of Napoleon Bonaparte, who were to become the catalysts for Mexican independence.

In 1808, the detested Carlos IV abdicated and was succeeded by his son, Fernando VII. Lured to Paris by Napoleon, both were imprisoned and replaced on the Spanish throne by Napoleon's brother, Joseph, whose "reign" was supported only by French bayonets. The resulting power vacuum in Madrid threw Mexico and all of Spain's American colonies into turmoil. For two years the various factions—the *gachupines* and the *criollos*, the liberals and conservatives—debated whether to maintain their allegiance to an imprisoned king or to rule themselves in his stead. Cells of independence-minded creoles sprang up in the major towns, and the one in the city of Querétaro included a liberal priest from the town of Dolores who had endeared himself to his Indian and *mestizo* parishioners: Miguel de Hidalgo. On September 16, 1810, as a Spanish force moved toward Querétaro to arrest Father Hidalgo and other conspirators, the priest rang the bells of the church in Dolores to assemble his parishioners and declared that the moment had come to take up arms against their oppressors. The date of the famous *Grito*, or cry, of Dolores, has been observed ever since as Mexico's independence day.

As with the U.S. War of Independence, the struggle in Mexico was to be long, bloody, tedious and marked by discouraging reverses that would continue for 11 years. Father Hidalgo quickly assembled a rag-tag "army" of peasants who, motivated by a quest for social liberation as much as for independence, eagerly followed their creole leader. The rebels marched inexorably southward, gaining momentum, defeating the better-armed and trained but hopelessly outnumbered Spaniards. Yet, on the very threshold of Mexico City, Hidalgo lost his nerve and retreated. He would never regain the momentum. The Spanish counterattacked and defeated the rebel army at the Battle of Calderón, and Hidalgo fled to the northern mountains. There a trusted comrade betrayed him and other rebel leaders to the Spanish, who captured them. On July 31, 1811, the father of Mexican independence was defrocked and executed by firing squad in Chihuahua, and his head was sent to Guanajuato, where it remained on public display until independence was achieved.

However, the Spanish soon learned that the cause of independence did not die with Hidalgo. Another creole priest, José María Morelos, a man with more military skills than Hidalgo, raised a guerrilla army and took the offensive. Like Hidalgo before him, Morelos enjoyed the initiative for a time, scoring a succession of victories before he, too, was betrayed, captured and shot in 1815. Yet, still more leaders arose to take up the cause.

Meanwhile, the fall of Napoleon and the restoration of Fernando VII to the throne eliminated the issue of who was in charge in Madrid, but by then the movement for independence had taken on a life of its own. Fernando VII dispatched more troops to quell the uprising and, in a Byzantine maneuver, even negotiated with Mexican conservatives a scheme by which Fernando would leave Madrid and become the king of an independent Mexico. This occurred after Spanish liberals had forced him to swear to a constitution he abhorred. A pivotal moment in the war came when Agustín Iturbide, a competent officer in the Spanish army, defected and took up the cause of independence. He issued a decree, called the *Plan de Iguala*, under which an independent Mexico would be governed either by Fernando or another European monarch, the *gachupines* and *criollos* would become social equals, and the church would retain its Privileges. The two principal rebel generals, Vicente Guerrero and Guadalupe Victoria, embraced the plan, and one by one the major cities fell in behind. Finally, faced with the inevitable, the newly arrived Spanish viceroy also accepted the *Plan de Iguala*,

and on September 27, 1821, the Spanish abandoned Mexico City to Iturbide's army—300 years and one month after Cortés had taken it from Cuauhtémoc.

The Post-Independence Period

Just as the colonial period lasted exactly 300 years, the post-independence period would span 99, from 1821, when Iturbide triumphantly entered Mexico City, until 1920, when another military hero, Alvaro Obregón, would assume the presidency and begin to consolidate the gains of the Revolution. Those 99 years would prove to be the bloodiest and most contentious in the country's history, being marked by intrigue, betrayal, dictatorships and civil war. Few of the key players of this period would die quietly in their beds of old age.

The struggle for independence had found the various segments of Mexican society—the Privileged creoles, the *mestizos* and the Indians—fighting together in a peculiar alliance against a common enemy. With the departure of the Spaniards, however, the alliance became unraveled and friction inevitably developed among the classes. Moreover, as they fled, the *gachupines* took with them what little treasure remained, leaving the new country virtually bankrupt. Compounding Mexico's travails, the Spanish did not bequeath a strong governmental infrastructure the Mexicans could build upon for self-rule. As was the case in other emerging Latin American republics, such as Chile and Colombia, Mexico's first century and be-

General Agustín Iturbide

Mexico

Mexico City street scene in the early 19th century

yond would be marked by a struggle between the forces of conservatism—the landed gentry and the clergy—and liberalism patterned after the ideals of the French and American revolutions.

The Liberals, understandably in the majority, counted on the support of the *mestizo* and Indian masses, whose cause they ostensibly championed. Fiercely anticlerical, the Liberals nonetheless were pragmatic enough to recognize that the devoutly Catholic masses would never accept such a radical concept as Protestantism. The Liberals' opposition to the properties and Privileges of the church led to the embrace of Freemasonry, a secret society with ancient roots in Europe and the Near East that remains influential among the governing elite to this day.

Unfortunately for the Liberals, the concept of Jeffersonian democracy was to prove unfeasible in a land where the vast majority of the population was illiterate, where there was no democratic tradition

to build upon and where the lines of communication were too primitive for effective centralized government. That situation suited the outnumbered Conservatives just fine, many of them being local *caciques*, or strongmen, who wanted no interference from Mexico City. Also unfortunately for the Liberals, the generals who held the genuine power, backed by the cannon, the musket and the bayonet, opted to side with the Conservatives because it was they who possessed what wealth the country still had. The generals, quite simply, were bought off, rewarded for their services with land and treasure. As many a Mexican leader would discover over the next century, the lifespan of the generals' loyalty coincided with that of the payroll.

Iturbide, the conquering hero of the moment but also a man of unbridled ambition and pretentiousness, soon "amended" the *Plan de Iguala*. Instead of a European monarch, he himself would become emperor of Mexico, and he had the military forces to

enforce that decision. The country was to witness the tragicomic spectacle of a woefully expensive coronation that the country could ill afford. Iturbide proved a less able administrator than he had a military commander, however. After a little more than a year, his governmental ineptitude, coupled with his profligate spending on the ridiculous trappings of monarchy, left the government bankrupt. That meant, of course, that he couldn't pay the army, which quickly overthrew him and sent the hemisphere's first "emperor" into exile. When he returned uninvited in 1823, he was arrested and shot.

With the fall of Iturbide, Mexico at last became a republic, the Liberals came to power, and in 1824 they promulgated the first of Mexico's three reasonably enlightened constitutions. Guadalupe Victoria (the inspirational *nom de guerre* of Félix Fernández) became the first president, and he was succeeded in 1828 by the third great military hero of independence, Vi-

232

cente Guerrero. Alas, as was the case with Iturbide before them, their proficiency on the battlefield proved of little value in the halls of government. Both were crude, abrasive men who alienated their own congress as well as the Conservatives. Mexico dissolved into chaos and in 1830 the Conservatives seized power in a *coup d'etat*. When Guerrero fled and took to the field to combat the usurpers, the deposed president was betrayed, captured and shot, like Hidalgo and Morelos before him. Also like Morelos, a southern state later was named in his honor.

Into this volatile situation was to stride a charismatic figure who was to dominate the country off and on for the next 30 years: Antonio López de Santa Anna. A former Spanish officer who, like Iturbide,

General Antonio López de Santa Anna

had joined the independence movement, Santa Anna was the quintessential Latin American *caudillo*, the charismatic man on horseback who rules with an iron fist to maintain order. At the time of the Conservative coup, he was the commander of the garrison in Vera Cruz (today spelled Veracruz) where the all-important customs house was located. Santa Anna rebelled against the Conservative government in 1832. By the end of the year the grateful Liberals ill-advisedly made him president and Valentín Gómez Farías, a Zacatecan who would be the guiding force of Mexican Liberalism for 30 years, vice president. On the four occasions he would enjoy the supreme power of the republic, Santa Anna followed a curious practice of retiring to his *hacienda* in Vera Cruz and leaving the day-to-day responsibilities of governing the country to surrogates until

such time as the situation demanded his strong hand.

Betraying the Liberals who had mistakenly hailed him as their champion, Santa Anna dissolved the Constitution of 1824, assumed dictatorial powers, and began calling himself the "Napoleon of the West." Liberals in the state of Zacatecas rose in revolt, and Santa Anna mercilessly suppressed them. Then the Anglo-American settlers of the far northern province of Texas, unaccustomed to being ruled by despots, also rebelled. In what is now a legendary epic in Texas history, Santa Anna marched into Texas in 1836 with an army of 6,000 men, killed the 187-man garrison at the mission fortress of the Alamo in San Antonio de Bexar after a desperate and bloody battle, ordered the execution of the 300 Texans who had surrendered the fort at Goliad, then swept eastward almost to the border of Louisiana. There he was defeated and captured by the army of General Sam Houston at the Battle of San Jacinto.

Houston, himself as skilled at politics as he was at war, bartered Santa Anna for Texan independence rather than hanging him, then sent the defeated dictator to Washington to meet with President Andrew Jackson. Santa Anna returned to Mexico in disgrace, retired again to his *hacienda*, and waited patiently for his country's call.

It came in 1838, when the French landed an invasion force to impose collection of debts. In the ensuing battle, Santa Anna's leg was shot off by a French cannon ball, and again he became a national hero. His leg was ceremoniously buried in the cathedral in Mexico City and in 1841, at the height of the latest Liberal-Conservative power struggle, he again became dictator. An efficient tax-collector, he was an equally extravagant spender. As had happened to Iturbide, the army deposed him in 1844 when he was unable to meet its payroll and sent him into exile in Cuba.

Meanwhile, a border dispute with the United States erupted into full-scale war in 1846, and Santa Anna was recalled from exile to take the field against the invaders from the north. Cunning as ever, Santa Anna slipped through the U.S. naval blockade by convincing American agents that he would make peace if he returned to Mexico. Instead, he was named acting president and took up arms against the Americans. Defeated by General Zachary Taylor at the Battle of Buena Vista near the city of Saltillo in February 1847, Santa Anna nonetheless sent back dispatches to Mexico City declaring that he had won a resounding victory.

Returning to the capital a hero, he again assumed dictatorial powers. He next opposed General Winfield Scott's army,

which had landed in Vera Cruz and was marching on Mexico City. Again Santa Anna was ignominiously defeated, and the capital fell to the Americans. Under the resulting Treaty of Guadalupe-Hidalgo, Mexico ceded nearly half its territory, from Texas to California. In return, the United States paid Mexico $15 million—a welcome deposit for the bankrupt treasury. Santa Anna again went into exile, this time to Venezuela.

There followed a few years of stable and efficient Liberal civilian governments, but in 1853 Santa Anna, this time the champion of the Conservatives, again was placed in power by *coup d'etat*. To raise money, he sold off another tract of land to the United States—the Gadsden Purchase, in what is today southern Arizona and New Mexico—for $10 million.

Of course, he quickly and frivolously squandered the money. The Liberals, under the leadership of Ignacio Comonfort, rebelled against the dictator and published the *Plan de Ayutla*, which called for

Benito Juárez

the drafting of a new constitution. Santa Anna fell from power for the fourth and final time in 1855 and spent most of the rest of his life in Cuba. Eventually allowed to return, he died in poverty and obscurity in 1876.

Mexico's second Liberal constitution was promulgated in 1857 under the presidency of Comonfort, but it was so anti-clerical that the archbishop threatened to excommunicate anyone who took the required oath. By January 1858, the Conservatives had again overthrown the government, but this time the two sides found themselves in full-scale civil war, which was to last for three years and leave the

Mexico

country torn apart. Two Liberal champions emerged during the conflict who would later play decisive roles in Mexican history.

One was a full-blooded Zapotec Indian who was governor of Oaxaca: Benito Juárez. It was he who would become the moral and spiritual guardian of Liberalism and social justice and become revered as the greatest of Mexico's leaders. The other was a *mestizo* guerrilla leader who would betray the cause of reform and become one of Mexico's most reviled villains: Porfirio Díaz.

After Comonfort was deposed, Juárez was named president and removed the constitutionalist government to the north, where it enjoyed the support of the United States. The Liberals won the civil war, and on January 11, 1861, Juárez became the newest hero to triumphantly enter Mexico City, but in keeping with his humble image he did so in a plain black carriage. He was reelected president, but the Conservatives were not yet ready to admit defeat. They resurrected the old idea of in-

Emperor Maximilian of Mexico

stalling a European monarch on a Mexican throne, and they found a willing ally in France's Emperor Napoleon III.

Emboldened by the Americans' distraction with their own civil war, Napoleon landed an army at Vera Cruz and began the traditional march of conquerors to Mexico City. But at Puebla, the stubborn Mexican defenders dealt the French a stinging defeat on May 5, 1862, still commemorated as a national holiday—*el Cinco de Mayo*. The victory was fleeting, however, and the French soon captured the capital. Juárez again fled to the north with his government. In his place the Conservatives invited Archduke Maximilian, brother of the Hapsburg emperor of Austria, to reign as Mexico's second emperor.

Maximilian and his wife, Carlotta, a member of the Belgian royal family, are two of history's truly tragic figures. The Conservatives duped Maximilian into believing that he had been elected emperor in a plebiscite, and he and Carlotta arrived in Mexico expecting to be treated as beloved sovereigns. Instead, they found the country at civil war over his intervention. Ironically, Maximilian was himself something of a liberal, and he shocked the Conservatives by implementing some of the very reforms the Liberals had advocated. The Conservatives soon cooled toward their new emperor, and the *Juarista* army began scoring victories over the French and Conservative forces. With the end of the U.S. Civil War, the U.S. government warned Napoleon III to remove its forces from Mexico or the United States would intervene to enforce the Monroe Doctrine. To compound the woes of the beleaguered Maximilian, Carlotta began showing signs of mental instability. She was evacuated to Europe, where she sought unsuccessfully to win an audience with Napoleon III. Faced with the threat of war with the United States and lack of success on the battlefield, Napoleon III abandoned Maximilian to his fate. After a final defeat at Querétaro, the emperor and his army surrendered. Maximilian and two of his generals were executed by firing squad a few days later on June 19, 1867, atop the Hill of Bells, today a national landmark. Carlotta spent the remaining 60 years of her life in insanity.

Once again, Juárez triumphantly entered Mexico City and was soon reelected to a third term. By most accounts, the Juárez presidency was the most honorable and enlightened in Mexico's troubled history, before or since. There was no shameless self-enrichment such as Santa Anna and others had engaged in. The industrial base began to grow, and railroads were built. Juárez also began to implement the reforms of the Constitution of 1857, and he devoted special attention to secular ed-

General Porfirio Díaz

ucation, particularly for the hapless Indians who had long been treated as third-class citizens. This, of course, alienated Juárez from even the Liberal creoles. Moreover, in the name of economy and to guard against the praetorianism that had been the bane of Mexico since independence, Juárez had brusquely cashiered most of the officers and soldiers from the army with scant compensation for their services during 10 years of civil war. There were the inevitable military rebellions, which Juárez crushed as ruthlessly as his predecessors had. In the 1867 election, Juárez was opposed by one of his own generals, Porfirio Díaz.

Juárez was elected to a fourth term in 1871, which raised accusations that he hoped to become merely another dictator. In reality, the 1871 election was quite fair by Mexican standards, and Juárez failed to receive a majority, so his election was decided by Congress. Alas, Juárez died suddenly of a heart attack on July 18, 1872, and with him died Mexico's greatest hope for democracy with social reform. Vice President Sebastián Lerdo de Tejada, a respected and honest intellectual, succeeded him and was elected to a full term that fall, but when he chose to run again in 1876 Díaz issued a *pronunciamiento* that cynically purported to uphold the Liberal cause of "effective suffrage, no re-election." After a brief military struggle, the *Porfirista* forces captured the capital and forced Lerdo into exile. Díaz became provisional president, ushering in the longest dictatorship in Mexican history.

The Díaz dictatorship was a veritable yin-yang dichotomy of good and evil, darkness and light. On the one hand, Mexico was to experience unprecedented modernization and economic development during the 35 years he would control the country. On the other, Díaz ruled in the style of the classic Latin American *caudillo*, enjoying absolute power through a principle called *pan o palo* (bread or club). Díaz could be exceedingly generous in return for whole-hearted support, but those who refused his good offices faced imprisonment, economic deprivation, or worse. Turning his back on the Liberal principle of nationalism, he opened the doors to massive foreign investment, chiefly U.S. and British, which capitalized the country and expanded the middle class but left much of Mexico's land and wealth in foreign hands. Himself a *mestizo*, Díaz nonetheless abandoned Juárez's goal of improving the lot of the Indians, who were to continue to languish in the feudalism to which they had been consigned since the Conquest. Díaz surrounded himself with a cadre of creole technocrats, called *científicos*, who managed the economy *so* efficiently that in 1894 Mexico recorded the first budget surplus in its history. The dictator poured much of this revenue into much-needed public works projects and into the beautification of Mexico City, which he wanted to rival the grand capitals of Europe.

Because he had come to power on a platform opposing reelection, Díaz cleverly chose one of his sycophants, Manuel González, to be "elected" in 1880. During his single term, which of course was overshadowed by Díaz, González engaged in corruption on an unprecedented scale, even for Mexico. By 1884, the public was only too happy to forget about Díaz's supposed opposition to reelection and clamored for him to retake the presidency. He maintained himself in power thereafter through six rigged elections, in some of

which he awarded himself a unanimous vote! In 1904, he also extended the presidential term to six years. He concentrated all the patronage in his own hands, and enjoyed such power that he literally designated every state governor and member of Congress. Employing a system of divide-and-conquer, he pitted various factions against each other, and if one faction became too strong for his liking, he would undermine it by throwing his support to another. He did much the same thing with the officials in his government, so great was his fear of possible usurpation.

So jealous was he of possible rivals, he made absolutely no preparations for an eventual successor. By the time of his last "election" in 1910, he was 80 years old and showing signs of senility, raising concerns among the ruling elite. But there also was a restiveness among the lower classes who had been bypassed in the economic development of the Díaz years. Mexico was a social powder keg.

The spark that was to set off the inevitable explosion came from an unlikely source, a short, unassuming young man from a wealthy creole ranching family in the state of Coahuila: Francisco I. Madero. Díaz had indicated in an interview with a U.S. correspondent that he would not seek reelection in 1910, a statement that had been intended to mollify the democratic sensibilities of the U.S. government but which soon became reported in Mexico. Díaz then reneged on his promise not to stand again, and the idealistic Madero announced his own candidacy against him. Díaz at first tolerated the opposition of this seemingly insignificant upstart in order to perpetuate the myth of Porfirian democracy, but Madero's campaign appearances began attracting large, enthusiastic audiences. Madero was arrested on a trumped-up charge that he was conspiring to overthrow the regime, and he was kept behind bars until after Díaz had safely "reelected" himself. Symbolically, Díaz's latest power play had coincided with his grandiose centennial celebration of Father Hidalgo's *Grito de Dolores*.

Released from jail, Madero fled to the United States and issued a *pronunciamiento*. Suddenly there were spontaneous demonstrations against the dictatorship. Reentering Mexico, Madero found influential people flocking to his standard, but he also found himself the champion of the lower classes. Among his most important supporters was a legendary bandit from Chihuahua who had become a revolutionary: Francisco "Pancho" Villa. Meanwhile, in the southern state of Morelos, Emiliano Zapata organized a peasant army that seized the lands of the *hacendados* and engaged in battle with Díaz's federal army. The Mexican Revolution had begun.

Francisco "Pancho" Villa

Emiliano Zapata

Francisco I. Madero

Mexico

Within months, the 35-year-old dictatorship began collapsing like the house of cards it was. When Villa's forces captured the border city of Ciudad Juárez in May 1911, Díaz made the traditional "withdrawal" from the treasury, fled to Vera Cruz and took ship to France. He died in Paris four years later. Madero, meanwhile, became the latest hero to enter the capital to the cheers of the masses.

Unfortunately, for all his noble ideals, Madero was no Benito Juárez. He proved an inept administrator and was easily manipulated by his family and their friends, some of whom had been among Díaz's *científicos*. The masses who had joined his movement expecting genuine social revolution were soon disillusioned. But a graver threat came in the traditional form of military uprisings, this time by counterrevolutionary *Porfiristas*. The Revolution took on the aspect of a free-for-all, with Villa and Zapata battling the counterrevolutionaries in the name of social justice and Madero's creole generals fighting essentially for themselves. The U.S. ambassador, meanwhile, angered by Madero's reversal of Díaz's *carte blanche* to foreign business interests, threw his support behind the counterrevolutionaries. Faced with the possibility of military defeat, Madero entrusted the defense of his government to a general he believed to be loyal: Victoriano Huerta. But in February 1913, with the complicity of the U.S. ambassador, Huerta arrested Madero and Vice President Pino Suárez and ordered them shot, allegedly while trying to escape. Huerta then seized the presidency for himself through a Machiavellian manipulation of the constitution.

Huerta, an alcoholic and drug addict and one of the most treacherous and repugnant figures in Latin American history, immediately found himself faced with formidable opposition. He had arrested Villa shortly before Madero's death, but the wily bandit bribed his way free and fled to the north. After Madero's murder became common knowledge, both Villa and Zapata took to the field against Huerta. In Coahuila, Governor Venustiano Carranza refused to recognize Huerta's regime and in time became the acknowledged leader of the constitutionalist forces. In Sonora, a laborer-turned-businessman-turned-general, Alvaro Obregón, raised yet another army to oppose the usurper.

Meanwhile, Woodrow Wilson became the U.S. president, and Huerta's naked power grab offended Wilson's democratic principles. He replaced the U.S. ambassador with one who applied pressure on the dictator. When Wilson learned a shipment of German arms was en route to Mexico, he ordered the Marines to seize the port of Vera Cruz in April 1914 to pre-

Venustiano Carranza

vent the guns from reaching Huerta. This intervention backfired, however, causing the various warring factions to unite temporarily in their denunciation of this new *gringo* invasion, even as the constitutionalists accepted shipments of U.S. arms.

In one of the most glorious and celebrated periods of Mexican history, the twin northern armies of Villa and Obregón literally raced each other southward, taking city after city from Huerta's forces, while Zapata's revolutionaries fought their way north toward the capital. In August 1914—the very month that Europe exploded into full-scale war—Huerta fled Mexico City and made his way to Texas, where he drank himself to death a year later.

Álvaro Obregón

All three revolutionary armies converged on the capital, and for a few days there was near-anarchy. Order was restored as the various leaders met to discuss how Mexico was to be ruled, but peace was not yet at hand. Much to the displeasure of Villa and Zapata, Carranza was elected provisional president, and the two revolutionaries took to the field once again. This time, however, Villa met his match in Obregón, who employed modern concepts from the battlefields of Europe, such as massed machine guns and barbed wire, to decimate Villa's once-invincible cavalry at Celaya. Driven farther north, Villa was outflanked when President Wilson allowed constitutionalist forces to use Texas railroads for troop movements. Enraged, Villa captured some American engineers and had them shot, and in March 1916 he sacked the border town of Columbus, New Mexico, killing 19 Americans. Wilson ordered General John J. Pershing into Chihuahua in pursuit of Villa, a hopeless mission which, once again, served only to unite the warring factions against the invading *gringos*.

Even as the bloodshed droned on, Carranza summoned a constitutional convention that assembled in Querétaro in December 1916 and early the next year finalized the country's third liberal constitution. Unlike the earlier organic laws, this one guaranteed the rights of labor and decreed that property rights were secondary to the public good. The Constitution of 1917, which has decidedly socialist overtones, remains the oldest basic law in effect in Latin America. The constitution should be Carranza's legacy, but he is remembered as much for the rampant corruption that went on during his administration as for his role in the creation of a new Mexico.

The Mexican Revolution, which by most estimates claimed about 1 million lives, slowly wound down. A Carranza officer betrayed and assassinated Zapata in 1919. His armed struggle died with him, although the Morelos peasants were permitted to retain the lands they had seized from the *hacendados*. Villa, meanwhile, was bribed into passivity with an amnesty and a huge *hacienda* in Durango. Though he never took up arms again, he remained such a threatening force that he, too, was assassinated in 1923. In 1920, when Carranza sought to circumvent his own constitution's ban on reelection by hand-picking a puppet successor, Obregón and others turned against him. He was forced to abandon the capital and, a few days later, was murdered in his sleep by a trusted lieutenant. Obregón's army became the latest to enter Mexico City in triumph, and Obregón was duly elected president and took office in November

1920. After 10 years of Revolution, Mexico was at peace.

The Post-Revolutionary Period

Obregón, unlike earlier conquering generals who became president, proved both an able and enlightened leader, the best since Juárez. There was some of the inevitable corruption, but nothing on the scale of Díaz. Himself a former laborer who became a businessman before the call to arms, Obregón was friendly to labor but chose not to enforce some of the more radical aspects of the new constitution. He did, however, begin a modest land-redistribution program, Primarily to the Indian communal plots, called *ejidos.* He also allowed unprecedented press freedom and adhered to the constitution by stepping aside at the end of his term in 1924—although he essentially dictated who his successor would be.

Largely because of Obregón's guidance during those first critical post-revolutionary years, Mexico embarked on a nominally democratic path with guarantees of civil liberties, rather than embracing the totalitarian experiment of the Bolsheviks who had seized power in Russia the same year the Mexican constitution was drafted. And in 1924, the very year Lenin died and was succeeded by Stalin, Obregón duly relinquished power to another revolutionary general, Plutarco Elías Calles. Although this new president was to succumb to the temptations of near-absolute power, he was certainly no Stalin.

Calles served only one term, but he was destined to wield the actual power for 10 years. His administration basically was a continuation of Obregón's, with whom he maintained a close, harmonious personal relationship. It was suggested that the two men essentially were co-presidents. Calles, however, was even less committed to the social goals of the Revolution than was Obregón, and he slowed even the modest land distribution program.

On the subject of the church, however, Calles was deeply committed to the anticlerical principles that had been embodied in all three liberal constitutions. Both he and Obregón were practicing Freemasons, who are decidedly anti-Catholic and whose influence was believed to be even stronger after the Revolution. When the church opposed Calles' programs, he began enforcing all the radical anticlerical provisions of the constitution. The church's property, even the actual church buildings, were expropriated; priests were forbidden from engaging in political activity or even from wearing clerical garb on the street; foreign priests were expelled, and members of the clergy were required to register with the government. The clergy literally went on strike in 1926, refusing to say Mass for three years. Some fanatical Catholic laymen, called *cristeros,* engaged in acts of terrorism. Church-state relations remained hostile for decades. Not until 1993 did Mexico establish diplomatic relations with the Vatican.

As the election of 1928 approached, Calles and Obregón found themselves unwilling to turn over power to a third man, so the constitution was amended to allow Obregón to run for a second term. Another amendment lengthened the presidential term, as Díaz had done, from four to six years. Obregón was elected over token opposition, but just three weeks later, on July 17, he was shot to death while dining in a restaurant by a young artist who apparently was a *cristero* acting on his

Lázaro Cárdenas

own initiative. An eminent intellectual, Emilio Portes Gil, was named interim president until another election could be held in 1929, although it was Calles who actually held the power. During this brief interregnum, however, an institution was established that was to be the dominant force in Mexican political life for the next 71 years. Calles and Portes Gil organized a new political party, the National Revolutionary Party, or *PNR,* that incorporated the revolutionary sectors of *campesinos,* or peasants, and organized labor under its umbrella. Its name would be changed in 1938 to the Party of the Mexican Revolution and yet again in 1946 to its current name, the Institutional Revolutionary Party, or *PRI.* Its candidate in 1929, Pascual Ortiz Rubio, won a suspiciously lopsided victory, a phenomenon that would be repeated over and over again.

Ortiz Rubio's three-year presidency is remembered as little more than a footnote because it was Calles who was really in charge. His control was so complete that when, in 1932, the president fired some officials who enjoyed Calles' support, Calles merely summoned a news conference to announce that Ortiz Rubio had resigned. The hapless president had no choice but to comply. Calles hand-picked Abelardo Rodríguez to fill out the last two years of what was to have been Obregón's term, then likewise designated a well-respected, 39-year-old former revolutionary general, Lázaro Cárdenas, as the official party's candidate for the 1934 election.

Cárdenas won by the predictable landslide, but before long the left-leaning president and the quasi-fascist Calles clashed over policy. A bloodless power struggle ensued, but this time it was Cárdenas who prevailed.

The Cárdenas administration is generally regarded as the most honest and socially conscious of the post-revolutionary period. During his six years in power, Cárdenas redistributed 45 million acres of land to the peasants, compared with 19 million that had been distributed from 1920–1934. He also gave unprecedented moral and official support to organized labor. He refused to recognize the government of the victorious Generalísimo Francisco Franco at the end of the Spanish Civil War and gave refuge to thousands of defeated Republicans. But the act for which Cárdenas is best remembered was the nationalization of foreign oil companies in 1937 after the companies refused the government's terms for settling a prolonged strike. Today, despite the privatization trend sweeping Latin America, oil drilling, refining and fuel retailing remain in the hands of the state monopoly, *Petroleos Mexicanos,* or *Pemex.*

Despite the near-absolute power Mexican presidents enjoy, there was less abuse under Cárdenas than under many of his predecessors or successors. Press freedom continued to grow, and Cárdenas tolerated the establishment of a conservative opposition movement, the National Action Party, or *PAN,* in 1939. It also was Cárdenas who finally and irrevocably established the revolutionary principle of "no reelection" by stepping aside at the end of his *sexenio,* or six-year term. Although he was to remain a respected and influential voice in Mexican politics until his death in 1970, Cárdenas made no effort to remain the power behind the throne as Calles and others had done.

Mexico

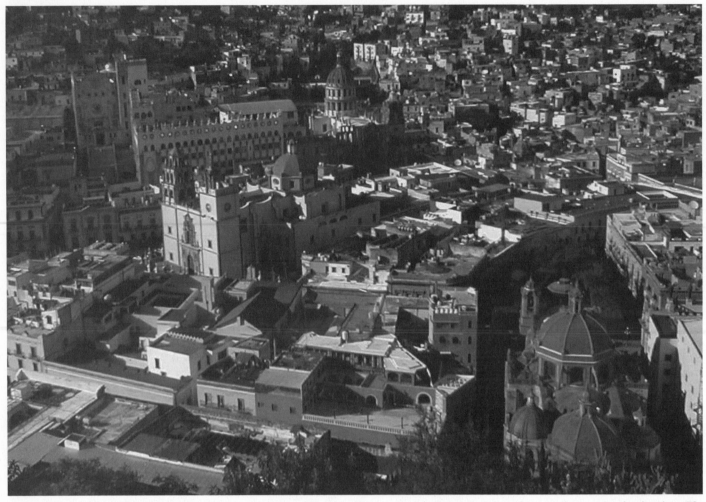

A panoramic view of the beautiful colonial city of Guanajuato, still a center of silver mining and a popular tourist destination. The triangular park in the right foreground is the *Jardín de la Unión*; the University of Guanajuato, one of the oldest and most prestigious learning institutions in Mexico, is the large white building on the hill at upper left. *Photo by the author.*

However, Cárdenas chose to continue, and thus perpetuate, the decidedly undemocratic practice of Obregón and Calles of hand-picking his successor. Referred to in Mexico as *el dedazo*, or the tap of the finger, this practice was followed by all of Cárdenas' successors until Ernesto Zedillo disavowed it in 1999. By tradition, the incumbent conferred in secret about a year before the election with former presidents and a handful of top party leaders to discuss a list of possible candidates. At this stage, the heir apparent was referred to as *el tapado*, or the hidden one, whose identity became the focus of intense speculation by the public and the press. When the president announced his decision, the designated candidate was hailed by all sectors of the party and pro-*PRI* newspapers as a near-messiah and acclaimed as the greatest possible choice. The process more closely resembled the selection of a new pope by the College of Cardinals than the nomination of a presidential candidate in a supposedly democratic system; all that was missing was the emission of white smoke from the presidential palace to announce that a choice had been made. Some scholars have suggested the *PRI*'s selection process was based upon Masonic rites.

Cárdenas' choice was yet another revolutionary general, Manuel Ávila Camacho, who had been Cárdenas' defense secretary. This surprised many, because Ávila Camacho was far to the right of Cárdenas. Moreover, he was a devout Catholic, which represented a sharp break with the anti-clericalism of the past. This transition estabÁlished a precedent that would be seen again in the ensuing decades of alternating between presidents that were leftist and centrist, also between presidents who were dynamic and passive. Under Ávila Camacho, land redistribution slowed to a glacial pace. But World War II was to result in an economic boom for Mexico, which joined the Allies and declared war on Germany and Japan. Mexican industries churned out war supplies that were exported to the United States; relations in general between the United States and Mexico, strained since the beginning of the Revolution, finally began to improve. Ávila Camacho hosted President Franklin D. Roosevelt at a meeting in Monterrey in 1943, the first time a sitting U.S. president had crossed the southern border.

As his successor in 1946 Ávila Camacho picked Miguel Alemán, his *secretario de gobernación*, or interior minister, the most powerful post in the cabinet, one that is roughly the combined equivalent of the secretary of the interior and White House chief of staff in the U.S. system. Whoever holds it is automatically placed on the "short list" to be nominated for president. Unlike earlier elections, however, this time there was a serious opposition candidate in the form of Foreign Minister Ezequiel Padilla, who was disgruntled over not being selected himself. Alemán, of course, was declared the winner with 80% of the vote. How honest that vote count was remains questionable, but for Mexico even 20% for an opposition candidate was extraordinary. The transition

238

Manuel Avila Camacho

was a watershed in modern Mexican history because Ávila Camacho was to be the last general to serve as president.

Like Ávila Camacho, Alemán was a centrist who merely give lip service to the socialist Principles of the Revolution, but he was more dynamic and more of a visionary than his predecessor. The Mexican economy was still growing, and Alemán chose to devote much of the increased revenues to mammoth public works projects like highways and dams. He also embarked on the greatest building program since the days of Díaz, and one of the chief beneficiaries of this program was the National Autonomous University of Mexico, or *UNAM*. Moreover, Alemán greatly improved the efficiency of state-owned enterprises like *Pemex*. On the negative side, corruption reappeared on a scale reminiscent of the days of Carranza and Díaz. The president himself escaped scandal, but it was noted that he and many of his appointees left office far wealthier than they had been before.

Apparently in response to the public discontent over the corruption, Alemán chose his interior secretary, Adolfo Ruíz Cortines, as the *PRI* presidential candidate in 1952. Once again, however, a *PRI* defector, a wealthy businessman and former general named Miguel Henríquez Guzmán, launched a serious independent candidacy. Ruíz Cortines supposedly defeated the popular Henríquez and minor candidates with 77% of the vote—still questionable, but it would be the smallest percentage the *PRI* would admit to for 36 years.

Ruíz Cortines restored an atmosphere of integrity to the presidency. Lacking Alemán's flamboyance and charisma, he often was derided as colorless. But he proved an aggressive, if not demonstrative, reformer. While Alemán had constructed grand projects, Ruíz Cortines focused on roads, irrigation, schools and hospitals. Among his lasting achievements was extending the suffrage to women in 1953, and in his last year in office Mexico became for the first time a net exporter of food.

Ruíz Cortines selected his young labor secretary, Adolfo López Mateos, as the *PRI* candidate in 1958. The *PAN* for the first time mounted a reasonably serious challenge, but López Mateos won by the usual landslide, about 90%. López Mateos swung the pendulum back to the left and toward more dynamic leadership. As labor minister he had earned the respect of the unions, and there were fewer strikes during his *sexenio* than in the previous three. Land distribution, which had tapered off steadily under his three predecessors, picked up dramatically. López Mateos parceled out about 22 million acres, making him second only to Cárdenas.

The pendulum then swung sharply back toward conservatism and drabness. As his successor, López Mateos picked his interior secretary, Gustavo Díaz Ordáz, a homely, most unpresidential-looking choice. For the first time, the *PAN* garnered more than 1 million votes in the 1964 election, and its percentage rose to just above 10%. There was nothing particularly breathtaking in the achievements of Díaz Ordáz other than the sports complex that was built for the 1968 Olympic Games. On the very eve of the games, however, something occurred that was to haunt the president until his death. The student unrest that had spread across Europe and the United States in 1968 arrived in Mexico that summer. Federal troops occupied the *UNAM* to quell a lengthy student strike. On the night of October 2, when students staged a peaceful demonstration in the Plaza de Tlatelolco in Mexico City, troops opened fire on the pre-

text that snipers had fired on them. Little or no evidence supports this, but as many as 300 people were killed, hundreds more wounded and more than 1,000 arrested. It was the greatest outbreak of violence since the *cristero* revolt of the 1920s. More than 30 years later, the "Tlatelolco Massacre" remains a national controversy, with questions still unanswered.

Ironically, the man who was responsible for crushing the protests, Interior Secretary Luis Echeverría, was the man Díaz Ordáz selected to succeed him in 1970. This time the *PAN*'s percentage of the vote edged up to 13%. As if to atone for his role in the Tlatelolco incident, Echeverría swung the pendulum dramatically back to the left. Early in his term he freed hundreds of students who had been jailed for two years. He angered the United States by establishing diplomatic relations with the People's Republic of China and by speaking out against the war in Vietnam. He made a point of expressing support for Cuba's Fidel Castro and welcomed Castro on a state visit to Mexico. He refused to recognize the government of General Augusto Pinochet after the 1973 coup that overthrew and killed Marxist President Salvador Allende in Chile, and he granted asylum to thousands of Chilean leftists. He ordered his U.N. delegate to support a resolution condemning Zionism as racism, but when U.S. Jews launched a boycott of Mexican resorts, he abruptly reversed course. He made pretensions about being a leader of the so-called "Nonaligned Movement" and even sought to become U.N. secretary-general upon his retirement.

On the whole, Echeverría can be described as a fountain of hollow rhetoric. He denounced capitalism, and increased the number of state-owned enterprises from 50 to 750, but pragmatically did little to interfere with free enterprise in Mexico. He talked about democratizing the *PRI*, but didn't follow through. He encouraged the

Former President López Portillo and family

Mexico

creation of left-wing publications, but when the leftist editor of the daily *Excélsior*, Julio Scherer García, became too critical for his taste, Echeverría used his influence to have him fired. Scherer then launched a weekly newsmagazine, *Proceso*, which the president tried to strangle at birth by refusing to sell Scherer government-subsidized newsprint. *Proceso* survived, however, and today is the leading news weekly. Four months before he left office in 1976, Echeverría set a precedent for future presidents by making a dramatic economic move and leaving the consequences to his successor: he devalued the peso, from 12.5 to 20 to the dollar. He also bequeathed a 50% unemployment/underemployment rate and a 22% inflation rate.

That successor would be Echeverría's finance secretary, José López Portillo, who was elected without any meaningful opposition when the *PAN* refused to field a candidate in 1976 to protest what it called, not incorrectly, *PRI* electoral manipulations. In keeping with tradition, López Portillo swung the pendulum back to the right. The major departure from his predecessor's policy was to stop baiting big business, international lending institutions and the United States. He met with President Jimmy Carter, who was sworn in six weeks after himself, in Washington early in their terms and agreed to an emergency sale of Mexican natural gas to help the United States cope with the brutally cold winter of 1977. He also became the first Mexican president to address the U.S. Congress, to which he delivered a fatherly lecture about being good neighbors. Carter would later reciprocate the visit and become the first U.S. president to address the Mexican Congress—in Spanish. López Portillo later would exchange visits with Carter's successor, Ronald Reagan. López Portillo did not, however, distance himself from Fidel Castro. He also lent moral and financial support to the *Sandinista* regime in Nicaragua, which came to power on his watch in 1979, and opposed Reagan's support for right-wing regimes in El Salvador and Guatemala.

Still, he wisely mended fences with the International Monetary Fund and major foreign banks and succeeded in reassuring them that Mexico was a sound credit risk again. In this he was aided by the discovery in the early 1970s of vast deposits of petroleum, by some estimates rivaling the reserves of Saudi Arabia, in the southern states of Tabasco and Chiapas. *Pemex* brought the fields on line just in time to take full advantage of OPEC's quadrupling of the world market price for oil. Mexico opted not to join OPEC, but the revenue from petroleum sales began to fill government coffers. López Portillo, like a poor man who has suddenly won the

Former President de la Madrid and family

lottery, went on a wild spending spree. When the money ran out, he merely borrowed more from abroad on the assumption that the petroleum gravy train would rumble on indefinitely. He would leave office before the full weight of his folly came crashing down upon his successor.

So, too, would the massive corruption committed by López Portillo and his top officials on a scale unseen since the time of Alemán. He became the embodiment of an old Mexican quip about the president: "The first two years he talks about corruption, the next two years he does nothing and the last two years he takes all he can." In López Portillo's case, he acquired a palatial estate called Dog Hill, with five mansions, swimming pools, stables, tennis courts and a gymnasium. On the positive side, he finally moved to give opposition parties a somewhat greater voice, while, of course, not actually jeopardizing the *PRI*'s grip on power. In the 1960s, the opposition had been reserved a maximum of 20 seats in the 197-seat Chamber of Deputies, the lower house of Congress, distributed by proportional representation. López Portillo enlarged the chamber to 400 seats, of which up to 100 could go to the opposition.

In 1982, López Portillo's final year in office, the world price of oil plummeted and Mexico found itself in deep financial trouble. López Portillo was forced to implement a drastic—and exceedingly unpopular—austerity program that threw about 1 million bureaucrats out of work. He also was forced to devalue the peso again. In the midst of this crisis, he broke with convention by selecting as his successor his secretary of planning and budget, Miguel de la Madrid. This also shattered the long-accepted tradition of never picking a *PRI* candidate who speaks English. Not only that, de la Madrid had earned a master's degree in public administration from Harvard. It was, moreover, to establish a new trend of selecting presidents who are tech-

nocrats who have never held elective office, reminiscent of Díaz's *científicos*, except that these new ones received their training in the United States.

In the July 1982 election, de la Madrid reportedly received 74.4% to 14% for the *PAN* candidate and 5.8% for the candidate of a coalition of left-wing parties. Just two weeks before he left office, López Portillo did something that not even the leftist Echeverría had dared to do—he nationalized the banks. On December 1, 1982, he turned over the mess he had created to de la Madrid and retired to Dog Hill. He was held in low esteem in public opinion right up until his death on February 17, 2004—and beyond.

De la Madrid was left to cope with the country's gravest economic crisis since the Depression of the 1930s. In 1983, inflation was 60%, and the foreign debt continued to mushroom, from $65 billion in 1983 to $105 billion in 1988—among the greatest per capita debts in the world. Even as the president struggled to cope with this daunting challenge, the country was hammered by a dual blow in 1985. OPEC slashed the price of petroleum by about two thirds, from roughly $30 to $10 per barrel, which completely pulled the rug out from under the debt-ridden economy.

Even nature seemed to be against Mexico; a disastrous earthquake struck Mexico City that year, killing an estimated 10,000 people and causing $3.5 billion in property damage—much of which was attributed to shoddy construction of government-sponsored projects. The peso began to plummet against the dollar, and the country faced the kind of hyperinflation that had once plagued Argentina, Brazil and Peru. Inflation soared to more than 100% on de la Madrid's watch, and the peso dropped from 24.5 to the dollar to 2,800 by 1990.

Compounding the dilemma was Mexico's burgeoning birthrate of 3.2% annually. Even in the boom times the economy had barely been able to absorb the young new workers flooding the labor market, but in these lean times the situation became especially desperate. The cardboard shantytowns on the outskirts of Mexico City grew larger and larger, and more Mexicans than ever were seeking the traditional escape route from their misery—illegal entry into the United States. This, of course, served to strain bilateral relations.

Desperate times do indeed call for desperate measures, and de la Madrid employed them. He allowed the price of Mexican crude oil to "float" instead of pegging it at an artificial price. He also began to sell off some of the government-owned enterprises whose payrolls had become bloated from *PRI* patronage. Attempts to renegotiate the foreign debt satisfied neither Mexico nor its creditors. Finally, de la Madrid succeeded in obtaining a $3.5 billion "bridging" loan from the Reagan administration in 1988.

As if de la Madrid did not have enough problems, early in his administration he was faced with still another—a scandal that erupted over the corruption committed under his predecessor. Among the high-level López Portillo officials accused of financial wrongdoing were the head of *Pemex*, who could not account for a missing 300,000 barrels of oil. Perhaps the most egregious case, one that especially outraged the public, was that of the Mexico City police chief, who had built himself an unbelievably ostentatious estate complete with air-conditioned doghouses! The chief was prosecuted and his property was expropriated and opened to the public as a "museum of corruption." López Portillo himself managed to escape prosecution (no such action had ever been taken against a former head of state since the Revolution), but the damage to his reputation wrought by his shameless nest-feathering was irreparable and today, even in death, he remains pariah.

The lean economic times and the publicizing of outrageous cases of corruption took a serious toll on the *PRI*. Up to that point, the *PRI* not only had won every presidential election since 1929, but it had never lost an election for a state governorship or a federal Senate seat and rarely lost at any level. Now, for the first time, the *PAN* began winning municipal elections and even won some directly elected seats in the Chamber of Deputies, not merely the scraps the *PRI* reserved for the opposition under proportional representation.

In the 1988 presidential election, the *PRI* was to face the greatest threat to its power in its 60-year history, not from the right, but from the left. Cuauhtémoc Cárdenas, son of the revered former president and himself a member of the *PRI*, abandoned the party to organize a new left-wing movement, the Party of the Democratic Revolution, or *PRD*. As his successor, de la Madrid selected another technocrat who, like himself, spoke fluent English, was schooled at Harvard and had never held an elective office: Carlos Salinas de Gortari. The *PAN*, meanwhile, launched its most determined effort to date with the candidacy of Manuel Clouthier, a wealthy landowner from Sinaloa.

Polls showed that Salinas not only might fail to win an absolute majority, but even more unthinkable, might actually lose to Cárdenas. The campaign was the most contentious in living memory, and the actual election on July 6 remains the most controversial. As the polls had indicated, on election night early returns showed Cárdenas closing on Salinas. Then, suddenly, it was reported that the vote count had been delayed by a computer breakdown. Federal troops seized the ballot boxes. The results weren't announced until September 10, and it was reported that Salinas had neatly received a bare majority of 50.36% to 31.06% for Cárdenas and 16.81% for Clouthier. Both opposition parties cried foul, but Salinas was duly sworn in on December 1 under a cloud of suspicion and illegitimacy that haunts him to this day.

Just as Echeverría had sought to atone for the Tlatelolco Massacre by tilting heavily to the left, so Salinas attempted to neutralize the outrage over his suspicious election victory by portraying himself as a political reformer. The timing of the Salinas reforms, beginning in 1989, was especially symbolic. *Perestroika* and *glasnost* were in full flower in the Soviet Union; the democracy movement was underway in China, although it was to be crushed that June; the Berlin Wall came tumbling down in November, and the autocratic regime of Romania's Nicolae Ceaucescu came to a bloody end in December. Moreover, one Latin American dictatorship after another had given way to multi-party democracy.

With the temper of these times, Mexico's monopolistic political system suddenly looked as out of place as a man with his fly open at an elegant dinner party. Salinas put out the word that at least some elections must be fair and clean, if only to keep up appearances. As a result, the *PAN* began winning state governorships, first Guanajuato, then Baja California Norte, Jalisco and Chihuahua. Both the *PAN* and the *PRD* began winning more directly elected seats in the Chamber of Deputies, and even the *PRI*'s monopoly in the 64-member Senate was finally broken.

Perhaps just as important as the electoral reforms, however, was the relaxation of controls on the media. Salinas abolished *Pipsa*, the government newsprint monopoly that offered paper at subsidized prices but which often had withheld it from overly critical publications. The virtual monopoly enjoyed by the giant pro-*PRI* television network *Televisa* also came to an end as rival network *TV Azteca* went on the air, although it, too, had pro-*PRI* owners. As a consequence, reporting became both more aggressive and more critical. Salinas, and the so-called "dinosaurs," or traditionalists within the *PRI*, soon discovered what Mikhail Gorbachev was to learn: that reforms after decades of repression gain momentum and take on a life of their own; once the forces of openness are placed in motion, they cannot be reversed without a violent reaction.

Meanwhile, Salinas sought to cope with the economic crisis he had inherited from his predecessor. He negotiated another "bailout" loan in 1990 from President George H. W. Bush, with whom he met several times and enjoyed a satisfactory working relationship. In addition, Salinas embraced the Latin American trend toward privatization of state-owned enterprises. The Mexican Revolution was essentially dead. In its place was a stampede toward free-market capitalism. No longer were foreign, particularly U.S., business-

Former President Salinas de Gortari and family

Mexico

men viewed as bogeymen. Assembly plants, called *maquiladoras,* sprang up along the northern border. Hundreds of thousands of Mexicans found jobs in them, at wages well below U.S. levels but far above what they had before—nothing.

Slowly the economy began to improve, and Bush and Salinas discussed a grand scheme designed to benefit both economies—a North American Free Trade Agreement (NAFTA) that would encompass Canada, the United States and Mexico. NAFTA became a hot political issue in the U.S. presidential election of 1992, with organized labor vehemently opposed to it. But after some vacillation, Democratic candidate Bill Clinton also endorsed the concept. The independent candidate that year, tycoon H. Ross Perot, warned that NAFTA would create "a giant sucking sound" as U.S. jobs disappeared south of the border. After Clinton's victory, the U.S. Senate ratified the treaty in late 1993—after the Canadian Parliament and Mexican Congress already had done so—and it took effect on January 1, 1994.

Modeled loosely after the European Common Market, in theory NAFTA benefits all three countries by eliminating tariffs, thereby stimulating trade and, indirectly, production. There has, indeed, been an explosion of trade. Tractor trailers flow in an endless stream across the Rio Grande in both directions, although in those heading north illegal drugs frequently ride piggy-back with legitimate cargo. The boom in northern Mexico was to be cut short, however, by yet another disastrous peso devaluation.

By the 1994 elections, Salinas' reforms had ricocheted on him, and the *PRI* was split more than ever between the reformers and the "dinosaurs." The traditionalists contemptuously regarded the reformers, most of whom had held only appointed offices by virtue of their advanced degrees, many of them from the United States, as upstarts who had not paid the necessary dues by coming up through party ranks. Despite his reforms, Salinas was not about to abandon the practice of the *dedazo.* According to tradition, he met privately in September 1993 with a handful of influential party leaders before announcing he had selected yet another technocrat with a U.S. doctorate, Luis Donaldo Colosio, as the *PRI* candidate. Though he was a technocrat, the party elders regarded him as harmless and pledged to support him.

But Colosio soon demonstrated that he was his own man, not Salinas'. He campaigned as a populist and drew large, enthusiastic crowds, which led to a falling out with Salinas. The rift may have been Colosio's doom. On March 23, 1994, while pressing the flesh with a crowd of cheer-

**Former President
Ernesto Zedillo Ponce de León**

ing supporters in Tijuana, Baja California Norte, Colosio was shot in the head by a man wielding a pistol and died on the spot. The killing sent shock waves through Mexico, because although violence is relatively commonplace in local politics, this was the highest-level assassination since the murder of President-elect Obregón in 1928. The lone gunman was apprehended, convicted and sentenced to 45 years in prison (Mexico does not have the death penalty), and although he never implicated anyone else in the assassination, there remains a widespread public belief that the killing was the result of a conspiracy.

Stunned, *PRI* officials met again with Salinas, who chose yet another technocrat, the Yale-educated Ernesto Zedillo Ponce de León. While Colosio had been perceived as shy, Zedillo was seen as colorless and reclusive. He had a flat, uninspiring speaking voice and initially showed no talent for leadership. He had spent his 21 years with the party hidden away from the public in various bureaucratic assignments. He received coaching to improve his style, but with dire results. In the spirit of Salinas' reforms, he agreed to meet the *PRD's* Cárdenas and the *PAN* candidate, Diego Fernández de Cevallos, in a televised debate; his performance was disastrous. Polls after the event showed Fernández leading by 20%.

The well-oiled *PRI* machinery rushed to Zedillo's rescue. Although the "dinosaurs" were lukewarm about having a fourth Ivy League-trained bureaucrat as the party nominee, they rallied behind him

to ensure victory through the *PRI's* time-honored methods. Zedillo likely would have won the August 21 vote even without creative vote counting, but like Salinas, he reportedly—and suspiciously—received the magic 50% majority. Fernández supposedly received 26%, while Cárdenas dropped to 17%. The *PAN* and the *PRD* made significant gains in the Congress. The *PRI* won an even 300 of the 500 seats in the Chamber of Deputies, while the *PAN* total rose to 119, the Workers Party (*PT*) had 10 and the *PRD* 7. In the expanded Senate, the *PRI* had 95 of the 128 seats, the *PAN* 25 and the *PRD* 8.

Like Echeverría before him, Salinas decided in the waning days of his administration to devalue the peso and let Zedillo deal with the consequences. The consequences were terrible; the economic recovery collapsed virtually overnight and the country plunged once again into recession. The trauma of this latest downturn on the newly emerging middle class was to have long-lasting political fallout for the *PRI.* Even today, young urban professionals from different states tell this author that they vote for the *PAN* because of Carlos Salinas.

Even before Zedillo could take office on December 1, 1994, the country would be shocked by yet another assassination, one that shook the government and the *PRI* to their very foundations. On September 28, *PRI* Secretary General José Francisco Ruíz Massieu, the No. 2 man in the party and a leader in the reform faction, was gunned down. Salinas, whose sister was once married to the slain politician, appointed Ruíz Massieu's brother Mario to investigate the murder. A few months later, after Zedillo had taken office, Mario Ruíz Massieu resigned, alleging that the *PRI* was obstructing the investigation. Ostensibly to ensure a non-partisan investigation, Zedillo appointed as attorney general a *PAN* loyalist, Antonio Lozano. In February 1995, Lozano stunned the nation again by ordering the arrest of former President Salinas' brother, Raúl, on charges of masterminding the Ruíz Massieu murder.

A month later, Carlos Salinas—disgraced as much by his brother's arrest as by the recession already being blamed on him—absconded from the country, first to the United States, then to Canada, and finally to Ireland, which has no extradition treaty with Mexico. He remains a pariah in Mexico to this day, while the Ruíz Massieu assassination and the Salinas brothers' alleged links to it, as well as revelations they may have been linked to drug traffickers, remain grist for the Mexican media. In January 1999, Raúl Salinas was convicted of the murder and sentenced to 50 years' imprisonment. In June 2005, a three-judge appeal panel shocked the country by overturning the conviction. He walked out of prison a few days later.

The Political Earthquake of 1997

Mexico embarked on an uncharted political course with the midterm elections of July 6, 1997. At stake were all 500 deputies in the lower house of Congress, 300 of them elected directly by district and 200 by proportional representation, and 32 of the 128 senators, allocated by proportional representation. The *PRI* would have had to poll at least 42.2% to retain its absolute majority in the Chamber of Deputies, but it received only 39%.

Of the 300 deputies elected directly, the *PRI* won 164, the *PRD* won 70, the *PAN* took 65, and the *PT* had one. Proportionally, the *PRI* received 39% of the vote, *PAN* 27% and the *PRD* 25.5%. When the complicated formula was put into effect, the *PRI* fell about 10 seats short of a majority. Its majority in the Senate remained secure.

Buffeted from right and left, the *PRI* also took an unprecedented drubbing in local races. In Mexico City, where the mayor was elected directly for the first time rather than appointed by the president, Cuauhtémoc Cárdenas, the *PRD* presidential candidate in 1988 and 1994, received a landslide victory, polling 47.1% of the vote.

Of the six governorships at stake in the election, the *PAN* won decisive victories in both Nuevo León (Monterrey) and Querétaro. Those triumphs brought to six the number of states *PAN* had wrested from the *PRI* since 1989, after President Salinas' electoral reforms were implemented. The *PRI* retained San Luis Potosí and Colima states, but the *PAN* claimed fraud cost it the governorship of Sonora, which borders Arizona, and of Campeche, in the southeast.

Yet the election, which this author observed in Monterrey, apparently was fair. Elections are now conducted under the auspices of the Federal Electoral Institute *(IFE)*, an independent, non-partisan entity, not a creature of *PRI* patronage as was the case in the past; each state has a similar body. Since 1994, each voter has a plastic ID card with photo and thumbprint, which is matched against a master list in each polling station. Each party is entitled to five accredited poll watchers at each station. Voters mark their ballots in secret, free from intimidation by *PRI* operatives. After a voter casts his ballot, his thumb is marked with indelible ink to thwart Chicago-style multiple voting. Alcohol sales are banned not only on election day but on election eve.

The business newspaper *El Financiero* had perhaps the most succinct headline the morning after the election: "END TO 70 YEARS OF HEGEMONY." Julio Cas-

Headlines in the Monterrey newspaper *El Norte* the morning of July 7, 1997, declare the opposition *PAN* candidate, Fernando Canales, the winner of the Nuevo León governor's race, as well as announcing that the opposition parties have broken the *PRI*'s domination of Congress and that the *PRD*'s Cuauhtémoc Cárdenas has won the mayor's race in Mexico City.

trillón, one of the victorious *PAN* candidates for national deputy from Nuevo León, had a prophetic assessment. "This is the death of the one-party system," he proclaimed during an interview with me.

The election went beyond leaving with an opposition-controlled Congress, however. Mexico's electoral map now showed a troubling polarization between north and south, rich and poor, right and left, which

Mexico

continues today. The *PAN* was clearly on the ascendancy in the prosperous northern half of the country, where jobs were generated by ubiquitous *maquiladora* assembly plants. I was stunned by the increased affluence I found in Monterrey since my last visit 14 years earlier. With prosperity, it seems, had come political conservatism. The farther south one goes, however, the worse the poverty and the greater the voting strength of the *PRD*.

For the first year after the historic 1997 elections, the *PAN* and the *PRD* put aside their obvious ideological differences to join forces to wrest control of key committees in the Chamber of Deputies from the *PRI*.

Cárdenas took office as mayor of Mexico City in December 1997, but the euphoria of victory abruptly gave way to the grim realities of governing the world's most populous city. The extent of *PRI* patronage and corruption proved to be even more mind-boggling than had been imagined. The outgoing *PRI* officials had erased the hard drives of all the computers—except for the computers that had mysteriously vanished. The erasures apparently were less an act of sour-grapes sabotage by the losers than a matter of destroying evidence of malfeasance. Meanwhile, scandal after scandal dominated newscasts and the front pages of newspapers throughout the country in 1998, most of them involving *PRI* officials or wealthy patrons.

But the worst was yet to come. In March 1998, President Zedillo startled the Chamber of Deputies with a cavalier proposal for the government to assume $65 billion in bad debts from the 1994–95 economic crisis. The debts were held by the Bank Savings Protection Fund, the equivalent of the U.S. Federal Deposit Insurance Corporation, known by the acronym *Fobaproa*. Zedillo's plan amounted to a massive bailout of banks that went under during the crisis, with the taxpayers footing the bill. Soon, however, investigative journalists and opposition congressmen began disclosing that many of the bad debts resulted from incredibly stupid loans to multi-millionaires for high-risk ventures. Many of those businessmen, it turned out, had contributed millions to the *PRI*'s 1994 campaign chest.

The public outrage was immediate and intense. For months, the opposition *PAN* and *PRD* deputies joined forces to keep Zedillo's bailout bill hostage in the lower house, while the government made lame efforts to assuage public opinion by arresting more than 180 businessmen for fraudulent loans. The logjam was broken when the *PAN* struck a compromise with the *PRI* on the 1999 budget, by which $55 billion of the *Fobaproa* debt would be converted into public debt. The *PRD* denounced the bailout as a travesty, ending the cooperation between the two opposition parties.

Prelude to 2000

With the *Fobaproa* scandal reverberating in the background, Mexicans elected 17 of their 31 governors in 1998 and 1999. With the electoral reforms firmly in place, the outcomes were no longer a foregone conclusion. This author drove to Zacatecas to cover that election as a free-lance journalist. There, a former *PRI* whip in the Chamber of Deputies, Ricardo Monreal, had bolted the party and was the candidate for the *PRD*, while the *PRI* nominated a long-time party hack. The race was symbolic because Zacatecas had long been a faithful *PRI* stronghold. Monreal won a decisive victory, 43% to 36%, despite evidence of *PRI* vote-buying. That same day, the *PRI* easily held onto the governorship of Durango, and made history in Chihuahua with the first *recapturing* of a governorship from the *PAN*, which had won there in 1992.

A month later, the *PAN* captured the governorship of Aguascalientes for the first time. The same day, the *PRI*'s Miguel Alemán, son and namesake of the former president, won by a large margin in Veracruz, while the *PRI* held onto the governorship of Oaxaca against a determined *PRD* challenge. The *PRD* claimed fraud.

The *PRI* retained the governorships of Tamaulipas in October 1998 and of Puebla and Sinaloa in November. But in tiny Tlaxcala, a former *PRI* loyalist, Alfonso Sánchez Anaya, ran as the *PRD* candidate and pulled off a narrow upset victory, 45% to 43%.

Guerrero and Baja California Sur voted in February 1999; both were battles between the *PRI* and *PRD*. In Guerrero, the *PRI* candidate was declared the winner by 49% to 47%. The *PRD* cried foul, alleging the *PRI* had swapped votes for groceries. But in Baja California Sur, the *PRD*'s Leonel Cota Montana won by a landslide 55% to 36%.

Two weeks later, the *PRI* won in Hidalgo and even in Quintana Roo, where the incumbent *PRI* governor, Mario Villanueva Madrid, was under federal investigation for drug trafficking. In both states, the two opposition parties had failed to present a united front, thus dividing the opposition vote and assuring the *PRI* easy wins. As a bizarre anticlimax to the Quintana Roo election, Governor Villanueva absconded the day before the inauguration of his successor and disappeared. For two years he was an international fugitive before being arrested in Cancún in his home state in May 2001. (In 2010, he was extradited to the United States.)

In July 1999, the *PRI* benefited from a divided opposition to retain the governorship of the populous state of Mexico behind the candidacy of Arturo Montiel,

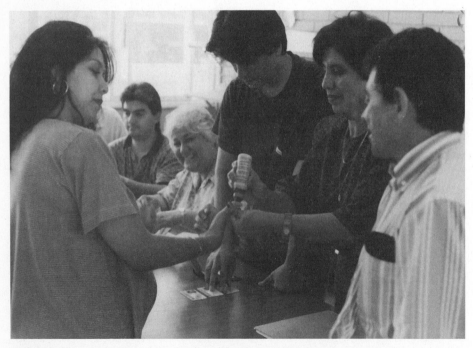

A poll-watcher applies indelible ink to the thumb of a woman in Monterrey after she cast her ballots in the historic 1997 congressional elections, one of the many safeguards now in effect to prevent electoral fraud. The ruling *PRI* lost its majority in the lower house of Congress for the first time.   *Photo by the author*

Thousands packed the Plaza de Armas in Zacatecas for the closing rally of the *PRD* gubernatorial candidate, Ricardo Monreal, in July 1998.
Photo by the author

The pre-election issue of the weekly newsmagazine *Proceso* carries irreverent caricatures of the three major candidates. At left is Vicente Fox, a Coca-Cola in one hand and an obscene gesture in place of his trademark "*Ya*" sign in the other; around his neck is a cross, symbolizing his devout Catholicism. In the middle is Francisco Labastida, carrying an enormous forefinger representing "*el dedazo*," meaning he was the favored candidate of President Ernesto Zedillo. On his lapel button is the unpopular former president, Carlos Salinas de Gortari. At right is Cuauhtémoc Cárdenas, portrayed as a moralistic reformer.

while in Nayarit the *PAN*, *PRD*, and *PT* put aside their ideological differences to field a single candidate, who won, 50% to 44%. The *PRI* defeated an opposition coalition in Coahuila that September.

Thus, voters sent mixed signals in the governorship races of 1998–99. The major psychological winner was the *PRD*, which went into the races with no state governorships and emerged with three, Zacatecas, Tlaxcala and Baja California Sur. The *PAN* didn't quite break even, losing a large, powerful state (Chihuahua) while picking up a smaller, but still influential one (Aguascalientes). An opposition alliance won the governorship of Nayarit but lost in Coahuila. The *PRI* could console itself that it won 13 of the 17 governorships, including the recapturing of Chihuahua, and that it still controlled 21 of the 31, but there was no escaping the mathematics that it suffered a net loss of four states and saw its electoral strength eroded in several more. Of the three parties, it clearly was the major loser.

The Elections of 2000

One of the most pivotal events in 20th century Mexico occurred in October 1998 when President Zedillo publicly disavowed the *dedazo*, or tap, by which for 65 years the incumbent president had personally designated the next *PRI* candidate.

Seven candidates expressed interest in the *PRI* nomination, but the list soon winnowed to four: Manuel Bartlett, former governor of Puebla and interior secretary under de la Madrid, closely identified with the party's "dinosaur" faction; Humberto Roque Villanueva, a former *PRI* chief; Interior Secretary Francisco Labastida, a former governor of Sinaloa, considered a reformist and unquestionably Zedillo's preferred choice; and Tabasco Governor Roberto Madrazo, a dinosaur.

Meanwhile, the *PRD*'s presumed candidate, Mexico City Mayor Cárdenas, who had been the frontrunner for president in most opinion polls throughout 1998, began to suffer a decline in public esteem for his perceived lack of progress. In 1999, a new book alleged Cárdenas had met secretly with Carlos Salinas shortly after the highly suspect 1988 election and agreed not to challenge Salinas' stolen victory.

The *PRI*'s National Political Council (*CNP*) approved the primary election process over a party convention and set November 7 as the date for the primary. The nominee would not be elected directly; the nomination would go to the candidate who polled a plurality of the vote in the largest number of the country's 300 districts for the Chamber of Deputies. The primary was opened to all voters regardless of party affiliation, apparently be-

Mexico

cause the *PRI* does not have party membership cards. The *CNP* required public officials to resign their posts first.

Labastida, Zedillo's favorite, scored a landslide victory, which attracted worldwide media attention. He received 5.3 million votes, or 55% of the 9.7 million votes cast, and in the vote that really mattered, carried 274 of the 300 districts for the Chamber of Deputies. Madrazo finished second and Bartlett third. The *dedazo*, it appeared, was not quite dead after all.

Mexico had never seen the likes of the campaign for the July 2, 2000 presidential election. Guanajuato Governor Vicente Fox of the *PAN* had replaced Cárdenas as the frontrunner in all major polls. But once Labastida's landslide primary victory was a fact, he emerged as the front-runner. Attempts to forge an alliance between Fox and Cárdenas failed. Neither man, each known for an oversized ego, was willing to yield to the other.

Fox chiseled away at Labastida's lead, and the race became essentially a contest between them. The Green Party (*PVEM*) forged a coalition with the *PAN* called the Alliance for Change. Later, the candidate of the small but venerable Authentic Party of the Mexican Revolution (*PARM*) also withdrew and endorsed Fox. The *PRD*, meanwhile, formed a coalition with the *PT* and two smaller left-wing parties.

Fox closed the gap with an April 25 debate, in which the flamboyant Fox was widely seen as the victor over Labastida and Cárdenas. His unorthodox campaign style, heretofore unknown to Mexicans, struck a responsive chord. The six-foot, six-inch Fox enhanced his image by wearing cowboy boots.

In June, Labastida (and Cárdenas) accused Fox of illegally accepting foreign campaign contributions, which Fox adamantly denied. (The *IFE* later confirmed they were true and levied a heavy fine on the *PAN*). Labastida even suggested that the devoutly Catholic Fox would impose his religious beliefs on the country.

This author drove to Mexico to cover the final days of the campaign for several newspapers. Convinced that Fox was where the story was, I attended Fox's closing rally in a soccer stadium in León, in his home state of Guanajuato. "If you are tired of the *PRI*, if you are sick of the corruption, if you want a government that is pluralist and inclusive, the only choice is to vote for the Alliance for Change!" he shouted. "Give me 10 seconds of your time, and I will give you six years working to give you a Mexico of grand opportunities!" The crowd cheered as though Mexico had won the World Cup.

If the mid-term elections of 1997 were a political earthquake, the elections of 2000 were a tidal wave. I observed some of the

After the results began coming in, jubilant young supporters of *PAN* candidate Vicente Fox congregate in Avenida Venustiana Carranza in Saltillo to celebrate his victory—and the *PRI*'s first presidential defeat in 71 years.

Photo by the author

voting Sunday morning in Guanajuato, and was struck by a new feature: There were plastic curtains on the voting booths to ensure secrecy. On the booths were the words, "The vote is free and secret."

I drove north to Saltillo, Coahuila, arriving precisely as the polls closed at 8 p.m. On my car radio I heard the news that was once unimaginable: Exit polls showed Fox with 44%, Labastida with 38%, Cárdenas with 16%. Two hours later, Fox's stunning and historic victory became assured. Along Saltillo's Boulevard Venustiano Carranza, thousands of jubilant *Panistas* honked horns, waved banners and posters and flashed the two-fingered symbol for Fox's campaign slogan, *"Ya!"* ("Right now!") There was a far larger explosion of jubilation around the Angel of Independence monument along the Paseo de la Reforma in Mexico City. It was a euphoria I had witnessed in 1989 when Patricio Aylwin was elected president of Chile to end the 16-year dictatorship of Augusto Pinochet. For Mexico's opposition, the wait had been 71 years.

At midnight, a dour President Zedillo addressed his countrymen on television and acknowledged that "it appears unquestionable that the next president will be Licenciado Vicente Fox Quesada." He graciously congratulated Fox on his victory and pledged his cooperation for a smooth transition, but not as graciously

spent considerably more time praising Labastida, reminding his viewers what a positive force the *PRI* had been and pledging that the party would remain a vital force in the life of the nation. Soon thereafter, Fox appeared, and graciously praised Zedillo and Labastida. Ironically, July 2 also had been the victor's 58th birthday.

Mexico awoke not to a hangover but what seemed like another impossible dream. Not only had Fox carried 21 of the 31 states, but the *PAN* had near-parity with the *PRI* in Congress. Cárdenas carried only two states—Baja California Sur and his home state of Michoacán. To make the *PAN*'s night complete, it picked up the governorship of the southern state of Morelos (the state of Emiliano Zapata) with 58% of the vote. It was the first time the *PAN* had won a governorship outside of its power base in the north.

Meanwhile, the *PRD* candidate for mayor of Mexico City, Andrés Manuel López Obrador, narrowly won with 38% of the vote.

Overnight, Mexico had been turned upside down, and a shell-shocked *PRI* began taking stock of the situation and wondering what the future would bring. One of my final images before leaving Mexico was a car with a sign painted on its back window that largely summed up the feelings of a decisive plurality of Mexicans:

246

"GANO PAN, GANO MEXICO" ("PAN WON, MEXICO WON").

Final official tabulations by the nonpartisan *IFE* were:

Fox	15,988,740	42.52%
Labastida	13,576,385	36.0%
Cárdenas	6,259,048	16.64%

A total of 37,603,924 Mexicans had voted, a respectable turnout of 63.97%. The breakdown in the lower house after the allocation of the 200 seats by proportional representation was: The *PAN*, 208, and its partner, the *PVEM*, 15, for a total of 223 for the Alliance for Change, 27 seats short of a majority; the *PRI*, 209; the *PRD*, 52; the *PT*, 8; the Convergence for Democracy, 3; the Nationalist Society, 3; and the Social Alliance, 2. The breakdown of the 128 Senate seats was 58 for the *PRI*, 53 for the *PAN* and the *PVEM* and 17 for the *PRD*.

The new president was born on a ranch in Guanajuato; his father was of U.S. descent. He received a Jesuit higher education, then went into the family's business. He ran a boot manufacturing company and a frozen fruit and vegetable firm as well as becoming chief of Coca-Cola's Latin American division. He was elected to the Chamber of Deputies in 1988, and was instrumental in passing a constitutional amendment to allow citizens with one foreign-born parent to be elected president; previously, both parents had to be born in Mexico. Fox was elected governor in 1995. and had a solid record of achievement as governor of Guanajuato. Despite his devout Catholicism, he was Mexico's first divorced president.

A New Era Begins

Vicente Fox was inaugurated on December 1, 2000. The inaugural ceremony was attended by such ideologically diverse personalities as Cuban President Fidel Castro, Colombian Nobel Laureate Gabriel García Márquez, U.S. Secretary of State Madeleine Albright and Microsoft chairman Bill Gates.

After receiving the presidential sash from Zedillo, Fox, still wearing cowboy boots, kept a campaign promise by ordering an army withdrawal from Chiapas as his first official act. (see Armed Rebellions). He then did something no *PRI* president could have done: He went to the Basilica of Our Lady of Guadalupe to offer thanks to Mexico's patron saint.

He proposed a breathtaking list of reforms: amending the constitution to permit referenda; a crackdown on corruption; greater environmental protection; streamlining, but not privatizing, *Pemex*; strengthening U.S.-style judicial review over laws

The front page of the Saltillo, Coahuila, daily newspaper *Vanguardia* proclaiming the stunning and decisive victory of Vicente Fox in the July 2, 2000, presidential election.

passed by Congress; a code of ethics for cabinet secretaries; increased availability to university scholarships; increased incentives for savings and investments; greater government support for small businesses; universal health care; greater autonomy for the states; and the Indian rights bill demanded by the *Zapatistas*.

As foreign secretary, Fox appointed Jorge Castañeda, the noted political scien-

Mexico

tist; as attorney general, General Rafael Macedo, the army's prosecutor, who had a reputation for incorruptibility; as interior secretary, the *PAN*'s leader in Congress, Santiago Creel.

Mexican-U.S. relations improved dramatically. Fox met with the new U.S. president, George W. Bush, on Fox's ranch. It was historic symbolism that for the first time ever, a U.S. president opted to make his first foreign visit to Mexico. The two businesslike conservatives with ranching backgrounds got along well and discussed trade, drugs, immigration and energy. Even before he became president, Fox made regular appearances on U.S. interview programs.

Fox made a symbolic gesture by opening the presidential palace of Los Pinos for the first time to the public. That gesture was to boomerang on him, however, when the media reported that the towels in the presidential bathrooms cost $400 and that the remote-controlled curtains cost $17,000. The media immediately labeled the first Fox mini-scandal "Towelgate."

Mexicans learned that their new president was serious about cracking down on corruption. He fired 12 high-ranking government officials after they were caught taking bribes in a sting operation.

Fox obtained congressional support for his Indian rights bill, but he found less enthusiasm when he introduced an ambitious tax reform plan. He argued that the plan would encourage investments, create jobs and help redistribute wealth. The Green Party broke with Fox over the tax reform scheme. Congress finally passed a watered-down version that focused on luxury taxes.

Fox averted a possible personal scandal by marrying his press spokeswoman, Martha Sahagún, on July 2, 2001, his 59th birthday and the first anniversary of his election victory. The nature of their relationship had been the subject of gossip for years, and she was known to be living in Los Pinos. It was reportedly she who had ordered the controversial towels and curtains. The press was not kind to the first lady, criticizing her actions and her taste.

In politics, the *PRI* continued to be plagued with problems since its defeat. An internecine battle for control ensued between the reformers and the dinosaurs, and the party's separation from the reins of power has stripped it of its most powerful tool—patronage. It also continued to lose governorships, beginning with Chiapas to the *PRD*.

In Tabasco, Governor Roberto Madrazo, in true dinosaur fashion, hand-picked the *PRI* candidate to succeed him, Manuel Andrade. In the October 2000 election, Andrade was declared the winner, 44% to 43%, over the *PRD*'s Raúl Ojeda. The *PRD*

appealed the decision to the *IFE*, citing the usual evidence of *PRI* vote-buying. Just three days before Andrade's inauguration, the *IFE* made the unprecedented decision to nullify the election results. The decision threw Tabasco into turmoil. A new election was held in August 2001. Andrade won narrowly, 50.5% to 46%, apparently fairly.

The *PAN* won the Yucatán governorship for the first time in May 2001, bringing to eight the number of states it controlled. That July, the *PAN* easily retained control of the governorship of Baja California Norte for a third straight term. In November 2001, the *PRI* lost the governorship of Michoacán. Lázaro Cárdenas Batel of the *PRD*, son of Cuauhtémoc and grandson and namesake of the illustrious former president, defeated the *PRI* candidate 41.8% to 36.7%. The victory brought to five the number of states, plus the Federal District, that the *PRD* controlled. President Fox himself attended Cárdenas' inauguration.

Fox had promised a fact-finding commission to investigate disappearances during the 1960s and 1970s, but took no action until the high-profile murder in October 2001 of Digna Ortíz, a prominent human rights lawyer. He then commissioned the human rights ombudsman to prepare a report on past abuses, which could only prove an embarrassment to the *PRI*. The 3,000-page report concluded that 532 people who disappeared during that period had been illegally detained by security forces, including the military, and that 275 were murdered and their bodies disposed of. Fox appointed an independent truth commission to investigate the abuses, ostensibly to bring those responsible to justice. In June 2002, he ordered the declassification and release of 80 million intelligence files from the *PRI* period.

Oddly, however, Fox opposed resuming an inquiry into the 1968 Tlatelolco Massacre, saying it was time to focus on the future, not the past. The Supreme Court disagreed in 2002 and upheld a lower court decision that had overturned a decision by the justice ministry that the statute of limitations precluded an investigation.

That July, former President Luis Echeverría (1970–76), then 80, was summoned before the commission and spent six hours being interrogated about Tlatelolco, which occurred while he was interior secretary, and about atrocities committed during his term as president, especially the so-called "Corpus Christi Day Massacre" on June 10, 1971, in which an undetermined number of leftists was slain. He refused to answer, saying he would give his responses in writing. The prosecutor then gave Echeverría 186 written questions to respond to; Echeverría re-

fused to comply. Never before had a president or former president been held accountable for his actions.

A year later, on October 2, 2003, the 35th anniversary of the Tlateloleo massacre, declassified documents confirmed that the government had placed 360 snipers around the plaza and had opened fire on the demonstrators. A lower court dismissed the charges against Echeverría in the Corpus Christi Massacre in 2004, ruling that the statute of limitations had expired, but federal prosecutors appealed. In 2005, the Supreme Court ruled 3–2 that Echeverría could be tried, writing that the statute of limitations had to be dated to 1976, when he left office. He was eventually arrested on June 30, 2006, and placed under house arrest awaiting trial. But a week later, a federal judge dismissed the charges, saying the 30-year statute of limitations had expired.

The commission released its long-awaited report to the public in 2006, days before Fox left office. It concluded that officials at the highest level in the administrations of Díaz Ordaz, Echeverría and López Portillo had engaged in a systemized plan to exterminate people it considered "ideological opponents" and bluntly accused them of "crimes against humanity" and of "genocide." It was the first time the Mexican government had ever assigned responsibility to itself for wrongdoing. Echeverría was later recharged and remains under house arrest.

Fox visited Cuba in 2002, which seemingly continued Mexico's tradition of friendship with the Castro regime. Foreign Minister Castañeda stated in Havana that Mexico, as before, would not support a perennial resolution brought before the U.N. Human Rights Commission in Geneva urging Cuba to allow greater freedom of expression. But Fox outraged Castro—and the Mexican left—by meeting with Cuban dissidents. Relations were strained further when more than 20 dissidents invaded the Mexican Embassy in Havana (see Cuba).

Relations with Cuba came close to the breaking point that April. First, Fox hosted a U.N. conference on poverty in Monterrey, which Castro decided to attend at the last minute. Castro left in a huff on the first day of the conference after making his speech, accusing Fox of pressuring him into leaving before President Bush arrived, which Fox denied. A few days later, in Geneva, Mexico not only voted for the resolution critical of Cuba's human rights record, it co-sponsored it! An outraged Castro broke with diplomatic courtesy and released a secretly recorded tape of his conversation with Fox concerning the Monterrey poverty summit that corroborated Castro's contention that Fox had pressured him into leaving; basically, Castro called Fox a liar.

The Mexican left rallied to Castro's side; the Mexican Senate even denied Fox permission for a trip he had scheduled to the United States and Canada. Fox was humiliated, and argued that the Senate's action would damage Mexico's international prestige. But the *PRI* had its revenge for the corruption probe, petty as it was. Fox replaced the ambassador to Cuba, apparently because he was considered too friendly to the dictatorial regime for his taste. His removal represented a major shift in foreign policy.

In politics, the power struggle between the dinosaurs and the reformers within the *PRI* erupted with a fury during the election for the new party president in 2002. Madrazo, as expected, was the candidate of the dinosaurs (who, not surprisingly, prefer the term *"tradicionalistas,")* while Beatríz Paredes, speaker of the Chamber of Deputies, was the choice of the reform wing. During and after the bitter campaign, the two rivals came close to disemboweling their party. About 3 million *Pristas* voted, and the count was so close the final results weren't announced until March. Madrazo was declared the winner by a slim 52,000-vote margin, or 1.7 percentage points.

The *PRD* also elected a new leader in a campaign that also was rambunctious but less acrimonious. Former interim Mexico City Mayor Rosario Robles was declared the winner with 60.8%.

An event that had been intended to be spiritual turned out to be political. On July 31, 2002, Pope John Paul II arrived in Mexico for his fifth visit to formally canonize the Indian peasant Juan Diego, to whom the Virgin of Guadalupe reportedly appeared in 1521 (see The Colonial Period). In the ceremony at the Shrine of Guadalupe, Fox broke with Mexico's longstanding anticlerical tradition and knelt and kissed the pope's ring. Perhaps more significantly, so did Mexico state Governor Arturo Montiel—a *Prista*. Fox made history again when John Paul II died in 2005, becoming the first Mexican president to attend a papal funeral.

The U.S. invasion of Iraq in 2003 strained the warm relations between Fox and Bush. Mexico held one of Latin America's two rotating seats on the U.N. Security Council, and Mexico sided with France, a permanent member of the Security Council, in denying U.N. authorization for the United States to attack Iraq if Saddam Hussein did not account for weapons of mass destruction. Mexico was one of the members that refused to commit itself to a U.S. resolution calling for use of force. Fox stated he favored the disarmament of Iraq but preferred to exhaust

diplomatic means to accomplish it. The United States was forced to withdraw the resolution and invade Iraq without a U.N. blessing.

Citing his frustration over relations with the United States, Foreign Minister Castañeda resigned and was replaced by Economy Minister Luis Ernesto Derbéz.

The gridlock between Fox's *PAN* and the opposition majority in Congress led the president to make a plaintive plea for multipartisan cooperation for the good of the nation in his annual congressional address on September 1, 2002. There were three positive developments: First, the parties for the first time agreed to rotate the speakership of the Chamber of Deputies among the three major parties during that session. Second, both houses passed Mexico's first genuine civil service law, which creates a five-tiered system of government employees free from the political patronage that the *PRI* had used and abused for so long. Third, Congress enacted a U.S.-style freedom-of-information act that gives citizens—and especially journalists—unprecedented access to government records.

2003 Midterm Elections

All the parties knew they faced high stakes in the midterm elections on July 6, 2003. The *PAN* came under investigation for allegedly receiving $14,000 in illegal funds from the United States for Fox's 2000 presidential campaign. The Federal

Electoral Institute *(IFE)* verified a number of irregularities, and fined the *PAN* $32 million.

In the *PRI*, the dinosaurs' Madrazo pulled off a skillful, but politically unwise, power play when he packed the party's list of candidates for the 200 federal deputies chosen through proportional representation with his own supporters. The outraged reformists cried foul.

At stake were all 500 members of the Chamber of Deputies, 300 of them directly elected from districts and 200 by proportional representation, and six governorships: Campeche, Colima, Nuevo León, Querétaro, San Luis Potosí and Sonora.

Fox hoped to win an outright majority in both houses of Congress; even just increasing the *PAN*'s number of seats could be interpreted as approval of his presidency. The *PAN* scented blood in Sonora, where polls showed a dead heat between the *PRI*'s Eduardo Bours and the *PAN*'s Ramón Corral. This author reported on the midterm elections from Sonora.

The results of the nationwide voting were a cruel blow to Fox's quixotic dreams of a majority in the lower house. Not only did the *PAN* fail to win a majority and increase its number of seats, but it *lost* 51 of the 206 seats it had. The *PRI* rebounded by slightly increasing its representation. The major winner was the *PRD*, which doubled the size of its delegation.

A dejected Fox acknowledged, "Once again, it is apparent that no single political force will have a majority in the Cham-

An enterprising woman sells iced *horchata*, a sweet rice-based beverage, and *duros*, a fried chip made from flour, outside a polling station set up in a *Pemex* station in Hermosillo, Sonora, on July 6, 2003. Hundreds of people were still waiting in sweltering heat to use one voting booth when the polls closed, but the voting continued.

Photo by the author

Mexico

An elderly *Panista* participates in premature street celebrations in Hermosillo, Sonora on election night, July 6, 2003.
Photo by Sherre Amire

A scuffle breaks out on election night along Calle Rosales in Hermosillo, Sonora, between supporters of rival gubernatorial candidates Eduardo Bours of the *PRI* and Ramón Corral of the *PAN*, as a news photographer records the melee. Bours was the eventual winner of the cliffhanger election. *Photo by the author*

ber of Deputies." I couldn't help but recall how an equally despondent Zedillo, three years earlier, had conceded that Fox had won the presidency. Such is the ebb and flow of democracy. "The work now begins to build a consensus among us." He also focused on another significant outcome of the elections: the disturbingly low turnout of only 41%. "We hear the voices of those who did not express themselves at the polls," he said. "We all understand your silence."

In terms of raw votes, the *PRI* had received 34.4%, the *PAN* 30.5%, the *PRD* 17.1%. The *IFE* released its final tally on the 300 directly elected seats: 163 for the *PRI*, 67 for the *PAN*, 56 for the *PRD*. After the complex formula was applied for the allocation of the 200 seats by proportional representation, the *PRI* increased its delegation from 211 to 224, 26 short of a majority. The *PAN* wound up with 155 seats, while the *PRD* jumped from 50 seats to 96. The Green Party *(PVEM)* won 15 seats through proportional representation, about the same as before. The *PT* won only 2.4% of the vote and eight seats.

The *PAN* suffered another blow with the loss of Nuevo León, 56.4%–33.9%. About the only cause the *PAN* had for cheer on election night was that it captured the governorship of San Luis Potosí for the first time, 44%–37%, and it retained the governorship of Querétaro. In Campeche, the *PRI* pulled off a narrow victory. The *PRI* also retained Colima.

Sonora provided the country with some high political drama for a few days. On election night in Hermosillo, I witnessed a bizarre spectacle on the streets, as throngs of enthusiastic *Panistas* and *Priistas* both celebrated their perceived victory. The confusion was compounded by the extra editions of the two morning newspapers, which hit the streets about 10 p.m. with conflicting headlines about who was ahead. In front of the University of Sonora, *pristas* and *panistas* waved banners and taunted each other. It was like downtown Dallas the night before a Texas-Oklahoma game. Some scuffles inevitably broke out. Police arrived to maintain order. I was then convinced that the much-criticized 48-hour dry law in effect in Mexico on

election day and the day before is not such a bad idea.

On July 12, the *CEE* declared Bours the winner, 372,467 to 364,544.

The Ahumada Affair

By early 2004, it appeared from the polls that Mexico City Mayor Andrés Manuel López Obrador not only was the favorite for the *PRD* presidential nomination but that he was the frontrunner to win the 2006 election. Suddenly, he became the latest politician to confront a scandal.

Carlos Ahumada was a wealthy, politically connected businessman who had lucrative paving contracts with the Mexico City government under López Obrador's

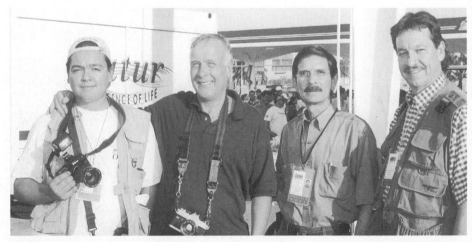

The author, second from left, with three photographers from the Hermosillo, Sonora, daily, *El Imparcial,* at a polling station on election day, July 6, 2003. *Photo by Sherre Amire*

predecessor. He videotaped himself offering a bribe to René Bejerano, the *PRD* floor leader in the Federal District's legislature. The videotape was leaked to the media, and the country was treated to images of Bejerano stuffing money into his suit. Two days earlier, similar videotapes showed Mexico City's Finance Secretary Gustavo Ponce living it up gambling at a Las Vegas casino.

The mayor fired Ponce, who was then arrested. Bejerano insisted he had been collecting a "campaign donation" from Ahumada for a *PRD* legislative candidate, something that was itself illegal. Ahumada told the media that the city government had extorted the money from him.

The Ahumada affair became an international incident when Ahumada fled to Cuba. Ahumada was arrested in April and deported to Mexico, but not before the Cuban government announced that Ahumada had "confessed" on videotape that the Fox administration had concocted the bribe in an attempt to damage López Obrador politically. Cuba had its revenge for Fox supporting the U.N. vote against Cuba.

Fox denied the allegation, recalled the Mexican ambassador to Cuba, expelled the Cuban ambassador and declared the Cuban Embassy's political officer *persona non grata*. It seemed for a time that Mexico might break diplomatic relations with its old friend, but the two foreign ministers met and re-established ambassador-level relations.

Wrangling over Immigration

U.S.-Mexican relations remained problematical in 2005 and 2006 over immigration and with mutual finger-pointing over the alarming increase in drug-related violence on the Mexican side of the border (see Other Current Issues: Drugs).

Bush and Fox had once been in accord on immigration, but Fox's proposal for free immigration across the border went nowhere in the U.S. Congress. Bush then advocated a compromise that would allow Mexicans who are offered jobs to work in the United States for up to three years, but they would not be eligible for U.S. citizenship and would be required to return to Mexico.

Fox grudgingly endorsed the watered-down plan and lobbied the U.S. Congress for its passage, but Congress demurred. Then Bush announced the extension of a wall along the California-Baja California border and pushed for legislation requiring states to require proof of citizenship to obtain drivers licenses. The two measures were ostensibly aimed at thwarting terrorists from crossing the border, but they offended Fox and Mexicans in gen-

Former President Vicente Fox Quesada

eral. Fox's government sent a formal letter of protest regarding the wall.

Next, Fox generated international media attention with an injudicious remark to a group of visiting Texas businessmen in 2005. Voicing frustration over the lack of progress on the immigration issue, he said Mexican immigrants traditionally have taken jobs that "not even blacks want to do." That sparked a firestorm of criticism from U.S. black organizations, and provided grist for satirists and cartoonists on both sides of the border. Fox said he regretted that his remarks had been "misinterpreted," but did not apologize. The Mexicans themselves rallied behind their president; to them, he had merely spoken the truth.

In 2006, a bill was introduced in the U.S. House of Representatives that would make it a felony to hire illegal immigrants. Bush, meanwhile, proposed a controversial plan that would permit up to 400,000 "guest workers" a year and eventually make 11 million illegals eligible for citizenship, which members of his own party rejected as tantamount to an amnesty. On May 1, 2006, illegal immigrants—Mexicans and others—staged a one-day walk-out in the United States, refusing to work to dramatize the role they play in the U.S. economy. It coincided with a one-day *"no gringo"* sympathy boycott of U.S. goods and companies in Mexico.

Drugs also strained Mexican-U.S. relations. In 2006, the Mexican Congress passed a bill that would have legalized possession of five grams of marijuana, 500 milligrams of cocaine, 25 milligrams of heroin and small amounts of some hallu-

cinogens such as peyote. The rationale was a sound one: To have the Mexican authorities divert more of their limited resources toward the traffickers instead of wasting their time busting penny-ante users. Fox declared he would sign it into law, generating headlines on both sides of the border. The U.S. government leaned heavily on Fox to veto it, arguing that such legalization would lead to "drug tourism" across the border. Fox sent the measure back to Congress, where it died.

Jockeying for 2006

López Obrador remained high in the polls, but his legal problems continued. He stood accused of contempt of court in 2001 for refusing to halt work on a road across expropriated private land that he insisted was needed for access to a public hospital. Then Fox's attorney general's office said López Obrador faced prosecution also for refusing to obey a court order to reinstate 39 city employees who were terminated when he became mayor in 2000 and to pay them back wages.

The mayor responded that the charges were politically motivated. Faced with a possible congressional vote stripping him of his immunity, he defiantly called a mass demonstration in August 2004 to declare his presidential candidacy. As trivial as the charges were, they could have forced him from office and disqualified him from running for any public office if he were convicted.

The *PAN* had its own problems. In May 2004, Energy Secretary Calderón angrily resigned a day after Fox had publicly chastised him for attending a political rally in Guadalajara at which the governor of Jalisco endorsed Calderón for the *PAN* presidential nomination, even though Calderón had not yet declared his candidacy. Fox declared that he expected his cabinet secretaries to occupy themselves with their duties. In his resignation letter, Calderón called Fox's remarks "unjust and excessive."

As always, governor's races in the two years prior to presidential election were closely watched as gauges of the three parties' strength. Chihuahua was an especially crucial battleground, as the only state that the *PRI* had recaptured from the *PAN*. The PRD was defending Zacatecas for the first time. The *PAN* was defending Aguascalientes for the first time, while the *PRI* faced a strong challenge from a peculiar *PRD-PAN* coalition in Oaxaca.

In the balloting on July 4, which this author observed in Zacatecas, voters opted for the status quo in all three states. In Chihuahua, José Reyes Baeza, the candidate of a *PRI*-led alliance, won with 57%. In Durango, the *PRI* candidate, Ismael

Mexico

About 40,000 people turned out for the *"Fiesta del Triunfo,"* the closing rally for winning *PRI* gubernatorial candidate Jose Reyes Baéza, outside the Palacio de Gobierno in Chihuahua on June 30, 2004. National *PRI* President Roberto Madrazo appeared at the rally. *Photo by the author*

Hernández, received 56%. In Zacatecas, the *PRD* candidate, Amalia García, a federal deputy, received 46%.

The *PAN's* Luis Armando won easily in Aguascalientes a month later. But the Oaxaca campaign turned violent the week before the election. The *PRI's* Ulises Ruíz claimed victory, 47% to 45% for Gabino Cué of the *PRD-PAN* alliance. Cué claimed vote fraud had cost him the election. Ruíz belongs to the dinosaur faction.

The *PRI* took some satisfaction over the victory of Jorge Hank Rhon, a controversial racetrack owner with alleged indirect ties to the Tijuana drug cartel, in the Tijuana mayor's race. The city, and the state of Baja California Norte, are *PAN* strongholds.

In September 2004, the *PRI* marked another Pyrrhic victory in the Veracruz governor's race, where the *PRI's* Fidel Herrera defeated the *PAN* candidate by less than one percentage point, with just 34.5% of the vote. In 1998, the *PRI* had won by 20 points in what had been one of its bastions. The *PRI* easily retained the governorships of its stronghold states of Tamaulipas and Puebla that November and even recaptured Tlaxcala from the *PRD*, which ran a poor third.

In February 2005 the *PRD* held onto Baja California Sur and the *PRI* to Quintana Roo. But in poverty-stricken Guerrero, the *PRI* lost for the first time. Like Oaxaca, there was some pre-election violence, but the *PRD* candidate, Zeferino Torrreblanca, a popular former mayor of Acapulco and a successful businessman with a centrist platform, received 55%. His victory more than made up for the *PRD's*

loss of tiny Tlaxcala. The *PRI* retained the governorship of Hidalgo.

When the *PRI* governor of Colima was killed in a plane crash, a special election was called. The *PRI's* Silverio Cavazos defeated the *PAN* candidate by about the same percentages as in 2003.

On July 3, 2005, the *PRI's* Ney González recaptured the governorship of Nayarit it

had lost in 1999 to an opposition coalition, winning with a 46% plurality against the *PRD* candidate's 42.7%. That same day, the *PRI* retained the state of Mexico, where Enrique Peña Nieto received 47.6%.

In September, the *PRI's* Humberto Moreira received a landslide 55.5% in Coahuila.

Governor-elect Amalia Garcia of the *PRD* addresses cheering supporters on election night in Zacatecas July 4, 2004. *Photo by the author*

Mexico City's main thoroughfare, *Paseo de la Reforma*

The *"Desafuero"* Controversy

The lingering controversy over López Obrador's supposed contempt of court and its effect on his presidential ambitions dominated Mexicans' attention in 2005. What amounted to an impeachment effort in Congress led to an unholy alliance between the *PRI* and the *PAN*, both of which feared López Obrador would win. But to disqualify him for such a picayunish charge smacked of political opportunism at best and antidemocratic machinations, reminiscent of the old-style trickery of the *PRI*, at worst.

López Obrador called for "civil resistance" if he were arrested, throwing down the gauntlet to the Congress with a threat of public unrest if what was considered the will of the people—his people—were thwarted. Polls showed upwards of 80% of Mexicans opposed his prosecution. He declared he would campaign from a jail cell if necessary.

Unintimidated, the Chamber of Deputies voted 360–127, along party lines, for *el desafuero* to strip López Obrador of his immunity, paving the way for his removal from office pending trial. Pro-López Obrador demonstrators, 150,000 strong, filled the streets before the vote, while *"no al desafuero"* posters filled the capital.

Legal authorities disagreed over whether or not the congressional vote meant López Obrador could continue serving as mayor. The two sides were involved in a literal Mexican standoff. Fox ruled out a presidential pardon, however, Interior Secretary Creel—who hoped to be the *PAN* nominee—hinted at a "political solution." The mayor appeared before a judge and posted a token amount for bail. The judge, like Pontius Pilate, sent the case back to prosecutors because of a legal technicality.

A "silent march" in support of the mayor in April drew 1 million people. Finally, Fox capitulated by firing Attorney General Rafael Macedo de la Concha, the leading advocate for prosecuting López Obrador. Basically, Fox sacrificed Macedo on the altar of public opinion, replacing him with Daniel Cabeza de Vaca, who dropped the case against López Obrador. Both López Obrador and Fox issued conciliatory statements, and the country breathed a sigh of relief. The two men even had an amicable meeting in the Los Pinos presidential residence.

López Obrador resigned as mayor on July 31 to devote himself full-time to his presidential campaign.

Burros graze along a desert highway between Saltillo and Zacatecas.

Photo by the author

Mexico

The Elections of 2006

For the remainder of 2005 and the first few months of 2006, it seemed a foregone conclusion that López Obrador would coast into Los Pinos. It helped that both the *PRI* and the *PAN* were beset by intra-party rivalries.

In the *PAN*, Fox made no secret that Creel was his anointed heir apparent—a *PAN* version of the *dedazo*. But neither counted on the groundswell of support for the renegade Calderón, who was as charismatic a campaigner as Creel was lackluster. A member of the party's so-called traditionalist wing, Calderón, who holds a graduate degree in public administration from Harvard, had proven himself an able problem-solver as energy minister. Moreover, polls showed Creel running a poor third behind López Obrador and the *PRI*'s Madrazo. Calderón swept the three party primaries that won him the nomination. Fox and Creel dutifully closed ranks behind their party's standard-bearer.

The battle for the *PRI* nomination was not as gentlemanly. The reformist wing coalesced around the candidacy of outgoing Mexico state Governor Arturo Montiel. Madrazo received the nomination, but the bitterness of the mudslinging Madrazo-Montiel battle left unhealed wounds.

This time, the small Green Party allied itself with the *PRI* instead of the *PAN*.

As often happens with frontrunners with huge leads, López Obrador had nowhere to go but down once he had actual challengers questioning his record and his proposals and advancing their own. Calderón edged past Madrazo in the polls, and by April he had moved into a statistical tie with López Obrador. Calderón challenged López Obrador's vague populist rhetoric and launched a media blitz warning that López Obrador would ruin Mexico the way Hugo Chávez had ruined Venezuela. Calderón probably was aided as well by the rapidly expanding economy, which benefits the party in power.

López Obrador's most dangerous opponent was himself. His populist rhetoric continued to excite his core constituency of the poor, but to Mexico's growing middle class it lacked specifics and seemed harsh, demagogic—even scary. Moreover, his constant ridiculing of Fox backfired; the president still enjoyed an approval rating of about 60%. Finally, the overconfident López Obrador, the political equivalent of Aesop's hare, refused to participate in a televised debate in April with Calderón, Madrazo and three minor candidates. He apparently hoped Calderón and Madrazo would disembowel each other, but to many voters his refusal to debate came across as cowardly, arrogant or both. He participated in a second debate, but the damage proved irrevocable.

The major candidates all sounded the same major themes: maintaining good relations with the United States but demanding a better U.S. immigration policy; combating corruption; improving education; investing the windfall from high petroleum prices wisely. Probably the major source of disagreement was Calderón's and Madrazo's call for joint ventures between *Pemex* and foreign firms to exploit deep offshore oil deposits in the Gulf, an idea that was anathema to López Obrador. They also had different approaches to the drug war. López Obrador advocated a greater role for the military; Calderón said he would extradite more kingpins to the United States; Madrazo called for stiffer sentences.

This author observed the July 2 election in the state of Morelos, which was also electing a governor, as were Jalisco and Guanajuato. Morelos was especially interesting because it had elected its first *PAN* governor, Sergio Estrada, in 2000, but in 2004 he was indicted for collusion with the Juárez drug cartel. The legislature had failed by one vote to strip him of his immunity from prosecution. The Federal District also elected a new chief of government.

Voter turnout was 58.61%. The vote count was so close between Calderón and López Obrador that both men claimed victory, but the *IFE* said it would have to recount the votes from each precinct beginning July 5. The following day, it released its breathtakingly close official final tally:

Calderón	15,000,284	35.89%
López Obrador	14,756,350	35.31%
Madrazo	9,301,441	22.26%
Others:	1,828,643	4.37%
Null:	904,604	2.16%

López Obrador refused to concede, alleging vote fraud despite a lack of concrete evidence, and said he would challenge the results before the Supreme Electoral Tribunal, which had until September 6 to issue a final ruling.

In the Congress, there was a dramatic new party lineup. The once-omnipotent *PRI* dropped from first place to third in both houses. In the Senate, it decreased from 58 to 27 seats and from 203 to only 49 in the Chamber of Deputies. The *PAN* thus emerged as the largest bloc in both houses, even though it, too, lost seats. It dropped from 48 to 43 seats in the Senate and from 148 to 141 in the lower house. The *PRD* and its allied parties were the major winners, increasing from 15 to 26 seats in the Senate and from 97 to 110 in the Chamber.

The *PAN* held on to the governorships of all three states, winning easily in Guanajuato, where Juan Manuel Oliva received 59%. But it faced stiffer competition in the other two. In Jalisco, Emilio González had a winning plurality of only 45.2%.

In Morelos, despite Estrada's drug scandal, the *PAN*'s Marco Adame received 36% to 32% for the *PRD* candidate and 24.1% for that of the *PRI*-Green coalition. In 2000, Estrada had received 57%.

In the Federal District, the *PRD*'s Marcelo Ebrard was elected mayor, considered by many the second most powerful post in the country, with 47%.

A map of Mexico's states published in *El Universal* showed graphically just how divided Mexico had become. While the United States has so-called red states and blue states, Mexico's states are literally red (*PRI*), blue (*PAN*) or yellow (*PRD*), the parties' official colors. The electoral map in the presidential race showed Mexico painted almost exclusively blue north of Mexico City, and almost solidly yellow to the south and east. In the north, López Obrador carried only Zacatecas, Nayarit and Baja California Sur; in the south, Calderón carried only Puebla and Yucatán. The *PRI*'s Madrazo did not carry a single state, not even his home state of Tabasco! Calderón carried 16 states, López Obrador carried 15 and the Federal District.

Besides appealing to the Federal Electoral Tribunal, or *Trife*, López Obrador continued to cry fraud and to use inflammatory rhetoric against Calderón, Fox and even the *IFE*, which in the past had backed the *PRD*'s claims of *PRI* fraud in some state elections. Such "proof" of fraud that the *PRD* finally produced turned out to be bogus.

López Obrador then incited his followers to take to the streets in what he called a campaign of "civil resistance" that could only be interpreted as an effort to intimidate the *Trife* into invalidating the results and calling for a new election. If the *Trife* could not reach a decision by September 6, it would have to do just that, and the badly fragmented Congress would have to name an interim president. He twice filled the Zócalo in Mexico City with hundreds of thousands of *peeredistas*. Throughout August, they camped out in the Zócalo and staged demonstrations throughout the country; this author observed one in Saltillo. On September 1, *PRD* congressmen, in an antidemocratic power play, prevented Fox from delivering his annual state of the union address to Congress.

The *Trife* painstakingly examined returns from tens of thousands of disputed

The headlines of newspapers the day after the July 2, 2006 presidential election reflect the uncertainty of the outcome. *Reforma's* headline says, "And the winner is. . ." *El Universal* says "Fighting for every vote." *Excélsior's* says simply, "Who?"

polling places. It was eerily reminiscent of the disputed 2000 presidential election in the United States, where the Supreme Court ultimately decided who had won Florida and thus the election. But the U.S. Supreme Court was split 5–4. On September 5, the seven *Trife* members announced their *unanimous* conclusion. They had disallowed about 220,000 contested ballots,

but that only shrank Calderón's winning margin by a few thousand votes. Calderón, they ruled, had won the election by 233,831 votes, or .56 percentage points, of the 41.8 million votes cast.

Still, López Obrador refused to concede. He threatened to continue the "civil resistance" and to establish a "shadow government." His supporters remained in the

Zócalo, where on September 16, Independence Day, he declared himself "president-elect" and appointed a 12-member "cabinet." Once again, Fox was prevented from following tradition of speaking in the Zócalo on Independence Day.

Gradually, López Obrador's defiance of Mexico's painfully constructed new democratic institutions began to lose steam.

Mexico

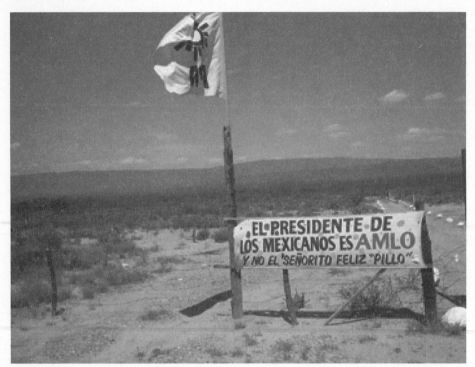

A *PRD* banner in the Coahuila desert protesting the official vote count awarding the 2006 presidential election to the *PAN*'s Felipe Calderón reads, "The president of the Mexicans is AMLO (Andés Manuel López Obrador) and not the happy queer Little Felipe."

Photo by the author

The small Convergence Party, the *PRD*'s coalition partner, announced it accepted the *Trife*'s decision. *PRD* leaders like Cárdenas, who actually *had* been robbed of an election in 1988, told López Obrador it was time to concede. The crowds of protesters began to dwindle.

But López Obrador defiantly claimed he was the legitimate president-elect. His poor sportsmanship and antidemocratic demeanor began to grate on the Mexicans' nerves; a poll by the newspaper *Reforma* showed that if there were a new election, he would receive only 30%, down five points from his showing on July 2. In an actual bellwether, the *PRD* candidate for governor of López Obrador's home state of Tabasco, who had been favored to win, lost badly to the *PRI*'s Andrés Granier on October 15. López Obrador had campaigned energetically on Ojeda's behalf, and his defeat was widely viewed as a backlash against López Obrador's behavior.

Die-hard *PRD* congressmen then threatened to prevent Calderón from taking the oath in Congress on December 1, camping out in the Chamber of Deputies and attempting to block the doors, *PAN* congressmen seized the chamber in a show of force. Fistfights broke out and *PRD* congressmen threw chairs and cans at the *panistas*, an unparliamentary melee that was shown on television around the world.

Once again, Fox sought to avoid confrontation. In an unprecedented midnight ceremony at Los Pinos, he surrendered the presidential sash. Constitutionally, the president must be sworn in before Congress, so for nine hours Mexico was without a president. Calderón and Fox arrived through a back door to the Chamber of Deputies and went to the podium amid catcalls from the *peeredistas*. Calderón quickly took the oath, then hurried off to deliver his inaugural address at a heavily guarded auditorium across town. The foreign representatives in the gallery, including former President George H. W. Bush and California Governor Arnold Schwarzenegger from the United States, President Álvaro Uribe of Colombia and the prince of Asturias from Spain, were there only minutes as the spectacle of bedlam unfolded below. It was not Mexico's finest hour.

A year later, López Obrador was still claiming to be the legitimate president, and he authored a bitter book, *El mafia nos robó la elección (The Mafia Stole the Election from Us)*. He was still able to muster a few thousand demonstrators to the Zócalo on the first anniversary of the election, but a poll by *Reforma* indicated that only 61% of the people who voted for him would do so again. He became such an embarrassment that *PRD* gubernatorial candidates have eschewed his support.

The Calderón Presidency

A serious domestic crisis Calderón inherited from Fox was a near-insurrection in the state of Oaxaca that had left several people dead. It began as a strike by teachers demanding higher pay in May 2006. The teachers occupied the Zócalo in the state capital until they were forcibly removed in June by the unpopular *PRI* governor, Ulises Ruíz, who had narrowly defeated his *PRD* rival in 2004 in an election still considered fraudulent. Other sectors joined the teachers to form the Popular Assembly of the Peoples of Oaxaca *(APPO)*, headed by Flavio Sosa. *APPO* demanded Ruíz's resignation. The protests became so violent in October and November with acts of arson and vandalism of public buildings that Fox dispatched 4,000 federal police to maintain order.

Fox, and now Calderón, depended on the *PRI* bloc in Congress to pass legislation. The Oaxaca crisis thus led to an unholy alliance between the *PAN* and the *PRI* in the name of expediency. In one of his first acts as president, Calderón ordered Sosa's arrest.

Calderón's unspoken alliance with the *PRI* led to the election of *PRI* members as speaker of the Chamber of Deputies and president of the Senate, and he named a few *pristas* to cabinet posts. This coalition in all but name reaped legislative fruit. In March 2007, Calderón got through Congress the pension reform plan Fox had tried but failed to enact. Even the *PRD*, which opposed the pension reform, supported Calderón's electoral and judicial reforms. However, when it came to reorganizing *Pemex* or privatizing electricity, the *PRI* and *PRD* remained united against Calderón. As under Fox, Mexico continued to be ruled by consensus, but Calderón showed himself more skillful than Fox in reaching that consensus.

An important moment in the history of the *PRI* came in 2007 with the election of Beatríz Paredes, a reformer, to succeed Madrazo as party president.

The immigration issue continued to strain relations with the United States. The long-awaited immigration "reform" compromise reached in the U.S. Congress in 2007, heralded by such polar opposites as President Bush and Senator Ted Kennedy, came under attack from Republicans, Democrats and Mexicans alike. Republicans saw it as tantamount to an amnesty for illegal immigrants. Democrats feared it would threaten organized labor and divide families. Mexicans saw it as demeaning. The issue was so volatile that the Miss USA contestant was booed by the audience at the pageant held in Mexico City.

Mexico

President Felipe de Jesús Calderón

The *PRI* finally savored a triumph in May 2007 when it recaptured the governorship of Yucatán from the *PAN* under the candidacy of 34-year-old Ivonne Ortega, who received 49.9% of the vote. She is the state's first woman governor.

Tijuana Mayor Jorge Hank Rhon hoped to reclaim the Baja California Norte government for the *PRI* after 18 years of *PAN* control, but the *PAN*'s José Guadalupe Osuna bested him in August, 50.4% to 44%.

The *PRD* retained the governorship of Michoacán in November behind the candidacy of Leonel Godoy Rangel, who received 38%.

In 2007 and 2008, Calderón was preoccupied with three transcendental reforms Fox tried and failed to enact: tax reform, judicial reform and energy reform, "energy" being a euphemism for oil and gas. Using his horse-trading skills, Calderón forged a congressional consensus with the *PRI* and even some legislators from the badly divided *PRD*, which is now torn between the sour-grapes faction loyal to López Obrador that opposes Calderón at every turn, and the moderates willing to work toward the good of the country.

In September 2007, Congress overwhelmingly approved the historic tax reform package, badly needed because petroleum production, which had provided 40% of federal government revenue, was expected to begin declining sharply over the coming decade. It had already dropped 10% in three years, to 3.3 million barrels per day. The tax package included a corporate income tax of 16.5%, going up to 17.5% in three years, which pleased the left. It also raised gasoline taxes. The overhaul increases the non-petroleum revenue from 10% of GDP to 12% by the end of Calderón's term in 2012, and it will bring in $10.3 billion in

2019. It also provides *Pemex*, the state-owned oil monopoly, with reinvestment funds for new exploration.

As a tradeoff to ensure *PRD* support, Calderón agreed to a campaign reform measure that includes an institutional overhaul of the Federal Electoral Institute *(IFE)*, which the *PRD* blamed for López Obrador's defeat, a merciful reduction of the year-long presidential campaign period by half and strict limits on campaign advertising.

Congress approved an historic constitutional amendment in 2008 overhauling the judicial and legal systems from top to bottom, including open instead of closed trials, in which judges hear oral testimony instead of documented evidence. Criminal suspects were given the presumption of innocence. Once again, Calderón compromised with the left and human rights advocates by abandoning a provision that would have allowed police to enter a home without a warrant. Retained was a provision that will allow prosecutors to hold "organized crime" suspects for 80 days without charges.

Calderón finally had success with energy reform. Because Mexico must export crude oil and then must re-import 40% of its refined fuel, Calderón proposed allowing *Pemex* to sign contracts with private firms—interpreted as foreign firms—to build refineries and storage facilities. He also proposed contracting with private firms to exploit deep offshore deposits to extend Mexico's dwindling reserves.

It seemed pragmatic, but there is no more sacred cow in Mexico than *Pemex*. López Obrador and the sour-grapes faction of the *PRD* denounced the move. As usual, he threatened to mobilize mass demonstrations. Showing its antidemocratic proclivities once again, the sour-grapes faction seized both houses of Congress to block discussion of the bill. But on October 29, 2008, Congress passed it with the support of *PRI* lawmakers.

Mexico's interior, or government secretary is traditionally regarded as the second most powerful person in the country. On November 4, 2008, Interior Secretary Juan Carrillo Mourino and two former officials died when their government jet crashed in Mexico City. Calderón appointed an obscure attorney, Fernando Francisco Gómez, to succeed him.

The new U.S. president, Barack Obama, made his first state visit to Mexico in April 2009, en route to the Summit of the Americas. He and Calderón discussed the alarming drug violence, which claimed 5,400 lives in Mexico in 2008, and Calderón urged Obama to crack down on the legal sale of firearms to drug traffickers on the U.S. side of the border. Obama agreed that

reinstituting a ban on the sale of assault weapons could help stem the flow of arms to the cartels, who are better armed than the authorities. He also endorsed the concept of a hemispheric treaty to combat arms trafficking. Obama pledged to continue Bush's partnership with Mexico in the fight against the cartels, telling Calderón, "You can't fight this war with just one hand."

The thorny issue of immigration came up, but Obama stated adamantly that nothing would be done before the end of the year.

Calderón's Midterm Setback

Mexico's political landscape was shaken up once again in the midterm elections on July 5, 2009, which this author covered as a freelance journalist from Monterrey. The *PRI* staged a stunning comeback from near-oblivion to emerge once again as the largest bloc in the Chamber of Deputies. The *PAN* fell from first to second place in the lower house, and the *PRD* dropped to a distant third.

A jubilant Beatríz Paredes said the *PRI*'s alliance with the Green Party *(PVEM)* would give their alliance a working majority. She said the election results show "Mexico is a country in search of proposals, in search of solutions, in search of methods." By overseeing the *PRI*'s comeback, Paredes has emerged as the party's frontrunner for president in 2012. By contrast, the *PAN* president, Germán Martínez, resigned the day after the election as a result of his party's drubbing at the polls.

In terms of raw votes, the *PRI* received 36.5% of the 21.6 million votes cast, the *PAN* received 27.8%, the *PRD* 12.2% and the *PVEM*, 6.7%. In "fifth place" were null or blank ballots, totaling 1.3 million or 6 percent, double the percentage in previous elections. Minor parties made up the remainder. Turnout was an anemic 44 percent, but still up from 42 percent in the last midterm elections in 2003.

In the new Chamber of Deputies, the *PRI* won 233 seats, up from 106, and the *PVEM* won 22, up from 17, a potential working majority of 255. The *PAN* fell from 206 seats to 146, and the *PRD* from 127 seats to 72.

The *PAN* also was dealt serious psychological blows in the governor's races, losing Querétaro, which it had held for 12 years, and San Luis Potosí, which it won for the first time in 2003. It failed a second time to recapture Nuevo León, and lost control of the state legislature. The only bright spot for the *PAN* was winning Sonora for the first time after two near misses, and retaining the mayoralty of

Mexico

EL NORTE

LUNES

6 de Julio
del 2009
Monterrey, N.L.
México

$ 12.(

124 págin
8 seccior
Año LX
Número 25,7

www.elnorte.com

Gana Rodrigo la Gubernatura de NL; llegan tres Alcaldes menores de 35

Toca a los jóvenes

The Monterrey daily *El Norte* reports the election victory of the *PRI*'s Rodrigo Molina for governor of Nuevo León and the *PRI*'s stunning comeback in the midterm congressional elections of July 5, 2009.

Monterrey. The *PRI* easily retained the governorships of Campeche and Colima.

In San Luis Potosí, the *PRI*'s Fernando Toranzo received a landslide 54%. In Querétaro, the *PRI*'s José Calzada won with 49%. The *PRI*'s Rodrigo Molina received 49% in Nuevo León. In the country's most dramatic contest, in Sonora, which borders Arizona, the *PAN*'s Guillermo Padrés Elias defeated his second cousin, the *PRI*'s Alfonso Elias Serrano, 48% to 43%.

Addressing the nation, Calderón congratulated voters for participating and said, "Today, our political process is more open than ever. Democracy always has the last word. This election has given us another opportunity to improve the electoral system, to give us a country that is distinct and better." Without mentioning the *PRI*, he called for "collaboration and

co-responsibility to confront the great challenges facing the country. We will work together for the good of the country, for education, health, the environment and security."

Contrary to expectations, the elections were not marred by the drug-related violence that has become the country's major political issue, along with the slowdown in economic growth. The violence has created a climate of fear (see Other Current Issues: Drugs). The army had dispatched 8,500 troops to safeguard the election, 3,500 for ballot security and 5,000 to prevent violence. The election was marred only by the usual charges that the *PRI* was bribing voters with groceries in states it controlled. It is significant that while millions of voters turned back to the *PRI*, 1.3 million others registered their disgust by casting null ballots or by staying home.

Mexico 2010. . .

Recession and violence have continued to preoccupy Calderón and his countrymen since the elections. Although the *PRI* has not been openly obstructionist, neither has it made life easy for the president. In his state of the nation message on September 1, 2009, Calderón outlined 10 more reforms, including expansion of the energy and tax reforms already passed. His proposed labor reforms, designed to curb the power of the unions, met with a frosty reception, as labor is a sacred cow for both the *PRI* and *PRD*. He had better luck with tax reform. In an apparent effort to appease the *PRI*, Calderón proposed an increase in the income tax on the wealthy from 28% to 30%. The opposition parties still balked at the idea of allowing contracts between Pemex and foreign firms

A father in Monterrey gives his daughter a lesson in democracy on July 5, 2009 in the election for governor of Nuevo León. *Photo by the author*

that allow incentives based on production. But with oil production declining by another 10% in 2009, deep offshore wells are the only way to prolong Mexico's oil production, which continues to account for 40% of federal revenue. If the current production decline continues, Mexico will become an oil importer by 2017.

The number of drug-related murders doubled in 2009 to almost 10,000, while Ciudad Juárez, Chihuahua, officially became the world's most dangerous city and is currently patrolled by 10,000 army troops (see Other Current Issues—Drugs). The victims include operatives of rival drug cartels, policemen, soldiers, journalists and, increasingly, politicians.

Among them were Armando Chavarría, president of the Guerrero state legislature, gunned down in August 2009. The highest-profile incident was the disappearance of Diego Fernández de Cevallos, a former senator and the 1994 *PAN* presidential candidate, who was apparently abducted from his ranch in Querétaro on May 14, 2010. Drug traffickers were suspected, although the motive was unclear, and his family asked the government to suspend its investigation, which it did, compounding the mystery. When this book went to press, Fernández had not been found—alive or dead. Five journalists also had been murdered by mid-year, most of them gruesomely.

Mexico's booming economy ground to a halt with the U.S. recession, which reduced both Mexican exports to the north and the vital remittances from Mexicans working there who were laid off. The vital tourism industry, also affected by the recession, suffered two other blows in 2009: The almost daily reporting on spectacular drug-related killings and massacres, and an outbreak of swine flu in Mexico, both of which led the U.S. State Department to issue travel advisories. The GDP shrank by 6.5% and tourism by 15% in 2009. For the first quarter of 2010, the GDP loss had at least slowed to –0.35%.

The Federal District's legislature made news around the world in December 2009 by legalizing same-sex unions, something unheard of even in anti-clerical Mexico. It took effect in March. Several state legislatures quickly amended their constitutions to ban the practice.

The violence along the border and immigration continue to dominate Mexico's relations with the United States. Very little of the U.S. aid pledged under the Merida Initiative has been disbursed. Secretary of State Hillary Clinton visited Mexico in March and pledged an additional $331 million, but to be spent on social programs and to help upgrade the judicial system. The Mexican government pressed for more stringent control of southbound traffic to curtail the flow of illegal weapons,

and the Obama administration complied with stepped-up inspections.

The immigration issue splashed back into headlines in both countries on April 23 when Arizona Governor Jan Brewer signed a controversial new law that requires aliens to carry proof of their immigration status at all times and allows police to detain people suspected of being in the United States illegally. The law was prompted by an alarming increase in common crime, allegedly committed by illegal immigrants. Mexicans on both sides of the border denounced the law, saying it encourages racial profiling, and there were demonstrations against it in several U.S. states. Obama called it "misguided." Polls, however, showed a majority of Americans, and even a sizable minority of Hispanics, agreed with the law.

The Arizona law overshadowed Calderón's state visit to Washington on May 19–20. Obama feted Calderón at a state dinner, and repeated his opposition to the law. The next day, Calderón addressed a poorly attended joint session of Congress in Spanish and repeated his fear that the law would be used to discriminate against law-abiding Mexicans. On the drug issue, Democrats applauded when he urged Congress to reinstate a ban on automatic assault weapons that had expired, while most Republicans remained silent. Thousands of these weapons have been smuggled across the border to drug traffickers.

In politics, this is the important bellwether year in which 12 of the 31 states elect their governors. In the past, the elections were spread out through the latter half of the year, but for the first time they were all held the same day, July 4. The states are Aguascalientes, Chihuahua, Durango, Hidalgo, Oaxaca, Puebla, Quintana Roo, Sinaloa, Tamaulipas, Tlaxcala, Veracruz and Zacatecas. Drug-related violence dominated the races in Chihuahua and Sinaloa, where the *PRI* was facing stiff challenges from the *PAN*. But the race that drew the most interest was in Oaxaca. Once again, the *PRD* and *PAN* put aside their ideological differences to field a unified candidacy behind Gabino Cué, who narrowly lost the disputed 2004 election, against the *PRI*'s Eviel Pérez Magaña.

Also of interest was the campaigning on behalf of *PRI* candidates by Mexico State Governor Enrique Peña Nieto, who has emerged as the leader of the dinosaur faction and was collecting IOUs for an anticipated run for president in 2012.

The results on July 4 were a validation of the *PRI*'s dramatic comeback the year before. It won nine of the 12 contested governorships, retaining six—Chihuahua, Durango, Hidalgo, Quintana Roo, Tamaulipas and Veracruz—and recapturing Aguascalientes and Tlaxcala from the *PAN* and

Mexico

Zacatecas from the *PRD*. But the three gains were offset by first-ever losses in Oaxaca, Puebla and Sinaloa; in all three, the *PAN* and *PRD* had forged cross-ideological alliances to offset the *PRI*'s numerical superiority. In Oaxaca, Cué won by a convincing majority of 56%. It could be argued that the three states the *PRI* lost were for local rather than national issues and personalities. It will be interesting to see whether the *PAN* and *PRD* can govern effectively together now that they have won.

Other Current Issues

Drugs

Given the geographic reality of Mexico's 2,000-mile border with the United States, it was inevitable that Mexico would become a conduit in the traffic of illegal drugs from Colombia to the United States. It is estimated that 70%–80% of the cocaine and heroin entering the United States crosses that border. In addition, vast quantities of Mexican-grown marijuana also stream across the border, as do methamphetamines. It was also inevitable that domestic drug cartels would arise in Mexico, further corrupting already corrupt governmental and law enforcement institutions.

Until 1997 there were three major drug cartels operating in northern Mexico: the Gulf Cartel on the eastern flank, based in Matamoros, Tamaulipas, and headed by Juan García Abregu; the Juárez Cartel, based in Ciudad Juárez in Chihuahua and headed by Amado Carrillo Fuentes; and the Tijuana Cartel in Baja California Norte, run by the Arellano Félix brothers, Ramón, Benjamín, Eduardo, Francisco Javier and Francisco Rafael. Of these five brothers—there were a total of 10 siblings—Benjamín was considered the brains behind the business, while Ramón was a bloodthirsty enforcer who himself died in a hail of bullets in 2002.

These three groups had unofficially "divided" the 1,200-mile U.S. border into operational zones. Friction between them erupted into gangland-style violence, which has reached epic proportions. In one legendary case, a lieutenant of the Arellano Félixes infiltrated the Juárez Cartel in 1989, seduced the wife of a Carrillo Fuentes lieutenant, persuaded her to withdraw $7 million from her husband's account, then killed her and sent her head to her husband in a box. He also reportedly threw the couple's two children to their deaths from a bridge in Caracas, Venezuela.

Another still-infamous incident was a 1993 shootout in the Guadalajara airport in which Cardinal Juan Jesús Posadas Ocampo was killed, supposedly in the crossfire. Some theories still contend that he was in fact a target because he knew too much of official complicity in the drug trade, and his death remains controversial to this day. Francisco Rafael Arellano Félix was convicted of his role in the archbishop's death, as was Joaquín Guzmán of the rival gang. Guzmán escaped in early 2001; Francisco Rafael Arellano Félix remains in prison.

In 1996, the Gulf Cartel was beheaded when García Abregu was extradited to the United States and sentenced to 11 life terms by a federal court in Houston. He was known for his high-level influence, among others, it is reported, with Raúl Salinas, brother of the former president, and former federal prosecutor Mario Ruíz Massieu.

In July 1997, Carrillo Fuentes, nicknamed "Lord of the Skies" because of his use of aging jetliners to ferry massive amounts of cocaine from Colombia and believed to have the largest of the three cartels, died while undergoing clandestine plastic surgery to alter his appearance. Reports surfaced in some Mexican media that his death was a "hit" by a rival drug gang, probably the Tijuana Cartel. Although the report never was confirmed, two of his surgeons later were found tortured and killed; a third was granted protection in the United States, where he insisted to investigators that Carrillo Fuentes' death was, indeed, due to nothing more than a botched procedure.

Carrillo Fuentes' brother, Vicente, for a time assumed leadership of the cartel, but he lacked his brother's genius for organization, logistics and control. The dead kingpin was not even in his grave before a monumental turf war erupted between his cartel and that of the Arellano Félix brothers. Both Juárez and Tijuana became war zones, and still are. Most killings are in imaginatively gruesome gangland fashion by strangulation, suffocation with plastic bags or multiple gunshot wounds. The bodies frequently were burned, dismembered or beheaded and found stuffed into suitcases, oil drums or automobile trunks. The violence continues to be beyond the capability of federal, state or local police to contend with.

For a time, the Tijuana Cartel gained the upper hand. It was the richest, most powerful, most feared and most bloodthirsty of the cartels. The Arellano Félix brothers maintained their power over public officials with a Godfather-like carrot-or-stick tactic called *"plata o plomo"* ("silver or lead"). They were Mexico's most wanted criminals, and Ramón was on the FBI's 10 Most Wanted List.

The heat on the cartel intensified when it committed a serious tactical error: it began shooting crusading journalists, like Benjamín Flores, the young publisher of a small daily newspaper in Sonora along the border with Arizona, who was gunned down outside his office in 1997. The same year, Jesús Blancornelas, publisher of *Zeta,* a weekly magazine in Tijuana that has been a nemesis of the Arellano Félixes, was critically wounded in an ambush that killed his bodyguard; one of the gunmen also was slain, and was identified as a hit man for the Tijuana Cartel. Other journalists vowed to create unbearable pressure on the Tijuana cartel. As one of them told this author, "They can't kill all of us."

Because of the endemic corruption that riddles government at all levels and the parallel law enforcement agencies, efforts to combat drug trafficking have sometimes taken on the semblance of a comic opera. Frequent changes of top law enforcement officials, for example, hamstrung any serious attempt to combat the drug cartels prior to 2000. Mexico had seven attorneys general in eight years during the 1990s.

In 1994, then-President Salinas established the Institute to Combat Drugs (*INCD*), the equivalent of the U.S. Drug Enforcement Administration, but it, too, has had a revolving door. One of its directors, Army General Jesús Gutiérrez Rebollo, was fired in 1997 and arrested, accused of taking bribes from Carrillo Fuentes. He was sentenced to 13 years and nine months in prison. Zedillo abolished the *INCD* and returned its functions to the attorney general's office.

President Bill Clinton made a largely cosmetic state visit to Mexico in 1997, his first, and he succeeded in ameliorating anti-U.S. feeling by acknowledging that the root of the drug trade was not Mexican greed but the insatiable demand for drugs in the United States. That good will evaporated in 1998 as a result of a secret three-year-long sting operation by U.S. agents to nab Mexican bankers involved in money laundering. "Operation Casablanca" involved U.S. agents acting clandestinely in Mexico without the knowledge or approval of Mexican authorities. The operation yielded 150 arrests and $110 million in laundered money, and three Mexican banks were indicted. Mexicans were outraged by what they regarded as a violation of their sovereignty. Clinton offered lukewarm apologies for the failure to consult the Mexicans, but there was an implicit unstated message: We don't trust you enough to tell you about undercover drug operations.

Clinton met with Zedillo in 1999 for a one-day summit in Yucatán that focused on drugs and trade. The two presidents worked out a new drug agreement that established performance measures of effectiveness (PMEs) for 16 areas of drug control—including reduction of demand in the United States. The United States also agreed to provide increased police training assistance. After the summit, Clinton recertified Mexico as an ally in the drug war.

In 2000, the newly inaugurated president, Vicente Fox, pledged a crackdown on corruption, which in Mexico is almost synonymous with drugs. In a meeting with his new U.S. counterpart, George W. Bush, in early 2001, Fox pledged heightened cooperation in the war on drugs, although like his predecessors he voiced his disapproval of the U.S. drug certification policy.

The Fox administration scored some significant victories. One was the capture of the fugitive former governor of Quintana Roo, Mario Villanueva, who allegedly aided the Juárez Cartel in smuggling 200 tons of cocaine into the United States. He had been on the run for two years. In 2010, he was extradited to the United States.

Mexican authorities also arrested 21 alleged members of the Gulf Cartel, by then headed by Osiel Cárdenas, among them one of the suspected kingpins, Gilberto García, known as *"El June."* In 2003 he was sentenced to eight years. Two months after García's arrest, Juan Manuel Garza, another of the alleged leaders of the Gulf Cartel, crossed the border from Reynosa into McAllen, Texas, and surrendered to the FBI.

Cárdenas himself, nicknamed *"El Loco"* because he is so brazen that he once confronted DEA agents and ordered them out of "his" territory, and 22 accomplices were apprehended in 2003 after a gun battle in Matamoros, across from Brownsville, Texas.

Drug-related violence erupted in Nuevo Laredo, and since then a new turf battle has raged there to fill the latest vacuum at the apex of the Gulf Cartel. By 2003, a band of deserters from the Mexican army, calling themselves *"Los Zetas,"* had become established in Nuevo Laredo and was fighting for a piece of the turf.

The Arellano Félix organization suffered two major blows in 2002. First, Ramón was killed in a shootout, supposedly with police, in Mazatlán. He killed the policeman who killed him in the exchange of gunfire. Because the body was quickly cremated, there was speculation as to whether the corpse was actually that of an imposter; it was reminiscent of the death of the Juárez Cartel's Carillo Fuentes in 1997.

A month later, Benjamín was arrested in a raid in Puebla. Benjamín confirmed it was Ramón who had been killed in Mazatlán. Police took blood and saliva samples from Benjamín, and DNA sam-

National University of Mexico Library

ples taken from blood on the clothes of the man killed in Mazatlán were a match.

There was a bizarre postscript to Ramón's death. The Associated Press, citing an anonymous "senior U.S. law enforcement official," reported that the police who killed Ramón were in fact part of a hit paid for by Ismael Zambada García, head of a new, rival cartel in Sinaloa. Officials declined to comment on the report—but did not deny it.

A judge ruled there was insufficient evidence to implicate Benjamín and his imprisoned brother, Rafael, in Archbishop Posadas Ocampo's death in 1993. Another judge dismissed a charge that Benjamín headed a drug-trafficking organization. Another brother, Eduardo, a surgeon, was thought to hold a leadership role. He remained at large until 2008.

With the seeming downfall of the Arellano Félix brothers and the decapitation of

the Gulf Cartel, the center of gravity in the drug trade shifted to Sinaloa—the original home of the Arellano Félixes. Sinaloa has a long history of involvement in the raising and trafficking of drugs dating to the 19th century, when Chinese immigrants raised poppies for the production of opium, much of which was smuggled to the United States.

At least two major, rival cartels then operated in Sinaloa. One is headed by the Guzmán brothers, Arturo, known as "the Chicken," and Joaquín, *"El Chapo,"* who was serving a 20-year sentence for the accidental shooting death of Archbishop Posadas Ocampo in 1993 before he escaped in 2001. He remains at large, but Arturo was arrested in 2001. Arturo is believed to be responsible for an elaborate 1,400-foot tunnel under the U.S. border. Joaquín is believed to be among the drug lords trying to fill the vacuum in Nuevo Laredo.

Mexico

The other cartel is headed by Ismael "El Mayo" Zambada García. He reportedly attempted to muscle in on the Arellano Félixes' Tijuana operations for at least a decade, fueling speculation he was responsible for Ramón's "execution" in Mazatlán. His organization became the target of a U.S.-Mexican investigation, code-named "Operation Trifecta" after the seizure of a 10-ton cocaine shipment at sea in 2001.

An exceptionally violent turf battle erupted between the two gangs. Within days of Ramón's death, a suspected Arellano Félix ally was gunned down, sparking a wave of gangland killings.

In 2003, Attorneys General John Ashcroft and Maceda de la Concha announced simultaneously in Washington and Mexico City a "significant victory" when Zambada García was named in an unsealed U.S. indictment, along with two of his lieutenants; all three remain at large, however. Ashcroft and Macedo also announced that Operation Trifecta had yielded 240 arrests and indictments.

President Bush announced in 2004 that the Arellano Félix and Carillo Fuentes organizations, and Mexicans Eduardo Arellano Félix, Francisco Javier Arellano Félix, and Armando Valencia Cornelio had been placed on a sanctions list, denying them access to U.S. financial institutions or from dealing with U.S. companies or individuals. U.S. authorities arrested Francisco Javier Arellano Félix, the youngest of the brothers, on a yacht off the California coast in 2006.

The two governments jointly launched a fugitive-hunting effort code-named Operation United Eagles in 2003. The biggest catch was Gilberto Higuera Guerrero, a former operative in the Tijuana Cartel who joined the Zambada gang in Sinaloa.

In a major, and frightening, development, Juan José Esparragoza, who had been operations chief of the Juárez Cartel, reportedly took over the leadership from Vicente Carrillo Fuentes and began building alliances. Carillo Fuentes went into hiding after his other brother, Rodolfo, was gunned down in 2004 in a hit reportedly ordered by the Guzmán gang. Nonetheless, Esparragoza persuaded the rival Guzmán and Zambada cartels in Sinaloa to put aside their differences and to join the Juárez Cartel. With Benjamín Arellano Félix of the Tijuana Cartel and Cárdenas of the Gulf Cartel both behind bars, this new alliance made the Juárez Cartel the largest in Mexico, and it began a two-front offensive against its rivals, with "El Mayo" Zambada the "general" in charge of battling the Tijuana Cartel for control of the drug routes into California and Arizona, and *"El Chapo"* Guzmán fighting the Gulf Cartel in Tamaulipas along the Texas border.

In an equally stunning development, Benjamín Arellano Félix and Cárdenas, jailed in the maximum-security La Palma federal prison near Mexico City, formed an unholy alliance of their own to defend their respective turfs against the onslaught from the Juárez-Sinaloa alliance. When the federal government got wind of their collusion, it launched a crackdown on the federal prison system, dispatching troops to surround La Palma. Cárdenas and Arellano Félix were separated, but not before their alliance was created.

This clash of titans has become spectacularly bloody, generating headlines on both sides of the border. Gangland-style killings remain a daily occurrence, but the victims are not always members of the two gangs; law enforcement officers, journalists and innocent bystanders die as well. The number of drug-related killings increased from 1,300 in 2005 to 2,100 in 2006. It would go much higher.

The main battlegrounds were once Matamoros, Nuevo Laredo and Ciudad Alemán, border cities in Tamaulipas, where *Los Zetas* were believed to have become enforcers for the Gulf Cartel. In a bold act that shocked both countries, six guards at the prison in Matamoros were seized by hit men when their shift ended in January 2005, handcuffed, riddled with bullets execution-style and left in a car outside town. The killings were reportedly retribution for the crackdown on the federal prisons, and were interpreted as a challenge by the drug lords to the national government itself. The killings were probably carried out by *Los Zetas*. President Fox sent army troops to cordon off the prison.

In Nuevo Laredo, the lawless atmosphere is reminiscent of the Capone-Moran rivalry in Chicago in the 1920s—only bloodier. In 2005, the Fox administration dispatched 600 heavily armed federal policemen there, then added army troops to a force of 700 to help patrol the city, one step short of declaring martial law. When the city finally filled the vacancy for police chief, the new chief was ambushed by drug traffickers and killed his first day on the job. His replacement soon resigned. The city still averages at least one drug-related murder a day.

The drug traffickers loathe—and fear—crusading journalists only slightly less than they do law enforcement officials who can't be bought. In 2004, for the first time, more journalists were slain in Mexico than in Colombia. According to the Paris-based Reporters Without Borders, only Iraq, Bangladesh and the Philippines recorded more journalists killed than did Mexico. By 2007, Mexico had become the second-most dangerous country for journalists after Iraq. Most of the killings are close to the border.

In Tijuana, Francisco Ortíz Franco, assistant editor of Jesús Blancornelas' crusading weekly *Zeta*, was gunned down in 2004. Two months later, Francisco Arratia Saldierna, a syndicated newspaper columnist in Matamoros who regularly attacked organized crime, was sadistically tortured and beaten to death. Gregorio Rodríguez, a photographer with a newspaper in Sinaloa, was murdered after he took a picture of a drug dealer.

In Nuevo Laredo, two well-known journalists, both of whom reported on the cartels, were murdered in 2004 and 2005. Roberto Mora, news editor of *El Mañana*, was stabbed to death, and Guadalupe García Escamilla, who hosted a radio crime program, was riddled with bullets outside the station and died 10 days later.

Mexican journalists and international journalism organizations demanded that the Fox administration do more to protect journalists and to apprehend their killers. Yet, in 2006, the offices of *El Mañana* in Nuevo Laredo were attacked with automatic weapons and grenades, and a reporter was critically wounded. The publisher announced that the paper would refrain from any further investigative reporting on the cartels.

After two grenade attacks on the office of *Cambio,* the evening daily in Hermosillo, Sonora, Mario Vásquez Raña, owner of the Editora Mexicana chain that owns *Cambio,* announced he was "temporarily" closing the newspaper to assure the safety of its employees. It was the first time drug traffickers had succeeding in actually putting a Mexican newspaper out of operation. In 2009, the office of *Televisa* in Monterrey was attacked with grenades and a high-powered weapon, but there were no casualties. Much the same happened in 2009 with the powerful Mexico City newspaper *Reforma* and its sister paper in Monterrey, *El Norte*. Their publisher, Alejandro Junco de la Vega, went into self-imposed exile in the United States because of death threats.

The cartels have even targeted musicians who have popularized the so-called drug ballads, or *narco-corridos;* 13 were killed in 2007 alone (see Culture).

President Felipe Calderón, who took office on December 1, 2006, has been even tougher on the drug gangs than Fox had been. Days after his inauguration, he dispatched 7,000 federal troops to his home state of Michoacán, where a turf battle between the Gulf and Sinaloa cartels killed 600 people in 2006; decapitations are a favorite method there of sending "messages." Alfonso Barajas, or "Ugly Poncho," a leader of the Gulf cartel, was arrested.

In 2007, Calderón dispatched another 3,300 troops to Tijuana, where they supplanted the local police. They even confiscated the weapons of the police to conduct ballistic tests to determine if they had been used in drug-related murders. In 2008, Calderón sent another 2,000 troops to Ciudad Juárez and 2,700 into Sinaloa, bringing to 24,000 the number of troops deployed against the cartels. Mexico began to resemble Colombia.

In two stunning developments, Calderón extradited Osiel Cárdenas and three other kingpins to the United States. He also beefed up and reorganized the new Federal Investigative Agency, or *AFI*, the Mexican equivalent of the FBI, and transferred it from the Justice Ministry to the new Public Security Ministry. The ministry has 30,000 troops under its control.

Calderón and Bush met in Mérida, Yucatán, in March 2007, where they discussed increased U.S. drug aid. Bush asked Congress to approve a $500-million-a-year aid package for three years to provide Mexico with sophisticated technology to aid in the drug war. Congress showed the same enthusiasm it did for Bush's immigration plan. It finally approved an initial $194 million of a $1.4 billion aid plan in late 2008, just before Bush left office. Secretary of State Condoleezza Rice, Defense Secretary Robert Gates, Attorney General Michael Mukasey and Homeland Security officials met with their Mexican counterparts for the first session of the high-level policy group established in the "Merida Initiative."

In April 2007, Benjamín Arellano Félix was sentenced to five years on weapons charges in Mexico. That November, his brother Francisco Javier was sentenced to life without parole in San Diego after entering a guilty plea in exchange for his life. He admitted to numerous murders and issued a surprisingly remorseful letter asking for forgiveness. Although Benjamín is serving time in Mexico, U.S. authorities are seeking his extradition.

By 2007, there were indications that the bilateral crackdown against the cartels was having an effect. According to the U.S. DEA, the street price of cocaine had jumped 44% in the first three quarters, that of methamphetamines 73%.

The authorities enjoyed another major success in January 2008 with the arrest of Alfredo Beltrán Leyva, believed to be Guzmán's enforcer and to be behind shipments of tons of cocaine to the United States.

The cartels' response was a counteroffensive at the highest levels of law enforcement. In May 2008, Edgar Millán Gómez, the acting national police chief, was assassinated, shot nine times as he arrived at his home. Although wounded himself, his bodyguard apprehended the gunman. The killing was believed to have been ordered in reprisal for the arrest of

Alfredo Beltrán Leyva by his brother, Arturo. The next day, the head of Mexico City's investigative police was murdered. Other recent victims have included the director of organized crime investigation in Mexico City and the deputy police chief in Ciudad Juárez.

Coincidentally, Guzmán's son was slain the same day as Millán Gómez, supposedly by elements of the Juárez Cartel.

That October, Ismael Zambada's brother, Jesús, and 15 other members of the Sinaloa Cartel were arrested after a gun battle with police in Mexico City. Jesús is also suspected of involvement in the Millán Gómez assassination.

Four days after Zambada's arrest, authorities arrested the elusive Eduardo Arrellano Félix after a gun battle at a Tijuana residence. The DEA had tipped off Mexican authorities. He is the last of the brothers active in the cartel to be captured or killed, but it is believed the brothers' role in the cartel has been carved up between their nephew, Luis Fernando Sánchez Arrellano, and Eduardo García Simental. García Simental's brother, Teodoro, split off from the Tijuana Cartel and went off on his own, forging an alliance with the Sinaloa Cartel.

In another example of cartel fragmentation, Arturo Beltrán Leyva split off from the Sinaloa Cartel in 2008 and established his own, entering into an alliance with *Los Zetas* in Tamaulipas and setting up operations in the state of Morelos. He quickly became one of the three most-wanted men in Mexico—but not for long. On December 16, 2009, he and six of his bodyguards died in a 90-minute gun battle with army troops in a house in Cuernavaca, Morelos. The government scored another major success in January 2010 with the arrest of Teodoro García Simental. So much for branching off on your own.

The government's spectacular successes against cartels at war with the Sinaloa Cartel have led Calderón's critics to suggest darkly that his administration is in league with the Sinaloa organization. Indeed, raids and arrests against Sinaloa kingpins seem suspiciously under-represented compared with those against other drug cartels. What is possible is that the government has struck a Faustian deal by which the Sinaloa Cartel provides investigators with vital intelligence against its rivals, benefiting both parties. If so, it will be interesting to see what will happen when Sinaloa is the last cartel standing.

Meanwhile, a frightening new variable in this already crowded field is a group calling itself *La Familia*, which thus far operates exclusively in Michoacán—Calderón's home state. Besides specializing in methamphetamines, it has diversified into extortion. The night before Independence

Day in September 2008, eight people were killed and at least 100 wounded when suspected *La Familia* members tossed grenades into a crowd of revelers in Morelia, the state capital, apparently just to instill terror. They succeeded, but they also sparked further outrage. By September 2009, there were indications the cartel was trying to reach an accommodation with the government; Calderón responded to the feelers with another crackdown, dispatching 5,000 troops to the state.

By 2008, the violence nationwide had become so alarming that Mexico resembled the sectarian warfare in Iraq, only the killings were even more grisly. Calderón submitted a new security plan to Congress that would streamline coordination among the various civilian and military agencies and zero in on corruption. He also summoned a hemispheric drug summit attended by representatives of 34 countries, among them OAS Secretary-General José Miguel Insulza and U.S. Attorney General Mukasey. Calderón urged a "continental front" to combat the drug trade from cultivation to demand on the streets of the United States. Among the bad news the participants heard: the Colombian deputy defense minister reported that the Revolutionary Armed Forces of Colombia *(FARC)* was now selling cocaine and methamphetamines directly to the Mexican cartels.

The border area has essentially become a war zone. In 2008, the death toll in Mexico from drug-related violence was about 4,500, half the figure of 9,226 civilians killed in Iraq that year. By 2009, the Mexican death toll was 9,635 compared with 4,497 civilian deaths in Iraq.

The slaughter of journalists also continues. Eleven were murdered in Mexico in 2009, making it the most dangerous country for journalism in Latin America, and bringing to 62 the number of journalists killed since 2000; five more were murdered in just the first four months of 2010.

Juárez has now eclipsed the other Mexican cities as a slaughterhouse. In 2009, it officially became the world's most dangerous city, with about 2,750 drug-related murders, an average of 12 a day. It is now patrolled by 10,000 federal police and troops, who have been accused of various abuses. By mid-2010, the death toll appeared destined to go higher this year. In January, 16 teenagers at a New Year's party were slain in what appeared to be a case of mistaken identity. In March, a pregnant U.S. consulate official, her husband and another consular employee became victims, which made headlines in both countries. The woman and her husband were U.S. citizens, and the mayor of Ciudad Juárez said it appeared they were tar-

Mexico

geted by drug traffickers. The husband worked for the El Paso sheriff's department. Calderón visited the city three times that month, but the carnage has continued.

The Environment

Mexico City faces an air pollution crisis that is one of the worst of any of the world's major cities. Because the capital is located in a "bowl" surrounded by high mountains, with a population of 20 million and 3 million cars and trucks, there is literally no air circulation for about eight months a year. *Pemex*, the state-controlled petroleum monopoly, was notorious for producing poorly refined, pollutant-laden (particularly sulfur) gasoline, but unleaded fuel has become commonplace, which has led to a dramatic improvement in air quality. The Environment Ministry issued new guidelines in June 2005 aimed at providing even cleaner-burning gasoline and diesel fuel by 2008.

But smog remains a serious problem in the capital. The No. 1 diseases among the young are respiratory (chronic and debilitating). The response under a succession of presidential administrations has been inadequate. Factories have been suspended from operation, and autos (both domestic and foreign) are allotted certain days of the week on which they may be operated.

Mexico City's pollution is made worse by hundreds of tons of human and animal waste which, untreated, is dumped outside the city. It dries, and when the wind blows, it is picked up as a fine dust, further choking the air. Because of this and other pollution problems, educated and wealthy people have left the city for places such as San Luís Potosí and Cuernavaca.

Another environmental concern that has only recently attracted governmental attention is the alarming rate of deforestation through illegal logging. The Environment Ministry estimates that 1.3 million acres of forest are lost to illegal logging each year, even in the 133,000-acre preserve of El Rosario in the state of Michoacán, where the monarch butterflies spend the winter. In 2005, the winter population of the butterflies was only about a fourth what it was the year before. In December 2004, the ministry announced that 103 people had been arrested that year for illegal logging, triple the number of the year before, and that sophisticated surveillance had been undertaken to detect the poaching.

Until the government crackdown, the only effort to stem the logging had come from environmental activists, who often were met with violence and questionable charges brought by powerful local *caciques*, or political bosses. Perhaps the

best-known group is the Peasant Ecologists of the Sierra Petatlán, in the state of Guerrero. Under national and international pressure, President Vicente Fox intervened to free two of the group's activists in 2001 after they were arrested on what were apparently trumped-up drug and weapons possession charges. Another member of the group, Felipe Arreaga, was arrested in November 2004 on questionable murder charges; domestic and international rights and environmental groups have demanded his release. In May 2005, yet another of the group's leaders, Albertano Penalosa, narrowly escaped death in an ambush that killed two of his sons, aged 19 and 9. The international environmental group Greenpeace estimates that 40% of the forest in the Sierra Petatlán was logged out between 1992 and 2000.

Also endangered is the Lacandón rainforest in the south, considered by ecologists to be the most biologically diverse jungle in the hemisphere after the Amazon, which also is threatened by illegal logging (see Brazil).

In a positive development, a private campaign by the U.S. group Nature Conservancy and Pronature of Mexico raised $3 million in 2004 purchase 370,000 acres of rain forest in Yucatán, which was added to the existing 1.8-million-acre Calakmul Biosphere Reserve. It was the largest private conservation project in Mexican history.

Mexico is believed to be home to 10 percent of all wildlife species on Earth.

Armed Rebellions

For all its corruption and political violence, Mexico had not experienced actual armed insurrection since the Revolution. Thus, the country was shocked on New Year's Day 1994 when an organized band of rebels calling itself the *Zapatista* National Liberation Army (*EZLN*) launched a bloody offensive against federal institutions in Chiapas state. The group proclaimed itself the champion of the poor southern peasants, most of them full-blooded Indians, much like the revolutionary hero Emiliano Zapata after whom it is named.

Disputes between the wealthy ranchers and the impoverished masses had been festering in Chiapas for 175 years. The *EZLN*, whose strength was variously estimated at 200 to 2,000, denounced alleged electoral fraud by which the *PRI* had won the governorship of Chiapas. The army was sent in and for 10 days there was some skirmishing in which about 145 people were killed on both sides. Then the government and the rebels agreed to negotiate.

What followed was a media circus. The *EZLN* leader who emerged as its negotia-

tor went by the *nom de guerre* "Subcomandante Marcos," who always appeared in ski mask and with bandoliers containing ammunition incompatible with the shotgun he brandished. This "guerrilla" subsequently was identified as Rafael Sebastián Guillén, son of a wealthy Caucasian family in Tampico in far-off northern Mexico and a former *Sandinista* activist. The unmasking of Subcomandante Marcos largely undermined the credibility of the *EZLN*.

Nonetheless, the *Zapatistas* made up in media savvy what they lacked in military expertise and proved to be skilled in public relations. At first, they aroused sympathy, but support waned in 1995 after the government engaged in a public relations counteroffensive that blamed the rebels for frightening off foreign investments, thus contributing to the crippling recession. For the most part, the *EZLN* has engaged in what one political scientist wryly labeled "guerrilla theater."

Not so with a second group that burst on the scene—also in the south—in 1996. On June 28, peasants in Guerrero state held a memorial service to commemorate the first anniversary of the massacre of 17 peasants by Guerrero police. Dozens of hooded men and women showed up at the service, calling themselves the Popular Revolutionary Army (*ERP*). Unlike the *EZLN*, this group appeared to be well armed with AK-47s and clad more like serious guerrillas, with boots instead of sandals, for example.

Alarmed, President Zedillo dispatched thousands of troops to Guerrero, angering local officials who said the president was "militarizing" the state. Like Chiapas, Guerrero is sharply divided between extreme wealth (Acapulco and other posh Pacific resorts are in Guerrero) and abject poverty. It was the site of a minor insurgency in the 1960s and 1970s, led by the legendary, Robin Hood-like outlaw, Lucio Cabañas, who eventually was slain by security forces. The Organization of American States sent a team of human rights workers to investigate charges of rights abuses in the state.

That August, the *ERP* stunned the country with a series of well-coordinated attacks against military garrisons and police stations, not only in Guerrero but in Chiapas and Oaxaca as well. They killed at least 18 people, including two civilians.

Since its first spectacular strikes, the *ERP* seemed to fade into the background. Unlike the *EZLN*, the *ERP* has called for the violent overthrow of the government and showed no appetite for negotiation. Also unlike the *EZLN*, it has failed to win public support, judging from opinion polls. Subcomandante Marcos himself distanced the *EZLN* from the new group,

A newly paved stretch of Highway 59 vaults through La Muralla, a notch-shaped pass through the rugged volcanic mountains north of Saltillo, Coahuila. *Photo by the author*

saying, "You fight for power. We fight for democracy, liberty and justice."

In February 1996, the government and the *EZLN* reached a tentative agreement in the town of San Andrés de Larrainzar, called the San Andrés accords, that would grant the Indians in the south greater autonomy from the institutionalized state and local governments, almost all of them controlled by the *PRI*. The *Zapatistas* broke off from talks the following September, alleging the government was dragging its feet in implementing the accords. For 15 months the talks were in limbo; it took a shocking tragedy to get things moving again.

On December 22, 1997, about 70 armed members of a *PRI*-affiliated paramilitary group in Chiapas entered the village of Acteal, about 12 miles north of San Cristóbal de las Casas. Without provocation, they shot anyone who presented a target—men, women, children, even infants in their mothers' arms. People were gunned down as they desperately attempted to flee, others as they huddled in a church, an atrocity reminiscent of My Lai during the Vietnam War or the "ethnic cleansing" in the Balkans. When the firing stopped, 45 Indian peasants had been slain, all but nine of them women or children; four of the women were pregnant. At least 25 others were wounded.

The massacre made international headlines and presented Zedillo with a public relations nightmare. With considerable understatement, the president denounced

the massacre as a "cruel, absurd criminal act." In a clumsy effort at damage control, "investigators" from Mexico City hurried to Acteal and initially offered the lame explanation that the massacre had been motivated by a local family feud.

There was a time, before the emergence of viable opposition parties and press reforms, that the *PRI*'s version would have been accepted. Mexico's independent media and foreign journalists, however, interviewed survivors and reported that the gunmen, armed with AK-47s and dressed in blue uniforms, were members of a *PRI* paramilitary group from a neighboring village. One survivor said the gunmen fired in the direction of crying children. Eventually, more than 30 men either were arrested, including a *PRI* mayor, or surrendered. Like the victims, the killers were Indians. The motive for the killings, they explained, was that the villagers were *Zapatista* sympathizers—including, presumably, the slain infants and fetuses.

The opposition *PRD* demanded the resignations of Interior Minister Emilio Chuayffet and the *PRI* governor of Chiapas, Julio César Ruíz Ferro. Zedillo soon sacrificed his No. 2 man on the altar of public opinion and replaced him with Francisco Labastida. Ruíz Ferro yielded to public pressure and resigned.

According to subsequent press reports, such killings of peasants by *PRI*-linked paramilitaries had occurred regularly on a smaller scale in Chiapas, but the Acteal massacre shocked the nation and the

world and forced Zedillo to take action. Among other things, he pledged to reduce the army presence in Chiapas (the army was suspected of providing sophisticated weapons to the paramilitaries) and to crack down on paramilitary groups. Most importantly, he introduced sweeping constitutional reforms to Congress in an effort to jump-start the San Andrés accords. His proposal would have recognized the rights of Mexico's 9 million indigenous people and permit them greater autonomy.

The rebels denounced the initiative as providing "the peace of tombs." Moreover, some lawmakers in the *PRI* and the *PAN* opposed the proposal as giving in too much to the rebels, while the *PRD* faulted it for not going far enough. To be enacted, the proposal would have to receive a two-thirds vote of Congress and ratification of 16 of the 31 state legislatures, a goal that seemed all but unattainable. If it failed, of course, Zedillo at least could say, "Well, I tried."

Apparently, he didn't try hard enough. A clash between army troops and a resurgent *EPR* in Guerrero in May 1998 left 11 civilians dead. Three days later, in Chiapas, there occurred the worst violence since the so-called peace process began. The *EZLN* ambushed a combined army-police patrol and in the ensuing clash eight rebels and one policeman were killed.

Soon thereafter, Mary Robinson, the U.N. commissioner for human rights, rebuked the Mexican government for its alleged rights abuses in Chiapas. U.N. Secretary-General Kofi Annan touched off a diplomatic furor when he suggested the United Nations should play a role in the peace process. Mexico swiftly and vigorously denounced any outside interference. Annan quickly backed off, but visited Mexico to meet with Zedillo and Mexican human rights groups. Although Chiapas was not on the formal agenda, the two leaders discussed it at length. In the end, Annan said the government should exert more effort, but he also urged the rebels to return to the negotiating table, invoking the chiché, "It takes two to tango."

It appeared the "tango" might resume in November 1998 when 29 *Zapatista* delegates showed up in their trademark ski masks for a government-initiated meeting in San Cristóbal de las Casas; Marcos was not among them. The government delegation included six congressmen from all three major parties. The rebels soon dashed any hopes the talks might resume in earnest. They accused the congressmen of being "racists" and refused to return to the bargaining table until the government met the five demands that led to the collapse of the talks two years earlier, including release of *EZLN* prisoners, democratic reforms, disbanding of paramilitary

Mexico

groups and demilitarization of much of southern Mexico.

In April 1999, a potentially explosive incident ended peacefully. About 1,000 unarmed *Zapatistas* came down from the hills and "reoccupied" the city hall in San Andrés de Larrainzar, site of the first talks. The 150 outnumbered state policemen wisely fell back without opening fire. A few days later, 300 state policemen expelled the few remaining *Zapatistas* without violence or arrests.

For his part, Marcos finally came out of hiding in May 1999 for the first time in 18 months, attending a meeting in the Chiapas village of La Realidad.

The peace process remained moribund until after the 2000 presidential election, and it took the election of the conservative *PAN* candidate, Vicente Fox, followed a month later by the election of *PRD* candidate Pedro Salazar for governor of Chiapas, to get it moving again. Fox's first official act after being inaugurated on December 1, 2000, was to fulfill a campaign pledge to order the withdrawal of army troops from Chiapas as a sign of good faith. Fox also introduced a constitutional amendment to Congress in December that would accede to one of the *Zapatistas'* demands, to grant greater autonomy to Mexico's indigenous citizens. With the detested *PRI* out of power both in Mexico City and in Chiapas, and a president in power who seemed serious about peace, the ball was then in Marcos' court. He was now dealing with a president who was at least as astute a public relations practitioner as himself.

What occurred next was typical of Marcos' theatrics, and it garnered worldwide media attention. The *Zapatistas* staged a "caravan" to the capital in March 2001, which the media quickly labeled the "Zapatour." Their stated goal was to lobby Congress directly for the indigenous rights bill. Traveling in trucks and buses, and leaving their weapons at home, Marcos and 23 other *EZLN* members and their entourage traveled through 12 states, receiving tumultuous welcomes from the impoverished Indians along the way, before arriving in the capital. They asked permission to lobby the Chamber of Deputies. Fox agreed, although legislators of his own party adamantly opposed the idea.

The *Zapatistas* remained in the capital for 18 days before they received the invitation to address the lower house. The *EZLN* leaders delivered not strident demands, but respectful requests to the country's lawmakers during a meeting of several hours that was broadcast on national television; the always unpredictable Marcos did not appear. The army, meanwhile, dismantled its last bases in Chiapas.

Congress then debated the indigenous rights bill in earnest. The original bill was based on the accords reached by the *EZLN* and the government in 1996 in San Andrés de Larrainzar. But *PRI* legislators grumbled that the bill infringed on the traditional authority of state governors, while *Panistas* complained it conceded too much to the *Zapatistas*. The Senate unanimously approved an amended version, and the Chamber of Deputies passed it, 386–60. This time the opposition came from the *PRD* and the *PT* on the left, because of language that stressed the preeminence of national sovereignty over indigenous rights. The *EZLN* also opposed the watered-down version because it eliminated the guarantee of rights over land, water and mineral resources.

In July 2001, Michoacán became the 16th state to ratify the amendment. It took effect on August 15, with the *EZLN* still complaining about "betrayal." The law was challenged, but the Supreme Court ruled 8–3 that it lacked jurisdiction over constitutional amendments.

The world heard little more from the *Zapatistas* until 2005, when Marcos declared a "red alert" and ordered *Zapatista* fighters to assemble in their bases. They announced they would create a new political movement, composed of peasant Indians, laborers and students, and they would begin participating in the mainstream political system.

In 2006, Marcos resurfaced and announced his latest public relations-gimmick: a six-month motorbike tour of Mexico all the way to the U.S. border to coincide with the Mexican presidential campaign. (He quickly abandoned his bike for a car). He addressed a rally of thousands in San Cristóbal de las Casas, where he said the *Zapatista* movement was part of a groundswell of indigenous political muscle in Latin America. However, the *Zapatistas* declined to participate in the election. Instead, Marcos condemned all the major candidates, and called the *PRD*'s Andrés Manuel López

Obrador a "traitor." But there has been no violence.

The new president, Felipe Calderón of the *PAN*, found himself faced with a new armed group, calling itself the Popular Revolutionary Army. In September 2007, the group took responsibility for six bombings of oil and gas pipelines in the state of Veracrúz, which caused massive disruptions in supply and temporarily closed 1,500 factories. Little is known about the group. In April 2008, it offered to call a cease-fire in return for establishing a commission to investigate its supposed grievances against the government. Calderón refused.

Culture: Appropriately symbolizing Mexico's ethnic composition is a park in Mexico City called *La Plaza de las Tres Culturas*. In Mexico as much as anywhere in the New World, the blending of the Spanish and Indian produced a third, separate race, the *mestizo*, which predominates today.

The giant of Spanish America in more ways than population size, Mexico had a rich cultural heritage centuries before the Spanish Conquest. The Aztec, Mayan, Toltec, Mixtec and other indigenous civilizations all have contributed much to Mexican folklore. Just as the mixing of bloods created a new race, so did the infusion of Spanish art, music, literature, food, and architecture, give rise to a new, discrete culture. It is Mexico's culture that most North Americans erroneously associate with all of Latin America: *mariachi* music, a spicy rice, bean and tortilla diet, red-tiled roofs and white stuccoed walls.

After independence, cultural development was slow owing to political instability, the crippling civil war between Liberals and Conservatives from 1857–61, the subsequent French intervention and general inattention to public education. Despite the Porfirio Díaz dictatorship rather than because of it, the late 19th and early

Cancún, on the northeastern tip of the Yucatán Peninsula   *Courtesy: Ann and Martin Shuey*

266

20th centuries were marked by the emergence of a distinctly Mexican literature. The most prominent writers of this period were Amado Nervo, Ramón López Velarde and Manuel Gutiérrez Nájera.

The demarcation line of Mexican culture, however, was the Revolution of 1910–20. Besides forever changing the political fabric of the country, the Revolution gave birth to a movement in realist art, appropriately called "revolutionary art," music and literature. Two classic revolutionary novels are Mariano Azuela's *Los de abajo* (1916), and Martín Luís Guzmán's *El aguila y la serpiente* ("The Eagle and the Serpent," 1928), both of which focus on social issues. The poetry of Alfonso Reyes, José Gorostiza and Jaime Torres Bodet and the novels of Agustín Yáñez also are identified with the post-revolutionary period.

Mexico's best-known novelists of the second half of the 20th century are Juan Rulfo (1917–86), best remembered for *Pedro Páramo*, and Carlos Fuentes (1928–), whose classic remains *El gringo viejo*, adapted into the 1989 motion picture *The Old Gringo* with Gregory Peck and Jane Fonda. The acknowledged master of the short story was Juan José Arreola (1921–2001), a friend of Rulfo's, who developed a half-prose, half-poetry genre called *varia invención*, after the title of one of his stories. He published 16 books of stories, probably the most renowned being *La feria* and *Bestiario*.

But the titan of modern Mexican literature was the poet Octavio Paz (1914–98), who received the Nobel Prize in 1990, the fifth and most recent Latin American to be so honored. His verse was a critical, brutally honest examination of Mexico's hybrid Spanish-Indian culture, which alienated him from many of his leftist intellectual contemporaries. Yet, when he died at age 84 in April 1998, his former detractors heaped praise on him, and the government accorded him a state funeral.

The premier figures of post-revolutionary art were Diego Rivera (1886–1957), José Clemente Orozco (1883–1949) and David Alfaro Siqueiros (1896–1974), whose heroic murals epitomize the social struggle of the Revolution. Rivera and Orozco also were at home in the *avant-garde* art crowd of 1920s Paris, and were friends of Pablo Picasso, the influence of whose abstractionism can be detected in their paintings. Siqueiros, a combat veteran of the Revolution, lived and painted for a time in Los Angeles, and fought on the republican side during the Spanish Civil War.

One of Rivera's four wives, Frida Kahlo (1907–54), carved out an international reputation as an artist in her own right and has posthumously become a feminist cultural icon in Europe and the United States. She was the subject of a 2002 U.S. motion picture, *Frida,* starring Mexican actress Salma Hayek (see next page).

Probably Mexico's best-known artist today is the painter and sculptor Francisco Toledo, famed for his erotic shaman-based figures.

In photography, the premier figure was the internationally renowned Manuel Alvarez Bravo (1902–2002), whose photos ranged from street scenes to nude women.

Mexican music of the post-revolutionary period was dominated by Carlos Chávez, who founded the national symphony orchestra in 1928 and whose classical compositions were drawn from Mexico's Indian heritage.

Popular music is characterized both by the *ranchero* style, a guitar-based sound that celebrates Mexico's *vaqueros,* (cowboys), through corridos, or ballads, and the quintessentially Mexican *mariachis*.

Mexico has long had a thriving popular music industry, one that blends the sounds of traditional Mexican music with the internationalized Latino sounds of the Caribbean. Mexican singers have achieved renown throughout Latin America and in the United States.

One of Mexico's leading pop icons is Gloria Trevi, the so-called "Madonna of Mexico." However, she has been more like the Michael Jackson of Mexico. For five years, she and her lover-manager were the focus of a tawdry international investigation of alleged kidnapping and raping of underage girls. She was jailed in Brazil (where she mysteriously became pregnant and gave birth) and extradited to Mexico, where she was finally acquitted by a judge in September 2004 in a court proceeding broadcast on national television. It generated much the same excitement as Michael Jackson's molestation trial and acquittal in the United States. She was 36 at the time of the acquittal and resumed her singing career.

A relatively new Mexican band, called RBD, has an enthusiastic following throughout Latin America and the Mexican community in the United States.

An interesting trend since the 1990s has been the singers specializing in the so-called "narco-corridos," inspired by the drug-related violence along the border. In 2007, 13 such singers were murdered, apparently by the drug cartels, including Sergio Gómez and Valentín Elizalde.

Mexico City has a robust theatrical community, though the works of its playwrights to date have been primarily for domestic consumption.

Mexican cinema, on the other hand, developed parallel with that of the United States, and Mexican films have been exported for several decades now. Many Mexican film stars went on to successful careers in Hollywood, such as Dolores del Río, Ramón Navarro, Anthony Quinn and Ricardo Montalbán.

But arguably Mexico's most revered film legend was María Félix (1914–2002), perhaps because she eschewed moving to Hollywood and devoted her career to her native country. Known as the "Marilyn Monroe of Mexico," she made 47 films between 1942 and 1970 and was a national icon. Her death in April 2002 brought thousands of mourners to the Palacio de Bellas Artes in Mexico City; President Vicente Fox extolled her as "a great shrine to our country."

Mexican cinema continues to thrive with several films that have achieved international acclaim in recent years. In 2001, for example, there were *De la calle, (On the street),* directed by newcomer Gerardo Tort, which is a searing glimpse of the lives of Mexico's street urchins; and *Amores perros (Love's a Bitch).* Another, and more controversial film that won notice abroad in 2002—and outraged the Roman Catholic hierarchy in Mexico—was *El crimen de Padre Amaro (The Crime of Father Amaro).* Adapted from a Portuguese novel, it is the story of a priest who seduces a 16-year-old girl. Another hit abroad was *Y tu mamá también (And Your Mama, Too.)*

Cinema also has been boosted by a new generation of actors, some of whom have also made their marks in Hollywood. One is Salma Hayek, who was nominated for an Academy Award in 2003 for her title role in the U.S. movie *Frida,* based on the life of artist Frida Kahlo. Another is Gael García, who starred in *Amores perros, Y tu mamá también* and *Padre Amaro.* Both have become international sex symbols; in fact, the media have nicknamed García "Sex-Mex." García's co-star in *Y tu mamá también,* Diego Luna, later co-starred with Robert Duval and Kevin Costner in *Open Range.*

Mexico's television industry has been characterized by a mix of public-private cooperation. The privately owned *Televisa* network is today one of the world's largest, and Mexican programs, chiefly *telenovelas,* are the most popular in Latin America. By the mid-1990s, a new privately owned channel, *TV Azteca,* was making inroads with daring new *telenovelas* that dealt frankly with formerly taboo subjects, such as women's sexuality and official corruption. Some programs began eclipsing *Televisa*'s in the ratings.

The Mexican press is nominally independent, but for more than 60 years the Mexican government controlled the supply of newsprint through a subsidized public entity called *Pipsa*. This allowed the *PRI* to wield a powerful cudgel against overly critical newspapers, which often would find their supply of paper cut off. Meaningful reform came with the Salinas administration of 1988–94, but intimida-

Mexico

Frida Kahlo in 1932, sitting beneath her self-portrait

tion of the press continues. Mexico now exceeds Colombia in the number of journalists murdered each year in Latin America. The press remains largely unbowed, however. About 30 dailies are published in the capital. The paper once regarded as the most prestigious was *Excélsior*, a cooperative owned by its employees, but in recent years its ties to the *PRI* have hurt the paper's credibility and its bottom line.

Diego Rivera

The workers voted in June 2002 to sell the paper because of declining revenues—and lost wages. Newspapers with greater circulation and with better reputations of independence and aggressive reporting today are *El Universal* and *Reforma*.

Mexico has a more vigorous provincial press than do most Latin American countries; in fact, it is these smaller papers in the interior that frequently are the targets of violence by drug traffickers or corrupt local politicians or police officials who themselves have been targeted by aggressive reporters. Probably the most prestigious of these provincial papers is *El Norte* of Monterrey, owned by *Reforma*.

Mexico also has a sizable magazine industry, producing slick, high-quality, full-color magazines comparable with those in the United States or Europe. Probably the magazine most read abroad is the left-of-center *Proceso*, launched by Julio Scherer García in 1976 after the thin-skinned President Echeverría forced him from the editorship of *Excélsior* for his critical reporting and editorials.

The new role of the Mexican media in exposing corruption cannot be understated. Many, if not most, of the allegations of wrongdoing stem from journalistic rather than official investigations. A decade ago, this would have been unheard of. The government used the newsprint monopoly as a carrot and stick to keep the print media in line. The owners of the television giant Televisa, meanwhile, were loyal *PRI* partisans. The termination of the newsprint monopoly and the diversification of television with the new network, *TV Azteca*, with the resulting increase in aggressive, investigative journalism, has been as significant a factor in curtailing the power of the once omnipotent *PRI* as has the rising electoral strength of the opposition parties. In fact, some have viewed the two parallel developments as a chicken-and-egg analogy— which led to what?

At the same time, investigative journalism in Mexico remains a notoriously high-risk endeavor. Journalists investigating links between drug traffickers and public officials have been murdered or intimidated at an alarming rate since 1997, and by 2004 the number of journalists killed in Mexico was the fourth highest in the world, exceeding the number in Colombia for the first time. By 2007, it had become the second-deadliest country for journalists in the world after Iraq (see Other Current Problems—Drugs). This is not to say that all Mexican journalists are martyrs and saints, however. For decades, government officials and *PRI* leaders routinely paid bribes to low-paid reporters to ensure favorable news coverage, or—even better—no news coverage. This tawdry

practice has been reduced with the election of opposition governors and an opposition president in 2000.

In addition, it must be conceded that too many Mexican journalists are overly subjective in their reporting and are not above slanting or even distorting the facts to make a story fit into that medium's particular agenda. Still, the fearless reporting of such Mexico City newspapers as *Reforma* and *El Universal*, as well as that of numerous feisty newspapers and magazines along the U.S. border, is a refreshing change from the old days when the press was either cowed or bought, and it has sent many a corrupt official scurrying for cover like cockroaches from a bright light.

Economy: The Mexican economy is divided into three major sectors: agriculture (20%), industry (30%) and services (50%), a pattern generally associated with advanced nations.

The industrial sector, formerly centered around Mexico City and Monterrey, now is more clustered generally throughout the north, based on factories, called *maquiladoras*, that assemble finished products for export; most are owned by U.S. companies, though joint ventures have become more common. Consequently, the standard of living is significantly higher in the north than in the still-impoverished south.

The quasi-socialist nature of the economy during the seven decades of domination of the *PRI*, and especially after the expropriation of foreign-owned oil companies in 1938, hung a "not welcome" sign for foreign investors. For decades, foreign nationals or businesses could own only a 49% share of real estate or a business. After the 1960s, government participation in industry increased under the *PRI*, which viewed this as a means of extending party power, but was accompanied by inefficiency and corruption. In the 1990s, this was reversed under former President Salinas. By 1993, more than 363 state-owned companies had been sold or shut down, bringing the government (and *PRI*) more than $22 billion.

The *maquiladora* movement greatly stimulated national development, at least in the north. Mexico's hourly wage was less than half that of the United States, and the workforce was literate. The lure of assembling finished goods just across the border at bargain-basement prices was irresistible to U.S. corporations. Of course, it was anathema to organized labor in the United States. The *maquiladoras* led to a veritable boom along the border, and stimulated growth of a middle class. (By 2000, *maquiladoras* accounted for about 48% of Mexico's exports, compared with 10% for oil exports).

The erstwhile silver mining boom town of Real de Catorce in San Luis Potosí State, abandoned in 1909, has become a popular tourist destination and movie location in recent years.
Photo by the author

The North American Free Trade Agreement (NAFTA) of 1994 accelerated the boom and unquestionably helped the country emerge from the disastrous peso devaluation that year. By 2003, however, Mexico had lost more than 300 companies to China. The NAFTA-generated boom in the north shrank the unemployment rate, from 5.5% in 1996, to 2.3% in 2000, the lowest (officially) in Latin America.

Petroleum remains the only major government monopoly, but it was a hotbed of *PRI* labor and management corruption. For a time there was talk of privatizing *Pemex*, which controls production from the wellhead to distribution at the gasoline station, but public opinion was so vehemently opposed to it that not even the conservative, pro-business government of Vicente Fox pursued it. *Pemex* still accounts for about 40% of the federal government's revenue.

In the 1980s, *Pemex* departed from production of sulphur-laden, sub-quality gasoline to include unleaded gasoline that meets U.S. standards in order to accommodate a burgeoning tourist trade.

Pemex currently is faced with the need to invest in discovery and deep-sea drilling as its existing fields become depleted. Production in 2004 was 3.59 million barrels per day, but as expected, this dropped to 3.42 million in 2007. In 2009, it was only 2.6 million. Mexico remains the world's sixth-largest exporter of crude oil, although it lacks sufficient refining capacity to meet more than 60% of its fuel needs. Current reserves are estimated at 16–19 billion barrels, a dramatic drop from more

than 28 billion in 1999. *Pemex* lacks deep-sea recovery technology, but contracting with foreign oil firms, even if it means keeping Mexico an exporter rather than an importer, is a political taboo in Mexico. If production continues to decline at the current rate, Mexico will become an oil importer by 2017.

President Felipe Calderón introduced an energy-reform package in April 2008 that would open up *Pemex* to private investors for deep-sea exploration and refining. Despite fierce opposition from the left, Congress approved it a few months later (see History).

Tourism has long been a major economic pillar. Various resorts offer complete package vacations to winter-weary neighbors to the north seeking the warm sun. The popularity of these soared in the late 1980s and 1990s as the peso plummeted in value against the dollar. Tourism suffered briefly from the September 11, 2001, terrorist attacks; it has also suffered from drug-related violence along the border and by a new requirement begun in 2005 that Americans have passports to travel to and from Canada, Mexico, and several Caribbean countries. According to the World Tourism Organization, Mexico was the world's seventh most popular destination in 2007, with 21.4 million visitors from abroad. It increased to 22.6 million in 2008, although dropping to ninth place. With the recession of 2008–09 and an outbreak of swine flu in 2009, it suffered a 5% drop in 2009, to 21.5 million visitors, 10th place in the world. Tourism

brought in $13.3 billion in foreign exchange in 2008, only $11.3 billion in 2009, a precipitous 15% drop.

Agriculture is limited by a lack of arable land and division of what there is into small parcels. The official policy of the government after the Revolution favored redistribution of land, much of it into communal plots called *ejidos*, but the program moved forward at a glacial pace. In 2006, agriculture accounted for only 4% of GDP, and Mexico remains a net food importer.

In 1993, Mexico's economy appeared to be blooming, but it was an illusion caused by increased U.S investment in anticipation of the results of the NAFTA treaty. Mexico printed more pesos, and foreign investors in Mexican bonds demanded more and more interest, as high as 33% per annum to compensate for what they decided was greater risk.

The break came in December 1994, when the peso was devalued by 20% and then allowed to "float" four days later, which led to its decline of 50% by early 1995. The stock and bond markets panicked, contributing to the decline of the peso. The IMF revealed that before the devaluation, individuals and institutions quietly moved $6.7 billion out of Mexico.

President Clinton proposed massive bailout loans to Mexico totaling $13.5 billion, which he got despite widespread opposition in Congress. More than 16,000 businesses ceased operation and more than 2 million Mexicans lost their jobs in 1995. Banks foreclosed on mortgages and repossessed autos at a record rate; more than 12% of bank loans were in default (the rate was about 1.2% in the U.S.).

The loans were guaranteed by the Mexican equivalent of the Federal Deposit Insurance Corporation, known as *Fobaproa*. An organization of creditors, *El Barzón*, correctly charged that the aid being received by Mexico was being used to help depositors, not debtors. *Fobaproa* became the focus of a major political scandal in 1998 when it was learned that many of the failed banks had made risky loans to *PRI* political cronies (see History).

In 1997, amid much media hype, Mexico repaid the last installment of the $13.5 billion loan Clinton had authorized, two years ahead of schedule. What Mexico downplayed was the fact that the loan was repaid by borrowing the necessary amount from European sources.

After 1994–95 crisis, the economy rebounded into one of the healthiest in Latin America, weathering both the drop in oil prices in 1998 and the Brazilian market panic of January 1999.

The drop in oil prices was probably responsible for a decline in GDP growth from 7% in 1997 to 4.8% in 1998 to 3.4% in

Mexico

Except for the automobiles and the 21st century clothing, this cobblestoned plaza in Zacatecas looks much as it did in colonial times.   *Photo by the author*

1999. Growth shot back up to 7.2% for 2000, thanks largely to the continued high price of oil. But the U.S. recession in 2001 and the September 11 terrorist attacks that year proved a double whammy for the Mexican economy. The recession caused trade to plummet, and the terrorist attacks caused a general decrease in tourism, compounded in Mexico's case by the inconveniences caused by tightened security along the border.

Consequently, GDP for 2001 declined by –0.3% and grew by only 0.9% in 2002, not enough to keep up with the growth in the labor market. In 2003, the economy grew by 1.3%, still sluggish. In his state of the nation address to Congress in 2004, a contrite President Fox admitted that the economy had not performed as he had hoped. Growth in 2004 was a more encouraging 4.4% and was about the same in 2005, the result of the spike in world oil prices.

The Fox administration privatized the telecommunications system and in 2005 sold off Mexicana, a state-owned airline.

Growth has steadily tapered off under Calderón: 4.9% in 2006, 3.2% in 2007 and 1.4% in 2008. The drop in oil prices from $140 a barrel in mid-2008 to only $70 in mid-2009, coupled with the global recession, sent the economy into a tailspin. The GDP shrank by –6.5% in 2009. It shrank another –0.35% in the first quarter of 2010. Unemployment grew from 4% in 2008 to 5.6% in 2009.

Inflation, meanwhile, declined gradually from 18.6% in 1998 to 13.7% in 2001 to only 3.2% in 2005 and 3.4% in 2006. However, higher prices for corn pushed consumer prices higher in 2007. With the recession, inflation fell from 6.5% in 2008 to 3.6% in 2009.

One of the mainstays of the Mexican economy for years has been the remittances that Mexican workers abroad, whether legal or illegal, mostly in the United States, send home to their families. Remittances in 2003 totaled $6.3 billion, for the first time surpassing direct foreign investment, which was $5.2 billion, or tourism, which was $4.9 billion. Remittances were second only to oil sales, which were $8 billion. By 2006, remittances were estimated at $23 billion and peaked at $26.07 billion in 2007. They fell 3.6% in 2008, to $25.14 billion, indicative of the beginning of the recession in the United States. Estimates for 2009 are only

$21.27 billion, the lowest since 2005, a 14% drop.

The Future: Vicente Fox assured himself of a place in Mexican—and world—history by breaking the *PRI*'s stranglehold on the presidency and ushering in a multiparty democracy. His successor, Felipe Calderón, the youngest president since Lázaro Cárdenas, has proven more successful than Fox in working with the still-fragmented Congress to pass monumental reforms in taxation and the judiciary. Mexico has one of the most stable economies in Latin America, even with the current global recession.

Yet, Mexico is a country in crisis because of rampant drug-related violence that now takes more civilian lives than does the war in Iraq, almost 10,000 in 2009. These powerful drug cartels constitute a greater threat to government institutions than the *Zapatista* guerrillas could ever have hoped to. To date, the government does not appear to be winning in its offensive against them. The U.S. Joint Forces Command issued a report in November 2008 that adjudged Pakistan and Mexico as two countries on the brink of "a rapid and sudden collapse." Pakistan perhaps; Mexican institutions, although riddled with corruption and under incredible stress, are not likely to "collapse," but the battle will be long and bloody and require determined leadership.

Surprisingly and alarmingly, for the first time since the first *Latinobarómetro* poll in 1996, when 53% of Mexicans agreed that democracy is preferable to any other form of government, Mexico ranked at the *bottom* of the 18-nation survey in 2009; only 42% said they thought democracy was the best form of government.

With the political shakeup from the July 5, 2009 midterm election, the *PRI* has had much greater influence over Calderón's legislative agenda than it had in the first half of his term. This also makes *PRI* President Beatríz Paredes the power behind the throne, even though she herself is not a member of Congress. By bringing her party back from the brink of political oblivion, she is a likely *PRI* candidate for president in 2012, and unless she does something to alienate voters like López Obrador did, she could well become Mexico's first woman president. A member of the *PRI*'s reformist faction, however, she faces a likely primary challenge from Mexico State Governor Enrique Peña Nieto, of the dinosaur faction. Both campaigned for *PRI* candidates in the 12 governors' races on July 4, collecting political IOUs.

If she prevails, will she be up to the daunting challenges that Calderón will inevitably bequeath to his successor in just two more years?

Nicaragua

A Saturday afternoon native dance in the countryside

Area: 49,163 square miles.

Population: 6.0 million (2010 estimate).

Capital City: Managua (population 1.7 million).

Climate: Tropical, with distinct wet and dry seasons. Rainfall is heavier on the Atlantic coast, with the heaviest downpours from May to December.

Neighboring Countries: Honduras (North); Costa Rica (South).

Official Language: Spanish.

Other Principal Tongues: English, Indian dialects.

Ethnic Background: *Mestizo* (A mixture of Spanish and Indian, 69%), Caucasian (17%), Negro (9%), Amerindian (5%).

Principal Religion: Roman Catholic Christianity.

Chief Commercial Products: Cotton, coffee, bananas, sugar.

Currency: Córdoba

Gross Domestic Product: US $6.372 billion in 2009 ($1,062 per capita).

Former Colonial Status: Spanish Colony (1519–1821).

Independence Date: September 15, 1821.

Chief of State: Daniel Ortega Saavedra (b. November 11, 1945), president (since January 10, 2007).

National Flag: Blue, white and blue horizontal stripes with a coat of arms on the white stripe.

Nicaragua is the largest and most sparsely settled of the Central American republics. It has three distinct geographic regions: a triangular mountain extension of the Honduran highlands, with its apex reaching to the San Juan River valley on the Costa Rican frontier; a narrow Pacific coastal plain containing two large lakes (Managua, 32 miles long and Nicaragua, 92 miles long); there is a wider Atlantic coastal plain.

The Pacific plain is part of a trough that runs from the Gulf of Fonseca in the northwest through the two scenic lakes and the San Juan River valley to the Atlantic. This is one of the most promising sites for a new interoceanic canal. There is considerable volcanic activity in the northwestern part of this region. Three volcanoes reaching to some 5,000 feet

have emerged from Lake Nicaragua, another stands majestically on the north shore of Lake Managua and some 20 more lie formidably between the lakes and the Gulf of Fonseca. The moist easterly winds from the Caribbean Sea drench the San Juan River valley and the Atlantic coastal plains, which are heavily forested.

The Pacific coastal plains receive less rainfall and in some parts require flood control and irrigation for agriculture. The majority of Nicaragua's population is found between the western slope of the highlands and the Pacific Ocean. The few settlements on the Atlantic coast were founded by the British and the population in this region is predominantly of African-West Indian origin, with a few pockets of native Miskito Indians.

History: The Spanish conquerors reached Nicaragua from Panama in 1519. They found a fairly dense population of agricultural Maya Indians on the shores of Lake Nicaragua, from whom gold ornaments were acquired. The Spaniards returned in 1524 and founded settlements at

271

Nicaragua

Granada and León. By 1570 the flow of gold had ceased, most of the settlers left and the two towns were put under the administration of the captaincy-general of Guatemala.

León, more accessible to the sea, was chosen as the administrative center rather than the larger and more wealthy Granada. The eastern coast was entirely neglected by the Spanish—the towns of Bluefields and Greytown (San Juan del Norte) were established by British loggers cutting mahogany and other valuable timber. By the time of independence, the Lake Nicaragua basin was the site of productive sugar and indigo plantations and the town of Granada was the center of political Conservatism. León, the center of less valuable grain and food production and capital of the province, was the seat of anti-clerical political Liberalism.

Independence came to Nicaragua as a by-product of the movements in Mexico and in the South American states. Through the actions of Guatemala, Nicaragua joined Mexico under Iturbide and became a member of the Central American Confederation, but withdrew from it in 1838. The Liberal-Conservative conflict that marked the period was manifested in Nicaragua by an as-yet unsettled feud between Granada and León.

British interests established a protectorate over the Atlantic region, known as the Autonomous Kingdom of Miskitia, which was not incorporated into the national territory until 1860. During the 1850s and 1860s, Commodore Cornelius Vanderbilt's transit company became involved in ferrying California-bound gold prospectors across Nicaragua, and the Liberals of León invited William Walker, a U.S. soldier of fortune, to head up their army to crush the Granada Conservatives. At the same time, there were conflicts of British and North American interests who backed the various factions.

Walker's successes in León were such that Vanderbilt was induced to aid the Conservatives of Granada. Walker finally was captured and executed in 1860 and the Conservatives established their dominance, which endured for 30 years. They quelled numerous uprisings, installed their presidents and gave the country a semblance of stable government. The cultivation of coffee and bananas was started, gold production was resumed and a few immigrants arrived from Europe.

Factional quarrels among the Conservatives made possible a Liberal coup in 1893 and the seizure of power by youthful José Santos Zelaya. Sixteen years of tyrannical misrule by Santos Zelaya became notorious both at home and abroad. He persecuted his Conservative enemies, betrayed his Liberal supporters and systematically looted both public and private funds. He maintained his position with a ruthless system of spies and police, suppressing all critics. Despite his misrule, the economy prospered, railroads were built and public schools were increased.

His execution of two U.S. adventurers aroused the U.S. government and the dictator fled into exile in 1909. This left the country in a state of near anarchy—the government was bankrupt and foreign creditors threatened intervention. The Conservatives appealed to Washington to intervene while New York financiers bought up foreign bonds and installed economic supervisors to manage the Nicaraguan economy and ensure repayment of their investments.

Liberals revolted in 1912 against a situation in which their country was the ward of foreign banks in. U.S. Marines landed, suppressed the revolt and became involved in a 20-year war for the elimination of banditry and the establishment of a stable government. While Washington supported the Conservatives, Mexico supported Liberals in a see-saw contest. Larger forces of Marines were introduced in 1927 to control the country; the United States tried to resolve the internal Liberal-Conservative conflict through supposedly free and democratic elections. A guerrilla leader fighting against the Marines became a legendary figure in Nicaragua and most of Central America: Augusto César Sandino, a colorful character sporting a 10-gallon hat and six-shooter.

The Somoza Dynasty

U.S. forces left Nicaragua in 1933, with the government in the hands of a Liberal president, Juan Sacasa, and a peace guaranteed by a Marine-trained police force, the *Guardia Nacional*, under the command of Anastasio "Tacho" Somoza. By 1934 it was obvious that true power lay with the *Guardia* and its commander. Sandino still maintained his guerrilla forces, but had agreed to a cease-fire once the Marines had gone. The government accepted a sweeping amnesty for Sandino's men, additionally offering them land and jobs.

Then the Nicaraguan Congress voted to raise the salary of Sandino's 100-man personal guard while reducing the pay of the military. But not all of Sandino's followers had turned in their arms. The *Guardia*

272

Augusto César Sandino

decided that Sandino had to be eliminated. A supposedly innocent President Sacasa invited Sandino to the presidential palace to discuss outstanding issues, where there were several meetings. But after a farewell supper, the *Guardia* met Sandino at the gate and took him and his men to the airfield, where they were executed and secretly buried.

Anastasio Somoza ruled until his assassination in 1955 and Congress named his son, Luis, to the presidency, which he occupied until 1963. The elections that year were relatively quiet and honest.

In 1967, Luis Somoza's younger brother, Anastasio "Tachito" Somoza Debayle, a West Point graduate, became the third member of the family to occupy the presidency. Barred by law from succeeding himself, Somoza created a caretaker three-man *junta* in 1971 to rule until 1974, when he was "elected" to a second term with 91.7% of the vote. Somoza was a "Liberal" in name only. Nine small opposition parties were barred from the election.

Somoza's second term would be his last. Resentment against the regime grew as increasing numbers of Nicaraguans objected to his heavy-handed tactics and greed. His brutal treatment of political opponents convinced many that the regime would never tolerate democratic elections in the country. The business community was bitter and angry with Somoza's levying of kickbacks on the major commercial transactions conducted in the country. Residents of Managua were outraged by the *junta*'s blatant misuse of international aid earmarked for the city's reconstruction following a disastrous 1972 earthquake. Most Liberals and leftists were offended by the strongman's ostentatious display of wealth: his family owned a half billion dollars worth of investments and 8,260 square miles of Nicaragua, while 200,000 peasants were landless.

Revolution

For the first time, opponents of the regime united, joined by one thing: anti-Somoza feelings (but little else). A broad-based coalition—ranging from Marxist guerrillas to conservative business leaders—was formed. While the business sector continued its strikes to dry up the economy, the guerrillas battled the *Guardia.*

Many moderate opposition groups, wittingly or unwittingly, joined together with the Sandinista National Liberation Front (*FSLN*), named after the legendary nationalist guerrilla leader of the 1930s. The *FSLN,* founded in the 1960s under the auspices of Fidel Castro, grew rapidly when Anastasio Somoza became president. His brutal and corrupt rule pumped new life into the guerrilla movement. As the *Sandinistas* gained strength from association by non-communist elements, Somoza retaliated with sweeping attacks against rural peasants suspected of aiding the guerrillas, which backfired against the regime. Mass support for the *FSLN* developed further following the 1972 earthquake that leveled Managua when it became known that Somoza was pocketing some of the international relief funds and buying up Managua real estate at firesale prices.

While the *Guardia* enjoyed a 4–1 manpower edge, the *Sandinistas* and associates nonetheless boasted a force of 3,000 members by 1978. It was actually divided into three groups: two openly Marxist and a third—by far the largest—consisting of socialists and non-Marxist leftist trade unionists, Catholic Church members and a sprinkling of businessmen. Known as the *Terceristas* (Third Force), this last group is best remembered for its daring 1978 occupation of the National Palace in Managua.

Collapse of the Regime

The crucial jolt in the long train of events leading to the overthrow of the Somoza regime came in January 1978, when assassins gunned down Pedro Joaquín Chamorro, longtime Conservative Party critic and publisher of the nation's leading newspaper, *La Prensa.* Although the identity of the killers remains unknown, most Nicaraguans attributed the murder to Somoza. Chamorro was widely respected—10,000 attended his funeral—and his death quickly touched off three days of bloody demonstrations throughout the nation. The *Guardia* responded in a heavy-handed manner; its ruthless mop-up operations in five major cities left 3,000 dead.

The Chamorro murder, combined with the *Guardia*'s indiscriminate killings, cost the regime the vital support of business leaders who then called for a general strike to demand Somoza's resignation. The strike brought more reprisals. As the death toll mounted, the United States proposed a referendum to test national support for the Somoza regime. Somoza quickly rejected the idea, saying, "If they want me to leave Nicaragua, they'll only get me out by force."

The *Sandinistas* were only too willing to oblige him. During its final two years, the Somoza regime was under attack throughout the country. The only significant Nicaraguan sector that continued to support the dictatorship was, as always, the *Guardia.* Meanwhile, the guerrillas continued to score important victories in rural areas, while major power groups in the cities were becoming more militant in their opposition to Somoza. One by one, rural areas fell under rebel control and by the spring of 1979 it was clear that Somoza could not endure.

Still, he refused to budge. Secluded in his Managua bunker—a grim reminder of the last days of World War II in Berlin—Somoza continued to direct the military activities of his *Guardia.* Curiously, Somoza made the same tactical error committed by Hitler during the battle for Stalingrad: He ordered heavy bombing of civilian areas in order to deny the enemy food and shelter. In both cases, the bombed-out buildings provided ideal concealment from which the defenders could fight back. In Nicaragua, the *Guardia*'s bombing of populated

Anastasio Somoza Debayle

Nicaragua

Sandinistas celebrate Somoza's overthrow, 1979

areas killed virtually no guerrillas—it merely solidified public opinion against Somoza.

Along with the heavy shelling of civilian areas, Somoza also ordered the summary execution of suspected opponents of his regime. Many of these were youths, whose blindfolded and bound bodies were often found strewn along the shores of Lake Managua. During the final two years of fighting, thousands were killed and left homeless.

By late May 1979, ranking members of the regime began to flee the country. Somoza himself finally abandoned his bunker and flew to the United States, where he boarded a luxury yacht for a leisurely trip to Paraguay, to be given refuge by the Stroessner regime of that country. He left hapless caretakers in charge. Thus ended one of the most durable dictatorships—46 years—in Latin American history.

He lasted only 14 months in Paraguay, however, before he was gunned down by three persons reported to be Argentine guerrillas. He had become depressed, drank to excess and grew fat. Before his death, he was involved in a much-publicized love affair with a former Miss Paraguay—who also happened to be the mistress of Stroessner's son-in-law.

The Sandinista Era

On July 19, 1979, the *Sandinistas* took control of Managua—and a *new* revolution was about to start. Their noncommunist allies in the revolution found themselves with little power within the new government.

After Somoza's ouster, the country was administered by a three-member *junta* called the Revolutionary Junta Government (*JRG*). One of the three was Violeta Barrios de Chamorro, widow of the assassinated journalist. This group, in turn, followed policy directives established by a nine-member *Sandinista* National Directorate, controlled by the *FSLN*. Power was shared with a Council of State, a *Sandinista*-dominated legislative body of 47 members representing various political and economic groups as well as the armed forces and the *FSLN*.

Although the Marxist influence was clearly in evidence—especially in the schools, the armed forces and the media— the government was initially primarily nationalistic. But in international relations, Nicaragua quickly joined the nonaligned bloc of Third World nations and establishwd close ties with communist-bloc nations. The regime refused to condemn the Soviet invasion of Afghanistan and in 1982 supported Argentina's invasion of the British Falkland Islands. Trade pacts were signed with various communist nations, including Bulgaria, East Germany, the Soviet Union and Cuba.

Relations became particularly close with the Castro's Cuba. Almost all communist *Sandinista* leaders visited Havana and in mid-1980 Fidel Castro was guest of honor in Managua for the revolution's first anniversary celebration. As many as 6,000 Cuban "advisers" were stationed in Nicaragua; hundreds of Nicaraguan youths were sent to Cuba for educational programs that stressed Marxism.

Although the Carter administration applauded the fall of Somoza and pledged to work with the new regime, the *Sandinistas'* increased ties with communist nations soon led to strained relations with the United States. Some powerful members of the U.S. Congress regarded the *Sandinista* regime as a threat to Central America. Although the Carter administration provided some financial aid to Nicaragua in the hope of strengthening the pro-democratic forces, the new Reagan administration responded with a tough stance against what it concluded was a Soviet-sponsored client state within Central America.

Thus, Washington suspended all aid to Nicaragua in the spring of 1981 after the State Department accused the *Sandinistas* of aiding leftist guerrillas in El Salvador. In late 1981, the Reagan administration again denounced Nicaragua for "arms trafficking to El Salvador," and for building the largest military force "in the history of Central America." In early 1982, Reagan lectured Nicaragua's new ambassador to the United States against "adopting alien influence and philosophies in the hemisphere."

The Pentagon unveiled CIA aerial photos in 1982 to prove that Cuba and the Soviet Union were providing sophisticated military equipment to Nicaragua. Newly enlarged Nicaraguan airfields could be used for bombing raids against the Panama Canal, according to some U.S. officials. Several days later, a badly informed U.S. State Department staged a highly publicized press conference to display a Nicaraguan guerrilla who had been captured in El Salvador. But when the cameras started rolling, the Nicaraguan coolly accused his captors of torture. Highly embarrassed State Department officials promptly deported the man to Nicaragua (where he received a hero's welcome). Nicaraguan strongman Daniel Ortega Saavedra called an urgent meeting of the U.N. Security Council to protest "aggressive and destabilizing acts" by the United States against his country. In 1982, Washington accused Nicaragua of firing on a U.S. helicopter over international waters near the Nicaraguan coast (the United States then recognized a 12-mile territorial limit; Nicaragua claimed 200 miles).

The "Stolen" Revolution

What had been envisioned by in some U.S. circles as a pluralistic revolution in Nicaragua was an illusion. Many elements joined together in the anti-Somoza struggle, but only one had cohesiveness: the *FSLN*. At first, other groups were allowed to participate, but in 1982–83 the true nature of the *FSLN* became apparent. Although U.S. conservatives charged that the *Sandinistas* "stole" the revolution, in fact the *Sandinistas* simply filled a political vacuum and then refused to share it.

In 1984, Ortega was elected president by a predictably wide margin. The opposition was divided and denied access to the media.

During more than 10 years in power, the *Sandinista* regime generated widespread disillusionment and disappointment. Anti-*Sandinista* rallies and meetings were broken up and were later totally prohibited. A prominent leftist within the regime resigned, accusing the *Sandinistas* of planting "a reign of terror . . . a Soviet style Stalinist regime in Nicaragua."

The press that was not directly seized by the government was regularly harassed; *La Prensa* soon became the only non-government newspaper that quickly came to face daily government inspection and approval. Mrs. Chamorro, the publisher, resigned from the *junta* as a result. International credit evaporated as the United States withdrew loan promises and private foreign banks balked at extensions of credit. Somoza had emptied he treasury, compounding the problems of the fledgling government.

Human rights violations sharply increased. Ultimately, an estimated 10,000 people, including former Somoza supporters and former members of the *Guardia*, were jailed and other opponents were sent into exile. A dispute between the government and the Miskito Indians (who had been given a large measure of independence under Somoza) was provoked when the Miskitos were accused of aiding counter-revolutionary Somoza exiles living in Honduras. When the government attempted to resettle about 10,000 tribe members away from border areas, an estimated 20,000 fled to Honduras, from

where they started to harass the *Sandinistas*. The government responded by raiding Miskito settlements along the border, leaving an estimated 105 dead. This would lead in the future to an alliance between the Indians and the "*Contras.*"

Relations were strained with the Catholic Church durung a visit by Pope John Paul II in 1982. The pope was heckled by Sandinista hardliners while delivering Mass, and he publicly scolded priests who were serving in the *Sandinista* government in violation of his order against priests serving in secular political posts.

In 1985, Reagan requested military aid for the *Contras* ("antis"), a loosely organized but relatively effective opposition to the regime. It had been armed by the CIA. The Democratic-controlled House refused, but did allow $14 million for "humanitarian" aid. Ortega, meanwhile, received pledges of $200 million from Moscow. Reagan imposed a total economic embargo on Nicaragua, and his advisers worked out a secret deal that almost proved the undoing of the Reagan presidency. Arms were illegally sold to Iran, then at war with Iraq, in exchange for Iran's influence in freeing American citizens held hostage by the Iranian-backed Hezbollah guerrillas in Lebanon. The profits from the arms sales were secretly channeled to the *Contras* in defiance of the congressional ban. When the "Iran-Contra affair" became public, Congress held investigatory hearings. Reagan denied knowledge of the deal, but contritely assumed responsibility.

The state-controlled economy ultimately shrank to about one-third of the level it had been before *Sandinista* control. Crops were not harvested because of military pressures and the unwillingness of farmers to accept artificially low prices. Foreign aid dried up by 1987, when the final stages of a precipitous decline was underway in the former Soviet Union and its

client, Cuba. Shortages were rampant and housing was shabby and crumbling.

A last-ditch effort was made to overcome the *Contras* located in neighboring Honduras in 1988; the *Sandinista* effort was repulsed when two battalions of U.S. troops were sent to that country.

The Arias Plan

Costa Rican President Oscar Arias offered to broker a Central America-wide peace agreement, for which he would receive the Nobel Peace Prize. Signed by the leaders of Costa Rica, El Salvador, Guatemala, Honduras and Nicaragua meeting in Guatemala City on August 7, 1987, the Arias Plan obligated the *Sandinistas* to negotiate a cease-fire with the *Contras*, allow freedom of the press and other media, cease political repression and allow free, open and democratic elections. Support of rebel forces in adjoining nations would be banned. It further provided for monitoring of all requirements by national conciliation commissions that would include opposition figures, Catholic Church officials and Inter-American Human Rights Commission representatives.

Ortega signed the agreement. Negotiations with the *Contras* and internal opposition groups began in October 1987. They broke down immediately when the *Sandinistas* abruptly announced that "there will never, at any time or any place, be any direct *political* dialogue with the *Contras*." The impasse continued until Cardinal Obando y Bravo volunteered to mediate talks between the parties. His efforts were short-lived: the *Sandinistas* were firm in their ultimatum that they would only accept a military surrender from the *Contras*, not discuss politics. The cardinal walked out in disgust in January 1988, accusing the *Sandinistas* of negotiating in bad faith.

La Prensa and *Radio Católico* were allowed to resume their activities in Octo-

Daniel Ortega exhorts a group of students about the spirit of the *Sandinista* revolution

Nicaragua

Signing of the Summit Agreement

ber 1987, but were again shut down for 15 days in the spring of 1988.

The *Sandinistas* declared a unilateral cease-fire in 1988, *not* because of the Arias peace plan, but because of dire economic conditions within Nicaragua. The cease-fire was extended into 1990.

In 1989, the new Bush administration didn't even bother to ask for military assistance for the *Contras*, settling for more humanitarian aid. Faced with economic and political bankruptcy, the *Sandinistas* engaged in a transparent effort to rig elections set for February 25, 1990.

Chamorro Upsets Ortega

It was clear that the *Sandinistas* were uneasy about the outcome. A cease-fire with the *Contras* was canceled, but the half-hearted military effort that followed was ineffective. Ortega took to the campaign trail. He discarded his khakis and appeared in a variety of costumes and said anything to please everybody, swinging his hips to rock music. Television and newspapers were full of propaganda extolling the party. The *FSLN* outspent the opposition, the National Opposition Union (*UNO*), by at least 10–1.

The *UNO* candidate was Violeta Chamorro, widow of the publisher slain in 1978 under the Somoza regime. *Sandinista* efforts were stepped up, including crude efforts such as bludgeoning those attending opposition rallies.

A Washington Post-ABC poll published predicted a *Sandinista* triumph by a margin of 48% to 32%, although the pollsters issued strong disclaimers as to its accuracy. Chamorro and the *UNO* won by 55.2% to 40.8%! Even the White House was startled. Also surprisingly, Ortega meekly conceded defeat and congratulated Chamorro. She was sworn in on April 25, making

history as the first elected woman president in Latin America.

After Chamorro's inaugural, Nicaragua's slim hope for improved conditions evaporated. Much to the dismay of the *UNO*, she appointed Humberto Ortega, Daniel's brother, to continue as defense minister. However, she reduced the army from about 80,000 to zero on the grounds that it was no longer needed. There remained shadowy, informal armed forces, used to protect property seized by the *Sandinistas* by "law" between the time of Chamorro's election and the time she assumed office. The *UNO* coalition in the National Assembly soon turned on Chamorro, claiming she had betrayed her mandate.

The disbanding of the army and of the *Contras* added tremendously (almost 100,000) to unemployment, which rose to more than 50%. Few exiles returned; the wealthy ones in particular, who took much of their money with them, remained outside the country. Conditions on farms, prosperous in the 1970s, were dreadful. Many that were split up and given to peasants and *Sandinista* fighters were idle.

Lower-level *Sandinistas* deserted the *FSLN*, as did former low-income supporters of the movement. The more affluent *Sandinistas* clung tenaciously to the property they had acquired during their years in power.

With the *Sandinistas* in charge of the army, the police and the judiciary, Nicaragua was far from democratic. The president ignored the Assembly and formed an "inner cabinet" to rule the nation. She particularly relied on her son-in-law, Antonio Lacayo, in making crucial decisions that favored the top-drawer *Sandinistas*. The *Sandinista*-controlled Supreme Court nullified all actions of the National Assembly after September 2, 1992, on the dubious

grounds that on that date it lacked a quorum! Its ruling was ignored.

The U.S. Congress appropriated $104 million in aid for Nicaragua, to be released in 1992, contingent upon the firing of army commander Ortega, discharge of the police chief, judicial reform, and compensation for seized U.S. property. Chamorro did fire the police chief and said she would "discuss" compensation of U.S. owners. President Bush reluctantly released $50 million after his 1992 re-election defeat.

Following President Bill Clinton's inauguration, Nicaraguan officials intensely lobbied the U.S. Congress for release of the remainder. The Clinton administration sent the funds, citing "important strides that have been made by the Nicaraguan government." An offended senator charged that the money was sent to a "government of thugs."

The Chamorro government promised that Humberto Ortega would leave as army commander—in late 1995, by retirement. Continued U.S. pressure resulted in Ortega's removal in 1994; he was put under house arrest because of alleged involvement in a 1990 crime.

Six years after being elected by hopeful Nicaraguans who had "voted with their stomachs," Chamorro had done little to raise Nicaragua out of its abject poverty.

The Alemán Presidency

Sensing an opportunity for a comeback, Ortega announced his candidacy for the October 1996 presidential election. He entered the race an underdog behind the popular and conservative former mayor of Managua, Arnoldo Alemán, the candidate of the Liberal Alliance. Gone were Ortega's *Sandinista* uniform and his Marxist rhetoric, which he realized had helped defeat him in 1990. Six weeks before the election, the *Sandinistas* even softened the lyrics of their truculent anthem, removing the reference to "the Yankees, enemies of mankind."

Opinion polls indicated that the rehabilitated Ortega, preaching a more social democratic gospel, was running even with Alemán. With 23 candidates, there appeared little likelihood that anyone could garner the necessary 45% to avoid a runoff. But once again, the Nicaraguan voters startled prognosticators by giving Alemán a decisive first-round victory of 48.4% to Ortega's 38.6%—even less than Ortega had obtained in 1990.

Ortega immediately—and unconvincingly—cried fraud. A delegation of OAS observers—including longtime *Sandinista* apologist Jimmy Carter and former Secretary of State James Baker—concluded there was no evidence of major irregularities. Carter persuaded his friend Ortega to accept the results rather than resorting to mass protests as he had threatened to do.

Where Chamorro had pragmatically and almost with flattery sought to placate the *Sandinistas* whom she knew could easily overthrow her, Alemán was confrontational. But then, he had a personal score to settle. A onetime Somoza supporter, Alemán had five farms confiscated by the *Sandinistas* in the 1980s. In 1989, while he was under house arrest, the *Sandinistas* refused even to allow him to accompany his wife, who was dying of cancer, to a hospital.

A lawyer, Alemán was elected mayor of Managua in the same 1990 election that brought Chamorro to power. He compiled an impressive record of achievement in the capital, which still felt the effects of the 1972 earthquake. He improved the traffic engineering system, beautified the city and removed the *Sandinistas*' revolutionary art from walls and billboards.

Alemán was inaugurated on January 10, 1997 for a term that had been reduced to five years, marking the first time in Nicaraguan history that one duly elected civilian president had succeeded another. Alemán delivered a conciliatory inaugural address, offering dialogue with the archrival *Sandinistas*. At first, the *Sandinistas* resisted his overtures and continued their bombastic threats to take to the streets. Yet, perhaps faced with the reality that they could no longer marshal that kind of public support, the Ortega brothers met privately with Alemán.

Alemán promised to reverse the *Sandinistas*' opposition to free-market capitalism and to make Nicaragua more attractive to foreign investors in order to bring in desperately needed capital. He also proposed expanding the free-trade zone Chamorro established in 1992, which attracted Mexican-style *maquiladora* assembly plants, mostly for apparel. His most controversial and divisive proposal was the plan to return land expropriated by the *Sandinistas* to its former owners, compensating the new owners with government bonds.

After months of bickering between the Liberals and the *FSLN*, the two parties came to realize the delay in resolving the title issue was hurting Nicaragua economically by discouraging foreign investment. Moreover, the United States was leaning on Alemán to resolve the issue because of the thousands of Nicaraguans displaced by the Revolution who were residing in the United States. The National Assembly approved, 70–4, a compromise measure that essentially verified the current ownership of most of the 1 million hectares the *Sandinistas* had seized. The new law granted title to those who received rural plots of less than 35 hectares or urban plots

of less than 100 square meters. About 5,000 pre-revolutionary landowners thus were frustrated in their hopes of getting their property back.

In 1998, the *Sandinistas* continued to suffer reversals of fortune. The official *FSLN* newspaper *Barricada*, which had been the pro-Somoza daily *Noticias* before it was expropriated in 1979, succumbed to the loss of government subsidies and ceased publication. Its editors accused the Alemán government of retribution through the withholding of government advertising, a time-honored practice of Latin American strongmen, but their protests carried a hollow ring given the *Sandinistas*' own intimidation and censorship of the independent media when they were in power. *Barricada* subsequently reopened in 2000 as a weekly. Later its name was changed to the less combative *Visión Sandinista*.

Another blow, which threatened the very unity of the *FSLN*, came as a bombshell. Ortega's 30-year-old stepdaughter, Zoilamérica Narváez, accused him in an interview in a daily newsletter of having sexually abused her for years, beginning when she was 11 and continuing into the years that he was president. Narvaez's estranged husband, Alejandro Bendaña, like her a committed *Sandinista* and Ortega's former deputy foreign minister, denounced his former boss' "abuse of power."

Ortega adamantly denied the accusation, as did his common-law wife, Rosario Murillo, Narváez's mother. Ortega supporters denounced the charges as "politically motivated" and even accused Narváez of participating in a CIA plot to undermine Ortega. The leader of the Liberals in the Assembly accused Ortega of hiding behind his legislative immunity and called on him to resign. With the storm of controversy swirling around him, Ortega called for party unity. It worked; he was re-elected as *Sandinista* leader. Almost simultaneously, Narváez filed a civil suit against him and also accused high-level *Sandinistas* of aiding and abetting in the sex abuse. Ortega claimed parliamentary immunity, and for weeks the Nicaraguan media reported almost daily "no-I-didn't-yes-you-did" exchanges between Ortega and Narváez.

Ortega attempted to divert attention from the sex scandal. In a mass demonstration, he called Alemán a "dictator" because of his move to re-establish a state security agency similar to that of the Somoza period. Ortega hinted darkly that if the president threatened human rights—as though he himself hadn't—the *Sandinistas* would be called upon "to take up arms." Alemán responded by calling on Ortega to "bury forever the hatchet of war and the rifle of death and let Nicaragua emerge from the poverty in which he left it."

In 1998, Alemán faced a greater adversary even than Ortega: Hurricane Mitch. The storm killed 2,863 Nicaraguans, 948 were missing and more than 867,000 were affected. Seventy-one bridges were destroyed, 70% of the roads were damaged and 30% of the banana crop was wiped out; Mitch also wiped out any hopes of immediate economic recovery. International relief aid poured in to alleviate the appalling human suffering.

Although there was no evidence that this president profited from the disaster as Somoza had in 1972, Alemán was accused of enriching himself while on the public payroll. In 1999, Comptroller General Agustín Jarquín, a member of the Social Christian Party and a longtime political rival of Alemán's, issued a report alleging the president had increased his personal wealth by 900% between 1990, when he was elected mayor of Managua, and 1997, his first full year as president. Alemán maintained the increase had come from property in Nicaragua and Miami that he had inherited from his parents and from his wife's family. He countered that Jarquín was merely out to get him.

Alemán counterattacked when the national police chief, before a crowd of journalists, arrested Jarquín and a well-known television journalist on supposed fraud charges. An appeals court subsequently dismissed the charges.

The Power-Sharing Accord

A major political development occurred in June 1999 whose long-term implications are still being felt. The long-antagonistic Liberals and *Sandinistas* suddenly concluded an agreement by which they

Former President Arnoldo Alemán

Nicaragua

Street scene in Bluefields on the Caribbean Sea

would cooperate in governing the country and would apportion seats on the Supreme Court and the electoral council between them. The agreement also would have the effect of reducing the number of frivolous individual presidential candidacies. On the surface, it seemed a welcome respite from the partisan bickering that had plagued the country. However, the minor parties charged—with some degree of justification—that the new pact was designed merely to divide the country's political spoils between the two major parties and exclude all others from a place at the public trough. Similar bipartisan pacts had existed in Colombia and Venezuela.

As Alemán neared the end of his term, he could point to a dramatically improving economy as foreign investment poured into the country and shopping malls began to spring up, a sign of a growing consumer economy. But the charges of corruption took a toll on his popularity and even his control over his party. A poll showed that 88% of Nicaraguans believed Alemán was corrupt.

Moreover, members of Alemán's party, now called the Constitutionalist Liberal Party (*PLC*), criticized his autocratic method of hand-picking party candidates for the 2000 municipal elections. They also alleged that his call for a constitutional convention was aimed at allowing him to run for re-election. Defense Minister Antonio Alvarado resigned over these issues. In the end, there was no constitutional convention, so Alemán was barred from seeking re-election.

The effect of the unholy political pact between the *PLC* and the *FSLN*, two parties with decidedly undemocratic ancestries, was seen clearly in the 2000 municipal elections. The two major parties, through questionable challenging of the

signatures of voters on party registration petitions, disqualified all parties but themselves from participating. In the voting, the *FSLN* won 11 of the 17 departments, and captured the mayoralty of Managua under the candidacy of Herty Lewites, one of the party's moderates.

The Elections of 2001

The *PLC* and the *FSLN* continued their heavy-handed treatment of other parties in the 2001 presidential race. Through their control of the Electoral Council, they denied registration to Jarquín's Social

Christian Party, the National Unity Movement of former army commander Joaquín Cuadra and the fledgling party organized by former Defense Minister Alvarado, among others. Only the venerable Conservative Party was allowed to compete with the two major parties.

Denied registration for his own party, Jarquín challenged Ortega for the *FSLN* nomination. But the *Sandinistas* stuck with Ortega. The *PLC*, meanwhile, nominated former Vice President Enrique Bolaños, 73, who had resigned to make the run. The Conservatives' standard-bearer was Noel Vidaurre.

When Ortega began his fourth campaign for the presidency, polls again showed he had a better than even chance to stage a comeback. Bolaños, who himself enjoyed a reputation for personal honesty, was tarnished by his association with the unpopular Alemán.

Ortega broadened his political base by enticing prominent former *Sandinista* opponents to join his new coalition, called the Convergence. Chief among them was Jarquín, whom Ortega persuaded to become his running mate. Ortega also sought to sanitize his former guerrilla image even more than he had in 1996, abandoning the familiar black and red *Sandinista* colors in favor of the less threatening pink, and as a campaign slogan he adopted, "The Path to Love." He embraced the Liberals' free-market policies, and he even pledged to continue the Liberals' close ties with the United States. His victory appeared all but certain.

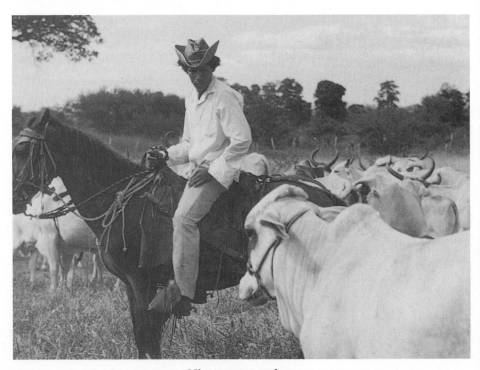

Nicaraguan cowboy

But as the November 4 election drew ever nearer, Ortega's lead in the polls shrank. Meanwhile, Vidaurre, reportedly under U.S. pressure not to divide the anti-*Sandinista* vote, withdrew. After the September 11 terrorist attacks on the United States, Ortega vowed to cooperate in the war against terrorism. Bolaños aired embarrassing television ads that showed then-President Ortega embracing Libyan leader Muammar Qadhafi and Iraqi dictator Saddam Hussein, both suspected of supporting Islamic terrorism. Ortega was stung further when two of his erstwhile protégés, Sergio Ramirez, who had been his vice president, and Father Ernesto Cardenal, his foreign minister, announced they would boycott the election, saying neither Ortega nor Bolaños was "worthy."

The U.S. ambassador, in a startling breach of protocol, appeared openly at Bolaños rallies and said in interviews that an Ortega victory could jeopardize the future of U.S. aid. Even Florida Gov. Jeb Bush, brother of the U.S. president, got into the act by urging the thousands of resident Nicaraguans in Florida to vote for Bolaños.

Nicaraguan voters once again confounded the pollsters and handed Ortega his third successive humiliating defeat, 56% to 43.5%, prompting jubilant Liberals to take to the streets chanting, "Three strikes, you're out!" Ortega once again graciously conceded defeat, and an equally magnanimous Bolaños praised the *Sandinistas* as "worthy opponents."

The Liberals retained their majority in the 90-seat Assembly with 49 seats to 40 for the *Sandinistas* and one for the Conservatives. In addition, under the Liberal-*Sandinista* pact, the retiring president (Alemán) and the losing presidential candidate (Ortega) both received seats in the Assembly—thus assuring Ortega continued immunity from his stepdaughter's molestation charges and Alemán from charges of illegal enrichment. Ortega later renounced his immunity—once the statute of limitations for prosecuting rape had expired.

The Bolaños Presidency

Bolaños was inaugurated on January 10, 2002. Almost immediately, he launched an anti-corruption campaign that soon had him at odds with his predecessor. Alemán was charged with involvement in a $1.5 million embezzlement scheme at the state-owned television station. Bolaños sought to have Alemán, who had been elected president of the National Assembly, stripped of his legislative immunity. Alemán lashed out at Bolaños as "inept" and called the investigation a "witch hunt" that was "politically motivated."

In 2002, prosecutors unveiled additional evidence against Alemán and his associates of mind-boggling proportions. They allegedly had channeled nearly $100 million in public funds to a phantom foundation in Panama. At a time when Nicaragua was desperately trying to emerge from its economic straits, the revelations that its president and his cronies may have enriched themselves on such a scale stirred outrage. It also deepened the schism between the Bolaños faction of the *PLC* and the so-called *Arnoldistas*.

Yet, Bolaños stepped up his pressure on the Assembly to strip Alemán of his immunity, and the *Sandinistas*—among them, ironically, Ortega—joined that chorus. But the *Arnoldistas* enjoyed a one-seat majority, and they stonewalled the attempts to prosecute their leader. As the damning evidence and the public outrage mounted,

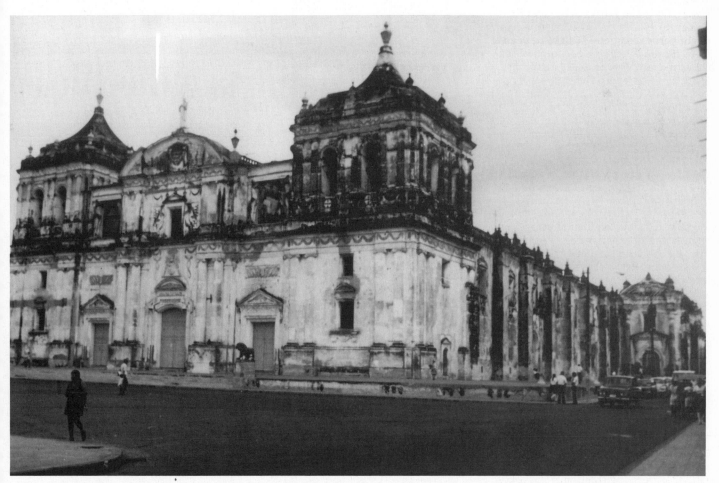

The Metropolitan Cathedral of León, considered the finest examples of colonial architecture in Central America

Nicaragua

however, Alemán's support eroded. The Bolaños faction and the *FSLN* mustered 47 votes to remove Alemán as Assembly president; 44 *Arnoldistas* boycotted the session.

Bolaños suddenly found himself entangled in his own anti-corruption net when a prosecutor—who admitted being a friend of Alemán's—filed charges accusing the president of having illegally channeled foreign donations into his 2001 campaign fund. Like Alemán, Bolaños maintained his innocence and dismissed the charges as politically motivated, but unlike Alemán he voluntarily renounced his executive immunity and vowed to clear his name.

Several members of Alemán's family and former associates were charged on various counts of embezzlement and money-laundering. Among those implicated was his daughter, María Dolores, who also enjoyed immunity as a member of the Assembly. In December 2002, the Assembly finally stripped Alemán of his immunity. He appeared in court the next day, claiming he still enjoyed immunity as a member of the largely ceremonial Central American Parliament.

In 2003, some of the accused were tried, although Alemán remained under house arrest on his ranch, refusing to answer prosecutors' questions. Prosecutors raised new charges that he stole another $113 million from the treasury, theft on a Somoza-sized scale. The *PLC* was hopelessly rent, with 38 Assembly members abandoning Bolaños, leaving him with only 10 loyal members.

Alemán was eventually convicted and sentenced to 20 years. In March 2004, he went to prison, but continued to direct the *Arnoldistas*, who remain fanatically loyal to him. Meanwhile, the United States and Panama both sought his extradition for money laundering, but in 2006 a Nicaraguan court rejected their petitions.

In a Machiavellian maneuver similar to the power-sharing accord of 1999, the *Sandinistas* and *Arnoldistas* joined in an improbable joint effort in 2004 to form a special legislative committee to decide whether to impeach Bolaños on the old charge of receiving foreign campaign contributions. Between them, they had far more than the 60% needed for removal. Bolaños, hopelessly outnumbered in the Assembly, lashed out at both Alemán and Ortega, accusing them of "a plot to carry out a *coup d'etat*." The move was motivated, apparently, by revenge on the part of the *Arnoldistas* and by fear on the part of the *Sandinistas*, who no doubt wondered whether the president would look next at their own sins.

Under pressure from both the United States and the OAS, which warned against removing a constitutional president for politically motivated, trumped-up charges, the *FSLN* and the *PLC* backed off, but in 2005 they enacted a new law that curtailed Bolaños' appointment powers, especially the appointment of judges. The crisis eased when Ortega suddenly declared he would support Bolaños remaining in office until the end of his term.

The *FSLN* was once again the major winner in the 2004 municipal elections, retaining the mayoralty of Managua and winning in all the major cities.

The skyrocketing cost of petroleum in 2005 sparked violent protests when Bolaños announced an increase in bus fares from 15 to 18 cents. When Bolaños attempted to address the thousands of student and peasant protesters, he was met with a barrage of rocks. The high fuel prices also led the Spanish-owned power company to seek, and receive, an 11.3% increase in electric rates, which Bolaños restricted to major users. The resulting outcry prompted Bolaños to decree a state of economic emergency in May, which restricted the right of protest. He rescinded the decree three days later.

In October 2005, after bitter debate, the Assembly approved, 49–37, Nicaragua's participation in the Central American Free Trade Agreement (CAFTA) with the United States. The *Sandinistas* opposed it, and Ortega took part in demonstrations against it. Nicaragua's participation took effect on April 1, 2006.

Also in 2006, a feasibility study was begun to resurrect a dream dating to colonial times—a canal across Nicaragua. The proposed sea-level canal would cost $18 billion and would connect the San Juan River with Lake Nicaragua and the lake with the Pacific, a total of about 173 miles. It would be wider and deeper than the existing Panama Canal, to accommodate large modern cargo ships that are too large for the Panama Canal. Construction would take 12 years.

Former President Enrique Bolaños

Ortega Returns to Power

As the country geared up for the November 5, 2006 presidential and legislative elections, both major parties found themselves with serious divisions. Herty Lewites, the popular former mayor of Managua, challenged Ortega for the *FSLN* nomination and criticized the power-sharing accord. Ortega demonstrated his latent Marxist-Leninist tendencies by expelling Lewites from the party; so much for pink. Lewites launched the Herty 2006 Alliance. The *Sandinistas* became further fragmented when Ortega's former vice president, Edén Pastora, declared his own candidacy.

The *PLC*, meanwhile, also remained split between the pro- and anti-Alemán factions. When Bolaños' presidency secretary, Eduardo Montealegre, announced his intention to run, the *arnoldistas* expelled him from the *PLC* just as the *Sandinistas* had expelled Lewites. He, too, formed a new movement called the Nicaraguan Liberal Alliance, or *ALN*, and formed a coalition with the old Conservative Party. The *arnoldistas* nominated José Rizo, a former vice president, as the *PLC* candidate.

Under a new election law that Ortega and Alemán had hatched between them, a candidate now needed only 40% instead of 45% to avoid a runoff, or only 35% if a candidate had a five-point lead.

Suddenly, Lewites died of a heart attack in July, which threw the entire election into turmoil. His party chose his running mate, Edmundo Jarquín, a former official of the Inter-American Development Bank, to replace him. Unlike Lewites, Jarquín was not an experienced campaigner, nor a popular elected official. The question was whether Lewites' followers would stay

with Jarquín, drift into the camp of Montealegre, like Lewites a renegade reformer, or go with ideology and return to the *Sandinista* fold and Ortega.

Ortega once again scented victory, and he was more determined than ever to come across as a pussycat instead of a jaguar. He adopted the tune of John Lennon's "Give Peace a Chance" as his campaign anthem, which seemed peculiar as Nicaragua had been at peace for 16 years. He mended fences with the Catholic Church, promising to oppose abortion even to protect the life of the mother, and he frequently invoked the name of God in his speeches. He even chose a former *Contra*, Jaime Morales, as his running mate.

The U.S. Embassy made little secret of its support for Montealegre, although its efforts were far less overt than they had been for Bolaños in 2001. Still, there were thinly veiled threats that an Ortega victory could mean an end to U.S. aid.

Nonetheless, Ortega renounced his earlier opposition to Nicaragua's participation in CAFTA, insisted he welcomed foreign investment and downplayed the obvious enthusiasm of Venezuelan President Hugo Chávez for his candidacy.

On November 5, the voters ended the suspense:

Ortega	854,316	38.07%
Montealegre	650,879	29.0%
Rizo	588,304	26.51%
Jarquín	144,596	6.44%
Pastora	6,120	.27%

Montealegre and Ortega held an amicable meeting in which they pledged to work together to create jobs and to reduce Nicaragua's grinding poverty, still endemic after 11 years of *Sandinista* rule and 16 years under three non-*Sandinista* presidents.

The new Assembly was even more fragmented than before, with the *FSLN* winning a plurality of 38 of the 90 elected seats. The *PLC* won 25, Montealegre's *ALN* won 22 and Jarquín's Sandinista Reform Movement *(MRS)* took 5. The fact that former President Bolaños and Montealegre, the presidential runner-up, also were entitled to seats further complicated matters for Ortega.

Ortega, who turned 61 six days after his victory, was sworn in on January 10, 2007. Both Chávez and Bolivian President Evo Morales attended the inauguration. The United States, as usual, sent a mere Cabinet member, Health and Human Services Secretary Michael Leavitt, who met with Ortega and assured him, "Our desire is to work with you." He pledged aid to establish a regional health training facility in Nicaragua, while Chávez promised cut-rate petroleum and fertilizer and said he would pay for 32 badly needed electric generating plants.

President Daniel Ortega Saavedra

For a time, Ortega maintained a delicate balancing act between his old friends in Cuba and his new ones in Caracas on the one hand, and his old nemesis in Washington on the other. He even landed a pledge of $350 million from Iran for port construction, while receiving disaster aid from the United States in 2007. He interjected himself into the Colombian-Ecuadorian border incident in March 2008 on the side of Ecuador (see Colombia and Ecuador), for reasons that were unclear other than ideological kinship with Ecuador's President Rafaél Correa and Nicaragua's long-standing territorial dispute with Colombia over San Andrés Island.

Any further doubts about the unholy alliance Ortega and Alemán had reached in 1999 were dispelled when Ortega succeeded in circumventing the courts by joining with the *arnoldistas* in the Assembly to reduce Alemán's sentence from 20 to five years. He was released from prison but remained under house arrest.

Once back in power, Ortega morphed back into the hardline, Marxist-Leninist Cold Warrior of the 1980s. He brought Nicaragua into *ALBA*, Chávez's anti-U.S. bloc, with Cuba, Venezuela and Bolivia. The old truculent anthems of the 1980s began playing again at *FSLN* rallies. He ordered formation of what have been used as goon squads, funded with Venezuelan money, to intimidate opponents and dissenters.

Dogged by polls that showed his popularity plummeting to 20%, Ortega has demonstrated his true antidemocratic colors by harassing political opponents and opposition media, by preventing opposition parties from competing in the November 9, 2008 municipal elections, and then by rigging that election so blatantly that it brought world-wide condemnation—except from Ortega's allies in Cuba, Venezuela, Bolivia and Ecuador.

Nicaragua

First, Ortega used hurricane damage as a pretext to delay local elections in April 2008 along the Caribbean coast, which sparked riots. Next, he stacked the Supreme Electoral Council, designed to be a neutral, independent body and which certified his 2006 election, with loyal *Sandinistas*. That council then disqualified both Jarquín's *MRS* and Montealegre's *ALN* from participating in the municipal elections; it also disqualified the Conservative Party. His party disqualified, Montealegre reconciled with the *PLC* and became its candidate for mayor of Managua.

In October 2008, the government announced it was investigating two prominent groups that have been critical of Ortega for alleged money laundering: the Center of Media Investigations, headed by Carlos Chamorro Barrios, son of former President Violeta Chamorro; and the Autonomous Women's Movement, which had criticized Ortega for opposing abortion even to save the life of the mother, calling it a betrayal of *Sandinista* principles. Their offices were raided. The government also threatened Ernesto Cardenal, the most prominent *FSLN* defector, with legal difficulties after he called Ortega a "thief" and his government a "monarchy."

The municipal elections were the predictable sham. To allay a resounding rebuke predicted by polls, Ortega refused accreditation to the OAS, the European Union and the Carter Center from serving as outside observers, as they had in 1990 and every election since; Ortega publicly

admitted he blamed the OAS for his 1990 defeat. He also prevented the Nicaraguan watchdog group, Transparency and Ethics, from monitoring the voting and the count.

On election day, Transparency and Ethics volunteers posted themselves outside polling places and alleged irregularities at one third of them, including the early closing of some polling stations. Polls had showed Montealegre leading the *FSLN*'s Alexis Argüello, a former world boxing champion. But on election night, non-*FSLN* members of the electoral council were expelled from the vote counting, which continued in secret. In the city of León, thousands of ballots marked for Liberal candidates were found in the city dump.

The official results: The *FSLN* won in 94 of the 146 municipalities, and Argüello won in Managua with 51.5% of the vote. Montealegre claimed his independent tally showed him winning handily, and he demanded a recount. His supporters took to the streets, only to be met by *Sandinista* goons wielding clubs and machetes; they also fired home-made mortar rounds at the opposition protesters, while police stood by passively. The electoral council agreed to a recount—which took place behind closed doors and independent observers were barred. The results of the "recount" were predictable. The EU expressed its disgust with Ortega's dictatorial behavior by suspending desperately needed aid, which amounted to a third of the budget. Ortega continues to rely on the largess of Venezuela's Chávez.

Recent Developments

Ortega turned the clock back to the Cold War on the international stage. He appointed his former foreign minister, Miguel D'Escoto, an unmellowed Revolutionary Theology defrocked priest, as ambassador to the United Nations, just as Nicaragua's turn came to hold the General Assembly presidency. D'Escoto has used the presidency as a pulpit to harangue the United States for a litany of real or imagined sins, alienating himself and Nicaragua from Secretary-General Ban Ki-moon.

Nor has Ortega made an effort to seek improved relations with the new U.S. president, Barack Obama. At the Fifth Summit of the Americas in Port-of-Spain, Trinidad, in April 2009, Ortega made a spectacle of himself with a 50-minute, *yanqui*-baiting diatribe, reciting a shopworn list of complaints dating back to the 19th century, as Obama listened indulgently. Ortega even attacked the summit itself because of the exclusion of Cuba, "whose crime has been that of fighting for independence, fighting for sovereignty of the peoples. I don't feel comfortable attending this summit. I cannot feel comfortable by being here. I feel ashamed of the fact that I'm participating at this summit with the absence of Cuba."

Pressed later to comment on Ortega's speech, Obama said, "To move forward, we cannot let ourselves be prisoners of past disagreements. I'm grateful that President Ortega did not blame me for things that happened when I was three months old. Too often, an opportunity to build a fresh partnership of the Americas has been undermined by stale debates. We've all heard these arguments before."

Managua Mayor Argüello was found dead on July 1, 2009 of what was described as a self-inflicted gun shot wound to the heart, but there were allegations of foul play.

In his latest anti-democratic power play, Ortega pulled a legal sleight-of-hand in October 2009 to get the Supreme Court to nullify the restriction on immediate re-election, which would allow him to run again without first obtaining a constitutional amendment. In November, tens of thousands of anti-Ortega demonstrators filled the streets of Managua to protest the move; tens of thousands of Ortega's supporters counter-demonstrated. In December, the Assembly passed a resolution renouncing what it called the court's "psuedo-ruling" and declaring that Ortega is not eligible to run again.

Even if Ortega succeeds in defying the Assembly and gets on the ballot, it is questionable whether he could win an *honest* vote count. A year-end poll by CID-Gallup

Traditional Dance

put his approval rating at 22%, and another in May 2010 showed that 56% believe his candidacy would have a negative impact on the country (see The Future).

Culture: Though a substantial number of Nicaraguans lead a modern, urban life comparable to that of the large cities of Latin America, the majority live in rural simplicity and poverty. The culture closely resembles that of the rest of the Central American states.

The music of the people, derived from their Spanish-Moorish conquerors, is used to accompany a wide variety of local dances and festivals. It was possible to see the latest dramatic and musical productions professionally performed in the busy capital of Managua, and after a short journey to also view a traditional *mestizo* comedy quaintly performed in a combination of *Hahuatl* (an Indian dialect), Spanish and *Mangue*, another Indian dialect.

Under the *Sandinistas*, most education heavily stressed communist principles and ideals—all alien to a basically politically unskilled people who are seldom politically intelligent and aware. Culturally, Nicaragua is currently (except in the rural countryside) a desert.

Nicaragua contributed one of the world's foremost poets, Rubén Dario (1867–1916).

Economy: Although Nicaragua is largely based on agriculture, which employed 65% of the work force, the increased development of light industry before the revolution gave Nicaragua's economy a degree of hope for a broader base than was found in most other Latin American countries. Underpopulated and with many unexploited natural resources, the nation has a substantial potential for tremendous economic growth with proper management.

Nicaragua's most important farm commodities are produced in the western region. Rich in volcanic soils, this section is the source of cotton, coffee and sugar. The cattle industry has also expanded in the west. The eastern region is largely devoted to banana production. Nationalization of large producing farms during the *Sandinista* era did not contribute to their efficiency, and the breakup of some into smaller peasant farms actually seriously lowered production.

The U.S. commercial embargo on Nicaragua in the 1980s had a devastating effect. The closing of U.S. ports and a ban on technological imports all but shut down the economy. As in Cuba, Soviet limitations on its economic aid to socialist countries added a somber note to Nicaragua's possibilities for development. During 1986–90, virtually all that was exported was bananas, sold to the Soviet Union and Eastern Europe at inflated prices.

The Chamorro government, hamstrung by the ever-present threat of the *Sandinista* military, accomplished little at reducing unemployment and underemployment, which totaled more than 65%. President Arnoldo Alemán moved more aggressively to bring Nicaragua in line with International Monetary Fund demands and to make the country more attractive to foreign investors. GDP growth was a respectable 5% in 1997. Meanwhile, the IMF extended Nicaragua a three-year, $136 million loan package and praised Alemán for stabilizing the currency and reducing the bloated, featherbedded bureaucracy. The World Bank also granted a $70 million loan to help transform the financial sector from the old Marxist system.

Hurricane Mitch caused billions of dollars in damage to the economic infrastructure in 1998, a blow the country could ill afford and which added another $300 million to the already oppressive $6.2 billion external debt. Surprisingly, however, Mitch did not derail the expanding economy. GDP growth was still 4% for 1998 and 6.2% for 1999. In 2000 it had tapered off slightly to 5.0%. It was 2.5% in 2001 and only 1% in 2002 and 1.4% in 2003.

President Enrique Bolaños claimed a better economic record, with growth in 2004 and 2005 running at about 4% and 3.9% in 2006. Bolaños signed, and the Assembly ratified, the Dominican Republic-Central American Free Trade Agreement with the United States in 2005. It took effect on April 1, 2006.

Nicaragua's per capita income fell lower than Haiti's in 1997, to $436, making it for the first time the poorest country in the Western Hemisphere. By 2002 it had dropped even lower, to $370, compared with $440 for Haiti. It has since moved past Haiti again, to about $980.

Economic growth has dropped under Ortega's second administration, to 3.2% in 2007 and 2008. With the global recession, it dropped by –2.9% in 2009. Meanwhile, inflation has soared under Ortega, from 9.45% in 2006 to 19.9% in 2008. With the recession, it dropped to 4.3% in 2009.

Unemployment has fluctuated for years. In 2009 it was officially only 5.9%, although another 46.5% are underemployed.

Nicaragua has long been saddled with one of the highest per capita foreign debts in the world, a dubious distinction exacerbated by Hurricane Mitch. In 2004, Nicaragua was on the list of 18 heavily indebted nations provided with debt forgiveness by the so-called Paris Club. But in 2008, public debt was still 74.8% of GDP; in 2009, it rose to 87%, 12th highest in the world.

Like Mexico and other Central American countries, Nicaragua depends heavily on remittances from Nicaraguans working abroad, mostly in the United States.

Remittances have increased from $655.5 million in 2006 to $768 million in 2009, about 12% of GDP.

The Future: For the past three decades, Nicaragua has been whipsawed from corrupt right-wing dictatorship to corrupt left-wing dictatorship to inept and corrupt democracy and back to a repressive left-wing dictatorship, as if on an amusement park ride—only there is nothing amusing about it.

Whatever his shortcomings, Daniel Ortega, now 64, balding and with a heart condition, could at least be given credit as a determined cuss, rising Phoenix-like from the ashes of three successive defeats to regain the presidency in 2007. But Ortega hoodwinked his countrymen into giving him a 38% winning plurality, convincing them that he was a different man from the fire-breathing Stalinist of the 1980s. His actions during his two and a half years in power have shown him to be the unreconstructed *yanqui*-hating Cold Warrior he was then. He has alienated the United States and the European Union in favor of dubious alliances with Cuba and Venezuela, even as economic growth dropped to a pitiful 2% for 2008 and shrank by –2.9% in 2009.

Nicaraguans' commitment to democracy also has been on a roller-coaster ride. In 1996, in the first annual *Latinobarómetro* survey of Latin American countries, 59% of Nicaraguans said they agreed that democracy is preferable to any other form of government. By 2004, that figure had dropped to 39%, tying with Paraguay for the lowest in Latin America. Perhaps because of the spectacle of seeing the disgraced former President Alemán going to jail, coupled with an improving economy, support for democracy rebounded to 57% in 2005, 56% in 2006 and 61% in 2007. In 2008, it dropped back to 58%, and that was even before the stolen municipal elections in November. In 2009, it dropped to 55%

At the same time, Nicaraguans who believe that authoritarianism is sometimes preferable to democracy has roller-coasted from 14% in 1996 to 22% in 2001 to 8% in 2008 to 10% in 2009.

Alas, authoritarianism is what they now have under Ortega. He is attempting to circumvent the constitution to run for immediate re-election in 2011, and he now has the legislative and judicial branches at loggerheads on the issue, with the Supreme Court saying he can and the Assembly refusing to recognize that decision.

Even if he does run, polls show his approval ratings at about 22%. Will he try to rig the 2011 election like he did the 2008 municipal elections? If he does, Nicaragua could well see a return to the violence of the 1970s and '80s.

The Republic of Panama

The almost completed Panama Canal—final blasting of a channel, October 1913

Area: 28,745 square miles.

Population: 3,410,676 (2010 est.).

Capital City: Panama City (Pop. 700,000).

Climate: Tropical, with clearly marked wet and dry seasons. The heaviest rainfall is from May to December.

Neighboring Countries: Colombia (southeast); Costa Rica (northwest).

Official Language: Spanish.

Other Principal Tongue: English.

Ethnic Background: Mulatto (mixed African and European, 72%); African (14%); European (12%); Indians and other (2%).

Principal Religion: Roman Catholic Christianity.

Chief Commercial Products: Bananas, shrimp and apparel.

Currency: Balboa (in reality, the U.S. dollar is the legal tender).

Gross Domestic Product: U.S. $25.04 billion in 2009 ($7,342 per capita).

Former Colonial Status: Spanish Colony (1519–1821), Province of Colombia (1821–1903).

Independence Date: November 3, 1903.

Chief of State: Ricardo Martinelli Fabrega (b. March 11, 1952), president (since July 1, 2009)

National Flag: A rectangle of four quarters; white with a blue star, blue, white with a red star, red.

Panama is a very narrow isthmus, 480 miles long and varying in width from 37 to 110 miles, connecting North and South America. Mountainous throughout, the highest elevation is the volcano Baru (11,397 feet) near the Costa Rican border. The Talamanca range continues southeast at an average elevation of 3,000 feet until it drops into the sea just west of Panama City. The San Blas range, rising east of Colón, runs southeast into Colombia; again the average elevation is 3,000 feet. A third range appears along the Pacific coast east of Panama City and runs southeast into Colombia. Both coasts have narrow plains cut by numerous small rivers running into the sea.

Lying in the tropical rainbelt, Panama's Atlantic coast receives up to 150 inches of rainfall—the Pacific coast receives about 100 inches. The dry season, or "summer," runs from December to April. Four fifths of Panama's territory is covered with jungle and one half lies outside effective control by the Panamanian government. The principal reason for Panama's existence as a nation and the principal source of its earnings is the geographical accident of the north-south gap between the Talamanca and San Blas ranges, which permitted the construction of a canal between the Atlantic and Pacific oceans. Now the site of the Panama Canal and the nation's major cities, more than half the population is found in a narrow corridor and along the Pacific coast west of the gap.

History: Columbus discovered Panama in 1498–1500 and called it Veraguas. It assumed importance in 1513 when Vasco Nuñez de Balboa discovered the Pacific. Panama City was established on the Pacific coast in 1518 and connected to three Caribbean ports by trails and rivers.

Nombre de Dios (Name of God) and Portobelo were the principal Atlantic ports maintained by the Spanish. Panama became the base for the outfitting of expeditions into Peru and Central America; it later was a major link in the route over which the wealth of the region was shipped to Spain. This wealth, and Panama's strategic importance, attracted pirates, buccaneers and foreign armies.

The British privateer Sir Francis Drake burned Nombre de Dios in 1573 and 1598; Henry Morgan raided the isthmus, looting and burning Panama City in 1617; British Admiral Edward Vernon captured Portobelo in 1739 and San Lorenzo in 1740. Spain abandoned the Panamanian route in 1746 in favor of the trip around Cape Horn at the tip of Argentina and Chile to reach its colonies in western Latin America.

For nearly 100 years Panama was bypassed by trade and ignored during the wars for independence in Mexico and South America. Panama became a province of Colombia. The discovery of gold in California brought renewed interest in quick transit from the Atlantic to the Pacific coast of the United States. A railroad was constructed between 1850 and 1853, and the De Lesseps Company of France started work on a canal in 1882. The work was abandoned in 1893, in part because of yellow fever epidemics, and in 1904 the United States acquired the assets of the bankrupt company.

There ensued three years of fruitless negotiations between the United States and Colombia. Colombia was gripped by civil war during the period. Philippe Jean Bunau-Varilla, the French agent of the defunct canal company, with the knowledge of the United States, engineered a revolution in Panama with the understanding that the United States would intervene to establish Panama as an independent state and that U.S. financial interests would acquire the right to complete the interoceanic canal across the isthmus. President Theodore Roosevelt recognized the independence of Panama three days after its proclamation on November 3, 1903.

Treaty negotiations between the United States and Panama were brief. Bunau-Varilla represented Panama, and the two sides quickly reached an agreement giving the United States virtually sovereign rights "in perpetuity" over the Canal Zone, a 10-mile-wide swath of Panamanian territory from coast to coast. Panamanians were horrified when confronted with Bunau-Varilla's *fait accompli*, but there was little they could do. Construction on the canal started shortly thereafter—as did 70 years of wrangling between the United States and the Republic of Panama over the sovereignty issue. In August 1914, the 400-year-old dream of Spanish, French, British and North American adventurers was accomplished when a vessel sailed through the completed canal from the Atlantic to the Pacific Ocean.

Panama's political history as an independent state was in keeping with the pattern of the Central American and Caribbean nations. Power lay in the hands of a small, elite Caucasian group that exploited the geographic situation for its personal benefit. The population at the time of independence was concentrated in the terminal cities of the trans-isthmian railroad and dependent upon commerce for its income. The influx of labor for the

Panama's Declaration of Independence

Panama

El Casco Viejo, **the old part of Panama City**

construction completely overwhelmed the administrative capabilities of the small nation. A pattern ensued in which actual power was in the hands of the *Guardia Nacional*, whose head was infrequently the actual chief of state; more often he ruled through a figurehead president.

U.S. Patrimony

The United States took what measures it deemed necessary to achieve its purposes while Panama elected or appointed one ineffective government after another. The Panama Railroad, the United Fruit Company, which had established banana plantations during the late 1800s, and the Panama Canal Company, in consort with a small group of Panamanian families, exercised effective political and economic power in Panama. The steady influx of wealth supported a booming economy through the 1940s. Following World War II, the growing population exceeded the service demands of commerce and Panama began to feel the effects of 50 years of lack of direction and failure to invest its earnings in substantial industrial ventures.

Into this volatile political environment there appeared a charismatic and demagogic figure who was to dominate Panamanian politics for the next half-century—and even beyond his death: Arnulfo Arias. The founder of the ultra-nationalist *Panameñista* Party, Arias exploited his people's near-xenophobic dislike of foreigners. He lashed out not only at the United States and the "Zonians" who enjoyed their suburban tropical paradise, but foreign immigrants as well, particularly those from Asia. On those rare occasions when the *Guardia Nacional* allowed Panamanians to vote in fair elections, Arias and his party did well—*too* well, for the *Guardia* and the elite. He was elected president in 1940 and in 1948, only to be deposed by the *Guardia* both times. He won again—and was deposed again—in 1968 and probably won two other elections, in 1964 and 1984, but was denied victory through creative vote-counting.

As the military, in league with the tiny clique of oligarchs, was the actual power in the country, it "elected" one of its own, Police Chief José Antonio Remón, as president in 1952. Oddly enough, Remón was to prove one of Panama's more enlight-

ened rulers, instituting long-overdue social reform, which estranged him from the oligarchy, and cracking down on the more overt corruption. He also was friendlier to the United States than many of his predecessors had been, *too* friendly for some Panamanians. Nonetheless, his more rational policy succeeded in obtaining an increase in the rent for the Canal Zone in 1955 from a paltry $430,000 (it had been only $250,000 until 1939!) to a still-ridiculous $1.9 million. Remón was assassinated that same year, but whether his killers were motivated by social reactionism or anti-Americanism never has been determined.

Remón's antithesis, Ernesto de la Guardia, was elected president in a reasonably fair count in 1956 and began making strident demands on the United States. The war over the Suez Canal that year helped further fan Panamanian passions. Some of the demands were quite legitimate, such as elimination of the inequitable wage scales between Zonian and Panamanian canal employees. President Eisenhower, who had served in Panama as a young Army officer in the early 1920s, acceded to the wage demands, as well as to a demand to allow the Panamanian flag to fly in the Zone. But it seemed the more the Americans conceded, the more antagonistic the de la Guardia government became. On Panamanian Independence Day in 1959, a well-orchestrated mob sought to "invade" the Zone, forcing U.S. troops to deter them with fixed bayonets. Ultra-nationalists and pro-Castro students exploited the incident for propaganda purposes. If nothing else, de la Guardia earned one important distinction for a Panamanian president: he served out his elected four-year term.

A far more moderate figure (and a member of the oligarchy), Roberto Chiari, was elected president in 1960 in what probably was the cleanest election Panama would ever have until 1994. Chiari enjoyed an amicable relationship with President Kennedy, and followed an anti-Castro line pleasing to Washington.

Nonetheless, toward the end of Chiari's term there occurred the worst incident of violence yet between Americans and Panamanians. In January 1964, foolhardy Zonian students at Balboa High School tore down the Panamanian flag flying next to the U.S. flag in front of the school and desecrated it. As word got out, Panamanians exploded in fury, and rioters flooded into the Zone, separated from Panama City only by the broad Fourth of July Avenue. In the resulting violence, 23 Panamanians and six Americans, most of them soldiers, were killed. Chiari broke diplomatic relations with the United States, and President Lyndon B. Johnson was faced with his first foreign policy crisis since succeeding the assassinated Kennedy two months earlier. Panama renamed Fourth of July Avenue *Avenida de los Mártires* (Avenue of the Martyrs), and to this day there are ceremonies marking each anniversary of the deadly riots.

In the election of May 1964, Chiari's cousin and fellow oligarch, Marco Aurelio Robles, narrowly defeated the fiery Arias, though the vote counting remains suspect to this day. Robles re-established relations with Washington which, still shaken by the riots, began negotiating seriously about changes to the 1903 canal treaty. Robles withdrew government sanctioning on anti-U.S. demonstrations, and relations gradually improved—for a time.

The 1968 Coup

In the May 1968 elections, the perennial Arias won by a convincing margin that could not be denied. He was duly inaugurated on September 1, but just 11 days into his term, the *Guardia* overthrew him for a third time, ushering in 21 years of despotic military rule as heavy-handed as any in Latin America. For the first 13 of those years, absolute power rested with Colonel

President Jimmy Carter looks on as Panama's Omar Torrijos signs the 1977 Panama Canal Treaty

Omar Torrijos, who later promoted himself to brigadier general, a flamboyant and charismatic figure in the classic style of the Latin American *caudillo*.

Torrijos became a hero to the long-suppressed lower class as he established what amounted to a Panamanian version of a dictatorship of the proletariat. Political activity ceased, and a puppet legislative assembly rubber-stamped Torrijos' dictates. The egomaniacal Torrijos even had his heroic image emblazoned in a new frieze work on the legislative palace. Press freedom vanished as the government expropriated three newspapers owned by Arias' brother, Harmodio, and blackmailed the owner of the venerable and respected *La Estrella de Panama* into becoming a sycophantish parrot of the government line.

Critics of the regime were tortured, and more than a few took a one-way helicopter ride over the Pacific Ocean. Those too prominent to kill were hustled off into exile, often after being beaten as a farewell gesture. Torrijos re-established diplomatic relations with Cuba, and engaged in *gringo*-baiting on a scale not seen since de la Guardia. He attacked traditional corruption long practiced by the elite, but a newer, more sinister version with ties to Colombian drug traffickers soon arose. Torrijos implemented lax banking regulations that attracted branches of major banks from every continent, while the drug traffickers found Panama a veritable paradise for money-laundering.

The New Canal Treaties

National politics was dominated in the 1970s by the lingering dispute with the United States over the canal. Most of this centered around the 1903 treaty that granted the United States virtual sovereignty "in perpetuity" over the 530-square-mile Canal Zone. Widespread resentment against what was regarded as an outdated treaty unified most Panamanian political factions in demanding a new treaty. Key changes sought by Panama included (1) increased rental payments, (2) a large-scale reduction of U.S. military presence in the zone, (3) a greater Panamanian role in operating the canal and (4) recognition of complete Panamanian sovereignty over the zone.

Although there was an effort to place some nationals in management positions within the Canal Company, Panamanians insisted they could, and should, be allowed an even greater role in running their nation's major industry. Panamani-

Brigadier General Omar Torrijos

Panama

The Panama Canal at Miraflores locks

ans employed in the Canal Zone were usually given menial tasks at low wages. Since its opening in 1914, the canal was operated almost entirely by U.S. staff and supervisors. The zone itself resembled a "company town" as residents were provided with cradle-to-grave programs such as free schooling and medical care.

Because the 1903 treaty granted the United States territorial supremacy over the Zone, Panama said the corridor represented a virtual foreign nation in its midst. It was a valid point. Zonians paid U.S. taxes. The Zone had its own police force. It had a U.S. federal district court, which was part of the 5th Circuit. It had U.S. post offices, although the Zone actually had its own postage stamps. Democrats in the Zone elected delegates to their party's national conventions. Panamanians could even be "deported" from the zone. It contended that U.S. control was a form of colonialism and insisted the 1903 treaty had to be replaced since it was forced on the tiny nation by U.S. "big stick" gunboat diplomacy. Interestingly, however, Americans born in the Zone were entitled to dual nationality. One was now-Senator John McCain.

An eight-point agenda for negotiators was signed early in 1974, during the waning days of the Nixon administration, and talks began shortly thereafter. The negotiations were continued into the Ford administration, and while they were not exactly secret, the administration certainly kept them low-key. In 1976, the canal talks became a campaign issue when Ronald Rea-

gan, running for the Republican nomination against President Ford, assailed Ford for negotiating to surrender the vital U.S.-controlled waterway to a "tinpot dictator." Ford clumsily denied that he intended to give up the canal, an assertion that immediately drew the ire of the Panamanians. Caught between a domestic political dilemma and an international powder keg, Ford then backtracked and acknowledged that canal negotiations were underway, but he denounced Reagan as "irresponsible" for opposing them. Ford narrowly defeated Reagan for the nomination, but lost the general election to Democrat Jimmy Carter.

Shortly after his inauguration in 1977, Carter gave a high priority to a new canal treaty. Ambassador Sol M. Linowitz was appointed to join Ellsworth Bunker as chief U.S. negotiators, and talks resumed in February 1977.

Completed in August, the new accord consisted of two separate treaties. The first one would permanently guarantee the canal's neutrality and use by all nations. In case of emergency, however, U.S. warships would be given priority over commercial traffic.

The second accord detailed a timetable for gradual transfer of the canal and the Zone from the United States to Panama. At noon on December 31, 1999, Panama would gain control of the whole works. Annual payments to Panama would also be boosted at once from $2.3 million to an estimated $60 million.

Although the two treaties incorporated a number of Panamanian demands, they

left unsettled the question of a larger, deeper sea-level canal that Carter said would be needed before the year 2000. The present facility employs the use of time-consuming locks. The Navy's largest warships and the new generation of super-tankers are too large to pass through the canal's locks. The waterway is also subject to congestion. Both traffic and tonnage had been rising, placing additional burdens on the canal's facilities.

The new treaties were signed with a flourish when leaders from 23 Latin American nations gathered in Washington in September 1977 to witness the historic event. Still, the festive occasion could not hide the fact that the treaties faced a tough fight—both in the U.S. Senate (where critics said Washington gave up too much) and in Panama (where critics said Washington gave up too *little*).

The first test came in Panama, where the treaties were submitted to a national referendum. Despite vocal protests from both leftists and conservatives—who insisted that Torrijos should have held out for more money plus an earlier U.S. withdrawal—the treaties were approved by a comfortable 2–1 margin.

Attention next turned to Washington; for ratification, the agreements needed support from two thirds of the Senate—a tall order for an accord that public opinion polls said was still opposed by a majority of Americans. A campaign by retired and active high government figures was mounted in favor of the treaties. Ten weeks of debate ensued. Seventy-nine

Panama

amendments were offered. The first treaty was approved in March by 68–32—just one vote more than the necessary two thirds. To gain approval, however, the president had to agree to an amendment permitting U.S. military intervention in Panama should the canal be closed for any reason, including a strike or even technical problems. This amendment caused an immediate uproar in Panama. Nationalists protested that it was not only an affront to Panamanian dignity, but would violate previous U.S.-Latin American agreements that specifically prohibited the concept of unilateral intervention. As the Senate prepared to vote on the second treaty, Torrijos—subjected to a blast of pressure from critics at home—sent a message to 115 world leaders saying Panama could not accept the amendment.

In an 11th-hour attempt to save 14 years of painful negotiations, the White House and Senate leaders agreed to a new provision that promised that the United States would not interfere with Panama's "internal affairs" or "political independence." The lawmakers, obviously tired of the whole matter, voted in April by the same 68–32 margin in favor of the second treaty.

Behind the scenes, Carter had persuaded Torrijos that U.S. Senate ratification of the treaties would be impossible unless he sanitized his odious dictatorship. Torrijos pragmatically agreed to permit competitive elections and to ease restrictions on freedom of expression and of the press, which Carter trumpeted as proof of Torrijos' commitment to democracy. The seemingly close relationship between the U.S. president, who assailed right-wing Latin American military strongmen for their human rights abuses, and the Panamanian dictator who ordered the murders of political dissidents and confiscated newspapers, was most peculiar.

This author was in Panama in June 1978 when Carter visited Panama to sign the instruments of ratification. At the public ceremony, Carter thrilled the Panamanian crowd by delivering a conciliatory address in his broken Spanish, in which he promised *"no intervención."* Torrijos, by contrast, was a disgrace. On this highly significant occasion in the life of his country, the representative of Panama was so drunk that his speech was badly slurred and he had to brace himself against the podium to keep from falling.

On October 1, 1979, an enormous Panamanian flag was raised atop Ancon Hill, which looms above Panama City and was the site of the U.S. Southern Command headquarters, and titular Panamanian sovereignty over the Canal Zone became a reality. Meanwhile, as window dressing, exiles were allowed to return. A new, more liberal press law was enacted, though the

Arístedes Royo

confiscated newspapers remained in government hands and *La Estrella* remained a faithful mouthpiece underneath its Sword of Damocles. The military established the Revolutionary Democratic Party (*PRD*) as its civilian political façade. In 1980, an ostensible "election" was held in which numerous parties participated, but the winner was predictable: Arístides Royo, candidate of the *PRD*.

That same year, a group of anti-Torrijos businessmen and intellectuals, headed by Roberto Eisenmann, who had been in exile for four years, put the new press law to the test by establishing a new daily newspaper, *La Prensa*, which soon became a constant irritant to the regime with its investigative reporting of government corruption, biting editorials and iconoclastically satirical cartoons.

Numerous problems faced strongman Torrijos and his protégé, President Royo. Many of the financial benefits expected to flow into Panama as a result of the new treaties were slow to materialize. In 1980 unemployment grew to 20% and growing inflation touched off two days of general strikes that crippled 80% of the country's industries.

The election of Ronald Reagan in 1980 caused shock waves in Panama, where Torrijos feared that the new president might try to sabotage the canal treaties. Given Reagan's long-standing opposition to the pacts, Panama felt it necessary to safeguard its position by obtaining (with the help of Cuba) a seat on the U.N. Security Council in 1980.

The Panamanian political landscape was altered abruptly and dramatically on July 31, 1981, when Torrijos was killed in a plane crash while on an inspection of *Guardia* units in western Panama. Bad weather was cited as the official cause of the crash, though persistent rumors began

circulating almost immediately that it was no accident. Fidel Castro, of course, immediately accused the CIA, then headed by Reagan protégé William Casey, of rubbing out his friend. Torrijos, or what little remained of him, was buried in an elaborate mausoleum on the parade ground of the former U.S. Army installation of Fort Amador. There was a frenzied outpouring of grief for the man who, whatever his shortcomings, had succeeded in reasserting Panamanian sovereignty over the Canal Zone.

Command of the *Guardia* passed initially to Brigadier General Rubén Paredes, and democratic forces held their breath to see what course post-Torrijos Panama would take. Almost a year to the day after Torrijos' death, they found out. On July 30, 1982, Panama experienced a veritable night of the long knives as the military launched a widespread crackdown on dissent. President Royo was summoned to military headquarters and informed that he was resigning for "health reasons"; he readily complied. At the same time, a goon squad invaded the offices of *La Prensa*, vandalized it and beat several of its employees, including women. The paper was padlocked for several days; other independent publications and radio stations also were silenced.

Noriega Comes to Power

After two years of a behind-the-scenes power struggle, command of the *Guardia*, which had been renamed the Panama Defense Forces (*FDP*), passed to one of the most sinister figures in recent Latin American history: Colonel Manuel Noriega. The longtime chief of the *Guardia's* G-2, or intelligence section, Noriega was no charismatic *caudillo* like Torrijos. He was squat and ugly, with a face heavily scarred by acne, which led his many detractors to give him the uncharitable sobriquet "*Cara de Piña*," or "Pineapple Face." Where Torrijos had enjoyed the popularity of the masses, Noriega would rule by raw fear.

Noriega was an alumnus of the U.S. Army's School of the Americas, then located at Fort Gulick, Panama, and had become a paid CIA operative. But he also acted as a double agent, providing intelligence to the Soviets and Cubans. Even more sinister, he enriched himself by providing protection to the Medellín Cartel of Colombia, which used Panama as a safe haven for its cocaine trafficking and money laundering. When this author served Army Reserve tours at the Southern Command in the 1970s and 1980s, Noriega's activities were well known, and his ascension to power was seen as the worst possible scenario. As *La Prensa's* Eisenmann later told me, the difference

Panama

between Torrijos and Noriega was that Torrijos merely ordered people tortured and murdered; Noriega participated in the torturing and killing and enjoyed it.

Noriega soon demonstrated the extent of his commitment to Torrijos' promise to Carter to ease human rights restrictions. In 1984, he dutifully held open presidential elections for an expanded five-year term. As its candidate, the military-backed *PRD* selected Nicolás Ardito Barletta, a respected economist and graduate of the University of Chicago. The *Panameñistas* again nominated the resilient Arias, by then 83. When early tabulations, which were monitored by international observers, showed an unmistakable trend in favor of Arias, the *FDP* abruptly impounded the ballot boxes and continued the vote counting in secret. By independent estimates, Arias would have received a plurality of between 25,000 and 50,000 votes out of 900,000 cast, but through the *FDP*'s creative vote counting, Barletta was declared the winner by 1,700 votes.

Public opposition to Noriega's heavy-handed rule intensified. A curious coalition of the wealthy elite, leftist intellectuals and housewives took to the streets waving white handkerchiefs. Some of the demonstrations were broken up by truncheon-wielding goon squads from *FDP*-backed groups euphemistically named "Dignity Battalions." Not all opponents of the regime fared that well, however.

One of the most prominent Noriega critics was Dr. Hugo Spadafora, a physician who once had served as Torrijos' vice minister of health. He had served both the Nicaraguan *Sandinistas* in their struggle against Somoza and then, when he became disillusioned with their human rights abuses once in power, he lent his support to the *Contras*. He contributed a regular column to *La Prensa*, in which he vilified the Noriega dictatorship, and he announced he would return to Panama from Costa Rica to lead an opposition movement. He never made it. In September 1985, his bus was stopped when it crossed the border and, according to witnesses, he was forcibly removed. Days later, his decapitated body was found stuffed in a mailbag in Costa Rica; the body bore unmistakable evidence of hideous torture.

The Spadafora murder backfired on Noriega the same way the murder of journalist Pedro Joaquín Chamorro had served as the catalyst for the downfall of Nicaragua's Somoza. News of this atrocious crime made headlines around the world, and domestic and international pressure mounted on the regime. A half-hearted investigation concluded that the murder had occurred in Costa Rica and that Panamanian authorities had no juris-

diction. The Costa Ricans disputed that claim, which only served to fuel the mounting public indignation in Panama. Trying to appease public opinion, President Barletta publicly vowed to bring the killers to justice, a declaration he had foolishly made without consulting with Noriega. Like so many of his predecessors, the president was summoned to military headquarters and was informed he would not leave the building unless he resigned; he did. He was succeeded by the vice president, Eric Arturo Delvalle.

General Manuel Antonio Noriega

This author was stationed in Panama during the first half of 1986, when the outcry over the Spadafora murder reached a crescendo. The regime's response to the protests was to cow the opposition with death threats. Graffiti accusing Eisenmann of "treason" appeared all over Panama City, and the editor fled again to Miami for his life. That June, Pulitzer Prize-winning reporter Seymour Hersh of the *New York Times* reported what insiders in Panama had known for years, that Noriega was involved in drug trafficking and that he was a double agent. I watched with amazement as a State Department spokesman testified on television before a congressional committee that there was no evidence to support Hersh's charges; apparently they hadn't been reading the military's intelligence cables for the past 10 years! Eventually, the U.S. government acknowledged that Noriega had once

been a paid informant and was heavily involved in drug trafficking.

Noriega, of course, played the nationalist card, accusing the *gringos* of trying to undermine him. But in June 1987, one of his own former minions, Colonel Roberto Díaz Herrera, told the press not only that Noriega was a drug trafficker but that he had ordered Torrijos' fatal plane crash. The opposition press gleefully published the charges. On July 26, 1987, Noriega cracked down hard. Díaz was arrested, and *La Prensa* and several other opposition papers and radio stations were shut down. The Reagan administration ostracized the Noriega regime economically. In February 1988, President Delvalle attempted to salvage the country's devastated economy and to restore some degree of respect in the eyes of the world by firing Noriega as *FDP* commander. Noriega, of course, immediately fired Delvalle; Education Minister Manuel Solis Palma was installed to keep the president's chair warm until Barletta's term expired in 1989. That same year, a U.S. grand jury indicted Noriega on drug trafficking charges.

Incredibly, in May 1989, Noriega went ahead with another showcase election, as though anyone still believed Panama was a democracy. Arias had died in exile in Miami the previous August, and the *Panameñistas*, now renamed *Arnulfistas*, nominated a portly and uninspiring doctor, Guillermo Endara, as the sacrificial lamb to head a coalition opposition ticket. The *PRD* nominated Carlos Duque, a member of the family that published the regime's faithful mascot newspaper, *La Estrella*. Perhaps the most enduring image of this sham campaign was an attack on an opposition rally by Dignity Battalion goons. Guillermo Ford, one of the opposition's two vice presidential candidates, was badly beaten, and international news photographers and cameramen recorded him fleeing for his life, his white *guayabera* shirt drenched bright red with his own blood; these images were carried around the world.

International observers were present for election day. In a replay of the 1984 electoral farce, early returns showed Endara winning by a landslide, and once again the *FDP* halted the vote counting. This time, however, the observers knew Endara had won, so instead of merely proclaiming Duque the winner, the government nullified the election results. The justification: "Foreign interference"! When the term to which Barletta had been "elected" in 1984 expired on September 1, the Council of State, composed entirely of *FDP* officers and their *PRD* lapdogs, designated a close associate of Noriega's, Francisco Rodríguez, as the newest figurehead president.

Operation "Just Cause"

Relations between the United States and Panama deteriorated after the 1989 "election." Noriega suppressed a coup attempt by a group of *FDP* officers in October; they were summarily executed. The CIA made an abortive attempt to abduct Noriega, while President George H. W. Bush (who as CIA director in 1976 had been Noriega's "boss") issued an executive order banning Panamanian registered ships from entering U.S. ports. As Panama was second only to Liberia in the number of registries in world shipping, the order had potentially disastrous implications.

The bombastic Noriega soon proved to be his own worst enemy. Wielding a machete before a howling crowd of his adherents, he publicly "declared war" on the United States. In December, there were two separate incidents of off-duty U.S. service personnel—and one of their wives—being beaten by goons, and one U.S. serviceman was shot to death at a roadblock.

Faced with these provocations, Bush ordered the bombing of Noriega's headquarters on December 20, 1989, which was followed by an invasion by 9,500 U.S.-based paratroopers and Army Rangers in what was labeled Operation "Just Cause."

Army forces stationed in Panama also moved to seize key installations. There were casualties on both sides as the *FDP* and the Dignity Battalions offered some futile resistance. Within days, order was restored, and for once, U.S. troops were actually cheered by the Panamanians, a stark contrast to the riots of 1964. The day after the invasion, Endara was inaugurated as president. Panamanians suddenly found themselves with more individual freedom than they ever had experienced. *La Prensa* and other closed media reopened, the confiscated newspapers were returned to the widow and children of Harmodio Arias, the *FDP* was disbanded and replaced with a more benign civilian constabulary, and the country began building for the future.

Noriega went into hiding, changing his location every few hours. He obtained refuge in the residence of the papal nuncio. A U.S. psychological warfare unit, in a move considered shrewd by some and crude by others, placed powerful loudspeakers outside the building and broadcast heavy-metal rock at an overwhelming volume at the occupants of the building. The horrified nuncio told Noriega that the residence would be moved across the street and Noriega would not be welcome. Gloomily, the beaten man

surrendered, to be taken to the United States with the assurance of no death penalty. He was sentenced to 40 years in 1992 and remains behind bars.

Endara unsuccessfully tried to maintain a low profile to disguise his lack of talent. An opposition newspaper ridiculed him as "a non-musician leading an orchestra that does not play." Endara shrugged off chronic unemployment and rampant corruption as normal occurrences. By 1993 his government became a caretaker; influential cabinet members resigned to take part in 1994 presidential elections.

Ernesto Pérez Balladares

At the turn of the year, the organization that had supported Noriega, the *PRD*, nominated Ernesto Pérez Balladares, a former Citi-bank official with a U.S. education, as its presidential candidate. He carefully distanced himself from Noriega, and won the election against a divided opposition. Running a strong second was Mireya Moscoso, the young widow of Arnulfo Arias, running as the *Arnulfista* candidate.

In 1996, U.S. newspapers reported that Pérez Balladares had received funds from drug traffickers for his presidential campaign. The president threatened not to extend the work permit of a Peruvian investigative journalist, Gustavo Gorriti, working at *La Prensa*, accusing him of "masterminding a conspiracy" to undermine his government. A few days later, however, the president publicly confessed that the charges were true but insisted he had not known.

In 1997, *La Prensa* reported that Pérez Balladares had delayed passage of a new antitrust law to give his cousin time to acquire control of a second television station. This time the president revoked Gorriti's work permit, becoming the center of a storm of international condemnation from journalism organizations and human rights groups. He finally relented and agreed to extend Gorriti's work permit.

Other critics accused the president of nepotism and cronyism. International shipping companies expressed concerns that as the day inched closer for Panama to take over canal operations, Pérez Balladares was appointing friends and relatives to the Panama Canal Commission, now fully Panamanian. Even members of the president's own party criticized the appointments.

Panamanian officials resorted to yet another time-honored counterattack against media criticism: libel suits. Unlike the United States, Latin American countries have loosely defined defamation laws that allow public officials to sue for the expression of critical opinions; Panamanian officials under both Endara and Pérez Bal-

Far from the capital's cosmopolitan life: Cuna Indians of the San Blas Islands

Panama

ladares resorted to it; Endara once sued a political cartoonist!

On the positive side, Pérez Balladares put the economy on a solid footing, nationally and internationally, through privatization and fiscal discipline and through a new bank law to curtail the laundering of drug money, thus improving the country's image abroad.

Panama marked a major milestone in September 1997 when the U.S. Southern Command moved its headquarters from Quarry Heights to Miami, turning over the long-time U.S. nerve center atop Ancon Hill on the edge of Panama City to the Panamanians. Albrook Air Base also reverted to Panamanian control. Another milestone in the transfer of the former Canal Zone to Panama came in 1999 when the U.S. Army departed Fort Clayton for the last time, ending a U.S. military presence of 96 years. The Americans' departure also was a reminder that the payroll of the U.S. bases, which once pumped $370 million into the economy, was drying up.

Mireya Moscoso

Pérez Balladares became the fourth Latin American president to seek to amend the constitution to permit him to run for immediate re-election. Constitutional amendments require only a majority vote in the National Assembly, then approval by the electorate. In a referendum in August 1998, a resounding 64% voted "no" to Pérez Balladares' attempt to succeed himself, leaving the field wide open.

The *arnulfistas* again coalesced around Moscoso. The *PRD* decided to play the dynasty card as well by nominating Martín Torrijos, the 35-year-old illegitimate son of the former strongman, a businessman who earned an economics degree from Texas A&M and once managed a McDonald's franchise in Chicago.

The two candidates both pledged to maintain the canal efficiently and fairly, for the benefit of all nations. About the only issue that divided them was Moscoso vowed to attack the rampant corruption that had been evident under Pérez Balladares; what could Torrijos say? Torrijos chided Moscoso for her lack of formal training; she had studied interior design at a junior college in Miami. Of course, she had another, unspoken handicap in a *macho* society: her gender.

But the underdog woman suddenly pulled abreast of Torrijos in the polls. In a pathetic attempt to minimize a possible bandwagon effect, *PRD* loyalists bought up 20,000 copies of *La Prensa*, which carried a poll showing Moscoso ahead, and destroyed them.

On election day, May 2, 1999, Moscoso received a clear plurality of 44% to Torri-

jos' 38% and 18% for a third candidate. With voter turnout 75%, her mandate was solid despite lacking a majority. The combined anti-*PRD* vote represented a dramatic rebuke to the ruling party. Both Pérez Balladares and Torrijos graciously conceded defeat. Moscoso joined a growing number of Latin American presidents elected on their second try.

Thus, from the grave, Arnulfo Arias finally achieved a sweet triumph, as his widow defeated the son of the man who had overthrown him in 1968. Moscoso, 52, had married Arias in exile in 1969, when he was 67 and she was 22, and was with him until his death in 1988. Very possibly it was his memory and his populist message, which she exploited, coupled with disturbingly high unemployment of 12.8%, that was responsible for her victory.

Moscoso was sworn in as Panama's first woman president on September 1, 1999, the 31st anniversary of her late husband's ill-fated inauguration in 1968. Moscoso was only the second elected female president in Latin America, after Nicaragua's Violeta Chamorro.

It was an ugly transition. Pérez Balladares had packed the Supreme Court with last-minute appointees, denied public funds for the open-air inaugural ceremony Moscoso had requested at a stadium, and even ramrodded legislation through the lame-duck Assembly that restricted presidential powers. Pérez Balladares declined to attend the inauguration to place the presidential sash on his successor's shoulders as is traditional.

Moscoso received a sweet consolation for her predecessor's ungentlemanly actions when two small parties, Solidarity and National Liberal, withdrew from their coalition with the *PRD* and joined the *Panameñista Party* in a new coalition, giving it a one-seat majority in the 71-seat National Assembly.

Because of Y2K fears, the date for the ceremony transferring control of the canal was moved from December 31 to December 14, 1999. Representing the United States, appropriately enough, was former President Jimmy Carter, who had signed the new treaties in 1977. With his and Moscoso's signatures, Panama at last enjoyed full sovereignty over its territory and over the canal.

In 2001, a two-year, $300 million project was completed that widened the Gaillard Cut, the "ditch" section of the canal, by 40 yards, increasing its traffic potential by 20 percent. The following year, canal tolls were raised 8%, the first increase since the Panamanian takeover; they were increased another 4% in 2003—the centennial year of the Bunau-Varilla Treaty. The pricing system also was changed from a per-ton basis to the type of ship and cargo.

Former President Mireya Moscoso

The increases were deemed necessary to keep the canal competitive.

The country experienced a catharsis of sorts in 2002 when a special "truth commission" on disappearances and mysterious deaths during the 1968–89 military regimes presented its report to Moscoso. The commission investigated 168 cases and reached conclusions on 110. Of those, 70 were found to be assassinations of political dissidents, most of them during the Torrijos period. Another 40 remain unsolved.

The remainder of Moscoso's presidency was marred by various allegations of corruption, which proved an albatross around the *Panameñista* Party's neck in the next election. One that continues to embroil the country revolved around allegations that *panameñista* legislators accepted bribes from a consortium seeking to build the so-called Multimodal Industrial and Service Center *(CEMIS)* at the old U.S. military airfield of France Field, near Colón.

In the waning days of her administration, Moscoso provoked a diplomatic row with Cuba. The Cuban government told Moscoso it understood she was considering pardoning four Cuban exiles imprisoned in Panama for planning an assassination attempt on Fidel Castro there in 2000 and warned that it would sever diplomatic relations if she did. Moscoso denied such plans, condemned Cuba for its language, recalled Panama's ambassador to Cuba and ordered the Cuban ambassador to leave Panama. Six days before leaving office, she abruptly pardoned the four for "humanitarian" reasons, saying she feared her successor would extradite them to Cuba, where they would be executed. Cuba broke diplomatic relations,

Panama

calling Moscoso an "accomplice and protector of terrorism" and the pardons "repugnant and treacherous."

The most notorious of the four men is Luis Posada Carriles, who in 1985 escaped from prison in Venezuela where he was awaiting retrial for masterminding the bombing of a Cuban airliner in 1976 that killed 73 people. Consequently, Venezuela also severed diplomatic relations with Panama because of the pardons. Posada eventually turned up in Miami, where he was arrested in 2005, not on a fugitive warrant but for entering the country illegally. Cuba and Venezuela demanded he be extradited to Venezuela. Posada Carilles was indicted in 2009 by a U.S. grand jury and was scheduled to go on trial in 2010. (see Cuba).

Martín Torrijos

Martín Torrijos, still just 39, announced his second bid for the presidency in the May 2004 election. He received the *PRD*'s nomination and that of the Popular Party, the descendant of the Christian Democrats, forming an alliance called *Patria Nueva*. The *Panameñistas* nominated Moscoso's personal choice, Foreign Minister José Miguel Alemán, who formed an alliance with two other parties called *Visión de País*. Former President Endara also entered the race as candidate of a movement called *Solidaridad*. Rounding out the field was Ricardo Martinelli, a multimillionaire supermarket magnate, of *Cambio Democrático*.

Torrijos promised to clean up the endemic corruption (neglecting to mention that it had been also rife in the Pérez Balladares administration, in which he served as a deputy government and justice minister). Unlike his father, he was not a *gringo*-baiter. Educated at Texas A&M, he was a practical businessman and advocated a free-trade agreement with the United States. He even cleaned up the *PRD*'s image for his generation of voters by purging it of some of the unsavory elements left over from the dictatorship. He was endorsed by the popular singer-actor Rubén Blades (see Culture).

On May 2, 76.9% of Panamanians voted, slightly more than in 1999. The results:

Torrijos	711,447	47.7%
Endara	462,766	30.9%
Alemán	245,845	16.6%
Martinelli	79,595	5.3%

The Cuban pardons overshadowed the September 1, 2004 inauguration of Torrijos, who called them "unacceptable," and he restored diplomatic relations with both Cuba and Venezuela soon after taking office. Despite the tension, Moscoso was far

Former President Martín Torrijos

more gracious to Torrijos at his inauguration than Pérez Balladares had been to her. She also had the satisfaction of serving out her full term, something her late husband was denied three times—the last time by the father of the man who succeeded her.

Two months after Moscoso left office, the electoral tribunal revoked her immunity from prosecution. She was asked to account for the alleged disappearance of $70 million in public funds during her presidency. She called the charges politically motivated, even though she brazenly admitted spending $3 million, which she said was justified—to maintain her image!

Torrijos took a businesslike approach to solving pressing economic problems. Although the economy was showing encouraging growth (see Economy), he inherited a huge budget deficit, a crushing public debt and a bloated public pension system that was $100 million in the red. Torrijos raised taxes, and his plan to increase the retirement age for men from 62 to 65 and to raise social security contributions led to violent protests, mostly by teachers and construction workers, in 2005. Nonetheless, the National Assembly approved the changes 43–30. The reforms allow Panama to borrow money at lower interest rates.

Torrijos then turned to expansion of the canal. He called a referendum, held on October 22, 2006, on whether or not to invest $5.2 billion to build a new set of wider, deeper locks on each coast; instead of creating new reservoirs, the water would be recycled. About $2.3 billion would be borrowed, the rest raised by increased canal tolls. The project is expected to take seven years and create up to 9,000 jobs at its peak. Critics warned of environmental dangers and cost overruns, and a former canal authority director said it would be far less costly to transship cargo

by land between superports on each coast for the 300 "post-Panamax" ships that are too large to transit the canal. Voter turnout was a disappointing 43% of the 2.1 million eligible, but the voters approved expansion by a resounding 76.3%.

Work formally began with a ceremony on September 3, 2007, when part of a hill alongside the Gaillard Cut was blasted away. Torrijos and former President Carter attended the ceremony.

Torrijos entered into free-trade talks with the United States, which broke down when Panamanian producers of pork, chicken and rice complained that they could be undermined by cheaper U.S. imports. President Bush visited Panama in 2005. In their meeting, Bush and Torrijos agreed to push ahead with their bilateral trade talks. Panama is not included in the recently created Dominican Republic-Central American Free Trade Agreement.

Torrijos and Bush the FTA in a meeting in Washington in June 2007 and the Panamanian National Assembly approved it in July, but a new glitch arose when the National Assembly elected as its president Pedro Miguel González Pinzón, who was wanted in the United States in connection with the shooting deaths of two U.S. Army sergeants in 1992 during the visit of the first President Bush. González Pinzón was acquitted of the charges in Panama in 1997. The U.S. Congress balked on approval of the FTA. Torrijos wanted González Pinzón to step down for the good of the country, but the *PRD*'s left wing argued it would be an infringement of national dignity to yield to U.S. pressure. González Pinzón agreed not to seek another term as Assembly president when his term expired. Although he has now been replaced, the U.S. Congress still not approved the FTA as of mid-2010.

Meanwhile, one Panamanian the United States did hold, Manuel Noriega, completed his prison sentence in 2007. Panama had sought his extradition, but Torrijos thought better of it, because Panamanian law prohibits extradition, and Noriega was still wanted in France (see Recent Developments).

Ricardo Martinelli

With a booming economy and a popular president, the *PRD* should have been favored to hold power in the 2009 presidential election. But the *PRD* unwisely nominated Balbina Herrera, the housing minister and a member of the left wing of the party, who had an unsavory reputation as a Noriega protégé. Endara again quixotically entered the race as an independent. But instead of the usual fragmentation, the *Panameñistas* and other opposition parties rallied around the *Cambio Democrático* of

Panama

Ricardo Martinelli, 57, owner of the Super 99 supermarket chain, who had placed a poor fourth in the 2004 race.

Martinelli campaigned as a centrist and as an outsider, pledging to combat the corruption that had plagued the administrations of both the *PRD* and the *Panameñistas*. Like Ross Perot, he said he would use his skills as a successful businessman to run the country more efficiently. This time Blades, who served at Torrijos' tourism minister, endorsed Martinelli, whom polls showed the heavy favorite.

Herrera futilely tried to use Martinelli's reported net worth of $400 million against him, and she argued that his plan to cut the corporate income tax rate was a blatant conflict of interest. But the voters liked the message of the handsome businessman with the take-charge attitude, and on May 3, 74% of them went to the polls to deliver their mandate:

Martinelli	952,333	60.1%
Herrera	597,227	37.5%
Endara	36,867	2.0%

It was the first time since the establishment of democracy that a candidate had won with an absolute majority. Martinelli, son of Italian immigrants, became the third consecutive president to win on his second try, and the latest to have been educated in the United States; he earned a bachelor's of business administration from the University of Arkansas. His victory was a stunning deviation from the trend of leftist victories from Guatemala to Uruguay in recent years.

Martinelli's *Cambio* won only 14 of the 71 National Assembly seats, while the *PRD* won 26 and the *Panamañistas*, 22.

Panama's inauguration day was advanced from September 1 to July 1.

President Ricardo Martinelli

Carlota—a Panamanian beauty in native costume

Recent Developments

In July 2009, the Supreme Court agreed to re-open, after four years, the investigation into the *CEMIS* scandal. By mid-2010, it was threatening to involve prominent members of both major parties, including former Presidents Moscoso of the *Panameñistas* and Pérez Balladares of the *PRD*, as well as *PRD* presidential candidate Herrera.

Former President Endara died of a heart attack from complications of kidney failure on September 28, 2009, at the age of 73. He received a state funeral at the Metropolitan Cathedral.

Panama has been spared the political hot potato of what to do with Noriega, whose U.S. prison term ended in 2007 but who had remained behind bars pending a French extradition request. His U.S. attorneys requested that he be allowed to return to Panama, citing his status as a prisoner of war under the Geneva Convention. Noriega faces murder charges in Panama, but because of his age he would be allowed to serve any sentence under house arrest. He turned 76 on February 11, 2010. Federal judges denied his request, and the U.S. Supreme Court declined in January 2010 to hear his appeal. U.S. Secretary of State Hillary Clinton finally signed the French extradition request on April 26. He arrived in France the next day; his attorneys were not even notified the request had been signed. He faces money-laundering charges in France, less serious than murder, but he

would serve his sentence in prison and will likely die there.

Culture: Panama's culture is a reflection of its unique geographical situation as a crossroads of both terrestrial and maritime traffic between two oceans and two continents. There is a polyglot of ethnic groups, not one of which predominates: the indigenous Indians, many of them unassimilated, such as the Cuna tribe of the San Blas Islands on the Caribbean coast that contributed the distinctive *mola* tapestries that have become so identifiable with Panamanian culture; the Caucasians, not merely Spanish descendants but the scions of latter-day European, Arab and Jewish immigrants who today account for a disproportionate share of the country's wealth and political power; the *mestizos*, who outnumber the first two groups; blacks and mulattos, who are about equal in number to the *mestizos*, descended not from slaves as in Brazil, but from workers imported from the British West Indies to help construct the canal; and the sizable community of Orientals, principally Chinese, who have filtered into the country in the decades since the completion of the canal.

Because of this, Panama boasts a distinctive culture, particularly in its folk music, dances and costumes that its tourist industry has helped to preserve. In popular music it also has made some contributions. Its best-known singer, Rubén Blades, won a following in Latin America before appearing in a number of U.S.

movies and receiving a U.S. Grammy Award. He ran for president of Panama in 1994 but ran third with 18% of the vote.

Literacy is relatively high in Panama, but the small population has not been sufficient to support much book or magazine publishing. Panama boasts one of Latin America's oldest daily newspapers, *La Estrella de Panamá*, founded in 1853. Unfortunately, *La Estrella's* owners were blackmailed into editorial support for dictators Torrijos and later Noriega, and the paper has never fully recovered from its reputation as a sycophant.

Until the U.S. invasion of 1989 that brought down the Noriega dictatorship, aggressive and critical journalism in Panama was a risky business. *El Panamá América*, expropriated from Harmodio Arias by Torrijos in 1968, was restored to his family and remains the second-leading daily. The country's leading daily, *La Prensa*, was established in 1980 by Roberto Eisenmann and courageously stood up to both the Torrijos and Noriega dictatorships. For this it was repeatedly vandalized and finally closed in 1987. The month after the U.S. invasion, its repaired presses began rolling again.

Economy: Panama's economy is based on trade brought to it by an accident of geography. Farm output is unable to feed the population; the major source of income (about 20% of the gross national product) is tied to the Canal. The Torrijos regime sought to diversify the economy, and established incentives to make Panama an international banking center. Passage of the Panama Canal treaties has had the effect of stimulating new industrial investments. An oil pipeline enables the transport of crude by supertankers ocean-to-ocean, compensating for their inability to fit through the narrow canal, providing substantial revenues to Panama.

Much of the impetus for Panama becoming a major international banking center in the 1970s and 1980s stemmed from a Swiss-style banking law that made Panama a favored spot for the laundering of illegal drug money. Not until 1997 did Panama make a concerted effort to change the law and remove this stigma.

The prodigious economic spinoff from the canal, including the thousands of jobs generated by the canal itself and the numerous U.S. military bases, gave Panama among the highest standards of living in Latin America, although income inequality was the second-worst in Latin America in 2008; 28.6% of Panamanians still lived in poverty in 2006.

Panama has avoided the hyperinflation that has plagued so many of its neighbors. The reason: The official currency is called the Balboa, but in reality the U.S. dollar is the country's legal tender, which is a boon for international banking and provides monetary stability. (Panama has its own coins, which are identical in size and weight with U.S. denominations and thus are interchangeable in vending machines.) Largely because of the dollar-based economy, inflation has remained manageable. For that reason, Ecuador and El Salvador have emulated Panama by replacing their currency with the dollar.

One of the country's greatest economic success stories is the Colón Free Zone, on the Caribbean side, created in 1948. It imports and re-exports products from all over the world and is now the second-largest free-trade zone in the world after Hong Kong. It accounts for more than $16 billion of imports and re-exports annually as of 2010, $1.3 billion of which is pumped into the Panamanian economy.

On the negative side, Panama has one of the most cumbersome national debts per capita in the world. In 2009, the public debt was estimated at 49.5% of GDP.

The Panamanian takeover of the canal on December 31, 1999, was historic, and while it was no economic panacea, Panama's stewardship has been far more successful than anticipated. When Panama took over, it generated $500 million in revenue; in 2005, it was $1.2 billion, with an operating profit of $183 million. In 2008, revenue hit a record $2.007 billion in the fiscal year that ends on September 30, but it declined to $1.96 billion in 2009 because the global recession reduced traffic. In the first quarter of the 2010 fiscal year, transits were down 4% but revenue still showed a 3.1% increase over the same period in 2009, $360 million. Total revenue for the 2010 fiscal year was projected to be $2.02 billion. The canal still averages about 14,000 transits annually, and accounts for 4% of all ocean-going trade.

Because 19% of cargo ships are too large to transit the century-old locks, President Martín Torrijos called for reinvesting $5.3 billion in expanding the canal to increase its capacity, which Panamanian approved in a referendum in late 2006.

Panama's GDP growth in 2002 was only 0.9%, but it rebounded to 4.3% in 2003, 6.2% in 2004 and 6.9% in 2005. Since then, its growth has been at boom levels, and among the highest in Latin America: 8.7% in 2006, 11.5% in 2007, 9.2% in 2008. While most Latin American countries saw GDP decline from the 2008–09 global recession, Panama's still grew by 2.4% in 2009.

Key to the boom has been an enormous influx of foreign investment, which grew from 16% of GDP in 2006 to 24.9% in 2008. Occidental Petroleum and Qatar Petroleum are planning to build a $7 billion oil refinery at Puerto Armuelles on the Pacific coast, while the Chinese are planning a huge new port on the Caribbean side. A British firm is planning to turn the former Howard Air Force Base into an industrial facility, while Donald Trump has plans to build a high-rise hotel and resort.

The boom has reduced chronically high unemployment, which was 8.6% in 2007 and 5.6% in 2008. With the recession, it rose to 7.2% in 2009. Inflation in 2008 was 8.8% and 2.3% in 2009.

With the boom has come increased international pressure for Panama to tighten regulations of its banks, which are seen as money launderers, much like those in the Cayman Islands. President Ricardo Martinelli is responding to the pressure, but slowly, lest he derail the gravy train and appear to be caving in to foreigners.

The Future: Panama has become something of a Latin American success story since the fall of the Noriega dictatorship. Its economy is booming, and it has peacefully transferred power four times among competing parties.

The canal remains Panama's greatest hope for continued economic growth, and hopefully the $5.3 billion expansion will be completed in time for the centennial of the canal's opening, in 2014.

President Ricardo Martinelli, who took office on July 1, 2009, represents a fresh face and a fresh approach, a successful, multi-millionaire businessman from outside the two major political movements. He has inherited an enviable economy, and he promises to use his business skills to run the country efficiently, but he needs to address Panama's three greatest remaining concerns: institutionalized corruption, a crushing public debt, and one of the most inequitable income distributions in Latin America. If he can accomplish that, then his movement, *Cambio Democrático* (Democratic Change), will live up to its Obamaesque name.

Washing clothes at an outdoor sluice

The Republic of Paraguay

The unspoiled beauty of a whitewater river in Paraguay

Area: 157,047 square miles.

Population: 6.4 million (2010 estimate).

Capital City: Asunción (Pop. 1.2 million in 2002; estimated 1.8 million in metropolitan area).

Climate: The eastern section (*Oriental*) lies in a temperate zone; the western (*Occidental*) section is hot and oppressive. Rainfall is heaviest from February to May; most of Paraguay receives adequate water except for the western plains.

Neighboring Countries: Brazil (East and Northeast); Argentina (South); Bolivia (West and Northwest).

Official Language: Spanish.

Other Principal Tongues: Guaraní, a native Indian dialect, spoken as a first language by half the population.

Ethnic Background: *Mestizo* (mixed Spanish and Guaraní ancestry).

Principal Religion: Roman Catholic Christianity.

Chief Commercial Products: Cotton, soybean, timber, vegetable oils, coffee, light manufactured goods.

Currency: Guaraní.

Gross Domestic Product: U.S. $13.77 billion in 2009 ($2,221 per capita).

Former Colonial Status: Spanish Crown Colony (1537–1811).

Independence Date: May 14, 1811.

Chief of State: Fernando Armindo Lugo Méndez (b. May 30, 1951), president (since August 15, 2008)

National Flag: Red, white and blue horizontal stripes. The white stripe displays the national seal on one side and the words *Paz y Justicia* (Peace and Justice) on the opposite side. This is the only flag in the world having different sides.

Although Paraguay is landlocked, he Paraná River forms part of the boundary with Argentina and Brazil and links Paraguay with the Atlantic. The north to south Paraguay River, a Paraná tributary, divides the country into two regions with very different characters. Paraguay's third important river, the Pilcomayo, forms the southwest frontier with Argentina and joins the Paraguay opposite Asunción.

The eastern (*Oriental*) region of Paraguay, between the Paraguay and the Paraná rivers, is referred to as Paraguay proper. Containing approximately 40% of the nation's territory, the *Oriental* has fertile rolling plains with scattered hills in the south central portion, rising to the Amabay Mountains (2,700 feet) in the northeast along the Brazilian border. This is the most densely populated region of Paraguay.

The western (*Occidental*) region of the nation, commonly called the *Chaco*, is a hot, grassy prairie, interspersed with stands of hardwood known as *quebracho* (axe-breaker). Crossed by numerous unnavigable streams, its underground water is too salty for irrigation or human consumption; until recently this region was largely uninhabited. Today, through the impounding of rainwater, the Chaco is dotted with cattle ranches and the *quebracho* is harvested for tannin.

History: The history of Paraguay centers on the capital, Asunción, and on the villages within a 60-mile radius around that city on the eastern side of the Paraguay River. To the primitive people who roamed the area prior to the Spanish conquest, the lush plains lying between the Paraguay and the Paraná rivers were their traditional Garden of Eden. Of the many tribes which resided here, most were of the Tupi-Guaraní linguistic group. An amiable people, living by trapping, fishing and simple plantings, they offered little opposition to the Spaniards who explored the Paraná valley and established a fort at Asunción on August 15, 1537, some 70 years prior to the first English settlement in North America.

Though neglected by the Spanish crown, the colony prospered and at the end of 20 years boasted 1,500 Spanish residents, a cathedral, a textile mill and a growing cattle industry. For two centuries, Asunción and its pleasant valley developed slowly while serving as the seat of Spanish authority in South America east of the Andes Mountains and south of the Portuguese colony in Brazil.

From Asunción, expeditions founded the cities of Santa Fé, Corrientes and Buenos Aires. Beginning in 1588, a company of Jesuit missionaries gathered some 100,000 Indians into mission villages and taught them better methods of farming, stock raising and handicrafts. The Jesuits protected their wards against enslavement by civil governors, settlers and Brazilian slave hunters; in the process, they helped to hold Paraguay and Uruguay for the Spanish. Unfortunately for the colony, the Jesuits were expelled in 1767.

Paraguay's transition from colonial status to independence was swift and unspectacular. In 1810, following the declaration of independence by Buenos Aires, Paraguay was invited to join with the Argentine ex-colony. The invitation was rejected and in 1811 Paraguay defeated a force sent from Buenos Aires to compel acceptance of Argentine leadership. A congress declared Paraguay to be a free and independent state and a five-man ruling council was established.

Dissension erupted; in 1814 a hopelessly deadlocked Congress voted full dictatorial powers to Dr. José Gaspar Rodríguez de Francia, who ruled until 1840. Austere, frugal, honest, dedicated and brutally cruel, he set the dictatorial pattern that persisted until 1989. Francia introduced improved methods in agriculture and in stock raising and was able to force the Paraguayan soil to produce more than ever before. Although dissent was ruthlessly suppressed, Paraguay was well ordered and well fed.

Francia's death created a power vacuum and a year of turmoil. The man who came to power, Carlos Antonio López, imposed a constitution, but one that let him

rule with the same autocratic powers that Francia had. López established trade and diplomatic relations with other countries and groomed his son, Francisco Solano López, to succeed him.

The son enjoyed playing soldier and built up Paraguay's army. After he succeeded his father, he gave himself the rank of *mariscal* (field marshal) and looked around for someone to fight. He foolishly declared war on Brazil, Argentina and Uruguay in 1865, a decision that was to decimate the country's male population. In the bloody, five-year War of the Triple Alliance, Paraguay's three enemies invaded the country and engaged in what today would be called genocide. Of a population of 520,000, at least 300,000 Paraguayans were slaughtered; only 28,746 males survived. It was a demographic cataclysm from which it took the country generations to recover. "Mariscal" López, for whom the main boulevard of Asunción is named today, was himself killed in the Battle of Cerro Corá with the Brazilians in 1870, which ended the pointless struggle, the costliest in the history of post-colonial South America. It says something of the Paraguayan mentality that Solano López still is revered as a national hero, as is Francia.

Between 1870 and 1932 Paraguay slowly recovered and remained at peace with its neighbors. However, internal turmoil persisted and presidents were put in office by gunplay rather than by elections. From 1870

until 1954, Paraguay had 39 presidents, most of whom were jailed, murdered or exiled before they completed their term. As in many Latin American countries, the Conservative and Liberal parties competed for power, but there was little alternation between them; the Conservatives ruled from 1870–1904, when the Liberals gained power in a modest social revolution and governed until 1936. Economically, there was some progress. Immigrants from Italy, Spain, Germany and Argentina developed the agriculture, stock raising and forestry industries. Of the 800,000 population in 1928, the majority were illiterate and landless; profits from agriculture and industry went to foreign owners, mostly Argentine.

The Paraguay-Bolivia border remained undefined after the war of 1870. A humiliated Paraguay sought to extend its barren Chaco territory. In the 1920s, it granted a concession to Canadian Mennonites to establish a colony in the Chaco, called Filadelfia, which is still there today and accounts for more than half the country's dairy products. Bolivia sought access to the Atlantic via ports on the Paraguay River. War broke out in 1932, ending in a 1935 truce that awarded Paraguay about 20,000 square miles at a cost of 36,000 dead, and a seriously damaged economy. Six of the Chaco War's heroes later became president.

A revolt by Chaco War veterans in 1936 brought Colonel Rafael Franco into the presidency. Like his Spanish namesake who took power that very year, Franco

Paraguay

initiated a quasi-fascist economic system that would endure for 50 years. He was deposed in 1937 by Félix Paiva, and a decade of upheaval ensued. Paiva allowed nominally democratic elections in 1939, which the Liberals won behind the candidacy of General Estigarribia, a Chaco War hero. But Estigarribia perished in a plane crash in 1940 and his war minister, Higinio Morínigo, seized power and ruled as dictator for eight years.

In 1947, the old Conservative Party renamed itself the National Republican Association, popularly called the *Colorado* Party, and staged a coup that toppled the dictatorship and began an unbroken period of party dominance that continued until 2008. Five presidents came and went during the next three years, until the election of the *Colorados'* Federico Cháves in 1950.

The Stroessner Era, 1954–89

In July 1954, the army revolted against Cháves and installed General Alfredo Stroessner, son of a Bavarian brewing company accountant and the daughter of a wealthy Paraguayan family. He was "re-elected" to the presidency by a large vote seven times, serving for 35 years. Although he initially allowed opposition elements to contest elections, they were eliminated by 1963. He later allowed the Liberal Party to field candidates in the elections in 1973 and 1978, but the outcomes of all the elections during his rule were preordained.

In 1973, for example, Stroessner received 681,306 votes over his opponent, Gustavo Riart of the Liberal Party, who got 198,096. Abstentions and blank ballots accounted for 35%. Since Stroessner's *Colorado* Party won a majority of the viotes, it was by law entitled to two thirds of the seats in Congress. The remaining one third was assigned to the opposition by a prescribed formula.

General Alfredo Stroessner

Two small opposition groups were similar in outlook to the *Colorados*, favoring free enterprise with minimal state intervention in the economy. However, the Liberals favored a more democratic government. Whenever any individual appeared to gain *too much* popularity during Stroessner's years, he was either jailed, exiled or simply disappeared.

With solid military backing, Stroessner ruled Paraguay as his personal fiefdom. He emphasized political stability, road construction and a strong stand against communism. Living standards rose slowly but steadily during his tenure. Political stability also attracted foreign investment.

Relations with the Catholic Church were generally poor, particularly when Stroessner sought to undermine the church's Marandú rural public housing program. Supported with funds obtained in the United States, the effort attempted to provide the nation's 100,000 impoverished Indian population with medical, legal and economic assistance. The conservative elite viewed such attempts to help the Indians as a "communist conspiracy." Five Jesuit priests in the movement were deported and others were jailed. (Even as recently as April 2005, the democratically elected Paraguayan Congress rejected a bill that would have established a 114,000-hectare reserve for the nomadic Ayoreo tribe in the Chaco, the last tribe outside the Amazon to have resisted contact with outsiders.)

Stroessner ruled by "state of siege" legislation that suspended constitutional guarantees. It was renewed every 90 days.

Corruption within the ruling *Colorado* Party was reported by the independent newspaper *ABC Color*, by some radio stations and by the Paraguayan Episcopal Conference in late 1984. The first two were closed down and the latter was ignored.

Stroessner was elected to his eighth term by a majority of 89% in 1988, at the age of 75. There were the usual irregularities and voter apathy. The *Colorado* Party became divided over the issue of a transition. The *tradicionalistas* wanted the aging dictator to step aside, while the *oficialistas* (also called *militantes*) thought Stroessner, barring ill health, should remain in office. The matter was postponed by Stroessner's candidacy for re-election. When *Radio Ñandutí* became too vocal, it was jammed.

Stroessner Falls

When Stroessner disappeared for 10 days in 1988 there were rumors he had died. He underwent prostate surgery at an undisclosed location; his recovery was slow. Sensing the time was right, the commander-in-chief of the military, General Andrés Rodríguez, staged a coup in February 1989, exiling the now-feeble

Stroessner to Brazil without opposition. Low estimates of deaths during the coup were 50, high ones 300. An era had ended.

Taking the opposition by surprise, Rodríguez announced elections for May 1, 1989; Rodríguez became the *Colorado* candidate, assuring his election to a four-year term. He projected the image of a populist in contrast to the aloof, distant Stroessner.

Things didn't really change in Paraguay. Rodríguez received more than 74% of the vote, and the *Colorado* Party received the usual two thirds of the seats in both houses iof Congress. Power struggles erupted within the party occurred between the "democratic" faction and the slightly more conservative "traditionalists." Rodríguez favored the former, even though his daughter was married to Stroessner's son.

Under Stroessner and Rodríguez, Paraguay was a giant fencing operation, the largest in Latin America. If one wanted to buy or sell anything that had been stolen, Paraguay was (and still is, to a large degree) the place to go. Rodríguez was reported to have ties to the drug trade, including to the infamous Auguste Joseph Ricord of *The French Connection* infamy, who sought refuge in Paraguay in the 1970s; the obvious protection he received was a bone of contention between Paraguay and the United States, which sought his extradition.

The smuggling enterprise was shaken in 1992 when a whistle-blowing colonel disclosed that the army had a virtual monopoly on fencing expensive, stolen cars. Surprisingly, Rodríguez removed four top officers, probably to avoid a charge that he was also involved.

Rodríguez, who was in ill health anyway, was barred by the new 1992 constitution from re-election, so he retired to a palatial estate. When journalists asked him how he could build such an estate on his salary as a general or president, he replied arrogantly that it was from the money he had saved by giving up smoking! He did not quit soon enough; he died of cancer in 1997.

Juan Carlos Wasmosy

In late 1992, preparing for primary and general elections, the *Colorados* again became badly divided. The "democratic" faction prevailed and nominated Juan Carlos Wasmosy, a civil engineer and businessman. The conservatives, who had backed a charismatic army general named Lino Oviedo, ultimately supported Wasmosy. There are still suspicions that Wasmosy and Oviedo both stuffed ballot boxes, but Wasmosy's people managed to stuff more than did Oviedo's. Wasmosy was then opposed by two candidates in the May 1993 general

Children celebrate Independence Day in a small town

election—Domingo Laino, long-time leader of the Authentic Radical Liberal Party *(PLRA)*, and Guillermo Caballero Vargas of the National Encounter Party. Wasmosy won an expanded five-year term with more than 40% of the vote after campaigning on promises to improve the economy and employment. As an encouraging sign of increased pluralization and decentralization, the governors of the 17 departments were elected directly for the first time, and the Liberals captured Central Department, where Asunción is located.

The Oviedo Factor

The military promised to continue "cogoverning" with the *Colorado* Party. But the main political parties agreed upon a "governability pact" that excluded the police and military from party membership. Its signing was postponed, however, after attacks by *Colorado* supporters on opposition legislators.

A Liberal politician exposed the existence of secret police files in 1992 containing facts behind the disappearance of some 15,000 people during the Stroessner years. It also allegedly contained evidence of the existence of Operation Condor, a cooperative effort against leftists by Paraguay, Chile, Argentina and Uruguay during the 1980s that arranged disappearances of undesired people.

Democratic forces held their breath in April 1996 when General Oviedo publicly called for Wasmosy to resign. It amounted to an attempted coup, but the rest of the armed forces failed to move against the civilian president. Wasmosy then summoned Oviedo to his office and ordered him to retire, promising him the cabinet post of defense secretary. For 27 tense hours, Oviedo demurred, provoking fears of a throwback to Paraguay's bad old days of military strongmen. In the end, he relented and retired, but public protests against his accepting the cabinet post led Wasmosy to withdraw the offer. Paraguay, at least, appeared to have established civilian control over the military. Wasmosy went even further that December, cashiering 207 cavalry officers who he said had supported Oviedo's short-lived rebellion. A judge overturned Wasmosy's order a month later, citing insufficient evidence. An appeals court overturned the judge's decision and Wasmosy signed a decree dismissing the officers. Once again, civilian authority prevailed.

The Oviedo saga continued, however. In the *Colorado* primary in September 1997, Oviedo won the nomination for the May 10, 1998, presidential election. This infuriated Wasmosy, and their relations went from poor to deplorable. Oviedo accused the president of incompetence and corruption; Wasmosy, falling back on his authority as commander-in-chief, ordered the general arrested for insubordination. Oviedo was a fugitive for 42 days before turning himself in. Wasmosy placed him under house arrest for 30 days.

Legal battles ensued between the two men in both civilian and military courts. In December 1997, the nation's top electoral court rejected a plea from Wasmosy to disqualify Oviedo as the *Colorado* candidate. There was another coup scare in January 1998 when, after a judge indicated he might order Oviedo's release because he had never been formally charged, tanks began rumbling in the streets. The military claimed it was merely a practice for a ceremony. A determined Wasmosy assembled a special military tribunal that ordered Oviedo jailed for an "indefinite" term for his abortive 1996 coup. The tribunal then sentenced Oviedo, still a presidential candidate, to 10 years.

When it became apparent Wasmosy might not be able legally to strip Oviedo of the nomination, and faced with polls that showed the Guaraní-speaking Oviedo leading, the president pondered a decidedly undemocratic move: to postpone the election. Paraguay's *Mercosur* partners quickly reminded Wasmosy that democratic government was a condition of membership. The United States also issued a warning against postponement. Wasmosy was rescued from the role of antidemocrat when the Supreme Court voted 5–4 to uphold Oviedo's prison term, effectively disqualifying his candidacy.

Oviedo vowed to campaign from jail, but the party, facing reality, nominated

Lino Oviedo still maintains his own Web page

Paraguay

Former President Raúl Cubas

A Paraguayan *alza prima* pulled by an ox.

Oviedo's running mate, Raúl Cubas, a businessman. To mollify the Wasmosy faction, they agreed on Luis María Argaña as the new vice-presidential candidate. The 11th-hour termination of Oviedo's candidacy gave a boost to the perennial standard-bearer of the Liberals, Domingo Laino, running this time as candidate of the Democratic Alliance coalition. Now it was the *Colorado*s who called for a postponement of the election.

It was just as well for them the vote wasn't delayed. Cubas received 54% to Laino's 42%; the Democratic Alliance claimed fraud, a charge that was largely unsubstantiated. Days before the election, Cubas declared that if the *Colorado*s won, "Free, in jail, or wherever he is, Oviedo will have political power." He was to make good on that promise soon after his inauguration on August 15, 1998.

Assassination, Impeachment, Aftermath

Cubas' seven months in office were marked by Byzantine political intrigues that culminated in a high-level assassination, the president's impeachment and then his resignation and the ignominious flights into exile of both Cubas and Oviedo. These events sorely tested whether this fledgling democracy would long endure.

Three days after his inauguration, Cubas pardoned Oviedo, which led to jubilant demonstrations by the general's supporters, who chanted, *"Lino presidente!"* Cubas then appointed a new military tribunal, packed with Oviedo sympathizers, which dismissed all charges against the general. This brash action plunged Paraguay into a constitutional crisis, pitting the executive branch against both the legislative and judicial branches; under Stroessner's rule, of course, it would have been a short-lived contest. Congress threatened Cubas with impeachment.

In December 1998, the Supreme Court ruled Cubas' pardon and the military tribunal unconstitutional and ordered Oviedo re-incarcerated. Cubas ignored the order, creating a deep schism within the ranks of the *Colorado* Party. Heading the anti-Oviedo faction was Vice President Argaña, who prevailed in a vote by the *Colorado* leadership days later to expel Oviedo from the party. The president and vice president had not even been on speaking terms since their inauguration.

By February, there were rampant rumors that Cubas was planning a Fujimori-style military takeover, which he denied.

On February 11, the lower house of Congress voted 71–37 to charge Cubas with abuse of power for his actions the previous August—just two votes shy of the two-thirds-plus-one-vote majority needed for impeachment. Several *Colorado* deputies joined with the opposition Liberals. To further complicate this Byzantine spectacle, the armed forces high command—loyal to Oviedo—dismissed the air force generals who had refused to participate in Oviedo's barracks revolt in 1996.

As this political drama reached a climax, Vice President Argaña was assassinated in broad daylight on March 23, 1999, as he arrived at work. A vehicle containing three or four men in camouflage fatigues curbed Argaña's jeep. One threw a grenade, while others opened fire, hitting Argaña in the heart. He died at the scene. His driver also was killed and his bodyguard gravely wounded. The killing threw the country into even greater turmoil and brought international denunciations. Both Cubas and Oviedo issued statements denouncing their rival's murder, but not before thousands of Argaña's supporters took to the streets in protest; security forces opened fire, leaving seven people dead.

The next day, the Chamber of Deputies overwhelmingly voted to impeach Cubas. The anti-Cubas *Colorado*s and opposition Liberals did not come across as champions of democracy, however; at least one pro-Cubas *Colorado* deputy was roughed up when he arrived at the Congress and prevented from entering. The Senate took the case up immediately. Conviction and removal were certain.

On March 28, Cubas abruptly resigned and boarded a waiting Brazilian air force plane that flew him into a comfortable exile at a beach house in southern Brazil. Oviedo flew to Buenos Aires, where he was briefly detained for lacking immigration papers. Within a day, Argentina granted him asylum, which precluded extradition. Paraguay requested it anyway.

Senate President Luis Angel González Macchi, next in the line of succession after the president and vice president, was sworn in as interim president hours after Cubas' resignation. The army pledged him its crucial support. The new president, a former professional basketball player who had an unspectacular career as a legislator, appointed a new cabinet that included Argaña's brother and even some ministers from the opposition Liberal and National Encounter parties. Such power-sharing was unprecedented in the 52 years the *Colorado* Party had been entrenched in power.

The new government announced it would hold a presidential election in six months and that a Liberal would be the running mate of the *Colorado* candidate. Later, the Supreme Court ruled that González Macchi could serve the remainder of Cubas' five-year term.

Paraguay recalled its ambassador from Argentina after President Carlos Menem's government refused to extradite Oviedo. Paraguay recalled its envoy from Uruguay, which refused to extradite Cubas' defense minister, José Segovia Boltes, in connection with the Argaña assassination. In October, the election to succeed Menem in Argentina was won by Fernando de la Rua, who had pledged to extradite Oviedo. Sensing he had overstayed his welcome, the wily general vanished before de la Rua's inauguration.

Just after New Year's Day, 2000, Oviedo resurfaced, brazenly holding a news conference with a handful of reporters at an undisclosed location in rural Paraguay, which was reported by media throughout Latin America (this author read about it in Chilean newspapers and saw it on television there). He maintained his innocence and alleged that his enemies had murdered Argaña to discredit him. Cocky as ever, he boasted again that he would one day return as the people's champion.

Oviedo supporters in the military, the police and the Congress gave the country—and the world community—a scare in May 2000 when three armored cars parked in front of the legislative palace and fired two shots at the building. A standoff ensued, as military unit commanders declared their support for González Macchi, who declared a 30-day state of siege. Denunciations of the revolt poured in from the United States and neighboring democracies. The next morning, about 25 soldiers, a few retired officers, 12 policemen and three pro-Oviedo congressmen surrendered. The president of the Congress claimed that documents found after the revolt indicated that the mutineers planned to assassinate several *Colorado* Party leaders, including González Macchi and vice-presidential candidate Félix Argaña, the 42-year-old son of the slain vice president, who was running to fill his father's vacant seat in an August election. Oviedo sent a communiqué from his hideout to the newspaper *ABC Color* denying he was involved.

The whereabouts of the elusive general became a national—and international—obsession. Besides Paraguay and Bolivia, Oviedo sightings were reported in Brazil, which turned out to be correct. In June 2000, acting on information from Paraguayan intelligence authorities who had been tapping and tracing Oviedo's phone calls to supporters back home, Brazilian police arrested him in a posh apartment in Foz do Iguaçu, across the border from Ciudad del Este. Police found a .38 pistol, which allowed them to charge him with illegal weapons possession.

He was in jail for 18 months until December 2001, when the Brazilian Supreme Court unanimously rejected Paraguay's extradition request as "politically motivated" and ordered Oviedo released. The Paraguayan government was furious. A jubilant and boastful Oviedo vowed to return to Paraguay and run for president again.

**Former President
Luis Angel González Macchi**

In domestic politics, González Macchi's tenuous coalition with the Liberals fell apart in 2000 after the Liberals decided to return to their role as an opposition party to protest corruption. The bone of contention between the two parties was a reform bill that would have streamlined and depoliticized Paraguay's cumbersome bureaucracy, which sucks up more than 80% of the national budget. Hard-line *Colorado*s had resisted the reforms because patronage is a traditional tool by which the party has ensured support. The president also sought to privatize inefficient state-owned companies, which sparked a protest in front of the legislative palace by state workers and by landless peasants demanding free land.

After the *Colorado*-Liberal alliance fell apart, the two parties fielded separate candidates in the special election to fill the vacancy in the vice presidency. The *Colorado*s nominated Argaña's son, Félix, seemingly an unbeatable choice. But the political establishment was stunned when the Liberal candidate, Julio César "Yoyito" Franco, narrowly defeated Argaña. It was the *Colorado*s' first national-level defeat, a political event virtually on a par with the defeat of the *PRI* in Mexico's presidential election the month before.

With the opposition in the vice presidency, pressure increased on the unpopular—and unelected—González Macchi to step aside. His position was not helped by the continued deterioration of an already sour economy, nor by the embarrassing revelation that his personal BMW, worth about $130,000 but for which he reportedly paid only $80,000, apparently had been stolen in Brazil and smuggled into Paraguay.

The water control spillways at Yacyretá

Paraguay

For the second year in a row, the United States "decertified" Paraguay in 2000 as an ally in the war on drugs, citing inaction at countering rampant smuggling. Paraguay's remote Chaco region is an important way station in smuggling coca from neighboring Bolivia. The United States was also displeased when Paraguay reestablished diplomatic relations with Cuba in 1999 after a 38-year break, the last South American nation to do so. The United States recertified Paraguay in 2001.

Paraguay, which has a large Arab community, primarily Lebanese and Jordanians, was in the international spotlight following the September 11, 2001 terrorist attacks in the United States. Paraguayan police raided several Arab-owned businesses in Ciudad del Este, notorious as a smuggling center because of the porous borders with Brazil and Argentina, and detained several people. Police seized evidence of links with the Iranian-backed terrorist group Hezbollah, although not with al-Qaeda. Even before 9/11, the U.S. State Department had identified the so-called "Tri-Border" area as a hotbed of Islamic extremists.

González Macchi became even more unpopular in 2002 by declaring a state of emergency after anti-government demonstrations in three cities that left two people dead. He blamed the disturbances on Oviedo supporters and accused Vice President Franco of collaborating with them to bring down his government—an implausible scenario. Franco called for González Macchi's resignation, and mass protests continued.

Former President Cubas voluntarily returned to Paraguay in 2002 and placed himself at the disposition of the courts. He was placed under house arrest, then released pending trial. He settled on a ranch in the Chaco. In 2007, a judge acquitted him of all charges. He then sought to claim his lifetime non-voting Senate seat as a former president, but the Senate never brought his request to a vote.

González Macchi faced an impeachment trial in 2003 over the stolen BMW and for allegedly mishandling $16 million in state funds, but he was acquitted.

Nicanor Duarte Frutos

Nicanor Duarte Frutos, 46, a lawyer and former journalist from the reformist wing of the party, who had served capably as education minister under both Wasmosy and González Macchi, won the *Colorado* primary for the April 2003 presidential election. As his running mate he chose Luis Castiglioni.

After two straight defeats, Laino stepped aside in favor of Vice President Franco for the *PLRA* nomination. Pedro Fadul, a

banker, ran as the candidate of a new movement called *Patria Querida* (Beloved Fatherland). Oviedo hand-picked another lackey named Guillermo Sánchez to run as the stand-in as candidate of his whimsically named *Unión Nacional de Ciudadanos Eticos* (National Union of Ethical Citizens), or *UNACE.*

By 2003, the *Colorado* Party had been in power continuously longer than any party in the world save the North Korean Communist Party, which has ruled since 1945; the Chinese Communist Party came to power two years after the *Colorados* did. Given the unpopularity of González Macchi and the 2000 election victory of Vice President Franco, it seemed logical that 2003 would be the year the opposition finally broke the *Colorados'* 56-year grip on power. Logical in any other democracy, perhaps. The fragmented field of candidates divided the opposition vote, and Paraguay, like Mexico and Panama, does not have runoff elections; a simple plurality wins. Moreover, all the candidates vowed to combat corruption.

Turnout was 64.5% of the 2.4 million registered voters, despite the fact that voting is mandatory, possibly a reflection of the widespread disenchantment with the democratic process in Paraguay (see The Future). In the end, voters opted for the status quo:

Duarte Frutos	574,232	37.1%
Franco	370,348	24%
Fadul	328,916	21.3%
Sánchez	208,391	13.5%

The *Colorados* had little cause for gloating. They won the presidency by the smallest percentage yet, and lost their Senate majority for the first time. The Liberals also won the governorship of Caaguazú for the first time and retained the governorship of Central Department. Oviedo was an even bigger loser, given his stand-in's poor showing. Oviedo congratulated Duarte from his refuge in Brazil, but he ordered the *UNACE* bloc in Congress not to join with the *Colorados* to form a majority coalition but to remain in opposition. *UNACE,* the *PLRA, Patria Querida* and National Encounter formed an uneasy but majority opposition coalition.

Duarte Frutos, the first president born after the Colorado takeover in 1947, soon stepped on toes, vowing to overhaul the customs and internal revenue services, both notoriously corrupt and riddled with political patronage, which put him on an inevitable collision course with the *oficialista* wing of the party. He publicly vilified the country's Catholic priests as "a bunch of hypocrites" who, he charged, "had manipulated the faith" in favor of Fadul's candidacy.

Duarte Frutos and Castiglioni were inaugurated on August 15, 2003, inheriting a bankrupt government, a stagnant economy, a $2.2 billion public debt and a population that had begun to long for the comparatively prosperous and stable days of dictatorship. The much-reviled outgoing president was not even invited to place the presidential sash on his shoulders. Duarte sounded a populist theme, not only reiterating his vow to fight the "mafia" that controls smuggling and piracy, but also the "unproductive local oligarchy, who want the government to remain the lackey of its privileges."

Duarte Frutos met with President George W. Bush soon after the inauguration, the first Paraguayan president to visit the White House. Bush was not pleased that Paraguay rejected a U.S. request to send a contingent of troops to Iraq, as the Dominican Republic, El Salvador, Honduras and Nicaragua did. Paraguay also abstained on the vote before the U.N. Human Rights Commission in Geneva in April 2004 to condemn Cuba for human rights violations. A large number of Paraguayans now study medicine in Cuba, while Cuba has sent many doctors to provide medical care in rural Paraguay.

Duarte Frutos seemed eager to back up his populist rhetoric against the "oligarchy." During González Macchi's tenure, a group of armed peasants invaded a large estate near San Lorenzo and established a colony called Marquetalia, named after the Colombian town where the Revolutionary Armed Forces of Colombia *(FARC)* was formed. Duarte Frutos expropriated 25,000 hectares (62,000 acres) and issued titles to 1,300 peasant families, telegraphing that the way to obtain free land was to arm oneself and become a squatter on someone else's property and

Former President Nicanor Duarte Frutos

302

the government would back him up. Emboldened peasants invaded another 60 estates in 2004. There are an estimated 300,000 landless peasants, and by some non-governmental estimates, 1% of the population owns 80% of the land.

He also kept his promise to crack down on corruption, especially smuggling, and at the end of his first year the government reported that customs collections were up by 89%.

Former President González Macchi, still a pariah, was tried but acquitted of illegally diverting $16 million into a New York bank account. He and his wife went on trial over an unexplained $1 million in a Swiss bank account. They were convicted, but an appeals court threw out the convictions.

Meanwhile, the restless ghost of the assassinated Argaña returned to haunt Paraguay. Oviedo embarked on a public relations campaign to clear his name in the murder, and found an ally in the daily newspaper *ABC Color* and the Brazilian newsmagazine *Isto É*. The paper quoted the chauffeur who survived the shooting as saying that Argaña had died of cancer the night before and the assassination was staged by the Argaña faction to discredit Oviedo. *Isto É* contended that Duarte Frutos, then head of the Colorado Party, was a party to this conspiracy. Another conspiracy theory floating about the country is that Argaña's own children rubbed out their ill father in an intra-family estate dispute. Casting doubts on the conspiracy theories is the news videotape shot immediately after the shooting, which shows Argaña's body covered in blood, which would have been impossible if he had died the night before. The news footage also shows the body limp when it was placed on a stretcher.

Oviedo announced he would return to Paraguay in June 2004 to face the accusations, but only after several pro-Oviedo lawmakers met with Duarte to extract certain "guarantees." The president shouted that he would not tolerate anyone "destabilizing" the country. Oviedo kept his promise and returned, turning himself in to authorities. He was held in a military jail awaiting trial. In February 2005, he was cleared of charges that he had tried to overthrow González Macchi, but that December, an appeals court denied his release in the case involving the demonstrators killed after Argaña's assassination. Questions about his role in the Argaña assassination continued to hang over him as well. In 2006, the Supreme Court, in a 7–2 decision, reversed the ruling clearing him of charges in the 1996 coup attempt and ruled he had to serve the remainder of his 10-year prison term. He remained behind bars at the Viña Cué military prison until

he was paroled in September 2007 and made plans to run for president.

In 2004 and 2005, the attention of Paraguayans shifted to an alarming increase in street crime and kidnappings, something they never experienced during Stroessner's iron-fisted regime. The climate of fear had political repercussions. The highest-profile kidnapping was that of former President Cubas' 31-year-old daughter, Cecilia, abducted in broad daylight near her home in September 2004. Raúl Cubas paid an $800,000 ransom, while Paraguayans demonstrated for his daughter's release and put up "Free Cecilia" posters. Her decomposed body was found in February 2005, buried under a house near Asunción. Paraguayans, long inured to non-violent corruption, were horrified, and the national police were criticized for failing to save her after receiving a credible tip as to her whereabouts.

Osmar Martínez, leader of a tiny leftist group, *Patria Libre*, which is thought to have contacts with the *FARC* guerrillas of Colombia, was arrested in connection with Cubas' death. The *FARC* denied involvement with the kidnapping and murder. So did *Patria Libre*, which claimed it was a scapegoat to justify political repression. Duarte Frutos vowed to use the army if necessary to combat crime, and he promised to recruit 12,000 more policemen, without explaining how he would pay for them. Martínez and other members of *Patria Libre* were convicted and sentenced to long prison terms.

A peculiar issue arose in 2005. In 2000, the Paraguayan government had endorsed the sale 1.5 million acres of land around Puerto Casado in the eastern Chaco to the Unification Church of the Rev. Sun Myung Moon, the messianic Korean. The understanding was that the church's practitioners would develop the area, creating jobs. By 2005, however, the Paraguayan residents of Puerto Casado complained that not only had nothing been done but that they were denied entry to the vast tract to collect firewood. They demanded that Congress expropriate part of the tract for the local people. Congress enacted, and Duarte Frutos signed, an expropriation totaling about 115,000 acres.

An era in Paraguayan history ended on August 16, 2006, when Stroessner died in his exile in Brazil. He was 93. He was buried in Brasilia, although the Brazilian government let it be known it considered this a "transitory" burial until he could eventually be disinterred and buried in Paraguay—as though he would contaminate Brazilian soil. Stroessner's family sought unsuccessfully to persuade the Paraguayan government to allow his remains to be buried in his native soil—shabby treatment from his fellow *Colorados*.

Duarte Frutos, notorious for abrasive comments, brought negative international publicity to himself in 2007 with a tasteless, sexist remark he made in Guaraní at the dedication of a low-income housing project. He was accompanied by his social action minister, Judith Andrashko, whom he defended against recent criticism. He said her critics were always "hammering" her, using the Guaraní word *"apatuka,"* which also has a sexual connotation. Duarte Frutos then asked if there were men in the audience who would volunteer to "hammer her where it would do some good and put her in a good mood." Women's groups and media commentators assailed the president for the remark. The president did not apologize, but neither did Andrashko resign.

Paraguay achieved more international notoriety in 2008 when the United Nations announced that it was the second-largest producer of marijuana in the world in 2006, with 5,900 metric tons out of 41,400 tons worldwide; Mexico was first with 7,400 tons. Paraguayan soil is deemed ideal for growing cannabis. That dubious distinction could help explain the improvement in Paraguay's GDP growth in recent years (see Economy).

Lugo Makes History—
and Creates Scandal

The campaign for the April 20, 2008 presidential election turned into an even greater free-for-all than the one in 2003, thanks to a bitter intra-party turf war between two strong *Colorado* candidates, the release from jail of Oviedo and the sudden groundswell of popular support for a populist dark horse who vowed to shake up the system.

Vice President Castiglioni, a pro-American with the nickname "Johnny Bravo," resigned to seek the *Colorado* nomination in a primary in December 2007. Duarte Frutos let it be known his choice was, ironically, a woman, Education Minister Blanca Ovelar de Duarte, whose husband is no relation to the president.

A bitter primary battle between the Castiglioni and the Duarte Frutos-Ovelar factions ensued. Castiglioni said he would not support Ovelar in the general election if she won the nomination. The primary was so close that the counting took a month. Ovelar won by a razor-thin 45.04% to 44.5%. A bitter Castiglioni refused to accept defeat and threatened to contest her victory in court, claiming 30,000 of her votes were fraudulent. But her nomination was affirmed.

The expected *PLRA* standard bearer was Federico Franco, governor of Central Department in which the capital is located and brother of former Vice President Julio

Paraguay

César Franco, the party's 2003 candidate. But polls suggested a charismatic political newcomer could end the *Colorados'* 60-year reign: Fernando Lugo, 56, a bearded priest and former bishop and revolution theologist who had championed the cause of land reform and expressed admiration for Venezuela's Hugo Chávez.

As bishop of San Pedro, Lugo became popular with landless peasants. Because of his political activities, the church removed him as bishop, a post he had held for 11 years. In 2006, Lugo sought to resign from the priesthood, both because the Vatican prohibits priests from holding civil public office, and because the Paraguayan constitution prohibits priests from serving as president. He established a political movement called *Teko joja*, Guaraní for justice and equality.

In a party convention in 2007, the Liberals *(PLRA)* stunned Franco by narrowly voting to abandon his candidacy in favor of Lugo's. However, the convention expressed a condition that the vice-presidential candidate be a Liberal. The new Lugo-Franco coalition was named the Patriotic Alliance for Change. Lugo suddenly backed away from his earlier pro-Chávez comments.

The enigmatic Oviedo sought and received the *UNACE* nomination. Now, at last, Paraguayans would see whether his popularity could live up to his boasting. Fadul once again stood as the candidate of *Patria Querida*. Three minor candidates rounded out the field.

Voter turnout on April 20 was 65.6%. The historic results:

Lugo	766,502	42.3%
Ovelar	573,995	31.8%
Oviedo	411,034	22.8%
Fadul	41,004	2.5%

Thus, 61 years of *Colorado* Party rule, the longest of any non-Communist party in the world, came to an end with Lugo's inauguration on August 15, 2008. Duarte Frutos assumed his non-voting Senate seat for life as a former president.

The new Congress is as fragmented as the old one. The *Colorados* won 15 of the 45 Senate seats, followed by the *PLRA* with 14; Oviedo's *UNACE*, 9; *Patria Querida*, 4; and Lugo's *Teko joja*, 1 (Lugo did not actively field a slate). In the 80-seat Chamber of Deputies, the *Colorados* have 29, the Liberals 26, *UNACE* 16, *Patria Querida* 3 and *Teko joja*, 1.

Lugo broke with the past by appointing a member of the Aché tribe, Margarita Mbywangi, as minister of indigenous affairs. He also sacked the military high command. She was soon forced to resign over allegations she showed favoritism to her own tribe at the expense of others.

In this cartoon circulating on the Internet, a journalist asks, "President Lugo, women keep appearing who say they are the mothers of your children. Excuse me for asking, but didn't you take any precautions?" Lugo replies, "Nooo, please, that's against the principles of the church."

Speaking of indigenous affairs, Paraguayans were unprepared for the scandal that exploded around their new president after he had been in office only eight months. In April 2009, Viviana Carrillo, 26, announced she was filing a paternity suit against Lugo, claiming he had fathered her child born in 2007 while he was still a bishop. Evidently the affair began when she was 16. The president acknowledged in passing in a televised Holy Week address that he is the father.

A week later, another woman, Benigna Lequizamón, 27, publicly alleged that Bishop Lugo had fathered her child, born in 2002. One day later, Hortensia Morán, 39, an activist in Lugo's political movement, claimed he had fathered her child born 16 months earlier, but she said she was not filing a paternity suit because the child was "the result of unconditional love." Lugo neither admitted nor denied his paternity of the other two children, but the scandal made news around the world and brought scorn upon the former bishop who could not control his libido.

Lugo's supporters praised his candor in admitting paternity and said it proved he was a champion of transparency; his women and children's affairs minister, Liz Torres, raised eyebrows by declaring, "This is the Paraguay we all want." Not surprisingly, *Colorados* countered that if he were so candid and transparent, why did he wait until he was sued to admit the paternity of Carrillo's child? The bishop of Asunción called on him to assume the necessary responsibilities if he were the father of the other children.

At that point, the president began exhibiting strange, erratic behavior. He canceled a trip to Washington, apparently not wanting to face international media scrutiny over the paternity allegations.

Shortly after insisting that he would be making "gradual" cabinet changes, he abruptly fired and replaced four cabinet members—from the same faction of the *PLRA*—as though that would help resolve the crisis.

Lugo attended a summit of *ALBA*, the left-wing, anti-U.S. group established by Venezuela's Chávez that also includes Cuba, Bolivia, Nicaragua and Honduras. Lugo denied media reports—and contradicted his own chief of staff—that he had concluded an energy treaty with Venezuela by which Paraguay would purchase cut-rate priced oil. Lugo called the reports "laughable," even as Chief of Staff Miguel López Perito announced it had been submitted to Congress for study and approval and *ABC Color* carried the text of the treaty and reported that the Venezuelan Congress had already approved it! The Paraguayan Congress, meanwhile, claimed it had not received it, adding to the confusion. Opponents warned that Paraguay was surrendering its sovereignty to Venezuela.

López Perito became so frustrated with the president that he submitted his resignation, then withdrew it. Lugo's relations with Vice President Franco also were reported to be strained.

Recent Developments

A fourth woman, Teresa Rojas, came forward in 2009 to allege that Padre Fernando had "fathered" her now 20-year-old daughter, Fatima. Lugo has not acknowledged his paternity, but he attended Fatima's wedding and appointed her husband to a government job with the legal department of the Yacyretá Binational Enterprise, raising accusations of nepotism. Lugo's own niece stated publicly that it was common knowledge in their family that Fatima was Lugo's daughter.

The self-styled Paraguayan People's Army *(EPP)*, a radical offshoot of *Patria Libre*, the group blamed for Cecilia Cubas' death in 2005, splashed into the public consciousness in 2008 with a series of kidnappings. In October 2009, it kidnapped a prominent rancher, Fidel Zavala. The specter of a guerrilla insurgency created a public outcry, and by the first week of November there were rumors of an imminent military coup. Lugo issued a statement, through the armed forces, denying the rumors. But the next day he stunned the country by firing his army, navy and air force commanders, and two days later, the commander of the armed forces. Over the next three months, he cashiered more than 60 other mid-ranking officers, which led the opposition to charge he was trying to pack the armed forces hierarchy, Chávez-like, with officers sympathetic with his leftist philosophy.

Unlike Cubas, Zavala was released underweight but unharmed in January 2010 after his family, who had urged the government not to interfere, paid a ransom reported to be $550,000. Zavala's release was the cause of national celebration.

But the *EPP* returned to the headlines in April by attacking a cattle ranch and killing a policeman and three ranch workers. On April 24, Lugo declared a 30-day state of exception in five departments, which permitted warrantless arrests and allowed the army to be utilized. Lugo dispatched 1,000 troops to the five departments to augment a force of 3,000 national police. There was a tragic-comic incident when soldiers, acting on a tip that *EPP* members may be in a building, raided a police station. The two sides narrowly avoided a firefight. Security forces also accidentally raided a *quinceañera*, or coming-out party. When the state of exception expired in May, the security forces could claim only one arrest, of a suspected *EPP* logistician, and that was outside the five departments.

It appeared Lugo could claim a diplomatic triumph in late 2009 by extracting an agreement from Brazilian President Da Silva to triple the royalties Paraguay receives from the Itaipu hydroelectric dam. When this book went to press, however, the Brazilian Congress still had not ratified it, and it appeared Brazil was reneging on a promise to build a power grid.

Lugo also placed himself in the forefront of international efforts in late 2009 to restore deposed Honduran President Manuel Zelaya to power. Lugo has refused to recognize the government of the newly elected Honduran president, Porfirio Lobo Sosa.

In early 2010, Lugo's approval rating was about 50%, and the opposition in Congress was blocking all his major proposals.

Culture: Paraguay's unique culture is a product of geography and politics. Landlocked and cut off from contact with the outside world by a series of 19th century strongmen, Paraguay developed differently from its sister republics. To begin with, the indigenous inhabitants, the Guaraní, were culturally different from tribes on the fringes of the continent. Just as it took a special breed of native to subsist in this hot, dry climate, so it took a special breed of Spaniard to eschew the relative comforts of either coast to pioneer this inhospitable land.

Along with such pioneers came Jesuit priests, who effectively ran the colony in the 16th and 17th centuries, until the Spanish Crown expelled them. The ruins of their mini-civilization can be seen near modern-day Encarnación. Some scholars attribute the Paraguayan trait of obse-

Augusto Roa Bastos

quiousness to authority to this long-ago Jesuit influence, which inspired the motion picture, *The Mission*.

Although Roman Catholicism remains the predominant religion, Paraguay's liberal immigration laws and tolerance of other religions has attracted various Protestant sects. In the 1920s, Mennonite pioneers from Canada established the settlement of Filadelfia in the Chaco, and they still account for a disproportionate amount of the country's dairy production. Jews and Jehovah's Witnesses came to Paraguay from less tolerant Argentina. The Assembly of God has grown in size in recent years and is building a huge new complex, and the Unification Church of the Rev. Sun Myung Moon purchased a tract of land near Puerto Casado.

Because Paraguayan leaders placed little value on education, and in no small part because of the genocide committed during the War of the Triple Alliance of 1865–70, Paraguay never developed a European-based literary, artistic or musical tradition as did its neighbors. Paraguayan culture is derived almost wholly from the Guaraní, whose language still thrives and is now in written form; half the population learns Guaraní before Spanish. Several unassimilated Indian tribes still exist in Paraguay, providing tourists with cheap trinkets. But it is from the Guaranís that Paraguay developed the beautiful lacework that is so identified with the country.

Probably the most identifiable element of Paraguayan culture, however, is its lovely harp-based folk music. During the Stroessner regime, law dictated that 50% of the music played on radio had to be domestic. One Paraguayan folk song in particular, *Recuerdos de Ypacaraí*, is so well known that guitarists or pianists can play it from memory in restaurants or piano bars from Mexico City to Buenos Aires to Madrid.

Paraguay's most internationally renowned literary figure—indeed, the only

Paraguay

one—of the 20th century was Augusto Roa Bastos (1917–2005). He served as a medic during the 1932–35 Chaco War with Bolivia. Because of his leftist sympathies and his irreverence toward authority, Roa Bastos voluntarily went into exile in 1947, living and writing abroad for 49 years, first in Argentina, then France, and finally Spain, returning to Paraguay to live in 1996 and dying in Asunción. Unlike many writers who live in exile, however, Roa Bastos did not lose his Paraguayan identity, and he wrote primarily about his homeland. He was known for his use of basing his fiction on historical figures. His best-known work was the novel *Yo, el Supremo (I, the Supreme)*, published in 1974, which was based on the 19th century Paraguayan dictator José Gaspar Rodríguez de Francia (see History). Two other works, *El Hijo de Hombre (Son of Man)*, a 1960 collection of short stories, and *El Baldío (Vagabond)*, a novel published in 1966, were biting observations on Paraguay's often tragic history. Another, *Vigilia del Almirante (Vigil of the Admiral)*, a novel about Columbus, was published in 1992 to mark the 500th anniversary of the European discovery of the New World. His works were translated into 25 languages. He received Spain's prestigious Cervantes Prize in Literature in 1989, and he was often mentioned as a possible Nobel Laureate.

As in many of the Latin American republics, dictatorship and illiteracy combined forces to stifle the development of viable independent newspapers. A few dailies are published, but only in Asunción. One was the official *Colorado* Party mouthpiece, *Patria*, which has since ceased publication. Beginning in the late 1970s the others courageously exposed the endemic corruption of the Stroessner regime—although they wisely avoided mentioning the president by name. The country's leading daily is *ABC Color*, founded by businessman Aldo Zucolillo in 1967, which became more and more critical of the dictatorship, until Stroessner ordered it closed in 1984. It didn't reopen until immediately after Stroessner's overthrow five years later. Other leading dailies are *Diario Popular*, *La Nación* and *Ultima Hora*.

Economy: The eastern (*Oriental*) region of Paraguay, with its favorable climate, is the country's primary source of economic wealth. The arid western (*Occidental* or *Chaco*) region was once a wasteland, but in recent years the Mennonite colonies in the Chaco have produced more than half the country's dairy products and a growing percentage of its beef. Approximately 26% of Paraguay's GDP is from agriculture, with cattle raising and soybeans the leading exports. Forestry once employed

half the workforce, but the forests have been largely logged out, with little attention given to reforestation; the government now prohibits export of raw timber, focusing on finished wood products like furniture.

Paraguay's foreign trade is primarily with Brazil, the United States, Argentina, the United Kingdom and Germany; other exports include vegetable oils, grains, cotton, leather goods and tobacco.

The economy boomed in the 1970s and 1980s, bolstered by work on a huge hydroelectric dam: Itaipú (financed by Brazil). Paraguay is selling its share of electricity to Brazil. A contract was let for the construction of a second dam, Yacyretá, downstream on the Paraná River, financed by Argentina. This is the longest river dam in the world. It is now producing an abundance of electrical power. Hydroelectric power is a leading export. However, Paraguay agreed to sell the energy to Brazil below market cost, something President Fernando Lugo began trying to renegotiate in 2008, asking Brazil for an additional $2 billion annually. Brazilian President Lula da Silva finally agreed in 2009 to triple Paraguay's royalties, but the Brazilian Congress has stalled on ratification.

Because of Paraguay's landlocked isolation, and its juxtaposition between two powerful neighbors, smuggling has traditionally been a major pillar of the economy. In recent years, traditional smuggling has been expanded to include drug trafficking, money laundering, gunrunning and copyright and trademark infringement. The United States at one point threatened Paraguay with economic sanctions because of the piracy of intellectual properties.

When Raúl Cubas assumed the presidency in 1998, he inherited a dismal economy and a budget deficit that totaled about 4% of the GDP of $10 billion. He attempted to crack down on long-accepted tax evasion and black marketeering. He estimated that as much as 55% of taxes were not being paid (the figure today is estimated at 70%).

Paraguay is one of the few remaining countries with diplomatic relations with Taiwan, but it paid off in 1999 when an appreciative Taiwan lent Paraguay $400 million, which kept the country afloat. President Nicanor Duarte Frutos, obtained a $73 million loan from the IMF, which prevented a possible default on the foreign debt.

Paraguay's GDP shrank for six out of eight years between 1995 and 2002. In 2002 it shrank by –2.3%, but showed positive growth of 2.6% in 2003, 3.9% in 2004 and 2.9% in 2005. It jumped to 4.3% in 2006, 6.4% in 2007 and 5.5% in 2008, a boom by Paraguayan standards. The improvement

was attributed to high world prices for commodities exported by Paraguay, especially soybeans. But the global recession caused GDP to contract again, by –3.5%, in 2009.

Per capita income declined from a peak of $1,793 in 1996 to only $1,019 in 2003. It increased to $1,670 in 2007 and $2,110 in 2008, but Paraguay was still the fifth-poorest country among the 20 Latin American republics, ahead of Haiti, Nicaragua, Honduras and neighboring Bolivia. In 2008, 19.4% of Paraguayans lived below the poverty line, and UNICEF reported that one child in seven suffers from chronic malnutrition. With the improving economy, unemployment declined to 5.7% in 2008, but underemployment may be as high as 35%. These factors account for Paraguay's traditional public discontent. With the recession, unemployment climbed to 7.9% in 2009.

Inflation increased from only 2.8% in 2004 to 11% in 2008, but with the recession it fell back to 1.9% in 2009.

An increasingly important economic pillar is the remittances sent by expatriates working abroad, primarily in Brazil, Argentina and Spain, to family members in Paraguay. Remittances in 2006 were estimated at $650 million, or about 8% of GDP. They were expected to top $1 billion in 2008, but the global recession was expected to have a tremendous impact in 2009. Unemployment in Spain was 18%, and many Paraguayans were repatriating.

The Future: The election of Fernando Lugo in 2008, ending 61 years of *Colorado* Party rule, was as historic as Vicente Fox's victory in Mexico in 2000 that ended 71 years of *PRI* domination. Like his predecessor and like all his opponents, Lugo pledged to crack down on the endemic corruption that is a leech on the struggling economy. Paraguayans have heard it all before. In 2008, Transparency International rated Paraguay the fourth most corrupt of the 20 Latin American republics. In 2009, Lugo's first full year in office, Paraguay slid back to the *third* most corrupt, ahead of Haiti and Venezuela. So much for promises. In addition to corruption, Lugo is dealing with a tawdry sex scandal.

It is difficult to blame the long-suffering Paraguayans for being cynical about their 21-year-old democracy. The periodic *Latinobarómetro* survey of 17 (now 18) Latin American countries for *The Economist* shows that the percentage of Paraguayans who think democracy is preferable to any other form of government plummeted from 59% in 1996 to just 32% in 2005, lower than any other nation in the survey; the 27-point drop was the greatest of any nation. It was still just 33% in 2007; only Guatemala, at 32%, was lower. With the election of Lugo in 2008, the percentage jumped to 53%; the 20-point one-year increase was the greatest in Latin America. But in 2009, in the wake of Lugo's paternity scandal and his lackluster, even bizarre, administrative performance, it slipped back to 46%. Only Ecuador and Mexico were lower.

Meanwhile, the percentage of Paraguayans who believe an authoritarian government can be preferable to a democracy "under certain circumstances" increased from 26% in 1996 to 44% in 2005, by far the highest percentage in Latin America. The percentage dropped to 36% in 2007 and 29% in 2008, then rose to 31% in 2009, still the highest of any nation in the survey.

This author lived in Paraguay from 1977–79, during the Stroessner era, and I was struck by the Paraguayans' traditional obsequiousness to authority and the reverence they still bestow upon their *caudillos* of yesteryear, like Francia and Francisco Solano López—and now Stroessner. Before his death, there were bumper stickers in Paraguay that said, "1954–1989—*yo era felíz y no lo sabía*" (I was happy and didn't know it). Now his grandson is active in the *Colorado* Party and is a senator.

Paraguayans had the opportunity in 2008 to return to strongman rule by voting for Lino Oviedo. But as with the once-popular former Guatemalan strongman Efraín Ríos Montt, who ran for president in 2003, when push came to shove and the voters really had to choose, Oviedo ran a poor third with 22.8% of the vote.

Instead, they put their hope and faith in Lugo, in the belief that not being a *Colorado* or a member of the privileged elite that had long controlled the country, and by having been a priest and bishop, he would be clean, moral, honest and represent genuine change. Not only are they shocked that their president violated his priestly vows of chastity to allegedly father at least three children out of wedlock and began one affair with a 16-year-old girl, but he has proved an erratic decision-maker and an indecisive administrator. He also has made a Faustian deal with Venezuela's Hugo Chávez for low-price oil that worries his countrymen.

Alas, Lugo appears to be merely Paraguay's latest disillusionment.

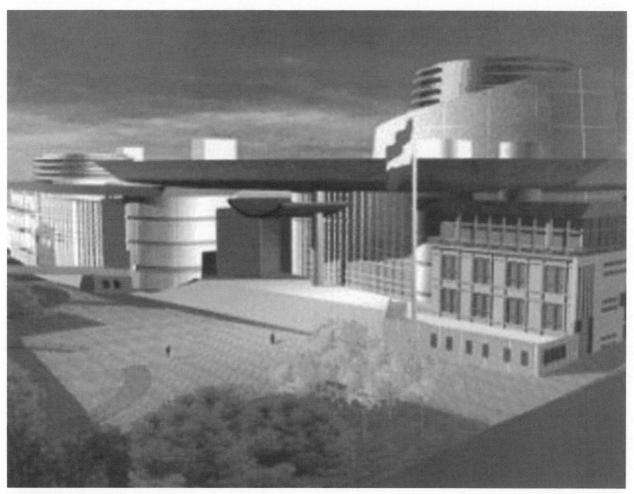

An architect's sketch of Paraguay's new Congress building, which opened in June 2003. The government of Taiwan contributed $22 million toward its construction.

Peru

Peruvian school girls in Lima

Area: 482,122 square miles.

Population: 29.9 milliion (2010 estimate).

Capital City: Lima (Pop. 7.8 million, 2006 estimate).

Climate: The eastern lowlands are hot and humid; the coast is arid and mild; the highlands are increasingly temperate as the altitude rises.

Neighboring Countries: Ecuador (northwest); Colombia (northeast); Brazil (east); Chile (south).

Official Language: Spanish.

Other Principal Tongues: Quechua and Aymara.

Ethnic Background: *Mestizo* (a mixture of Indian and Spanish ancestry) and pure Indian, 88%; European, mostly Spanish, 12%.

Principal Religion: Roman Catholic Christianity.

Chief Commercial Products: Fish, fishmeal, cotton, sugar, copper, silver, lead, crude petroleum.

Currency: Sol.

Gross Domestic Product: U.S. $128.9 billion in 2009 ($4,311 per capita).

Former Colonial Status: Spanish Colony (1532–1821).

Independence Date: July 21, 1821.

Chief of State: Alan Gabriel Ludwig García Pérez (b. May 23, 1949), president (since July 28, 2006).

National Flag: Red, white and red vertical stripes.

Peru sits astride the majestic Andes mountains. The Sierra (upland plateau) is at an average invigorating elevation of 13,000 feet from which ranges of high peaks emerge. The highest, Huascarán, is 22,334 feet; 10 others exceed 20,000 feet and there are many volcanoes in the southern region. The Sierra occupies about one fourth of Peru's surface and is home to more than 60% of the population.

The Sierra is cut and crisscrossed with rivers; those flowing to the west frequently disappear in the desert before reaching the Pacific Ocean; rivers flowing to the east drop into the tropical jungles of the Amazon basin. Some of the eastern rivers have cut scenic gorges into the Sierra 5,000 feet in depth, with tropical climates and vegetation at the lower levels. The Pacific coastal shelf is a narrow ribbon of desert except for a few river valleys where there is sufficient water for irrigation.

The eastern slope of the Andes, known as the *selva* (jungle) contains over 60% of Peru's land and about 14% of the population. There are few roads into this region; travel is along the river valleys.

This area's resources are great, but inaccessibility hampers their exploitation. Peru's climate varies with altitude—tropical in the lowlands, it becomes temperate above the elevation of 3,000 feet and cold above 10,000–12,000 feet, with snow and bitter frost throughout the year on the highest peaks of the Andes. People with respiratory or coronary difficulties dare not venture into these heights—the air is too "thin" to support any but the hardiest of lives.

History: Peru has been host to civilized people from about the 3rd century A.D. Artistically sophisticated people left pottery and textiles of excellent quality in the southern region that date from the 3rd to the 7th centuries. More primitive people lived in the vicinity of Lima, and a highly skilled culture existed in the north. The southern culture spread to the Sierra and gave rise to the Aymara society at Tiahuanaco, east of Lake Titicaca in the 10th to the 13th centuries. The Inca civilization began to develop in the Cuzco basin about the 11th century and by the end of the 15th century dominated the Andean Sierra and the Pacific shelf from Colombia to the Central Valley of Chile. At the time of the Spanish invasion, a division had split the Inca rulers. The legitimate Inca Huáscar ruled the south from Cuzco while his half-brother, Atahualpa, ruled the northern provinces from Quito as a usurper challenging the legitimacy of Huáscar (see Ecuador).

When the explorers Francisco Pizarro and Diego de Almagro landed their small Spanish force in Ecuador in 1531, Atahualpa—apparently seeking allies to assist in his fight against his half-brother—allowed the Spaniards to reach the Sierra. The outnumbered Spanish tricked Atahualpa into an ambush, held him for ransom and killed him after it was paid. As Atahualpa had ordered the assassination of Huáscar, and his person was considered divine by the Incas, no one in the vast empire dared to raise a finger against the Spaniards as long as the emperor was a prisoner. Unopposed, the Spaniards moved into the interior of Peru, occupying the most strategic cities and, after the death of Atahualpa, ruled through puppet Incas until they felt strong enough to proclaim Spain's sovereignty.

Pizarro withdrew from Cuzco, the sacred capital of the Inca empire in 1535 and

Atahaulpa is ambushed by Spanish troops

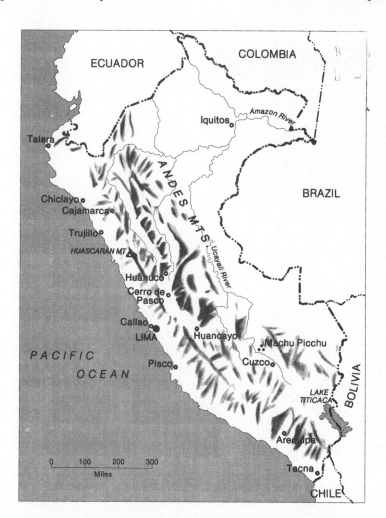

founded Lima near the coast. Almagro was sent to conquer Chile, but the arid territory and Indian hostility forced him to return to Lima. A brief struggle for power followed and first Almagro and then Pizarro were killed. Spanish authorities intervened, restored peace and began organizing the new rich colony. Francisco de Toledo, one of the best viceroys Spain ever had, established a firm basis for colonial power. He ruled from 1568 to 1582, adopted many Inca traditions like the "*mita*" (annually every male member of the Inca empires had to work free for the emperor during a few months) for Spain's benefit, and the colony prospered. By the middle of the 17th century, Lima was a splendid city with cathedrals, palaces and a university and the viceroyalty of Peru had become the political and strategic center of the Spanish empire in South America.

Exasperated by the exploitation of the Indians in the mining area, a descendant of the last Inca adopted the name of Tupac Amaru in 1780 and raised the banner of rebellion. Intelligently, he appealed to the creoles (people of Peruvian mixed Spanish-Indian blood), ratified his Catholic faith and proclaimed that he was not fighting against the king, but against his "corrupt officials." The rebellion spread rapidly, but Tupac's Indian followers killed Spaniards and creoles indiscriminately. The alliance of both, plus the condemnation of the Catholic Church, sealed his fate. Thousands of Indians rallied

Peru

around Spanish authorities (a testimony to Spain's colonial policies) and Tupac was defeated, captured and publicly executed. The rebellion, however, left a lingering fear among the creoles. As in Mexico and Cuba, they remained lukewarm toward an anti-Spanish struggle that could trigger another Indian uprising. The initiative for independence had to come from *outside*.

The arrival of General José de San Martín and his small army of Argentinians and Chileans opened the period of armed insurrection. Unable to defeat the Spaniards, who were supported by many

Tupac Amaru

creoles, San Martín awaited the arrival of General Simón Bolívar, whose victorious army was marching south from Venezuela and Colombia. After meeting with *el Libertador* in Guayaquil and failing to reach an agreement on the impending campaign, a disillusioned San Martín retired to private life. Bolívar and his second-in-command, Antonio José de Sucre, opened the campaign against colonial authorities and in 1824 the battle of Ayacucho put an end to Spanish dominion in South America.

After the battle, Bolívar made an energetic attempt to organize the country. Taxes were cut, convents were turned into schools and the most glaring abuses against the Indians were suppressed. Elected president-for-life, Bolívar could have accomplished much more, but growing resistance on the part of alarmed and conservative Peruvian creoles, and the progressive disintegration of his "Great Colombia" (the union of Venezuela, Colombia, and Ecuador) forced him to leave Peru in 1826. A period of relative stability followed while most of the government and military forces concentrated on solidifying a union with Bolivia in a "Confederation of the North." Unfortunately, Chile considered that union as a threat to its future and invaded Bolivia. Chilean victory at the battle of Yungay forced the con-

federation to break up. The defeat plunged Peru into political turmoil until 1844, when a capable man, Ramón Castilla, seized power. President Castilla, who served until 1850 and again from 1855–60, united the country, mediated differences between the pro-church Conservatives and the anti-clerical Liberals, established government services, abolished black slavery, ended forced tribute from the Indians and built a few schools.

The national economy, however, was restored by sea birds, whose mountains of dung (guano) on the offshore islands, were highly sought after in European fertilizer markets. The guano trade led to an economic boom and also led to the discovery of nitrate deposits in the southern deserts; the extraction of the mineral was largely in British hands.

The period following Castilla's rule was one of tension and war. Nine presidents occupied the office between 1862 and 1885, of which only two completed their terms. The most competent was Manuel Pardo (1872–76), Peru's first civilian president and founder of the *Civilista* Party. A war with Spain (1862–66) and the War of the Pacific with Chile (1879–83) were brought on by the prosperity that Peru was enjoying. Spain sought to recover its past grandeur and lost; Chile, with British connivance, sought the wealth of the desert nitrate fields and won.

The War of the Pacific was a disaster for Peru—thousands of lives were lost, much property was destroyed, some territory and the port of Arica were ceded to Chile, and the national economy was reduced to a shambles. Huge foreign debts were accumulated, the nitrate beds were lost and the guano deposits were almost exhausted.

British interests funded the foreign debt in exchange for the national railways, the steamers of scenic Lake Titicaca, the exploitation of remaining guano deposits, free use of ports and other trade privileges. Peru's recovery was slow, but a measure of peace and order was established and trade resumed under a succession of *Civilista* presidents.

The major event of the early 20th century was the dictatorship of Augusto B. Leguía (1919–30). Energetic and able, he gave impetus to mining and agriculture and restored Peru's international credit. Leguía called his regime "A New Fatherland," adopted a modern constitution and freed the church from state patronage. Initially an honest administrator, he succumbed to graft and corruption under the temptation of loans proffered by the U.S. banks during the 1920s. When the inevitable protests arose, there was wholesale jailing of critics, restriction of the press and the closing of universities.

By 1930, the Peruvian people were fed up with Leguía's despotism and the economic crisis caused by the worldwide depression. A revolt caused Leguía to flee; he was captured on the high seas and imprisoned on one of the offshore islands, where he died.

APRA is Founded

During the last decade of the 19th century, there developed a movement for liberal reforms in Peru's higher society. Led by Manuel González Prada, a respected intellectual, demands were made to end feudalism, traditionalism and clericalism, which González Prada declared enslaved the people to a handful of powerful men. Among the students attracted to González Prada was Victor Rául Haya de la Torre, a leader in the demand for educational reforms, who founded the American Popular Revolutionary Alliance (*APRA*) in 1924. It remains one of the major political institutions today.

Anti-communist, with ideas borrowed from Russian, Mexican and European models, *APRA* sought to integrate the Indians into Peru's social and economic structure and to terminate the monopoly of political power that had been held by the landowners and the clergy for more than 400 years. During the dictatorship of Leguía, *APRA* grew and became the spokesman for the Indians in the Sierra as well as for urban workers.

APRA won the 1931 elections, but Haya de la Torre was jailed and the party outlawed. The resulting revolts were savagely repressed, and Peru's second dictatorship of the 20th century was launched. Marshal Oscar Benavides ruled somewhat moderately until 1939.

Manuel Prado, a moderate, was president from 1939–45. He made progress in trade, public health, education and sanitation, but simultaneously repressed all popular challengers to the landowner-clergy domination of political power. His successor came to office by a change of *APRA* tactics; reorganizing as the People's Party, *APRA* supported the most liberal of the candidates, hoping to secure congressional seats and cabinet positions.

The *APRA* success in this effort brought on a conservative coup headed by General Manuel Odría, who ruled from 1948–56. No pretense of democracy was maintained; restoring order and suppressing *APRA*, the army ruled with firmness. From a managerial standpoint, the regime gave a good account of itself, restoring confidence in Peruvian industry. Legal elections again returned Prado to leadership, but conditions did not remain stable. When *APRA* won substantial gains in 1962 elections, the army again intervened

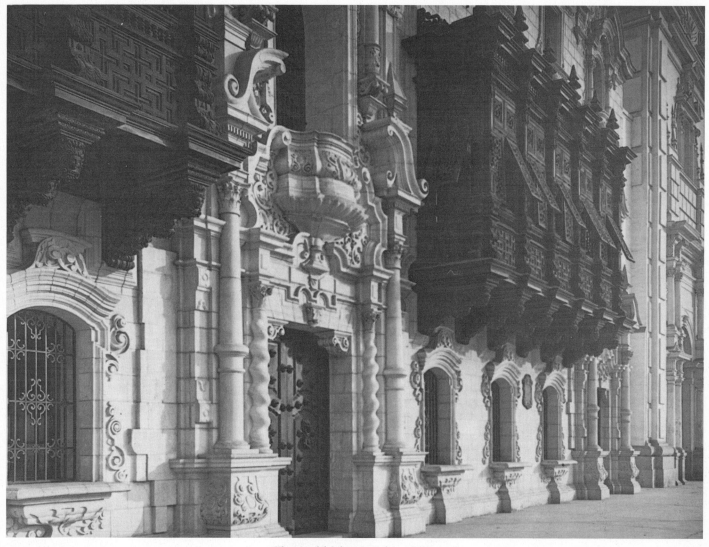

The Archbishop's Palace, Lima

by setting aside the results; in more carefully staged elections in 1963, Fernando Belaúnde Terry of the center-right Popular Action Party (*PAP*) won a bare plurality and was named president.

Leftist Military Rule, 1968–80

Charging that the nation's political leaders were insensitive to the needs of the masses, a military *junta* ousted Belaúnde in 1968 and replaced him with General Juan Velasco Alvarado, who served as president for the next seven years. The new regime promised to end the traditional political and economic control of Peru by the "top 40 families" and foreign corporations through a program of "social democracy," patterned loosely on the Yugoslav model, which (they said) would guide the nation on a path between capitalism and communism.

The first phase of the program, largely achieved by 1975, called for state control of strategic sectors of the economy. Thus, the regime nationalized the fishing industry, banks, communications facilities, most of the news media and U.S.-owned mining operations. A unique feature of the Inca Plan required major industries to grant half-ownership to the workers.

A cornerstone of the economic plan was one of the most extensive land reform programs in Latin America. Before the military seized power, fully 90% of all farmland was owned by just 2% of the population. To break the power of the landed aristocracy, the military seized 25 million acres from large private estates and redistributed them to worker-owned cooperatives and to peasant families.

In foreign affairs, the military government was nationalistic and leftist. Diplomatic ties were extended to many non-aligned and communist nations and Peru became the second nation in the Western Hemisphere to import Soviet weapons and advisers. At international confer-

ences, Peru was a major advocate of Third World causes as well as a frequent critic of U.S. economic power.

These policies naturally strained relations with the United States. Although Peru agreed to pay for some of the seized property, the prices were largely dictated by the *junta*. A low point in U.S.-Peruvian relations came in late 1974 when the *junta* ousted 137 members of the Peace Corps and several U.S. Embassy officials on charges of spying for the CIA.

By combining a nationalistic foreign policy with a state-controlled economy, the *junta* hoped to build what it described as a "new Peruvian man." To speed up the process, the government expanded education programs, increased per capita incomes, promised to spend new oil revenues on social programs and to turn over farms and factories to workers. The expected popular support, however, failed to materialize. Farm workers who received land bitterly opposed sharing their

Peru

gains with landless peasants. Factory workers continued to strike as often against state-owned industries as they had against the former owners. Part of the problem was rooted in the *junta*'s attempts to run Peru like a military barracks.

Congress was closed, most political parties were banned, and civilians were excluded from key government jobs. Professional organizations and free labor movements were suppressed and the press was censored. Compounding Peru's troubles were collapse of the fishmeal industry (the offshore anchovies disappeared), a plunge in world copper prices and the failure of new oil wells (in which the regime had gambled $1.5 billion) to produce as expected.

The government's economic program scared away badly needed foreign investment and poor management resulted in lowered production in nationalized industries. Benefits of the military revolution failed to filter down to the lower classes; unemployment and inflation cut the living standards of the people.

Velasco Alvarado, partially disabled from circulatory problems and a mild stroke, increasingly ruled by decree, jailing or exiling his critics. When he turned his wrath against fellow military officers, the armed forced finally stepped in and deposed him in a bloodless coup in 1975.

General Francisco Morales Bermúdez

Named as new president was General Francisco Morales Bermúdez, a moderate and former prime minister. Although he pledged to follow the basic goals of the previous regime, he further stated that the revolution had entered a more conservative "consolidation phase." Faced with a bankrupt treasury, the regime turned away from a policy of rigid state control of industry. A number of major businesses (including the key fishing industry), nationalized by the previous administration, were returned to their former owners. At the same time, the role and power of labor unions were reduced.

Nevertheless, Peru's economy continued to decline during 1977. Hoping to prevent further labor unrest and related political violence, the *junta* announced that plans were being made to surrender power to constitutional government. The first election was set for June 1978, when voters would name delegates to an assembly to rewrite the constitution. Under the plan, an elected president and congress would take control of the country by 1980. However, the military stipulated that the new constitution must embody basic nationalistic principles of the present government which had stressed social reforms and nationalization of major industries.

As an initial step toward the restoration of democracy, voters went to the polls for the first time in 11 years to elect representatives to a 100-seat Constituent Assembly, which drafted he new constitution. The biggest winner, with nearly 40% of the vote, was *APRA*, which campaigned on a slightly left-of-center platform. In second place were the leftists representing six Marxist parties with nearly 28%. The conservatives and moderates, led by the Popular Christian Party, had 27%.

Panoramic view of Lima with the broad Avenida Alfonso Ugarte in the foreground

312

Peru

Return to Democracy

When presidential elections were held in May 1980, former President Belaúnde of the *PAP* won easily over 11 other candidates with 43% of the vote. *APRA* was second with 26%, while extremist parties fared poorly.

Belaúnde became Peru's 102nd president, ending 12 years of military rule. The generals refused to attend the inauguration. Because his *PAP* won only 27 of the 60 Senate seats and 95 of the 180 seats in the Chamber of Deputies, Belaúnde had to have the cooperation of *APRA* and the *PCP*. The new administration promised to respect the new constitution, to create an independent judiciary, to promote human rights, to ensure freedom of the press (including return of newspapers and TV stations taken over by the previous military regimes), and to encourage economic development. Programs for construction of roads, housing, increased farm production and water resources and for nurturing foreign investments (especially in oil production) were given high priority.

The Belaúnde administration faced severe political and economic problems, the aftermath of the military regimes' wasteful spending on failed social programs and unnecessary Soviet arms, which brought the nation to the brink of insolvency. Austerity measures were taken to lower inflation and to stimulate financial investments for economic growth.

As usual, the real burden for these reforms fell most heavily on the poor and middle class; the cost of living rose sharply while real wages dropped. Strikes closed down mines, mills, oil installations and schools as workers protested rising prices and clamored for wage increases to catch up with galloping inflation. The volatile atmosphere heated up in 1981 when acts of terrorism became commonplace.

An important diplomatic event occurred for Peru in 1981 when Javier Pérez de Cuellar was named to a five-year term as secretary-general of the United Nations.

Terrorism-Counter-Terrorism

Peru's democracy remained frail, but Belaúnde assured the public that the military would not attempt another coup. This was put to a severe test, however, by the activities of Maoist guerrilla bands calling themselves *Sendero Luminoso* ("Shining Path." The movement consisted of cells rather than organized larger forces, making it extremely hard to deal with. Founded about 1970 by a philosophy professor, Abimael Guzmán (b. 1935) of the University of Huamanga, in Ayacucho State, it spread quickly to colleges and

High school girls in a mountain village

universities of the highlands, attracting many of Indian ancestry. Its actions, and the government's struggle against it, killed more than 25,000 people.

Guzmán, who went by the *nom de guerre* Presidente Gonzalo, went into hiding in 1975 but remained active. From sketchy accounts of his rigid beliefs and behavior (traditionalist Stalinist, Maoist communism) it was suspected that he was mentally deranged, becoming the leader of a mass cult that he mesmerized. One observer aptly called him "a Charlie Manson with an army to back him up."

Terrorism was committed not only by the *Sendero Luminoso* but also by elite military units sent to the impoverished region inhabited mostly by Indians. A group based in urban areas, the Tupac Amaru Revolutionary Movement, joined in the anti-government effort in 1984; it was named after the 18th century Peruvian Indian who revolted against Spanish rule. It used pipe bombs and heavier explosives to make life in Lima miserable. The city came to be surrounded in the 1980s by "suburbs" of countless shacks and shanties where more than 8 million settled. It was easy in such a setting to bomb strategic locations—banks, businesses, embassies and the presidential palace—and disappear.

Further complicating life in Peru was the entry of coca production in the Upper Huallaga Valley, which for a time became the source of 75% of coca used to produce cocaine. The hirelings of drug traffickers were merciless and sometimes posed as revolutionaries to divert attention from their actual purposes.

Belaúnde rapidly declined in popularity (from 70% in 1980 to 20% in 1984). By mid-1984 the annual inflation rate reached 120% and Peru looked toward the presi-

dential elections of 1985 with a mixture of hope and despair.

The First García Presidency

APRA candidate Alan García received 46% of the votes in April 1985, and the candidate of the United Left (which included Communist elements), Alfonso Barrantes, popular mayor of Lima, got 21%. In order to discourage voter turnout, both the Shining Path and Tupac Amaru terrorists issued death threats; the Shining Path actually amputated the fingers of peasants to prevent them from voting. Police and military security at the polls was tight.

According to the constitution, if no candidate obtains more than 50% of the votes, a second (runoff) election is obligatory. Before the runoff date was determined, *senderistas* gravely wounded the president of the Electoral Tribunal. Days later, Barrantes, probably trying to avoid a further decline of leftist votes, withdrew from the runoff.

García, just 36, took the oath of office in July 1985. He immediately made dramatic and controversial promises. He stated that no more than an amount corresponding to 10% of Peru's export income would be used to "repay" a foreign debt of almost $16 billion, knowing that such an amount wouldn't even pay the interest on the indebtedness. Peru's international bond rating suffered.

In order to deal with police and army corruption, García fired or retired top figures in both organizations. He declared a state of emergency as lawlessness increased in Lima, ordering armored units from the military to patrol the streets. An American oil company was nationalized (assets: $400 million) without compensa-

Peru

tion. The United States cut off aid as required by law. A new unit of currency, the *inti*, was introduced, a devaluation of 64 to 1 of the *sol*. It was later devalued several more times.

Conditions deteriorated after 1986. The *senderistas* promoted simultaneous riots at three prisons. The army responded by executing almost 200 prisoners after they had surrendered. The *senderistas* threatened to kill 10 *APRA* leaders for each guerrilla slain. Three universities were raided by 4,000 troops, who seized *senderista* propaganda, violating the traditional security of education institutions. Violence escalated, with the guerrillas resorting to tying bombs to children and burros to carry them to their target. The army's response was equally brutal.

There would have been a military coup, but the military didn't want to inherit an ungovernable country. Much of Peru came under martial law. The *senderistas* then retreated to the upper Huallaga Valley in the northeast, where most of the coca is grown. They imposed a 10% "sales tax" on the farmers "for protection." Because of their hatred for foreigners, the tourist trade all but dried up. The *senderistas* frequently bombed Lima's power grid, reducing power to three hours a day, if any. Polls showed more than half of Peruvians would leave the country if they could.

García nationalized banks and insurance companies in 1987, creating economic havoc. Having defaulted on its external loans, Peru was on a cash-in-advance basis. As many as 50 ships at a time would lie at port, laden with food, but awaiting payment in hard currency before unloading—while Peruvians went hungry. After García left office, evidence surfaced that he had received a kickback for depositing Peru's reserves in BCCI, a shady bank that became the target of an international investigation, and from the construction of an Italian-built electric rail line. The charges were filed in 1992 but García fled into self-imposed exile in Colombia and stayed there for nine years—until the statute of limitations had expired.

The Fujimori Era

When 1990 elections approached, it was generally assumed they would result in another traditional party victory. Polls showed the well-known novelist, Mario Vargas Llosa, the likely winner. But a surprise appeared on the horizon: Alberto Fujimori, an engineer and the soft-spoken son of Japanese immigrants, supported by a substantial number of Protestant evangelicals, entered the contest under the *Cambio '90* ("Change '90") banner. His

supporters, going from door to door extolling his virtues, were persuasive. His popularity swelled from 3% to 60% in the runoff a few months later.

A small element within the military, foreseeing Fujimori's victory, attempted a coup just before the elections, replete with a plan to murder him. It failed; his intelligence received word of its time and place.

Following his inauguration on July 28, 1990—his 5nd birthday—Fujimori dismissed the top echelon of the navy and air force, then the army. He turned inward, trusting no one with basic decisions and policy. He ordered the reorganized military to renew a campaign against the *senderistas* and armed rural peasants.

The *senderistas*, with their strength about 15,000, launched a campaign in 1992 to gain control of Lima. Arms and munitions supplies via Colombia had become unreliable and they needed the support of the vast number of poor people surrounding the city in slums. At the same time, it became evident to Fujimori that the National Assembly, dominated by the traditional political elite, was obstructing him at every turn. He dismissed the body, as well as members of the judiciary, and assumed personal control by decree in April. He had the backing of the military for this so-called "self-coup."

Under pressure from Washington and the OAS, Fujimori called for elections in late 1992. The *senderistas* attempted to disrupt them, but two months before the contest, Guzmán and other key members were nabbed by the military and police in a posh Lima apartment. Because he avoided publicity and pictures, little was known of Guzmán; he turned out to be an obese, psoriasis-ridden, ordinary-looking person with remarkable powers of persuasion, not unlike Charles Manson and David Koresh. Violence had become an end, not a means, for his followers, who engaged in the worst sort of torture, maiming, mutilation and murder of innocent victims. He was sentenced to a 40-year prison term. His capture inspired the novel and movie, *The Dancer Upstairs*.

Fujimori and his supporters drafted a new constitution, which voters approved in 1993 by a narrow margin.

Fujimori's harsh measures began to bear fruit. Violence dwindled to less than 25% of what it had been in 1993. The *senderistas* were reduced to a hard core of fewer than 1,000 who opposed Guzmán's surprising support from his jail cell of the new constitution.

Fujimori's popularity soared. *Cambio '90* changed its name to *Nueva Majoría Cambio '90* ("New Majority for Change 90") for the 1995 elections. Meanwhile, discord surfaced in the presidential mansion. Fujimori and his wife, Susana Higuchi, sep-

Alberto Fujimori

arated. Forming a new political party, Harmony 21st Century, she announced she would run for president. The National Election Board declared most of the signatures on her application invalid; she accused it of "techno-fraud."

Fifteen candidates filed for president in 1995, including former U.N. Secretary-General Javier Pérez de Cuellar. Higuchi aligned herself with the Police-Military Front. She and her husband divorced soon thereafter. Fujimori won 64% of the vote, and his party was assured of a comfortable margin in Congress. He acquired the nickname "Chinochet," a reference to his Asian heritage and the name of Chile's General Pinochet. He declared that Peru needed order, discipline, the principle of authority, sound leadership and administration and honesty. He provided all but the last.

In 1995, Peru fought a brief but bloody war with neighboring Ecuador over a border dispute that had simmered since 1942 (see Ecuador).

The Fujimori government soon faced a new guerrilla threat in 1996 from its other active guerrilla group, the Tupac Amaru Revolutionary Movement (*MRTA*). It differs from the *senderistas* in that it is urban-based and far less bloodthirsty. On December 17, 1996, it raided a Christmas party at the Japanese ambassador's residence in Lima and took more than 400 diplomats and government officials hostage. The *MRTA* demanded release of prisoners, and gradually it released most of the hostages as tense negotiations unfolded.

The siege attracted worldwide media coverage. After four months, only 73 hostages remained in the compound, but Fujimori steadfastly refused to cave in to the demand to release prisoners. The standoff continued until April 22, 1997, when Peruvian commandos, acting on intelligence that the rebels were engaged in a soccer game, stormed the compound and killed all 14 of the remaining guerrillas, at a loss of only two commandos and one hostage, a Supreme Court justice. There was evidence that at least two women guerrillas attempted to surrender but were gunned down in cold blood, charges the government denied. The operation, and questions about whether guerrillas were summarily executed, later returned to haunt Fujimori.

Fujimori sent up a trial balloon on the possibility of his running for a third consecutive term in 2000, on the pretext that his first election in 1990 had predated the new constitution. The Constitutional Tribunal rejected the idea. Fujimori merely cajoled Congress, controlled by his allies, to remove three of the tribunal's justices.

By 1997, Fujimori's tendency to play fast and loose with the constitution and with basic civil liberties erupted into a major scandal, which the opposition and its media allies exploited. A female army sergeant assigned to intelligence alleged in a televised interview that she had been tortured and another woman sergeant, Mariela Barreto, murdered for leaking information that military intelligence was wiretapping Fujimori's opponents in Congress and the media and threatening some with physical violence.

When Barreto's dismembered body was found, the public outcry reached a crescendo against the president and the two men who it was widely believed were ruling Peru with him as a triumvirate: intelligence chief Vladimiro Montesinos and General Nicolás Hermoza, chairman of the joint chiefs of staff. Foreign Minister Francisco Tudela, who had been one of the hostages held by the Tupac Amaru guerrillas, resigned to protest the government wiretapping campaign.

The embattled Fujimori responded to the crisis by revoking the Peruvian citizenship of Baruch Ivcher, the Israeli-born owner of *Frecuencia Latina* (Channel 2), the station that televised the interview, a flagrant violation of the constitution. Through a legal maneuver, control of the station passed to two pro-Fujimori shareholders. Spontaneous demonstrations erupted, and volunteers camped out at *Frecuencia Latina* to prevent an armed takeover by security forces. Fujimori's public approval rating nosedived to 19%, the lowest of his seven years in office.

There was more to come. For years, since Fujimori first ran in 1990, there had been rumors that he had been born in Japan and was thus constitutionally ineligible to serve as president. In 1997, *Caretas*, the country's most respected weekly newsmagazine, published documents that disputed Fujimori's claim he had been born in Miraflores in 1938. The media reprinted reproductions of the birth certificate, in which the place of birth obviously had been clumsily erased and the words "Miraflores, Lima" written over the erasure in a different handwriting. Other documents arose, such as Fujimori's mother claiming two children when she immigrated in 1934; Fujimori is her second son. It boiled down to Fujimori's word against the media's. Of course, there was no contest as to who would prevail.

Next came a showdown between Fujimori and the military. Fujimori published a book on the siege of the Japanese ambassador's residence, in which he played up his own role and downplayed that of Hermoza. In an apparent test of his authority, Hermoza summoned all the country's generals to Lima, ostensibly for his birthday party, sparking rumors of an imminent coup. Fujimori quickly ordered the generals back to their posts; just as quickly, they went. Once again, the feisty little president had prevailed in a test of wills.

Fujimori recuperated some of the fading esteem of his people by once again doing battle with a common enemy, not terrorists, but Mother Nature. *El Niño*, the periodic weather phenomenon that affects climate worldwide but which reserves its greatest fury for Peru, returned with a vengeance in December 1997 and continued for months. Flooding destroyed whole villages and killed about 300 people. Fujimori, a professional engineer, went to the affected areas and took per-

Machu Picchu   Courtesy: Heather Marion

Peru

sonal charge of the efforts to contain the floodwaters. To Fujimori's critics, this was micromanagement at best and shameless grandstanding and exploitation of a tragedy at worst, but it was a take-charge gesture that was typically Fujimori.

In 1998, a popular movement called the Democratic Forum, backed by Fujimori's congressional opposition, collected 1.45 million signatures on a petition demanding a referendum on the issue of whether Fujimori could run again. The petition was presented to the electoral board, which voted 4–1 that only the Congress—controlled, of course, by Fujimori allies—could approve a referendum.

Congress voted down the referendum. Pro-Fujimori and opposition legislators almost came to blows. Police cordoned off the Congress building to repel demonstrators who chanted, "Death to the dictatorship." The vote effectively removed any remaining obstacle to a third-term bid except for one—the Peruvian voters themselves.

In 1999 Fujimoro signed the long-sought peace agreement with Ecuador's President Jamil Mahuad in Brasilia. They dedicated the first border marker in January 2000 and signed bilateral economic development accords in Washington in February (see Ecuador).

On a darker note, Fujimori's government renewed its persecution of exiled television station owner Baruch Ivcher. In December 1998, a Lima court issued arrest warrants for Ivcher, his wife and daughter for allegedly altering the registration forms for his television station. Apparently stung by his growing image as a bully, Fujimori then shifted course and sought to reach an out-of-court settlement, arguing that the case was merely a legal battle between Ivcher and the pro-Fujimori shareholders who controlled the station. When the negotiations broke down, Ivcher took the case before the Inter-American Human Rights Commission, an organ of the OAS. The commission forwarded the case to the Inter-American Court of Human Rights. Fujimori resolved the matter in 1999 in typical fashion: He simply withdrew Peru from the Court of Human Rights. Ivcher remained abroad.

The "Elections" of 2000

The opposition grudgingly accepted Congress' refusal to call a referendum on a third term and set out to defeat the president the only way left: at the ballot box in April 2000. But three strong candidates emerged against him, dividing the opposition.

The early favorite was Lima Mayor Alberto Andrade, of *APRA*, who won a landslide re-election victory of 65% in 1998

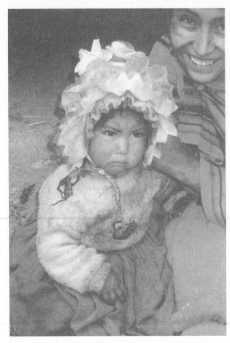

Mother and child in Andean village

against a Fujimori ally. Then a second candidate, Luis Casteñeda, who had earned high marks as head of the social security system, moved up even in the polls to Andrade. Fujimori held a strong first place in the polls, but not the 50% needed to avoid a runoff.

Suddenly, the fourth-ranking candidate, Alejandro Toledo, a 54-year-old economist of pure Indian descent, broke from the rear of the pack and moved up on the outside, emerging as the man for Fujimori to beat. The media made much of Toledo's humble farming background and how he had once shined shoes before going on to earn a doctorate at Stanford and to become an official at the World Bank.

Tension mounted as the opposition, the media and international election monitors uncovered evidence that machinery was in place for vote-rigging. Fujimori insisted the vote would be clean, but he denied the opposition access to the state-owned media, and thugs repeatedly pelted opposition rallies with rocks; no arrests were made. Opposition candidates were also the targets of scurrilous stories in tabloid newspapers.

The day after the election, it seemed that the worst fears would come to pass. Despite exit polls that showed Fujimori well short of a majority, the first "official" count—suspiciously delayed until April 10—showed Fujimori a hair short of a majority, 49.6%; Toledo was a strong second with 40.6%. It was apparent that as the count progressed, the president would go over the 50% mark. As the tedious count progressed, reports surfaced of such irregularities as soldiers preventing people

from voting, ballots with Toledo's name torn off the bottom, pre-filled ballots, and Fujimori campaign officials inserting votes into the electoral commission's computer via an Internet café.

Protests erupted, and the United States and other democracies warned Fujimori they would take a dim view of a fraudulent election. Then, as if by magic, election officials "revised" the final vote count, giving Fujimori 49.89%, just 20,000 short of a majority. Toledo obtained 40.15%.

The opposition took heart from Fujimori's failure to steal the election outright and even more from the results in the congressional election. Fujimori's *Perú 2000* party lost its absolute majority, dropping from 67 seats in the 120-member Congress to 51. Toledo's *Perú Posible* was second with 28 seats. The opposition alleged that Fujimori loyalists were offering $50,000 bribes for legislators to join an alliance with *Perú 2000*.

The eyes of the world were focused on the May 28 runoff, as it seemed obvious Fujimori did not intend to allow a trifle like the will of the people to stand in the way of his retaining power. The domestic watchdog *Transparencia* and observers from the OAS and the Atlanta-based Carter Center all concluded it would be impossible to guarantee a fair and honest vote. Toledo proclaimed he would withdraw from the race unless the vote were postponed until June to allow experts time to ensure there would not be the kinds of computer problems and irregularities that marred the first round. The international observers soon joined Toledo's call for a postponement. But Fujimori refused, countering that Toledo merely feared defeat.

Toledo withdrew, saying he refused to lend the appearance of legitimacy to a fraudulent election. Then the OAS and the Carter Center pulled out their observers, saying they could not guarantee the integrity of the vote unless it were delayed. The OAS mission declared that the process "was far from free and fair." The day before the election, this author spoke with Jimmy Carter in Venezuela, which had just postponed its election because of technical problems. "In Venezuela, the election has been postponed, but with integrity," he said. "In Peru, the election has been allowed to proceed without postponement, but without integrity."

The Clinton administration warned Fujimori that Peru could face economic sanctions. Street violence broke out as Toledo supporters attacked Fujimori campaign offices. Toledo at first called on his voters to boycott the election, but the $33 fine for failing to vote is too stiff for most Peruvians. He then called on them to deface their ballots by writing, "No to fraud!"

Fabián Salazar, a columnist for the newspaper *La República,* was given video-tapes from contacts in the National Intelligence Service that showed Montesinos instructing the head of the electoral commission how to rig the congressional elections to deny seats to certain candidates. As Salazar was viewing the tapes in his office, security agents broke in, confiscated the tapes and sawed Salazar's arm to the bone.

The outcome on May 28 was a foregone conclusion. Fujimori received only a bare majority of 51.1%. Toledo received 17.4%, and 30.3% of the ballots were voided as Toledo had requested.

The U.S. State Department quickly branded Fujimori's victory as "illegitimate," and the presidents of several Latin American countries expressed their concern. Toledo flew to Madrid to ask for support from Spanish President José María Aznar for a new election.

The tarnished election also headed the agenda of a meeting of OAS foreign ministers in Canada. But the Latin American representatives had no stomach for the U.S. position for strong hemispheric action. What emerged was a lukewarm resolution to conduct a fact-finding mission to Peru to study ways to "strengthen democracy" there. There was no mention of sanctions or new elections.

Fujimori Falls

Fujimori was inaugurated for his third term on July 28, 2000, an event largely snubbed by the international community and vigorously protested in the streets of Lima. Only two presidents, from neighboring Ecuador and Bolivia, attended, compared with nine in 1995. On inauguration eve, Toledo marshaled 80,000 demonstrators for a non-violent protest.

Inauguration day was uglier, as riot police dispersed protesters with tear gas, which wafted toward the presidential palace and into the nostrils of the dignitaries. Uglier still, a bank was torched, and six security guards died in the blaze; each side blamed the other. In his address, Fujimori ignored mention of the democratic reforms he had promised the OAS, focusing instead on economic growth. Meanwhile, as expected, several independent congressmen were "persuaded" to join the pro-Fujimori bloc, giving it a slim 63–57 majority.

For seven weeks, the protesters remained in the streets; usually the protests were non-violent. Among the demonstrators' symbolic protests in front of the presidential palace: Washing the Peruvian flag in a tub of soap and water; using fumigation guns to spray the "rats" in the palace, and surrounding the palace with yellow

police tape that bore the legend, "Caution! Mafia at work!" It was clever and effective non-violent protest in the best tradition of Gandhi and Martin Luther King. Still, the entrenched Fujimori hung tough.

Then in September, evidence became public that Montesinos may have been responsible for the transfer of arms through Peru to the *FARC* guerrillas in Colombia, which brought increased U.S. pressure on Fujimori. Then a television station broadcast a clandestine videotape of Montesinos attempting to bribe a congressman in the anti-Fujimori faction into switching sides.

The resulting domestic and international pressure finally proved too much. Fujimori stunned the nation in a televised address by announcing he would disband Montesinos' National Intelligence Service (whose Spanish acronym, *SIN,* is amusingly allegorical in English) and that he would call a new election—in which he would not be a candidate! He began talks with the opposition, brokered by the OAS, to effect a transition. Fujimori angered the opposition by agreeing to a new election on April 8, 2001, with the new president to succeed him on July 28, but only if the Congress approved an expanded amnesty law to protect members of the armed forces from prosecution in other than human rights cases. The opposition refused, and it prevailed. Many in the opposition preferred Fujimori's immediate resignation, which the president at first rejected, and they made the resignation of Montesinos the *sine qua non* for continued dialogue.

The nation was shocked again by the news that Montesinos had fled to Panama, Latin America's traditional dumping ground for unpopular and venal political figures. Fujimori had just "fired" him under mounting pressure, but his escape smacked of collusion. Others were relieved he was gone. Montesinos sought political asylum in Panama, which demurred, despite pressure from the United States and some Latin American countries to allow him to remain, thus removing the possibility of his continuing as a player in Peru's complex power game.

With his tourist visa expiring and no charges awaiting him in Peru, Montesinos returned to Peru just as suddenly and as unexpectedly as he had left, precipitating a domestic crisis. Rumors flew that the armed forces chiefs, known to owe their first loyalty to Montesinos, were planning a *coup d'etat.* Fujimori went on television to assure the country that he was in "total control" of the armed forces. Montesinos went into hiding, and Fujimori made a publicized effort to "find" his intelligence chief, although most Peruvians believed the president actually was harboring him.

The opposition demanded Fujimori's resignation. Even First Vice President Francisco Tudela, long a Fujimori ally, resigned in protest—a decision he may have regretted a month later. Fujimori sought to mollify public opinion by firing the heads of the three armed forces, all Montesinos loyalists. But his new army commander also was a *montesinista.*

For eight months, Montesinos' whereabouts became an international guessing game; he was reported in the Galapagos Islands of Ecuador, then Costa Rica, then Aruba; in January 2001, he was believed to have returned to Peru. By November, reports circulated in the media that Montesinos and Fujimori had been involved in money laundering, arms dealing and drug trafficking. A federal prosecutor alleged that Montesinos had $48 million in Swiss bank accounts (his monthly salary was just $337). By early 2001, an investigation raised that figure to $70 million, and further probing brought evidence that Montesinos may have amassed as much as $264 million. Evidence surfaced later that some of the money may have been laundered by two front companies that had been set up in Singapore—by Fujimori.

On November 13, 2000, Fujimori flew to Brunei for a meeting of the Asia-Pacific Economic Cooperation (APEC) conference. By then, defections from Fujimori's bloc in Congress had given the opposition control. Hours after Fujimori departed, Congress deposed his loyal speaker and replaced her with Valentín Paniagua from the now-tiny Popular Action Party. The country was jolted yet again on November 17, when Fujimori absconded to Japan, his family's homeland. Three days later, he faxed his resignation to Congress—which rejected it. Instead, Congress voted 62–9 to remove him from office as "permanently morally unfit."

At first, Second Vice President Ricardo Márquez, a *fujimorista,* sought to exercise his constitutional right to succeed the ousted president, but Congress appointed Paniagua as interim president. He vowed a "total house-cleaning" and appointed the respected former U.N. Secretary-General Javier Pérez de Cuellar as prime minister. Another positive step: *Frecuencia Latina* was restored to its rightful owner, Baruch Ivcher, and the media were given free rein to report on the upcoming election campaign. Congress also restored the three judges Fujimori had sacked from the Constitutional Tribunal.

Thus, one of the most intriguing eras of *personalismo* in 20th century Latin American history came to an end. In February 2001, Congress formally charged Fujimori with dereliction of duty and other specifications. But Japan granted him citizenship

Peru

and refused to extradite him. Nonetheless, Fujimori remained as much a fugitive as Montesinos, unable to travel to countries that have extradition treaties with Peru.

He then faced murder charges at home. According to a former Japanese hostage, three of the guerrillas slain in the 1997 commando raid on the Japanese ambassador's residence were seen alive after the raid in commando custody. Fujimori had boasted of his micromanagement of that raid, making it unlikely that the prisoners could have been killed without his approval. It was a shabby end for a man once hailed as the country's savior.

Investigators then seized from Montesinos' home about 2,400 videotapes on which the intelligence chief had unabashedly chronicled his bribes of a dazzling array of officials. Many of the so-called *"Vladivideos"* were released to the media, which kept the public spellbound—and further outraged.

Peruvian authorities then received word that Montesinos was in hiding in Venezuela, which the government of President Hugo Chávez denied for months. The Peruvians also learned that Montesinos had a secret bank account in Miami and asked the U.S. FBI to monitor it. Acting on irrefutable evidence from the FBI, the Peruvians confronted the Chávez government with the evidence of Montesinos' whereabouts, and in June 2001, Venezuelan intelligence officials arrested Montesinos in Caracas. Ironically, the Peruvian president-elect, Toledo, was in Caracas for the 13th Andean Summit, where Chávez announced Montesinos' arrest.

Montesinos was hustled back to Lima, not on an extradition request, but as an undocumented alien! His appearance in court, in handcuffs and bulletproof vest, was a hemispheric media event, and the Peruvian public waited expectantly for new revelations of Montesinos' perfidy like they would an unfolding *telenovela*. Besides the money laundering, drug trafficking and arms smuggling charges, Montesinos also faced a murder charge in the death of the whistle-blowing female army sergeant in 1997.

New Election, New President

Ten candidates presented themselves for the April 2001 election, including Toledo. Perhaps the most surprising postulant was former President García, who had returned home after nine years of self-imposed exile in Colombia—just after the statute of limitations on his kickback charges had expired. At first, the García candidacy on the APRA ticket was dismissed as a joke, a relic of the dreadful days of guerrilla warfare and hyperinfla-

tion. It seemed a foregone conclusion that the two candidates who would face each other in the runoff would be Toledo, candidate of *Perú Posible*, and Lourdes Flores, a veteran congresswoman from the conservative Popular Christian Party.

Suddenly, polls showed García closing in on Flores for the No. 2 spot. That sent a chill through domestic and international financial circles; as president, García had limited debt repayment to 10% of exports, sparking the hyperinflation that Fujimori was elected to combat. Nonetheless, García, an eloquent stump speaker, remained popular with the country's poor majority, who did not feel they had benefited appreciably from 10 years of *fujimorismo*. Still, he pragmatically toned down his fiery populist rhetoric so as not to frighten foreign investors and the ruling elite.

García also was aided by Toledo and Flores, who hurled mud at each other. Toledo was accused of fathering a child out of wedlock and refusing to take a paternity test. Also, *Caretas* magazine reproduced a medical report showing he had tested positive for cocaine in 1998; Toledo countered that the *SIN* had abducted him and framed him.

Peruvians should have become inured to shocks by this time, but they received another on April 8. Toledo led the field with 36.5%, less than he had received the year before in the first round against Fujimori. García won the runoff spot 26% to Flores' 24%. In the June 3 runoff, Toledo defeated García by a slim 52% to 48%, making history as Peru's first full-blooded Indian president.

Toledo's Troubled Presidency

Toledo was inaugurated on July 28, 2001. In his address, he pledged to combat the corruption left by Fujimori; to restructure the armed forces and police in the wake of Montesinos' departure; to create 400,000 jobs; and to continue cooperating with the United States in the war against drugs. In a symbolic demonstration of pride in his roots, Toledo participated in an Inca "inauguration" ceremony at the ruins of Machu Picchu.

Peru moved toward a catharsis to cleanse itself of the Fujimori legacy, which the disgraced former president continued to defend from his safe haven in Japan. Montesinos admitted Fujimori had ordered him to pay hundreds of thousands of dollars in bribes to key members of Congress to secure his re-election in 2000. He even named the members who had accepted the bribes, including several who had just been elected again.

Congress voted unanimously to strip Fujimori of his immunity from prosecution. Then the attorney general filed formal

murder charges against him for his alleged knowledge and approval of two massacres of dissidents: the so-called "barbecue massacre" in the Lima neighborhood of Barrio Alto in 1991 that left 15 people dead, and another in 1992, in which 10 were killed. The massacres allegedly were committed by an infamous paramilitary death squad known as the "Colina Group." Fujimori also was charged with complicity in the 1997 murder and dismemberment of Mariela Barreto, the whistle-blowing intelligence service sergeant.

A judge issued an international arrest warrant for Fujimori. Japan, however, continued to deny his extradition, which strained relations. Congress, meanwhile, questioned the disappearance of $372 million, $260 million of which apparently went into accounts controlled by Montesinos. Another international warrant was issued against Fujimori in 2002 for an alleged $15 million payoff to Montesinos. Fujimori also was charged with ordering the bribes of members of Congress to pave the way for his re-election.

Next, prosecutors cited forensic evidence that eight of the 14 guerrillas slain in the recapturing of the Japanese ambassador's residence in 1997 had been shot execution-style, not in combat as had been reported at the time. In 2003, Interpol added Fujimori to its 10 Most Wanted list.

Montesinos faced as many as 70 trials. His first conviction, of becoming intelligence chief in an illegal manner, was handed down in 2002. He was sentenced to nine years. In 2003 he was convicted of influence peddling and sentenced to five years, then he was convicted of embezzlement and sentenced to eight.

Meanwhile, former army commander Nicolás Hermoza, the third man in the so-called "triumvirate" with Fujimori and Montesinos, was convicted in 2005 of illegally amassing a $22 million fortune and sentenced to eight years.

The Truth and Reconciliation Commission, which had been appointed by interim President Paniagua, began public hearings in 2002 into human rights abuses committed during the 1980s and '90s. Peruvians were presented with horror stories of past atrocities. A team from the commission flew to Tokyo to interrogate Fujimori himself, who refused to meet with them.

Peruvians were abruptly reminded of another past horror that had led to the atrocities when, in March 2002, a powerful car bomb exploded near the U.S. Embassy in Lima on the eve of a one-day visit by U.S. President George W. Bush, the first visit by a U.S. president. Ten people were killed and 30 injured. Police arrested four members of *Sendero Luminoso* in connection with the bombing.

The prospect of renewed violence by the once-feared group, whose size was estimated variously at 175 to 700, sent a chill through the country. So did the decision by the Supreme Court in 2003 to overturn the conviction of *Sendero Luminoso* leader Guzmán. He was retried in 2004, but that ended in a mistrial. He was tried a third time, and in 2006 he was convicted and sentenced to life in prison. Ironically, his cell is close to Montesino's.

Toledo's honeymoon with the Congress and the public was brief. Despite the fact that the economy was showing a brisk growth rate (see Economy), demonstrators took to the streets in 2002 to denounce Toledo for failing to ease unemployment. His job approval rating plummeted to 25%, compared with 59% in August 2001.

Toledo contributed to his own image problem, coming across as inarticulate, unpunctual and indecisive. He changed prime ministers, interior ministers and finance ministers with bewildering regularity, and he replaced technocrats with political hacks. Street protests in the capital and elsewhere became a regular occurrence.

His efforts at privatization also came under attack. In 2002, he dispatched troops and riot police to Arequipa to quell violent protests against plans to privatize two local electric companies. Toledo declared a 30-day state of siege, which prompted his interior minister to resign. By the time the rioting died down a week later, two people had been killed and 200 injured. Toledo backed down and called off the sale of the companies.

Former President Fernando Belaúnde, the acknowledged patriarch of Peru's new democracy, died June 4, 2002, at the age of 89. Toledo declared three days of national mourning and tearfully praised his predecessor as a "paradigm of democracy."

As a means of enhancing decentralization, Congress created 25 new federal-style regional governments. Elections for these new governorships and legislative assemblies were held in November 2002. Toledo's *Perú Posible* party won only one governorship. *APRA* won 11 and independent candidates won 13.

In a separate development, Toledo publicly acknowledged just two days before the election that confirmed what had been alleged by a former lover and widely believed by the public: that he was the father of a 14-year-old girl born out of wedlock.

Despite Peru's boasting the fastest economic growth rate in Latin America, large sectors of the work force continued to grumble that they were not feeling any of the benefits of it. In 2003, teachers walked out on strike, and hundreds literally camped outside the Congress to demand

Former President Alejandro Toledo

an increase in their $190-a-month salaries. The government offered them a $29-a-month raise, which they rejected. Farmers, angered by taxes and by low prices they blamed on cheap imports, erected barricades on the 1,500-mile Peruvian segment of the Pan-American Highway, disrupting commerce and stranding travelers. Simultaneously, civil servants, health care workers and judicial employees went out on strike.

Toledo responded with another 30-day state of emergency. Troops and police forcibly but peaceably evicted the teachers from the Congress. Troops opened fire on protesting students in the southeastern city of Puno, killing one and wounding 36. The government claimed that *senderistas* had instigated the violence.

Peace returned as the government and teachers reached a compromise on a salary increase to $350 a month. Largely as a public relations gesture, Toledo and his top cabinet ministers reduced their salaries by 30%.

Toledo did little to enhance his popularity with his opulent lifestyle. He used the presidential jet to deliver the commencement address at his alma mater, Stanford, in 2003, which cost $100,000, when the university had provided first-class commercial tickets. Toledo's response to his growing unpopularity: another cabinet shuffle! By August 2003, Toledo's approval rating had dropped to 12%, the lowest of any Latin American president; even Fujimori's was 31%! Toledo's popularity soon would drop even lower.

The Peruvian government stubbornly filed a 700-page extradition request with Japan in 2003, naming Fujimori as the intellectual author of the 1991 "barbecue massacre." Japan still took no action, while Fujimori brazenly announced his intention to run for president in 2006—even though he has been barred from holding office until 2010. In 2005, Fujimori's brother and two sisters were arrested on charges that they has embezzled $21 million from a private charity.

The Truth and Reconciliation Commission presented its long-awaited report to Toledo in August 2003. It had spent two years and $13 million interviewing 17,000 witnesses and unearthing mass graves. Perhaps its most surprising conclusion was that 69,000 people had been killed during the guerrilla wars of the 1980s and '90s, more than twice as many as the 30,000 that had been generally believed. The commission laid the greatest blame for the deaths at the feet of *Sendero Luminoso*, but also faulted the security services for human rights violations. It criticized the governments of former presidents Belaúnde and García as inept and for not responding forcefully enough, and Fujimori's for responding *too* forcefully.

Faced with an approval rating that had sunk to 6%, the last thing Toledo needed was yet another scandal. But in 2005, a judge ordered the arrest of Toledo's sister, Margarita, and 25 others for allegedly falsifying voters' signatures on the petitions to qualify *Perú Posible* for the ballot in the 2000 election. A local TV station aired yet another embarrassing video showing Toledo congratulating followers for collecting the signatures. An investigation produced evidence that 78% of the party's 520,000 signatures were forged. Toledo neither admitted nor denied the allegations. His only response: another cabinet shuffle.

A congressional committee, on a 3–2 vote, concluded that Toledo was the "co-author" of the forgery scheme. This constituted grounds for impeachment and removal, but Congress voted instead, 57–48, to forward the charges to a prosecutor for Toledo to face criminal charges. Because the president enjoyed immunity, the effect was to allow Toledo to serve out the remaining 14 months of his term.

In the drug war, the United Nations released figures showing that coca production in Peru had soared by 55% in 2004. Although the report conceded that Peru has eradicated more than 26,000 acres of coca, 42,000 acres of new coca were planted. Experts theorized that the crackdown on coca cultivation in Colombia had forced producers to shift operations to Peru, Ecuador and Bolivia. The U.S. government reported that coca production in Peru was up another 38% in 2005.

Peru

In 2005, Peru became the 13th nation to sign a bilateral free-trade agreement with the United States; trade between Peru and the United States totaled about $6 billion in 2005. Colombia signed one soon thereafter, and Ecuador was negotiating one. This technically undermined the purpose of the Andean Pact, from which Venezuela's Chávez angrily withdrew to protest the Peruvian and Colombian decisions.

On November 7, 2005, the ever-enigmatic Fujimori, then 67, splashed back into the world headlines when he abandoned his safe haven in Japan and arrived unexpectedly in Santiago, Chile, where he apparently planned to set up a base from which to negotiate his return to Peru. Fujimori evidently believed the Chilean government would look tolerantly upon his presence, as it had fugitive former Argentine President Carlos Menem (see Argentina). He seriously miscalculated; Chilean authorities arrested him immediately, and a judge denied him bail pending Peru's request to extradite him on 12 counts of corruption and human rights violations. He was freed in May 2006, but was prohibited from leaving Chile until the extradition process was completed, which took more than a year.

García's Dramatic Comeback

The campaign for the April 9, 2006, presidential election was in many ways a replay of the one in 2001: A plethora of candidates, but only three major ones, two of them who also ran in 2001; a surprise finish in the first round; and a close, dramatic runoff. The two holdovers were former President García of the *APRA*, and Lourdes Flores, the conservative whom García had narrowly nudged out of the runoff.

The long-shot outsider this time was retired army Lieutenant Colonel Ollanta Humala, 43, a leftist nationalist who modeled himself after Venezuela's Chávez and professed admiration for the policies of former military strongman Juan Velasco Alvarado, who ruled from 1968–75. Like Chávez, Humala had participated in a coup attempt while in uniform, a failed attempt to oust Fujimori in 2000; he received an amnesty in 2001, then retired. In August 2005, a poll gave him only 5%, but by December, he had 23%, just behind front-runner Flores. Chávez openly endorsed Humala and compared him to Bolivia's new leftist president, Evo Morales. Toledo recalled Peru's ambassador from Caracas and accused Chávez of "meddling" in Peruvian politics. Humala called the action "desperation" by the ruling elite.

Suddenly the bombastic Fujimori, still under house arrest in Chile, declared his intention to run, even though he was

In this editorial cartoon, President Toledo asks God, "Father, why have You forsaken me?" God replies: "Because of incompetence, frivolousness, insecurity, lying, erratic behavior, irresponsibility, indecisiveness, nepotism, for being dumb, for being a bad father. . ."

barred from holding office until at least 2011. His daughter and other supporters filed the papers in Lima to have him on the ballot, and incredibly, a poll showed him with 15% support. But the electoral commission rejected his candidacy. Fujimori appealed, to no avail. In the end, his hastily created movement, Alliance for the Future, fielded Martha Chávez, a former president of the Congress, as his stand-in candidate. Her running mate was Fujimori's younger brother, Santiago.

Polls hinted that it would be a two-person race between Flores and Humala. Suddenly, just as he had in 2001, the populist García moved up on the outside. Turnout was 88.7%. Once again, García surprised everyone and Flores was again left on the outside looking in. The results:

Humala	3,758,258	30.6%
García	2,985,858	24.3%
Flores	2,925,280	23.8%
Chávez	912,420	7.4%

In the simultaneous elections for the new Congress, Humala's Union for Peru obtained the most seats, 45 out of 120. *APRA* was second with 36, and Flores' National Unity won 17. Fujimori's Alliance for the Future won 13; one of them went to Fujimori's daughter, Keiko.

If the prospect of a García presidency frightened the business elite, the U.S. government, international lenders and foreign investors, the idea of a Humala presidency gave them cardiac arrest. Flores' voters, and those of the other losing candidates who comprised more than 20% of the April 9 votes, agonized over whether to vote for a disgraced former president who had wrecked the economy or a left-wing ideologue who wanted to implement the same type of repressive revolutionary regime Chávez had imposed on Venezuela.

García downplayed his past, and while Humala frightened moderate voters by likening himself to Chávez or Morales,

García now portrayed himself as a pragmatic populist like Brazil's Lula da Silva or Chile's Socialist president, Michelle Bachelet. While Humala promised greater state control of the economy, García said he would continue Toledo's free-market policies that had given Peru among the highest growth rates in Latin America. García said he would move forward with the free-trade agreement (FTA) with the United States; Humala vowed to scuttle it.

If García's closet was full of skeletons, Humala had some of his own. Charges surfaced that Humala was responsible for human rights abuses during the dirty war against the *senderistas*, and that his abortive coup in 2000 was a diversion designed to help Montesinos flee the country; from his jail cell, Montesinos confirmed the allegations. Humala's brother, leader of a bizarre quasi-fascist paramilitary group, was in jail for leading an attack in 2005 that left four policemen dead. Their father also was notorious for his weird racial philosophy.

Even though millions of voters must have held their noses when they voted in the June 4 runoff, turnout was an impressive 87.7%. The percentages were almost identical to the 2001 runoff, only the loser in 2001 had become the winner in 2006:

García	6,965,017	52.6%
Humala	6,270,080	47.4%

The sigh of relief could be heard all the way from Washington.

Even before García's inauguration, he pledged an austerity program, including a reduction in the salaries of all elected officials from the president on down, which he kept. He criticized Toledo for hiring several new government consultants in the 11th hour of his term and terminated them.

García was sworn in on July 28, 2006. At the time, his approval rating was only 50%, but with the popular austerity measures—which critics dismissed as populist window dressing—at the end of his first 100 days it was 60%. Besides the salary reductions, he grounded the presidential jet and traveled by coach class.

Ironically, he left in place many of the policies of the detested Toledo, and even appointed Toledo's former finance minister, Pedro-Pablo Kuczynski, as prime minister for a time. He further assuaged the fears of the business elite and foreign investors by appointing Luis Carranza, a banker and mainstream economist, as finance minister. García flew to Washington to meet with President Bush, and he lobbied the new Democratic-controlled Congress to ratify the FTA. It was a far cry from the bogeyman of the in 1990s.

Some of his measures have been controversial, such as imposing the death penalty for terrorists and for pedophiles who murder children. He courageously faced the wrath of the powerful teachers' union, part of his constituency, by implementing teacher evaluations as part of badly needed educational reform. In their first exams in 2007, the teachers scored abysmally.

Precisely as had happened with Toledo, García has presided over one of the fastest growing economies in Latin America, 7.6% in 2006, 8.9% in 2007 and 9.8% in 2008, coupled with 2% inflation in 2007 and a five-point drop in the poverty rate. Yet, just like Toledo, his countrymen have not appreciated him for it. On the first anniversary of his inauguration, his approval rating had plunged to 32%, and by August 2009 it was 27%.

The U.S. Congress ratified the U.S.-Peruvian free-trade agreement in December 2007, and President Bush signed it into law. Congress and Bush also extended the Andean Trade Preferences Act, by which Peru and neighboring countries enjoy preferential access to the U.S. market.

In 2007, García renounced a 50-year-old agreement with Chile delineating their maritime boundary. He published a map claiming a triangular tract, rich in fish, totaling 14,630 square miles (see Chile). Chile withdrew its ambassador, and García promised to take the case before the International Court of Justice in The Hague, Netherlands.

For 16 months, the extradition request for Fujimori wound through the Chilean courts. In September 2007, the Supreme Court ordered Fujimori handed over to Peru to face seven specific charges, including the two Colina Group massacres of 1991 and 1992. The ruling thus established an important new precedent for Latin America, where several countries have unsuccessfully sought extradition of venal or bloodthirsty former leaders.

The head of the national police flew to Santiago, and one day later the still-

President Alan Gabriel Ludwig García

pugnacious former president was back in Lima. In the first of many pending cases against him, Fujimori pleaded guilty to ordering an illegal search of Montesinos' house. In December 2007, he was sentenced to six years; the Supreme Court upheld the sentence in April 2008, thus ending the possibility of his running for president in 2011.

Fujimori then went on trial for his involvement in 25 murders carried out by the Colina Group, including the infamous "barbecue massacre." Ninety witnesses testified during the 16-month trial. On April 7, 2009, a three-judge panel of the Supreme Court found him guilty and sentenced him to another 25 years—one year for each victim? Fujimori showed no emotion when the verdict and sentence were read, but human rights advocates in Peru and abroad reacted with glee, while *fujimoristas* expressed outrage. His daughter Keiko, declared, "We're going into the streets to demonstrate our open support for the best president this country has ever had, for the president who saved Peru from terrorism."

That terrorism could be making a comeback. In October 2008, Shining Path guerrillas ambushed an army convoy in Tayacaia Province with a roadside bomb, killing 12 soldiers and two civilians. In April 2009, another *senderista* ambush left 14 soldiers dead. Guerrilla casualties were not known. Two soldiers and at least four *senderistas* died in a firefight in August 2009. *Senderistas* shot down an air force helicopter that was trying to rescue three soldiers wounded in an ambush in September, killing two crewmen. Like the *FARC* in Colombia, the *senderistas* are now

known to have struck a partnership with Peruvian drug dealers, which provides the drug dealers with protection and the guerrillas with ample funds.

The *senderistas* are not the only threat to García. Widespread public protests against his policies, some of them violent, led the president to declare states of emergency. The first was in the provinces of Amazonas, Loreto and Cuzco in August 2008 after Indians blockaded roads to protest the sale of their lands for oil and gas pipelines. Another was in the southern province of Tacna in November.

The latest corruption scandal broke in October 2008 when an investigative television program aired a video that showed prominent *APRA* officials apparently accepting bribes from a small Norwegian oil exploration company. García's cabinet, including Prime Minister Jorge del Castillo, resigned en masse. García's approval rating nosedived to 20%. Castillo was replaced by Yehude Simón, the popular governor of Lambayeque Province, who served time in jail for his membership in the *MRTA* and became a born-again Christian.

García hosted the 2008 forum of the Asia-Pacific Economic Cooperation (APEC) in Lima in November 2008. He used the occasion to sign a FTA with Chinese President Hu Jintao. The forum took a strong stand against trade protectionism.

Recent Developments

Fujimori faced his final two trials in 2009. In July, he was convicted and sentenced to seven and a half years for paying Montesinos a $15 million bonus from

Peru

the treasury. As his fourth and final trial was beginning in September, Fujimori pleaded guilty to authorizing illegal wiretaps and bribing journalists during his 2000 re-election campaign. He was sentenced to six years and ordered to pay $8.4 million in fines.

Relations with Chile became strained again in November 2009 when a Peruvian air force officer who had been assigned to the Peruvian Embassy in Santiago was arrested and confessed to selling secrets to Chile. Two other officers were arrested as accomplices. Coincidentally, the news broke while García and Chilean President Michele Bachelet were both attending the latest APEC summit in Singapore. García abruptly canceled a scheduled workshop with Bachelet and flew home, calling Chile a "pseudo-republic" that has "an inferiority complex" if it must resort to buying state secrets. Bachelet retorted that García's remarks were "offensive and haughty." Peruvian Foreign Minister José Antonio García Belaunde discussed the matter in Singapore with his Chilean counterpart, Mario Fernández, and promised he would send him the evidence after the summit. Back in Santiago, the Chilean Foreign Ministry adamantly denied the charges, saying tersely, "Chile does not spy." Since then, the controversy appears to have died down, with García saying he did not want it to disrupt relations.

Peru's relations with the United States, however, have grown increasingly warm, something few would have thought imaginable given García's past rhetoric. García has been one of the few remaining U.S. allies in Latin America under both Bush and Obama. He was one of only four Latin American presidents to join Obama in recognizing the legitimacy of the Honduran election in 2009 to replace the deposed President Manuel Zelaya. Obama hosted García at the White House on June 1, 2010, where García voiced support for Obama's nuclear non-proliferation initiative aimed at Iran. Secretary of State Hillary Clinton met with García a few days later in Lima, which was hosting the 40th OAS General Assembly.

Catholic University released a poll in March 2010 showing that García's approval rating had improved to 39%, astronomical by Peruvian standards for a president after almost four years in office. Who do Peruvians want to replace him a year before the April 10, 2011 election? A CPI poll in March 2010 showed Lima Mayor Luis Castañeda in first place with 24%, Fujimori's 35-year-old daughter Keiko second with 18.9%, leftist Ollanta Humala third with 10.7% and former President Toledo fourth with 8.2%. Two-time loser Lourdes Flores was running fifth, so she dropped out and opted to run for mayor of Lima. As of June, an Ipsos Apoyo poll reported virtually the same results: Casteñeda 22%, Fujimori 18%, Humala and Toledo tied at 13% (see The Future).

Culture: The legacy of the Incas is evident in Peruvian folklore, art, music and architecture. Most of the population is full-blooded Indian today, and Quechua is the first language of millions of Peruvians. Still, the inevitable hybridization with Spanish culture produced something that is uniquely Peruvian.

Because Peru, like Mexico (New Spain), was a full-fledged viceroyalty that yielded dazzling amounts of gold and silver, the Spanish crown placed a higher value on this colony than on most. Consequently, a strong creole culture developed and along with it a literary tradition. Peruvian literary activity, however, never matched that of, say, Argentina or Chile. One of the most influential writers of the late 19th and early 20th centuries was Manuel González Prada, a journalist, poet and essayist who labored for reform and influenced later generations of idealistic Peruvian writers.

Many of Peru's best-known writers of the first half of the 20th century found their inspiration in politics, including the poet César Vallejo and the Marxist essayist José Carlos Mariátegui, who, like González Prada, was an major force in the *aprista* movement. The most acclaimed novelists of that period and later years have all stressed indigenous themes, such as Ciro Alegría, Julio Ramón Ribeyra and José María Arguedas.

Without question Peru's most prominent contemporary writer is Mario Vargas Llosa (b. 1936). He earned a doctorate in Madrid, and consequently his works are more cosmopolitan than those of his predecessors. His best-known novel, translated into several languages and the recipient of numerous international garlands, remains *La guerra del fin del mundo (The War of the End of the World)* (1981). One of his plays, *La señorita de Tacna* (1981), also has been translated into English and other languages and received favorable reviews when performed on Broadway.

Vargas Llosa was Fujimori's opponent in the 1990 presidential election, and his electoral loss was seen as a victory for Peruvian—and Latin American—literature. His 2000 novel *La fiesta del chivo (The Feast of the Goat)*, which was about the assassination of Dominican dictator Rafael Leonidas Trujillo in 1961, was made into an English-language film by his cousin, director Luis Llosa (see below). In 2003, he published *El paraíso en la otra esquina (The Way to Paradise)* and in 2006 he published his latest novel, *Las travesuras de una niña mala (The Mischief of a Bad Girl)*, his first-

Mario Vargas Llosa

ever love story. In November 2001, President Alejandro Toledo garlanded Vargas Llosa with the Order of the Sun, Peru's highest honor.

Peruvians are as fanatically devoted to their two native musical styles, *música criolla* and Peruvian waltzes, as Argentines are to the tango. The same is true of the national folk dance, the *marinera*, subject of an annual festival in Ayacucho. Until her death in 1983, the singer Chabuca Grande conveyed these distinctly Peruvian sounds to audiences throughout Latin America.

Peruvian theater, cinema and television still lag behind those of such countries as Mexico and Argentina, though some works and artists have achieved recognition abroad. Peru is producing more of its own *telenovelas*, and in 2005 it released Latin America's animated 3-D motion picture, *Piratas de Callao* (Pirates of Callao), produced by Hernán Garrido-Lecca, which has been distributed throughout Latin America as well as to the United States and China.

Peruvian cinema also is achieving international acclaim through the talents of director Claudia Llosa (b. 1976), Vargas Llosa's niece. Her 2005 film, *Madeinusa*, was named Best Latin American Movie at both the Málaga (Spain) and Mar del Plata (Argentina) film festivals and was selected for showing at the Sundance Film Festival in the United States, among other international awards. Her second film, *La teta asustada (Milk of Sorrows)*, an examination of the psychological impact on Peruvian women of the guerrilla wars of the 1970s and '80s, became the first Peruvian film nominated for the U.S. Academy Award for Best Foreign Film in 2010. It won a total of nine international awards, including the Golden Bear at the 2009 Berlin International Film Festival, the Grand Coral Prize in the Havana Film Festival and Spain's Goya Award for Best Spanish-Language Foreign Film.

Another Peruvian director, Luis Llosa, cousin of both Mario Vargas Llosa and Claudia Llosa, achieved fame in the

A religious procession in rural Peru

United States with his English-language films in the 1990s. Among others, he has directed Sandra Bullock in *Fire on the Amazon* (1993), Tom Berenger in *Sniper* (1993), Sylvester Stallone and Sharon Stone in *The Specialist* (1994) and Jennifer López in *Anaconda* (1997). In 2005, he brought his cousin's novel *The Feast of the Goat* to the screen; he directed and co-authored the screenplay with Vargas Llosa. In recent years he has devoted himself primarily to producing or directing *telenovelas*, most recently the popular *Condesa por amor*, produced in Venezuela and filmed in the Dominican Republic.

Peru can claim to be one of the birthplaces of Latin American journalism. Even before independence, the literary journal *Mercurio Peruano* appeared in 1791. The leading contemporary daily, *El Comercio*, (see below) was founded in 1839, losing to Chile's *El Mercurio* by two years the distinction of being Latin America's oldest continuously published newspaper. For most of Peru's troubled history, press freedom either was nonexistent or severely limited. During the peculiar social experi-

mentation of the 1968–80 military regime, the major dailies were expropriated and turned over to various "social organizations," such as teachers and labor unions. The result was a journalistic disaster, and the first act of President Belaúnde when he returned to power in 1980 was to restore the newspapers to their rightful owners. Numerous dailies of stature, plus the usual sleazy tabloids, are published in the capital. A newspaper that has come to rival *El Comercio* in journalistic prestige since the restoration of democracy is the pro-*Aprista La República*. Some dailies also are published in the major provincial capitals. There also is a thriving magazine industry, the highest quality probably being *Caretas* and *Oiga*.

Like the press in most Latin American countries, New York-based freedom House rates the Peruvian press as only "partly free," even since the fall of Fujimori. A reminder of why came in January 2010, when Alejandro Carrascal Carrasco, editor of a weekly newspaper in the Amazonian city of Bagua, became the latest Latin American journalist jailed for *de-*

sacato, or defamation, of an elected official (see Latin America today). He published a series of exposés in 2005 that alleged corruption in a local public education institute. He was convicted and sentenced to a year in jail, which was denounced by international journalism organizations.

Peruvian cuisine is unique, owing to the great variety of seafood provided by the Humboldt Current and the cornucopia of foodstuffs from tropical and Andean ecospheres. Peruvian restaurants have begun cropping up in major cities in Europe and North America. The best-known Peruvian dish abroad is *ceviche* (also spelled *cebiche*), raw fish marinated in lime juice. Pisco, a potent liquor distilled from grapes, is mixed with lime juice, sugar and egg whites to create the Pisco sour, one of South America's favorite cocktails.

Economy: Extraction and marketing of natural resources from mountain areas and the adjacent sea have long been the cornerstone of the Peruvian economy. Because the arid Pacific shelf and the high Andes restrict agricultural output, recent

Peru

efforts have been made to open the eastern Andean slopes for farming. Water from the eastern slopes is also being used to irrigate former arid regions.

The ambitious land reform program implemented by the military government of 1968–80 provided for the seizure of virtually all of the nation's large farms and their conversion into huge cooperatives rather than small, unproductive peasant plots. Relying on material incentives (profits were to go to the workers), the program was designed to increase farm output and bring—for the first time—larger numbers of peasants into the national money economy. However, because of poor management and a breakdown in the food distribution system, the land reform program fell far short of expectations.

In 1981, Occidental Petroleum reported that new oil fields had been discovered in Peru's Amazon basin. Peru then reported early in 1982 that its proven oil reserves increased to 900 million barrels.

The inflation rate in 1989 was about 2,800%, creating labor unrest and an economically ruinous strike by the miners. President Alan García began privatizing the nation's industry—the military had taken over more than 150 industries while in power. Peru's foreign debt was about $20 billion. To aid in its slow economic recovery, and under strict austerity requirements, the IMF in 1984 extended loans to the government; however, this was half as much as Peru hoped to receive.

When García demurred on payment of Peru's debts in the late 1980s, the IMF declared Peru ineligible to receive further loans, and all other lenders followed suit. This left the nation on a cash-in-advance status—an economic impossibility in a day and age when spare parts, machinery and manufacturing facilities are so vital to growth. It further meant that no government would honor Peruvian currency; the only substitute was foreign currency deposited in a foreign bank in advance to pay for imports.

This was reversed under President Alberto Fujimori. Peru again became creditworthy and received aid and investment from a number of sources. Approval of the constitution in late 1993 boosted available lending sources considerably.

Peru is the world's leading producer of raw coca leaf, from which refined cocaine is made, and second after Colombia in production of cocaine. Chewed by the Indians for millennia as a mild anesthetic to allay hunger, coca thrives in the remote Andean valleys. Illegal coca exports once accounted for an estimated $1 billion a year. But in 1996, Fujimori ordered his air force to begin shooting down planes crossing the border that refused to identify themselves. Total coca acreage that year dropped 18% as peasants willingly accepted a government plan, backed by $45 million in U.S. aid, that provided them with incentives to switch to such alternative crops as coffee, cocoa, yucca and peanuts.

Fujimori's much-touted privatization plan, his conquest of hyperinflation and his successful campaign to lure more foreign investors to Peru, received high marks in international financial circles, but they did little to alleviate Peru's grinding poverty. With the modernization that inevitably comes with privatization, industrial jobs were cut by the thousands. The streamlining of the bloated bureaucracy threw middle-class Peruvians out of work as well. The construction boom was concentrated in affluent sections of Lima, with little or no trickle-down effect. Meanwhile, the elimination of government subsidies drove up utility prices, which hit the poor the hardest.

Figures for real GDP were discouraging for several years. From a peak of $65.2 billion in 1997, which was a robust 7% growth from 1996, real GDP dropped to $51.6 billion in 1999. Per capita income also declined, from $2,675 in 1997 to $2,074 in 2001.

Despite the political uncertainty in 2000, real GDP grew by 3.1%, but it slowed to 0.6% in 2001, apparently because foreign investors held back to see what would happen when the dust from Fujimori's fall had settled.

Fujimori's successor, Alejandro Toledo, had a doctorate in economics from Stanford and was once a World Bank official. He was elected on a moderately leftist platform, but he surrounded himself with a retinue of U.S.-trained economists like himself, not unlike the "Chicago Boys" in Chile during the Pinochet years.

The new team had cause for boasting. Peru's GDP growth for 2002 was 5.2%, the highest in Latin America, while inflation was only about 1.2%. The growth in 2003 was 3.8%, and in 2004 it was 5.07%; only Chile and Argentina recorded faster growth. For 2005 it was even higher, 6.7%, ahead of Chile and behind only Argentina and the Dominican Republic.

García made a comeback in the 2006 election, but disavowed his fiery populism and pragmatically continued Toledo's policies. As a result, Peru's economy continues to boom, growing 7.6% in 2006, 8.9% in 2007 and 9.8% in 2008. With the global recession, it still showed growth of 0.9% in 2009, compared to losses recorded by most Latin American countries.

Exports increased by about a third in 2004, one of the highest increases in the world, and by 2006 Peru had an $8.8 billion balance of payments surplus. Inflation, meanwhile was only 1.2% in 2004, 1.5% in 2005 and 2% in 2007. It rose to 6.7% in 2008, then fell back to 1.2% in 2009.

Despite all these encouraging factors, critics on the left complain that the impressive economic growth has not trickled down to the poor. However, the pov-

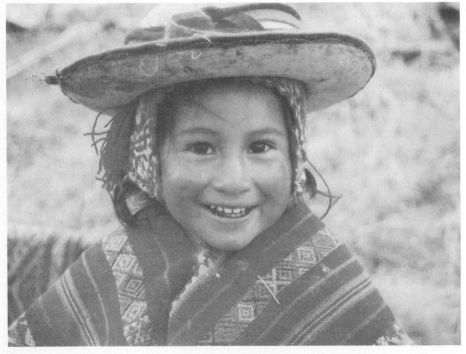

Smile in the Andes

erty rate under Toledo declined from 54% to 44.5% of the population by 2006. In 2007, under García, it reportedly dropped four more points. Unemployment was down to 8.4% in metropolitan Lima in 2008, although underemployment in the country is a nagging problem despite the boom. With the global recession, it rose from 8.1% in 2008 to 9.0% in 2009.

In 2003, Peru signed a free-trade agreement (FTA) with the *Mercosur* trade bloc (Argentina, Brazil, Paraguay and Uruguay), with tariff barriers to be gradually eliminated over a period of 13 years. In 2005, it signed a FTA with the United States, one with Chile in 2006 and one with China in 2008 (see History). China is now Peru's second-largest trading partner after the United States, accounting for 15.2% of exports in 2008.

Much of the credit for the recent boom goes to the mining sector, which remains Peru's greatest export earner, accounting for 62% in 2006. Peru ranks No. 2 in the world in silver production, No. 3 in zinc, No. 4 in lead and No. 6 in gold and copper. High world market prices in these metals have been a much-needed godsend for the economy. So has the demand for natural gas, which Peru plans to begin exporting.

Peru was awash with good economic news in 2005. Argentina, Brazil, Chile and Uruguay announced plans to begin buying $2.5 billion worth of gas from its new *Mercosur* partner, via a new pipeline to be built to Chile. Peru has estimated gas reserves of 13 trillion cubic feet in its Camisea field in the Amazon jungle in the south. Also, the U.S. oil company Petro-Tech announced it had discovered an offshore field containing 10–50 million barrels of light crude, the largest discovery in Peru in 30 years. The Spanish oil and gas company Repsol YPF announced discovery of a smaller but onshore field in the Amazon jungle in the north that contains 70 million barrels of heavy crude, which is more difficult to refine than light crude. The discoveries coincided with the record high price of oil on international markets. Peru's known oil reserves are 320 million barrels.

Another economic activity that shows enormous potential in the coming years is increased cultivation of sugar cane to produce ethanol for export. In 2006, it was estimated that private investors will be adding 25,000 acres of new sugar cultivation per year. A Spanish company is building a $90 million ethanol plant; a Texas firm plans to raise 23,000 acres of sugar cane and produce 120 million liters of ethanol annually. With the new FTA with the United States, Peru can export ethanol to the United States for 54 cents a gallon less than Brazil's ethanol.

Peru's tourism industry also is booming, with 1.8 million visitors in 2006. Much of Peru's popularity is because of ancient Inca sites like Cuzco and Machu Picchu, but ecotourism to the Amazon rainforest is also growing in popularity. Tourism was disrupted in 2010 by the worst El Niño since 1998–98. Floods left 3,900 tourists stranded at Machu Picchu.

The Future: Peru had one of Latin America's fastest GDP growth rates before the current global economic slowdown (8.9% in 2007 and 9.8% in 2008) and among the lowest inflation rates (2% in 2007 and 6.4% in 2008). Even with the recession, the economy still grew somewhat in 2009, while those of most other Latin American nations, shrank. Yet, Peruvians revile both Presidents Alejandro Toledo and his successor, Alan García, who has continued to preside over this growth. Toledo's approval rating bottomed out at 9%; García's is now about 39%.

If this seems incongruous, it is. Why, then, does it happen? Perhaps in part because the expanding economy has not trickled down to benefit the impoverished masses; 44% of the population still lives below the poverty line. But also, Peruvians are notoriously impatient for results. Ominously, in *The Economist's* annual *Latinobarómetro* survey, the percentage of Peruvians who believe democracy is preferable to any other form of government dropped from 63% in 1996 to just 40% in 2005. The 23-point drop was exceeded only by Paraguay's. By 2009, it was back up to 52%.

Just as ominously, 13% in 1996 agreed with the statement that authoritarianism is acceptable under certain circumstances; by 2008, it had ridden to 20%. Could they have been nostalgic about Alberto Fujimori? It dropped back to 16% in 2009.

It must be remembered that it was García's wretched performance that led desperate Peruvians to elect Fujimori in the first place in 1990. But in 1990 the economy under García was a shambles, while today it is booming.

Fujimori, now 72, will be in prison in 2011. His daughter, Keiko, just 35, who earned a business degree from Boston University and is married to an American, is running for president in his stead and is currently a strong second place in the polls. She has already promised to pardon her father if elected. The current frontrunner is still the popular Lima Mayor Luis Castañeda, 65, who is expected to have García's support. His approval rating in Lima is 73%.

Ollanta Humala, the left-wing disciple of Hugo Chávez who narrowly lost to García in 2006, is tied for third place with Toledo. They and their supporters will prove the kingmakers—or queenmakers—if there is a runoff between Castañeda and Keiko Fujimori. If the *Sendero Luminoso* guerrillas do become a nuisance again, the prospect of a Fujimori in the presidential palace may not be that far-fetched.

One thing learned from the past two elections is that in Peru, last-minute surprises are the norm. It is far too early for predictions.

Yucay Sacred Valley

Photo by Susan L. Thompson

Suriname

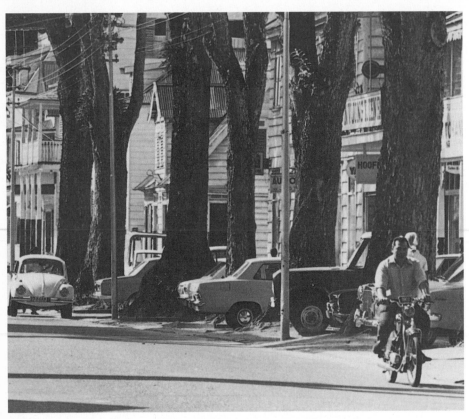

Street scene in the old section of Paramaribo

Area: 70,000 square miles.

Population: 486,618 (2010 estimate)

Capital City: Paramaribo (Pop. 250,000, estimated).

Climate: Rainy, hot and humid.

Neighboring Countries: Guyana (West); French Guiana (Southeast); Brazil (South).

Official Language: Dutch.

Other Principal Tongues: English, Spanish, Hindi, Javanese, Chinese and a local pidgin dialect called alternately *Sranan Tongo, Taki-Taki* or *Surinamese*.

Ethnic Background: Hindustani, 37%; creole (a person of mixed African and other ancestry) 31%; Asian, 15.3%; Bush Negro, 10.3%; Amerindian 2.6%; European and other, 3.8%. Figures are approximate.

Principal Religions: Hinduism, Roman Catholic Christianity, Islam, Protestant Christianity.

Chief Commercial Products: Refined aluminum ore, bauxite, aluminum, timber, rice, sugar, shrimp and citrus fruits.

Currency: Suriname Guilder.

Gross Domestic Product: U.S. $3.184 billion in 2009, estimated ($6,543 per capita)

Former Colonial Status: English Colony (1652–67); Dutch Colony (1667–1799); English-controlled (1799–1815); colony of the Netherlands (1815–1948); self-governing component of the Dutch Realm (1948–75).

Independence Date: November 25, 1975.

Chief of State: Runaldo Venetiaan (b. June 18, 1936), president (since August 12, 2000).

National Flag: Two green horizontal stripes, top and bottom, red horizontal stripe in the center, divided from the green by narrow white stripes; a gold five-pointed star is centered in the red stripe.

Separated from neighboring Guyana and French Guiana by large rivers, Suriname lies on the northeast coast of South America. Its 230-mile coastline is rather flat, a strip of marshy land lying mostly below sea level, which needs a series of dikes and canals to hold off the encroaching waters of the Atlantic Ocean. Along this fertile coast and stretching back about 50 of its 300 miles an inland extension is found where about 90% of the country's population lives.

Back from the coastal area, the land turns gradually into a grassland, becoming hilly and then densely forested with some 2,000 varieties of trees, 90% of the land area. This is a broad plateau land that reaches its highest point in the Wilhelmina Mountains. The land then dips down into the dense growth of the tropical rain forest where there are found hundreds of varieties of jungle birds, howler monkeys and all manner of wildlife typical to Brazil. In the interior is the 600-square-mile W.J. van Blommestein Meer (lake), which provides hydroelectric power for the bauxite industry located downriver.

History: Although in 1499 the Spanish touched along the coast of what is now Suriname, no attempt at colonization was made. European explorers generally ignored the entire region—the land was not inviting and there were not wealthy native empires to subjugate or loot for the motherlands. Toward the close of the 16th century, the Dutch appeared on the coast, but the first large-scale colonization efforts were made in the early 1650s by the English governor of Barbados, who became the region's first governor. These English colonists established successful sugarcane plantations.

In 1667 the Dutch received Suriname from the English in exchange for the colony of New Netherlands (now New York). Early in the 1680s, workers were brought from Africa to work in the fields since there were few local natives.

The territory again fell to the British during the Napoleonic Wars (1799–1815); a series of agreements between the three powers established the whole of Guiana, as it was then called, into British Guiana (now Guyana), Dutch Guiana (now Suriname) and French Guiana. The latter of these later became infamous for its offshore penal colony, Devil's Island.

The Netherlands emancipated the slaves in 1863 and many of them settled on small farms to cultivate their own produce. This created an immediate and critical labor shortage, which caused the Dutch to import cheap labor from India in the 1870s and from Java in the 1880s.

The territory was slow to develop any political awareness, but since World War II, Far Eastern groups have become increasingly insistent on playing a greater role in the destiny of the land in which they live. This has created a bitter rivalry between the largely agricultural creoles and the prosperous, business-oriented East Indians. The colony became a self-governing component of the Netherlands in 1948 and adopted the name Suriname. After 1950 it controlled its affairs with the exception of defense and foreign relations.

Border clashes between Suriname and the soon-to-be independent British Guiana (Guyana) occurred in 1970. Early in 1973, serious unrest erupted when the government refused to pay increased wages to trade union members. A bloody strike lasted for more than a month before order was restored.

Elections in 1973 for the Legislative Assembly resulted in a victory for an alliance of parties favoring independence. Known as the National Party Coalition (of which the strongest force is the National Party), it gained 13 seats. The Progressive Reform Party won three; this victory by the black-dominated National Party ended a long period of political control by a coalition of East Indians and Chinese.

With the National Party Coalition victory, the colony moved a step closer to independence. Although the Dutch appeared anxious to leave, the large East Indian (Hindustani) population feared that independence would bring serious racial problems similar to those that erupted in neighboring Guyana. The specter of violence soon sparked a mass migration to the Netherlands as independence approached. Nearly a quarter of the population (140,000) fled Suriname.

Despite the damaging exodus, Suriname gained full independence after 308 years of colonial rule on November 25, 1975; the Netherlands agreed to help the new nation adjust to its status by giving it $100 million a year for the next decade—one of the most generous foreign aid programs on a per capita basis in history.

The new minister-president, Henck Arron, urged the nation's former residents to return. The appeal was sincere, as most of those who left were educated and skilled workers; their departure created a severe "brain-drain" for the new nation.

The principal political-economic controversy was whether the aluminum industry should be nationalized or remain in private hands, thus encouraging additional foreign investment? Although Arron's regime was initially leftist, it refrained from nationalization. Further complicating the political scene were ethnic differences and fears. The East Indian and Asiatic communities feared a black-dominated, oppressive regime.

Arron's policies gradually moderated and relative tranquility prevailed. But economic stability was in reality based on the $100 million annual Dutch subsidy; vital aluminum production was steadily declining. In 1980, however, non-commissioned officers ousted the government when it refused to allow them to form a Dutch-style military union. A nine-member National Revolutionary Council (RNC) was formed and backed the election of a government headed by Chin-A-Sen. The military, however, retained actual power; Lieutenant Colonel Desi Bouterse emerged as its leader.

In December 1982 there was an attempted right-wing coup that led to assassinations of 22 military and civilian opponents of Bouterse. This "December Massacre" remains controversial to this day and is one of Bouterse's lingering political liabilities.

The Dutch suspended aid and conditions rapidly worsened. Bouterse enlarged the military and conditions became ex-

tremely tense. He established close relations with Cuba, to the extent that Cuba was viewed as a threat. The government was largely incompetent and inefficient. The "Cuban connection" was brief, ending after the United States invaded Grenada in 1983 (see Grenada).

Economically smarting because of the withdrawal of Dutch aid and lower world prices for aluminum products, Suriname announced a plan for "a return to democ-

racy" in 1984. A 31-member National Assembly consisting of 14 military officers, 11 trade unionists and six from the private sector were to draft a new constitution. The move did not satisfy the Dutch. Bouterse launched a mass political movement, *Stanvaaste*, in a move apparently intended to dominate any future democratically elected administration.

A U.N. report released in 1985 accused the military of involvement in political murders and "suicides."

In 1986, Ronnie Brunswijk (*Bruns*-veek) a Maroon (a descendant of escaped slaves) and former army sergeant, capitalized on the discontent of his people, about 50,000 strong, over the idea of being resettled in towns. They were used to living deep in the interior jungle, speaking their own language. The government had controlled little outside the capital. A group called the Jungle Commando began an armed resistance. The United Nations condemned fighting tactics of both sides, but the response was, "when you fight, there will be victims."

Beset with this internal revolt in the interior and pressures from Washington, Bouterse called for elections to an Assembly to be held in November 1987. Balloting was enthusiastic and the National

Suriname

Lt. Col. Desi Bouterse

President Runaldo Venetiaan

Front for Democracy and Development, a coalition of three ethnic groups, won 41 of the 51 seats. It elected Ramsewak Shankar president for a five-year term in early 1988. Actual power, however, remained with Bouterse and the 7,000-man military until moves got underway to pass control to the civilian government. It was unable, however, to militarily best Brunswijk and his followers.

The Dutch, denying aid under the 1975 treaty, continued to exert pressure on Suriname to settle its internal rivalries. Finally, the two factions reached a vague but written agreement for a truce in 1988. Bouterse alleged that the negotiations failed to end the rebellion. Many Maroons had fled to French Guiana to escape the conflict. The Dutch restored aid in generous amounts, but not enough to suit some Surinamese, particularly the military.

The Maroons began returning after assurances that the army would not occupy their traditional territories in the interior. Brunswijk, feeling safe, entered Paramaribo in March 1990 under a flag of truce. Feeling that at last his opportunity had arrived, Bouterse had the army arrest him. This was when the extent of Brunswijk's power (or lack thereof) was felt first-hand.

The following evening, all electrical power in Paramaribo was out; this included vitally needed sources to process aluminum. The Jungle Commando force announced that power would stay off until its leader was freed. President Ramsewak Shankar *ordered* Bouterse to release Brunswijk. After a few hours, Bouterse did so, steaming with resentment. The lights were promptly turned on.

In 1990, an investigation revealed Suriname was an important link in the Colombia-to-Europe cocaine traffic; both Bouterse and Brunswijk were accused of being heavily involved. When the drugs started reaching the Netherlands, the Dutch brought pressure, but Bouterse simply threw out President Shankar in a bloodless coup on Christmas Eve 1990 that was labeled the "Telephone Coup" because the president was told over the telephone to resign. The Dutch *again* suspended their aid.

Elections in 1991 resulted in the coalition selection of Runaldo Venetiaan, former education minister, as president, after five months of wheeling and dealing. Continued Dutch pressure brought about Bouterse's resignation as commander-in-chief in 1992. As the government gained control over the military, it was also possible in 1992 to negotiate with the Surinamese Liberation Army (Maroon) and *Tucayana Amazonica* (native Indian) rebel movements, leading to a cease-fire in 1992.

Even though Venetiaan's coalition was successful in elections held in May 1996, Bouterse's National Democratic Party *(NDP)* was the single most popular party.

Not unexpectedly, in elections held in September 1996, Jules Wijdenbosch of the *NDP* was elected president. Venetiaan's New Front had won 24 of the 51 seats in the National Assembly in May general elections, falling short of the two-thirds majority needed to form a government. Thus, the choice for president fell to the United People's Conference (comprising members of the National Assembly and regional and district councils). By a vote of 438–407, Wijdenbosch won.

Wijdenbosch's *NDP* and its coalition partner, the Movement of Freedom and Democracy (*BVD*), initially held a majority of 29 seats in the National Assembly, but the coalition began showing signs of strain in 1997 when the president fired Fi-

Former President Jules Wijdenbosch

nance Minister Motilal Mungra of the *BVD* for criticizing government policy. The schism became more pronounced when Bouterse was charged in absentia in the Netherlands with drug smuggling and the Wijdenbosch government adopted an aggressive response toward the mother country, which still provided Suriname with $65 million a year in aid.

In 1998, four of the five members of the *BVD* abandoned the coalition to protest what they deemed the government's inclination toward dictatorship and for failing to consult with the *BVD* members on policy matters.

Bouterse, meanwhile, now a lumber executive, denied the Dutch charges that he had smuggled 1.3 tons of cocaine into Europe and had ties to Colombian cartels. He announced in 1997 that he was considering running for president in 2001 and that he wanted to wean Suriname away from Dutch aid.

Bouterse was placed on the Interpol wanted list, and he was arrested in Trinidad in July 1998. But that country rejected a Dutch extradition request, and Bouterse returned to Suriname, where he continued to serve in Wijdenbosch's government with the euphemistic title of "presidential aide." In 1999, a court in The Hague issued a summons for Bouterse to appear for trial in March, but he ignored the order; not even his attorney appeared to offer a defense. Apparently to appease the Dutch, whose aid was still welcome, Wijdenbosch fired Bouterse. The Dutch court then began trying Bouterse in absentia, and he was convicted, sentenced to 16 years in prison and fined the equivalent of $2.17 million.

To compound Bouterse's legal problems, in 1999 the families of 15 of the dissidents slain after the 1982 coup attempt

Suriname

Boats tied up on the banks of the river at Paramaribo

Paramaribo's *De West*, March 28, 1990: "Military authority criticizes Government's position." Insert shows Ronnie Brunswijk.

filed a complaint with an Amsterdam court because Dutch prosecutors had not investigated the deaths. In 2000, a Dutch appeals court ruled that prosecutors did have jurisdiction to investigate on the grounds that the 1982 killings constitute crimes against humanity.

Bouterse then faced an international arrest warrant, much as did Chile's former strongman Augusto Pinochet, but in 2001 the Netherlands High Court dismissed the suit on the grounds that Dutch courts have no jurisdiction over Suriname and because Bouterse is neither a Dutch citizen nor a resident of the Netherlands. The court also ruled that Bouterse could not be tried under a U.N. convention against torture that went into effect seven years after the 1981 incident. However, in 2004 a Surinamese prosecutor announced that he would try Bouterse and 25 others for murder in the 15 deaths.

In May 1999, violent street protests erupted against Wijdenbosch's handling of the economy, especially drastic price increases and a precipitous drop in the exchange rate of the guilder. The opposition mustered 27 votes in the 51-seat National Assembly for a no-confidence motion against the president. Wijdenbosch refused to resign, and the constitution is ambiguous as to whether he could be removed. The consensus was that the National Assembly could call new elections by a two-thirds vote, or 34 members; Wijdenbosch's *NDP* had been reduced by defections to 16 seats, not quite enough to block the effort. In an attempt to defuse the move to unseat him, Wijdenbosch announced he would call for new elections no later than May 2000, a year ahead of schedule.

Efforts by the opposition to replace Wijdenbosch with an interim president failed, so Wijdenbosch limped along as a lameduck president for a full year.

The May 25, 2000, election, in which 23 parties competed and 72% of the 265,000 registered voters participated, was a stinging rebuke both to him and to Bouterse. The New Front of former President Venetiaan won 33 of the 51 Assembly seats, one short of the two thirds needed to name a new president outright. Bouterse's Millennium Combination was second with 10 seats, while Wijdenbosch's Democratic National Platform 2000 won only three.

Venetiaan was inaugurated for a five-year term on August 12, 2000. He immediately inherited an international crisis from Wijdenbosch. Just days after the election, the outgoing government ordered a Canadian offshore oil rig towed from the disputed zone with Guyana at the mouth of the Corantijn River. Both countries moved troops to the area, as diplomats negotiated a peaceful solution. The dispute

Suriname

lingered for seven years, until a U.N. commission awarded most of the disputed area to Guyana (see Guyana).

Internally, the issue of land rights for the black Maroons and indigenous Indian tribes (see Culture) resurfaced in 2004. A legal representative of the Association of Village Leaders of Suriname appeared at a two-week meeting of the Permanent U.N. Forum on Indigenous Issues in New York to complain that mining operations had encroached upon the traditional lands of the Maroons and Indians. She said the government had done little to implement the guarantees contained in the 1992 peace agreement that ended the rebellion.

Despite the murder charges pending against him for the 1982 massacre of his political opponents and his Dutch conviction for cocaine smuggling, Bouterse announced that he was standing for president again in the general elections of May 25, 2005, as the standard bearer of the *NDP*. Venetiaan coyly avoided saying whether he would seek re-election. In the voting, Venetiaan's New Front again emerged with the most seats, 24, nine fewer than before and two short of a simple majority, much less the two-thirds majority needed to elect the president. Bouterse's *NDP* jumped from seven to 15 seats, while Wijdenbosch's latest vehicle, the People's Alliance for Development, won only six. A new political organization representing the ethnic Maroons, the A-Combination, led by Bouterse's old nemesis Ronnie Brunswijk, won five seats and quickly agreed to join the New Front in a coalition. That still left the New Front five seats short of what it needed to elect a president, whether Venetiaan or someone else. Venetiaan had little choice but to swallow his pride and ask Bouterse to join his coalition; Bouterse refused.

Before the Assembly met to vote, Bouterse withdrew his name and the *NDP* named his running mate, Rabin Parmessar, as its candidate. As expected, no candidate received the needed 34 votes, so the choice fell once again to the 895-member United People's Conference as it did in 1996. Venetiaan was re-elected with a majority of 62.9% on August 3 and was inaugurated on August 12, 2005.

The long-delayed prosecution of Bouterse and others in the 1982 "December Massacre" began more or less in earnest in November 2007, when a court-martial subpoenaed him and 25 others. After months of pretrial wrangling, before a court that met only once a month, the actual trial began in April 2008. Several military witnesses have implicated Bouterse, now 64, in the massacre, but he continued to deny it. The trial was stopped for a time, then resumed in November 2009 after six witnesses were brought from the

Netherlands. When this book went to press, there was still no verdict.

Culture: The majority of the people are found along the coastal, agricultural zone. Of this group, about a third live in the capital and chief port of Paramaribo, a picturesque city with palm-lined streets and colorful market areas.

The creole population is well represented in the civil service and mining industries; the East Indians tend to concentrate in commerce and farming activities. There are also about 12,000 native Indians in the Arawak, Carib, Trio and Wayana tribes. There are about 50,000 Surinamese descended from African slaves, called Maroons, who prefer to live in the interior.

Dutch is the official language, and there is a literacy rate of about 80%. Although most students of higher education go to the Netherlands, there are law and medical faculties in Paramaribo. Suriname boasts a cultural center, museums, active theatrical groups, a well known philharmonic orchestra and a modern sports stadium.

Economy: Alumina, aluminum and bauxite, the ore of aluminum, account for as much as 5% of the country's exports and some 90% of its tax revenues. The leading bauxite firm is U.S.-owned Suralco, a subsidiary of Alcoa. Although some bauxite is processed locally, aluminum is now shipped in a finished or semi-finished state to the United States. Panaram, the center of the vital industry, receives its hydroelectric power from Lake van Blommestein.

Offshore and onshore petroleum deposits have tremendous economic potential; onshore deposits in the Guyana Plateau are estimated at 15 billion barrels. In 2004, the state-owned oil firm, Staatsolie, was pumping 12,000 barrels a day from the Tambaredjo Field, and its refinery capacity is 7,000 bpd, but it was investing $350 million to expand production to 18,000 bpd by 2012 and to expand refinery capacity. Current production meets domestic demands, but in 2004 it signed contracts with Spanish and Danish firms to explore for oil in a 7,200-square-mile tract bordering the Tambaredjo Field, which could allow Suriname to become a net exporter. The resolution of the maritime dispute with Guyana (see History) could benefit both nations.

There are few roads; rivers and aircraft provide most of the transportation. The majority of the people are employed in agriculture. The major cash crops are timber, citrus fruits, sugarcane, bananas and corn. Rice is the chief crop and food staple, accounting for half of all land under cultivation and is the source of valuable

export income. Major problems facing the economy are high inflation and unemployment. The government is increasing its economic ties with Colombia, Venezuela and Brazil; with the aid of Venezuela it is hoped that new bauxite mines can be developed in the southern part of the country.

In 2002, the government granted permits to a Canadian company to mine gold. The mine was expected to produce 6.7 tons of gold per year for eight years.

President Ronald Venetiaan devalued the guilder in 1993, which brought needed monetary stability, and by the end of his term in 1996 he had brought rampant inflation down to single digits.

In 2001, the economy grew by a sluggish 1.9%. In 2003, growth was a robust 13.2%, which tapered off to 6.2% in 2004 and 4.8% in 2006. It rose slightly to 5.3% in 2007 and 6% in 2008. Much of the growth was attributed to the high world market price for gold, bauxite and alumina, but the global recession caused GDP to shrink by –2.3% in 2009. Unemployment has been steady at about 9.5% for the past five years.

The Future: Suriname, underpopulated and underdeveloped, is a land with great economic potential from natural resources and, recently, from ecotourism. At a time of skyrocketing petroleum prices, it could experience a veritable economic boom.

But it must get a handle on its turbulent political situation. The confusing results of the May 25, 2005 election were not a step in the right direction, but at least the re-election of President Venetiaan represented stability.

The other remaining doubt is whether Bouterse will be convicted of the 15 killings in 1982. The date December 8, 1982 is the Surinamese equivalent of September 11, 2001, despite the relatively small death toll. Suriname needs a catharsis.

Fishing off the coast of Suriname

The Republic of Trinidad and Tobago

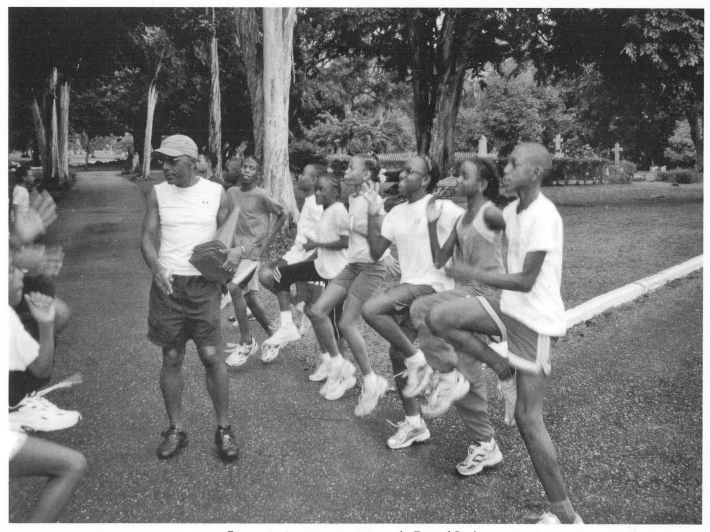

Cross-country runners warm up in Port of Spain

Area: 1,864 square miles.

Population: 1,228,691 (2010 estimate).

Capital City: Port of Spain (Pop. 49,031, 2000 census).

Climate: Tropically hot and humid. The heaviest rainfall occurs from May to December.

Neighboring Countries: Trinidad forms the eastern edge of a shelf surrounding the Gulf of Paria on Venezuela's northeast coast, separated from the mainland by narrow channels. Tobago lies 18 miles north of Trinidad.

Official Language: English.

Other Principal Tongues: Hindi, French and Spanish.

Ethnic Background: African Negroid (43%), Asiatic (40%), European and other (17%).

Principal Religion: Protestant Christianity.

Chief Commercial Products: Petroleum, natural gas (including liquefied), chemicals, tourism.

Currency: Trinidad Dollar.

Gross Domestic Product: U.S. $23.27 billion in 2009, estimated ($18,931 per capita).

Former Colonial Status: Spanish Colony (1498–1797); British Colony (1797–1962).

Independence Date: August 31, 1962.

Chief of State: George Maxwell Richards, president (since March 17, 2003).

Head of Government: Kamla Persad-Bissessar (b. April 22, 1952), prime minister (since May 26, 2010).

National Flag: A diagonal black stripe bordered with white on a red field.

Trinidad and Tobago both have mountainous spines representing rounded extensions of the Venezuelan coastal ranges. Trinidad's mountains lie along the north coast. Plains extend to the south, rimmed with low, rolling hills. Petroleum and the famed asphalt lake are found in the south of the island. Tobago's mountains on the north are skirted with coral-dotted shelves. Trinidad's soils are rich and well suited to sugar and other crops. Sea breezes moderate the tropical climate and the annual rainfall of 65 inches is evenly distributed. Trinidad's asphalt has been of commercial significance since the colonial period. The more recent discovery of oil and gas has fostered industrial development. Trinidad and Tobago's population is primarily African and Asian, with smaller groups of cosmopolitan people of Spanish, French and English ancestry.

History: Trinidad was discovered by Columbus in 1498 and colonized by the Spanish in the early 1500s. During the French Revolution, a large number of French families were settled on the land that in 1797 was captured from Spain by British forces. Ceded to Britain in 1802, Trinidad was joined by Tobago as a colonial unit in 1889.

The history of the dual-island nation has been rather uneventful. Administered as a British Crown Colony until 1962, its early value was in asphalt and sugar. Slaves had been introduced by the Span-

Trinidad and Tobago

ish to work sugar and indigo plantations, and the British continued to add slaves until 1834. With the abolition of slavery, indentured East Indians and Chinese laborers were imported to perform the manual labor. The black and East Indian communities remain the country's two principal ethnic and political groups. The decline of sugar markets hurt the island's economy, but the existence of asphalt and (later) petroleum cushioned the shock and led to a transformation of the economy.

The leasing of bases to the United States during World War II bolstered the economy. The transformation of Trinidad and Tobago from colonial dependency was relatively untroubled. Initially incorporated into the West Indian Federation, its reluctance to tie its healthy economy to the poorer island dependencies was a major factor in the demise of the Federation.

The United States was drawn into the final phases of the negotiations for independence when Prime Minister Eric Williams sought the U.S. base at Chaguaramas as the site for a new capital city. The United States released part of the site in 1960, with the remainder reverting to Trinidad in 1977.

Independence was attained in 1962, and Williams became prime minister. Parliament consists of an elected House of Representatives, which chooses the prime minister, and an elected Senate. Initially, Queen Elizabeth II was chief of state.

When opposition parties boycotted the May 1971 elections to protest voting procedures, Williams' People's National Movement won all 36 seats in the House of Representatives. Although generally a capable leader, Williams' popularity fell because of his heavy-handed methods. A major crisis developed in 1970 when labor unrest and rioting led to a mutiny by sections of the small army. Williams used government forces in 1975 to quell violent strikes by petroleum and sugar workers.

The dispute soon erupted into a more general strike, joined by transport and electrical workers. Williams jailed key opposition leaders. Despite growing hostility by labor members and some sectors of the business community, Williams' political control remained firm, bolstered by the "mini-boom" caused by the enormous increases in oil prices.

The nation became a republic on August 1, 1976. Although the new constitution severed all ties to Great Britain, the country retains its membership in the British Commonwealth. Named as first president was Governor General Sir Ellis Clarke.

In the general elections held in September 1976, Williams won another five-year term when his People's National Movement (PNM) won 24 of the 36 seats in the House of Representatives. The Democratic Action Congress, traditionally the main opposition party, won only two seats, while a new Marxist-Leninist labor-oriented United Labor Front (UPF) won 10.

Despite the steady flow of oil revenues, stubbornly high unemployment fueled social unrest and persistent criticism of Williams. He died in 1981 at the age of 69. George Chambers, the minister of agriculture, was designated Williams' successor.

In November 1981 elections, six parties vied for the 36 parliamentary seats. Due to the splintered opposition, the PNM scored a major victory, winning 26 seats by the largest margin of votes in the nation's history (219,000).

Relations with Jamaica and Barbados, which had deteriorated in 1982 because of a trade war within the Caribbean Community, became further strained in late 1983 when Trinidad and Tobago opposed the multinational invasion of Grenada. A multi-nation Caribbean organization to promote free trade had been created in 1979, which Trinidad and Tobago joined. At its meeting in mid-1986, Chambers joined with the other chiefs of state in criticizing the United States' Caribbean Basin Initiative because of its import restrictions on Caribbean products, principally textiles, footwear and oil products.

The collapse of international petroleum prices presented severe economic problems during 1984–87. The sugar industry also became non-existent except for production to meet local needs. The government started importing crude oil for refining because of decreased local production. Despite this, in the 1980s Trinidad and To-bago had one of the higher per capita annual incomes in the area.

The National Alliance for Reconstruction (NAR) led by Arthur Robinson won 33 of 36 seats in 1986 elections, ending the PNM's grip on power. Austerity and high unemployment led to an attempted coup in mid-1990 by a black Muslim group called Jamaat al-Muslimeen. The prime minister was shot and beaten before the loyal army ended the affair, in which 24 people died. The courts gave amnesty to the rebels, much to the government's displeasure.

In late 1991, the PNM returned to power with 21 seats. Patrick Manning, the new prime minister, stressed economic improvement and lowered black-Indian tensions.

The pendulum swung again in 1995, this time in favor of the Indian community, when the United National Congress (UNC) won a two-seat majority and elected Basdeo Panday as prime minister. He pledged to be "the leader of all the people," but blacks still feared Indian domination. Panday also was faced with a burgeoning crime rate, a divided judiciary and police corruption related to drug trafficking. Trinidad made interna-

332

Carnival in Port of Spain

tional headlines in 1999, and brought condemnation from human rights groups, when it hanged nine convicted murderers, justified as a deterrent to rising crime. The public seemed to approve of the hard-line policy.

Trinidadian courts have continued to hand down death sentences, although the crime wave has continued, as have international protests. In 2002, the Inter-American Court of Human Rights, an arm of the Organization of American States to which Trinidad and Tobago belongs, ordered the country not to carry out the executions of 31 men and one women on the grounds that their rights had been violated.

Panday's UNC was narrowly returned to power in general elections in December 2000, winning 19 of the 36 seats to 16 for the PNM, still led by Manning. The NAR won the remaining seat.

In his second term, Panday created a business-friendly environment that attracted new foreign investment. But critics, including three of his own cabinet ministers, complained he was becoming *too* friendly with business. Rumors circulated of kickbacks from an airport construction project. In 2001, Attorney General Ramesh Maharaj and two other cabinet ministers publicly alleged corruption within the government. Panday fired Maharaj in October, precipitating a crisis that Panday unwisely sought to resolve

by dissolving Parliament and calling a new election for December, only a year after being returned to power. The election results led to a constitutional crisis when the UNC and the PNM each won 18 seats.

Panday and Manning struck a deal by which they would let President Robinson of the PAR, usually only a figurehead, decide who would be prime minister, who would then head a unity government. Robinson, who like Manning is black, chose Manning to head the government, giving only a vague explanation for his reasons. A miffed Panday then reneged on his promise to cooperate in a unity government.

Parliament did not meet until April 2002, barely beating a six-month deadline that would have forced a new election. For two days, Parliament deadlocked on the election of a speaker, and the tension between the two parties—and hence the two ethnic groups—threatened to turn ugly.

In August 2002, Panday dissolved Parliament and called elections for October, the third in three years. The campaign was predictably bitter, with the PNM pointing to the criminal charges that Panday allegedly had a secret London bank account in which he had allegedly stashed hundreds of thousands of dollars and the UNC running advertisements linking Manning to the black Muslim terrorist group that had attempted the 1990 coup.

A woman also alleged that Manning had fathered her 2-year-old daughter. In the balloting, voters gave the PNM 51% of the popular vote and a majority of 20 of the 36 seats, although the PNM won two constituencies by margins of only 244 and 247 votes. Turnout was 69.8%.

Panday, then almost 70, announced he would step down as leader of the opposition. However, he reneged.

In 2003, Parliament elected George Maxwell Richards, 71, a former dean of the University of the West Indies who is of African descent, to succeed Robinson as president. Richards, who is not a member of either party, pledged he would govern without regard to race.

In May 2005, Panday, his wife, his former works minister and a businessmen were arrested and charged with offering or accepting a $45,600 bribe for the airport construction contract. Thousands of UNC supporters demonstrated in support of Panday, who at first refused to post bail. After eight days, however, he paid the equivalent of $104,000 in bail and was released from jail pending trial. He later was charged in connection with the secret London bank account.

The UNC has been in turmoil since then. In September 2005, Panday anointed Winston Dookeran to succeed him as political leader of the party, although Panday remained party chairman and resisted calls to step down as leader of the opposition. A power struggle then developed between the Panday and Dookeran factions.

On April 24, 2006, Panday, then 73, was convicted of fraud in connection with the secret bank account and sentenced to two

Ex-Prime Minister Patrick Manning

Trinidad and Tobago

President George Maxwell Richards

Prime Minister Kamla Persad-Bissessar

years at hard labor, although four days later he was released from jail because of ill health. President Richards revoked Panday's title as leader of the opposition and named the UNC's deputy political leader, Kamla Persad-Bissessar, 54, a former attorney general, as the new opposition leader. This caused a serious rift within the UNC, with Panday seeking to reclaim the title of opposition leader.

Manning called elections for an expanded 41-seat House of Representatives on November 5, 2007. Manning and the PNM received a decisive mandate this time, with 26 seats to 15 for the UNC. Voter turnout was 66%, about the same as 2002.

In December 2008, Manning went to Cuba for surgery for a malignant tumor in his kidney, returning to work in January 2009.

In 2008, the already high murder rate soared by 38% to 550 homicides, or about 42 per 100,000, the third highest in the world after Honduras and Venezuela that year.

In January 2010, the simmering rivalry between Panday and Persad-Bissessar for the UNC leadership came to a showdown when Panday challenged her leadership in a vote of the party's legislators, which Persad-Bissessar won overwhelmingly.

Apparently believing the divided and scandal-plagued UNC was mortally wounded, Manning called an early snap election on May 24. Voter turnout was 80% of the 1.3 million registered voters. In a stunning upset, the UNC-led coalition

called People's Partnership won 29 of the 41 seats. Manning conceded on television, saying, "I take full responsibility for the defeat." Two days later, Persad-Bissessar, 58, was sworn in as Trinidad and Tobago's first female prime minister.

Culture: The people of Trinidad and Tobago, about 45% of black ancestry and 35% East Indian (Gujerat) have remained distinct ethnic groups, but managed social and political integration during the period of British rule. Thus, people with many customs and origins live without restrictions of cultural variety. The Europeans find expression in sports clubs and in their business occupations.

The African element has acquired renown for its calypso music. The people learned that through hours of heating, tempering and pounding that the steel oil drums from World War II could be tuned into unique musical instruments that are world-familiar today. Although most speak English, it is with a unique lilt. Religious expression is unhampered, with popular participation in the *Carnival* of the Christians as well as the Islamic festival of Hosein.

Probably Trinidad's most noted calypso musician was Rupert Grant (1914–61), better known by the stage name Lord Invader. He is best remembered for the songs "Don't Stop the Carnival," which he recorded in 1939 and which was later recorded by Harry Belafonte, and "Rum and Coca-Cola," which became a hit by the Andrews Sisters in the 1940s and was the object of a successful copyright suit by Grant.

Trinidadians felt a sense of pride in 2001 when Vidiadhar Surajprasad (V.S.) Naipaul, a Trinidad-born novelist, was named recipient of the Nobel Prize for Literature, only the second West Indian to be so honored. Their pride was muted somewhat by the fact that Naipaul had spent 50 of his 69 years in Britain and has ridiculed his homeland as "primitive." Scion of a literary family, Naipaul attended Oxford and opted to stay in Britain, vowing to "beat them (the British) at their own lan-

Rural scene

guage." Yet, he used Trinidad as the setting for some of his novels, which include *A House for Mr. Biswas, The Suffrage of Elvira, The Mimic Men, Guerrillas,* and *In a Free State;* his first published novel, *The Mystic Masseur,* was made into a movie in 2001 and the filming was in Trinidad. The Nobel committee praised the iconoclastic Naipaul for his "incorruptible scrutiny" of the post-colonial West Indes, but he also had attracted notoriety for his attacks on Islam and for ridiculing such literary greats as C.S. Forrester and James Joyce.

Economy: Although the nation contains rich soils and agriculture is important, the economy is based on oil and natural gas production. The only Caribbean country with oil deposits, Trinidad and Tobago was at one time the hemisphere's third-largest oil exporting nation. This has been declining since 1982, but in 2002 still accounted for 26.3% of GDP. Oil production rose for the first time in four years in 1984, allowing the government to purchase the assets of the Texaco-Trinidad, Inc. petroleum operation before the world price of oil plummeted in the mid-1980s.

The picture had brightened by 1996, when unemployment dropped from 21.5% to 16.5%, and inflation fell from 13% to 3.5%.

The government has since offered tax advantages to oil firms to encourage exploration. Liquefied natural gas (LNG) is increasingly being exploited and exported; the United States obtains 75% of its imported LNG from Trinidad and Tobago.

In 2002, Prime Minister Patrick Manning announced plans for a gas pipe-line under the Caribbean with branches to Cuba, Puerto Rico, Barbados, Guadaloupe, Martinique, Antigua and St. Kitts. The project cost $500 million.

Trinidad and Tobago is also the world's leading exporter of methanol and ammonia. In 2006, a Trinidad-German consortium announced plans for a new $1.2 billion methanol plant.

During the days of the oil boom of the 1970s, per capita income was among the highest in the hemisphere, more than $7,000, but that plummeted to $3,800 at the depth of the recession of the late 1980s and early 1990s. By 2007, with the oil and chemical industries booming, it was $14,000 although as is the case in many oil-rich countries, it is not equitably distributed and it has led to a high cost of living for housing and basic goods.

A serious problem had been the external debt, which in 1999 stood at $1.42 billion, nearly 25% of GDP. It was still 26.7% of GDP in 2009.

Trinidad and Tobago has gone from boom to bust back to boom. Real GDP declined for eight consecutive years, from 1988–95. Growth averaged only 3%–4% from 1996–98, but was a robust 7.1% in 1999 and 6.9% in 2000. In 2001, it was 3.3% and in 2002, 2.7%. Growth picked up again, hitting 6.5% in 2004 and 7% in 2005, mostly because of the high price of crude oil. It was 12.2% in 2006, but dropped back to a still-healthy 5.5% in 2007, then fell to 3.5% in 2008 because of the fall in oil prices and the beginning of the global recession. In 2009, GDP shrank by –3.5%.

Unemployment has fallen from 8.4% in 2004 to 5.3% in 2008, but with the recession iut was back up to 7.5% in 2009.

Inflation increased from 5.6% in 2004 to 10% in 2006 to 12% in 2008. With the recession, it dropped to 7.6% in 2009.

Tourism, now principally on Tobago, would provide more profits than drug trafficking and would help diversify the oil-and-gas-dependent economy, but as in Jamaica, tourists are shunning this would-be tropical paradise because of an alarmingly high crime rate. In 2008, Trinidad and Tobago recorded 550 homicides or 55 per 100,000, the third-highest in the world that year, higher even than Jamaica. Both the United States and Great Britain issued travel advisories for the country.

The Future: The UNC's upset in the snap elections of May 24, 2010, and the ascension of Kamla Persad-Bessessar as the country's first woman prime minister has opened a new and uncertain chapter in the country's history. From all accounts, she is a capable and determined woman, a former teacher with degrees from Trinidad and Britain who became an attorney and rose through her party's ranks. She will now have to demonstrate how well she can walk the tightrope of power in her racially divided and crime-ridden nation.

Jesuit Ruin of Trinidad

The Oriental (Eastern) Republic of Uruguay

Gauchos **enjoy folk music in the countryside**

Area: 72,150 square miles.

Population: 3,510,386 (2010 estimate)

Capital City: Montevideo (Pop. 1,325,000 in 2004)

Climate: Temperate throughout the year. There is a warm season from November to April and a milder season from May through October. Rainfall is moderate and evenly distributed.

Neighboring Countries: Brazil (north); Argentina (west)

Official Language: Spanish.

Other Principal Tongues: Portuguese and English.

Ethnic Background: European (90%), *mestizo* (a mixture of European and Indian ancestry, 10%).

Principal Religion: Roman Catholic Christianity.

Chief Commercial Products: Hides, leather products, beef and other meat, wool, fish, rice.

Currency: New Peso.

Gross Domestic Product: U.S. $31.98 billion in 2009, estimated ($9,110 per capita).

Former Colonial Status: Spanish Colony (1624–80); contested between Spain and Portugal (1680–1806); captured by Great Britain (1806–07); War for Independence (1807–20); Portuguese Brazilian Colony (1820–25); contested between Brazil and Argentina (1825–28).

Independence Date: Independence was proclaimed on August 25, 1825, but Uruguay did not actually become independent until August 27, 1828, when a treaty was signed with Brazil and Ar-

gentina as a result of British intervention in the dispute between Uruguay's two neighboring countries.

Chief of State: José Alberto "El Pepe" Mujica Cordano (b. May 20, 1935), president (since March 1, 2010).

National Flag: Four blue and five white horizontal stripes; a rising sun of 16 alternating straight and wavy rays on a white square is in the upper left hand part of the flag.

Uruguay, the second smallest of the South American countries, is a land of rolling hills covered with lush grasses and a few scattered forests. The highest elevation is about 2,000 feet; the country is crossed by numerous small streams and is bounded by the Atlantic and several large rivers. The estuary of the Río de la Plata and the Uruguay River, separating Uruguay from Argentina, are navigable and provide an important means of transportation. The River Negro, which arises in Brazil and crosses Uruguay from northeast to southwest is also navigable for some distance.

The rich, black soils produce a high quality of grasses, which have encouraged cattle and sheep raising. Equally suited to agriculture, less than 10% of the land is used for farming. The climate is mild, though damp. Winter (June–August) temperatures average 57° to 60° F., with occasional frosts; summer (December–February) temperatures average 75° to 79° F. Rainfall is evenly distributed during the

year, averaging 40 inches annually. Nature and history have caused Uruguay to become a pastoral country.

History: The Spanish explorers of the Río de la Plata in the 16th century passed up the hills of Uruguay as unlikely to have treasure in gold and precious stones. The warlike Charrúa Indians also discouraged invasion. Military expeditions against the Indians were uniformly unsuccessful, but Jesuit and Franciscan missionaries were able to establish missions in 1624. Cattle are supposed to have been introduced by Hernando Arias in 1580 during one of the unsuccessful military expeditions. A counter-invasion by the Portuguese from Brazil came in 1680, following slave raids on the missions and cattle roundups of the wild herds that roamed the grasslands.

The Portuguese founded Colonia as a rival to Spanish Buenos Aires. The remainder of Uruguay's colonial history is one of war between the Spanish and Portuguese contenders for control of the La Plata River. Montevideo was planned by the Portuguese, built by the Spanish and taken by the British in 1806, but abandoned in 1807 when an attack on Buenos Aires failed. A Brazilian attack in 1811 was resisted by the Uruguayan cattleman and patriot José Artigas, who declared Uruguay's independence.

The struggle continued until 1820 when Montevideo fell to the Brazilians, and Artigas fled to Paraguay where he died in a comfortable self-imposed exile. A group of

Uruguay

33 exiles returned from Buenos Aires to take up the cause in 1825, and with Argentine assistance, they defeated the Brazilians at Ituzaingo in 1827 (the city of Treinte y Tres is named in honor of that band of exiles). At this point, Great Britain intervened. Both Brazil and Argentina renounced their claims and Uruguay became independent in fact on August 27, 1828.

The settlement of Uruguay proceeded slowly from the first missionary stations. The *gauchos* (cowboys) who hunted the cattle in the 17th and 18th centuries were nomads and not interested in the land. Slaughtering the cattle for hides, they sold their wares to merchants from Argentina. By the time of independence, the nomads had disappeared and large ranches had taken up the land. Farming was practiced only around Montevideo, where a market for produce was assured. Following independence, Italian and Spanish immigrants settled in the farming belt where their descendants still live today.

The early history of the republic was a chaotic period of civil war as the factions fought for power. Two parties emerged—the *Blanco* (White), representing conservative ranchers, and the *Colorado* (Red), favoring liberal reforms. The parties and politics established in the 1830s have been hardened in more than 150 years of combat and still persist today. A 10-year civil war was fought between the factions with support from other powers that intervened, including French, English and Italian. The foreign intervention terminated with the unseating of Argentine dictator Rosas in 1852; however, the Uruguayans continued the civil war for another 10 years.

Further strife in 1863 led to Brazilian support for a *Colorado* despot who unseated his *Blanco* opponent in 1865. The Paraguayan dictator Francisco Solano-Lopez came to the aid of the *Blancos*, precipitating the Triple Alliance (Argentina, Brazil and Uruguay) war against Paraguay. The defeat of Paraguay left the *Colorados* in power, which they retained for nearly a century except for the military period.

The year 1870 marked a turning point in Uruguayan history. The rancher with his *gaucho* army was out of place. The demand for better quality meat, hides and wool required more modern methods and business-like management of the huge estates. Railroads were built, European immigrants settled in the cities and a middle class mercantile society developed. Clashes continued between the two parties through the remainder of the 19th century, but a growing group of responsible citizens emerged. Three *Colorado* dictators ruled from 1875 to 1890 with some degree of moderation. Two more ruled from 1890 to 1896 with such disregard for the law

that civil war again broke out, resulting in the division of the country into *Colorado* and *Blanco* provinces. This uneasy arrangement lasted until 1903 and the election of Uruguay's foremost statesman and leader, José Batlle y Ordóñez.

The Batlle Era

Uruguay's 20th century history has been dominated by Batlle—who assumed the leadership of a bankrupt, battle-torn and

divided nation—even after his death. His first term, 1903–07, was spent in crushing civil war, uniting the country and securing popular support for sane, democratic government. From 1911–15 he campaigned for his plan, which included replacing the powerful presidency with a council, an idea based loosely on the Swiss model but unheard of in Latin America. He encountered considerable opposition, but by 1917 a new constitution was adopted, and full franchise and progressive social legislation was enacted. Using the editorial pages of *El Día*, Montevideo's leading newspaper, Batlle pleaded his case and educated the people. By the time of his death in 1929, Uruguay was the most literate, democratic, well-fed state in Latin America. Batlle's unique plural executive system was in use until 1933.

Batlle's reforms did not, however, create the economic base needed to support the welfare state he had created. The next two presidents tried to carry out his programs, but they were restricted by the nine-member national council that wielded considerable power. Social and economic reforms were completely stopped when Uruguay went into an economic depression with the rest of the world in 1931.

Uruguay

Confusion, near-anarchy and no progress marked the years 1931–51, replete with military dictators and corruption. Batlle's plural executive form of government was readopted as a result of a plebiscite in 1951 and its nine members functioned as the executive arm of government until March 1967. The long-dominant *Colorados* again were returned to power, but high inflation and other economic woes led to disenchantment. In the 1958 elections, the *Blancos* won for the first time since 1865. They were reelected in 1962. However, they proved no more capable of dealing with the economic crisis than had the *Colorados*, in no small part because neither party had the courage to deal with the bloated bureaucracy and overly generous retirement system that the welfare state had wrought.

In desperate need of dynamic leadership, Uruguayans voted overwhelmingly to return to a presidential executive in elections and a plebiscite in 1966. The *Colorados*, in the minority for eight years, elected a former air force general, Oscar D. Gestido, to the presidency, bypassing Jorge Batlle, grand-nephew of the reformer. When Gestido died in 1967, he was succeeded by the vice president, Jorge Pacheco Areco, a civilian. Encumbered by an inefficient bureaucracy and runaway inflation, and lacking forceful leadership abilities, Pacheco proved no more capable than his predecessor in solving economic stagnation, corruption and rising urban terrorism by the *Tupamaros*—Latin America's most infamous urban guerrilla force in the 1960s.

Promising law and order and economic reform, the *Colorados* received another mandate in 1971 with the presidential candidacy of Juan María Bordaberry. Most of the president's program was soon blocked in the Congress, however, where he lacked a majority.

The *Tupamaros* achieved international notoriety by kidnapping and murdering an agricultural official with the U.S. Embassy, Dan Mitrione, whom the *Tupamaros* alleged was a CIA agent who was training the Uruguayan security forces in torture techniques. As the *Tupamaros* increased their terrorism, and under U.S. pressure because of the Mitrione incident, Bordaberry turned to a new power source: the armed forces. With stunning efficiency, the military systematically routed some 2,000 guerrillas by early 1973. Then, instead of returning to the barracks, the military demanded major reforms in the nation's welfare programs, which it believed had been the basis for rampant political corruption and economic decay.

Military Rule, 1973–85

On February 8, 1973, the armed forces staged a *coup d'etat*. The generals agreed to allow Bordaberry to remain in office, provided he agreed to governmental reform and a crackdown on the *Tupamaros*. He did. Backed by the armed forces, Bordaberry dissolved Congress, banned eight political parties, closed the nation's only university, broke up labor unions, instituted strict press censorship and jailed 6,000 political opponents. Under the new order, all power was vested in the military-controlled Council of the Nation, which ruled by decree. The Mitrione incident and the subsequent *coup* inspired the Costa-Gavras film, "State of Siege."

Bordaberry decided he wanted to become president-for-life with the military backing him in 1977, but the military, favoring a gradual return to democracy, ousted him in a bloodless coup in 1976. An interim president was named, who was chief of a 27-member Council of State formed to replace the dissolved Congress.

Under the military's master plan, the new president was to serve for three years, at which time a duly elected president would serve another five years. Full democracy would then be restored at the end of this eight-year period. Further, the military was prepared to purge top leaders from the *Colorado* and *Blanco* parties before they would be permitted to participate in elections set for 1984. All other parties would be banned.

The master plan went awry, however, when the new president unexpectedly refused to issue a decree abolishing the nation's top political leadership. The military ousted *him* and, after consultation with top conservatives, the generals recruited a new civilian president, Dr. Aparicio Méndez. Méndez dutifully canceled the political rights of 1,000 leaders from all existing parties for a 15-year period.

In foreign affairs, the military government received increased criticism for its violation of human rights. In 1980, the *junta*, ruling through a civilian "front" administration, felt secure enough to submit a new constitution for popular approval. Although it provided for free congressional elections, it also established a National Security Council, empowered with final approval of almost all governmental activity and limited the presidential election to a *single* candidate approved by the military. On November 30, 1980, the voters rejected the constitution by a margin of 58% to 42%—to the utter amazement of the *junta*.

Rival factions divided the military: hardliners urged an end to the liberalization policy; others focused on the power struggle to name the presidential candidate. Meanwhile, *Blanco* and *Colorado* leaders demanded removal of a ban on political activity and restoration of a free press. Despite these appeals and the plebiscite, the military did not intend to surrender control, as more than 1,200 political prisoners languished in jail.

Transition to Democracy

General Gregorio Álvarez, former army commander, was appointed president and began preliminary discussions with the political leaders of the two traditional parties for free general elections in 1984, prior to March 1985 when his "term" expired. Negotiations stalled on the issue of membership of the commission to set rules for political activity and for framing a constitution to be submitted to a national referendum. The armed forces wanted guarantees that they would enjoy sufficient power under the democratic regime, but the opposition insisted that the army's place is in the barracks. The armed forces hinted at the necessity of a "transitional period" between the military regime and return to democracy. Most political parties had either opposed the idea or stressed the brevity of such a "transitional period."

Sanguinetti and Lacalle

Held on November 25, 1984, the elections resulted in the victory of Julio María Sanguinetti, the *Colorado* candidate, who received 39% of the vote; the *Colorados* also won a plurality in both houses of the National Assembly. Democracy was restored officially when the Assembly convened on February 15, 1985, and Sanguinetti was inaugurated on March 1 for a five-year term.

As in most of Latin America, the new president, considered a centrist, had to face the rising expectations of a population free of military rule, the political inexperience of many of his advisers and a serious economic situation. In 1985 strikes multiplied—including one that paralyzed Montevideo's port. The government suspended the activities of two banks, and reassured the public that the "restlessness" of the armed forces, provoked by a cut in the military budget and investigations into the actions of the past military regime, would be peacefully solved.

An avowed agnostic in a nominally Catholic but traditionally secular country, Sanguinetti once stirred controversy by not kneeling to kiss the ring of Pope John Paul II during a papal visit.

A delicate matter was resolved in 1986: what to do with the military, which, as in other Latin American countries, had committed numerous human rights violations. To try them would be an invitation to a military takeover. An oral agreement was reached prior to the return to civilian rule that there would be no trials of either *Tupamaros* or the military. A reluctant but practical Assembly passed a general amnesty measure at Sanguinetti's request. The military then publicly acknowledged that some officers had committed "transgressions of human rights."

The amnesty enraged human rights advocates and survivors of 50,000 persons who were slain or "disappeared." The matter was settled in 1989 when in a referendum the amnesty was upheld by a margin of 57% to 43%.

A moderate *Colorado* candidate was expected to win 1989 elections, but Luis Lacalle of the *Blanco* Party captured a plurality of 37%. He had entered into a preelection coalition with the leftist *Frente Amplio* (Broad Front), the candidate of which received 21% of the vote. Thus a loose combination of leftists, including Communists, became a force to be reckoned with in Uruguayan politics, and it remains so today.

Although nominally leftist, Lacalle followed a program of privatization of government enterprises, arousing opposition from surplus employees of these industries. Privatization of the telephone system was halted by a 1992 referendum, in which 72% opposed the measure.

Lacalle made Uruguay a charter member of *Mercosur*, the free-trade bloc with Argentina, Brazil and Paraguay. High inflation plagued Uruguay in 1993–94, which led to voter discontent.

The 1994 election was virtually a three-way tie and left no party with a mandate. Former President Sanguinetti was returned to the presidency with a bare plurality of 34.3%. The *Blanco* Party's Alberto Volonte was second with 33%. The Broad Front, an alliance of the left-wing Progressive Encounter with the Socialists and Communists, fielded Montevideo Mayor Tabaré Vázquez, an oncologist, who received 32.8%, the left's strongest showing yet. The traditional two-party dominance of Uruguayan politics effectively ended.

Largely because the vote had become so fragmented, the Assembly introduced a *segunda vuelta*, or runoff, for future presidential elections. Sanguinetti's second term was marked by continued emphasis on trade, especially within *Mercosur*. The economy experienced modest growth until late in his term, when the economic woes of neighboring Argentina and Brazil proved contagious.

Jorge Batlle

About half the country's 2.4 million voters participated in the party primaries in 1999 and a clear plurality, just over 37%, voted in the *Colorado* primary. The winner was Senator Jorge Batlle, grand-nephew of the party's illustrious founder and son of Luis Batlle, who served twice as presi-

Former President Jorge Batlle

dent, in 1947–51 and 1954–58. A former journalist, Batlle had failed in four earlier presidential bids.

Making his second bid, Vázquez received about 80% of the vote in the Progressive Encounter primary, while former President Lacalle easily won the *Blanco* primary.

Once again, the old Communist and Socialist parties coalesced around the Progressive Encounter to form the Broad Front. In the first round of voting on October 31, Vázquez scored a convincing first-place finish, with 39.8%, to 32.7% for Batlle and 22.2% for Lacalle. Moreover, the Broad Front stunned the two traditional parties by emerging as the largest force in the new Congress, winning 40 of 99 seats in the Chamber of Representatives and 12 of the 30 Senate seats. Voter turnout was 91.8%.

Clearly, the left wing had come a long way since the 1973 coup, but the prospect of a Vázquez presidency alarmed the political establishment. The defeated Lacalle swallowed his pride and endorsed Batlle, who pledged to continue Sanguinetti's moderate free-market reforms and derided the "crazy ideas" of his leftist opponent. In the November runoff, the results were:

Batlle	1,138,067	53.9%
Vázquez	972,197	46.1%

Thus, on his fifth try for the presidency, Batlle was inaugurated on March 1, 2000, at the age of 72. With 40% of the seats in both houses, the Broad Front forced the traditionally rival *Colorados* and *Blancos* to

form a legislative marriage of convenience. This formal coalition ended in 2002 when the *Blanco* cabinet ministers resigned, but the two parties continued to present a united front in the Assembly.

The Batlle government at first resisted the hemispheric trend toward wholesale privatization, then reluctantly began making moves to reform the bloated public sector in order to appease the International Monetary Fund (see Economy).

Batlle found himself in the maelstrom an international controversy in 2002. Uruguay co-sponsored a resolution before the U.N. Human Rights Commission that called upon Cuba to democratize and to respect human rights. When Cuban President Fidel Castro lashed out and called Batlle a "lackey" of the United States, Batlle broke diplomatic relations with Cuba, which had been restored in 1986 after a 25-year break (see Cuba).

Uruguay faced the same type of socioeconomic crisis that led to the chaos in Argentina in 2001. In July 2002, the government had issued a surprise decision to let the peso float, and it plummeted from 17 to the dollar to 28. When Uruguayans began withdrawing their savings in a panic, and bank deposits dropped from $13 billion at the end of 2001 to just $8.8 billion, Batlle declared a "temporary" bank holiday. Violence and looting broke out in August in Montevideo. The Bush administration authorized a $1.5 billion emergency loan, the first time Bush had approved a direct loan to a Latin American country. Within days, the loan was repaid when the IMF approved a $3.8 billion loan.

The economic crisis continued into 2003, and despite international predictions of a default, Uruguay serviced its debt through painful austerity measures that led to more street protests, but that even the opposition Broad Front proclaimed necessary.

Faced with grim economic choices, the *Blancos* and *Colorados* boldly voted to slaughter the sacred cow of state-owned monopolies by approving a bill in 2003 that dismantled the inefficient state oil monopoly, *ANCAP*, and opened it up to badly needed foreign investors. But the Broad Front had enough votes to force a referendum on the law on December 7, 2003. In a replay of the 1992 referendum on telephone privatization, 62% of the electorate voted to repeal the privatization.

Vázquez Prevails

In 2004, the Broad Front renominated Vázquez, the *Colorados* nominated former Interior Minister Guillermo Stirling, and the *Blancos* rejected former President Lacalle in favor of Jorge Larrañaga, a former governor and senator. By then the econ-

Uruguay

omy was rebounding, but it was too late for either of the now-discredited major parties, especially the *Colorados*.

Like Presidents Ricardo Lagos of Chile and Luiz Inácio da Silva of Brazil, Vázquez suddenly moderated his long-standing socialist rhetoric and emerged as a pragmatic, statesmanlike figure. He rejected a radical approach, pledging to couple an emphasis on social programs with moderate economic policies. It was a message the recession-weary Uruguayans, who were still reluctant to scrap their overly generous social welfare system, wanted to hear. The result was a stunning first-round victory for Vázquez:

Vázquez	1,121,622	50.5%
Larrañag	762,715	34.3%
Stirling	230,434	10.4%

Vázquez was inaugurated on March 1, 2005, Uruguay's first leftist president; the 170-year grip on power by the *Colorados* and the *Blancos* was finally broken. The Broad Front also emerged with a working majority in the Assembly. The inauguration proved a fiesta for the South American left. Cuba's Castro was uncharacteristically absent, but Vázquez's first act as president was to restore diplomatic relations with Cuba, three years after Batlle's spat with Castro.

In keeping with his campaign promises, Vázquez, himself a physician, announced a $100 million social program to provide medical care and nutrition. At the same time, he continued the grudging efforts toward, if not outright privatization, a mixed economy that has created partnerships between the state and private indus-

try. It was much the approach he followed as mayor of Montevideo. He also has succeeded in satisfying the IMF and the World Bank (see Economy).

Following the lead of Argentina and Chile, Vázquez made an effort for Uruguay to come to terms with the human rights abuses of the 1973–85 dictatorship. He struck a deal with the military by which he agreed to abide by the amnesty law, while the military would cooperate in recovering the bodies of those who disappeared during the dictatorship to give their families some closure.

But the amnesty deal did not exempt civilians. In November 2006, former President Bordaberry, then 78, who abetted the military seizure of 1973 and ruled as a dictator, and his foreign minister, Juan Blanco, were arrested on the order of a judge who was investigating the 1976 murders in Buenos Aires of two exiled leftist legislators, Senator Zelmar Micheneli and Deputy Héctor Gutiérrez, and two *Tupamaro* rebels. Commented President Vázquez, *"Habló la justicia"* (Justice has spoken).

Justice spoke slowly. They were jailed for several weeks before being placed under house arrest to await trial. The charges were expanded to include 14 murders. Like the Pinochet case in Chile, the case involved two and a half years of legal wrangling. Bordaberry was sent back to jail in April 2009, after which he was hospitalized for a severe respiratory condition. He turned 81 in June. The trial resumed, and on February 9, 2010, the judge found Bordaberry guilty of the two homicides, of nine disappearances and of "crimes against the constitution." He was sentenced to 30 years.

In economics, Vázquez proved to be a pragmatist like Brazil's da Silva, rather than a fire-breathing Marxist like Venezuela's Chávez, which confounded some hardliners in his own movement while delighting the middle class and the IMF. He followed Batlle's prudent policies that had begun to extract Uruguay from its devastating recession; in 2005 the country recorded GDP growth of 6.6%, and in 2008, it was 8.5%, among the highest in Latin America.

Uruguay allowed firms from Spain and Finland to invest $1.5 billion in two huge paper mills on the Río Plata, the largest single foreign investment in Uruguayan history. But the projects elicited concerns about pollution from greens in Vázquez's coalition as well as from the Argentines across the river, who feared dioxin contamination. Argentine protesters blocked a border bridge for two months in 2006. The Spanish firm then abandoned the project. The Finnish firm "finished" its mill in 2007, as 20,000 Argentines protested the formal opening on their side of the river. The plant is expected to add 1.6% to GDP and increase export revenue by 15%.

In 2006, Uruguay paid a $630 million installment to the IMF nine months ahead of schedule, saving $8.4 million in interest payments. Moreover, Finance Minister Danilo Astori hinted publicly at something that is heresy for Latin American leftists: possibly leaving *Mercosur* to enter a more lucrative free-trade agreement with the United States. Ironically, Vázquez had joined Venezuela's Chávez in hamstringing the U.S.-sponsored Free Trade Area of the Americas (FTAA) at the Summit of the Americas in Argentina two months earlier, and Chávez had just brought Venezuela into *Mercosur*.

Vázquez upped the ante even further in 2007 when Uruguay signed a trade and investment framework agreement with the United States, the first step toward a free-trade agreement (FTA). Moreover, Uruguay was one of five countries on President Bush's goodwill tour of Latin America in March. The two presidents had an amicable meeting, at which free trade was tops on the agenda. Chávez timed an anti-Bush rally in Buenos Aires the same day. Uruguay and the United States signed two more protocols in advance of a FTA in October 2008, but it has not yet been finalized.

Vázquez visited Washington in September 2009 and met with Secretary of State Hillary Clinton. He echoed her criticism of Venezuela's arms buildup, saying, "We believe that it is quite inconvenient to the region to devote such significant economic resources toward purchasing arms."

Vázquez angered women's rights advocates, part of his core constituency, in No-

Uruguay

Former President Tabaré Vázquez
Source: BBC

vember 2008 when he vetoed a bill to permit abortion in the first trimester, a rarity in Latin America. The Assembly had narrowly passed the measure, although the Roman Catholic bishop threatened legislators who supported it with excommunication. The physician-president said he opposed abortion "philosophically and biologically." The Assembly made global news again in September 2009 by passing Latin America's first same-sex adoption law.

The Elections of 2009

As his chosen successor, Vázquez endorsed Finance Minister Astori, who was challenged by Senator José Mujica, a former *Tupamaro* guerrilla who spent 14 years in prison before and during the military regime. In party primaries on June 28, 2009, Mujica, 74, narrowly defeated Astori. The same day, in the *Blanco* primary, former President Lacalle, 68, defeated Senator Jorge Larrañaga, the party's 2005 standard bearer, by a comfortable margin. The *Colorados* nominated the jailed former President Bordaberry's son, Pedro, 49, who has been proclaiming his father's innocence. Two minor candidates were also on the ballot.

In the first round on October 25, turnout was 89.9% of the 2,563,250 registered voters. The results:

Mujica	1,105,262	47.96%
Lacalle	669,942	29.07%
Bordaberry	392,307	17.02%

Bordaberry conceded defeat and immediately announced he was throwing his support to Lacalle for the November 29 runoff. But Mujica's huge lead proved insurmountable. In the runoff, the turnout was 89.2%. The results:

Mujica	1,197,638	52.4%
Lacalle	994,510	43.5%
Blank	53,100	2.3%
Null	40,103	1.75%

In the General Assembly, the Broad Front holds a one-seat majority in both houses. In the Senate, the Broad Front has 16 seats to 9 for the *Blancos* and 5 for the *Colorados*. In the Chamber of Deputies, the Broad Front has 50 seats, the *Blancos* 30, the *Colorados* 17 and the Independent Party, 2.

Mujica, who made news when he announced that he owns no property other than a 1987 Volkswagen Beetle and that his bank accounts and other property are in his wife's name, may be officially the world's poorest chief of state. He was inaugurated on March 1, 2010. The oldest elected president in Latin America, he turned 75 on May 20. He was expected to continue Vázquez's prudent, center-left course.

Culture: Almost entirely Caucasian, Uruguay in many ways resembles an extension of Europe, and this certainly is true in its culture. Like Chile, highly literate and prosperous Uruguay has made cultural contributions far out of proportion to its small size. Also as in Chile, this cultural development was made possible by a climate of political stability and virtually unlimited freedom of expression.

Uruguay's contributions to art and music are not insignificant, but it is in the field of literature that the country has attained its greatest recognition beyond its borders. One of the most distinguished writers was José Enrique Rodó, whose 1900 essay, *Ariel*, extolled Latin American culture and denounced the United States as lacking in appreciation for cultural values. Needless to say, this essay was revered by latter-day Marxists and *dependentistas* throughout Latin America.

Regarded as leading representatives of the romantic period in Uruguay were the novelists Eduardo Acevedo Díaz and Carlos Reyes; the poet Juan Zorilla de San Martín bridged the gap between romanticism and modernism. Two women of the post-modernist period, Delmira Agustini and Juana de Ibarbourou, also achieved international recognition.

Some of Uruguay's leading contemporary writers abandoned the country during the military regime of 1973–85, the two best known being the novelists Juan Carlos Onetti (1909–1994) and Mario Benedetti (1920–2009).

Onetti's first novel, *El pozo (The Pit)*, was considered a trend setter in Latin American literature. Taking a technique from Faulkner, whom he admired, Onetti created the fictional town of Santa María in his 1950 novel *La vida breve (The Short Life)* and used it in several of his 25 novels. He was jailed by the military regime, and when he was released, he spent the rest of his life in Spain, refusing even to visit

President José Mujica

Uruguay after the return to democracy. He received Spain's prestigious Cervantes Prize in 1980.

Benedetti was a poet, novelist, playwright and journalist. He wrote two plays and 11 novels, perhaps the best known being *La tregua (The Truce)* in 1960, later made into a movie, and *El cumpleaños de Juan Ángel (Juan Ángel's Birthday)* in 1971. He, too, was jailed by the military and went into exile in Argentina, Peru, Cuba and Spain, but he returned to Uruguay after the restoration of democracy and died in Montevideo on May 17, 2009.

Uruguayan journalism is highly developed but also highly politicized. The leading daily remains *El Día*, founded in 1886 by the future President of the Republic José Ordóñez y Batlle as a mouthpiece for his *Colorado* Party, which it still is today. Ordóñez's picture remains on the editorial page like the image of a patron saint. The *Blanco* Party has its own organ, *El País*, founded in 1918. The third major daily is *El Diario*, also pro-*Blanco*.

Economy: Uruguay's economy is almost totally dependent on its cattle and sheep-raising industry, which accounts for more than 40% of all exports. Because of heavy taxation on farm products, as well as inefficient state management of the economy, the gross national product actually declined between 1955 and 1975. Inflation has also been a serious problem. Prices rose by an incredible 1,200% in the decade following 1968. To help control inflation, the government imposed new tax and credit policies. Steps were also taken to increase farm output, stimulate exports and begin offshore oil exploration.

Economic growth declined for several years during the country's economic cri-

341

Uruguay

sis of 1999–2002 (see History). Real GDP shrank by –3.2% in 1999, –1.3% in 2000, –3.4% in 2001 and –10.8% in 2002. It finally grew by 2.5% in 2003 and 12.3% in 2004, but that did not even recover the ground lost during the recession. It then grew steadily for four years: 6.6% in 2005, 7% in 2006, 7.2% in 2007 and 8.5% in 2008. With the global recession, it shrank again by –2.5% in 2009.

Unemployment has remained stubbornly in the double-digits for several years and peaked at 20% in 2002 during the economic crisis. It was still 10.8% in 2006. Inflation dropped from 5.1% in 2000 to 4.5% in 2001, then spiraled back to 26% in 2002. It fell back to 8.5% in 2007 and 5.8% in 2008. With the recession, it climbed back to 9.3% in 2009.

Much of the blame for the 1999–2002 crisis could be placed on the dire economic situation in neighboring Argentina. Argentines who once crowded the beautiful beaches at Punta del Este stayed home in droves in the summer of 2002. Even worse, they began withdrawing millions they had deposited in Uruguayan banks for safekeeping. The crucial beef industry was simultaneously affected by an outbreak of mad cow disease, which caused exports to nosedive.

Uruguay's seemingly enviable cradle-to-the-grave social welfare system and generous retirement benefits helped give Uruguay one of the hemisphere's best standards of living for decades, and the per capita income for years was second only to Argentina's among the Latin American republics. It was $6,300 in 1998, but it dropped steadily during the devastating recession of 1999–2002. The per capita income of $3,300 in 2004 ranked seventh in the region, and in 2004. The situation has

improved dramatically. Uruguay's per capita income of $6,380 in 2007 and $8,260 in 2008 ranked fourth in Latin America, behind Chile, Mexico and Venezuela.

But the long-cherished social welfare system has come at a high price; external debt in 1999 was $6.3 billion, about 30% of GDP, even then a heavy burden for such a small country, and by the end of 2004 it was about 90% of GDP, the ninth highest in the world. It declined to 57% by 2008 and 52.9% in 2009.

In 2002, the international rating for Uruguayan bonds was reduced, thus making it more costly to borrow money. The Batlle administration responded with an economic austerity plan, which included privatization of state-owned utilities, telecommunications, airports and even highways, and a cut in the bloated civil service pensions. Batlle also promised to reduce the budget deficit, which was 4.2% of GDP in 2001, to 2.5% in 2002 and to balance the budget by 2004. The move was popular with the International Monetary Fund, which approved $743 million in loans in March 2002, another for $1.5 billion in May and $3.8 billion in August. Uruguay and the IMF agreed to restructure its bond indebtedness, thus extending the term of its bonds. But a law privatizing the state-owned oil company, *ANCAP*, proved unpopular with the voters; 62% of them voted to repeal it in a referendum on December 7, 2003.

Despite his leftist tilt, President Tabaré Vázquez bent over backward before his election in 2004 to reassure foreign investors and creditors that he would honor Uruguay's debt commitment (about $11 billion when he took office in March 2005), and he moderated his long-standing opposition to free trade. Thus, he more

closely resembled Brazilian President Luiz Inácio da Silva and former Chilean President Roberto Lagos, two socialists who pragmatically moved to the center, than the confrontationist Presidents Néstor Kirchner of Argentina and Hugo Chávez of Venezuela.

His pragmatism paid off, literally; in 2005, the IMF approved a $1.13 billion loan and the World Bank approved an $800 million, five-year loan to help the country recover from the recession. In 2006, Uruguay paid $630 million to the IMF ahead of schedule and paid another $1.1 billion in 2007.

Vázquez's successor in 2010, José Mujica, is a former *Tupamaro* guerrilla who, like Vázquez, has mellowed in recent years. He was not expected to radically change his predecessor's prudent and pragmatic policies.

The Future: Uruguay is the embodiment of Churchill's comment that democracy is the worst possible form of government—except for all the others. Uruguayans have been reluctant to abandon their cherished welfare state and state-owned monopolies, which had become luxuries the economy could not afford. They punished any party at the polls that sought to do so.

Dr. Tabaré Vázquez and now José Mujica finally succeeded in accomplishing at the ballot box what the *Tupamaros* failed to do with terror—bring the left to power and break the grip of the two traditional parties. But like so many other erstwhile Latin American left-wing firebrands, they moderated their Marxist rhetoric and eschewed a radical approach. Vázquez embraced the pragmatic socialism of Brazil's Lula da Silva, rather than the meat-ax Marxism of Venezuela's Hugo Chávez. His performance as president was impressive. He reassured foreign investors and attracted new industry—despite environmental risks. He repaid IMF loan installments ahead of schedule. The economy has shown encouraging growth on his watch. At the same time, he has sought justice for the human rights abuses of the military regime.

His five-year drew to a close just as the global recession shrank the Uruguayan economy in 2009 after four years of solid growth. Mujica, 75, was not Vázquez's choice to succeed him, and he was considered more of a leftist hardliner than Vázquez. But he seemed to downplay such suggestions on the campaign trail. Although he ius unlikely to upset Vázquez's successful economic apple cart, it isn't clears whether he'll maintain the current amicable relationship with the United States or bring Uruguay into the orbit iof Hugo Chávez, something his predecessor studiously avoided.

The Bolivarian Republic of Venezuela

Caracas and the mountains

Area: 352,150 square miles.

Population: 27,223,228 million (2010 estimate).

Capital City: Caracas (Pop. 5 million, estimated).

Climate: Tropical in the coastal lowlands, increasingly temperate at higher elevations in the interior. Heaviest rainfall is from June to December.

Neighboring Countries: Guyana (East); Brazil (Southeast and South); Colombia (Southwest and West); Trinidad and Tobago are islands lying a short distance from the northeast coast.

Venezuela

Official Language: Spanish
Other Principal Tongue: English.
Ethnic Background: Mulatto-*mestizo* (mixed European, African and Indian ancestry, 83%); European (10%); African (5%); Indian (2%).
Principal Religion: Roman Catholic Christianity.
Chief Commercial Products: Petroleum and petroleum products, aluminum, alumina and bauxite, agricultural products, small manufactured products.
Currency: Bolívar.
Gross Domestic Product: U.S. $357.6 billion in 2009 ($13,136 per capita).
Former Colonial Status: Spanish Colony (1498–1811).
Independence Date: July 5, 1811. Venezuela seceded from *Gran Colombia*, also known as New Granada, on September 22, 1811.
Chief of State: Hugo Chávez Frías (b. July 28, 1954), president (since February 2, 1999).
National Flag: Yellow, blue and red horizontal stripes with seven yellow stars in a semi-circle on the red stripe.

Venezuela has four distinct geographic regions: the Venezuelan Highlands to the west and along the coast, the Maracaibo Lowlands around freshwater Lake Maracaibo, the *Llanos* or plains of the Orinoco River and the Guiana Highlands. The Venezuelan Highlands are an extension of the eastern mountains of Colombia and are Venezuela's most densely populated region, with Caracas, Maracay and Valencia located in the fertile inter-mountain basins. The northern slope of the Highlands is relatively arid, but the basins receive adequate rainfall and because of elevation, are temperate and suited to agriculture.

The Maracaibo Lowlands, encircled by mountains, are windless and one of the hottest regions in South America, famous for the great lake (129 miles long and 60 miles wide) under whose water are some of the most extensive oil deposits in the world. Rainfall in this region is heavy along the slopes of the highlands, gradually diminishing toward the coast.

The *Llanos* of the Orinoco are the great treeless plains of the Orinoco River valley, which run east and west between the Venezuelan Highlands and the Guiana Highlands. Extending some 600 miles in length and 200 miles across, these plains are low and wet; intersected with slow moving streams, this region has been plagued with periodic floods and drought, but the poor soil has supported cattle raising. Presently, the government is undertaking flood control and irrigation projects to make this land available for agriculture and to support the development of new breeds of cattle.

The Guiana Highlands, south of the Orinoco, comprise more than half of Venezuela's territory. Rising in steep cliffs from the *Llanos*, this area is a flat tableland that extends to the Brazilian border. Heavily forested in part, it contains vast deposits of iron ore and bauxite. Gold and diamonds also exist in this region, which has been explored only superficially.

History: At the time of the Spanish conquest, Venezuela was inhabited by warlike tribes of Carib and Arawak Indians who offered brave but ineffective resistance to the invaders. The first landing was in the Gulf of Paria, where pearls were discovered. Under Spanish direction, Indian divers soon stripped the beds of the Gulf. The first settlement was established at Cumaná in 1520, with additional settlements at Coro (1520), Barquismeto (1551), Valencia (1555) and Caracas (1567).

Indians were utilized to pan the rivers for gold, but the results were disappointing and the settlers turned to agriculture. The wealth found in Peru and Mexico caused the Spanish government to lose interest in Venezuela, and options to explore its potential were leased to Dutch and German adventurers. The Spanish settlers gradually consolidated their small holdings, but it was nearly a century later before a serious attempt was made to explore the interior. The enslaved Indian laborers perished on the coastal plantations, and black slaves were imported from Africa to work the sugar and indigo crops. The neglected planters, with little merchandise to ship to the Spanish markets and forbidden to trade with the growing American markets, revolted against Spanish authority in 1796.

Two additional abortive attempts to set up an independent government were made in 1806 and 1811 under the leadership of Francisco de Miranda. At his urging, a republican congress declared independence on July 5, 1811, but the so-called First Republic lasted only a year. Venezuela's national hero, Simón Bolívar, took up the struggle and fought a limited, but deceptive, guerrilla war against local armies in the pay of Spain until his capture of Angostura in 1817. Here he was joined by British veterans of the Peninsular War in Spain and by cattlemen from the *Llanos* with whom he made a dramatic march on Bogotá. The Spanish were finally expelled from northern Latin America in 1819 and the country achieved full independence, becoming a part of the Republic of Gran Colombia, led by President Simón Bolívar and Vice President Francisco de Paula Santander, and including present-day Colombia and Ecuador. Dissension and the subsequent illness of Bolívar led to the dissolution of Gran Colombia; Venezuela withdrew in 1830.

General José Antonio Páez, the country's first president and a hero of independence, dominated Venezuelan politics from 1830 to 1848. He later returned as a dictator from 1861 to 1863. A capable and popular leader, he was effective in restoring order to war-torn Venezuela and in the establishment of governmental services and control. He was followed in 1848 by 13 years of repressive dictatorship by the Monagas brothers, who forced him into exile.

Returning to the *Llanos* in 1861, Páez raised another force of cattlemen to regain power in Venezuela. He ruled for two years, but was less tolerant of opposition than he had been during his first tenure; he was ousted in 1863 and intermittent civil war wracked the country until 1870 as young liberals fought conservatives.

Antonio Guzmán Blanco emerged from the chaos of civil strife; as strongman, he served as president or ruled through puppets for 18 years. Well educated, arrogant and completely unscrupulous, he enforced honesty among his ministers while converting a substantial part of the national treasury to his personal use. A careless despot who enjoyed living in Paris, he left his office in the hands of a puppet once too often and was overthrown in 1888.

Eleven years of confusion ensued, punctuated by violence and short-term presidents. An illiterate soldier of fortune who had been exiled to Colombia, Cipriano Castro, captured the presidency with the help of a private army in 1899. His nine-year rule was certainly the most repressive in Venezuela's troubled history. His high-handed dealing with European powers resulted in a blockade of the Venezuelan coastline by British, German and Italian naval units. After intervention by President Theodore Roosevelt, the matter was settled by arbitration. Castro turned the government over in 1909 to Juan Vincente Gómez, who ruled until 1935.

Gómez gave Venezuela its most able and its most savage administration. Oil had been discovered and he arranged lucrative contracts with American, British and Dutch interests for extraction and processing. Simultaneously, he fostered agriculture and public works, established sound foreign relations and paid off the national debt. He also mechanized the army to support his regime and built a personal fortune. By comparison with his predecessors, Gómez left Venezuela in a prosperous condition when he died, but totally bereft of qualified leaders to administer the wealth which he had accumulated or to control the army which he had enlarged and modernized.

From 1935 to 1948 a series of moderate, but ineffective presidents occupied the office; during this period, political parties were allowed to organize, the largest being *Acción Democrática* (Democratic Action), a popular, leftist party that had attempted to consolidate rural labor into a mass organization. Fearful of a rigged election in 1945, the party revolted and named Rómulo Betancourt as provisional president.

Venezuelans were delighted with democratic government, and action was taken to recover some of the wealth from Gómez's estate and from others who had privately benefited during his rule. In the first free and honest elections in Venezuela's history, Rómulo Gallegos, a well-known novelist, was chosen as president in 1947. Moving too fast to accomplish his goals, he frightened the army, which feared loss of its power and position in the government; he was ousted by a coup within three months of his inauguration. The army declared that it would save the country from communism, and exiled Gallegos and Betancourt, establishing another dictatorship under General Marcos Pérez Jiménez. He loosed a reign of terror and with reckless abandon spent the income from oil on public works in the city of Caracas and on poorly planned industrial ventures, with a handsome cut to friends and to the army. By late 1957 Venezuelans had had enough—resistance increased to the point that even the pampered army refused to oppose the popular will. Pérez Jiménez fled in January 1958, and a combined military and civilian committee took over the government.

Democracy Takes Root

Three moderate parties vigorously competed for the presidency in free elections that December: Democratic Action, or *AD*; the Democratic Republican Union (*URD*), and a social Christian movement with a cumbersome name that is better known by the acronym *COPEI*. The *AD*'s Betancourt was returned to the presidency with a 47% plurality and was sworn in for a five-year term on February 13, 1959, beginning an unbroken line of nine presidential administrations that has continued to the present, an enviable record of stability for Latin America.

An enlightened leader, Betancourt oversaw the adoption of a liberal constitution in 1961, but he also had to deal with a leftist insurgency incited by Cuba's Fidel Castro. Nonetheless, left-wing political parties such as the Movement to Socialism (*MAS*) were allowed to compete under Betancourt's tolerant constitution. One of the fundamental tenets of that document, designed to guard against another Gómez or Pérez Jiménez, was that no president could be re-elected for 10 years after leaving office. The popular Betancourt was

succeeded in 1964 by Raúl Leoni, also of *AD*, who received a 33% plurality.

In the December 1968 election, *COPEI*'s Rafael Caldera was elected with only a 29% plurality. Caldera was instrumental in establishing the Organization of Petroleum Exporting Countries (OPEC).

AD was returned to power in 1973 elections in which Carlos Andrés Pérez won a landslide (by Venezuelan standards) 48% of the vote over his principal opponent. Both candidates had run on almost identical center-left platforms. Voters firmly rejected both the radical left and right—the Marxist-Socialist candidate received only 4.2% of the vote and the right-wing candidate, a former associate of Pérez Jiménez, got less than 1%. In congressional races, *AD* won 24 of 49 seats in the Senate and 102 out of 200 seats in the Chamber of Deputies. Pérez launched new, ambitious programs in agriculture and education, which amazed even his own supporters.

Venezuela took charge of the U.S.-operated iron mines near Ciudad Guyana in 1975. The nationalization of the oil industry, occurred at the beginning of 1976. The 40 private firms, most of them U.S.-based, were granted compensation of $1.2 billion, which Venezuela asserted was equal to the book value of their assets. The companies claimed the true value to be between $3.5 and $5 billion.

Although Pérez maintained that nationalization of the oil industry would make Venezuelans "masters of their destiny," the nation continued to depend heavily on foreign oil companies to refine, transport and market the oil. In addition, the oil firms provided technical assistance to the state-owned oil organization, *Petroven*. Ironically, the fees charged by the private oil firms for these services were almost as high as the profits made by them before nationalization. Such a lucrative arrangement led to criticism of the Pérez administration by those who claimed that "oil nationalization needs more nationalization."

In 1973, when it joined OPEC in raising prices by more than 400%, Venezuela experienced windfall profits. With its oil income rising from $2 billion in 1972 to $10.4 billion in 1974 and $14.5 billion in 1983, Venezuela earned more from oil during the two years following the price hike than in the previous 56 years it had been exporting oil.

The gush of petrodollars swamped the nation with more money than it could realistically absorb. To control the resulting inflation, which rose from the usual rate of 2–3% to 20% in 1974, the government channeled half the money out of the country. Some was invested in international lending agencies while some was lent to developing nations, particularly in the Caribbean. To further reduce the cash inflow, and to conserve the nation's dwindling oil reserves (then estimated at 12–15 billion barrels), Venezuela cut production from an average of 3.3 million barrels a day in 1973 to 2.2 million barrels in 1976.

Oil income vastly increased Venezuelan influence in Latin America. By raising contributions (and therefore voting power) in international lending organizations, Pérez hoped to make these agencies less subject to "humiliating vetoes" of loans to nations out of favor with the United States. Venezuela also helped to finance the establishment of cartels—such as in banana and coffee production and marketing—so that developing nations could charge more for raw materials sold to industrialized countries.

In foreign relations, Venezuela became an advocate for Third World causes and for Latin American economic independence. Pérez also played a major role in advocating greater respect for human rights in the region, and condemned the use of torture by the military regime in Chile.

The house in Caracas where Simón Bolívar, *"El Libertador,"* was born.
Photo by the author

Venezuela

Caracas boasts an ultra-modern skyline, but the makeshift vendors' stalls in the foreground are a reminder of the disparity between the elite and the poor in Venezuela.
Photo by the author

Relations with the United States remained cordial. In 1977, Pérez visited the United States, where he praised the Carter administration's campaign for greater respect for human rights in Latin America. Carter gave Venezuela high marks for its refusal to join a 1973 OPEC oil embargo against the United States arising out of the Arab-Israeli conflict, and for shipping extra quantities of oil to North America during the unusually cold winter of 1976–77.

Venezuela had one of the highest per capita incomes in Latin America, but most of that was concentrated in the upper class (5%) and the middle class (15%), both of which literally went on a spending spree. Signs of the "good life" abounded—swimming pools, comfortable homes and beach villas. A 350% tax on luxury cars didn't slow demand. Although domestic car production reached record levels, there was a waiting list for buyers.

In this jewel of opulence, fully 80% of the people lived in poverty (and still do), with malnutrition afflicting half the nation's people. Almost none of the oil money filtered down to the poor. Pérez warned, "Our country is rich, but our people are poor." Ironically, at the time he was one of the "fat cat" class engaged in open thievery.

The search for jobs and a better life lured 80% of the nation's population to urban areas, where they settled in filthy slums surrounding major cities. This caused not only a costly drop in farm output and a jump in food prices, but created immense problems of how to provide basic services to this population encircling the cities. More than 70% of the population of Caracas, then and now, lives in sordid *ranchos*, where even the police hesitate to go, in sharp contrast to the gleaming skyscrapers of the city. Incentives encour-

aging slum dwellers to move back to the country failed.

Investment during the first Pérez administration centered on the oil, steel and electrical industries, traditional sources of income for the super-rich of Venezuela.

In 1978, Venezuela suffered its largest balance of payments deficit in its history ($1.7 billion). Exports (mostly oil) were down 7.5% from the previous year. During the five years Pérez was in office, imports rose by more than 230%.

As is often common during periods of rapid economic expansion, there was also widespread government fraud, inefficiency, administrative waste and a decrease in social services. Living standards actually declined for the lower-income masses. Although Pérez boasted that unemployment had been largely eliminated, the inflation rate ranged between 10% (officially) and 20% (more accurate). Urban residents also complained of overcrowded schools, shortages of water and electric power and declining quality of health facilities.

Increased economic problems set the stage for the 1978 presidential elections, when voters turned to the COPEI's Luis Herrera Campíns, who won with 46.6% of the 5.5 million votes cast. The *AD*'s candidate trailed with 43%. During the campaign, Herrera Campíns repeatedly charged that the nation's oil income had been squandered through government corruption, waste and deficit spending.

The new president, a former journalist, was widely regarded as an intellectual. He promised to emphasize state development of major industries while also encouraging greater private investments. He also pledged to pay more attention to the problems of the poor as well as to expand the nation's school system. Herrera Campíns also made an effort to diversify the economy from its over-dependence on oil.

He criticized the Reagan administration for its policies for its "treatment" of Nicaragua, its support of the right-wing government in El Salvador and for its backing of Britain in the Falkland Islands invasion by Argentina in 1982.

A burning issue was Venezuela's long-simmering border dispute with neighboring Guyana. Venezuela claimed a full five eighths of Guyana's territory! There was strong anti-British feeling in Venezuela—exacerbated by the Falklands dispute. British warships shelled Venezuela's ports early in the 20th century when Venezuela failed to repay loans to British banks. Herrera Campíns wanted to settle the border dispute through negotiation. However, the amount of territory claimed made a solution almost impossible to reach. The area claimed is rich in timber—and potentially rich in oil, minerals and precious gems.

Venezuela's oil wealth attracted a flood of immigrants from its poorer neighbors. Efforts to register the newcomers were inadequate. The ethnic makeup of the country was also altered by the presence of more than 1 million European and Arab immigrants, who worked in the technological aspects of petroleum production.

By 1981, it was clear Venezuela's governments had not been able to follow the wise advice of Rómulo Betancourt "to sow the oil," which meant to diversify the economy and avoid the country's increasing dependence on oil exports. Limited industrialization, declining agricultural production and a lack of serious planning made the economy highly vulnerable to any change in the price of oil.

Consequently, the oil gluts of 1979–80 and 1986–90 hit Venezuela hard. In 1982, the country suffered from a severe cash crisis produced by falling oil revenues, a sharp decline in international reserves and a lack of confidence of potential investors. The government re-evaluated its gold holdings and placed the state oil company under central bank jurisdiction. Unaccustomed to austerity, the Venezuelans reacted with mounting criticism to the erratic policies of the administration.

Presidential and congressional elections in 1983 demonstrated the general discontent with *COPEI*. Jaime Lusinchi, the presidential candidate of *AD*, won easily, receiving more than 50% of the vote over the respected former President Rafael Caldera of *COPEI*. *AD* also received a majority in Congress.

Lusinchi not only did not ease the austerity measures, he devalued the currency by almost half, increased fuel prices by more than 100% to eliminate what amounted to an annual subsidy of $85 million, and instituted temporary wage-price freezes in large sectors of the economy.

Venezuela placed a moratorium on the repayment of its foreign debt in 1983, but under pressure from international banks, it renegotiated the obligation and agreed in 1986 to resume payment. Although large reserves indicated the ability to maintain payments, at the same time the debt payment resumption was finally negotiated, Venezuelan oil was in the process of dropping from $28 per barrel to less than $10 in the face of increased Saudi Arabian and world production.

The 1988 presidential campaign was lively, but as usual there was little difference between the two powerful political parties. *COPEI* was still dogged by its association with the sharp economic drop in the early 1980s. Within *AD*, Lusinchi opposed the nomination of former President Pérez, but Pérez accurately accused the president of maintaining the illusion of prosperity by emptying the treasury. Pérez himself had been convicted of theft during his first term, but departed for Spain to avoid going to prison. The voters' memory didn't reach back that far, and he received a majority of 53%.

Lusinchi announced yet another moratorium on debt principal repayment shortly before leaving office. Pérez negotiated additional aid from the International Monetary Fund in return for imposing reforms, including a 90% increase in the price of gasoline (from 15 cents to 25 cents a gallon), a doubling of bus fares, unfreezing prices on almost everything and ending numerous subsidies.

Suddenly, the poor were faced with the brutal realization that the free lunch they had been enjoying was over. Riots broke out in Caracas in 1989 and quickly spread to other cities. Common criminals took advantage of the unrest to loot stores. Pérez declared martial law and ordered the army to crush the rioters. At least 300 people were killed and more than 2,000 injured in what came to be called the "*Caracazo*." It remains controversial to this day, just as the 1968 Tlatelolco Massacre is in Mexico.

Crisis and Corruption

Conditions deteriorated swiftly in 1988–89 in spite of nominally improved economic conditions. Caracas' homicide rate was more than 1,500 per year. Drug trafficking became rampant. Wages for all but the elite remained incredibly low. The mass of people enveloped by abject poverty began to fully realize who had benefited from more than a half century of oil exportation.

In 1992, Venezuela's once-admired democracy was shaken to its very foundations. There were two abortive military coups, one of which was nearly success-

ful but collapsed when commanders of key units failed to join the effort to oust Pérez. The instigator, a charismatic paratrooper named Lieutenant Colonel Hugo Chávez, was sentenced to two years in prison. The same year, Pérez was accused of pilfering $17 million in public funds. He issued a clumsy, unconvincing, almost arrogant denial, and public opinion turned harshly against him.

Pérez's party, his majority in the Congress and his hand-picked Supreme Court turned on him in 1993. Congress voted for impeachment, and he was forced to step down. The Senate appointed José Ramón Velásquez to head an interim government for the rest of his term. For good measure, Pérez was convicted in a criminal court and served 28 months in prison. In 1998, then 74, Pérez was again placed under house arrest when he and his mistress were charged with "illegal enrichment" for depositing large sums of undisclosed origin in U.S. banks.

In the 1993 elections, the voters rejected the two principal political parties, voting for Caldera, now 80, who had ended his association with *COPEI*. He was the candidate of a 17-party coalition, the *Convergencia Nacional* (*CN*—"National Convergence"). His first term had been uncontroversial and somewhat uneventful during a period of relative Venezuelan wealth. This time, he inherited an absolute nightmare when he took office in February 1994.

Despite decades of oil money, Venezuela was in dire financial straits. A controversial value added tax (VAT) was initially extended, then canceled because of popular opposition in 1994. The second-largest bank collapsed, with fallout in the form of

Former President Carlos Andrés Pérez

a run on all banks. The cause: massive thievery—83 were arrested.

Venezuela's years of drunken-sailor spending had given it a foreign debt in excess of $27 billion, more than half of GDP, which threatened the country with insolvency. The crisis was so severe that in 1996 Caldera was forced to sign a reform package with the IMF, something he once vowed he would never do. Among other things, the package eliminated the gasoline subsidy and abolished price controls. The measures were annoying to Venezuela's small, crybaby middle class but were especially painful to the poor, who accounted for 80% of the population.

The crisis lumbered on into 1997. The state-owned airline, *Viasa*, went bankrupt. At the end of the year, Caldera, the one-time populist, privatized the money-losing state-owned steel company, *Sidor*,

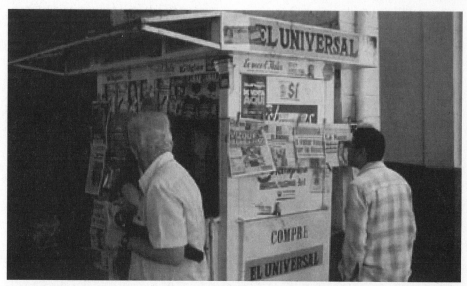

Pedestrians glance at the morning headlines at a news kiosk near Plaza de Bolívar in Caracas. Venezuela supports a multitude of newspapers and magazines, but press freedom has been under pressure under President Hugo Chávez. *Photo by the author*

Venezuela

and announced plans to sell off the state's aluminum company. In 1998, the government was hit with a new fiscal blow when the price of oil, on which the government pegs its budget estimates, suddenly dropped. The government had drawn up a $23 billion budget based on an estimate of $15.50 a barrel, but the price fell to $12.80. Moreover, despite efforts to reduce the size of the cumbersome bureaucracy (see Economy), the public payroll in 1997 actually *increased* by 4%! Inflation was reduced to a still-high 38% in 1997, the highest in Latin America, due mostly to a 75% pay increase for public employees.

The Elections of 1998

Like a retreaded tire, the second Caldera administration blew out and the country lumbered along for the last year of his term, as Venezuelans desperately searched for a mechanic. So eager were they for a fresh face offering dynamic new leadership that for a time it seemed they would entrust their future to Irene Sáez, the 1981 Miss Universe, who had compiled a respectable record as mayor of the Caracas suburb of Chacao. Polls showed the 35-year-old Sáez with a commanding lead, but her poll figures dropped when she failed to offer any substantive solutions for the country's ills; she was, it seemed, little more than a still pretty-face with name recognition.

Not so Hugo Chávez, leader of the abortive 1992 coup, who declared his own independent candidacy in early 1998 under the banner of the Fifth Republic Movement. His candidacy sent chills through the heavily entrenched political and economic establishments, but he soon gained a following among the downtrodden masses.

Chávez was a dynamic speaker, whose *macho*, charismatic mien and populist rhetoric were reminiscent of Latin American *caudillos* of old. Instead of a white horse and fringed epaulets, however, this late 20th-century savior had his red paratrooper's beret. Born into the middle class in 1954, he is the son of two schoolteachers. As a boy, he sold fruit on a street corner, and the army recruited him because of his skill as a baseball pitcher. Besides the appeal of his humble beginnings, his vow to clean up the country's cumbersome, corrupt political system, to wrest power away from the elite and to effect genuine socioeconomic reforms electrified Venezuela's destitute, long-suffering and resentful masses. As his bandwagon gained inertia, more alienated political groupings jumped aboard, forming an alliance called Patriotic Pole. At the same time, Chávez's open admiration for Fidel Castro alarmed the elite, as well as foreign investors.

The campaigns for the November 1998 congressional and regional elections and the December presidential election were the most bizarre of Venezuela's 40-year-old democracy. As Chávez's lead in the polls widened, the two traditional parties panicked and grasped for ways to stop this juggernaut. *COPEI* offered its nomination to Sáez, who foolishly accepted. Now identified with one of the establishment parties blamed for the country's woes, she fell even further behind Chávez. *AD*, meanwhile, showed initially nominated a 76-year-old party hack. Filling out the race was another independent, Henrique Salas, a respected 62-year-old businessman and Yale graduate, who formed a movement called Project Venezuela.

In the November 8 elections, Patriotic Pole became the largest force in the new Congress, winning 34% of the seats in the 48-member Senate and 189-member Chamber of Deputies. *AD* was a distant second with 22%; Salas' Project Venezuela won 12% of the seats, and *COPEI* won a pitiful 11%. Patriotic Pole also won seven of the 23 governorships; Chávez's father, also named Hugo, was elected governor of Barinas. *AD* fell from 11 governorships to eight.

Chávez then suddenly softened his fiery populist, anti-establishment rhetoric. Evidently aware that he was on the brink of full power, he seemed to be reassuring foreign investors and domestic financial kingpins on whose support he would depend to resuscitate the moribund economy.

In an unprecedented Machiavellian maneuver, *AD* and *COPEI* jettisoned their own candidates on November 20 and rallied behind Salas, who was second in the polls. Chávez sneered that this only proved that *AD* and *COPEI* had conspired all along to share power.

But this last-ditch ploy failed. On December 6, an uncharacteristically high 65% of the electorate turned out to vote. Chávez polled a landslide 56.5%, to 39.5% for Salas; Sáez was a microscopic third. The flamboyant Chávez suddenly appeared humble and conciliatory, and reached out to *AD* and *COPEI* for a consensus on how to solve the country's problems. He also reassured the business establishment that he did not seek to dismantle the capitalist system.

Even before the new Congress was installed, the president-elect declared his intention to call for a referendum dissolving Congress and the judiciary and calling for the installation of a constituent assembly to rewrite the 1961 constitution. The traditional parties vowed to block Chávez's initiative, prompting Chávez to denounce what he called a "conspiracy" and to threaten to dissolve Congress and rule by decree. It was to be the first of many bombastic threats to circumvent democratic institutions.

New President, New Constitution

Chávez was inaugurated on February 2, 1999. He reiterated his plans to scrap the constitution he had just sworn to uphold, deriding it as "moribund," and proclaimed what he called the "Bolivarian revolution." He set the date for the first of three referenda on constitutional reform. Among his proposals for the new basic law: removal of the ban against immediate re-election, saying he needed at least 10 years to put Venezuela's house in order.

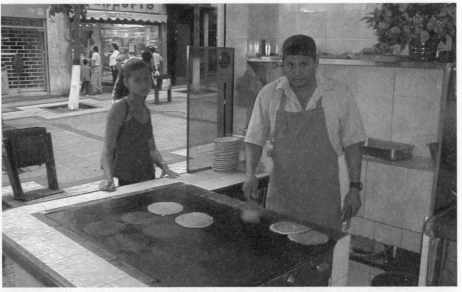

A short-order cook prepares a batch of *cachapas,* a popular corn-based Venezuelan pancake, at one of Caracas' many sidewalk cafes.   *Photo by the author*

348

Venezuela

The Cienpies Exchange, Caracas

Like a weary parent trying to placate a willful child, Congress acceded to Chávez's persistent demands and gave him the power to make sweeping economic decisions without congressional approval for six months.

In the April referendum, which had a 60% turnout, a stunning 90% voted "*sí*" for a constituent assembly. The election for the 131 members of the constituent assembly was held in July 1999. Predictably, 121 of the 131 members elected were members of Patriotic Pole, including Chávez's wife, Marisabel, and his brother.

In August, the assembly formally voted to strip Congress of its powers and sealed off the gold-domed capitol building, which sparked protests by Chávez opponents. Several opposition members of Congress scaled the fence around the *Capitolio* in defiance of the assembly's decision, while pro- and anti-Chávez factions clashed in the street outside. Violence appeared imminent.

The Catholic Church mediated a peaceful solution, preventing another bloody *Caracazo* that would have benefited neither side. The agreement stipulated that Congress would continue to serve as the law-making body, including the power to approve the budget, until after the referendum on the new constitution. (Chávez later broke that promise.)

The assembly soon renewed its attack on the judiciary. It appointed a special judicial investigative committee, which summarily removed 130 judges who had been under investigation for bribery and other sins. Few had any sympathy for the sacked judges, as the judiciary had become notoriously corrupt, but the lack of due process was troubling. The Supreme Court meekly upheld the judges' dismissal.

The assembly moved like a steamroller on the new constitution. The final document had Chávez's fingerprints all over it. It renamed the country the Bolivarian Republic of Venezuela. It established a new 165-member unicameral National Assembly, abolishing the Senate. The presidential term was increased from five to six years, and immediate re-election was permitted. The president was to enjoy far greater authority than under the old constitution. The state and local governments were replaced by regional and municipal councils. Active-duty members of the military were given the right to vote for the first time. There was no prohibition against abortion, which drew fire from the Catholic Church. It reduced the work week from 48 to 40 hours, which upset businessmen. It declared that Venezuelans have a right to "free, truthful, uncensored information," but left unsaid who would determine what is "truthful," a clause seen as an attempt to silence Chávez's critics in the media. The cries of naysayers that the new organic law was drafted too hastily and concentrated too much power in the president's hands were drowned out in an avalanche of public approval. On December 15, 1999, voters overwhelmingly ratified it.

Renewed Mandate

The constituent assembly abolished the old Congress and the Supreme Court, then created a 23-member standing committee, nicknamed the "*Congresillo*," to act as the legislative authority pending the election of the new National Assembly. Elected president of the *Congresillo* was Luis Miquilena, a close Chávez ally who was widely regarded as the second most powerful man in the country.

Chávez announced he would subject himself to the electorate under the new constitution to seek a renewed mandate. All other officials established under the new constitution would be selected in the same "*Megaelecciones*," scheduled for May 28, 2000.

In February 2000, the first schism appeared in Chávez's Bolivarian revolution. To mark the eighth anniversary of the 1992 coup attempt, three of Chávez's former comrades-in-arms broke with the president, accusing him of corruption and of betraying the goals of their revolutionary movement. Among them was Francisco Arias Cárdenas, governor of Zulia State, widely regarded as the intellectual author of the 1992 coup attempt. Though not as charismatic or brash as Chávez, Arias was generally respected for his more reasoned, moderate approach. To use a Steinbeckian metaphor, Arias played the role of George to Chávez's Lenny. An even unkinder metaphorical cut for Chávez came, symbolically, on March 15—the Ides of March—when Arias declared that he would run for president against his former friend and chief. A former mayor of Caracas, Claudio Fermín, also declared his candidacy.

Chávez wisely eschewed the intellectually superior Arias' invitation to a debate. Arias aired a television commercial in which he "debated" a hen, which represented his "chicken" opponent. A white hen became the unofficial symbol of the Arias campaign.

But there was an ominous cloud over the campaign. The five-member National Electoral Council, or *CNE*, all of them Chávez appointees, warned that it was unsure it could resolve computer problems in time for the election. The *CNE* blamed the problems on a U.S. firm that had the contract to tabulate the votes, while the company complained that the *CNE* had made 11,000 last-minute changes

President Hugo Chávez Frías

349

Venezuela

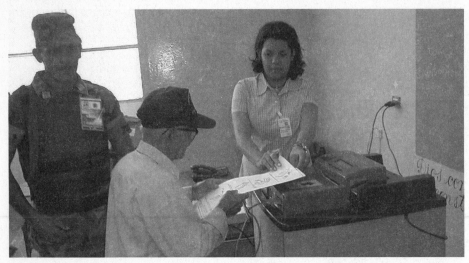

Under the watchful eye of a soldier assigned to maintain order, and with the assistance of a polling official, an elderly voter casts his ballot in a computerized tabulation machine in Caracas on July 30, 2000. Malfunctions in the machines delayed the voting for several hours past the scheduled time to close the polls.   *Photo by the author*

to the database. This prevented the company from having the flashcards needed to program the computers that would be used in more than half the 8,400 polling stations ready in time. Days before the election, Chávez dispatched an air force jet to Omaha, Nebraska, to receive the flashcards.

This was the milieu when this author flew to Caracas to cover the elections the following Sunday as a free-lance journalist. Arias had held his closing rally in the Avenida Bolívar the previous day, and Chávez's closing rally was in full sway that night, also in the Avenida Bolívar. The president's electrically charged voice sounded more like that of a soccer announcer than a politician. It was easy to understand from hearing him how he could so work up a crowd. The atmosphere at his rally resembled Mardi Gras more than a political event. A majority of those in the almost entirely working-class multitude—many of them wearing Chávez's trademark red beret—showed signs of advanced inebriation.

At noon the following day, the *CNE* postponed the election because of technical difficulties. Chávez and Arias both expressed support for the delay, although Arias demanded dismissal of the *CNE* for incompetence. Reaction I heard on the street ran the gamut from outrage to nonchalant acceptance.

Former U.S. President Jimmy Carter, who had become a sort of self-appointed guardian of Latin American democracy, held a news conference in Caracas to endorse the postponement which, he said, "was for a good reason." In response to my question, he drew a contrast with the

obviously rigged election in Peru that would be held the following day and predicted that the Venezuelan election ultimately would be held and would "accurately reflect the will of the Venezuelan people."

On one point, there was almost universal agreement: the *CNE* had botched its job. Chávez sacked the five members and replaced them, at Carter's suggestion, with a group less partisan and more representative. It contracted with a Spanish firm to conduct the election, and the new election was set for July 30, 2000.

Chávez was resoundingly re-elected with 59.2% of the vote, a mandate even greater than in 1998. His Fifth Republic Movement (*MVR*) received 57.6% of the votes for the new National Assembly, which translated into 92 of the 165 seats. That fell short of the two-thirds majority needed for constitutional amendments and confirmation of judicial appointments, but it gave Chávez the three-fifths majority needed to pass emergency legislation that would allow him to rule by decree. *AD* was second with 19.7%, giving it 35 seats. Arias' *Proyecto Venezuela* was a distant third with 4.9%, or eight seats, while *COPEI* was a poor fifth with a mere 2.4%, or four seats. The *MVR* and its ally, the Movement to Socialism (*MAS*), won 15 of the 23 governorships.

Dissent and Repression Grow

Chávez had to contend with such pressing domestic issues as declining living standards. One solution: Create a new labor organization to replace the Confederation of Venezuelan Workers (*CTV*), long

affiliated with the discredited *AD*. The new organization had the predictable name Bolivarian Workers' Force. As usual, he put the idea up for a vote by referendum, in December 2000. Critics warned that this was merely another attempt to concentrate more power in Chávez's own hands. Chávez received the expected lopsided majority for his plan, but he was stunned by the anemic 25% voter turnout. In municipal elections, the *MVR* won 40% of the seats.

Strikes protesting the state of the economy became common, as Chávez grew increasingly impatient with dissent, something he no doubt picked up from his friend in Havana. He long had assailed the Venezuelan press as controlled by the oligarchy. In one case of legalized suppression, Pablo López, editor of the gadfly Caracas weekly *La Razón*, went into exile in 2000 rather than face house arrest for charges he had defamed a wealthy friend and financial benefactor of Chávez's and Miquilena's. The judge had refused to allow López to introduce evidence that the articles published in *La Razón* about influence peddling were true. In many countries with a Hispanic legal tradition, truth is not a defense in libel or defamation cases; all that must be proven is that the plaintiff was offended. López's lawyer took his case to the Inter-American Commission on Human Rights (ICHR) in Washington, an organ of the Organization of American States. In 2001, the ICHR ruled in López's favor and ordered the Venezuelan government to stop persecuting him. Chávez responded that the matter is a judicial one, and López remains in self-imposed exile in Costa Rica.

Chávez also lashed out at the independent television station *Globovisión*, known for hard-hitting reporting that often embarrasses the government. The station was notified that it was being investigated under a broad provision of the new constitution that prohibits "false or misleading" information. This harassment was continuing in 2009 and 2010.

Rangel announced the establishment of pro-Chávez neighborhood groups called "Bolivarian Circles." Rangel denied they were patterned after Cuba's Committees for the Defense of the Revolution. Another parallel with Cuba was the application of a clause in the new constitution to teach "Bolivarian principles" in the public schools.

In a move reminiscent of Salvador Allende's land reform program in Chile, Chávez presented the deeds to 105,000 acres of idle land to small farmers in 2001, and he warned large landowners that they should "donate" unused land to the state for redistribution or face confiscation. Chávez touted his agrarian reform plan as a means of relieving the crowded, squalid conditions in the slums around Caracas, something chillingly reminiscent of the Khmer Rouge in Cambodia.

Chávez stunned the nation in 2001 with a list of 49 decrees affecting virtually all economic sectors, especially the all-important oil industry. One decree doubled royalties on foreign oil companies from 16.5% to 30%, a move that would drive away badly needed capital investment. This action had the unintended effect of forging an unlikely alliance between *Fedecamaras*, the country's main business lobby, led by Pedro Carmona, and the *CTV*, whose president, Carlos Ortega, had defeated Chávez's hand-picked candidate.

Venezuela became irrevocably polarized between passionate pro-Chávez and anti-Chávez camps. The president's approval ratings slipped below 50% for the first time, and few Venezuelans remained ambivalent about Chávez and his revolution. *Fedecamaras* and the *CTV* called for a 12-hour general strike. Chávez ridiculed the strike and its organizers, but millions participated in the stoppage.

By 2002, there was growing dissent as well within the ranks of the military, which had become riddled with corruption as the administrator of Chávez's $100 million social program, *Plan Bolívar 2000*. The president was acutely embarrassed by revelations that his hand-picked army commander had pocketed millions from the fund; Chávez fired him. Yet, when the auditor-general uncovered still more examples of embezzlement of funds destined for the poor, Chávez responded by firing the auditor-general.

Chávez's popularity dropped to 30%, and anti-Chávez demonstrations and pro-Chávez counter-demonstrations became commonplace. Suddenly, Chávez began to sound conciliatory. In a televised address, he agreed to moderate some of his more radical economic decrees. He called for understanding from the opposition, and said he hoped he could "sheath my sword." He attempted to mend fences with the church. He even condemned Colombia's *FARC* guerrillas. But this era of good feeling proved fleeting.

Events unfolded quickly and dramatically in 2002 after Chávez fired General Gaucaipuro Lameda as president of the state-owned oil company, *Petroleos de Venezuela* (*PDVSA*) and replaced him with a leftist economist. *PDVSA* white-collar workers protested with marches, but held off on calling a strike that would halt oil exports.

Then two high-ranking officers, Vice Admiral Carlos Molina Tamayo and Air Force General Roman Gómez Ruíz, publicly declared their opposition to their commander-in-chief for what they re-

Thousands of jubilant supporters of President Hugo Chávez crowd under the balcony of the Miraflores Palace in Caracas late on July 30, 2000, to hear him proclaim his landslide re-election victory. *Photo by the author*

garded as corruption and mismanagement of the armed forces; Gómez Ruíz called on Chávez to resign.

Rumors of an imminent coup began to fly, and the media reported that dissident officers had approached U.S. diplomats for support. The State Department expressed its firm support for democratic in-

stitutions. The crisis escalated in March when *Fedecamaras* and the *CTV* issued a plan for a post-Chávez Venezuela. The protests at *PDVSA* continued, threatening to upset the world oil market; production dropped by 450,000 barrels a day—about 20%. Venezuelans and the world watched anxiously to see what would happen next.

The Caracas daily *El Universal* reports the landslide reelection victory of President Chávez on July 30, 2000.

351

Venezuela

Coup and Counter-Coup

In April, *Fedecamaras* and the *CTV* declared a one-day general strike, which was so successful it was extended indefinitely—meaning, until Chávez resigned. When 150,000 people poured into the streets to demand Chávez's resignation, pro-Chávez goons opened fire on them, killing 17 and wounding at least 100. The armed forces high command declared later that Chávez had ordered them to implement *"Plan Ávila,"* the code name for the use of deadly force to protect the Miraflores Palace, but that they had refused to fire on unarmed civilians; a leaked audiotape corroborated their account.

After midnight on April 12, 2002, the generals acted, using the violence against the peaceful demonstrators as justification to restore order. The president was taken into "protective custody" on the island of La Orchila; accounts leaked later to the media revealed that Chávez broke into tears when he surrendered. By Chávez's own account later, he was told to sign a resignation statement, but he refused. Nonetheless, General Efraín Vásquez, the army commander, announced that Chávez had stepped down. As interim president, the military named *Fedecamaras'* Pedro Carmona. Meanwhile, the U.S. State Department issued a statement, which would later backfire, suggesting that the forcible removal of Chávez was the will of the Venezuelan people. The United States also sought to allay an OAS resolution denouncing "the alteration of the constitutional order," but in the end it supported it.

Carmona unwisely said he was abrogating Chávez's 1999 constitution and dissolving the Assembly and the Supreme Court; he called for new congressional elections in eight months. This was too much even for those delighted by Chávez's ouster, and it brought international rebuke—even from the Bush administration, which directed its ambassador to try to dissuade Carmona. Mexican President Vicente Fox refused to recognize the interim government. To make matters worse, Carmona did not name any representatives of the *CTV* in his interim cabinet. Within hours, the new "government" unraveled.

On April 13, hundreds of thousands of furious *chavistas* poured into the streets around the country and rioted to demand Chávez's reinstatement. Fighting broke out, and at least 50 people were killed and hundreds injured. Some of the *chavistas'* rage was directed against the opposition media. Suddenly, a schism appeared within the ranks of the armed forces, which had been thought to be almost solidly opposed to Chávez. Loyalist mid-ranking unit commanders rebelled against the rebellion and stormed the Miraflores Palace; among them were the paratroopers, whence Chávez had sprung. That night, Carmona resigned; to fill the power vacuum, the high command agreed to allow Chávez's vice president, Diosdado Cabello, to take charge until Chávez returned. Carmona was placed under house arrest. An estimated 80 officers also were detained.

On April 14, Chávez was back in power. Although brief, his forcible removal marked only the third military coup in more than 20 years of democratic reforms in Latin America, following that in Haiti in 1991 and Ecuador in 2000. In the days following the coup and counter-coup, Chávez appeared chastened and, again, conciliatory. "Let's put our house in order," he said, and he promised not to seek revenge. He lamented having "sown hatred." He accepted the resignations of the entire *PDVSA* board and said that he was willing to compromise to settle the dispute with the *PDVSA* management.

Oil production soon returned to normal. Chávez appointed Ali Rodríguez, the OPEC secretary-general and a former Venezuelan oil minister, as president of *PDVSA*. He also replaced Vice President Cabello with Defense Minister Rangel, and relieved Vásquez from command of the army.

The U.S. government denied abetting the coup attempt. Then-security adviser Condoleezza Rice did little to quell international suspicions when she stated in a televised interview that she hoped Chávez had received the "message" of the Venezuelan people and that he "takes advantage of this opportunity to right his own ship, which has been moving, frankly, in the wrong direction for quite a long time."

Political Stalemate

OAS Secretary-General Cesar Gaviría, a former Colombian president, met with Chávez and leaders of the umbrella opposition body, Democratic Coordinator, urging them to effect a reconciliation. But the opposition remained intransigent. Chávez invited former President Carter to Caracas to broker an agreement, but those talks ended in failure.

Then Chávez's dropped the conciliatory tone and vilified those who instigated the coup as "Nazis." In a separate development, Carmona escaped from house arrest and sought asylum at the Colombian Embassy. Colombian President Pastrana, no doubt delighted to repay Chávez for his support of the *FARC*, granted it. Carlos Fernández succeeded him as *Fedecamaras* president.

Then Chávez, who was himself once jailed for leading a coup attempt, sought to prosecute four officers involved in the coup against *him*. The officers—two navy admirals and an army and an air force general—appealed to the Supreme Court to block their trial, arguing that Chávez's own constitution makes it lawful to disobey orders from an authoritarian government, in this case, an order to fire on unarmed civilians. They also argued that they had acted to prevent anarchy when they believed Chávez had resigned. The court, packed with Chávez appointees, nonetheless voted 11–8 to dismiss the charges, citing insufficient evidence. Furious Chávez supporters tried to storm the court building but were repulsed by security forces. Surprisingly, Chávez accepted the decision and appealed to his supporters to "swallow the decision like a fish with bones."

Animated by the court decision, the opposition filed criminal charges against Chávez, including abuse of power and accepting illegal campaign contributions. Chávez also was criticized by international journalism organizations for his harsh rhetoric against the opposition media and for the alarming number of physical attacks on journalists.

Chávez next found himself in a test of wills with Alfredo Peña, the opposition mayor of Caracas. Chávez accused the Caracas police of treating pro-Chávez demonstrators more harshly than anti-Chávez demonstrators; Peña alleged that his police were ambushed by *chavistas* when they responded to a disturbance call. In retaliation, Chávez grounded Peña's helicopter. Fighting broke out between the police and *chavistas*. Pro-Chávez policemen began a strike, dividing the police force and exacerbating an already volatile situation.

Chávez invited international representatives to mediate a solution between him and the so-called Democratic Coordinator. Representatives of the United Nations, the OAS and the Carter Center attmpted to jump-start the dialogue. Chávez reiterated that he was agreeable to a recall referendum, but not before August 2003, the midpoint of his term, as specified in the constitution. The talks failed.

Events turned uglier in November 2002 when the opposition staged a march to the *CNE* to present petitions containing 2 million signatures calling for a referendum on December 4. *Chavistas* attacked the marchers, and Caracas police intervened. In the resulting melee, dozens of people were injured, more than 20 by gunfire.

Chávez refused to call the referendum. Tensions between the pro-Chávez and anti-Chávez factions of the police force erupted into violence that left two people dead and dozens wounded. Chávez ordered a federal takeover of the Caracas police force, sending in national guardsmen to augment the police. Demonstrators banging pots and pans, Latin America's traditional *cacerolazo* form of non-violent protest, filled the streets almost daily, and violence erupted. Venezuela appeared on the brink of anarchy.

General Strike

Fedecamaras and the *CTV* called for an indefinite general strike, to begin December 2, 2002. At first it was not universally observed and the vital oil industry continued functioning. The government proclaimed the strike a failure. But it continued day after day, and the economy soon felt the pinch. On December 6, *chavista* gunmen fired into an opposition rally, killing three and wounding 28. *Chavistas* also stepped up their vandalism against *Globovisión* and other anti-Chávez media, egged on by the president. Yet, Chávez disavowed the violence.

Rebels then seized a government oil tanker; Chávez ordered the navy to retake it. By the fourth day, striking port workers had brought oil exports from the world's fifth-largest producer almost to a halt. Production dropped from 3 million barrels a day to 400,000, then to 200,000; the world oil market shivered. The price of crude jumped accordingly, to more than $30 a barrel. Chávez assailed the opposition as "fascists," "traitors," "terrorists," "saboteurs," "coup-plotters" and "hijackers." He broke off the OAS-sponsored negotiations until the strike ended, and used foreign reserves to import food, medicine and, ironically, fuel.

The nation remained paralyzed for weeks. Neither side budged, and the economy languished. The opposition now set February 2, 2003, as a date for the referendum. Gavíria, Carter, the Bush administration and the European Union all advocated early elections as the only way to defuse the crisis. Chávez left the door open to negotiations over a *binding* referendum after August 2003, but refused to resign under duress. The divided army backed Chávez, saying the strike was threatening the national well-being.

In January 2003, with street violence continuing, Chávez flew to New York to meet with U.N. Secretary-General Kofi Annan to discuss a diplomatic solution. Meanwhile, newly inaugurated Brazilian President Luiz Inácio da Silva offered his intercession and invited the United States, Spain, Portugal, Chile and Mexico to form a "Friends of Venezuela" group to mediate an end to the crisis. Annan agreed to send an emissary. Carter returned and met with both sides and with Gavíria against the backdrop of violent demonstrations.

Suddenly, the general strike lost its steam as small businesses, faced with bankruptcy, began reopening. By the end of January, oil production was back up to about 1 million barrels a day. Private banks reopened on February 3. The same week, the non-oil sector was operating normally. Chávez claimed victory and threatened to prosecute the strike's organizers. In reality, there were no winners, as the strike had cost $6 billion and left the economy in a shambles (see Economy), not to mention the lives lost. Perhaps Finance Minister Tobías Nobrega summed it up best when he called the 61-day general strike a "kamikaze attack."

The Recall Movement

The opposition returned to petition-gathering, this time claiming 4 million signatures. Chávez hung tough, saying there could be no vote before August 19, 2003.

Gavíria and the "Friends of Venezuela" finally persuaded the two sides to agree to an eight-point resolution that renounced violence. It also called for the government to respect freedom of expression and for the media to show restraint in their rhetoric. But the deal quickly unraveled.

The opposition threatened to resume the general strike, and international condemnation poured in on Chávez. The president accused the United States and Spain of siding with the opposition and even reprimanded Gavíria, who had spent three months patiently trying to effect an agreement, for meddling in Venezuela's internal affairs!

The logjam again appeared to break in April when the two sides finally agreed on the terms for a referendum. The opposition agreed to wait until after August 19, 2003 (in reality, there was no other choice),

and Chávez pledged not to try to delay the vote and to resign if he lost. However, he said the signatures collected earlier were invalid and that the opposition would have to go through the petition process again after August 19. Chávez soon reneged on the agreement, raising a new condition that the opposition's elected officials also face a recall referendum.

In May, the two sides finally signed an agreement on a referendum, for both Chávez and some opposition legislators. Moreover, the National Assembly, in which the *chavistas* enjoyed a small majority, would have to appoint a new *CNE*. Chávez suddenly reneged again, arguing that the terms did not specify that he *must* call a referendum.

Still, the Democratic Coordinator pressed on with plans for a binding referendum, which would require 20%, not just 10%, of the more than 12 million registered voters, or 2,436,083 valid signatures. The turnout would have to be at least 25% and the votes to remove Chávez would need to match or exceed the 3.76 million votes Chávez received in his 2000 re-election. Also key would be the date. If held before August 19, 2004, the fourth anniversary of Chávez's re-election, the *CNE* would be required to call a new election within 30 days. If after that date, Vice President Rangel would serve out the remainder of his term.

On August 20, 2003, one day after the mid-point of Chávez's term, the Democratic Coordinator presented the *CNE* with petitions containing 3.4 million signatures. Chávez declared the signatures invalid, not explaining how he could know that, and ridiculed his opponents as "crazy."

The Supreme Tribunal appointed a new five-member *CNE*, approved by Chávez,

Oil derricks, Lake Maracaibo

Venezuela

the Democratic Coordinator, Gaviría and the United States. The members were seen as balanced, two pro-Chávez, two favoring the opposition and one neutral. Soon, however, it became apparent that the "neutral" member was in the government's corner.

The *CNE* ruled that the petitions were invalid because the signatures were collected *before* the August 19 mid-point. It said the Democratic Coordinator would have to collect the needed signatures again during a four-day window, a hurdle the *CNE* perhaps believed to be insurmountable, but in November the opposition succeeded in collecting 3.4 million signatures.

The *CNE* stalled until March 2004, when it ruled that only 1.83 million signatures were valid, 140,000 were invalid and 1.1 million more were in doubt. Changing the rules in the middle of the game, the *CNE* announced that the Democratic Coordinator had the burden of confirming the signatures of enough of the questioned signatures to reach the necessary number, or about 600,000, and gave it four days to do so. Riots erupted throughout the country, which left six people dead.

The Democratic Coordinator appealed to the Supreme Tribunal's electoral chamber. In a stunning decision, the chamber upheld the validity of the petitions and ruled that a recall election must be held. The government appealed to the Supreme Tribunal's constitutionality chamber, which just as quickly overturned the electoral chamber's decision. Apparently miffed by the unpredictability of the Supreme Tribunal, Chávez introduced a bill that would allow him to increase the size of the court from 20 justices to 32 and would reduce the requirement for Assembly confirmation from two-thirds (which Chávez did not have) to a simple majority (which he barely had). Despite a filibuster, this it passed.

The two sides agreed on the four-day verification window, during which signers were required to come forward and verify their signatures. Again the Democratic Coordinator presented its petitions to the *CNE*, and again the country and the world held their breaths. This time, although it disallowed about 110,000 signatures the opposition insisted were valid, the *CNE* could not escape reality. On June 3, it announced that the Democratic Coordinator had collected 2,451,821 valid signatures—15,738 more than required.

Instead of his usual defiance, Chávez accepted the *CNE*'s conclusion and insisted that he "welcomes the challenge" of the recall election. His followers were less conciliatory and went on a violent rampage in Caracas, attacking Mayor Peña's office and the offices of several opposition media.

The *CNE* arbitrarily postponed the agreed date one week to August 15, so the new computer system could be in place. After a tempestuous but relatively non-violent campaign, hundreds of international observers and foreign journalists observed the climax of the two-year-long recall effort. A total of 70% of Venezuela's 14 million registered voters participated, voting "*Sí*" to remove Chávez, or "*No*." The results stunned both sides:

Sí	3,989,008	40.74%
No	5,800,629	59.25%

In a replay of two earlier election nights in 1998 and 2000, Chávez claimed victory before jubilant supporters at the Miraflores Palace. Becoming a bit messianic, he declared that "the will of the people is the will of God."

The opposition suffered another stinging defeat in state and municipal elections in October 2004, losing control of Caracas and losing 20 of the 23 state governorships.

The Screws Tighten

The opposition eventually accepted its defeat, and for the first time in more than two years it seemed peace would return. Those hopes were suddenly jarred on November 19, 2004, when a car bomb killed Danilo Anderson, the prosecutor in charge of the cases against about 400 opposition figures implicated in the 2002 coup attempt.

Two brothers who are former policemen and their cousin were arrested and charged with planting the bomb. They were convicted in 2005 and sentenced to terms of from 27 to 30 years. In November 2005, four other people were arrested as the "intellectual authors" of the murder. These included Nelson Mezerhane, a respected banker and co-owner of *Globovisión*, and Patricia Poleo, editor of the opposition newspaper *El Nuevo País*. All proclaimed their innocence, and international journalism organizations questioned whether the charges against Poleo and Mezerhane were trumped up to intimidate the opposition media.

Chávez consolidated more and more power in his hands. A new law placed municipal and state police forces under unified national—meaning his—control. The addition of 12 new justices to the Supreme Court took effect in December 2004. He appointed another loyalist to the *CNE*, giving it a lop-sided 4–1 majority. He stepped up seizures of privately owned rural land under the 2001 land reform act. He ingratiated himself to the armed forces with a 50–60% pay increase.

Chávez also tightened the screws on privately owned broadcast stations with

the Radio and Television Social Responsibility Law, which has such vague language that domestic and international media organizations and even the OAS's Inter-American Human Rights Commission denounced it as an attempt to censor content. The law, ostensibly designed to protect children, states that images of sex or violence, including news coverage of violent demonstrations, cannot be aired between 7 a.m. and 11 p.m. It also provides for 70 minutes of government programming per week. Violators can be fined or have their licenses revoked for carrying programming that is deemed slanderous, that "incites disruption of public order" or that is "contrary to national security," all defined by the government on a case-by-case basis.

Several journalists were charged with violations. The government's taxing agency levied fines against several anti-Chávez television stations, not under the terms of the new law but for allegedly airing opposition propaganda for free during the general strike of 2002–03 and for back taxes. The stations appealed, and eventually the amount of back taxes was reduced.

Equally onerous were Chávez's revisions to the penal code, which in effect outlawed peaceful dissent. It subjects journalists to up to 12 months in jail for criminal defamation, which is loosely defined, and five years for "causing panic" by disseminating "false information," not just by the mass media but by e-mail or other means; the presumption of innocence in such cases was eliminated. Demonstrators engaging in banging pots and pans, the traditional Latin American *cacerolazo*, could be arrested for "intimidating" public officials.

Next, Chávez got his government into the mass media business itself with the creation of a regional all-news television channel, *Telesur*, in conjunction with the friendly governments of Argentina and Uruguay; Brazil and Cuba provide technical support. It began operation in 2005. While Chávez extolled the channel as a counterweight to the domination of U.S. and European all-news channels, critics complained it carried little more than left-wing, anti-U.S. propaganda.

Chávez also tightened the screws on domestic and foreign businesses. He greatly increased the government's role in the private sector through the creation of more than 65,000 cooperatives, euphemistically named "social production companies," and new laws mandated that private companies be "co-managed," meaning that workers have a greater share in decision-making. Companies that do not embrace "co-management" have been denied government contracts, and the mandate has continued to widen to include more companies.

In 2005, Chávez stunned foreign oil companies by announcing on his weekly television program that they would be required to sign new contracts with the government or leave the country by January 1, 2006. This raised serious legal questions about breach of contract. Chávez said under the new contracts, taxes would be raised from 34% to 50% and royalties to the government from 1% to 30%. With oil selling then for $50 a barrel, the companies still stood to benefit, so they grudgingly agreed.

The last remaining political check on Chávez's growing power—the opposition in the National Assembly—was eliminated in the congressional elections of December 2005. It wasn't a power grab by Chávez, but a rather a surrender of it by the major opposition parties, which boycotted the election. The *AD, COPEI* and Project Venezuela complained that the fingerprint-reading machines used to confirm voters' identification were synchronized with the vote-counting machines so that it would be possible to match a person with how he or she voted. (There already were suspicions that businessmen who voted to recall Chávez in 2004 were being denied government services.) The *CNE* agreed to turn off the fingerprint machines, but the opposition then called for a delay in the election, which the government refused. The result: Chávez's Fifth Republic Movement and its allies won all 167 seats in the expanded Assembly. Chávez could then amend his constitution at will.

Venezuelan-U.S. relations continued to deteriorate. In May 2005, the United States arrested Luis Posada Carriles, an anti-Castro Cuban exile who bribed his way out of a Venezuelan prison in 1985. Posada was awaiting retrial for the bombing of a Cuban airliner off Barbados in 1976 that killed 73 people. Venezuela requested his extradition, after assuring the United States that Posada would not be sent to Cuba, where he almost certainly would be shot. Chávez threatened to close the Venezuelan embassy in Washington if Posada were not extradited, but backed off. The United States refused extradition on the grounds that the request did not contain the required evidence against Posada, who already had been acquitted in Venezuela of the bombing. Posada is scheduled to go on trial for perjury in the United States in late 2010 (see Cuba).

Chávez announced in 2005 that he planned to begin talks with Iran for a Venezuelan nuclear program. That was too much even for friendly Brazil, which said it would not cooperate in helping Venezuela establish a nuclear program if Iran were involved.

Chávez then complained that the United States was not keeping its agreement to supply spare parts for Venezuela's fleet of 21 F-16 fighter aircraft, and he threatened to contribute some of the jets to Cuba and China. The U.S. Embassy responded that it had documentary proof that spare parts were in fact being delivered, and reminded Venezuela that such transfer of technology to third countries would violate the terms of the sale. Venezuela had purchased the F-16s in 1983.

The United States escalated the conflict in 2006 when it invoked its legal rights to refuse a license for Spain to sell to Venezuela 12 Spanish transport and surveillance aircraft that contained U.S. parts. The deal was worth $2 billion for Spain.

Chávez angrily responded with a thinly veiled threat—which he was later to repeat often—to stop oil exports to the United States. It was not an idle threat; Venezuela is the United States' fourth-largest supplier of oil, amounting to 1.5 million barrels a day, about 13% of the total. Venezuela also has 70% ownership in Citgo, which owns three refineries and 14,000 stations in the United States. Chávez has threatened to shut down Citgo and to find other buyers for the oil now sold to the United States. However, Venezuela cannot afford to reduce its exports by 13% overnight, and the United States could retaliate with a food embargo; one fourth of Venezuela's food imports are from the United States.

In 2006, Chávez said he would begin buying fighter aircraft from Russia. In addition to the 100,000 AK-47 and AK-103 assault rifles that began arriving from Russia in April, Chávez announced that the first factory in South America to manufacture the popular Kalashnikov rifles would be built in Venezuela.

The Election of 2006

Two years after being trounced in the recall referendum, the opposition to Chávez was still in disarray. The various groups were at odds over whether they should contest the December 3, 2006 presidential election or boycott it, and if they opted to contest it, who their candidate should be. They agreed that more than one candidate was a recipe for defeat. By August, they had agreed to try to defeat Chávez at the ballot box, perhaps because their last boycott only produced a Cuban-style one-party Congress. Opinion polls confirmed that their chances of unseating Chávez were as quixotic as they had been in 2004.

Three political veterans expressed interest in taking on the increasingly dictatorial president: Manuel Rosales, the popular governor of Zulia State of the *Un Tiempo*

Nuevo party; Teodoro Petkoff, a moderate leftist former planning minister and the publisher of the nettlesome opposition newspaper *Tal Cual*; and Julio Borges, head of a center-right movement called Justice First. Ultimately, the opposition coalesced around Rosales.

Rosales attacked Chávez where he was most vulnerable: corruption, which had worsened in the eight years since Chávez was first elected on a promise to clean up the corruption of the past, and violent crime, which had become of epidemic proportions. He chided Chávez for squandering billions of dollars in aid to try to secure a seat on the U.N. Security Council (see Hugo Chávez: An International Loose Cannon) instead of using it to reduce unemployment and build needed housing. He promised to channel 20% of oil revenue directly to the poor through the use of a debit card.

Chávez reminded voters of the billions of dollars in oil profits he *had* channeled into such social programs as subsidized groceries for the poor and free universities. He vowed to consolidate his revolution and implement what he called "21st century socialism." The Chávez campaign was embarrassed by the release of a clandestine video that showed Rafael Ramírez, head of *PDVSA*, threatening to fire employees who did not support Chávez.

In the end, there were no surprises. About 75% of the 15.9 million eligible voters turned out. The results:

Chávez	7,309,080	63.1%
Rosales	4,292,466	36.9%

Rosales conceded defeat (he lost every state, even Zulia) but promised to try to keep the opposition intact and to defend Venezuelan democracy, or what was left of it. Chávez hailed his victory as one for his socialist revolution, saying "socialism is love" and "a new era has begun."

Third Term

Even before his third inauguration, Chávez unveiled some chilling details of his "new era," things he hadn't outlined *before* the election. Although he insisted he would respect private property, he contended that democracy is incompatible with capitalism. He proposed merging his Fifth Republic Movement and the other groups of his Patriotic Pole into one homogenous political party—under his control, of course. The Communist Party and other groups balked at this plan, but Chávez forged the United Socialist Party.

Chávez also announced that the license for privately owned Radio Caracas Television, or *RCTV*, the oldest and most

Venezuela

Hugo Chávez: An International Loose Cannon

Hugo Chávez has sought to make Venezuela—in reality, himself—a player on the world stage. Beginning in 2000, he made it a point to make high-profile visits to rogue states and leaders like Iraq's Saddam Hussein, Libya's Muammar Qadhafi and Iran's Mahmoud Ahmadinejad. Ostensibly for bilateral talks among OPEC members, the trips' primary purpose was for Chávez to poke his finger in the eye of the United States.

At an OPEC summit Chávez hosted in Caracas in 2000, his was the loudest voice in favor of curtailing production to drive up oil prices—then $30 a barrel, the highest since Gulf War I. Every $1 increase in the price of a barrel added $1 billion a year to his government's revenue, which he has used to fund his "social revolution" at home and to buy influence abroad. He sells oil at discount prices to Cuba, Nicaragua and other allies.

Chávez idolizes Fidel Castro, who celebrated his 75th birthday in Caracas with Chávez. When Castro fell gravely ill in 2006, Chávez regularly came to his bedside.

Chávez strained relations with both Colombia and Peru in 2001. Venezuela arrested, then released, a guerrilla from the National Liberation Army (ELN) of Colombia wanted in an airplane hijacking. Chávez is known to be sympathetic to the ELN and to the Revolutionary Armed Forces of Colombia FARC. Diego Serna, a member of the FARC, admitted in a television interview in Colombia that he had helped provide security for Chávez during a state visit to Colombia. Even more embarrassing, a captured video showed Chávez and Serna together.

Chávez adamantly denied reports in 2001 that the fugitive former Peruvian intelligence chief, Vladimiro Montesinos, was hiding in Venezuela (see Peru). Only when Peruvian authorities presented him with conclusive evidence from the U.S. FBI that Montesinos was, in fact, in the country did Chávez order Montesinos arrested and flown back to Peru. Each country temporarily withdrew its ambassador from the other.

Chávez again relished being in the international spotlight at the Third Summit of the Americas in Quebec in 2001, where he was the only one of the 34 heads of state who opposed the idea of a Free Trade Area of the Americas (FTAA). He argued that subregional integration should come first, and warned of U.S. domination of the FTAA. He also

irked his fellow presidents by balking at the requirement that signatories to the FTAA be "representative democracies;" he said he preferred the term "participatory democracy," which could be more loosely construed. U.S. President George W. Bush snubbed Chávez by avoiding a one-on-one meeting.

Then came September 11, 2001. Chávez dutifully denounced the terrorist attacks on the United States as "abominable," but Chávez defended his close ties with Iraq, Iran and Libya, calling them "our brothers and partners."

Chávez next irritated the French by expressing his concern over the welfare of the notorious Venezuelan-born terrorist Ilyich Ramírez, better known by the sobriquet Carlos the Jackal, who was incarcerated in a French prison after two decades as an international fugitive.

He criticized the U.S. bombing campaign in Afghanistan as "using terror to fight terror." The U.S. State Department responded that it was "surprised and deeply disappointed" by the remark, a diplomatic euphemism that meant U.S. policymakers were mad as hell. The United States recalled its ambassador. Relations were strained again in 2003 when Chávez condemned the U.S. invasion of Iraq. Media reports also circulated that the large Arab community on the Venezuelan island of Margarita had become a haven for Hamas and Hezbollah terrorists.

Chávez declined to give the traditional address by heads of state at the United Nations in 2003, claiming there was a plot to kill him in New York. Besides, he said, the addresses served no purpose and he called them a "dialogue of the deaf."

In 2003, it was Chile's turn to become annoyed with Chávez's loose tongue. He commented that he dreamed of one day visiting a Bolivian beach, a reference to Bolivia's ongoing quest to regain the seacoast it lost to Chile in the 1979–84 War of the Pacific (see Bolivia, Chile). Chile protested the comment and recalled its ambassador.

In 2004, Colombia announced it had arrested Rodrigo Granda, considered the FARC's "foreign minister," in the Colombian city of Cucuta. Chávez charged that Granda had been abducted in Caracas and whisked across the border by Venezuelan national guardsmen who, Chávez said, had been "bribed" by the Colombian government. President Álvaro Uribe called the payment for Granda's abduc-

tion a "reward." Chávez denounced Colombia's violation of Venezuelan sovereignty and demanded an apology from Uribe, who not only refused but accused Chávez of having harbored a representative of a known terrorist organization, threatening Colombia's security. Chávez recalled his ambassador and canceled a bilateral agreement to build a $200 million gas pipeline. Eight national guardsmen were arrested and charged with treason. The two presidents met in Caracas and announced that the crisis had been resolved, that the pipeline deal was back on, and that Venezuela was mindful of Colombia's security concerns. There still was no apology from Uribe.

Relations with Spain improved immediately with the election victory of José Luis Rodríguez Zapatero's Socialist Party in 2004. Zapatero turned foreign policy 180 degrees from that of his conservative predecessor, José María Aznar, whom Chávez accused of complicity in the 2002 coup attempt. Zapatero signed a $1.7 billion arms deal by which Venezuela purchased four coastal patrol ships, four corvettes, 10 transport planes and two surveillance planes. The two leaders also announced that Spain would sell Venezuela an oil tanker and that Repsol, Spain's oil company, would increase its investments in Venezuela. The United States later blocked the sale of the planes by a NATO ally.

The announcement that Venezuela was buying 100,000 AK-47 and AK-103 assault rifles and 40 Mi-35 assault helicopters from Russia drew a quick protest to Russia from U.S. Secretary of State Condoleezza Rice (whom Chávez deridingly referred to as "Condolencia"). Rice called Chávez a "negative force" in the region. Meanwhile, Defense Secretary Donald Rumsfeld questioned during a visit to Brazil why Venezuela needs 100,000 assault rifles and suggested they would wind up in the hands of the Colombian rebels. In 2008, Russia also agreed to sell Venezuela three submarines.

At the Fourth Summit of the Americas in Mar del Plata, Argentina in 2005, Chávez was instrumental in dashing President Bush's hopes of implementing the FTAA. He gloated that he had dealt the FTAA a "knockout." He was joined by the four members of Mercosur—Argentina, Brazil, Paraguay and Uruguay. Chávez brought Venezuela into Mercosur, seen a challenge to Brazil's da Silva for regional leadership. Mexico's Vicente

Fox, one of the leaders at the summit who supported the FTAA, suggested that the 29 pro-FTAA countries could proceed without the other five, which led Chávez after the sum-mit to accuse Fox of selling out to the United States. Fox demanded an apology; Chávez withdrew his ambassador to Mexico temporarily.

Between 2005 and 2009, Chávez's regional influence was boosted by the election victories in Bolivia of Evo Morales, who had promised to join with Cuba and Venezuela as part of a "Bolivarian alternative;" of Manuel Zelaya in Honduras; of Daniel Ortega in Nicaragua; of Rafael Correa in Ecuador; of Fernando Lugo in Paraguay; and of Mauricio Funes in El Salvador. Chávez had openly endorsed all of them.

But when he tried the same thing in Peru, it blew up in his face. Chávez enthusiastically supported left-wing candidate Ollanta Humala in Peru's 2006 presidential election. Chávez even ridiculed Humala's two major opponents, calling former President Alan García a "thief" and a "crook" and conservative Lourdes Flores "the candidate of the oligarchy." He even suggested he would break diplomatic relations if García won. García, Flores and President Toledo denounced what they called Chávez's interference in domestic Peruvian politics, and Toledo recalled his ambassador to Venezuela. Humala ran first in the election, but narrowly lost to García in the runoff; Chávez's interference was widely viewed as the deciding factor that cost Humala the election.

Chávez's scuttling of the FTAA also backfired on him. In 2005 and 2006, Colombia and Peru, two of Venezuela's Andean Pact partners, signed lucrative bilateral free-trade agreements with the United States. A furious Chávez withdrew Venezuela from the Andean Pact.

Chávez openly uses Venezuela's oil wealth to extend his regional influence, offering discounted fuel to Caribbean countries in exchange for their votes on international bodies. He sought to embarrass the United States by offering to provide discounted heating oil to the poor residents of the Bronx and Boston during the bitterly cold weather in 2005–06. His generosity abroad has caused grumbling among his supporters at home, however.

In 2006, Chávez did an about-face and attended the "dialogue of the deaf" at the United Nations. In his address to the General Assembly, he sparked global controversy once again by referring to President Bush as "the devil." An-gry Americans boycotted Venezuelan-owned Citgo. Chávez also announced he wanted Venezuela to receive one of Latin America's two rotating seats on the U.N. Security Council, making no secret of the fact he intended to use it to oppose the United States. Guatemala was already in line for the seat, and the contest caused serious intra-regional tension; Chávez called in his IOUs from countries on which he had lavished foreign aid. After more than 20 inconclusive ballots in the General Assembly, the Latin American ambassadors settled on Panama as a compromise.

Chávez visited Argentina and Bolivia in 2007 in an obvious attempt to steal the limelight during President Bush's visits to Brazil, Uruguay and Colombia. He addressed large, anti-American rallies; Bush ignored him.

Chávez further alienated himself from his old friend da Silva during an energy conference Chávez hosted in Caracas in 2007. Da Silva supported Bush's proposal to use arable land in Latin America for sugar cane to produce biofuels such as ethanol, for export and to reduce dependence on imported petroleum. Chávez, who depends on oil exports to fund his socialist revolution and as a cudgel to intimidate other countries, ridiculed the idea, saying it would remove land from cultivation to feed the poor, the argument of Fidel Castro. Da Silva countered that Latin America has sufficient arable land for both food and ethanol.

Chávez's defense of North Korea's and Iran's nuclear programs has caused even his Latin American sympathizers to cringe.

After bringing Venezuela into *Mercosur* with much fanfare, Chávez failed to attend the *Mercosur* summit in Asunción in 2007; instead, he went to Russia and Iran on an arms shopping trip.

Chávez next managed to alienate himself from the friendly government of Spain. During the Ibero-American Summit in Santiago, Chile, in 2007, Chávez railed in undiplomatic language against former Spanish President Aznar, whom he was still accusing of complicity in the 2002 coup attempt, calling him among other things a "fascist." That proved too much even for Chávez's friend Zapatero, who came to the defense of his predecessor and arch-rival and admonished Chávez for using such language against a chief of government who had been duly elected by the Spanish people. Chávez repeatedly tried to interrupt Zapatero, until Spain's King Juan Carlos finally told Chávez, "*Por qué no te callas?*" ("Why don't you shut up?") Chávez threatened to break diplomatic relations with the best friend he has in the European Union. Of course, he did not.

When Venezuelan voters in 2007 rejected Chávez's proposed constitutional changes that would have allowed him to keep running indefinitely, Zapatero's foreign minister praised Venezuelans for their "democratic maturity."

The U.S. Justice Department charged a Venezuelan businessman, Guido Antonioni Wilson, who lives in Miami, and three others of illegally carrying $800,000 in cash at Chávez's behest to Buenos Aires to contribute to the 2007 presidential campaign of Cristina Fernández, wife of outgoing President Kirchner (see Argentina).

Chávez's brashness almost led to war with Colombia in 2008, when Colombia launched a raid on a *FARC* camp just across the border in Ecuador. President Correa moved 3,200 troops to the border, whereupon Chávez went on television to order the defense minister to move 10 battalions to the Colombian border. Chávez, Correa and Uribe met in the Dominican Republic to resolve the matter without bloodshed.

However, Colombia turned over to Interpol several laptop computers confiscated from the *FARC* camp which, among other things, reportedly prove that Chávez has channeled $300 million to the *FARC*, despite Chávez's many denials. Interpol's experts verified that the files on the laptops had not been tampered with. Chávez called the Interpol report a "clown show."

Even before the border incident, Chávez had shocked the EU by asking it to remove the *FARC* from its list of terrorist organizations.

When Bolivia expelled the U.S. Ambassador in September 2008, Chávez impetuously expelled the U.S. ambassador from Caracas in "solidarity" with Bolivia, prompting the United States to expel the Venezuelan ambassador. Relations remained frozen for the remainder of Bush's term—and beyond. In January 2009, he just as impetuously expelled the Israeli ambassador and broke diplomatic relations with Israel over the Israeli invasion of Gaza. Israel quickly returned the favor.

Chávez hosted a visit by Russian President Dmitri Medvedev in November 2008, and the two countries' navies held joint exercises for the first time, much to the annoyance of the Bush administration. In April 2009, Venezuela acquired Russian surface-to-air missiles.

Venezuela

As usual, Chávez engaged in grandstanding at the Fifth Summit of the Americas in Port-of-Spain, Trinidad, in April 2009. There was speculation on whether he would meet with the new U.S. president, Democrat Barack Obama, whom he already had called "ignorant" and said has "the same stench as Bush." Chávez interrupted a plenary session by approaching Obama and, as the cameras rolled, presented him a copy of a leftist book, *Latin America's Open Veins—Five Hundred Years of the Pillage of a Continent* by Uruguayan author Eduardo Galeano. An awkward-looking Obama shook his hand and thanked him. Twice Chávez told Obama in English at the summit, "I want to be your friend." Chávez also approached Secretary of State Hillary Clinton to voice his willingness to restore ambassadorial-level relations. Clinton and her State Department spokesman responded coolly. Later, the State Department announced it "welcomes" the restoration. Ambassadors were eventually exchanged in late June.

At a post-summit news conference, Obama insisted he wanted to be an equal partner with Latin America, but he chided Chávez for his tendency to play to the TV cameras and for years of "inflammatory" rhetoric toward the United States. Ultimately, he said, "The test for all of us is not simply words but also deeds."

Chávez took the lead international role in demanding the reinstatement of his ally, Honduran President Manuel Zelaya, who was deposed on June 28, 2009, for allegedly attempting to impose a new, Chávez-style constitution. He failed, but he has succeeded in preventing his allies from recognizing the elected government of Zelaya's successor, Porfirio Lobo Sosa.

Chávez visited Russia, Iran, Syria and six other countries in September 2009. In Syria, he accused Israel of "genocide." In Iran, President Mahmoud Ahmadinejad agreed to provide Venezuela with nuclear technology while Chávez agreed to provide Iran with gasoline if the rest of the world applied sanctions against Iran for refusing to abandon its nuclear program. In Russia, he obtained a $2.2 billion credit to buy tanks, short-range missiles and air-defense radar, which promptly led Secretary Clinton to accuse Chávez of starting what could be a regional "arms race." She repeated the charge at the 40th OAS General Assembly in Lima, Peru, in June 2010.

popular station in the country, would not be renewed when it expired on May 27, 2007. He made no secret of the fact the non-renewal was retribution for the station's outspoken opposition to him and for what Chávez alleged was its complicity in the 2002 coup. His announcement met swift criticism from international journalism organizations and from OAS Secretary-General José Miguel Insulza of Chile, who termed it a form of censorship. Chávez responded by calling Insulza, himself a leftist of long standing and whom Venezuela had supported for the post, an "idiot." The heretofore friendly governments of Brazil and Chile concurred with Insulza, however.

At midnight on May 27, 2007, *RCTV*'s signal went black, and a few seconds later the new station was on the air on that channel, opening with a pro-Chávez anthem. Unexpectedly, thousands of demonstrators, mostly students, took to the streets in Caracas and other cities to protest the closure. Police opened fire with tear gas and plastic bullets, injuring several. Two days of rioting ensued. The protests prompted Chávez to call a counter-demonstration in support of the closure.

RCTV's closure left *Globovisión* as the only openly anti-Chávez station, and the station's management vowed it would not be intimidated. Chávez hinted he might not wait for *Globovisión*'s license to expire, saying he has the power to close media that "incite unrest." *RCTV* soon returned as a cable and satellite channel, but could claim only 40% of its previous audience.

Sadly, the decision not to renew *RCTV*'s license has led two other privately owned channels, *Televen* and *Venevisión*, to practice self-censorship to avoid the same fate. Both toned down their criticism of Chávez.

Next, Chávez said he planned to renationalize the electric and telecommunications utilities, something he had not advocated during the campaign. Without explanation, he abruptly removed Vice President Rangel, perhaps because his prominence in the socialist movement rivaled his own. He replaced him with Jorge Rodríguez, head of the *CNE*, seen as even more devoted to Chávez.

He was sworn in on January 10, 2007, declaring "fatherland, socialism, or death!" He quickly announced more features of his "new era:" nationalizing foreign-owned refineries and natural gas operations, and constitutional amendments that would curb the powers of state and local officials and, more ominously, permit his indefinite re-election. Finally, he asked his rubber-stamp National Assembly for the power to rule by decree. For the first time, he declared himself a "communist" and said he had been one since 2002, something else he had neglected to mention before the election. Polls showed a majority of Venezuelans oppose a Cuban-style totalitarian regime. Jesus Christ, he argued, was "an authentic communist."

In January 2007, the National Assembly dutifully gave Chávez the power to rule by decree for 18 months. Venezuela thus officially came under one-man rule. One of his first acts was to purchase the 28.5% stake of the U.S. firm Verizon in Venezuela's largest telephone company, *CANTV*, for $572 million. Chávez had accused *CANTV* of tapping his telephone conversations.

The government also applied more pressure on its critics in the print media. In 2007, Laureano Márquez, one of the country's most popular humorists, wrote a satirical editorial in Petkoff's newspaper *Tal Cual* that lampooned the suggestion attributed to Chávez's nine-year-old daughter, Rosines, to change the national coat of arms to show a horse galloping to the left instead of to the right. In the editorial, Márquez asked Rosines to suggest changing the horse to a faithful golden retriever or to a tortoise "to symbolize our sluggishness in everything." A judge, citing child-protection laws, imposed an $18,600 fine on *Tal Cual's* publishing company for "violating the honor, reputation and privacy" of the girl. The judge fined Márquez separately. Márquez ridiculed the government for its sensitivity to traditional satire.

Chávez announced Venezuela's withdrawal from both the World Bank and the IMF in 2007. Venezuela had already paid its debts to the two institutions.

Then he announced the government was assuming operational control from Exxon Mobil, Conoco Phillips, Chevron, British Petroleum, Norway's Statoil and France's Total over the exploitation of the tar deposits of the Orinoco Belt. The companies were converting 600,000 barrels of heavy crude a day into synthetic oil. They were told they would have to agree to harsh new contractual terms if they wanted to remain in the country. Exxon Mobil and Conoco-Philips refused, although the others agreed. In 2008, Exxon Mobil fought back, obtaining a court injunction freezing $12 billion in *PDVSA* assets in the United States, Great Britain and the Netherlands to recover what it said it had lost from Venezuela's breach of contract. Chávez, as usual, threatened to cut off the flow of oil to the United States. In September 2008, Congress passed a new law that also expropriated the foreign companies' filling stations and a fleet of 1,200 trucks.

Meanwhile, a 500-page blueprint for a new education system was leaked to the press. It is unmistakably patterned on the Cuban model, with the purpose of indoctrinating children in Marxist ideology.

Chávez pursued his plans to revamp his own constitution to consolidate his personal power even more and to advance his "21st century socialism." The National Assembly approved a bewildering 69 constitutional amendments, among them extending the presidential term from six to seven years and allowing indefinite re-election. Elected state and municipal governments would have to share power with so-called regional councils, appointed by the president. The Central Bank would lose its autonomy to him. He would be able to expropriate private property by decree and to declare an open-ended state of emergency and suspend civil liberties, including presumption of innocence and the right to fair trial. Domestic and international human rights groups labeled the power-grab for what it was, a move toward absolute dictatorship.

December 2, 2007, was set as the date for the referendum. The 69 amendments were lumped together in two separate "blocks." Venezuelans again found themselves in a campaign that turned violent when chavistas opened fire on an opposition rally of 80,000 students in November; eight were wounded.

Chávez, long accustomed to lop-sided election and referendum victories, was confident this one would be no different. But only 45% of the electorate turned out to vote, handing him—and an anxious world—a stunning surprise:

	"Block A"	
Sí	4,379,392	49.29%
No	4,504,354	50.71%

	"Block B"	
Sí	4,335,136	48.94%
No	4,522,332	50.06%

Chávez said he accepted the will of the voters, claiming that it proved that Venezuela is a genuine democracy. He even admitted he had tried to push the country too far too fast, and said his revolution would focus on "three Rs: revision, rectification and relaunching." He reshuffled his cabinet and once again ejected his vice president, Jorge Rodríguez, replacing him with Ramón Alonso Carrizales, a retired colonel and a member of the Socialist Party.

Several factors contributed to Chávez's first electoral defeat. One was resentment over his suspension of the highly popular RCTV. Another is the frightening crime wave that has continued for years; in 2006, Venezuela's murder rate of 49 per 100,000 inhabitants was second-highest in the

world after El Salvador. Another was the perception that Venezuela's vast oil riches had done little to alleviate the grinding poverty despite Chávez's new social programs. The individual components of his coalition, such as long-time Communists and Socialists, balked at his plan for an umbrella organization under his control. Finally, many Venezuelans simply don't want a dictatorship.

Chávez's self-professed mellowing has slowed, but not stopped, his move toward "21st century socialism." In 2008, he renationalized Sidor, the steel complex that had been run by an Argentine-Italian consortium. The nationalization, ironically, strained relations with Argentina; he ignored his friend, former President Néstor Kirchner, who had lobbied him not to do it.

In 2008, Human Rights Watch, the hemispheric ombudsman group, released a 267-page report critical of Venezuela's growing repression. Speaking in Caracas, José Miguel Vivanco, the Chilean executive director of the group, said, "During this decade, democracy and its key institutions have become seriously weakened, judicial power has lost independence, civil society has less space, the news media, too, and the unions—the big, strong ones—cannot exercise their rights." As though to verify Vivanco's point, Chávez expelled him.

Chávez also came under criticism from Poland's Nobel Peace Laureate, Lech Walesa. Speaking in Warsaw, Walesa said, "I am the best proof that communism failed because it is a bad system, and introducing it there (Venezuela) is the biggest mistake of the region." Walesa then canceled a speech at a pro-democracy forum in Venezuela sponsored by Chávez critics when the Venezuelan government said it could not guarantee his security.

Venezuelans went to the polls again on November 23, 2008 to elect 22 state governors and 330 mayors and municipal councils. Turnout was 55%. Chávez's electoral machinery "disqualified" some of the opposition's strongest candidates on flimsy pretexts, and during the campaign Chávez made naked threats against the opposition. In one state, he even threatened to call out his tanks if the "oligarchy" won.

But voters chafed at such intimidation. Chavistas won 17 of the governorships, but the opposition took cheer from winning the two largest states, Zulia and Miranda, and the Caracas mayoralty. It also won the governorships of Carabobo, Táchira and Nueva Esparta, meaning that a majority of Venezuela's population would be governed by the opposition. Two of Chávez's past presidential opponents won office, Henrique Salas as governor of Carabobo, with a three-point plurality, and Manuel

Rosales as mayor of Maracaibo, with a 60% majority. Antonio Ledezma won the mayoralty of Caracas with 52.4% of the vote over Manuel Silva, a hand-picked Chávez protégé. Perhaps the most humiliating—and ominous—loss for the chavistas was the mayoralty of Sucre, which contains some of Caracas' sprawling suburban slums and which had been a bastion of regime support.

A tally of the popular vote for the 22 governorships and Caracas shows that the chavistas still won a majority of the 10.22 million votes cast, 53.1% to 43.2% for the opposition and 3.4% for independents, but that was a dramatic drop from the 59% he received in 2000 or the 2004 recall referendum or the 63% he received in 2006.

Chávez claimed the elections were a victory for his revolution, but there was no misreading the results as anything but a trend toward the opposition. He responded in two ways: Six days after the elections, he announced that he was "open" to the idea of another referendum to lift the ban on term limits; the Assembly quickly acted on his cue. The second was to place several of the functions of the Caracas municipal government under federal—meaning his—control. The police were nationalized, as well as a sports stadium and a parking lot that were important revenue sources for the city.

When Ledezma took office, he was appalled at the degree of featherbedding he found in the municipal government, with thousands of employees on the government payroll—including a suspicious number of beautiful young women—who apparently did no work. When he announced their contracts would not be renewed, hundreds staged an occupation of city hall. Chávez blamed Ledezma for creating the problem.

The new referendum on term limits was held February 15, 2009. This time, Chávez took no chances. The media blitz in favor of a "Sí" vote was of Orwellian proportions. He mobilized the workers of PDVSA and the state-owned telephone company, making it clear their jobs depended on a favorable outcome. This time the turnout was 70.3% and the outcome was more to his liking:

Sí	6,316,482	54.85%
No	5,193,839	45.15%

Chávez made the usual victory speech from the window of the Miraflores Palace, but once again, there was no escaping the reality that his winning percentage, despite the heavy turnout, was far less than what he was accustomed to, and the results showed that Venezuelans are as polarized as ever.

Venezuela

During the first half of 2009, Chávez was forced to slow down, but not stop, his nationalizations because the price of oil had dropped below $70 a barrel from a high of $140 the previous July. He expropriated a Cargill rice mill, but was forced to abandon a $1.2 billion takeover of Spain's Banco de Santander branch. Incredibly, even as he continued nationalizations, Chávez has invited foreign oil companies to make bids for exploration!

In the next move to suppress opposition, the government ordered Manuel Rosales, his 2006 election opponent and the newly elected mayor of Maracaibo, to appear in court in March 2009 on charges that he had illegally enriched himself while serving as governor of Zulia. Rosales denied the charges, went into hiding, and in April sought political asylum in Peru, which granted it.

Recent Developments

When the United States and Colombia announced in August 2009 that Colombia would allow U.S. forces use of seven Colombian military bases, Chávez denounced the deal as a "declaration of war" and threatened to sever diplomatic relations with Colombia (see Colombia). He didn't, but he began restricting trade with Colombia. Argentina agreed to replace the sale of $1.1 billion in Venezuelan goods that had once been sold to Colombia, and he restricted Colombian imports by 70%.

In early September, Chávez made a nine-country tour of Iran, Syria, Russia, Libya, Algeria, Turkmenistan, Belarus, Italy and Spain. Returning home, he proudly announced that Venezuela had obtained a $2.2 billion arms-purchasing credit from Russia and would buy, among other items, 92 T-72 tanks and short-range missiles with a 55-mile range, as well as an anti-aircraft system with a 185-mile range. The arms deal was obviously in response to the U.S.-Colombian base deal. U.S. Secretary of State Hillary Clinton used a meeting with visiting Uruguayan President Vázquez, heretofore a Chávez ally, to denounce what she called a regional "arms race." Vázquez agreed with Clinton, saying Latin America would be better served channeling its resources to social problems rather than weapons.

Tension mounted along the two countries' border, and hostilities appeared imminent. In August, Colombia said it had captured shoulder-fired anti-tank rockets from *FARC* guerrillas that had been traced to Venezuela. On October 28, Venezuela announced it had arrested two Colombians who allegedly were spying for Colombia's Administrative Department of Security, or *DAS*. The *DAS* denied the

charges, saying it does not conduct operations outside Colombia. Five days later, two Venezuelan national guardsmen were killed on the Venezuelan side of the border. Four suspects were arrested, who Vice President Ramón Carrizalez alleged were right-wing Colombian paramilitaries. The same week, Venezuela announced the discovery of 10 bodies on the Venezuelan side; Colombia said they were a kidnapped amateur soccer team, while Venezuela said they were paramilitaries. He accused the Colombian government of using the paramilitaries to destabilize Venezuela. Venezuela closed two of the bridges on the border, which disrupted commerce.

Carrizalez resigned as vice president and defense minister in January 2010 for "purely personal reasons."

Domestically, Chávez has continued moving Venezuela inexorably toward a Cuban-style dictatorship. In August 2009, Diosdado Cabello, former vice president and now the minister of public works and housing, who oversees broadcasting and is widely regarded as the second most powerful man in the country, announced that he was not renewing the broadcast licenses of 34 privately owned radio stations, ostensibly because their owners had had a case of mass amnesia and all neglected to complete the proper paperwork. The owners protested they had tried for two years to seek guidance on what kind of paperwork was required but that the government ignored them.

The announced closures led to mass anti-Chávez demonstrations, not only in Venezuela but in Colombia, Honduras, the United States and Europe. Cabello responded to the demonstrations by announcing that an additional 29 stations would be closed! He also filed another legal complaint against the beleaguered *Globovisión*, saying that during its coverage of the demonstrations it had carried tickers at the bottom of the screen calling for a coup. Pro-Chávez goons vandalized the station; Chávez unconvincingly condemned the attack.

The radio station closures were soon followed by a new media law that tightens the provisions of the current law. Among other provisions, the surviving private radio stations could not share national news but could only report local news. On January 23, 2010, *RCTV* was also barred from cable TV after it refused to adhere to a new regulation that cable channels also must carry Chávez speeches live. Its second closure also drew protest rallies.

The government went after *Globovisión* again in March. First, it arrested Oswaldo Álvarez Paz, former governor of Zulia and a presidential candidate in 1993. Álvarez Paz said in an interview on *Globovisión* that Venezuela had become a haven for narcotraffickers and that it was secretly supporting the Marxist rebels in Colombia. He was charged with conspiracy against the government, public incitement to commit a crime and spreading false information.

Two weeks later, Guillermo Zuloaga, president of *Globovisión*, also was arrested for allegedly disseminating false information that created panic. How? By criticizing Chávez during a meeting of the Inter American Press Association in Aruba, saying he was seeking to divide Venezuelans and suppress freedom of expression. His house also was raided twice for evidence that he had hunted endangered species; no evidence was found. He was also charged with stockpiling 24 cars to sell them for a profit. The IAPA condemned Zuloaga's arrest.

The OAS' Inter-American Commission on Human Rights denounced both arrests. In February, the commission issued a 319-page report accusing Venezuela of "routinely" committing human rights violations and of persecuting people for their political beliefs.

In May, the government dropped the conspiracy charge—the most serious—against Álvarez Paz. The remaining two charges remain. *Globovisión* was facing a total of 40 civil complaints. Zuloaga disappeared in June and was believed to have left the country.

The National Assembly was also discussing extending regulation to Internet content to prevent "false" information, with the government deciding what is false.

In November, the National Assembly passed a new electoral law that will give the party with the highest percentage of the votes a disproportionately large share of Assembly seats and delegates to the *CNE*, not the Assembly, the reapportionment of congressional districts. The *CNE* conducted the redistricting in January 2010, which critics allege was a gerrymander to favor Chávez's movement.

The Assembly also passed in 2009 a new education law that appears to be a Cuban-style effort to shape the thinking of the next generation of Venezuelans.

These moves toward increased authoritarianism, as well as the 2.9% decline in GDP caused by stagnant world oil prices and the global recession, have taken a toll on Chávez's popularity. By the beginning of 2010, his approval rating had slipped to 46%, and 66% of poll respondents said they did not want him to be elected again in 2012. Perhaps to boost his chances going into congressional elections scheduled for September, he decreed a 10% devaluation in January, which has given the economy a short-term boost by making Venezuelan goods cheaper abroad.

Culture: Venezuela's ethnic make up is an intriguing blend of European, Indian, *mestizo*, black and mulatto. The crippling succession of dictatorships took a heavy toll on cultural development, however.

Its two most distinguished men of letters both spent many of their most productive years abroad. The 19th century intellectual and writer Andrés Bello (1781–1865), left Venezuela at the age of 19 in 1810, then spent 19 years in London and the remainder of his life in Chile.

In the 20th century, Rómulo Gallegos (1884–1969) spent two decades in Spain during the Gómez dictatorship. His best known novel, *Doña Bárbara*, was published in 1929—in Madrid, not in Caracas. Two more of Gallegos' best known works were written in Barcelona: *Cantaclaro* (1934) and *Canaima* (1935). Returning to Venezuela after Gómez's death in 1935, Gallegos wrote *Pobre negro* (1937) *and El forestero* (1942), but they never achieved the critical acclaim of his novels written in Spain. Perhaps that was because he was more absorbed by his political activities; he was elected president of the republic in 1948 (see History). He went into exile again during the Pérez Jiménez dictatorship of the 1950s, this time to Mexico. The Romulo Gallegos International Novel Prize, now one of the most prestigious in Latin America, was created in his honor in 1965.

In art, Venezuela has produced a few figures with a regional reputation, but in classical music and theater it still largely borrows from abroad.

In popular music, however, Venezuela has produced at least two singers who have achieved acclaim throughout Latin America and beyond. One is a regional megastar of pop-rock, José Luís Rodrí-guez (b. 1943), also known by the sobriquet *El Puma*. He recorded his first hit in Venezuela in 1978 and for more than two decades has remained one of Latin America's most popular crooners. His three-volume *"Inolvidable"* album, released between 1997 and 2001, has been among his most popular.

The other singer is Simón Díaz (b. 1928), who specializes in the genre of the *tonadas*, or Venezuelan folk ballads. He has composed and sung hundreds of *tonadas*, which celebrate the bygone lifestyle of the farmers and cowboys of Venezuela's high plains, much as Woody Guthrie did with his folk ballads about the common man in the United States. His signature song is a love ballad, *"Caballo viejo,"* which the French group Gypsy Kings co-opted for its international smash hit *"Bamboleo"* in 1989. Díaz later received a copyright infringement settlement. Long a popular television personality in Venezuela, Díaz became famous throughout Latin America, and in 2004 he released a CD in the United States, *"Mis canciones."* In 2009, he received the Latin Grammy Lifetime Achievement Award.

Venezuela's fledgling film industry continues to show promise, and a few Venezuelan *telenovelas* are marketed abroad.

Beauty contests are a national passion in Venezuela, where special schools that groom young women for competition, and plastic surgeons who enhance their looks, have become thriving industries. Five Venezuelans have won the Miss World title since its inception in 1951, the most recent in 1995. Four Venezuelans have won the Miss Universe title since it was created in 1953, in 1979, 1981, 1986 and 1996. One, Irene Sáez (1981), later went into politics and ran for president in 1998 (see History).

The absence of free expression before the advent of democracy in 1958 also ham-strung the press. Press freedom caused the number of newspapers and magazines to mushroom. The capital's two prestigious dailies are the venerable *El Universal*, founded in 1909, and *El Nacional*, which dates to 1943. High-quality magazines include *Resúmen*, *Momento*, *Bohemia*, *Elite*, *Auténtico* and *Zeta*. However, freedom of the press has come under increasing attack from President Hugo Chávez, and the New York-based freedom House rates Venezuela as one of two Latin American countries in 2009 where the press is "not free"; Cuba is the other.

Economy: Venezuela's economy is completely dominated by petroleum production. Oil revenues account for about half of all government income and 90% of the nation's exports; Venezuela is the world's fifth-largest oil producer and the fourth-largest exporter of oil to the United States.

Extracting oil from the tar-like deposits of the Orinoco oil belt led to an $8 billion project to develop those resources. A large field was discovered in the eastern state of Monagas with an estimated 8.6 billion barrels in 1987. Total reserves, including "heavy" oil, are about 300 billion barrels. In 2003, the state oil company announced the discovery of still another new field in Monagas containing an estimated 350 million barrels of light crude and 870 million cubic feet of natural gas.

There has been renewed oil drilling in the Maracaibo area. Twenty-one years after Venezuela nationalized its oil industry, it began inviting oil companies to come back in 1996 to explore in promising areas. But President Hugo Chávez, elected in 1998, reneged on those contracts in 2007 and demanded tough new terms that Exxon Mobil and ConoicoPhillips refused to accept (see History).

Venezuela's bloated, featherbedded, inefficient and corrupt bureaucracy became the horror story of Latin America. The bureaucracy was padded with phantom employees and real employees who were notoriously lazy and inefficient. This discouraged foreign investors and lenders and drove up inflation. Despite President Caldera's effort to reduce the public sector, the workforce actually *increased* by 50,000 in 1997. Why? Because of decentralization, laid-off federal workers entered the payrolls of state and local governments. Another reason was the traditional dark side of democracy: spoils and patronage. To gain or keep power, politicians swap jobs for votes.

Chávez was elected in 1998 to rescue the economy and battle the corruption that was such a drain. Economic statistics confirmed the severity of the crisis he inherited. Real GDP growth in 1997 was an illusionarily rosy 5.1%, but that gain fol-

Angel Falls

Venezuela

lowed negative growth of –0.4% the year before. In 1998, the year of the free-fall in world oil prices, growth declined by –0.3%, and in 1999, Chávez's first full year in office, it plummeted by a devastating –6.1% despite skyrocketing oil prices. In 2000, Venezuela showed positive growth of only 3.2%, almost entirely the result of the continued high price of oil on the international markets, but it was not enough to overcome the losses of the previous three years.

Growth in 2001 was 3%, but in 2002, largely because of the abortive coup and a crippling general strike (see History), GDP fell again by –8.9%. Growth in 2003 was about 9% and in 2004 was a robust 17.9%, the highest in Latin America. Growth has since continued at 9.3% in 2005 and 10.3% in 2006, again the highest in Latin America, but this growth was the result of the spiraling world price of petroleum. Growth was still 8.4% in 2007, but tapered off to 4.8% in 2008 as the price of oil plummeted late in the year. In 2009, GDP shrank by –2.9%, the worst year since 2002.

Unemployment remained stubbornly in the double digits from 1997 to 2005, peaking at 20% in 2003. It fell to 8.9% in 2006 and 8.5% in 2008. With the global recession, it climbed to 10.9% in 2009.

Inflation declined from a paycheck-stealing 103.2% in 1996 to 12% in 2001. In 2003 it was back up to 27.1%, the highest in Latin America. It has remained high: 17% in 2006, 22.5% in 2007, 31% in 2008 and 27.1% in 2009—again the highest in Latin America.

Oil wealth once gave Venezuela among the highest standards of living in the region, but inflation and negative economic growth have steadily eroded it. In 2008 its per capita income of $9,230 was the third-highest of the 20 Latin American republics after Mexico and Chile, but it is inequitably distributed; nearly 40% of the population live below the poverty line. The public debt rose from 29% of GDP when Chávez became president to 39% in 2005, but is has tapered off to 13.8% in 2009.

Three decades after oil production was nationalized, the state oil company, *PDVSA*, has become increasingly dependent on foreign companies once again to maintain production, which in 2008 was 2.643 million barrels per day, the fifth-highest in the world. Part of the reason for this is that Chávez largely politicized *PVDSA* after the crippling general strike of 2002–03; he fired more than 40% of *PDVSA* managers and workers and replaced them with political loyalists.

The change has not improved efficiency. *PDVSA* has entered into joint ventures with U.S., British, Dutch, Spanish and Brazilian oil firms to try to bring production up to 5 million bpd by 2009. However,

Chávez's government abruptly canceled existing contracts in 2005 and 2007 and forced foreign companies to sign new ones on even more favorable terms for the government, which led Exxon Mobil to obtain an injunction freezing $12 billion in *PDVSA* assets (see History). After his re-election in 2006, Chávez announced plans for a greater government stake in the foreign-owned refineries. He also announced plans to nationalize the electricity and telecommunications sectors.

With the price of oil at $70 per barrel in mid-2006, it became economically feasible to exploit the heavy crude in the Orinoco tar belt. Natural gas production is expected to increase as well. In mid-2008, oil skyrocketed to $140 a barrel, which prompted more drunken-sailor spending by Chávez for his foreign adventures. But the boom quickly turned to bust as the price of oil plummeted to a low as $37 a barrel by the end of 2008. As this book went to press in July 2010, it had stabilized at about $70, not enough to finance the president's grandiose foreign and domestic agenda. The government offered new leases in the Orinoco in 2009, but not on attractive terms. Still, it had some takers.

The Future: Venezuela is beyond any further doubt a one-man dictatorship, under the control of an elected despot in the mold of Argentina's Juan Perón, another charismatic military man who touted himself as the champion of the poor and then used legal and economic maneuvers to harass and intimidate political opponents and the independent opposition media. Hugo Chávez has consolidated his power so that the government, the United Socialist Party, the military, the state-owned oil company *PDVSA* and an increasing number of mass media outlets and small businesses are all firmly in his grasp. This absolute control is reminiscent of Louis XIV, who declared, *"L'etat c'est moi."*

Chávez is tightening the screws on the private radio stations, *Globovisión*, cable TV channels, the Internet and independent print media as well, some of which are also showing signs of practicing self-censorship. His attorney general coined a new oxymoron in 2009: "Regulated free expression." The crackdown on peaceful forms of protest, such as the traditional banging of pots and pans, is equally disturbing. That leaves Chávez's opponents little recourse except violent protest, as happened after *RCTV* was removed from the air in 2007.

Chávez has failed to deliver on two promises that brought him to power: to reduce poverty and corruption. In 2006, it was estimated that 33.9% of Venezuelans were "poor" and 23.2% were "extremely poor." He has used the country's oil wealth

to provide some social services and make-work projects, but unemployment remains stubbornly high in a country awash with oil wealth. Part of the reason for this is that Chávez squanders billions of that wealth on "foreign aid" designed to extend his regional—and global—influence.

For the past four years, Transparency International has rated Venezuela the second-most corrupt country in Latin America behind Haiti, and in 2009 it ranked 162nd out of 180 countries in the world.

These are hardly records of achievement for Chávez, and they no doubt help explain why his approval rating was 46% at the beginning of 2010, down from 62% a year earlier.

Interestingly, support for democracy remains high in Venezuela. In the perennial *Latinobarómetro* survey of 17 countries for *The Economist*, 62% of Venezuelans in 1996 said they believed that democracy was preferable to any other form of government. By 2005, it had risen to 78%. In 2008 it was 82% and in 2009, 84%, the highest in Latin America. By the same token, the percentage of those who believe that an authoritarian form of government is sometimes preferable to democracy has declined, from 19% in 1996 to 7% in 2009. Does this 84% support for democracy mean Venezuelans are satisfied with the system they have—or wistful over the one they would *like* to have?

Venezuela has become a classic "tyranny of the majority." An Associated Press poll shortly before the 2006 election showed that 84% of Venezuelans do not want a Cuban-style dictatorship. Like Perón, or Louisiana's Huey P. Long, Chávez does not realize that in a democracy, the losers are still entitled to civil liberties, the right of dissent and a free press.

With his popularity dimming, and his oil revenues shrinking, he may find September's congressional elections his stiffest challenge yet, if the opposition can present a united front. And even if he loses the next presidential election in 2012, would he really relinquish power? Not likely. If it comes down to it, are we likely to see something along the lines of Fujimori's rigged re-election in Peru in 2000?

**Wall of the Thousand Columns
(top of the Auyán-Tepui)**

362

HAITI

DOMINICAN REPUBLIC

PUERTO RICO

CARIBBEAN SEA

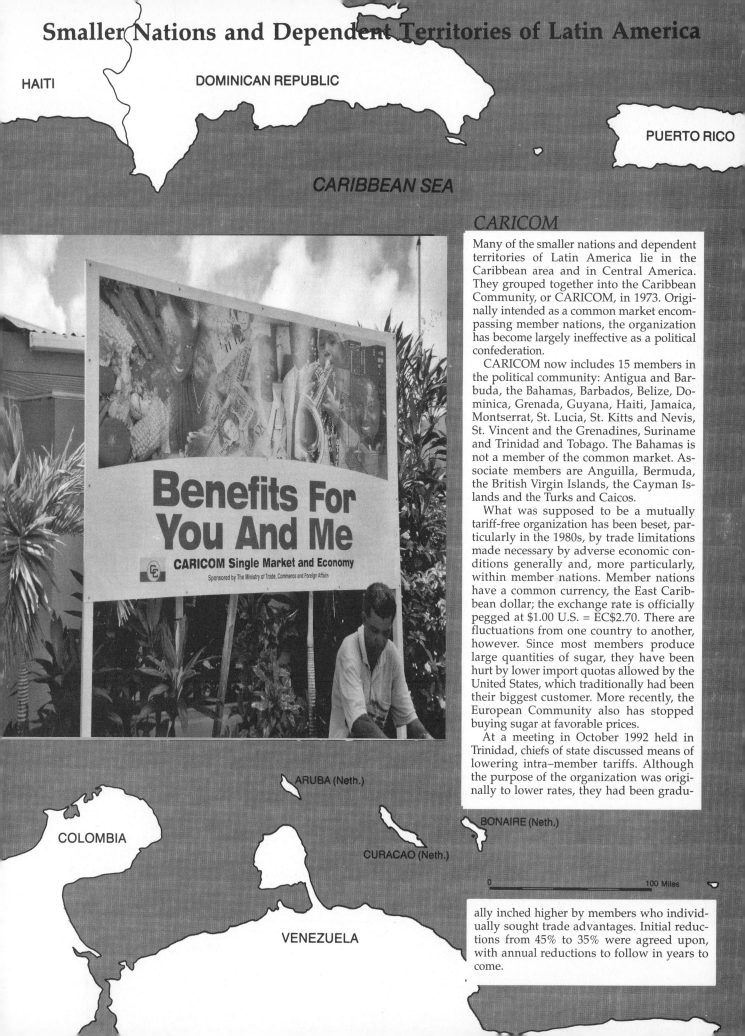

CARICOM

Many of the smaller nations and dependent territories of Latin America lie in the Caribbean area and in Central America. They grouped together into the Caribbean Community, or CARICOM, in 1973. Originally intended as a common market encompassing member nations, the organization has become largely ineffective as a political confederation.

CARICOM now includes 15 members in the political community: Antigua and Barbuda, the Bahamas, Barbados, Belize, Dominica, Grenada, Guyana, Haiti, Jamaica, Montserrat, St. Lucia, St. Kitts and Nevis, St. Vincent and the Grenadines, Suriname and Trinidad and Tobago. The Bahamas is not a member of the common market. Associate members are Anguilla, Bermuda, the British Virgin Islands, the Cayman Islands and the Turks and Caicos.

What was supposed to be a mutually tariff-free organization has been beset, particularly in the 1980s, by trade limitations made necessary by adverse economic conditions generally and, more particularly, within member nations. Member nations have a common currency, the East Caribbean dollar; the exchange rate is officially pegged at $1.00 U.S. = EC$2.70. There are fluctuations from one country to another, however. Since most members produce large quantities of sugar, they have been hurt by lower import quotas allowed by the United States, which traditionally had been their biggest customer. More recently, the European Community also has stopped buying sugar at favorable prices.

At a meeting in October 1992 held in Trinidad, chiefs of state discussed means of lowering intra–member tariffs. Although the purpose of the organization was originally to lower rates, they had been gradu-

ARUBA (Neth.)

BONAIRE (Neth.)

COLOMBIA

CURACAO (Neth.)

0   100 Miles

ally inched higher by members who individually sought trade advantages. Initial reductions from 45% to 35% were agreed upon, with annual reductions to follow in years to come.

VENEZUELA

BRITISH VIRGIN ISLANDS

ST. THOMAS

ST. JOHN

U. S. VIRGIN ISLANDS

ST. CROIX

ANGUILLA

ST. MARTIN

ST. BARTHELEMY (Fr.)

ATLANTIC

SABA (Neth.)

ST. EUSTATIUS (Neth.)

BARBUDA

OCEAN

ST. KITTS

NEVIS

ANTIGUA

REDONDA

MONTSERRAT

GUADELOUPE

MARIE GALANTE

DOMINICA

MARTINIQUE

ST. LUCIA

Plans were made in 1993 for a pact between member nations that would provide for taxation of income at the place of its origin rather than the location where it is received; the agreement has not been finalized. Further complicating the economic picture has been the NAFTA treaty (Mexico, U.S., Canada) and the General Agreement on Tariffs and Trade (GATT), both lowering and/or abolishing tariffs.

Because of the relative political stability of most CARICOM countries and the success with offshore banking on many of them, they tended to enjoy favorable credit ratings, which led many of them to overborrow and to become heavily indebted. Of the 10 countries in the world with the highest debt as percentage of GDP in 2004, six are CARICOM members. In order of percentage, they are Guyana, St. Kitts and Nevis, Antigua and Barbuda, Dominica, Grenada and Belize.

Most of the members are heavily dependent on tourism for foreign exchange, and thus suffered from the fall in tourism following the September 11, 2001 terrorist attacks on the United States. That sector has recovered, but violent crime is frightening away tourists from such idyllic destinations as Barbados, St. Kitts and Nevis, and Trinidad and Tobago.

In 2001, 12 of the English-speaking countries and dependencies signed a treaty to establish the Caribbean Court of Justice in Port-of-Spain, Trinidad, which would replace the British Privy Council as the region's court of last resort. The court was formally established on April 16, 2005, although only two of the signatories, Barbados and Guyana, have enacted the necessary legislation to forward cases to the new court.

SOVEREIGN NATIONS
Antigua and Barbuda (Independent November 1, 1981)
The Bahamas (Independent July 10, 1973)
Barbados (Independent November 30, 1966)
Grenada (Independent February 7, 1974)
Dominica (Independent November 3, 1978)
St. Kitts and Nevis (Independent September 19, 1983)
St. Lucia (Independent February 22, 1979)
St. Vincent and the Grenadine (Independent October 27, 1979)

THE DEPENDENT TERRITORIES
British Virgin Islands (colony)
Anguilla (British Crown colony)
Cayman Islands (British colony)

ST. VINCENT

BARBADOS

GRENADINES

GRENADA

Falkland Islands (British colony)
Turks and Caicos (British colony)
Montserrat (British colony)
French Guiana (French overseas department)
Guadeloupe (French overseas department)
Martinique (French overseas department)
Puerto Rico (U.S. commonwealth)
U.S. Virgin Islands (territory)

TO

TRINIDAD

The Commonwealth of the Bahamas

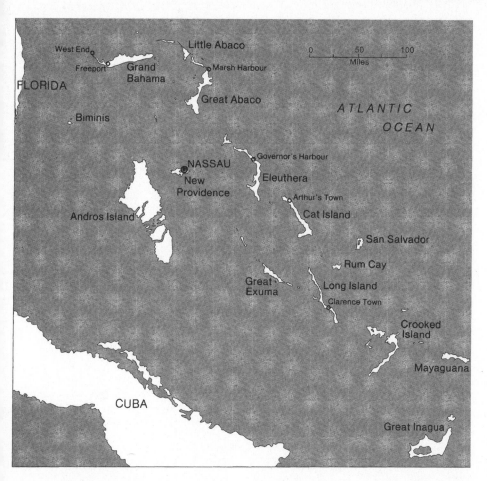

Like the fragments of a broken piece of pottery, the Bahama Islands spread their natural beauty over about 100,000 square miles of ocean, making a gently curving arc 700 miles long from a point off the Florida coast down to the islands of Cuba, Haiti and the Dominican Republic. Only 35 of the islands are inhabited, with New Providence Island having more than half of the nation's population.

History: In October 1492 Christopher Columbus first sighted his New World at the island he promptly named San Salvador—"the Savior"—lying on the eastern edge of the island group. The Arawak Indians who populated these islands were exterminated over a brief period of years by Spanish slave traders, who shipped them off to the large Spanish-owned islands to work on the sugarcane plantations.

Thinly populated, the islands were virtually ignored for a century and a half until 1647 when a former governor of the English island of Bermuda sailed south and landed on the long, narrow strip of land called Eleuthera. He and his party were seeking greater religious freedom than was found on Bermuda. In the late 1930s and early 1940s the tourist boom started; today the islands receive more than a million and a half vacationers annually.

The Progressive Liberal Party (PLP) was formed in 1953 by Bahamians (pronounced Ba-haim-yans) who resisted rule by a small group of businessmen then in control of political and economic life on the islands ("The Bay Street Boys"). Continually gaining strength, the PLP was voted into office in 1967, and in 1972 it won 29 of 38 seats in the House of Assembly.

In July 1977, Bahamians voted in the island's first elections since independence in 1973. Although Prime Minister Lynden O. Pindling ("Black Moses") had been severely criticized for his economic policies, voters gave his PLP 31 of the 38 House seats. The government's "black power" image hurt the all-important tourist industry.

Pindling followed a trend found throughout the Caribbean: increased state control over the economy. The government forced many businesses to hire local workers to replace foreigners. New taxes were placed on foreign workers and on the sale of property to non-Bahamians. The government claimed that these programs produced a black middle class.

One impact of these measures was an end to the Bahamas' former status as a tax-free haven for the rich. Many of the so-called suitcase companies moved from the Bahamas to the Cayman Islands, where taxes remain low.

General elections in mid-1982 saw Prime Minister Pindling's PLP win with 53% of the vote and a majority in the House of Assembly. A similar victory occurred in 1987, despite repeated accusations that the prime minister was involved in drug trafficking, including eyewitness testimony linking him to Everette Bannister. The latter was known as "Mr. Fixit" of the Bahamas, and widely suspected as a drug smuggler.

Prime Minister Hubert A. Ingraham

Bahamas

Former Prime Minister Perry Christie

In August 1992, elections resulted in victory for the opposition Free National Movement (FNM) and selection of Hubert Ingraham as prime minister, ending the 27-year rule of Pindling. An investigation of corruption in state owned enterprises during the Pindling years ensued. Ingraham's government also has stressed economic development through inviting foreign investment. The FNM was returned to power in general elections in March 1997, winning 35 seats to only four for the PLP.

In the general elections of May 2002, the PLP returned to power, winning 29 of 40 seats. Perry Christie became prime minister.

The pendulum swung back in the next elections on May 2, 2007. The FNM accused the PLP of corruption and of making it too easy for foreigners to buy the limited amount of land in the Bahamas. The FNM won 23 seats to 18 for the PLP.

Culture: The people of the Bahamas, approximately 90% of whom are of African ancestry, are good-humored and generally prosperous. Most derive their living from the tourist trade. Among their many festivals is a special holiday—Junkanoo—a carnival not unlike the New Orleans Mardi Gras, which takes place during Christmas week. A sportsman's paradise, the islands provide excellent fishing, first-rate golf courses, a lively night life, visiting ballet companies, concerts and other theatrical productions. Goombay is a musical sound which is exclusively Bahamian; it blends a combination of goatskin drums, maracas and saws scraped with nails. The rhythm is fast-paced, exciting and non-stop.

Economy: Tourism is the number one industry, accounting for 60% of GDP. Most visitors are from the United States on excursion cruises out of Miami who stay one or two days. Europeans, who stay for an average of two weeks, spend much more, and strong efforts are being made to cultivate this trade. New hotels and vacation facilities have been constructed in the "outer" islands. Tourism could be negatively affected by a new U.S. regulation in 2005 requiring U.S. citizens to have a passport to visit the Bahamas.

Ranking second to tourism is the international banking industry (15% of GDP), with more than 350 banks located on the islands. Because there is no income tax and great secrecy of financial transactions, the Bahamas has traditionally been a major tax haven and scene of widespread "laundering" of money from illegal drugs. The government has attempted to broaden the base of the economy by lowering import duties and other attractive incentives. Production of bauxite is important. Oil refining and transshipment from large ships to smaller vessels at new terminals is a major source of income, together with cement production.

Another source of income is "dummy" registration of ships, which can be returned to U.S. registry in the event of a war. Better terms are being offered than those of Liberia; Bahamian registry includes huge supertankers. Commercial fishing is also being expanded. Lavish and lively gambling casinos, in operation around the clock, see millions of dollars changing hands each week, but they have felt the effect of U.S. state lotteries and legalized gambling.

Although new building developments are encroaching on the limited arable farmlands, "double cropping" each year in this warm climate makes most food plentiful, but imports have increased. Citrus fruit groves have replaced dairy farming as the most important sector of agriculture. Huge groves were planted to take advantage of severe frosts in Florida in the 1980s. Oranges, limes and other tropical fruit are plentiful and some are shipped to the United States. Other major exports include rum and salt.

Limitations on the economy include the presence of a large number of unskilled Haitians requiring high levels of social services.

The Bahamas posted a GDP in 2007 of $6.586 billion. The growth rate was 2.8% in 2007 and 1.5% in 2008. With the global recession, which always impacts tourism heavily, the economy shrank by –4.0% for 2009.

The Future: Blessed with the highest annual per capita income in the Western Hemisphere after the United States and Canada, the Bahamas is highly prosperous; this does not include a considerable amount of money generated by illicit drug trafficking. As in most prosperous places of the world, prices are high, including items that attract tourists.

Flamingos at Nassau's Ardastra Gardens

Barbados

Former Prime Minister Owen Arthur

Area: 166 square miles.

Population: 285,653 (2010 estimate).

Capital City: Bridgetown (Pop. 96,578 in 2006).

Climate: Tropical, but pleasant, with moderate rainfall from June to December.

Ethnic Background: African (77%); mixed races (17%); European (6%).

Chief Commercial Products: Sugar, molasses, rum.

Gross Domestic Product: U.S.$3.637 billion in 2009 ($12,732 per capita in 2009).

Former Colonial Status: Colony of Great Britain, 1627–1966.

Independence Date: November 30, 1966.

Chief of State: Queen Elizabeth II of Great Britain, represented by Governor General Sir Clifford Straughn Husbands.

Head of Government: David John Howard Thompson (b. December 25, 1961), prime minister (since January 16, 2008).

Barbados is an island 21 miles in length and 14.5 miles at its greatest width, lying in the Atlantic Ocean 100 miles east of the Lesser Antilles. The island is surrounded by colorful coral reefs and has but one natural harbor, Carlisle Bay, on the southwestern coast; the island's high elevation is Mt. Hillaby (1,115 feet) on the northern part. The land slopes to the south in gentle terraces. Temperatures of the tropical climate are moderated by sea breezes. Fertile soils and adequate rainfall have favored sugar production.

History: Barbados was occupied by the British in 1625 and remained continuously in British control until its independence in 1966. Until the mid-19th century, sugar produced great wealth for the planters. The abolition of slavery in 1838 disturbed, but did not destroy, the island's economy. By comparison with other West Indian islands, Barbados' history has been tranquil. Riots occurred in 1876 and in 1937 because of efforts to federate the island with other British possessions. Ministerial government with partial self-rule was granted in 1954 by Britain. In 1961 Barbados became internally self-governing within the British Commonwealth. Full independence was achieved in 1966. The House of Assembly is the second-oldest legislative body in the Western Hemisphere, having first met in 1639.

Elections in 1971 were won by Prime Minister Errol Walton Barrow's Democratic Labor Party. Disturbed by the decline in the national economy, voters in 1976 turned to the Barbados Labor Party headed by J.M.G. (Tom) Adams. But in 1986 elections, in the presence of a declining economy, the people again turned to Barrow, who won a landslide victory in mid-1986, but died in June 1987. He was succeeded by his deputy, Erskine Sandiford.

Winning half the vote in January 1991, the DLP captured 18 of the 28 seats in the House of Assembly. Sandiford, who continued as prime minister, had promised to carry out the policies of his predecessor. The BLP had revitalized itself under the

leadership of Owen Arthur since 1993 and promised competition based on the flagging economy in the next election.

Tax reforms, including a value-added tax, highlighted 1993, as did the development of tax reductions and incentives intended to boost export of small manufactured goods, including clothing.

In elections held in September 1994, the BLP ended the eight-year rule of the DLP winning 18 of the 28 seats in the House of Assembly, and Arthur became prime minister. Arthur and the BLP won a landslide re-election victory in January 1999, winning 26 seats. Two seats were added to the Assembly before the May 21, 2003 elections, which the BLP won again, taking 23 of the 30 seats.

Crime has become such a serious problem, threatening the vital tourism industry, that the Arthur government has followed Trinidad and Tobago's and Jamaica's lead in reinstating death by hanging. The last hanging was in 1984, but the British Privy Council, which has a five-judge panel that hears Caribbean appeals, commuted several sentences. In response, on April 16, 2005, 12 Caribbean members of the British Commonwealth established a new Caribbean appeals court of last resort, which will sit in Port-of-Spain Trinidad that will replace the Privy Council. So far, only Barbados and Guyana have ratified this change.

In February 2005, Prime Minister Arthur went a step further and advocated abolishing Barbados' recognition of the queen as chief of state and establishing a

Barbados

**Prime Minister
David John Howard Thompson**

republic. He said the change would be submitted to voters in a referendum.

That referendum was to have been held concurrently with the general election for a new House of Assembly on January 15, 2008, but was postponed. In the parliamentary elections, the DLP was returned to power after 14 years, winning 20 of the 30 seats. David Thompson, 46, who held several cabinet posts under Sandiford, was sworn in as prime minister the next day.

Thompson announced in May 2010 he was stepping aside pending the results of medical treatments abroad for an undisclosed illness. Deputy Prime Minister and Attorney General Freundel Stuart is governing in his absense.

Culture: The people of Barbados are descendants of British colonists and African slaves. They have a typically West Indian culture with a blend of English tradition. Their rhythmic dances and Calypso music, backed by steel drum bands (see Trinidad and Tobago), are in strange contrast to their love of cricket, always the joy of the British upper classes, but in Barbados the game of the people. African influence is as dominant as British, except in political and economic institutions, where the latter is maintained. Barbados is densely populated, with more than 1,500 people per square mile.

Economy: Sugar production and tourism account for a large percentage of the nation's foreign exchange earnings. Fish, fruit and beef output barely meet domestic needs of the nation, one of the world's most densely populated regions. In addition, a lack of mineral wealth hampers economic growth. To help reduce unemployment and racial tensions, the government has been making a concerted effort to involve its large, literate (97% adult literacy rate) black population in tourism to

offset a decline in sugar production. Production of sugar has been steadily declining in the face of falling world prices.

The tourism boom of the 1990s has made Barbados a relatively prosperous little country, with an estimated per capita income in 2001 of $9,444, well above that of most of the 20 "Latin" republics. GDP grew by 3.7% in 2000, well above the 0.7% annual population growth rate. But it declined by .6% in 2001 and another 0.4% in 2002, reflecting the global drop in tourism in the wake of the September 11, 2001 terrorist attacks on the United States. It grew by 3.4% in 2004, 4.1% in 2005 and 3.9% in 2006, 3.3% in 2007 and 1.5% in 2008. With the global recession, it declined by –2.8% in 2009.

Unemployment remains stubbornly high, although the rate of 9.8% in 2004 was a record low. The income tax rate, 25%, is one of the highest in the region.

Tourism, which now accounts for three-fourths of GDP, helps offset the serious balance of trade deficit. In 2006, Barbados imported $1.586 billion in goods and exported only $285 million.

The Future: Persistent unemployment has made crime a perennial problem. Tourism has not grown as rapidly as might be expected because of this. Establishing a republic may give Barbadians a greater sense of identity, but it has not solved their economic problems.

The Village of Bathsheba

Grenada

Area: 133 square miles, including the islets of Carricou and Petit Martinique in the Grenadines.

Population: 107,818 in 2010 (estimated).

Capital City: St. George's (Pop. 34,000, est.).

Climate: Tropically rainy and dry, hot, with prevailing ocean breezes.

Official Language: English.

Ethnic Background: African.

Chief Commercial Products: Nutmeg, tropical agricultural products.

Gross Domestic Product: $691 million in 2009, estimated ($6,409 per capita).

Former Colonial Status: Ruled alternately by French and British, 1650–1783; colony of Great Britain, 1783–1974.

Independence Date: February 7, 1974.

Chief of State: Queen Elizabeth II of Great Britain, represented by Governor-General Carlyle Arnold Glean.

Head of Government: Tillman Thomas (b. June 13, 1945), prime minister (since July 9, 2008).

Former Prime Minister Keith Mitchell

Like a large pearl, Grenada (pronounced Greh-NAY-dah) is the southernmost of the Windward Island chain, lying peacefully at the edge of the Caribbean Sea and the Atlantic Ocean. Blessed with beautiful beaches, clear water and a pleasant (but tropical) climate, the island is 21 miles long from north to south and only 12 miles horizontally at its widest point. Grenada has heavily wooded mountains watered by many streams that feed the quiet, lush valleys. There is the calm of smooth beaches and the rockbound coasts where the surf pounds and churns endlessly.

History: Discovered in 1498 by Columbus, Grenada was originally inhabited by the Carib Indians. In the 1650s the island was colonized by the French, who established large tobacco plantations. England acquired Grenada in 1763 by the Treaty of Paris, under which (among other exchanges of territory) France ceded Canada to the English. The new rulers of the island imported slaves from Africa to work the sugarcane plantations.

For over 200 years, Grenada basked peacefully in obscurity, harvesting its crops and almost oblivious to the rest of the world. During this period it was administered as a separate British Colony until its membership in the short-lived West Indian Federation (1958–72). The federation collapsed partly because one key member, Trinidad, did not want to tie its own healthy economy to that of its poorer federation neighbors.

Elections held in 1972 brought an overwhelming victory to the Grenada United Labor Party of Premier Eric Gairy (13 out of 15 seats in the House of Representatives), whose major platform during the election was the complete independence of the island nation. As a result of talks in London soon afterward, a constitutional conference was set for May 1973.

Grenada gained its independence in 1974. The most prominent figure in the nation's politics since 1962, Gairy continued to control Grenada through his domination of powerful labor unions. However, his corrupt and brutal rule generated widespread resentment at home, while abroad he generated notoriety over his stated belief in UFOs. Opponents, led by the "new left" black-power New Jewel Movement, ousted him in 1979.

The new regime, headed by London-educated Maurice Bishop, 34, promptly dissolved Parliament and promised a new constitution that would make the island a "socialist democracy." Although it restricted personal liberties (no press free-dom, no elections), the regime somewhat improved living conditions for the poor. Private enterprise remained largely intact.

In foreign affairs, Bishop embraced the Castro regime. Cuba responded with technical and military assistance for Grenada's new "People's Revolutionary Army."

The Reagan administration viewed the Grenada regime as a tool of Moscow via Cuba and imposed a blackout of the island. The government collapsed and anarchy ensued which was ended when a force of U.S. Marines and troops from other Caribbean nations and territories invaded. Several hundred Cuban troops were taken prisoner and returned to Cuba; vast amounts of Soviet and Cuban military equipment was found. The occupying force was withdrawn after elections were held in December 1984.

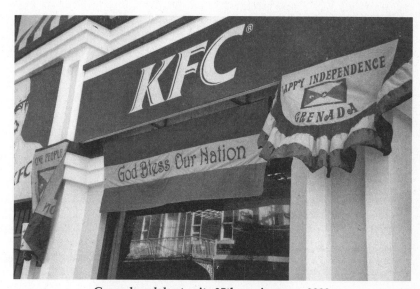

Grenada celebrates its 35th anniversary, 2009

369

Grenada

Prime Minister Tillman Thomas

Herbert Blaize, leader of the New National Party, was selected prime minister over a coalition government that split in 1989; Blaize died shortly thereafter. Inconclusive elections in 1990 resulted in Nicholas Braithwaite being selected to lead another coalition government. He stumbled badly in 1993, failing to find economic measures acceptable to the media and people, and he resigned on February 1, 1995. In June elections, the New National Party (NNP) led by former Works and Communications Minister Keith Mitchell, defeated the NDC, taking eight of the 15 seats in the House of Representatives.

As prime minister, Mitchell embarked on a successful campaign to lure foreign investors to the island, but there were signs that his government corrupted itself in the awarding of public works contracts. When two of his ministers defected to the opposition in late 1998 over the allegations of corruption, Mitchell lost his one-seat majority and was forced to call general elections 18 months early. On January 18, 1999, voters resoundingly indicated they were more concerned about the jobs Mitchell had brought to the island than with the corruption charges: The NNP won all 15 seats in the House. Mitchell himself received 89% in his district. The leader of one opposition party complained that with the snap election and short six-week campaign, "We were caught with our pants down."

In the next election on November 27, 2003, and the NNP was returned to power but with only a one-seat majority of 8–7.

Grenada was hit harder than any other country by Hurricane Ivan in September 2004, the most powerful storm in the Caribbean in at least 20 years. An estimated 85% of the homes and other buildings on the island, including Mitchell's home and the prison, were destroyed or damaged.

Mitchell waited the maximum five years before calling the latest election on July 8, 2008, probably because of a sluggish economy that actually shrank in 2006 (see Economy). The NDC's leader, Tillman Thomas, promised to lead Grenada out of the "disaster" he said Mitchell had created. The NDC won 11 of the 15 seats, and Thomas, a 63-year-old attorney who had been jailed by Maurice Bishop, became prime minister the following day. He promised to practice the "politics of inclusion."

Culture: The people of Grenada, 95% of whom are black or mulatto, are a fun-loving and hard-working group. Grenada's capital and main port, St. George's, rises steeply from the bay and the red-roofed houses are painted in pastel shades of pink and green. Nightlife in the city is often punctuated by continuous music from colorful Calypso bands.

Economy: Grenada is called the Isle of Spice, and for centuries its economy has been based on its nutmeg. It is presently the world's second-largest exporter of this product. Other exports include bananas, sugar, cacao and mace. The tourist industry is vital to the island's economic health. Most exports go to EC countries. An annual U.S. assistance package will be necessary indefinitely. Grenada and the Windward Islands were greatly favored by EC import limitations on bananas from other Caribbean sources.

GDP grew by only 0.6% in 2002, due in part to the general downturn in tourism following the September 11, 2001, terrorist attacks on the United States. Grenada has a public debt that in 2004 was 112% of GDP, the eighth highest in the world. The devastation of Hurricane Ivan in September 2004 was an economic catastrophe from which Grenada may take several years to recover.

The economy shrank by –1.1% in 2006, then grew by 4.3% in 2007 and 3.7% in 2008. Then global recession caused it to decline in 2009 by –04.0%.

The Future: The sluggish economy and corruption remain problems that need to be addressed by the new prime minister, Tillman Thomas.

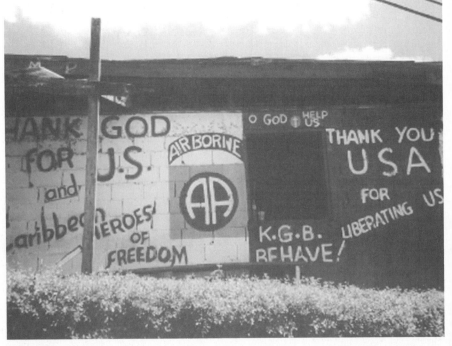

Mixed feelings still exist concerning U.S. invasion in 1983

Photo by Susan L. Thompson

370

THE DEPENDENT TERRITORIES

The dependencies in the Western Hemisphere have a wide variety of relationships with the nations controlling them. Those of Great Britain have various degrees of internal self-government. In the Caribbean area, the British attempt to unite several territories into the West Indian Federation failed, and Barbados, Guyana and Jamaica became sovereign nations shortly thereafter.

The islands of Guadeloupe and Martinique, and mainland French Guiana, are governed as *départments* of France. The Netherlands Antilles are internally self-governing. Puerto Rico is a commonwealth within the United States that possesses internal autonomy, and the U.S. Virgin Islands are federally administered territories of the United States. The Falkland Islands, lying off the coast of Argentina, are governed by the British and claimed by the Argentines.

Fort-de-France, Martinique; Mt. Pelee looms behind the capital. *Photo by Miller B. Spangler*

British dependencies

CAYMAN, TURKS AND CAICOS ISLANDS

Area: 269 square miles.
Population: 28,000 (estimated).
Administrative Capital: Georgetown (Pop. 4,700, estimated).
Heads of Government: Stuart Jack (Caymans); Gordon Wetherell (Turks and Caicos), governors.

These two groups of islands were administered by the Governor of Jamaica until 1962 when they were placed under the British Colonial Office. With the closing of the Colonial Office, administration passed to the Commonwealth Relations Office. The Cayman Islands lie midway between Jamaica and the western tip of Cuba. Turks and Caicos Islands are geographically a portion of the Bahamas. There are some 35 small islands in these groups, of which only eight are populated. The predominantly black and mulatto people eke a meager existence from fishing and the production of salt. Because of their limited resources, these islands cannot sustain themselves as independent nations. The Cayman Islands have become increasingly popular as a tax haven since the Bahamian government ended tax exempt status there for foreign corporations. There are numerous banks catering to "commerce," which means "laundering" money, the source of which is desired to be secret—usually narcotics. Crime associated with drug trade is increasing sharply. There are 532 banks, 80 of which actually have offices in the islands—one for every 53 people; more than 25,000 companies are registered to do business.

A five-member executive council is elected in the Caymans; political activity is minimal. Turks and Caicos Islands have a 20-member Legislative Council and an eight-member executive council.

FALKLAND ISLANDS

Area: 4,618 square miles.
Population: 3,140 (2008 estimate).
Administrative Capital: Port Stanley
Head of Government: Tim Thorogood, chief executive (since 2008).

The Falkland Islands are made up of two large and 200 small islands, treeless, desolate and windswept, which lie off the southern tip of Argentina in the Atlantic Ocean.

The British discovered and named the islands in 1690; the French established a small colony on one of the larger islands in 1764 and the British started a settlement on the other large island in the following year. France gave up its possession to Spain in 1767 and the Spanish drove the British from the island they occupied. The territory was abandoned by the Spanish in 1811, and Argentina, after gaining independence, established a small colony on the islands in 1824. This settlement was destroyed by the U.S. Navy in 1831 in retaliation for Argentine harassment of whaling ships from Boston.

The British again gained possession of the islands in 1833 and have held them since that time. Argentina claims the islands based on its effort of 1824. Originally of strategic importance because of their closeness to the Atlantic-Pacific sea route around the Cape, with the opening of the Panama Canal their value greatly decreased. However, the British Navy successfully struck from the islands against the German Navy in both world wars.

The islands are an economic liability to Britain, but are still a symbol of its sovereignty, not to be relinquished. When Argentina suddenly invaded the Falklands in April 1982, Britain met the challenge head on . . . successfully. A later dispute was resolved when Britain and Argentina agreed upon a joint, 200-mile fishing boundary around the islands calculated to exclude Japan, Russia and Taiwan.

Development of oil deposits within the 200-mile radius, and a new Argentine constitution reaffirming sovereignty over what it calls the *Islas Malvinas*, have created problems that will be difficult to solve.

A new constitution went into effect on January 1, 2009.

French dependencies

FRENCH GUIANA

Area: 34,740 square miles.
Population: 221,500 (2010 estimate).
Administrative Capital: Cayenne (Pop. 61,550, 2006 estimate).
Head of Government: Rodolphe Alexandre, regional president (since 2010).

French Guiana lies on the north coast of South America, north of Brazil and east of Suriname. The land consists of fertile, low plains along the coast, rising to the Tumuc-Humac Mountains on the Brazilian frontier. The Isles of Salut (Enfant Perdu, Remire and Ile du Diable—Devil's Island), lying off the coast, form part of the territory administered as a French *département*. The climate is tropical, with an average temperature of 80°F. The rainy season is from November to July, with the heaviest downfall in May.

Guiana was awarded to France in 1667, attacked by the British in the same year, taken by the Dutch in 1676 and retaken by France in the same year. In 1809 it was seized by a joint British-Portuguese effort based in Brazil, and remained under Brazilian occupation until 1817, when the French regained control. Gold was discovered in 1853, inspiring disputes with Brazil and Suriname which were not set-tled until 1915. The colony is best known for its infamous prison colony, which was closed in 1945.

Guiana has fertile soils, 750,000 acres of land suitable for stock raising, vast resources of timber and coastal waters abounding in shrimp and fish. However, only some 12,000 acres are cultivated and most foodstuffs are imported. The population consists of creoles (descended from African black ancestors), Europeans, Chinese and a few native Indians. The principal products are shrimp, gold, hardwood and rum. French Guiana has adequate resources to support itself as an independent state, but little or no effort has been made to exploit these resources.

For a brief interval, French Guiana loomed in France as a 20th century *El Dorado*. During a three-day visit to Guiana in 1975, Olivier Stirn, minister of territories, announced a resettlement plan for the French colony, one part of which would initially require 10,000 settlers to develop a pulp and lumber industry. The plan was adversely received by Guiana local leadership and was condemned by 11 Caribbean chiefs of state. Nevertheless, French immigration to the territory proceeded. A satellite-launching base was constructed at Kourou, and continental French now constitute about a third of the population of Guiana. They have gathered in an ultra-conservative political movement, the *Front National*, and, of course, oppose independence; the local movement for this faded quickly.

Political expression is mainly through the Guianese Socialist Party affiliated with the Socialist Party in France and the opposition Rally for the Republic, a Gaullist party affiliated with that of France. Guiana is one of 26 regions of France, called an overseas department, governed by a regional president with the advice and consent of a General Council and a Regional Council.

Vast unused resources remain under the dense rain forest that covers more than 70% of the land area. Intense farming is done by the industrious Hmong people of Laos who were transplanted here more than three decades ago. Timber and fish are the most important exports. Hydroelectric installations completed in 1993 provide all electricity needed, albeit at a substantial cost in local animal and bird life. As in so many other tropical settings of the region, social and economic unrest is at a high level and probably has no "cure."

GUADELOUPE

Area: 657 square miles.
Population: 448,700 (2006 estimate).
Administrative Capital: Basse-Terre (Pop. 44,864).
Head of Government: Jacques Gillot, president of the Regional Council (since 2001).

Guadeloupe consists of two islands separated by a narrow channel. Five small French islands in the Lesser Antilles are administered as a part of the Department of Guadeloupe (Marie Galante, Les Saintes, Desirade, St. Barthelemy and one-half of St. Martin).

Guadeloupe dependencies are occupied by the white descendants of Norman and Breton fishermen (and pirates) who settled there 300 years ago—the population is predominantly of mixed European and African derivation. The climate is tropical, with the rainy season extending from July to December.

Guadeloupe's principal products are bananas, sugar, rum, coffee, cocoa and tourism. Although this is an island of call for Caribbean cruises, it has excellent accommodations for extended vacations. The balance of trade is unfavorable and the *département* has little hope for independence.

The people are apparently content with a Regional Council and a General Council, the latter of which exercises executive power. Elections are on a party basis and are spirited; the one in 1992 had to be voided because of "irregularities." The right wing prevailed in a re-run.

A new World Trade Center opened on Guadeloupe in 1994 and is the seat of numerous efforts to boost Euro-Caribbean trade.

372

MARTINIQUE

Area: 420 square miles.
Population: 401,000 (2007 estimate).
Administrative Capital: Fort-de-France (Pop. 120,000, estimated).
Head of Government: Alfred Marie-Jeanne, regional president (since 1998).

Martinique has been in French possession since 1635 except for two short periods of British occupation. Mountainous, with Mt. Pelee reaching 4,800 feet, its climate is tropical; the rainy season extends from July to December; violent hurricanes are frequent during this period. An eruption of Mt. Pelee in 1906 killed 10,000 people. The population is predominantly of mixed European and African origin.

Martinique's principal products are sugar, rum, bananas and other tropical fruits. This island also is an attractive tourist haven, with modern facilities available widely. Cattle raising is a steady industry, but presently produces enough for local consumption only.

Netherlands dependencies

NETHERLANDS ANTILLES

Area: 395 square miles.
Population: 183,000 (2005 estimate).
Administrative Capital: Willemstad (Pop. 75,000, estimated).

The Netherlands Antilles consist of two groups of three islands each—one group lies off the north coast of Venezuela; the other lies just east of the Virgin Islands. Fully autonomous in internal affairs since 1954, the islands are organized into four self-governing communities—Aruba, Bonaire, Curaçao, and the Leeward Islands (southern portion of St. Martin, St. Eustatius and Saba). The population consists of about one third European ancestry and two thirds of mixed blood. Dutch is the official language. Spanish, English and a local *lingua franca* called Papamiento are also spoken. All of the islands are popular calls for cruise ships, and have, with the exception of St. Eustatius and Saba, have good facilities for extended vacations.

The economy of the Netherlands Antilles is based on the large oil refineries on Curaçao and Aruba. Almost all articles for consumption must be imported because fishing does not fill local needs and an arid climate coupled with poor soil do not support agriculture. The islands of Bonaire, St. Martin, St. Eustatius and Saba are of little economic importance. Despite some discontent among the non-European population, it is not likely that the islands will seek independence. Aruba was granted separate status from the other islands in 1986, with full independence set for 1996.

The lingering question of independence was probably laid to rest by balloting in 1993 on Curaçao and in 1994 on the remaining islands. Voters chose to remain a Dutch territory by a large majority, rejecting even the semi-independence that had been granted to Aruba. They undoubtedly wished a continuation of benefits derived from an annual Dutch subsidy of U.S. $160 million. Aruba, originally scheduled to become completely independent in 1996, instead continues in "special status."

The island of Curaçao has evidently been chosen as a drug outlet by Colombian, Surinamese and Dutch traffickers—rivals and their hired thugs fought pitched battles in late 1993.

Willemstad, Curaçao

United States dependencies

El Morro fortress for centuries guarded the entrance to the harbor at San Juan.

PUERTO RICO

Area: 3,423 square miles.
Population: 3,977,663 (2010 est.).
Capital: San Juan (Pop. 2,450,292 in 2000, greater metropolitan area).
Gross domestic product: $87.79 billion in 2009 ($22,071 per capita).
Head of Government: Luis Guillermo Fortuño Burset (b. October 31, 1960) governor (since January 2, 2009).

The easternmost and smallest island of the Greater Antilles, Puerto Rico is somewhat rectangular in shape, measuring 111 miles from east to west and about 36 miles north to south at its widest point; it includes four offshore islands, two of which are populated. Centrally located at almost the middle of approximately 7,000 tropical islands, most of them very tiny, hardly more than atolls, much of the island is mountainous or hilly—three quarters of the terrain is too steep for large-scale, mechanized cultivation. Puerto Rico is a *commonwealth* of the United States—while not a state, it is legally within the territorial jurisdiction of the U.S. The people are by language and culture part of the Caribbean and Latin America. Since it is not a state, Puerto Rico has no voting rep-

resentation in Congress, but does have an elected resident commissioner with a four-year term who holds a seat, can speak out on issues, but does not have a vote. Otherwise, he enjoys the same privileges and immunities of other congressmen.

History: Columbus discovered Puerto Rico in 1493. There were at least three native cultures on the island, mostly of Arawak origin from the South American mainland. They were a peaceful group, quickly enslaved by the Spaniards and

eventually died out as a race. Columbus claimed the island for Spain and named it San Juan Bautista (St. John the Baptist). After many years of colonization, the island was given the name Puerto Rico (Rich Port) and its capital city became San Juan.

Its first governor was Juan Ponce de León, who was later to discover Florida in his fabled search for the Fountain of Youth. Almost from the time of early colonization, Puerto Rico was a military target due to its strategic location. The

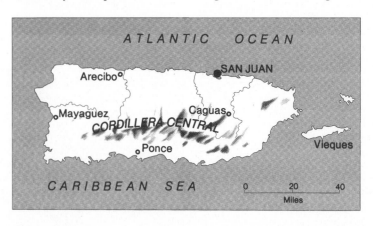

374

French, British and Dutch were repelled over the centuries and massive fortifications were erected by Spain to guard the harbor at San Juan.

The 18th century was rather uneventful, and during Latin American wars for independence, Puerto Rico remained faithful to Spain. Sugar, tobacco and coffee produced on the island found a ready market in the United States, as did its flourishing rum industry. Toward the middle of the 19th century, Puerto Rican social consciousness came slowly to life. In 1868 there was a revolution against Spain, which was quickly snuffed out.

Slavery was abolished in 1873. As the 19th century came to a close, Spain granted Puerto Rico broad powers of self-rule, but only days after the new government assumed its duties the Spanish-American war broke out. The U.S. public had been appalled by the stories of harsh treatment of Cuban revolutionaries, which caused a growing anti-Spanish sentiment in the United States, carefully fed by the press, which printed sensational stories of supposed atrocities. After the battleship *U.S.S. Maine* was mysteriously blown up in Havana harbor on February 15, 1898, the United States declared war on Spain. One of the operations was the invasion of Puerto Rico by American forces under General Nelson A. Miles the following July.

The treaty of peace signed in Paris in December after the brief conflict forced Spain to withdraw from Cuba, and ceded to the United States were Puerto Rico, Guam and the Philippines. The Spanish-American War established the United States as a world power. A military government was set up in Puerto Rico, and in 1900 the first civil government was established. It gave the U.S. government full control over island affairs, with the president appointing the governor, the members of the Executive Council (legislature) and the island's Supreme Court. Members of the House of Delegates, which functioned as a second legislative branch, were popularly elected. All trade barriers with the United States were removed as Puerto Rico was placed within existing U.S. tariff walls. The island, the Philippines and Guam, were collectively designated an "unincorporated territory."

With the advent of civil government, men were again allowed the right to vote as they had under Spain. Also, the island was exempted from paying federal taxes; duties and excise taxes collected in Puerto Rico on foreign products and on Puerto Rican products sold in the United States were handed over to the island treasury. Between 1900 and 1925, foreign trade increased from $16 million to $178 million annually; it now more than $14 billion. A

corresponding population increase occurred: from some 950,000 in 1905 to 1.3 million in 1921.

The school system expanded rapidly, reducing illiteracy from about 90% to less than 50%. A more worrisome condition was the gradual concentration of wealth in fewer hands. Two half-mile tunnels were opened in 1909 through the mountains that provided irrigation for the south side of the island, very dry due to the constant trade winds. On the eve of World War I, Congress granted U.S. citizenship to Puerto Ricans and replaced the appointed Executive Council with a popularly elected Senate. However, the island remained exempt from federal taxes and was allowed to design its own tax system and raise its own revenues. Trade with the United States grew by leaps and bounds so that the island became one of the top consumers of U.S. goods in Latin America.

When the United States declared war on Germany in 1917, the Selective Service Act was extended to Puerto Rico by request of the island's government and some 18,000 men were inducted into service.

During the first decades of the 20th century, Puerto Rico developed its sugar production, but most of the profits went to absentee landlords in the United States. By the time of the Great Depression of 1929, there was mass unemployment, malnutrition and deteriorating health conditions. By 1930, unemployment stood at a frightening 60%. When the Roosevelt administration came into office in 1933, it extended a large measure of relief to the stricken island. Because of the dire conditions, a strong nationalist movement emerged seeking complete independence. The movement reached its peak in 1937, when police fired on a nationalist demonstration in the southern city of Ponce, killing 20 people.

Commonwealth Status

Puerto Rico played an important defense role in the Caribbean region during World War II. President Truman appointed a Puerto Rican governor for the island in 1946 and one year later signed a law permitting it to elect its own governor. In 1948, voters elected Luis Muñoz-Marín of the Popular Democratic Party (PDP). In 1950, U.S. Congress allowed the island to draft its own constitution, which was approved with amendments by the Congress and then ratified in a plebiscite in 1952. Governor Muñoz-Marín claimed the constitutional process and plebiscite were an act of self-determination, thus marking an end to American colonial rule. The Commonwealth was officially established on July 25, 1952, the 54th anniversary of the day the U.S. forces landed in 1898.

Despite the move toward self-determination, a small but aggressive minority of "nationalists" still clamored for full independence, eventually resorting to terrorism. A band of nationalists attempted to assassinate President Truman in a bloody shootout in Washington in 1951. Three years later, nationalist terrorists opened fire from the gallery of the U.S. House of Representatives, wounding five congressmen. Militant nationalism resurfaced in the 1970s with the creation of the so-called Armed Forces of National Liberation, or *FALN*. Between 1974 and 1983, the *FALN* was believed responsible for 130 terrorist bombings in the continental United States that killed six people and wounded dozens of others. The worst bombing, on a tavern in New York's Greenwich Village in 1975, killed four.

Muñoz-Marín laid the foundations for the industrial development of the island, aided by important incentives at home and aggressive promotion abroad. The program, called "Operation Bootstrap," was one of the 20th century's great success stories—Puerto Rico's economy was transformed from one based on a single crop (sugar) to a broadly based manufacturing one, creating a strong middle class and one of the highest standards of living in all of Latin America. Per capita income has increased geometrically since 1940. Further, university and college enrollment soared from about 5,000 students in 1945 to about 150,000 by the mid-1980s.

In a 1967 plebiscite, 60% of the voters favored continuation and improvement of the commonwealth status with the United States while 38% voted for statehood. The major independence groups boycotted the plebiscite. The pro-statehood New Progressive Party (PNP) won the governor-

Former Governor Pedro J. Rosselló

Puerto Rico

Street scene in Ponce, Puerto Rico's second largest city

Photo by Miller B. Spangler

ship in 1968, winning again in 1976 and 1980. The pro-commonwealth *PDP* won in 1972, 1984 and 1988. These frequent changes in power produced a virtual stalemate on the political status of the island. This still goes on; the effect is to discourage investment in job producing facilities in Puerto Rico.

In spite of then-President George H. W. Bush's support for Puerto Rican statehood, the matter was bottled up in Congress in 1989–91; the Republicans did not wish to give Democrats an opportunity to tighten their hold on both houses of Congress. In a gesture of defiance, Puerto Rico enacted a measure providing that Spanish was the only official language. It was later repealed by a measure in 1993 recognizing both Spanish and English. Only the wealthy and middle-class are genuinely bilingual.

Roselló and Referendums

In the 1992 elections, the *PNP* and its candidate for governor, Pedro J. Rosselló, again ran on a platform advocating statehood. The *PDP* favored continuing commonwealth status, and was soundly trounced in its worst defeat in its 44-year history. The victors held another referendum (non-binding) on statehood in November 1993. Fully 73% of the electorate participated and the result was 48.4% for commonwealth status and 46.2% for an

application for statehood. Less than 5% favored independence. Rosselló, ignoring the result, and insisted that the struggle for statehood would go on.

Rosselló was reelected in 1996, which he interpreted as a mandate to continue his quest for statehood. Responding to his persistent efforts, the U.S. House of Representatives voted in 1998 for a *binding* referendum that ostensibly would decide the issue once and for all; the measure passed by only one vote, however, and the Senate failed to follow up.

Marking the 100th anniversary of U.S. occupation in July 1998, Rosselló then called for yet another non-binding referendum for December. Five options were listed on the complicated ballot: statehood, independence, an ambiguous "free association," continued commonwealth and "none of the above." The opposition *PDP*, however, advocated instead what it called an "enhanced commonwealth" by which Puerto Rico could enter into treaties with other nations and would have the power to annul federal laws, definitely the best of both worlds but which likely would never win congressional approval. As its "enhanced commonwealth" was not on the ballot, the *PDP* campaigned vigorously for "none of the above." The 1998 referendum was a near-duplicate of the 1993 plebiscite, only this time "none of the above" won a slim but absolute majority of 50.2%, while the vote for state-

hood was virtually unchanged at 46.5%. Independence received 2.5%, "free association" 0.3% and commonwealth only 0.1%. This sent the ambiguous message that Puerto Ricans were ready to change their status, but didn't yet know what that status should be.

Meanwhile, a corruption scandal exploded in 1999 that tarnished Rosselló's reputation and credibility and proved a major political liability for the *PNP* in the 2000 elections. The former comptroller of the San Juan AIDS Institute—an entity Rosselló had approved in 1987 when he was health director of San Juan—pleaded guilty to conspiracy and testified that $2.2 million in federal funds intended for AIDS victims had been diverted to the political campaigns of both the *PNP* and *PDP*, including Rosselló, who allegedly received $250,000 for his 1992 campaign. Rosselló dismissed the allegations as a "character assassination." Although the governor himself was never indicted, he underwent the ignominy of appearing on the witness stand in the trials that ended in 2000 with the convictions of two high-ranking officials.

Then, in August 2000, 18 *PNP* officials, including two mayors, were indicted on federal charges that they received $800,000 in campaign donations in exchange for $56 million in government contracts. Several of them also were convicted in 2001.

Rosselló also stood accused by pro-*PDP* newspapers of employing the time-honored cudgel of Latin American dictators of withholding government advertising from them. *El Nuevo Día*, which lost its government advertising after several investigative articles on corruption, sued the government in 1997. In 1999, the paper and the government reached a settlement by which the government restored the advertising, established a policy for distributing advertising fairly and expressed its respect for press freedom, but while the paper granted the government discounted rates.

In 1999, President Clinton sparked controversy by granting clemency to 12 convicted members of the *FALN* and another militant group, the *Macheteros*, or machete wielders, in exchange for their promise to renounce terrorism. None had been convicted of any of the bombings of the 1970s and '80s, but on charges of seditious conspiracy and weapons possession. Nine of the prisoners accepted the clemency offer, and returned to heroes' welcomes in Puerto Rico. Even Governor Rosselló supported Clinton's offer. Not so the Republican-controlled Congress, which passed a stinging censure resolution against the president for his perceived softness on terrorists. Other critics alleged the clemency bid was designed to help Hillary Clinton win Puerto Rican votes in her successful campaign for the U.S. Senate from New York in 2000.

Independence activists seized the national spotlight again in 1999 and 2000 with their support for the 9,100 residents of the island of Vieques, who were protesting the island's use by the U.S. Navy as a bombing and gunnery range. The Navy had bombarded Vieques since 1941, but residents now complained that they were endangered by the exercises and by unexploded ordnance. Public protests began when a resident of the island was killed by a stray bomb in 1999. President Clinton announced a five-year withdrawal plan to placate the islanders. But they were not placated. In 2000, 200 residents staged a nonviolent occupation of the range, forcing federal agents to take them into custody for trespassing on federal property. The occupation and arrests became the focus of national and international media attention.

More protesters were arrested in 2001, while others sought redress in federal court to enjoin the Navy from using the range. But a federal court ruled in favor of the Navy, which resumed target practice. Even pro-commonwealth Puerto Ricans were offended by the Navy's arrogance. The Rev. Al Sharpton, a controversial civil rights activist from New York City, who like Mrs. Clinton was believed to be cur-

Former Governor Sila María Calderón

rying favor among Puerto Rican voters there for his presidential run, was among several protesters arrested on Vieques for trespassing on the range.

A referendum was held in July 2001, in which the island's residents voted 68% for the Navy to leave immediately. President George W. Bush announced that the Navy would abandon Vieques in 2003—not soon enough for many critics.

First Woman Governor

The corruption scandals of the Rosselló administration forced him to decide, wisely, not to seek a third term. Instead, the wounded *PNP* nominated Carlos Pesquera, a former secretary of transportation and public works, while the *PDP* nominated a woman, Sila María Calderón; the Puerto Rican Independence Party (*PIP*) nominated Rubén Berrios.

The Vieques issue overshadowed the campaign, with Pesquera largely avoiding it, Berrios trumpeting it and Calderón making only vague statements in support of the island's residents. An extraneous issue was interjected into the campaign when a pro-statehood federal judge in San Juan ruled in favor of 11 residents who demanded the right to vote in the U.S. presidential election between Al Gore and George W. Bush. The *PDP* and the *PIP* challenged the ruling, and the 1st U.S. Circuit Court of Appeals in Boston ruled that Puerto Ricans did not have that constitutional right.

The gubernatorial election was another reminder of how divided Puerto Ricans are on the statehood issue, and the results were a virtual replay of the 1998 referendum: Calderón narrowly won with 48.5% of the vote to 46.1% for Pesquera and 4.9%

for Berrios. The *PDP* also won clear majorities in the House and Senate. However, the *PNP's* Jorge Santini recaptured the mayoralty of San Juan after 12 years of *PDP* control, making him a rising star in the party.

After her inauguration on January 2, 2001, as Puerto Rico's first woman governor, Calderón suddenly became far more strident in demanding that the Navy leave Vieques. She discussed the issue with President Bush in Washington soon after his own inauguration.

The Vieques controversy continued to simmer for two years. In 2002, the Navy notified Calderón that it would resume bombing exercises on the island, which brought a tart rebuke from the governor. But in October, the Navy did an about-face and announced that it would abandon Vieques the following May. It kept its word, and on May 1, 2003, the Navy's bombing range—along with six decades' worth of unexploded ordnance—reverted to Puerto Rican control. Jubilant celebrations, some of which turned ugly, marked the transition. Calderón sought federal help in cleaning up the old bombing range.

The commonwealth-statehood-independence debate continued to raise controversy between elections and referenda; even license plates became an issue. The new license plates issued under the Calderón administration contained the legend, "Free Associated State." Both the *PNP* and the *PIP* denounced the plates as a *PDP* political statement.

2004 Electoral Deadlock

Governor Calderón opted not to seek re-election in 2004, and the *PDP* nomination went to Aníbal Acevedo Vila, Puerto Rico's resident commissioner to the U.S. Congress. Despite the past scandals, the *PNP* nominated former Governor Rosselló instead of Pesquera. The *PIP* again ran Berrios. Acevedo scored points by raising the corruption issue and by promising to come to terms with the alarming increase in crime that was frightening and angering Puerto Ricans. Calderón had been compelled to put the National Guard on the streets of San Juan in 2004 to complement the police force. By year's end, Puerto Rico experienced a record 789 murders, up from 780 the year before.

Puerto Ricans had become accustomed to closely divided elections, but the November 2, 2004 contest was closer than ever. In the preliminary vote count, Acevedo led Roselló by a mere 3,880 votes out of 1,990,372 cast. Acevedo received 48.38% to Rosello's 48.18%. By law, when the difference is less than 0.5 percentage points, a recount is mandatory. The results of the

Puerto Rico

Former Governor Aníbal Acevedo Vila
Source: BBC

recount by the elections commission reconfirmed Acevedo's razor-thin margin:

Acevedo	963,303	48.40%
Roselló	959,737	48.22%
Berrios	54,551	2.74%

In an eerie replay of the contested 2000 presidential vote count in Florida, the *PNP* disputed about 7,000 ballots that had been ambiguously marked for both the *PIP* as a party and for Acevedo for governor. Roselló went to U.S. district court in San Juan to have the votes disallowed. The *PDP* argued in the commonwealth court system that the ballots were valid votes for Acevedo. The Puerto Rico Supreme Court ruled that the ballots should be counted, while the federal judge said they should be counted pending his review of them. The *PDP* appealed to the 1st Circuit Court of Appeals in Boston, arguing that the election was a commonwealth, not federal, matter. A three-judge panel agreed that the Puerto Rico Supreme Court has jurisdiction over elections. On December 28, just five days before the inauguration, the elections commission certified Acevedo's 3,566-vote margin.

Roselló grudgingly said he would not contest the election further, but added that he still considered the election results "irregular and unjust." He could console himself that Acevedo had a legislature with a *PNP* majority of 18 of the 27 Senate seats and 34 of 51 House seats. A Roselló protégé, Luis Fortuño, was narrowly elected the new resident commissioner to Washington. It is the first time the governor and commissioner have been from different parties.

At his January 2, 2005, inauguration, Acevedo called for an end to the partisan bitterness that has so sharply divided Puerto Ricans. He also declared that he favored a U.S. withdrawal from Iraq within six months. At the time, 23 Puerto Ricans had been killed in the war.

In March, Acevedo laid off more than 23,000 public employees in an effort to reduce a mounting budget deficit. In April, the *PNP*-controlled legislature passed a vague law that called on Washington to abide by any future decision by Puerto Ricans on the island's status. Acevedo vetoed it.

The crisis surrounding the $740 million deficit continued, as the *PDP* governor and *PNP*-controlled legislature deadlocked on a solution and each blamed the other for the gridlock. On May 1, 2006, the commonwealth officially ran out of money, and about 100,000 public employees, including 40,000 teachers, were furloughed indefinitely. The impasse was temporarily resolved when the legislature approved, and Acevedo signed, an emergency loan measure designed to keep the governing running until the end of the fiscal year on June 30.

The 2008 Election

Acevedo ran for re-election in 2008, and he endorsed Democratic presidential candidate Barack Obama. But in March 2008, Acevedo and 12 others were charged in federal court with 19 counts of conspiracy to violate U.S. campaign finance laws and of giving false statements to the FBI. He was not jailed, although five of the suspects were arrested and appeared in court in handcuffs. They were accused of illegally raising money to pay off Acevedo's campaign debts. Acevedo maintained his innocence and claimed he was being persecuted by federal authorities because he criticized an FBI raid in 2005 in which a Puerto Rican nationalist activist was killed. He refused to resign or abandon his re-election bid.

Besides the pending charges, Acevedo was haunted during the campaign by a miserable economic record that actually saw a decline in the island's GDP in 2007 and 2008 (see Economy).

Fortuño, the resident commissioner to Washington, defeated former Governor Roselló in a *PNP* primary in March with almost 60% of the vote. The *PIP* nominated Edwin Irizarry Mora, while the "Puerto Ricans for Puerto Rico Party" fielded Rogelio Figueroa. The outcome of the voting on November 4, 2008:

Fortuño	1,014,852	52.8%
Acevedo	793,753	41.3%
Figueroa	53,033	2.8%
Irizarry	39,170	2.0%

Fortuño's winning margin of 220,000 votes was the largest in the commonwealth's history. His handpicked choice for resident commissioner, Attorney General Pedro Pierluisi, also was elected. In-

Governor Luis Guillermo Fortuño

credibly, the *PNP* swept all the Senate seats with 81.5% of the vote and almost all the House seats with 72.5%, but by law the opposition is guaranteed representation. The *PNP* thus has 22 of the 27 Senate seats and 37 of the 51 House seats.

Fortuño, who holds a bachelor's degree from Georgetown University and a law degree from the University of Virginia, was inaugurated on January 2, 2009.

Puerto Ricans of all parties were understandably electrified in May 2009 when President Obama nominated Sonia Sotomayor, an appeals court judge of Puerto Rican parentage, to the U.S. Supreme Court. Sotomayor herself was born in the Bronx, New York, and was educated at Princeton and Yale. The Senate confirmed her on August 6.

Faced with a huge $3.2 billion budget deficit when he took office, Fortuño ordered a 10% cut in non-essential government spending, mostly perks like vehicles and cell phones. But when he announced plans to lay off almost 17,000 government employees, thousands of civil servants, students and clergymen staged a one-day general strike in October 2009. Fortuño's office issued a statement arguing that 70% of the commonwealth's budget goes for employee salaries and that Puerto Rico has a higher proportion of government workers per capita than any of the 50 states. The layoffs compounded an unemployment rate estimated at 15%, a result of the global and U.S. recessions.

Culture: For centuries the Spanish presence in Puerto Rico left an indelible imprint on the island, but it also has been a true melting pot, a blend of the Spanish with Indians and Africans. Color lines are thus blurred and racial tensions hardly exist.

The abundant literature of Puerto Rico emphasizes its colonial past and the island's fight to retain its Hispanic identity. Leading authors include Luis Rafael Sánchez, Pedro Juan Soto, José Luis González and Enrique Laguerre.

In art, José Campeche (1752–1809) produced some magnificent portraits and points of historical and religious themes. Francisco Oller (1833–1917) was influenced by the great figures of French impressionism—two of his paintings hang in the Louvre Museum in Paris. Today the island is particularly strong in silk screening and plastic arts, with recognized masters such as Lorenzo Homar, Rafael Tufiño, Julio Rosado del Valle, Manuel Hernández Acevedo, Carlos Raquel Rivera and later, Antonio Martorell, Myrna Baez and Luis Hernández Cruz. Also, Francisco Rodón has emerged as one of Latin America's leading portrait artists.

In the mainland United States, Puerto Rican performers in the movies, popular music, television and legitimate theater have included José Ferrer, Rita Moreno, Chita Rivera, Raúl Julia, Erik Estrada, Justino Díaz and Pablo Elvira, to mention only a few.

In recent years, Puerto Rican salsa singers like Ricky Martin have carved out a niche in U.S. and Latin American popular music. A new, underground musical genre on the island is called "raggaeton,"

a peculiar combination of Latin and hip-hop. Tego Calderón was the first raggaeton singer to sign a contract with a U.S. recording label, in 2005.

Puerto Rico's favorite sport is baseball, and it has contributed many dozens of players to the major leagues—in 1984 Willie Hernández of the Detroit Tigers was the American League's Most Valuable Player. The unforgettable Pittsburgh Pirate Roberto Clemente shares company in Baseball's Hall of Fame with such greats as Babe Ruth and Hank Aaron.

On the bleak side, Puerto Rican slums and housing projects are comparable to the worst in the United States. The murder rate rose to more than any of the 50 states during the 1990s (but not as high as Washington, D.C.), forcing the Governor Roselló in 1993 and Governor Calderón in 2004 to call out the National Guard with assault weapons to reduce street violence. Most of it is related to drug trafficking and use. It has grown even worse; in 2004, the island recorded 200 homicides more than New York City, which has twice the population.

Economy: Although the Puerto Rican economy is reasonably strong, it has its problems. The main pillar of the economy is manufacturing. The island has nearly 2,000 plants, the majority of which are

subsidiaries of U.S. companies attracted to Puerto Rico mainly because of tax advantages. The 1987 tax reforms, however, altered these incentives. These industries are geared to producing export items—the famous Bacardi Rum, for example, is produced on the island. Puerto Rico is a favorite location for U.S. pharmaceutical manufacturers because of particular tax advantages derived from locating on the island.

With industrialization, agricultural production, the dominant sector of the economy, commenced a decline starting in the 1950s. Agricultural workers first went to San Juan and then immigrated to the United States in search of jobs. As a result, about 3 million people of Puerto Rican heritage are now living in the United States.

Tourism, after manufacturing and agriculture, has been one of the mainstays of the economy. It now stands seriously threatened by crime directly connected to a burgeoning drug traffic from Colombia to the United States. It is relatively easy to get cocaine to the island and difficult to prevent it from entering the mainland United States since Puerto Ricans are citizens and need pass no more than the security check for weapons on flights to the United States, particularly New York. An area in which there could be much im-

PUERTO RICO

provement is government employment: fully 28% of the people work for the government, a figure about 15% too high, at an enormous, unnecessary cost.

If Puerto Rico were independent, its per capita income of about $17,800 would be the highest in Latin America. In relative terms, that is only about one third the per capita income of the U.S. mainland, but it is five times as much as Puerto Rico's closest sovereign neighbor, the Dominican Republic. Because wages are so much higher than in other Caribbean countries, however, Puerto Rico is at a disadvantage in the competition for tourism.

Nonetheless, economic growth has been lackluster in recent years. In 2006, growth was only 0.5%; it declined by –1.8% in 2007, –2.0% in 2008 and –3.2% in 2009.

Although Puerto Ricans pay no federal income tax, they qualify for welfare and unemployment benefits; unemployment is about 14%, compared with less than 9% on the U.S. mainland. Moreover, the island receives about $10 billion in aid from the mainland. In other words, the Puerto Ricans have the best of both worlds, which helps explain why a clear majority of them continues to eschew both statehood and independence.

The Future: Luis Fortuño's landslide victory for governor in 2008 was probably due more to the federal charges hanging over Governor Acevedo and to Acevedo's miserable economic record rather than to any groundswell of support for statehood, the *PNP*'s overriding cause. However, now that she has been confirmed as a U.S. Supreme Court justice, it will be interesting to see whether the surge of pride by Puerto Ricans has an unintended side effect of increased support for statehood, in both Puerto Rico and Washington, even though Sotomayor herself was not born on the island.

U.S. VIRGIN ISLANDS

Area: 132 square miles
Population: 109,755 (2010 est.).
Administrative Capital: Charlotte Amalie (Pop. 19,000, 2004 estimate).
Head of Government: John de Jongh, governor (since 2006).

The U.S Virgin Islands lie about 40 miles east of Puerto Rico and consist of three major islands (St. Croix, St. Johns and St. Thomas) and some 50 small islands and cays, mostly uninhabited. The islands were acquired by purchase from Denmark in 1917 and are administered as a Federal Territory by the U.S. Department of the Interior. Although voters turned down a proposed new constitution in 1978, attempts are being made to write a new charter. Most residents seem to prefer commonwealth status—rather than independence or statehood—with the United States.

The islands are hilly, with arable land given to small farms. The climate is tropical, with a May to November rainy season.

The population is about 20% North American and European descent; the remainder is of African and mixed heritage. The principal products for export are rum and bay rum, the fragrant distilled oil of the bayberry leaf. Cattle raising and truck farming are important for local consumption. The islands do not possess resources adequate for support as an independent entity.

Prosperity in the 1970s brought a tremendous influx of immigrants—now only about 40% of the islanders are natives. The ethnic derivation of these "newcomers" was about 75% black from neighboring Caribbean nations, including Haitians, and 25% white U.S. mainlanders. Because the Virgin Islands in the past relied prin-

cipally on rum taxes for government expenses, tax changes have seriously undermined this scheme. The response was increased taxes on just about everything in the last several years—very unpopular to say the least. Tourism has been a mainstay of the economy and is being promoted. Unemployment remains very low by Caribbean standards—about 5%.

After an unsuccessful run in 2002, John de Jongh was elected governor in 2006.

A referendum of the islands' future relationship with the United States was held in late 1993 after being postponed because of a hurricane. Ninety percent voted for continued or enhanced status—the status quo. But only 27% of the electorate bothered to participate in the balloting; it thus did not meet validation requirements

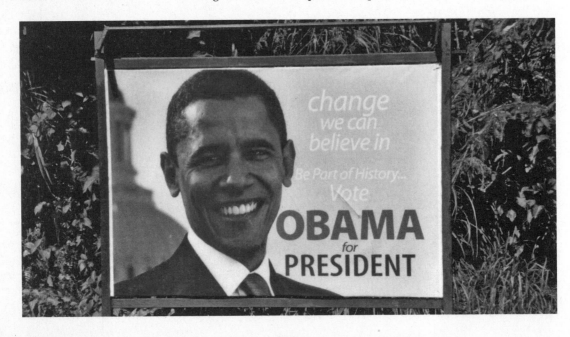

Selected Bibliography of Key English Language Sources

WEB SITES
Useful General Web Sites:
www.un.org (Web site for United Nations. Many links.)
www.unsystem.or (Official UN website)
http://europa.eu.int (EU server site)
www.oecd.org/daf/cmis/fdi/statist.htm (OECD site)
www.wto.org (World Trade Organization site)
www.worldbank.org/html/Welcome.html (World Bank news, publications with links to other financial institutions)
www.ceip.org (Carnegie Endowment for International Peace, using a fully integrated Web-database system)
www.cia.gov/index.html (Central Intelligence Agency)
www.odci.gov/cia (Includes useful CIA publications, such as *The World Factbook* and maps)
www.state.gov/www/ind.html (U.S. Department of State, including country reports)
http://usinfo.state.gov (U.S. Department of State)
lcweb2.loc.gov/frd/cs/cshome.html (Library of Congress with coverage of over 100 countries)
www.embassy.org/embassies (A site with links to all embassy web sites in Washington D.C.)
www.psr.keele.ac.uk\official.htm (Collective site for governments and international organizations)
www.desdecuba.com/generationy/

Newspapers, Journals and Television with good coverage on Latin American affairs:
www.chicagotribune.com (Named best overall U.S. newspaper online service for newspapers with circulation over 100,000.)
www.csmonitor.com (*Christian Science Monitor.* Named best overall U.S. newspaper online service for newspapers with circulation under 100,000.)
www.dallasnews.com (*The Dallas Morning News*)
www.diariolasamericas.com (*Diario las Américas*, Miami)
www.economist.com (British weekly news magazine)
www.miami.com/mld/miamiherald/news/world/americas/ (*The Miami Herald*)
www.nytimes.com
www.washingtonpost.com
www.washingtontimes.com
www.foreignaffairs.org (One of best-known international affairs journal)
www.cnn.com (Latest news with external links)
www.news.BBC.co.uk (British Broadcasting Corporation site)
www.c-span.org (Includes C-SPAN International)

www.sun-sentinel.com (South Florida Sun-Sentinel, Fort Lauderdale)

General
Adelman, Jeremy, ed. *Colonial Legacies: the Problem of Persistence in Latin American History.* New York: Routledge, 1999.
Alcántara Sáez, Manuel, ed. *Politicians and Politics in Latin America.* Boulder, CO: Lynne Rienner, 2008.
Álvarez, Sonia E. *Cultures of Politics, Politics of Cultures: Revisioning Latin American Social Movements.* Boulder, CO: Westview Press, 1998.
Appelbaum, Nancy P., Anne S. Macpherson, and Karin Alejandra Rosemblatt, eds. *Race and Nation in Modern Latin America.* Chapel Hill: University of North Carolina Press, 2003.
Arnson, Cynthia. *Comparative Peace Processes in Latin America.* Stanford, CA: Stanford University Press, 1999.
Atkins, G. Pope. *Latin America and the Caribbean in the International System.* Boulder, CO: Westview Press, 1998.
Atkins, G. Pope. *Latin America in the International Political System.* Boulder, CO: Westview Press, 3rd. ed. 1995.
Barham, Bradford L. and Oliver T. Coomes. *Prosperity's Promise: the Amazon Rubber Boom and Distorted Economic Development.* Boulder, CO: Westview Press, 1996.
Barton, Jonathan R. *A Political Geography of Latin America.* London: Rutledge, 1997.
Beezley, William H. and Linda Curcio-Nagy, eds. *Latin American Popular Culture: an Introduction.* Wilmington, DE: Scholarly Resources, 2000.
Berg, Janine, Christoph Ernst and Peter Auer. *Meeting the Employment Challenge: Argentina, Brazil and Mexico in the Global Economy.* Boulder, CO: Lynne Rienner, 2006.
Bethell, Leslie, ed. *A Cultural History of Latin America: Literature, Music and the Visual Arts in the 19th and 20th Century.* New York: Cambridge University Press, 1998.
Bethell, Leslie, ed. Latin America since 1930. New York: Cambridge University Press, 1994.
Black, Jan Knippers, ed. *Latin America: Its Problems and Its Promise.* (3rd Edition) Boulder, CO: Westview Press, 1998.
Blake, Charles H. *Politics in Latin America.* St. Charles, Il: Houghton Mifflin, 2004.
Bonilla, Frank, et al., eds. *Borderless Borders: U.S. Latinos, Latin Americans, and the Paradox of Interdependence.* Philadelphia, PA: Temple University Press, 1998.
Britton, John A. *The United States and Latin America: a Select Bibliography.* Langham, MD: Scarecrow Press, 1997.
Brysk, Alison. *From Tribal Village to Global Village: Indian Rights and International*

Relations in Latin America. Stanford, CA: Stanford University Press, 2000.
Bulmer-Thomas, Victor. *The Economic History of Latin America since Independence.* New York: Cambridge University Press, 1994.
Burkholder, Mark A. and Lyman L. Johnson. *Colonial Latin America.* New York: Oxford University Press, 3rd ed. 1998.
Castañeda, Jorge G. *Utopia Unarmed: the Latin American Left after the Cold War.* New York: Random House, 1993.
Centeno, Miguel Angel, *Blood and Debt: War and the Nation-State in Latin America.* University Park: The Pennsylvania State University Press, 2002.
Chasteen, John Charles. *Born in Blood and Fire: a Concise History of Latin America.* New York: W.W. Norton & Company, 2000.
Chomsky, Noam. *Latin America: from Colonization to Globalization.* Hoboken, NJ: Ocean Press, 1999.
Chong, Nilda and Francia Baez. *Latino Culture: A Dynamic Force in the Changing American Workplace.* Yarmouth, ME: Intercultural Press, 2005.
Cleary, Edward L. and Timothy J. Steigenga, eds. *Resurgent Voices in Latin America: Indigenous Peoples, Political Mobilization and Religious Change.* New Brunswick: Rutgers University Press, 2004.
Cockcroft, James D. *Latin America: History, Politics, and U.S. Policy.* Chicago, IL: Nelson-Hall, 2nd ed. 1996.
Cooper, Andrew F. and Jorge Heine, eds., *Which Way Latin America? Hemispheric Politics Meets Globalization.* Washington: The Brookings Institution Press, 2009.
Craske, Nikki. *Women and Politics in Latin America.* Piscataway, NJ: Rutgers University Press, 1999.
Davis, Darien J. *Slavery and Beyond: the African Impact on Latin America and the Caribbean.* Wilmington, DE: SR Books, 1995.
Dealy, Glen Caudill, *The Latin Americans: Spirit & Ethos.* Boulder, CO: Westview Press, 1992.
De la Campa, Romban. *Latin Americanism.* Minneapolis, MN: University of Minnesota Press, 1999.
Dent, David W. *Monroe's Ghosts.* Westport, CT: Greenwood Publishing Group, 1999.
Diamond, Larry et al. *Democracy in Developing Countries: Latin America.* Boulder, CO: Lynne Rienner, 1999.
Dominguez, Jorge I. and Michael Shifter, eds., *Constructing Democratic Governance in Latin America,* 2nd Ed. Baltimore: The Johns Hopkins University Press, 2003.
Dominguez, Jorge I. *Democratic Politics in Latin America and the Caribbean.* Baltimore, MD: Johns Hopkins University Press, 1998.
Dominguez, Jorge I., ed. *Latin America's International Relations and Their Domestic*

Consequences: War and Peace, Dependency and Autonomy, Integration and Disintegration. New York: Garland Publishing, 1994.

Dominguez, Jorge I., ed. *Race and Ethnicity in Latin America.* New York: Garland Publishing, 1994.

Early, Edwin. *A History Atlas of South America.* Old Tappan, NJ: Macmillan Publishing Company, 1998.

Ellis, R. Evan, *China in Latin America: the Whats and Wherefores.* Boulder, CO: Lynne Rienner, 2009.

Fagg, John E. *Latin America: a General History.* New York: Macmillan Publishing Company, 3rd ed 1977.

Fauriol, Georges A. *Fast Forward: Latin America on the Edge of the Twenty-First Century.* New Brunswick, NJ: 1997.

Ferman, Claudia, ed. The Postmodern in Latin America Cultural Narratives: Collected Essays and Interviews. New York: Garland Publishing, 1996.

Ferreira, Leonardo. Centuries of Silence: The Story of Latin American Journalism. Westport, CT: Praeger, 2006.

Fitch, John S. *The Armed Forces and Democracy in Latin America.* Baltimore, MD: Johns Hopkins University Press, 1998.

Foders, Frederico and Manfred Feldsieper, eds. *The Transformation of Latin America.* Northampton, MA: Edward Elgar Publishing, 1999.

Foster, Dean. *The Global Etiquette Guide To Mexico and Latin America.* New York: John Wiley & Sons, Inc, 2002.

Fowler, Will, ed. *Ideologues and Ideologies in Latin America.* Westport, CT: Greenwood Publishing Group, 1997.

Franco, Jean, et al. *Profane Passions: Politics and Culture in the Americas.* Durham, NC: Duke University Press, 1999.

Garreton, Manual Antonia et al. *Latin America in the Twenty-First Century: Toward a New Sociopolitical Matrix.* Boulder, CO: Lynne Rienner, 2003.

Garreton, Manuel Antonia and Edward Newman, eds. *Democracy in Latin America.* Washington D.C.: Brookings, 2002.

Gilderhus, Mark T., et al., eds. *The Second Century: U.S.-Latin American Relations since 1889.* Wilmington, DE: Scholarly Resources, 1999.

Gill, Anthony. *Rendering Unto Caesar: The Catholic Church and the State in Latin America.* Chicago: University of Chicago Press, 1998.

Goodwin, Paul Jr. *Latin America* (10th Ed). Guilford, CT: The Dushkin Publishing Group, Inc., 2003.

Graham, Carol . and Eduardo Lora, eds., *Paradox and Perception: Measuring Quality of Life in Latin America.* Washington: The Brookings Institution Press, 2009.

Green, Roy E., ed. *The Enterprise for the Americas Initiative: Issues and Prospects for a Free Trade Agreement in the Western Hemisphere.* New York: Praeger, 1993.

Gutteridge, William F. *Latin America and the Caribbean: Prospects for Democracy.* Brookfield, VT: Ashgate Publishing Company, 1997.

Gwynne, Robert N. *Latin America Transformed: Globalization and Modernity.* New York: Oxford University Press, 1999.

Halebsky, Sandor and Richard L. Harris, eds. *Capital, Power, and Inequality in Latin America.* Boulder, CO: Westview Press, 1995.

Hamill, Hugh M., ed. Caudillos: *Dictators in Spanish America.* Norman, University of Oklahoma Press, 1992.

Harris, Richard L. and Jorge Nef, eds. *Capital, Power and Inequality in Latin America and the Caribbean, New Edition.* Lanham, MD: Lexington Books, 2008.

Hartlyn, Jonathan et al. Eds. *The United States and Latin America in the 1990s: Beyond the Cold War.* Chapel Hill: The University of North Carolina Press, 1992.

Harvey, Robert. *Liberators: Latin America's Struggle for Independence.* New York: The Overlook Press, 2000.

Henderson, James D., et al. *A Reference Guide to Latin American History.* Armonk, NY: M.E. Sharpe, 2000.

Hillman, Richard S., ed. *Understanding Contemporary Latin America*, 3rd ed. Boulder, CO: Lynne Rienner Publishers, 2005.

Hofman, André A. *The Economic Development of Latin America in the Twentieth Century.* Northampton, MA: Edward Elgar Publishing, 2000.

Howe, Brendan, Vesselin Popovski and Mark Notaras, eds., *Democracy in the South: Participation, the State and the People.* Washington: The Brookings Institution Press, 2010.

Jackiewicz, Edward L., and Fernando J. Bosco, eds. *Placing Latin America: Contemporary Themes in Human Geography.* Boulder, CO: Lynne Rienner Publishers, 2008.

Jorge, Antonio, et al., eds. *Capital Markets, Growth and Economic Policy in Latin America.* Westport, CT: Greenwood Publishing Group, 2000.

Kanellos, Nicolas and Cristela Perez. *Chronology of Hispanic-American History.* Detroit, MI: Gale Research, 1995.

Keen, Benjamin and Mark Wasserman. *A History of Latin America* (6th Edition). Boston: Houghton Mifflin Company, 2000.

Kelly, Philip. *Checkerboards & Scatterbelts: The Geopolitics of South America.* Austin: The University of Texas Press, 1997.

Landau, Saul. *The Guerrilla Wars of Central America: Nicaragua, El Salvador, and Guatemala.* New York: Saint Martin's Press, 1993.

Langley, Lester D. *The Americas in the Age of Revolution: 1750–1850.* New Haven, CT: Yale University Press, 1996.

Logan, Samuel, *This is for the Mara Salvatrucha—Inside the MS-13, America's Most Violent Gang.* New York: Hyperion Books, 2009.

Lombardi, Cathryn L. and John V. *Latin-American History. A Teaching Atlas.* Madison, WI: The University of Wisconsin Press, 1983.

Loveman, Brian. *For la Patria: Politics and the Armed Forces in Latin America.* Scholarly Resources, 1999.

Lowenthal, Abraham F., Theodore J. Piccone and Lawrence Whitehead, eds. *The Obama Administration and the Americas: Agenda for Change.* Washington: Brookings Institution Press, 2009.

Lynch, John, ed. *Latin American Revolutions, 1808–1826: Old and New World Origins.* Norman, OK: University of Oklahoma Press, 1994.

MacDonald, Scott B. and Georges A. Fauriol. *Fast Forward: Latin America on the Edge of the Twenty-First Century.* Piscataway, NJ: Transaction Publishers, 1998.

Mace, Gordon, Jean-Philippe Thérien and Paul A. Haslam, eds. *Governing the Americas: Assessing Multilateral Institutions.* Boulder, CO: Lynne Rienner, 2007.

Mainwaring, Scott, ed. *Presidentialism and Democracy in Latin America.* New York: Cambridge University Press, 1997.

Maldifassi, José and Pier A. Abetti. *Defense Industries in Latin American Countries: Argentina, Brazil, and Chile.* New York: Praeger, 1994.

Manzetti, Luigi. *Privatization South American Style.* New York: Oxford University Press, 2000.

Margheritis, Ana, ed. *Latin American Democracies in the New Global Economy.* North South Center Press, Miami: University of Miami, 2003.

Márquez, Ivan, ed. *Contemporary Latin American Social and Political Thought: An Anthology.* Lanham, MD: Rowman Littlefield Publishers, 2008.

Martz, John D., ed. *United States Policy in Latin America: a Decade of Crisis and Challenge.* Lincoln, NE: University of Nebraska Press, 1995.

Mendez, Juan E., et al., eds. *The (Un)Rule of Law and the Underprivileged in Latin America.* Notre Dame, IN: Notre Dame Press, 1999.

Millett, Richard L. and Michael Gold-Biss, eds. *Beyond Praetorianism: The Latin American Military in Transition.* North South Center Press, University of Miami, 1996.

Mills, Kenneth and William B. Taylor, eds. *Colonial Spanish America: a Documentary History.* Wilmington, DE: Scholarly Resources, 1998.

Morales, Juan Antonio and Gary McMahon, eds. *Economic Policy and the Transition to Democracy: the Latin American Experience.* New York: Saint Martin's Press, 1996.

Morley, Samuel A. *Poverty and Inequality in Latin America: the Impact of Adjustment and Recovery in the 1980s.* Baltimore,

MD: Johns Hopkins University Press, 1995.

O'Brien, Thomas F. Century of U.S. Capitalism in Latin America. Albuquerque, NM: University of New Mexico Press, 1999.

Oppenheimer, Andres. Saving the Americas: The Dangerous Decline of Latin America and What the U.S. Must Do. Mexico City: Random House Mondadori, 2007.

Orr, Bernadette M, and Cruz. Americas: Study Guide. New York: Oxford University Press, 1993.

Park, James William. Latin American Underdevelopment: a History of Perspectives in the United States, 1870–1965. Baton Rouge, LA: Louisiana State University Press, 1995.

Payne, Leigh A. Uncivil Movements: the Armed Right Wing and Democracy in Latin America. Baltimore, MD: Johns Hopkins University Press, 2000.

Peeler, John. Building Democracy in Latin America. Boulder, CO: Lynne Rienner Publishers, 1998.

Peeler, John. Building Democracy in Latin America. Third Edition. Boulder, CO: Lynne Rienner, 2008.

Peruzzotti, Enrique and Catalina Smulovitz, eds. Enforcing the Rule of Law: Social Accountability in the New Latin American Democracies. Pittsburgh: University of Pittsburgh Press, 2006.

Ramsey, Russell, Guardians of the Other Americas: Essays on the Military Forces of Latin America. Lanham, MD: University Press of America, Inc., 1997.

Roberts, Paul. The Capitalist Revolution in Latin America. New York: Oxford University Press, 1997.

Rochlin, James F. Vanguard Revolutionaries in Latin America: Peru, Colombia, Mexico. Boulder, CO: Lynne Rienner, 2003.

Roseberry, William, ed. Coffee, Society, and Power in Latin America. Baltimore, MD: Johns Hopkins University Press, 1995.

Rosenberg, Kincaid and Logan, eds. Americas, an Anthology. New York: Oxford University Press, 1992.

Rosenberg, Tina. Children of Cain. New York: Penguin Books, 1991.

Scheina, Robert L., Latin America's Wars (Vol. 1)—The Age of the Caudillo, 1791–1899. Washington: Brassey's Inc., 2003.

Sáez, Manuel Alcántara. Politicians and Politics in Latin America. Boulder, CO: Lynne Rienner, 2007.

Schoultz, Lars. Beneath The United States: A History of US Policy Toward Latin America. Cambridge: Harvard University Press, 1998.

Schoultz, Lars, et al., eds. Security, Democracy, and Development in U.S.-Latin American Relations. North South Center Press, University of Miami, 1996.

Schwaller, John F., et al., eds. The Church in Colonial Latin America. Wilmington, DE: Scholarly Resources, 2000.

Silva, Patricio, ed. The Soldier and the State in South America. Great Britain: Palgrave, 2001.

Skidmore, Thomas and Smith, Peter. Modern Latin America. (7th Edition). New York: Oxford University Press, 2009.

Smith, Gaddis. The Last Years of the Monroe Doctrine: 1945–1993. New York: Hill & Wang/Farrar, Straus & Giroux, 1994.

Smith, Peter H. Democracy In Latin America. Oxford: Oxford University Press. 2005.

Smith, Peter H. Talons of the Eagle: Dynamics of U.S.-Latin America Relations. New York: Oxford University Press, 1996.

Smith, William C., ed. Politics, Social Change, and Economic Restructuring in Latin America. Coral Gables, FL: University of Miami, North/South Center Press, 1997.

Stahler-Sholk, Richard, Harry E. Vanden and Glen David Kuecker, eds. Latin American Social Movements in the Twenty-first Century: Resistance, Power and Democracy. Lanham, MD: Rowman Littlefield Publishers, 2008.

Stallings, Barbara and Wilson Peres. Growth, Equity and Employment: the Impact of the Economic Reforms in Latin America and the Caribbean. Washington, DC: Brookings Institution Press, 2000.

Stephenson, Skye. Understanding Spanish-Speaking South Americans: Bridging Hemispheres. Yarmouth, ME: Intercultural Press, 2003.

Swenson, Russell G. and Susana C. Lemozy, eds. Democratización de la función de inteligencia: El nexo de la cultura nacional y la inteligencia estratégica. Washington: National Defense Intelligence College, 2009.

Taylor, Lance, ed. After Neoliberalism: What Next for Latin America? Ann Arbor, MI: University of Michigan Press, 1998.

Tenenbaum, Barbara A. Encyclopedia of Latin American History and Culture. New York: Scribner, 1996.

Thorp, Rosemary. Progress, Poverty and Exclusion: an Economic History of Latin America in the 20th Century. Washington, DC: Inter-American Development Bank, 1998.

Tulchin, Joseph S., and Ralph H. Espach, eds. Combating Corruption in Latin America. Baltimore: Woodrow Wilson Center Press, 2000.

Tulchin, Joseph S. and Ralph H. Espach, eds. Latin America in the New International System. Boulder, CO: Lynne Rienner, 2001.

Tulchin, Joseph. S. and Meg Ruthenberg. Citizenship in Latin America. Boulder, CO: Lynne Rienner, 2007.

Turner, Barry. Latin America Profiled: Essential Facts on Society, Business and Politics in Latin America. New York: Saint Martin's Press, 2000.

Ungar, Mark. Elusive Reform: Democracy and the Rule of Law in Latin America. Boulder, CO: Lynne Rienner, 2002.

Valtmeyer, Henry and James F. Petras. Dynamics of Social Change in Latin America. New York: Saint Martin's Press, 2000.

Vanden, Harry E. And Gary Prevost, Politics of Latin America. New York: Oxford University Press, 2008.

Vargas Llosa, Alvaro. Liberty For Latin America. New York: Farrar, Strauss and Giroux, 2005.

Vera, Leonardo. Stabilization and Growth in Latin America: a Critique and Reconciliation. New York: Saint Martin's Press, 2000.

Von Mettenheim, Kurt and James M. Malloy. Deepening Democracy in Latin America. Pittsburgh, PA: University of Pittsburgh Press, 1998.

Wiarda, Howard J., The Soul of Latin America: The Cultural and Political Tradition. New Haven: Yale University Press, 2001.

Youngers, Coletta A. and Rosin, Eileen, eds. Drugs and Democracy in Latin America. The Impact of U.S. Policy. Boulder, CO: Lynne Rienner, 2004.

Andes Region

Crandall, Russell, et al, eds. The Andes in Focus: Security, Democracy, and Economic Reform. Boulder, CO: Lynne Rienner, 2005.

Caribbean

Allahar, Anton, ed. Caribbean Charisma: Reflections on Leadership, Legitimacy, and Populist Politics. Boulder, CO: Lynne Rienner, 2001.

Beckles, Hilary M. and Verene Shepherd, eds. Caribbean Freedom: Economy and Society from Emancipation to the Present. Princeton, NJ: Markus Wiener Publishers, 1998.

Braveboy-Wagner, Jacqueline and Dennis J. Gayle, eds. Caribbean Public Policy Issues of the 1990s. Boulder, CO: Westview Press, 1997.

Braveboy-Wagner, Jacqueline, et al. The Caribbean in the Pacific Century: Prospects for Caribbean-Pacific Cooperation. Boulder, CO: Lynne Rienner Publishers, 1993.

Braveboy-Wagner, Jacqueline A. The Caribbean in World Affairs: the Foreign Policies of the English-Speaking States. Boulder, CO: Westview Press, 2000.

Carvajal, Manuel J. The Caribbean, 1975–1980: a Bibliography of Economic and Rural Development. Lanham, MD: Scarecrow Press, 1993.

Craton, Michael. Empire, Enslavement and Freedom in the Caribbean. Princeton, NJ: Markus Wiener Publishers, 1997.

Desch, Michael C., et al., eds. From Pirates to Drug Lords: the Post-Cold War Caribbean Security Environment. Albany, NY: State University of New York Press, 1998.

Dominguez, Jorge I., ed. Democracy in the Caribbean: Political, Economic, and Social Perspectives. Baltimore, MD: Johns Hopkins University Press, 1993.

Dominguez, Jorge I. Democratic Politics in Latin America and the Caribbean. Baltimore, MD: Johns Hopkins University Press, 1998.

Granberry, Julian, ed. *An Encyclopaedia Caribbeana: a Research Guide*. Detroit, MI: Omnigraphics, 2000.

Griffith, Ivelaw L. *The Political Economy of Drugs in the Caribbean*. New York: Saint Martin's Press, 2000.

Griffith, Ivelaw L. *The Quest for Security in the Caribbean: Problems and Promises in Subordinate States*. Armonk, NY: M.E. Sharpe, 1993.

Grugel, Jean. *Politics and Development in the Caribbean Basin: Central America and the Caribbean in the New World Order*. Bloomington, IN: Indiana University Press, 1995.

Hillman, Richard S. and Thomas D'Agostino, eds. *Understanding the Contemporary Caribbean*. Boulder, CO: Lynne Rienner, 2003.

Maingot, Anthony P. *The United States and the Caribbean: Challenges of an Asymmetrical Relationship*. Boulder, CO: Westview Press, 1994.

Marshall, Don D. *Caribbean Political Economy at the Crossroads: NAFTA and Regional Developmentalism*. New York: Saint Martin's Press, 1998.

Meditz, Sandra W. and Dennis M. Hanratty. *Islands of the Commonwealth of the Caribbean: a Regional Study*. Washington, DC: U.S. GPO, 1989.

Palmer, Ransford W., ed. *U.S.-Caribbean Relations: Their Impact on Peoples and Cultures*. Westport, CT: Greenwood Publishing Group, 1998.

Payne, Anthony and Paul Sutton, eds. *Modern Caribbean Politics*. Baltimore, MD: Johns Hopkins University Press, 1993.

Portes, Alejandro, ed. *The Urban Caribbean: Transition to the New Global Economy*. Baltimore, MD: Johns Hopkins University Press, 1997.

Sheperd, Verene, ed. *Women in Caribbean History*. Princeton, NJ: Markus Wiener Publishers, 1999.

Smith, Robert Freeman. *The Caribbean World and the United States: Mixing Rum and Coca-Cola*. Boston, MA: Twayne Publishers, 1994.

Stallings, Barbara and Wilson Peres. *Growth, Equity and Employment: the Impact of the Economic Reforms in Latin America and the Caribbean*. Washington, DC: Brookings Institution Press, 2000.

Taylor, Patrick. *Nation Dance: Religion, Identity and Cultural Difference in the Caribbean*. Bloomington, IN: Indiana University Press, 2000.

Tulchin, Joseph S. and Ralph H. Espach, eds. *Security in the Caribbean Basin: the Challenge of Regional Cooperation*. Boulder, CO: Lynne Rienner Publishers, 2000.

Central America

Alexander, Robert J. *Presidents of Central America, Mexico, Cuba and Hispaniola: Conversations and Correspondence*. New York: Praeger, 1995.

Booth, John A. and Thomas W. Walker. *Understanding Central America*. (3rd Edition) Boulder, CO: Westview Press, 1999.

Brockett, Charles D. *Land, Power and Poverty: Agrarian Transformation and Political Conflict in Central America*. Boulder, CO: Westview Press, 1998.

Coatsworth, John H. *Central America and the United States: the Clients and the Colossus*. Boston, MA: Twayne Publishers, 1994.

Dominguez, Jorge I., ed. *Democratic Transitions in Central America*. Gainesville, FL: University Press of Florida, 1997.

Foster, Lynn V. *A Brief History of Central America*. New York: Facts on File, 2000.

Krenn, Michael L. *The Chains of Interdependence: U.S. Policy toward Central America, 1945–1954*. Armonk, NY: M.E. Sharpe, 1996.

Langley, Lester D. and Thomas Schoonover. *The Banana Men: American Mercenaries and Entrepreneurs in Central America, 1880–1930*. Lexington, KY: University Press of Kentucky, 1995.

Lentner, Howard H. *State Formation in Central America: the Struggle for Autonomy, Development, and Democracy*. Westport, CT: Greenwood Publishing Publishing, 1993.

LeoGrande, William M. *Our Own Backyard: the United States in Central America, 1977–1992*. Chapel Hill, NC: University of North Carolina Press, 1998.

Logan, Samuel, *This is for the Mara Salvatrucha—Inside the MS-13, America's Most Violent Gang*. New York: Hyperion Books, 2009.

Meara, William R. *Contra Cross: Insurgency and Tyranny in Central America, 1979–1989*. Annapolis: Naval Institute Press, 2006.

Moreno, Dario. *The Struggle for Peace in Central America*. Gainesville, FL: University Press of Florida, 1994.

Paige, Jeffery M. *Coffee and Power: Revolution and the Rise of Democracy in Central America*. Cambridge, MA: Harvard University Press, 1997.

Scott, Peter D. *Cocaine Politics: Drugs, Armies and the CIA in Central America*. Berkeley, CA: University of California Press, 1998.

Torres-Rivas, Edelberto. *History and Society in Central America*. Austin, TX: University of Texas Press, 1993.

Walker, Thomas W. and Ariel C. Armony, eds. *Repression, Resistance and Democratic Transition in Central America*. Wilmington, DE: Scholarly Resources, 2000.

Weaver, Frederick Stirton. *Inside the Volcano: the History and Political Economy of Central America*. Boulder, CO: Westview Press, 1994.

Woodward, Ralph L. Jr. *Central America: a Nation Divided*. New York: Oxford University Press, 1999.

Argentina

Adelman, Jeremy. *Republic of Capital: Buenos Aires and the Legal Transformation of the Atlantic World*. Stanford, CA: Stanford University Press, 1999.

Alonso, Paula. *Between Revolution and the Ballot Box: the Origins of the Argentine Radical Party*. New York: Cambridge University Press, 2000.

Armory, Ariel C. *Argentina, the United States, and the Anti-Communist Crusade in Central America*. Athens, OH: Ohio University Press, 1997.

Balze, Felipe A.M. de la. *Remaking the Argentine Economy*. New York: Council on Foreign Relations, 1995.

Berg, Janine, Christoph Ernst and Peter Auer. *Meeting the Employment Challenge: Argentina, Brazil and Mexico in the Global Economy*. Boulder, CO: Lynne Rienner, 2006.

Biggins, Alan. *Argentina*. Santa Barbara, CA: ABC-CLIO, 1991.

Cavarozzi, Marcelo. *Argentina*. Boulder, CO: Westview Press, 1999.

Deutsch, Sandra McGee and Ronald H. Dolkart, eds. *The Argentine Right: Its History and Intellectual Origins, 1910 to the Present*. Wilmington, DE: Scholarly Resources, 1993.

Epstein, Edward and David Pion-Berlin. *Broken Promises? The Argentine Crisis and Argentine Democracy*. Boulder, CO: Lynne Rienner Publishers, 2008.

Erro, Davide G. *Resolving the Argentine Paradox: Politics and Development, 1966–1992*. Boulder, CO: Lynne Rienner Publishers, 1993.

Escude, Carlos. *Foreign Policy Theory in Menem's Argentina*. Gainesville, FL: University Press of Florida, 1997.

Feitlowitz, Marguerite. *A Lexicon of Terror: Argentina and the Legacies of Torture*. New York: Oxford University Press, 1998.

Foster, David W. and Melissa F. Lockhart. *Culture and Customs of Argentina*. Westport, CT: Greenwood Publishing Group, 1998.

Hinton, Mercedes S. *The State on the Streets: Police and Politics in Argentina and Brazil*. Boulder, CO: Lynne Rienner, 2006.

Horvath, Laszlo. *A Half Century of Peronism, 1943–1993: an International Bibliography*. Stanford, CA: Hoover Institution Press, 1993.

Ivereigh, Austen. *Catholicism and Politics in Argentina, 1810–1960*. New York: Saint Martin's Press, 1995.

Keeling, David J. *Contemporary Argentina: a Geographical Perspective*. Boulder, CO: Westview Press, 1997.

Manzetti, Luigi. *Institutions, Parties, and Coalitions in Argentine Politics*. Pittsburgh, PA: University of Pittsburgh Press, 1993.

Munck, Gerardo L. *Authoritarianism and Democratization: Soldiers and Workers in Argentina, 1976–1983.* University Park, PA: Pennsylvania State University Press, 1998.

Rein, Monica. Translated by Martha Grenzeback. *Politics and Education in Argentina, 1946–1962.* Armonk, NY: M.E. Sharpe, 1998.

Rock, David. *Authoritarian Argentina: the Nationalist Movement, Its History and Its Impact.* Berkeley, CA: University of California Press, 1993.

Sawers, Larry. *The Other Argentina: the Interior and National Development.* Boulder, CO: Westview Press, 1996.

Shumway, Nicolas. *The Invention of Argentina.* Berkeley, CA: University of California Press, 1996.

Tulchin, Joseph S., ed. *Argentina: the Challenge of Modernization.* Wilmington, DE: Scholarly Resources, 1998.

Barbados

Beckles, Hilary McD. *A History of Barbados: from Amerindian Settlement to Nation-State.* New York: Cambridge University Press, 1990.

Belize

Merrill, Tim L., ed. *Guyana and Belize: Country Studies.* Washington, DC: U.S. GPO, 2nd ed. 1993.

Sutherland, Anne. *The Making of Belize: Globalization in the Margins.* Westport, CT: Greenwood Publishing Group, 1998.

Wright, Peggy and Brian E. Coutts. *Belize.* Santa Barbara, CA: ABC-CLIO, 2nd ed. 1993.

Bolivia

Gallo, Carmenza. *Taxes and State Power: Political Instability in Bolivia, 1900–1950.* Philadelphia, PA: Temple University Press, 1991.

Gill, Lesley. *Teetering on the Rim: Global Restructuring, Daily Life and the Armed Retreat of the Bolivian State.* New York: Columbia University Press, 2000.

Hudson, Rex A. and Dennis M. Hanratty, eds. *Bolivia: a Country Study.* Washington, DC: U.S. GPO, 3rd ed. 1991.

Lehman, Kenneth D. *Bolivia and the United States: a Limited Partnership.* Athens, GA: University of Georgia Press, 1999.

Leons, Madeline B. and Harry Sanabria, eds. *Coca, Cocaine, and the Bolivian Reality.* Albany, NY: State University of New York Press, 1997.

Morales, Waltraud. *Bolivia: Land of Struggle.* Boulder, CO: Westview Press, 1992.

Morales, Waltraud Q. *A Brief History of Bolivia.* New York: Checkmark Books, 2004.

Brazil

Baronov, David. *The Abolition of Slavery in Brazil: the "Liberation" of Africans through the Emancipation of Capital.* Westport, CT: Greenwood Publishing Group, 2000.

Berg, Janine, Christoph Ernst and Peter Auer. *Meeting the Employment Challenge: Argentina, Brazil and Mexico in the Global Economy.* Boulder, CO: Lynne Rienner, 2006.

Boer, Werner. *The Brazilian Economy: Growth and Development.* Boulder, CO: Lynne Rienner, 2007.

Boxer, C.R. *The Golden Age of Brazil: Growing Pains of a Colonial Society.* New York: Saint Martin's Press, 1995.

Brainard, Lael and Leonardo Martínez-Díaz, eds., *Brazil as an Economic Superpower?* Washington: The Brookings Institution Press, 2009.

Bresser-Pereira, Luiz Carlos. *Economic Crisis and State Reform in Brazil: Toward a New Interpretation of Latin America.* Boulder, CO: Lynne Rienner Publishers, 1996.

Bresser-Pereira, Luiz Carlos. *Developing Brazil: Overcoming the Failure of the Washington Consensus.* Boulder, CO: Lynne Rienner Publishers, 2005.

Burns, E. Bradford. *A History of Brazil.* New York: Columbia University Press, 3rd ed. 1993.

Capistrano de Abreu, João. *Chapters in Brazil's Colonial History, 1500–1800.* New York: Oxford University Press, 1997.

Cavalcanti, Clovis de Vasconcelos, ed. *The Environment, Sustainable Development and Public Policies: Building Sustainability in Brazil.* Northampton, MA: Edward Elgar Publishing, 2000.

Cavaliero, Roderick. *The Independence of Brazil.* New York: Saint Martin's Press, 1993.

Chaffee, Wilber A. *Desenvolvimento: Politics and Economy in Brazil.* Boulder, CO: Lynne Rienner Publishers, 1997.

De la Barra, Ximena and Richard A. Dello Buono. *Latin America after the Neoliberal Debacle: Another Region is Possible.* Lanham, MD: Rowman Littlefield Publishers, 2008.

Eakin, Marshall C. *Brazil: Once and Future Country.* New York: Saint Martin's Press, 1997.

Fausto, Boris. *A Concise History of Brazil.* New York: Cambridge University Press, 1999.

Goertzel, Ted G. *Fernando Henrique Cardoso: Reinventing Democracy in Brazil.* Boulder, CO: Lynne Rienner Publishers, 1999.

Gordon, Lincoln. *Brazil's Second Chance. En Route toward the First World.* Washington, D.C.: Brookings, 2003.

Hanchard, Michael. *Racial Politics in Contemporary Brazil.* Durham, NC: Duke University Press, 1999.

Hecht, Tobias. *At Home in the Street: Street Children in Northeast Brazil.* New York: Cambridge University Press, 1998.

Hinton, Mercedes S. *The State on the Streets: Police and Politics in Argentina and Brazil.* Boulder, CO: Lynne Rienner, 2006.

Hudson, Rex A., ed. *Brazil: a Country Study.* Washington, DC: U.S. GPO, 5th ed. 1998.

Hunter, Wendy. *Eroding Military Influence in Brazil: Politicians against Soldiers.* Chapel Hill, NC: University of North Carolina Press, 1997.

Kingstone, Peter R. and Timothy J. Powers, eds. *Democratic Brazil: Actors, Institutions and Processes.* Pittsburgh, PA: University of Pittsburgh Press, 2000.

Kinzo, Maria, ed. *Brazil under Democracy. Economy, Polity, and Society since 1985.* Washington, D.C.: Brookings, 2003.

Lesser, Jeff. *Negotiating National Identity: Immigrants, Minorities, and the Struggle for Ethnicity in Brazil.* Durham, NC: Duke University Press, 1999.

Levine, Robert M. *Brazilian Legacies.* Armonk, NY: M.E. Sharpe, 1997.

Levine, Robert M. and John J. Crocitti, eds. *The Brazil Reader: History, Culture, Politics.* Durham, NC: Duke University Press, 1999.

Levine, Robert M. *Father of the Poor? Vargas and His Era.* New York: Cambridge University Press, 1998.

Mainwaring, Scott. *Rethinking Party Systems in the Third Wave of Democratization: the Case of Brazil.* Stanford, CA: Stanford University Press, 1999.

Matos, Carolina. *Journalism and Political Democracy in Brazil.* Lanham, MD: Lexington Books, 2008.

Page, Joseph A. *The Brazilians.* Reading, MA: Addison-Wesley, 1995.

Power, Timothy J. *The Political Right in Postauthoritarian Brazil: Elites, Institutions and Democratization.* University Park, PA: Pennsylvania State University Press, 2000.

Purcell, Susan K. *Brazil under Cardoso.* Boulder, CO: Lynne Rienner Publishers, 1997.

Reiter, Bernd. *Negotiating Democracy in Brazil: The Politics of Exclusion.* Boulder, CO: Lynne Rienner Publishers, 2009.

Ribeiro, Darcy and Gregory Rabassa. *The Brazilian People: the Formation and Meaning of Brazil.* Gainesville, FL: University Press of Florida, 2000.

Robinson, Roger. *Brazil.* Des Plaines, IL: Heinemann Library, 1999.

Roett, Riordan, *The New Brazil.* Washington: The Brookings Institution Press, 2010.

Skidmore, Thomas E. *Brazil: Five Centuries of Change.* New York: Oxford University Press, 1999.

Topik, Steven C. *Trade and Gunboats: the United States and Brazil in the Age of Empire.* Stanford, CA: Stanford University Press, 2000.

Von Mettenheim, Kurt. *The Brazilian Voter: Mass Politics in Democratic Transition.* Pittsburgh, PA: University of Pittsburgh Press, 1995.

Weyland, Kurt Gerhard. *Democracy without Equity: Failures of Reform in Brazil.*

Pittsburgh, PA: University of Pittsburgh Press, 1996.

Willumsen, Maria J., ed. *The Brazilian Economy: Structure and Performance*. Coral Gables, FL: University of Miami, North/South Center Press, 1997.

Chile

Bosworth, Barry P., ed. *The Chilean Economy: Policy and Challenges*. Washington, DC: Brookings Institution Press, 1994.

Collier, Simon and William F. Sater. *A History of Chile, 1808–1994*. New York: Cambridge University Press, 1996

Constanble, Pamela and Arturo Valenzuela. *A Nation of Enemies: Chile under Pinochet*. New York: W.W. Norton, 1993.

Davis, Madeleine, ed. *The Pinochet Case*. Washington, D.C.: Brookings, 2003.

Franceschet, Susan. *Women and Politics in Chile*. Boulder, CO: Lynne Rienner, 2005.

Hachette, Dominique and Rolf Luders. *Privatization in Chile: an Economic Appraisal*. San Francisco, CA: ICS Press, 1993.

Franceschet, Susan. *Women and Politics in Chile*. Boulder, CO: Lynne Rienner, 2005.

Hojman, David E. *Chile: the Political Economy of Development and Democracy in the 1990s*. Pittsburgh, PA: University of Pittsburgh Press, 1993.

Hudson, Rex A., ed. *Chile: a Country Study*. Washington, DC: U.S. GPO, 3rd ed. 1994.

Huneeus, Carlos. *The Pinochet Regime*. Boulder, CO: Lynne Rienner, 2007.

Lomnitz, Larissa Adler and Ana Melnick. *Chile's Political Culture and Parties: an Anthropological Explanation*. Notre Dame, IN: University of Notre Dame Press, 2000.

Lonregan, John B. *Legislative Institutions and Ideology in Chile*. New York: Cambridge University Press, 2000.

Monteon, Michael. *Chile and the Great Depression: the Politics of Underdevelopment, 1927–1948*. Tempe, AZ: Arizona State University, Center for Latin American Studies, 1998.

Oppenheim, Lois Hecht. *Politics in Chile: Democracy, Authoritarianism, and the Search for Development*. Boulder, CO: Westview Press, 2nd ed. 1998.

Oxhorn, Philip. *Organizing Civil Society: the Popular Sectors and the Struggle for Democracy in Chile*. University Park, PA: Pennsylvania State University Press, 1995.

Petras, James, et. al. *Democracy and Poverty in Chile: the Limits to Electoral Politics*. Boulder, CO: Westview Press, 1994.

Pietrobelli, Carlo. *Industry, Competitiveness and Technological Capabilities in Chile: a New Tiger from Latin America*. New York: Saint Martin's Press, 1998.

Puryear, Jeffrey. *Thinking Politics: Intellectuals and Democracy in Chile, 1973–1988*.

Baltimore, MD: Johns Hopkins University Press, 1994.

Quereshi, Lubna Z. *Nixon, Kissinger and Allende: U.S. Involvement in the 1973 Coup in Chile*. Lanham, MD: Lexington Books, 2008.

Roberts, Kenneth M. *Deepening Democracy? The Modern Left and Social Movements in Chile and Peru*. Stanford, CA: Stanford University Press, 1999.

Siavelis, Peter. *The President and Congress in Post-Authoritarian Chile: Institutional Constraints to Democratic Consolidation*. University Park, PA: Pennsylvania State University Press, 1999.

Sigmund, Paul E. *The United States and Democracy in Chile*. Baltimore, MD: Johns Hopkins University Press, 1993.

Silva, Eduardo. *The State and Capital in Chile: Business Elites, Technocrats, and Market Economics*. Boulder, CO: Westview Press, 1996.

Solimano, Andres. *Distributive Justice and Economic Development: the Case of Chile and Developing Countries*. Ann Arbor, MI: University of Michigan Press, 2000.

Spooner, Mary Helen. *Soldiers in a Narrow Land: the Pinochet Regime in Chile*. Berkeley, CA: University of California Press, 1994.

Valdes, Juan Gabriel. *Pinochet's Economists: the Chicago School in Chile*. New York: Cambridge University Press, 1995.

Verdugo, Patricia. *Chile, Pinochet, and the Caravan of Death*. Boulder, CO: Lynne Rienner, 2001.

Wheelan, James R., *Out of the Ashes: Life, Death and Transfiguration of Democracy in Chile, 1833–1988*. Washington: Regnery Gateway, 1989.

Colombia

Ardila Galvia, Constanza. *The Heart of the War in Colombia*. London: Latin American Bureau, 2002.

Brittain, James J. *Revolutionary Social Change in Colombia: The Origin and Direction of the FARC-EP*. London: Pluto Press, 2010.

Bouvier, Virginia M., ed. *Building Peace in a Time of War*. United States Institute for Peace Press, 2009.

Crandall, Russell. *Driven By Drugs: U.S. Policy Toward Colombia*. Boulder, CO: Lynne Reinner, 2002.

Davis, Robert H. *Historical Dictionary of Colombia*. Lanham, MD: Scarecrow Press, 2nd ed. 1993.

Drexler, Robert W. *Colombia and the United States: Narcotics Traffic and a Failed Foreign Policy*. Jefferson, NC: McFarland & Company, 1997.

Duzan, Maria Jimena. Translated and edited by Peter Eisner. *Death Beat: a Colombian Journalist's Life inside the Cocaine Wars*. New York: HarperCollins, 1994.

Gonsalves, Marc, Tom Howes, Keith Stansell and Gary Brozek, *Out of Captiv-*

ity: Surviving 1,967 Days in the Colombian Jungle. New York: Harper Collins, 2009.

Hanratty, Dennis M. and Sandra W. Meditz, eds. *Colombia: a Country Study*. Washington, DC: U.S. GPO, 4th ed. 1990.

Hristov, Jasmin. *Blood and Capital: The Paramilitarization of Colombia*. Athens: Ohio University Press, 2009.

Kirk, Robin. *More Terrible Than Death: Massacres, Drugs, and America's War in Colombia*. New York: Public Affairs, 2003.

Kline, Harvey F. *Colombia: Democracy under Assault*. Boulder, CO: Westview Press, 2nd ed. 1995.

Kline, Harvey F. *State Building and Conflict Resolution in Colombia, 1986–1994*. Tuscaloosa, AL: University of Alabama Press, 1999.

McFarlane, Anthony. *Colombia before Independence: Economy, Society, and Politics under Bourbon Rule*. New York: Cambridge University Press, 1993.

Menzel, Sewall H. *Cocaine Quagmire: Implementing the U.S. Anti-Drug Policy in the North Andes-Colombia*. Lanham, MD: University Press of America, 1997.

Mohan, Rakesh. *Understanding the Developing Metropolis: Lessons from the Study of Bogota and Cali, Colombia*. New York: Oxford University Press, 1994.

Posada-Carbo, Eduardo. *Colombia*. New York: Saint Martin's Press, 1997.

Rabasa, Angel and Peter Chalk. *Colombian Labyrinth: The Synergy of Drugs and Insurgency and Its Implications for Regional Stability*. Santa Monica: Rand Corp, 2001.

Rausch, Jane M. *The Llanos Frontier in Colombian History, 1830–1930*. Albuquerque, NM: University of New Mexico Press, 1993.

Safford, Frank and Marco Palacios. *Colombia: Fragmented Land, Divided Society*. New York: Oxford University Press, 2002.

Thorpe, Rosemary. *Economic Management and Economic Development in Peru and Colombia*. Pittsburgh, PA: University of Press, 1991.

Thoumi, Francisco E. *Political Economy and Illegal Drugs in Colombia*. Boulder, CO: Lynne Rienner Publishers, 1995.

Wade, Peter. *Blackness and Race Mixture: the Dynamics of Racial Identity in Colombia*. Baltimore, MD: Johns Hopkins University Press, 1993.

Costa Rica

Basok, Tanya. *Keeping Heads above Water: Salvadorean Refuges in Costa Rica*. Toronto: University of Toronto Press, 1993.

Biesanz, Mavis H., Richard Biesanz and Karen Z. Biesanz. *The Ticos: Culture and Social Change in Costa Rica*. Boulder, CO: Lynne Rienner, 1999.

Booth, John A. *Costa Rica: Quest for Democracy*. Boulder, CO: Westview Press, 1998.

Colesberry, Adrian and Brass McLean. *Costa Rica: the Last Country the Gods Made*. Helena, MT: Falcon Press, 1993.

Creedman, Theodore S. *Historical Dictionary of Costa Rica*. Lanham, MD: Scarecrow Press, 2nd ed. 1991.

Edelman, Marc. *Peasants against Globalization: Rural Social Movements in Costa Rica*. Stanford, CA: Stanford University Press, 2000.

Helmuth, Chalene. *Culture and Customs of Costa Rica*. Westport, CT: Greenwood Publishing Group, 2000.

Honey, Martha. *Hostile Acts: U.S. Policy in Costa Rica in the 1980s*. Gainesville, FL: University of Florida Press, 1994.

Miller, Eugene D. *A Holy Alliance? The Church and the Left in Costa Rica, 1932–1948*. Armonk, NY: M.E. Sharpe, 1996.

Rottenberg, Simon, ed. *Costa Rica and Uruguay*. New York: Oxford University Press, 1993.

Stansifer, Charles L. *Costa Rica*. Santa Barbara, CA: ABC-CLIO, 1991.

Wilson, Bruce M. *Costa Rica: Politics, Economics, and Democracy*. Boulder, CO: Lynne Rienner Publishers, 1998.

Yashar, Deborah J. *Demanding Democracy: Reform and Reaction in Costa Rica and Guatemala, 1870s–1950s*. Stanford, CA: Stanford University Press, 1997.

Cuba

Arbdeya, Jesus. Translated by Rafael Betancourt. *The Cuban Counterrevolution*. Athens, OH: Ohio University Press, 2000.

Baloyara, Enrique and James A. Morris. *Conflict and Change in Cuba*. Albuquerque, NM: University of New Mexico Press, 1993.

Benjamin-Alvarado, Jonathan. *Power to the People: Energy and the Cuban Nuclear Program*. New York: Routledge, 2000.

Blight, James G, et al. *Cuba on the Brink: Castro, the Missile Crisis, and the Soviet Collapse*. New York: Pantheon Books, 1993.

Bunck, Julie Marie. *Fidel Castro and the Quest for a Revolutionary Culture in Cuba*. University Park, PA: Pennsylvania State University, 1994.

Corbett, Ben. *This is Cuba*. Boulder, CO: Westview, 2002.

Diaz-Briquets, Sergio and Jorge Perez-Lopez. *Conquering Nature: the Environmental Legacy of Socialism in Cuba*. Pittsburgh, PA: University of Pittsburgh Press, 2000.

Fernandez, Damian J. *Cuba and the Politics of Passion*. Austin, TX: University of Texas Press, 2000.

Fursenko, Alexandr and Timothy J. Naftali. *"One Hell of a Gamble": Khrushchev, Castro and Kennedy, 1958–1964*. New York: W.W. Norton & Company, 1997.

Gonzalez, Edward and McCarthy, Kevin F. *Cuba After Castro. Legacies, Challenges,*

and Impediments. Santa Monica, CA: Rand, 2004.

Gott, Richard. *Cuba: A New History*. New Haven: Yale University, 2004.

Halperin, Maurice. *Return to Havana: the Decline of Cuban Society under Castro*. Nashville, TN: Vanderbilt University Press, 1994.

Hernandez, José M. *Cuba and the United States: Intervention and Militarism, 1868–1933*. Austin, TX: University of Texas Press, 1993.

Huddleston, Vicki and Carlos Pascual, *Learning to Salsa: New Steps in U.S.-Cuba Relations*.

Washington: The Brookings Institution Press, 2010.

Ibarra, Jorge. *Prologue to Revolution: Cuba, 1898–1958*. Boulder, CO: Lynne Rienner Publishers, 1998.

James, Ian Michael. *Ninety Miles: Cuban Journeys in the Age of Castro*. Lanham, MD: Lexington Books, 2008.

Jordan, David C. *Revolutionary Cuba and the End of the Cold War*. Lanham, MD: University Press of America, 1993.

Kirk, John M. *Canada-Cuba Relations: the Other Good Neighbor Policy*. Gainesville, FL: University Press of Florida, 1997.

Klepak, Hal. *Cuba's Military 1990–2005: Revolutionary Soldiers During Counter-Revolutionary Times*. New York: Palgrave MacMillan, 2005.

Kornbluh, Peter, ed. *Bay of Pigs Declassified: the Secret CIA Report*. New York: New Press, 1998.

Leonard, Thomas M. *Castro and the Cuban Revolution*. Westport, CT: Greenwood Publishing Group, 1999.

Luis, Julio Garcia. *Cuban Revolution Reader: a Documented History of 40 Years of the Cuban Revolution*. Hoboken, NJ: Ocean Press, 2000.

Mesa-Largo, Carmelo, ed. *Cuba after the Cold War*. Pittsburgh, PA: University of Pittsburgh Press, 1993.

Moses, Catherine. *Real Life in Castro's Cuba*. Wilmington, DE: Scholarly Resources, 2000.

Oppenheimer, Andres, *Castro's Final Hour: The Secret Story Behind the Coming Downfall of Communist Cuba*. New York: Simon & Schuster, 1992.

Paterson, Thomas G. *Contesting Castro: the United States and the Triumph of the Cuban Revolution*. New York: Oxford University Press, 1994.

Perez, Louis A., Jr. *On Becoming Cuban: Identity, Nationality and Culture*. Chapel Hill, NC: University of North Carolina Press, 1999.

Perez, Louis A., Jr., *Cuba: Between Reform and Revolution*. New York: Oxford University Press, 2005.

Perez-Lopez, Jorge F. *Cuba at a Crossroads: Politics and Economics after the Fourth Party Congress*. Gainesville, FL: University of Florida Press, 1994.

Perez-Lopez, Jorge F. *Cuba's Second Economy: from behind the Scenes to Center*

State. New Brunswick, NJ: Transaction Publishers, 1995.

Perez-Stable, Marifeli. *The Cuban Revolution: Origins, Course, and Legacy*. New York: Oxford University Press, 2nd ed. 1999.

Purcell, Susan Kaufman and David Rothkopf, eds. *Cuba: the Contours of Change*. Boulder, CO: Lynne Rienner Publishers, 2000.

Quirk, Robert E. *Fidel Castro*. New York: W.W. Norton, 1993.

Ritter, Archibald R.M. and John M. Kirk, eds. *Cuba in the International System: Normalization and Integration*. New York: Saint Martin's Press, 1995.

Roy, Joaquín. *Cuba, the United States, and the Helms-Burton Doctrine: International Reactions*. Gainesville, FL: University Press of Florida, 2000.

Santi, Enrico Mario, ed. *Cuban Studies XXIV*. Pittsburgh, PA: University of Pittsburgh Press, 1994.

Schwab, Peter. *Cuba: Confronting the U.S. Embargo*. New York: Saint Martin's Press, 2000.

Schulz, Donald E. *Cuba and the Future*. Westport, CT: Greenwood Press, 1994.

Skoug, Kenneth N. *The United States and Cuba under Reagan and Shultz: a Foreign Service Officer Reports*. New York: Praeger, 1996.

Stubbs, Jean, et al. *Cuba*. Santa Barbara, CA: ABC-CLIO, 1996.

Suchlicki, Jaime. *Cuba: from Columbus to Castro and Beyond*. McLean, VA: Brassey's, Inc.: 4th ed. 1997.

Szulc, Tad. *Fidel. A Critical Portrait*. NY: Avon Books, 1986.

Tulchin, Joseph S., et al., eds. *Cuba and the Caribbean: Regional Issues and Trends in the Post-Cold War Era*. Wilmington, DE: Scholarly Resources, 1997.

Dominican Republic

Atkins, G. Pope. *The Dominican Republic and the United States: from Imperialism to Transnationalism*. Athens, GA: University of Georgia Press, 1998.

Baud, Michiel. *Peasants and Tobacco in the Dominican Republic, 1870–1930*. Knoxville, TN: University of Tennessee Press, 1995.

Haggerty, Richard A., ed. *Dominican Republic and Haiti: Country Studies*. Washington, DC: U.S. GPO, 2nd ed. 1991.

Hall, Michael R. *Sugar and Power in the Dominican Republic: Eisenhower, Kennedy and the Trujillos*. Westport, CT: Greenwood Publishing Group, 2000.

Hartlyn, Jonathan. *The Struggle for Democratic Politics in the Dominican Republic, 1961–1996*. Chapel Hill, NC: University of North Carolina Press, 1998.

Howard, David. *Dominican Republic: a Guide to the People, Politics and Culture*. Northampton, MA: Interlink Publishing Group, 1999.

Roorda, Eric. *The Dictator Next Door: the Good Neighbor Policy and the Trujillo Re-*

gime in the Dominican Republic, 1930–1945. Durham, NC: Duke University Press, 1998.

Sagás, Ernesto. Race and Politics in the Dominican Republic. Gainesville, FL: University Press of Florida, 2000.

Ecuador

Alchon, Suzanne Austin. Native Society and Disease in Colonial Ecuador. New York: Cambridge University Press, 1991.

De la Torre, Carlos. Populist Seduction in Latin America: the Ecuadorian Experience. Athens, OH: Ohio University Press, 2000.

Gerlach, Allen. Indians, Oil, and Politics: A Recent History of Ecuador. Wilmington: Scholarly Resources, Inc, 2003.

Goffin, Alvin M. The Rise of Protestant Evangelism in Ecuador, 1895–1990. Gainesville, FL: University Press of Florida, 1994.

Hanratty, Dennis M., ed. Ecuador: a Country Study. Washington, DC: U.S. GPO, 3rd ed. 1991.

Herz, Monica and J.P. Nogueira. Ecuador vs. Peru: Peacemaking Amid Rivalry. Boulder, CO: Lynne Rienner, 2002.

Hey, Jeanne A.K. Theories of Dependent Foreign Policy and the Case of Ecuador in the 1980s. Athens, OH: Ohio University Press, 1995.

Isaacs, Anita. The Politics of Military Rule and Transition in Ecuador, 1972–92. Pittsburgh, PA: University of Pittsburgh Press, 1993.

Muratorio, Blanca. The Life and Times of Grandfather Alonso: Culture and History in the Upper Amazon. New Brunswick, NJ: Rutgers University Press, 1991.

Roitman, Karem. Race, Power and Ethnicity in Ecuador: The Manipulation of the Mestizaje. Boulder, CO: First Forum Press, 2009.

Selverston-Scher, Melina. Ethnopolitics in Ecuador: Indigenous Rights and the Strengthening of Democracy. North South Center Press, Miami: University of Miami, 2001.

El Salvador

Angel, José, et al. Strategy and Tactics of the Salvadoran FMLN Guerrillas: Last Battle of the Cold War, Blueprint for Future Conflicts. New York: Praeger, 1995.

Beirne, Charles Joseph. Jesuit Education and Social Change in El Salvador. New York: Garland Publishing, 1996.

Didion, Joan. Salvador. New York: Vintage, 1994.

Doggett, Martha. Death Foretold: the Jesuit Murders in El Salvador. Washington, DC: Georgetown University Press, 1993.

Grenier, Yvon. The Emergence of Insurgency in El Salvador: Ideology and Political Will. Pittsburgh, PA: University of Pittsburgh Press, 1999.

Haggerty, Richard A., ed. El Salvador: a Country Study. Washington, DC: U.S. GPO, 2nd ed. 1990.

Hammond, John L. Fighting to Learn: Popular Education and Guerrilla War in El Salvador. New Brunswick, NJ: Rutgers University Press, 1998.

Hassett, John and Hugh Lacey, eds. Toward a Society that Serves Its People: the Intellectual Contribution of El Salvador's Murdered Jesuits. Washington, DC: Georgetown University Press, 1991.

Marenn, M.J. Salvador's Children: a Song for Survival. Columbus, OH: Ohio State University, 1993.

Pelupessy, Wim. The Limits of Economic Reform in El Salvador. New York: Saint Martin's Press, 1997.

Popkin, Margaret L. Peace without Justice: Obstacles to Building the Rule of Law in El Salvador. University Park, PA: Pennsylvania State University, 2000.

Quizar, Robin O. My Turn to Weep: Salvadoran Women in Costa Rica. Westport, CT: Greenwood Publishing Group, 1998.

Ucles, Mario L. Translated by Amelia F. Shogun. El Salvador in the 1980's: Counterinsurgency and Revolution. Philadelphia, PA: Temple University Press, 1996.

Williams, Philip J. Militarization and Demilitarization in El Salvador's Transition to Democracy. Pittsburgh, PA: University of Pittsburgh Press, 1998.

Wood, Elisabeth Jean. Insurgent Collective Action and Civil War in El Salvador. Cambridge: Cambridge University Press, 2003.

Grenada

Heine, Jorge, ed. A Revolution Aborted: the Lessons of Grenada. Pittsburgh, PA: University of Pittsburgh Press, 1990.

Guatemala

Benz, Stephen Connely. Guatemalan Journey. Austin: University of Texas Press, 1996.

Dosal, Paul J. Doing Business with the Dictators: a Political History of the United Fruit in Guatemala, 1899–1944. Wilmington, DE: Scholarly Resources, 1993.

Dosal, Paul J. Power in Transition: The Rise of Guatemala's Industrial Oligarchy, 1871–1994. New York: Praeger, 1995.

Goldman, Francisco, The Art of Political Murder: Who Killed the Bishop? New York: Grove Press, 2007.

Grandin, Greg. The Blood of Guatemala: a History of Race and Nation. Durham, NC: Duke University Press, 2000.

Handy, Jim. Revolution in the Countryside: Rural Conflict and Agrarian Reform in Guatemala, 1944–1954. Chapel Hill, NC: University of North Carolina Press, 1994.

Hendrickson, Carol. Weaving Identities: Construction of Dress and Self in a Highland Guatemalan Town. Austin: University of Texas Press, 1995.

Jonas, Susanne. Of Centaurs and Doves: Guatemala's Peace Process. Boulder, CO: Westview Press, 2000.

Jones, Oakah L. Guatemala in the Spanish Colonial Period. Norman, OK: University of Oklahoma Press, 1994.

Levenson-Estrada, Deborah. Trade Unionists against Terror: Guatemala City, 1954–1985. Chapel Hill, NC: University of North Carolina Press, 1994.

Lovell, George W. A Beauty That Hurts: Life and Death in Guatemala. Austin, TX: University of Texas Press, rev. ed 2000.

McCleary, Rachel M. Dictating Democracy: Guatemala and the End of Violent Revolution. Gainesville, FL: University Press of Florida, 1999.

McCreery, David. Rural Guatemala, 1760–1940. Stanford, CA: Stanford University Press, 1994.

Nelson, Diane M. A Finger in the Wound: Body Politics in Quincentennial Guatemala. Berkeley, CA: University of California Press, 1999.

Perera, Victor. Unfinished Conquest: the Guatemalan Tragedy. Berkeley, CA: University of California Press, 1993.

Schirmer, Jennifer. The Guatemalan Military Project: a Violence Called Democracy. Philadelphia, PA: University of Pennsylvania Press, 1998.

Shea, Maureen E. Culture and Customs of Guatemala. Westport, CT: Greenwood Publishing Group, 2000.

Stanley, William. Enabling Peace in Guatemala: The Story of MINGUA. Boulder, CO: Lynne Rienner, 2009.

Stoll, David. Between Two Armies: in the Ixil Towns of Guatemala. New York: Columbia University Press, 1993.

Stoll, David. Rigoberta Menchu and the Story of All Poor Guatemalans. Boulder, CO: Westview Press, 1998.

Trudeau, Robert H. Guatemalan Politics: the Popular Struggle for Democracy. Boulder, CO: Lynne Rienner Publishers, 1993.

Wilkinson, Daniel. Silence On The Mountain: Stories of Terror, Betrayal, and Forgetting in Guatemala. Boston: Houghton Mifflin Company, 2002.

Woodward, Ralph Lee. Guatemala. Santa Barbara, CA: ABC-CLIO, rev. ed. 1992.

Woodward, Ralph Lee. Rafael Carrera and the Emergence of the Republic of Guatemala. Athens, GA: University of Georgia Press, 1993.

Yashar, Deborah J. Demanding Democracy: Reform and Reaction in Costa Rica and Guatemala., 1850s–1950s. Stanford, CA: Stanford University Press, 1997.

Zimmerman, Marc. Literature and Resistance in Guatemala: Textual Modes and Cultural Politics from El Señor Presidente to Rigoberta Menchu. Athens, OH: Ohio University Press, 1995.

Guyana

Da Costa, Emilia Viotti. Crowns of Glory, Tears of Blood: the Demerara Slave Rebel-

lion of 1823. New York: Oxford University Press, 1994.

Gibson, Kean. *The Cycle of Racial Oppression in Guyana.* Lanham, MD: University Press of America, 2003.

Merrill, Tim L., ed. *Guyana and Belize: Country Studies.* Washington, DC: U.S. GPO, 2nd ed. 1993.

Williams, Brackette F. *Stains on My Name, War in My Veins: Guyana and the Politics of Struggle.* Durham, NC: Duke University Press, 1991.

Williams, David P., et al., eds. *Privatization vs. Community: the Rise and Fall of Industrial Welfare in Guyana.* Lanham, MD: Rowman & Littlefield, 1998.

Haiti

Chambers, Frances, ed. *Haiti.* Santa Barbara, CA: ABC-CLIO, 2nd ed. 1994.

Fatton, Robert Jr. *Haiti's Predatory Republic: The Unending Transition to Democracy.* Boulder, CO: Lynne Rienner, 2002.

Fatton, Robert Jr. *The Roots of Haitian Despotism.* Boulder, CO: Lynne Rienner Publishers, 2007.

Gibbons, Elizabeth D. *Sanctions in Haiti: Human Rights and Democracy under Assault.* Westport, CT: Greenwood Publishing Group, 1999.

Fatton, Robert Jr.. *Haiti's Predatory Republic: The Unending Transition to Democracy.* Boulder: Lynne Reinner Publishing, 2002.

Fatton, Robert Jr. *The Roots of Haitian Despotism.* Boulder, CO: Lynne Rienner, 2007.

Haggerty, Richard A., ed. *Dominican Republic and Haiti: Country Studies.* Washington, DC: U.S. GPO, 2nd ed, 1991.

Hein, Robert Debs and Hein, Nancy Gordon. Revised and Expanded by Hein, Michael. *Written in Blood. The Story of the Haitian People 1492–1995.* Lanham, MD: University Press of America, 1996.

Kumar, Chetan. *Building Peace in Haiti.* Boulder, CO: Lynne Rienner Publishers, 1998.

Laguerre, Michel S. *The Military Society in Haiti.* Knoxville, TN: University of Tennessee Press, 1993.

Langley, Lester D. *The Americas in the Age of Revolution, 1750–1850.* New Haven, CT: Yale University Press, 1996.

Perusse, Roland I. *Haitian Democracy Restored, 1991–1995.* Lanham, MD: University Press of America, 1995.

Rotberg, Robert I., ed. *Haiti Renewed: Political and Economic Prospects.* Washington, DC: Brookings Institution Press, 1997.

Stotzky, Irwin P. *Silencing Guns in Haiti: the Promise of Deliberative Democracy.* Chicago: University of Chicago Press, 1997.

Weinstein, Brian and Aaron Segal. *Haiti: the Failure of Politics.* New York: Praeger, 1992.

Zephir, Flore. *Haitian Immigrants in Black America: a Sociological and Sociolinguistic Portrait.* Westport, CT: Bergin & Garvey, 1996.

Honduras

Euraque, Dario A. *Region and State in Honduras, 1870–1972: Reinterpreting the "Banana Republic."* Chapel Hill, NC: University of North Carolina Press, 1996.

Merrill, Tim L. *Honduras: a Country Study.* Washington, DC: U.S. GPO, 3rd ed. 1995.

Meyer, Harvey Kessler and Jessie H. Meyer. *Historical Dictionary of Honduras.* Lanham, MD: Scarecrow Press, 2nd ed. 1994.

Jamaica

Butler, Kathleen Mary. *The Economics of Emancipation: Jamaica and Barbados, 1823–1843.* Chapel Hill, NC: University of North Carolina Press, 1995.

Gray, Obika. *Radicalism and Social Change in Jamaica, 1960–1972.* Knoxville, TN: University of Tennessee Press, 1991.

Heuman, Gad. *The Killing Time: the Morant Bay Rebellion in Jamaica.* Knoxville, TN: University of Tennessee Press, 1994.

Hewan, Clinton G. *Jamaica and the United States Caribbean Basin Initiative: Showpiece or Failure?* New York: Peter Lang Publishing, 1994.

Ingram, K.E. *Jamaica.* Santa Barbara, CA: ABC-CLIO, Inc., revised ed. 1997.

Keith, Nelson W. and Novella Z. Keith. *The Social Origins of Democratic Socialism in Jamaica.* Philadelphia, PA: Temple University Press, 1992.

Lundy, Patricia. *Debt and Adjustment: Social and Environmental Consequences in Jamaica.* Brookfield, VT: Ashgate, 1999.

Mordecai, Martin and Pamela Mordecai. *Culture and Customs of Jamaica.* Westport, CT: Greenwood Publishing Group, 2000.

Moser, Caroline and Jeremy Holland. *Urban Poverty and Violence in Jamaica.* Washington, DC: The World Bank, 1997.

Payne, Anthony J. *Politics in Jamaica.* New York: Saint Martin's Press, rev. ed. 1994.

Zips, Werner. Translated by Shelley L. Frisch. *Black Rebels: African-Caribbean Freedom Fighters in Jamaica.* Princeton, NJ: Markus Wiener Publishers, 1999.

Mexico

Alonso, Ana Maria. *Thread of Blood: Colonialism, Revolution, and Gender on Mexico's Northern Frontier.* Tucson, AZ: University of Arizona Press, 1995.

Aspe, Pedro. *Economic Transformation in the Mexican Way.* Cambridge, MA: MIT Press, 1993.

Berg, Janine, Christoph Ernst and Peter Auer. *Meeting the Employment Challenge: Argentina, Brazil and Mexico in the Global Economy.* Boulder, CO: Lynne Rienner, 2006.

Bondi, Loretta. *Beyond the Border and Across the Atlantic. Mexico's Foreign and Security Policy Post-September 11.* Washington: Brookings, 2004.

Bosworth, Barry P., et al., eds. *Coming Together? Mexico-U.S. Relations.* Washington, DC: Brookings Institution Press, 1997.

Britton, John A. *Revolution and Ideology: Images of the Mexican Revolution and the United States.* Lexington, KY: University Press of Kentucky, 1995.

Brunk, Samuel. *Emiliano Zapata: Revolution and Betrayal in Mexico.* Albuquerque, NW: University of New Mexico Press, 1995.

Bulmer-Thomas, Victor, et al., eds. *Mexico and the North American Free Trade Agreement: Who Will Benefit?* New York: Saint Martin's Press, 1994.

Butler, Edgar. *Mexico and Mexico City in the World Economy.* Boulder, CO: Westview Press, 2000.

Camp, Roderic A., *Politics in Mexico: The Democratic Consolidation.* New York: Oxford Universiuty Press, 2006.

Castañeda, Jorge G. *The Mexican Shock: Its Meaning for the U.S.* New York: New Press, 1995.

Chand, Vikram K. *Mexico's Political Awakening.* Notre Dame, IN: University of Notre Dame Press, 2000.

Clough-Riquelme, Jane. *Equity and Sustainable Development: Reflections from the U.S.-Mexico Border.* Boulder, CO: Lynne Rienner, 2006.

Cope, R. Douglas. *The Limits of Racial Domination: Plebeian Society in Colonial Mexico City, 1660–1720.* Madison, WI: University of Wisconsin Press, 1994.

Cornelius, Wayne A., and Jessica M. Lewis, eds. *Impacts of Border Enforcement on Mexican Migration: The View from Sending Communities.* Boulder, CO: Lynne Rienner, 2007.

Crandall, Russell, et al, eds. *Mexico's Democracy at Work: Political and Economic Dynamics.* Boulder, CO: Lynne Rienner, 2004.

Davidow, Jeffrey. *The U.S. and Mexico: The Bear and the Porcupine.* Markus Weiner, 2004.

Davis, Diane E. *Urban Leviathan: Mexico City in the Twentieth Century.* Philadelphia, PA: Temple University Press, 1994.

Dominguez, Jorge I. and James A. McCann. *Democratizating Mexico: Public Opinion and Electoral Choices.* Baltimore, MD: Johns Hopkins University Press, 1996.

Dominguez, Jorge I. and Alejandro Poire, eds. *Toward Mexico's Democratization: Parties, Campaigns, Elections and Public Opinion.* New York: Routledge, 1999.

Edmonds-Poli, Emily and David A. Shirk. *Contemporary Mexican Politics.* Lanham, MD: Rowman Littlefield Publishers, 2008.

..r, John S.D. *Intervention! The .. States and the Mexican Revolution, ..13–1917*. New York: W.W. Norton, 1993.

Erfani, Julie A. *The Paradox of the Mexican State: Rereading Sovereignty from Independence to NAFTA*. Boulder, CO: Lynne Rienner Publishers, 1995.

Fehrenbach, T.R. *Fire and Blood: a History of Mexico*. New York: Da Capo Press, 1995.

Foster, Lynn V. *A Brief History of Mexico*. New York: Facts on File, 1997.

Garber, Peter M., ed. *The Mexico-U.S. Free Trade Agreement*. Cambridge, MA: MIT Press, 1994.

Gledhill, John. *Neoliberalism, Transnationalism and Rural Poverty: a Case Study of Michoacan, Mexico*. Boulder, CO: Westview Press, 1995.

Grayson, George W. *Oil and Mexican Foreign Policy*. Pittsburgh: University of Pittsburgh Press, 1988.

Hamnett, Brian. *Juarez*. White Plains, NY: Longman Publishing, 1994.

Harvey, Neil, ed. *Mexico: Dilemmas of Transition*. London: British Academic Press, 1993.

Homedes, Núria, and Antonio Ugalde, eds. *Decentralizing Health Services in Mexico*. Boulder, CO: Lynne Rienner, 2006.

Johns, Christina Jacqueline. *The Origins of Violence in Mexican Society*. New York: Praeger, 1995.

Jones, Richard C. *Ambivalent Journey: U.S. Migration and Economic Mobility in North-Central Mexico*. Tucson, AZ: University of Arizona Press, 1995.

Katz, Friedrich. *The Life and Times of Pancho Villa*. Stanford, CA: Stanford University Press, 1998.

Krauze, Enrique. *Mexico-Biography of Power: a History of Modern Mexico, 1810–1996*. New York: HarperCollins Publishers, 1997.

Krooth, Richard. *Mexico, NAFTA and the Hardships of Progress: Historical Patterns and Shifting Methods of Oppression*. Jefferson, NC: McFarland & Company, 1995.

Markiewicz, Dana. *The Mexican Revolution and the Limits of Agrarian Reform, 1915–1946*. Boulder, CO: Lynne Rienner Publishers, 1993.

Merrell, Floyd. *The Mexicans. A Sense of Culture*. Boulder, Co: Westview, 2003.

Merrill, Tim L. and Ramon Miro, eds. *Mexico: a Country Study*. Washington, DC: U.S. GPO, 4th ed. 1997.

Meyer, Michael C., et al. *The Course of Mexican History*. New York: Oxford University Press, 1998.

Middlebrook, Keven J., ed. *Dilemmas of Political Change in Mexico*. Washington: Brookings, 2004.

Morris, Stephen D. *Political Corruption in Mexico: The Impact of Democratization*. Boulder, CO: Lynne Rienner Publishers, 2009.

Oppenheimer, Andres. *Bordering on Chaos: Guerrillas, Stockbrokers, Politicians and Mexico's Violent Struggle*. New York: Little, Brown, 1996.

Peters, Enrique Dussel. *Polarizing Mexico: the Impact of Liberalization Strategy*. Boulder, CO: Lynne Rienner Publishers, 2000.

Preson, Julia and Dillon, Samuel. *Opening Mexico: The Making of a Democracy*. New York: Farrar, Straus and Giroux, 2004.

Purcell, Susan K. and Luis Rubio, eds. *Mexico under Zedillo*. Boulder, CO: Lynne Rienner Publishers, 1998.

Rodriguez, Victoria E. and Peter M. Ward. *Opposition Government in Mexico*. Albuquerque, NM: University of New Mexico Press, 1995.

Roett, Riordan, ed. *Political and Economic Liberalization in Mexico: at a Critical Juncture?* Boulder, CO: Lynne Rienner Publishers, 1993.

Rubio, Luis and Purcell, Susan Kaufman, eds. *Mexico Under Fox*. Boulder, CO: Lynne Rienner, 2004.

Ruíz, Ramon E. *On the Rim of Mexico: Encounters of the Rich and Poor*. Boulder, CO: Westview Press, 1998.

Schulz, Donald E. and Edward J. Williams, eds. *Mexico Faces the 21st Century*. Westport, CT: Greenwood Publishing Group, 1995.

Sernau, Scott. *Economies of Exclusion: Underclass Poverty and Labor Market Change in Mexico*. New York: Praeger, 1994.

Shirk, David A. *Mexico's New Politics: The PAN and Democratic Change*. Boulder, CO: Lynne Rienner, 2004.

Staudt, Kathleen A. *Free Trade? Informal Economies at the U.S.-Mexican Border*. Philadelphia, PA: Temple University Press, 1998.

Thomas, Hugh. *Conquest: Montezuma, Cortes, and the Fall of Old Mexico*. New York: Simon & Schuster, 1994.

Tulchin, Joseph S. and Andrew D. Selee, eds. *Mexico's Politics and Society in Transition*. Boulder, CO: Lynne Rienner, 2002.

Wise, Carol. *The Post-NAFTA Political Economy: Mexico and the Western Hemisphere*. University Park, PA: Pennsylvania State University Press, 1998.

Womack, John Jr. *Rebellion in Chiapas: an Historical Reader*. New York: New Press, 1999.

Netherlands Antilles

Brown, Enid. *Suriname and the Netherlands Antilles: an Annotated English-Language Bibliography*. Lanham, MD: Scarecrow Press, 1992.

Sedoc-Dahlberg, Betty, ed. *The Dutch Caribbean: Prospects for Democracy*. New York: Gordon and Breach, 1990.

Nicaragua

Biondi-Morra, Brizio N. *Hungry Dream: the Failure of Food Policy in Revolutionary Nicaragua, 1979–1990*. Ithaca, NY: Cornell University Press, 1993.

Gambone, Michael D. *Eisenhower, Somoza and the Cold War in Nicaragua, 1953–1961*. Westport, CT: Greenwood Publishing Group, 1997.

Hale, Charles R. *Resistance and Contradiction: Miskitu Indians and the Nicaraguan State, 1894–1987*. Stanford, CA: Stanford University Press, 1994.

Kagan, Robert. *A Twilight Struggle: American Power and Nicaragua, 1977–1990*. New York: Free Press, 1996.

Luciak, Ilja A. *The Sandinista Legacy: Lessons from a Political Economy in Transition*. Gainesville, FL: University Press of Florida, 1995.

Merrill, Tim L., ed. *Nicaragua: a Country Study*. Washington, DC: U.S. GPO, 3rd ed. 1994.

Miranda, Roger and William Ratliff. *The Civil War in Nicaragua: Inside the Sandinistas*. New Brunswick, NJ: Transaction, 1993.

Prevost, Gary. *The Undermining of the Sandinista Revolution*. New York: Saint Martin's Press, 1997.

Randall, Margaret. *Sandino's Daughters: Feminism in Nicaragua*. New Brunswick, NJ: Rutgers University Press, 1994.

Ryan, David. *US-Sandinista Diplomatic Relations: Voice of Intolerance*. New York: Saint Martin's Press, 1995.

Sabia, Debra. *Contradiction and Conflict: the Popular Church in Nicaragua*. Tuscaloosa, AL: University of Alabama Press, 1997.

Spalding, Rose J. *Capitalists and Revolution in Nicaragua: Opposition and Accommodation, 1979–1993*. Chapel Hill, NC: University of North Carolina Press, 1994.

Vanden, Harry E. and Garry Prevost. *Democracy and Socialism in Sandinista Nicaragua*. Boulder, CO: Lynne Rienner Publishers, 1993.

Walker, Thomas W. *Nicaragua. Living in the Shadow of the Eagle*. Boulder, Co: Westview, 2003.

Walker, Thomas W., ed. *Nicaragua without Illusions: Regime Transition and Structural Adjustment in the 1990s*. Wilmington, DE: Scholarly Resources, 1997.

Walter, Knut. *The Regime of Anastasio Somoza, 1936–1956*. Chapel Hill, NC: University of North Carolina Press, 1993.

Whisnant, David E. *Rascally Signs in Sacred Places: the Politics of Culture in Nicaragua*. Chapel Hill, NC: University of North Carolina Press, 1995.

Panama

Conniff, Michael L. *Panama and the United States: the Forced Alliance*. Athens, GA: University of Georgia Press, 1992.

Donnelly, Thomas, et al. *Operation Just Cause: the Storming of Panama*. New York: Lexington Books, 1991.

Guevara Mann, Carlos. *Panamanian Militarism: a Historical Perspective*. Athens, OH: Ohio University Press, 1996.

Johns, Christina Jacqueline and P. Ward Johnson. *State Crime, the Media, and the*

Invasion of Panama. New York: Praeger, 1994.

Leonard, Thomas M. *Panama, the Canal and the United States: a Guide to Issues and References.* Claremont, CA: Regina Books, 1993.

Major, John. *Prize Possession: the United States and the Panama Canal, 1903–1979.* New York: Cambridge University Press, 1993.

Meditz, Sandra W. and Dennis M. Hanratty, eds. *Panama: a Country Study.* Washington, DC: U.S. GPO, 4th ed. 1989.

Noriega, Manuel and Peter Eisner. *America's Prisoner: the Memoirs of Manuel Noriega.* New York: Random House, 1997.

Pearcy, Thomas L. *We Answer Only to God: Politics and the Military in Panama, 1903–1947.* Albuquerque, NM: University of New Mexico Press, 1998.

Perez, Orlando J., ed. *Post-Invasion Panama: the Challenges of Democratization in the New World Order.* Lanham, MD: Lexington Books, 2000.

Ward, Christopher. *Imperial Panama: Commerce and Conflict in Isthmian America, 1550–1800.* Albuquerque, NM: University of New Mexico, 1993.

Paraguay

Gimlette, John, *At the Tomb of the Inflatable Pig: Travels Through Paraguay.* New York: Alfred A. Knopf, 2003.

Hanratty, Dennis and Sandra W. Meditz, eds. *Paraguay: a Country Study.* Washington, DC: U.S. GPO, 2nd ed. 1990.

Kracy, Hendrick, and Thomas Whigham, eds., *I Die With My Country: Perspectives on the Paraguayan War, 1864–70.* Lincoln: University of Nebraska Press, 2004.

Lambert, Peter and Andrew Nickson, eds. *Transition to Democracy in Paraguay.* New York: Saint Martin's Press, 1997.

Leis, Paul H. *Political Parties and Generations in Paraguay's Liberal Era, 1869–1940.* Chapel Hill, NC: University of North Carolina Press, 1993.

Miranda, Carlos R. *The Stroessner Era: Authoritarian Rule in Paraguay.* Boulder, CO: Westview Press, 1990.

Mora, Frank O. and Jerry W. Cooney. *Paraguay and the United States: Distant Allies.* Athens: The University of Georga Press, 2007.

Nickson, R. Andrew. *Historical Dictionary of Paraguay.* Lanham, MD: Scarecrow Press, 2nd ed. 1993.

Whigham, Thomas, *The Paraguayan War (Vol. 1)—Causes and Early Conduct.* Lincoln: University of Nebraska Press, 2002.

Peru

Cameron, Maxwell, A. *Democracy and Authoritarianism in Peru: Political Coalitions and Social Change.* New York: Saint Martin's Press, 1994.

Clayton, Lawrence A. *Peru and the United States: the Condor and the Eagle.* Athens, GA: University of Georgia Press, 1999.

Gootenberg, Paul. *Imagining Development: Economic Ideas in Peru's "Fictitious Prosperity" of Guano, 1840–1880.* Berkeley, CA: University of California Press, 1993.

Gorriti, Gustavo. *The Shining Path: a History of the Millenarian War in Peru.* Chapel Hill, NC: University of North Carolina Press, 1999.

Hudson, Rex A., ed. *Peru: a Country Study.* Washington, DC: U.S. GPO, 1993.

Jacobsen, Nils. *Mirages of Transition: the Peruvian Altiplano, 1780–1930.* Berkeley, CA: University of California Press, 1993.

Kirk, Robin. *The Monkey's Paw, New Chronicles From Peru.* Amherst: University of Massachusetts Press, 1997.

Klaren, Peter Flindell. *Peru: Society and Nationhood in the Andes.* New York: Oxford University Press, 2000.

Lockhart, James. *Spanish Peru, 1532–1560: a Social History.* Madison, WI: University of Wisconsin Press, 1994.

Masterson, Daniel M. *Militarism and Politics in Latin America: Peru from Sanchez Cerro to Sendero Luminoso.* Westport, CT: Greenwood Publishing Publishing, 1991.

Palmer, David Scott, ed. *The Shining Path of Peru.* New York: Saint Martin's Press, 1992.

Peña, Milagros. *Theologies and Liberation in Peru: the Role of Ideas in Social Movement.* Philadelphia, PA: Temple University Press, 1995.

Quiroz, Alfonso W. *Domestic and Foreign Finance in Modern Peru, 1850–1950: Financing Visions of Development.* Pittsburgh, PA: University of Pittsburgh Press, 1993.

Roberts, Kenneth M. *Deepening Democracy? The Modern Left and Social Movements in Chile and Peru.* Stanford, CA: Stanford University Press, 1999.

Seligmann, Linda J. *Between Reform and Revolution: Political Struggles in the Peruvian Andes, 1969–1991.* Stanford, CA: Stanford University Press, 1995.

Sheahan, John. *Searching for a Better Society: the Peruvian Economy from 1950.* University Park, PA: Pennsylvania State University Press, 1999.

Starn, Orin, Carlos Ivan Degregori, and Robin Kirk, eds. *The Peru Reader: History, Culture, Politics.* Durham: Duke University Press, 1995.

Stern, Steve J. *Peru's Indian Peoples and the Challenge of Spanish Conquest: Huamanga to 1640.* Madison, WI: University of Wisconsin Press, 2nd ed. 1993.

Stern, Steve J., ed., *Shining And Other Paths.* Durham: Duke University Press, 1998.

Tarazona-Sevillano, Gabriela. *Sendero Luminoso and the Threat of Narcoterrorism.* New York: Praeger, 1990.

Tulchin, Joseph S. and Gary Bland, eds. *Peru in Crisis: Dictatorship or Democracy?* Boulder, CO: Lynne Rienner Publishers, 1994.

Watters, R.F. *Poverty and Peasantry in Peru's Southern Andes, 1963–90.* Pitts-burgh, PA: University of Pittsburg, Press, 1994.

Puerto Rico

Acosta-Belén, Edna, and Carlos E. Santiago. *Puerto Ricans in the United States: A Contemporary Portrait.* Boulder, CO: Lynne Rienner, 2006.

Dietz, James L. *Puerto Rico: Negotiating Development and Change.* Boulder, CO: Lynne Rienner, 2003.

Suriname

Brown, Enid. *Suriname and the Netherlands Antilles: an Annotated English-Language Bibliography.* Lanham, MD: Scarecrow Press, 1992.

Dew, Edward M. *The Trouble in Suriname, 1975–1993.* New York: Praeger, 1994.

Hoefte, Rosemarijn. *In Place of Slavery: a Social History of British Indian and Javanese Laborers in Suriname.* Gainesville, FL: University Press of Florida, 1998.

Hoefte, Rosemarijn. *Suriname.* Santa Barbara, CA: ABC-CLIO, 1991.

Trinidad and Tobago

Anthony, Michael. *Historical Dictionary of Trinidad and Tobago.* Lanham, MD: Scarecrow Press, 1997.

Regis, Louis. *The Political Calypso: True Opposition in Trinidad and Tobago, 1962–1987.* Gainesville, FL: University Press of Florida, 1998.

Yelvington, Kelvin A. *Trinidad Ethnicity.* Knoxville, TN: University of Tennessee Press, 1993.

Uruguay

Gillespie, Charles Guy. *Negotiating Democracy: Politicians and Generals in Uruguay.* New York: Cambridge University Press, 1991.

Gonzalez, Luis E. *Political Structures and Democracy in Uruguay.* Notre Dame, IN: University of Notre Dame Press, 1991.

Hudson, Rex A. and Sandra W. Meditz, eds. *Uruguay: a Country Study.* Washington, DC: U.S. GPO, 2nd ed. 1992.

Preeg, Ernest H. *From Here to Free Trade: Essays in Post-Uruguay Round Trade Strategy.* Chicago: University of Chicago Press, 1998.

Rottenberg, Simon, ed. *Costa Rica and Uruguay.* New York: Oxford University Press, 1993.

Sosnowski, Saul. *Repression, Exile, and Democracy: Uruguayan Culture.* Durham, NC: Duke University Press, 1992.

Venezuela

Canache, Damarys J. and Michael R. Kulisheck, eds. *Reinventing Legitimacy: Democracy and Political Change in Venezuela.* Westport, CT: Greenwood Publishing Group, 1998.

Coppedge, Michael. *Strong Parties and Lame Ducks: Presidential Partyarchy and*

...alism in Venezuela. Stanford, CA: ...ford University Press, 1994.

...onil, Fernando. *Magical State: Nature, Money and Modernity in Venezuela*. Chicago: University of Chicago Press, 1997.

Ellner, Steve and Hellinger, Daniel, eds. *Venezuelan Politics in the Chávez Era: Class, Polarization, and Conflict*. Boulder, CO: Lynne Rienner, 2004.

Ellner, Steve and Miguel Tinker Salas, eds. *Venezuela: Hugo Chávez and the Decline of an "Exceptional Democracy."* Rowman & Littlefield Publishers, Inc: Lanham. 2007.

Ellner, Steve. *Rethinking Venezuelan Politics: Class, Conflict and the Chavez Phenomenon*. Boulder, CO: Lynne Reinner Publishers, 2008.

Enright, Michael J., et al. *Venezuela: the Challenge of Competitiveness*. New York: Saint Martin's Press, 1996.

Golinger, Eva. *The Chavez Code: Cracking U.S. Intervention in Venezuela*. Northampton, MA: Olive Branch Press, 2006.

Goodman, Louis W., et al., eds. *Lessons of the Venezuelan Experience*. Baltimore, MD: Johns Hopkins University Press, 1995.

Gott, Richard. *In The Shadow of the Liberator: Hugo Chávez and the Transformation of Venezuela*. Verso Press: London, 2000.

Gott, Richard. *Hugo Chavez and the Bolivarian Revolution*. London/New York: Verso, 2005

Haggerty, Richard A. *Venezuela: a Country Study*. Washington, DC: U.S. GPO, 4th ed. 1993.

Hillman, Richard S. *Democracy for the Privileged: Crisis and Transition in Venezuela*. Boulder, CO: Lynne Rienner, 1994.

Kozloff, Nikolas. *Hugo Chavez: Oil, Politics, and the Challenge to the U.S.* New York: Palgrave MacMillan, 2006.

Nelson, Brian A. *The Silence and the Scorpion: The Coup Against Chavez and the Making of Modern Venezuela*. New York: Nation Books, 2009.

Rudolph, Donna K. and G.A. Rudolph. *Historical Dictionary of Venezuela*. Lanham, MD: Scarecrow Press, 1996.

Schoen, Douglas, and Michael Rowan. *The Threat Closer to Home: Hugo Chávez and the War Against America*. Free Press, 2009.

Wilpert, Gregory. *Changing Venezuela By Taking Power: The History and Policies of the Chavez Government*. London/New York: Verso, 2007.

A Peruvian Indian and his llama keep a lonely vigil in some of the highest country in the western Andes